VATICAN COUNCIL II

The Conciliar and Post Conciliar Documents

This edition authorized for distribution in the following areas only: North America, the Caribbean, South America, the Philippines and Japan.

Also available in the Vatican Collection series:

Volume 2: VATICAN COUNCIL II
        More Postconciliar Documents

In preparation:

Volume 3: MAJOR PAPAL DOCUMENTS,
        (John XXIII to John Paul II)

Mary Bold

VATICAN COUNCIL II

The Conciliar and Post Conciliar Documents

General Editor,
AUSTIN FLANNERY, O.P.

1988 Revised Edition

COSTELLO PUBLISHING COMPANY
Northport, New York

Nihil Obstat: Reverend Francis X. Glimm, S.T.L.
Censor Librorum
July 25, 1975

Imprimatur ✠ Walter P. Kellenberg, D.D.
Bishop of Rockville Centre
August 12, 1975

Vatican Collection
Volume 1

VATICAN II
THE CONCILIAR AND POST CONCILIAR DOCUMENTS

Eighth printing, June 1987

Library of Congress Catalog Card Number: 75-18840

International Standard Book Number: 0-918344-15-8

Copyright © 1975, 1984, and 1987 by Harry J. Costello and Reverend
Austin Flannery, O.P.

Printed in the United States of America

Costello Publishing Company, Inc.
P.O. Box 9
Northport, New York 11768

Table of Contents

1. For easier reference, all Documents are numbered consecutively and are referred to subsequently as D.1, D.2, etc.
2. When referring to an official Roman Document, it is customary to indicate: (a) its provenance (e.g., The Second Council of the Vatican, here referred to as Vatican II, or the Vatican department which issued it, such as the Sacred Congregation of Rites, here abbreviated to S.C.R.); (b) the first words of the original document, usually Latin (e.g., *Sacrosanctum concilium*); and (c) the date of its publication. As a help to the reader, these details are added underneath each title in the Table of Contents and at the commencement of each Document.
3. An alphabetically arranged key to the abbreviations used for Vatican departments is given after the Table of Contents.

vii

ABBREVIATIONS FOR VATICAN CONGREGATIONS AND OTHER DEPARTMENTS

C.C.P.A	Council for the Church's Public Affairs (split off from the Secretariat of State in 1967)
C.L.	Council for the Laity
C.P.I.C.L.	Consilium for the Proper Implementation of the Constitution on the Sacred Liturgy
C.R.R.J.	Committee for Religious Relations with the Jews
P.C.I.S.C.	Pontifical Council for the Instruments of Social Communication
S.A.P.	Sacred Apostolic Penitentiary
S.C.B.	Sacred Congregation for Bishops
S.C.C.	Sacred Congregation for the Clergy
S.C.C.E.	Sacred Congregation for Catholic Education
S.C.C.S.	Sacred Congregation for the Causes of the Saints (Sacred Congregation of Rites was split in 1969 into this and S.C.D.W., q.v.)
S.C.D.F.	Sacred Congregation for the Doctrine of the Faith (had been called S.S.C.H.O. until 1965: see A. 20)
S.C.D.S.	Sacred Congregation for the Discipline of the Sacraments (merged with S.C.D.W. to form S.C.S.D.W., q.v., in 1975)
S.C.D.W.	Sacred Congregation for Divine Worship (had been part of S.C.R. [q.v.] until 1969: see A. 26): merged with S.C.D.S. to form S.C.S.D.W., q.v., in 1975)
S.C.E.P.	Sacred Congregation for the Evangelization of Peoples, or Propaganda Fide
S.C.O.C.	Sacred Congregation for the Oriental Churches
S.C.R.	Sacred Congregation of Rites (in 1969 split into S.C.D.W. and S.C.C.S. See A. 26)
S.C.Rel.	Sacred Congregation for Religious (known as S.C.R.S.I. after 1967: see A. 24)
S.C.R.S.I.	Sacred Congregation for Religious and Secular Institutes (see previous entry)
S.C.S.D.W.	Sacred Congregation for the Sacraments and Divine Worship (S.C.D.S. and S.C.D.W. merged to form this in 1975: see A 34a)
S.P.U.C.	Secretariat for the Promotion of the Unity of Christians
S.S.	Secretariat of State, or Papal Secretariat (See note on C.C.P.A.)
S.S.C.H.O.	Supreme Sacred Congregation of the Holy Office (see S.C.D.F.)
S.T.A.S.	Supreme Tribunal of the Apostolic Signature
S.U.	Secretariat for Unbelievers

OTHER ABBREVIATIONS (BIBLIOGRAPHICAL AND OF THE DOCUMENTS OF VATICAN II)

A	Appendix: used here when referring to documents listed in the appendix, "Descriptive catalogue of the more important post-conciliar documents."
A.A.	*Apostolicam actuositatem*: The Decree on the Apostolate of the Laity
A.A.S.	*Acta Apostolicae Sedis*, the Vatican gazette, published a varying number of times each year. Carries the original text (mostly Latin) of the more important Vatican documents.
A.G.D.	*Ad gentes divinitus*: The Decree on the Church's Missionary Activity
A.S.S.	*Acta Sanctae Sedis*: title of A.A.S. up to 1 January, 1909
C.C.L.	Corpus Christianorum, Series Latina (Collected Works of Christian Writers, Latin Series)
C.D.	*Christus Dominus;* The Decree on the Pastoral Office of Bishops in the Church.
C.I.C.	*Codex Juris Canonici*: The Code of Canon Law.
Const.	Constitution
C.R.M.	*Commentarium pro Religiosis et Missionariis*: Commentary for Religious and Missionaries, a quarterly review published in Rome.
C.S.E.L.	*Corpus Scriptorum Ecclesiasticorum Latinorum.* Vienna, 1866 ff. (Collected Works of Latin Church Writers)
C.T.S.	Catholic Truth Society, London
D	Document: used here when referring to the documents published in the present collection, e.g. D.*1*, D.*2*, etc.
Denz.	H. Denzinger, *Enchiridion Symbolorum*, 32nd edition, 1963 (Collection of more important Church Documents)
Denz. Schon.	New edition of Denzinger, edited by A. Schönmetzer.
D.H.	*Dignitatis humanae;* The Declaration on Religious Liberty
D.V.	*Dei verbum*: The Dogmatic Constitution on Divine Revelation
Funk	F. X. Funk, *Patres Apostolici*, two volumes, Tubingen, 1901
G.C.S.	*Die Grieschischen Christlichen Schriftsteller der ersten drei Jahrhunderte* (Greek Christian authors of the first three centuries; in fact the

	series extends further.) Edited in Berlin since 1897.
G.E.	*Gravissimum educationis*: The Declaration on Christian Education
G.S.	*Gaudium et spes*: The Pastoral Constitution on the Church in the Modern World
I.M.	*Inter mirifica*: The Decree on the Means of Social Communication
L.G.	*Lumen gentium*: The Dogmatic Constitution on the Church
Mansi	J. D. Mansi, *Sacrorum conciliorum nova et amplissima collectio,* thirty-one volumes, (1757–1798)
M.G.	Migne, Greek; same as P.G.
M.L.	Migne, Latin; same as P.L.
N.A.	*Nostra aetate*: The Declaration on the Church's Realtions with non-Christian Religions
Notitiae	A monthly, organ of the Sacred Congregation for Divine Worship, Vatican City
O.E.	*Orientalium ecclesiarum*: The Decree on the Catholic Oriental Churches
Oss. Rom.	*Osservatore Romano,* Vatican daily, published in Italian. English version, with same title, published weekly.
O.T.	*Optatam totius*: The Decree on the Training of Priests
P.C.	*Perfectae caritatis*: The Decree on the Up-to-date Renewal of Religious Life
P.G.	J. P. Migne, *Patrologia Graeca,* 161 volumes, 1857–1865
P.L.	J. P. Migne, *Patrologia Latina,* 217 volumes, 1878–1890.
P.O.	*Presbyterorum ordinis*: The Decree on the Life and Ministry of Priests
S.C.	*Sacrosanctum concilium*: The Constitution on the Sacred Liturgy.
S.Ch.	Sources Chretienne (Christian Sources), edited by H. deLubac and J. Danielou, Paris
Sess.	Session (of an ecumenical council)
Summa Theol	*Summa Theologiae,* by St. Thomas Aquinas
U.R.	*Unitatis redintegratio*: The Decree on Ecumenism.

ABBREVIATIONS OF THE BOOKS OF THE BIBLE

Acts The Acts of the Apostles
Am. Amos
Apoc. Apocalypse (Revelation)
Bar. Baruch
Cant. Canticle of Canticles
    (S. of S.)
1 Chr. 1 Chronicles (Paralip.)
2 Chr. 2 Chronicles (Paralip.)
Col. Colossians
1 Cor. 1 Corinthians
2 Cor. 2 Corinthians
Dan. Daniel
Dt. Deuteronomy
Ec. Ecclesiastes
Eccl. Ecclesiasticus (Sirach)
Eph. Ephesians
1 Esd. 1 Esdras
2 Esd. 2 Esdras
Est. Esther
Ex. Exodus
Ezel. Ezekiel
Ezra Ezra
Gal. Galatians
Gen. Genesis
Hab. Habakkuk
Hag. Haggai (Aggeus)
Heb. Hebrews
Hos. Hosea (Osee)
Is. Isaiah
Jas. James
Jdt. Judith
Jer. Jeremiah
Jg. Judges
Jl. Joel
Jn. John (Gospel)
1 Jn. 1 John (Epistle)
2 Jn. 2 John
3 Jn. 3 John
Job Job
Jon. Jonah
Jos. Joshua
Jude Jude
1 Kg. 1 Kings

2 Kg. 2 Kings
Lam. Lamentations
Lev. Leviticus
Lk. Luke
1 Macc. 1 Maccabees
2 Macc. 2 Maccabees
Mal. Malachi
Mic. Micah
Mk. Mark
Mt. Matthew
Nah. Nahum
Neh. Nehemiah
Num. Numbers
Ob. Obadiah (Abdias)
Os. Osee (Hosea)
1 Paralip. 1 Paralipomenon
    (1 Chronicles)
2 Paralip. 2 Paralipomenon
    (2 Chronicles)
1 Pet. 1 Peter
2 Pet. 2 Peter
Phil. Philippians
Philem. Philemon
Pr. Proverbs
Ps. Psalms
Rev. Revelation (Apocalypse)
Rom. Romans
Ru. Ruth
1 Sam. 1 Samuel
2 Sam. 2 Samuel
Sir. Sirach (Ecclesiasticus)
S. of S. Song of Solomon
    (Canticle of Canticles)
Soph. Sophoniah (Zephaniah)
1 Th. 1 Thessalonians
2 Th. 2 Thessalonians
1 Tim. 1 Timothy
2 Tim. 2 Timothy
Tit. Titus
Tob. Tobit (Tobias)
Wis. Wisdom of Solomon
Zech. Zechariah
Zeph. Zephaniah (Sophoniah)

EDITOR'S NOTE ON THE SECOND EDITION

I am grateful to the readers who suggested improvements in the rendering of more difficult terms and to those who pointed out minor errors. I am particularly grateful to the readers who drew my attention to two instances of the omission of a line of text—publishers and printers are all to painfully aware of how this can happen!

On page 360, the ten words following the word 'Lord' in the next to last line of paragraph 9, had been omitted, as had the thirteen words on page 800, line 6, paragraph 2.

We had intended to add more recent post-conciliar documents to this volume, making extra space available by omitting some of the less important documents included in the first volume. Unfortunately, this has not been possible. The proposed omissions would have necessitated resetting the book, thus increasing the cost to a degree far in excess of that made necessary by current high inflation. Nor did it prove feasible to add the new material to the present volume, for with nearly 1100 it is already at the outer limits of our printers binding capacity. It is almost twice the size of the average 'blockbuster'.

We decided to put the new post-conciliar material into a second volume. Details are given on the back cover of this volume. We are preparing a third volume, which will contain all other major papal documents and documents promulgated by the Roman congregations.

Austin Flannery, O.P.
15 October 1980

INTRODUCTION

Why a new edition of the documents of Vatican II? For eighteen years I have been involved in the translation and publication of official Church documents, including those of Vatican II and its aftermath, and I have long felt that there is need for a volume containing not only the sixteen Council documents, but also as useful a selection as possible of the relevant subsequent official documents, those which dot the i's and cross the t's, as it were, of the sixteen.

It might have been physically possible to have included all the postconciliar documents in one book, but it would have been an excessively large book—or couple of books —and would in any case have been less than helpful for the general reader. It seemed more feasible and more helpful to attempt to meet the needs of the average priest, religious or lay person who might find themselves asking: "Where can I lay my hands on that second directory on ecumenism?" or, "Where can I get those documents on mixed marriages?" or, "Wasn't there something in the last year or two about subdeacons?" or, "Isn't the Index abolished—or is it?"

One knows, of course, that there are many, perhaps very many priests, religious and lay people who, since the controversies of the sixties, are unlikely to lose any sleep over the location of a Roman document—any Roman document! In fact they may find the mere mention of a Roman document a soporific. For some of them the phrase, "Roma locuta, causa finita: Rome has spoken, the case is finished," may have taken on a new and cynical meaning, best rendered perhaps by "Rome has spoken, that's one more subject buried."

That is a pity, and they are themselves the poorer.

I have tried to include all documents of general interest which form part of the postconciliar process. Many of them are not easily available. I have also added in an appendix a descriptive catalogue of a much more ample selection of postconciliar documents.

The postconciliar documents on the liturgy presented by far the greatest difficulty. Well over a hundred of them have been issued since the beginning of 1964, some of them short, some of them very long. A book limited to a collection of these documents would have to be somewhat selective to be manageable. Much more drastic selectivity is called for in a more general collection, such as the present one. In the introduction to the section on liturgy, I explain how the selection was made.

There are other documents which are not of immediate concern to all the members of the Church, but only to certain categories of members, to whom in fact they are relatively accessible. Here too I have been selective. Thus, I have omitted documents on clerical formation and several documents listing special faculties granted to bishops and to religious superiors.

This volume contains documents which might be described as organically linked with the conciliar process. During the course of the Vatican Council, and after it had finished, a number of bodies were formally entrusted with the task of working out the detailed application of the principles and directives agreed at the Council. Many of them were brought into existence solely for this purpose and, their work done, have since ceased to exist. Some of the work, naturally, was shared with existing Roman congregations. (For details, see Appendix—hereafter referred to simply as A.—numbers 17, 18, 21, 22, 24, 28.) It is the documents produced in this way which I describe as being organically linked with the conciliar process. They are printed after the conciliar documents to which they relate, and in chronological order.

The descriptive catalogue in the Appendix lists two hundred and fifty of the more important postconciliar documents. Those included in the present volume are marked with an asterisk. The descriptive catalogue, one hopes, offers a general view of the scope and development of the official blueprints for renewal in the Church. In many instances, it also offers an adequate synopsis or brief indication of the contents of documents not published in the present collection. It gives full details of the titles and dates of all documents and of where their originals may be found.

The official Latin text of the council documents is that prepared by the General Secretariat of the Second Vatican Council. They have been published in the *Acta Apostolicae Sedis*, the official Vatican gazette. They have also been published in the official collection published 11 October, 1966, by the Secretariat under the title: *Sacrosanctum Oecumeni-*

cum Concilium Vaticanum II: Constitutiones, Decreta, Declarationes. We have followed the order of that publication. The main source for the originals of postconciliar documents is the *Acta Apostolicae Sedis*, but we have also had recourse to *Commentarium pro Religiosis* and *Notitiae* (see Other Abbreviations) and the other publications listed in A. 101 to 122.

A constantly augmented collection of conciliar and postconciliar documents in their original languages and in Italian translation is published by Edizioni Dehoniane, Bologna, Italy. It is called *Enchiridion Vaticanum: Documenti, Il Concilio Vaticano II*. A collection of postconciliar documents is being published in several volumes by Les Editions Fides of Montreal, Canada, and Les Editions du Cerf, Paris, France, in the original languages and in French translation. It is called: *Pour construire L'Eglise Nouvelle: Normes d'application du Concile Vatican II et documents complementaries*. A well-known French translation of the council documents is published by Editions du Centurion, Paris, France: *Concile Oecumenique Vatican II: Documents Conciliares*, in four volumes. We have compared our translations of the council documents with the Italian and French versions mentioned above and with Father Walter Abbott's and other English versions.

I wish to thank those who have given us permission to use translations already published elsewhere. Most of the translations, however, were prepared under our own auspices, and these we have checked with the Italian versions published in *Enchiridion Vaticanum* and in the *Osservatore Romano*, and with the French versions published in the Fides and Cerf publication mentioned above.

The council documents are printed in the order of their promulgation, which is the order adopted by the official Latin publication listed above. This volume omits the Apostolic Constitution convening the council and the Apostolic Letter closing it. It also omits the papal addresses at the beginning and end of each session of the council and the papal addresses delivered during sessions. They are important documents, are included in the official Latin volume listed above, and they belong to the *Acta Conciliaria: conciliar proceedings*. For all that, they are not council documents, do not have the same importance or interest as the postconciliar documents which form part of the postconciliar process, and are easily accessible in Father Abbott's edition of the council documents. Their inclusion would have considerably increased the size of the present volume.

PRACTICAL POINTS TO REMEMBER IN USING THIS VOLUME

1. All documents are numbered consecutively. Larger documents have their own internal system of numbering, of paragraphs, sections or chapters. By combining the two (our own numbering on the documents and the documents' internal system of numbering) we have devised a simple system of reference. For example, D. *1*, 26, means Document no. 1 (The Constitution on the Sacred Liturgy), paragraph 26.

2. Documents in the descriptive catalogue (Appendix) are referred to as, for example, A. 35: Appendix, document no. 35.

3. If a reader comes across a reference in Latin to a document, the Latin will very often be the first words of the Latin original—it is a common way of referring to ecclesiastical documents. If he consults the Index of First Words of Documents at the end of this volume he will discover at once if it is listed in the descriptive catalogue or if it is one of the documents printed in this volume.

4. Each council document begins with the sonorous phrase: "Paul Bishop, Servant of the Servants of God, Together with the Council Fathers, For a permanent record." Each council document ends in the following fashion: "What has been set down in this (Constitution, Decree, Declaration) has been accepted by the Fathers of the Sacred Council in its entirety and in all its parts. And, together with the Venerable Council Fathers, we by the apostolic power granted to us by Christ, approve, decree and establish it, and we order that what has thus been established in synod be promulgated, for the glory of God." Then follow the place and date of promulgation: "Given at Rome, at St. Peter's, . . ." and the following: "I Paul, Bishop of the Catholic Church." The signatures of the other Fathers then follow. To save space, the above have been omitted from this volume, but the date of the promulgation of each document is given under its title.

5. The postconciliar documents also have a more elaborate introduction, giving the name of the Vatican depart-

ment issuing the document, and at the end the date, place of promulgation and the signatures of the prefect and Secretary of the department. We give the date of promulgation and the initials of the Roman department under the title of each document. The names of the Prefect and Secretary are omitted, however.

AUSTIN FLANNERY, O.P.
Editor of monthly review *Doctrine and Life*

Editor's note on second printing.

I have taken advantage of this second printing to correct errors which reviewers and readers have kindly pointed out. I have also made certain other changes and improvements. There are a number of changes in Father Clifford Howell's translation of the Constitution on the Roman Missal and of the Instruction which he himself had made but which had reached me too late for the first printing. They have been incorporated in this printing.

I have abandoned the rather cumbersome method of numeration used in *Eucharisticum mysterium* (it had been used in earlier editions of the English version), replacing it with the numeration used in the Latin original in the *Acta Apostolicae sedis.*

Further revision and updating will have to await the more thorough-going revision which a new edition would entail.

A. F.

Editor's note on the fourth printing, 1984.

The present edition incorporates a number of changes in liturgical documents to bring them in line with the "New Code Of Canon Law." It also has corrected a number of minor errors which readers have brought to my attention.

Austin Flannery, O.P.
Editor of monthly review
Doctrine and Life

PREFACE

It is a privilege to introduce by this brief prefatory note a major work of scholarship and of contribution to the bibliography and documentation on Vatican Council II.

The compendium is a unique collection of translations into English of Council documents, together with selected subsequent Roman documents which amplify, elucidate or apply the major themes of the Vatican Council constitutions, decrees and other major pronouncements.

The plan of the present book is simplicity itself and designed for the maximum service of the careful student or casual reader. Most of the collected translations of Council documents which have appeared in English have appeared in separate pamphlets or almost scattered and unrelated brochures. They have, moreover, appeared with little or no part of the subsequent official documentation which provides them with their context and something of the possibility of their intelligent implementation. In the present case we have a book which gives us each document in lucid, perceptive translation, followed by the more important subsequent official documentation; the document on the Liturgy, so often left hanging in the air, is brought down to cases and practice by many of the official instructions which followed upon it, notably those which admit of general application. The same principle of selectivity, yet comprehensiveness, has been followed in the choice of subsequent authoritative documents to follow up the documents on Ecumenism, the Religious Life, and others.

The critical apparatus of the volume makes for handiness and ready reference. The numbering of the documents is not the least of the features for which scholars will be deeply indebted to those who have planned this volume, a volume, I repeat, which is unique in its form and its excellency among books published in the English-speaking world and, so far as the present writer knows, in any other language.

The need for the book is crucial, not only for readers of English but for scholars generally. The immediate translations of the various Council documents were, of course, greatly needed as soon as possible after the publication of the original documents. But the very rapidity with which they appeared made them perhaps necessarily but certainly excessively hasty because of their frequent infelicities, not to say inaccuracies, in translation. The result was that their true worth was necessarily transient and, in some cases, they failed to communicate the permanent doctrinal and spiritual richness which the present translation, free from the journalistic touch inevitable in first translations and characterized by sober second thoughts and carefully measured words, manages to communicate admirably and effectively. In any case, the initial hasty translations are now largely superseded and the time has come for a work with an air of permanence, completeness and academic thoroughness.

A further limitation of some of the earlier translations is happily missing from the present work. In these first versions the Council documents were frequently accompanied by commentary or reactions usually friendly and helpful to further lines of independent thought, but frequently irrelevant and even confusing to one seeking to learn exactly what the Council *said* rather than what someone outside the Council *thought* about the matter. This new and extremely useful book suffers from no such obscurities or digressions; it is *the* collection of Council documents and their authentic interpretation that is indispensable for the serious student. If the volume is overdue, it is only because its preparation took as much time and work as has gone into the finished product. It deserves a wide and warm reception in libraries, at the hands of individual readers and wherever the message of the Council is needed and welcomed.

John Cardinal Wright

Vatican City, 1 October, 1974

1

THE CONSTITUTION ON THE SACRED LITURGY[a]

Sacrosanctum Concilium, 4 December, 1963

INTRODUCTION

1. The sacred Council has set out to impart an ever-increasing vigor to the Christian life of the faithful; to adapt more closely to the needs of our age those institutions which are subject to change; to foster whatever can promote union among all who believe in Christ; to strengthen whatever can help to call all mankind into the Church's fold. Accordingly it sees particularly cogent reasons for undertaking the reform and promotion of the liturgy.

2. For it is the liturgy through which, especially in the divine sacrifice of the Eucharist, "the work of our redemption is accomplished,"[1] and it is through the liturgy, especially, that the faithful are enabled to express in their lives and manifest to others the mystery of Christ and the real nature of the true Church. The Church is essentially both human and divine, visible but endowed with invisible realities, zealous in action and dedicated to contemplation, present in the world, but as a pilgrim, so constituted that in her the human is directed toward and subordinated to the divine, the visible to the invisible, action to contemplation, and this present world to that city yet to come, the object of our quest.[2] The liturgy daily builds up those who are in the Church, making of them a holy temple of the Lord, a dwelling-place for God in the Spirit,[3] to the mature mea-

---

a. This translation was made by the late Joseph Rodgers, bishop of Killaloe. It owes a great deal to the translation made by Clifford Howell, s.j. For this edition it has been considerably revised by A.F. The constitution was promulgated on 4 December, 1963.
1. Secret prayer of 9th Sunday after Pentecost.
2. Cf. Heb. 13:14.
3. Cf. Eph. 2:21-22.

1

sure of the fullness of Christ.[4] At the same time it marvelously increases their power to preach Christ and thus show forth the Church, a sign lifted up among the nations,[5] to those who are outside, a sign under which the scattered children of God may be gathered together[6] until there is one fold and one shepherd.[7]

3. That is why the sacred Council judges that the following principles concerning the promotion and reform of the liturgy should be called to mind, and that practical norms should be established.

Among these principles and norms there are some which can and should be applied both to the Roman rite and also to all the other rites. The practical norms which follow, however, should be taken as applying only to the Roman rite except for those which, in the very nature of things, affect other rites as well.

4. Finally, in faithful obedience to tradition, the sacred Council declares that Holy Mother Church holds all lawfully recognized rites to be of equal right and dignity; that she wishes to preserve them in the future and to foster them in every way. The Council also desires that, where necessary, the rites be revised carefully in the light of sound tradition, and that they be given new vigor to meet present-day circumstances and needs.

4. Cf. Eph. 4:13.
5. Cf. Jn. 11:12.
6. Cf Jn. 11:52.
7. Cf. Jn. 10:16.

CHAPTER I

GENERAL PRINCIPLES FOR THE RESTORATION AND PROMOTION OF THE SACRED LITURGY

I. THE NATURE OF THE SACRED LITURGY AND ITS IMPORTANCE IN THE LIFE OF THE CHURCH

5. God who "wills that all men be saved and come to the knowledge of the truth" (1 Tim. 2:4), "who in many times and various ways spoke of old to the fathers through the prophets" (Heb. 1:1), when the fullness of time had come sent his Son, the Word made flesh, anointed by the Holy Spirit, to preach the Gospel to the poor, to heal the contrite of heart,[8] to be a bodily and spiritual medicine:[9] the Mediator between God and man.[10] For his humanity united with the Person of the Word was the instrument of our salvation. Therefore, "in Christ the perfect achievement of our reconciliation came forth and the fullness of divine worship was given to us."[11]

The wonderful works of God among the people of the Old Testament were but a prelude to the work of Christ Our Lord in redeeming mankind and giving perfect glory to God. He achieved his task principally by the paschal mystery of his blessed passion, resurrection from the dead, and glorious ascension, whereby "dying, he destroyed our death, and rising, restored our life."[12] For it was from the side of Christ as he slept the sleep of death upon the cross that there came forth "the wondrous sacrament of the whole Church."[13]

8. Cf. Is. 61:1; Lk. 4–18.
9. Cf. St. Ignatius of Antioch: *Ad Ephesios*, 7:2.
10. Cf. 1 Tim. 2:5.
11. *Sacramentarium Veronese* (Leonianum).
12. Easter Preface of the Roman Missal.
13. Prayer before Second Lesson of Holy Saturday (Roman Missal, before restoration).

3

6. Accordingly, just as Christ was sent by the Father so also he sent the apostles, filled with the Holy Spirit. This he did so that they might preach the Gospel to every creature[14] and proclaim that the Son of God by his death and resurrection had freed us from the power of Satan[15] and from death, and brought us into the Kingdom of his Father. But he also willed that the work of salvation which they preached should be set in train through the sacrifice and sacraments, around which the entire liturgical life revolves. Thus by Baptism men are grafted into the paschal mystery of Christ; they die with him, are buried with him, and rise with him.[16] They receive the spirit of adoption as sons "in which we cry, Abba, Father" (Rom. 8:15) and thus become true adorers such as the Father seeks.[17] In like manner as often as they eat the Supper of the Lord they proclaim the death of the Lord until he comes.[18] That was why on the very day of Pentecost when the Church appeared before the world those "who received the word" of Peter "were baptized." And "they continued steadfastly in the teaching of the apostles and in the communion of the breaking of bread and in prayers . . . praising God and being in favor with all the people" (Acts 2:41–47). From that time onward the Church has never failed to come together to celebrate the paschal mystery, reading those things "which were in all the scriptures concerning him" (Lk. 24:27), celebrating the Eucharist in which "the victory and triumph of his death are again made present,"[19] and at the same time "giving thanks to God for his inexpressible gift" (2 Cor. 9:15) in Christ Jesus, "in praise of his glory" (Eph. 1:12) through the power of the Holy Spirit.

7. To accomplish so great a work Christ is always present in his Church, especially in her liturgical celebrations. He is present in the Sacrifice of the Mass not only in the person of his minister, "the same now offering, through the ministry of priests, who formerly offered himself on the

14. Cf. Mk. 16:15.
15. Cf. Acts 26:18.
16. Cf. Rom. 6:4; Eph. 2:6; Col 3:1; 2 Tim. 2:11.
17. Cf. Jn. 4–23.
18. Cf. 1 Cor. 2:26.
19. Council of Trent, Session 23: Decree on the Holy Eucharist, ch. 5.

cross,"[20] but especially in the eucharistic species. By his power he is present in the sacraments so that when anybody baptizes it is really Christ himself who baptizes.[21] He is present in his word since it is he himself who speaks when the holy scriptures are read in the Church. Lastly, he is present when the Church prays and sings, for he has promised "where two or three are gathered together in my name there am I in the midst of them" (Mt. 18:20).

Christ, indeed, always associates the Church with himself in this great work in which God is perfectly glorified and men are sanctified. The Church is his beloved Bride who calls to her Lord, and through him offers worship to the eternal Father.

The liturgy, then, is rightly seen as an exercise of the priestly office of Jesus Christ. It involves the presentation of man's sanctification under the guise of signs perceptible by the senses and its accomplishment in ways appropriate to each of these signs. In it full public worship is performed by the Mystical Body of Jesus Christ, that is, by the Head and his members.

From this it follows that every liturgical celebration, because it is an action of Christ the Priest and of his Body, which is the Church, is a sacred action surpassing all others. No other action of the Church can equal its efficacy by the same title and to the same degree.[b]

8. In the earthly liturgy we take part in a foretaste of that heavenly liturgy which is celebrated in the Holy City of Jerusalem toward which we journey as pilgrims, where Christ is sitting at the right hand of God, Minister of the holies and of the true tabernacle.[22] With all the warriors of the heavenly army we sing a hymn of glory to the Lord; venerating the memory of the saints, we hope for some part and fellowship with them; we eagerly await the Saviour, Our Lord Jesus Christ, until he our life shall appear and we too will appear with him in glory.[23]

---

20. Council of Trent, Session 22: Doctrine on the Holy Sacrifice of the Mass, ch. 2.
21. Cf. St. Augustine, *Tractatus in Ioannem VI*, ch. 1, n. 7.
b. The sense of these words is that no other action can lay claim to derive its value from so close a relation to the action of Christ or to procure such rich fruits.
22. Cf. Apoc. 21:2; Col. 3:1; Heb. 8:2.
23. Cf. Phil. 3:20; Col. 3:4.

9. The sacred liturgy does not exhaust the entire activity of the Church. Before men can come to the liturgy they must be called to faith and to conversion. "How then are they to call upon him in whom they have not believed? And how are they to believe in him of whom they have not heard? And how are they to hear without a preacher? And how are men to preach unless they be sent?" (Rom. 10:14–15).

Therefore the Church announces the good tidings of salvation to those who do not believe, so that all men may know the one true God and Jesus Christ whom he has sent and may be converted from their ways, doing penance.[24] To believers also the Church must ever preach faith and penance; she must prepare them for the sacraments, teach them to observe all that Christ has commanded,[25] and encourage them to engage in all the works of charity, piety and the apostolate, thus making it clear that Christ's faithful, though not of this world, are to be the lights of the world and are to glorify the Father before men.

10. Nevertheless the liturgy is the summit toward which the activity of the Church is directed; it is also the fount from which all her power flows. For the goal of apostolic endeavor is that all who are made sons of God by faith and baptism should come together to praise God in the midst of his Church, to take part in the Sacrifice and to eat the Lord's Supper.

The liturgy, in its turn, moves the faithful filled with "the paschal sacraments" to be "one in holiness";[26] it prays that "they hold fast in their lives to what they have grasped by their faith."[27] The renewal in the Eucharist of the covenant between the Lord and man draws the faithful and sets them aflame with Christ's insistent love. From the liturgy, therefore, and especially from the Eucharist, grace is poured forth upon us as from a fountain, and the sanctification of men in Christ and the glorification of God to which all other activities of the Church are directed, as toward their end, are achieved with maximum effectiveness.

11. But in order that the liturgy may be able to produce its full effects it is necessary that the faithful come to it with proper dispositions, that their minds be attuned to

24. Cf. Jn. 17:3; Lk. 24:27; Acts 2:38.
25. Cf. Mt. 28:20.
26. Postcommunion for both Masses of Easter Sunday.
27. Collect for Mass of Tuesday of Easter Week.

their voices, and that they cooperate with heavenly grace lest they receive it in vain.[28] Pastors of souls must, therefore, realize that, when the liturgy is celebrated, something more is required than the laws governing valid and lawful celebration. It is their duty also to ensure that the faithful take part fully aware of what they are doing, actively engaged in the rite and enriched by it.

12. The spiritual life, however, is not limited solely to participation in the liturgy. The Christian is indeed called to pray with others, but he must also enter into his bedroom to pray to his Father in secret;[29] furthermore, according to the teaching of the apostle, he must pray without ceasing.[30] We also learn from the same apostle that we must always carry around in our bodies the dying of Jesus, so that the life also of Jesus may be made manifest in our mortal Flesh.[31] That is why we beg the Lord in the Sacrifice of the Mass that "receiving the offering of the Spiritual Victim" he may fashion us for himself "as an eternal gift."[32]

13. Popular devotions of the Christian people, provided they conform to the laws and norms of the Church, are to be highly recommended, especially where they are ordered by the Apostolic See.

Devotions proper to individual churches also have a special dignity if they are undertaken by order of the bishops according to customs or books lawfully approved.

But such devotions should be so drawn up that they harmonize with the liturgical seasons, accord with the sacred liturgy, are in some way derived from it, and lead the people to it, since in fact the liturgy by its very nature is far superior to any of them.

II. THE PROMOTION OF LITURGICAL INSTRUCTION AND ACTIVE PARTICIPATION

14. Mother Church earnestly desires that all the faithful should be led to that full, conscious, and active participation in liturgical celebrations which is demanded by the very nature of the liturgy, and to which the Christian people, "a chosen race, a royal priesthood, a holy nation, a re-

---

28. Cf. 2 Cor. 6:1.
29. Cf. Mt. 6:6.
30. Cf. 1 Th. 5:17.
31. Cf. 2 Cor. 4:10–11.
32. Secret for Monday of Pentecost Week.

deemed people" (1 Pet. 2:9, 4–5) have a right and obligation by reason of their baptism.

In the restoration and promotion of the sacred liturgy the full and active participation by all the people is the aim to be considered before all else, for it is the primary and indispensable source from which the faithful are to derive the true Christian spirit. Therefore, in all their apostolic activity, pastors of souls should energetically set about achieving it through the requisite pedagogy.

Yet it would be futile to entertain any hope of realizing this unless pastors of souls, in the first place, themselves become fully imbued with the spirit and power of the liturgy and capable of giving instruction about it. Thus it is absolutely essential, first of all, that steps be taken to ensure the liturgical training of the clergy. For that reason the sacred Council has decided on the following enactments:

15. Professors who are appointed to teach liturgy in seminaries, religious houses of studies, and theological faculties, must be properly trained for their work in institutes which specialize in this subject.

16. The study of sacred liturgy is to be ranked among the compulsory and major courses in seminaries and religious houses of studies. In theological faculties is it to rank among the principal courses. It is to be taught under its theological, historical, spiritual, pastoral, and juridical aspects. In addition, those who teach other subjects, especially dogmatic theology, sacred scripture, spiritual and pastoral theology, should—each of them submitting to the exigencies of his own discipline—expound the mystery of Christ and the history of salvation in a manner that will clearly set forth the connection between their subjects and the liturgy, and the unity which underlies all priestly training.

17. In seminaries and religious houses, clerics shall be given a liturgical formation in their spiritual lives. For this they will need a proper initiation, enabling them to understand the sacred rites and participate in them wholeheartedly. They will also need to celebrate the sacred mysteries and popular devotions which are imbued with the spirit of the sacred liturgy. Likewise they must learn to observe the liturgical laws so that life in seminaries and religious institutes may be thoroughly influenced by the liturgical spirit.

18. Priests, both secular and religious, who are already working in the Lord's vineyard, are to be helped by every suitable means to a fuller understanding of what they are

about when they perform sacred rites, to live the liturgical life and to share it with the faithful entrusted to their care.

19. With zeal and patience pastors of souls must promote the liturgical instruction of the faithful and also their active participation, both internal and external, taking into account their age, condition, way of life and standard of religious culture. By so doing pastors will be fulfilling one of the chief duties of a faithful dispenser of the mysteries of God, and in this matter they must lead their flock not only by word but also by example.

20. Transmission of the sacred rites by radio and television, especially in the case of Mass, shall be done with delicacy and dignity. A suitable person, appointed by the bishops, should direct it and have the responsibility for it.

III. THE REFORM OF THE SACRED LITURGY

21. In order that the Christian people may more certainly derive an abundance of graces from the sacred liturgy, holy Mother Church desires to undertake with great care a general restoration of the liturgy itself. For the liturgy is made up of unchangeable elements divinely instituted, and of elements subject to change. These latter not only may be changed but ought to be changed with the passage of time, if they have suffered from the intrusion of anything out of harmony with the inner nature of the liturgy or have become less suitable. In this restoration both texts and rites should be drawn up so as to express more clearly the holy things which they signify. The Christian people, as far as is possible, should be able to understand them with ease and take part in them fully, actively, and as a community.

Therefore, the sacred Council establishes the following general norms:

A. General Norms

22. (1) Regulation of the sacred liturgy depends solely on the authority of the Church, that is, on the Apostolic See, and, as laws may determine, on the bishop.

(2) In virtue of power conceded by law, the regulation of the liturgy within certain defined limites belongs also to various kinds of bishops' conferences, legitimately established, with competence in given territories.

(3) Therefore no other person, not even a priest, may

add, remove, or change anything in the liturgy on his own authority.

23. In order that sound tradition be retained, and yet the way remain open to legitimate progress, a careful investigation—theological, historical, and pastoral—should always be made into each part of the liturgy which is to be revised. Furthermore the general laws governing the structure and meaning of the liturgy must be studied in conjunction with the experience derived from recent liturgical reforms and from the indults granted to various places.

Finally, there must be no innovations unless the good of the Church genuinely and certainly requires them, and care must be taken that any new forms adopted should in some way grow organically from forms already existing.

As far as possible, notable differences between the rites used in adjacent regions should be avoided.

24. Sacred scripture is of the greatest importance in the celebration of the liturgy. For it is from it that lessons are read and explained in the homily, and psalms are sung. It is from the scriptures that the prayers, collects, and hymns draw their inspiration and their force, and that actions and signs derive their meaning. Hence in order to achieve the restoration, progress, and adaptation of the sacred liturgy it is essential to promote that sweet and living love for sacred scripture to which the venerable tradition of Eastern and Western rites gives testimony.

25. The liturgical books are to be revised as soon as possible. Experts are to be employed on this task, and bishops from various parts of the world are to be consulted.

B. Norms Drawn from the Hierarchic and Communal Nature of the Liturgy

26. Liturgical services are not private functions but are celebrations of the Church which is "the sacrament of unity," namely, "the holy people united and arranged under their bishops."[33]

Therefore, liturgical services pertain to the whole Body of the Church. They manifest it, and have effects upon it. But they also touch individual members of the Church in different ways, depending on their orders, their role in the liturgical services, and their actual participation in them.

33. St. Cyprian, "On the Unity of the Catholic Church," 7; cf. Letter 66, n. 8, 3.

27. It must be emphasized that rites which are meant to be celebrated in common, with the faithful present and actively participating, should as far as possible be celebrated in that way rather than by an individual and quasi-privately.

This applies with special force to the celebration of Mass (even though every Mass has of itself a public and social nature) and to the administration of the sacraments.

28. In liturgical celebrations each person, minister, or layman who has an office to perform, should carry out all and only those parts which pertain to his office by the nature of the rite and the norms of the liturgy.

29. Servers, readers, commentators, and members of the choir also exercise a genuine liturgical function. They ought, therefore, to discharge their offices with the sincere piety and decorum demanded by so exalted a ministry and rightly expected of them by God's people.

Consequently they must all be deeply imbued with the spirit of the liturgy, each in his own measure, and they must be trained to perform their functions in a correct and orderly manner.

30. To promote active participation, the people should be encouraged to take part by means of acclamations, responses, psalms, antiphons, hymns, as well as by actions, gestures and bodily attitudes. And at the proper time a reverent silence should be observed.

31. When the liturgical books are being revised, the people's parts must be carefully indicated by the rubrics.

32. In the liturgy, apart from the distinctions arising from liturgical function or sacred orders and apart from the honors due to civil authorities in accordance with liturgical law, no special exception is to be made for any private persons or classes of persons whether in the ceremonies or by external display.

C. Norms Based on the Educative and Pastoral Nature of the Liturgy

33. Although the sacred liturgy is principally the worship of the divine majesty it likewise contains much instruction for the faithful.[34] For in the liturgy God speaks to his peo-

34. Cf. Council of Trent, Session 22: Doctrine on the Holy Sacrifice of the Mass, ch. 8.

ple, and Christ is still proclaiming his Gospel. And the people reply to God both by song and prayer.

Moreover the prayers addressed to God by the priest who, in the person of Christ, presides over the assembly, are said in the name of the entire holy people and of all present. And the visible signs which the sacred liturgy uses to signify invisible divine things have been chosen by Christ or by the Church. Thus not only when things are read "which were written for our instruction" (Rom. 15:4), but also when the Church prays or sings or acts, the faith of those taking part is nourished, and their minds are raised to God so that they may offer him their spiritual homage[c] and receive his grace more abundantly.

Therefore in the revision of the liturgy the following general norms should be observed:

34. The rites should be distinguished by a noble simplicity. They should be short, clear, and free from useless repetitions. They should be within the people's powers of comprehension, and normally should not require much explanation.

35. That the intimate connection between rite and words may be apparent in the liturgy:

(1) In sacred celebrations a more ample, more varied, and more suitable reading from sacred scripture should be restored.

(2) The most suitable place for a sermon ought to be indicated in the rubrics, for a sermon is part of the liturgical action whenever a rite involves one. The ministry of preaching is to be fulfilled most faithfully and carefully. The sermon, moreover, should draw its content mainly from scriptural and liturgical sources, for it is the proclamation of God's wonderful works in the history of salvation, which is the mystery of Christ ever made present and active in us, especially in the celebration of the liturgy.

(3) Instruction which is more explicitly liturgical should also be given in a variety of ways. If necessary, short directives to be spoken by the priest or competent minister should be provided within the rites themselves. But

c. The Latin has *rationabile obsequium*, which is often translated as "rational service" or "reasonable service" or "the worship which reason requires." We here follow the authoritative French version, *hommage spirituel*, of the *Centre de Pastorale Liturgique*.

they should be given only at suitable moments and in prescribed words or their equivalent.

(4) Bible services should be encouraged, especially on the vigils of the more solemn feasts, on some weekdays of Advent and Lent, and on Sundays and holidays, especially in places where no priest is available. In this case a deacon or some other person authorized by the bishop should preside over the celebration.

36. (1) The use of the Latin language, with due respect to particular law, is to be preserved in the Latin rites. (2) But since the use of the vernacular,[d] whether in the Mass, the administration of the sacraments, or in other parts of the liturgy, may frequently be of great advantage to the people, a wider use may be made of it, especially in readings, directives and in some prayers and chants. Regulations governing this will be given separately in subsequent chapters.

(3) These norms being observed, it is for the competent territorial ecclesiastical authority mentioned in Article 22:2, to decide whether, and to what extent, the vernacular language is to be used. Its decrees have to be approved, that is, confirmed, by the Apostolic See. Where circumstances warrant it, it is to consult with bishops of neighboring regions which have the same language.

(4) Translations from the Latin for use in the liturgy must be approved by the competent territorial ecclesiastical authority already mentioned.

D. Norms for Adapting the Liturgy to the Temperament and Traditions of Peoples

37. Even in the liturgy the Church does not wish to impose a rigid uniformity in matters which do not involve the faith or the good of the whole community. Rather does she respect and foster the qualities and talents of the various races and nations. Anything in these people's way of life which is not indissolubly bound up with superstition and error she studies with sympathy, and, if possible, preserves intact. She sometimes even admits such things into the liturgy itself, provided they harmonize with its true and authentic spirit.

d. See "The Postconciliar Documents on the Liturgy: Introduction," *The Growth of the Vernacular.*

38. Provided that the substantial unity of the Roman rite is preserved, provision shall be made, when revising the liturgical books, for legitimate variations and adaptations to different groups, regions and peoples, especially in mission countries. This should be borne in mind when drawing up the rites and determining rubrics.

39. Within the limits set by the typical editions of the liturgical books it shall be for the competent territorial ecclesiastical authority mentioned in Article 22:2, to specify adaptations, especially as regards the administration of the sacraments, sacramentals, processions, liturgical language, sacred music and the arts, according, however, to the fundamental norms laid down in this Constitution.

40. In some places and circumstances, however, an even more radical adaptation of the liturgy is needed, and this entails greater difficulties. For this reason:

(1) The competent territorial ecclesiastical authority mentioned in Article 22:2, must in this matter, carefully and prudently consider which elements from the traditions and cultures of individual peoples might appropriately be admitted into divine worship. Adaptations which are considered useful or necessary should then be submitted to the Holy See, by whose consent they may be introduced.

(2) To ensure that adaptations may be made with all the circumspection necessary, the Apostolic See will grant power to this same territorial ecclesiastical authority to permit and to direct, as the case requires, the necessary preliminary experiments over a determined period of time among certain groups suitable for the purpose.

(3) Because liturgical laws usually involve special difficulties with respect to adaptation, especially in mission lands, men who are experts in the matters in question must be employed to formulate them.

E. Promotion of the Liturgical Life in Diocese and Parish

41. The bishop is to be considered as the High Priest of his flock from whom the life in Christ of his faithful is in some way derived and upon whom it in some way depends.

Therefore all should hold in the greatest esteem the liturgical life of the diocese centered around the bishop, especially in his cathedral church. They must be convinced that the principal manifestation of the Church consists in the full, active participation of all God's holy people in the same liturgical celebrations, especially in the same Eucharist, in one prayer, at one altar, at which the bishop presides, surrounded by his college of priests and by his ministers.[35]

42. But as it is impossible for the bishop always and everywhere to preside over the whole flock in his church, he must of necessity establish groupings of the faithful; and, among these, parishes, set up locally under a pastor who takes the place of the bishop, are the most important, for in some way they represent the visible Church constituted throughout the world.

Therefore the liturgical life of the parish and its relation to the bishop must be fostered in the spirit and practice of the laity and clergy. Efforts must also be made to encourage a sense of community within the parish, above all in the common celebration of the Sunday Mass.

F. Promotion of Pastoral Liturgical Action

43. Zeal for the promotion and restoration of the sacred liturgy is rightly held to be a sign of the providential dispositions of God in our time, and as a movement of the Holy Spirit in his Church. It is today a distinguishing mark of the life of the Church, and, indeed, of the whole tenor of contemporary religious thought and action.

Therefore, so that this pastoral liturgical action may become still more vigorous in the Church the sacred Council decrees:

44. It is desirable that the competent territorial ecclesiastical authority mentioned in Article 22:2 set up a liturgical commission to be assisted by experts in liturgical science, sacred music, art and pastoral practice. As far as possible the commission should be aided by some kind of Institute for Pastoral Liturgy, consisting of people who are eminent in these matters, not excluding laymen, if circumstances so demand. It will be the task of this commission, under the direction of the above-mentioned competent territorial ecclesiastical authority (see Article 22:2), to regulate pastoral liturgical action throughout the territory, and to promote studies and necessary experiments whenever there is a question of adaptations to be proposed to the Holy See.

35. Cf. St. Ignatius of Antioch: *Magnesians*, 7; *Philadelphians*, 4; *Smyrnaeans*, 8.

45. For the same reason every diocese is to have a commission on the sacred liturgy, under the direction of the bishop, for promoting the liturgical apostolate.

Sometimes it may be expedient that several dioceses should form between them one single commission which will be able to promote the liturgy by common consultation.

46. In addition to the commission on sacred liturgy, every diocese, as far as possible, should have commissions for sacred music and sacred art.

These three commissions must work in the closest collaboration. Indeed it will often be best to fuse the three of them into one single commission.

CHAPTER II

THE MOST SACRED MYSTERY OF THE EUCHARIST

47. At the Last Supper, on the night he was betrayed, our Savior instituted the eucharistic sacrifice of his Body and Blood. This he did in order to perpetuate the sacrifice of the Cross throughout the ages until he should come again, and so to entrust to his beloved Spouse, the Church, a memorial of his death and resurrection: a sacrament of love, a sign of unity, a bond of charity,[36] a paschal banquet in which Christ is consumed, the mind is filled with grace, and a pledge of future glory is given to us.[37]

48. The Church, therefore, earnestly desires that Christ's faithful, when present at this mystery of faith, should not be there as strangers or silent spectators. On the contrary, through a good understanding of the rites and prayers they should take part in the sacred action, conscious of what they are doing, with devotion and full collaboration. They

36. Cf. St. Augustine, *Tractatus in Ioannis Evangelium*, ch. 6, n. 13.
37. Roman Breviary: Feast of Corpus Christi, Second Vespers, Antiphon to Magnificat.

should be instructed by God's word, and be nourished at the table of the Lord's Body. They should give thanks to God. Offering the immaculate victim, not only through the hands of the priest but also together with him, they should learn to offer themselves. Through Christ, the Mediator,[38] they should be drawn day by day into ever more perfect union with God and each other, so that finally God may be all in all.

49. For this reason the sacred Council having in mind those Masses which are celebrated with the faithful assisting, especially on Sundays and holidays of obligation, has made the following decrees so that the sacrifice of the Mass, even in the ritual forms (of its celebration) may have full pastoral efficacy.

DECREES

50. The rite of the Mass is to be revised in such a way that the intrinsic nature and purpose of its several parts, as well as the connection between them, may be more clearly manifested, and that devout and active participation by the faithful may be more easily achieved.

For this purpose the rites are to be simplified, due care being taken to preserve their substance. Parts which with the passage of time came to be duplicated, or were added with little advantage, are to be omitted. Other parts which suffered loss through accidents of history are to be restored to the vigor they had in the days of the holy Fathers, as may seem useful or necessary.[e]

51. The treasures of the Bible are to be opened up more lavishly so that a richer fare may be provided for the faithful at the table of God's word.[f] In this way a more representative part of the sacred scriptures will be read to the people in the course of a prescribed number of years.

52. By means of the homily the mysteries of the faith and the guiding principles of the Christian life are expound-

38. Cf. St. Cyril of Alexandria: "Commentary on the Gospel of St. John," Book 11, ch. 11–12.

e. Over the next eleven years the revised rites were published. See A. 55, 61, 64, 65, 68, 70, 72, 74, 76, 109, 112, 114, 138.

f. The directives for the revised series of readings were promulgated 25 May, 1969. Volume I of the new Lectionary itself was published, in Latin, on 30 September 1970, and the remaining two volumes in 1971 and 1972. Many vernacular publications of the Lectionary—following the directives of 25 May 1969—appeared earlier.

ed from the sacred text during the course of the liturgical year. The homily, therefore, is to be highly esteemed as part of the liturgy itself. In fact at those Masses which are celebrated on Sundays and holidays of obligation, with the people assisting, it should not be omitted except for a serious reason.

53. The "common prayer" or "prayer of the faithful" is to be restored after the gospel and homily, especially on Sundays and holidays of obligation. By this prayer in which the people are to take part, intercession will be made for holy Church, for the civil authorities, for those oppressed by various needs, for all mankind, and for the salvation of the entire world.[39]

54. A suitable place may be allotted to the vernacular in Masses which are celebrated with the people, especially in the readings and "the common prayer," and also, as local conditions may warrant, in those parts which pertain to the people, according to the rules laid down in Article 36 of this Constitution.

Nevertheless care must be taken to ensure that the faithful may also be able to say or sing together in Latin those parts of the Ordinary of the Mass which pertain to them.

Wherever a more extended use of the vernacular in the Mass seems desirable, the regulation laid down in Article 40 of this Constitution is to be observed.[g]

55. The more perfect form of participation in the Mass whereby the faithful, after the priest's communion, receive the Lord's Body from the same sacrifice, is warmly recommended.

The dogmatic principles which were laid down by the Council of Trent remaining intact,[40] communion under both kinds may be granted when the bishops think fit, not only to clerics and religious but also to the laity, in cases to be determined by the Apostolic See. For example,

To the newly ordained in the Mass of their ordination;
To the newly professed in the Mass of their religious profession;
To the newly baptized in the Mass which follows their baptism.

39. Cf. 1 Tim. 2:1–2.
g. See "The Postconciliar Document on the Liturgy: Introduction," *The Growth of the Vernacular.*
40. Council of Trent, Session 21: On Communion under Both Species, ch. 1–3.

56. The two parts which in a sense go to make up the Mass, viz. the liturgy of the word and the eucharistic liturgy, are so closely connected with each other that they form but one single act of worship. Accordingly this sacred Synod strongly urges pastors of souls that, when instructing the faithful, they insistently teach them to take their part in the entire Mass, especially on Sundays and holidays of obligation.

57. (1) Concelebration whereby the unity of the priesthood is appropriately manifested has remained in use to this day in the Church both in the East and in the West. For this reason it has seemed good to the Council to extend permission for celebration to the following cases:

1. (a) On the Thursday of the Lord's Supper (not only at the Mass of the Chrism, but also at the evening Mass.

(b) At Masses during Councils, Bishops' Conferences and Synods.

(c) At the Mass for the Blessing of an abbot.

2. Also, with permission of the Ordinary, to whom it belongs to decide whether concelebration is opportune:

(a) at conventual Mass, and at the principal Mass in churches, when the needs of the faithful do not require that all the priests available should celebrate individually;

(b) at Mass celebrated at any kind of priests' meetings whether the priests be secular or religious.

(2) 1. The regulation, however, of the discipline of concelebration in the diocese pertains to the bishop.

2. Each priest shall always retain his right to celebrate Mass individually, though not at the same time in the same church as a concelebrated Mass nor on the Thursday of the Lord's Supper.

58. A new rite for concelebration is to be drawn up and inserted into the Pontifical and into the Roman Missal.

CHAPTER III

THE OTHER SACRAMENTS AND THE SACRAMENTALS

59. The purpose of the sacraments is to sanctify men, to build up the Body of Christ, and, finally, to give worship to God. Because they are signs they also instruct. They not only presuppose faith, but by words and objects they also nourish, strengthen, and express it. That is why they are called "sacraments of faith." They do, indeed, confer grace, but, in addition, the very act of celebrating them most effectively disposes the faithful to receive this grace to their profit, to worship God duly, and to practise charity.

It is, therefore, of the greatest importance that the faithful should easily understand the sacramental signs, and should eagerly frequent those sacraments which were instituted to nourish the Christian life.

60. Holy Mother Church has, moreover, instituted sacramentals. These are sacred signs which bear a resemblance to the sacraments. They signify effects, particularly of a spiritual nature, which are obtained through the Church's intercession. By them men are disposed to receive the chief effect of the sacraments, and various occasions in life are rendered holy.

61. Thus, for well-disposed members of the faithful the liturgy of the sacraments and sacramentals sanctifies almost every event of their lives with the divine grace which flows from the paschal mystery of the Passion, Death and Resurrection of Christ. From this source all sacraments and sacramentals draw their power. There is scarcely any proper use of material things which cannot thus be directed toward the sanctification of men and the praise of God.

62. With the passage of time, however, there have crept into the rites of the sacraments and sacramentals certain features which have rendered their nature and purpose far from clear to the people of today. Hence some changes are necessary to adapt them to present-day needs.[h] For that reason the sacred Council decrees as follows concerning their revision:

h. See footnote (e) above.

63. Because the use of the vernacular[1] in the administration of the sacraments and sacramentals can often be of very great help to the people, this use is to be extended according to the following norms:

(a) In the administration of the sacraments and sacramentals the vernacular may be used according to the norm of Article 36.

(b) The competent territorial ecclesiastical authority designated in Article 22:2 of this Constitution shall forthwith prepare, in accordance with the new edition of the Roman Ritual, local rituals adapted linguistically and otherwise to the needs of the different regions. These rituals, on authentication by the Apostolic See, are to be followed in the regions in question. But in drawing up those rituals or particular collections of rites, the instructions prefixed to the individual rites in the Roman Ritual, whether they be pastoral and rubrical or whether they have a special social import, shall not be omitted.

64. The catechumenate for adults, comprising several distinct steps, is to be restored and brought into use at the discretion of the local ordinary. By this means the time of the catechumenate, which is intended as a period of suitable instruction, may be sanctified by sacred rites to be celebrated at successive intervals of time.

65. In mission countries, in addition to what is furnished by the Christian tradition, those elements of initiation rites may be admitted which are already in use among some peoples insofar as they can be adapted to the Christian ritual in accordance with Articles 37–40 of this Constitution.

66. Both rites for the baptism of adults are to be revised, not only the simpler rite but also, taking into consideration the restored catechumenate, the more solemn rite. A special Mass "For the conferring of Baptism" is to be inserted into the Roman Missal.

67. The rite for the baptism of infants is to be revised, its revision taking into account the fact that those to be baptized are infants. The roles of parents and godparents, and also their duties, should be brought out more clearly in the rite itself.

68. The baptismal rite should contain variants, to be used at the discretion of the local ordinary when a large number

i. See "The Postconciliar Documents on the Liturgy: Introduction." *The Growth of the Vernacular.*

are to be baptized. Likewise a shorter rite is to be drawn up, especially for mission countries which catechists, and also the faithful in general, may use when there is danger of death and neither priest nor deacon is available.

69. In place of the rite called "Rite for supplying what was omitted in the baptism of an infant" a new rite is to be drawn up. This rite should indicate more fittingly and clearly that the infant baptized by the short rite has already been received into the Church.

So also a new rite is to be drawn up for converts who have already been validly baptized. It should indicate that they are now admitted to communion with the Church.

70. Baptismal water, outside of paschal time, may be blessed within the rite of Baptism itself by an approved shorter formula.

71. The rite of Confirmation is to be revised also so that the intimate connection of this sacrament with the whole of the Christian initiation may more clearly appear. For this reason the renewal of baptismal promises should fittingly precede the reception of this sacrament.

Confirmation may be conferred within Mass when convenient. For conferring outside Mass, a formula introducing the rite should be drawn up.

72. The rite and formulae of Penance are to be revised so that they more clearly express both the nature and effect of the sacrament.

73. "Extreme Unction," which may also and more fittingly be called "Anointing of the Sick," is not a sacrament for those only who are at the point of death. Hence, as soon as anyone of the faithful begins to be in danger of death from sickness or old age, the fitting time for him to receive this sacrament has certainly already arrived.

74. In addition to the separate rites for Anointing of the Sick and for Viaticum, a continuous rite shall be prepared in which a sick man is anointed after he has made his confession and before he receives Viaticum.

75. The number of the anointings is to be adapted to the occasion, and the prayers which belong to the rite of Anointing are to be revised so as to correspond to the varying conditions of the sick who receive the sacrament.

76. Both the ceremonies and texts of the Ordination rites are to be revised. The addresses given by the bishop at the beginning of each ordination or consecration may be in the vernacular.

In the consecration of a bishop the laying on of hands may be done by all the bishops present.

77. The Marriage rite now found in the Roman Ritual is to be revised and enriched so that it will more clearly signify the grace of the sacrament and will emphasize the spouses' duties.

"If any regions use other praiseworthy customs and ceremonies when celebrating the sacrament of Matrimony the sacred Synod earnestly desires that these by all means be retained."[41]

Moreover, an ecclesiastical authority having the territorial competence described in Article 22:2 of this Constitution is free to draw up its own rite suited to its people and region, according to the provisions of Article 63, but on the express condition that the priest assisting at the marriage ask for and obtain the consent of the contracting parties.

78. Matrimony is normally to be celebrated within the Mass after the reading of the gospel and the homily and before "the prayer of the faithful." The prayer for the bride, duly amended to remind both spouses of their equal obligation of mutual fidelity, may be said in the vernacular.

But if the sacrament of Matrimony is celebrated apart from Mass, the epistle and gospel from the nuptial Mass are to be read at the beginning of the rite, and the blessing should always be given to the spouses.

79. The sacramentals are to be revised, account being taken of the primary principle of enabling the faithful to participate intelligently, actively, and easily. The circumstances of our times must also be considered. When rituals are being revised as laid down in Article 63, new sacramentals may also be added as necessity requires.

Reserved blessings shall be very few. Reservations shall be in favor only of bishops or ordinaries.

Provision should be made for the administration of some sacramentals, at least in special circumstances and at the discretion of the ordinary, by qualified lay persons.

80. The rite of the Consecration of Virgins contained in the Roman Pontifical is to be revised.

Moreover a rite of religious profession and renewal of vows shall be drawn in order to achieve greater unity, sobriety, and dignity. Apart from special exceptions granted

41. Council of Trent, Session 24: On Reform, ch. 1. Cf. Roman Ritual, Title 8, ch. 2, n. 6.

by law, this rite should be adopted by those who make their profession or renewal of vows within the Mass.

It is recommended that religious profession be made within the Mass.

81. Funeral rites should express more clearly the paschal character of Christian death, and should correspond more closely to the circumstances and traditions found in various regions. This also applies to the liturgical color to be used.

82. The rite for the Burial of Infants is to be revised, and a special Mass for the occasion should be provided.

Chapter IV

THE DIVINE OFFICE

83. Jesus Christ, High Priest of the New and Eternal Covenant, taking human nature, introduced into this earthly exile that hymn which is sung throughout all ages in the halls of heaven. He attaches to himself the entire community of mankind and has them join him in singing his divine song of praise.

For he continues his priestly work through his Church. The Church, by celebrating the Eucharist and by other means, especially the celebration of the divine office, is ceaselessly engaged in praising the Lord and interceding for the salvation of the entire world.

84. The divine office, in keeping with ancient Christian tradition, is so devised that the whole course of the day and night is made holy by the praise of God. Therefore, when this wonderful song of praise is correctly celebrated by priests and others deputed to it by the Church, or by the faithful praying together with a priest in the approved form, then it is truly the voice of the Bride herself addressed to her Bridegroom. It is the very prayer which Christ himself together with his Body addresses to the Father.

85. Hence all who take part in the divine office are not

only performing a duty for the Church, they are also sharing in what is the greatest honor for Christ's Bride; for by offering these praises to God they are standing before God's throne in the name of the Church, their Mother.

86. Priests who are engaged in the sacred pastoral ministry will pray the divine office the more fervently, the more alive they are to the need to heed St. Paul's exhortation, "Pray without ceasing" (1 Th. 5:17). For only the Lord, who said, "Without me you can do nothing," can make their work effective and fruitful. That is why the apostles when instituting deacons said, "We will devote ourselves to prayer and to the ministry of the word" (Acts 6:4).

87. In order that the divine office may be better and more perfectly prayed, whether by priests or by other members of the Church, in existing circumstances, the sacred Council, continuing the restoration so happily begun by the Apostolic See, decrees as follows concerning the office of the Roman rite:

88. Since the purpose of the office is to sanctify the day, the traditional sequence of the hours is to be restored so that, as far as possible, they may again become also in fact what they have been in name.[j] At the same time account must be taken of the conditions of modern life in which those who are engaged in apostolic work must live.

89. Therefore, in the revision of the office these norms are to be observed:

(a) By the venerable tradition of the universal Church, Lauds as morning prayer, and Vespers as evening prayer, are the two hinges on which the daily office turns. They must be considered as the chief hours and are to be celebrated as such.

(b) Compline is to be drawn up so as suitably to mark the close of the day.

(c) The hour called Matins, although it should retain the character of nocturnal prayer when recited in choir, shall be so adapted that it may be recited at any hour of the

j. By the time of Vatican II and for a long time previously, clerics had been little mindful of the time-sequence of the divine office. It was not uncommon to recite all of the day's office at the beginning or at the end of the day. Thus evening prayer might be said in the morning, or at midday; morning prayer, in fact, was very commonly prayed on the previous evening. Pious books recommended it as a prudent measure.

day, and it shall be made up of fewer psalms and longer readings.

(d) The hour of Prime is to be suppressed.

(e) In choir the minor hours of Terce, Sect, and None are to be observed. Outside of choir it will be lawful to select any one of the three most suited to the time of the day.

90. The divine office, because it is the public prayer of the Church, is a source of piety and a nourishment for personal prayer. For this reason, priests and others who take part in the divine office are earnestly exhorted in the Lord to attune their minds to their voices when praying it. To achieve this more fully, they should take steps to improve their understanding of the liturgy and of the Bible, especially of the psalms. When the Roman office is being revised, its venerable centuries-old treasures are to be so adapted that those to whom it is handed on may profit from it more fully and more easily.

91. So that it may be possible in practice to observe the course of the hours proposed in Article 89, the psalms are no longer to be distributed throughout one week but through a longer period of time.[k]

The task of revising the psalter, already happily begun, is to be finished as soon as possible. It shall take into account the style of Christian Latin, the liturgical use of the psalms —including the singing of the psalms—and the entire traditin of the Latin Church.

92. As regards the readings, the following points shall be observed:

(a) Readings from sacred scripture shall be so arranged that the riches of the divine word may be easily accessible in more abundant measure;

(b) Readings taken from the works of the fathers, doctors, and ecclesiastical writers shall be better selected;

(c) The accounts of the martyrdom or lives of the saints are to be made historically accurate.

93. Hymns are to be restored to their original form, as far as may be desirable. They are to be purged of whatever smacks of mythology or accords ill with Christian piety. Also, as occasion may warrant, other selections are to be made from the treasury of hymns.

94. So that the day may be truly sanctified and that the

k. In the new breviary, the psalms are distributed over four weeks.

hours themselves may be recited with spiritual advantage, it is best that each of them be prayed at the time which corresponds most closely with its true canonical time.

95. Communities obliged to choral office are bound to celebrate the office in choir every day in addition to the conventual Mass. In particular:

(a) Orders of canons, monks, and nuns, and of other regulars bound by law or constitutions to choral office, must say the entire office;

(b) Cathedral or collegiate chapters are bound to recite those parts of the office imposed on them by general or particular law;

(c) All members of the above communities who are in major orders or who are solemnly professed, except for lay brothers, are bound to recite individually those canonical hours which they do not pray in choir.

96. Clerics not bound to office in choir, but who are in major orders, are bound to pray the entire office every day, either in common or individually, as laid down in Article 89.

97. The rubrics shall determine when it is appropriate to substitute a liturgical service for the divine office.

In particular cases, and for adequate reasons, ordinaries may dispense their subjects, wholly or in part, from the obligation of reciting the divine office, or they may change it to another obligation.

98. Any religious who in virtue of their constitutions recite parts of the divine office, are thereby joining in the public prayer of the Church.

The same can be said of those who, in virtue of their constitutions, recite any "little office", provided it be drawn up after the pattern of the divine office, and be duly approved.[1]

99. Since the divine office is the voice of the Church, that is, of the whole mystical body publicly praising God, it is recommended that clerics who are not obliged to attend office in choir, especially priests who live together or who assemble for any purpose, should pray at least some part of the divine office in common.

All who pray the divine office, whether in choir or in

1. Since the publication of the Constitution and especially since the publication of the new breviary, almost all religious have taken on the divine office, or part of it, in place of the "little offices."

common, should fulfil the task entrusted to them as perfectly as possible. This refers not only to the internal devotion of mind but also to the external manner of celebration.

It is, moreover, fitting that whenever possible the office be sung, both in choir and in common.[m]

100. Pastors of souls should see to it that the principal hours, especially Vespers, are celebrated in common in church on Sundays and on the more solemn feasts. The laity, too, are encouraged to recite the divine office, either with the priests, or among themselves, or even individually.

101. (1) In accordance with the age-old tradition of the Latin rite, the Latin language is to be retained by clerics in the divine office.[n] But in individual cases the ordinary has the power to grant the use of a vernacular translation to those clerics for whom the use of Latin constitutes a grave obstacle to their praying the office properly. The vernacular version, however, must be one that is drawn up in accordance with the provisions of Article 36.

(2) The competent superior has the power to grant the use of the vernacular for the divine office, even in choir, to religious, including men who are not clerics. The vernacular version, however, must be one that is approved.

(3) Any cleric bound to the divine office fulfils his obligation if he prays the office in the vernacular together with a group of the faithful or with those mentioned in par. 2, above, provided that the text used has been approved.

Chapter V

THE LITURGICAL YEAR

102. Holy Mother Church believes that it is for her to celebrate the saving work of her divine Spouse in a sacred commemoration on certain days throughout the course of

m. The difference here between "in choir" and "in common" is a legal one.
n. See "The Postconciliar Documents on the Liturgy: Introduction," *The Growth of the Vernacular.*

the year. Once each week, on the day which she has called the Lord's Day, she keeps the memory of the Lord's resurrection. She also celebrates it once every year, together with his blessed passion, at Easter, that most solemn of all feasts.

In the course of the year, moreover, she unfolds the whole mystery of Christ from the incarnation and nativity to the ascension, to Pentecost and the expectation of the blessed hope of the coming of the Lord.

Thus recalling the mysteries of the redemption, she opens up to the faithful the riches of her Lord's powers and merits, so that these are in some way made present for all time; the faithful lay hold of them and are filled with saving grace.

103. In celebrating this annual cycle of the mysteries of Christ, Holy Church honors the Blessed Mary, Mother of God, with a special love. She is inseparably linked with her son's saving work. In her the Church admires and exalts the most excellent fruit of redemption, and joyfully contemplates, as in a faultless image, that which she herself desires and hopes wholly to be.

104. The Church has also included in the annual cycle memorial days of the martyrs and other saints. Raised up to perfection by the manifold grace of God and already in possession of eternal salvation, they sing God's perfect praise in heaven and pray for us. By celebrating their anniversaries the Church proclaims achievement of the paschal mystery in the saints who have suffered and have been glorified with Christ. She proposes them to the faithful as examples who draw all men to the Father through Christ, and through their merits she begs for God's favors.

105. Finally, in the various seasons of the year and in keeping with her traditional discipline, the Church completes the formation of the faithful by means of pious practices for soul and body, by instruction, prayer, and works of penance and mercy.

Accordingly the sacred Council has decided to decree as follows:

106. By a tradition handed down from the apostles, which took its origin from the very day of Christ's resurrection, the Church celebrates the paschal mystery every seventh day, which day is appropriately called the Lord's Day or Sunday. For on this day Christ's faithful are bound to come together into one place. They should listen to the word of God and take part in the Eucharist, thus calling to

mind the passion, resurrection, and glory of the Lord Jesus, and giving thanks to God who "has begotten them again, through the resurrection of Christ from the dead, unto a living hope" (1 Pet. 1:3). The Lord's Day is the original feast day, and it should be proposed to the faithful and taught to them so that it may become in fact a day of joy and of freedom from work. Other celebrations, unless they be truly of the greatest importance, shall not have precedence over Sunday, which is the foundation and kernel of the whole liturgical year.

107. The liturgical year is to be revised so that the traditional customs and discipline of the sacred seasons shall be preserved or restored to suit the conditions of modern times. Their specific character is to be retained so that they duly nourish the piety of the faithful who celebrate the mysteries of the Christian redemption and, above all, the paschal mystery. If certain adaptations are necessary because of local conditions, they are to be made in accordance with the provisions of Articles 39 and 40.

108. The minds of the faithful should be directed primarily toward the feasts of the Lord whereby the mysteries of salvation are celebrated throughout the year. For this reason, the Proper of the Time shall be given due preference over the feasts of the saints so that the entire cycle of the mysteries of salvation may be suitably recalled.

109. The two elements which are especially characteristic of Lent—the recalling of baptism or the preparation for it, and penance—should be given greater emphasis in the liturgy and in liturgical catechesis. It is by means of them that the Church prepares the faithful for the celebration of Easter, while they hear God's word more frequently and devote more time to prayer.

(a) More use is to be made of the baptismal features which are proper to the Lenten liturgy. Some of them which were part of an earlier tradition are to be restored where opportune.

(b) The same may be said of the penitential elements. But catechesis, as well as pointing out the social consequences of sin, must impress on the minds of the faithful the distinctive character of penance as a detestation of sin because it is an offense against God. The role of the Church in penitential practices is not to be passed over, and the need to pray for sinners should be emphasized.

110. During Lent, penance should be not only internal

and individual but also external and social. The practice of penance should be encouraged in ways suited to the present day, to different regions, and to individual circumstances. It should be recommended by the authorities mentioned in Article 22.

But the paschal fast must be kept sacred. It should be celebrated everywhere on Good Friday, and where possible should be prolonged throughout Holy Saturday so that the faithful may attain the joys of the Sunday of the resurrection with uplifted and responsive minds.

111. The saints have been traditionally honored in the Church, and their authentic relics and images held in veneration. For the feasts of the saints proclaim the wonderful works of Christ in his servants and offer to the faithful fitting examples for their imitation.

Lest the feasts of the saints should take precedence over the feasts which commemorate the very mysteries of salvation, many of them should be left to be celebrated by a particular Church, or nation, or family of religious. Only those should be extended to the universal Church which commemorate saints who are truly of universal importance.

CHAPTER VI

SACRED MUSIC

112. The musical tradition of the universal Church is a treasure of inestimable value, greater even than that of any other art. The main reason for this pre-eminence is that, as a combination of sacred music and words, it forms a necessary or integral part of the solemn liturgy.

Sacred scripture, indeed, has bestowed praise upon sacred song.[42] So have the Fathers of the Church and the Roman pontiffs who in more recent times, led by St. Pius X, have explained more precisely the ministerial function exercised by sacred music in the service of the Lord.

42. Cf. Eph. 5:19; Col. 3:16.

Therefore sacred music is to be considered the more holy, the more closely connected it is with the liturgical action, whether making prayer more pleasing, promoting unity of minds, or conferring greater solemnity upon the sacred rites. The Church, indeed, approves of all forms of true art which have the requisite qualities, and admits them into divine worship.

Accordingly, the sacred Council, keeping to the norms and precepts of ecclesiastical tradition and discipline and having regard to the purpose of sacred music, which is the glory of God and the sanctification of the faithful, decrees as follows:

113. Liturgical worship is given a more noble form when the divine offices are celebrated solemnly in song with the assistance of sacred ministers and the active participation of the people.

As regards the language° to be used, the provisions of Article 36 are to be observed; for the Mass, Article 54; for the sacraments, Article 63; for the divine office, Article 101.

114. The treasury of sacred music is to be preserved and cultivated with great care. Choirs must be assiduously developed, especially in cathedral churches. Bishops and other pastors of souls must take great care to ensure that whenever the sacred action is to be accompanied by chant, the whole body of the faithful may be able to contribute that active participation which is rightly theirs, as laid down in Articles 28 and 30.

115. Great importance is to be attached to the teaching and practice of music in seminaries, in the novitiates and houses of studies of religious of both sexes, and also in other Catholic institutions and schools. To impart this instruction teachers are to be carefully trained and put in charge of the teaching of sacred music.

It is desirable also that higher institutes of sacred music be established whenever possible.

Composers and singers, especially boys, must also be given a genuine liturgical training.

116. The Church recognizes Gregorian chant as being specially suited to the Roman liturgy. Therefore, other things being equal, it should be given pride of place in liturgical services.

o. See "The Postconciliar Documents on the Liturgy: Introduction," *The Growth of the Vernacular.*

Other kinds of sacred music, especially polyphony, are by no means excluded from liturgical celebrations so long as they accord with the spirit of the liturgical action as laid down in Article 30.

117. The typical edition of the books of Gregorian chant is to be completed. In addition a more critical edition is to be prepared of those books already published since the restoration by St. Pius X.

It is desirable also that an edition be prepared containing simpler melodies for use in smaller churches.

118. Religious singing by the faithful is to be intelligently fostered so that in devotions and sacred exercises as well as in liturgical services, the voices of the faithful may be heard, in conformity with the norms and requirements of the rubrics.

119. In certain countries, especially in mission lands, there are people who have their own musical tradition, and this plays a great part in their religious and social life. For this reason their music should be held in proper esteem and a suitable place is to be given to it, not only in forming their religious sense but also in adapting worship to their native genius, as indicated in Articles 39 and 40.

Therefore, in the musical training of missionaries, great care should be taken to see that they become competent in promoting the traditional music of those peoples both in the schools and in sacred services, as far as may be practicable.

120. The pipe organ is to be held in high esteem in the Latin Chruch, for it is the traditional musical instrument, the sound of which can add a wonderful splendor to the Church's ceremonies and powerfully lifts up men's minds to God and higher things.

But other instruments also may be admitted for use in divine worship, in the judgment and with the consent of the competent territorial authority as laid down in Articles 22: 2, 37 and 40. This may be done, however, only on condition that the instruments are suitable, or can be made suitable, for sacred use; that they accord with the dignity of the temple, and that they truly contribute to the edification of the faithful.

121. Composers, animated by the Christian spirit, should accept that it pertains to their vocation to cultivate sacred music and increase its store of treasures.

Let them produce compositions which have the qualities proper to genuine sacred music, and which can be sung not only by large choirs but also by smaller choirs, and which make possible the active participation of the whole congregation.

The texts intended to be sung must always be in conformity with Catholic doctrine. Indeed, they should be drawn chiefly from the sacred scripture and from liturgical sources.

CHAPTER VII

SACRED ART AND SACRED FURNISHINGS

122. The fine arts are rightly classed among the noblest activities of man's genius; this is especially true of religious art and of its highest manifestation, sacred art. Of their nature the arts are directed toward expressing in some way the infinite beauty of God in works made by human hands. Their dedication to the increase of God's praise and of his glory is more complete, the more exclusively they are devoted to turning men's minds devoutly toward God.

For that reason holy Mother Church has always been the patron of the fine arts and has ever sought their noble ministry, to the end especially that all things set apart for use in divine worship should be worthy, becoming, and beautiful, signs and symbols of things supernatural. And to this end she has trained artists. In fact the Church has, with good reason, always claimed the right to pass judgment on the arts, deciding which of the works of artists are in accordance with faith, piety, and the laws religiously handed down, and are to be considered suitable for sacred use.

The Church has been particularly careful to see that sacred furnishings should worthily and beautifully serve the dignity of worship. She has admitted changes in material, style, or ornamentation prompted by the progress of technical arts with the passage of time.

Wherefore it has pleased the Fathers to issue the following decrees on these matters:

123. The Church has not adopted any particular style of art as her own. She has admitted styles from every period, in keeping with the natural characteristics and conditions of peoples and the needs of the various rites. Thus in the course of the centuries she has brought into existence a treasury of art which must be preserved with every care. The art of our own times from every race and country shall also be given free scope in the Church, provided it bring to the task the reverence and honor due to the sacred buildings and rites. Thus it is enabled to join its voice to that wonderful chorus of praise in honor of the Catholic faith sung by great men in past ages.

124. Ordinaries are to take care that in encouraging and favoring truly sacred art, they should seek for noble beauty rather than sumptuous display. The same principle applies also to sacred vestments and ornaments.

Bishops should be careful to ensure that works of art which are repugnant to faith, morals, and Christian piety, and which offend true religious sense either by depraved forms or through lack of artistic merit or because of mediocrity or pretense, be removed from the house of God and from other sacred places.

And when churches are to be built, let great care be taken that they be suitable for the celebration of liturgical services and for the active participation of the faithful.

125. The practice of placing sacred images in churches so that they be venerated by the faithful is to be maintained. Nevertheless their number should be moderate and their relative positions should reflect right order. For otherwise the Christian people may find them incongruous and they may foster devotion of doubtful orthodoxy.

126. When passing judgment on works of art, local ordinaries should ask the opinion of the diocesan commission on sacred art and—when occasion demands—the opinions of others who are experts, and the commissions mentioned in Articles 44, 45 and 46.

Ordinaries should ensure that sacred furnishings and works of value are not disposed of or destroyed, for they are ornaments in God's house.

127. Bishops, either personally or through suitable priests who are gifted with a knowledge and love of art, should have a special concern for artists, so as to imbue them with the spirit of sacred art and of the sacred liturgy.

It is also desirable that schools or academies of sacred art should be established in those parts of the world where they would be useful for the training of artists.

All artists who, prompted by their talents, desire to serve God's glory in holy Church should ever remember that they are engaged in a kind of holy imitation of God the Creator: that they are concerned with works destined to be used in Catholic worship, for the edification of the faithful and to foster their piety and religious formation.

128. The canons and ecclesiastical statutes which govern the provision of external things which pertain to sacred worship should be revised as soon as possible, together with the liturgical books, as laid down in Article 25. These laws refer especially to the worthy and well-planned construction of sacred buildings, the shape and construction of altars, the nobility, placing, and security of the eucharistic tabernacle, the suitability and dignity of the bapistry, the proper ordering of sacred images, and the scheme of decoration and embellishment. Laws which seem less suited to the reformed liturgy should be amended or abolished. Those which are helpful are to be retained, or introduced if lacking.

In this matter, especially as regards the material and form of sacred furnishing and vestments, in accordance with Article 22 of this Constitution, powers are given to territorial episcopal conferences to adapt such things to the needs and customs of their different regions.

129. During their philosophical and theological studies, clerics are to be taught about the history and development of sacred art, and about the basic principles which govern the production of its works. Thus they will be able to appreciate and preserve the Church's ancient monuments, and be able to aid by good advice artists who are engaged in producing works of art.

130. It is fitting that the use of pontificals be reserved to those ecclesiastical persons who have episcopal rank or some particular jurisdiction.

A DECLARATION OF THE SECOND VATICAN ECUMENICAL COUNCIL ON REVISION OF THE CALENDAR

The Sacred Second Vatican Ecumenical Council, recognizing the importance of the wishes expressed by many concerning the assignment of the feast of Easter to a fixed Sunday and concerning an unchanging calendar, having carefully considered the results that could follow from the introduction of a new calendar, declares as follows:

1. The sacred Council is not opposed to assigning the feast of Easter to a fixed Sunday in the Gregorian Calendar, provided those whom it may concern give their assent, especially the brethren who are not in communion with the Apostolic See.

2. The sacred Council likewise declares that it does not oppose efforts designed to introduce a perpetual calendar into civil society.

But among the various systems which are being devised with a view to establishing a perpetual calendar and introducing it into civil life, those and only those are unopposed by the Church which retain and safeguard a seven-day week, with Sunday, without the introduction of any days outside the week, so that the succession of weeks may be left intact, unless in the judgment of the Apostolic See there are extremely weighty reasons to the contrary.

THE POSTCONCILIAR DOCUMENTS ON THE LITURGY

INTRODUCTION

The number of postconciliar documents on the liturgy is very great, greater than in any other postconciliar area. Almost half of the documents listed in the descriptive catalogue of documents in this volume deal with liturgy—close to one hundred and twenty out of two hundred and fifty. Even in a volume devoted exclusively to liturgy, selectivity would have been necessary. Much greater selectivity was needed in this present volume, otherwise there would have been room for little else.

It was this that led the editor to make what at first may seem a surprising decision: to omit the most important category of postconciliar liturgical documents, the introductions to the new liturgical books—to the breviary, the sacramental rituals, the lectionary, the funeral rites, etc. One would of course have included them in a collection limited to the postconciliar liturgical documents. However, granted the constraints imposed in this present collection, it seemed reasonable to omit them, especially since they are otherwise easily accessible in good English translations. What this volume does offer is a complementary selection of other important documents which are not readily available.

We have, however, compromised to the extent of including the apostolic constitution on the revised Roman Missal, the General Instruction on the Roman Missal, and the more recent "On Holy Communion and the Worship of the Eucharist outside of the Mass." The reason for making these exceptions is the great and daily importance of the Eucharist in the life of the Christian.

The other documents omitted from this section fall into two main categories: documents of interest to a limited number of people, and documents or portions of documents of purely temporary interest.

To the first category belong documents on the translation and publication of liturgical books and documents, for example, on vestments and on naming the bishop in the eucharistic prayers.

Two kinds of documents, or portions of documents, are to be found in the second category. To the first kind belong documents or portions of documents which prescribed changes introduced into the liturgy between 1964 and 1974 on a purely temporary basis, "pending the completion of the reform," or pending the availability of the new liturgical books. With the completion of the reform, the documents prescribing these temporary measures become of mere historic interest.

THE GROWTH OF THE VERNACULAR

The second kind of document or portion of document in this latter category deals with liturgical questions the treatment of which evolved or even changed in the course of a few years. One such question was that of the vernacular. The Constitution on the Sacred Liturgy had allowed a very restricted use of the vernacular in the Mass (see D. *1*, 36, 54), but left the way open for an appeal by hierarchies to the Holy See for more radical concessions (*ibid*, 40). The Constitution also allowed ordinaries to grant permission to individual clerics to recite the office in the vernacular if they found it very difficult to recite in Latin (see D. *1*, 101, par. 1). But Latin had to be used by religious clerics for recitation of the divine office in common or in choir (*ibid*.). Further, the Instruction *Inter oecumenici* (D. *3*) made it obligatory for publishers to print the Latin text *as well* when publishing translations of the altar missal and of the breviary for the use of clerics (nos. 57 and 89).

However, restrictions on the use of the vernacular were progressively lifted in the face of representations by hierarchies from all over the world, until by 1971 the use of the vernacular in public Masses was left entirely to the judgment of episcopal conferences, to the judgment of individual priests for private Masses, and of the ordinary for divine office, in private, in common or in choir. (See A. 144.)

Strangely enough, the ruling that translations of the breviary had to carry the Latin text as well was not formally revoked, but it was no longer applied after a while. The ruling on missals was modified on 10 November, 1969 (see A. 71).

EVOLUTION

The building or reconstructing of churches or oratories for the new liturgy was treated in the Constitution on the Sacred Liturgy (D. *1*, 122 to 130), in the Instruction, *Inter oecumenici* (D. *2*, 90 to 99), the Instruction, *Eucharisticum mysterium* (D. *10*, 52 to 57), The General Instruction on the Roman Missal (D. *14*, 253 to 280) and in "Holy Communion and the Worship of the Eucharistic Mystery outside of Mass" (D. *22*, 9 to 11). The definitive statement is in the General Instruction on the Roman Missal, and it is included in this collection. The section in the Constitution on the Liturgy is included, being a statement of principle, and the short treatment of the tabernacle in the last of these documents is included also. The other two are omitted.

We have likewise omitted lists of concessions of holy communion under both kinds, for example, which were subsequently enlarged.

GENERAL INSTRUCTION ON THE ROMAN MISSAL

There is a point of some importance to be noted with regard to the General Instruction on the Roman Missal. It was first published in Latin on 6 April, 1969, and translations were made available subsequently (see A. 66). It was again published as part of the new Latin Roman Missal, *Missale Romanum*, on 26 March, 1970 (see A. 72 and 112; D. *13*). This edition, which replaces the previous one, differs in many respects from it. The differences are described in *Notitiae*, 1970, pp. 169 to 190. Later again, the abolition of minor orders and of the sub-diaconate (see D. 29, A. 170) on 15 August, 1972, necessitated further changes in the General Instruction. These are described in *Notitiae* 1973, pp. 34 to 38 (see A. 81).

Our translation is made from the 1970 Latin original, but with the changes prescribed by the Sacred Congregation for Divine Worship (*Notitiae, loc. cit.*). The Congregation prescribed that where paragraphs are omitted, the numbering of subsequent paragraphs is not changed, but remains as it was previously. Thus, paragraphs 142 to 152 are omitted, but the paragraph which thus immediately follows number 141 is numbered 153. Similarly, paragraph 301 is omitted, but the paragraph following it retains its previous numeration, 302. Our translation adheres to these instructions.

2

MOTU PROPRIO ON THE SACRED LITURGY[a]

Sacram Liturgiam, 25 January, 1962

There is abundant evidence of the constant solicitude of Our predecessors and Ourselves, and of the bishops of the Church, for the preservation, the improvement and—where needful—the reform of the sacred liturgy. Many and well-known published documents testify to it. A more recent indication is the Constitution on the Sacred Liturgy, which was approved almost unanimously by the Second Ecumenical Council of the Vatican, and which We promulgated in solemn session on 4 December, 1963.

The reason for this solicitude is that "in the earthly liturgy we take part in a foretaste of that heavenly liturgy which is celebrated in the holy city of Jerusalem, toward which we journey as pilgrims, where Christ is sitting at the right hand of God, minister of the holies and of the true tabernacle. With all the warriors of the heavenly army we sing a hymn to the Lord's glory: venerating the memory of the saints, we hope for some part and fellowship with them; we eagerly await the Saviour, the Lord Jesus Christ, until he, our life, shall appear and we too will appear with him in glory" (Constitution on the Sacred Liturgy, no. 8).

And so it is that the faithful, when they thus worship God, the source and model of all holiness, are themselves drawn and, as it were, impelled to holiness; though still earthbound pilgrims, they become "imitators of the heavenly Sion" (Lauds hymn, feast of the Dedication of a Church.)

In the light of this, it is easy to see why We so much want to see all Christians, and especially all priests, study the Constitution on the Liturgy and be prepared to put it

a. Translated by A.F., Latin text in *AAS* 56, pp. 139–144. Articles 3 to 9 have been omitted.

41

wholeheartedly and loyally into execution as soon as it comes into force. In the nature of the case, there is need for the immediate implementation of the prescription bearing on the knowledge and the promulgation of the liturgical laws. For this reason We appeal insistently to bishops of dioceses to set at once about teaching their people the power and the interior worth of the sacred liturgy, taking into account their age, condition in life, and standard of religious culture. They should avail of the help of their priests, "the dispensers of the mysteries of Christ" (1 Cor. 4:1). Their shared knowledge will enable the faithful to take part in the religious services together, devoutly, and with body and soul (see Constitution, no. 19).

It is obvious, at the same time, that several prescriptions of the Constitution need time for their implementation: certain rites have to be revised and new editions of the liturgical books prepared. To ensure that this work will be carried out with the requisite wisdom and prudence, We have set up a special commission[b] whose principal task it will be to see to the proper implementation of the Constitution.

However, there are certain prescriptions of the Constitution which can be implemented at once. It is Our wish that these come into force without delay, so that the faithful will no longer be deprived of the spiritual benefits which are expected from them.

b. The special commission was later named The Consilium for the Implementation of the Constitution on the Sacred Liturgy. The Latin word "consilium" means "advice," "counsel," or "a group of advisers." This is the sense in which the word is used here. We have retained the Latin word, since neither council, counsel, committee, nor commission conveys quite the sense of the Latin.

Archbishop A. Bugnini, who was secretary of the Consilium since its foundation and up to recently was secretary of the Sacred Congregation for Divine Worship, says that the Consilium was set up on 3 December, 1974 (*Notitiae*, 1973, p. 395). However, presumably in the absence of any other documentation on its inception, this present Motu Proprio and the date of its publication have usually been associated subsequently with the inauguration of the Consilium (see D 3, 2).

The Consilium ceased to have an independent existence on 8 May, 1969, when Pope Paul VI, by his Apostolic Constitution, *Sacra Rituum*, made it part of the new Sacred Congregation for Divine Worship, which he set up by the same Apostolic Constitution. The Pope directed that the Consilium would persist as a special commission of the Congregation until the reform of the liturgy should be completed, retaining is members and consulters (see *AAS* 61, (1969) pp. 299 and 301).

Therefore, with Our apostolic authority, and by means of this *Motu Proprio*, We order and decree that, from the coming first Sunday of Lent, which this year [1964] falls on 16 February, when the *vacatio legis*c shall have been terminated, the following prescriptions shall come into force:

1. It is Our wish that seminaries, houses of study of religious orders, and faculties of theology set at once about implementing in their curricula the prescriptions of Articles 15, 16 and 17 on the teaching of the liturgy, in such wise that they will be able to carry them out properly and diligently from the beginning of the next scholastic year.

2. We also decree that, in accordance with the prescriptions of Articles 45 and 46, a commission be set up in every diocese whose task it will be, under the direction of the bishop, to promote the liturgy and understanding of the liturgy.

It is advisable that, in some cases, several dioceses should come together and share a common commission.

Further, as far as possible, in every diocese two other commissions should be set up, one for sacred music and one for sacred art.

In many cases it will be convenient to unify those three diocesan commissions.

. . .

10. According to Article 22:2, the care of the liturgy is, within certain limits, vested in territorial episcopal conferences of various types. We lay down that the word "territorial" is for the time being to be taken to mean "national."

As well as residential bishops, all those who are mentioned in Canon 292 of the Code of Canon Law can take part in these national conferences; with the right to vote. Further, coadjutor and auxiliary bishops can also be called to these conferences.

In these assemblies, a two-thirds majority by secret ballot is required for the making of legitimate decrees.

11. Lastly, We would draw attention to the fact that, apart from the innovations which We have introduced in this apostolic letter, and apart from other changes whose implementation We have anticipated, the regulation of the sacred liturgy is vested exclusively in the Church: that is to say, in

c. *Vacatio legis* is a technical term denoting a period of time between the promulgation of a law and the date appointed when it comes into force.

this Apostolic See and, in the measure allowed by the law, in the bishop. For this reason, nobody else, not even a priest, is entitled to add, subtract or change anything in the liturgy (see Constitution, Article 22:1, 3).

We ordain that all that We have laid down in this *motu proprio* is to stand and is to be observed, no matter what else may stand contrary to it.

3

INSTRUCTION ON THE PROPER IMPLEMENTATION OF THE CONSTITUTION ON THE SACRED LITURGY[a]

S.C.R., *Inter Oecumenici*, 26 September, 1964

NATURE OF THIS INSTRUCTION

1. It is only fitting that the Constitution on the Sacred Liturgy should be among the first fruits of the Second Ecumenical Council of the Vatican, since it regulates the Church's noblest activities. It will yield fruit more abundantly the more profoundly pastors and the faithful are truly imbued with its spirit and the more willingly they implement it.

2. The Consilium for the Implementation of the Constitution on the Sacred Liturgy which Pope Paul VI established by the *Motu Proprio, Sacram Liturgiam* (25 January, 1964)[b] has energetically set about the task confided to it: the faithful execution of the prescriptions of the Constitution and of the *Motu Proprio,* their interpretation and implementation.

3. It is of the greatest importance that, from the beginning, these documents should be rightly implemented everywhere and that all possible doubts as to their interpretation should be eliminated. It is for this reason that the Consilium, on the instructions of the Holy Father, has prepared the present Instruction. It defines more clearly the competence of episcopal conferences in liturgical matters, it makes more specific what was expressed in general terms in both documents, it permits, or decrees, certain changes which can be introduced prior to the revision of the liturgical books.

a. Translated by A.F., Latin text in *AAS* 56, pp. 877–900. The following articles have been omitted: 30, 36, 40, 42, 43, 48–76, 78, 84–99.
b. See D2, note b.

PRINCIPLES TO BE BORNE IN MIND

4. The practical directives which now follow have for their object to make the liturgy correspond more perfectly with the mind of the Council—to promote, that is to say, the active participation of the faithful. Further, the general reform of the liturgy will be better received by the faithful if it is accomplished gradually, and if it is proposed and explained to them properly by their pastors.

5. First of all, however, it is essential that everybody be persuaded that the scope of the Constitution on the Sacred Liturgy is not limited merely to the changing of liturgical rites and texts. Rather its aim is to foster the formation of the faithful and that pastoral activity of which the liturgy is the summit and source (see Const., Art. 10). The changes in the liturgy which have already been introduced, or which will be introduced later, have this same end in view.

6. The thrust of pastoral activity which is centered on the liturgy is to give expression to the Paschal Mystery in people's lives. It was in the Paschal Mystery that the Son of God incarnate, having been obedient unto the death of the 'cross, was raised so high by his resurrection and ascension that he was able to share his own divine life with the world, in such wise that men who had been dead to sin and were now made like to Christ "may not now live to themselves, but unto him who died for them, and rose again" (2 Cor. 5:15).

This is accomplished by faith and by the sacraments of faith—especially, that is to say, by baptism (see Const., Art. 6), by the sacred mystery of the Eucharist, the pivot of all the other sacraments and sacramentals (see Const., Art. 47), and also by the cycle of celebrations in which, throughout the Church's year, the paschal mystery of Christ is unfolded (see Const., Art. 102–107).

7. Consequently, even though the liturgy is not the whole of the Church's activity (see Const., Art. 9), great care must be taken that pastoral work be properly linked with it. At the same time, the liturgical apostolate must not be exercised separately and, as it were, in a vacuum. It should be closely linked with other pastoral activities.

It is especially necessary that there be close links between liturgy, catechesis, religious instruction and preaching.

8. Bishops and their helpers in the priesthood, therefore,

should set great store by their whole liturgy-centered apostolate. Thus the faithful too, by perfect participation in the liturgy will receive the divine life abundantly and, having become Christ's leaven and the salt of the earth, they will announce and transmit it to others.

CERTAIN GENERAL NORMS

HOW THESE NORMS WILL APPLY

9. The practical norms contained in the Constitution and in this Instruction as well as the changes which, even prior to the reform of the liturgical books, are by this same Instruction permitted or decreed, all apply solely to the Roman rite. However, they may be adopted by the other Latin rites, due allowance being made for the demands of the law.

10. Whatever measures this Instruction submits to the jurisdiction of the competent territorial ecclesiastical authority, it is this same authority, alone, which can and must put them into effect, by legitimate decrees.

In every case, the time and circumstances in which decrees become binding must be indicated. A sufficient interval of time should be allowed for notification of the faithful and for instructing them in the observance of the decrees.

LITURGICAL FORMATION OF THE CLERGY
(Const., Art. 15, 16, 18)

11. With regard to the liturgical formation of the clergy:
(a) Theological faculties are to have a chair of liturgy, so that all students may be properly instructed in the liturgy; local ordinaries and major religious superiors should see to the provision, as soon as possible, of properly trained professors of liturgy in seminaries and in houses of study for religious;
(b) Professors who are given charge of courses in sacred

liturgy must be trained, as soon as possible, in accordance with Article 15 of the Constitution.

(c) Where possible, institutes of pastoral liturgy must be set up for further training of the clergy, especially of those who are already engaged in the apostolate.

12. Liturgy courses must be of appropriate duration, to be decided by the responsible authority, and must follow a proper method, in accordance with Article 15 of the Constitution.

13. Liturgical ceremonies should be celebrated with the utmost perfection. For this reason:

(a) The rubrics are to be observed carefully and the ceremonies to be performed with dignity, under the watchful scrutiny of the ecclesiastical superiors. They should be practised beforehand.

(b) Each cleric should frequently exercise the liturgical activities proper to his order: the activities, that is to say, of deacon, subdeacon, acolyte, reader and, further, commentator and chanter.[c]

(c) Churches and oratories, church furnishings and vestments should be examples of genuine Christian art, including modern art.[d]

LITURGICAL FORMATION OF THE SPIRITUAL LIFE OF THE CLERGY (Const., Art. 17)

14. In seminaries and in studentates for religious, the Constitution on the Sacred Liturgy must be fully implemented, in accordance with the directives of the Holy See, and through the combined efforts of superiors and teachers; this to the end that the clerical students be taught to take part fully in the liturgical ceremonies and to draw from

c. When this document was promulgated, the sub-diaconate was a "major order" and the offices of acolyte and reader were "minor orders," though this terminology had already been dropped in the document. Eight years later, however, the sub-diaconate ceased to exist as a major order (it was in fact abolished altogether) and the other two were reduced to the status of "ministries," pertaining not to the clerical state but to the lay state. The functions of the sub-deacon were divided between the two of them. (see D30).

d. The meaning is not that modern art is merely permissible, but that just as in older churches one would expect to find genuine Christian art *of that time*, so in a modern church one would expect to find genuine Christian *modern* art.

them nourishment both for their own spiritual lives and for communication to others later. They should be properly initiated into the liturgy by the following means: by recommending to them, and by stocking their libraries with, a sufficient quantity of books which treat of the liturgy under its theological and spiritual aspects especially; by means of meditations and sermons drawn primarily from sacred scripture and from the liturgy (see Const., Art. 35:2); by communal practice of the traditional customs of the Christian life, in conformity with the liturgical seasons.

15. The daily celebration of the Eucharist, which is the center of the spiritual life, should take the form best adapted to the condition of the participants (see Const., Art. 19).

On Sundays and on the greater feasts Mass should be sung and all those who are not away should take part. There should be a homily and, as far as possible, those who are not priests should receive Holy Communion. Priests who are not needed for individual Masses for the faithful may concelebrate, especially on the more solemn feasts, after the new rite shall have been published.[e]

It is desirable that seminaries should take part in the eucharistic celebration with the bishop in the cathedral, at least on the great feasts (see Const., Art. 41)

16. It is very desirable that clerical students who are not yet bound to the divine office should recite or sing Lauds in common daily as morning prayer and Vespers as evening prayer, or Compline at the end of the day. As far as possible, the professors themselves should take part in this common exercise. Further, clerics who are in sacred orders should be given sufficient time for the recitation of the divine office through the day.

It is very desirable that, when possible, seminarians should sing Vespers in the cathedral, at least on the great feasts.

17. Devotions which owe their origin to the customs or the laws of a locality or institute should be accorded due reverence. Care should be taken, however, especially if they are performed in common, that they be in keeping with the liturgy, in accordance with Article 13 of the Constitution, and that they take account of the liturgical seasons.

e. The new rite for concelebration was published on 7 March, 1965.

LITURGICAL FORMATION OF RELIGIOUS

18. What has been said in the foregoing articles about the spiritual formation of the clergy must be applied to religious men and women.

LITURGICAL FORMATION OF THE FAITHFUL
(Const., Art. 19)

19. Pastors of souls are to make it their business to implement, with care and patience, the precepts of the Constitution on the instruction of the faithful in the liturgy, and on their active participation in it, internally and externally, "taking into account their age and condition, their way of life and standard of religious culture" (Const., Art. 19). They should take special care that members of religious associations for layfolk be instructed in the liturgy and take an active part in it. It is the role of such associations to share more intimately in the life of the Church and to assist pastors in organizing the liturgical life of the parish (see Const., Art. 42).

THE COMPETENT AUTHORITY IN LITURGICAL MATTERS (Const., Art. 22)

20. It belongs to the Church's authority to regulate the sacred liturgy. Nobody, therefore, is allowed to proceed on his own initiative in this domain, for this would be to the detriment of the liturgy itself, more often than not, and of the reform which the competent authority has to carry out.

21. It is for the Holy See to reform and to approve liturgical books for general use, to regulate the sacred liturgy for the universal Church, to approve or confirm the 'Acts' and deliberations of the territorial authorities and to receive the proposals or petitions of these same territorial authorities.

22. It is for the bishop to regulate the liturgy in his own diocese, in accordance with the norms and the spirit of the Constitution on Sacred Liturgy, the decrees of the Holy See and of the competent territorial authority.

23. For the time being the various types of territorial conferences of bishops which are invested with authority to regulate the liturgy, according to Article 22:2 of the Constitution, are to be understood to be the following:

(a) either the conference of all the bishops of o.
tion, in accordance with the *Motu Proprio, Sacram L.*
turgiam, no. 10;

(b) or a conference, already legitimately constituted, embracing the bishops, or the bishops and other local ordinaries, of several nations;

(c) or a conference, yet to be constituted, with the consent of the Holy See, of bishops, or of bishops and other local ordinaries, of several nations. Such a solution is envisaged especially where the bishops in each nation are so few that it would be better for the bishops of nations which share the same language and the same civil culture to form one conference.

If, however, a particular local situation seems to demand a different solution, the matter should be referred to the Holy See.

24. The following must be invited to such conferences:

(a) Residential bishops;

(b) Abbots and prelates *nullius;*

(c) Vicars and Prefects Apostolic;

(d) Apostolic administrators of dioceses who have been permanently appointed;

(e) all other local ordinaries, with the exception of Vicars General.

Coadjutor and auxiliary bishops may be invited to attend by the president, with the consent of the majority of those present who have deliberative votes.

25. Unless special local conditions legitimately demand another solution, a conference is to be called together:

(a) by its respective president, when there is a question of a conference already legitimately constituted;

(b) otherwise, by the archbishop or the bishop who has the legal right of precedence.

26. The president, with the consent of the Fathers, is to decide the order of the business to be transacted, he opens the meeting, transfers it, prorogues and closes it.

27. All those mentioned in number 24 have deliberative votes, not excluding co-adjutor and auxiliary bishops, unless the document by which the meeting is convened expressly states otherwise.

28. For the legitimate enactment of decrees, a two-thirds majority, by secret vote, is required.

29. When the "Acts" of a territorial conference of bish-

...mes of those who were present at the confer-

...account of the proceedings,

...he results of the voting on each decree.

Tw...copies of the "Acts," signed by the president and secretary of the conference, and properly sealed, must be sent to the Consilium for the Implementation of the Constitution on Sacred Liturgy.

• • •

31. The decrees of the territorial conferences which need the approval, or confirmation, of the Holy See must not be promulgated or implemented until they have received it.

DIVISION OF LITURGICAL FUNCTIONS TO BE OBSERVED (Const., Art. 28)

32. If the parts which belong to the choir and the people are chanted or recited by them, they must not be said privately by the celebrant.

33. Similarly, the celebrant must not say privately the readings which are read or sung by the competent minister or the altarserver.

NOT RESPECTING PERSONS (Const., Art. 32)

34. Bishops—or, if it seems opportune, regional or national episcopal conferences—are to see to the implementation, in their territories, of the prescription of the holy Council which forbids the according of special honours, either in ceremonies or by external display, to private persons or to social classes.

35. For the rest, in liturgical ceremonies, and especially in the celebration of Mass and in the administration of the sacraments and of the sacramentals, pastors should, with prudence and charity, see to it that the equality of all the faithful is expressed, even externally, and that any appearance of money-making is avoided.

BIBLE SERVICES (Const., Art. 35:4)

37. Where there is a shortage of priests, if there is no priest to celebrate Mass on a Sunday or Holy Day of obligation, a Bible service is recommended, subject to the judg-

ment of the local ordinary, under the presidency of a deacon or a layman deputed for the task.

The structure of this Bible service is to be the same as that of the liturgy of the Word at Mass: the Epistle and Gospel of the day's Mass are generally read in the vernacular; chants, especially from the psalms, being sung at the beginning of the service and during it. The person who presides should preach, if he is a deacon; if he is not a deacon, he should read a homily chosen by the bishop or the parish priest. The service should terminate with "the community prayer," or "the prayer of the faithful," and the Lord's prayer.

38. It is fitting that Bible services on the vigils of great feasts, on certain ferial days of Lent and Advent, on Sundays and feastdays, should also have the same structure as the liturgy of the Word at Mass, though it is quite permissible to have only one reading.

If there is more than one reading, however, the reading from the Old Testament normally precedes the reading from the New Testament, and the reading of the Gospel is the culmination of the serivce; when this is done, the sequence of salvation history is perceived more clearly.

39. In order that these services be performed with dignity and reverence, the diocesan liturgical commissions will give whatever assistance is needed.

THE VERNACULAR AND MIGRANTS

41. Wherever there is a group of people who share a language other than that of the region in which they find themselves—as happens especially with emigrants, in "personal" parishes and such like—it is permissible to use the language they know, in liturgical ceremonies, provided one has the consent of the local ordinary and provided the version used has been legitimately approved by the competent territorial ecclesiastical authority for that language.

REGIONAL LITURGICAL COMMISSIONS
(Const., Art. 44)

44. When a territorial authority sets up a liturgical commission, it must be drawn from the ranks of the bishops themselves, as far as possible; alternatively, it may comprise one or more bishops, with the addition of priests who are

expert in liturgy and pastoral matters, and who have been selected by name for this office.

It is fitting that the members of this commission, and its consultors, should meet several times a year, for discussion.

45. The terrtorial authority may fittingly entrust the following matters to such a commission:

(a) The promotion of investigations and experiments, in accordance with Article 40, pars 1 and 2, of the Constitution.

(b) The promotion of practical initiatives, in the territory as a whole, for fostering the liturgy and the implementation of the Constitution on sacred liturgy.

(c) The preparation of the investigations and the assistance needed for the implementation of the decrees of the plenary assembly of bishops.

(d) The direction of the pastoral liturgical programme of the region as a whole, the superintendence of the implementation of the decrees of the assembly of bishops, and reporting on this to the assembly.

(e) The promotion of frequent contacts with groups in the same territory which are concerned with the Bible, catechetics, pastoral matters, music, sacred art. They should foster similar contacts with every manner of pious associations of the laity. They should also promote initiatives in common with all these groups.

46. The members of the institute of pastoral liturgy, and the experts who are selected to assist the liturgical commission, must not refuse requests by individual bishops for assistance in the more effective promotion of the liturgical apostolate in their own territories.

THE DIOCESAN LITURGICAL COMMISSION
(Const., Art. 45)

47. The diocesan liturgical commission, under the guidance of the bishop:

(a) must acquaint themselves with the state of pastoral liturgical activity in the diocese;

(b) must diligently implement what has been proposed by the competent authority, at the same time acquainting themselves with investigations and initiatives which have been undertaken elsewhere in the same field;

(c) in individual cases, or even for the diocese as a whole, they must suggest opportune plans for the progress of pastoral liturgical action; they must indicate, and even select, suitable people who can, as occasion offers, assist the clergy in this matter; they must propose whatever material helps they deem necessary;

(d) they must suggest and promote practical initiatives which can contribute to the progress of the liturgy, with an eye to assisting, especially, the priests who are already engaged in the apostolate;

(e) they must see to it that, in the diocese, all initiatives directed towards the promotion of the liturgy are in mutual accord and that the different groups help one another, in a manner analogous to what was described for the liturgical commission attached to the assembly of bishops (no. 45 e).

SACRAMENTALS
(Const., Art. 79)

77. The blessings which are listed in the Roman Ritual, tit. IX, c. 9, 10, 11, and which up to now, have been reserved, may henceforth be given by any priest, except for the following: the blessing of bells for use in a church or an oratory (c. 9, n. 11), of the foundation stone of a church (c. 9, n. 16), of a new church or public oratory (c. 9, n. 17), of an antimension (c. 9, n. 21), of a new cemetery (c. 9, n. 22). Papal blessings are also excepted (c. 10, nn.1–3), and the blessing and erection of the Stations of the Cross (c. 11, n. 1), which are reserved to the bishop.

THE FACULTY OF DISPENSING FROM THE DIVINE OFFICE (Const., Art. 97)

79. The faculty, which has been given to all ordinaries, of dispensing their subjects, in individual cases and for a just cause, from the whole or part of the obligation to the Divine Office, or of changing it to another obligation, is extended to major superiors of non-exempt clerical institutes, and of societies of clerics who live in common without vows.

THE LITTLE OFFICES (Const., Art. 98)

80. No little office is to be regarded as having been drawn up after the pattern of the Divine Office unless it comprises psalms, readings, hymns and prayers, and unless

it has some pattern of day-hours and is in some measure of conformity with the liturgical seasons.

81. For the time being, those little offices which have already been legitimately approved can be used in the Church's public worship, provided they have been drawn up according to the requirements outlined in number 80. (See D1, 98, note *b*.)

New little offices, however, require the approval of the Holy See before they can be used in the Church's public worship.

82. When the text of a little office is translated into the vernacular, with a view to using it in the Church's public worship, it must be approved by the competent territorial ecclesiastical authority, whose 'Acts' must be approved by the Holy See.

83. When there is question of granting permission to use a vernacular version of the little office to those who are obliged to it by their constitutions, or when there is question of dispensing them from their obligation or of changing it for another obligation, the competent authority is the individual subject's ordinary, or major superior.

4

DECREE ON CONCELEBRATION AND COMMUNION UNDER BOTH SPECIES[a]

S.C.R., *Ecclesiae Semper,* 7 March, 1965

Whenever the Church has been engaged in the regulation and reformation of the celebration of the sacred mysteries, it has always taken care that the rites themselves should also manifest to best advantage the inexhaustible riches of Christ which they contain and which they communicate to those who are well disposed, thus facilitating their impregnation of the souls and lives of the faithful who take part in them.

When it is the celebration of the Eucharist which is in question, however, the Church is particularly attentive to this point. It arranges and regulates the different forms of eucharistic celebration to the end that they might express the various aspects of the sacrifice of the Eucharist and impress them on the faithful.

In every type of Mass, no matter how simple, all the qualities and properties are to be found which, of its very nature, necessarily form part of the holy sacrifice of the Mass. Among them, however, the following are particularly to be noted:

In the first place, the unity of the sacrifice of the cross: inasmuch as a multiplicity of Masses represent but the one and only sacrifice of Christ[1] and owe their sacrificial character to the fact that they are a memorial of the bloody immolation accomplished on the cross, whose fruits are received through this unbloody immolation.

a. Translated by A.F. from the Latin text as published in the *Ritus Servandus in Concelebratione Missae et Ritus Communionis sub utraque specie,* editio typica, Vatican Polyglot Press, 1965. Latin text of decree in *AAS* 57 (1965), pp. 410–412.
1. See Council of Trent, Session 23: ch. 1.

Secondly, the unity of the priesthood: the priests who celebrate Mass are indeed many, but they are but ministers of Christ, who exercises his priesthood through them and, to this end, makes each of them a sharer in a very special way in his own priesthood by means of the sacrament of Orders. It follows that when, singly, they offer the sacrifice, all of them do so by the power of the same priesthood. They act in the place (*in persona . . . agunt*) of the high priest, for whom the consecration of the sacrament of his Body and Blood is effected through the ministry of one priest as fully as through the ministry of several.[2]

Lastly, the action of the entire people of God appears with greater clarity. Every Mass is the celebration of that sacrament by which the Church lives and grows continuously[3] and in which its Church's own nature is especially manifested.[4] For this reason it is, more than any of the other liturgical actions,[5] an action of the entire people of God, hierarchically organized, and acting hierarchically.

These three characteristics are found in every Mass, but they are more vividly apparent in the rite by which several priests concelebrate the same Mass.

In this manner of celebrating Mass, several priests act together with one will and one voice, by the power of the same priesthood and in the place of the high priest, together they consecrate and offer the one sacrifice, in one sacramental act, and together they participate in it.

Consequently, when the sacrifice is thus celebrated, the faithful are taking an active part, aware of what they are doing, and as befits a community, the principal manifestation of the Church is realized[6]—especially if the bishop is presiding—in unity of sacrifice and priesthood, in one sole act of thanksgiving, around one sole altar, with ministers and holy people.

Thus it is that the rite of concelebration expresses and inculcates vividly truths of great moment for the spiritual and pastoral lives of priests and the Christian formation of the faithful.

2. See S.T. Thomas Aquinas. *Summa Theol.*, III, q. 82, a. 2, ad 2 and 3 (the editio typica refers to article 3, but this would appear to be a mistake).
3. See Constitution on the Church, (D. *28*), Art. 26.
4. See Constitution on the Liturgy, (D. *1*), Art. 2 and 41.
5. See Constitution on the Liturgy, Art. 26.
6. See Constitution on the Liturgy, Art. 41.

For these reasons, much more than for merely practical considerations, concelebration of the mystery of the Eucharist has existed in the Church from antiquity, in different forms, and has survived to our own day, evolving differently, in both East and West.

It was for these same reasons that liturgical experts had been pursuing researches into the matter, submitting requests that permission for concelebration be extended and that the rite be reformed.

Finally, the Second Vatican Council, having considered the matter carefully, had extended the faculty of concelebrating to a number of cases and had ordered the preparation of a new rite of concelebration, to be inserted into the Pontifical and the Roman Missal.[7] Consequently, after he had solemnly approved and proclaimed the Constitution on Sacred Liturgy, His Holiness Pope Paul VI commissioned the Consilium charged with the implementation of the constitution to prepare a rite of concelebration as soon as possible. While the rite was being prepared, it was several times examined by the members and consultors of the Consilium and was considerably revised. Finally, the Consilium unanimously ratified it on 19 June 1964, ordaining that, if the Holy Father approved, it should be experimented with in different parts of the world and in varying circumstances before being definitively approved.

The Concilium for the Implementation of the Constitution on the Sacred Liturgy, in accordance with the wishes of the council, also prepared a rite for the administration of Communion under both species and it defined the occasions and the manner in which clergy, religious and laity may receive the Eucharist under both species.

For some months a number of experiments were carried out, with excellent results, with regard to the rites both of concelebration and of Communion under both species, all over the world. When the secretary had received reports and comments on these experiments, both rites were submitted to a final revision in the light of the experience gained and were submitted to the Holy Father by Cardinal Giacomo Lercaro, President of the Consilium.

The Holy Father considered the two rites very carefully, with the assistance both of the Consilium and of the Sacred Congregation of Rites, and he approved and confirmed

7. See Constitution on the Liturgy, Art. 57 and 58.

them, *speciali modo,* in their entirety and in all parts, in virtue of his authority, in an audience with Cardinal Arcadio Maria Larraona, Prefect of the Sacred Congregation of Rites. He ordered it to be published and to be observed by everybody from Holy Thursday, 16 April, 1965, and to be accurately transcribed into the Pontifical and Missal.

5

DECREE ON THE ADMINISTRATION OF HOLY COMMUNION IN HOSPITALS[a]

S.C.R., *Cum Hac Nostra Aetate,* 14 February, 1966

Nowadays it is customary to administer Holy Communion frequently, even daily, to patients in hospitals. However, this can cause inconvenience because of the way hospitals are constructed and because of their internal regimes. The Sacred Congregation of Rites has decided that the prescriptions of the Roman Ritual, Title 5, ch. 4, no. 28, should be changed as follows, so as to make it possible to administer communion to a large number of patients easily and quickly:

1. In a hospital in which there is only one building and which has an oratory, the priest administering Holy Communion should recite in the oratory all the prayers prescribed by the ritual to be said before and after communion of the sick. He should then distribute Holy Communion to the individual patients in their own rooms, using the formula for communion.

2. In a hospital in which there are several buildings, the Blessed Sacrament should be reverently taken from the oratory to a table placed in a proper and suitable place in each building. The priest should there recite the prayers before and after communion and then distribute Holy Communion as was said above.

a. Translated by A.F., Latin text in *AAS* 58 (1966), pp. 525–526.

6

APOSTOLIC CONSTITUTION ON THE REVISION OF INDULGENCES[a]

Paul VI, *Indulgentiarum Doctrina*, 1 January, 1967

INDULGENCES ARE FOUNDED IN DIVINE REVELATION

1. The doctrine of indulgences and their practice have been in force for many centuries in the Catholic Church. They would appear to be solidly founded on divine Revelation,[1] handed down "from the apostles." This (tradition ". . . makes progress in the Church, with the help of the Holy Spirit," and "as the centuries go by, the Church is always advancing towards the plenitude of divine truth, until eventually the words of God are fulfilled in her."[2]

If we wish to understand exactly the doctrine of indulgences and its benefits in practice, we must remember truths which the whole Church, enlightened by God's word, has always believed. These truths have been taught by the bishops, who are the successors of the apostles, and by the Roman Pontiffs, who, as successors of St. Peter, are first and foremost among the bishops. They have taught these truths by means of their pastoral practice as well as in documents setting forth doctrine. They have done it throughout the centuries to this day.

a. Translated by Francis Ripley, published by CTS, London, Reproduced with permission, Latin text in *AAS* 59 (1967) pp. 5–24.
1. Cf. Council of Trent, Session 25, Decree on Indulgences: *Denz.* (Denzinger-Schonmetzer) 1835; cf. Mt. 28:18.
2. Vatican II, Dogmatic Constitution on Divine Revelation, n. 8: *AAS* 58 (1966), p. 821; cf. Vatican I, Dogmatic Constitution on the Catholic Faith, ch. 4: *Denz.* 3020.

SIN MUST BE EXPIATED

2. The truth has been divinely revealed that sins are followed by punishments. God's holiness and justice inflict them. Sins must be expiated. This may be done on this earth through the sorrows, miseries and trials of this life and, above all, through death.[3] Otherwise the expiation must be made in the next life through fire and torments or *purifying* punishments.[4] This is why the faithful have always been convinced that the paths of evil are strewn with many stumbling blocks. They bring to those who follow them adversities, bitterness and harm.[5]

The punishments with which we are concerned here are imposed by God's judgment, which is just and merciful. The reasons for their imposition are that our souls need to be purified, the holiness of the moral order needs to be strengthened and God's glory must be restored to its full majesty. In fact, every sin upsets the universal order God, in his indescribable wisdom and limitless love, has established. Further, every sin does immense harm to the sinner himself and to the community of men. Throughout history Christians have always believed that sin is not only a breaking of God's law but that it shows contempt for or disregard of the friendship between God and man. The latter is not always directly evident.[6] Further, they have believed that sin is a real offense against God, the effect of which cannot be estimated. Again, it is a display of ingratitude, a rejection of the love God has shown us through Jesus Christ. He called his disciples friends, not servants.[7]

3. Cf. Gen. 3:16-19, Lk. 19:41-44; Rom. 2:9; 1 Cor. 11:30. Cf. St. Augustine, *Enarr. in Ps.* 58, 1, 13: *CCL* 39, p. 739: *PL* 36, 701; St. Thomas, *Summa Theol. I-II*, q. 87, a. 1.
4. Cf. Mt. 25:41-42; Mk. 9:42-43;Jn. 5:28-29; Rom. 2:9; Gal. 6:68. Cf. Council of Lyons II, Session 4, *Profession of faith of Michael Palaeologus: Denz.* 856-858; Council of Florence, Decree for the Greeks: *Denz.* 1304-1306; St. Augustine, *Enchiridion* 66, 17, ed. Scheel, Tubingen 1930, p. 42: *PL* 40, 263.
5. Cf. *Hermae pastor,* Mand. 6, 1, 3: Funk, *Patres Apostolici* I, p. 487.
6. Cf. Is. 1:2-3; also Dt. 8:11, 32:15 ff.; Ps. 105:21, 118 *passim;* Wis. 7:14; Is. 17:10, 44:21; Jer. 33:8; Ezek. 20:27. Cf. Vatican II, Dogmatic Constitution on Divine Revelation, n. 2: *AAS* 58 (1966), p. 818; cf. also ibid., n. 21, pp. 827-828.
7. Cf. Jn. 15:14-15. Cf. Vatican II, Pastoral Constitution on the Church in the Modern World, n. 22: *AAS* 58 (1966), p. 1042; Decree on the Missionary Activity of the Church, n. 13: *AAS* 58 (1966), p. 962.

WHAT EXPIATION INVOLVES

3. The full taking away and, as it is called, reparation of sins requires two things. Firstly, friendship with God must be restored. Amends must be made for offending his wisdom and goodness. This is done by a sincere conversion of mind. Secondly, all the personal and social values, as well as those that are universal, which sin has lessened or destroyed must be fully made good. This is done in two ways. The first is by freely making reparation, which involves punishment. The second is by accepting the punishments God's just and most holy wisdom has appointed. From this the holiness and splendor of his glory shine out through the world. The very facts that punishment for sin exists and that it is so severe make it possible for us to understand how foolish and malicious sin is and how harmful its consequences are.

The doctrine of purgatory clearly demonstrates that even when the guilt of sin has been taken away, punishment for it or the consequences of it may remain to be expiated or cleansed.[8] They often are. In fact, in purgatory the souls of those "who died in the charity of God and truly repentant, but who had not made satisfaction with adequate penance for their sins and omissions"[9] are cleansed after death with punishments designed to purge away their debt. All this is gathered also from the prayers of the liturgy Christian people, admitted to holy communion, have addressed to God since very ancient times: "may we who are justly punished for our sins be freed through your mercy and for the glory of your name."[10]

All men who walk this earth commit at least venial and so-called daily sins.[11] All, therefore, need God's mercy to set them free from sin's penal consequences.

---

8. Cf. Num. 20:12, 27:13–14; 2 Kg. 12:13–14; also Innocent IV, *Instructio pro Graecis: Denz.* 838. Cf. Council of Trent, Session 6, Can. 30: *Denz.* 1580; also *Denz.* 1689, 1693. Cf. St. Augustine, *In Iohannis Evangelium Tractatus* 124, 5: *CCL* 36, pp. 683–684: *PL* 35, 1972–1973.
9. Council of Lyons II, Session 4: *Denz.* 856.
10. Cf. Septuagesima Sunday, *Oratio;* Monday after First Sunday in Lent, *Oratio super populum;* Third Sunday in Lent, *Postcommunio.*
11. Cf. Jas. 3:2; 1 Jn. 1:8; the Council of Carthage gave a commentary on this text for which see *Denz.* 228; Cf. Council of Trent, Session 6, Decree on Justification, ch. 2: *Denz.* 1537. Cf. Vatican II, Dogmatic Constitution on the Church, n. 40: *AAS* 57 (1965), p. 45.

Chapter II

THE COMMUNION OF SAINTS

4. By the hidden and kindly mystery of God's will a supernatural solidarity reigns among men. A consequence of this is that the sin of one person harms other people just as one person's holiness helps others.[12] In this way Christian believers help each other to reach their supernatural destiny. We can see evidence of this solidarity in the fact that Adam's sin is passed on through propagation to all men. But the greatest and most perfect source, foundation and example of this supernatural solidarity is Christ himself. God has called us to communion with him.[13]

5. Indeed, Christ "committed no sin," "suffered for us,"[14] "was wounded for our transgressions, he was bruised for our iniquities . . . and with his stripes we are healed."[15]

Following in Christ's steps,[16] those who believe in him have always tried to help one another along the path which leads to the heavenly Father, through prayer, the exchange of spiritual goods and penitential expiation. The more they have been immersed in the fervor of love, the more they have imitated Christ in his sufferings. They have carried their crosses to make expiation for their own sins and the sins of others. They were convinced that they could help their brothers to obtain salvation from God who is the Father of mercies.[17] This is the very ancient dogma called

12. Cf. St. Augustine, *De bapt. contra Donat.* I, 28: *PL* 43, 124.
13. Cf. Jn. 15:5; 1 Cor. 12:27; also 1 Cor. 1:9, 10:17; Eph. 1:20–23, 4:4. Cf. Vatican II, Dogmatic Constitution on the Church, n. 7: *AAS* 57 (1965), pp. 10–11. Cf. Pius XII, Encycl. *Mystici Corporis: Denz.* 3813: *AAS* 35 (1943), pp. 230–231. Cf. St. Augustine, *Enarr. in Ps.* 90, 1: *CCL* 39, p. 1266: *PL* 37, 1159.
14. Cf. 1 Pet. 2:21–22.
15. Cf. Is. 53:4–6 with 1 Pet. 2:21–25; also Jn. 1:29; Rom. 4:25, 5:9 ff.; 1 Cor. 15:3; 2 Cor. 5:21; Gal. 1:4; Eph. 1:7 ff.; Heb. 1:3 etc.; 1 Jn. 3:5.
16. Cf. 1 Pet. 2:21.
17. Cf. Col. 1:24. Cf. Clement of Alexandria, *Quis dives salvetur* 42: *GCS* Clement 3, p. 190: *PG* 9, 650 also St. Cyprian, *De lapsis* 17, 36: *CSEL* 3(1), pp. 249–250, 263: *PL* 4, 495, 508. Cf. St. Jerome, *Contra Vigilantium* 6: *PL* 23, 359; St. Basil the Great, *Homilia in martyrem Julittam* 9: *PG* 31, 258–259; St. John Chrysostom, *Epist. ad Philipp.* 1, 3, 3: *PG* 62, 203; St. Thomas, *Summa Theol.* I–II, q. 87, a .8.

the Communion of Saints.[18] It means that the life of each individual son of God is joined in Christ and through Christ by a wonderful link to the life of all his other Christian brethren. Together they form the supernatural unity of Christ's Mystical Body so that, as it were, a single mystical person is formed.[19]

THE TREASURY OF THE CHURCH

The "treasury of the Church"[20] is explained like this. We certainly should not think of it as being the sum total of the material goods which have accumulated during the course of the centuries. On the contrary the "treasury of the Church" is the infinite value, which can never be exhausted, which Christ's merits have before God. They were offered so that the whole of mankind could be set free from sin and attain communion with the Father. In Christ, the Redeemer himself, the satisfactions and merits of his Redemption exist and find their efficacy.[21] This treasury includes as well the prayers and good works of the Blessed Virgin Mary. They are truly immense, unfathomable and even pristine in their value before God. In the treasury, too, are the prayers and good works of all the saints, all those who have followed in the footsteps of Christ the Lord and by his grace have made their lives holy and carried out the mission the Father entrusted to them. In this way they attained their own salvation and at the same time cooperated in saving their brothers in the unity of the Mystical Body.

CONSEQUENCE OF THE DOCTRINE OF THE MYSTICAL BODY

"All who belong to Christ and are in possession of his Spirit, combine to make one Church with a cohesion that depends on him (cf. Eph. 4:16). The union of the living with their brethren who have fallen asleep in Christ is not

18. Cf. Leo XIII, Encycl. *Mirae caritatis: Acta Leonis XIII* 22 (1902), p. 129: *Denz.* 3363.
19. Cf. 1 Cor. 12:12–13. Cf. Pius XII, Encycl. *Mystici Corporis: AAS* 35 (1943), p. 218; St. Thomas, *Summa Theol.* III, q. 48, a. 2, q. 49, a. 1.
20. Cf. Clement VI, Jubilee Bull *Unigenitus Dei Filius: Denz.* 1025, 1026, 1027. Cf. Sixtus IV, Encycl. *Romani Pontificis: Denz.* 1406. Cf. Leo X, Decree *Cum postquam: Denz.* 1448; cf. *Denz.* 1467, 2641.
21. Cf. Heb. 7:23–25, 9:11–28.

broken; the Church has rather believed through the ages that it gains strength from the sharing of spiritual benefits. The great intimacy of the union of those in heaven with Christ, gives extra steadiness in holiness to the whole Church . . . and makes a manifold contribution to the extension of her building (cf. 1 Cor. 12:12–27). Now that they are welcomed in their own country and at home with the Lord (cf. 2 Cor. 5:8), through him, with him and in him they intercede unremittingly with the Father on our behalf, offering the merit they acquired on earth through Christ Jesus, the one and only mediator between God and man (cf. 1 Tim. 2:5), when they were at God's service in all things, and in their flesh were completing what is lacking in Christ's afflictions for the sake of his Body, the Church (cf. Col. 1:24). Their brotherly care is the greatest help to our weakness."[22]

For these reasons a perennial link of charity exists between the faithful who have already reached their heavenly home, those who are expiating their sins in purgatory and those who are still pilgrims on earth. Between them there is, too, an abundant exchange of all the goods by which divine justice is placated as expiation is made for all the sins of the whole of the Mystical Body. This is how God's mercy is led to forgiveness and it becomes possible for sinners who have repented sincerely, to share, as soon as they are capable of it, in the full enjoyment of the benefits of God's family.

CHAPTER III

THE CHURCH APPLIES THE FRUITS OF CHRIST'S REDEMPTION

6. The Church has known these truths ever since it came into existence. It formulated them and devised various ways of applying the fruits of Christ's redemption to the individual faithful. It also led them to cooperate in the salvation of

22. Vatican II, Dogmatic Constitution on the Church, (D.28), n. 49.

their brothers. The purpose was that the whole body of the Church might be prepared in justice and holiness for the complete realization of God's kingdom, when he will be all things to all men.

In fact the apostles themselves urged their disciples to pray that sinners might be saved.[23] This very ancient practice of the Church has happily lasted,[24] particularly in the practice of penitents begging the whole community's prayers,[25] and in helping the dead with intercessions, especially through the offering of the Eucharistic Sacrifice.[26] From the most ancient times in the Church good works were also offered to God for the salvation of sinners, particularly the works which human weakness finds hard.[27] Because the sufferings of the martyrs for the faith and for God's law were thought to be very valuable, penitents used to turn to the martyrs to be helped by their merits to obtain a more speedy reconcilation from the bishops.[28] Indeed, the prayers and good works of holy people were regarded as of such great value that it could be asserted that the penitent was washed, cleansed and redeemed with the help of the entire Christian people.[29]

However, the belief was not that individual members of the Church worked for the remission of their brethren's sins by their own merits alone but that the whole Church as a single body united to Christ its Head was bringing about satisfaction.[30]

The Church of the Fathers was fully convinced that it

23. Cf. Jas. 5:16; 1 Jn. 5:16.
24. Cf. St. Clement of Rome, *Ad Cor.* 56, 1: Funk, *Patres Apostolici* I, p. 171; *Martyrium S. Polycarpi* 8, 1: Funk, *Patres Apostolici* I, pp. 321, 323.
25. Cf. Sozomenus, *Hist. Eccl.* 7, 16: *PG* 67, 1462.
26. Cf. St. Cyril of Jerusalem, *Catechesis* 23 (*mystag.* 5), 9, 10: *PG* 33, 1115, 1118; St. Augustine, *Confessiones* 9, 12, 32: *PL* 32, 777; and 9, 11, 27: *PL* 32, 775: *Sermones* 172, 2: *PL* 38, 936; *De cura pro mortuis gerenda* 1, 3: *PL* 40, 593.
27. Cf. Clement of Alexandria, *Quis dives salvetur* 42: *CGS* 17, pp. 189–190: *PG* 9, 651.
28. Cf. Tertullian, *Ad Martyras* 1, 6: *CCL* 1, p. 3: *PL* 1, 695. Cf. St. Cyprian, *Epist.* 18 (alias: 12), 1: *CSEL* 3(2), pp. 523–524: *PL* 4, 265; cf. *Epist.* 19 (alias: 13), 2: *CSEL* 3(2), p. 525: *PL* 4, 267. Also Euebius of Caesarea, *Hist. Eccl.* 1, 6, 42: *CGS* Eus. 2, 2, 610; *PG* 20, 614–615.
29. Cf. St. Ambrose, *De paenitentia* 1, 15: *PL* 16, 511.
30. Cf. Tertullian, *De paenitentia* 10, 5–6: *CCL* 1, p. 337: *PL* 1, 1356. Cf. St. Augustine, *Enarr. in Ps.* 85, 1: *CCL* 39, pp. 1176–1177: *PL* 37, 1082.

was carrying on the work of salvation in community and under the authority of the pastors appointed by the Holy Spirit as bishops to rule God's Church.[31] So the bishops made a prudent judgment about these questions. They decided on the way and the extent to which satisfaction was to be made. Indeed, they allowed the canonical penances to be replaced by other works which may have been easier but which would be useful for the good of all and suitable to promote piety. These works were performed by the penitents themselves and sometimes by other members of the Church.[32]

CHAPTER IV

HOW INDULGENCES DEVELOPED FROM THE CANONICAL PENANCES

7. The conviction was present in the Church that the pastors of the Lord's flock could set the individual free from the vestiges of sin by applying to him the merits of Christ and of the saints. In the course of the centuries and under the influence of the Holy Spirit's continuous inspiration of the People of God this conviction led to the practice of indulgences. It was a progression in the Church's doctrine and discipline rather than a change.[33] From the roots of Revelation something had grown up, a new privilege which

31. Cf. Acts 20:28; also Council of Trent, Session 23, Decree on the Sacrament of Order, ch. 4: *Denz.* 1768; Vatican I, Session 4, Dogmatic Constitution on the Church, ch. 3: *Denz.* 3061: Vatican II, Dogmatic Constitution on the Church, n. 20: *AAS* 57 (1965), p. 23. Cf. St. Ignatius of Antioch, *Ad Smyrn.* 8, 1: Funk, *Patres Apostolici* I, p. 283.
32. Cf. Council of Nicaea I, Can. 12: Mansi, *SS. Conciliorum collectio* 2, 674; Council of Neocaesarea, Can. 3: *loc. cit.* 540. Cf. also St. Innocent I, *Epist.* 25, 7, 10: *PL* 20, 559: St. Leo the Great, *Epist.* 159, 6: *PL* 54, 1138; St. Basil the Great, *Epist.* 217 (Can. 3), 74; *PG* 32, 803; St. Ambrose, *De paenitentia* 1, 15 (see note 29 above).
33. Cf. St. Vincent of Lerins, *Commonitorium primum* 23: *PL* 50, 667–668.

was for the benefit of the faithful and the whole Church.

The use of indulgences spread gradually. It became a very clear element in the history of the Church when the Popes decreed that certain works which were suitable for promoting the common good of the Church "could replace all penitential practices"[34] and that the faithful who were "genuinely sorry for and had confessed their sins" and done such works were granted "by almighty God's mercy and . . . trusting in his Apostles merits and authority" and "by virtue of the fullness of the apostolic power" "not only full and abundant forgiveness, but the most complete forgiveness possible for their sins."[35]

For "God's only-begotten Son . . . has won a treasure for the militant Church . . . he has entrusted it to blessed Peter, the key-bearer of heaven, and to his successors who are Christ's vicars on earth, so that they may distribute it to the faithful for their salvation. They may apply it with mercy for reasonable causes to all who have repented for and have confessed their sins. At times they may remit completely, and at other times only partially, the temporal punishment due to sin in a general as well as in special ways (insofar as they judge it to be fitting in the sight of the Lord). The merits of the Blessed Mother of God and of all the elect . . . are known to add further to this treasure."[36]

WHAT INDULGENCES ARE: THE CHURCH'S AUTHORITATIVE INTERVENTION

8. The taking away of the temporal punishment due to sins when their guilt has already been forgiven has been called specifically "indulgence."[37]

While it has something in common with other ways of eliminating the vestiges of sin, an indulgence is clearly different from them.

In fact, in granting an indulgence the Church uses its power as minister of Christ's Redemption. It not only prays. It intervenes with its authority to dispense to the faithful, provided they have the right dispositions, the trea-

34. Cf. Council of Claremont, Can. 2: Mansi, SS. Conciliorum collectio 20, 816.
35. Cf. Boniface VIII, Bull Antiquorum habet: Denz. 868.
36. Clement VI, Jubilee Bull Uniguenitus Dei Filius: Denz. 1025, 1026, 1027.
37. Cf. Leo X, Decree Cum postquam: Denz. 1447–1448.

sury of satisfaction which Christ and the saints won for the remission of temporal punishment.[38]

The authorities of the Church have two aims in granting indulgences. The first is to help the faithful to expiate their sins. The second is to encourage them to do works of piety, penitence and charity, particularly those which lead to growth in faith and which help the common good.[39]

Further, if the faithful offer indulgences by way of intercession for the dead they cultivate charity in an excellent way. While they raise their minds in heaven they bring a wiser order into the things of this world.

INDULGENCES HAVE BEEN ABUSED IN THE PAST

The teaching authority, the Magisterium of the Church, has defended and explained the teaching about indulgences in various documents.[40] Unfortunately, the practice of indulgences has on occasions been improperly applied. This has been either through "untimely and superfluous indulgences" which humiliated the power of the keys and weakened penitential satisfaction[41] or it has been through the collection of "unlawful profits" which blasphemously took away the good name of indulgences.[42] The Church deplored and corrected these improper uses. It "teaches and commands that the usage of indulgences—a usage most beneficial to Christians and approved by the authority of the Sacred Councils—should be kept in the Church; and it condemns with anathema those who say that indulgences are useless or that the Church does not have the power to grant them."[43]

38. Cf. Paul VI, Letter *Sacrosancta Portiunculae: AAS* 58 (1966), pp. 633–634.
39. Cf. Paul VI, Letter cited: p. 632.
40. Clement VI, Jubilee Bull *Uniguenitus Dei Filius: Denz.* 1026; Letter *Super quibusdam: Denz.* 1059. Martin V, Bull *Inter cunctas: Denz.* 1266. Sixtus IV, Bull *Salvator noster: Denz.* 1398; Encly. *Romani Pontificis provida: Denz.* 1405–1406. Leo X, Bull *Exsurge Domine: Denz.* 1467–1472. Pius VI, Constitution *Auctorem fidei,* prop. 40, 41, 42: *Denz.* 2640, 2641, 2642. Pius XI, Indiction of the extraordinary holy year: *AAS* 25 (1933), p. 8; Indiction of the universal Jubilee, *AAS* (1949), pp. 258–259.
41. Cf. Lateran Council IV, ch. 62: *Denz.* 819.
42. Cf. Council of Trent, Decree on Indulgences: *Denz.* 1835.
43. Cf. ibid.

THE BENEFITS OF INDULGENCES

9. At the present day also, then, the Church invites all its children to think over and weigh up in their minds as well as they can how the use of indulgences benefits their lives and all Christian society.

We recall briefly the most important considerations. First, the practice of indulgences is beneficial because it teaches us to "know and see that it is evil and bitter for us to forsake . . . the Lord our God."[44] Really, when they gain indulgences the faithful understand that by their own powers they could not remedy the harm they have done to themselves and to the whole community by their sin. They are therefore moved to a salutary humility.

Further, the use of indulgences shows us how closely we are united to each other in Christ. It emphasizes, too, how the supernatural life of each can help others and thus unite them more easily and more closely with the Father. The use of indulgences, therefore, effectively influences charity in us. That charity is demonstrated in an outstanding way when we offer indulgences to help our brethren who rest in Christ.

10. Moreover, the religious practice of indulgences arouses again confidence and hope that we can be fully reconciled with the Father. But it does not do this in a way which would justify negligence of any kind or in the slightest manner lessen the effort one has to make to acquire the dispositions that are needed for full communion with God. While it is true that indulgences are free gifts, they are granted only on fixed conditions for the living as well as for the dead. To gain indulgences the work prescribed must be done. But that is not all. The faithful must have the dispositions that are necessary. These are that they must love God, hate sin, trust in Christ's merits, and believe firmly in the great help they obtain from the Communion of Saints.

In addition, we ought not to forget that when they try to gain indulgences the faithful submit with docility to the lawful pastors of the Church. Above all, they acknowledge the authority of the successor of Blessed Peter, the keybearer of heaven. To them the Saviour himself entrusted the task of feeding his flock and ruling his Church.

44. Jer. 2:19.

The beneficial institution of indulgences therefore does its part in bringing it about that the Church might be presented to Christ without spot or wrinkle but holy and without blemish,[45] excellently united with Christ in the supernatural bond of charity. By means of indulgences those members of the Church who are enduring their purification are united more speedily to the members who are in heaven the unity of the faith and of the knowledge of the Son of God, to mature manhood, to the measure of the stature of the fullness of Christ."[46]

INDULGENCES DO NOT LESSEN THE IMPORTANCE AND VALUE OF SACRAMENTS

11. Supported by these truths, holy Mother Church again recommends the practice of indulgences to the faithful. It has been very dear to Christian people for many centuries as well as in our own day. Experience proves this. Still, the Church does not intend in any way to lessen the value of other means of holiness and purification. First and foremost among these are the Sacrifice of the Mass and the Sacraments, especially the Sacrament of Penance. Neither does the Church reduce the importance of the many helps which are called sacramentals nor of the works of piety, penitence and charity. All these things have one thing in common: they make people holy and purify them all the more effectively according to the closeness of their union with Christ the Head and with the Body of the Church by charity. Indulgences also confirm the preeminence of charity in the Christian life. This is because indulgences cannot be gained without a sincere conversion of outlook and unity with God. The doing of the prescribed works is added to these things. The order of charity is preserved in this way. The remission of punishment by distribution from the Church's treasury is incorporated into it.

The Church recommends its faithful not to abandon or neglect the holy traditions of those who have gone before. They should be welcomed in a religious spirit as a precious treasure of the Catholic family and esteemed as such. At the same time all are left free to use these means of purification and sanctification with the holy freedom of God's children. Still, the Church reminds them constantly of the

45. Cf. Eph. 5:27.
46. Eph. 4:13.

things which should be given preference because they are necessary or at least better and more efficacious helps in the task of winning salvation.[47]

In order to give greater dignity and appreciation to the use of indulgences holy Mother Church has thought it fitting to introduce some innovations into the discipline of indulgences. Therefore new rules are being published.

CHAPTER V

12. The rules which follow introduce appropriate variations in the discipline of indulgences. They take into consideration the proposals made by the Conferences of Bishops.

The rulings of the Code of Canon Law and of the Decrees of the Holy See about indulgences remain unchanged except insofar as they differ from these new rules.

Three considerations have been given special attention in drawing up these new standards. First, a new measurement had to be laid down for partial indulgences. Second, the number of plenary indulgences had to be considerably reduced. Third, a simpler and more dignified statement was needed for the so-called "real" and "local" indulgences.

NEW RULES FOR PARTIAL INDULGENCES

Concerning partial indulgences, the way they have been determined hitherto, by days and years, is abolished. Instead a new standard for measuring them has been laid down. It takes into account the action itself of the faithful Christian who does the work to which the indulgence is attached.

The faithful can obtain by their acts—apart from the merit which is the principal fruit of the act—removal of temporal punishment, and this to a greater degree according to the love of the one who performs the act and the val-

47. Cf. St. Thomas Aquinas, *In Quat. Sent.* dist. 20, q, 1, a. 2, 3, ad 2 (*Suppl.* q. 25, a. 2, ad 2).

ue of the act itself. In view of these facts it has been thought appropriate that this remission of temporal punishment which the Christian faithful gain through an action should serve as the measurement for the remission of punishment that the authority of the Church adds by way of partial indulgence.

FEWER PLENARY INDULGENCES

In order that the faithful may esteem plenary indulgences more, it has been thought proper to reduce their number appropriately. This will help people to gain them with right dispositions. The more indulgences are multiplied, the less they are esteemed. What is offered too abundantly is not sufficiently appreciated. Besides, many of the faithful need considerable time to prepare themselves properly to gain a plenary indulgence.

INDULGENCES NOT ATTACHED TO THINGS AND PLACES

The number of "real" and "local" indulgences has been considerably reduced and their designations abolished. The purpose of this change is to make it clearer that indulgences are attached to what the faithful do, and not to things or places which are only the occasion for gaining the indulgences. In fact, members of pious Associations can gain the indulgences proper to their Associations without being bound to use special things.

NORMS

1. An indulgence is a remission before God of the temporal punishment due to sins whose guilt has already been forgiven, which the faithful Christian who is duly disposed gains under certain defined conditions through the Church's help when, as minister of Redemption, she dispenses and applies with authority the treasury of the satisfaction won by Christ and the saints.

2. An indulgence is partial or plenary according as it removes either part or all of the temporal punishment due to sin.

3. Partial as well as plenary indulgences can always be applied to the dead by way of prayer.

4. From now on a partial indulgence will be indicated only with the words "partial indulgence" without any determination of days or years.

5. The faithful who at least with a contrite heart perform an action to which a partial indulgence is attached obtain, in addition to the remission of temporal punishment merited by the action itself, an equal remission of punishment through the Church's intervention.

6. A plenary indulgence can be gained only once a day, except for the provisions stated in n. 18 below for those who are "on the point of death."

A partial indulgence can be gained more than once a day, unless there is an explicit direction to the contrary.

7. The requirements for gaining a plenary indulgence are: the indulgenced work must be performed and three conditions fulfilled. These are: (a) sacramental confession, (b) eucharistic communion, (c) prayer for the Pope's intentions. Further, it is necessary to be free from all attachment to any sin at all, even venial sin.

If this condition is not complete or if the conditions laid down are not fulfilled (except as provided in n. 11 for those who are "impeded"), the indulgence gained will be only partial.

8. The three conditions may be fulfilled several days before or after the prescribed work has been performed. However, it is appropriate that communion be received and the prayers for the Pope's intention be said on the same day the work is performed.

9. One sacramental confession suffices to gain several plenary indulgences. But for each plenary indulgence communion must be received and prayers for the Pope's intentions must be said.

10. One *Our Father* and one *Hail Mary* fully satisfy the condition of praying for the Pope's intentions; nevertheless, if a person wishes to substitute some other prayer according to his own piety and devotion towards the Pope he is free to do so.

11. The faculty granted by Canon 935 of the Code of Canon Law to confessors to change either the required work or the prescribed conditions (for gaining indulgences) for those who are "impeded" (i.e., unable to perform them because of some lawful impediment) is not changed. But local ordinaries can grant permission to gain a plenary indulgence without an actual confession and communion to

those of their canonical subjects for whom confession and communion are impossible or at least very difficult where they live, provided they are sorry for their sins and intend to receive these sacraments as soon as possible.

12. To make it clear that indulgences are attached to the actions of the faithful (even though they may sometimes be linked with some thing or place) the division of indulgences into "personal," "real" and "local" is abolished.

13. The *Enchiridion Indulgentiarum* (collection of indulgenced prayers and works) is to be revised. The purpose of the revision will be to attach indulgences only to the most important prayers and works of piety, charity and penance.

14. The lists and summaries of indulgences special to Religious Orders, Congregations, Societies of those living in community without vows, secular Institutes and the pious Associations of the faithful are to be revised as soon as possible. When this is done plenary indulgences may be gained only on set days appointed by the Holy See after considering the proposals made by the Superior General, or, in the case of pious Associations, of the local ordinary.

15. A plenary indulgence, applicable only to the dead, can be gained in all churches and public oratories (and in semi-public oratories by those who have the right to use them) on November 2.

In addition, a plenary indulgence can be gained twice a year in parish churches. This is on the feast of the church's Titular and on August 2, the date of the "Portiuncula," or on some other more suitable day to be determined by the ordinary.

All the indulgences mentioned above can be gained either on the set day or, with the ordinary's consent, on the Sunday before or the Sunday after.

Other indulgences attached to churches and oratories are to be revised as soon as possible.

16. The work prescribed for gaining a plenary indulgence connected with a church or oratory is a devout visit during which an *Our Father* and *Creed* are recited.

17. The faithful who use with devotion an object of piety (crucifix, cross, rosary, scapular or medal) after it has been duly blessed by any priest, can gain a partial indulgence.

But if this object of piety is blessed by the Pope or any bishop, the faithful who use it with devotion can also gain a plenary indulgence on the feast of the Apostles Peter and

Paul, provided they also make a profession of faith using any approved formula.

18. When one of the faithful is in danger of death and no priest is available to administer the sacraments to him with the apostolic blessing, to which a plenary indulgence is attached (according to Canon 468, par. 2 of the Code of Canon Law), holy Mother Church still grants a plenary indulgence to be gained at the moment of death, on condition that they are properly disposed and have been in the habit of reciting some prayers during their lifetime. The practice of using a crucifix or cross while gaining this plenary indulgence is praiseworthy.

This plenary indulgence at the point of death can be gained by the faithful even if they have already gained another plenary indulgence on the same day.

19. The rules set out for plenary indulgences, especially those referred to in n. 6, apply also to what have been known up to now as the *toties quoties* plenary indulgences.

20. Holy Mother Church is extremely concerned for the faithful departed. She has decided to intercede for them to the fullest extent in every Mass and abrogates every special privilege in this matter.*

These new regulations for gaining indulgences will become valid three months from the date of publication of this Constitution in the *Acta Apostolicae Sedis* (i.e., 30 April 1967).

The indulgences which have been attached to objects of piety, which are not mentioned above, end three months after the date of publication of this Constitution in the *Acta Apostolicae Sedis* (i.e., 30 April 1967).

The revisions referred to in n. 14 and n. 15 must be submitted within a year to the Sacred Apostolic Penitentiary. Two years after the date of this Constitution, indulgences which have not been confirmed will become null and void.

We will that these statutes and prescriptions of ours be

* The revised *Enchiridion Indulgentiarum* referred to in n. 13 (See A. 104) has a considerably expanded set of norms, 36 in all (pp. 17-25). The additional norms come mostly from canon law and describe the powers of different ecclesiastical authorities to grant indulgences and the powers of a confessor to change the regulations. They outline the subjective dispositions needed to gain an indulgence, the manner of reciting the prescribed prayers. They state that nobody can gain an indulgence for another living person, nor for an action to which he is obliged. One can, however, gain an indulgence attached to a prayer or action prescribed as penance in confession. (Ed.)

put in force now and remain in force for the future, notwithstanding, if it is necessary so to state, the constitutions and apostolic directives published by our predecessors or any other prescriptions even if they might be worthy of special mention and derogation.

7

INSTRUCTION ON MUSIC IN THE LITURGY[a]

S.C.R., *Musicam Sacram,* 5 March, 1967

PREFACE

1. Sacred music, in those aspects which concern the liturgical renewal, was carefully considered by the Second Vatican Ecumenical Council. It explained its role in divine services, issued a number of principles and laws on this subject in the Constitution on the Liturgy, and devoted to it an entire chapter of the same Constitution.

2. The decisions of the Council have already begun to be put into effect in the recently undertaken liturgical renewal. But the new norms concerning the arrangement of the sacred rites and the active participation of the faithful have given rise to several problems regarding sacred music and its ministerial role. These problems appear to be able to be solved by expounding more fully certain relevant principles of the Constitution on the Liturgy.

3. Therefore the Consilium set up to implement the Constitution on the Liturgy, on the instructions of the Holy Father, has carefully considered these questions and prepared the present Instruction. This does not, however, gather together all the legislation on sacred music; it only establishes the principal norms which seem to be more necessary for our own day. It is, as it were, a continuation and complement of the preceding Instruction of this Sacred Congregation, prepared by this same Consilium on 26 September 1964, for the correct implementation of the Liturgy Constitution.

4. It is to be hoped that pastors of souls, musicians and the faithful will gladly accept these norms and put them

a. Translation issued by the Congregation. Latin text in *AAS* 59 (1967), pp. 300–320.

into practice, uniting their efforts to attain the true purpose of sacred music, "which is the glory of God and the sanctification of the faithful."[1]

(a) By sacred music is understood that which, being created for the celebration of divine worship, is endowed with a certain holy sincerity of form.[2]

(b) The following come under the title of *sacred music* here: Gregorian chant, sacred polyphony in its various forms both ancient and modern, sacred music for the organ and other approved instruments, and sacred popular music, be it liturgical or simply religious.[3]

I. SOME GENERAL NORMS

5. Liturgical worship is given a more noble form when it is celebrated in song, with the ministers of each degree fulfilling their ministry and the people participating in it.[4]

Indeed, through this form, prayer is expressed in a more attractive way, the mystery of the liturgy, with its hierarchical and community nature, is more openly shown, the unity of hearts is more profoundly achieved by the union of voices, minds are more easily raised to heavenly things by the beauty of the sacred rites, and the whole celebration more clearly prefigures that heavenly liturgy which is enacted in the holy city of Jerusalem.

Pastors of souls will therefore do all they can to achieve this form of celebration.

They will try to work out how that assignment of different parts to be performed and duties to be fulfilled, which characterizes sung celebrations, may be transferred even to celebrations which are not sung, but at which the people are present. Above all one must take particular care that the necessary ministers are obtained and that these are suitable, and that the active participation of the people is encouraged.

The practical preparation for each liturgical celebration should be done in a spirit of cooperation by all parties concerned, under the guidance of the rector of the church, whether it be in ritual, pastoral or musical matters.

6. The proper arrangement of a liturgical celebration re-

---

1. Constitution on the Liturgy, Art. 112.
2. Cf. St. Pius X, *Motu Proprio 'Tra le sollecitudini,'* n. 2.
3. Cf. Instruction of the S.C.R., 3 September 1958, n. 4.
4. Cf. Constitution on the Liturgy, Art. 113.

quires the due assignment and performance of certain functions, by which "each person, minister or layman, should carry out all and only those parts which pertain to his office by the nature of the rite and the norms of the liturgy."[5] This also demands that the meaning and proper nature of each part and of each song be carefully observed. To attain this, those parts especially should be sung which by their very nature require to be sung, using the kind and form of music which is proper to their character.

7. Between the solemn, fuller form of liturgical celebration, in which everything that demands singing is in fact sung, and the simplest form, in which singing is not used, there can be various degrees according to the greater or lesser place allotted to singing. However, in selecting the parts which are to be sung, one should start with those that are by their nature of greater importance, and especially those which are to be sung by the priest or by the ministers, with the people replying, or those which are to be sung by the priest and people together. The other parts may be gradually added according as they are proper to the people alone or to the choir alone.

8. Whenever, for a liturgical service which is to be celebrated in sung form, one can make a choice between various people, it is desirable that those who are known to be more proficient in singing be given preference; this is especially the case in more solemn liturgical celebrations and in those which either require more difficult singing, or are transmitted by radio or television.[6]

If, however, a choice of this kind cannot be made, and the priest or minister does not possess a voice suitable for the proper execution of the singing, he can render without singing one or more of the more difficult parts which concern him, reciting them in a loud and distinct voice. However, this must not be done merely for the convenience of the priest or minister.

9. In selecting the kind of sacred music to be used, whether it be for the choir or for the people, the capacities of those who are to sing the music must be taken into account. No kind of sacred music is prohibited from liturgical actions by the Church as long as it corresponds to the spirit of the liturgical celebration itself and the nature of its indi-

5. Constitution on the Liturgy, Art. 28.
6. Instruction of the S.C.R., 3 September 1958, n. 95.

vidual parts,[7] and does not hinder the active participation of the people.[8]

10. In order that the faithful may actively participate more willingly and with greater benefit, it is fitting that the format of the celebration and the degree of participation in it should be varied as much as possible, according to the solemnity of the day and the nature of the congregation present.

11. It should be borne in mind that the true solemnity of liturgical worship depends less on a more ornate form of singing and a more magnificent ceremonial than on its worthy and religious celebration, which takes into account the integrity of the liturgical celebration itself, and the performance of each of its parts according to their own particular nature. To have a more ornate form of singing and a more magnificent ceremonial is at times desirable when there are the resources available to carry them out properly; on the other hand it would be contrary to the true solemnity of the liturgy if this were to lead to a part of the action being omitted, changed, or improperly performed.

12. It is for the Holy See alone to determine the more important general principles which are, as it were, the basis of sacred music, according to the norms handed down, but especially according to the Constitution on the Liturgy. Direction in this matter, within the limits laid down, also belongs to the competent territorial Episcopal Conferences of various kinds, which have been legitimately constituted, and to the individual bishop.[9]

13. Liturgical services are celebrations of the Church, that is, of the holy people, united under and directed by the bishop or priest.[10] The priest and his ministers, because of the sacred order they have received, hold a special place in these celebrations, as do also—by reason of the ministry they perform—the servers, readers, commentators and those in the choir.[11]

14. The priest, acting in the person of Christ, presides over the gathered assembly. Since the prayers which are said or sung by him aloud are proclaimed in the name of

7. Cf. Constitution on the Liturgy, Art. 116.
8. Cf. Constitution on the Liturgy, Art. 28.
9. Cf. Constitution on the Liturgy, Art. 22.
10. Cf. Constitution on the Liturgy, Art. 26 and 41–32; Constitution on the Church, Art. 28.
11. Cf. Constitution on the Liturgy, Art. 29.

the entire holy people and of all present,[12] they should be devoutly listened to by all.

15. The faithful fulfil their liturgical role by making that full, conscious and active participation which is demanded by the nature of the liturgy itself and which is, by reason of baptism, the right and duty of the Christian people.[13] This participation

(a) Should be above all internal, in the sense that by it the faithful join their mind to what they pronounce or hear, and cooperate with heavenly grace,[14]

(b) Must be, on the other hand, external also, that is, such as to show the internal participation by gestures and bodily attitudes, by the acclamations, responses and singing.[15]

The faithful should also be taught to unite themselves interiorly to what the ministers or choir sing, so that by listening to them they may raise their minds to God.

16. One cannot find anything more religious and more joyful in sacred celebrations than a whole congregation expressing its faith and devotion in song. Therefore the active participation of the whole people, which is shown in singing, is to be carefully promoted as follows:

(a) It should first of all include acclamations, responses to the greetings of the priest and ministers and to the prayers of litany form, and also antiphons and psalms, refrains or repeated responses, hymns and canticles.[16]

(b) Through suitable instruction and practices, the people should be gradually led to a fuller—indeed, to a complete—participation in those parts of the singing which pertain to them.

(c) Some of the people's song, however, especially if the faithful have not yet been sufficiently instructed, or if musical settings for several voices are used, can be handed over to the choir alone, provided that the people are not excluded from those parts that concern them. But the usage of entrusting to the choir alone the entire singing of the whole Proper and of the whole Ordinary, to the complete exclusion of the people's participation in the singing, is to be deprecated.

12. Cf. Constitution on the Liturgy, Art. 33.
13. Cf. Constitution on the Liturgy, Art. 14.
14. Cf. Constitution on the Liturgy, Art. 11.
15. Cf. Constitution on the Liturgy, Art. 30.
16. Cf. Constitution on the Liturgy, Art. 30.

17. At the proper times, all should observe a reverent silence.[17] Through it the faithful are not only not considered as extraneous or dumb spectators at the liturgical service, but are associated more intimately in the mystery that is being celebrated, thanks to that interior disposition which derives from the word of God that they have heard, from the songs and prayers that have been uttered, and from spiritual union with the priest in the parts that he says or sings himself.

18. Among the faithful, special attention must be given to the instruction in sacred singing of members of lay religious societies, so that they may support and promote the participation of the people more effectively.[18] The formation of the whole people in singing, should be seriously and patiently undertaken together with liturgical instruction, according to the age, status and way of life of the faithful, and the degree of their religious culture; this should be done even from the first years of education in elementary schools.[19]

19. Because of the liturgical ministry it performs, the choir—or the *Capella musica,* or *schola cantorum*—deserves particular mention. Its role has become something of yet greater importance and weight by reason of the norms of the Council concerning the liturgical renewal. Its duty is, in effect, to ensure the proper performance of the parts which belong to it, according to the different kinds of music sung, and to encourage the active participation of the faithful in the singing. Therefore:

(a) There should be choirs, or *Capellae,* or *scholae cantorum,* especially in cathedrals and other major churches, in seminaries and religious houses of studies, and they should be carefully encouraged.

(b) It would also be desirable for similar choirs to be set up in smaller churches.

20. Large choirs (*Capellae musicae*) existing in basilicas, cathedrals, monasteries and other major churches, which have in the course of centuries earned for themselves high renown by preserving and developing a musical heritage of inestimable value, should be retained for sacred celebra-

17. Cf. Constitution on the Liturgy, Art. 30.
18. Cf. Instruction of the S.C.R., 26 September 1964, (D.3), nn. 19 and 59.
19. Cf. Constitution on the Liturgy, Art. 19; Instruction of the S.C.R., 3 September 1958, nn. 106–8.

tions of a more elaborate kind, according to their own traditional norms, recognized and approved by the Ordinary.

However, the directors of these choirs and the rectors of the churches should take care that the people always associate themselves with the singing by performing at least the easier sections of those parts which belong to them.

21. Provision should be made for at least one or two properly trained singers, especially where there is no possibility of setting up even a small choir. The singer will present some simpler musical settings, with the people taking part, and can lead and support the faithful as far as is needed. The presence of such a singer is desirable even in churches which have a choir, for those celebrations in which the choir cannot take part but which may fittingly be performed with some solemnity and therefore with singing.

22. The choir can consist, according to the customs of each country and other circumstances, of either men and boys, or men and boys only, or men and women, or even, where there is a genuine case for it, of women only.

23. Taking into account the layout of each church, the choir should be placed in such a way:

(a) That its nature should be clearly apparent—namely, that it is a part of the whole congregation, and that it fulfils a special role;

(b) That it is easier for it to fulfil its liturgical function;[20]

(c) That each of its members may be able to participate easily in the Mass, that is to say by sacramental participation.

Whenever the choir also includes women, it should be placed outside the sanctuary (*presbyterium*).

24. Besides musical formation, suitable liturgical and spiritual formation must also be given to the members of the choir, in such a way that the proper performance of their liturgical role will not only enhance the beauty of the celebration and be an excellent example for the faithful, but will bring spiritual benefit to the choir-members themselves.

25. In order that this technical and spiritual formation may more easily be obtained, the diocesan, national and international associations of sacred music should offer their

20. Cf. *Inter Oecumenici*, (D.3), (Nn. 84 to 99 omitted in this collection; point covered in D. *13*, 274: Ed.)

services, especially those that have been approved and several times commended by the Holy See.

26. The priest, the sacred ministers and the servers, the reader and those in the choir, and also the commentator, should perform the parts assigned to them in a way which is comprehensible to the people, in order that the responses of the people, when the rite requires it, may be made easy and spontaneous. It is desirable that the priest, and the ministers of every degree, should join their voices to the voice of the whole faithful in those parts which concern the people.[21]

27. For the celebration of the Eucharist with the people, especially on Sundays and feast days, a form of sung Mass (*Missa in cantu*) is to be preferred as much as possible, even several times on the same day.

28. The distinction between solemn, sung and read Mass, sanctioned by the Instruction of 1958 (n. 3), is retained, according to the traditional liturgical laws at present in force. However, for the sung Mass (*Missa cantata*), different degrees of participation are put forward here for reasons of pastoral usefulness, so that it may become easier to make the celebration of Mass more beautiful by singing, according to the capabilities of each congregation.

These degrees are so arranged that the first may be used even by itself, but the second and third, wholly or partially, may never be used without the first. In this way the faithful will be continually led towards an ever greater participation in the singing.

29. The following belong to the first degree:

(a) *In the entrance rites*:

the greeting of the priest together with the reply of the people; the prayer.

(b) *In the Liturgy of the Word*:

the acclamations at the Gospel.

(c) *In the Eucharistic Liturgy*:

the prayer over the offerings; the preface with its dialogue and the *Sanctus*; the final doxology of the Canon; the Lord's prayer with its introduction and embolism; the *Pax Domini;* the prayer after the Communion; the formulas of dismissal.

30. The following belong to the second degree:

---

21. Cf. *Inter Oecumenici*, (Nn. 48 to 76 omitted in this collection; points covered in D. *13*, ch. 2: Ed.)

(a) the *Kyrie, Gloria* and *Agnus Dei;*

(b) the Creed;

(c) the prayer of the faithful.

31. The following belong to the third degree:

(a) the songs at the Entrance and Communion processions;

(b) the songs after the Lesson or Epistle;

(c) the Alleluia before the Gospel;

(d) the song at the Offertory;

(e) the readings of Sacred Scripture, unless it seems more suitable to proclaim them without singing.

32. The custom legitimately in use in certain places and widely confirmed by indults, of substituting other songs for the songs given in the *Graduale* for the Entrance, Offertory and Communion, can be retained according to the judgment of the competent territorial authority, as long as songs of this sort are in keeping with the parts of the Mass, with the feast or with the liturgical season. It is for the same territorial authority to approve the texts of these songs.

33. It is desirable that the assembly of the faithful should participate in the songs of the Proper as much as possible, especially through simple responses and other suitable settings.

The song after the lessons, be it in the form of gradual or responsorial psalm, has a special importance among the songs of the Proper. By its very nature, it forms part of the Liturgy, of the Word. It should be performed with all seated and listening to it—and, what is more, participating in it as far as possible.

34. The songs which are called the "Ordinary of the Mass," if they are sung by musical settings written for several voices may be performed by the choir according to the customary norms, either *a capella*, or with instrumental accompaniment, as long as the people are not completely excluded from taking part in the singing.

In other cases, the parts of the Ordinary of the Mass can be divided between the choir and the people or even between two sections of the people themselves: one can alternate by verses, or one can follow other suitable divisions which divide the text into larger sections. In these cases, the following points are to be noted: it is preferable that the *Creed,* since it is a formula of profession of faith, should be sung by all, or in such a way as to permit a fitting participation by the faithful; it is preferable that the *Sanctus,* as the concluding acclamation of the Preface, should normally be sung by the whole congregation together with the priest; the *Agnus Dei* may be repeated as often as necessary, especially in concelebrations, where it accompanies the Fraction; it is desirable that the people should participate in this song, as least by the final invocation.

35. The Lord's Prayer is best performed by the people together with the priest.[22]

If it is sung in Latin, the melodies already legitimately existing should be used; if, however, it is sung in the vernacular, the settings are to be approved by the competent territorial authority.

36. There is no reason why some of the Proper or Ordinary should not be sung in said Masses. Moreover, some other song can also, on occasions, be sung at the beginning, at the Offertory, at the Communion and at the end of Mass. It is not sufficient, however, that these songs be merely "Eucharistic"—they must be in keeping with the parts of the Mass, with the feast, or with the liturgical season.

II. THE SINGING OF THE DIVINE OFFICE

37. The sung celebration of the Divine Office is the form which best accords with the nature of this prayer. It expresses its solemnity in a fuller way and expresses a deeper union of hearts in performing the praises of God. That is why, in accordance with the wish of the Constitution on the Liturgy,[23] this sung form is strongly recommended to those who celebrate the Office in choir or in common.

For it is desirable that at least some part of the Divine Office, especially the principal Hours, namely Lauds and Vespers, should be performed in sung form by these people, at least on Sundays and feast days.

Other clerics also, who live in common for the purpose of studies, or who meet for retreats or other purposes, will sanctify their meetings in a very fitting way if they celebrate some parts of the Divine Office in sung form.

38. When the Divine Office is to be celebrated in sung form, a principle of "progressive" solemnity can be used, inasmuch as those parts which lend themselves more directly to a sung form, e.g. dialogues, hymns, verses and canticles, may be sung, and the rest recited. This does not

22. Cf. *Inter Oecumenici*, n. 48.
23. Cf. Constitution on the Liturgy, Art. 99.

change the rules at present in force for those obliged to choir, nor does it change particular indults.

39. One will invite the faithful, ensuring that they receive the requisite instruction, to celebrate in common on Sundays and feast days certain parts of the Divine Office, especially Vespers, or, according to the customs of the particular area and assembly, other Hours. In general, the faithful, particularly the more educated, should be led by suitable teaching, to understand the psalms in a Christian sense and use them in their own prayers, so that they may gradually acquire a stronger taste for the use of the public prayer of the Church.

40. The members of Institutes professing the evangelical virtues should be given special instruction of this type, so that they may draw from it more abundant riches for the development of their spiritual life. It is desirable also that they should participate more fully in the public prayer of the Church by performing the principal Hours of the Office in sung form, as far as possible.

41. In accordance with the norm of the Constitution on the Liturgy and the centuries-old tradition of the Latin rite, the Latin language is to be retained for clerics celebrating the Divine Office in choir.[24] Since however the same Liturgy Constitution[25] concedes the use of the vernacular in the Divine Office both by the faithful and by nuns and other members of Institutes professing the evangelical virtues, who are not clerics, due care should be taken that melodies are prepared which may be used in the singing of the Divine Office in the vernacular.

III. SACRED MUSIC IN THE CELEBRATION OF THE SACRAMENTS AND SACRAMENTALS, IN SPECIAL FUNCTIONS OF THE LITURGICAL YEAR, IN CELEBRATIONS OF THE WORD OF GOD, AND IN POPULAR DEVOTIONS

42. The Council laid down in principle that whenever a rite, in keeping with its character, allows a celebration in common with the attendance and active participation of the faithful, this is to be preferred to an individual and quasi-private celebration of the rite.[26] It follows logically from

24. Cf. Constitution on the Liturgy, Art. 101:1.
25. Cf. Constitution on the Liturgy, Art. 101:2, 3.
26. Constitution on the Liturgy, Art. 27.

this that singing is of great importance since it more clearly demonstrates the 'ecclesial' aspect of the celebration.

43. Certain celebrations of the Sacraments and Sacramentals, which have a special importance in the life of the whole parish community, such as confirmation, sacred ordinations, matrimony, the consecration of a church or altar, funerals, etc., should be performed in sung form as far as possible, so that even the solemnity of the rite will contribute to its greater pastoral effectiveness. Nevertheless, the introduction into the celebration of anything which is merely secular, or which is hardly compatible with divine worship, under the guise of solemnity should be carefully avoided: this applies particularly to the celebration of marriages.

44. Similarly, celebrations which are singled out by the liturgy in the course of the liturgical year as being of special importance, may be solemnized by singing. In a very special way, the sacred rites of Holy Week should be given due solemnity, since these lead the faithful to the center of the liturgical year and of the liturgy itself through the celebration of the Paschal Mystery.

45. For the liturgy of the Sacraments and Sacramentals, and for other special celebrations of the liturgical year, suitable melodies should be provided, which can encourage a celebration in a more solemn form, even in the vernacular, depending on the capabilities of individual congregations and in accordance with the norms of the competent authority.

46. Sacred music is also very effective in fostering the devotion of the faithful in celebrations of the word of God, and in popular devotions.

In the celebrations of the word of God,[27] let the Liturgy of the Word in the Mass[28] be taken as a model. In all popular devotions the psalms will be especially useful, and also works of sacred music drawn from both the old and the more recent heritage of sacred music, popular religious songs, and the playing of the organ, or of other instruments characteristic of a particular people.

Moreover, in these same popular devotions, and especially in celebrations of the word of God, it is excellent to include as well some of those musical works which, although they no longer have a place in the liturgy, can nevertheless

27. Cf. *Inter Oecumenici*, nn. 37–9.
28. Cf. *Inter Oecumenici*, n. 37.

foster a religious spirit and encourage meditation on the sacred mystery.[29]

IV. THE LANGUAGE TO BE USED IN SUNG LITURGICAL CELEBRATIONS, AND ON PRESERVING THE HERITAGE OF SACRED MUSIC

47. According to the Constitution on the Liturgy, "the use of the Latin language, with due respect to particular law, is to be preserved in the Latin rites."[30]

However, since "the use of the vernacular may frequently be of great advantage to the people"[31] "it is for the competent territorial ecclesiastical authority to decide whether, and to what extent, the vernacular language is to be used. Its decrees have to be approved, that is, confirmed by the Apostolic See."[32]

In observing these norms exactly, one will therefore employ that form of participation which best matches the capabilities of each congregation.

Pastors of souls should take care that besides the vernacular "the faithful may also be able to say or sing together in Latin those parts of the Ordinary of the Mass which pertain to them."[33]

48. Where the vernacular has been introduced into the celebration of Mass,, the local Ordinaries will judge whether it may be opportune to preserve one or more Masses celebrated in Latin—especially sung Masses (*Missae in cantu*)—in certain churches, above all in large cities, where many come together with faithful of different languages.

49. As regards the use of Latin or the mother tongue in the sacred celebrations carried out in seminaries, the norms of the Sacred Congregation of Seminaries and Universities concerning the liturgical formation of the students should be observed.

The members of Institutes professing the evangelical virtues should observe, in this matter, the norms contained in the Apostolic Letter *Sacrificium Laudis* of 15 August 1966 besides the Instruction on the language to be used by religious in celebrating the Divine Office and conventual or

29. Cf. below, n. 53.
30. Constitution on the Liturgy, Art. 36:1.
31. Constitution on the Liturgy, Art. 36:2.
32. Constitution on the Liturgy, Art. 36:3.
33. Constitution on the Liturgy, Art. 54; *Inter Oecumenici*, n. 59.

community Mass, given by this Sacred Congregation of Rites on 23 November 1965.

50. In sung liturgical services celebrated in Latin:

(a) Gregorian chant, as proper to the Roman liturgy, should be given pride of place, other things being equal.[34] Its melodies, contained in the "typical" editions, should be used, to the extent that this is possible.

(b) "It is also desirable that an edition be prepared containing simpler melodies, for use in smaller churches."[35]

(c) Other musical settings, written for one or more voices, be they taken from the traditional heritage or from new works, should be held in honor, encouraged and used as the occasion demands.[36]

51. Pastors of souls, having taken into consideration pastoral usefulness and the character of their own language, should see whether parts of the heritage of sacred music, written in previous centuries for Latin texts, could also be conveniently used, not only in liturgical celebrations in Latin, but also in those performed in the vernacular. There is nothing to prevent different parts in one and the same celebration being sung in different languages.

52. In order to preserve the heritage of sacred music and genuinely promote the new forms of sacred singing, "great importance is to be attached to the teaching and practice of music in seminaries, in the novitiates and houses of study of religious of both sexes, and also in other Catholic institutes and schools," especially in those higher institutes intended specially for this.[37] Above all, the study and practice of Gregorian chant is to be promoted, because, with its special characteristics, it is a basis of great importance for the development of sacred music.

53. New works of sacred music should conform faithfully to the principles and norms set out above. In this way they will have "the qualities proper to genuine sacred music, being within the capacities not merely of large choirs, but of smaller choirs, facilitating the participation of all the faithful."[38]

As regards the heritage that has been handed down, those parts which correspond to the needs of the renewed

34. Cf. Constitution on the Liturgy, Art. 116.
35. Constitution on the Liturgy, Art. 117.
36. Cf. Constitution on the Liturgy, Art. 116.
37. Constitution on the Liturgy, Art. 115.
38. Constitution on the Liturgy, Art. 121.

liturgy should first be brought to light. Competent experts in this field must then carefully consider whether other parts can be adapted to the same needs. As for those pieces which do not correspond to the nature of the liturgy or cannot be harmonized with the pastoral celebration of the liturgy—they may be profitably transferred to popular devotions, especially to celebrations of the word of God.[39]

V. PREPARING MELODIES FOR VERNACULAR TEXTS

54. In preparing popular versions of those parts which will be set to melodies, and especially of the Psalter, experts should take care that fidelity to the Latin text is suitably harmonized with applicability of the vernacular text to musical settings. The nature and laws of each language must be respected, and the features and special characteristics of each people must be taken into consideration: all this, together with the laws of sacred music, should be carefully considered by musicians in the preparation of the new melodies.

The competent territorial authority will therefore ensure that in the commission entrusted with the composition of versions for the people, there are experts in the subjects already mentioned as well as in Latin and the vernacular; from the outset of the work, they must combine their efforts.

55. It will be for the competent territorial authority to decide whether certain vernacular texts set to music which have been handed down from former times, can in fact be used, even though they may not conform in all details with the legitimately approved versions of the liturgical texts.

56. Among the melodies to be composed for the people's texts, those which belong to the priest and ministers are particularly important, whether they sing them alone, or whether they sing them together with the people, or whether they sing them in "dialogue" with the people. In composing these, musicians will consider whether the traditional melodies of the Latin liturgy, which are used for this purpose, can inspire the melody to be used for the same texts in the vernacular.

57. New melodies to be used by the priests and ministers

39. Cf. above, n. 46.

must be approved by the competent territorial authority.[40]

58. Those Episcopal Conferences whom it may concern, will ensure that for one and the same language, used in different regions, there will be a single translation. It is also desirable that as far as possible, there should be one or more common melodies for the parts which concern the priest and ministers, and for the responses and acclamations of the people, so that the common participation of those who use the same language may be encouraged.

59. Musicians will enter on this new work with the desire to continue that tradition which has furnished the Church, in her divine worship, with a truly abundant heritage. Let them examine the works of the past, their types and characteristics, but let them also pay careful attention to the new laws and requirements of the liturgy, so that "new forms may in some way grow organically from forms that already exist,"[41] and the new work will form a new part in the musical heritage of the Church, not unworthy of its past.

60. The new melodies for the vernacular texts certainly need to undergo a period of experimentation in order that they may attain a sufficient maturity and perfection. However, anything done in churches, even if only for experimental purposes, which is unbecoming to the holiness of the place, the dignity of the liturgy and the devotion of the faithful, must be avoided.

61. Adapting sacred music for those regions which possess a musical tradition of their own, especially mission areas,[42] will require a very specialized preparation by the experts. It will be a question in fact of how to harmonize the sense of the sacred with the spirit, traditions and characteristic expressions proper to each of these peoples. Those who work in this field should have a sufficient knowledge both of the liturgy and musical tradition of the Church, and of the language, popular songs and other characteristic expressions of the people for whose benefit they are working.

VI. SACRED INSTRUMENTAL MUSIC

62. Musical instruments can be very useful in sacred celebrations, whether they accompany the singing or whether they are played as solo instruments.

40. Cf. *Inter Oecumenici*, n. 42.
41. Constitution on the Liturgy, Art. 23.
42. Cf. Constitution on the Liturgy, Art. 119.

"The pipe organ is to be held in high esteem in the Latin Church, since it is its traditional instrument, the sound of which can add a wonderful splendor to the Church's ceremonies and powerfully lift up men's minds to God and higher things.

"The use of other instruments may also be admitted in divine worship, given the decision and consent of the competent territorial authority, provided that the instruments are suitable for sacred use, or can be adapted to it, that they are in keeping with the dignity of the temple, and truly contribute to the edification of the faithful."[43]

63. In premitting and using musical instruments, the culture and traditions of individual peoples must be taken into account. However, those instruments which are, by common opinion and use, suitable for secular music only, are to be altogether prohibited from every liturgical celebration and from popular devotions.[44]

Any musical instrument permitted in divine worship should be used in such a way that it meets the needs of the liturgical celebration, and is in the interests both of the beauty of worship and the edification of the faithful.

64. The use of musical instruments to accompany the singing can act as a support to the voices, render participation easier, and achieve a deeper union in the assembly. However, their sound should not so overwhelm the voices that it is difficult to make out the text; and when some part is proclaimed aloud by the priest or a minister by virtue of his role, they should be silent.

65. In sung or said Masses, the organ, or other instrument legitimately admitted, can be used to accompany the singing of the choir and the people; it can also be played solo at the beginning before the priest reaches the altar, at the Offertory, at the Communion, and at the end of Mass.

The same rule, with the necessary adaptations, can be applied to other sacred celebrations.

66. The playing of these same instruments as solos is not permitted in Advent, Lent, during the Sacred Triduum and in the Offices and Masses of the Dead.

67. It is highly desirable that organists and other musicians should not only possess the skill to play properly the instrument entrusted to them: they should also enter into and be thoroughly aware of the spirit of the liturgy, so that

43. Constitution on the Liturgy, Art. 120.
44. Cf. Instruction of the S.C.R., 3 September 1958, n. 70.

even when playing *ex tempore*, they will enrich the sacred celebration according to the true nature of each of its parts, and encourage the participation of the faithful.[45]

VII. THE COMMISSIONS SET UP FOR THE PROMOTION OF SACRED MUSIC

68. The diocesan Commissions for sacred music are of most valuable assistance in promoting sacred music together with pastoral liturgical action in the diocese.

Therefore they should exist as far as possible in each diocese, and should unite their efforts with those of the liturgical Commission.

It will often be commendable for the two Commissions to be combined into one, and consist of persons who are expert in both subjects. In this way progress will be easier.

It is highly recommended that, where it appears to be more effective, several dioceses of the same region should set up a single Commission, which will establish a common plan of action and gather together their forces more fruitfully.

69. The Liturgical Commission, to be set up by the Episcopal Conference as judged opportune,[46] should also be responsible for sacred music; it should therefore also consist of experts in this field. It is useful, however, for such a Commission to confer not only with the diocesan Commissions, but also with other societies which may be involved in musical matters in the same region. This also applies to the pastoral liturgical Institute mentioned in art. 44 of the Constitution.

In the audience granted on 9 February, 1967 to His Eminence Arcadio M. Cardinal Larraona, Prefect of the Sacred Congregation of Rites, His Holiness Pope Paul VI approved and confirmed the present Instruction by his authority, ordered it to be published and at the same time established that it should come into force on Pentecost Sunday, 14 May, 1967.

45. Cf. above, n. 24.
46. Cf. Constitution on the Liturgy, Art. 44.

8

SECOND INSTRUCTION ON THE PROPER IMPLEMENTATION OF THE CONSTITUTION ON THE SACRED LITURGY[a]

S.C.R., *Tres Abhinc Annos,* 4 May, 1967

Three years ago, on 26 September 1964, the Sacred Congregation of Rites issued the Instruction, *Inter Oecumenici,* which prescribed a number of changes in the sacred rites. The changes became mandatory on 7 March 1965, and they were the first fruits, as it were, of the general reform of the liturgy envisaged by the Council's Constitution.

That these changes had already begun to bear fruit was made abundantly clear by the reports sent in by many bishops. These disclosed that the participation of the faithful in the sacred liturgy, especially in the holy sacrifice of the Mass, had everywhere increased and had become more conscious and more active.

The bishops have proposed several other changes designed to increase the faithful's participation and to make the rites, especially the rites of the Mass, clearer and more intelligible. Their recommendations were first sent to the Consilium for the Proper Implementation of the Constitution on the Sacred Liturgy and were then examined and weighed both by the Consilium and by the Sacred Congregation of Rites.

It was not possible, at any rate for the present, to introduce all the changes proposed. It was, however, felt that one could at once introduce some of the proposals which had pastoral reasons to recommend them and which do not seem to be out of harmony with the eventual and definitive

a. Translated by A.F. The Instruction is sometimes referred to by the first words of the Latin original, but also as "The Second Instruction" or *Instructio altera.* Latin text in *AAS* 59 (1967), pp. 442–448.

reform of the liturgy. These are changes which are deemed to contribute to the gradual process of reforming the liturgy and, on the other hand, they can be put into effect by simple rubrical indications, without changing the existing liturgical books.

It seems necessary to take this opportunity of recalling to mind the capital principle of ecclesiastical discipline which was solemnly reiterated by the Constitution on the Sacred Liturgy: "regulation of the sacred liturgy depends solely on the authority of the Church. . . . Therefore no other person, even if he be a priest, may add, remove or change anything in the liturgy on his own authority" (Art 22:1, 3).

Ordinaries, whether local or religious, should be mindful therefore of their grave obligation before the Lord to see that this law is exactly observed. It is of the greatest importance in the structures and life of the Church, and clergy and laity should willingly conform to it.

The law is necessary for the spiritual growth and welfare of each individual; it is also necessary if the members of the same local community are to live together in the Lord in harmony, helping each other by good example; it is further necessary in view of the grave obligation that is imposed on all communities to cooperate for the good of the entire Church, especially at the present time when a good or evil occurrence in one local community quickly has repercussions on the entire family of God.

All should bear in mind St. Paul's admonition: "For God is not a God of confusion but of peace" (1 Cor. 14:33).

The following adaptations and changes are prescribed, to the end that the reform of the liturgy may, progressively, be brought to a satisfactory conclusion.

(The remainder of this Instruction is omitted in accordance with the principles outlined in the Introduction to this section.—Ed.)

9

INSTRUCTION ON THE WORSHIP OF THE EUCHARISTIC MYSTERY[a]

S.C.R., *Eucharisticum Mysterium,* 25 May, 1967

Introduction

1. RECENT DOCUMENTS OF THE CHURCH CON-CERNING THE MYSTERY OF THE EUCHARIST

The mystery of the Eucharist is the true center of the sacred liturgy and indeed of the whole Christian life. Consequently the Church, guided by the Holy Spirit, continually seeks to understand and to live the Eucharist more fully.

In our own day the Second Vatican Council has stressed several important aspects of this mystery.

In the Constitution on the Liturgy the Council recalled certain facts about the nature and importance of the Eucharist.[1] It established principles for the reform of the rites of the sacrifice of the Mass so as to encourage the full and active participation of the faithful in the celebration of this mystery.[2] It also extended the practice of concelebration and communion under both kinds.[3]

In the Constitution on the Church the Council showed the close and necessary connection between the Eucharist and the mystery of the Church.[4] Other documents of the Council frequently stressed the important role of the eucharistic mystery in the life of the faithful.[5] They showed its

a. Translation issued by the Congregation. Latin text in *AAS* 59 (1967), pp. 539–573.
1. Constitution on the Liturgy, nn. 2, 41, 47: *AAS* 56 (1964), pp. 97–98, 111, 113.
2. Ibid., nn. 48–54, 56: *AAS* 56 (1964), pp. 113–115.
3. Ibid., nn. 55, 57: *AAS* 56 (1964), pp. 115–116.
4. Constitution on the Church, nn. 3, 7, 11, 26, 50: *AAS* 57 (1955), pp. 6, 9–11, 15–16, 31–32, 33–36, 55–57.
5. Decree on Ecumenism, 2, 15: *AAS* 57 (1965), pp. 91–92, 101–102; Decree on the Pastorial Office of Bishops in the Church, nn. 15, 30: *AAS* 58 (1966), pp. 679–680, 688–689; Decree on the Ministry and Life of Priests, nn. 2, 5–8, 13–14, 18: *AAS* 58 (1966), pp. 991–993, 997–1005, 1011–14, 1018–19.

power to reveal the meaning of man's work, and indeed of all created nature, since in it "natural elements, refined by man, are changed into the glorified Body and Blood."[6]

Pope Pius XII had prepared the way for many of these statements of the Council, especially in the Encyclical Letter *Mediator Dei*,[7] while Pope Paul VI in the Encyclical Letter *Mysterium Fidei*[8] has recalled the importance of certain aspects of eucharistic doctrine, of the real presence of Christ in particular and the worship due to this sacrament even outside the Mass.

2. THE NEED TO RETAIN AN OVERALL VIEW OF THE TEACHING CONTAINED IN THESE DOCUMENTS

In recent years, then, certain aspects of the traditional teaching on this mystery have been the subject of deeper reflection throughout the Church, and have been presented with new zeal for the greater spiritual benefit of the faithful. Undertakings and research in various fields, particularly the liturgical and biblical, have greatly assisted this process.

From the doctrine contained in these documents it is necessary to formulate practical norms which will show the Christian people how to act in regard to this sacrament so as to pursue that knowledge and holiness which the Council has set before the Church.

It is important that the mystery of the Eucharist should shine out before the eyes of the faithful in its true light. It should be considered in all its different aspects, and the real relationships which, as the Church teaches, are known to exist between these various aspects of the mystery should be so understood by the faithful as to be reflected in their lives.

3. THE PRINCIPAL POINTS OF DOCTRINE IN THESE DOCUMENTS

Among the doctrinal principles concerning the Eucharist formulated in these documents of the Church, the following

6. Pastoral Constitution on the Church in the Modern World, n. 38: *AAS* 58 (1966), pp. 1055–56.
7. *AAS* 39 (1947), pp. 547–572; cf. Address to those who took part in the International Conference on Pastoral Liturgy held at Assisi, 22 Sept. 1956: *AAS* 48 (1956), pp. 715–724.
8. *AAS* 57 (1965), pp. 753–774.

should be noted as having a bearing upon the attitude of Christians towards this mystery, and, therefore, as falling within the scope of this Instruction.

a. "The Son of God in the human nature which he united to himself redeemed man and transformed him into a new creation by overcoming death through his own death and resurrection (cf. Gal. 6:15; 2 Cor. 5:17). For by giving his spirit he mystically established as his body his breathren gathered from all nations. In that body the life of Christ is communicated to those who believe; for through the sacraments they are joined in a mysterious yet real way to the Christ who suffered and is glorified."[9]

Therefore "Our Saviour at the Last Supper on the night when he was betrayed instituted the eucharistic sacrifice of his Body and Blood so that he might perpetuate the sacrifice of the cross throughout the centuries till his coming. He thus entrusted to the Church, his beloved spouse, a memorial of his death and resurrection: a sacrament of love, a sign of unity, a bond of charity, a paschal meal in which Christ is eaten, the mind filled with grace and a pledge of future glory given to us."[10]

Hence the Mass, the Lord's Supper, is at the same time and inseparably:

a sacrifice in which the sacrifice of the cross is perpetuated;

a memorial of the death and resurrection of the Lord, who said "do this in memory of me" (Lk. 22:19);

a sacred banquet in which, through the communion of the Body and Blood of the Lord, the People of God share the benefits of the Paschal Sacrifice, renew the New Covenant which God has made with man once for all through the Blood of Christ, and in faith and hope foreshadow and anticipate the eschatological banquet in the kingdom of the Father, proclaiming the Lord's death "till his coming."[11]

b. In the Mass, therefore, the sacrifice and sacred meal belong to the same mystery—so much so that they are linked by the closest bond.

For in the sacrifice of the Mass Our Lord is immolated

---

9. Constitution on the Church, n. 7: *AAS* 57 (1965), p. 9.
10. Constitution on the Liturgy, n. 47: *AAS* 56 (1964), p. 113.
11. Constitution on the Liturgy, nn. 6, 10, 47, 106: *AAS* 56 (1964), pp. 100, 102, 113, 126; Decree on the Ministry and Life of Priests, n. 4: *AAS* (1965), pp. 995–997.

when "he begins to be present sacramentally as the spiritual food of the faithful under the appearances of bread and wine."[12] It was for this purpose that Christ entrusted this sacrifice to the Church, that the faithful might share in it both spiritually, by faith and charity, and sacramentally, through the banquet of Holy Communion. Participation in the Lord's Supper is always communion with Christ offering himself for us as a sacrifice to the Father.[13]

c. The celebration of the Eucharist which takes place at Mass is the action not only of Christ, but also of the Church. For in it Christ perpetuates in an unbloody manner the sacrifice offered on the cross,[14] offering himself to the Father for the world's salvation through the ministry of priests.[15] The Church, the spouse and minister of Christ, performs together with him the role of priest and victim, offers him to the Father and at the same time makes a total offering of herself together with him.

Thus, the Church, especially in the great Eucharistic Prayer, together with Christ, gives thanks to the Father in the Holy Spirit for all the blessings which ge gives to men in creation and especially in the Paschal Mystery, and prays to him for the coming of his kingdom.[16]

d. Hence no Mass, indeed no liturgical action, is a purely private action, but rather a celebration of the Church as a society composed of different orders and ministries in which each member acts according to his own order and role.[17]

e. The celebration of the Eucharist in the sacrifice of the Mass is the origin and consummation of the worship shown to the Eucharist outside Mass. Not only are the sacred species which remain after the Mass derived from the

12. Paul VI, Encyclical Letter, *Mysterium Fidei: AAS* 57 (1965), p. 762.

13. Pius XII, Encyclical Letter, *Mediator Dei: AAS* 39 (1947), pp. 564–566.

14. Constitution on the Liturgy, n. 47: *AAS* 56 (1964), p. 113.

15. Council of Trent, Session 22; Decree on the Mass, ch. 1; *Denz.* 938 (1741).

16. Constitution on the Church, n. 11: *AAS* 57 (1965), pp. 15–16; Constitution on the Liturgy, nn. 47–48: *AAS* 56 (1964), p. 113; Decree on the Ministry and Life of Priests, n. 2, 5: *AAS* 58 (1966), pp. 991–993, 997–999; Pius XII, Encyclical Letter, *Mediator Dei: AAS* 39 (1947), p. 552; Paul VI, Encyclical Letter, *Mysterium Fidei: AAS* 57 (1965), p. 761.

17. Constitution on the Liturgy, n. 26–28: *AAS* 56 (1964), p. 107; and below n. 44.

Mass, but they are preserved so that those of the faithful who cannot come to Mass may be united to Christ, and his sacrifice celebrated in the Mass, through sacramental communion received with the right dispositions.[18]

Consequently the eucharistic sacrifice is the source and the summit of the whole of the Church's worship and of the Christian life.[19] The faithful participate more fully in this sacrament of thanksgiving, propitiation, petition and praise, not only when they whole-heartedly offer the sacred victim, and in it themselves, to the Father with the priest, but also when they receive this same victim sacramentally.

f. There should be no doubt in anyone's mind "that all the faithful ought to show to this most holy sacrament the worship which is due to the true God, as has always been the custom of the Catholic Church. Nor is it to be adored any the less because it was instituted by Christ to be eaten."[20] For even in the reserved sacrament he is to be adored[21] because he is substantially present there through that conversion of bread and wine which, as the Council of Trent tells us,[22] is most aptly named transubstantiation.

g. The mystery of the Eucharist should therefore be considered in all its fullness, not only in the celebration of Mass but also in devotion to the sacred species which remain after Mass and are reserved to extend the grace of the sacrifice.[23]

These are the principles from which practical rules are to

18. Cf. below, n. 49.
19. Constitution on the Church, n. 11: *AAS* 57 (1965), pp. 15–16; Constitution on the Liturgy, n. 41: *AAS* 56 (1964), p. 111; Decree on the Ministry and Life of Priests, n. 2, 5, 6: *AAS* 58 (1966), pp. 991–993; 997–999, 999–1001; Decree on Ecumenism, n. 15: *AAS* 57 (1965), pp. 101–102.
20. Council of Trent, Session 13; Decree on the Eucharist, ch. 5; *Denz.* 878 (1643).
21. Paul VI, Encyclical Letter, *Mysterium Fidei: AAS* 57 (1965), pp. 769–770; Pius XII, Encylical Letter, *Mediator Dei: AAS* 39 (1947), p. 569.
22. Council of Trent, Session 13: Decree on the Eucharist, ch. 4: *Denz* 877 (1642); *can. 2; Denz.* 884 (1642).
23. Cf. the above-mentioned documents insofar as they deal with the sacrifice of the Mass; besides the following, which deal with both aspects of the mystery: Decree on the Ministry and Life of Priests, nn. 5, 18: *AAS* 58 (1966), pp. 997–999, 1018–19; Paul VI, Encyclical Letter, *Mediator Dei: AAS* 39 (1947), pp. 547–572; Address to those who took part in the International Conference on Pastoral Liturgy held at Assisi, 22 Sept. 1956: *AAS* 48 (1956), pp. 715–724.

be drawn to govern devotion due to the sacrament outside Mass and its proper relation to the right ordering of the sacrifice of the Mass according to the mind of the Second Vatican Council and the other documents of the Apostolic See on this subject.[24]

4. The General Intention of This Instruction

For this reason the Consilium set up to implement the Constitution on the Liturgy, on the instructions of His Holiness Pope Paul VI, has prepared an Instruction setting out such practical rules of this nature as may be suitable for the present situation.

The particular purpose of these rules is not only to emphasize the general principles of how to instruct the people in the Eucharist, but also to make more readily intelligible the signs by which the Eucharist is celebrated as the memorial of the Lord and worshipped as a permanent sacrament in the Church.

For although this sacrament has this supreme and unique feature, that the author of holiness is himself present in it, nevertheless, in common with the other sacraments, it is the symbol of a sacred reality and the visible form of an invisible grace.[25] Consequently the more intelligible the signs by which it is celebrated and worshipped, the more firmly and effectively it will enter into the minds and lives of the faithful.[26]

24. Cf. Paul VI, Encyclical Letter, *Mysterium Fidei: AAS* 57 (1965), pp. 769–772; Pius XII, Encyclical Letter, *Mediator Dei: AAS* 39 (1947), pp. 547–572; S.C.R., Instruction *De Musica Sacra,* 3 Sept. 1958: *AAS* 50 (1958), pp. 630–663; Instruction *Inter Oecumenici,* 26 Sept. 1964: *AAS* 56 (1964), pp. 877–900.
25. Council of Trent, Session 13: Decree on the Eucharist, ch. 4: *Denz.* 876 (1639). Cf. also St. Thomas Aquinas, *Summa Theol.,* III, q. 60, a. 1.
26. Constitution on the Liturgy, nn. 33, 59; *AAS* 56 (1964), pp. 108–109, 116.

CHAPTER I

SOME GENERAL PRINCIPLES OF PARTICULAR IMPORTANCE IN INSTRUCTING THE PEOPLE OF GOD IN THE MYSTERY OF THE EUCHARIST

5. What Is Required of Pastors Who Are to Give Instruction About This Mystery

Suitable catechesis is essential if the mystery of the Eucharist is to take deeper root in the minds and lives of the faithful.

To convey this instruction properly, pastors should not only bear in mind the many aspects of the Church's teaching, as contained in the documents of the magisterium, but in their hearts and in their lives they must endeavour to penetrate more deeply the Church's spirit in this matter[27] (*spiritum Ecclesiae . . . altius penetrare*). Only then will they readily perceive which of the many facets of this mystery best suits the needs of the faithful at any one time.

While recalling all that was said above in n. 3, one should take special note of what follows below.

6. The Mystery of the Eucharist as the Center of the Entire Life of the Church

The catechesis of the eucharistic mystery should aim to help the faithful to realize that the celebration of the Eucharist is the true center of the whole Christian life both for the universal Church and for the local congregation of that Church. For "the other sacraments, as indeed every ministry of the Church and every work of the apostolate, are linked with the Eucharist and are directed towards it. For the Eucharist contains the entire spiritual good of the Church, namely, Christ himself, our Passover and living bread, offering through his flesh, living and life-giving in the Spirit, life to men who are thus invited and led on to offer themselves, their labors and all created things together with him."[28]

---

27. Ibid., nn. 14, 17–18: *AAS* 56 (1964), pp. 104, 105.
28. Decree on the Ministry and Life of Priests, n. 5: *AAS* 58 (1966), p. 997.

The Eucharist both perfectly signifies and wonderfully effects that sharing in God's life and unity of God's people by which the Church exists.[29] It is the summit of both the action by which God sanctifies the world in Christ, and the worship which men offer to Christ and which through him they offer to the Father in the Spirit.[30] Its celebration "is the supreme means by which the faithful come to express in their lives and to manifest to others the mystery of Christ and the true nature of the Church."[31]

7. The Mystery of the Eucharist as the Focal Point of the Local Church

It is through the Eucharist that "the Church continually lives and grows. This Church of Christ is truly present in all legitimate local congregations of the faithful which, united with their pastors, are called churches in the New Testament. These are, each in its own region, the new people, called by God in the Holy Spirit and in all fullness (cf. 1 Th. 1:5). In them the faithful are gathered by the preaching of Christ's Gospel and the mystery of the Lord's Supper is celebrated, 'so that through the Body and Blood of the Lord the whole brotherhood is united.' "[32] "Every gathering around the altar under the sacred ministry of the bishop"[33] or of a priest who takes the place of the bishop[34] "is a sign of that charity and 'unity of the Mystical Body, without which there can be no salvation' "[35] In these communities, though they may often be small and poor or living amongst the 'diaspora,' Christ is present, by whose power the one, holy, catholic and apostolic Church is united. For 'the partaking of the Body and Blood of Christ has no less an effect than to change us into what we have received.' "[36,37]

---

29. Constitution on the Church, n. 11: *AAS* 57 (1965), pp. 15–16; Decree on Ecumenism, nn. 2, 15; *AAS* 57 (1965), pp. 91–92, 101–102.
30. Constitution on the Liturgy, n. 10: *AAS* 56 (1964), p. 102.
31. Ibid., n. 2: *AAS* 56 (1964), pp. 97–98; cf. also n. 41: *AAS* 56 (1964), p. 111.
32. Mozarabic Prayer: PL 96, 759B.
33. Constitution on the Church, n. 26: *AAS* 57 (1965), p. 31.
34. Constitution on the Liturgy, n. 42: *AAS* 56 (1964), p. 111–112.
35. Cf. St. Thomas Aquinas, *Summa Theol.*, III, q. 73, a. 3.
36. St. Leo the Great, *Sermones*, 63, 7: *PL* 54, 357C.
37. Constitution on the Church, n. 26: *AAS* 57 (1965), pp. 31–32.

8. The Eucharistic Mystery and Christian Unity

In addition to those things which concern the ecclesial community and the individual faithful, pastors should pay particular attention to that part of her doctrine in which the Church teaches that the memorial of the Lord, celebrated according to his will, signifies and effects the unity of all who believe in him.[38]

As the Decree on Ecumenism of the Second Vatican Council declares,[39] the faithful should be led to a proper appreciation of the values which are preserved in the eucharistic tradition according to which our brethren of the other Christian confessions have continued to celebrate the Lord's Supper. For while "they call to mind the death and resurrection of the Lord in the Holy Supper, they profess that it signifies life in communion with Christ and await his coming in glory."[40] But those who have preserved the sacrament of Order, "united with the bishop, have aceess to God the Father through the Son, the Word incarnate, who suffered and is glorified, by the outpouring of the Holy Spirit, and attain communion with the Blessed Trinity, becoming 'sharers in the divine nature' (2 Pet. 1:4). And so through the celebration of the Lord's Eucharist in these individual churches the Church of God is built up and grows, and their communion is manifested through concelebration."[41]

It is above all in the celebration of the mystery of unity that all Christians should be filled with sorrow at the divisions which separate them. They should therefore pray earnestly to God that all disciples of Christ may daily come closer to a proper understanding of the mystery of the Eucharist according to his mind, and may so celebrate it as to become sharers in the Body of Christ, and so become one body (cf. 1 Cor. 10:17) "linked by the very bonds by which he wishes it to be constituted."[42]

---

38. Constitution on the Church, nn. 3, 7, 11, 26: *AAS* 57 (1965), pp. 6, 9–11, 15–16, 31–32; Decree on Ecumenism, n. 2: *AAS* 57 (1965), pp. 91–92.
39. Ibid., nn. 15, 22: *AAS* 57 (1965), pp. 101–102, 105–106.
40. Ibid., n. 22: *AAS* 57 (1965), p. 106.
41. Ibid., n. 15: *AAS* 57 (1965), p. 102.
42. Paul VI, Encyclical Letter, *Mysterium Fidei: AAS* 57 (1965), p. 773.

9. The Different Modes of Christ's Presence

In order that they should achieve a deeper understanding of the mystery of the Eucharist, the faithful should be instructed in the principal ways in which the Lord is present to his Church in liturgical celebrations.[43]

He is always present in a body of the faithful gathered in his name (cf. Mt. 18:20). He is present, too, in his Word, for it is he who speaks when the Scriptures are read in the Church.

In the sacrifice of the Eucharist he is present both in the person of the minister, "the same now offering through the ministry of the priest who formerly offered himself on the cross,"[44] and above all under the species of the Eucharist.[45] For in this sacrament Christ is present in a unique way, whole and entire, God and man, substantially and permanently. This presence of Christ under the species "is called 'real' not in an exclusive sense, as if the other kinds of presence were not real, but *par excellence*."[46]

10. The Connection Between the Liturgy of the Word and the Liturgy of the Eucharist

Pastors should therefore "carefully teach the faithful to participate in the whole Mass," showing the close connection between the liturgy of the Word and the celebration of the Lord's Supper, so that they can see clearly how the two constitute a single act of worship.[47] For "the teaching of the Word is necessary for the very administration of the sacraments, in as much as they are sacraments of faith, which is born of the Word and fed by it."[48] This is especially true of the celebration of Mass, in which it is the purpose of the liturgy of the Word to develop the close connection between the preaching and hearing of the Word of God and the eucharistic mystery.[49]

43. Constitution on the Liturgy, n. 7: *AAS* 56 (1964), pp. 100–101.
44. Council of Trent, Session 22: Decree on the Mass, ch. 2: *Denz.* 940 (1743).
45. Constitution on the Liturgy, n. 7: *AAS* 56 (1964), pp. 100–101.
46. Paul VI, Encyclical Letter, *Mysterium Fidei: AAS* 57 (1965), p. 764.
47. Cf. Constitution on the Liturgy, n. 56: *AAS* 56 (1964), p. 115.
48. Ibid., *AAS* (1965), pp. 14–15; Decree on the Ministry and Life of Priests, n. 4: *AAS* 58 (1966), pp. 995–997.
49. Ibid., n. 4: *AAS* 58 (1966), pp. 995–997; cf. also n. 3 of this Instruction.

When therefore the faithful hear the Word of God, they should realize that the wonders it proclaims culminate in the Paschal Mystery, of which the memorial is sacramentally celebrated in the Mass. In this way the faithful will be nourished by the Word of God which they have received and in a spirit of thanksgiving will be led on to a fruitful participation in the mysteries of salvation. Thus the Church is nourished by the bread of life which she finds the table both of the Word of God and of the Body of Christ.[50]

11. The Priesthood Common to All the Faithful and the Ministerial Priesthood in the Celebration of the Eucharist

The more clearly the faithful understand the place they occupy in the liturgical community and the part they have to play in the eucharistic action, the more conscious and fruitful will be the active participation which is proper to that community.[51]

Catechetical instruction should therefore explain the doctrine of the royal priesthood to which the faithful are consecrated by rebirth and the anointing of the Holy Spirit.[52]

Moreover there should also be further explanation of the role in the celebration of the Eucharist of the ministerial priesthood which differs from the common priesthood of the faithful in essence and not merely in degree.[53] The part played by others who exercise a ministry in the Eucharist should also be explained.[54]

12. The Nature of Active Participation in the Mass

It should be made clear that all who gather for the Eucharist constitute that holy people which, together with the ministers, plays its part in the sacred action. It is in-

50. Constitution on Divine Revelation, n. 21: AAS 58 (1966), pp. 87–88.
51. Constitution on the Liturgy, nn. 14, 26, 30, 38: AAS 56 (1964), pp. 104, 107, 108, 110.
52. Constitution on the Church, n. 10: AAS 57 (1965), pp. 14–15; Decree on the Ministry and Life of Priests, n. 2: AAS 58 (1966), pp. 991–993; Paul VI, Encyclical Letter, Mysterium Fidei: AAS 57 (1965), p. 761.
53. Constitution on the Church, n. 10: AAS 57 (1965), pp. 14–15; Decree on the Ministry and Life of Priests, nn. 2, 5: AAS 58 (1966), pp. 991–993, 997–999.
54. Constitution on the Liturgy, nn. 28–29: AAS 56 (1964), pp. 107–108.

deed the priest alone, who, acting in the person of
Christ, consecrates the bread and wine, but the role
of the faithful in the Eucharist is to recall the passion, resurrection and glorification of the Lord, to give
thanks to God, and to offer the immaculate victim not only
through the hands of the priest, but also together with him;
and finally, by receiving the Body of the Lord, to perfect
that communion with God and among themselves which
should be the product of participation in the sacrifice of the
Mass.[55] For the faithful achieve a more perfect participation in the Mass when, with proper dispositions, they receive the Body of the Lord sacramentally in the Mass itself,
in obedience to his words "take and eat."[56]

Like the passion of Christ itself, this sacrifice, though offered for all, "has no effect except in those united to the
passion of Christ by faith and charity . . . To these things
it brings a greater or less benefit in proportion to their
devotion."[57]

All these things should be explained to the faithful, so
that they may take an active part in the celebration of the
Mass both by their personal devotion and by joining in the
external rites, according to the principles laid down in the
Constitution on the Liturgy,[58] which have been further determined by the Instruction *Inter Oecumenici* of 26 September 1964 and the Instruction *Musicam Sacram* of 5
March 1967,[59] and through the Instruction *Tres abhinc annos* of 4 May 1967.

13. The Influence of the Eucharist on the Daily Lives of the Faithful

What the faithful have received by faith and sacrament
in the celebration of the Eucharist should have its effect on
their way of life. They should seek to live joyfully and
gratefully by the strength of this heavenly food, sharing in
the death and resurrection of the Lord. And so everyone
who has participated in the Mass should be "eager to do
good works, to please God, and to live honestl-, devoted to
the Church, putting into practice what he has learnt, and

55. Ibid., nn. 48, 106: *AAS* 56 (19( ), pp. 113, 126.
56. Ibid., n. 55: *AAS* 56 (1964), p. 115.
57. St. Thomas Aquinas, *Summa Theol.*, III, q. 79, a. 7, ad 2.
58. Constitution on the Liturgy, nn. 26–32: *AAS* 56 (1964), pp.
107–108.
59. Cf. S.C.R., Instruction *Musicam Sacram*, 5 March 1967: AAS 59
(1967), pp. 300–320.

growing in piety."[60] He will seek to fill the world with the Spirit of Christ and "in all things, in the very midst of human affairs" to become a witness of Christ.[61]

For no "Christian community can be built up unless it has as its basis and pivot the celebration of the holy Eucharist. It is from this therefore that any attempt to form a community must begin."[62]

14. Teaching Children About the Mass

Those who have charge of the religious instruction of children, especially parents, parish priests and teachers, should be careful when they are introducing them gradually to the mystery of salvation,[63] to give emphasis to instruction on the Mass. Instruction about the Eucharist, while being suited to the age and abilities of the children, should aim to convey the meaning of the Mass through the principal rites and prayers. It should also explain the place of the Mass in participation in the life of the Church.[64]

All this should be borne in mind especially when children are being prepared for first communion so that the first communion may be seen as the full incorporation into the Body of Christ.

15. Catechesis of the Mass Should Take the Rites and Prayers as Its Starting-Point

The Council of Trent prescribes that pastors should frequently "either themselves or through others, expound some part of what is read at Mass and, among other things, explain something of the mystery of this sacrament."[65]

60. Hippolytus, *Traditio Apostolica*, 21: ed. B. Botte, 1963, pp. 58–59; cf. Constitution on the Liturgy, nn. 9, 10: *AAS* 56 (1964), pp. 101–102; Decree on the Apostolate of Lay People, n. 3: *AAS* 58 (1966), pp. 839–840; Decree on the Church's Missionary Activity, n. 39: *AAS* 58 (1966), pp. 986–987; Decree on the Ministry and Life of Priests, n. 5: *AAS* 58 (1966), pp. 997–999.

61. Pastoral Constitution on the Church in the Modern World, n. 43: *AAS* 58 (1966), p. 1063.

62. Decree on the Ministry and Life of Priests, n. 6: *AAS* 58 (1966), p. 1063.

63. Declaration on Christian Education, n. 2: *AAS* 58 (1966), pp. 730–731.

64. Decree on the Ministry and Life of Priests, n. 5: *AAS* 58 (1966), pp. 997–998.

65. Council of Trent, Session 22: Decree on the Mass, ch. 8: *Denz.* 946 (1749).

Pastors should therefore gently lead the faithful to a full understanding of this mystery of faith by suitable catechesis. This should take as its starting point the mysteries of the liturgical year and the rites and prayers which are part of the celebration. It should clarify their meaning and especially that of the great eucharistic prayer, and should lead the people to a profound understanding of the mystery which these signify and accomplish.

CHAPTER II

THE CELEBRATION OF THE MEMORIAL OF THE LORD

I. SOME GENERAL NORMS REGARDING THE CELEBRATION OF THE MEMORIAL OF THE LORD IN THE COMMUNITY OF THE FAITHFUL

16. The Common Unity to Be Shown in the Celebration

Since through baptism "there is neither Jew nor Greek, slave nor free-man, male nor female," but all are one in Christ Jesus (cf. Gal. 3:28), the assembly which most fully portrays the nature of the Church and its role in the Eucharist is that which gathers together the faithful, men and women, of every age and walk of life.

The unity of this community, having its origin in the one bread in which all share (cf. 1 Cor. 10:17), is arranged in hierarchial order. For this reason it is necessary that "each person, performing his role as a minister or as one of the faithful, should do all that the nature of the action and the liturgical norms require of him, and only that."[66]

The outstanding example of this unity may be seen "in the full and active participation of the entire people of God . . . in the same Eucharist, in a single prayer, around the one altar where the bishop presides, accompanied by his priests and ministers."[67]

---

66. Constitution on the Liturgy, n. 28: *AAS* 56 (1964), p. 107.
67. Ibid., n. 41: *AAS* 56 (1964), p. 111; cf. Constitution on the Church, n. 26: *AAS* 57 (1964), pp. 31–32.

17. The Community Should Not Be Disrupted, and the Faithful's Attention Diverted

In liturgical celebrations, the community should not be disrupted or be distracted from its common purpose. Care then must be taken not to have two liturgical celebrations at the same time in the same church, since it distracts the people's attention.

This is above all true of the celebration of the Eucharist. That is why that disruption of the congregation is to be assidiously avoided, which, when Mass is celebrated with the people on Sundays and feast days, is caused by the simultaneous celebration of Masses in the same church.

As far as possible it should be avoided on other days as well. The best way of achieving this, is, in accordance with the law, for those priests to concelebrate who want to say Mass at the same time.[68] Likewise, when Mass is being celebrated for the people, in accordance with the public timetable of the church, baptisms, marriage, exhortations and the common or choral recitation of the Divine Office are to be avoided.

18. An Awareness of the Local and Universal Church Community Is to Be Fostered

In the celebration of the Eucharist, a sense of community should be encouraged. Each person will then feel himself united with his brethren in the communion of the Church, local and universal, and even in a way with all men. In the sacrifice of the Mass in fact, Christ offers himself for the salvation of the entire world. The congregation of the faithful is both type and sign of the union of the whole human race in Christ its Head.[69]

19. On Welcoming to the Local Celebration People from Elsewhere

When any of the faithful take part in a eucharistic celebration outside their own parish, they will follow the form of celebration used by the local community.

Pastors should do what they can to help faithful from other areas join in with the community. This is above all necessary in city churches and places where many of the

---

68. Cf. n. 47 of this Instruction.
69. Cf. Constitution on the Church, n. 3: *AAS* 57 (1965), p. 6.

faithful come on holiday. Where there are large numbers of emigrants or people of another language, pastors should provide them at least from time to time with the opportunity of participating in the Mass in the way which they are accustomed. "Steps should be taken, however, to enable the faithful to say or sing together in Latin those parts of the Mass which pertain to them."[70]

20. The Care to Be Taken by Ministers in Celebrating the Liturgy

To encourage the active participation of the people and to ensure that the celebrations are carried out as they should be, it is not sufficient for the ministers to content themselves with the exact fulfilment of their role according to the liturgical laws. It is also necessary that they should so celebrate the liturgy that by this very fact they convey an awareness of the meaning of the sacred actions.

The people have the right to be nourished by the proclamation of the Word of God, and by the minister's explanation of it. Priests, then, will not only give a homily whenever it is prescribed or seems suitable, but will ensure that whatever they or the ministers say or sing will be so clear that the faithful will be able to hear it easily and grasp its meaning; and they will in fact be spontaneously drawn to respond and participate.[71] The ministers should undergo a careful preparation for this, above all in seminaries and religious houses.

21. The Canon of the Mass

a. In Masses celebrated with the people, even when not concelebrated, it is permissible for the celebrant, if it seems oportune, to say the Canon aloud. In sung Masses (*Missae in cantu*) it is permissible for him to sing those parts of the Canon which are at present allowed to be sung in a concelebrated Mass (*Ritus servandus in concelebratione Missae*, nn. 39, 42) in accordance with the Instruction *Tres abhinc annos* of 4 May 1967, no. 10.

b. In printing the words of consecration the custom of printing them in a way different from the rest of the text should be maintained, in order that they may stand out more clearly.

70. Constitution on the Liturgy, n. 54: *AAS* 56 (1964), p. 115.
71. Ibid., n. 11: *AAS* 56 (1964), pp. 102–103.

22. The Mass on Radio and Television

When according to the mind of Art. 20 of the Constitution on the Liturgy, the Mass is televised or broadcast, local ordinaries must see to it that prayer and participation of the faithful do not suffer. It should be celebrated with such dignity and discretion as to be a model of the celebration of the sacred mystery in accordance with the laws of the liturgical renewal.[72]

23. Photographs During the Celebration of the Eucharist

Great care should be taken to ensure that liturgical celebrations, especially the Mass, are not disturbed or interrupted by the taking of photographs. Where there is good reason for taking them, the greatest discretion should be used and the norms laid down by the local ordinary should be observed.

24. The Importance of the Arrangement of Churches for Well-Ordered Celebrations

"The house of prayer where the most holy Eucharist is celebrated and preserved should be kept clean and in good order, suitable for prayer and sacred celebrations. It is there too that the faithful gather and find help and comfort in venerating the presence of the Son of God, our Saviour, offered for us on the altar of sacrifice."[73]

Pastors must realize then that the way the church is arranged greatly contributes to a worthy celebration and to the active participation of the people.

For this reason the directives and criteria given in the Instruction *Inter Oecumenici* should be followed regarding: the building of churches and adapting them to the renewed liturgy, the setting up and adorning of altars, the suitable arrangement of the seating for the celebrant and ministers, the correct place from which to give the readings, and the arrangement of the places for the faithful and the choir.

Above all, the main altar should be so placed and constructed that it is always seen to be the sign of Christ himself, the place at which the saving mysteries are carried out,

---

72. Cf. S.C.R., Instruction *Musicam Sacram*, 5 March 1967, (D.7), nn. 6, 8, 11.
73. Decree on the Ministry and Life of Priests, n. 5: *AAS* 58 (1966), p. 998.

and the center of the assembly, to which the greatest reverence is due.

In adapting churches, care will be taken not to destroy treasures of sacred art. If in the interests of liturgical renewal a local ordinary decides, having obtained the advice of experts and—if needs be—the consent of those whom it concerns, to remove some of those works of art from their present position, it should be done with prudence, and in such a way that even in their new surroundings they are well placed.

Pastors will recall that the material and appearance of vestments greatly contributes to the dignity of liturgical celebrations. "They should strive after noble beauty rather than sumptuous display."[74]

II. CELEBRATION ON SUNDAYS AND WEEKDAYS

25. The Celebration of the Eucharist on Sundays

Whenever the community gathers to celebrate the Eucharist, it announces the death and resurrection of the Lord, in the hope of his glorious return. The supreme manifestation of this is the Sunday assembly. This is the day of the week on which, by apostolic tradition, the Paschal Mystery is celebrated in the Eucharist in a special way.[75]

In order that the faithful may willingly fulfill the precept to sanctify this day and should understand why the Church should call them together to celebrate the Eucharist every Sunday, from the very outset of their Christian formation "Sunday should be presented to them as the primordial feast day,"[76] on which, assembled together, they are to hear the Word of God and take part in the Paschal Mystery.

Moreover, any endeavor that seeks to make Sunday a genuine "day of joy and rest from work"[77] should be encouraged."

26. The Celebration of Sunday Around the Bishop and in Parishes

It is fitting that the sense of ecclesial community, especially fostered and expressed by the celebration in common

74. Constitution on the Liturgy, n. 124: *AAS* 56 (1964), p. 131.
75. Ibid., nn. 6, 106: *AAS* 56 (1964), pp. 100, 126.
76. Ibid., n. 106: *AAS* 56 (1964), p. 126.
77. Ibid.

of Sunday Mass, should be encouraged both around the bishop, particularly in the cathedral church, and in the parish assembly, where the pastor takes the place of the bishop.[78]

It is important that the active participation of the entire people in the Sunday celebration, which is expressed in singing, should be assiduously promoted. In fact, sung Masses (*Missae in cantu*) should be preferred as far as possible.[79]

On Sundays and feast days above all, the celebrations which take place in other churches or oratories should be arranged in connection with the celebrations in the parish church so that they contribute to the general pastoral effort. It is preferable that small religious non-clerical communities and other similar communities, especially those that work in the parish, should take part in the parish Mass on these days.

As regards the time and number of Masses to be celebrated in parishes, the good of the parish community should be kept in mind and the number of Masses should not be so multiplied as to weaken the effectiveness of the pastoral effort: for example: if through the great number of Masses, only small groups of the faithful were to come to each of the Masses in a church that can hold a great number of people. Another example would be if, for the same reason, the priests were so overburdened by their work as to make it difficult for them to fulfil their ministry adequately.

27. Group Masses

In order to emphasize the value of the unity of the parish community in the celebration of the Eucharist on Sundays and feast days, Masses for particular groups, such as associations and societies, would be better held on weekdays, if possible. If it is not possible to transfer them to a weekday, one thould try to preserve the unity of the parish community by incorporating these particular groups into the parish celebrations on Sundays and feast days.

78. Constitution on the Liturgy, nn. 41–42: *AAS* 56 (1964), pp. 111–112; Constitution on the Church, n. 28: *AAS* 57 (1965), pp. 33–36; Decree on the Ministry and Life of Priests, n. 5: *AAS* 58 (1966), pp. 997–999.
79. Cf. S.C.R. Instruction *Musicam Sacram*, 5 March 1967, nn. 16, 27: *AAS* 59 (1967), pp. 305, 308.

28. Anticipating the Sunday Feast Day Masses on the Previous Evening

Where permission has been granted by the Apostolic See to fulfil the Sunday obligation on the preceding Saturday evening, pastors should explain the meaning of this permission carefully to the faithful and should ensure that the significance of Sunday is not thereby obscured. The purpose of this concession is in fact to enable the Christians of today to celebrate more easily the day of the resurrection of the Lord.

All concessions and contrary customs notwithstanding, when celebrated on Saturday this Mass may be celebrated only in the evening, at times determined by the local ordinary.

In these cases the Mass celebrated is that assigned in the calendar to Sunday, and the homily and prayers of the faithful are not to be omitted.

What has been said above is equally valid for the Mass on holidays of obligation, which for the same reason has been transferred to the preceding evening. The Mass celebrated on the evening before Pentecost Sunday is the present Mass of the Vigil, with the Creed. Likewise, the Mass celebrated on the evening of Christmas Eve is the Mass of the Vigil but with white vestments, the Alleluia and the Preface of the Nativity, as on the feast. Nevertheless it is not permitted to celebrate the Vigil Mass of Easter Sunday before dusk, or at least certainly not before sunset. This Mass is always that of the Easter Vigil, which, by reason of its special significance in the liturgical year and in the whole Christian life must be celebrated with the liturgical rites laid down for the vigil on this holy night.

The faithful who begin to celebrate the Sunday or holiday of obligation on the preceding evening, may go to communion at that Mass even if they have already received communion in the morning. Those who "have received communion during the Mass of the Easter Vigil, or during the Mass of the Lord's Nativity, may receive communion again at the second Paschal Mass and at one of the Masses on Christmas Day."[80] Likewise, "the faithful who go to communion at the Mass of Chrism on Maundy

Thursday, may again receive communion at the evening Mass on the same day," in accordance with the Instruction *Tres abhinc annos* of 4 May 1967, n. 14.

29. Masses Celebrated on Weekdays

The faithful should be invited to go to Mass frequently on weekdays, to go even daily in fact.

This is particularly recommended on those weekdays which should be celebrated with special care, above all in Lent and Advent, as also on lesser feasts of the Lord, and on certain feasts of the Blessed Virgin Mary or of saints who are particularly venerated in the universal or local Church.

30. Mass at Meetings and Gatherings of a Religious Character

It is very fitting that meetings or congresses which seek to develop the Christian life or apostolate, or which seek to promote religious studies, as also spiritual exercises and retreats of every kind, should be so arranged as to have their climax in the celebration of the Eucharist.

III. THE COMMUNION OF THE FAITHFUL

31. The Communion of the Faithful During Mass

Through sacramental communion the faithful take part more perfectly in the celebration of the Eucharist. It is strongly recommended that they should normally receive it during the Mass and at that point of the celebration which is prescribed by the rite, namely, immediately after the communion of the celebrant.[81]

In order that, even through signs, the communion may be seen more clearly to be participation in the sacrifice which is being celebrated, care should be taken to enable the faithful to communicate with hosts consecrated during the Mass.[82]

It should above all belong to the celebrant priest to distribute communion; nor should the Mass continue until the

---

81. Constitution on the Liturgy, n. 55: *AAS* 56 (1964), p. 115.
82. Ibid., n. 55: *AAS* 56 (1964), p. 115; *Missale Romanum*, Ritus Servandus in Celebratione Missae, 27 June 1965, n. 7.

communion of the faithful is over. Other priests or deacons will help the priest, if need be.[83]

32. Communion Under Both Kinds

Holy Communion, considered as a sign, has a fuller form when it is received under both kinds. For under this form (leaving intact the principles of the Council of Trent,[84] by which under either species or kind there is received the true sacrament and Christ whole and entire), the sign of the eucharistic banquet appears more perfectly. Moreover, it is more clearly shown how the new and eternal Covenant is ratified in the Blood of the Lord, as it also expresses the relation of the eucharistic banquet to the eschatological banquet in the Kingdom of the Father (cf. Mt. 26:27–29).

(There followed a list of cases when communion under both kinds is permitted. We omit it, since the later and fuller list is given in D *12*, 242. There was also a reference to previous legislation[85]—Ed.)

33. Communion Outside Mass

a. It is necessary to accustom the faithful to receive communion during the actual celebration of the Eucharist. Even outside Mass, however, priests will not refuse to distribute communion to those who have good reason to ask for it.[86] By permission of the bishop of the place, according to the norm of the *Motu Proprio Pastorale Munus*, n. 4,[87] or by permission of the major superior of a religious institute according to the Rescript *Cum admotae*, Art. 1, n. 1, communion may be distributed even during the afternoon.

b. When, at the prescribed times, communion is distributed outside Mass, if it is judged suitable, a short Bible service may precede it, in accordance with the Instruction *'Inter Oecumenici'*, nn. 37 and 39.

c. If Mass cannot be celebrated because of a lack of priests, and communion is distributed by a minister who

83. Cf. S.C.R., Rubrics of the Breviary and *Missale Romanum*, 26 July 1960, n. 502; *AAS* 52 (1960), p. 680.
84. Session 21: Decree on Eucharistic Communion, ch. 1–3: *Denz.* 930–932 (1726–29).
85. *Ritus servandus in distributione communionis sub utraque specie*, 7 March 1965, n. 1.
86. Cf. Pius XII, Encyclical Letter, *Mediator Dei: AAS* 39 (1947).
87. Cf. *AAS* 56 (1954), p. 7; *AAS* 59 (1967), p. 374.

has the faculty to do this by indult from the Holy See, the rite laid down by the competent authority is to be followed.

34. The Way of Receiving Communion

a. In accordance with the custom of the Church, communion may be received by the faithful either kneeling or standing. One or the other way is to be chosen, according to the decision of the Episcopal Conference, bearing in mind all the circumstances, above all the number of the faithful and the arrangement of the churches. The faithful should willingly adopt the method indicated by their pastors, so that communion may truly be a sign of the brotherly union of all those who share in the same table of the Lord.

b. When the faithful communicate kneeling, no other sign of reverence towards the Blessed Sacrament is required, since kneeling is itself a sign of adoration.

When they receive communion standing, it is strongly recommended that, coming up in procession, they should make a sign of reverence before receiving the Blessed Sacrament. This should be done at the right time and place, so that the order of people going to and from communion should not be disrupted.

35. Communion and the Sacrament of Penance

The Eucharist is also presented to the faithful "as a medicine, by which we are freed from our daily faults and preserved from mortal sin;"[88] they should be shown how to make use of the penitential parts of the liturgy of the Mass. "The precept 'let a man examine himself' (1 Cor. 11:28) should be called to mind for those who wish to receive communion. The custom of the Church declares this to be necessary, so that no one who is conscious of having committed mortal sin, even if he believes himself to be contrite, should approach the holy Eucharist without first making a sacramental confession."[89] "If someone finds himself in a case of necessity, however, and there is no confessor to

---

88. Council of Trent, Session 13: Decree on the Eucharist, ch. 2: *Denz.* 875 (1638); cf. also Session 22: Decree on the Mass, ch. 1–2: *Denz.* 938 (1740), 940 (1743).
89. Council of Trent, Session 13; Decree on the Eucharist, ch. 7: *Denz.* 880 (1646–47).

whom he can go, then he should first make an act of perfect contrition."[90]

The faithful are to be constantly encouraged to accustom themselves to going to confession outside the celebration of Mass, and especially at the prescribed times. In this way, the sacrament of Penance will be administered calmly and with genuine profit, and will not interfere with participation in the Mass. Those who receive communion daily or very frequently, should be counselled to go to confession at times suitable to the individual case.

36. Communion in Circumstances of Particular Solemnity

It is very fitting that, whenever the faithful are setting out on a new state of life or a new way of working in the vineyard of the Lord, they should take part of the sacrifice through sacramental communion in order to dedicate themselves again to God and to renew their covenant with him.

This can well be done, for example: by the assembly of the faithful, when they renew their baptismal vows at the Easter Vigil; by young people, when they do likewise before the Church, in a manner in keeping with their age; by bride and bridegroom, when they are united in the sacrament of marriage; by those who dedicate themselves to God, when they take their vows or make their solemn commitment; and by the faithful, when they are to devote themselves to apostolic tasks.

37. Frequent and Daily Communion

Since "it is clear that the frequent or daily reception of the Blessed Eucharist increases union with Christ, nourishes the spiritual life more abundantly, strengthens the soul in virtue and gives the communicant a stronger pledge of eternal happiness, parish priests, confessors and preachers will frequently and zealously exhort the Christian people to this holy and salutary practice."[91]

90. *CIC*, can. 859.
91. S.C. of the Council, Decree on the daily reception of communion, 20 Dec. 1905, n. 6: *AAS* 38 (1905–06), pp. 401 seq.; Pius XII, Encyclical Letter, *Mediator Dei: AAS* 39 (1947), p. 565.

38. Private Prayer After Communion

On those who receive the Body and Blood of Christ, the gift of the Spirit is poured out abundantly like living water (cf. John 7:37–39), provided that this Body and Blood have been received sacramentally and spiritually, namely, by that faith which operates through charity.[92]

But union with Christ, to which the sacrament itself is directed, is not to be limited to the duration of the celebration of the eucharist; it is to be prolonged into the entire Christian life, in such a way that the Christian faithful, contemplating unceasingly the gift they have received, may make their life a continual thanksgiving under the guidance of the Holy Spirit and may produce fruits of greater charity.

In order to remain more easily in this thanksgiving which is offered to God in an eminent way in the Mass, those who have been nourished by holy communion should be encouraged to remain for a while in prayer.[93]

39. Viaticum

Communion given as Viaticum should be considered as a special sign of participation in the mystery celebrated in the Mass, the mystery of the death of the Lord and his passage to the Father. By it, strengthened by the Body of Christ, the Christian is endowed with the pledge of the resurrection in his passage from this life.

Therefore, the faithful who are in danger of death from any cause whatsoever are obliged to receive holy communion.[94] Pastors must ensure that the administration of this sacrament is not delayed, but that the faithful are nourished by it while still in full possession of their faculties.[95]

Even if the faithful have already communicated on the same day, it is earnestly recommended that when they are in danger of death, they should again receive communion.

92. Cf. Council of Trent, Session 13: Decree on the Eucharist, ch. 8: Denz. 881 (1648).
93. Cf. Pius XII, Encyclical Letter, Mediator Dei: AAS 39 (1947), p. 566.
94. Cf. CIC, can. 864, 1.
95. Cf. CIC, can. 865.

40. Communion of Those Who Cannot Go to Church

It is fitting that care should be taken to provide the nourishment of the Eucharist for those who are prevented from attending its celebration in the community. They will thus feel themselves united to this community and substained by the love of their brethren.

Pastors of souls will take every care to make it possible for the sick and aged to receive the Eucharist frequently, even if they are not gravely ill or in danger of death. In fact, if possible, this could be done every day, and should be done in paschal time especially. Communion may be taken to these people at any time of the day.

41. Communion Under the Species of Wine Alone

In case of necessity, depending on the judgment of the bishop, it is permitted to give the Eucharist under the species of wine alone to those who are unable to receive it under the species of bread.

In this case it is permissible, with the consent of the local ordinary, to celebrate in the house of the sick person.

If, however, Mass is not celebrated in the presence of the sick person, the Blood of the Lord should be kept in a properly covered chalice and placed in the tabernacle after Mass. It should be taken to the sick person only if contained in a vessel which is closed in such a way as to eliminate all danger of spilling. When the sacrament is administered, that method should be chosen from the possible ones given in the *Ritus servandus in distributione communionis sub utraque specie* which is most suited to the case. When communion has been given, should some of the precious Blood still remain, then it should be consumed by the minister; he will also carry out the normal ablutions.

IV. THE CELEBRATION OF THE EUCHARIST IN THE LIFE AND MINISTRY OF BISHOPS AND PRIESTS

42. The Celebration of the Eucharist in the Life and Ministry of Bishops

The celebration of the Eucharist expresses in a particular way the public social nature of the liturgical actions of the Church, "which is the sacrament of unity, namely, a holy people united and ordered under its bishops."[96]

In consequence, "the bishop, endowed with the fullness of the sacrament of Order, is the steward of the grace of the supreme priesthood, above all in the Eucharist, which he offers himself or causes to be offered. . . . But every legitimate celebration of the Eucharist is regulated by the bishop. For to him is entrusted the task of offering Christian worship to the majesty of God and of directing it according to the Lord's commandments and the Church's laws, further determined for his diocese by his own decisions."[97] The Church is most perfectly displayed in its hierarchic structure in that celebration of the Eucharist at which the bishop presides, surrounded by his priests and ministers, with the active participation of the whole people of God.[98]

43. Priests Should Take Their Proper Role in the Celebration of the Eucharist

In the celebration of the Eucharist, priests also are deputed to perform a specific function by reason of a special sacrament, namely, holy Orders. For they too "as ministers of the sacred mysteries, especially in the sacrifice of the Mass . . . act in the person of Christ in a special way."[99] It is, therefore, fitting that, for the sake of the symbolism, they participate in the Eucharist by exercising the order proper to them,[100] by celebrating or concelebrating the Mass, and not by limiting themselves to communicating like the laity.

---

96. Constitution on the Liturgy, n. 26: *AAS* 56 (1964), p. 107.
97. Constitution on the Church, n. 26: *AAS* 57 (1965), pp. 31–32.
98. Constitution on the Liturgy, n. 41: *AAS* 56 (1964), p. 111.
99. Decree on the Ministry and Life of Priests, n. 13: *AAS* 58 (1966), p. 1011; cf. Constitution on the Church, n. 28: *AAS* 57 (1965), p. 33–36.
100. Constitution on the Liturgy, n. 28: *AAS* 56 (1964), p. 107.

44. The Daily Celebration of Mass

"In the mystery of the eucharistic sacrifice, in which the priest exercises his highest function, the work of our redemption is continually accomplished. Daily celebration of Mass, therefore, is most earnestly recommended, since, even if the faithful cannot be present, it remains an action of Christ and the Church,"[101] an action in which the priest is always acting for the salvation of the people.

45. The Laws of the Church Must Be Faithfully Observed in Celebrating Mass

In the celebration of the Eucharist above all, no one, not even a priest, may on his own authority add, omit, or change anything in the liturgy. Only the supreme authority of the Church, and, according to the provisions of the law, the bishop and Episcopal Conferences, may do this.[102] Priests should, therefore, ensure that they so preside over the celebration of the Eucharist that the faithful know that they are attending not a rite established on private initiative,[103] but the Church's public worship, the regulation of which was entrusted by Christ to the apostles and their successors.

46. Pastoral Considerations as the Criterion by Which to Choose Between Different Forms of Celebration

"Care must be taken that in a liturgical action not only are the laws for a valid and licit celebration observed, but also that the faithful consciously, actively and fruitfully participate in it."[104] From among the forms of celebration permitted by the law, priests should, therefore, endeavour to choose in each instance those which seem most suited to the needs of the faithful and favourable to their full participation.

101. Decree on the Ministry and Life of Priests, n. 13: *AAS* 58 (1966), pp. 1011–12; cf. Paul VI, Encyclical Letter, *Mysterium Fidei: AAS* 57 (1965), p. 782.
102. Constitution on the Liturgy, n. 22:3: *AAS* 56 (1964), p. 106.
103. Cf. St. Thomas Aquinas, *Summa Theol.*, II–II, q. 93, a. 1.
104. Constitution on the Liturgy, n. 11: *AAS* 56 (1964), pp. 102–103; cf. also n. 48, ibid., p. 113.

47. Concelebration

Concelebration of the Eucharist aptly demonstrates the unity of the sacrifice and of the priesthood. Moreover, whenever the faithful take an active part, the unity of the People of God is strikingly manifested,[105] particularly if the bishop presides.[106]

Concelebration both symbolizes and strengthens the brotherly bond of the priesthood, because "by virtue of the ordination to the priesthood which they have in common, all are bound together in an intimate brotherhood."[107]

Therefore, unless it conflicts with the needs of the faithful, which must always be consulted with the deepest pastoral concern, and although every priest retains the right to celebrate alone, it is desirable that priests should celebrate the Eucharist in this eminent manner. This applies both to communities of priests and to groups which gather on particular occasions, as also to all similar circumstances. Those who live in community or serve the same church should welcome visiting priests into their concelebration.

The competent superiors should, therefore, facilitate, and indeed positively encourage concelebration, whenever pastoral needs or other reasonable motives do not prevent it.

The faculty to concelebrate also applies to the principal Masses in Churches and public and semi-public oratories of seminaries, colleges and ecclesiastical institutes, and also of religious orders and societies of clergy living in community without vows. However, where there is a great number of priests, the competent superior may give permission for concelebration to take place even several times on the same day, though at different times or in different places.

48. The Bread for Concelebration

If a large host is used for concelebration, as permitted in the *Ritus servandus in concelebratione Missae*, n. 17, care

105. Constitution on the Liturgy, n. 57: *AAS* 56 (1964), pp. 115–116; S.C.R., General Decree, *Ecclesiae Semper*, 7 March 1965: *AAS* 57 (1965), pp. 410–412.
106. Constitution on the Liturgy, n. 41: *AAS* 56 (1964), p. 111; Constitution on the Church, n. 28: *AAS* 57 (1965), pp. 33–36; Decree on the Ministry and Life of Priests, n. 7: *AAS* 58 (1966), 1001–03.
107. Constitution on the Church, n. 28: *AAS* 57 (1965), p. 35; cf. Decree on the Ministry and Life of Priests, n. 8: *AAS* (1966), pp. 1003–05.

must be taken that, in keeping with traditional usage, it should be of such a shape and appearance as befits so great a sacrament.

CHAPTER III

THE WORSHIP OF THE EUCHARIST AS A PERMANENT SACRAMENT

I. THE REASONS FOR RESERVING THE EUCHARIST; PRAYER BEFORE THE BLESSED SACRAMENT

49. The Reasons for Reserving the Eucharist Outside Mass

"It would be well to recall that the primary and original purpose of the reserving of the sacred species in church outside Mass is the administration of the Viaticum. Secondary ends are the distribution of communion outside Mass and the adoration of Our Lord Jesus Christ concealed beneath these same species."[108] For "the reservation of the sacred species for the sick . . . led to the praiseworthy custom of adoring the heavenly food which is preserved in churches. This practice of adoration has a valid and firm foundation,"[109] especially since belief in the real presence of the Lord has as its natural consequence the external and public manifestation of that belief.

50. Prayer Before the Blessed Sacrament

When the faithful adore Christ present in the sacrament, they should remember that this presence derives from the sacrifice and is directed towards both sacramental and spiritual communion.

108. S.C. of Sacraments, Instruction *Quam Plurimum*, 1 Oct. 1949: *AAS* 41 (1949), pp. 509–510; cf. Council of Trent, Session 13: Decree on Eucharist, ch. 4: *Denz.* 879 (1645); St. Pius X, Decree, *Sacra Tridentina Synodus*, 20 Dec. 1905: *Denz.* 1981 (3375).
109. Pius XII, Encyclical Letter, *Mediator Dei: AAS* 39 (1947), p. 569.

In consequence, the devotion which leads the faithful to visit the Blessed Sacrament draws them into an ever deeper participation in the Paschal Mystery. It leads them to respond gratefully to the gift of him who through his humanity constantly pours divine life into the members of his body.[110] Dwelling with Christ our Lord, they enjoy his intimate friendship and pour out their hearts before him for themselves and their dear ones, and pray for the peace and salvation of the world. They offer their entire lives with Christ to the Father in the Holy Spirit, and receive in this wonderful exchange an increase of faith, hope and charity. Thus they nourish those right dispositions which enable them with all due devotion to celebrate the memorial of the Lord and receive frequently the bread given us by the Father.

The faithful should therefore strive to worship Christ our Lord in the Blessed Sacrament, in harmony with their way of life. Pastors should exhort them to this, and set them a good example.[111]

51. The Faithful Should Have Easy Access to Churches

Pastors should see to it that all churches and public oratories where the Blessed Sacrament is reserved remain open for at least several hours in the morning and evening so that it may be easy for the faithful to pray before the Blessed Sacrament.

II. WHERE THE BLESSED SACRAMENT IS TO BE RESERVED

52. The Tabernacle

Where reservation of the Blessed Sacrament is permitted according to the provisions of the law, it may be reserved permanently or regularly only on one altar or in one place in the church.[112] Therefore, as a rule, each church should have only one tabernacle, and this tabernacle must be safe and inviolable.[113]

110. Decree on the Ministry and Life of Priests, n. 5: *AAS* 58 (1956), pp. 997–999.
111. Ibid., n. 18: *AAS* 58 (1966), pp. 1018–19.
112. Cf. *CIC*, can. 1268, par. 1.
113. S.C.R. Instruction *Inter Oecumenici*, 26 Sept. 1964, n. 95: *AAS* 56 (1964), p. 898; S.C. of Sacraments, Instruction *Nullo Umquam Tempore*, 28 May 1938, n. 4: *AAS* 30 (1938), pp. 199–200.

53. The Blessed Sacrament Chapel

The place in a church or oratory where the Blessed Sacrament is reserved in the tabernacle should be truly prominent. It ought to be suitable for private prayer so that the faithful may easily and fruitfully, by private devotion also, continue to honor our Lord in this sacrament.[114] It is therefore recommended that, as far as possible, the tabernacle be placed in a chapel distinct from the middle or central part of the church, above all in those churches where marriages and funerals take place frequently, and in places which are much visited for their artistic or historical treasures.

54. The Tabernacle in the Middle of the Altar or in Some Other Part of the Church

"The Blessed Sacrament should be reserved in a solid, inviolable tabernacle in the middle of the main altar or on a side altar, but in a truly prominent place. Alternatively, according to legitimate customs and in individual cases to be decided by the local ordinary, it may be placed in some other part of the church which is really worthy and properly equipped.

"Mass may be celebrated facing the people even though there is a tabernacle on the altar, provided this is small yet adequate."[115]

55. A Tabernacle on an Altar Where Mass Is Celebrated with a Congregation

In the celebration of Mass the principal modes of worship by which Christ is present to his Church[116] are gradually revealed. First of all, Christ is seen to be present among the faithful gathered in his name; then in his Word, as the Scriptures are read and explained; in the person of the minister; finally and in a unique way (*modo singulari*) under the species of the Eucharist. Consequently, by reason of the symbolism, it is more in keeping with the nature of

---

114. Cf. Decree on the Ministry and Life of Priests, n. 18: *AAS* 58 (1966), pp. 1018–19; Paul VI, Encyclical Letter, *Mysterium Fidei: AAS* 57 (1965), p. 771.
115. S.C.R. Instruction *Inter Oecumenici,* 26 Sept. 1964, n. 95: *AAS* 56 (1964), p. 898.
116. Cf. n. 9 above.

the celebration that the eucharistic presence of Christ, which is the fruit of the consecration and should be seen as such, should not be on the altar from the very beginning of Mass through the reservation of the sacred species in the tabernacle.

56. The Tabernacle in the Construction of New Churches and the Adaptation of Existing Churches and Altars

The principles stated in nn. 53 and 55 ought to be kept in mind in the building of new churches.

The adaptation of existing churches and altars may only take place according to the principles laid down in n. 24 of this Instruction.

57. The Means of Indicating the Presence of the Blessed Sacrament in the Tabernacle

Care should be taken that the presence of the Blessed Sacrament in the tabernacle is indicated to the faithful by a tabernacle veil or some other suitable means prescribed by the competent authority.

According to the traditional practice, a lamp should burn continually near the tabernacle as a sign of the honor paid to the Lord.[117]

III. EUCHARISTIC DEVOTIONS

58. Devotion, both private and public, towards the sacrament of the altar even outside Mass, provided it observes the norms laid down by the legitimate authority and those of the present Instruction, is highly recommended by the Church, since the eucharistic sacrifice is the source and summit of the whole Christian life.[118]

In determining the form of such devotions, account should be taken of the regulations of the Second Vatican Council concerning the relationship to be maintained between the liturgy and other, non-liturgical, celebrations. Especially important is the rule which states: "The liturgical seasons must be taken into account, and these devotions must harmonize with the liturgy, be in some way derived

117. Cf. C.I.C., can. 1271.
118. Constitution on the Church, n. 11: *AAS* 57 (1965), pp. 15–16.

from it and lead the people towards the liturgy as to something which of its nature is far superior to these
devotions."[119]

IV. PROCESSIONS OF THE BLESSED SACRAMENT

59. In processions in which the Blessed Sacrament is solemnly carried through the streets to the singing of hymns, especially on the feast of *Corpus Christi*, the Christian people
give public witness to their faith and devotion towards this
sacrament.

However, it is for the local ordinary to decide whether
such processions are opportune in present-day circumstances. He will also determine the place and form of such
processions, so that they may be conducted with dignity
and without deteriment to the reverence due to this sacrament.

V. EXPOSITION OF THE BLESSED SACRAMENT

60. The exposition of the Blessed Sacrament, for which either a monstrance or a ciborium may be used, stimulates
the faithful to an awareness of the marvellous presence of
Christ, and is an invitation to spiritual communion with
him. It is therefore an excellent encouragment to offer him
that worship in spirit and truth which is his due.

Care must be taken that during these expositions the
worship given to the Blessed Sacrament should be seen, by
signs, in its relation to the Mass. It is necessary then that
when the exposition in question is solemn and prolonged, it
should be begun at the end of the Mass in which the host to
be exposed has been consecrated. The Mass ends with the
Benedicamus Domino and the blessing is omitted. In the
decoration which accompanies exposition,[120] one must
carefully avoid anything which could obscure the desire of
Christ in instituting the Eucharist; for he instituted it above
all with the purpose of nourishing, healing and sustaining
us.[121]

119. Constitution on the Liturgy, n. 13: *AAS* 56 (1964), p. 103.
120. Cf. n. 62 below.
121. Cf. St. Pius X, Decree, *Sacra Tridentina Synodus*, 20 Dec. 1905:
Denz. 1918 (3375).

61. It Is Forbidden to Celebrate Mass Before the Blessed Sacrament Exposed

While the Blessed Sacrament is exposed, the celebration of Mass in the same area of the Church (*eadem aula ecclesiae*) is forbidden, all concessions and contrary customs valid up to the present time, even those worthy of special mention, notwithstanding.

This is because, besides the reasons given in n. 55 of this Instruction, the celebration of the Mystery of the Eucharist includes in a more perfect way that spiritual communion to which exposition should lead the faithful. Therefore there is no need for this further help.

If exposition of the Blessed Sacrament is prolonged for a day, or for several successive days, it should be interrupted during the celebration of the Mass, unless it is celebrated in a chapel apart from the exposition area and some at least of the faithful remain in adoration.

In places where the interruption of a long-established contrary custom would upset the faithful, local ordinaries should establish a suitable but not over-long period of time, in order that this norm may be explained to the faithful before coming into effect.

62. How the Rite of Exposition Is to Be Carried Out

If the exposition is only to be a short one, then the monstrance or ciborium should be placed on the altar table. If exposition is over a longer period, then a throne may be used, placed in a prominent position; care should be taken, however, that it is not too high or far away.

During the exposition everything should be so arranged that the faithful can devote themselves attentively in prayer to Christ our Lord.

To foster personal prayer, there may be readings from the Scriptures together with a homily, or brief exhortations which lead to a better understanding of the mystery of the Eucharist. It is also good for the faithful to respond to the Word of God in song. It is necessary that there should be periods of silence at suitable times.

At the end of the exposition, Benediction with the Blessed Sacrament is given.

If the vernacular is used, instead of singing the *Tantum Ergo* before the blessing, another eucharistic hymn may be used, as laid down by the Episcopal Conference.

63. Solemn Annual Exposition

In churches where the Blessed Sacrament is normally reserved, there could be a period of solemn exposition each year, even if it were not strictly continuous, giving the local community the opportunity to adore and meditate on this mystery more deeply and fervently.

Exposition of this kind should only be held if it is seen that there will be a reasonable number of the faithful, by consent of the local ordinary and according to the law.

64. Prolonged Exposition

For any grave and general need, the local ordinary can order that there should be prayer before the Blessed Sacrament exposed over a long period, and which can be strictly continuous, in those churches where there are large numbers of the faithful.

65. Interrupting Exposition

Where, due to the fact that there is not a suitable number of faithful for the adoration of the Blessed Sacrament, continuous exposition is not possible, it is permissable to replace the host in the tabernacle, at prearranged and publicized times. This should not be done however more than twice in a day, for example, at midday and at night.

This reposition may be carried out in the more simple way and without singing: the priest dressed in cotta and stole, having adored the Blessed Sacrament for a short time, replaces it in the tabernacle. In the same way, at a set time, the Blessed Sacrament is again exposed: the priest retires after a short period of adoration.

66. Exposition for Short Periods

Even brief exposition of the Blessed Sacrament held in accordance with the law should be so arranged that before the blessing with the Blessed Sacrament reasonable time is provided for readings of the Word of God, hymns, prayers and silent prayer, as circumstances permit.

Local ordinaries will make certain that these expositions of the Blessed Sacrament are always and everywhere carried out with due reverence.

Exposition merely for the purpose of giving Benediction after Mass is forbidden.

VI. EUCHARISTIC CONGRESSES

67. In Eucharistic Congresses Christians seek to understand this mystery more deeply through a consideration of its many aspects (cf. above, n. 3). But they should celebrate it in accordance with the norms of the Second Vatican Council and should venerate it through devotions and private prayer, *especially by solemn processions,* in such a way that all these forms of devotion find their climax in the solemn celebration of Mass.

For the duration of the Eucharistic Congress of an entire region, it is fitting that some churches should be reserved for perpetual adoration.

10

APOSTOLIC CONSTITUTION ON THE ROMAN MISSAL[a]

Paul VI, *Missale Romanum,* 3 April, 1969

The Roman Missal, promulgated by our predecessor St. Pius V in the Year of our Lord 1570 by decree of the Council of Trent,[1] is universally acknowledged to be among the most useful of the many fruits which that Council brought forth for the good of the whole Church of Christ. Throughout four centuries not only did the priests of the Roman rite use it as a guide to the way in which they should celebrate the Eucharistic Sacrifice, but also the heralds of the Gospel introduced it into almost every country of the world. Countless saintly men have drawn rich nourishment for their spiritual lives from its scripture readings and prayers, most of which were arranged in due order by St. Gregory the Great.

In recent times, however, there has been at work with ever increasing intensity among the faithful a liturgical renewal which our predecessor Pius XII described as a manifest sign of God's benign providence towards the present generation of mankind, and as a movement of the Holy Spirit bringing grace to his Church.[2] This movement of renewal has made it abundantly clear that in certain respects the texts of the Roman Missal now stand in need of revision and simplification. The process was in fact begun by our predecessor in his restoration of the Paschal Vigil and the Restored Order of Holy Week,[3] whereby he took the

a. Translated by Clifford Howell, S.J., published by CTS, London, reproduced with permission. Latin text in Roman missal, *Missale Romanum.*
1. Apostolic Constitution, *Quo primum,* 14 July 1570.
2. Pius XII, Discourse to the participants in the First International Congress of Pastoral Liturgy, Assisi, 22 Sept. 1956; *AAS* 48 (1956), p. 712.
3. Sacred Congregation of Rites, Decree *Dominicae Resurrectionis,* 9 Feb. 1951: AAS 43 (1951) pp. 128 ff.; Decree *Maxima Redemptionis nostrae mysteria,* 16 Nov. 1955: AAS 47 (1955), pp. 838 ff.

first steps towards the adaptation of the Roman Missal to the new outlook and spiritual mentality of our own times.

The recently concluded Second Ecumenical Council of the Vatican, by its Constitution *Sacrosanctum Concilium*, laid the foundations for the general revision of the Roman Missal. The Council has decreed that "both texts and rites should be drawn up so that they express more clearly the holy things which they signify";[4] that "the rite of the Mass is to be revised in such a way that the intrinsic nature and purpose of its several parts, as also the connection between them, may be more clearly manifested and that devout and active participation by the people may be more easily achieved";[5] further, that "the treasures of the Bible are to be opened up more fully, so that richer fare may be provided for the faithful at the table of God's word";[6] and finally that "a new rite for concelebration is to be drawn up and inserted into the Pontifical and into the Roman Missal."[7]

However, no one should think that this renewal of the Roman Missal has taken place all of a sudden and without adequate preparation; rather has the way to its achievement been well prepared by progress in liturgical studies made during the past four centuries. Quite soon after the Council of Trent, as is apparent from the Apostolic Constitution *Quo Primum* of our predecessor St. Pius V, the study and comparison of ancient manuscripts available in the Vatican Library and elsewhere contributed not a little to the revision of the Missal. Since that time many other very ancient liturgical texts have been discovered and published, and texts from the oriental churches have also been studied. Many have expressed the desire that the riches of faith and doctrine contained in these texts should no longer remain hidden in the darkness of library cupboards and shelves, but should be brought out into the light to warm the hearts and enlighten the minds of the Christian peoples.

We wish now to sketch, at least in outline, the main features of the newly revised Roman Missal.

We begin by drawing attention to the *Institutio Generalis* or "General Instruction" which serves as a preface to the whole book. This not only gives new regulations for cele-

4. Constitution on the Sacred Liturgy, Art. 21.
5. Ibid., Art. 50.
6. Ibid., Art. 51.
7. Ibid., Art. 58.

brating the Eucharistic Sacrifice, but also explains the functions and duties of each participant, and describes the material things and spatial arrangements required for the sacred celebration.

The most remarkable of the new features are those which concern the great Eucharistic Prayer, as it is called nowadays. In the Roman rite the first part of this prayer, known as the Preface, has indeed acquired many different texts in the course of the centuries; but the second part, known as the Canon, assumed an unchanging form about the fourth or fifth century. By contrast, the oriental liturgies have ever admitted a certain variety in their anaphoras (prayers expressing the sacrificial offering).

Besides enriching the Eucharistic Prayer by providing a larger selection of Prefaces (some drawn from the more ancient traditions of the Roman Church and some newly composed) we have decided now to add three more Canons (anaphoras) for use in that prayer. Their purpose is to emphasize different aspects of the mystery of salvation, and to express a variety of motives for giving thanks to God. But for pastoral reasons, and so as to facilitate concelebration, we have ordered that the words of our Lord shall be the same in all forms of the Canon. In every Eucharistic Prayer, therefore, we wish these words to be as follows: Over the bread: "Take this, all of you, and eat it; this is my Body which will be given up for you." Over the wine: "Take this, all of you, and drink from it; this is the cup of my Blood, the Blood of the new and everlasting covenant. It will be shed for you and for all men so that sins may be forgiven. Do this in memory of me." The words, "The mystery of faith," spoken by the priest are to be taken out of the context of the words spoken by our Lord, and used instead to introduce an acclamation by the faithful.

As regards the Order of the Mass, "the rites have been simplified, due care having been taken to preserve their substance.[8] Elements which, with the passage of time, came to be duplicated or were added with but little advantage have now been discarded,"[9] especially in the rites concerned with the preparation of the bread and wine, the Breaking of Bread, and the Communion. On the other hand, certain "elements which have suffered injury through accidents of history are now restored to the vigor which

8. Ibid., Art. 50.
9. Ibid., Art. 50.

they had in the days of the holy Fathers."[10] Among these are the Homily,[11] the Prayer of the Faithful,[12] and the Penitential Rite of reconciliation with God and the brethren which once more has its due significance.

The Second Vatican Council also decreed that "a more representative portion of the holy scriptures should be read to the people in the course of a prescribed number of years."[13] Accordingly the repertoire of scripture passages which are to be read has been drawn up in a cycle of three years. In addition, the Epistle and Gospel on Sundays and Feast Days are to be preceded by a reading taken from the Old Testament—except during Eastertide when it shall be from the Acts of the Apostles. In this way the continuity of development in the history of salvation will become more clearly apparent and be expressed in the very words of divine revelation. This ample provision of biblical readings by which the major part of holy scripture will be proposed to the faithful on Sundays and Feast Days will be supplemented by further extracts from the sacred books to be read on other days.

All these various ordinances are intended to stimulate ever more intensely among the faithful that hunger for the word of God[14] which, under the guidance of the Holy Spirit, is urging the people of the New Testament towards the goal of perfect unity within the Church. We cherish the firm hope that, through the influence of these new arrangements, both priests and people will together prepare themselves more effectively for the celebration of the Lord's Supper and, at the same time, will daily receive increasing nourishment from the word of God through more intensive reflection on holy scripture. Thus, in accordance with the exhortation of the Second Vatican Council, the sacred writings will be recognized by all as the unfailing source of the spiritual life, the basis of all Christian instruction, and the very kernel of theological study.

The revision of the Roman Missal has not been limited to changes in the three main constituents of the Mass already mentioned, namely the Eucharistic Prayer, the Order of Mass and the scripture readings. Besides these, other ele-

10. Ibid., Art. 50.
11. Ibid., Art. 52.
12. Ibid., Art. 53.
13. Ibid., Art. 51.
14. Amos 8:11.

ments of it have been thoroughly investigated and considerably modified. These are the proper of the Season, the Proper of the Saints, the Common of the Saints, the Ritual Masses for particular occasions, and the Votive Masses. In all of these special attention has been given to the Collects. Their number has been increased so that they may better correspond with the needs of our own times, and the older Collects have been critically examined and amended in the light of their original texts. The revision has made it possible to provide different Collects every day for the weekdays of the main liturgical seasons. Advent, Christmastide, Lent and Eastertide.

As regards other parts of the Roman Missal, the text and music of the *Graduale Romanum* have been left unchanged for use when they are sung. But so as to provide some more easily intelligible texts, the Responsorial Psalm, so often the subject of comments by St. Augustine and St. Leo, has been restored to use; and, for Masses celebrated without singing, the Antiphons for the Entrance and Communion have been revised according to need.

In conclusion, among various points explained in this Instruction about the Roman Missal, there is one which we now intend to enforce and accomplish. When our predecessor St. Pius V published the first edition of the *Missale Romanum*, he presented it to the Christian people both as an instrument of liturgical unity and as a witness to the truth and devotion of the new Church's worship. Although we have admitted into this new Missal that "provision for the legitimate variations and adaptations to different groups, regions and peoples" decreed by the Second Vatican Council,[15] we now express a similar hope that this book will be received by the faithful as an aid whereby all can witness to each other and strengthen the one faith common to all, since it enables one and the same prayer, expressed in so many different languages, to ascend to the heavenly Father through our High Priest Jesus Christ in the Holy Spirit—a prayer more fragrant than any incense.

It is our will that these decisions and ordinances should be firm and effective now and in future, notwithstanding any Constitutions and Apostolic Ordinances made by our predecessors, and all other decrees including those deserving of special mention, no matter of what kind.

15. Constitution on the Sacred Liturgy, Art. 38.

11

INSTRUCTION ON MASSES FOR SPECIAL GROUPS[a]

S.C.D.W., *Actio Pastoralis Ecclesiae*, 15 May, 1969

One of the principal objectives of the Church's pastoral activity is to educate the faithful to become part of the ecclesial community so that everyone, above all in liturgical celebrations, will feel at one with his brothers and in communion with the universal and local Church. The liturgical assembly is presided over by the person empowered to unite, guide, instruct and sanctify God's people. It is a sign and instrument of the unity of all men, and above all of the Church with Christ (cf. Constitution on the Sacred Liturgy, n. 83).

This is especially true of the common celebration of the Eucharist, above all on Sundays, with the bishop or in the parochial assembly where the pastor takes the place of the bishop.

Smaller groups can also be the object of pastoral care. The aim is not to create a separate, privileged class, but hopefully to deepen and intensify the Christian life of a group, in keeping with their needs and their stage of development. It achieves this by taking advantage of the opportunities which emanate from a common spiritual or apostolic commitment and from the desire for mutual edification.

Experience shows the efficacy of pastoral activity in these gatherings. If they are well directed and thought out, rather than damaging the unity of the parish, they benefit its missionary action by bringing some people closer and by deepening the formation of others.

Their vitality stems from the fact that the common study of Christian truth and the equally common effort to conform one's own existence and behavior to this are joined in

a. Translation issued by Vatican Press office. *AAS* 61 (1969), pp. 806–811.

this coming-together in prayer. These prayer reunions are carried out in a manner and form consonant with the gathering, especially in the reading and meditating on the word of God and often in the eucharistic celebration, which becomes the culmination and crowning point of the reunion.

The desire to have the eucharistic celebration at these gatherings is particularly felt today. Therefore, it seemed appropriate to give some norms which may regulate such a celebration, so that it may be carried out with order, propriety and serenity, with a spiritual advantage for the participants and with respect for its essential character of sacred and religious worship.

1. It pertains to the bishop to examine accurately the circumstances in order to judge whether in each case pastoral reasons dictate a eucharistic celebration, or if instead it would be better to suggest another religious celebration.

2. The special gatherings for which permission can be given to celebrate the Eucharist are:

(a) Gatherings for retreat, religious or pastoral studies, for one or more days, or for meetings of the lay apostolate or similar associations.

(b) Meetings for pastoral motives in certain sections of the parish.

(c) Gatherings of young people or of persons of the same condition or formation, who periodically come together for religious formation or instruction adapted to their mentality.

(d) Family gatherings around the sick or aged who cannot leave their house and who otherwise would never participate in the eucharistic celebration. Included with these are friends and those who look after the sick.

(e) Those gathered together for a wake or for some other exceptional religious occasion.

3. Normally, the Eucharist for special gatherings is celebrated in a sacred place.

4. The norm in Canon 822, par. 4, of the Code of Canon Law and n. 7 of the first part of the motu proprio *Pastorale Munus*, 30 November 1963, still hold. The permission to celebrate the Eucharist for special gatherings, outside of a sacred place, can be given only by the local ordinary. In cases of celebrations in private houses or institutes, he will give this permission only if the group gathers where there is no chapel or oratory and only if this is a fitting place for

such a celebration. Celebrations in bedrooms are always excluded.

However, in searching for spacious and decorous places, some families should not be preferred towards others. This would only resuscitate, under another form, the privilege class system which was disapproved of in the liturgical constitution (n. 32).

5. The basic principles, delineated in the *Instruction on Eucharistic Worship* (n. 3), should be kept in mind, especially the following:

(a) The sacrifice and the sacred meal belong to the same mystery, to such an extent that they are linked to one another by a very close theological and sacramental bond.

(b) No Mass may be considered as an exclusive action of a particular group, but as a celebration of the Church, in which the priest, exercising his office, presides as a minister of the Church over the entire liturgical action.

(c) Everything should be disposed in such a way that, in the selection of a place, in the attitude of the persons, and in the use of things, true worship is rendered to the sacrament of the Eucharist.

6. In order to achieve a celebration corresponding to circumstances and environment, the single parts should be well organized, keeping in mind the following norms and principles:

(a) In the fullest way possible, participation of the faithful should be encouraged, according to the particular circumstances.

(b) The celebration can be preceded by a period of meditation on holy scripture or of instruction on spiritual things, adapted to the characteristics of the gathering.

(c) Besides an initial admonition, the celebrant can briefly introduce the liturgy of the word before the readings and the eucharistic liturgy before the preface, and also intervene again before the dismissal. Any other interruption is excluded during the eucharistic liturgy.

(d) With the exception of the following norms (cf. f and h below) and the role of the commentator during the celebration, the faithful will refrain from any interventions in the way of reflections, exhortations and the like.

(e) In the liturgy of the word readings adapted to the particular celebration can be chosen from approved lectionaries.

(f) The readings which precede the gospel should be read by one of the participants (man or woman); the gospel, however, must be proclaimed by the priest or deacon.

(g) In the homily the priest should recall the particular character of the celebration, and its link with the local and universal Church.

(h) The prayer of the faithful can be adapted to the circumstances. The general intentions for the Church, the world, brothers in need and the assembly should not be entirely omitted. A particular intention, properly prepared can be proposed by the participants.

7. A more complete and perfect participation in the celebration is had with eucharistic communion. For communion under both species the disposition in the *Instruction on Eucharistic Worship* must be adhered to (cf. n. 32). This type of communion is excluded when Mass is celebrated in houses. Giving communion to oneself and receiving it in the hand are likewise excluded.

8. In order to favor the participation of those present the use of song, in some circumstances, would be useful. Also in this regard, the norms regarding song and music in sacred celebrations should be observed, avoiding that which is contrary to the holiness of the rite and to the piety of the participants.

9. The above-indicated adaptations, introduced exclusively for these cases, are not to be introduced in celebrations done in church for the entire community of the faithful.

10. For celebrations of the Eucharist for special gatherings outside of a sacred place, especially in private houses, these conditions are required:

(a) The faculty (cf. n. 4 above) may not be given for Sundays and holidays of obligation.

(b) The necessity of obtaining the permission of the local ordinary should always be kept in mind. If the celebrant is not the pastor, the pastor should be notified. These, then, will give a report to the bishop concerning the celebrations.

(c) the norms for eucharistic fast should be observed; in no way can the Eucharist be preceded by an agape. If one should follow it will not be at the same table on which the Eucharist is celebrated.

(d) Bread for the Eucharist remains unleavened bread,

the only kind permitted in the Latin Church and not without grave reasons. It will be confected in the customary form.

(e) The celebration should not occur late in the night.

(f) Even in gatherings with family ties no one is to be excluded who desires to participate.

11. To safeguard the success of these celebrations and to obtain a greater spiritual efficaciousness, they should be well prepared and always celebrated with dignity and sacredness. Attention must be given to the form, and the more fitting elements should be chosen with respect for liturgical norms. Therefore:

(a) The texts of the Mass should be taken from the missal or from approved supplements. Every change (except for what has been said in n. 6h) is arbitrary and therefore rejected.

(b) The furnishings of the altar (cross, altar cloth, candles, missal, purificator, corporal, hand towel and communion plate), the sacred vessels (chalice, paten, pyx), the vestments (amice, alb, cincture, stole and chasuble) should be, in number, form and quality, as desired by present legislation.

(c) The ritual gestures and the ceremonies of the celebrant, as well as the attitude of the participants, should be those prescribed for the normal eucharistic celebration.

Pastors in charge of the faithful are encouraged to consider and deepen the spiritual and formative values of these celebrations. They are valid only if they direct the participants to a greater awareness of the Christian mystery, to an insertion in the ecclesial community and its worship and to the faithful exercise of charity and the apostolate.

In our day and age there are those who think they are up-to-date only when they can show off novelty, often bizarre, or devise arbitrary forms of liturgical celebrations. Priests, religious and diocesan, considerate of the true welfare of the faithful, realize that only in a generous and unyielding fidelity to the will of the Church, expressed in its directives, norms and structures, lies the secret of a lasting and sanctifying pastoral success.

Those who wander from this line, even if it is alluring, finish in creating bewilderment in the faithful. At the same time they are killing and rendering sterile their sacerdotal ministry.

This Instruction, prepared at the request of higher authority by the Sacred Congregation for Divine Worship, will regulate every type of Mass celebrated in special gatherings *until the Apostolic See disposes otherwise.*

12

INSTRUCTION ON THE MANNER OF DISTRIBUTING HOLY COMMUNION[a]

S.C.D.W., *Memoriale Domini*, 29 May, 1969

When the Church celebrates the memorial of the Lord it affirms by the very rite itself its faith in Christ and its adoration of him, Christ present in the sacrifice and given as food to those who share the eucharistic table.

For this reason it is a matter of great concern to the Church that the Eucharist be celebrated and shared with the greatest dignity and fruitfulness. It preserves intact the already developed tradition which has come down to us, its riches having passed into the usage and the life of the Church. The pages of history show that the celebration and the receptions of the Eucharist have taken various forms. In our own day the rites for the celebration of the Eucharist have been changed in many and important ways, bringing them more into line with modern man's spiritual and psychological needs. Further, a change has taken place in the discipline governing the laity's participation in the sacrament. Holy communion under two kinds, bread and wine, has been reintroduced. It had once been common in the Latin Church too, but had subsequently been progressively abandoned. This state of affairs had become general by the time of the Council of Trent, which sanctioned and defended it by dogmatic teaching as being suited to the conditions of that time.[1]

These changes have made of the eucharistic banquet and the faithful fulfilment of Christ's command a clearer and more vital symbol. At the same time in recent years a fuller sharing in the eucharistic celebration through sacramental

a. This, and the portion of the Letter following it, were translated by A.F. from *AAS* 61 (1969), pp. 541–547.
1. Cf. Council of Trent, Session 21, The Doctrine of Communion under Both Kinds: *Denz.* 1726–1727.

communion has here and there evoked the desire to return to the ancient usage of depositing the eucharistic bread in the hand of the communicant, he himself then communicating, placing it in his mouth.

Indeed, in certain communities and in certain places this practice has been introduced without prior approval having been requested of the Holy See, and, at times, without any attempt to prepare the faithful adequately.

It is certainly true that ancient usage once allowed the faithful to take this divine food in their hands and to place it in their mouths themselves. It is also true that in very ancient times they were allowed to take the Blessed Sacrament with them from the place where the holy sacrifice was celebrated. This was principally so as to be able to give themselves Viaticum in case they had to face death for their faith.

However, the Church's prescriptions and the evidence of the Fathers make it abundantly clear that the greatest reverence was shown the Blessed Sacrament, and that people acted with the greatest prudence. Thus, "let nobody . . . eat that flesh without first adoring it."[2] As a person takes (the Blessed Sacrament) he is warned: " . . . receive it: be careful lest you lose any of it."[3] "For it is the Body of Christ."[4]

Further, the care and the ministry of the Body and Blood of Christ was specially committed to sacred ministers or to men specially designated for this purpose: "When the president has recited the prayers and all the people have uttered an acclamation, those whom we call deacons distribute to all those present the bread and wine for which thanks have been given, and they take them to those who are absent."[5]

Soon the task of taking the Blessed Eucharist to those absent was confided to the sacred ministers alone, so as the better to ensure the respect due to the sacrament and to meet the needs of the faithful. Later, with a deepening understanding of the truth of the eucharistic mystery, of its power and of the presence of Christ in it, there came a greater feeling of reverence towards this sacrament and a deeper humility was felt to be demanded when receiving it. Thus the custom was established of the minister placing a

2. St. Augustine, *On the Psalms*, 98, 9.
3. St. Cyril of Jerusalem, *Mystagogic Catechesis*, V, 21.
4. Hippolytus, *Apostolic Tradition*, n. 37.
5. Justin, *Apologia*, 1, 65.

particle of consecrated bread on the tongue of the communi-cant.

This method of distributing holy communion must be re-tained, taking the present situation of the Church in the en-tire world into account, not merely because it has many centuries of tradition behind it, but especially because it ex-presses the faithful's reverence for the Eucharist. The cus-tom does not detract in any way from the personal dignity of those who approach this great sacrament: it is part of that preparation that is needed for the most fruitful recep-tion of the Body of the Lord.[6]

This reverence shows that it is not a sharing in "ordinary bread and wine"[7] that is involved, but in the Body and Blood of the Lord, through which "The people of God share the benefits of the Paschal Sacrifice, renew the New Covenant which God has made with man once for all through the Blood of Christ, and in faith and hope foresha-dow and anticipate the eschatological banquet in the king-dom of the Father."[8]

Further, the practice which must be considered tradition-al ensures, more effectively, that holy communion is distrib-uted with the proper respect, decorum and dignity. It re-moves the danger of profanation of the sacred species, in which "in a unique way, Christ, God and man, is pre-sent whole and entire, substantially and continually."[9] Last-ly, it ensures that diligent carefulness about the fragments of consecrated bread which the Church has always recom-mended: "What you have allowed to drop, think of it as though you had lost one of your own members."[10]

When therefore a small number of episcopal conferences and some individual bishops asked that the practice of plac-ing the consecrated hosts in the people's hands be permitted in their territories, the Holy Father decided that all the bishops of the Latin Church should be asked if they thought it opportune to introduce this rite. A change in a matter of such moment, based on a most ancient and vener-able tradition, does not merely affect discipline. It carries certain dangers with it which may arise from the new man-ner of administering holy communion: the danger of a loss

6. See St. Augustine, *On the Psalms*, 98, 9.
7. See Justin, *Apologia*, 1, 66.
8. Instruction *Eucharisticum Mysterium*, n. 3.
9. Ibid., n. 9.
10. St. Cyril of Jerusalem, *Mystagogic Catechesis*, V, 21.

of reverence for the august sacrament of the altar, of profanation, of adulterating the true doctrine.

Three questions were asked of the bishops, and the replies received by 12 March 1969 were as follows:

1. Do you think that attention should be paid to the desire that, over and above the traditional manner, the rite of receiving holy communion on the hand should be admitted?

Yes: 597
No: 1,233
Yes, but with reservations: 315
Invalid votes: 20

2. Is it your wish that this new rite be first tried in small communities, with the consent of the bishop?

Yes: 751
No: 1,215
Invalid votes, 70

3. Do you think that the faithful will receive this new rite gladly, after a proper catechetical preparation?

Yes: 835
No: 1,185
Invalid votes: 128

From the returns it is clear that the vast majority of bishops believe that the present discipline should not be changed, and that if it were, the change would be offensive to the sentiments and the spiritual culture of these bishops and of many of the faithful.

Therefore, taking into account the remarks and the advice of those whom "the Holy Spirit has placed to rule over" the Churches,[11] in view of the gravity of the matter and the force of the arguments put forward, the Holy Father has decided not to change the existing way of administering holy communion to the faithful.

The Apostolic See therefore emphatically urges bishops, priests and laity to obey carefully the law which is still valid and which has again been confirmed. It urges them to take account of the judgment given by the majority of Catholic bishops, of the rite now in use in the liturgy, of the common good of the Church.

Where a contrary usage, that of placing holy communion on the hand, prevails, the Holy See—wishing to help them fulfil their task, often difficult as it is nowadays—lays on those conferences the task of weighing carefully whatever

11. See Acts 20:28.

special circumstances may exist there, taking care to avoid any risk of lack of respect or of false opinions with regard to the Blessed Eucharist, and to avoid any other ill effects that may follow.

In such cases, episcopal conferences should examine matters carefully and should make whatever decisions, by a secret vote and with a two-thirds majority, are needed to regulate matters. Their decisions should be sent to Rome to receive the necessary confirmation,[12] accompanied with a detailed account of the reasons which led them to take those decisions. The Holy See will examine each case carefully, taking into account the links between the different local churches and between each of them and the Universal Church, in order to promote the common good and the edification of all, and that mutual good example may increase faith and piety.

Note: in the *Acta Apostolicae Sedis* (pp. 546–547) the Instruction was accompanied by a sample of the letter (in French) which is sent to hierarchies who ask for and are granted permission to introduce the practice of holy communion on the hand. The letter laid down the following regulations:

1. The new method of administering communion should not be imposed in a way that would exclude the traditional usage. . . .

2. The rite of communion in the hand must be introduced tactfully. In effect, since human attitudes are in question, it is linked with the sensibility of the person receiving communion. It should therefore be introduced gradually, beginning with better-educated and better-prepared groups. It is, above all, necessary that an adequate catechesis prepares the way so that the faithful will understand the significance of the action and will perform it with the respect due to the sacrament. The result of this catechesis should be to remove any suggestion of wavering on the part of the Church in its faith in the eucharistic presence, and also to remove any danger or even suggestion of profanation.

3. The fact that the lay person is now able to receive holy communion in the hand should not suggest to him that this is ordinary bread, or just any sacred object. Rather ought it to strengthen his sense of his dignity as a member of the Mystical Body of Christ, of which baptism and the

12. See Vatican II Decree *Christus Dominus*, n. 38, par. 4.

grace of the Eucharist make him a part. He will thus experience an increase of faith in the great reality of the Body and Blood of the Lord which he touches with his hands. His respectful attitude should be proportionate to what he is doing.

4. With regard to the manner of administering the sacrament, one may follow the traditional method, which emphasized the ministerial function of the priest or deacon, in having them place the host in the hand of the communicant. One may also adopt a simpler method, allowing the communicant himself to take the host from the ciborium. In either case, the communicant ought to consume the host before returning to his place, and the minister's role will be emphasized by his saying, "The Body of Christ," to which the communicant responds, "Amen."

5. No matter which method is adopted, one will be careful not to allow any fragment of the host to fall. . . .

6. When the communion is distributed under both kinds, it is never permitted to place in the hands of the communicants hosts which have first been placed in the Blood of the Lord.

7. Bishops who have been permitted to introduce the new rite of communion are asked to send a report to the congregation, six months hence, on the outcome.

13

GENERAL INSTRUCTION ON THE ROMAN MISSAL[a]

FOREWORD

1. When Christ the Lord desired to celebrate with his disciples the Paschal Supper at which he instituted the sacrifice of his Body and Blood, he ordered the preparation of "a large upper room furnished with couches" (Lk. 22:12). The Church has ever taken this behest as applying to herself. Accordingly she has drawn up for the eucharistic celebration rules which concern the disposition of men's hearts and also such things as the place, the rites and the texts to be used. The norms which are now to come into force by order of the Second Vatican Council, and the new Missal which the Church of the Roman rite is henceforth to use in the celebration of Mass, are a fresh proof of the Church's solicitude for her faith and her unchanging love for the eucharistic mystery. In addition, even some new features which have been introduced, testify to her abiding and constant tradition.

Witness to unchanging Faith

2. The sacrificial character of the Mass was solemnly defined by the Council of Trent in accordance with the universal tradition of the Church.[1] The Second Vatican Council has enunciated this same teaching once again, and made this highly significant comment: "At the Last Supper our Saviour instituted the eucharistic sacrifice of his Body and Blood. He did this in order to perpetuate the sacrifice of the Cross until he should come again; and he wished to entrust

a. Translated by Clifford Howell, S.J. from the text in the Roman Missal (1970) and with the changes necessitated by the abolition of the subdiaconate and minor orders. Published by CTS, London, Reproduced with permission.
1. Session 22, 17 Sept. 1562.

154

to his beloved spouse, the Church, a memorial of his death and resurrection."[2] The Council's teaching on this point finds an enduring expression in the texts of the Mass. A sentence from the Leonine sacramentary: "Whenever the memorial of this sacrifice is celebrated, the work of our redemption is accomplished"[3] expresses succinctly the very doctrine set forth anew in suitable and accurate terms in the Eucharistic Prayers. In these the priest, during the anamnesis (prayer of remembrance), addresses himself to God in the name of all the people; he gives thanks to God and offers to him a holy and living sacrifice, the Church's offering, the Victim whose death has reconciled man with God;[4] he prays that the Body and Blood of Christ may be the acceptable sacrifice which brings salvation to the whole world.[5]

Thus in the new Missal the Church's rule of worship corresponds with her unchanging rule of faith. From this we learn that the sacrifice of the Cross and its sacramental renewal in the Mass are, apart from the difference in the manner of offering, one and the same sacrifice; it is this sacramental renewal which Christ the Lord instituted at the Last Supper and commanded his apostles to celebrate in his memory. The Mass is therefore a sacrifice of praise, of thanksgiving, of propitiation and of satisfaction.

3. In the celebration of Mass there is proclaimed the wonderful mystery of the real presence of Christ our Lord under the eucharistic species. The Second Vatican Council[6] and other magisterial pronouncements of the Church[7] have confirmed this truth in the same sense and the same words as those in which the Council of Trent defined it as an article of faith.[8] It is proclaimed not only by the words of consecration whereby Christ becomes present through an essential change in the elements, but also by the

2. Constitution on the Sacred Liturgy, Art. 47; cf. Dogmatic Constitution on the Church, nn. 3, 28; Décree on the Ministry and Life of Priests, nn. 2, 4, 5.
3. *Sacramentarium Veronense*, ed. C. Mohlberg, n .93.
4. Eucharistic Prayer III.
5. Eucharistic Prayer IV.
6. Constitution on the Sacred Liturgy Arts. 7, 47; Decree on the Ministry and Life of Priests, nn. 5, 18.
7. Pius XII, *Humani generis;* Paul VI, *Mysterium fidei; Solemnis professio fidei;* S.C.R. Instruction *Eucharisticum mysterium*, 25 May 1967, (D.9), nn. 3 f., 9.
8. Session 13, 11 Oct. 1551.

meaning of the celebration and the several external manifestations of deep reverence and adoration occurring during the course of the eucharistic liturgy. It is this same belief which leads the Christian people to adore the wonderful sacrament by special acts of veneration on Maundy Thursday and on the Solemnity of the Body and Blood of Christ (Corpus Christi).

4. The nature of the ministerial priesthood of the celebrant who offers the sacrifice in the person of Christ, and who presides over the holy people, is clearly manifested not only by the way in which the rite is conducted, but also by the prominent position and unique functions allotted to the priest. These are explained more fully in the Preface of the Chrism Mass on Maundy Thursday, the day on which the institution of the priesthood is commemorated. This Preface mentions how the priestly powers are conferred by the imposition of hands, and it describes the various duties of the priestly ministry whereby the power of Christ High Priest of the New Testament, is continued.

5. But the very nature of the ministerial priesthood sheds light upon another kind of priesthood of great dignity, namely, the royal priesthood of the faithful whose spiritual sacrifice is accomplished through the ministry of the priest in union with the sacrifice of Christ, the One Mediator.[9] For the celebration of the Eucharist is an act of the whole Church. Everyone at Mass is to do all of, but only, those parts which pertain to his office according to his status within the people of God. A consequence of this principle is that certain features of the celebration are now receiving greater attention than was formerly accorded to them during some of the preceding centuries. The celebrating people are in fact the people of God, purchased by the Blood of Christ, convened by their Lord, nourished by his word, a people called on to lay before God the entreaties of all mankind. They are a people who give thanks to God for the mystery of salvation in Christ by offering his sacrifice; a people who grow together in unity by being united with his Body and Blood, a people, holy by origin, who continually grow in holiness by active, conscious and fruitful participation in the eucharistic mystery.[10]

9. Decree on the Ministry and Life of Priests, n. 2.
10. Constitution on the Sacred Liturgy, Art. 11.

Continuity in Tradition

6. When issuing decrees that the Order of the Mass should be revised, the Second Vatican Council ruled, among other things, that certain rites were "to be restored to the vigor which they had in the days of the holy Fathers."[11] These are the very words used by St. Pius V in his Apostolic Constitution *Quo primum* whereby he promulgated the Tridentine Missal of 1570. The employment of the very same words indicates that the two Missals, though separated in time by four centuries, are nevertheless inspired by and embody one and the same tradition. Reflection on the basic content of this tradition will show that the new Missal is a considerable improvement on the old one.

7. In those troubled days St. Pius V was unwilling to make any changes in the rites except minor ones; he was intent on preserving more recent tradition, because at that time attacks were being made on the doctrine that the Mass is a sacrifice, that its ministers are priests, and that Christ is really and abidingly present under the eucharistic species. In point of fact the Missal of 1570 differs very little indeed from the first printed Missal which dates from the year 1474, and this in turn follows very closely a Mass book dating back to the time of Pope Innocent III. Moreover the manuscripts then available in the Vatican Library, though providing evidence to justify a few textual improvements, could offer nothing useful for any "research into the ancient and approved authors" except for some liturgical commentaries dating from the Middle Ages.

8. By contrast, today the "norms of the holy Fathers" which the revisors of St. Pius V's Missal were trying to follow, can now be ascertained far more completely and certainly as the fruit of innumerable scientific researches. The first printed edition of the Gregorian Sacramentary came out in 1571; soon after that the ancient Roman and Ambrosian Sacramentaries were published in several critical editions. These were followed by editions of old Spanish and Gallican liturgical books. As a result of all this work, many texts of no small spiritual value, previously unknown, were brought to light.

In like manner the liturgical traditions of the early centu-

11. Ibid., Art. 50.

ries before the Eastern and Western rites took definite shape are much better known today because so many early liturgical documents have been discovered.

Finally there has been great progress in patristic studies, and this has cast much light on the theology of the eucharistic mystery from the teachings of the leading Fathers of Christian antiquity, such as Irenaeus, Ambrose, Cyril of Jerusalem and John Chrysostom.

9. Following "the norms of the holy Fathers" does not, therefore, mean preserving only what we have received from our most recent ancestors. It means understanding and evaluating all the periods of time and ways of thought in which the one faith of the Church has been expressed in terms of the widely differing human cultures formerly obtaining in the Semitic, Greek and Latin worlds. Such a wide perspective enables us to appreciate how marvellously the Holy Spirit has endowed the people of God with an astonishing fidelity in preserving unchanged the deposit of faith, notwithstanding an immense variety in prayers and rites.

Adaptation to new Circumstances

10. The new Missal, therefore, is a witness to the Church's way of prayer, and it preserves the deposit of faith handed down to us through the more recent Councils. But at the same time it is a very important step forward in liturgical tradition. When the Fathers of the Second Vatican Council repeated the dogmatic pronouncements of the Council of Trent, they were speaking in a profoundly different epoch of the world's history. For this reason they were in a position to put forward in the pastoral sphere proposals and directives which, four centuries ago, could hardly have been imagined.

11. The Council of Trent had recognized the great catechetical values contained in the celebration of Mass, but was not in a position then to draw the practical conclusions which naturally would have followed. Many of the Fathers did indeed urge that permission should be granted for the use of living languages in celebrating the Mass. But the circumstances prevailing in those days forced the Council to a conclusion incompatible with that desire, namely, that there was an imperative need to emphasize once again a traditional doctrine of the Church. This was the doctrine that the eucharistic Sacrifice is in the first place an action of

Christ himself, and that its intrinsic efficacy is independent of the manner in which the faithful take part in it. The Council decided, therefore, in firm and carefully weighed words, that "Although the Mass contains much valuable instruction for the faithful, the Fathers do not think it expedient to allow it generally to be celebrated in the vernacular language."[12] The Council condemned also those who maintained that "the rite of the Roman Church in which the Canon and the words of consecration are said inaudibly is to be reprobated" or "that the Mass must be said in the vernacular."[13] Even so, although the Council at that time forbade the use of the vernacular in the Mass, it ordered pastors of souls to make up for this by suitable instructions: "Lest the flock of Christ should go hungry . . . this Sacred Synod commands pastors and all who have care of souls frequently to explain, during Mass, something of what is read at Mass either personally or through others; and they should expound, among other matters, something about the mystery of this most holy sacrifice, especially on Sundays and Feast Days."[14]

12. When the Second Vatican Council assembled with the aim of adapting the Church to the needs of today's apostolate, it considered thoroughly, as the Council of Trent had done, the catechetical and pastoral character of the sacred liturgy.[15] Since no Catholic would now deny the legitimacy and efficacy of a liturgical rite celebrated in Latin, the Council could now concede that "the use of the mother tongue can frequently be of great advantage to the people,"[16] and it gave permission for such use. The enthusiastic welcome given in every country to this permission has in fact led to the situation in which, under the guidance of the bishops and of the Apostolic See, all liturgical functions in which the people take part may now be celebrated in the vernacular so that the mystery being celebrated may be the better understood.

13. The use of the mother tongue is indeed an important means for imparting instruction about the sacred mysteries celebrated in the liturgy; but it is not the only means. Hence the Second Vatican Council has also insisted that

12. Session 22, Doctrine on the Sacrifice of the Mass, Cap. 8.
13. Ibid., Cap. 9
14. Ibid., Cap. 8.
15. Constitution on the Sacred Liturgy, Art. 33.
16. Ibid., Art. 36.

certain decisions of the Council of Trent, hitherto some-what neglected, are now to be implemented. Among these are the homily which must be delivered on Sundays and Feast Days[17] and the possibility of inserting a few words of instruction here and there within the sacred rites themselves.[18] The Council has also laid special stress on "that more perfect form of participation in the Mass where-by the faithful, after the priest's Communion, receive the Lord's Body from the same sacrifice."[19] In this way yet an-other desire of the Council of Trent will be realized in practice, namely that "in every Mass the faithful who are present should take part, not only by their spiritual disposi-tions, but also by sacramental reception of the Eucharist."[20]

14. In the same spirit and with the same pastoral con-cern, the Second Vatican Council has reconsidered the rul-ing of the Council of Trent about Communion under both kinds. In our own day no one disputes the doctrinal princi-ples which legitimize the reception of Communion under the species of bread only; hence the Council is in a position to allow Communion under both species in certain circum-stances, because this provides a special opportunity for the faithful to achieve a deeper understanding of the mystery in which they participate through the increased clarity of the sacramental sign.[21]

15. In this way the Church, as the teacher of truth, re-mains faithful to her task of preserving "the old," that is, the deposit of faith; at the same time she fulfils her other task of considering and wisely making use of "the new" (cf. Mt. 13:52).

One section of the new Missal adapts the prayers of the Church more suitably to the needs of our own times. This is exemplified chiefly in the Masses conjoined with the cele-bration of sacraments and sacramentals, and in those for particular intentions. In these Masses old and new elements are harmoniously blended. While many of the texts are de-rived unchanged from the most ancient traditions of the Church, some have been adapted to contemporary needs and circumstances; yet others are completely new, drawing on the thoughts and even the very words of recent conciliar

17. Ibid., Art. 52.
18. Ibid., Art. 35, n. 2.
19. Ibid., Art. 55.
20. Session 22, Doctrine on the Sacrifice of the Mass, Cap. 6.
21. Constitution on the Sacred Liturgy, Art. 55.

documents. These last are exemplified in the prayers for the Church, for the laity, for the sanctification of human work, for the community of all nations, and for particular needs which have come to the fore in our own day.

To change a phrase or two here and there in the venerable treasury of prayers inherited from the past so as to relate them to present-day circumstances is in no way to undervalue them. Such changes have been made so that the mode of expression may be in harmony with that of modern theology and with the facts of contemporary Church discipline. That is why some phrases concerning the estimation and use of earthly things or the external forms of penance formerly in vogue in the Church have been altered.

In this way the liturgical norms of the Council of Trent have in many respects been fulfilled and perfected by those of the Second Vatican Council. The latter Council has in fact brought to fruition previous efforts to lead the faithful closer to the liturgy—efforts made throughout the past four centuries but especially in more recent times in consequence of the liturgical initiatives of St. Pius X and his successors.

CHAPTER I

IMPORTANCE AND DIGNITY OF THE EUCHARISTIC CELEBRATION

1. The celebration of the Mass, as an action of Christ and the people of God hierarchically ordered, is the center of the whole Christian life for the universal Church, the local Church and for each and every one of the faithful.[1] For therein is the culminating action whereby God sanctifies the world in Christ and men worship the Father as they adore

1. Constitution on the Sacred Liturgy, Art. 41; Dogmatic Constitution on the Church, n. 11; Decree on the Ministry and Life of Priests, nn. 2, 5, 6; Decree on the Pastoral Office of Bishops in the Church, n. 30; Decree on Ecumenism, n. 15; S.C.R. Instruction *Eucharisticum mysterium*, 25 May 1967, nn. 3e, 6.

...1 through Christ the Son of God.[2] The mysteries of
...an's redemption are in some way made present through-
...ut the course of the year by the celebration of Mass.[3] All
other sacred celebrations and the activities of the Christian
life are related to the Mass; they spring forth from it and
culminate in it.[4]

2. It is therefore of the greatest importance that the celebration of the Mass, the Lord's Supper, be so arranged that
everybody—ministers and people—may take their own
proper part in it. For thus they will more abundantly draw
from it those fruits[5] which our Lord intended them to derive when he instituted the Eucharist as the sacrifice of his
Body and Blood and entrusted it to his beloved spouse, the
Church, as a memorial of his death and resurrection.[6]

3. The best way to achieve this will be to consider the
particular character and circumstances of the community,
and then to organize the details of the celebration in a way
that will lead them to full, active and conscious participation. This implies a participation that will involve them in
both body and soul, and which will inspire them with faith,
hope and charity. This is what the Church desires; this is
what the nature of the celebration demands; it is this to
which the faithful have both the right and duty by reason
of their baptism.[7]

4. It is indeed the presence and active participation of the
faithful which most clearly manifests the ecclesial nature of
the celebrations;[8] yet even when Mass is celebrated without
them, as is sometimes unavoidable, it nevertheless retains
its dignity and saving power because it is the action of
Christ and his Church[9] in which the priest always acts for
the salvation of the people.

5. The celebration of the Eucharist, as also of the entire
liturgy, is carried out by means of signs perceptible to the
senses—signs by means of which faith is nourished,
strengthened and expressed.[10] Hence all possible care

2. Constitution on the Sacred Liturgy, Art. 10.
3. Ibid., Art. 102.
4. Ibid., Art. 10; Decree on the Ministry and Life of Priests, n. 5.
Constitution on the Sacred Liturgy, Art. 10.
5. Constitution on the Sacred Liturgy, Arts. 14, 19, 26, 28, 30.
6. Ibid. Art. 47.
7. Ibid. Art. 14.
8. Ibid. Art. 41.
9. Decree on the Ministry and Life of Priests, n. 13.
10. Constitution on the Sacred Liturgy, Art. 59.

should be taken that, from the rites and ceremonies proposed by the Church, those should be chosen which, in view of individual and local circumstances, will best foster active participation and meet the needs of the faithful.

6. The aims of this General Instruction are to give the basic principles for the worthy celebration of the Eucharist and the regulations governing each form of celebration. However, as the Constitution on Sacred Liturgy has envisaged, Bishops' Conferences are empowered to lay down for those under their jurisdiction norms which accord with traditions and temperaments of their people and suit local groups.[11]

CHAPTER II

STRUCTURE, COMPONENT ELEMENTS AND PARTS OF THE MASS

I. THE STRUCTURE OF THE MASS AS A WHOLE

7. In the Mass or Lord's Supper the people of God are called together into one place where the priest presides over them and acts in the person of Christ. They assemble to celebrate the Memorial of the Lord, which is the sacrifice of the Eucharist.[12] Hence the promise of Christ: "Wherever two or three are gathered together in my name, there am I in the midst of them" (Mt. 18:20) applies in a special way to this gathering of the local church. For in the celebration of the Mass whereby the sacrifice of the Cross is perpetuated,[13] Christ is really present in the very community which has gathered in his name, the person of his minister, and also substantially and continuously under the eucharistic species.[14]

11. Constitution on the Sacred Liturgy, Arts. 37–40.
12. Decree on the Ministry and Life of Priests, n. 5; Constitution on the Sacred Liturgy, Art. 33.
13. Council of Trent, Session 22, c. 1; cf. Paul VI, Solemn Profession of Faith, 30 June 1968.
14. Constitution on the Sacred Liturgy, Art. 7; Paul VI, Encyclical *Mysterium fidei*, 3 Sept. 1965; S.C.R. Instruction *Eucharisticum mysterium*, 25 May 1967, n. 9.

8. The Mass is made up of two parts, the Liturgy of the Word and the Liturgy of the Eucharist. They are so closely connected with each other that together they constitute but one single act of worship.[15] In the Mass both the table of God's word and the table of Christ's body are prepared, so that from them the faithful may be instructed and nourished.[16] There are also some introductory and concluding rites.

II. Individual Parts of the Mass

The Reading and Explanation of God's Word

9. When the sacred scriptures are read in church, God himself is speaking to his people, and Christ, present in his word, is proclaiming his Gospel.

Hence the readings from God's word are among the most important elements in the liturgy, and all who are present should listen to them with reverence. The word of God in the scripture readings is indeed addressed to all men of all times and can be understood by them; yet its power to influence men is increased if it be given a living explanation by means of a homily which should be ranked as an integral part of the liturgical action.[17]

The Prayers and Other Items Allotted to the Priest

10. Among the items which the priest has to do, the most important is the Eucharistic Prayer, climax of the entire celebration; next come those prayers known as the Collect, Prayer over the Gifts, and Postcommunion. These are prayers which the celebrant, presiding over the assembly in the person of Christ, addresses to God in the name of the entire holy people and of all present.[18] With good reason, therefore, they are called "presidential prayers."

11. The priest as president issues instructions and words of introduction and conclusion as provided in the rite. Of their nature, these instructions need not be issued in the exact words of the missal. It can be helpful, at least in certain cases, to change them so as to communicate better. The priest is also to

---

15. Constitution on the Sacred Liturgy, Art. 56; S.C.R. Instruction *Eucharisticum mysterium*, 25 May 1967, n. 10.
16. Constitution on the Sacred Liturgy, Arts. 48, 51; Constitution on Divine Revelation, n. 21; Decree on the Ministry and Life of Priests, n. 4.
17. Constitution on the Sacred Liturgy, Arts. 7, 33, 52.
18. Ibid., Art. 33.

proclaim God's word, and give a blessing at the end of Mass. At its beginning he may speak to the people briefly about the Mass of the day; before the Liturgy of the Word he may introduce the Readings; before the Preface he may say something about the Eucharistic Prayer. Before the people are dismissed he may add some remarks which bring the whole celebration to its close.

12. The very nature of the presidential prayers requires that they be spoken audibly and clearly, and everyone should listen to them with close attention.[19] During these prayers, therefore, no other prayers, no singing, no playing of the organ or other musical instruments is allowed.

13. The priest, however, does not pray only as president and in the name of the whole community. Sometimes he prays in his personal capacity so as to perform his functions with more careful attention and devotion. Prayers of this kind are said inaudibly.

Other Items Occurring Within the Mass

14. Because the celebration of Mass is of its nature a community activity,[20] the dialogues between celebrant and people, as also the acclamations, are of considerable importance.[21] They are not only external signs of celebration in common, but also engender and foster union between celebrant and people.

15. The people's acclamations and their answers to the priest's greetings and presidential prayers constitute that minimum of active participation which is to be given by the congregation in every form of Mass; at least this much active participation is required to express and to foster the unity of communal action.[22]

16. Other parts which conduce to the same end, and which therefore are allotted to the people, are the Penitential act, the Profession of Faith (Creed), the Prayer of the Faithful and the Lord's Prayer.

17. Of the remaining items in Mass:

(a) There are some which in themselves constitute a rite or action. These are the *Gloria* hymn, the Responsorial Psalm, the Alleluia and verse before the Gospel, the *Sanctus*, the Ac-

19. S.C.R. Instruction on Sacred Music, 5 March 1967.
20. Constitution on the Sacred Liturgy, Arts. 26, 27; S.C.R. Instruction *Eucharisticum mysterium*, 25 May 1967, n. 3d.
21. Constitution on the Sacred Liturgy, Art. 30.
22. S.C.R. Instruction on Sacred Music, 5 March 1967, n. 16a.

clamation after the Consecration, and the singing after the Communion.

(b) Others, however, are but accompaniments to some action, exemplified by the Antiphons at the Entrance, the Offertory and the Communion, and the singing during the Breaking of Bread *(Agnus Dei)*.

The Manner in Which Texts Are to Be Sung or Said

18. The style of utterance of the priest's texts, those of his assistants and of the congregation should be suited to the nature of the text concerned, according as it is a reading, a prayer, a directive, an acclamation or a hymn; it should take into account also the form of the celebration and its degree of solemnity. The characteristics of the different languages and the sensibilities of the different peoples also have a bearing on this matter. Hence, in the rubrics and directions which follow, the verb "to say" should be understood as meaning "to sing" or "to speak" according to the principle just explained.

The Importance of Singing

19. The Apostle exhorts the faithful assembled in expectation of their Lord's return to sing together, "psalms, hymns and spiritual canticles:" (Col. 3:16). For singing is an expression of joy (cf. Acts 2:46). That is why St. Augustine very rightly says "it is natural for a lover to sing,[23] and an ancient proverb tells us "he who sings well is praying twice over." Although it is not necessary that every singable text should in fact be sung, it is eminently desirable that extensive use be made of singing in the course of celebration. The dispositions and capabilities of each congregation should, of course, be taken into account.

When deciding which parts of the Mass are actually to be sung, preference should be given to those which are more important, especially those which the priest or one of his assistants is to sing in alternation with the people, or which he and they are to sing together.[24]

Since nowadays the faithful of different languages come together with ever-increasing frequency, it is desirable that all should be able to sing together in Latin at least some

23. Sermons 336, 1; *PL* 38, 1472.
24. S.C.R. Instruction on Sacred Music, 5 March 1967, nn. 7, 16.

parts of the Order of Mass, especially the Creed and the Lord's Prayer. The easiest musical settings should be used.[25]

Gestures and Bodily Postures

20. A bodily posture common to all who are present is a sign of their unity with each other as a congregation; it expresses the mental attitude and dispositions of those taking part and enhances them.[26]

21. To achieve this bodily posture the faithful should heed the directions given to them in the course of the celebration by the deacon, the priest or other assistant. Unless some contrary instruction has been given, they should in all forms of Mass stand from the moment when the priest enters or reaches the altar until the end of Collect; also at the *Alleluia* before the Gospel; during the Gospel itself, the Creed and the Prayer of the Faithful; in addition from the Prayer over the Gifts until the end of Mass except where indicated below.

They should sit during the readings which precede the Gospel and during the Responsorial Psalm; for the homily, and during the Preparation of the Gifts; also, when it seems fitting, during the silence which follows the distribution of Communion. But, unless impeded by lack of space, density of the crowd or other reasonable cause, they should kneel down for the Consecration.

However, it is for the Bishops' Conference to adapt the postures and gestures here described as suitable for the Roman Mass, so that they accord with the sensibilities of their own people,[27] yet remain suited to the meaning and purpose of each part of the Mass.

22. Among the gestures or actions should be accounted the Entrance Procession of the priest, the manner in which gifts are brought to the altar, and the Communion Procession. These actions should be performed with solemnity and accompanied by the kind of singing which is relevant to their nature.

25. Constitution on the Sacred Liturgy, Art. 54; S.C.R. Instruction *Inter Oecumenici*, Art. 59. S.C.R. Instruction on Sacred Music, Art. 47.
26. Constitution on the Sacred Liturgy, Art. 30.
27. Ibid., Art. 39.

Silence

23. Meaningful silence is an element in celebration which must be given its due place.[28] The meaning will vary according to the point in the celebration at which it occurs. In the Penitential Act and the pause before the Collect the people should turn their thoughts within themselves; after the readings and the homily they should meditate on what they have heard; after the Communion they should praise God and pray in their hearts.

A. Individual Parts of the Mass

A. The Introductory Rites

24. The items which precede the Liturgy of the Word, namely, the Antiphon at the Entrance, the Greeting, the Penitential Act, the *Kyrie, Gloria* and Collect serve as an opening, introduction and preparation.

Their purpose is to help the faithful who have come together in one place to make themselves into a worshipping community and to engender the dispositions they should have when listening to God's word and celebrating the Eucharist.

The Antiphon at the Entrance

25. Once the people have assembled and while the priest and his assistants are coming in, the Antiphon at the Entrance is sung or said. Its purpose is to open up the celebration, to foster union among the people, to direct their minds to the sacred mystery being celebrated, and to accompany the incoming procession.

26. It is to be performed by the choir and people in alternation, or by a cantor and people in like manner, or even by the people alone or the choir alone. Available for use are the antiphon and appropriate psalm given in the Roman Gradual or the Simple Gradual, or else some other sung item such as a hymn suited to the day or season having a text approved by the Bishops' Conference.

If there is no singing during the procession, the antiphon given in the Missal should be recited by all the faithful together, or by some of them, or by a reader or, as a last resort, by the priest himself after the greeting.

28. Ibid., Art. 30; S.C.R. Instruction on Sacred Music, Art. 17.

Salutation of Altar and People

27. When the priest and his assistants have entered the sanctuary, they venerate the altar. Priest and deacon do this by kissing the altar, and the priest incenses it if the occasion warrants this.

28. As soon as the Antiphon at the Entrance is finished, the priest and all the faithful make the Sign of the Cross together. Then the priest, by his greeting, reminds the assembled people that the Lord is present among them. This greeting and the people's reply express the mystery of the Church formally assembled.

The Penitential Act

29. After the greeting, the priest may briefly introduce the people to the Mass of the day, or he may delegate a suitable assistant to do this. Then he invites the community to join in a Penitential Act, which consists of an acknowledgement by all of their sinfulness. The priest concludes it by praying for God's forgiveness.

The Appeal for Mercy

30. After the Penitential Act comes the Appeal for Mercy, the *Kyrie*, unless this has already been included within the Penitential Act itself. Of its nature it is a cry of the people to God for his mercy, and so should normally be sung by everybody, the people, choir and cantor all having part in it.

Usually each invocation is sung twice, but there may be further repetitions and also brief text-insertions (tropes) if these seem called for by the nature of the language, the music, or other circumstances of the celebration. If the *Kyrie* is not sung it is to be said.

The Gloria in Excelsis

31. The *Gloria* is a very ancient and venerable hymn by which the Church, gathered together in the Holy Spirit, offers praise and entreaty to God the Father and to the Lamb. It should be sung by the whole congregation, or else by them in alternation with the choir, or by the choir itself. When it is not sung it should be recited by all together or in alternation. It is to be sung or said on the Sundays outside

Advent and Lent, on Solemnities and Feast Days, and at specially solemn celebrations.

The Collect

32. Next the priest invites the people to prayer; he and all present remain silent for a few moments, reflecting that they stand in the presence of God. Each formulates mentally his own intentions. Then the priest says the prayer of the day which goes by the name of "Collect." By this prayer the special characteristics of the celebration are expressed, and the prayer of all is directed in the words of the priest to God the Father, through Christ, in the Holy Spirit.

The people join in this prayer mentally, express their assent to it and make it their own by their acclamation: *Amen*.

In each Mass only one Collect is to be said; the same rule applies to the Prayer over the Gifts and to the Postcommunion.

The Collect is to be said with the long conclusion as follows:

If it is directed to the Father: *Through our Lord Jesus Christ your Son who lives and reigns with you in the untiy of the Holy Spirit, God, for ever and ever.*

If directed to the Father but with mention of the Son towards its end: *Who lives and reigns with you in the unity of the Holy Spirit, God, for ever and ever.*

If it is directed to the Son: *You who live and reign with God the Father in the untiy of the Holy Spirit, God, for ever and ever.*

But the Prayer over the Gifts and the Postcommunion are terminated by the shorter conclusions: if directed to the Father: *Through Christ our Lord.* If it is directed to the Father, but the Son is mentioned towards the end: *Who lives and reigns with you for ever and ever.*

If it is directed to the Son: *You live and reign for ever and ever.*

B. The Liturgy of the Word

33. The most important part of the Liturgy of the Word consists of the readings from sacred scripture and the songs occurring between them. The homily, the Profession of Faith (Creed) and the Prayer of the Faithful develop and conclude it. In the readings, which are interpreted by the

homily, God speaks to his people,[29] reveals to them the mysteries of redemption and salvation, and provides them with spiritual nourishment; and Christ himself, in the form of his word, is present in the midst of the faithful.[30] The people appropriate this divine word to themselves by their singing, and testify their fidelity to God's word by their profession of faith. Strengthened by the word of God they intercede, in the Prayer of the Faithful, for the needs of the entire Church and for the salvation of the whole world.

The Scripture Readings

34. In the readings, the table of God's word is laid before the people and the treasures of the Bible are opened to them.[31] By tradition the reading of the extracts from scripture is not a presidential function, but that of an assistant. Hence the deacon—or, if no deacon is present, some other priest—should read the Gospel. A lector reads the other extracts. But if neither deacon nor any other priest is available, the Gospel is to be read by the celebrant.[32]

35. The liturgy itself teaches that the greatest reverence is to be shown towards the reading of the Gospel, for it assigns to the Gospel more particular marks of honor than it does to the other readings. The minister deputed to announce it prepares himself for his task by prayer, or seeks a blessing; the faithful, by their acclamation, recognize that Christ has come to speak to them, and they stand erect while listening to his Gospel. Marks of honor are said also to the book itself.

The Chants Between the Readings

36. After the first reading comes the Responsorial Psalm or Gradual, which is an integral part of the Liturgy of the Word. Normally the psalm is taken from the Lectionary, for the texts in it have been chosen so as to have some bearing on the particular reading. The selection of the psalm is therefore dependent on the selection of the reading. However, to make it easier for the people to sing a responsory to the psalm verses, certain psalms and responsor-

---

29. Constitution on the Sacred Liturgy, Art. 33.
30. Ibid., Art. 7.
31. Ibid., Art. 51.
32. S.C.R Instruction *Inter Oecumenici,* 26 Sept. 1964, n. 50.

ies have been chosen for use throughout the different seasons of the year and for the feasts of particular classes of saints. These may be used instead of the psalms given in the Lectionary, provided that the psalm is in fact sung.

The cantor (or psalmist) sings the verses of the psalm from the ambo or some other suitable place. The people sit and listen to him, but take their due part by singing the responsory between the verses, unless the psalm is sung "directly," that is, without any responsory. If the psalm is to be sung, it may be the one given in the Lectionary, but may instead be taken from the *Graduale Romanum*: or it may be the responsorial or *Alleluia* psalm given in the Simple Gradual, as indicated in those books.

37. After the second reading comes the *Alleluia* or other chant according to the liturgical season.

(a) The *Alleluia* is sung during all seasons except Lent. It is intoned by all present, by the cantor or by the choir, and on certain occasions it may be repeated. The verses are taken either from the Lectionary or from the Gradual.

(b) The other chant is the verse before the Gospel, though it may be another psalm (known as the Tract) as given in the Lectionary or in the Gradual.

38. When there is only one reading before the Gospel:

(a) during seasons when the *Alleluia* is said, the chant may be one of the *Alleluia* psalms, or else a psalm and *Alleluia* with its verse, or else a psalm by itself or even an *Alleluia* by itself.

(b) during the season when *Alleluia* is not to be said this chant may be a psalm or else the verse before the Gospel.

39. If the Responsorial Psalm is not going to be sung, it is said. If the *Alleluia* or verse before the Gospel are not sung, they may be omitted.

40. Except on Easter Sunday and Whit Sunday the Sequences are optional.

The Homily

41. The homily is part of the liturgy and is strongly recommended,[33] for it is a necessary source of nourishment for the Christian life. Ideally its content should be an exposition of the scripture readings or of some particular aspect of them, or of some other text taken from the Order or the Proper of the Mass

33. Constitution on the Sacred Liturgy, Art. 52.

for the day, having regard for the mystery being celebrated or the special needs of those who hear it.[34]

42. On Sundays and holidays of Obligation there is to be a homily at every Mass celebrated with the people and it may not be omitted save for a grave reason; on other days a homily is recommended, especially on the weekdays of Advent, Lent and Eastertide, as also on other occasions when there is a large congregation.[35]

The Profession of Faith

43. The purpose of the Profession of Faith (or Creed) is to express the assent and response of the people to the scripture reading and homily they have just heard, and to recall to them the main truths of the faith, before they begin to celebrate the Eucharist.

44. The Creed is to be said by priest and people together on Sundays and solemn feasts; it may also be said on other specially solemn occasions. If sung, it should normally be done by all together or in alternation.

The Prayer of the Faithful

45. In the Prayer of the Faithful (General Intercession, or Bidding Prayer) the people exercise their priestly function by praying for all mankind. It is desirable that a prayer of this type be normally included in Masses celebrated with the people, so that they may pray for Holy Church, for those in authority, for those oppressed by various needs, for all mankind, and for the salvation of the entire world.[36]

46. The sequence of intentions is usually as follows:

(a) for the needs of the Church,

(b) for civil authorities and for the salvation of the whole world,

(c) for those oppressed by any kind of need,

(d) for the local community.

However, on special occasions, such as in Masses conjoined with Confirmations, Weddings or Funerals, the list of intentions may be concerned more explicitly with the particular occasion.

47. It is the function of the priest to preside over this

---

34. S.C.R. Instruction *Inter Oecumenici*, n. 54.
35. Ibid., n. 53.
36. Constitution on the Sacred Liturgy, Art. 53.

prayer; he introduces it with a brief invitation and concludes it with a prayer. The intentions themselves are best proposed by a deacon, a cantor, or some other assistant.[37] The community as a whole expresses its prayer either by a common response after each petition, or else by a silent prayer.

C. The Liturgy of the Eucharist

48. Christ our Lord instituted the paschal sacrifice and meal at the Last Supper. In this the sacrifice of the Cross is continually made present in the Church whenever the priest, who represents Christ our Lord, does what Christ himself did and commanded his disciples to do in memory of himself.[38]

Christ took bread and the cup, prayed the thanksgiving, broke the bread and gave to his disciples saying: "Take, eat and drink; this is my Body, this is the cup of my Blood. Do this in memory of me." The Church has arranged the celebration of the Eucharist so that its several parts correspond with the words and actions of Christ.

(a) In the Preparation of the Gifts there are brought to the altar bread, and wine with water, the very same elements which Christ took into his hands.

(b) In the Eucharistic Prayer God is thanked for the whole work of redemption, and the gifts become the Body and Blood of Christ.

(c) In the breaking of one bread the unity of the faithful is signified, and in Communion they receive the Body and Blood of the Lord as the apostles once did from the hands of Christ himself.

The Preparation of the Gifts

49. At the beginning of the eucharistic liturgy, the bread and wine destined to become the Body and Blood of Christ are brought to the altar. First of all the altar, which is the table of the Lord,[39] is made ready as the central point of the whole eucharistic liturgy. The corporal, purificator, chalice, unless it is prepared at the side table, and Missal are carried

---

37. S.C.R. Instruction *Inter Oecumenici*, Art. 56.
38. Constitution on the Sacred Liturgy, Art. 47; S.C.R. Instruction *Eucharisticum mysterium*, n. 3a, b.
39. S.C.R. Instruction *Inter Oecumenici* n. 91; S.C.R. Instruction *Eucharisticum mysterium*.

to it and put in position.

Then the gifts are brought up to the altar. It is both meaningful and desirable that the faithful should bring up the bread and wine; the priest or the deacon receive them at some suitable point, and place them on the altar. While doing this the priest says some prescribed prayers. Although nowadays the faithful do not provide from their own homes the bread and wine destined for use in the liturgy, as they did in former times, the ritual of carrying them up to the altar is still meaningful and of spiritual value.

Money and other gifts for the poor or for the Church may be collected from the faithful and carried to the altar; but these should not be put on the altar itself; they can be deposited in some other convenient place.

50. The Offertory Antiphon is intended to accompany the procession in which the gifts are carried to the sanctuary, and the singing should go on at least until they have been put on the altar. The regulations governing this singing are the same as those already given for the Antiphon at the Entrance, n. 26. But if there is not going to be any singing, this antiphon may be omitted.

51. The gifts, now in position, and the altar itself may be incensed as a sign that the offering and prayer of the Church are to rise in God's sight like the smoke of incense. The priest and people may also be incensed by a deacon or one of the observers after the incensation of the gifts and the altar.

52. Then the priest washes his hands as a symbol of his desire for inward purification.

53. When these rites have been performed the Preparation of the gifts is concluded by an invitation to the people to pray with the priest, and by the Prayer over the Gifts which leads into the Eucharistic Prayer.

The Eucharistic Prayer

54. The Eucharistic Prayer, which now begins, is the climax and the very heart of the entire celebration, a prayer of thanksgiving and sanctification. The priest invites the people to raise their hearts to God in praise and thanks, and associates them with himself in the prayer which he addresses to God the Father, through Jesus Christ, in the name of the whole community. The meaning of the prayer is that all the faithful now gathered together unite them-

selves with Christ in praising the wonderful works of God and in offering sacrifice.

55. The constituent parts which together make up a Eucharistic Prayer may be listed as follows:

(a) *Thanksgiving*. This finds its clearent expression in the Preface, wherein the priest, in the name of all the people of God, offers praise and thanksgiving to God the Father for the whole work of redemption or for some particular aspect of it, according to the day, feast or season.

(b) *Acclamation*. In this the entire congregation, in union with the heavenly powers, sings or says the *Sanctus*. This acclamation is an integral part of the Eucharistic Prayer itself, and the voices of all should join in with that of the priest.

(c) *Epiclesis*. This is a special petition by the Church that the power of God should intervene to consecrate the gifts proffered by mankind, so that they may become the Body and Blood of Christ, and that the immaculate Victim may be the source of salvation to those who share in Communion.

(d) *The Institution Narrative and Consecration*. Through the words and actions of Christ there is accomplished the very sacrifice which he himself instituted at the Last Supper when, under the species of bread and wine, he offered his Body and Blood and gave them to his apostles to eat and drink, commanding them in turn to perform this same sacred mystery.

(e) *Anamnesis*. In this prayer of remembrance the Church, fulfilling the command she has received from her Lord through the apostles, celebrates the memorial of Christ, calling to mind especially his blessed passion, his glorious resurrection and his ascent to heaven.

(f) *Oblation*. It is through this very memorial that the Church—in particular the Church here and now assembled —offers the immaculate Victim to God the Father, in the Holy Spirit. The Church strives also that the faithful should not only offer the immaculate Victim but should learn to offer themselves; through Christ their Mediator they should be drawn day by day into an ever more perfect union with God and with each other, so that finally God may be all in all.[40]

---

40. Constitution on the Sacred Liturgy, Art. 48; Decree on the Ministry and Life of Priests, Art. 5. S.C.R. Instruction *Eucharisticum mysterium*, Art. 12.

(g) *Intercessions*. These express the truth that the Eucharist is celebrated in union with the whole Church in heaven and on earth, and that the sacrifice is offered for her and for all her members living and dead, since all of them are called to share in the redemption and salvation acquired through the Body and Blood of Christ.

(h) *Doxology*. The end of the Eucharistic Prayer is an expression of the praise of God, and is emphasized and concluded by the people's acclamation.

The importance of the Eucharistic Prayer demands that all should listen to it in reverent silence, making it their own by joining in those acclamations which the course of the rite provides for them.

The Communion Rite

56. Since the celebration of the Eucharist is a paschal meal it implies that the faithful in good dispositions should heed the Lord's command by receiving the Body and Blood of Christ as their spiritual nourishment.[41] This is the purpose of the Breaking of Bread and other preparatory rites which lead up to the Communion of the faithful.

(a) *The Lord's Prayer*. In this we ask for our daily bread which, for Christians, means also the eucharistic bread; we beg forgiveness of our sins, so that those to whom the Holy Things are given may in truth be holy. The priest invites the people to pray, and all should say this prayer with him. He alone adds the Embolism which the people conclude with a doxology or acclamation of praise. "Embolism" is the name given to the prayer which develops the thought of the last petition of the Lord's Prayer; it asks that the whole community of the faithful may be freed from every kind of evil. The invitation, the prayer itself, the Embolism, the Doxology and concluding acclamation by the people should be sung or spoken aloud.

(b) *The Rite of Peace*. By word and gesture the people pray for peace and unity in the Church and the whole human family, and express their love for one another before they share the one bread. Practical details of the way in which this is to be done are to be settled by the local Bishops' Conference in accordance with the sensibilities and conventions of the people.

(c) *The Breaking of Bread*. In the days of the apostles

41. S.C.R. Instruction *Eucharisticum mysterium*, Arts. 12, 33a.

Christ's action in breaking bread at the Last Supper suggested the name then given to the whole eucharistic celebration. The purpose of breaking the bread is not merely practical; it is also intended to convey a meaning. It means that through Communion we, though many in number, become one body because we eat the one Bread of Life which is Christ (1 Cor. 10:17).

(d) *The Commingling.* The priest drops a part of the host into the chalice.

(e) *Agnus Dei.* During the breaking of bread and the commingling the invocation "Lamb of God" is usually sung by the choir or the cantor with the people responding. If it is not sung, it should be said aloud. The invocation may be repeated as often as is needed to cover the whole action of bread-breaking, but on the last occasion it always has the conclusion "Grant us peace."

(f) *Private Preparation of the Priest.* That he may receive the Body and Blood of Christ fruitfully the priest prepares himself in silent prayer. The people also should pray in silence.

(g) *Invitation.* The priest shows to the faithful the eucharistic Bread which they are to receive in Communion, and invites them to the table of the Lord. Together with them he expresses, in words from the Gospel, sentiments of humility.

(h) *Distribution of Communion.* It is important that the hosts given to the faithful should be those consecrated in that same Mass, and that on authorized occasions they should also share in the chalice. The reason is that their participation in the sacrifice then and there being celebrated is more visibly manifested.[42]

(i) *Singing at Communion.* While the priest and people are receiving the Sacrament, the Communion Antiphon is sung. Its purpose is to express the spiritual union of the communicants by the union of their voices, to show forth their joy, and to make it clear that the Communion Procession is a fraternal occasion. The singing should begin when the priest receives Communion, and should continue as long as may seem desirable during the Communion of the people. If there is going to be a hymn after the distribution is finished, the singing during the distribution may well be curtailed.

---

42. S.C.R. Instruction *Eucharisticum mysterium,* n. 31, 32. On receiving Holy Communion a second time on the same day, see the Code of Canon Law, canon 917.

For the singing at Communion there are several possibilities; the antiphon given in the *Graduale Romanum* may be used, with or without a psalm; or else the antiphon with a psalm, taken from the Simple Gradual; or any suitable hymn which has the approval of the Bishops' Conference. The choir may sing alone (as in a Motet), or the people may sing and be assisted by choir or cantor.

If there is to be no singing during the Communion Procession, the antiphon given in the Missal should be said by the faithful, by a group or a cantor. As a last resort the antiphon should be said by the priest after his own Communion but before he distributes to the people.

(j) *The Pause*. When feasible there should be a pause after the distribution of Communion. During this the priest and people pray for a while in silence. As an alternative the whole community may sing a hymn or psalm of praise during the pause.

(k) *The Postcommunion*. In this the priest prays that the celebration of the sacred mystery may bring forth its due effects. The people associate themselves with this prayer by adding their *Amen*.

D. The Concluding Rites

57. The Mass is brought to an end thus:

(a) The priest greets the people and gives them his blessing. On certain days and particular occasions he may expand this by including a special prayer over the people and a more solemn form of blessing.

(b) Finally comes the formal dismissal of the people who may now return to their daily lives of good works, praising and blessing God.

CHAPTER III

FUNCTIONS AND MINISTRIES IN THE MASS

58. In the community which assembles to celebrate Mass everyone has the right and duty to take an active part, though the ways in which individuals do so will differ ac-

cording to the status and function of each.[48] Each one, whether cleric or layman, should do all of, but only, those parts pertaining to his office,[44] so that, from the very way in which the celebration is organized, the Church may be seen to consist of different orders and ministries.

I. FUNCTIONS AND MINISTRIES OF THOSE IN SACRED ORDERS

59. Every legitimate celebration of the Eucharist takes place under the authority of the bishop who presides over it in person or else through priests who are his helpers.[45]

If the bishop himself is present at a Mass in which the faithful take part, it is fitting that he should preside, and should associate other priests with himself, preferably by concelebration. The motive for this is not to increase the external solemnity of the rite, but to show forth in clearer light the mystery of the Church, which is the sacrament of unity.[46]

However, if the bishop is not personally celebrating the Eucharist but delegates another to do so, it is fitting that he should at least preside over the Liturgy of the Word, and should give the blessing at the end of Mass.

60. In virtue of his ordination the priest is the member of the community of the faithful who possesses the power to offer sacrifice in the person of Christ.[47] It is his function, therefore, to preside over the community; it is for him to lead their prayer, to proclaim to them the good news of salvation and to associate the people with himself in offering the sacrifice to God the Father through Christ in the Holy Spirit; he distributes to his brethren the Bread of eternal life, and himself receives it with them. Hence, when he celebrates the Eucharist, he is to serve God and the people with dignity and humility, and by his general behavior and the manner in which he utters the sacred words he should make the faithful realize the presence of the living Christ.

61. Among those who serve at the altar the first in rank is the deacon, whose order has ever been held in honor

43. Constitution on the Sacred Liturgy, Arts. 14, 26.
44. Ibid., Art. 28.
45. Dogmatic Constitution on the Church, n. 26, 28; Constitution on the Sacred Liturgy, Art. 42.
46. Constitution on the Sacred Liturgy, Art. 26.
47. Decree on the Ministry and Life of Priests, n. 2; Dogmatic Constitution on the Church, n. 28.

from the earliest days of the Church. At Mass he has duties proper to his order; his task is to proclaim the Gospel and on certain occasions to preach God's word; he leads the Prayer of the Faithful, assists the priest in distributing Holy Communion, especially by administering the chalice. Sometimes he also gives indications to the people about their gestures and movements.

II. THE FUNCTIONS AND OFFICE OF GOD'S PEOPLE

62. In the celebration of Mass the faithful constitute the sacred assembly, a chosen race, a royal priesthood, a consecrated nation, a people set apart that they may give thanks to God and offer the immaculate Victim, not only through the hands of the priest but also with him, learning also to offer themselves.[48] They should endeavor to express all this by sincere piety and loving regard for their brethren who are taking part in the same celebration.

Hence they should avoid every kind of individualism or discord, remembering that they all have the same Father in heaven and that they are in consequence brethren of one another.

From this it follows that they should appear as one body, whether they are listening to God's word or taking part in prayers or singing, and especially when together they offer the sacrifice and share in the Lord's table. This unity is most fittingly manifested when the people make gestures or take up common postures all together. And let them not be unwilling to serve God's people with joy whenever they are asked to perform some special function during the celebration.

63. Within the body of the faithful the choir (schola) has its own particular liturgical functions to fulfil. These are to give an adequate performance of the Proper according to the nature of each part, and to give a lead in congregational singing.[49] What is here said about the choir applies, also, with the needed qualifications, to all others involved in the music of the liturgy, especially to the organist.

64. There should be a cantor or choirmaster to direct and support the congregational singing. Indeed, if there is no

---

48. Constitution on the Sacred Liturgy, Art. 48. S.C.R. Instruction *Eucharisticum mysterium* n. 12.
49. S.C.R. Instruction on Sacred Music, n. 19.

the cantor should take the lead in singing all the ensuring that the people sing their own parts.[50]

III. SPECIAL MINISTRIES

65. "Acolyte" is a title properly belonging to one who has been officially commissioned to serve at the altar and to assist the priest and the deacon. The acolyte's tasks are to prepare the altar and the sacred vessels, and in certain circumstances to distribute Holy Communion to the people. In so doing he is acting as the "minister extraordinary" of the Eucharist.

66. "Lector" is a title properly belonging to one who has been officially commissioned to read passages from holy scripture other than those taken from the Gospels. He may also announce the intentions in the Prayer of the Faithful, and, if there is no psalmist, he should recite the psalm between the readings.

The lector has his own particular functions in the Mass, and it is he who should fulfil them even though ministers of higher rank may be present.

So that the faithful may derive a keen appreciation of holy scripture by listening to the readings[51] it is very necessary that those who read it to them, whether commissioned lectors or not, should be competent for their task and carefully prepared for it.

The Bishops' Conference may permit a woman to read those scripture passages which precede the Gospel, and to give out the intentions in the Prayer of the Faithful. It is for them also to specify the place whence she may most suitably announce God's word to the people.[52]

67. The task of the psalmist is to sing the psalm or other biblical canticle which may occur between the readings. If he is to do this well he must master the art of psalmody, and of correct and articulate pronunciation.

68. Of others who have special tasks, some perform them within the sanctuary, others outside it. The former include those who have been designated extraordinary ministers of Holy Communion, those who carry the Missal, the Cross, the candles, the bread, the wine, the water and the thurible. Among the latter are:

50. Ibid., n. 21.
51. Constitution on the Sacred Liturgy, Art. 54.
52. S.C.D.W., Third Instruction *Liturgiae Instauratione*, 5 Sept. 1970, n. 7.

(a) The commentator who gives explanations and directions to the people that they may be drawn into the celebration and better understand what is happening. His interventions must be carefully prepared and kept short. When performing his function the commentator should stand in some suitable place in front of the people. It is less fitting that he stand at the ambo.

(b) The ushers who, in some places, meet people at the door of the church, conduct them to their places, and marshall them if there are processions.

(c) Those who take up collections in church.

69. Especially in large churches or communities, it is recommended that someone be appointed to see that liturgical celebrations are well organized, and to ensure that all who are involved in them should perform their function in a dignified, efficient and reverent way.

70. All the ministries below those proper to the deacon may be performed by laymen, whether they have been commissioned for any office or not. Those ministries which are performed outside the sanctuary may be entrusted to women if this be judged prudent by the priest in charge of the church. The provisions of n. 66 about the place whence the scriptures are to be read should be taken into account.

71. If there are present several who are capable of fulfilling some particular ministry, there is no reason why the various functions should not be shared among them. For example, one deacon could undertake whatever parts have to be sung by a deacon, while another would do whatever has to be done at the altar. If there are several readings, these could be distributed among several commissioned lectors, and so on.

72. If there is but one server at a Mass celebrated with a congregation, he may do all the various ministries required.

73. The ceremonies, as also the musical and pastoral arrangements, for every liturgical celebration, should be prepared with care and the cooperation of those concerned. They should work together under the leadership of the rector of the church and should take into account the wishes of the people concerning the parts which pertain to the congregation.

Chapter IV

VARIOUS FORMS OF CELEBRATION

74. Among the different ways of celebrating Mass in the local church, the most important, because the most meaningful, is that wherein the bishop presides over his priests and other ministers[53] with the people taking their full and active part. This is the way in which the Church is most clearly and visibly manifested.

75. A Mass celebrated with any community is of great value, especially if it be the community of a parish, for this represents the universal Church at a given time and place. The parochial Mass on Sunday is an outstanding example of this truth.[54]

76. Some religious communities celebrate a "Conventual Mass" as part of their daily divine Office; others have a "Community Mass." Although neither of these has a specific form of celebration, it is most fitting that they be celebrated in song, with full participation of all members of the monastic or conventual community. Individuals, moreover, should exercise the ministry proper to their order. Thus any priests who are not required for pastoral reasons to celebrate on their own would laudably concelebrate if this be possible.[55] All priest members of the community who have to celebrate individually for the faithful may concelebrate the conventual or community Mass that same day. [See D 16—Ed.]

(Nn. 77 to 141, inclusive, are omitted: they are detailed directives on the celebration of Mass. Nn. 142 to 152, inclusive, are omitted for the reasons explained in n. a, *The General Instruction on the Roman Missal*, p. 154.—Ed.)

53. Constitution on the Sacred Liturgy, Art. 41.
54. Constitution on the Sacred Liturgy, Art. 42: S.C.R. Instruction *Eucharisticum mysterium*, n. 26; Dogmatic Constitution on the Church, n. 28; Decree on the Ministry and Life of Priests, n. 5.
55. S.C.R. Instruction *Eucharisticum mysterium*, n. 47.

I. CONCELEBRATED MASS

Introduction

153. Concelebration expresses clearly the unity of the priesthood, of sacrifice, and of the entire people of God. It is prescribed by the rite itself at the ordination of a bishop and of a priest and at the Chrism Mass. It is recommended, however, unless the benefit of Christ's faithful requires or suggests otherwise:

(a) On Maundy Thursday, at the Evening Mass.[56]

(b) At Masses at Councils, Meetings of Bishops and Synods.

(c) At a Mass for the Blessing of an Abbot.

(d) At the Conventual Mass and the principal Mass of any church or oratory.

(e) At any Mass to be celebrated when a number of priests, diocesan or religious, are holding a meeting.[57]

154. When priests are very numerous the competent superior may allow several concelebrated Masses on the same day provided they are at different times or in different sacred places.[58]

155. The actual conduct of concelebrated Masses is subject to the bishop throughout his diocese, including those in the churches and oratories of exempt religious.[59]

156. No one will ever be allowed to join in a concelebration after the Mass has begun.[60]

157. A concelebration in which priests of a diocese concelebrate with their own bishop is to be held in high esteem. Examples are the Chrism Mass on Maundy Thursday, or a Mass celebrated at a Synod or a pastoral visitation. Concelebration is to be recommended whenever priests have a meeting with their own bishop as, for example, when they are making a retreat together or have assembled for some other spiritual purpose. On such occasions the meaning of

---

56. Ibid., n. 26; Instruction on Sacred Music, n. 15, 27.
57. Constitution on the Sacred Liturgy, Art. 57.
58. S.C.R. Instruction *Eucharisticum mysterium*, n. 47.
59. Cf. *Ritus servandus in concelebratione Missae* n. 3.
60. Ibid., n. 8.

concelebration as a sign on unity of the priesthood and of the Church is shown forth with special clarity.[61]

158. For some reasonable cause, such as the significance of the rite or feast, it is lawful to celebrate (or concelebrate) more than once in the day as follows:

(a) A priest who has concelebrated at the Chrism Mass on Maundy Thursday may again celebrate or concelebrate at the Evening Mass.

(b) A priest who has celebrated or concelebrated at the Paschal Vigil may again celebrate or concelebrate on Easter Sunday.

(c) At Christmas every priest may celebrate or concelebrate three Masses, provided that each Mass takes place at its own proper time.

(d) A priest who has celebrated at a Synod, a pastoral visitation or a meeting of priests with their bishop may also celebrate again if this would be of service to the faithful and provided the bishop agrees to it.[62] The same applies to a meeting of religious with their own ordinary or with his delegate. [See D 16—Ed.]

(Nn. 159 to 239, inclusive, are omitted: they are detailed directives on the celebration of Mass.—Ed.)

Communion Under Both Kinds[b]

240. The meaning of Communion is signified as clearly as possible when it is given under both kinds. In this form the meal-aspect of the Eucharist is more fully manifested, and Christ's intention that the new and eternal Covenant should be ratified in his Blood is better expressed. Also the connection between the eucharistic meal and the heavenly banquet in the Father's kingdom[63] becomes easier to see.

241. Pastors of souls should therefore strive that the faithful who receive or see the reception of Communion under both kinds should be thoroughly instructed in the Catholic doctrines about Communion as expounded by the Council of Trent.

First, they should be reminded that, according to the Catholic faith, Christ is received whole and entire in a complete sacrament even when people communicate under one

61. S.C.R. Decree *Ecclesiae Semper*, 7 March 1965: AAS 57 (1965), pp. 410–412: S.C.R. Instruction *Eucharisticum mysterium*, n. 47.
62. Cf. *Ritus servandus concelebratione Missae*, n. 9.
b. See also D14.
63. S.C.R. Instruction *Eucharisticum mysterium*, n. 32.

kind only. And they are not thereby deprived of any grace necessary for salvation.[64]

Further, it should be explained to them that the Church, when specifying how sacraments are to be administered, has the power to make laws about sacraments and to change these laws so long as the changes do not affect the very nature of the sacrament. The Church makes use of this power whenever she judges that reverence for the sacrament or the spiritual good of the faithful requires changes in view of particular circumstances of time and place.[65] The faithful also should be encouraged to desire Communion under both kinds in which the meaning of the eucharistic banquet is more fully signified.

242. With the bishop's approval and after due instruction the following persons may receive Communion from the chalice:[66]

(1) Newly baptized adults in the Mass following their Baptism; newly confirmed adults in the Mass following their Confirmation; baptized persons who are being received into full communion with the Church.

(2) The bridegroom and bride at their Nuptial Mass.

(3) Deacons at their ordination Mass.

(4) An abbess in the Mass wherein she is blessed; virgins at the Mass of their consecration; professed religious and their parents, close relatives and other members of their community in the Mass wherein they make their first, renewed or perpetual religious profession on condition that the profession is made during Mass.

(5) Lay missionaries at the Mass in which they are publicly assigned to their missionary task; others who, during Mass, are entrusted by the Church with some special mission.

(6) A sick person, and all who are present when Viaticum is given in a Mass celebrated in the sick person's home.

(7) The deacon and others who have special ministries in a Mass celebrated with singing.

(8) When there is concelebration:

(a) all who perform a genuine liturgical ministry in concelebration; and all seminarians who are present.

(b) all members of institutes professing the evangeli-

---

64. Council of Trent, Session 21, Decree on Communion, c. 1–3.
65. Ibid., c. 2.
66. S.C.R. Instruction *Eucharisticum mysterium*, n. 32.

cal counsels, and other societies whose members dedicate themselves to God by religious vows or promises, provided that the Mass be in their own church or chapel; in addition, all those who live in the houses of these institutes and societies.

(9) Priests who are present at important celebrations and yet are not able personally to celebrate or concelebrate.

(10) All who are making a retreat or some other form of spiritual exercise, in a Mass specially celebrated for those taking part; all who attend a meeting of pastoral commission, in a Mass which they celebrate in common.

(11) Those mentioned in 2 and 4 above, at Masses celebrating their jubilees.

(12) Godparents, parents, spouses and lay catechists of a newly baptized adult, during the Mass of Initiation.

(13) Parents, relatives and special benefactors of a newly ordained priest at his first Mass.

(14) Members of the Community at a Conventual or Community Mass as described in n. 76 of this Instruction.

(Nn. 243 to 252, inclusive, are omitted: they are detailed directives on the manner of distributing Holy Communion. —Ed.)

CHAPTER V

THE ARRANGEMENT AND DECORATION OF CHURCHES FOR THE CELEBRATION OF THE EUCHARIST

I. GENERAL PRINCIPLES

253. To celebrate the Eucharist God's people normally assemble in a church or, if this is not possible, in some other

place fit for such a sacred occasion. The church (or other place) should therefore be suitable for the ceremonies and such as to encourage the people to take their full part. Buildings and appurtenances for divine worship ought to be beautiful and symbolic.[67]

254. The Church always presses into her service the arts cultivated by the various nations and wishes to give them a place in her worship.[68] While preserving artistic treasures of former times[69] and adapting them to current needs she also encourages new developments in the arts.[70]

Artists are trained and works of art are selected by the Church so that faith and piety may be fostered by good and appropriate art.[71]

255. All churches are to be solemnly dedicated or at least blessed. Cathedrals and parochial churches, however, are always to be dedicated. The faithful should hold their diocesan cathedral and their parish church in high esteem, and recognize them as signifying that spiritual Church which they are committed to build up and extend by their own vocation as Christians.

II. ARRANGEMENT OF A CHURCH FOR THE SACRED ASSEMBLY

257. The people of God, when assembled for Mass, has an organic and hierarchical structure which is manifested in the various actions and different functions performed during Mass. Hence the shape of the church ought in some way to suggest the form of the assembly and the different functions of its members; and each one who has an office to perform should find its arrangements convenient.

The body of the faithful and the choir should be placed where they can easily take their due part.[73]

67. Constitution on the Sacred Liturgy, Arts. 122–124; Decree on Ministry and Life of Priests, n. 5; S.C.R. Instruction *Inter Oecumenici*, n. 90; *Eucharisticum mysterium*.
68. Constitution on the Sacred Liturgy, Art. 123.
69. S.C.R. Instruction *Eucharisticum mysterium*, n. 24.
70. Constitution on the Sacred Liturgy, Arts. 123, 129. S.C.R. Instruction *Inter Oecumenici*, n. 13.
71. Constitution on the Sacred Liturgy, Art. 123.
72. Constitution on the Sacred Liturgy, Art. 126.
73. S.C.R. Instruction *Inter Oecumenici*, n. 97–98.

The priest and the servers should have places in the sanctuary, that is, the part of the church which indicates what they have to do, whether presiding over the prayer, announcing the word of God or ministering at the altar.

Though these spatial arrangements should express the structure of the community and the different functions within it, they should also bring everyone together in a way which shows that the Church is one. The building and its decor should foster devotion and reflect the sacredness of the ceremonies for which it is the setting.

III. THE SANCTUARY

258. The sanctuary should be distinguished from the rest of the church by some feature such as a raised floor, special shape or decoration. It should be large enough for the sacred rites to be performed without difficulty.[74]

IV. THE ALTAR

259. The altar on which the sacrifice of the Cross is made present under sacramental signs is also the Lord's table which the people are invited to share when they come to Mass. It is also the center from which thanksgiving is offered to God through celebration of the Eucharist.[75]

260. In a consecrated building the altar on which the Eucharist is celebrated may be fixed or movable; in any other place, especially if Mass is not normally celebrated there, a convenient table may be used, but it must be covered with a cloth and a corporal.

261. An altar is said to be fixed if it is in fact fixed to the floor so that it cannot be moved; it is said to be movable if it can in fact be moved.

262. Normally a church should have a fixed and dedicated altar, freestanding, away from any wall, so that the priest can walk all around it and can celebrate facing the people. It should be in a position such that the entire congregation will naturally focus their attention on it.[76]

263. The table of a fixed altar should be made of natural stone; this accords with age-long practice of the Church and

74. Ibid., n. 91.
75. S.C.R. Instruction *Eucharisticum mysterium,* n. 24.
76. S.C.R. Instruction *Inter Oecumenici,* n. 91.

its own symbolic meaning. Nevertheless the Bishops' Conference may authorize the use of some other generally accepted and solid material susceptible of good workmanship. The structure supporting the table may be of any material so long as it is solid and durable.

264. A movable altar may be made from any material which is solid and dignified, suitable for liturgical use and acceptable to local traditions and culture.

265. Both fixed and movable altars should be dedicated in accordance with the rites provided in the liturgical books; it suffices merely to bless a movable altar, however.

266. The custom of putting relics of saints under an altar to be dedicated is to be retained. But it is important to verify the authenticity of such relics.

267. Other altars should be few in number; in new churches they should be located in chapels somewhat apart from the nave of the church.[77]

V. ADORNMENT OF ALTARS

268. Out of reverence for the Mass which is both sacrifice and sacred meal the altar must be covered with at least one cloth. Its shape, size and ornamentation should be in keeping with the structure of the altar.

269. In all liturgical celebrations candles are required to express reverence and to indicate the various degrees of solemnity. These may be put on the altar or placed near it as may best suit the structure of the altar and the character of the sanctuary. The candles must not impede the people's view of the altar or of anything placed on it.

270. A cross, easily visible to the people, should be on the altar or somewhere not far from it.

VI. THE CELEBRANT'S CHAIR AND OTHER SEATS

271. The celebrant's chair should draw attention to his office of presiding over the community and leading its prayer. Hence the place for it is the apex of the sanctuary, facing the

77. S.C.R. Instruction *Inter Oecumenici*, n. 93.

people. But the shape of the building or other circumstances may militate against this position; for example, the distance between priest and people may then be so great as to make contact between them difficult. The priest's chair must not look like a throne. Seats for others with special duties in the sanctuary should be in places convenient for their functions.[78]

VII. THE AMBO, OR PLACE FOR PROCLAIMING GOD'S WORD

272. The dignity of God's word requires that some fitting place be provided whence it may be proclaimed; it should be a place on which the people would naturally concentrate their attention during the Liturgy of the Word.[79]

Normally this place should be a fixed ambo, not a mere portable lectern. As dictated by the shape of the church, the ambo should be put where those who read from it can be easily heard and seen by all.

From the ambo are proclaimed the readings at Mass, the Responsorial Psalm and the *Exultet* of the Paschal Vigil. But it may also be used for the homily and for the Prayer of the Faithful. It is not fitting that the commentator, cantor or choirmaster should make use of it.

VIII. PLACES FOR THE FAITHFUL

273. Much care should be devoted to the places for the people, so that by seeing and understanding the sacred ceremonies they may take their full active part in them. Normally benches or chairs should be provided for the faithful, but the custom of reserving particular places for private individuals is not approved.[80] The chairs or benches should be so arranged that the people may easily assume the different postures required in the course of the celebration, and should find no difficulty in going to Communion.

If there are acoustic problems a public address system should be installed so that the people may not only see but also hear the priest and others who have special functions.

78. Ibid., n. 92.
79. Ibid., n. 96.
80. Constitution on the Sacred Liturgy, Art. 32; S.C.R. Instruction *Inter Oecumenici*, n. 98.

IX. SITUATION OF THE CHOIR, ORGAN AND OTHER MUSICAL INSTRUMENTS

274. As the shape of the church will best permit, the choir should occupy a place which clearly shows what it is, namely, a section of the assembled community which has a special task. From where it is situated the choir should be able to fulfil its own liturgical function, to take a full active part in the Mass, and to receive Communion without inconvenience.[81]

275. The organ and other lawfully approved musical instruments should be located where they can support both choral and congregational singing and also be heard properly when played alone.

X. RESERVATION OF THE BLESSED SACRAMENT

276. It is strongly recommended that the Blessed Sacrament be reserved in a special chapel well suited for private adoration and prayer, apart from the nave.[82] But if the plan of the church or legitimate local custom impedes this, then the Sacrament should be kept on an altar or elsewhere in the church in a place of honor suitably adorned.[83]

277. The Blessed Sacrament is to be reserved in only one tabernacle which is immovable and made of solid and non-transparent material and which can be locked in a way which gives the greatest possible security against the danger of profanation. For this reason there should normally be only one tabernacle in each church.[84]

XI. IMAGES DISPLAYED FOR VENERATION BY THE FAITHFUL

278. From the very earliest days of the Church there has been a tradition whereby images of our Lord, his holy Mother, and of saints are displayed in churches for the veneration of the faithful. But there should not be too many such images, lest they distract the people's attention from the ceremonies, and those which are there ought to conform to a correct order

81. S.C.R. Instruction on Sacred Music, 5 March 1967, n. 23.
82. S.C.R. Instruction *Eucharisticum mysterium*, n. 53.
83. Ibid., n. 54; S.C.R. Instruction *Inter Oecumenici*, n. 95.
84. S.C.R. Instruction *Eucharisticum mysterium*, n. 52; *Inter Oecumenici*, n. 95; S.C.D.S. Instruction *Nullo umquam tempore*, 28 May 1938, n. 4: *AAS* (1938), pp. 199–200.
85. Constitution on the Sacred Liturgy, Art. 125.

of prominence." There should not be more than one image of any particular saint. In the adornment and appointments of a church as far as images are concerned, it is the piety of the entire community which should be the first consideration.

XII. THE GENERAL ARRANGEMENT OF THE CHURCH

279. Church decor should aim at noble simplicity rather than at ostentatious magnificence. The style of decorations should suit the materials used. Decorations should convey instruction besides enhancing the dignity of the building as a whole.

280. Arrangements in the nave of the church and its annexes should conform to modern requirements. Hence it is not enough to provide the immediate prerequisites for liturgical celebrations; there must also be the amenities normally found in any building wherein any considerable number of people are wont to congregate.

CHAPTER VI

REQUISITES FOR CELEBRATING MASS

I. BREAD AND WINE

281. Following the example of Christ, the Church has ever made use of bread and wine with water when celebrating the Lord's Supper.

282. The bread for the Eucharist must be fresh, made only from wheat and it must be unleavened in accordance with the ancient tradition of the Latin Church.

283. That the bread may effectively signify the meaning it is intended to convey, it must really look like food. Hence bread used for the Eucharist, even though unleavened and of the traditional shape, ought to be made in such a way that the priest, when celebrating with a congregation, can break it into pieces and distribute these to at least some of the faithful. Additional small hosts are not thereby excluded if the number of communicants or some other pastoral reason makes them necessary.

The action of breaking the bread, which in apostolic times prompted the very name then used for the Mass, has an important significance; it means that all are united in mutual love through the one bread, since this one bread is shared among many brethren.

284. The wine used to celebrate the Eucharist must be made from the fruit of the vine (cf. Lk. 22:18), natural and pure, unmixed with anything else.

285. Care must be taken to ensure that the bread and wine destined for the Eucharist are kept in good condition; the wine must not be allowed to go sour, nor the bread to become corrupt or so stale that it can be broken only with difficulty.

286. If the priest should discover, after the Consecration or when receiving Communion, that water has been poured into the chalice instead of wine, he should pour that water into some other vessel, put wine and a little water into the chalice, and consecrete it. He says only that part of the consecration narrative which applies to the chalice, and is not obliged to consecrate bread again.

II. SACRED FURNISHINGS IN GENERAL

287. Not only for the building of a church, but also for its furnishing, the Church is willing to accept the artistic style of any culture. She will permit adaptations to suit the religious outlook and customs of the various peoples provided only that they be compatible with the liturgical purposes for which the furnishings are designed.[86]

In this context also the emphasis should be on that noble simplicity which it is possible to combine admirably with true art.

288. Besides the materials traditionally used for liturgical furnishings, other modern materials may be employed provided that they also are durable and are considered worthy for use in divine worship. Decisions on these points lie with the local Bishops' Conference.

III. SACRED VESSELS

289. Among the various things needed for celebrating Mass none is more important than the chalice and paten

---

86. Constitution on the Sacred Liturgy, Art. 128; S.C.R. Instruction *Eucharisticum mysterium,* n. 24.

used for the offering and consecration of bread and wine and their distribution in Holy Communion.

290. The sacred vessels should be made of materials which are solid and esteemed as valuable in the regions where they are to be used. Which these are should be decided by the local Bishops' Conference. They should give preference to materials which do not easily break or deteriorate.

291. Every chalice or other vessel destined to contain the Precious Blood should have a cup made from some material which is impermeable to liquids. The foot, however, can be made of anything solid and worthy of its purpose.

292. Whatever is destined to hold the Sacred Host, such as a paten, communion bowl, pyx or monstrance, may be made from any material locally held in esteem as suitable for use in worship—for example, ebony and certain hardwoods.

293. When consecrating bread for priest, servers and people one may use a single large paten or communion bowl.

294. If sacred vessels are made from metal liable to become tarnished, they should be gold-plated inside. But this is not necessary if the metal is both precious and immune from oxidation.

295. When designing sacred vessels the artist may do it according to the taste and customs of the various regional cultures, so long as the result is suitable for liturgical use.

296. When sacred vessels are blessed or consecrated the rites prescribed in the liturgical books are to be followed.

IV. SACRED VESTMENTS

297. Not all the members of the Church, the Body of Christ, have the same functions to fulfil. That there are different ministries performed in the course of a celebration is made clear by the use of different vestments. These signify the role proper to each person who has a special part in the rite, and they help to make the ceremonies beautiful and solemn.

298. The vestment common to all ministers is the alb, gathered at the waist by a girdle unless it has been tailored to make a girdle unnecessary. If the alb does not cover the ordinary neckwear, an amice should be put on before it. A cassock and surplice may be used instead of an alb except when a chasuble or dalmatic is to be worn, or when a stole will be used instead of a dalmatic.

299. When celebrating Mass or any other liturgical service directly connected with it, the priest, unless otherwise directed, is to wear a chasuble over his alb and stole.

300. The dalmatic, worn over the alb and stole, is the vestment proper to the deacon.

301. Ministers below the rank of deacon may wear the alb or other vestment approved in the region.

302. The priest wears his stole round his neck, hanging down in front. The deacon wears his stole over his left shoulder, falling diagonally to the right-hand side of his waist where it is secured.

303. The priest wears a cope in processions and certain other liturgical actions when this is indicated in their respective rubrics.

304. Bishops' Conferences may determine and propose to the Holy See any adaptations in the shape or style of vestments which they consider desirable by reason of local customs or needs.[87]

305. Besides the materials traditionally used for making sacred vestments, natural fabrics from each region are admissible, as also artificial fabrics which accord with the dignity of the sacred action and of those who are to wear the vestments. It is for the Bishops' Conference to decide on these matters.[88]

306. The beauty and dignity of liturgical vestments is to be sought in the excellence of their material and the elegance of their cut, rather than in an abundance of adventitious ornamentation. Any images, symbols or figures employed in decorating vestments should be sacred in character and exclude anything inappropriate.

307. The use of vestments of various colors has two purposes: one is to express some aspect of the particular mystery of faith being celebrated, and the other is to give a sense of progress or development of the Christian life in the course of the liturgical year.

308. The colors of the vestments used on any occasion should follow long-standing custom, namely:

(a) White for the offices and Masses of Christmastide and Eastertide; for the feasts and memorials of the Lord other than those concerning his passion; for feasts and memorials of the Blessed Virgin Mary, of the angels, of

87. Constitution on the Sacred Liturgy, Art. 128.
88. Constitution on the Sacred Liturgy, Art. 128.

saints who were not martyrs; on the feasts of All Saints (Nov. 1), St. John the Baptist (June 24), St. John the Evangelist (Dec. 27), St. Peter's Chair (Feb. 22) and the Conversion of St. Paul (Jan. 25).

(b) Red is used for Passion Sunday, Good Friday, Whit Sunday, and commemorations of the Lord's passion; on days commemorating the martyrdoms of apostles, evangelists and other martyrs.

(c) Green is used in the offices and Masses of those times of the year which are not particular seasons.

(d) Purple is used during Advent and Lent. This color may also be used in offices and Masses for the Dead.

(e) Black may be used in Masses for the Dead.

(f) Rose-colored vestments are allowed on the Sundays known as "Gaudete" and "Laetare" (the third in Advent and the fourth in Lent).

Nevertheless Bishops' Conferences may determine and propose to the Holy See changes in these customs if they judge that a different selection of colors would better suit the needs and tastes of their people.

309. On festive occasions the very best vestments may be worn even if they are not of the color of the day.

310. Ritual Masses are celebrated in their own color, or in white or festive; Masses for various needs and occasions are celebrated in the color proper to the day or the season or in violet, if they are of a penitential nature, such as numbers 23, 28, 40 for example. Votive Masses may be celebrated in the color which best suits the character of the chosen Mass, or in the color of the day or the season.

V. OTHER REQUISITES FOR USE IN CHURCH

311. Not only the sacred vessels and vestments mentioned above, but also everything else destined for use in the liturgy or admitted into the church for any purpose ought to be worthy of such acceptance and fitted for the use to which it is put.

312. Even concerning things of small importance every effort should be made to ensure that the canons of art are followed. The aim should be to combine a noble simplicity with immaculate cleanliness.

CHAPTER VII

CHOICE OF TEXTS FOR CELEBRATING MASS

313. The pastoral effect of any celebration is enhanced if the readings, prayers and chants are suited as well as possible to the needs, spiritual preparation and receptivity of those who are to take part. This aim can be achieved by the intelligent use of the considerable freedom of choice described in what follows.

When preparing a Mass the priest ought to consider the spiritual good of the people rather than his own preferences. He should remember also that the choice of the various parts can best be made in consultation with the ministers and servers who have roles to play in the celebration, and with members of the congregation as regards the parts which directly concern them.

Since so many choices are now possible, it is necessary to make sure that the deacon, lector, psalmist, cantor, commentator and choir should all know beforehand what they have to do. Nothing should be left for a hurried last-minute decision. A well-considered and carefully prepared celebration can do much to dispose the faithful to take their full parts in the Mass.

I. CHOICE OF MASS FORMULA

314. On great feasts the priest is obliged to follow the calendar of the church in which he is celebrating.

315. On Sundays, weekdays of Advent, Christmastide, Lent and Eastertide and on feasts and obligatory memorials:

(a) if the Mass is to be celebrated with a congregation the priest is to follow the calendar of the church in which he is celebrating.

(b) if the Mass is to be celebrated without a congregation he may follow either the calendar of the church or else the calendar he normally follows.

316. On optional memorials:

(a) on the weekdays of Advent from 17th till 24th December, during the octave of Christmas, on the weekdays of Lent except Ash Wednesday, and during Holy Week, the priest is to say the Mass of the day. He may, however, use the Collect of an optional memorial occurring in the General Calendar so long as it does not fall on Ash Wednesday or a day of Holy Week.

(b) on the days of Advent prior to December 17th, and on the weekdays of Christmastide and Eastertide, the priest may choose the Mass of the day, or the Mass of the saint, or of one of the saints commemorated that day, or of a saint mentioned in that day's Martyrology.

(c) throughout the rest of the year the priest may choose the Mass of the weekday, of the optional memorial, of any saint mentioned in the day's Martyrology, a Mass for various needs and occasions, or a votive Mass.

If he is celebrating with a congregation he should consider the spiritual good of the faithful, and beware of imposing his own preference. He should take special care not to omit too frequently or without sufficient reason the readings given in the Lectionary for weekdays, for the Church desires that richer fare be offered to the faithful at the table of God's word.[89]

For the same reason he should be moderate in the use of Masses for the Dead, for every Mass is offered for both living and dead, and every Eucharistic Prayer contains a Memento for the Dead.

Wherever optional memorials of the Blessed Virgin or of the saints are dear to the people, at least one Mass of these should be celebrated so as to satisfy the legitimate demands of their piety.

When the choice lies between an optional memorial in the General Calendar and one occurring in the calendar of a diocese or religious order, the particular calendar should have preference, all things being equal.

II. CHOICE OF INDIVIDUAL TEXTS

317. The following guidelines should be followed when choosing texts for the individual parts of Masses of the season or of the saints:

Readings

318. On Sundays and feasts three readings are provided, namely, from the Old Testament, from a writing by an apostle, and from a Gospel. By means of these the Christian people are led to an understanding of the continuity of God's wonderful plan of salvation.

89. Constitution on the Sacred Liturgy, Art. 51.

Hence it is very desirable that all three readings should in fact be used; nevertheless it is lawful in some places to use only two readings if the local Bishops' Conference has so decided for pastoral reasons. If a choice has to be made between the first and second reading, the principles of choice given in the Lectionary should be followed, and every effort be made to lead the people to a deeper understanding of holy scripture. It is not good always to choose the shorter or the easier text.

319. In the weekday lectionary there are readings for each day of every week throughout the year; hence normally these are the readings to be chosen when it is neither a solemnity nor feast.

But if the sequence of these readings during the week has been broken because of a feast or some special celebration, the priests should think over the readings for the entire week, and then decide either to include the omitted reading with the next one to occur, or else to substitute it for one of the remaining excerpts which seems less important.

In Masses celebrated for some special group the priest may choose whatever readings would be most suitable for the particular occasion, provided only that they are to be found somewhere in the approved Lectionary.

320. The Lectionary provides a special selection of scripture readings for Masses which include the celebration of some sacrament or sacramental or which are celebrated in certain particular circumstances.

They are included so that the faithful, by hearing distinctively pertinent extracts from the Bible may be led to a deeper understanding of the mystery in which they are taking part and may derive a more intense love for the word of God.

For these reasons the texts of readings ought to be chosen so that they accord with pastoral considerations, and yet are within the bounds of that freedom of selection which is now lawful.

Prayers

321. The reason why so many Prefaces are included in the Roman Missal is that they set forth in different ways the motives for the thanksgiving expressed in the Eucharistic Prayer; also they bring out more clearly various aspects of the mystery of salvation.

322. Eucharistic Prayers should be chosen with the following principles in mind:

(a) the first one, the Roman Canon, may be used on any occasion whatever. It is more appropriate on days for which a special *Communicantes* or *Hanc igitur* is provided, and on feasts of the apostles or the saints named in the Canon. It is a good choice for Sundays if one of the others is not preferred for pastoral reasons.

(b) the second Eucharistic Prayer, because of certain characteristics, is best used on weekdays or in special circumstances. Though it has a Preface of its own, it may nevertheless be used with other Prefaces, especially those which summarize the mystery of redemption, for example, a Sunday or a Common Preface.

When the Mass is to be offered for a dead person, one can insert into this prayer a special formula just before the Memento.

(c) The third Eucharistic Prayer can be used with any Preface. It is most suitable on Sundays or Feast Days. This prayer also has a special formula for a dead person, to be inserted in the place indicated by the rubric.

(d) The fourth Eucharistic Prayer is inseparable from its own Preface because it gives a conspectus of the whole history of salvation. It may be used whenever the Mass has no proper Preface.

No special formula for a dead person may be inserted into the Eucharistic Prayer because of its structure.

(e) The two Eucharistic Prayers having Prefaces of their own (second and fourth) may retain their Prefaces even when the Mass would otherwise have the seasonal Preface.

323. Unless otherwise indicated, the prayers which belong to the Mass being celebrated should be used. But in the Mass of a memorial the Collect may be proper or taken from the Common; the Prayer over the Gifts and the Postcommunion should be from the Common; but they may be from the weekday Mass of the current season if they are not proper.

In the weekday Masses throughout the year the prayers may be taken from the preceding Sunday or from any other Sunday of the Year, or else they may be taken from the collection of prayers for special intentions provided in the Missal. The priest, however, remains free to take only the Collect from these sources.

In this way a much wider choice of texts becomes available, and the prayers of the liturgical assembly can be enriched with ever fresh themes. It becomes possible also to take into account the particular needs of the faithful, the Church and the world. In major liturgical seasons this is already done in the prayers which the Missal provides for the weekdays of each season.

Singing

324. When choosing the chants between the readings, as also the Antiphons at the Entrance, Offertory and Communion, the guidelines given elsewhere in this Instruction should be followed.

325. In addition to all the above permissions about choosing texts, the Bishops' Conferences may also specify further adaptations of the laws governing choice of readings if they judge that special circumstances warrant it. But even then the chosen texts must be among those given in a lawfully approved Lectionary.

CHAPTER VIII

MASSES AND PRAYERS FOR PARTICULAR OCCASIONS, VOTIVE MASSES, AND MASSES FOR THE DEAD

I. MASSES FOR SPECIAL OCCASIONS AND VOTIVE MASSES

326. For well-disposed Catholics the liturgy of the sacrament and sacramentals brings God's blessings on almost every event of their lives; they are given access to the stream of divine grace which flows from the paschal mystery;[90]

90. Constitution on the Sacred Liturgy, Art. 61.

and the Eucharist is the sacrament of all sacraments. That is why the Missal provides Masses and prayers which can be used on various occasions of the Christian life and be offered for the needs of the Church, both universal and local, and for the whole world.

327. Because there is now so much freedom of choice for prayers and readings, votive Masses for special intentions should be used in moderation, and then only when the circumstances really call for them.

328. Apart from any explicit ruling to the contrary, the weekday readings and the chants between them may be used in Masses for special occasions if they are deemed suitable.

329. Masses for special occasions are of three kinds:

(a) Ritual Masses linked with the administration of a sacrament or sacramental.

(b) Masses for particular needs or intentions which are celebrated when required or periodically.

(c) Votive Masses of the Mysteries of Christ or in honor of the Blessed Virgin Mary or the saints. These may be celebrated at will, as prompted by the piety of the faithful.

330. Ritual Masses are forbidden on the Sundays of Advent, Lent and Eastertide, on solemn feasts, on Ash Wednesday and throughout Holy Week, as stated in the rubrics of the Ritual and the Missal.

331. From the Masses for various needs the competent authority may choose Mass texts for special days or times of intercession ordered by the Bishops' Conference during the course of the year.

332. If a serious need or some great pastoral opportunity should occur, a Mass appropriate to the occasion may be celebrated at the behest or with permission of the local ordinary on any day except the great feasts and the Sundays of Advent, Lent and Eastertide, Ash Wednesday and the days of Holy Week.

333. If a serious or great pastoral opportunity should occur on an obligatory memorial, a weekday of Advent, Christmastide or Eastertide (that is, on days when a votive Mass would normally be forbidden) an appropriate Mass may nevertheless be celebrated with the people if the rector of the church or even the celebrant himself should consider it justified.

334. On weekdays of the year, when the weekday office or an optional memorial may be celebrated, it is lawful to use any Mass formula or any prayer for a particular need, with

the exception of the Ritual Masses.

II. MASSES FOR THE DEAD

335. The Church offers the Paschal Sacrifice for the Dead so that, through the union of all with each other in Christ, the dead may be helped by prayers and the living may be consoled by hope.

336. Among Masses for the Dead it is the Funeral Mass which holds the first place in importance. It may be celebrated on any day which is neither a holiday of Obligation, the Thursday, Friday or Saturday of Holy Week, nor a Sunday in Advent, Lent or Eastertide.

337. A Mass for the Dead may be celebrated as soon as news of a death is received, on the day of final burial, and on the first anniversary. This holds good even during the Christmas octave, on an obligatory memorial and on any weekday which is neither Ash Wednesday nor a day in Holy Week. Other "daily" Masses for the dead may be said on days through the year on which there is an optional memorial or Mass of the day, provided the Mass is in fact offered for the dead.

338. At a Funeral Mass there should normally be a short homily, but it must not have the character of a panegyric. In other Masses celebrated with a congregation a homily is recommended.

339. When Mass is offered for a dead person the faithful, especially relatives, should be encouraged to share in the eucharistic sacrifice by receiving Communion.

340. If the Funeral Mass is to be followed at once by the burial its concluding rites are omitted; the Commendation or Farewell, which may be celebrated only when the body is present, takes place after the Postcommunion.

341. In a Mass for the Dead, especially if it be a Funeral Mass, the variable parts (Prayers, Readings, Bidding Prayer) should be chosen, as is only right, in the light of the pastoral benefit they may bring to the dead person, the family and the congregation there present.

Pastors of souls should also bear in mind their responsibility towards those who are at Mass and hearing the Gospel just because they have come to a funeral. They may be non-Catholics, or Catholics who seldom if ever come to Mass, or seem to have lost the faith altogether. A priest is a herald of Christ's Gospel for all men.

14

INSTRUCTION ON THE EXTENSION OF THE FACULTY TO ADMINISTER HOLY COMMUNION UNDER BOTH KINDS[a]

S.C.D.W., *Sacramentali Communione*, 29 June, 1970

Through sacramental communion the faithful take part more perfectly in the eucharistic celebration. This is the teaching of the entire tradition of the Church. By communion, in fact, the faithful share fully in the eucharistic sacrifice. In this way they are not limited to sharing in the sacrifice by faith and prayer, nor merely to spiritual communion with Christ offered on the altar, but they receive Christ himself sacramentally so as to receive more fully the fruits of this most holy sacrifice.

In order that the fullness of sign in the eucharistic banquet may be seen more clearly by the faithful,[1] the Second Vatican Ecumenical Council laid down that in certain cases —to be decided by the Holy See—the faithful should be able to receive holy communion under both kinds. This leaves intact the dogmatic principles recognized in the Council of Trent, by which it is taught that Christ whole and entire and the true sacrament[2] are also received under one species alone.[3]

This desire of the council has gradually been put into effect.[4] The preparation of the faithful has accompanied this gradual development, so that from this change in eccle-

---

a. Translation issued by the Congregation. *AAS* 62 (1970), pp. 664–667.
1. Cf. *Institutio generalis Missalis romani*, n. 240.
2. Cf. Council of Trent, Session 21: Decree, *De Communione eucharistica*, ch. 1–3; *Denz.* 929–932 (1725–29).
3. Cf. Constitution on the Liturgy, n. 55.
4. S.C.R., General Decree, *Ecclesiae Semper*, 7 March 1965: *AAS* 57 (1965), pp. 411–412; Instruction *Eucharisticum Mysterium*, 25 May 1967, n. 32: *AAS* 59 (1967), pp. 558–559; *Institutio generalis Missalis romani*, nn. 76, 242.

siastical discipline there should come ever more abundant fruits of devotion and spiritual growth.

As time has gone on it has been possible to witness an ever increasing desire that the number of cases, in which it is possible to administer communion under both kinds, should be further extended according to the needs of different regions and people.

REQUESTS HEEDED

Therefore this Sacred Congregation for Divine Worship, taking into account the requests of numerous bishops, and indeed of episcopal conferences, and the requests of the superiors of religious families, lays down, by mandate of his Holiness the Pope, all that follows regarding the faculty of distributing holy communion under both kinds:

1. Communion under both kinds may be distributed, in accordance with the judgment of the ordinary, in the cases determined by the Holy See—as given in the list adjoining this instruction.

2. Moreover, the episcopal conferences may decide to what extent, for what motives and in what conditions, ordinaries may concede communion under both kinds in other cases which have great importance for the spiritual life of a particular community or group of the faithful.

3. Within these limits, the ordinaries may indicate particular cases. This is on the condition, however, that the faculty should not be conceded indiscriminately, and that the celebration should be clearly indicated, together with those points to which particular attention must be paid. This faculty should not be granted on occasions where there are large numbers of communicants. The groups to whom the faculty is conceded should be adequately instructed on the significance of the rite.

4. The ordinary of the place may grant these faculties for all the churches and oratories in his territory; the religious ordinary for those houses dependent on him. It is for these to ensure that the norms given by the Holy See or by the episcopal conference should be observed. Before they grant the faculty, they should be sure that everything will be carried out in a way befitting the holiness of this sacrament.

5. Before the faithful are to receive communion under both kinds, they should be adequately instructed on the significance of the rite.

6. In order that communion under both kinds may be properly administered, care should be taken to maintain due reverence and to carry out the rite in the way described in nn. 244–51 of the General Instruction of the Roman Missal.

That method of distribution should be chosen which best ensures that communion is received with devotion and dignity, and also avoids the dangers of irreverence. The nature of each liturgical group, and the age, conditions, and preparation of those wishing to receive communion must also be taken into account.

DRINKING FROM THE CHALICE

Among the ways of distribution given by the Instruction of the Roman Missal, the reception of communion by drinking from the chalice itself certainly has pre-eminence. However, this method should only be chosen when everything can be carried out in an orderly fashion and without any danger of irreverence towards the blood of the Lord. If there are other priests present, or deacons or acolytes, they should therefore be asked to help by presenting the chalice. On the other hand, it does not seem that manner of distribution should be approved in which the chalice is passed from one to another, or in which the communicants come up directly to take the chalice themselves and receive the blood of the Lord. When the ministers mentioned above are not available, then if the communicants are few in number and communion is taken directly from the chalice, the same priest should distribute communion first under the species of bread and afterwards under the species of wine.

Otherwise the rite of communion under both kinds by intinction is to be preferred in order that practical difficulties may be avoided and that due reverence might the more aptly be given to the sacrament. In this way access to communion under both kinds is offered more easily and more safely to the faithful, whatever their age or condition, and at the same time the fullness of sign is preserved.

(For list of occasions on which Holy Communion under both kinds may be received, see D *13*, 242.—Ed.)

15

THIRD INSTRUCTION ON THE CORRECT IMPLEMENTATION OF THE CONSTITUTION ON THE SACRED LITURGY[a]

S.C.D.W., *Liturgiae Instaurationes*, 5 September, 1970

The reforms which have so far been put into effect in implementing the Liturgical Constitution of the Second Vatican Council have been concerned above all with the celebration of the eucharistic mystery "For the holy Eucharist contains the Church's entire spiritual good, that is, Christ himself, our passover and living bread. Through his very flesh made living and giving life by the Holy Spirit, he offers this life to men. They are thereby invited and led to offer themselves, their work, and all created things together with him.[1] In the same way, when the Church assembles to offer the sacrifice of the Mass according to the renewed form of celebration, it is made manifest that the Mass is the center of the Church's life. Thus the purpose of the reform of the rites is "to promote a pastoral action which has its summit and source in the sacred liturgy" and "to bring to life the paschal mystery of Christ."[2]

This work of renewal has been carried out, step by step, during the past six years; it has prepared the way for the passage from the former Mass liturgy to the renewed liturgy outlined in detail in the Roman Missal with the *Ordo Missae* and the General Instruction which it includes. Now it can be said that a new and promising future lies ahead for pastoral, liturgical action; the way is open to make full use of all the possibilities contained in the new Order of

a. Translation issued by the Congregation. *AAS* 62 (1970), pp. 692–704.
1. Decree on the Ministry and Life of Priests, n. 5: *AAS* 58 (1966), p. 997.
2. Cf. S.C.R., Instruction *Inter Oecumenici*, 26 Sept. 1964, nn. 5–6: *AAS* 56 (1964), p. 878.

Scripture Readings for the Mass and in the abundant variety of forms contained in the Roman Missal.

The wide choice of texts and the flexibility of the rubrics make it possible to adapt the celebration to the circumstances, the mentality and the preparation of the assembly. Thus there is no need to resort to arbitrary adaptations, which would only weaken the impact of the liturgy. The possibilities offered by the Church's reforms can make the celebration living, moving and spiritually effective.

The gradual introduction of the new liturgical forms has taken into consideration both the overall renewal program and the great variety of local conditions throughout the world. These new forms have been well received by the majority of the clergy and laity,[3] though here and there they have met with some resistance and impatience.

There were those who, for the sake of conserving ancient traditions, were unwilling to accept these reforms. There were others who, concerned with urgent pastoral needs, felt they could not wait for the definitive reform to be promulgated. As a result some individuals, acting on private initiative, arrived at hasty and sometimes unwise solutions, and made changes, additions or simplifications which at times went against the basic principles of the liturgy. This only troubled the faithful and impeded or made more difficult the progress of genuine renewal.

For these reasons many bishops, priests and laymen have asked the Holy See to intervene. They desired that the Church use her authority to keep and increase that fruitful union of minds and hearts which is the characteristic of the Christian family's encounter with God.

Such an intervention was not deemed advisable while the Consilium was engaged in bringing about and guiding the work of renewal. This can now be done on the basis of the final completion of this task.

First of all the bishops are called upon to exercise their responsibility. It is they whom the Holy Spirit has made rulers of the Church of God.[4] They are "the chief stewards of the mysteries of God, as governors, promotors and guardians of the whole liturgical life of the Church commit-

---

3. Cf. Paul VI, Address at a general audience, 20 Aug. 1969: *L'Osservatore Romano,* 21 August 1969.
4. Cf. Acts. 20:28.

ted to them."[5] It is their duty to guide, direct, stimulate and sometimes correct, but always to be shining examples in carrying out the genuine renewal of the liturgy. It must also be their concern that the whole body of the Church can move ahead with one mind, in the unity of charity, on the diocesan, national and international level. This work of the bishops is necessary and especially urgent in this case, because of the close relationship between liturgy and faith, so that what benefits the one, benefits the other.

With the help of their liturgical commissions, the bishops should be accurately informed about the religious and social conditions of the faithful committed to their care. In order to meet their spiritual needs in the best way possible, they should learn to make full use of the means offered by the rites. By thus evaluating the situation in their diocese, they will be able to note what helps and what hinders genuine renewal, and engage in the wise and prudent work of education and guidance, a work which both recognizes the real needs of the faithful and follows the guidelines laid down in the new liturgical laws.

A well-informed bishop will be a great help to the priests who must exercise their ministry in hierarchical fellowship with him.[6] His knowledge will make it easier for them to work together in obedience to him for the more perfect expression of divine worship and for the sanctification of souls.

It is the scope of this document to aid and encourage the bishops in putting into effect the liturgical norms, especially those contained in the General Instruction of the Roman Missal. In order to restore the orderly and disciplined celebration of the Eucharist, the center of the Church's life as "a sign of unity, a bond of charity,"[7] the following rules and guidelines should be kept in mind:

1. The recent reforms have simplified liturgical formulas, gestures and actions, according to the principle laid down in the Constitution on the Sacred Liturgy: "The rites should be distinguished by a noble simplicity; they should

---

5. Decree on the Pastoral Office of Bishops in the Church, n. 15: *AAS* 58 (1966), pp. 679–680; Constitution on the Sacred Liturgy, n. 22: *AAS* 56 (1964), p. 106.
6. Cf. Decree on the Ministry and Life of Priests, n. 15: *AAS* 58 (1966), pp. 1014–15.
7. Constitution on the Sacred Liturgy, n. 47: *AAS* 56 (1964), p. 113.

be short, clear and unencumbered by useless repetitions; they should be within the powers of comprehension of the people and normally should not require much explanation."[8] Yet this simplification must not go beyond certain limits. This would be to deprive the liturgy of the sacramental signs and special beauty necessary for the mystery of salvation to be really effective in the Christian community and to be rightly understood—with due instruction —under visible symbols.

Liturgical reform is not synonymous with so called *desacralization* and should not be the occasion for what is called the *secularization of the world.* Thus the liturgical rites must retain a dignified and sacred character.

The effectiveness of liturgical actions does not consist in the continual search for newer rites or simpler forms, but in an ever deeper insight into the word of God and the mystery which is celebrated. The presence of God will be ensured by following the rites of the Church rather than those inspired by a priest's individual preference.

The priest should realize that by imposing his own personal restoration of sacred rites he is offending the rights of the faithful and is introducing individualism and idiosyncrasy into celebrations which belong to the whole Church.

The ministry of the priest is the ministry of the whole Church, and it can be exercised only in obedience, in hierarchical fellowship, and in devotion to the service of God and of his brothers. The hierarchical structure of the liturgy, its sacramental power, and the respect due to the community of God's people require that the priest exercise his liturgical service as a "faithful minister and steward of the mysteries of God."[9] He should not add any rite which is not contained and authorized in the liturgical books.

2. Sacred scripture, above all the texts used in the liturgical assembly, enjoys a special dignity: in the readings, God speaks to his people, and Christ, present in his word, announces the good news of the gospel.[10] Therefore:

(a) The Liturgy of the Word should be conducted with the greatest reverence. Other readings, from past or present, sacred or profane authors, may never be substituted for the word of God. The purpose of the homily is to ex-

8. Ibid., n. 34: *AAS* 56 (1964), p. 109.
9. Cf. 1 Cor. 4:1.
10. Cf. Constitution on the Sacred Liturgy, nn. 7, 33: *AAS* 56 (1964), pp. 100–101, 108.

plain the readings and make them relevant for the present day. The homily is the task of the priest; the faithful should refrain from comments, dialogue, etc. It is not permissible to have only one reading.

(b) The Liturgy of the Word prepares for and leads into the Liturgy of the Eucharist, forming with it one act of worship.[11] The two parts should not be celebrated separately at different times or in difference places.

Special rules for the integrating of another liturgical action or part of the divine office into the Liturgy of the Word will be indicated in the relative liturgical books.

3. The liturgical texts composed by the Church also deserve the greatest respect. No one on his own authority may make changes, substitutions, additions or deletions in them.[12]

(a) This rule applies especially to the *Ordo Missae*. The formulas which it contains in the official translations may never be altered, not even when Mass is sung. However, some parts of the rite, namely the penitential rite, the Eucharistic Prayer, the acclamation of the people, the final blessing, can be chosen from various alternative formulas as indicated for each rite.

(b) The entrance and communion chants can be selected from the Roman Gradual, the Simple Gradual, the Roman Missal or from collections approved by episcopal conferences. In choosing hymns for Mass, episcopal conferences should consider not only their present-day suitability and the various circumstances of the celebration of Mass, but also the needs of the faithful who will sing them.

(c) All means must be used to promote singing by the people. New forms of music suited to different mentalities and to modern tastes should also be approved by the episcopal conference. The conference should indicate selections of hymns to be used in Masses for special groups, e.g. for young people or children; the words, melody and rhythm of these songs, and the instruments used for their accompaniment, should correspond with the sacred character of the Mass and the place of worship.

Though the Church does not exclude any kind of sacred

11. Cf. ibid., n. 56: *AAS* 56 (1964), p. 115.
12. Cf. ibid., n. 22, 3: *AAS* 56 (1964), p. 106.

music from the liturgy,[13] not every type of music, song or instrument is equally capable of stimulating prayer or expressing the mystery of Christ. Music during Mass must serve the worship of God, and thus should have qualities of holiness and good form,[14] should be suited to the liturgical action and the nature of each of its parts, should not impede the participation of the whole congregation,[15] and must direct the attention of mind and heart to the mystery which is being celebrated.

Episcopal conferences will determine more particular guidelines for liturgical music, or, if these do not obtain, local bishops may issue norms for their own diocese.[16] Great care should be given to the choice of musical instruments; these should be few in number, suited to the place and the congregation, should favor prayer and not be too loud.

(d) Great freedom of choice is given for selecting the prayers, especially on ferial days, when they may be taken from any one of the thirty-four Sunday Masses *per annum*, from the Masses for Special Occasions[17] or from the Votive Masses.

Furthermore, in translating these texts the episcopal conference can make use of the special norms used by the Consilium, on 25 January 1969, n. 34,[18] in the Instruction on vernacular liturgical translations for use with the people.

(e) With regard to the readings, besides those indicated for each Sunday, feast and ferial day, a wide choice of readings is given for the celebration of the sacraments and for special occasions. When Mass is celebrated with special groups, texts which are more suited to the group may be chosen, provided they are taken from an approved lectionary.[19]

13. Cf. S.C.R., Instruction *Musicam sacram,* 5 March 1967, n. 9; *AAS* 59 (1967), p. 303; Constitution on the Sacred Liturgy, n. 116: *AAS* 56 (1964), p. 131.
14. Cf. S.C.R., Instruction *Musicam sacram,* n. 4: *AAS* 59 (1967), p. 301.
15. Cf. Constitution on the Sacred Liturgy, nn. 119–120: *AAS* 56 (1964), p. 130.
16. Cf. S.C.R., Instruction *Musicam sacram,* n. 9: *AAS* 59 (1967), p. 303.
17. Cf. *Institutio generalis Missalis romani,* n. 323.
18. Cf. *Notitiae* 5 (1969), pp. 9–10; cf. also nn. 21–24: ibid., pp. 7–8.
19. Cf. S.C. for Divine Worship, Instruction *Actio Pastoralis,* 15 May 1969, n. 6e: *AAS* 61 (1969), p. 809.

(f) During the celebration of the Mass, the priest may say a few words to the people: at the beginning, before the readings, before the preface, and before he dismisses the people.[20] But he should abstain from adding comments during the Eucharistic Prayer. These words should be brief and to the point, and should be prepared beforehand. If other comments need to be made, these should be entrusted to the commentator ("leader"), but he should avoid all exaggeration and limit himself to what is necessary.

(g) In the Prayer of the Faithful, besides the petitions for the Church, the world and the needy, it is good to add some special intentions for the local community. Intentions should not be inserted into the Roman Canon at the remembrances of the living and the dead. These intentions should be prepared and written down beforehand in the style of the Prayer of the Faithful[21] and may be read by one or several members of the congregation.

If these possibilities are used judiciously, they give such a wide range of choice that the celebrant will have no need to resort to his own private adaptations. Priests should be led to prepare their celebration, taking into consideration the circumstances and spiritual needs of the faithful. They can thus be confident that they are acting within the bounds set by the General Instruction of the Missal.

4. The Eucharistic Prayer, of all the parts of the Mass, is assigned to the celebrant alone, because of his sacerdotal office.[22] Thus it is forbidden to have some part of it read by a minister of lower rank, by the congregation or by a lay person. This is against the hierarchical structure of the liturgy in which everyone must take part, fully carrying out only what is required of him.[23] Therefore the priest alone must say the whole of the Eucharistic Prayer.

5. The bread used for the celebration of the Eucharist is wheat bread, and, according to the ancient custom of the Latin Church, is unleavened.[24]

Though the nature of the sign demands that this bread appear as actual food which can be broken and shared among

20. Cf. *Institutio generalis Missalis romani*, n. 11.
21. Ibid., nn. 45–46.
22. Ibid., n. 10.
23. Cf. Constitution on the Sacred Liturgy, n. 28: *AAS* 56 (1964), p. 107.
24. Cf. *Institutio generalis Missalis romani*, n. 282.

brothers, it must *always* be made in the traditional form, in line with the General Instruction of the Missal.[25] This applies both to the individual hosts for the communion of the faithful and to the larger hosts which are broken up into smaller parts for distribution.

The necessity for the sign to be genuine applies more to the colour, taste and texture of the bread than to its shape. Out of reverence for the sacrament, every care and attention should be used in preparing the altar bread. It should be easy to break and should not be unpleasant for the faithful to eat. Bread which tastes of uncooked flour, or which becomes dry and inedible too quickly, must never be used.

The breaking of the consecrated bread and the receiving of the bread and wine, both at communion and in consuming what remains after communion, should be conducted with the greatest reverence.[26]

6. A more perfect sharing by the faithful in the sacramental sign comes in the receiving of communion under both kinds.[27] The occasions on which this may be done are enumerated in the General Instruction of the Roman Missal (n. 242) and in the Instruction of the Sacred Congregation of Divine Worship on extending the possibilities of communion under both kinds, *Sacramentali Communione*, of 29 June 1970. Therefore:

(a) Ordinaries, within the limits set by the episcopal conference, should not give general permission but should clearly state the occasions and celebrations in which it is given. They should avoid Masses when there may be a large number of communicants. The groups should be limited in number, well ordered and homogeneous.

(b) The faithful should be given careful instruction, so that when they receive communion under both kinds, they can fully understand its meaning.

(c) A priest, deacon or ordained acolyte should be present to offer the chalice to the communicants. In the absence of another minister the priest should follow the rite given in the General Instruction of the Roman Missal, n. 245.

The passing of the chalice from one communicant to another or the communicant himself taking the chalice di-

25. Ibid., n. 283.
26. Cf. S.C.R., Instruction *Eucharisticum mysterium*, 26 May 1967, n. 48: *AAS* 59 (1967), p. 566.
27. Cf. *Institutio generalis Missalis romani*, n. 240.

rectly are practices which are not approved. In these cases communion by intinction should be preferred.

(d) The office of administering communion belongs first to priests, then to deacons and, in some cases, to acolytes. The Holy See can grant permission for some other suitable person to carry out this office. Those who have not been appointed must not distribute communion or carry the Blessed Sacrament.

The manner of distributing communion should follow the prescriptions of the General Instruction of the Roman Missal (nn. 244–252) and the above-mentioned Instruction of 29 June 1970. If permission is given for administering communion in a different way, the conditions laid down by the Holy See should be observed.

(e) Where there is a lack of priests, the bishop may, with the permission of the Holy See, designate other persons, such as catechists in missionary countries, to celebrate the Liturgy of the Word and to distribute holy communion. They may never say the Eucharistic Prayer, but if they find it useful to read the narrative of the Last Supper, they should use it as a reading in the Liturgy of the Word. Thus such liturgical assemblies consist of the Liturgy of the Word, the recitation of the Lord's prayer and the distribution of holy communion with the prescribed rite.

(f) In whatever way communion is administered, it must be done in a dignified, reverent and orderly manner, avoiding any lessening of the respect due to the sacrament. Attention should be paid to the nature of each congregation, and to the age, condition and preparation of the communicants.[28]

7. The traditional liturgical norms of the Church prohibit women (young girls, married women, religious) from serving the priest at the altar, even in women's chapels, houses, convents, schools and institutes.

In accordance with the rules governing this matter; women may:

(a) Proclaim the scripture readings, with the exception of the gospel. Modern technical means should be used so that everyone can easily hear. Episcopal conferences may determine more concretely a suitable place from which women may read the word of God.

28. Cf. S.C. for Divine Worship, Instruction *Sacramentali Communione*, 29 June 1970, n. 6: *L'Osservatore Romano*, 3 September 1970.

(b) Offer the intentions for the Prayer of the Faithful.

(c) Lead the congregation's singing; play the organ and other approved instruments.

(d) Give the explanatory comments to help the people's understanding of the service.

(e) Fulfil certain offices of service to the faithful which in some places are usually entrusted to women, such as receiving the faithful at the doors of the church and directing them to their places, guiding them in processions and collecting their offerings in church.[29]

8. Special care and attention is due to the sacred vessels, vestments and church furnishings. If greater freedom is given for their material and design, it is to give different nations and different artists the widest possible scope for applying their talents to divine worship. However, the following should be kept in mind:

(a) Things which are used for worship must always be "durable, of good quality according to contemporary taste, and well adapted for sacred use."[30] Thus things in common, everyday use should not be employed.

(b) Chalices and patens should be consecrated by the bishop before they are used; he will judge whether or not they are suitable for the liturgy.

(c) "The vestment common to all ministers of whatever rank is the alb."[31] The practice of wearing only a stole over the monastic cowl or ordinary clerical clothes for concelebration is an abuse. It is forbidden to celebrate Mass or perform other sacred actions, such as the laying on of hands at ordinations, the administering of other sacraments or the giving of blessings, while wearing only a stole over non-clerical clothes.

(d) The episcopal conferences may decide whether materials other than those traditionally used may be employed for church furnishings and vestments. They should inform the Holy See of their decisions.[32]

Episcopal conferences may also propose to the Holy See adaptations in the design of sacred vestments in conformity with the needs and customs of their regions.[33]

29. Cf. *Institutio generalis Missalis romani*, n. 68.
30. Ibid., n. 288.
31. Ibid., n. 298.
32. Cf. Constitution on the Sacred Liturgy, n. 128: *AAS* 56 (1964), pp. 132–3.
33. Cf. *Institutio generalis Missalis romani*, n. 304.

9. The Eucharist is normally to be celebrated in a sacred place.[34] It is not allowed to celebrate Mass outside a church without a real need, according to the judgment of the local ordinary within his own diocese. If the ordinary gives permission, careful attention should be given to the choice of a suitable place and that the table is fitting for the eucharistic sacrifice. As far as possible, Mass should not be celebrated in refectories or on tables normally used for meals.

10. In applying the liturgical reform, bishops should give special attention to the fixed and dignified arrangement of the sacred place, especially its sanctuary, in accordance with the norms of the General Instruction of the Roman Missal[35] and the document *Eucharisticum Mysterium*.[36]

Temporary arrangements made in recent years should gradually be given a final form. Some of these provisional solutions, already reproved by the Consilium,[37] are still in use though they are liturgically and artistically unsatisfactory and render difficult the worthy celebration of Mass.

With the help of diocesan committees on liturgy and sacred art, and after consultation if necessary with other experts and the civil authorities, a detailed study should be made of new building projects, and a review of temporary arrangements, so that churches should be given a definitive arrangement which respects artistic monuments, adapting them as far as possible to present-day needs.

11. To make the reformed liturgy understood, a great deal of work still remains to be done in translating accurately and in publishing the new liturgical books in vernacular languages. They must be translated in their entirety and must replace all other special liturgical books previously in use.

If the episcopal conferences find it necessary and useful to add other formulas or make certain adaptations, these may be introduced, after securing the approval of the Holy See, and should be distinguished typographically from the translation of the official Latin text.

34. Ibid., n. 260.
35. Cf. nn. 153–280.
36. Cf. nn. 52–57: *AAS* 59 (1967), pp. 567–569.
37. Cf. Epistola Em. mi Cardinal I. Lercaro, Praesidis "Consilii ad exsequendam Constitutionem de sacra Liturgia", ad Praesides Conferentiarum Episcopalium, 30 June 1965: *Notitiae* 1 (1965), pp. 261–262.

It would be better not to hurry the work of translation. With the help of many experts, not only theologians and liturgists, but also writers and poets, the vernacular liturgical texts will be works of real literary merit and of enduring quality, whose harmony of style and expression will reflect the deeper riches of their content.[38]

In publishing the vernacular liturgical books, the tradition of not indicating the names of the authors and translators should be retained. These books are destined for the use of the Christian community. They are prepared and edited only with the mandate and authority of the hierarchy; they should not depend on the decisions of private individuals; this would harm the freedom of the Church and the dignity of her liturgy.

12. When liturgical experimentation is seen to be necessary or useful, permission will be granted in writing by this Sacred Congregation alone, with clearly defined norms and under the responsibility of the competent local authority.

With regard to the Mass, those faculties for conducting experiments which were granted in view of the reform of the rite are no longer valid. With the publication of the new Roman Missal, the norms and the form of the Mass are those given in the General Instruction and the *Ordo Missae*.

Adaptations already foreseen by the liturgical books should be defined more particularly by episcopal conferences and submitted to the Holy See for confirmation.

If wider adaptations are necessary, in accordance with n. 40 of the Constitution *Sacrosanctum Concilium*, the bishops should make a detailed study of the culture, traditions and special pastoral needs of their people. If they find there is need for some practical experimentation, this should be done within clearly defined limits. Experiments should be carried out by well-prepared groups, under the direction of men of judgment specially appointed for the task; they should not be made with large congregations, nor should they be given publicity; they should be few in number and carried out for periods of no longer than one year, after which a report should be made to the Holy See. The liturgical changes requested may not be put into effect while awaiting the reply of the Holy See. If changes are to be made in the structure of the rites or in the order of parts as given in the liturgical books, or if actions differing from the

38. Paul VI, *Allocutio ad Commissiones liturgicas Italiae,* 7 February 1969: *L'Osservatore Romano,* 8 February 1969.

traditional ones or new texts are to be introduced, a complete outline and program of the modifications should be proposed to the Holy See before any experiments are begun.

Such a procedure is required and demanded both by the Constitution *Sacrosanctum Concilium* and by the seriousness of the matter.[39]

13. Finally, it should be remembered that the liturgical renewal set by the Council affects the whole Church. It requires both theoretical and practical study in pastoral meetings, with a view to educating the faithful to make the liturgy a living, uplifting and central part of their lives.

The present reform offers liturgical prayer as it should be, flowing from centuries of living, spiritual tradition. The work of the whole people of God, structured in its variety of orders and ministries, should be visible in the way the reform is carried out.[40] For only in this unity of the whole body of the Church can the liturgy's efficacy and authority be guaranteed.

The pastors of the Church, by their willing fidelity to the norms and directives of the Church, and in a spirit of faith which abandons all personal and individual preferences, are in an especial way the ministers of the common liturgy. By their example, by their deep understanding, by their dauntless preaching, they can bring about that flowering growth which the renewal of the liturgy requires. They will listen to the needs of the present day in a way which is far from a secularism and arbitrary attitude which would seriously threaten the liturgical reform.

39. Cf. n. 40: *AAS* 56 (1964), p. 111.
40. Cf. *Institutio generalis Missalis romani*, n. 58.

16

DECLARATION ON CONCELEBRATION[a]

S.C.D.W., *In Celebratione Missae*, 7 August, 1972

Everyone has the right and duty, when sharing in the celebration of Mass "to play his proper role in accordance with the diversity of orders and functions . . . in such wise that the very ordering of the celebration will manifest the Church in its various ranks and ministries."[1] Priests, ordained by the special Sacrament of Orders, perform the function that is properly theirs in the celebration of Mass whenever, individually or with other priests, they effect and offer the sacrifice of Christ sacramentally and receive Holy Communion.[2]

It is fitting therefore that at Mass priests should celebrate or concelebrate, so as to play their part more fully and in the manner proper to themselves, and that they should not communicate merely, as do the laity.[3]

Since a number of problems have been posed about the interpretation of the General Instruction on the Roman Missal (numbers 76 and 158), the Sacred Congregation for Divine Worship makes the following declaration:

1. The members of chapters and communities of institutes of perfection whom pastoral care obliges to celebrate Mass for the faithful, may, on the same day, concelebrate at the conventual or community Mass.[4] The concelebration of the Eucharist in communities ought to be held in high esteem. Fraternal concelebration by priests symbolizes and strengthens the links which unite them with one another

---

a. The Latin text appeared in *AAS* 60 (1972), pp. 561–563. This translation is by A.F.
1. General Instruction on the Roman Missal, n. 58; Constitution on the Sacred Liturgy, n. 28.
2. S.C.R. Decree *Ecclesiae Semper*, 7 March 1965: *AAS* 57 (1965), pp. 410–411.
3. S.C.R. Instruction *Eucharisticum Mysterium*, 25 May 1967, n. 43.
4. General Instruction on the Roman Missal, n. 76.

and which unite the community.[5] This way of celebrating the sacrifice, with everybody taking part consciously, actively and in the way that is proper to him, sets the action of the community more clearly in relief and is a very special manifestation of the Church, showing the unity of sacrifice and priesthood in the unique act of thanksgiving around the same altar.[6]

2. When a priest, in conformity with number 158 of the General Instruction on the Roman Missal, concelebrates at the principal Mass on the occasion of a pastoral visitation or a special gathering of priests—for example, during a pastoral gathering, a congress or a pilgrimage—he may also celebrate for the good of the faithful.

3. The following however must be observed:

(a) Bishops and competent superiors[7] must see to it that in communities and at gatherings of priests, concelebration is performed with dignity and true piety. To ensure this, and to achieve their greater spiritual good, the liberty of the concelebrants must always be respected and their interior and exterior participation facilitated by organizing the celebration authentically and totally in accordance with the norms of the General Instruction on the Roman Missal. Each part of the Mass should be celebrated as its nature demands,[8] tasks and functions should be clearly defined and attention paid to the singing and to the moments of silence.

(b) Priests who celebrate Mass for the good of the faithful and who concelebrate at another Mass may on no account accept a stipend for the concelebrated Mass.

(c) While the excellence of concelebration as a manner of celebrating the Eucharist in communities is not to be denied, Mass without the participation of the faithful "remains at the same time the center of the entire Church and the heart of priestly existence.[9]

5. Dogmatic Constitution on the Church, n. 28; Decree on the Ministry and Life of Priests, n. 8.
6. S.C.R. Decree *Ecclesiae Semper,* 7 March 1965; Instruction *Eucharisticum Mysterium,* n. 47.
7. General Instruction on the Roman Missal, n. 155.
8. S.C.R. Instruction *Musicam Sacram,* 5 March 1967, n. 6.
9. The Synod of Bishops, *De Sacerdotio Ministeriali,* Part Two, n. 3. [This paragraph seems open to misinterpretation. The Latin is: *Quamvis concelebratio forma sit praeclara celebrationis eucharisticae in communitatibus habendae, ipsa quoque celebratio sine fidelium participatione "manet tamen centrum totius Ecclesiae et veluti cor*

For this reason, every priest ought to be allowed the right to celebrate Mass alone.[10] To ensure priests' liberty, everything should be made available to facilitate such celebrations: time should be set aside, there should be a place where single celebration is possible and an altar server should be at hand, and whatever else is needed should be made available.

---

existentiae sacerdotalis." The French translation in *Documentation catholique* (n. 1622, p. 1113) renders *forma praeclara* as *une maniere excellente,* which seems weaker than the context would warrant. But it is the quotation from the Synod's text which might most easily be misinterpreted. The meaning is *not* that it is only Mass celebrated without the participation of the faithful which is "the center of the entire Church and the heart of priestly existence"; this, of course, applies to all celebrations of the Eucharist, "even if the Eucharist should be celebrated without participation by the faithful," as the Synod's text puts it.—Editor.]

10. S.C.R. Instruction *Eucharisticum Mysterium,* n. 47.

17

INSTRUCTION ON FACILITATING SACRAMENTAL EUCHARISTIC COMMUNION IN PARTICULAR CIRCUMSTANCES[a]

S.C.D.S., *Immensae Caritatis*, 25 January, 1973

Christ the Lord has left to the Church, his spouse, a testament of his immense love. This wonderful gift of the Eucharist, which is the greatest gift of all, demands that such an important mystery should be increasingly better known and its saving power more fully shared. With the intention of fostering devotion to the Eucharist—the summit and center of Christian worship—the Church, moved by pastoral zeal and concern, has on more than one occasion issued suitable laws and appropriate documents.

Present-day conditions, however, demand that, while the utmost reverence owing to such a Sacrament[1] is constantly

a. Translation issued by the Vatican Press Office. Latin text in *AAS* 65 (1973), pp. 264–271.
1. Cf. Council of Trent, Session 13, *Decretum de SS. Eucharistiae Sacramento,* c. 7; D. 880 (1646–1647): "If it is not fitting for anyone to approach any sacred functions except in a state of holiness, then certainly to the extent that the holiness and godliness of this heavenly Sacrament is more and more known to the Christian, all the more must he take care that he does not come to receive it without great reverence and holiness, especially because of the fearful words of the Apostle which we read: "A person who eats and drinks without recognizing the Body of the Lord is eating and drinking his own condemnation" (1 Cor. 11:29). Thus the following precept should be recalled to the one desirous of receiving Holy Communion: "Let a man so examine himself" (1 Cor. 11:28). Ecclesiastical custom declares that the proving of one's self is necessary, so that no one, conscious of having committed mortal sin, through considering himself contrite, should approach the Holy Eucharist without first having made a sacramental confession. This holy Synod declares that this must perpetually be observed by all Christians, even by priests, whose duty it is to celebrate Mass, as long as there is an availability of confessors. If in the case of urgent

maintained, greater access to Holy Communion should be made possible so that the faithful, by sharing more fully in the fruits of the sacrifice of the Mass, might dedicate themselves more readily and effectively to God and to the good of the Church and of mankind.

First of all, provision must be made lest reception become impossible or difficult owing to a lack of a sufficient number of ministers. Provision must also be made lest the sick be deprived of such a great spiritual consolation by being impeded from receiving Holy Communion because of the law of fast, which they may not be able to observe, even though it be already very moderate. Finally, it seems appropriate to determine in which circumstances the faithful who ask to receive sacramental Communion a second time on the same day may be permitted fittingly to do so.

After a study of the recommendatins of certain episcopal conferences the following norms are issued in regard to:

(1) extraordinary ministers for the distribution of Holy Communion;

(2) a more extensive faculty of receiving Holy Communion twice in the same day;

(3) mitigation of the Eucharistic fast for the sick and elderly;

(4) the piety and reverence owing to the Blessed Sacrament whenever the Eucharist is placed in the hand of the communicant.

EXTRAORDINARY MINISTERS FOR DISTRIBUTION OF HOLY COMMUNION

There are various circumstances in which a lack of sufficient ministers for the distribution of Holy Communion can occur:

During Mass, because of the size of the congregation or a particular difficulty in which a celebrant finds himself; outside of Mass, when it is difficult because of distance to

necessity a priest will have celebrated without previous confession, he is to make a confession as soon as possible." Sacred Congregation of the Council, Decree *Sacra Tridentina Synodus* (20 December 1905): *ASS* 38 (1905–1906), pp. 400–406; Sacred Congregation for the Doctrine of the Faith, *Normae pastorales circa absolutionem sacramentalem generali modo impertiendam* (31 July 1972), Norm 1: *AAS* 64 (1972), p. 511.

take the sacred species, especially in the Viaticum, to the sick in danger of death, or when the very number of the sick, especially in hospitals and similar institutions, requires many ministers. Therefore, in order that the faithful, who are in the state of grace and who with an upright and pious disposition, wish to share in the Sacred Banquet, may not be deprived of this sacramental help and consolation, it has seemed appropriate to the Holy Father to establish extraordinary ministers, who may give Holy Communion to themselves and to other faithful under the following determined conditions:

1. Local ordinaries have the faculty to permit a suitable person individually chosen as an extraordinary minister for a specific occasion or for a time or, in the case of necessity, in some permanent way, either to give the Eucharist to himself or to other faithful and to take it to the sick who are confined to their homes. This faculty may be used whenever:

(a) there is no priest, deacon or acolyte;

(b) these are prevented from administering Holy Communion because of another pastoral ministry or because of ill health or advanced age;

(c) the number of faithful requesting Holy Communion is such that the celebration of Mass or the distribution of the Eucharist outside of Mass would be unduly prolonged.

2. Local ordinaries also have the faculty to permit individual priests exercising their sacred office to appoint a suitable person who in cases of genuine necessity would distribute Holy Communion for a specific occasion.

3. The above-mentioned local ordinaries can delegate these faculties to auxiliary bishops, episcopal vicars and episcopal delegates.

4. The suitable person to who numbers I and II refer shall be designated according to the following order: lector, student of major seminary, male religious, woman religious, catechist, Catholic man or woman. This order however can be changed according to the prudent judgment of the local ordinary.

5. In oratories of religious communities of either sex the office of distributing Holy Communion in the circumstances described in number (I) can fittingly be given to a male superior not having major orders or to a woman superior or to their respective vicars.

6. If time permits, it is fitting that the suitable person individually chosen by the local ordinary for administering Holy Communion, as well as the person appointed by a priest having the faculty spoken of in number II, should receive the mandate according to the rite annexed to this Instruction; they are to distribute Holy Communion according to the liturgical norms.

Since these faculties are granted only for the spiritual good of the faithful and for cases of genuine necessity, priests are to remember that they are not thereby excused from the task of distributing the Eucharist to the faithful who legitimately request it, and especially from taking and giving it to the sick.

The person who has been appointed to be an extraordinary minister of Holy Communion is necessarily to be duly instructed and should distinguish himself by his Christian life, faith and morals. Let him strive to be worthy of this great office; let him cultivate devotion to the Holy Eucharist and show himself as an example to the other faithful by his piety and reverence for this most holy Sacrament of the altar. Let no one be chosen whose selection may cause scandal among the faithful.

THE EXTENDED FACULTY FOR RECEIVING HOLY COMMUNION TWICE IN THE SAME DAY

According to the discipline currently in force, the faithful are permitted to receive Holy Communion a second time:

On the evening of Saturday or of the day preceding a holyday of obligation, when they intend to fulfil the precept of hearing Mass, even though they have already received Holy Communion in the morning of that same day.[2]
At the second Mass of Easter and at one of the Masses celebrated on Christmas Day, even if they have already received Holy Communion at the Mass of the Paschal Vigil or at the midnight Mass of Christmas.[3]
Likewise at the evening Mass of Holy Thursday, even if

2. Sacred Congregation of Rites, Instruction *Eucharisticum Mysterium* 25 May 1967, 28; *AAS* 59 (1967), p. 557.
3. Cf. Ibid.

they have received Holy Communion at the earlier Mass of the Chrism.[4]

Since, beyond these circumstances which have been mentioned, there are similar occasions which suggest that Holy Communion might fittingly be received twice in the same day, it is necessary here to determine more precisely the reasons for the new faculty.

The norm which the Church, a most provident Mother, has introduced according to venerable custom and included in canon law by which the faithful are permitted to receive Holy Communion only once a day, remains intact, nor is it permitted to be set aside merely from motives of devotion. To a simple desire for repeated reception of Holy Communion it should be answered that the power of the Sacrament by which faith, charity and the other virtues are nourished, strengthened and expressed is all the greater to the extent that one more devoutly approaches the sacred table.[5] For, from the liturgical celebration the faithful should go out to the works of charity, piety and apostolic action so that "they may hold fast by their conduct and life to what they have received by faith and the Sacrament."[6]

Special circumstances however can occur when the faithful who have already received Holy Communion that same day, or even priests who have already celebrated Mass, may be present at some community celebration. They may receive Holy Communion again in the following instances:

(1) At those Masses in which the Sacraments of Baptism, Confirmation, Anointing of the Sick, Sacred Orders and Matrimony are administered; also at a Mass at which First Communion is received.[7]

(2) At Masses at which a church or altar is consecrated; at Masses of religious profession or for the conferring of a "canonical mission."

(3) At the following Masses of the Dead: the funeral

4. Cf. Ibid.; Sacred Congregation of Rites, Instruction *Inter Oecumenici*, 26 September 1964, 60: *AAS* 56 (1964), p. 891; Instruction, *Tres abhinc annos*, 4 May 1967, 14: *AAS* 59 (1967), p. 445.
5. Cf. St. Thomas Aquinas, *Summa Theol.* III, q. 79, a. 7 ad 3 and a. 8 ad 1.
6. Sacred Congregation of Rites, Instruction *Eucharisticum Mysterium*, 25 May 1967, 13: *AAS* 59 (1967), p. 549.
7. Cf. *Institutio generalis Missalis Romani*, 329a, typical edition 1970, p. 90.

Mass, the Mass celebrated after notification of death, the Mass on the day of final burial and the Mass on the first anniversary.

(4) At the principal Mass celebrated in the cathedral or in the parish on the feast of Corpus Christi and on the day of a parochial visitation; at the Mass celebrated by the major superior of a religious community on the occasion of a canonical visitation, of special meetings or chapters.

(5) At the principal Mass of a Eucharistic or Marian Congress, whether international or national, regional or diocesan.

(6) At the principal Mass of any congress, sacred pilgrimage or preaching mission for the people.

(7) In the administration of Viaticum, in which Communion can also be given to the relatives and friends of the patient.

(8) Also Local Ordinaries may, besides those cases mentioned above, grant permission *ad actum* to receive Holy Communion twice in the same day, as often as they shall judge it truly justified by reason of genuinely special circumstances, according to the norm of this Instruction.

MITIGATION OF THE EUCHARISTIC FAST FOR THE SICK AND THE AGED

Above all it remains firmly decreed that a person to whom Viaticum is administered in danger of death is not bound by any law of fasting.[8] Likewise remaining in force is the concession already granted by Pius XII whereby "the sick, even if not confined to bed, can take non-alcoholic drinks and medicines in either liquid or solid form before the celebration of Mass and the reception of the Eucharist without any restriction of time."[9]

In the case of foods and drinks taken for the purpose of nutrition that tradition is to be respected according to which the Eucharist should be received, as Tertullian said, 'before any food'[10] so as to indicate the excellence of the sacramental food.

In order to appreciate the dignity of the Sacrament and

8. Cf. *CIC* 858, paragraph 1.
9. Motu Proprio, *Sacram Communionem,* 19 March 1957, 4; *AAS* 49 (1957), p. 178.
10. *Ad uxorem* 2, 5: *PL* 1, 1408.

to prepare with joy for the coming of the Lord, a time of silence and recollection before the reception of Holy Communion is opportune. In the case of the sick, however, it will be a sufficient sign of piety and reverence if, for a brief period of time, they turn their minds to the greatness of the mystery. The period of time of the Eucharistic fast or abstinence from food and alcoholic drink is reduced to approximately one quarter of an hour, for the following:

(1) The sick in hospitals or in their own homes, even if they are not confined to bed.

(2) The faithful advanced in age who must remain at home because of age or who are living in a home for the aged.

(3) Sick priests, even if not confined to bed, and elderly priests, who wish to celebrate Mass or receive Holy Communion.

(4) Persons looking after the sick and the aged as well as those relatives of the sick and aged wishing to receive Holy Communion with them, whenever they are unable to observe the fast of one hour without inconvenience. (See D. *20*, 24.)

PIETY AND REVERENCE TOWARDS THE BLESSED SACRAMENT WHEN THE EUCHARIST IS PLACED IN THE HANDS OF THE FAITHFUL

Since the Instruction *Memoriale Domini* was published three years ago, some episcopal conferences have sought the faculty from the Apostolic See to allow the minister of Holy Communion to place the Eucharistic species in the hands of the faithful. As that Instruction recalled, "the precepts of the Church and the documents of the Fathers amply testify that the deepest reverence and the greatest prudence have been shown with regard to the Holy Eucharist,"[11] and should continue to be shown. Especially in this manner of receiving Holy Communion some points indicated by experience should be most carefully observed.

Let the greatest diligence and care be taken particularly with regard to fragments which perhaps break off the hosts. This applies to the minister and to the recipient whenever the Sacred Host is placed in the hands of the communicant.

Before initiating the practice of giving Holy Communion

11. Sacred Congregation for Divine Worship, Instruction *Memoriale Domini*, 29 May 1969; *AAS* 61 (1969), p. 542.

in the hand a suitable instruction and catechesis of Catholic doctrine is necessary concerning both the real and permanent presence of Christ under the Eucharistic species and the reverence due to this Sacrament.[12] It is necessary to instruct the faithful that Jesus Christ is the Lord and Saviour and that the same worship and adoration given to God is owed to him present under the sacramental signs. Let the faithful be counselled therefore not to omit a sincere and fitting thanksgiving after the Eucharistic banquet, such as may accord with each one's particular ability, state and duties.[13] So that participation in this heavenly table may be altogether worthy and profitable, the value and effects deriving from it for both the individual and the community must be pointed out to the faithful in such a way that their familiar attitude reveals reverence, fosters that intimate love for the Father of the household who gives us "our daily bread"[14] and leads to a living relationship with Christ of whose flesh and blood we partake.[15]

12. Cf. Second Vatican Council, Constitution on the Sacred Liturgy, 7: *AAS* 56 (1969), pp. 100–101; Sacred Congregation of Rites, Instruction *Eucharisticum Mysterium*, 25 May 1967, 9: *AAS* 59 (1967), p. 547.
13. Paul VI, Address *Ad Membra Consilii Eucharisticis ex omnibus Nationibus conventibus moderandis habita: AAS* 64 (1972), p. 287.
14. Cf. Lk. 11:3
15. Cf. Heb. 2:14.

18

CIRCULAR LETTER ON THE EUCHARISTIC PRAYERS[a]

S.C.D.W., *Eucharistiae Participationem*, 27 April, 1973

1. The reform of the sacred liturgy and, especially, the recent revision of the Roman Missal as directed by the Second Vatican Council[1] have as their principal objective the promotion of the faithful's attentive, devout and active participation in the Eucharist.[2]

A notable feature of the revised missal promulgated by Pope Paul VI is that quite frequently it offers a wide choice of texts: of scripture readings, chants, prayers, people's acclamations, Presidential prayers and even eucharistic prayers. Three new eucharistic prayers are now in use, apart from the venerable Roman Canon.[3]

2. It was pastoral concern which motivated the provision of such a variety of texts and, indeed, the revision of the prayer formulae, a concern to achieve both variety and unity in liturgical prayer. By using the texts of the Roman Missal in the celebration of the Eucharist, the various Christian communities are enabled to feel that they form one Church which shares the same faith and the same prayer. They are also enabled, especially when the celebration is in the vernacular, to proclaim the one Christian mystery in various ways. Further, they can the more easily raise their hearts to the Lord in prayer and thanksgiving[4] and can take part in the celebration with greater spiritual profit.

3. Even though some years have elapsed since the pro-

---

a. The full title is 'A circular letter to the Presidents of Episcopal Conferences: *Litterae Circulares ad conferentiarum praesides de precibus eucharisticis*. It is put out by the Sacred Congregation for Divine Worship. The first words of the Latin text (by which such documents are frequently referred to) are *Eucharistiae participationem*. The translation is by A.F. *AAS* 65 (1973), pp. 340–347.

1. Constitution on the Liturgy, n. 48.
2. Paul VI, Apostolic Const. *Missale Romanum.*
3. Ibid.
4. General Introduction to the Roman Missal, n. 54.

mulgation of the new Roman Missal, it has not yet every-where been possible to use it to the fullest extent in celebrations with the people. In a number of countries the very considerable work of translation[5] has taken a good deal of time. Further, there has been ignorance at times about the possibilities offered of improving the pastoral effectiveness of liturgical celebration, and sufficient attention is not always given to the common spiritual good of congregations.[6]

4. In the meantime, many have manifested a desire for further adaptation of the eucharistic celebration by the composition of new formulae, not excluding new eucharistic prayers. They say that the choice of presidential prayers and of the four eucharistic prayers in the present Order of the Mass does not yet fully meet the needs of the diversity of congregations, regions and people. Thus this sacred congregation has frequently been asked to approve new texts of presidential and eucharistic prayers, or that others be permitted to grant them approval, texts more in keeping with modern modes of thought and speech.

Further, several authors, of different languages and in different countries, have in recent years published eucharistic prayers composed by themselves for scientific purposes. Furthermore priests frequently use these privately-composed texts in liturgical celebrations, in spite of the prohibitions of Vatican II[7] and of bishops.

5. Taking this into account, this sacred congregation, at the request of the Supreme Pontiff, studied carefully the question of the composition of new eucharistic prayers and of granting episcopal conferences the right to approve of them. It also studied other related questions and their implications and it took the advice of experts from different parts of the world.

The conclusions arrived at were submitted to the members of this congregation in plenary assembly, to other congregations whom it concerned, and to the Supreme Pontiff. After careful consideration of all aspects of the problem, it was decided that the time was not ripe for granting to episcopal conferences a general permission for the composition or approval of eucharistic prayers. Rather was it deemed

5. With regard to the principles governing translations, see *Notitiae*, no. 5, 1969, pp. 3–12.
6. General Instruction on the Roman Missal, n. 313.
7. See Constitution on the Liturgy, n. 22.

more opportune to emphasize the need for a more thorough-going catechesis on the nature and characteristics of the eucharistic prayer;[8] since it is the high point of the celebration it ought also to be the culmination of a more profound catechesis. Further, it was thought advisable to provide fuller instruction on the ways open to priests to promote full participation by the faithful, following the current liturgical norms and using the formulae offered in the Roman Missal.

6. Thus there are at present four eucharistic prayers, those in the revised Roman Missal. It is not permissible to use any other eucharistic prayer which had not been composed by permission of the Holy See or approved by it. Episcopal conferences and individual bishops are earnestly requested to use suitable arguments to persuade their priests to accept the single discipline of the Roman Church. This will both benefit the Church itself and be conducive to the proper ordering of the liturgical celebration.

The Apostolic See reserves to itself a matter of such importance as the regulation of the discipline of the eucharistic prayers, this for the sake of pastoral unity. If episcopal conferences, within the context of the unity of the Roman rite and in view of special circumstances, ask permission to compose and use new eucharistic prayers, such requests will be sympathetically considered. The Holy See will, however, set out the norms to be observed in each instance.

7. Having promulgated this decision, it seems useful to offer some observations which may make its sense clearer and its execution easier. Some of these relate to the nature and importance of the eucharistic prayer in liturgical tradition, especially Roman liturgical tradition. Others have to do with adapting the celebration to individual congregations, without in the least changing the text of the eucharistic prayer.

8. The eucharistic prayer is of its nature "the culmination of the entire celebration" and is "a prayer of thanksgiving and sanctification." Its purpose is that "the entire congregation of the faithful should unite with Christ in confessing the wonderful works of God and in offering sacrifice."[9] It is recited by the ministerial priest. His voice is at once that of God speaking to his people and that of the people raising

8. See *Notitiae*, no. 4, 1968, pp. 146–148; 148–155.
9. General Instruction on the Roman Missal, n. 54.

their souls to God. His voice alone should be heard, therefore, the congregation observing a religious silence.

There is in this prayer a catechetical element, which expresses whatever is characteristic of the feast being celebrated. But of greater importance is the element of thanksgiving for the whole mystery of salvation or for whatever aspect of it is being celebrated on any particular day or feast, at a particular time or in a particular rite.[10]

It was for this reason, and in order that worshippers might the better thank God and bless him, that in the revised Roman Missal "the number of prefaces has been increased. They have been taken from the ancient tradition of the Roman Church or have been newly composed. They have both set certain aspects of the mystery of salvation in stronger relief and have offered more and stronger motives for giving thanks."[11]

It is for this reason that the priest who presides over the eucharist is allowed briefly to introduce the eucharistic prayer,[12] outlining for the faithful the motives it offers for thanksgiving, adapting them to his congregation, helping them to realize that their own lines are involved in salvation history and thus to gain more benefit from the eucharistic celebration.

9. Then there is the element of petition or intercession. This is to be regarded as secondary both to the purpose of the eucharistic prayer and in its composition and structure. In the reformed liturgy this element finds expression particularly in the prayers of the faithful. Here prayers are offered for the Church, for all men and their needs, in a form that is freer and more easily adapted to circumstances. At the same time the new liturgical books offer forms of intercession to be inserted into the eucharistic prayers in a way suited to the structure of each. This can be done in certain celebrations, especially in ritual Masses.[13] In this way ac-

---

10. *Ibid.*, n. 55a.
11. Apost. Const., *Missale Romanum.*
12. See General Instruction on the Roman Missal, n. 11.
13. With regard to Euch. Prayer 1, besides the faculty of introducing names in the Memento, see special Memento for godparents in Masses for baptism of adults and the formula for *Hanc Igitur* in Masses from Easter Vigil to Second Sunday of Paschal time, for baptism of adults, for confirmation, ordination, marriage, profession, consecration of virgins. With regard to Canons 2, 3, 4, see Embolisms for adult baptised, for professions and consecrations of virgins.

count is taken of what is proper to a particular celebration and at the same time it is made clear that such a prayer is offered in communion with the universal Church.[14]

10. Apart from the variations mentioned above, whose object is to unite thanksgiving and intercession more closely with the celebration, there are other special formulae in the Roman tradition to be used on the principal solemnities "within the action." Their object is to set in clearer relief the memorial of the mystery of the Lord which is being celebrated.[15]

From this it is clear that it is part of the Roman tradition to lay great store by the immutability of texts and yet not to exclude changes where appropriate. If the faithful can join more easily in prayer with the celebrant because a text has become familiar to them from repetition, it is also true that variations in the text—but not frequent—can be welcome and helpful. They can attract attention, excite piety and impart a special tone to the prayer.

Nor is there any reason why episcopal conferences for their regions, bishops for their dioceses or the competent authorities for religious families should not make similar provision with regard to the variable elements mentioned above (numbers 8 to 10) and ask the Holy See for confirmation of them.

11. Great importance should be attached to the ecclesial dimension of the eucharistic celebration. While it is true that in the eucharistic celebration "the unity of the faithful is effected and symbolized: they constitute one body in Christ."[16] At the same time it is true that "the celebration of Mass is already in itself a profession of faith by which the entire Church understands and expresses itself."[17] All this appears clearly in the eucharistic prayer itself in which it is not an individual or a local community but "the one and only Catholic Church" present in every local Church[18] which addresses itself to God.

Where unapproved eucharistic prayers are used it often

14. General Instruction on the Roman Missal, n. 55g.
15. See proper *Communicantes* for Christmas and octave, for the Epiphany for Paschal time (from Paschal vigil to Second Sunday of Paschal time), for the Ascension and for Pentecost.
16. Constitution on the Church, no. 3.
17. Secretariate for Christian Unity, Instruction, *In quibus rerum circumstantiis*, 1 June, 1972 (DOCTRINE AND LIFE, August, 1972).
18. Constitution on the Church, n. 23.

happens that disquiet and dissensions break out among the priests and in the community. The eucharist ought rather to be a 'sign of unity' and a "bond of charity."[19] Many complain of the over-subjective character of such texts. It is indeed the right of those who take part in liturgical celebrations to expect that the eucharistic prayer which they ratify with their final *Amen* should not be interspersed with or totally imbued with the personal outlook of the person who wrote it or of the person who proclaims it.

Hence the necessity of using only those texts of the eucharistic prayer which have been approved by legitimate Church authority and which are clearly and fully ecclesial in character.

12. A closer adaptation of the celebration to differing congregations and differing circumstances will be called for in those portions and formulae of the liturgical action which allow variation or demand it. It is not always possible or desirable to effect such adaptation during the eucharistic prayer, granted its nature. The same is true of the catechetical element in the celebration.

13. First of all, when celebrants are preparing the liturgy or presiding at it, they should recall the faculty granted in the General Instruction to the Roman Missal[20] to select in certain cases the Mass formulae and the texts of various parts of the Mass, such as the readings, prayers and chants, so that they might correspond as far as possible to "the needs, the spiritual preparedness and the ability of the participants."[21] Nor must it be forgotten that other documents published since the appearance of the General Instruction offer other norms and suggestions for enlivening celebrations and making them pastorally effective.[22]

14. Among the elements which admit of fuller adaptation and which are within the power of each celebrant one should mention the admonitions, the homily, and the prayer of the faithful.

First, the admonitions. It is by means of the admonitions that the faithful are led to a fuller understanding of the sacred function or of certain of its parts, and to participate in

---

19. St. Augustine, *In Ioannis Evangelium*, 26.
20. General Instruction on the Roman Missal, n. 314–324.
21. Ibid., n. 313.
22. Sacred Congr. for Divine Worship, Instruction *Actio Pastoralis*, 15 May 1969; Instruction *Memoriale Domini* 29 May 1969; Instruction, *Memoriale Domini*, 29 June 1970.

them in accordance with their true spirit. The most important of these admonitions are those which the General Instruction on the Roman Missal invites the celebrant to compose and proclaim. He is thus invited to introduce the faithful to the day's Mass at the very beginning of the celebration; to introduce them to the liturgy of the word, before the readings; to the eucharistic prayer, before the preface. He is invited to bring the entire function to a conclusion, in his own words, before the dismissal.[23] But those admonitions are also important which are set out in the Order of the Mass itself before certain rites: before the penitential act, for example, or before the Lord's Prayer. Of their very nature it is not necessary that these admonitions be delivered word for word as they are in the missal. It may be advisable, at least in certain circumstances, to adapt them somewhat to this or that community. However, the admonitions must not be allowed to develop into sermons or homilies. Brevity must be cultivated and verbosity avoided: it would bore the participants.

15. Next comes the homily, which is "part of the liturgy itself."[24] In the homily the word of God which has been proclaimed in the liturgical assembly is explained to the community present, taking into account its capacity and way of life, and in the context of the actual celebration.

16. Lastly, stress must be laid on the prayers of the faithful, by which the congregation in a sense make their response to the word of God expounded to them and accepted by them. To make the prayers more effective, care must be taken that they be relevant to the particular assembly. In composing them that wise liberty should be employed which the nature of these prayers demands.

17. Certainly, if a celebration is to be really communal and is to come alive it requires—over and above the selection of its parts—that the celebrant and all others who have special parts to play should give careful thought to the different kinds of verbal communication with the congregation. These are the readings, the homily, the admonitions, the introductions, etc.[25]

When reciting the prayers, and especially the eucharistic prayers, the celebrant should avoid, on the one hand, a

23. General Instruction on the Roman Missal, n. 11.
24. Constitution on the Liturgy, n. 52.
25. General Instruction on the Roman Missal, n. 18.

mode of delivery which is dry and monotonous and, on the other, one which is too subjective and emotional. As the president over the function he must endeavour, whether reading, singing, or performing a liturgical action, to help the participants to form a true community which will celebrate and live the memorial of the Lord.

18. Then there is the sacred silence, which appeals to many and which must always be observed at set times and as part of the liturgical function.[26] Its purpose is that the full power of the words may be perceived and greater spiritual fruit be obtained from them. During the silences, the participants—each responding in his own way to the demands of the moment—will recollect themselves, reflect briefly on what has been read, or will praise and pray to God in their innermost spirit.[27]

19. In view of what has been said, it is to be hoped that pastors of souls, rather than introduce novelties in the texts or rites of the sacred actions, will zealously lead the faithful to greater understanding of the character, the structure and the elements of the celebration and especially of the eucharistic prayer, so that they will take part in the celebrations more fully and with greater awareness. The power of the liturgy does not consist merely in the novelty and the variety of the elements, but rather in a more profound sharing in the mystery of salvation, present and active in the liturgical action. Only in this way can the faithful, professing the same faith and offering to God the same prayer, save themselves and their brethren.

26. Constitution on the Liturgy, n. 30.
27. General Instruction on the Roman Missal, n. 23.

19

DECLARATION ON FIRST CONFESSION AND FIRST COMMUNION

S.C.C. and S.C.D.S., *Sanctus Pontifex,* 24 May, 1973

On 8 August 1910, St. Pius X laid down in the decree *Quam singulari (AAS.* 1910, pp. 577-583) that, in accordance with Canon 21 of the Fourth Council of the Lateran, children might receive the Sacraments of Penance and the Eucharist as soon as they had attained the use of reason. That prescription was applied throughout the Church and has borne and still bears abundant fruit in Christian life and spiritual perfection.

The note added to the general catechetical directory promulgated by the Sacred Congregation for the Clergy on 11 April 1971 *(AAS,* 1972, pp. 97-176) confirmed the custom of administering the Sacrament of Penance before the first communion of children. Its statement read as follows: "Taking everything into account, it would seem that one could not in principle abrogate a common and general practice except with the consent of the Holy See. Having consulted episcopal conferences the Holy See believes that it is proper to continue the Church's custom of placing first confession before first communion" (n. 5).

The same document took account of certain new practices which have been introduced in certain quarters, where it is permitted to receive first communion without first receiving the Sacrament of Penance. It allowed such practices to continue on a temporary basis, merely, "in consultation with the apostolic see in a spirit of communion with it" (ibid.).

After mature consideration and having taken account of the views of the bishops, the Sacred Congregation for the Discipline of the Sacraments and for the Clergy declares by this present document, with the approval of the Sovereign Pontiff, Paul VI, that these experiments, which have lasted for two years up to the end of the school year 1972-73, should cease and that everybody everywhere should conform to the decree *Quam singulari.*

20

ON HOLY COMMUNION AND THE WORSHIP OF THE EUCHARISTIC MYSTERY OUTSIDE OF MASS[a]

S.C.D.W., *Eucharistiae Sacramentum* 21 June, 1973

INTRODUCTORY OBSERVATIONS

I. THE RELATION BETWEEN THE WORSHIP OF THE BLESSED EUCHARIST OUTSIDE MASS AND THE EUCHARISTIC CELEBRATION

1. The celebration of the Eucharist is the center of the whole Christian life both for the universal Church and for the local congregations of that Church. For "the other sacraments, and indeed all ecclesiastical ministries and works of the apostolate are bound up with the Eucharist and are directed towards it. For in the most blessed Eucharist is contained the whole spiritual good of the Church, namely Christ himself our pasch and the living bread which gives life to men through his flesh—that flesh which is given life and gives life through the Holy Spirit. Thus men are invited and led, themselves, their labors and all creation with Christ."[1]

2. Moreover, "the celebration of the Eucharist in the sacrifice of the Mass is the origin and consummation of the worship shown to the Eucharist outside Mass."[2] For "in the sacrifice of the Mass Christ our Lord is immolated when he begins to be present sacramentally as the spiritual food of the faithful under the appearances of bread and wine," so also "when the sacrifice has been offered and the Eucharist

a. Translated by Dom Matthew Dillon, OSB, selected excerpts from the preface to *De sacra communione et de cultu mysterii eucharistici extra missam*, a liturgical book.
1. Vatican II, Decree on the Ministry and Life of Priests, n. 5.
2. S.C.R. Instruction *Eucharisticum mysterium*, n. 3e: *AAS* 59 (1967), p. 542.

is reserved in churches or oratories he is in truth Emmanuel, i.e. 'God with us.' For he is in our midst day and night, he dwells in us full of grace and truth."[3]

3. There can accordingly be no doubt "that all the faithful ought to show to this most holy sacrament the worship which is due to the true God, as has always been the custom of the Catholic Church. Nor is it to be adored any the less because it was instituted by Christ the Lord to be eaten."[4]

4. In order to direct and foster devotion to the Blessed Sacrament, the Eucharistic mystery must be considered in all its aspects, both in the celebration of Mass and in the devotion to the sacred species which remain after Mass and are reserved to extend the grace of the sacrifice.[5]

II. REASONS FOR THE RESERVATION OF THE EUCHARIST

5. The original and primary reason for the reservation of the Eucharist outside Mass is the administration of Viaticum: the distribution of Holy Communion and the adoration of our Lord Jesus Christ present in the Blessed Sacrament are derivative. For in fact the reservation of the sacred species for the benefit of the sick led to the admirable practice of adoring this heavenly food reserved in our churches. This practice of adoration is essentially proper and rational because faith in the real presence of our Lord spontaneously evokes a public and external manifestation of that faith.[6]

6. In the celebration of Mass the principal forms of Christ's presence in his Church are manifested progressively. First, he is present in the assembly of the faithful gathered together in his name; then he is present in his word when the Scriptures are read in the church and explained; likewise he is present in the person of the priest; finally and above all he is present under the eucharistic species. For in the sacrament of the Eucharist Christ is present, in a manner altogether unique, God and man, whole and entire, substantially and continuously. This presence of Christ under

3. Ibid., n. 3b, p. 541; Paul VI, Encyclical *Mysterium Fidei,* near end: *AAS* 57 (1965), p. 771.
4. S.C.R. Instruction *Eucharisticum mysterium,* n. 3f: *AAS* 59 (1967), p. 543.
5. Ibid., n. 3g, p. 543.
6. Cf. Ibid., n. 49, pp. 566–567.

the species "is called 'real' not in an exclusive sense, as if the other kinds of presence were not real, but par excellence."[7]

To ensure the full sacramental signification it is therefore more appropriate that when Mass is celebrated Christ should not, if this can be arranged, be eucharistically present on the altar from the beginning of Mass in the sacred species reserved in the tabernacle. For the eucharistic presence of Christ is the fruit of the consecration and should be recognized as such.[8]

7. Consecrated hosts in sufficient quantities to provide for the communion of the sick and of other members of the faithful should be frequently renewed and reserved in a pyx or ciborium.[9]

8. Pastors should ensure that, unless there is a grave reason against it, churches in which the blessed Sacrament is normally reserved should be open every day for at least some hours, at the most suitable times, so that the faithful may be easily able to pray before the blessed Sacrament.[10]

CHAPTER I

HOLY COMMUNION OUTSIDE MASS

I. THE RELATION BETWEEN HOLY COMMUNION OUTSIDE MASS AND THE SACRIFICE

13. By receiving Holy Communion during Mass we participate more perfectly in the celebration of the Eucharist. This is more clearly signified by this sacrament when the

7. Paul VI, Encyclical *Mysterium fidei: AAS* 57 (1965), p. 764 cf. S.C.R. Instruction *Eucharisticum mysterium,* n. 9: *AAS* 59 (1967), p. 547.
8. See S.C.R. Instruction *Eucharisticum mysterium,* n. 55: *AAS* 59 (1967), pp. 568–569.
9. See Roman Missal, General Instruction, nn. 285, 292.
10. See S.C.R. Instruction *Eucharisticum mysterium,* n. 51: *AAS* 59 (1967), p. 567.

faithful receive the Body of the Lord after the priest's communion from the same sacrifice.[1] Accordingly fresh hosts should, as a general rule, be consecrated in every celebration of the Eucharist for the communion of the faithful.

14. The faithful should be encouraged to receive Holy Communion during the celebration of the Eucharist.

However, priests should not refuse the faithful who, for a good reason, seek to receive Holy Communion outside Mass.

It is indeed eminently fitting that those who are unable to assist at the celebration of the Eucharist should receive the spiritual nourishment of the blessed Sacrament and in this way feel that they are united not only to the sacrifice of the Lord but also to the community, and are sustained by the charity of their brethren.

Pastors of souls should take care that the sick and the aged, even though they are not gravely ill or in imminent danger of death, should be given the opportunity to receive Holy Communion frequently, daily indeed if it is possible, especially during Eastertide. Those who are unable to receive the sacrament under the species of bread may receive Holy Communion under the species of wine alone.[3]

15. It should be carefully explained to the faithful that even when they receive Holy Communion outside Mass they are intimately united with the sacrifice which is the perpetuation of the sacrifice of the cross, and that they participate in the sacred banquet in which the people of God "by receiving the Body and Blood of the Lord share in the treasures of the paschal sacrifice, renew the covenant sealed by God once for all with men in the Blood of Christ, and prefigure and anticipate the heavenly banquet in the kingdom of the Father, proclaiming the death of the Lord until he comes again."[4]

II. THE TIMES AT WHICH HOLY COMMUNION MAY BE DISTRIBUTED OUTSIDE MASS

16. Holy Communion may be distributed outside Mass on any day and at any time of the day. It is desirable, however, that fixed times be appointed for the distribution of

1. See Vatican II, Constitution on the Sacred Liturgy, n. 55.
2. S.C.R. Instruction *Eucharisticum mysterium,* n. 33a: *AAS* 59 (1967), pp. 559–560.
3. Ibid., nn. 40–41, pp. 562–563.
4. Ibid., n. 3a, pp. 541–542.

Holy Communion, with due consideration for the convenience of the faithful, so that the ceremony may be conducted in a fuller form to the greater spiritual benefit of the faithful.

However:

(a) On Holy Thursday Holy Communion may be distributed only during Mass. It may be brought to the sick, however, at any time of the day.

(b) On Good Friday Holy Communion may be distributed only during the celebration of the Passion of our Lord. It may, however, be brought to the sick who are unable to attend the ceremony, at any time of the day.

(c) On Holy Saturday Holy Communion may be given only by way of Viaticum.[5]

III. THE MINISTER OF HOLY COMMUNION

17. It is primarily the function of priests and deacons to distribute Holy Communion to the faithful who seek it.[6] It is eminently fitting, therefore, that they should devote a reasonable part of their time in keeping with the needs of the faithful to this exercise of their ministry.

Acolytes duly appointed, moreover, may, as extraordinary ministers, distribute Holy Communion when no priest or deacon is available, when neither priest or deacon is able to distribute it on account of ill health or advanced age, or because of the pressure of other pastoral duties. Acolytes may similarly distribute Holy Communion when the number of the faithful approaching the altar is so large that the celebration of Mass or other sacred ceremony would be unduly prolonged.[7]

The local ordinary may give to other extraordinary ministers the faculty to distribute Holy Communion whenever this seems necessary for the pastoral good of the faithful, and when no priest, deacon or acolyte is available.[8]

---

5. See Roman Missal: Evening Mass on Holy Thursday; the Celebration of the Lord's Passion (Good Friday); Holy Saturday.
6. See S.C.R. Instruction *Eucharisticum mysterium*, n. 31: *AAS* 59 (1967), pp. 557–558.
7. See Paul VI, Apostolic Letter *Ministeria quaedam*, 15 Aug. 1972, (D.29) n. 6: *AAS* 64 (1972), p. 532.
8. See S.C.D.S. Instruction *Immensae caritatis*, 29 Jan. 1973, 1, I and II.

IV. WHERE HOLY COMMUNION MAY BE DISTRI-BUTED OUTSIDE MASS

18. As a general rule Holy Communion should be distributed outside Mass in a church or oratory in which Mass is habitually celebrated or the Blessed Sacrament is reserved, or in a church, oratory, or other place in which the local community habitually assembles for liturgical celebrations on Sundays or other days. But Holy Communion may be distributed in other places, not excluding private houses in the case of sick people, prisoners or other who cannot go out without danger or grave inconvenience.

. . . .

21. In administering Holy Communion the practice of placing the particle on the tongue of the recipient should be observed, as it is based on a long-standing tradition.

Episcopal conferences may, however, prescribe, subject to the confirmation of the Apostolic See, that in the region under their jurisdiction Holy Communion may be distributed by placing the consecrated host in the hand of the recipient, provided that there is no danger of a lack of reverence or of the propagation of false opinions about the blessed Sacrament in the minds of the faithful.[9]

The faithful should, however, be taught that Jesus Christ is our Lord and Saviour, and that we should offer to him, present in the Sacrament, the same worship of latria or adoration that we offer to God.[10]

In either case Holy Communion must be distributed by a lawful minister, who shall hold up the consecrated host before the communicant and administer it to him, pronouncing the formula "the Body of Christ" to which the communicant should reply *Amen*.

When Holy Communion is administered under the form of wine, the liturgical norms should be carefully observed.[11]

22. Any fragments of the host which may remain after the administration of Holy Communion should be reverently collected and placed in the pyx or in a bowl of water.

9. See S.C.D.W. Instruction *Memoriale Domini*, 29 May 1969: *AAS* 61 (1969), pp. 541–555.
10. See S.C.D.S. Instruction *Immensae caritatis*, 29 Jan. 1973, n. 4.
11. *AAS* 62 (1970), pp. 665–666.

Likewise if Holy Communion is administered under the form of wine the chalice or other vessel employed should be purified with water. The water used for this purification should be either drunk or poured away in some suitable place.

VI. DISPOSITION REQUIRED IN THOSE RECEIVING HOLY COMMUNION

23. The blessed Sacrament, by virtue of which the paschal mystery of Christ is ever present among men, is the source of all grace and of pardon for sins. But those who wish to receive the Body of the Lord in order to share in the fruits of the pashcal sacrament must approach it with a pure conscience and the proper dispositions. In particular the Church prescribes that "no one who is conscious of being guilty of mortal sin, however repentant he may feel, may receive Holy Communion until he has received sacramental absolution."[12]

If there is a grave reason and no opportunity of going to confession, a communicant should make an act of perfect contrition with the intention of confessing every mortal sin of which he or she is guilty as soon as possible.

Those who receive Holy Communion daily or very frequently should receive the sacrament of Penance at suitable times, according to their individual circumstances.

But the faithful should consider the blessed Sacrament as a remedy by which they are absolved from their daily venial faults and are preserved from mortal sin. They should appreciate the value of the penitential elements in the Liturgy and especially in the Mass.[13]

24. The faithful may not receive Holy Communion unless they have abstained for at least one hour from food and drink, with the sole exception of water and medicine.

People of advanced years, those who are ill and those who take care of them may receive Holy Communion even if they have partaken of food or drink during the course of the previous hour.

---

12. See Council of Trent, Session 13, Decree on the Eucharist, n. 7; ibid., Session 14, Canons on the Sacrament of Penance, n. 9; S.C.D.F. Pastoral Norms for Imparting General Sacramental Absolution, 16 June 1972, Introduction and n. 6: *AAS* 64 (1972), pp. 510, 512.
13. Cf. S.C.R. Instruction *Eucharisticum mysterium*, n. 35: *AAS* 59 (1967), p. 561.

25. Union with Christ, which is the object of the sacrament, should extend to the whole Christian life. The faithful, therefore, being ever mindful of the gift they have received, should live their daily lives in a spirit of gratitude under the guidance of the Holy Spirit and thus derive more abundant fruits of charity.

In order the better to maintain this spirit of gratitude, which is so admirably expressed to God in the Mass, it is recommended that all those who receive Holy Communion should spend some time in prayer afterwards.[15]

CHAPTER II

THE VARIOUS FORMS OF WORSHIP OF THE BLESSED SACRAMENT

79. Since the eucharistic sacrifice is the source and summit of the whole Christian life, devotion, both public and private, to the blessed Sacrament according to the norms laid down by legitimate authority is strongly recommended.

In determining the forms of such devotions attention should be paid to the liturgical seasons so that the devotion may be in harmony with the sacred liturgy, may draw their

14. Cf. S.C.D.S. Instruction *Immensae caritatis*, 29 Jan. 1973, n. 3.
15. Cf. S.C.R. Instruction *Eucharisticum mysterium*, n. 38: *AAS* 59 (1967), p. 562.

inspiration from it to some extent, and may lead the people towards it.[1]

80. When the faithful worship Christ in the blessed Sacrament they should recollect that this presence is derived from the sacrifice and evokes sacramental and spiritual communion. That piety, therefore, which moves the faithful to adore the blessed Sacrament inspires them also to participate more fully in the paschal mystery and to respond with grateful heart to Christ's gift of himself, who through his humanity is ever bestowing divine life on the members of his mystical body. Remaining closely united to Christ, they enjoy intimate familiarity with him and offer heart-felt prayer to him for themselves, for all those who are dear to them, for peace and for the salvation of the world, offering their entire lives with Christ to the Father in the Holy Spirit. From this admirable exchange they receive an increase of hope and charity. In this way they develop the right dispositions for celebrating the memorial of the Lord with fitting devotion and for receiving frequently the heavenly Bread which the Father has provided for us.

The faithful should, therefore, be zealous in keeping with their conditions of life, in their devotion to the blessed Sacrament.

Pastors should encourage them in this by their example and their teaching.[2]

81. Let them remember also that by prayer of this kind before Christ in the blessed Sacrament they prolong that union which they have achieved with him in Holy Communion, and renew the covenant which commits them to practice in their lives and conduct what they have received in faith in the celebration of the Eucharist and in the reception of the Sacrament. Let them strive, therefore, to live their whole lives joyously in the strength of this heavenly food, participating in the death and resurrection of the Lord. Each individual, therefore, should be eager to do good works and to please God, making it his aim to impregnate the world with the Christian spirit and to be a faithful witness to Christ in all things in the midst of human society.[3]

---

1. Cf. S.C.R. Instruction *Eucharisticum mysterium*, n. 58: *AAS* 59 (1967), p. 569.
2. Ibid., n. 50, p. 567.
3. Ibid., n. 13, p. 549.

I. EXPOSITION OF THE BLESSED SACRAMENT

A. Relation Between Exposition and Mass

82. Exposition of the blessed Sacrament, whether in a pyx or a monstrance, is a recognition of the wondrous presence of Christ in the sacrament and stimulates us to unite ourselves to him in a spiritual union which finds its culmination in sacramental communion. It is, accordingly, eminently in harmony with the worship which we owe him in spirit and in truth. Care must be taken that in exposition the worship of the blessed Sacrament should clearly express its relation to the Mass. In the arrangements of the exposition everything should be carefully excluded which might in any way obscure the intention of Christ, who instituted the Eucharist primarily in order to make himself available to us as food, as healing, and as consolation.[4]

83. While the blessed Sacrament is exposed the celebration of Mass in the same part of the church or oratory is forbidden.

This is because, in addition to the reasons given in n. 6, the celebration of the mystery of the Eucharist includes in a more perfect manner that spiritual communion to which exposition is intended to stimulate the faithful.

If exposition is prolonged for a day or for a number of successive days it should be interrupted during the celebration of Mass unless Mass is celebrated in a chapel apart from the exposition and some at least of the faithful remain in adoration.[5]

B. Some Points to Be Observed in Arranging Exposition

84. Genuflection on one knee is prescribed before the blessed Sacrament whether it be reserved in the tabernacle or exposed for public adoration.

85. For exposition of the blessed Sacrament in the monstrance four or six candles should be lighted, that is, as many as are used at Mass, and incense should be used. For exposition in the pyx only two candles should be lighted; incense may be used.

4. Ibid., n. 60, p. 570.
5. Ibid., n. 61, pp. 570–571.

Exposition Over a Longer Period

86. In churches and oratories in which the blessed Sacrament is reserved it is recommended that there should be a period of solemn exposition of the blessed Sacrament every year, even though it may not be entirely continuous, so that the local community may have the opportunity to meditate on the sacrament and adore it more fervently.

Such exposition should be arranged only if it is foreseen that there will be a suitable attendance of the faithful.[6]

87. In any grave and general need the local ordinary may direct that there be prayer before the blessed Sacrament exposed for a protracted period in those churches which are attended by larger numbers of the faithful.[7]

88. Where continuous adoration is not possible because there is not a sufficient number of the faithful available for adoration, it is permissible to replace the Sacrament in the tabernacle at times which have been prearranged and duly announced. This may be done not more than twice in the day—for example, at midday and at night.

The replacing of the blessed Sacrament may be done without undue ceremony: a priest or deacon wearing an alb or surplice and stole over his cassock, having adored the blessed Sacrament for a brief period and recited a prayer with the faithful, places the blessed Sacrament in the tabernacle. It will be exposed again in the same manner at the hour appointed.[8]

Brief Period of Exposition

89. Brief periods of exposition should be so arranged that before the blessing with the blessed Sacrament a fitting amount of time is allowed for readings of the word of God, for hymns, prayers, and for a period of silent prayer. Exposition merely for the purpose of imparting the blessing is forbidden.[9]

6. Ibid., n. 63, p. 571.
7. Ibid., n. 64, p. 572.
8. Ibid., n. 65, p. 572.
9. Ibid., n. 66, p. 572.

Adoration by Religious Communities

90. Religious communities and other pious associations who, according to their constitutions or the norms of their institute, practice perpetual adoration or adoration for protracted periods are earnestly recommended to perform this pious practice in the spirit of the sacred liturgy so that when the whole community participates in the adoration it may be carried out with sacred readings, with hymns and periods of reverential silence. In this way it will be more fruitful for the spiritual life of the community. Thus the spirit of unity and fraternity which the Eucharist signifies and effects will be promoted among the members of the religious community and the due worship of the Sacrament will be more fittingly exercised.

That form of adoration in which only one or two members of the community adore successively is also permissible and indeed highly commendable. In this way, in accordance with the rule of the institute approved by the Church, they offer adoration and prayer to Christ the Lord in the Sacrament in the name of the whole community.

21

DIRECTORY ON CHILDREN'S MASSES[a]

S.C.D.W., *Pueros Baptizatos,* 1 November, 1973

INTRODUCTION

1. The Church is bound to be specially concerned about the welfare of children who have been baptized but have not yet received Confirmation and the Eucharist, or who have only recently made their First Communion. They are growing up in a world which is not conducive to their spiritual welfare[1] and many parents do not take seriously the obligation they undertook, when their children were baptized, the obligation to bring them up as Christians.

2. The church is the place where children should receive a Christian education, but there is a problem here. Liturgical, and especially eucharistic celebrations, which of their very nature have an educative value,[2] are scarcely fully effective where children are concerned. The Mass may be in their own language, but the words and symbols used are not those which they can understand.

There are, of course, many things in their day-to-day life with adults which children do not always understand, and this does not make them disinterested. So one does not have to insist that every detail of liturgy be made completely comprehensible to them. All the same, it must surely be spiritually harmful to them to have the experience of going to church for years without ever understanding properly what is going on. Recent psychology has proved the profound influence that the religious experience of infancy and

---

a. Translation issued by the Vatican Press office. Latin text in *AAS* 66 (1974), pp. 30–46.
1. Cf. Sacred Congregation for the Clergy, *Directorium catechisticum generale,* n. 5: *AAS* 64 (1972), pp. 101–102.
2. Cf. Constitution on the Liturgy, n. 33.

early childhood has on the religious development of the individual.[3]

3. The Church, whose Master "took the little children in his arms and blessed them" (M. 10:16) cannot be content to leave such children to their own devices. The Second Vatican Council's Constitution on the Sacred Liturgy[4] spoke of the need to adapt the liturgy to various groups. Shortly after the Council, therefore, and especially at the First Synod of Bishops in Rome in 1967, very careful consideration was given to the question of helping children to take part in the liturgy. On that occasion the president of the Consilium for putting into effect the Constitution on the Liturgy said in his address that there could be no question "of composing a special rite, but rather of restricting, abbreviating or omitting certain elements, and of choosing suitable texts."[5]

4. The General Instruction in the 1969 revision of the Roman Missal set out in detail all the regulations concerning the celebration of the Eucharist with the people. Thereupon this Congregation, in response to repeated requests from all over the Catholic world, commenced work on preparing a special Directory for Children's Masses to serve as a kind of supplement to the General Instruction. Specialists in the field, men and women from nearly every country, cooperated in this work.

5. In this Directory, as in the General Instruction, certain adaptations are reserved to conferences of bishops or to individual bishops.[6]

When such conferences consider particular adaptations (which cannot be included in a general directory) necessary for children's Masses in their own territory, they should, in accordance with article 40 of the Constitution on the Liturgy, apply to the Holy See for permission to introduce them.

6. This Directory is concerned with children who have not yet reached the age of "pre-adolescence." It does not

3. Cf. Sacred Congregation for the Clergy, *Directorium catechisticum generale*, n. 78: *AAS* 64 (1972), pp. 146–147.
4. Cf. Constitution on the Liturgy, n. 38; cf. also Sacred Congregation for Divine Worship, Instruction *Actio pastoralis*, 15 May 1969: *AAS* 61 (1969), pp. 806–811.
5. Re the Liturgy in the First Synod of Bishops: *Notitiae* 3 (1967), p. 368.
6. Cf. below, nn. 19, 32, 33.

specifically mention physically or mentally handicapped children, for whom of course a greater degree of adaptation is often necessary.[7] All the same, the general principles which follow can also be made applicable to them.

7. Chapter One of this Directory (nn. 8-15) lays down the basic principles and discusses the various ways of helping children to understand the Mass. Chapter Two (nn. 16-19) deals briefly with adult Masses in which children also participate. Chapter three (nn. 20-54) deals more extensively with children's Masses in which some adults take part.

Chapter I

HELPING CHILDREN TO UNDERSTAND THE MASS LITURGY

8. A fully Christian life is unthinkable without participation in the celebration of the Eucharist. Hence the religious initiation of children should have the same object.[8] The Church, which baptizes infants and entrusts them with the gifts conferred by this sacrament, should make sure that they grow in communion with Christ and with the Christian community. The sign and pledge of this communion is to share in the eucharistic table, and children are either being prepared for this, or are being led to an ever-deeper understanding of what it means. Such liturgical and eucharistic formation must not be divorced from the child's general education as a human being and a Christian. It would be harmful if liturgical formation lacked this basis.

9. All those therefore who are concerned with education should work and plan together to ensure that the children, besides having some idea of God and the supernatural,

7. Cf. *Ordo Missae* with deaf and dumb children in Germany, 26 June 1970, approved and confirmed by this Congregation (Prot. n. 1546/70).
8. Cf. Constitution on the Liturgy, nn. 14, 19.

should also, in proportion to their years and degree of maturity as persons, have some experience of those human values which are involved in eucharistic celebration: e.g. acting together as a community, exchanging greetings, the capacity to listen, to forgive and to ask for forgiveness, the expression of gratitude, the experience of symbolic actions, conviviality, and festive celebration.[9]

The aim of eucharistic catechesis (see n. 12) will therefore be to cultivate these human values, so that the children's appreciation of Christian values and their celebration of the mystery of Christ will keep pace with their age and their psychological and social condition.[10]

10. The Christian family has the greatest part to play in teaching these human and Christian values.[11] Hence, even from the point of view of the liturgical formation of their children, it is very important to encourage the Christian education of parents and other educators.

In virtue of the obligation in conscience which they freely accepted at the baptism of their children, parents are bound to teach them step by step how to pray, by praying with them every day and encouraging them to pray by themselves.[12] Children who have been prepared in this way from their earliest years and who have had the opportunity of going to Mass with the family when they so wish, will readily begin to sing and pray in the liturgical assembly, and indeed will already be experiencing something of the meaning of the eucharistic mystery.

Parents of weak faith, but who nevertheless want their children to receive a Christian education, should at least be invited to communicate to their children those human values already mentioned, and to take part whenever they can in meetings for parents and the non-eucharistic celebrations that are organized for the children.

11. Moreover, the Christian communities to which the individual families belong or in which the children are living, have a duty towards the children baptized in their Church. A Christian community which bears witness to the gospel, lives out its fraternal charity, and actively celebrates

9. Cf. Sacred Congregation for the Clergy, *Directorium catechisticum generale*, n. 25: *AAS* 64 (1972), p. 114.
10. Cf. Declaration on Christian Education, n. 2.
11. Cf. ibid., n. 3.
12. Cf. Sacred Congregation for the Clergy, *Directorium catechisticum generale*, n. 78: *AAS* 64 (1972), p. 147.

the mysteries of Christ, is for the children that live there the best school of Christian and liturgical education.

Within a Christian community, sponsors or others involved and apostolic persons can be of great assistance in providing good catechetical instruction for the children of families which find it difficult to fulfil their role in Christian education.

Kindergartens, Catholic schools, and the various organizations for children are especially valuable in doing this kind of work.

12. Although the liturgy has an educative value of its own[13] even for children, it is important that the catechism classes given in schools and parishes include a catechesis on the Mass[14] with a view to encouraging a participation in it which is active, conscious and genuine.[15] Such catechesis must "obviously be geared to the age and intelligence of the children, and must be aimed at conveying through the principal rites and prayers the meaning of the Mass particularly as a sharing in the life of the Church."[16] This applies especially to the texts of the eucharistic prayer and to the acclamations through which the children take part in it.

The preparation of children for their First Communion deserves special consideration. It should be aimed not only at teaching them the truths of the faith concerning the Eucharist, but also at explaining how from now on they are going to be able to share the Eucharist actively with the people of God and have a share in the Lord's table and in the community of their fellow Christians. Prepared by Penance in proportion to their understandings, they are now going to be inserted fully into the body of Christ.

13. Celebrations of various kinds which help the children to understand some of the elements of liturgy (such as greeting, silence, community praise especially in song) have a great part to play in their liturgical formation and in preparing them for the liturgical life of the Church. Care must

13. Cf. Constitution on the Liturgy, n. 33.
14. Cf. Sacred Congregation of Rites, Instruction *Eucharisticum mysterium*, 25 May 1967, n. 14: *AAS* 59 (1967), p. 550.
15. Cf. Sacred Congregation for the Clergy, *Directorium catechisticum generale*, n. 25: *AAS* 64 (1972), p. 114.
16. Sacred Congregation of Rites, Instruction *Eucharisticum mysterium*, 25 May 1967, n. 14: *AAS* 59 (1967), p. 550; cf. also Sacred Congregation for the Clergy, *Directorium catechisticum generale*, n. 57: *AAS* 64 (1972), p. 131.

be taken, however, not to make celebrations of this sort excessively didactic in character.

14. In these celebrations more and more prominence should be given to the word of God according to the children's ability to understand. Indeed, as their spiritual capacity increases one could celebrate proper spiritual services with them, especially in Advent and Lent.[17] Such celebrations can do much to enhance their appreciation of the word of God.

15. Every liturgical and eucharistic instruction should always aim at making the daily life of the children conform more and more to the gospel. To say this is not to contradict anything that has been said above.

CHAPTER II

ADULT MASSES IN WHICH CHILDREN PARTICIPATE

16. In many places, especially on Sundays and feast days, parish Masses are celebrated in which quite a number of children participate together with a large number of adults. In such Masses the witness given by the adult faithful can have a great effect on the children, and the adults too can derive spiritual benefit from seeing for themselves the part which children have in the Christian community. To have children sharing in these Masses with their parents and other members of the family does much to foster a Christian spirit in these families.

Very small children[b] can be left in a separate room in the charge of parish helpers, for example, and brought in at the end of Mass for the blessing with the community.

---

17. Cf. Constitution on the Liturgy, n. 35, 4.
b. Sticklers for *verbal* accuracy and those who enjoy a quiet chuckle might like to know that a literal translation would be: "Infants who are unable or unwilling to take part in the Mass . . ." [Editor].

17. However, in Masses of this kind care must be taken not to allow the children to feel neglected because of their inability to participate in and understand what is being done and proclaimed in the celebration. At the very least some account must be taken of their presence, for example, by saying a special word to them at the beginning and at the end of the Mass and in some part of the homily.

Sometimes, perhaps, if the necessary facilities are available, it will be appropriate to have a special liturgy of the word and homily for the children in a separate place not too far distant from the main church. Then when the eucharistic liturgy begins they can be brought back to the place where in the meantime the adults have been celebrating their own liturgy of the word.

18. In these Masses it can be very useful to allocate certain duties to the children, for example, to bring forward the gifts, or to sing one or other of the chants of the Mass.

19. If there is a considerable amount of children present, arrangements should sometimes be made at these Masses to do even more to cater for their needs. The homily could be addressed to the children, but in such a way that the adults too can profit by it. Apart from the adaptations already permissible in the Order of Mass, one or the other of the special adaptations described below could be used, with the permission of the bishops, wherever children participate in adult Masses.

Chapter III

CHILDREN'S MASSES IN WHICH ONLY A FEW ADULTS PARTICIPATE

20. In addition to the Masses which children attend with their parents and other members of the family where this is possible—and it is not always possible—it is also recommended that Masses be celebrated with children only, especially on weekdays. At such Masses only a few adults will

be present. From the beginning of the reform of the liturgy it has been accepted by everyone that certain adaptations are necessary.[18]

These adaptations—the more general of them only—will be discussed below (nn. 38-54).

21. It must always be borne in mind that the eucharistic celebrations under discussion are intended to help the children along, so that they will be able to take part in adult Masses, especially those which the Christian community comes together to celebrate on Sundays.[19] Hence adaptations will be necessary on account of the age of the children, but this does not amount to composing rites which are altogether special[20] and which differ too much from the Order of Mass with the people. The various elements should always have the same thrust as that laid down in each instance in the General Instruction of the Roman Missal, even though for pastoral reasons one cannot always insist on absolute identity.

I. ROLES AND MINISTRIES IN THE CELEBRATION

22. In Masses celebrated with children the principles of active and conscious participation are if anything of even greater validity. Everything therefore must be done to increase and intensify this participation. As many children as possible must have a special part to play in the celebration: preparing the room and the altar (cf. n. 29), acting as cantors (cf. n. 24), singing in the choir, providing instrumental music (cf. n. 32), reading the lessons (cf. nn. 24 and 27), answering questions in the course of the homily (cf. n. 48), announcing the intentions of the bidding prayer, bringing the gifts to the altar, and doing other such things in accordance with local customs (cf. n. 34).

Some additions to the rite will sometimes prove useful in encouraging participation, e.g., the insertion of reasons for giving thanks before the priest begins the preface dialogue.

In all this it must be borne in mind that external acts are worthless and may even be harmful unless they help the children's internal participation. The sacred silence has its

18. Cf. n. 3 above.
19. Cf. Constitution on the Liturgy, nn. 42 and 106.
20. Cf. Rev. the Liturgy in the First Synod of Bishops: *Notitiae* 3 (1967), p. 368.

importance even in children's Masses (cf. n. 37). Great care must be taken not to let children forget that all forms of participation lead up to eucharistic communion, in which Christ's body and blood are received as spiritual nourishment.[22]

23. The priest who is celebrating Mass with children should be at pains to make the celebration a festive, fraternal and prayerful one.[23] This attitude on the part of the priest has a greater effect on the celebration than in Masses with adults. Everything depends on his personal preparation and on the way he conducts himself and addresses himself to the children.

He should give first consideration to the dignity, clarity and simplicity of his gesture. In speaking to the children he should express himself in a way which they can readily understand, but at the same time avoid forms of expression which are childish.

His *ad lib* instructions[23] should help the children to participate genuinely in the liturgy, and not merely didactic.

In order to get through to the children it will sometimes be useful for the priest to use his own words at the invitation to the act of penance, for example, or to the prayer over the gifts, the Lord's Prayer, the sign of peace, and communion.

24. Since the Eucharist is an act of the whole ecclesial community, the participation of some at least of the adults is desirable, so that they are not just spectators but actually pray the Mass with the children and give them every necessary help.

There is no reason why one of the adults should not preach a homily to the children after the gospel, especially if the priest has difficulty in adapting himself to the mentality of the children. This should be done with the consent of the parish priest or rector of the church and in accordance with the rules of the Sacred Congregation for the Clergy.

A diversity of ministerial roles should also be encouraged in children's Masses so that the celebration is seen to be a community one.[24] For example, lectors and cantors should be used, chosen either from among the children or the adults. A variety of voices will help to avoid tedium.

21. Cf. General Instruction of the Roman Missal, n. 56.
22. Cf. below, n. 37.
23. Cf. General Instruction of the Roman Missal, n. 11.
24. Cf. Constitution on the Liturgy, n. 28.

II. THE PLACE AND TIME OF CELEBRATION

25. The church is the primary place for a eucharistic celebration with children, and, if possible, a space within it should be carefully selected to suit the number of participants and the use they will need to make of it if their liturgy is to be lively and adapted to their age.

If the church does not meet these requirements, it will sometimes be advisable to celebrate a children's Mass elsewhere, but the place chosen should be a suitable one, worthy of the dignity of the Mass.[25]

26. The time chosen for a children's Mass should be one which best suits the circumstances in which they are living, namely, a time when they will be most receptive to the word of God and best able to celebrate the Eucharist.

27. Weekday Masses with children (for example in boarding schools) will certainly be more profitable and less open to the risk of boredom if they do not occur every day. Moreover, they can be better prepared if there is a longer interval of time between the celebrations.

Sometimes it is preferable to have community prayer to which the children can make their own spontaneous contribution, or a meditation in common, or a celebration of the word of God which continues the previous celebration of the Eucharist and prepares the children to participate more deeply in those which are to follow.

28. Attentive and conscious participation will be very difficult if too many children are celebrating the Eucharist at one time. If possible they should be split into a number of groups, not strictly in accordance with their age, but with regard to their progress in religious formation and their degree of catechetical instruction.

It would be best to invite these groups to take part in the sacrifice of the Mass on different days of the Week.

III. PREPARING THE CELEBRATION

29. Every eucharistic celebration with children should be carefully prepared well beforehand, especially with regard to the prayers, chants, readings, and bidding prayer. This preparation should be done in consultation with the adults and the children who are to exercise a special ministry in these Masses. If possible some of the children should have a part

25. Cf. General Instruction of the Roman Missal, n. 253.

in preparing and decorating the place of celebration and in preparing the chalice, paten and cruets. Without sacrificing interior participation, such acts can help to foster a sense of community celebration.

IV. SINGING AND MUSIC

30. Singing must be regarded as an asset to any celebration, and in view of the fondness children have for music, it is especially to be recommended in the celebration of children's Masses.[26] Attention must be given to the type of music characteristic of different countries and to the musical capabilities of the children present.

Where possible the acclamations, especially those which belong to the eucharistic prayer, should be sung rather than said.

31. To make it easier for the children to participate in the singing of the Gloria, Credo, Sanctus and Agnus Dei, popular adaptations of these texts with appropriate musical settings can be authorized by the competent authority, even though they do not adhere strictly to the liturgical text.[27]

32. In children's Masses, too, "the use of musical instruments can be very valuable,"[28] especially when played by the children themselves. They help to sustain the singing, evoke meditative prayer, and are particularly expressive of festive joy and the praise of God.

Care must always be taken not to allow the music to overshadow the singing, or to become a distraction rather than an edification to the children. It must also be confined to those intervals in the Mass when music is in place.

With these safeguards, and with due care and discretion, recorded music can also be used in children's Masses in accordance with the rules laid down by episcopal conferences.

V. GESTURE

33. Having regard to the nature of the liturgy as an action of the whole man, and with particular reference to the psychology of children, participation through gesture and bodily attitude is to be highly recommended in children's

---

26. Cf. ibid., n. 19.
27. Cf. Sacred Congregation of Rites, Instruction *Musicam sacram*, 5 March 1967, n. 55: *AAS* 59 (1967), p. 316.
28. Ibid., n. 62: *AAS* 59 (1967), p. 318.

Masses. One should keep in mind the age of the children and the dictates of local custom. Much depends not only on the gestures of the priest[29] but also on the behavior of the whole group.

Where, in accordance with the General Instruction in the Roman Missal, a particular conference of bishops adapts the gestures of the Mass to suit the mentality of the people,[30] it should also consider the special case of children, or even confine such adaptations to children's Masses only.

34. Among the actions which come under the heading of gestures, special mention should be made of processions and other actions involving physical movement.

An entrance procession of children with the priest can help them to realize that they are now forming themselves into a community.[31] The participation of at least some of the children in the gospel procession will make the presence of Christ proclaiming the word to his people more real to them. A procession of children with the chalice and the gifts more clearly expresses the purpose and meaning of the preparation of the gifts. An orderly communion procession is of great help in fostering the devotion of the children.

VI. VISUAL AIDS

35. The liturgy of the Mass contains in itself many visual elements which are of great importance to children. This applies especially to those visual elements particular to the various liturgical seasons: the adoration of the cross, the paschal candle, the lights carried on the feast of the Presentation of the Lord, and the various liturgical colors and ornaments.

Besides these visual elements which pertain to the actual celebration and the place of celebration, others may be introduced from time to time which will allow the children to see with their own eyes the wonderful works of God in creation and redemption, and their prayer will be assisted by what they see. Liturgy must never be presented as something arid and purely cerebral.

36. For the same reason the use of pictures done by the

---

29. Cf. above, n. 23.
30. Cf. General Instruction of the Roman Missal, n. 21.
31. Cf. ibid., n. 24.

children themselves can be of value—pictures, for example, illustrating the homily, the bidding prayer, or themes for prayer.

VII. SILENCE

37. "The silence is a part of the celebration and must be observed at the times indicated."[32] This is just as true of children's Masses, otherwise too much emphasis will be laid on external actions. Even children in their own small way are capable of meditative prayer. They will, of course, need a helping hand. At different times in the Mass (for example, after the Communion[33] or even after the homily) they will learn to recollect themselves, make a short meditation, or simply praise God and pray to him in their hearts.[34]

The liturical texts must be recited intelligibly, without haste, and with appropriate pauses. Even greater care is needed here than in adult Masses.

VIII. THE PARTS OF THE MASS

38. The general structure of the Mass which "consists of two parts, namely, the liturgy of the word and the eucharistic liturgy with the opening and concluding rites"[35] must always remain unchanged. However, in order that children, in their own way and in accordance with the laws of child psychology, may genuinely experience "the mystery of faith . . . through the rites and prayers,"[36] the undermentioned adaptations in the different parts of the celebration would seem to be necessary.

39. To prevent children's Masses from becoming altogether too different from adult Masses,[57] there are certain rites and texts which should never be adapted, such as "the acclamation and responses of the faithful to the priest's greetings,"[38] the Lord's prayer, and the trinitarian formula which concludes the priest's blessing at the end of Mass. The Apostles' Creed may be used (see n. 49), but the chil-

32. Ibid., n. 23.
33. Cf. Sacred Congregation of Rites, Instruction *Eucharisticum Mysterium,* 25 May 1967, n. 38: *AAS* 59 (1967), p. 562.
34. Cf. General Instruction of the Roman Missal, n. 23.
35. Ibid., n. 8.
36. Constitution on the Liturgy, n. 48.
37. Cf. above, n. 21.
38. General Instruction of the Roman Missal, n. 15.

dren should also gradually become acquainted with the Nicene Creed.

A. The Opening Rite

40. Since the opening rite of the Mass is intended "to make the assembled faithful into a community ready to listen to the word of God and to celebrate the Eucharist worthily,"[39] thought must be given to arousing this same disposition in the children. It must not be jeopardized by an excess of rites occurring at this point.

So it is sometimes permissible to omit one or other of the elements of the opening rite and perhaps to amplify some other element. There should always be at least one element of introduction ending with the opening prayer. In choosing particular elements, the aim should be to include each of them in turn. None should be consistently omitted.

B. The Reading and Explanation of the Word of God

41. Since the scripture readings constitute "the main part of the liturgy of the word,"[40] a children's Mass should never be without its Bible reading.

42. As to the number of readings on Sunday and feast-days, the decisions of the episcopal conferences should be adhered to. If the two or three readings appointed for Sundays or feasts can only be understood with difficulty by the children, then it is allowable to read only one or two of them. The gospel reading, however, should never be omitted.

43. If all the readings assigned to a particular day seem beyond the understanding of the children, a reading or readings may be chosen from the lectionary of the Roman Missal or straight from the Bible, bearing in mind the liturgical season. Episcopal conferences are encouraged to compile their own lectionaries for children's Masses.

Should it seem necessary for the sake of the understanding of the children to omit an occasional verse in the Bible reading, this should be done with caution so as not "to mutilate the sense of the passage or, to say, the stylistic nuances of the scripture,"[41]

39. Ibid., n. 24.
40. Ibid., n. 28.
41. M.R. Lectionary I, *De Ord. lectionum Missae, Praenotanda generalia*, n. 7d.

44. In choosing the readings the criterion should be quality rather than quantity. A shorter scripture reading is not always or necessarily easier for a child to understand than a longer one. All depends on the spiritual value it can have for the children.

45. Paraphrases of scripture should be avoided, since it is in the actual biblical text that "God is speaking to his people and Christ himself is present by his word in the midst of the faithful."[42] However, it is commendable to use versions which, perhaps, exist already and which the competent authority has sanctioned for catechetical purposes.

46. Between the readings psalm verses should be sung carefully selected to suit the children's understanding, or a psalm-type hymn, or an "Alleluia" with a simple versicle. A prayerful silence may sometimes take the place of a chant.

If only one reading is chosen, a hymn can be sung after the homily.

47. So that the children may read the Bible for themselves and appreciate more and more the dignity of the word of God, great store must be set on all those elements which help them to understand the readings.

Among these are the introductions to the readings[43] which help the children to listen to them well and fruitfully, either by explaining the context or introducing the actual text. In interpreting or illustrating the scripture readings in the Mass on a saint's day, something about the life of a saint can be mentioned not only in the homily, but also in the remarks before the Bible readings.

It can be useful for the children to take different parts in the reading of a scriptural passage where the text suggests this kind of treatment, as is in fact laid down for the reading of the Lord's Passion in Holy Week.

48. In all children's Masses a homily explaining the word of God is very important. It can sometimes take the form of a dialogue with the children, unless it is preferred that they listen in silence.

49. If the Creed occurs at the end of the liturgy of the word, the Apostles' Creed can be used since they are familiar with it in their catechism classes.

---

42. General Instruction of the Roman Missal, n. 33.
43. Ibid., n. 11.

C. The Presidential Prayers

50. When reciting the presidential prayers the priest must maintain contact with the children. He is therefore permitted to choose from the Roman Missal texts which are better suited to their needs. His choice, however, should take into account the liturgical season.

51. Sometimes the principle of selection will not meet the case, as the prayers were composed for adults, and children are not always able to recognize in them an expression of their own life and religious experience.[44] In that case the text of the Roman Missal prayers may be adapted to their needs, but the purpose and substance of these prayers should be preserved, and one should avoid anything that is alien to the literary genre of a presidential prayer, such as moral exhortation or excessively childish forms of expression.

52. In celebrating the Eucharist with children the most important thing will be the eucharistic prayer, the climax of the whole celebration.[45] Much will depend on the way the priest says this prayer[46] and the children participate in it by their attention and their acclamations.

The very attitude of mind demanded in this central point of the celebration, the tranquility and reverence with which everything is done, should make the children supremely aware of the real presence of Christ on the altar under the species of bread and wine, aware too of the offering of Christ and the giving of thanks through him, with him, and in him, and the offering of the whole Church which is then taking place as with Christ the faithful offer themselves and their life to the eternal Father in the Holy Spirit.

The four eucharistic prayers approved by the supreme authority for Masses with adults and authorized for liturgical use must be used for the time being, that is, until the Holy See makes other provisions for children's Masses.

D. The Rites Before Communion

53. After the eucharistic prayer must always follow the Lord's Prayer, the breaking of the bread, and the invitation

44. Consilium for Implementing the Constitution on the Liturgy, *Instruction sur la traduction des textes liturgiques pour la celebration avec le peuple,* 25 January 1969, n. 20: *Notitiae* 5 (1969), p. 7.
45. General Instruction of the Roman Missal, n. 54.
46. Cf. above, nn. 23 and 37.

to Communion,[47] since these elements are of supreme importance in the structure of this part of the Mass.

E. The Communion and the Rites Which Follow It

54. Everything must be done to ensure that children who have made their First Communion and who are rightly disposed approach the holy table in a tranquil and recollected frame of mind, so as to share fully in the eucharistic mystery. If possible, a Communion chant that is suitable for children should be sung during the procession.[48]

It is very important in children's Masses to say a few words before the final blessing.[49] Before being sent away children need a very brief reminder and practical application of what they have heard. Here is a special opportunity of making clear the connection between liturgy and life.

Now and again, to mark the liturgical season or the different stages in the life of the children, the priest should use one of the ampler forms of the blessing, always retaining the final trinitarian formula with the sign of the cross.[50]

55. Everything in this Directory is intended to help children to meet Christ with joy in the celebration of the Eucharist and to stand by him in the Father's presence.[51] Formed by a conscious and active participation in the eucharistic sacrifice and meal, they must daily learn to become better witnesses to Christ among their friends and peers, at home and outside the home, by living the faith "which operates through charity" (Gal. 5:6).

47. Cf. above, n. 23.
48. Cf. Sacred Congregation of Rites, Instruction *Musicam sacram*, 5 March 1967, n. 32: *AAS* 59 (1967), p. 309.
49. Cf. General Instruction of the Roman Missal, n. 11.
50. Cf. above, n. 39.
51. Cf. Roman Missal, Eucharistic Prayer II.

22

DECLARATION ON THE MEANING OF TRANSLATIONS OF SACRAMENTAL FORMULAE[a]

S.C.D.F., *Insauratio Liturgica*, 25 January, 1974

The liturgical reform which has been carried out in accordance with the Constitution of the Second Vatican Council has made certain changes in the essential formulae of the sacramental rites. These new expressions, like the other ones, have had to be translated into modern languages in such a way that the original sense finds expression

a. Translated by A.F. from the Latin text in *L'Osservatore Romano*, 30 October 1974. Some indication of the nature of the "difficulties" referred to in this declaration may be gleaned from a letter sent to the presidents of episcopal conferences by Cardinal Jean Villot, Secretary of State, and Archbishop A. Bugnini, Secretary of the Congregation for Divine Worship. The letter is dated 25 October 1973, and is published in *Notitiae*, January 1974 (No. 80), pp. 37–38. The letter would seem to acknowledge that it is not always possible fully to convey the sense of an original in translation. It does not quote the famous Italian adage, *traduttore traditore* (the translator is a traitor), but it does add the qualification, *quantum fieri poterit* (As far as possible), to its insistence that a translation of a sacramental formula must be faithful to the original. It also acknowledges a special difficulty in vetting translations into one of the languages less known in Europe—the languages other than English, French, German, Spanish, Dutch, Italian and Portuguese. It asks episcopal conferences seeking approval of translations into such languages to submit accurate explanations of the force and meaning of each word, using one of the languages listed above for this purpose. Lastly, it acknowledges that translations cannot always be literal: "If formulae pertaining to the essence of the sacraments are not translated literally, the reasons which make departure from the letter desirable must be explained, taking the Latin into account."
The letter explains that translations of the essential formulae of the sacraments are submitted to the Holy Father himself for approval and a note appended in *Notitiae (loc. cit)* explains that the experience of the past few years had led the Congregation for Divine Worship to single out the sacramental formulae for special care, they being the culmination of all sacramental celebrations.

in the idiom proper to each language. This has given rise to certain difficulties, which have come to light now that the translations have been sent by episcopal conferences to the Holy See for approval. In these circumstances, the Sacred Congregation for the Doctrine of the Faith again calls attention to the necessity that the essential formulae of the sacramental rites render faithfully the original sense of the Latin "typical text." With that in mind it declares:

When a vernacular translation of a sacramental formula is submitted to the Holy See for approval, it examines it carefully. When it is satisfied that it expresses the meaning intended by the Church, it approves and confirms it, stipulating, however, that it must be understood in accordance with the mind of the Church as expressed in the original Latin text.

23

LETTER TO BISHOPS ON THE MINIMUM REPERTOIRE OF PLAIN CHANT[a]

S.C.D.W., April, 1974

Eminence, Excellency,

Our congregation has prepared a booklet entitled, *Jubilate Deo,* which contains a minimum selection of sacred chants. This was done in response to a desire which the Holy Father had frequently expressed, that all the faithful should know at least some Latin Gregorian chants, such as, for example, the *Gloria,* the *Credo,* the *Sanctus* and the *Agnus Dei.*[1]

It gives me great pleasure to send you a copy of it, as a personal gift from His Holiness, Pope Paul VI. May I take this opportunity of recommending to your pastoral solicitude this new initiative, whose purpose is to facilitate the observance of the recommendation of the Second Vatican Council: ". . . steps must be taken to ensure that the faithful are able to say or chant together in Latin those parts of the ordinary of the Mass which pertain to them.[2]

In effect, when the faithful gather together for prayer they manifest at once the diversity of a people drawn "from every tribe, language and nation" (Ap. 5:9) and its unity in faith and charity. Their diversity is manifested in the

a. The following is a translation of a letter which was sent to all bishops and heads of religious orders, together with a book of Latin chants, *Jubilate Deo.* The letter was published in Latin in the April, 1974, issue of *Notitiae,* (pages 123–126) and in French in *La Documentation Catholique,* 2 June 1974. Our translation was made from the French (said by D.C. to be the original) by A.F.
1. See Address of Pope Paul VI at general audience, 22 August, 1973; address of Pope Paul VI to the 'Consociatio Internationalis Musicae Sacrae', 12 October 1973; Letter of Cardinal Jean Villot to the national assembly of the Italian Association of St. Cecilia, 30 September, 1973.
2. Constitution on the Liturgy, no. 54.

present multiplicity of liturgical languages and in the vernacular chants which, in the context of one shared faith, give expression to each people's religious sentiment in music drawn from its culture and traditions. On the other hand, their unity finds particularly apt and even sensible expression through the use of Latin Gregorian chant. Down the centuries, Gregorian chant has accompanied liturgical celebrations in the Roman rite, has nourished men's faith and has fostered their piety, while in the process achieving an artistic perfection which the Church rightly considers a patrimony of inestimable value and which the Council recognized as "the chant especially suited to the Roman liturgy."[3]

One of the objectives of the liturgical reform is to promote community singing in assemblies of the faithful, so that they might the better express the festive, communal and fraternal character of liturgical celebrations. In effect, "the liturgical action becomes more dignified when it is accompanied by chant, when each minister fulfils his own role and the faithful also take part.[4]

Those who are charged with responsibility for the liturgical reform are particularly anxious to achieve this difficult objective. To that end, the Sacred Congregation for Divine Worship appeals once again, as they have often done in the past, for the proper development of singing by the faithful.

VERNACULAR SINGING

Where vernacular singing is concerned, the liturgical reform offers "a challenge to the creativity and the pastoral zeal of every local church."[5] Poets and musicians are therefore to be encouraged to put their talents at the service of such a cause, so that a popular chant may emerge which is truly artistic, is worthy of the praise of God, of the liturgical action of which it forms part and of the faith which it expresses. The liturgical reform has opened up new perspectives for sacred music and for chant. "One hopes for a new flowering of the art of religious music in our time. Since the vernacular is admitted to worship in every

3. Ibid., no 116.
4. Instruction, *Musicam Sacram*, no. 5.
5. Ibid., no. 54; Address of Pope Paul to members of the Italian Association of St. Cecilia, 23 September, 1972.

country it ought not to be denied the beauty and the power of expression of religious music and appropriate chant.[6]

GREGORIAN CHANT

At the same time, the liturgical reform does not and indeed cannot deny the past. Rather does it "preserve and foster it with the greatest care."[7] It cultivates and transmits all that is in it of high religious, cultural and artistic worth and especially those elements which can express even externally the unity of believers.

This minimum repertoire of Gregorian chant has been prepared with that purpose in mind: to make it easier for Christians to achieve unity and spiritual harmony with their brothers and with the living tradition of the past. Hence it is that those who are trying to improve the quality of congregational singing cannot refuse to Gregorian chant the place which is due to it. And this becomes all the more imperative as we approach the Holy Year of 1975, during which the faithful of different languages, nations and origins, will find themselves side by side for the common celebration of the Lord.

Those who because of their special vocation in the Church need to have a deeper knowledge of sacred music ought to be particularly careful to observe a proper balance between popular chant and Gregorian chant. For this reason the Holy Father recommended that "Gregorian chant be preserved and be sung in monasteries, other religious houses and seminaries, as a special form of chanted prayer and as something of high cultural and pedagogic value."[8]

Further, the study and the performance of Gregorian chant remain "because of its special characteristics, a very useful foundation for the cultivation of sacred music."[9]

In presenting the Holy Father's gift to you, may I at the same time remind you of the desire which he has often expressed that the Conciliar constitution on the liturgy be increasingly better implemented. Would you therefore, in collaboration with the competent diocesan and national agencies for the liturgy, sacred music and catechetics, decide on

6. Address of Pope Paul to the 'Consociatio Internationalis Musicae Sacrae', 12 October 1973.
7. Constitution on the Liturgy, no. 114.
8. Letter of Cardinal Jean Villot to the National Assembly of the Italian Association of St. Cecilia, 30 September 1973.
9. Instruction, *Musicam Sacram*, no. 52.

the best ways of teaching the faithful the Latin chants of *Jubilate Deo* and of having them sing them, and also of promoting the preservation and execution of Gregorian chant in the communities mentioned above. You will thus be performing a new service for the Church in the domain of liturgical renewal.

The contents of this booklet may be reproduced free of charge. To help people understand these texts, one may add the normal vernacular translation.

24

APOSTOLIC LETTER CONCERNING MASS STIPENDS[a]

Paul VI, *Firma in Traditione*, 15 June, 1974

It is a long-established tradition in the Church that the faithful, desiring in a religious and ecclesial spirit to participate more intimately in the Eucharistic Sacrifice, add to it a form of sacrifice of their own by which they contribute in a particular way to the needs of the Church and especially to the sustenance of its ministers. This is in accord with the spirit of the Lord's saying: "The laborer is worthy of his hire," which the Apostle Paul recalls in the first letter to Timothy (5:18) and in the first letter to the Corinthians (9:7–14).

This practice by which the faithful unite themselves more closely with Christ offering himself as a victim, thus deriving more abundant fruit from the sacrifice, has not merely been approved but has been positively encouraged by the Church. It is regarded as a sign of the union of the baptized person with Christ and of the faithful with the priest who exercises his ministry for their good.

In order that this idea should be fully preserved while being protected from possible abuse, appropriate regulations have been laid down in the past. Their purpose is, further, to ensure that the worship which the faithful desire to offer generously to God should be conducted with due reverence and magnanimity.

It sometimes happens, however, that the passage of time and changes in human society render morally impossible, and consequently inequitable, the complete fulfilment of obligations which had been accepted with due consideration. For this reason the Church finds it necessary to recon-

a. Text from the English-language *L'Osservatore Romano,* 11 July 1974. The footnotes are by A.F.

sider such obligations while endeavoring to harmonize its own interests and the rights of donors.

With a view, especially, to determining in a uniform manner the norms of regulating Mass stipends—a grave and delicate matter—we issued a decree which was promulgated by the Secretariat of State, 29 November 1971: *AAS* 63 (1971), p. 841, whereby we reserved to ourself for the time being all questions referring to petitions for reductions, condonations, commutations of Mass stipends. All faculties conceded to any other person and in whatever manner were by this decree revoked as from 1 February 1972.

Since, however, the purposes for which this restriction was introduced have now been substantially achieved, we consider that it need no longer be maintained.

In order that an appropriate disposition in this matter should be established on new grounds and to preclude its obstruction by inexact interpretations based on what was lawful in the past, it has seemed good to revoke completely all former faculties.

At the same time, in order to provide in some measure for the problems which sometimes confront our brethren in the episcopate and keeping in mind the benefits which have resulted from the use of faculties granted to them by the Apostolic Letters *Pastorale Munus*: *AAS* 56 (1964), pp. 5–12, and *De Episcoporum Muneribus*: *AAS* 58 (1966), pp. 467–472, given motu proprio, we have deemed it fitting to grant certain faculties to those who share with us the Church's pastoral ministry.

Therefore, after mature reflection, from the plentitude of our apostolic power and motu proprio we declare and decree the following for the entire Church:

1. From 1 July 1974 the above-mentioned reservation in the notification of the Secretariat of State of 29 November 1971 ceases. For the same date the Sacred Congregations of the Roman Curia may resume their competence in these matters, observing, however, the new and more precise norms which have been communicated to them. Petitions, therefore, concerning these matters should henceforth be addressed to them.[b]

2. All previous faculties relating to Mass stipends, in whatever manner granted or sought, are definitively withdrawn as from the same date. There no longer exist, there-

b. Six Roman Congregations are empowered to deal, in different contexts, with problems arising with regard to stipends.

fore, faculties granted to any person, physical or moral, by us or by any of our predecessors, even if granted *vivae vocis oraculo,* or by the Roman Curia, or by any other authority, whether by way of privilege, indult, dispensation or in any other way, not excepting particular law. The same holds true for faculties obtained by way of communication or custom, including particular, centenary, and immemorial customs, or by way of prescription or in any other manner.

By reason of this revocation only the following faculties are henceforth valid:

(a) Faculties granted to the Sacred Congregations of the Roman Curia mentioned in n. 1 above;

(b) Faculties in the Motu Proprio *Pastorale Munus* and in the Lists of Faculties customarily given to local ordinaries and papal legates;

(c) New faculties contained in this Apostolic Letter, given motu proprio and mentioned here in n. 3.

3. We grant to all those mentioned in the Motu Proprio *Pastorale Munus* and in accordance with the conditions there stated the following faculties:

(a) The faculty of allowing priests who say two or three Masses on the same day in the diocese either to receive a stipend for each Mass, the stipends being allocated for purposes designated by the diocesan bishop, or to apply the Masses for intentions for which it would otherwise be necessary to seek a condonation or even only a reduction. This faculty does not apply to the concelebrated binations treated of in the Declaration of the Sacred Congregation for Divine Worship issued on 7 August 1972, n. 3b: *AAS* 64 (1972), pp. 561–563. Acceptance of a stipend for these Masses under any title is forbidden.

(b) The faculty of reducing in proportion to diminution of income[c] the obligation of Cathedral and Collegiate Chapters of offering Mass daily for benefactors. But at least one conventual Mass for benefactors must be offered each month.

(c) The faculty of transferring for a fitting reason[d] the

---

c. Diminution of income through inflation. Many such bequests for Masses are very ancient and the annual interest on them is of very little value in today's money. It is certain that the benefactors would not have wanted to saddle their beneficiaries with an onerous burden in return for derisory sums.

d. For example change of population, so that an old church has to be vacated; shortage of priests.

obligation of offering Masses to days, churches, altars other than those designated in the original foundation. These norms come into force on 1 July 1974.

We declare that the prescription of this Apostolic Letter, promulgated motu proprio, shall be strictly observed notwithstanding anything to the contrary, even though it be worthy of special mention.

25

NOTE ON THE OBLIGATION TO USE THE NEW ROMAN MISSAL

S.C.D.W., *Conferentiarum Episcopalium*[a], 28 October, 1974

This sacred congregation, in a Note published on 14 June, 1971, and approved by the Supreme Pontiff, defined the role of episcopal conferences in the preparation of vernacular versions of liturgical books and set out the regulations for obtaining their confirmation by the Holy See. Gradually, the employment of the vernacular versions spread everywhere to such an extent that, enough time having elapsed, it is clear that the work is almost complete.

With regard to the Roman Missal: when an episcopal conference has determined that a vernacular version of the Roman Missal—or of a part of it, such as the Order of the Mass—must be used in its territory, from then on Mass may not be celebrated, whether in Latin or in the vernacular, save according to the rite of the Roman Missal promulgated by the authority of Paul VI on 7 April, 1969.

With regard to the regulations issued by this sacred congregation in favor of priests who, on account of advanced years or infirm health, find it difficult to use the new Order of the Roman Missal or the Mass Lectionary: it is clear that an ordinary may grant permission to use, in whole or in part, the 1962 edition of the Roman Missal, with the changes introduced by the Decrees of 1965 and 1967.[b] But

a. Translated by A.F. from the Latin text in *Notitiae,* Nov. 1974, p. 353.
b. The Order of Mass and the rite to be observed in the celebration of Mass: *Ordo missae et ritus servandus in celebratione Missae* was published on 27 Jan. 1965. It incorporated the changes introduced in the Mass by the First General Instruction on the Implementation of the Constitution on the Sacred Liturgy, *Inter oecumenici.* "Changes to be made in the Order of the Mass: *Variationes in ordinem missae inducendae,*" was published on 18 May 1967. It added the changes introduced in the Mass by the Second General Instruction, *Tres abhinc annos.*

this permission can only be granted for Masses celebrated without a congregation. Ordinaries may not grant it for Masses celebrated with a congregation. Ordinaries, both religious and local, should rather endeavor to secure the acceptance of the Order of the Mass of the new Roman Missal by priests and laity. They should see to it that priests and laity, by dint of greater effort and with greater reverence comprehend the treasures of divine wisdom and of liturgical and pastoral teaching which it contains. What has been said does not apply to officially recognized non-Roman rites, but it does hold against any pretext of even an immemorial custom.

26

DECREE ON THE MEANS OF SOCIAL COMMUNICATION[a]

Vatican II, *Inter Mirifica*, 4 December, 1963

1. Man's genius has with God's help produced marvellous technical inventions from creation, especially in our times. The Church, our mother, is particularly interested in those which directly touch man's spirit and which have opened up new avenues of easy communication of all kinds of news, of ideas and orientations. Chief among them are those means of communication which of their nature can reach and influence not merely single individuals but the very masses and even the whole of human society. These are the press, the cinema, radio, television and others of a like nature. These can rightly be called "the means of social communication."

a. Translated by A.F. Useful guidance was provided by the Italian version in *Il Concilio Vaticano II* (Edizioni Dehoniane, Bologna, Italy) and by the French version by the late Father Emile Gabel, editor of *La Croix*, Paris, who had an expert knowledge of the decree *(Concile Oecumenique Vatican II) Documents Conciliares,* Editions du Centurion, Paris.) There is a special problem about the translation of parts of this decree, as with parts of *The Church in the Modern World*. It concerns the presence of modern non-theological ideas and terms for which Latin words or phrases have had to be coined or assembled. When a new word or phrase finds its way into a living language, usage is the main determinant of its meaning, "usage" being another way of saying that people use a particular phrase or word and give it a particular meaning. Etymology may play a part in this, but not necessarily, and its role is always subordinate to usage. It will not do the trick on its own. Etymologically, for example, there is no reason why "disc-jockey," "boycott," "movie," "star," should mean what they do. It was usage which decided this. What has happened, one presumes, in the case of certain Latin renderings of modern words and ideas in this decree, is that an expert or group of experts decided, when the decree was being put into Latin or earlier, that on etymological grounds these modern ideas and terms were to be rendered into Latin in a particular way. But in the absence of usage by a community sufficient to fix these meanings, the process can misfire. Thus, in the first paragraph of the decree, the Latin word *praecepta* is coupled with

2. The Church, our mother, knows that if these media are properly used they can be of considerable benefit to mankind. They contribute greatly to the enlargement and enrichment of men's minds and to the propagation and consolidation of the kingdom of God. But the Church also knows that man can use them in ways that are contrary to the Creator's design and damaging to himself. Indeed, she grieves with a mother's sorrow at the harm all too often inflicted on society by their misuse.

This Sacred Synod shares the solicitude of popes and bishops in a matter of such importance and feels that it is its duty to treat of the main problems posed by the means of social communication.

CHAPTER I

3. The Catholic Church was founded by Christ our Lord to bring salvation to all men. It feels obliged, therefore, to preach the gospel. In the same way, it believes that its task involves employing the means of social communication to

---

two other Latin words meaning "news" and "ideas" respectively. All three of them, the decree tells us, come to us via the press, radio, television, etc. But three different translations of the Latin—i.e. English, French and Italian—give respectively three different meanings to the word *praecepta*: "directives" (English—Abbott); *"insegnamenti"* (Italian—Dehoniane, meaning "teachings") and *"orientations"* (French—Gabel—but we also use it in English, meaning "directions" or "developments," e.g. in thought, in art, in culture). Any of the three can be justified on etymological grounds and, in the absence of the guidance provided by usage, there are no other grounds on which one can argue, except one's subjective feeling for what makes most sense. This is the way the translator settled the matter. The Latin title of the decree is: *Decretum de instrumentis communicationis socialis*. We have preferred to translate it as decree on the *means* of social communication, rather than *instruments* of social communication. The meaning may be the same, but the word "means" fits better into English usage. The word used as an alternative to *instrumentum* in the decree is *medium*, or its plural *media*. Whenever either of these two words *instrumentum* or *medium* is used on its own in the decree, I have translated them "media" or "medium." I felt that "means" on its own did not feel right, while the same applied to "media of social communication" or "instruments of social communication."

announce the good news of salvation and to teach men how to use them properly.

It is the Church's birthright to use and own any of these media which are necessary or useful for the formation of Christians and for pastoral activity. Pastors of souls have the task of instructing and directing the faithful how to use these media in a way that will ensure their own salvation and perfection and that of all mankind.

For the rest, it will be principally for laymen to animate these media with a Christian and human spirit and to ensure that they live up to humanity's hopes for them, in accordance with God's design.

4. If the media are to be correctly employed, it is essential that all who use them know the principles of the moral order and apply them faithfully in this domain. They should take into account, first of all, the subject-matter, or content, which each medium communicates in its own way. They should also take account of the circumstances in which the content is communicated—the purpose, that is to say, the people, the place, the time, etc. The circumstances can modify and even totally alter the morality of a production. In this regard, particular importance may attach to the manner in which any given medium achieves its effect. Its impact may be such that people, especially if they are insufficiently prepared, will only with difficulty advert to it, control it, or, if need be, reject it.

5. It is essential that all those involved should form a correct conscience on the use of the media, especially with regard to certain issues which are particularly controversial today.

The first of these issues is information, or the search for news and its publication. Because of the progress of modern society and the increasing interdependence of its members on one another, it is obvious that information is very useful and, for the most part, essential. If news or facts and happenings is communicated publicly and without delay, every individual will have permanent access to sufficient information and thus will be enabled to contribute effectively to the common good. Further, all of them will more easily be able to contribute in unison to the prosperity and the progress of society as a whole.

There exists therefore in human society a right to information on the subjects that are of concern to men either as individuals or as members of society, according to each man's circumstances. The proper exercise of this right demands that the content of the communication be true and—within the limits set by justice and charity—complete. Further, it should be communicated honestly and properly. This means that in the gathering and in the publication of news the moral law and the legitimate rights and dignity of man should be upheld. All knowledge is not profitable, but on the other hand "love builds" (1 Cor. 8:1).

6. The second question bears on the relation between the rights of art—to use a current expression—and the moral law. The controversies to which this problem increasingly gives rise frequently trace their origin to an erroneous understanding either of ethics or of esthetics. The Council proclaims that all must accept the absolute primacy of the objective moral order. It alone is superior to and is capable of harmonizing all forms of human activity, not excepting art, no matter how noble in themselves. Only the moral order touches man in the totality of his being as God's rational creature, called to a supernatural destiny. If the moral order is fully and faithfully observed, it leads man to full perfection and happiness.

7. Lastly, the chronicling, the description or the representation of moral evil can, with the help of the means of social communication and with suitable dramatization, lead to a deeper knowledge and analysis of man and to a manifestation of the true and the good in all their splendor. If, however, this is to be more profitable than harmful to souls, the moral law must be rigorously observed, especially when dealing with matters deserving of respect or with matters that lead all too easily to base desires in man wounded by original sin.

8. Public opinion exercises enormous influence nowadays over the lives, private or public, of all citizens, no matter what their walk in life. It is therefore necessary that all members of society meet the demands of justice and charity in this domain. They should help, through the means of social communication, in the formation and diffusion of sound public opinion.

9. Those who receive the means of social communication —readers, viewers, audiences—do so of their own free choice. Special obligations rest on them in consequence. A properly motivated selectivity would be wholly in favor of whatever excels in virtue, culture and art. Likewise, it would avoid whatever might be a cause or occasion of spir-

itual harm to the recipients or might be a source of danger to others through bad example; it would avoid whatever might hinder the communication of the good and facilitate the communication of what is evil. This last usually occurs when financial help is given to those who exploit the media solely for profit.

If they are to obey the moral law, those who use the media ought to keep themselves informed in good time about assessments arrived at by the authorities with competence in this sphere and to conform to them as a right conscience would dictate. They should take appropriate steps to direct and form their consciences so that they may more readily resist less wholesome influences and profit more fully from the good.

10. Those who are at the receiving end of the media, and especially the young, should learn moderation and discipline in their use of them. They should aim to understand fully what they see, hear and read. They should discuss them with their teachers and with experts in such matters and should learn to reach correct judgments. Parents on their part should remember that it is their duty to see that entertainments and publications which might endanger faith and morals do not enter their houses and that their children are not exposed to them elsewhere.

11. A special responsibility for the proper use of the means of social communication rests on journalists, writers, actors, designers, producers, exhibitors, distributors, operators, sellers, critics—all those, in a word, who are involved in the making and transmission of communications in any way whatever. It is clear that a very great responsibility rests on all of these people in today's world: they have power to direct mankind along a good path or an evil path by the information they impart and the pressure they exert.

It will be for them to regulate economic, political and artistic values in a way that will not conflict with the common good. To achieve this result more surely, they will do well to form professional organizations capable of imposing on their members—if necessary by a formal pledge to observe a moral code—a respect for the moral law in the problems they encounter and in their activities.

They should always be mindful of the fact that a very large proportion of their readership and audience are young people who are in need of publications and entertainments for wholesome amusement and inspiration. They should en-

sure that religious features are entrusted to serious and
competent persons and are handled with proper respect.

12. Civil authorities have particular responsibilities in
this field because of the common good, toward which these
media are oriented. It is for the civil authority, in its own
domain, to defend and safeguard—especially in relation to
the press—a true and just freedom of information, for the
progress of modern society demands it.

The civil authority should foster religious, cultural and
artistic values. It should guarantee to those who use the media the free exercise of their lawful rights. It is, further, the
duty of the civil authorities to give assistance to those projects which, although very useful, especially for the young,
could not succeed otherwise.

Finally, the civil authorities, which rightly regard the
well-being of the citizens as their concern, are also bound
to ensure, equitably and vigilantly, that public morality and
social progress are not gravely endangered through the misuse of these media. This they can achieve by promulgating
laws and tirelessly enforcing them. The liberty of individuals and groups is not in the least compromised by such vigilance, especially where serious guarantees cannot be given
by those who use these media professionally.

Special measures should be taken to protect adolescents
from publications and entertainments harmful to them.

CHAPTER II

13. All the members of the Church should make a concerted effort to ensure that the means of communication
are put at the service of the multiple forms of the apostolate without delay and as energetically as possible, where
and when they are needed. They should forestall projects
likely to prove harmful, especially in those regions where
moral and religious progress would require their intervention more urgently.

Pastors of souls should be particularly zealous in this

field, since it is closely linked with their task of preaching the Gospel. Laymen who work professionally in these media should endeavor to bear witness to Christ: first of all, by doing their work competently and in an apostolic spirit, secondly by collaborating directly, each one according to his ability, in the pastoral activity of the Church, making a technical, economic, cultural or artistic contribution.

14. First of all, a responsible press should be encouraged. If, however, one really wants to form readers in a truly Christian spirit, an authentically Catholic press ought to be established and supported. Such a press, whether it be established and directed by the ecclesiastical authorities or by individual Catholics, would have for its manifest purpose to form, to consolidate and to promote a public opinion in conformity with the natural law and with Catholic doctrines and directives. It would also publish news of the Church's life and informed comment on it. The faithful should be reminded of the need to read and circulate the Catholic press if they are to judge all events from a Christian standpoint.

The production and screening of films which provide wholesome entertainment and are worthwhile culturally and artistically should be promoted and effectively guaranteed, especially films destined for the young. This is best achieved by supporting and co-ordinating productions and projects by serious producers and distributors, by marking the launching of worthwhile films with favorable criticism or the awarding of prizes, by supporting and coordinating cinemas managed by Catholics and men of integrity.

Likewise, decent radio and television programs should be effectively supported, especially those suited to the family. Ample encouragement should be given to Catholic transmissions which invite listeners and viewers to share in the life of the Church and which convey religious truths. Catholic stations should be established where it is opportune. Their transmissions, however, should excel by technical perfection and by effectiveness.

The noble and ancient art of the theatre has been widely popularized by the means of social communication. One should take steps to ensure that it contributes to the human and moral formation of its audiences.

15. Priests, religious and laity should be trained at once to meet the needs described above. They should acquire the competence needed to use these media for the apostolate.

First, lay people must be given the necessary technical, doctrinal and moral formation. To this end, schools, institutes or faculties must be provided in sufficient number, where journalists, writers for films, radio and television, and anyone else concerned, may receive a complete formation, imbued with the Christian spirit and especially with the Church's social teaching. Actors should also be instructed and helped so that their gifts too can benefit society. Lastly, literary critics and critics of films, radio, television and the rest should be carefully prepared so that they will be fully competent in their respective spheres and will be trained and encouraged to give due consideration to morality in their critiques.

16. Those who receive the means of social communication differ in age and culture. Hence the need for instruction and practical experience tailored not merely to the character of each medium but to the needs of each group. They need the instruction and practical experience if they are to use the media properly. Projects designed to effect this, especially among the young, should be encouraged and multiplied in Catholic schools at all levels, in seminaries and lay apostolate associations and should be directed in accordance with the principles of Christian morality. For quicker results, Catholic teaching and regulations in this matter should be given and explained in the catechism.

17. It would be shameful if by their inactivity Catholics allowed the word of God to be silenced or obstructed by the technical difficulties which these media present and by their admittedly enormous cost. For this reason the Council reminds them that they have the obligation to sustain and assist Catholic newspapers, periodicals, film-projects, radio and television stations and programs. For the main aim of all these is to propagate and defend the truth and to secure the permeation of society by Christian values. At the same time it earnestly invites groups or individuals who wield influence in technology or the economic field to give generously of their resources and of their knowledge for the support of the media, provided they are at the service of authentic culture and of the apostolate.

18. To make the Church's multiple apostolate in the field of social communication more effective, a day is to be set aside each year in every diocese, at the bishop's discretion, on which the faithful will be reminded of their duties in

this domain. They should be asked to pray for the success of the Church's apostolate in this field and to contribute toward it, their contributions to be scrupulously employed for the support and the further development of the projects which the Church has initiated in view of the needs of the entire Church.

19. A special office of the Holy See is at the disposal of the Sovereign Pontiff in the exercise of his supreme pastoral responsibility for the means of social communication.[1]

20. It is for bishops to oversee activities and projects of this sort in their own dioceses, to promote and, where they touch the public apostolate, to regulate them, including those under the control of exempt religious.

21. An effective national apostolate requires acceptance of a common objective and the unification of effort. This Council therefore decides and ordains that national offices for the press, the cinema, radio and television be established everywhere and be properly supported. The main task of these offices will be the formation of a right conscience in the faithful in their use of the media and to encourage and regulate everything done by Catholics in this domain.

In each country, the direction of these offices is to be entrusted to episcopal commissions or bishops appointed to do the task. The offices should also have on their staffs laymen who are qualified in Catholic teaching and technically.

22. The influence of the means of social communication extends beyond national frontiers, making individuals citizens of the world, as it were. National projects should, consequently, cooperate with each other at international level. The offices mentioned in par. 21 should each collaborate closely with its corresponding international organization. These international organizations are approved by the Holy See alone and are responsible to it.

---

1. The Council Fathers, however, willingly grant the wish of the Secretariat for the Press and Entertainments and respectfully request the Supreme Pontiff to extend the duties and competence of this office to all the media of social communications, including the press, and to appoint experts to it, including laymen, from various countries. (Translator's note: this secretariat is the "office" referred to in the text. Pope Paul extended the competence of the secretariat as requested on 2 April 1964, by means of the *Motu Proprio, In Fructibus Multis.* The secretariat was renamed The Pontifical Commission for the Means of Social Communication. It was this body that published the instruction which follows the present decree.)

CONCLUSIONS

32. The Council expressly directs the commission of the Holy See referred to in par. 19 to publish a pastoral instruction, with the help of experts from various countries, to ensure that all the principles and rules of the Council on the means of social communication be put into effect.[b]

24. For the rest, the Council is confident that all the sons of the Church will welcome the principles and regulations contained in this decree and will observe them faithfully. Thus, they will not suffer damage as they use the media. Rather will the media, like salt and light, add savor to the earth and light to the world. Further, it invites all men of good will, especially those who control the media, to use them solely for the good of humanity, for its fate becomes more and more dependent on their right use. The name of the Lord will thus be glorified by these modern inventions as it was in former times by the masterpieces of art; as the apostle said: "Jesus Christ is the same yesterday, today, and for ever" (Heb. 13:8).

b. The instruction has since been prepared, and we print it immediately after the decree.

27

PASTORAL INSTRUCTION ON THE MEANS OF SOCIAL COMMUNICATION[a]

P.C.I.S.C., *Communio et Progressio,* 29 January, 1971

Foreword

1. The unity and advancement of men living in society: these are the chief aims of social communication and of all the means it uses. These means include the press, the cinema, radio and television. The constant improvement in the media puts them at the disposal of more and more people who in their daily lives make increasing use of them. More than ever before, the way men live and think is profoundly affected by the means of communication.

2. The Church sees these media as "gifts of God"[1] which, in accordance with his providential design, unite men in brotherhood and so help them to cooperate with his plan for their salvation.

A deeper and more penetrating understanding of social communication and of the contribution which the media it uses can make to modern society, can be derived from a number of documents issued by the Second Vatican Council. These are, notably, the Constitution on the Church in the World of Today,[2] the Decree on Ecumenism,[3] the Declaration on Religious Freedom,[4] the Decree on the Missionary Activity of the Church,[5] and the Decree on the Pastoral Duties of Bishops.[6] And, of course, there is a Decree

---

a. Translation prepared by the PCISC. Latin text in *AAS* 63 (1971), 593–656.

1. Encyclical of Pius XII *Miranda Prorsus, AAS* 44 (1957), p. 765.
2. *Gaudium et spes, AAS* 58 (1966), pp. 1025–1120.
3. *Unitatis redintegratio, AAS* 57 (1965), pp. 90–112.
4. *Dignitatis humanae, AAS* 58 (1966), pp. 929–946.
5. *Ad Gentes, AAS* 58 (1966), pp. 947–990.
6. *Christus Dominus, AAS* 58 (1966), pp. 673–696.

that is wholly devoted to a discussion of The Means of Social Communication.[7]

The deeper understanding based on the teaching and spirit of this Council will now guide Christians in thier attitudes to the media and will make them more eager to commit themselves in this field.

3. This Pastoral Instruction which is being published at the direction of the Second Vatican Council[8] sets out basic doctrinal principles and general pastoral guidelines. It carefully refrains from going into minute details on a subject which is continually changing and developing and which varies so much according to time and place.

4. It will therefore be the task of Bishops and their conference and, equally, of the Synods of the Eastern Churches, to consult experts and their diocesan, national and international councils. This should be done not only to implement this Instruction efficiently and in a spirit of collegiality, but also to discover the best way of explaining it and suiting it, as precisely as possible, to the needs of the people in their care. And while they do this, they will keep in mind the unity of the Church.

In this task Episcopal Conferences will rely on the professional assistance which priests, religious and laity can offer. For a proper use of the means of social communication is the responsibility of the entire People of God.

5. This Instruction, it is hoped, will be well received by all those who are professionally involved in the field of communications and, indeed, by all who in good will seek the progress of mankind. So, as a result of exchanges of views and cooperation with such men, the vast potential that lies in the means of social communication will be made good and this for the advancement of all.

7. *Inter mirifica, AAS* 56 (1964), pp. 145–157.
8. Cf. *Inter mirifica,* no. 23.

PART ONE

The Christian View of the Means of Social Communication: Basic Points of Doctrine

6. The means of social communication, even though they are addressed to individuals, reach and affect the whole of society.[9] They inform a vast public about what goes on in the world and about contemporary attitudes and they do it swiftly. That is why they are indispensable to the smooth functioning of modern society, with its complex and ever changing needs, and the continual and often close consultations all this involves. This exactly coincides with the Christian conception of how men should live together.

These technical advances have the high purpose of bringing men into closer contact with one another. By passing on knowledge of their common fears and hopes they help men to resolve them. A Christian estimate of the contribution that the media make to the well-being of mankind is rooted in this fundamental principle.

7. All over the world, men are at work on improving the conditions for human living and the latest scientific wonders and technical achievements play their part in this. The Christian vision of man, of his motives and of his history, sees in this development a response—though usually an unconscious one—to the divine command to "possess and master the world."[10] It also sees it as an act of cooperation in the divine work of creation and conservation.[11]

It is within this vision that the means of social communication fall into their proper place. They help men to share their knowledge and to unify their creative work. Indeed, by creating man in his own image, God has given him a share in his creative power. And so man is summoned to cooperate with his fellow men in building the earthly city.[12]

8. Social communications tend to multiply contacts within society and to deepen social consciousness. As a result

9. Cf. *Inter mirifica*, no. 1.
10. Gen. 1:26–28; cf. Gen 9:2–3; Wis. 9:2–3; *Gaudium et spes*, no. 34. (C.T.S. D 363).
11. Cf. *Gaudium et spes*, no. 34.
12. Cf. *Gaudium et spes*, no. 57.

the individual is bound more closely to his fellow men and can play his part in the unfolding of history as if led by the hand of God.[13] In the Christian faith, the unity and brotherhood of man are the chief aims of all communication and these find their source and model in the central mystery of the eternal communion between the Father, Son and Holy Spirit, who live a single divine life.

9. The means of social communication can contribute a great deal to human unity. If, however, men's minds and hearts are ill disposed, if good will is not there, this outpouring of technology may produce an opposite effect, so that there is less understanding and more discord, and as a result evils are multiplied. Too often we have to watch social communications used to contradict or corrupt the fundamental values of human life. The Christian considers these evils evidence of man's need to be redeemed and freed from that sin which entered human history with man's first fall.[14]

10. When, by his own fault, man turned away from his Creator, chaos succeeded crime and man became embroiled in discord and deadly fraternal strife.[15] He was no longer able to communicate with his fellow men. But for all that, God's love for man persisted, despite its rejection by man. It was he who made the first move to make contact with mankind[16] at the start of the history of salvation. In the fullness of time, he communicated his very self to man[17] and "the Word was made flesh."[18]

When, by his death and resurrection, Christ the Incarnate Son, the Word and Image of the invisible God,[19] set the human race free, he shared with everyone the truth and the life of God. And he did this more richly and lavishly than ever before. As the only mediator between the Father and mankind he made peace between God and man and laid the foundations of unity among men themselves.[20] From that moment, communication among men found its highest ideal and supreme example in God who had

13. Cf. ibid., no. 36; Encyclical of John XXIII, *Pacem in Terris,* *AAS* 55 (1963), p. 257 and *passim.* (C.T.S. S264).
14. Cf. Rom. 5:12–14.
15. Cf. Gen. 4:1–16; 11:1–9.
16. Cf. Gen. 3: 15; 9:17; 12:1–3.
17. Cf. Heb. 1:1–2.
18. Jn. 1:14.
19. Col. 1:15; 2 Cor. 4:4.
20. Cf. *Ad Gentes,* no. 3.

become man and brother. He ordered his disciples, always and everywhere,[21] to spread the good tidings "in the light of day" and "from the roof-tops."[22]

11. While he was on earth Christ revealed himself as the perfect communicator. Through his incarnation, he utterly identified himself with those who were to receive his communication, and he gave his message not only in words but in the whole manner of his life. He spoke from within, that is to say, from out of the press of his people. He preached the divine message without fear or compromise. He adjusted to his people's way of talking and to their patterns of thought. And he spoke out of the predicament of their time.

Communication is more than the expression of ideas and the indication of emotion. At its most profound level, it is the giving of self in love. Christ's communication was, in fact, spirit and life.[23] In the institution of the Holy Eucharist, Christ gave us the most perfect, most intimate form of communion between God and man possible in this life, and out of this, the deepest possible unity between men. Furthur, Christ communicated to us his life-giving Spirit, who brings all men together in unity.[24]

The Church is Christ's Mystical Body—the hidden completion of Christ glorified who "fills the whole creation."[25] As a result we move, within the Church and with the help of the word and the sacraments, toward the hope of that last unity where "God will be all in all."[26]

12. So, "among the marvellous technical inventions"[27] which foster communication among human beings, Christians find means that have been devised under God's Providence for the encouragement of social relations during their pilgrimage on earth. These means, in fact, serve to build new relationships, and to fashion a new language which permit men to know themselves better and to understand one another more easily. By this, men are led to a mutual understanding and shared ambition. And this, in turn, inclines them to justice and peace, to good will and

21. Mt. 28:19.
22. Mt. 10:27; Lk. 12:3.
23. Jn. 6:53.
24. Cf. *Lumen gentium, AAS* 57 (1965), no. 9, p. 14. (C.T.S. Do 349).
25. Eph. 1:23; 4:10.
26. 1 Cor. 15:28.
27. *Inter mirifica,* no. 1.

active charity, to mutual help, to love and, in the end, to communion. The means of communication, then, provide some of the most effective methods of cultivating that charity among men which is at once the cause and the expression of fellowship.

13. All men of good will, then, are impelled to work together to ensure that the media of communication do in fact contribute to the pursuit of truth and the speeding up of progress. The Christian will find in his faith an added incentive to do this. And the message of the Gospel thus spread will promote this idea—which is the brotherhood of man under the fatherhood of God.

Contact and cooperation among men depend, in the last resort, on man's free choice, which in its turn is affected by psychological, sociological and technical factors. And so the importance and ultimate significance of the media of communication depend upon the working of man's free choice in their use.

14. Since it is man himself who decides how the available means of communication shall be used, the moral principles at issue here are those based on a true interpretation of the dignity of man. And man, it should be recalled, must be accounted a member of the family of the adopted children of God. At the same time, these principles derive from the essential character of social communication and the innate qualities of the medium in question. This follows also from what is said in *Gaudium et spes:* "By the very nature of creation, material being is endowed with its own stability, truth, goodness, its own order and laws. These men must respect. . . ."[28]

15. Whoever wants to see the media take their allotted place in the history of Creation, in the Incarnation and Redemption, and to consider the morality that governs their use, must have a full and proper understanding of man. He must also have a sound knowledge both of the true nature of social communication and of the tools at its service.

"Communicators" are all those who actively employ the media. These have a duty in conscience to make themselves competent in the art of social communication in order to be effective in their work.[29] And as a man's influence on the process of communication grows, so does this duty. All

28. *Gaudium et spes,* no. 36.
29. Cf. ibid., no. 43.

this applies even more to those who have to instruct the tastes and judgements of others. It applies to those who have to teach the young or the uneducated. And it applies to all who can in any way enrich or impoverish man's nature, whether that man be a man alone or a man engulfed in a crowd.

"Recipients" are those who, for their own purpose, read, listen to, or view the various media. Everything possible should be done to enable these to know about the media. So they will be able to interpret their message accurately, to reap their benefit in full and play their part in the life of society. Only if this is done will the media function in the best possible way.

16. The total output of the media in any given area should be judged by the contribution it makes to the common good.[30] Its news, culture and entertainment should meet the growing needs of society. The news of something that has happened must be given and so too must the background of the event, so that people can understand society's problems and work for their solution. A proper balance must be kept not only between hard news, educational material and entertainment but also between the light and the more serious forms of that entertainment.

17. Every communication must comply with certain essential requirements, and these are sincerity, honesty and truthfulness. Good intentions and a clear conscience do not thereby make a communication sound and reliable. A communication must state the truth. It must accurately reflect the situation with all its implications. The moral worth and validity of any communication does not lie solely in its theme or intellectual content. The way in which it is presented, the way in which it is spoken and treated, and even the audience for which it is designed—all these factors must be taken into account.[31]

18. A deeper understanding and a greater sympathy between men, as well as fruitful cooperation in creative work, these are the marvellous benefits that should come from so-

30. The "common good" is defined in the Encyclical of John XXIII, *Mater et Magistra* (C.T.S. S259), as the "sum of those conditions of social life by which men can attain their perfection more fully and with greater ease." *AAS* 53 (1961), p. 417. See also *Pacem in Terris, AAS* 55 (1963), pp. 272–274; *Dignitatis humanae*, no. 6; *Gaudium et spes*, nos. 26 and 74.
31. Cf. *Inter mirifica*, no. 4.

cial communication. These are ideals which are completely in tune with the aims of the People of God. Indeed, they are strengthened and reinforced by them. "For the promotion of unity belongs to the innermost nature of the Church," since she is "by her relationship with Christ, both a sacramental sign and an instrument of intimate union with God, and of the unity of all mankind."[32]

32. *Gaudium et spes*, no. 42; *Lumen gentium*, no. **1.**

PART TWO

The Contribution of the Communications Media to Human Progress

CHAPTER I

THE WORK OF THE MEDIA IN HUMAN SOCIETY

19. The modern media of social communication offer men of today a great round table. At this they are in search of, and able to participate in, a world-wide exchange of brotherhood and cooperation. It is not surprising that this should be so, for the media are at the disposal of all and are channels for that very dialogue which they themselves stimulate. The torrent of information and opinion pouring through these channels makes every man a partner in the business of the human race. This interchange creates the proper conditions for that mutual and sympathetic understanding which leads to universal progress.

20. The swift advances of the means of social communication tear down the barriers that time and space have erected between men. They can make for greater understanding and closer unity. A mass of information is continually on the move to and from all parts of the world, and as a result men can learn what goes on and how other men live. Teaching at all levels has benefited by the use of these aids. The media plays their part in eliminating illiteracy and in providing both basic and furthur education. They can, very effectively, help people in developing countries to achieve progress and freedom. They can establish a measure of universal equality in which all men, whatever their place in society, can enjoy the delights of culture and leisure. They enrich men's minds. They help them to keep in touch with reality by providing the sights and sounds which are the very stuff of life. They bring faraway times and places within their grasp. And when illiteracy is widespread —and this is not in any way to question the validity of traditional cultures—citizens can quickly be put in touch with recent developments.

21. In the light of these advantages, the communications media can be seen as powerful instruments for progress. It is

true they present difficulties but these must be faced and overcome. Both the communicators and the recipients ought to be aware of their inherent dangers and difficulties. For instance, how can we ensure that this swift, haphazard and endless stream of news is properly evaluated and understood? The media are bound to seek a mass audience, and so they often adopt a neutral stance in order to avoid giving offense to any section of their audience. How, in a society that is committed to the rights of dissent, is the distinction between right and wrong, and true and false, to be made?

How in the face of competition to capture a large popular audience are the media to be prevented from appealing to and inflaming the less admirable tendencies in human nature? How can one avoid the concentration of the power to communicate in too few hands, so that any real dialogue is killed? How can one avoid allowing communications, made indirectly and through machinery, to weaken direct contact—especially when these communications take the form of pictures and images? When the media invite men to escape into fantasy, what can be done to bring them back to present reality? How can one stop the media encouraging mental idleness and passivity? And how can one be certain that the incessant appeal to emotion does not sap reason?

22. It is obvious that there has been a decline in moral standards in many areas of life today, and this decline is a source of profound concern to all honest men. It is easy to find evidence of decline in all the means of social communication. But how far these means must be blamed for the decline is open to question. Many responsible men hold that these means are only a reflection of what already exists in society. Others hold that they increase and spread those tendencies and that, by making them commonplace, lead to their gradual acceptance. And still others would put most of the blame squarely upon the means of social communication. What is certainly true is that the weakness lies in society itself and that the attempt to restore standards must involve the whole of society, its parents, teachers, pastors, and all who care about the common good. In this attempt the means of social communication have no small part to play. It is however impossible to put the means of social communication into a quite separate category from that of the everyday life and attitudes of the people.

23. In order that the benefits offered to society by social

communication can be better understood and used to the full and the incidental difficulties they present set aside, the chief aspects of the working of the media among men must be investigated.

I. PUBLIC OPINION

24. The means of social communication are a public forum where every man may exchange ideas. The public expression and the confrontation of different opinions that occur within this dialogue influence and enrich the development of society and further its progress.

25. Public opinion is an essential expression of human nature organized in a society. This opinion is formed in the following way. In everyone there is an innate disposition to give vent to opinions, attitudes and emotions in order to reach a general acceptance on convictions and customs. Pius XII describes public opinion as "the natural echo of actual events and situations as reflected more or less spontaneously in the minds and judgments of men."[33] So freedom of speech is a normal factor in the growth of public opinion which expresses the ideas and reactions of the more influential circles in a society defined by geography, culture and history.

26. If public opinion is to emerge in the proper manner, it is absolutely essential that there be freedom to express ideas and attitudes. In accordance with the express teaching of the Second Vatican Council it is necessary unequivocally to declare that freedom of speech for individuals and groups must be permitted so long as the common good and public morality be not endangered.[34] In order that men may usefully cooperate and further improve the life of the community, there must be freedom to assess and compare differing views which seem to have weight and validity. Within this free interplay of opinion, there exists a process of give and take, of acceptance or rejection, of compromise or compilation. And within this same process, the more valid ideas can gain ground, so that a concensus that will lead to common action becomes possible.

27. Communicators have therefore a most important

33. In his Allocution to Catholic Journalists on 17 February 1950. *AAS* 42 (1950), p. 251. See also *Gaudium et spes*, no. 59; *Pacem in Terris, AAS* 55 (1963), p. 283.
34. *Gaudium et spes*, no. 59.

part to play in forming public opinion. They have to gather up different views and compare them and transmit them so that people can understand and make a proper decision.

28. Every citizen is expected to play his part in the formation of public opinion. If needs be, he must do this through representatives who reflect his own views.[35] Those who exert influence because of the office they hold or because of their natural talent or for any other reason have an important part to play in forming public opinion: they help to do so whenever they express their views. The greater their quality of leadership, the greater is their responsibility to exert it in this way.

29. The process of promoting what is sometimes called a "propaganda campaign," with a view to influencing public opinion, is justified only when it serves the truth, when its objectives and methods accord with the dignity of man, and when it promotes causes that are in the public interest. These causes may concern either individuals or groups, one's own country or the world at large.

30. Some types of propaganda are inadmissible. These include those that harm the public interest or allow of no public reply. Any propaganda should be rejected which deliberately misrepresents the real situation, or distorts men's minds with half-truths, selective reporting, or serious omissions, and which diminishes man's legitimate freedom of decision. It is necessary to stress this because the power of propaganda is increasing. And its power is being augmented by the growth of behavioral sciences like that of psychology and of the technical resources at the disposal of the communications media.

31. Not every opinion that is given publicity should be taken as a true expression of that public opinion which is held by a significant number of people. A number of differing opinions can flourish at the same time in the same area, though, usually, one has a greater following than the others. The opinion of the majority, however, is not necessarily the best or closest to the truth.

Public opinion, moreover, changes often. The same idea sometimes gains and sometimes loses hold of the public. Because of this, it is prudent to maintain a certain detachment towards the opinions currently in public vogue. There may well be good reasons that require one to oppose them.

35. Cf. *Inter mirifica*, no. 8.

32. However, views openly and commonly expressed which reflect the aspirations of the people should always be carefully considered. This is especially binding on those in authority, whether civil or religious.

II. THE RIGHT TO BE INFORMED AND TO INFORM

33. If public opinion is to be properly formed, it is necessary that, right from the start, the public be given free access to both the sources and the channels of information and be allowed freely to express its own views. Freedom of opinion and the right to be informed go hand in hand. Pope John XXIII,[36] Pope Paul VI[37] and the Second Vatican Council[38] have all stressed this right to information which today is essential for the individual and for society in general.

A. Access to the Sources and Channels of News

34. Modern man cannot do without information that is full, consistent, accurate and true. Without it he cannot understand the perpetually changing world in which he lives, nor be able to adapt himself to the real situation. This adaptation calls for frequent decisions that should be made with a full knowledge of events. Only in this way can he assume a responsible and active role in his community and be a part of its ecomnomic, political, cultural and religious life.

With the right to be informed goes the duty to seek information. Information does not simply occur; it has to be sought. On the other hand, in order to get it, the man who wants information must have access to the varied means of social communication. In this way he can freely choose whatever means best suit his needs, both personal and social. It is futile to talk about the right to information if a variety of the sources for it are not made available.

35. Society, at all levels, requires information if it is to choose the right course. The community requires well-informed citizens. The right to information is not merely the

36. Cf. *Pacem in Terris, AAS* 55 (1963), p. 260.
37. Cf. the Allocution given on 17 April 1964 to 'Séminaire des Nations Unies sur la liberté de l'information,' *AAS* 56 (1964), pp. 387 ff.
38. Cf. *Inter mirifica,* nos. 5, 12.

prerogative of the individual, it is essential to the public interest.

36. Those whose job it is to give the news have a most difficult and responsible role to play. They face formidable obstacles and these obstacles will sometimes include persons interested in concealing the truth. This is especially the case for reporters who give close-up impressions of the news and who, in order to do this, often travel to the four corners of the earth to witness events as they actually happen.[39] At times they risk their lives and indeed a number of them have been killed in this line of duty.[40] The safety of such correspondents should be ensured in every possible way because of the service they render to man's right to know about what is happening. This is particularly true in the case of wars, which involve and concern the whole human race. So the Church utterly condemns the use of violence against newsmen or against anyone in any way involved in the passing on of news. For these persons vindicate and practise the right of finding out what is happening and of passing on this information to others.

37. It is hard for anyone to learn the whole truth and to pass this on to others, but newsmen face an additional problem. Of its nature, news is about what is new. So journalists deal with what has just happened and with what is of present interest. More than that, out of a mass of material they must select what they judge to be the significant facts that will concern their audience. So it can happen that the news reported is only a part of the whole and does not convey what is of real importance.

38. Communicators must give news that is up to the minute, complete and comprehensible. So more and more they have to seek out competent men for comments, background briefing and discussion. Often these comments are required immediately, sometimes even before the expected event has happened. Trustworthy men are rightly reluctant to make hasty or unprepared comments, preferring to wait until they have had a chance to study a situation in its context, and especially when they are in a position of responsibility or authority. And so because the media are impelled to demand quick comment, the initiative often passes to

39. Pius XII in an address given to American journalists on 21 July 1945. *L'Osservatore Romano*, 22 July 1945.
40. An address to a similar group on 27 April 1946. *L'Osservatore Romano*, 28 April 1946.

men who are less responsible and less well-informed, but who are more willing to oblige. Those acquainted with a given situation should try to prevent this happening. As far as they can, they should keep themselves up-to-date so that they themselves can reply and ensure that the public is properly informed.

39. Then there is another problem. Those who have to keep the public informed must give the news quickly if it is to appear fresh and interesting. Competition also obliges them to do this, and speed is often won at the price of accuracy. The communicator has also to know the tastes and cultural level of his public and to take into account its known preferences. And when he comes to present the news, it is in the face of such hazards that a communicator must remain faithful to the truth.

40. But as well as these problems which are inherent in the nature of the news and communications media, there is another. Communicators must hold the wandering attention of a harried and hurried public by vivid reporting. And yet they must not give way to the temptation of making the news sensational in such a way that they risk distorting it —by taking it out of context or by exaggerating it out of all proportion.

41. The recipients who piece together the news that comes to them in fragments may well end up with an unbalanced or distorted idea of the whole picture. To a certain extent, accuracy can be restored by the continuity of the flow from different sources, which must always be carefully assessed.

The recipients of information should have a clear conception of the predicament of those that purvey information. They should not look for a superhuman perfection in the communicators. What they do have a right and duty to expect, however, is that a rapid and clear correction should follow any mistake or misrepresentation that has found its way into a report. They are to protest whenever omissions or distortions occur. They are to protest whenever events have been reported out of context or in a biased manner. They are to protest whenever the significance of events has been wildly exaggerated or underplayed. This right should be guaranteed for recipients by agreement among the communicators themselves, and if this cannot be got, then by national law or international convention.

42. But the right to information is not limitless. It has to

be reconciled with other existing rights. There is the right of truth which guards the good name both of men and of societies. There is the right of privacy which protects the private life of families and individuals.[41] There is the right of secrecy which obtains if necessity or professional duty or the common good itself requires it. Indeed, whenever public good is at stake, discretion and discrimination and careful judgement should be used in the preparation of news.

43. The reporting of violence and brutality demands a special care and tact. There is no denying that human life is debased by violence and savagery and that such things happen in our own time and perhaps more now than ever before. It is possible to delineate all this violence and savagery so that men will recoil from it. But if these bloody events are too realistically described or too frequently dwelt upon, there is a danger of perverting the image of human life. It is also possible that such descriptions generate an attitude of mind and, according to many experts, a psychosis which escapes the control of the very forces that unleashed it. All this may leave violence and savagery as the accepted way of resolving conflict.

B. Freedom of Communication

44. This right to information is inseparable from freedom of communication. Social life depends on a continual interchange, both individual and collective, between people. This is necessary for mutual understanding and for cooperative creativity. When social intercourse makes use of the mass media, a new dimension is added. Then vast numbers of people get the chance to share in the life and progress of the community.

45. Because man is social by nature, he feels the need to express himself freely and to compare his views with those of other people. This applies today more than ever before, now that man's intellect and genius are often enough served more by team work than by individual effort. So the result is that when people follow their natural inclination to exchange ideas and declare their opinions, they are not merely making use of a right. They are also performing a social duty.

41. Information "should be communicated honestly and with propriety. This means that in the gathering and in the publication of news the moral law and the legitimate rights and dignity of man should be upheld." *Inter mirifica*, (D.26), no. 5.

46. Those societies which tolerate diverse component groups and are called "pluralist," can well understand the importance of the free flow of information and opinion that enables the citizens to play an active part in the community. Laws have been passed in such countries to guard this freedom. Moreover, the Universal Declaration of Human Rights has proclaimed this freedom to be fundamental and thereby implies that the same freedom is essential in the use of the means of social communication.

47. This freedom of communication also implies that individuals and groups must be free to seek out and spread information. It also means that they should have free access to the media. On the other hand, freedom of communication would benefit those who communicate news rather than those who receive it if this freedom existed without proper limits and without thought for those real and public needs upon which the right to information is based.

III. EDUCATION, CULTURE AND LEISURE

48. The means of social communication have an ever-growing role to play in the vast field of human education. In many places audio visual aids, the new video cassettes and the regular use of radio and television have become accepted teaching instruments. They make the work of experts in different fields accessible to more and more people. Elsewhere the means of social communication are used to complement the established ways of teaching. They also give opportunities for further education to adolescents and adults. In places where the educational facilities are inadequate, they can provide religious instruction and basic education; and they fight illiteracy. They are useful instruments for instructing people in agriculture, medicine, hygiene and in many forms of community development. As far as possible, this use of the media for education should have a creative quality and elicit an active response. In this way, the pupil is not only led to knowledge but learns to express himself by using the media.

49. Moreover, in a manner that is unique, the media, which are already a conspicuous element in daily life, bring artistic and cultural achievements within the orbit of a great part of the human race. And soon, perhaps, they will do the same for the whole of it. This is as authentic a mark of so-

cial progress as is the removal of economic and social inequality.

50. The media can deepen and enrich contemporary culture and communicators should recognize that everyone has
a right to this enrichment. They should not therefore hesitate to take the chance offered by the so-called "mass media" to reach great numbers of people. The media also
make it possible to cater for differing needs and interests
since, in a professional and attractive manner, they can produce the fruits of every type of artistic expression.

People, then, will find no difficulty in using the media to
deepen and refine their cultural life, as long as they supplement this use with the exercise of personal reflection and an
exchange of views with others.

51. An example of the cultural potential of the media
can be found in their service to the traditional folk arts of
countries where stories, plays, song and dance still express
an ancient national inheritance. Because of their modern
techniques, the media can make these achievements known
more widely. They can record them so that they can be
seen and heard again and again and make them accessible
even in districts where the old traditions have vanished. In
this way the media help to impress on a nation a proper
sense of its cultural identity and, by portraying that culture
they can, delight and enrich other cultures and countries as
well.

52. It should be recalled that many great works recognized as the products of genius, particularly in music, drama and literature, were first presented to the public as entertainment. So entertainment need not lack cultural
validity.[42]

Today, through the media, the noblest forms of artistic
expression offer true recreation—in the fullest sense of that
word—to more and more people. And there is more and
more call for this in our complex society.

Simple entertainment, too, has a value of its own. It
lightens the burden of daily problems and it occupies men's
leisure. The wide variety of productions that the media offer for these hours of leisure, is in fact a remarkable service
to mankind. But recipients should exercise self-control.
They must not allow themselves to be so beguiled by the

42. Cf. Encyclical of Pius XII *Miranda Prorsus*, *A.A.S.*, (1957, p.
765.

charms of the media's products or by the curiosity that these arouse that they neglect urgent duties or simply waste time.

53. The media are themselves new factors in contemporary culture, serving as they do large numbers of people at the same time. But as well as enriching culture, they can occasionally degrade it. They often play for the applause of the lowest cultural levels of their audience. And because they take so much of modern man's time, they can easily divert him from higher and more profitable cultural pursuits.

An unrelieved diet of productions geared to the lowest cultural level within a population would tend to debase the taste of those who have already attained a higher level. These dangers can be avoided if communicators really care about the well-being of culture and buttress their good intentions with a sound knowledge of the science of education. Moreover, it will be recalled that the media are perfectly capable of productions on the highest artistic level, and for the great majority these are not necessarily the most difficult to follow and to enjoy.

IV. FORMS OF ARTISTIC EXPRESSION

54. The media of social communication do more than present the traditional forms of artistic expression, they themselves create new ones. And now that the media cover the whole earth and multiply the opportunities for international cultural cooperation, especially in creative work using the talents of artists from many nations, it is only right that both communicators and recipients should seek to acquire a truly catholic taste, one that includes both the traditional and the latest forms of artistic expression, one that appreciates and understands the art forms of all nations, of all cultures and of all subcultures within the same areas of civilization.

55. Artistic expression both for its own excellence and for what it does for man should be highly appreciated. Of itself, beauty ennobles the mind that contemplates it. The work of the artist can also penetrate and illumine the deepest recesses of the human spirit. It can make spiritual reality immediate by expressing it in a way that the senses can comprehend. And as a result of this expression man comes to know himself better. This is not only a cultural benefit

but a moral and religious one as well. "It is a fact that when you writers and artists are able to reveal in the human condition, however lowly or sad it may be, a spark of goodness, at that very instant a glow of beauty pervades your whole work. We are not asking of you that you should play the part of moralists. We are only asking you to have confidence in your mysterious power of opening up the glorious regions of light that lie behind the mystery of man's life."[43]

56. Those who would truly understand the spirit of another age have to study not only its history, but also its literature and artefacts. And this is so because, in a very precise and lucid way, the creative arts are more revealing than conceptual descriptions of the character of people, of their aspirations, emotions and thoughts. Even when the artist takes flight from the tangible and solid world and pursues his creative fantasies, he can give priceless insight into the human condition. Stories fashioned out of imagination in which the artist creates characters that live and evolve in a world of fiction, these too communicate their special truth. Even though they are not real, they are realistic; for they are made of the very stuff of human life. They even affect those deep causes that rouse men to blaze with life.[44] For in the light they throw on these causes, the sensitive man may know them for what they are. And with this knowledge he can begin to foresee the direction that humanity will take.

57. Pope Pius XII taught that human life "certainly cannot be understood, at least when considering violent and serious conflicts, if one deliberately turns one's eyes from the crimes and evils from which they often have their origin. How then, can ideal films take this as their subject? The greatest poets and writers of all times have occupied themselves with this difficult and rough matter, and they will continue to do so in the future. . . . When the conflict with evil, not excluding cases when evil prevails for a while, is treated, within the context of a work as a whole, in an effort to understand life better, to see how it should be or-

43. Paul VI: Allocution given on 6 May 1967 to a large number of those who devote themselves to the theatre, the cinema, radio and television, and other media of social communication. *AAS* 59 (1967), p. 509.
44. Pius XII: Allocution given on 21 June 1955 to the patrons of the art of the cinema in Italy meeting in Rome. *AAS* 47 (1955), p. 509.

dered, or to show how man should conduct himself, how he should think and act with more consistency, then, in such cases, such matter can be chosen as an integral part of the development of the whole film."[45] Such a work would contribute to moral progress. Even though they are quite distinct, genuine artistic values do not clash with moral standards. Each, in fact, confirms the validity of the other.

58. Moral problems may, at times, arise in productions that deal with evil. For instance, these may occur when the audience is unable to grasp, as it should, the full implications of evil, either because its members are young and undeveloped or because their education is inadequate.

The artist is faced with life in its entirety, with its good as well as its bad aspects. Good sense and judgement are therefore called for when a work is destined for a large audience with different backgrounds. This is especially true when the subject is man confronted by evil.

V. ADVERTISING

59. The importance of advertising is steadily on the increase in modern society. It makes its presence felt everywhere; its influence is unavoidable. It offers real social benefits. It tells buyers of the goods and services available. It thus encourages the widest distribution of products, and in doing this it helps industry to develop and benefit the population. All this is to the good so long as there is respect for the buyer's liberty of choice, even though in trying to sell some particular object the advertiser makes it appear as a real need. Advertising too must respect the truth, taking into account accepted advertising conventions.

60. If harmful or utterly useless goods are touted to the public, if false assertions are made about the goods for sale, if less admirable human tendencies are exploited, those responsible for such advertising harm society and forfeit their good name and credibility. More than this, unremitting pressure to buy articles of luxury can arouse false wants that hurt both individuals and families by making them ignore what they really need. And those forms of advertising which, without shame, exploit the sexual instincts simply to make money or which seek to penetrate into the subcon-

45. Pius XII: Allocution given on 28 October 1955 to the patrons of the art of the cinema gathered in Rome for their International Convention. *AAS* 47 (1955), pp. 822–823.

scious recesses of the mind in a way that threatens the freedom of the individual, those forms of advertising must be shunned. It is therefore desirable that advertisers make definite rules for themselves lest their sales methods affront human dignity or harm the community.

61. It is true that a judicious use of advertising can stimulate developing countries to improve their standard of living. But serious harm can be done them if advertising and commercial pressure become so irresponsible that communities seek to rise from poverty to a reasonable standard of living are persuaded to seek this progress by satisfying wants that have been created artificially. The result of this is that they waste their resources and neglect their very needs, and genuine development falls behind.

62. In fact the vast sums of money spent in advertising threaten the very foundations of the mass media. People can get the impression that the instruments of communication exist solely to stimulate men's appetites so that these can be satisfied later by the acquisition of the things that have been advertised. Moreover, because of economic demands and pressures, the essential freedom of the media is at stake. Since advertising revenue is vital for these media, only those can ultimately survive which receive the greatest share of advertising outlays. Consequently, the door is open for monopolies to develop in the media which may impede the right to receive and give information and inhibit the exchange of views within the community. A variety of independent means of social communication must therefore be carefully safeguarded even if this requires legislative action. This will ensure that there is an equitable distribution of advertising revenue among the most deserving media of communication and prevent the lion's share from going to those that are already the most powerful.

Chapter II

THE MEDIA: THE BEST CONDITIONS FOR
THEIR PROPER WORKING

63. If the media of social communication are to give their best service to mankind, the importance of the human element must be recognized. This element plays a more decisive role than the most marvelous electronic and mechanical instruments by themselves. For the proper functioning of the media in society does not occur of its own accord. Both communicators and recipients, according to their own requirements, need a suitable grounding if full advantage is to be taken of the opportunities offered by these instruments. All should know what their particular role requires of them and then proceed to play it, both as individuals and members of society. Civil authorities, as well as religious leaders and educators, should play their part too so that the rich promise of the media may be effectively realized for the good of society.

I. TRAINING

64. A training that grounds a man in the basic principles governing the working of the media in human society, as explained above, is nowadays clearly necessary for all. If their character and function is understood, the means of communication genuinely enrich men's minds. On the other hand, men who do not sufficiently appreciate their importance may find their own liberty diminished.

Training should include a practical consideration of the special nature of each medium and of its status in the local community and how it can best be utilized. And this should be done with special reference to man and society.

A. The Recipients

65. Recipients need some basic training if they are to benefit to the full from what the instruments of social communication have to offer. This training is not merely for their personal advantage, but it should help them to make their contribution to the give-and-take of society as well as to the constructive work of the community. Such a training will also help them to discover the best way of achieving

these ends. It will help them to play their part in the process of striving for justice among nations and for the elimination of glaring inequalities between the richer and poorer countries.

66. For this they require a knowledge of the media that will keep pace with their maturing. And the process of education, which should be available to all, does not come to an end. It is to be supplemented continually by lectures and discussions, by special courses and study sessions that make use of the help of professionals in this field.

67. It is never too early to start encouraging in children artistic taste, a keen critical faculty and a sense of personal responsibility based on sound morality. They need all these so that they can use discrimination in choosing the publications, films and broadcasts that are set before them. This is necessary because the young are naturally vulnerable, but this self-discipline acquired in childhood will richly serve the adult too. Generosity and idealism are admirable qualities in young people, so are their frankness and sincerity. But these qualities, along with self-discipline, will only survive if they are guarded and fostered from an early age. This is why parents and teachers should urge children to make their own choice even if the educators should reserve at times the final decision to themselves. And if they find themselves forced to disapprove of the way their children are using some aspect of the media, they must clearly explain the reasons for their objections. Persuasion works better than prohibition, and this is especially true in education. Adults should realize that the psychology of children differs from that of adults. Because of this, programs that seem meaningless to them may be useful to children and even to teenagers. Young people can, without doubt, influence one another for the better when it comes to culture. Their very years serve as a passport to the new forms it takes, giving them an entrance to their own circle. There is ample evidence to prove how effective this can be.

68. It is useful for educators to take note of some of the broadcasts, films and publications that most interest the young in their care. They can then discuss them together, and this helps to develop the child's critical powers. As for the more difficult or even controversial artistic productions, here the parent should, at the right moment, help his children to discover the human values in the production and to

interpret its details within the context of the work as a whole.

69. This sort of training must be given a regular place in school curricula. It must be given and systematically, at every stage of education. In this way, young people can be helped gradually to develop a new perception in their interpretation of what is offered them by the press, the other media and the literary publishing houses. All this should be taught in study courses planned to include special sessions where the teacher can call on the help of professional communicators for lectures and for practical exercises.

70. It is obvious that parents and other educators cannot meet these obligations unless they themselves are reasonably well grounded in an understanding of the media. Here it must be remembered that parents who have not grown up to be at home with the media often find it harder to comprehend the language used than do the young people of today. Often parents are disturbed by the frankness with which the media treat every question, including the problems that face both the civil government and the Church. Naturally they wish their children to use the media in a proper manner. Nevertheless, let them trust the young because these have been born and have grown up in a different kind of society. Because of this, they are better forewarned and better forearmed to meet the pressures that come from every side.

B. The Communicators

71. Not a few communicators handle well the tools of their profession, but even so lack a deep understanding of the art of communicating with all it implies. It is obvious that the communicators who wish to excel in the media need a serious and specialized training in every aspect of their work. The growing practice of founding Communications Faculties in institutions of higher learning—faculties with authority to confer degrees—is a welcome development. For if communicators are to meet their professional obligations, they must have sound knowledge as well as experience.

72. In the training of a communicator human qualities as well as professional competence should be developed. Since the media of social communication are for mankind, communicators should be consumed by the desire to serve men. They can only achieve this if they really do know and love

their fellow man. The more communicators remember that beyond the lifeless instruments which pass on their words and images are countless living men and women, the more satisfaction they will get from their work and the better they will help others. The more they get to know their audience, the more they understand it and appreciate it, the more they will make what they communicate suit those who receive it. If they do this, they help to make the process of communication a communion of the spirit.

II. OPPORTUNITIES AND OBLIGATIONS

A. Communicators

73. Communicators breathe life into the dialogue that happens within the family of man. It is they who preside while the exchange proceeds around the vast "round table" that the media have made. Their vocation is nobly to promote the purpose of social communication. This purpose is to accelerate every sort of human progress and to increase cooperation among men until there exists a genuine communion among them.

74. When they come to choose the subjects for their productions, communicators will attempt to match all the needs of their public. They will be scrupulous in seeing that every relevant group is fairly represented. To do this, they have to try to foresee the kind of audience they serve. There should, accordingly, be close cooperation between communicators and recipients. Only in this way can these social communications set up a working and workable dialogue between free and adequately prepared people. And this dialogue must not ignore the age, culture and social background of the participants. The media of social communication are the right instruments for the propagation of this sort of interchange between men.

75. Pope Paul said of communicators that they are obliged to pay continual attention to and to carry on an uninterrupted observation of the external world: "You must continually stand at the window, open to the world; you are obliged to study the facts, the events, the opinions, the current interest, the thought of the surrounding environment."[46] Because factual information provides a pub-

---

46. Paul VI: Allocution given on 24 January 1969 to the Officers of the Catholic Association of Italian Journalists (U.C.S.I.). *L'Osservatore Romano,* 24 January 1969.

lic service, not only must news reporting keep to the facts, and bear down upon the most important of these, but the meaning of what it reports should be brought out by explanation. The real bearing of one item of news upon another should be pointed out, especially when different items reach the recipient without evidence of any discernible pattern. In this way the recipient will be able to use this information as a basis for his judgment and decision in matters affecting the community.

76. Communicators should not allow themselves to forget that the nature of the mass media makes their audience a vast one. While they must keep faith with their artistic integrity, they should at the same time remember both their power and the grave responsibilities it brings with it. For they have been given a rare chance to promote the happiness and progress of men. In their productions justice and integrity of judgment will impel artists to be concerned with the needs of minorities as well as with those of larger and more numerous groups. And if some of the means of social communication, whether by law or local practice, in fact enjoy a monopoly, then a scrupulous impartiality must be sought, since in such a situation the danger is that monologue may replace dialogue.

77. Communicators who debase their skills and their work for money, or for easy popularity and passing acclaim, are not only failing their public. In the end, they are demeaning their profession.

78. Critics have a commanding role in getting communicators to maintain the highest standards of integrity and service and continually to make progress. As they are themselves communicators, they provide the self-criticism within the profession. In this way they are able to protect creative artists from external pressures. They must be convinced that integrity and incorruptibility are the essence of their profession. They will be inspired by fidelity to truth and a passion for justice. In a cool and objective way, they should try to display both the strength and the weakness of the work under review so that the public can make its own fair judgment. The importance of their own creative art should not be underrated, especially when through their wide knowledge and their penetrating judgment they are able to discover in works of art meaning and riches that may have escaped even the artists themselves. Yet they should not at-

tract all the attention to themselves at the expense of the work under study.

79. The founding of professional associations for communicators is most valuable. They provide a forum where opinions and experiences can be exchanged. They form a basis for organized cooperation. They help in coping with the sort of difficulties that are inherent in the communicator's task.

These associations can draw up codes of ethics on a basis of principle and experience. Through the guidance they offer, these codes can help in producing work that meets the needs of social communication. Fundamentally, the codes of these associations ought to be positive. They should not be wholly preoccupied with forbidding; rather they should concentrate on how to improve what can be done for the communicators' fellow men.

80. In order to survive and to expand, the means of social communication require reliable financial backing. It therefore happens that communicators must at times, either directly or indirectly, seek funds from public or private sources. The men who provide these funds can powerfully influence the quality of the product. But they must be discerning in choosing which enterprises to support, and desire the good of mankind rather than financial advantage. As long as they bear in mind that the means of social communication are more than commercial enterprises, and are, in fact, at one and the same time, cultural and social services, these investors should not exercise any undue pressure that might distort the proper liberty of the communicators, the artists or what we have called the recipients.

B. Recipients

81. The recipients can do more to improve the quality of the media than is generally realized; so their responsibility to do this is all the greater. Whether or not the media can set up an authentic dialogue with society depends very largely upon these recipients. If they do not insist on expressing their views, if they are content with a merely passive role, all the efforts of the communicators to establish an uninhibited dialogue will be useless.

82. Recipients can be described as active when they know how to interpret communications accurately and so

can judge them in the light of their origin, background and total context. They will be active when they make their selection judiciously and critically, when they fill out incomplete information that comes their way with more news which they themselves have obtained from other sources, and finally, when they are ready to make their views heard in public, whether they agree, or partly agree, or totally disagree.

83. There is the obvious objection that there is little a man can do alone at the receiving end. This is unnecessarily pessimistic. Recipients can find strength in unity. There exists no reason why they should not work closely together. They can band themselves into associations, just as communicators have been advised to do. Their organizations need not be set up with the single end of giving expression to what the man in the street feels about the products of the media. They could just as well avail themselves of organizations that already exist and which have a wider scope but compatible aims.

III. COOPERATION

A. Cooperation Between Citizens and the Civil Authorities

84. The media are there for the good of everyone and to serve everyone. So, at once, they concern both citizens and public authorities. These authorities have the essential duty of maintaining freedom of speech and of seeing that the right conditions exist for it. Every individual must have the chance of following his informed judgment. Human dignity must be fully respected. The good of the country and the interest of international cooperation must both be given due consideration.

85. The well-being of society requires absolutely that individuals and groups be free to exercise initiative. It also requires that citizens exercise responsibility and self-control both as communicators and as recipients. With this end in view, voluntary associations may not only be desirable; they may even be essential.

86. The role of the civil authorities in this matter is essentially a positive one. Their chief task is not to create difficulties or to suppress, though at times corrective measures may become necessary. The Second Vatican Council explained that man's freedom is to be respected as far as pos-

sible, and curtailed only when and in so far as necessary.[47] Censorship therefore should only be used in the very last extremity. Moreover the civil authorities should respect the principle of subsidiarity which has often been affirmed in the official teaching of the Church, the gist of which is: "Let them not undertake to do themselves what can be done just as well, or even better, by individuals or private groups."

87. Therefore it is right that, in the light of these principles, freedom of communication and the right to be informed be established in law and guarded from excessive economic, political and ideological pressures that might weaken them. There should be legislation to guarantee to citizens the right to criticize the actual working of the communications media. This is particularly desirable where the media are conducted as a monopoly. This is all the more necessary if the monopoly is exercised by the civil authorities themselves.

It is undoubtedly the task of the law-makers to legislate about the media. In fact the media must have the support of law so that they can survive, and survive in a sufficient variety and independence in the face of the encroachment of economic interests that make for harmful concentration. Again, the good name of the private citizen and of minority groups needs the protection of the law. Cultural and human values require protection. Religious liberty in the use of the media should be guaranteed.

88. It is highly recommended that professionals in the media, or their institutions, set up councils on their own account. These will have their own statutes and will be concerned with all aspects of social communication. Representatives of the different sections of the population should be invited to sit on these councils. This, it is hoped, will eliminate the wrong sort of interference from state or economic interests. It will strengthen cooperation and fellow-feeling between communicators, and that will be to the benefit of the whole community.

In some cases, however, the state may have to intervene and set up these advisory boards to supervise the media. In these cases, the boards should be, by law, representative of all shades of the opinion within the community.

47. Cf. *Dignitatis humanae*, no. 7.

89. As far as possible, the law should protect the young from what can do them permanent psychological or moral harm. It is the task of legislation in this field to give the necessary support to the family and the school in educating the young.

90. Legislation should be encouraged to provide financial support to initiatives in the use of communications that clearly serve the general good. These would include organizations that provide information, specialist educational publications, films, and broadcasts, particularly when these are made for children. This support is more desirable when the initiatives have little hope of financial success. This encouragement also applies to feature films of high artistic quality and to publications and performances which are destined for a restricted public and which are therefore unlikely to pay their way.

91. The responsibility of civil authorities over the means of social communication is now world wide, for they have to guarantee the development of social communication for the good of all mankind, and this without selection or discrimination. This development can be secured by the use of international agreements including those that touch on the use of space satellites. In this way, all nations will be guaranteed a fair place within the dialogue and interplay of mankind.

B. Cooperation Between Nations

92. Those forms of aid which help emerging nations to develop their own means of social communication are of great importance among the many forms of international effort which the media demand. The lack of proper means of social communication is, in fact, a sign of slow development in a community, as well as being one of the causes of it. Without the use of modern techniques of social communication no country can provide its citizens with necessary information or proper education. This inability endangers political, social and economic progress.

93. "Development," said Pope Paul VI, "is the new name for peace."[48] Countries that are well equipped should pro-

48. Paul VI: Letter to the Honorable U Thant, Secretary General of the United Nations. *AAS* 58 (1966), p. 480. See also the Holy Father's Allocution to the delegates present at Milan for the second meeting of the Administrative Council of the United Nations' Program for Development. *AAS* 58 (1966), p. 589.

vide technical assistance to those which are not. This is as true in the field of social communication as in any other. The developed countries are to help in the training of professionals and provide the necessary equipment. Their responsibilities for the common good do not end at their national frontiers. They extend to the whole of mankind. This requirement is all the more pressing now that developments in the field are progressing so swiftly. Developing countries should be helped with training centers for social communication set up within their own boundaries. Otherwise the trainees may be forced wastefully to leave their own country. Such centers will prevent a "brain drain" from the developing countries.

94. It goes without saying that the aid given to developing countries can never be at the expense of their own cherished traditions, of their culture and art forms, for these are rich in human significance. Cultural cooperation is not the giving of alms. It is an exchange that is mutually advantageous.

95. In developing countries, particularly in those where illiteracy hinders progress, audio-visual means are very effective in spreading knowledge. These means can help to improve agriculture, industry, commerce, hygiene and public health. They can serve to develop the individual's personality, to strengthen family life, social relations, and civic responsibility. It is virtually impossible to do such works at a profit. It is therefore necessary to appeal to the generosity of private citizens and of private organizations in the richer countries as well as to the support of international bodies.

C. Cooperation Between Christians, All Believers and All Men of Goodwill

96. The means of social communication are not likely to achieve their purpose—which is actively to further human progress—unless they face the formidable problems besetting modern man and strengthen his hopes and lead to a concerted effort on the part of all who believe in the living God. This is especially true in the case of those who are united in the Sacrament of Baptism. So teaches the Second Vatican Council in the documents on Ecumenism and non-Christian Religions.[49]

49. Cf. *Unitatis redintegratio, AAS* 57 (1965), pp. 90–112. See also *Nostra aetate, AAS* 58 (1966), pp. 740–744. (C.T.S. Do 360).

97. As a result of the work of the communications media, Christians are better able to understand the state of contemporary world society, a society which is frequently alienated from God. Dramatists and journalists describe this alienation in significant terms—asserting human liberty with all the force of their genius and with all the depth of their thought. Their creative power and descriptive skill has our admiration and gratitude.[50]

98. When their faith gives them real inspiration, people of different religions can render notable service to social communications. This will do more than further human progress both social and cultural. It can under Divine Providence institute a universal dialogue on the highest level that can lead man to cherish and foster in his daily life his common brotherhood under the One Eternal God, the Father of All.

99. There is almost no end to the opportunities for such collaboration. Some are obvious: joint programs on radio and television; educational projects and services especially for parents and young people; meetings and discussions between professionals, perhaps at an international level; recognition of achievement in these fields by annual awards; cooperation in research in the media, especially in professional training and education. All these can help towards the fair and equal advancement of all people.

100. To make practical the possibilities that are inherent in the media there should be a joint program of action. Resources will have to be made available for this. As a practical step the Vatican Council suggested the establishment of World Communications Day. Every man who believes in God is invited to spend one particular day every year to pray and think about the future and the problems of the media. He is also invited to friendly meetings with the different sorts of professionals. In this way it should be possible to explore what projects can be started and what initiatives encouraged, whereby the media can be used to further the progress of mankind. The People of God (both pastors and laymen) commit themselves, in the fulfilment of these duties, to give support to the initiatives of men of goodwill everywhere, so that the means of social communication may be used for justice, peace, freedom and human progress.

---

50. This was expressed by the World Council of Churches in their "Instruction" issued at Uppsala in 1968, p. 381.

PART THREE

The Commitment of Catholics in the Media

101. By the Second Vatican Council Catholics have been asked to consider still more carefully and in the light of the Faith what new work and responsibility the modern means of social communication place upon them.

In the first part of this Instruction, we have suggested how the history of salvation implied a vital role for social communications in God's creative and redeeming work among men. In interpreting her responsibilities in this, the Church tries to give a coherent vision that will embrace both the Faith and the practical working of social communication. It is in this light that she will fulfil her divine mission which is the object of all her pastoral activity, and which has the dual aspect of helping men and of announcing the Good News.

The aspect of human advancement by the media has been generally discussed in the second part of this document. The specifically Christian and Catholic contribution to human advancement will be dealt with briefly in the following chapter of this third part, which is concerned with the role of the media in the life of Catholics.

CHAPTER I

THE CONTRIBUTION OF CATHOLICS TO SOCIAL COMMUNICATION

102. If Catholics are to be of service to the means of social communication and to act so that these may serve humanity's ends, it goes without saying that it is in the spiritual sphere that the Church can best help. The Church hopes that, as a result of her spiritual contribution, the basic na-

ture of social communication will be more clearly appreciated. The Church hopes, too, that the dignity of the human person, both communicator and recipient, will be better understood and respected. In this way this social interplay that makes neighbors of men can lead to true communion.

103. Therefore the active cooperation of Christians who are professionally competent in this field is a major service to social communication. The excellence which they bring to their professional duty is itself a powerful testimony to Christianity. Moreover, as members of companies or organizations without religious affiliations, they will bring to the fore a Christian point of view on all questions that exercise men in society. They can help news editors and newscasters not to overlook news items about religious life which will interest their audience. They can give the religious dimension to human life. It goes without saying that they are not at this work in order to dominate the media with their viewpoint. Rather they aim to give a service which will earn the sympathy of their colleagues simply by its quality.

104. Communicators have the right to expect the kind of spiritual help that meets the special needs of their important but difficult role.

It is a source of strength for Catholic communicators that they receive from the Church spiritual help to meet the needs of their important and difficult role.

105. Fully aware of the importance of their profession and of the special difficulties it involves, the Church is very willing to undertake a dialogue with all communicators of every religious persuasion. She would do this so that she may contribute to a common effort to solve the problems inherent in their task and do what is best for the benefit of man.

106. As representatives of the Church, bishops, priests, religious, and laity are increasingly asked to write in the press, or appear on radio and television, or to collaborate in filming. They are warmly urged to undertake this work, which has consequences that are far more important than is usually imagined. But the complexity of the media requires a sound knowledge of their impact and of the best way to use them. It is therefore the task of the national centers and of the specialized organizations to make certain that those who have to use the media receive sufficient and timely training.

107. The Church considers it to be one of her most urgent tasks to provide the means for training recipients in Christian principles. This also is a service to social communication. The well-trained recipient will be able to take part in the dialogue promoted by the media and will demand high quality in communications. Catholic schools and organizations cannot ignore the urgent duty they have in this field. These schools and institutions will take care to teach young people not only to be good Christians when they are recipients but also to be active in using all the aids to communication that lie within the media, now called the "total language." So, young people will be true citizens of that age of social communication which has already begun.

108. The whole question of social communications deserves attention from theologians, particularly in the areas of moral and pastoral theology. Religious education, too, ought to include instruction on the modern media and their principal implications. This will be more readily achieved when theologians have studied the suggestions in Part One of this Instruction and enriched them with their research and insight.

109. Parents, educators, priests and Christian organizations should encourage young people with the right qualities to take up a career in social communication. To do this and to provide properly trained candidates, funds are necessary. In developing areas, the national hierarchies should get financial help for the training of local candidates both in theory and practice.

110. Bishops, priests, religious and laity, all in their own ways, have a clear duty to contribute to Christian education in this field. They must make this contribution with the social teachings of the Church in mind.

They should of their own accord keep in touch with the latest developments in communications so as to be well informed themselves. Otherwise they will lack that familiarity with the media which actual use requires. Working with professional communicators, they will be wise to go more deeply into the problems presented by communicating through the media and to exchange their experiences and ideas.

111. If students for the priesthood and religious in training wish to be part of modern life and also to be at all effective in their apostolate, they should know how the media work upon the fabric of society, and also the technique of their

use. This knowledge should be an integral part of their ordinary education. Indeed, without this knowledge an effective apostolate is impossible in a society which is increasingly conditioned by the media.[51] It is also desirable that
priests and religious understand how public opinion and
popular attitudes come into being, so that they can suit
both the situation and the people of their time. They can
find the media of great help in their effort to announce the
Word of God to modern men. Students who show a special
gift in the handling of the media should be given higher
training.

112. Reviews of radio and television broadcasts, of films
and illustrated magazines can be of help in cultural and religious education. They will also help those who wish to
make a wise choice of what the media have to offer, particularly for the family. In this connection, particular attention should be paid to reviews that have real competence.
These include assessment of the worth, the morality and the
Christian value of films, broadcasts and writings issued under the pastoral care of bishops in different regions by specially appointed boards.

113. Catholic universities and educational institutions
should be more assiduous in the promotion of scientific
studies and research on social communications. They
should try to collate all the findings of research, themselves
play a part in this research, and make all of it available to
the service of Christian education. While they will need financial help from others for these projects, they in turn
should readily cooperate with other institutions.

51. Cf. The Sacred Congregation for Catholic Education, "The
Fundamental Characteristic of Priestly Education." *AAS* 62 (1970),
pp. 321–384. See especially par. 4 and no. 68.

CHAPTER II

THE CONTRIBUTION OF THE COMMUNICATIONS MEDIA TO CATHOLICS

I. PUBLIC OPINION AND A CLOSER COMMUNICATION IN THE LIFE OF THE CHURCH

114. The Church looks for ways of multiplying and strengthening the bonds of union between her members. For this reason, communication and dialogue among Catholics are indispensable. The Church lives her life in the midst of the whole community of man. She must therefore maintain contacts and lines of communication in order to keep a relationship with the whole human race. This is done both by giving information and by listening carefully to public opinion inside and outside the Church. Finally, by holding a continuous discussion with the contemporary world, she tries to help in solving the problems that men face at the present time.

A. Dialogue Within the Church

115. Since the Church is a living body, she needs public opinion in order to sustain a giving and taking between her members. Without this, she cannot advance in thought and action. "Something would be lacking in her life if she had no public opinion. Both pastors of souls and lay people would be to blame for this."[52]

116. Catholics should be fully aware of the real freedom to speak their minds which stems from a "feeling for the faith" and from love.

It stems from that feeling for the faith which is aroused and nourished by the spirit of truth in order that, under the guidance of the teaching Church which they accept with reverence, the People of God may cling unswervingly to the faith given to the early Church, with true judgment penetrate its meaning more deeply, and apply it more fully in their lives.[53]

52. Pius XII: Allocution given on 17 February 1950 to those who were in Rome to participate in the International Congress for Editors of Catholic Periodicals. *AAS* 42 (1950), p. 256.
53. Cf. *Lumen gentium*, no. 12.

This freedom also stems from love. For it is with love that the liberty of the People of God is raised to an intimate sharing in the freedom of Christ himself, who cleansed us from our sins, in order that we might be able freely to make judgments in accordance with the will of God.

Those who exercise authority in the Church will take care to ensure that there is responsible exchange of freely held and expressed opinion among the People of God. More than this, they will set up norms and conditions for this to take place.[54]

117. There is an enormous area where members of the Church can express their views on domestic issues. It must be taken that the truths of the faith express the essence of the Church and therefore do not leave room for arbitrary interpretations. Nonetheless, the Church moves with the movement of man. She therefore has to adapt herself to the special circumstances that arise out of time and place. She has to consider how the truths of the Faith may be explained in different times and cultures. She has to reach a multitude of decisions while adjusting her actions to the changes around her. While the individual Catholic follows the Magisterium, he can and should engage in free research so that he may better understand revealed truths or explain them to a society subject to incessant change.

This free dialogue within the Church does no injury to her unity and solidarity. It nurtures concord and the meeting of minds by permitting the free play of the variations of public opinion. But in order that this dialogue may go in the right direction it is essential that charity is in command even when there are differing views. Everyone in this dialogue should be animated by the desire to serve and to consolidate unity and cooperation. There should be a desire to build, not to destroy. There should be a deep love for the Church and a compelling desire for its unity. Christ made love the sign by which men can recognize his true Church and therefore his true followers.[55]

118. For this reason, a distinction must be borne in mind between, on the one hand, the area that is devoted to scientific investigation and, on the other, the area that concerns the teaching of the faithful. In the first, experts enjoy the

54. Cf. "Reflexions and Suggestions on Ecumenical Dialogue" (D.42).
55. Cf. Jn. 17:21.

freedom required by their work and are free to communicate to others, in books and commentaries, the fruits of their research. In the second, only those doctrines may be attributed to the Church which are declared to be such by her authentic Magisterium. These last, obviously, can be aired in public without fear of giving scandal.

It sometimes happens, however, because of the very nature of social communication, that new opinions circulating among theologians, at times, circulate too soon and in the wrong places. Such opinions, which must not be confused with the authentic doctrine of the Church, should be examined critically. It must also be remembered that the real significance of such theories is often badly distorted by popularization and by the style of presentation used in the media.

119. Since the development of public opinion within the Church is essential, individual Catholics have the right to all the information they need to play their active role in the life of the Church.

In practice this means that communications media must be available for the task. These should not only exist in sufficient number but also reach all the People of God. Where necessary, they may even be owned by the Church as long as they truly fulfil their purpose.

120. The normal flow of life and the smooth functioning of government within the Church require a steady two-way flow of information between the ecclesiastical authorities at all levels and the faithful as individuals and as organized groups. This applies to the whole world. To make this possible various institutions are required. These might include news agencies, official spokesmen, meeting facilities, pastoral councils—all properly financed.

121. On those occasions when the affairs of the Church require secrecy, the rules normal in civil affairs equally apply.

On the other hand, the spiritual riches which are an essential attribute of the Church demand that the news she gives out of her intentions as well as of her works be distinguished by integrity, truth and openness. When ecclesiastical authorities are unwilling to give information or are unable to do so, then rumor is unloosed, and rumor is not a bearer of the truth but carries dangerous half-truths. Secrecy should therefore be restricted to matters that involve the good name of individuals, or that touch upon the rights of people whether singly or collectively.

B. Dialogue Between the Church and the World

122. The Church does not speak and listen to her own members alone; her dialogue is with the whole world. By virtue of a divine command and by the right to knowledge possessed by the people whose lot she shares on earth, the Church is in duty bound publicly to communicate her belief and her way of life.[56] Moreover, as the Second Vatican Council teaches, she is "to read the signs of the times," for these, too, reveal the message of God and indicate the unfolding of the history of salvation under Divine Providence. This is another reason why the Church needs to know contemporary reactions to ideas and events, whether they be Catholic or not. The greater the extent to which the means of social communication reflect these reactions, the more do they contribute towards this knowledge required by the Church.

123. It is the mission of those with responsible positions in the Church to announce without fail or pause the full truth, by the means of social communication, so as to give a true picture of the Church and her life. Since the media are often the only channels of information that exist between the Church and the world, a failure to use them amounts to "burying the talent given by God."

The Church naturally expects news agencies to put out religious news with all the care and attention that the subject demands. On her part, the Church is consequently bound in duty to give complete and entirely accurate information to the news agencies so that they, in their turn, can carry out their task.

124. What was said above,[57] where commentaries on the news were discussed, equally applies when the news is about the Church. Responsible leaders in the Church should try in advance to be ready to deal with a difficult situation and should not abandon the initiative. Further, it is wise to see that important decisions and statements be made available in advance, using time embargo on publication. In this way, arrangements can be made in the interests of the Church for proper explanation and discussion.

125. The means of social communication help Catholics in three ways. They help the Church reveal herself to the modern world. They foster dialogue within the Church.

56. Cf. Mt. 28:19.
57. Cf. par. 38 above.

They make clear to the Church contemporary opinions and attitudes. For the Church has been ordered by God to give men the message of salvation in a language they can understand and to involve herself in the concerns of man.

II. THE USE OF THE MEDIA FOR GIVING THE GOOD NEWS

126. Christ commanded the apostles and their successors to "teach all nations,"[58] to be "the light of the world,"[59] and to announce the Good News in all places at all times. During his life on earth, Christ showed himself to be the perfect Communicator, while the Apostles used what means of social communication were available in their time. It is now necessary that the same message be carried by the means of social communication that are available today. Indeed, it would be difficult to suggest that Christ's command was being obeyed unless all the opportunities offered by the modern media to extend to vast numbers of people the announcement of his Good News were being used. Therefore the Second Vatican Council invited the People of God "to use effectively and at once the means of social communication zealously availing themselves of them for apostolic purposes."[60]

127. The necessity for doing this is quite obvious once it is realized that modern men are immersed in the tide of social communication when they are forming their profound convictions and adopting their attitudes. This is as true of religious convictions and attitudes as it is of any other sort.

128. The modern media offer new ways of confronting people with the message of the Gospel, of allowing Christians even when they are far away to share in sacred rites and worship and in ecclesiastical functions. In this way they can bind the Christian community closer together and invite everyone to participate in the intimate life of the Church. Of course, the mode of presentation has to suit the special nature of the medium being used. The media are not the same as a church pulpit. It cannot be overstressed that the standard of such presentations must at least equal in quality the other productions of the media.

129. The media are invaluable helps for Christian educa-

58. Mt. 28:19.
59. Mt. 5:14.
60. *Inter mirifica*, no. 13.

tion. They can call on the services of the greatest specialists in religious teaching, as well as of experts on all the questions that arise. The media have at their command all the technical facilities required for attractive and contemproary presentation. They can back up most effectively the personal work of the teacher day by day. Their resources make possible the radical changes that are required in the whole style of religious instruction today.

Since the instruments of social communication are the usual channels for giving the news and for voicing contemporary man's attitudes and views, they offer marvellous opportunities to all for considering the implications of their religious convictions through the discussion of events and problems of the day. The Christian can then apply these deepened convictions to his daily life.

130. People today have grown so used to the entertaining style and skilful presentation of communications by the media that they are intolerant of what is obviously inferior in any public presentation. The same applies if this be a religious occasion, such as, for example, a liturgical ceremony, a sermon or instruction in the Faith.

131. In order to make the teaching of Christianity more interesting and effective the media should be used as much as possible. Every effort should be made to use the most appropriate technique and style in fitting a communication to its medium.

132. The Church can use means of communication that are not under her control but which, under agreed conditions, are offered for her use. Where it is necessary, she may also herself own and administer means of communication. No hard and fast rules can here be laid down; the situation varies from place to place. Religious authorities will advise those who are involved in this apostolate what to do within the differing conditions of different countries. They should give this advice when they have consulted the local experts and, if it should be necessary, after seeking international advice.

133. Considerable financial resources are required if Catholics are to meet the different commitments to further human progress in the light of the Gospel, both by making their proper contribution to social communication and by using these God-given methods themselves. Catholics are called upon to consider their responsibilities in this field and to meet them with generosity "as it would ill become

the faithful to suffer the word of salvation to be confined and circumscribed."[61]

134. In view of the mounting importance of the means of social communication—to the life of mankind in general and of the Church in particular—the media should receive a great deal more emphasis than they presently get in the overall plans for pastoral action made by Episcopal Conferences. These plans should make the necessary funds available for use in the areas under their jurisdiction. Funds should also be made available for international cooperation.

CHAPTER III

THE ACTIVE COMMITMENT OF CATHOLICS IN THE DIFFERENT MEDIA

135. We have considered[62] what should be the right approach of dedicated Catholic communicators towards their work, an approach shared by colleagues, whatever the nature of their beliefs. For the Catholic, his Faith provides an extra incentive.

Then we dealt with the special duties of communicators working specifically as Catholics. In this we confined ourselves to general discussion, without dealing with the media one by one.[63]

Here we deal with the duties of Catholic communicators in each separate medium of social communication. These are duties that affect anyone who appears in the name of the Church, whether he appears in media that are officially Catholic or as a spokesman in some uncommitted institution that opens its facilities to the expression of a Catholic point of view.

I. THE PRINTED WORD

136. The Press, of its power and nature, is of towering importance. Because of its adaptability, because of its variety and of the number of its publications, it can go into de-

61. *Inter mirifica*, no. 17.
62. Cf. par. 102–113 above.
63. Cf. par. 126–134 above.

tail when reporting the news. It can also comment on the news and, without boring the reader, interpret it in a way that makes him think for himself. It is a most useful complement to the audio-visual means of communication. It is a most effective means of stimulating men's critical faculties and of helping them form their own opinions. Since it is able to deal with such a variety of material, and since it can so admirably encourage men to think, it has prime place in the promotion of social dialogue.

Moreover, today all the classics of religious literature are available to everybody in the form of paperbacks, booklets and every sort of leaflet. So also are the accepted masterpieces of every nation, scientific works and every sort of light reading that can provide pleasant relaxation. "Comics" and illustrated stories are not to be despised. They can for instance be used to illustrate the sacred scriptures and the lives of the saints. All these productions of the printing press deserve our interest and support.

137. The Catholic Press—and this includes reviews, magazines and periodicals—can be marvellously effective in bringing a knowledge of the Church to the world and a knowledge of the world to the Church. It does this by imparting information and by stimulating those processes by which public opinion is formed. There is, however, no advantage in founding new publications if quantity is achieved at the cost of quality and if the new injure the old.

138. That part of the Catholic Press which is of general interest publishes news and opinions and background articles about all the facets and problems and worries of modern life. This it does in the light of Christian principles. It is the task of the Catholic Press to balance, to complete and, if necessary, to correct the news and comments about religion and the Christian life. At one and the same time it will be a glass that reflects the world and a light to show it the way. It will be a forum, a meeting place for the exchange of views. This Press needs talented men and funds if its professional competence is to be above dispute.

139. The Catholic Press must be able to acquire suitable offices and the proper facilities for obtaining news reports and features. Otherwise, a Catholic-run Press cannot effectively promote dialogue inside the Church and between the Church and the outside world. It must also achieve professional standards in printing up-to-date, accurate and com-

prehensive news about the life of the Church. In the collecting, collating and passing on of the news throughout the world there is need for cooperation at the international level.

140. Catholics are encouraged to read Catholic publications regularly. Naturally these must deserve the name of being Catholic. It is hard to see how people can keep in touch with what is happening in the Church without the Catholic Press. Neither can people keep a Catholic attitude towards what happens in the world without the help of commentaries on the news written in the light of Christian principles. This is certainly not intended as an interference in the individual's right to read what he chooses. Still less is it intended as an interference with the freedom of expression of writers with different convictions, nor is it intended to discourage the diversity ordinarily taken for granted in a particular area. It is self-evident that Catholic writers must earn their popularity and following by the high standard of their work.

141. When the events of the day raise questions that touch fundamental Christian principles, the Catholic Press will try to interpret these in accordance with the Magisterium of the Church. Apart from this, clergy and laity will encourage a free expression of opinion and a wide variety of publications and points of view. They should do this because it will satisfy the different interests and concerns of readers, and because it contributes to the formation of public opinion in the Church and the world.[64] Those Catholic newspapers which are recognized as the official organs of the various authorities and institutions of the Church should always, in accordance with usual press practice, try to explain fully the thinking of the organization for which they are accepted as public spokesmen. In these newspapers, an unrestricted liberty of expression should be maintained in those pages where it is made quite clear that the editors are not committing themselves in a particular question that is still under discussion.

64. Cf. Par. 114–121 above, where dialogue in the Church is discussed. Cf. Paul VI: *Ecclesiam Suam* (C.T.S. Do 354). See also the outline of the principles for ecumenical dialogue in the document "Reflections and Suggestions on Ecumenical Dialogue" (D.*42*), especially nn. IV, 4b and IV, 5.

II. CINEMA

142. The Cinema is part of contemporary life. It exerts a strong influence on education, knowledge, culture and leisure. The artist finds in film a very effective means of expressing his interpretation of life, and one that well suits his times. The improvement of techniques that increase audience-participation and the general availability at low cost of filming and projecting equipment, presage an even wider use of films in the future. Because of all this, it is possible to derive a deeper appreciation and a richer cultural dividend from the film and filming.

143. These developments should be carefully studied in pastoral planning, for there are many openings for a greater use of this medium in pastoral action. There has been a growth of international cooperation in this field. And it is easier now to produce films that are completely adapted to various needs and circumstances and to project these, not only in large cinemas, but also in small halls and even in homes.

144. Many films have compellingly treated subjects that concern human progress or spiritual values. Such works deserve everyone's praise and support. The Catholic organizations specializing in films should be among the first to support them. They should also promote these films in an organized manner. In this connection, it will be recalled that among films which have been widely accepted as classics, many have dealt with specifically religious themes. This not only proves that the cinema is a proper vehicle for such noble themes, but it is a strong encouragement to produce films of this kind.

145. Catholic associations for the cinema should collaborate with their counterparts in the other media in endeavors to plan, produce, distribute and exhibit films imbued with religious principles. With discrimination, they should also use for religious teaching all the new developments in this field which make inexpensive productions possible. These include gramophone records, audio- and video-tape-recorders, video-cassettes and all the machines that record and play back either sound or static or moving images.

146. In regions where there is illiteracy, films can make a very effective contribution to the provision of basic education. They can also help in teaching religious truth. The il-

literate are profoundly affected by images and can readily grasp the facts and ideas presented through them. The media should be used effectively in the effort to promote human and religious progress. But, of course, the films chosen for use must be suited to the cultural traditions of the local population.

147. Those engaged in film-making must cope with considerable professional difficulties. So all Catholics, and in particular those who belong to associations concerned with the cinema, should readily establish and maintain contact with them. This friendliness will clearly demonstrate the high regard in which their work is held as an art, and so all will convince themselves that this product of man's ingenuity is outstandingly useful.

III. RADIO AND TELEVISION

148. Radio and Television have given society new patterns of communication. They have changed ways of life. Broadcasting stretches out, farther and farther, towards every corner of the earth. Instantaneous transmissions break through political and cultural barriers. What they have to say reaches men in their own homes. Broadcasters have access to the minds and hearts of everyone. Rapid technological advances, especially those that involve satellite transmissions and the recording and storage of programs, have done still more to free the media from the restrictions of time and space, and these promise still more effectiveness and influence. For the listener and viewer, radio and television open up the whole world of events, of culture and of entertainment. Television, especially, brings individuals and events before the general public, as though the viewers were actually present. And besides the established forms of artistic expression, broadcasters have created art forms of their own which can affect man in new ways.

149. The religious aspects of human life find a place in daily broadcasting, both on radio and on television.

150. Religious programs that utilize all the resources of radio and television enrich people's religious life and create new bonds between the faithful. They help in religious education and in the Church's active commitment in the world. They are bonds of union for those who cannot share physically in the life of the Church because of their sickness or old age. In addition they create new relationships between

the faithful and those people—and today they are legion—who have no affiliation with any Church and yet subconsciously seek spiritual nourishment. They carry the message of the Gospel to countries where the Church is not. The Church cannot afford to ignore such opportunities. On the contrary, she will make the fullest use of any fresh opportunities that the improvement of those instruments may disclose.

151. The transmission of the Mass and of other sacred rites is to be included in religious broadcasting. Both in their technical and in their religious aspects, such transmissions must be carefully prepared in advance. The vastness of the audience must be considered and, if transmissions cross national frontiers, so too must the religious sensitivities and conditions of other nations. How often such programs are transmitted and how long they should last must be decided upon in the light of the popular demand.

152. Sermons and homilies must be adapted to the nature of the medium that is used. Those who are given the task of preaching in this way should, therefore, be carefully chosen from among those who have a sound practical knowledge of the technique of broadcasting.

153. Religious broadcasts, such as newscasts, commentaries, reports and discussions, can contribute a great deal towards education and dialogue. What has already been said about the Catholic commitment in the press, applies here too. And here, also, the general rules for giving a fair hearing to different points of view are equally valid, especially when the medium in question enjoys, in practice, a monopoly in a given region.

154. Well-known Catholics who go on the air, whether they are clerical or lay, are automatically regarded as spokesmen of the Church. They must keep this in mind and try to avoid any confusion arising from this. Even so they will be conscious of the responisbility when they express their views, when they decide on the style of their broadcast, and indeed on their whole manner of behavior. If they can do so in time, they should consult competent ecclesiastical authorities.

155. Listeners and viewers will contribute to the betterment of religious programs by making their reactions known.

156. If the active presence of the Church in general and in religious programs is to be ensured, then a close collabo-

ration based on mutual trust must be established between the responsible Catholic authorities and the broadcasting companies.

157. In those countries where the Church is forbidden the use of the media of social communication, listening to foreign religious broadcasts may be the only way the faithful can learn about the life of the Universal Church and hear the Word of God. In the name of Christian solidarity, such a situation puts a grave obligation upon the Catholics of other countries. It is necessary to organize religious broadcasts that are specially suited to the needs of fellow Christians who suffer this sort of deprivation.

IV. THE THEATER

158. The theater is one of the most ancient and lively forms of human expression and communication. Even today it commands a large audience, not only of those who go to plays, but also of those who follow drama on radio and television. Moreover, many plays have been adapted for films.

159. The partnership of the theater with the mass media of communication has brought about forms of dramatic expression that, aptly, have been called "multi-media," and these add something of their own to the traditional theater. Using their different resources, these have created a kind of synthesis of the potentials of each of the media of communication.

160. Finally and most significantly, the contemporary theater is, without doubt, an experimental workshop for the expression of new, daring and challenging ideas about modern man and his predicament. The impact of all this goes far beyond the audience attending a particular play, which may be quite small. Ultimately it extends to all the media of communication.

161. The Church has always shown considerable interest in the theater which, in its origins, was closely connected with manifestations of religion. This ancient interest in the theater should be maintained by Christians today and full use be made of its possibilities. Playwrights should be encouraged and helped to set man's religious preoccupations on the platform of the public stage. This is often the first step in a much wider diffusion made possible by the communications media.

CHAPTER IV

EQUIPMENT, PERSONNEL AND ORGANIZATION

162. The place of the instruments of social communication in human destiny, the opportunities and the problems that they set before the Christian conscience, all this makes it essential that a way be found for a pastoral approach to this field. Trained and experienced men must be found for this work. The proper pastoral structures, with all the necessary funding, rights and resources, should also be set up.

Finally, special organizations should be devoted to the apostolate of each of the media.

163. This modern mission of the Church will mean a great deal to the faithful. They will offer their prayers and support so that she will be adequately equipped to fulfil it. The latest media of social communication are indispensable means for evangelization, and for enlightening the minds and hearts of men. They also contribute towards cooperation in furthering human progress by a Christian leavening of the social order.

164. The official Catholic organizations and enterprises that work in social communications with a pastoral end in view, should be able to call upon trained personnel. The training of laymen, priests and religious is to be given a high priority by those responsible for this work in the Church.

165. A careful appraisal of the entire range of the communications media, a prudent and well-informed planning for pastoral work and in every apostolic enterprise, all this is the rightful province of the ecclesiastical authorities. They, in their turn, should depend upon the advice of experts in the different branches of communication. According to the ground rule laid down in *Inter mirifica*, this duty devolves upon every bishop in every diocese,[65] upon a special commission of bishops or a bishop-delegate in each country[66] and, for the Universal Church, upon the Pontifical Commission for Social Communications.[67]

166. The different sorts of projects and organizations for the specialized apostolate in social communications should

65. Cf. *Inter mirifica*, n. 20.
66. Cf. ibid., n. 21.
67. Cf. ibid., n. 19.

everywhere be promoted and coordinated one with another.[68] The ecclesiastical authorities should encourage the free flowering of Catholic initiative in this, but they should retain guidance over those works which properly belong to the priestly ministry, and over those which—according to the circumstances of time and place—demand a commitment on the part of the hierarchy on behalf of the faithful.

167. The competent ecclesiastical authorities at all levels (mentioned in par. 165) will lend their full support to the preparation and celebration of World Communications Day. This day has been designed specially to honor the professionals in the media and to encourage their cooperation.[69] The ecclesiastical authorities will present regularly to the Episcopal Conferences projects for financing pastoral activity in the field of social communications.

168. The local hierarchies will take a keen interest in the apostolate of social communications. They will seek the advice of their priests and laity. Wherever possible, diocesan or, at least, inter-diocesan offices will be set up. One of the chief tasks of these is to organize this pastoral apostolate within the diocese, penetrating right down to parish level. Another task is to prepare for the celebration of World Communications Day (mentioned above) within the diocese.

169. A national office for the communications media should be set up in every country. It can be divided into specialized and reasonably autonomous departments for each of the media. Or it can have separate offices for the press, cinema and broadcasting that work closely together. In any case, the whole of this apostolate should be placed under a single, overall direction.[70]

170. It is the mission of the national and diocesan offices to stimulate, promote and harmonize Catholic activities in the field of social communications. They will take particular pains about the training of the faithful, clerical and lay, by means of organized courses, conferences, study sessions and critical assessments prepared by their experts, so that the faithful can use their own informed judgment. The offices will also be ready to give advice to producers engaged in

68. Cf. *Apostolicam actuostitatem*, nn. 19 and 21.
69. *Inter mirifica*, n. 18.
70. Cf. ibid., n. 21.

films, performances or broadcasts that concern religious subjects.

171. The national and diocesan offices will maintain
these contacts with the professional world of social communications. They will furnish the documentary material, the
advice and the pastoral assistance that professional communicators may require. They also are to organize World
Communications Day on the national level and organize the
collection of funds that the Decree of the Council suggests
should be made on that day.[71]

172. The national episocopal commission for social communications or the delegated bishop is in charge of the
direction of all the activities of the national offices. They
are to lay down general guidelines for the development of
the apostolate of social communications on the national level. They will keep in touch with the other national episcopal
commissions and collaborate with the Pontifical Commission for Social Communications. The status of this Commission is described in the Conciliar Decree *Inter
mirifica*[72] and in the Apostolic Letter, by Pope Paul VI, *In
Fructibus multis.*[73]

173. On continents or in regions where an Episcopal
Conference exists that embraces several countries, this Conference will have an office for social communications under
the overall direction of a bishop or a number of bishops.

174. Every diocese, all Episcopal Conferences or Bishops' Assemblies and the Holy See itself should each have its
own official and permanent spokesman or press officer to issue the news and give clear explanations of the documents
of the Church so that people can grasp precisely what is intended. These spokesmen will give, in full and without delay, information on the life and work of the Church in that
area for which they are responsible. It is highly recommended that individual dioceses and the more weighty
Catholic organizations also have their own permanent
spokesmen with the sort of duties explained above.

All these officials and, indeed, all those who are identified
with the Church in the mind of the public, should take into
account the principles of public relations. They should consider the sort of audience they are, at various times, ad-

71. Cf. *Inter mirifica*, n. 18.
72. Cf. ibid., n. 19.
73. Cf. *In Fructibus multis. AAS* 56 (1964), pp. 289–292.

dressing and establish a relationship that is based on mutual trust and understanding. This can only be maintained as long as people have a genuine regard and consideration for one another and a scrupulous respect for the truth.

175. It is not enough to have a public spokesman. There must be a continual two-way flow of news and information. On the one hand, this aims to present a true image of the Church in a way that makes it visible to all. On the other, this exchange reveals to the ecclesiastical authorities the surges, currents and ideas that stir the world of men. Clearly this calls for the cultivation of friendly relations based on mutual respect between the Church, people and groups. In this way continual exchanges can be fostered, with each side both giving and receiving.[74]

176. To make sure of an effective dialogue, both within the Church and with the outside world, on the subject of recent events and their religious significance, official news releases are indispensable. These will publicize relevant news-items as quickly as possible. The public, in this way, will get their information in good time. Needless to say, all the necessary means are to be used to make these releases absolutely accurate and so avoid the necessity for subsequent corrections. News flashes, telex, all the latest techniques will be used to convey precise meanings in the most dependable way.

177. Religious Orders and Congregations will give thought to the many pressing tasks of the Church in the field of social communications and consider what they themselves can do to fulfil them under their constitutions. Their own specialized institutions for social communications will collaborate with one another, and they will keep abreast of the overall pastoral planning of the diocesan offices, and of the national, continental or regional offices, since these are, usually, the competent bodies for the apostolate of social communications.

178. The national offices[75] and the corresponding central offices of the Religious Congregations will cooperate with the International Organization for the Press, (U.C.I.P.), for the Cinema, (O.C.I.C.), and for Radio and Television, (UNDA). This will be done in accord with the statutes of

74. Cf. par. 138–141 above.
75. Cf. par. 169 above.

these international organizations as approved by the Holy See.[76]

179. These international Catholic organizations for social communications—each in its own sphere and in a way that fits its statutes—will help the national professional bodies of Catholics who have given themselves to these tasks. The way to do this is to keep abreast of research and development in the media. They will foster mutual aid and international cooperation. They will keep themselves informed on Catholic activity in the field. They will prepare the coordination of international programs and projects. They will continually seek advice on the best ways to help developing countries. They will encourage fresh initiatives. They will produce and distribute films and recorded broadcasts and every sort of audiovisual material, including the printed word. They will do all this for the advancement of social progress and for the betterment of Catholic life. These international Catholic organizations are exhorted to undertake and to coordinate research for the solution of their common problems.

180. The Episcopal Conferences, through their specialized offices, and the Catholic professional associations, will assure for the international Catholic organization the funds necessary for doing this work.

Conclusion

181. The question is posed whether we are on the threshold of an utterly new sort of era in social communications or whether we face merely a change in degree and not in kind. There is no easy answer to this question and it continually increases in complexity. What is certain is that soon, due to the latest technical developments—especially those that concern communication satellites—sounds, images and the messages they bear will soon be reaching men, simultaneously, all over the world. It will be possible to record these and play them back at will—either for entertainment or for instruction. So it will be possible for all peoples to learn more of each other as a result of this real dialogue. They can then work together for the unity of mankind and the establishment of peace.

76. Cf. *Inter mirifica*, n. 22.

182. Suddenly, and in proportion with these changes, the responsibilities of the People of God will enormously increase. Never before will they have been offered such opportunities. It will be possible to ensure that the media promote the advancement of the whole human race and the development of those countries in what is called the "Third World." It will be possible to strengthen the brotherhood of man. And then the Good News can be given everywhere, bearing witness to Christ, the Savior.

183. This Pastoral Instruction lays down some guidelines chosen after consideration of the general situation that prevails in social communications. As things stand at present, it would not be reasonable to try to be more precise and detailed. The Christian outlook is based on certain immutable principles that are founded on that message of love which is the Gospel's Good News and upon the dignity of man, who has been called to be an adopted son of God. It is obvious that directions and practical applications, as well as pastoral guidelines, will have to be adapted to the different conditions that obtain in different places—depending on their degree of technical progress and their social situation. They will change too with the changing conditions of the media and of their inherent laws, and the future is certain to bring changes in this area of social communications. In so fluid a situation, it is clear that those who are responsible for pastoral planning must stay flexible and be always willing to try to keep pace with new discoveries in this field.

184. Even today there is a great deal that must still be learned about the present media and how the fullest use can be made of them, in education particularly, and indeed at every level. There is room for study, in much greater depth, of the effects of social communications on different cultural environments and on different types of people.

In order to be able to understand the functioning of the media of social communication within the family of man, and to comprehend both their potential and present performance, to reach a better assessment of their varying psychological and cultural effects, it is necessary to concentrate on a rigorous program of scientific research. Indeed, a much greater effort than that now being made is required of all the concerned parties in furthering this research.

Universities, whether of new or ancient foundation, have an open field before them. The problems they face are not only urgent; they are also fully consonant with the dignity of the traditional disciplines. For her part, the Church wishes to let researchers know how eager she is to learn from their work in all these areas and to follow out its practical conclusions. Thus she herself may the better serve the process of social communication and use its means to the best advantage of all men.

185. In this connection, it appears necessary to discover through scientific research the true effectiveness of the Church in the field of social communications. It will then be possible to deploy her resources so that they suit the importance of the tasks she faces throughout the world. Catholics will then find it easier to start new projects that match the ever-growing importance of the media.

186. In the meantime, faced by the most urgent need for making closer contact with the professionals in social communication, for engaging these men in dialogue, for making her contribution, and for urging all men to use the media to serve both the progress of man and the glory of God, the Church could no longer delay this Pastoral Instruction. The Pontifical Commission for Social Communications issues this Instruction in accordance with the mandate from the Second Vatican Council, but only after intensive consultations on a world-wide basis. It is hoped that this publication marks not so much the end of a phase as the start of a new one.

187. The People of God walk in history. As they—who are, essentially, both communicators and recipients—advance with their times, they look forward with confidence and even with enthusiasm to whatever the development of communications in a space age may have to offer.

28

DOGMATIC CONSTITUTION ON THE CHURCH

Vatican II, *Lumen Gentium*, 21 November, 1964

CHAPTER I[a]

THE MYSTERY OF THE CHURCH

1. Christ is the light of humanity; and it is, accordingly, the heart-felt desire of this sacred Council, being gathered together in the Holy Spirit, that, by proclaiming his Gospel to every creature (cf. Mk. 16:15), it may bring to all men that light of Christ which shines out visibly from the Church. Since the Church, in Christ, is in the nature of sacrament—a sign and instrument, that is, of communion with God and of unity among all men—she here purposes, for the benefit of the faithful and of the whole world, to set forth, as clearly as possible, and in the tradition laid down by earlier Councils, her own nature and universal mission. The condition of the modern world lends greater urgency to this duty of the Church; for, while men of the present day are drawn ever more closely together by social, technical and cultural bonds, it still remains for them to achieve full unity in Christ.

2. The eternal Father, in accordance with the utterly gratuitous and mysterious design of his wisdom and goodness, created the whole universe, and chose to raise up men to share in his own divine life; and when they had fallen in Adam, he did not abandon them, but at all times held out to them the means of salvation, bestowed in consideration of Christ, the Redeemer, "who is the image of the invisible God, the firstborn of every creature" all the elect the Father foreknew and predestined before time began "to become conformed to the image of his Son, that he should be the firstborn among

a. This chapter has been translated by Father Colman O'Neill, o.p.

many brethren" (Rom. 8:29). He determined to call together in a holy Church those who should believe in Christ. Already present in figure at the beginning of the world, this Church was prepared in marvellous fashion in the history of the people of Israel and in the old Alliance.[1] Established in this last age of the world, and made manifest in the outpouring of the Spirit, it will be brought to glorious completion at the end of time. At that moment, as the Fathers put it, all the just from the time of Adam, "from Abel, the just one, to the last of the elect"[2] will be gathered together with the Father in the universal Church.

3. The Son, accordingly, came, sent by the Father who, before the foundation of the world, chose us and predestined us in him for adoptive sonship. For it is in him that it pleased the Father to restore all things (cf. Eph. 1:4–5 and 10). To carry out the will of the Father Christ inaugurated the kingdom of heaven on earth and revealed to us his mystery; by his obedience he brought about our redemption. The Church—that is, the kingdom of Christ already present in mystery—grows visibly through the power of God in the world. The origin and growth of the Church are symbolized by the blood and water which flowed from the open side of the crucified Jesus (cf. Jn. 19:34), and are foretold in the words of the Lord referring to his death on the cross: "And I, if I be lifted up from the earth, will draw all men to myself" (Jn. 12:32; Gk.). As often as the sacrifice of the cross by which "Christ our Pasch is sacrificed" (1 Cor. 5:7) is celebrated on the altar, the work of our redemption is carried out. Likewise, in the sacrament of the eucharistic bread, the unity of believers, who from one body in Christ (cf. 1 Cor. 10:17), is both expressed and brought about. All men are called to this union with Christ, who is the light of the world, from whom we go forth, through whom we live, and towards whom our whole life is directed.

4. When the work which the Father gave the Son to do on earth (cf. Jn. 17:4) was accomplished, the Holy Spirit was sent on the day of Pentecost in order that he might

1. See St. Cyprian, Epist. 64, 4: *PL* 3, 1017, *CSEL* (Hartel) III B, p. 720; St. Hilary of Poitiers, *In* Mt. 23, 6: *PL* 9, 1047; St. Augustine, passim; St. Cyril of Alexandria, *Glaph. in Gen.* 2, 10: *PG* 69, 110A.
2. See St. Gregory the Great, Hom. *In Evang.* 19, 1: *PL* 76; 1154B; St. Augustine, *Serm.* 341, 9, 11: *PL* 39, 1499; St. John Damascene, *Adv. Iconocl.* 11: *PG* 96, 1357.

continually sanctify the Church, and that, consequently, those who believe might have access through Christ in one Spirit to the Father (cf. Eph. 2:18). He is the Spirit of life, the fountain of water springing up to eternal life (cf. Jn. 4:47; 7:38–39). To men, dead in sin, the Father gives life through him, until the day when, in Christ, he raises to life their mortal bodies (cf. Rom. 8:10–11). The Spirit dwells in the Church and in the hearts of the faithful, as in a temple (cf. 1 Cor. 3:16; 6:19). In them he prays and bears witness to their adoptive sonship (cf. Gal. 4:6; Rom. 8:15–16 and 26). Guiding the Church in the way of all truth (cf. Jn. 16:13) and unifying her in communion and in the works of ministry, he bestows upon her varied hierarchic and charismatic gifts, and in this way directs her; and he adorns her with his fruits (cf. Eph. 4:11–12; 1 Cor. 12:4; Gal. 5:22). By the power of the Gospel he permits the Church to keep the freshness of youth. Constantly he renews her and leads her to perfect union with her Spouse.[8] For the Spirit and the Bride both say to Jesus, the Lord: "Come!" (cf. Apoc. 22:17).

Hence the universal Church is seen to be "a people brought into unity from the unity of the Father, the Son and the Holy Spirit."[4]

5. The mystery of the holy Church is already brought to light in the way it was founded. For the Lord Jesus inaugurated his Church by preaching the Good News, that is, the coming of the kingdom of God, promised over the ages in the scriptures: "The time is fulfilled, and the kingdom of God is at hand" (Mk. 1:15; Mt. 4:17). This kingdom shone out before men in the word, in the works and in the presence of Christ. The word of the Lord is compared to a seed which is sown in a field (Mk. 4:14); those who hear it with faith and are numbered among the little flock of Christ (Lk. 12:32) have truly received the kingdom. Then, by its own power the seed sprouts and grows until the harvest (cf. Mk. 4:26–29). The miracles of Jesus also demonstrate that the kingdom has already come on earth: "If I cast out devils by the finger of God, then the kingdom of God has come upon you" (Lk. 11:20; cf. Matt. 12:28). But principally the kingdom is revealed in the person of

3. See St. Irenaeus, *Adv. Haer.* III, 24, 1: *PG* 7, 966B.
4. St. Cyprian, *De Orat. Dom.* 23: *PL* 4, 553; St. Augustine, *Serm.* 71, 20, 33: *PL* 38, 463; St. John Damascene, *Adv. Iconocl.* 12: *PG* 96, 1358D.

Christ himself, Son of God and Son of Man, who came "to serve and to give his life as a ransom for many" (Mk. 10:45).

When Jesus, having died on the cross for men, rose again from the dead, he was seen to be constituted as Lord, the Christ, and as Priest for ever (cf. Acts 2:36; Heb. 5:6; 7:17–21), and he poured out on his disciples the Spirit promised by the Father (cf. Acts 2:23). Henceforward the Church, endowed with the gifts of her founder and faithfully observing his precepts of charity, humility and self-denial, receives the mission of proclaiming and establishing among all peoples the kingdom of Christ and of God, and she is, on earth, the seed and the beginning of that kingdom. While she slowly grows to maturity, the Church longs for the completed kingdom and, with all her strength, hopes and desires to be united in glory with her king.

6. In the Old Testament the revelation of the kingdom is often made under the forms of symbols. In similar fashion the inner nature of the Church is now made known to us in various images. Taken either from the life of the shepherd or from cultivation of the land, from the art of building or from family life and marriage, these images have their preparation in the books of the prophets.

The Church is, accordingly, a sheepfold, the sole and necessary gateway to which is Christ (Jn. 10:1–10). It is also a flock, of which God foretold that he would himself be the shepherd (cf. Is. 40:11; Ex. 34:11 f.), and whose sheep, although watched over by human shepherds, are nevertheless at all times led and brought to pasture by Christ himself, the Good Shepherd and prince of shepherds (cf. Jn. 10:11; 1 Pet. 5:4), who gave his life for his sheep (cf. Jn. 10:11–16).

The Church is a cultivated field, the tillage of God (1 Cor. 3:9). On that land the ancient olive tree grows whose holy roots were the prophets and in which the reconciliation of Jews and Gentiles has been brought about and will be brought about again (Rom. 11:13–26). That land, like a choice vineyard, has been planted by the heavenly cultivator (Mt. 21:33–43; cf. Is. 5:1 f.). Yet the true vine is Christ who gives life and fruitfulness to the branches, that is, to us, who through the Church remain in Christ without whom we can do nothing (Jn. 15:1–5).

Often, too, the Church is called the building of God (1 Cor. 3:9). The Lord compared himself to the stone which

the builders rejected, but which was made into the corner-
stone (Mt. 21:42; cf. Acts 4:11; 1 Pet. 2:7; Ps. 117:22).
On this foundation the Church is built by the apostles (cf.
1 Cor. 3:11) and from it the Church receives solidity and
unity. This edifice has many names to describe it: the house
of God in which his family dwells; the household of God in
the Spirit (Eph. 2:19, 22); the dwelling-place of God
among men (Apoc. 21:3); and, especially, the holy temple.
This temple, symbolized in places of worship built out of
stone, is praised by the Fathers and, not without reason, is
compared in the liturgy to the Holy City, the New
Jerusalem.[5] As living stones we here on earth are built into
it (1 Pet. 2:5). It is this holy city that is seen by John as it
comes down out of heaven from God when the world is
made anew, prepared like a bride adorned for her husband
(Apoc. 21:1 f.).

The Church, further, which is called "that Jerusalem
which is above" and "our mother" (Gal. 4:26; cf. Apoc.
12:17), is described as the spotless spouse of the spotless
lamb (Apoc. 19:7; 21:2 and 9; 22:17). It is she whom
Christ "loved and for whom he delivered himself up that he
might sanctify her" (Eph. 5:26). It is she whom he unites
to himself by an unbreakable alliance, and whom he constantly "nourishes and cherishes" (Eph 5:29). It is she
whom, once purified, he willed to be joined to himself, subject in love and fidelity (cf. Eph. 5:24), and whom, finally,
he filled with heavenly gifts for all eternity, in order that we
may know the love of God and of Christ for us, a love
which surpasses all understanding (cf. Eph. 3:19). While
on earth she journeys in a foreign land away from the Lord
(cf. 2 Cor. 5:6), the Church sees herself as an exile. She
seeks and is concerned about those things which are above,
where Christ is seated at the right hand of God, where the
life of the Church is hidden with Christ in God until she
appears in glory with her Spouse (cf. Col. 3:1–4).

7. In the human nature united to himself, the son of God,
by overcoming death through his own death and resurrec-

---

5. See *Origen, In Mt.*, 16, 21: PG 13, 1443C; Tertullian, *Adv. Marc.*
3, 7: *PL* 2, 357C; *CSEL*, 47, 3, p. 386. For liturgical documents see
Sacramentorum Gregorianum: PL 78, 160B; C. Mohlberg, *Liber
Sacramentorum Romanae Ecclesiae*, Rome, 1960, p. 111, XC: 'Deus
qui ex omni coaptacione sanctorum aeternum condis habitacul-
um . . .'; the hymn *Urbs Jersusalem beata* in the monastic breviary
and the hymn *Coelestis Urbs Jerusalem* in the Roman breviary.

tion, redeemed man and changed him into a new creation (cf. Gal. 6:15; 2 Cor. 5:17). For by communicating his Spirit, Christ mystically constitutes as his body those brothers of his who are called together from every nation.

In that body the life of Christ is communicated to those who believe and who, through the sacraments, are united in a hidden and real way to Christ in his passion and glorification.[6] Through baptism we are formed in the likeness of Christ: "For in one Spirit we were all baptized into one body" (1 Cor. 12:13). In this sacred rite fellowship in Christ's death and resurrection is symbolized and is brought about: "For we were buried with him by means of baptism into death"; and if "we have been united with him in the likeness of his death, we shall be so in the likeness of his resurrection also" (Rom. 6:4–5). Really sharing in the body of the Lord in the breaking of the eucharistic bread, we are taken up into communion with him and with one another. "Because the bread is one, we, though many, are one body, all of us who partake of the one bread" (1 Cor. 10:17). In this way all of us are made members of his body (cf. 1 Cor. 12:27), "but severally members one of another" (Rom. 12:4).

As all the members of the human body, though they are many, form one body, so also are the faithful in Christ (cf. 1 Cor. 12:12). Also, in the building up of Christ's body there is engaged a diversity of members and functions. There is only one Spirit who, according to his own richness and the needs of the ministries, gives his different gifts for the welfare of the Church (cf. 1 Cor. 12:1–11). Among these gifts the primacy belongs to the grace of the apostles to whose authority the Spirit himself subjects even those who are endowed with charisms (cf. 1 Cor. 14). Giving the body unity through himself, both by his own power and by the interior union of the members, this same Spirit produces and stimulates love among the faithful. From this it follows that if one member suffers anything, all the members suffer with him, and if one member is honored, all the members together rejoice (cf. 1 Cor. 12:26).

The head of this body is Christ. He is the image of the invisible God and in him all things came into being. He is before all creatures and in him all things hold together. He is the head of the body which is the Church. He is the be-

6. See St. Thomas Aquinas, *Summa Theol.*, III q. 62, a. 5 ad 1.

ginning, the firstborn from the dead, that in all things he might hold the primacy (cf. Col. 1:15–18). By the greatness of his power he rules heaven and earth, and with his all-surpassing perfection and activity he fills the whole body with the riches of his glory (cf. Eph. 1:18–23).[7]

All the members must be formed in his likeness, until Christ be formed in them (cf. Gal. 4:19). For this reason we, who have been made like to him, who have died with him and risen with him, are taken up into the mysteries of his life, until we reign together with him (cf. Phil. 3:21; 2 Tim. 2:11; Eph. 2:6; Col. 2:12, etc.). On earth, still as pilgrims in a strange land, following in trial and in oppression the paths he trod, we are associated with his sufferings as the body with its head, suffering with him, that with him we may be glorified (cf. Rom. 8:17).

From him "the whole body, supplied and built up by joints and ligaments, attains a growth that is of God" (Col. 2:19). He continually provides in his body, that is, in the Church, for gifts of ministries through which, by his power, we serve each other unto salvation so that, carrying out the truth in love, we may through all things grow unto him who is our head (cf. Eph. 4:11–16, Gk.).

In order that we might be unceasingly renewed in him (cf. Eph. 4:23), he has shared with us his Spirit who, being one and the same in head and members, gives life to, unifies and moves the whole body. Consequently, his work could be compared by the Fathers to the function that the principle of life, the soul, fulfils in the human body.[8]

Christ loves the Church as his bride, having been established as the model of a man loving his wife as his own body (cf. Eph. 5:25–28); the Church, in her turn, is subject to her head (Eph. 5:23–24). "Because in him dwells all the fullness of the Godhead bodily" (Col. 2:9), he fills the Church, which is his body and his fullness, with his divine gifts (cf. Eph. 1:22–23) so that it may increase and attain to all the fullness of God (cf. Eph. 3:19).

---

7. See Pius XII, Encyclical Letter, *Mystici Corporis*, 29 June 1943: *AAS* 35 (1943), p. 208.

8. See Leo XIII, Encyclical Letter, *Divinum Illud*, 9 May 1897: *AAS* 29 (1896–97), p. 650. Pius XII, Encyclical Letter, *Mystici Corporis*, *loc. cit.*, pp. 219–220: *Denz.* 2288 (3608); St. Augustine, *Serm.* 268, 2: *PL* 38, 1232, *et alibi.* St. John Chrysostom, *In Eph.*, Hom. 9, 3: *PG.* 62, 72; Didymus of Alex., *Trin.* 2, 1: PG 39, 449; St. Thomas, *In Col.*, 1, 18, lect. 5: "*Sicut constituitur unum corpus ex unitate animae, ita Ecclesia ex unitate spiritus . . .*"

8. The one mediator, Christ, established and ever sustains here on earth his holy Church, the community of faith, hope and charity, as a visible organization[9] through which he communicates truth and grace to all men. But, the society structured with hierarchical organs and the mystical body of Christ, the visible society and the spiritual community, the earthly Church and the Church endowed with heavenly riches, are not to be thought of as two realities. On the contrary, they form one complex reality which comes together from a human and a divine element.[10] For this reason the Church is compared, not without significance, to the mystery of the incarnate Word. As the assumed nature, inseparably united to him, serves the divine Word as a living organ of salvation, so, in a somewhat similar way, does the social structure of the Church serve the Spirit of Christ who vivifies it, in the building up of the body (cf. Eph. 4:15).[11]

This is the sole Church of Christ which in the Creed we profess to be one, holy, catholic and apostolic,[12] which our Saviour, after his resurrection, entrusted to Peter's pastoral care (Jn. 21:17), commissioning him and the other apostles to extend and rule it (cf. Matt. 28:18, etc.), and which he raised up for all ages as "the pillar and mainstay of the truth" (1 Tim. 3:15). This Church, constituted and organized as a society in the present world, subsists in the Catholic Church, which is governed by the successor of Peter and by the bishops in communion with him.[18] Nevertheless, many elements of sanctification and of truth are found outside its visible confines. Since these are gifts belonging to the Church of Christ, they are forces impelling towards Catholic unity.

Just as Christ carried out the work of redemption in pov-

9. Leo XIII, Encycl. *Sapientiae Christianae*, 10 June 1890: *ASS* 22 (1889–90) p. 392; *Idem* Encycl. *Satis Cognitum*, 29 June 1896: *AAS* 28 (1895–96) pp. 710 and 724; Pius XII, Encycl. *Mystici Corporis*, *loc. cit.*, pp. 199–200.

10. See Pius XII, Encycl. *Mystici Corporis, loc cit.*, p. 221; *Idem,* Encycl. *Humani Generis*, 12 August 1950, *AAS* 42 (1950), p. 571.

11. Leo XIII, Encycl. *Satis Cognitum, loc cit.*, p. 713.

12. See Apostles' Creed: *Denz.* 6–9 (10–13); *Nicene-Const. Creed: Denz.* 86 (150), coll. *Prof. fidei Trid.: Denz.*) 994 and 999 (1862 and 1868).

13. It is called: "*Sancta (Catholica apostolica) Romana Ecclesia*" in the Tridentine Profession of Faith, *loc. cit.*, and the Vatican Council, Sess. III, Const. Dogm. *de fide cath.: Denz.* 1782 (3001).

erty and oppression, so the Church is called to follow the same path if she is to communicate the fruits of salvation to men. Christ Jesus, "though he was by nature God . . . emptied himself, taking the nature of a slave" (Phil. 2:6, 7), and "being rich, became poor" (2 Cor. 8:9) for our sake. Likewise, the Church, although she needs human resources to carry out her mission, is not set up to seek earthly glory, but to proclaim, and this by her own example, humility and self-denial. Christ was sent by the Father "to bring good news to the poor . . . to heal the contrite of heart" (Lk. 4:18), "to seek and to save what was lost" (Lk. 19:10). Similarly, the Church encompasses with her love all those who are afflicted by human misery and she reconizes in those who are poor and who suffer, the image of her poor and suffering founder. She does all in her power to relieve their need and in them she strives to serve Christ. Christ, "holy, innocent and undefiled" (Heb. 7:26) knew nothing of sin (2 Cor. 5:21), but came only to expiate the sins of the people (cf. Heb. 2:17). The Church, however, clasping sinners to her bosom, at once holy and always in need of purification, follows constantly the path of penance and renewal.

The Church, "like a stranger in a foreign land, presses forward amid the persecutions of the world and the consolations of God,"[14] announcing the cross and death of the Lord until he comes (cf. 1 Cor. 11:26). But by the power of the risen Lord she is given strength to overcome, in patience and in love, her sorrows and her difficulties, both those that are from within and those that are from without, so that she may reveal in the world, faithfully, however darkly, the mystery of her Lord until, in the consummation, it shall be manifested in full light.

14. St. Augustine. *Civ. Dei,* XVIII, 51, 2: *PL* 41, 614.

THE PEOPLE OF GOD

9. At all times and in every race, anyone who fears God and does what is right has been acceptable to him (cf. Acts 10:35). He has, however, willed to make men holy and save them, not as individuals without any bond or link between them, but rather to make them into a people who might acknowledge him and serve him in holiness. He therefore chose the Israelite race to be his own people and established a covenant with it. He gradually instructed this people—in its history manifesting both himself and the decree of his will—and made it holy unto himself. All these things, however, happened as a preparation and figure of that new and perfect covenant which was to be ratified in Christ, and of the fuller revelation which was to be given through the Word of God made flesh. "Behold the days are coming, says the Lord, when I will make a new covenant with the house of Israel and the house of Judah. . . I will put my law within them, and I will write it upon their hearts, and they shall be my people . . . For they shall all know me from the least of them to the greatest, says the Lord" (Jer. 31:31–34). Christ instituted this new covenant, namely the new covenant in his blood (cf. 1 Cor. 11:25); he called a race made up of Jews and Gentiles which would be one, not according to the flesh, but in the Spirit, and this race would be the new People of God. For those who believe in Christ, who are reborn, not from a corruptible seed, but from an incorruptible one through the word of the living God (cf. 1 Pet. 1:23), not from flesh, but from water and the Holy Spirit (cf. Jn. 3:5–6), are finally established as "a chosen race, a royal priesthood, a holy nation . . . who in times past were not a people, but now are the People of God" (1 Pet. 2:9–10).

That messianic people has as its head Christ, "who was delivered up for our sins and rose again for our justification" (Rom. 4:25), and now, having acquired the name which is above all names, reigns gloriously in heaven. The state of this people is that of the dignity and freedom of the

a. This chapter has been translated by Father Christopher O'Donnell, O.CARM.

sons of God, in whose hearts the Holy Spirit dwells as in a temple. Its law is the new commandment to love as Christ loved us (cf. Jn. 13:34). Its destiny is the kingdom of God which has been begun by God himself on earth and which must be further extended until it is brought to perfection by him at the end of time when Christ our life (cf. Col. 3:4), will appear and "creation itself also will be delivered from its slavery to corruption into the freedom of the glory of the sons of God" (Rom. 8:21). Hence that messianic people, although it does not actually include all men, and at times may appear as a small flock, is, however, a most sure seed of unity, hope and salvation for the whole human race. Established by Christ as a communion of life, love and truth, it is taken up by him also as the instrument for the salvation of all; as the light of the world and the salt of the earth (cf. Mt. 5:13–16) it is sent forth into the whole world.

As Israel according to the flesh which wandered in the desert was already called the Church of God (2 Esd. 13:1; cf. Num. 20:4; Deut. 23:1 ff.), so too, the new Israel, which advances in this present era in search of a future and permanent city (cf. Heb. 13:14), is called also the Church of Christ (cf. Mt. 16:18). It is Christ indeed who had purchased it with his own blood (cf. Acts 20:28); he has filled it with his Spirit; he has provided means adapted to its visible and social union. All those, who in faith look towards Jesus, the author of salvation and the principle of unity and peace, God has gathered together and established as the Church, that it may be for each and everyone the visible sacrament of this saving unity.[1] Destined to extend to all regions of the earth, it enters into human history, though it transcends at once all times and all racial boundaries. Advancing through trials and tribulations, the Chruch is strengthened by God's grace, promised to her by the Lord so that she may not waver from perfect fidelity, but remain the worthy bride of the Lord, ceaselessly renewing herself through the action of the Holy Spirit until, through the cross, she may attain to that light which knows no setting.

10. Christ the Lord, high priest taken from among men (cf. Heb. 5:1–5), made the new people "a kingdom of priests to God, his Father" (Apoc. 1:6; cf. 5:9–10). The baptized, by regeneration and the anointing of the Holy

---

1. See St. Cyprian, *Epist.* 69, 6: *PL* 3, 1142 B; Hartel 3 B, p. 754: *"inseparabile unitatis sacramentum."*

Spirit, are consecrated to be a spiritual house and a holy priesthood, that through all the works of Christian men they may offer spiritual sacrifices and proclaim the perfection of him who has called them out of darkness into his marvellous light (cf. 1 Pet. 2:4–10). Therefore all the disciples of Christ, persevering in prayer and praising God (cf. Acts 2:42–47), should present themselves as a sacrifice, living, holy and pleasing to God (cf. Rom. 12:1). They should everywhere on earth bear witness to Christ and give an answer to everyone who asks a reason for the hope of an eternal life which is theirs. (cf. 1 Pet. 3:15).

Though they differ essentially and not only in degree, the common priesthood of the faithful and the ministerial or hierarchical priesthood are none the less ordered one to another; each in its own proper way shares in the one priesthood of Christ.[2] The ministerial priest, by the sacred power that he has, forms and rules the priestly people; in the person of Christ he effects the eucharistic sacrifice and offers it to God in the name of all the people. The faithful indeed, by virtue of their royal priesthood, participate in the offering of the Eucharist.[3] They exercise that priesthood, too, by the reception of the sacraments, prayer and thanksgiving, the witness of a holy life, abnegation and active charity.

11. The sacred nature and organic structure of the priestly community is brought into operation through the sacraments and the exercise of virtues. Incorporated into the Church by Baptism, the faithful are appointed by their baptismal character to Christian religious worship; reborn as sons of God, they must profess before men the faith they have received from God through the Church.[4] By the sacrament of Confirmation they are more perfectly bound to the Church and are endowed with the special strength of the Holy Spirit. Hence they are, as true witnesses of Christ, more strictly obliged to spread the faith by word and deed.[5]

2. See Pius XII, Alloc. *Magnificate Dominum*, 2 Nov. 1954: *AAS* 46 (1954) p. 669. Litt. Encycl. *Mediator Dei*, 20 Nov. 1947: *AAS* 39 (1947) p. 555.
3. See Pius XI, Litt. Encycl. *Miserentissimus Redemptor*, 8 May 1928: *AAS* 20 (1928) p. 171; Pius XII, Alloc. *Vous nous avez*, 22 Sept. 1956: *AAS* 48 (1956) p. 714.
4. See St. Thomas, *Summa Theol.* III, q. 63, a. 2.
5. See St. Cyril of Jerusalem, *Catech.* 17, de Spiritu Sancto, II, 35–37: *PG* 33, 1009–1012. Nic. Cabasilas, *De Vita in Christo*, bk. III, *de utilitate chrismatis: PG* 150, 569–580. St. Thomas, *Summa Theol.* III, q. 65, a. 3 and q. 72, a. 1 and 5.

Taking part in the eucharistic sacrifice, the source and summit of the Christian life, they offer the divine victim to God and themselves along with it.[6] And so it is that, both in the offering and in Holy Communion, each in his own way, though not of course indiscriminately, has his own part to play in the liturgical action. Then, strengthened by the body of Christ in the eucharistic communion, they manifest in a concrete way that unity of the People of God which this holy sacrament aptly signifies and admirably realizes.

Those who approach the sacrament of Penance obtain pardon from God's mercy for the offense committed against him, and are, at the same time, reconciled with the Church which they have wounded by their sins and which by charity, by example and by prayer labors for their conversion. By the sacred anointing of the sick and the prayer of the priests the whole Church commends those who are ill to the suffering and glorified Lord that he may raise them up and save them (cf. Jas. 5:14–16). And indeed she exhorts them to contribute to the good of the People of God by freely uniting themselves to the passion and death of Christ (cf. Rom. 8:17; Col. 1:24; Tim. 2:11–12; 1 Pet. 4:13). Those among the faithful who have received Holy Orders are appointed to nourish the Church with the word and grace of God in the name of Christ. Finally, in virtue of the sacrament of Matrimony by which they signify and share (cf. Eph. 5:32) the mystery of the unity and faithful love between Christ and the Church, Christian married couples help one another to attain holiness in their married life and in the rearing of their children. Hence by reason of their state in life and of their position they have their own gifts in the People of God (cf. 1 Cor. 7:7).[7] From the marriage of Christians there comes the family in which new citizens of human society are born and, by the grace of the Holy Spirit in Baptism, those are made children of God so that the People of God may be perpetuated throughout the centuries. In what might be regarded as the domestic Church, the parents, by word and example, are the first heralds of the faith with regard to their children. They must

6. See Pius XII, Litt. Encycl. *Mediator Dei, loc. cit.*, especially p. 552 s.

7. 1 Cor. 7:7: *"Ununquisque proprium donum (idion charisma) habet ex Deo: alius quidem sic, alius vero sic."* See St. Augustine, *De Dono Persev.*, 14, 37: *PL* 45, 1015 s. *"Non tantum continentia Dei donum est, sed coniugatorum etiam castitas."*

foster the vocation which is proper to each child, and this with special care if it be to religion.

Strengthened by so many and such great means of salvation, all the faithful, whatever their condition or state—though each in his own way—are called by the Lord to that perfection of sanctity by which the Father himself is perfect.

12. The holy People of God shares also in Christ's prophetic office: it spreads abroad a living witness to him, especially by a life of faith and love and by offering to God a sacrifice of praise, the fruit of lips praising his name (cf. Heb. 13:15). The whole body of the faithful who have an anointing that comes from the holy one (cf. 1 Jn. 2:20 and 27) cannot err in matters of belief. This characteristic is shown in the supernatural appreciation of the faith (*sensus fidei*) * of the whole people, when, "from the bishops to the last of the faithful"[8] they manifest a universal consent in matters of faith and morals. By this appreciation of the faith, aroused and sustained by the Spirit of truth, the People of God, guided by the sacred teaching authority (*magisterium*), and obeying it, receives not the mere word of men, but truly the word of God (cf. 1 Th. 2:13), the faith once for all delivered to the saints (cf. Jude 3). The People unfailingly adheres to this faith, penetrates it more deeply with right judgment, and applies it more fully in daily life.

It is not only through the sacraments and the ministrations of the Church that the Holy Spirit makes holy the People, leads them and enriches them with his virtues. Allotting his gifts according as he wills (cf. Cor. 12:11), he also distributes special graces among the faithful of every rank. By these gifts he makes them fit and ready to undertake various tasks and offices for the renewal and building up of the Church, as it is written, "the manifestation of the Spirit is given to everyone for profit" (1 Cor. 12:7). Whether these charisms be very remarkable or more simple and widely diffused, they are to be received with thanksgiving and consolation since they are fitting and useful for the needs of the Church. Extraordinary gifts are not to be rashly desired, nor is it from them that the fruits of apostolic la-

---

* (The *sensus fidei* refers to the instinctive sensitivity and discrimination which the members of the Church possess in matters of faith. —Translator.)

8. See St. Augustine, *De Praed. Sanct.* 14, 27: PL 44, 980.

bors are to be presumptuously expected. Those who have charge over the Church should judge the genuineness and proper use of these gifts, through their office not indeed to extinguish the Spirit, but to test all things and hold fast to what is good. (cf. Th. 5:12 and 19–21).

13. All men are called to belong to the new People of God. This People therefore, whilst remaining one and only one, is to be spread throughout the whole world and to all ages in order that the design of God's will may be fulfilled: he made human nature one in the beginning and has decreed that all his children who were scattered should be finally gathered together as one (cf. John 11:52). It was for this purpose that God sent his Son, whom he appointed heir of all things (cf. Heb. 1:2), that he might be teacher, king and priest of all, the head of the new and universal People of God's sons. This, too, is why God sent the Spirit of his Son, the Lord and Giver of Life. The Spirit is, for the Church and for each and every believer, the principle of their union and unity in the teaching of the apostles and fellowship, in the breaking of bread and prayer (cf. Acts 2:42 Gk.).

The one People of God is accordingly present in all the nations of the earth, since its citizens, who are taken from all nations, are of a kingdom whose nature is not earthly but heavenly. All the faithful scattered throughout the world are in communion with each other in the Holy Spirit so that 'he who dwells in Rome knows those in most distant parts to be his members' (*qui Romae sedet, Indos scit membrum suum esse*).[9] Since the kingdom of Christ is not of this world (cf. Jn. 18:36), the Church or People of God which establishes this kingdom does not take away anything from the temporal welfare of any people. Rather she fosters and takes to herself, in so far as they are good, the abilities, the resources and customs of peoples. In so taking them to herself she purifies, strengthens and elevates them. The Church indeed is mindful that she must work with that king to whom the nations were given for an inheritance (cf. Ps. 2:8) and to whose city gifts are brought (cf. Ps. 71[72]: 10; Is. 60:4–7; Apoc. 21:24). This character of universality which adorns the People of God is a gift from the Lord himself whereby the Catholic Church ceaselessly and efficaciously seeks for the return of all humanity and all its

9. See St. John Chrysostom, *In Io.* Hom. 65, 1: *PG* 59, 361.

goods under Christ the Head in the unity of his Spirit.[10]

In virtue of this catholicity each part contributes its own gifts to other parts and to the whole Church, so that the whole and each of the parts are strengthened by the common sharing of all things and by the common effort to attain to fullness in unity. Hence it is that the People of God is not only an assembly of various peoples, but in itself is made up of different ranks. This diversity among its members is either by reason of their duties—some exercise the sacred ministry for the good of their brethren—or it is due to their condition and manner of life—many enter the religious state and, intending to sanctify by the narrower way, stimulate their brethren by their example. Holding a rightful place in the communion of the Church there are also particular Churches that retain their own traditions, without prejudice to the Chair of Peter which presides over the whole assembly of charity,[11] and protects their legitimate variety while at the same time taking care that these differences do not hinder unity, but rather contribute to it. Finally, between all the various parts of the Church there is a bond of close communion whereby spiritual riches, apostolic workers and temporal resources are shared. For the members of the People of God are called upon to share their goods, and the words of the apostle apply also to each of the Churches, 'according to the gift that each has received, administer it to one another as good stewards of the manifold grace of God' (1 Pet. 5:10).

All men are called to this catholic unity which prefigures and promotes universal peace. And in different ways to it belong, or are related: the Catholic faithful, others who believe in Christ, and finally all mankind, called by God's grace to salvation.

14. This holy Council first of all turns its attention to the Catholic faithful. Basing itself on scripture and tradition, it teaches that the Church, a pilgrim now on earth, is necessary for salvation: the one Christ is mediator and the way of salvation; he is present to us in his body which is the Church. He himself explicitly asserted the necessity of faith and baptism (cf. Mk. 16:16; Jn. 3:5), and thereby affirmed at the same time the necessity of the Church which

10. See St. Irenaeus, *Adv. Haer.* III, 16, 6; III, 22, 1–3; *PG* 7, 925, C-926 A and 955 C-958 A; Harvey 2, 87 s. and 120–123; Sagnard, ed. *Sources Chrét.*, pp. 290–292 and 372 ss.
11. See St. Ignatius Martyr, *Ad Rom.*, Praef.: ed. Funk, 1, p. 252.

men enter through baptism as through a door. Hence they could not be saved who, knowing that the Catholic Church was founded as necessary by God through Christ, would refuse either to enter it, or to remain in it.

Fully incorporated into the Church are those who, possessing the Spirit of Christ, accept all the means of salvation given to the Church together with her entire organization, and who—by the bonds constituted by the profession of faith, the sacraments, ecclesiastical government, and communion—are joined in the visible structure of the Church of Christ, who rules her through the Supreme Pontiff and the bishops. Even though incorporated into the Church, one who does not however persevere in charity is not saved. He remains indeed in the bosom of the Church, but "in body" not "in heart."[12] All children of the Church should nevertheless remember that their exalted condition results, not from their own merits, but from the grace of Christ. If they fail to respond in thought, word and deed to that grace, not only shall they not be saved, but they shall be the more severely judged.[13]

Catechumens who, moved by the Holy Spirit, desire with an explicit intention to be incorporated into the Church, are by that very intention joined to her. With love and solicitude mother Church already embraces them as her own.

15. The Church knows that she is joined in many ways to the baptized who are honored by the name of Christian, but who do not however profess the Catholic faith in its entirety or have not preserved unity or communion under the successor of Peter.[14] For there are many who hold sacred scripture in honor as a rule of faith and of life, who have a sincere religious zeal, who lovingly believe in God the Father Almighty and in Christ, the Son of God and the Saviour,[15] who are sealed by baptism which unites them to

12. See St. Augustine, *Bapt. C. Donat.* V. 28, 39: *PL* 43, 197: *"Certe manifestum est, id quod dicitur, in Ecclesia intus et foris, non in corpore cogitandum."* See *ibid.*, III, 19, 26: *col.* 152; V. 18, 24: col. 189; *In Io.* tract. 61, 2: *PL* 35, 1800, and often elsewhere.

13. See Lk. 12:48: *"Omni autem, cui multum datum est, multum quaeretur ab eo."* See also Mt. 5: 19–20; 7:21–22; 25:41–46; Jas. 2:14.

14. See Leo XIII, Epist. Apost. *Praeclara gratulationis,* 20 June 1894: *ASS* 26 (1893–94) p. 707.

15. See Leo XIII, Epist. Encycl. *Satis cognitum,* 29 June 1896: *ASS* 26 (1895–96) p. 738. Epist. Encycl. *Caritatis studium,* 25 July 1898: *ASS* 31(1898–99) p. 11. Pius XII, Radio Message *Nell alba,* 24 Dec. 1941: *AAS* 34 (1942) p. 21.

Christ, and who indeed recognize and receive other sacraments in their own Churches or ecclesiastical communities. Many of them possess the episcopate, celebrate the holy Eucharist and cultivate devotion to the Virgin Mother of God.[16] There is furthermore a sharing in prayer and spiritual benefits; these Christians are indeed in some real way joined to us in the Holy Spirit for, by his gifts and graces, his sanctifying power is also active in them and he has strengthened some of them even to the shedding of their blood. And so the Spirit stirs up desires and actions in all of Christ's disciples in order that all may be peaceably united, as Christ ordained, in one flock under one shepherd.[17] Mother Church never ceases to pray, hope and work that this may be achieved, and she exhorts her children to purification and renewal so that the sign of Christ may shine more brightly over the face of the Church.

16. Finally, those who have not yet received the Gospel are related to the People of God in various ways.[18] There is, first, that people to which the covenants and promises were made, and from which Christ was born according to the flesh (cf. Rom. 9:4–5): in view of the divine choice, they are a people most dear for the sake of the fathers, for the gifts of God are without repentance (cf. Rom. 11:29–29). But the plan of salvation also includes those who acknowledge the Creator, in the first place amongst whom are the Moslems: these profess to hold the faith of Abraham, and together with us they adore the one, merciful God, mankind's judge on the last day. Nor is God remote from those who in shadows and images seek the unknown God, since he gives to all men life and breath and all things (cf. Acts 17:25–28), and since the Saviour wills all men to be saved (cf. 1 Tim. 2:4). Those who, through no fault of their own, do not know the Gospel of Christ or his Church, but who nevertheless seek God with a sincere heart, and, moved by grace, try in their actions to do his will as they know it through the dictates of their conscience—those too may achieve eternal salvation.[19] Nor shall divine provi-

16. See Pius XI, Litt, Encycl. *Rerum Orientalium,* 8 Sept. 1928: *AAS* 20 (1928) p. 287. Pius XII, Litt. Encycl. *Orientalis Ecclesiae,* 9 April 1944: *AAS* 36 (1944) p. 137.
17. See Instr. of Sacred Cong. of the Holy Office, 20 Dec. 1949: *AAS* 42 (1950) p. 142.
18. See St. Thomas, *Summa Theol.* III, q. 8, a. 3, ad 1.
19. See *Epist.* of the Sacred Cong. of the Holy Office to the Archbishop of Boston: *Denz.* 3869–72.

dence deny the assistance necessary for salvation to those who, without any fault of theirs, have not yet arrived at an explicit knowledge of God, and who, not without grace, strive to lead a good life. Whatever good or truth is found amongst them is considered by the Church to be a preparation for the Gospel[20] and given by him who enlightens all men that they may at length have life. But very often, decieved by the Evil One, men have become vain in their reasonings, have exchanged the truth of God for a lie and served the world rather than the Creator (cf. Rom. 1:21 and 25). Or else, living and dying in this world without God, they are exposed to ultimate despair. Hence to procure the glory of God and the salvation of all these, the Church, mindful of the Lord's command, "preach the Gospel to every creature" (Mk. 16:16) takes zealous care to foster the missions.

17. As he had been sent by the Father, the Son himself sent the apostles (cf. Jn. 20:21) saying, "go, therefore, and make disciples of all nations, baptizing them in the name of the Father, and of the Son, and of the Holy Spirit, teaching them to observe all that I have commanded you; and behold I am with you all days even unto the consummation of the world" (Mt. 28:18–20). The Church has received this solemn command of Christ from the apostles, and she must fulfil it to the very ends of the earth (cf. Acts 1:8). Therefore, she makes the words of the apostle her own, "Woe to me if I do not preach the Gospel" (1 Cor. 9:16), and accordingly never ceases to send heralds of the Gospel until such time as the infant Churches are fully established, and can themselves continue the work of evangelization. For the Church is driven by the Holy Spirit to do her part for the full realization of the plan of God, who has constituted Christ as the source of salvation for the whole world. By her proclamation of the Gospel, she draws her hearers to receive and profess the faith, she prepares them for baptism, snatches them from the slavery of error, and she incorporates them into Christ so that in love for him they grow to full maturity. The effect of her work is that whatever good is found sown in the minds and hearts of men or in the rites and customs of peoples, these not only are preserved from destruction, but are purified, raised up, and

20. See Eusebius of Caesarea, *Praeparatio Evangelica*, I, 1: *PG* 21, 28 AB.

perfected for the glory of God, the confusion of the devil, and the happiness of man. Each disciple of Christ has the obligation of spreading the faith to the best of his ability.[21] But if any believer can baptize, it is for the priests to complete the building up of the body in the eucharistic sacrifice, thus fulfilling the words of the prophet, "From the rising of the sun, even to going down, my name is great among the gentiles. And in every place there is a sacrifice, and there is offered to my name a clean offering" (Mal. 1:11).[22] Thus the Church prays and likewise labors so that into the People of God, the Body of the Lord and the Temple of the Holy Spirit, may pass the fullness of the whole world, and that in Christ, the head of all things, all honor and glory may be rendered to the Creator, the Father of the universe.

Chapter III[a]

THE CHURCH IS HIERARCHICAL

18. In order to shepherd the People of God and to increase its numbers without cease, Christ the Lord set up in his Church a variety of offices which aim at the good of the whole body. The holders of office, who are invested with a sacred power, are, in fact, dedicated to promoting the interests of their brethren, so that all who belong to the People of God, and are consequently endowed with true Christian dignity, may, through their free and well-ordered efforts towards a common goal, attain to salvation.

This sacred synod, following in the steps of the First Vat-

---

21. See Benedict XV, Epist Apost. *Maximum illud: AAS* 11 (1919) p. 440, especially p. 451 ss Pius XI, Litt. Encycl. *Rerum Ecclesia: AAS* 18 (1926) pp. 68–69. Pius XII, Litt. Encycl. *Fidei Donum,* 21 April 1957: *AAS* 49 (1957) pp. 236–237.

22. See *Didachè,* 14: ed. Funk, 1, p. 32. St Justin, *Dial.* 41: *PG* 6, 564. St. Irenaeus, *Adv. Haer.* IV, 17, 5; *PG* 7, 1023; Harvey, 2, p. 199s. Council of Trent, Session 22, ch. 1: *Denz.* 939 (1742).

a. This chapter has been translated by Father Cornelius Williams, O.P.

ican Council, teaches and declares with it that Jesus Christ, the eternal pastor, set up the holy Church by entrusting the apostles with their mission as he himself had been sent by the Father (cf. Jn. 20:21). He willed that their successors, the bishops namely, should be the shepherds in his Church until the end of the world. In order that the episcopate itself, however, might be one and undivided he put Peter at the head of the other apostles, and in him he set up a lasting and visible source and foundation of the unity both of faith and of communion.[1] This teaching concerning the institution, the permanence, the nature and import of the sacred primacy of the Roman Pontiff and his infallible teaching office, the sacred synod proposes anew to be firmly believed by all the faithful, and, proceeding undeviatingly with this same undertaking, it proposes to proclaim publicly and enunciate clearly the doctrine concerning bishops, successors of the apostles, who together with Peter's successor, the Vicar of Christ[2] and the visible head of the whole Church, direct the house of the living God.

19. The Lord Jesus, having prayed at length to the Father, called to himself those whom he willed and appointed twelve to be with him, whom he might send to preach the kingdom of God (cf. Mk. 3:13–19; Mt. 10:1–42). These apostles (cf. Lk. 6:13) he constituted in the form of a college or permanent assembly, at the head of which he placed Peter, chosen from amongst them (cf. Jn. 21:15–17). He sent them first of all to the children of Israel and then to all peoples (cf. Rom. 1:16), so that, sharing in his power, they might make all peoples his disciples and sanctify and govern them (cf. Mt. 28:16–20; Mk. 16:15; Lk. 24:45–48; Jn. 20:21–23) and thus spread the Church and, administering it under the guidance of the Lord, shepherd it all days until the end of the world (cf. Mt. 28:20). They were fully confirmed in this mission on the day of Pentecost (cf. Acts 2:1–26) according to the promise of the Lord: "You shall receive power when the Holy Ghost descends upon you; and you shall be my witnesses both in Jerusalem and in all Judea and Samaria, and to the remotest part of the earth" (Acts 1:8). By preaching everywhere the Gospel (cf. Mk. 16:20), welcomed and received under the influence of the

1. Cf. Vatican Council I, Session IV, Const. Dogm. *Pastor aeternus: Denz.* 1821 (3050 f.).
2. Cf. Council of Florence, *Decretum pro Graecis: Denz.* 694 (1307) and Vatican Council I, ibid.: *Denz.* 1826 (3059).

Holy Spirit by those who hear it, the apostles gather together the universal Church, which the Lord founded upon the apostles and built upon blessed Peter their leader, the chief corner-stone being Christ Jesus himself (cf. Apoc. 21:14; Mt. 16:18; Eph. 2:20).[3]

20. That divine mission, which was committed by Christ to the apostles, is destined to last until the end of the world (cf. Mt. 28:20), since the Gospel, which they were charged to hand on, is, for the Church, the principle of all its life for all time. For that very reason the apostles were careful to appoint successors in this hierarchically constituted society.

In fact, not only had they various helpers in their ministry,[4] but, in order that the mission entrusted to them might be continued after their death, they consigned, by will and testament, as it were, to their immediate collaborators the duty of completing and consolidating the work they had begun,[5] urging them to tend to the whole flock, in which the Holy Spirit had appointed them to shepherd the Church of God (cf. Acts 20:28). They accordingly designated such men and then made the ruling that likewise on their death other proven men should take over their ministry.[6] Amongst those various offices which have been exercised in the Church from the earliest times the chief place, according to the witness of tradition, is held by the function of those who, through their appointment to the dignity and responsibility of bishop, and in virtue consequently of the unbroken succession, going back to the beginning,[7] are regarded as transmitters of the apostolic

3. Cf. *Liber sacramentorum* St. Gregory, Praef. in natali St. Mathiae et St. Thomae: *PL* 78, 51 and 152; cf. Cod. Vat. lat. 3548, f. 18. St. Hilary, *In Ps.* 67, 10: *PL* 9, 450; *CSEL* 22, p. 286. St. Jerome, *Adv. Iovin.* 1, 26: *PL* 23, 247 A. St. Augustine, *In Ps.* 86, 4: *PL* 37, 1103. St. Gregory, Martyr, *More. in Job*, XXVIII, V: *PL* 76, 455–456. Primasius, *Comm. in Apoc.*, V: *PL* 68, 924 BC. Paschasius Radb., *In Mt.* L. VIII, cap. 16: *PL* 120, 561 C. Cf. Leo XIII, *Et sane*, 17 Dec. 1888: *ASS* 21 (1888) p. 321.
4. Cf. Acts 6:2–6; 11:30; 13:1; 14:23; 20:17; 1 Th. 5:12–13; Phil. 1:1; Col. 4:11 and *passim*.
5. Cf. Acts 20:25:27; 2 Tim. 4:6 f.; in conjunction with 1 Tim. 5:22; 2 Tim. 2:2; Tit. 1:5; Clement of Rome, *Ad Cor.* 44, 3: ed. Funk, I, p. 156.
6. St. Clement of Rome, *Ad Cor.* 44, 2: ed. Funk, I, p. 154 f.
7. Cf. Tertullian, *Praescr. Haer.* 32: *PL* 2, 53.

line.[8] Thus, according to the testimony of St. Irenaeus, the apostolic tradition is manifested[9] and preserved[10] in the whole world by those who were made bishops by the apostles and by their successors down to our own time.

In that way, then, with priests and deacons as helpers,[11] the bishops received the charge of the community, presiding in God's stead over the flock[12] of which they are the shepherds in that they are teachers of doctrine, ministers of sacred worship and holders of office in government.[13] Moreover, just as the office which the Lord confided to Peter alone, as first of the apostles, destined to be transmitted to his successors, is a permanent one, so also endures the office, which the apostles received, of shepherding the Church, a charge destined to be exercised without interruption by the sacred order of bishops.[14] The sacred synod consequently teaches that the bishops have by divine institution taken the place of the apostles as pastors of the Church,[15] in such wise that whoever listens to them is listening to Christ and whoever despises them despises Christ and him who sent Christ (cf. Lk. 10:16).[16]

21. In the person of the bishops, then, to whom the priests render assistance, the Lord Jesus Christ, supreme high priest, is present in the midst of the faithful. Though seated at the right hand of God the Father, he is not absent

8. Cf. Tertullian, *Praescr. Haer.* 32: *PL* 2, 52 f. St. Ignatius, Martyr, *passim.*

9. Cf. St. Irenaeus, *Adv Haer.* III, 3, 1: *PG* 7, 848 A: Harvey 2, 8; Sagnard, p. 100 f.: "manifestatem."

10. Cf. St. Irenaeus, *Adv Haer.* III, 2, 2: *PG* 847: Harvey 2, 7; Sagnard, p. 100: "custoditur," cf. ib. IV, 26, 2; col. 1053; Harvey 2, 236, and IV, 33, 8; col. 1077; Harvey 2, 262.

11. St. Ignatius, Martyr, *Philad.,* Praef.: ed. Funk, I, p. 264.

12. St. Ignatius, Martyr, *Philad.,* 1, 1; *Magn.* 6, 1: ed. Funk, 264 and 234.

13. St. Clement of Rome, *loc cit.,* 42, 3–4; 44, 3–4; 57, 1–2: ed. Funk, I, 152, 156, 171. f. St. Ignatius, Martyr, *Philad.* 2; *Smyrn.* 8, *Magn.* 3; *Trall.* 7: ed Funk, I, p. 265 f.; 282; 232; 246 f. etc.; St. Justin, *Apol.,* 1, 65: *PG* 6, 428; St. Cyprian, *Epist., passim.*

14. Cf. Leo XIII, Encycl. *Satis cognitum,* 29 June 1896: *ASS* 28 (1895–1896) p. 732.

15. Cf. Council of Trent, Session 23, Decr. *de sacr. ordinis,* cap. 4: *Denz.* 960 (1768); Vatican Council I, Session 4, Const. Dogm. 1 *De Ecclesia Christi,* cap. 3: *Denz* 1828 (3061). Pius XII, Encycl. *Mystici Corporis,* 29 June 1943; *AAS* 35 (1943) pp. 209 and 212. *Code of Canon Law,* C.329 §1.

16. Cf. Leo XIII, Epist, *Et Sane,* 17 Dec. 1888: *ASS* 21 (1888) p. 32 f.

from the assembly of his pontiffs;[17] on the contrary indeed, it is above all through their signal service that he preaches the Word of God to all peoples and administers without cease to the faithful the sacraments of faith; that through their paternal care (cf. 1 Cor. 4:15) he incorporates, by a supernatural rebirth, new members into his body; that finally, through their wisdom and prudence he directs and guides the people of the New Testament on their journey towards eternal beatitude. Chosen to shepherd the Lord's flock, these pastors are servants of Christ and stewards of the mysteries of God (cf. 1 Cor. 4:1), to whom is entrusted the duty of affirming the Gospel of the grace of God (cf. Rom. 15:16; Acts 20:24), and of gloriously promulgating the Spirit and proclaiming justification (cf. 2 Cor. 3:8-9).

In order to fulfil such exalted functions, the apostles were endowed by Christ with a special outpouring of the Holy Spirit coming upon them (cf. Acts 1:8; 2:4; Jn. 20:22-23), and, by the imposition of hands, (cf. 1 Tim. 4:14; 2 Tim. 1:6-7) they passed on to their auxiliaries the gift of the Spirit, which is transmitted down to our day through episcopal consecration.[18] The holy synod teaches, moreover, that the fullness of the sacrament of Orders is conferred by episcopal consecration, that fullness, namely, which both in the liturgical tradition of the Church and in the language of the Fathers of the Church is called the high priesthood, the acme of the sacred ministry.[19] Now, episcopal consecration confers, together with the office of sanctifying, the duty also of teaching and ruling, which, however, of their very nature can be exercised only in hierarchical communion with the head and members of the college. In fact, from tradition, which is expressed especially in the liturgical rites and in the customs of both the Eastern and

17. Cf. St. Leo Martyr, *Serm.* 5, 3: *PL* 54, 154.
18. Council of Trent, Session 23, cap. 3 quotes the words of 2 Tim. 1:6-7 to show that in Orders we have a true sacrament: *Denz.* 959 (1766).
19. In *Trad. Apost.* 3, ed. Botte, *Sources Chr.*, pp. 27-30, a "primacy of the priesthood" is attributed to the bishop. Cf. *Sacramentarium Leonianum*, ed. C. Mohlberg, *Sacramentarium Veronense*, Rome, 1955, p. 119: "to the ministry of the high priesthood . . . Make the height of your mystery complete in your priests" . . . Do., *Liber Sacramentorum Romanae Ecclesiae*, Rome, 1960, pp. 121-122: "Grant them the episcopal throne, Lord, to rule your Church and all the people." Cf. *PL* 78. 224.

Western Church, it is abundantly clear that by the imposition of hands and through the words of the consecration, the grace of the Holy Spirit is given, [20] and a sacred character is impressed[21] in such wise that bishops, in a resplendent and visible manner, take the place of Christ himself, teacher, shepherd and priest, and act as his representatives (*in eius persona*).[22] It is the right of bishops to admit newly elected members into the episcopal body by means of the sacrament of Orders.

22. Just as, in accordance with the Lord's decree, St Peter and the rest of the apostles constitute a unique apostolic college, so in like fashion the Roman Pontiff, Peter's successor, and the bishops, the successors of the apostles, are related with and united to one another. Indeed, the very ancient discipline whereby the bishops installed throughout the whole world lived in communion with one another and with the Roman Pontiff in a bond of unity, charity and peace;[23] likewise the holding of councils[24] in order to settle conjointly,[25] in a decision rendered balanced and equitable by the advice of many, all questions of major importance;[26] all this points clearly to the collegiate character and structure of the episcopal order, and the holding of ecumenical councils in the course of the centuries bears this out unmistakably. Indeed, pointing to it also quite clearly is the custom, dating from very early times, of summoning a

20. *Trad Apost.* 2, ed. Botte, p. 27.
21. Council of Trent, Session 23, cap. 4, teaches that the sacrament of Orders imprints an indelible character: *Denz.* 960 (1767). Cf. John XXIII, Alloc. *Jubilate Deo*, 8 May 1960: *AAS* 52 (1960) p. 466. Paul VI homily in Vatican, 20 Oct. (1963), p. 1014.
22. St. Cyprian, *Epist.* 63, 14: *PL* 4, 386; Hartel, IIIB, p. 713: "The priest truly acts in the place of Christ." St. John Chrysostom, *In 2 Tim.* Hom. 2, 4: *PG* 62, 612: The priest is "symbolon" of Christ. St. Ambrose, *In Ps.* 38, 25–26: *PL* 14, 1051–52: *CSEL* 64, 203–204. Ambrosiaster, *In 1 Tim.* 5, 19: *PL* 17, 479C and *In Eph.* 4:11–12: col. 387C. Theodore of Mops., *Hom. Catech.*-XV, 21 and 24: ed. Tonneau, pp. 487 and 503. Hesych. of Jesus, *In Lev.* L. 2, 9, 23: *PG.* 93, 894B.
23. Cf. Eusebius, *Hist. Eccl.*, V, 24, 10: G.C.S. II, 1, p. 495: ed. Bardy, *Sources Chr.* II, p. 69. Dionysius, apud Eusebium, ib. VII, 5, 2: G.C.S. II, 2, p. 638 f.: Brady, II, p. 168 f.
24. Cf. Eusebius, *Hist. Eccl.*, concerning the ancient councils, V, 23–24: G.C.S. II, 1, p. 488 ff.; Bardy, II, p. 66 ff. and *passim.* Conc. Nicea, can. 5: *Conc. Oec. Decr.* p. 7.
25. Tertullian, *De Ieiunio*, 13: *PL* 2, 972B; *CSEL* 20, p. 292, lin. 13–16.
26. St. Cyprian, *Epist.* 56, 3: Hartel, IIIB, p. 650; Bayard, p. 154.

number of bishops to take part in the elevation of one newly chosen to the highest sacerdotal office. One is constituted a member of the episcopal body in virtue of the sacramental consecration and by the hierarchical communion with the head and members of the college.

The college or body of bishops has for all that no authority unless united with the Roman Pontiff, Peter's successor, as its head, whose primatial authority, let it be added, over all, whether pastors or faithful, remains in its integrity. For the Roman Pontiff, by reason of his office as Vicar of Christ, namely, and as pastor of the entire Church, has full, supreme and universal power over the whole Church, a power which he can always exercise unhindered. The order of bishops is the successor to the college of the apostles in their role as teachers and pastors, and in it the apostolic college is perpetuated. Together with their head, the Supreme Pontiff, and never apart from him, they have supreme and full authority over the universal Church;[27] but this power cannot be exercised without the agreement of the Roman Pontiff. The Lord made Peter alone the rock-foundation and the holder of the keys of the Church (cf. Mt. 16:18-19), and constituted him shepherd of his whole flock (cf. Jn. 21:15 ff.). It is clear, however, that the office of binding and loosing which was given to Peter (Mt. 16:19), was also assigned to the college of the apostles united to its head (Mt. 18:18; 28:16-20).[28] This college, in so far as it is composed of many members, is the expression of the multifariousness and universality of the People of God; and of the unity of the flock of Christ, in so far as it is assembled under one head. In it the bishops, whilst loyally respecting the primacy and pre-eminence of their head, exercise their own proper authority for the good of their faithful, indeed even for the good of the whole Church, the organic structure and harmony of which are strengthened by the continued influence of the Holy Spirit. The supreme authority over the whole Church, which this college possesses, is exercised in a solemn way in an ecumenical council. There never is an ecumenical council which is not confirmed or at least recognized as such by Peter's successor.

27. Cf. Zinelli's *Relatio* on Vatican Council I: Mansi 52, 1109C.
28. Cf. Vatican Council I, Schema on the Dogm. Const. II, *de Ecclesia Christi*, c. 4: Mansi 53, 310. Cf. Kleutgen's *Relatio* on the reformed schema: Mansi 53, 321 B-322 B and Zinelli's *Declaratio*: Mansi 52, 111: A. See also St. Leo, Martyr, *Serm.* 4. 3: *PL* 54, 151A.

And it is the prerogative of the Roman Pontiff to convoke such councils, to preside over them and to confirm them.[29] This same collegiate power can be exercised in union with the pope by the bishops while living in different parts of the world, provided the head of the college summon them to collegiate action, or at least approve or freely admit the corporate action of the unassembled bishops, so that a truly collegiate act may result.

23. Collegiate unity is also apparent in the mutual relations of each bishop to individual dioceses and with the universal Church. The Roman Pontiff, as the successor of Peter, is the perpetual and visible source and foundation of the unity both of the bishops and of the whole company of the faithful.[30] The individual bishops are the visible source and foundation of unity in their own particular Churches,[31] which are constituted after the model of the universal Church; it is in these and formed out of them that the one and unique Catholic Church exists.[32] And for that reason precisely each bishop represents his own Church, whereas all, together with the pope, represent the whole Church in a bond of peace, love and unity.

Individual bishops, in so far as they are set over particular Churches, exercise their pastoral office over the portion of the People of God assigned to them, not over other Churches nor the Church universal. But in so far as they are members of the episcopal college and legitimate successors of the apostles, by Christ's arrangement and decree,[33] each is bound to have such care and solicitude for the whole Church which, though it be not exercised by any act of jurisdiction, does for all that redound in an eminent degree to the advantage of the universal Church. For all the bishops have the obligation of fostering and safeguarding the unity of the faith and of upholding the discipline which is common to the whole Church; of schooling the faithful in a love of the whole Mystical Body of Christ and, in a

29. Cf. Code of Canon Law, c. 227.
30. Cf. Vatican Council I, Const. Dogm. *Pastor aeternus: Denz.* 1821 (3050 f.).
31. Cf. St. Cyprian, *Epst.* 66, 8: Hartel, III, 2, p. 733: "The bishop in the Church and the Church in the bishop."
32. Cf. St. Cyprian, *Epist.* 55, 24: Hartel, p. 642, lin. 13: "One Church throughout the world divided into many members." *Epist.* 36, 4: Hartel, p. 575, lin. 20–21.
33. Pius XII, Encycl. *Fidei Donum,* 21 April 1957: *ASS* 49 (1957) p. 237.

special way, of the poor, the suffering, and those who are undergoing persecution for the sake of justice (cf. Mt. 5:10); finally, of promoting all that type of active apostolate which is common to the whole Church, especially in order that the faith may increase and the light of truth may rise in its fullness on all men. Besides, it is an established fact of experience that, in ruling well their own Churches as portions of the universal Church, they contribute efficaciously to the welfare of the whole Mystical Body, which, from another point of view, is a corporate body of Churches.[34]

The task of announcing the Gospel in the whole world belongs to the body of pastors, to whom, as a group, Christ gave a general injunction and imposed a general obligation, to which already Pope Celestine called the attention of the Fathers of the Council of Ephesus.[35] Consequently, the bishops, each for his own part, in so far as the due performance of their own duty permits, are obliged to enter into collaboration with one another and with Peter's successor, to whom, in a special way, the noble task of propagating the Christian name was entrusted.[36] Thus, they should come to the aid of the missions by every means in their power, supplying both harvest workers and also spiritual and material aids, either directly and personally themselves, or by arousing the fervent cooperation of the faithful. Lastly, in accordance with the venerable example of former times, bishops should gladly extend their fraternal assistance, in the fellowship of an all-pervading charity, to other Churches, especially to neighboring ones and to those most in need of help.

It has come about through divine providence that, in the course of time, different Churches set up in various places by the apostles and their successors joined together in a multiplicity of organically united groups which, whilst safeguarding the unity of the faith and the unique divine structure of the universal Church, have their own discipline, en-

---

34. Cf. St. Hilary of Poit., *In Ps.* 14, 3: *PL* 9, 206; *CSEL* 22, p. 86. St. Gregory, Martyr, *Moral.* IV, 7, 12: *PL* 75, 643C. PS.-BASIL, *In Is.* 15, 296: *PG* 30, 637C.

35. St. Celestine, *Epist.* 18, 1–2, to the Council of Ephesus: *PL* 50, 505 AB; Schwartz, *Acta Conc. Oec.* I, 1, 1, p. 22. Cf. Benedict XV, Apost Letter *Maximum illud: AAS* 11 (1919) p. 440. Pius XI Encycl. *Rerum Ecclesiae*, 28 Feb. 1926: *AAS* 18 (1926) p. 69. Pius XII, Encycl. *Fidei Donum*, loc. cit.

36. Leo XIII, Encycl. *Grande munus*, 30 Sept. 1880: *ASS* 13 (1880) p. 145. Cf. Code of Canon Law, c. 1327; c. 1350 par. 2.

joy their own liturgical usage and inherit a theological and spiritual patrimony. Some of these, notably the ancient patriarchal Churches, as mothers in the faith, gave birth to other daughter-Churches, as it were, and down to our own days they are linked with these by bonds of a more intimate charity in what pertains to the sacramental life and in a mutual respect for rights and obligations.[87] This multiplicity of local Churches, unified in a common effort, shows all the more resplendently the catholicity of the undivided Church. In a like fashion the episcopal conferences at the present time are in a position to contribute in many and fruitful ways to the concrete realization of the collegiate spirit.

24. The bishops, in as much as they are the successors of the apostles, receive from the Lord, to whom all power is given in heaven and on earth, the mission of teaching all peoples, and of preaching the Gospel to every creature, so that all men may attain to salvation through faith, baptism and the observance of the commandments (cf. Mt. 28:18; Mk. 16:15-16; Acts 26:17 f.). For the carrying out of this mission Christ promised the Holy Spirit to the apostles and sent him from heaven on the day of Pentecost, so that through his power they might be witnesses to him in the remotest parts of the earth, before nations and peoples and kings (cf. Acts 1:8; 2:1 ff.; 9:15). That office, however, which the Lord committed to the pastors of his people, is, in the strict sense of the term, a service, which is called very expressively in sacred scripture a *diakonia* or ministry (cf. Acts 1:17 and 25; 21:19; Rom. 11:13; 1 Tim. 1:12).

The canonical mission of the bishops, on the other hand, can be made by legitimate customs that have not been revoked by the supreme and universal authority of the Church, or by laws made or acknowledged by the same authority, or directly by Peter's successor himself. Should he object or refuse the apostolic communion, then bishops cannot be admitted to office.[38]

---

37. On the rights of patriarchal Sees, cf. Council of Nicea, can. 6 concerning Alexandria and Antioch, can. 7 on Jerusalem: *Conc. Oec. Decr.*, p. 8 Lateran Council IV in the year 1215, Constit. V: *De dignitate Patriarcharum:* ibid. p. 212. Council of Ferr.-Florence: ibid. p. 504.
38. Code of Canon Law for the Oriental Church, c. 216-314: on patriarchs; c. 324-339: on greater archbishops; c. 362-391: on other dignitaries; in general, c. 238 par. 3; 216; 240; 251: on the nomination of bishops by the patriarch.

25. Among the more important duties of bishops that of preaching the Gospel has pride of place.[39] For the bishops and heralds of the faith, who draw new disciples to Christ; they are authentic teachers, that is, teachers endowed with the authority of Christ, who preach the faith to the people assigned to them, the faith which is destined to inform their thinking and direct their conduct; and under the light of the Holy Spirit they make that faith shine forth, drawing from the storehouse of revelation new things and old (cf. Mt. 13:52); they make it bear fruit and with watchfulness they ward off whatever errors threaten their flock (cf. 2 Tim. 4:14). Bishops who teach in communion with the Roman Pontiff are to be revered by all as witnesses of divine and Catholic truth; the faithful, for their part, are obliged to submit to their bishops' decision, made in the name of Christ, in matters of faith and morals, and to adhere to it with a ready and respectful allegiance of mind. This loyal submission of the will and intellect must be given, in a special way, to the authentic teaching authority of the Roman Pontiff, even when he does not speak *ex cathedra* in such wise, indeed, that his supreme teaching authority be acknowledged with respect, and that one sincerely adhere to decisions made by him, conformably with his manifest mind and intention, which is made known principally either by the character of the documents in question, or by the frequency with which a certain doctrine is proposed, or by the manner in which the doctrine is formulated.

Although the bishops, taken individually, do not enjoy the privilege of infallibility, they do, however, proclaim infallibly the doctrine of Christ on the following conditions: namely, when, even though dispersed throughout the world but preserving for all that amongst themselves and with Peter's successor the bond of communion, in their authoritative teaching concerning matters of faith and morals, they are in agreement that a particular teaching is to be held definitively and absolutely. This is still more clearly the

39. Cf. Council of Trent, *Decr. de reform.*, Session V, c. 2; n. 9, and Session XXIV, can. 4; *Conc. Oecr.* pp. 645 and 739.
40. Cf. Vatican Council I, Const. Dogm. *Dei Filius*, 3: *Denz.* 1712 (3011). Cf. the note added to schema I *de Eccl.* (taken from St. Rob. Bellarmine): Mansi 51, 579C; also the revised schema of Const. II *de Ecclesia Christi,* with Kleutgen's commentary: Mansi 53, 313 AB. Pius IX, Letter *Tuas libenter: Denz.* 1683 (2879).

case when, assembled in an ecumenical council, they are, for the universal Church, teachers of and judges in matters of faith and morals, whose decisions must be adhered to with the loyal and obedient assent of faith.[41]

This infallibility, however, with which the divine redeemer wished to endow his Church in defining doctrine pertaining to faith and morals, is co-extensive with the deposit of revelation, which must be religiously guarded and loyally and courageously expounded. The Roman Pontiff, head of the college of bishops, enjoys this infallibility in virtue of his office, when, as supreme pastor and teacher of all the faithful—who confirms his brethren in the faith (cf. Lk. 22:32)—he proclaims in an absolute decision a doctrine pertaining to faith or morals.[42] For that reason his definitions are rightly said to be irreformable by their very nature and not by reason of the assent of the Church, in as much as they were made with the assistance of the Holy Spirit promised to him in the person of blessed Peter himself; and as a consequence they are in no way in need of the approval of others, and do not admit of appeal to any other tribunal. For in such a case the Roman Pontiff does not utter a pronouncement as a private person, but rather does he expound and defend the teaching of the Catholic faith as the supreme teacher of the universal Church, in whom the Church's charism of infallibility is present in a singular way.[43] The infallibility promised to the Church is also present in the body of bishops when, together with Peter's successor, they exercise the supreme teaching office. Now, the assent of the Church can never be lacking to such definitions on account of the same Holy Spirit's influence, through which Christ's whole flock is maintained in the unity of the faith and makes progress in it.[44]

Furthermore, when the Roman Pontiff, or the body of bishops together with him, define a doctrine, they make the definition in conformity with revelation itself, to which all are bound to adhere and to which they are obliged to submit; and this revelation is transmitted integrally either in written form or in oral tradition through the legitimate suc-

41. Code of Canon Law, c. 1322–1323.
42. Cf. Vatican Council I, Const. Dogm. *Pastor aeternus: Denz* 1839 (3074).
43. Cf. Gasser's explanation of Vatican Council I: Mansi 52, 1213 AC.
44. Gasser, ibid: Mansi 1214 A.

cession of bishops and above all through the watchful concern of the Roman Pontiff himself; and through the light of the Spirit of truth it is scrupulously preserved in the Church and unerringly explained.[45] The Roman Pontiff and the bishops, by reason of their office and the seriousness of the matter, apply themselves with zeal to the work of enquiring by every suitable means into this revelation and of giving apt expression to its contents;[46] they do not, however, admit any new public revelation as pertaining to the divine deposit of faith.[47]

26. The bishop, invested with the fullness of the sacrament of Orders, is "the steward of the grace of the supreme priesthood,"[48] above all in the Eucharist, which he himself offers, or ensures that it is offered,[49] from which the Church ever derives its life and on which it thrives. This Church of Christ is really present in all legitimately organized local groups of the faithful, which, in so far as they are united to their pastors, are also quite appropriately called Churches in the New Testament.[50] For these are in fact, in their own localities, the new people called by God, in the power of the Holy Spirit and as the result of full conviction (cf. 1 Thess. 1:5). In them the faithful are gathered together through the preaching of the Gospel of Christ, and the mystery of the Lord's Supper is celebrated "so that, by means of the flesh and blood of the Lord the whole brotherhood of the Body may be welded together."[51] In each altar community, under the sacred ministry of the bishop,[52] a manifest symbol is to be seen of that charity and "unity of the mystical body, without which there can be no salvation."[53] In these communities, though they may often be small and poor, or existing in the diaspora, Christ is present through whose power and influence the One, Holy, Catholic and Apostolic Church is constituted.[54] For "the

45. Gasser, ibid.: Mansi 1215 CD, 1216–1217 A.
46. Gasser, ibid.: Mansi 1213.
47. Vatican Council I, Const. Dogm. *Pastor aeternus*, 4: *Denz.* 1836 (3070).
48. Prayer of episcopal consecration in the Byzantine rite: *Euchologion to mega*, Rome, 1873, p. 139.
49. Cf. St. Ignatius, Martyr, *Smyrn.* 8, 1: ed. Funk, I, p. 282.
50. Cf. Acts 8:1; 14:22–23; 20:17 and *passim*.
51. Mozarabic prayer: *PL* 96, 759 B.
52. Cf. St. Ignatius, Martyr, *Smyrn.* 8, 1: ed. Funk, I, p. 282.
53. St. Thomas, *Summa Theol.*, III, q. 73, a. 3.
54. Cf. St. Augustine, *C. Faustum*, 12, 20: *PL* 42, 265; *Serm.* 57, 7: *PL* 38, 389, etc.

sharing in the body and blood of Christ has no other effect than to accomplish our transformation into that which we receive."[55]

Moreover, every legitimate celebration of the Eucharist is regulated by the bishop, to whom is confided the duty of presenting to the divine majesty the cult of the Christian religion and of ordering it in accordance with the Lord's injunctions and the Church's regulations, as further defined for the diocese by his particular decision.

Thus the bishops, by praying and toiling for the people, apportion in many different forms and without stint that which flows from the abundance of Christ's holiness. By the ministry of the word they impart to those who believe the strength of God unto salvation (cf. Rom. 1:16), and through the sacraments, the frequent and fruitful distribution of which they regulate by their authority,[56] they sanctify the faithful. They control the conferring of Baptism, through which a sharing in the priesthood of Christ is granted. They are the original ministers of Confirmation; it is they who confer sacred Orders and regulate the discipline of Penance, and who diligently exhort and instruct their flocks to take the part that is theirs, in a spirit of faith and reverence, in the liturgy and above all in the holy sacrifice of the Mass. Finally, by the example of their manner of life they should exercise a powerful influence for good on those over whom they are placed, by abstaining from all wrong doing in their conduct, and, as far as they are able, with the help of the Lord, changing it for the better, so that together with the flock entrusted to them, they may attain to eternal life.[57]

27. The bishops, as vicars and legates of Christ, govern the particular Churches assigned to them[58] by their counsels, exhortations and example, but over and above that also by the authority and sacred power which indeed they exercise exclusively for the spiritual development of their

55. St. Leo, Martyr, *Serm.* 63, 7: *PL* 54, 357C.
56. *Traditio Apostolica* of Hippolytus, 2–3: ed. Botte, pp. 26–30.
57. Cf. the text of the *examen* at the beginning of the consecration of bishops, and the *Prayer* at the end of the Mass of the same consecration, after the *Te Deum.*
58. Benedict XIV, Br. *Romana Ecclesia,* 5 Oct. 1752 par. 1: *Bullarium Benedicti XIV,* t. IV, Rome, 1758, 21: "A bishop bears the likeness of Christ, it is his office that he is performing." Pius XII, Encycl. *Mystici Corporis, loc. cit.,* p. 211: "They feed and rule the flocks assigned to each individually."

flock in truth and holiness, keeping in mind that he who is greater should become as the lesser, and he who is the leader as the servant (cf. Lk. 22:26–27). This power, which they exercise personally in the name of Christ, is proper, ordinary and immediate, although its exercise is ultimately controlled by the supreme authority of the Church and can be confined within certain limits should the usefulness of the Church and the faithful require that. In virtue of this power bishops have a sacred right and a duty before the Lord of legislating for and of passing judgment on their subjects, as well as of regulating everything that concerns the good order of divine worship and of the apostolate.

The pastoral charge, that is, the permanent and daily care of their sheep, is entrusted to them fully; nor are they to be regarded as vicars of the Roman Pontiff; for they exercise the power which they possess in their own right and are called in the truest sense of the term prelates of the people whom they govern.[59] Consequently their authority, far from being damaged by the supreme and universal power, is much rather defended, upheld and strengthened by it,[60] since the Holy Spirit preserves unfailingly that form of government which was set up by Christ the Lord in his Church.

Sent as he is by the Father to govern his family, a bishop should keep before his eyes the example of the Good Shepherd, who came not to be waited upon but to serve (cf. Mt. 20:28; Mk. 10:45) and to lay down his life for his sheep (cf. Jn. 10:11). Taken from among men and oppressed by the weakness that surrounds him, he can compassionate those who are ignorant and erring (cf. Heb. 5:1–2). He should not refuse to listen to his subjects whose welfare he promotes as of his very own children and whom he urges to collaborate readily with him. Destined to render an account for their souls to God (cf. Heb. 13:17), by prayer, preaching and all good works of charity he should be solicitous both for their welfare and for that too of those who do not belong to the unique flock, but whom he should regard as en-

59. Leo XIII, Encycl. Satis cognitum, 29 June 1896: ASS 28 (1895–1896) p. 732: Letter Officio sanctissimo, 22 Dec. 1887: ASS 20 (1887) p. 264. Pius IX, Apost. Letter to bishops of Germany, 12 March 1875 and Consist. Alloc., 15 March 1875: Denz. 3112–3117, only in new ed.
60. Vatican Council I, Dogm. Const. Pastor aeternus, 3: Denz. 1828 (3061). Cf. Zinelli's Relatio: Mansi 42, 1114 D.

trusted to him in the Lord. Since, like St Paul, he is in duty bound to everyone, he should be eager to preach the Gospel to all (cf. Rom. 1:14–15), and to spur his faithful on to apostolic and missionary activity. As to the faithful, they should be closely attached to the bishop as the Church is to Jesus Christ, and as Jesus Christ is to the Father, so that all things may conspire towards harmonious unity,[61] and bring forth abundant fruit unto the glory of God (cf. 2 Cor. 4:15).

28. Christ, whom the Father hallowed and sent into the world (Jn. 10:36), has, through his apostles, made their successors, the bishops namely,[62] sharers in his consecration and mission; and these, in their turn, duly entrusted in varying degrees various members of the Church with the office of their ministry. Thus the divinely instituted ecclesiastical ministry is exercised in different degrees by those who even from ancient times have been called bishops, priests and deacons.[63] Whilst not having the supreme degree of the pontifical office, and notwithstanding the fact that they depend on the bishops in the exercise of their own proper power, the priests are for all that associated with them by reason of their sacerdotal dignity;[64] and in virtue of the sacrament of Orders,[65] after the image of Christ, the supreme and eternal priest (Heb. 5:1–10; 7:24; 9:11–28), they are consecrated in order to preach the Gospel and shepherd the faithful as well as to celebrate divine worship as true priests of the New Testament.[66] On the level of their own ministry sharing in the unique office of Christ, the mediator, (1 Tim. 2:5), they announce to all the word of God. However, it is in the eucharistic cult or in the eucharistic assembly of the faithful (*synaxis*) that they exercise in a supreme degree their sacred functions; there, act-

---

61. Cf. St. Ignatius, Martyr, *Ad Ephes.* 5, 1: ed. Funk, 1, p. 216.
62. Cf. St. Ignatius, Martyr, *Ad Ephes.* 6, 1: ed. Funk I, p. 218.
63. Cf. Council of Trent, Session 23, *De sacr, ordinis,* cap. 2: *Denz.* 958 (1765), and can. 6: *Denz.* 966 (1776).
64. Cf. Innocent I, *Epist. ad Decentium: PL* 20, 554A; Mansi 3, 1029; *Denz.* 98 (215): "Presbyters, although they are *priests* of the second rank, do not possess the *high degree* of the pontificate." St. Cyprian, *Epist.* 61, 3: ed. Hartel, p. 696.
65. Cf. Council of Trent, *loc. cit., Denz.* 956a–968 (1763–1778), and specifically can. 7: *Denz.* 967 (1777). Pius XIII, Const. Apost. *Sacramentum ordinis: Denz.* 2301 (3857–61).
66. Cf. Innocent I, *loc. cit.* St. Gregory Naz., *Apol.* II, 22: *PG* 35, 432B. PS.-Dionysius, *Eccl. Hier.,* 1, 2: *PG* 3, 372D.

ing in the person of Christ[67] and proclaiming his mystery, they unite the votive offerings of the faithful to the sacrifice of Christ their head, and in the sacrifice of the Mass they make present again and apply, until the coming of the Lord (cf. 1 Cor. 11:26), the unique sacrifice of the New Testament, that namely of Christ offering himself once for all a spotless victim to the Father (cf. Heb. 9:11–28).[68] And on behalf of the faithful who are moved to sorrow or are stricken with sickness they exercise in an eminent degree a ministry of reconciliation and comfort, whilst they carry the needs and supplications of the faithful to God the Father (cf. Heb. 5:1–4). Exercising, within the limits of the authority which is theirs, the office of Christ, the Shepherd and Head,[69] they assemble the family of God as a brotherhood fired with a single ideal,[70] and through Christ in the Spirit they lead it to God the Father. In the midst of the flock they adore him in spirit and in truth (cf. Jn. 4:24). In short, they labor in preaching and instruction (cf. 1 Tim. 5:17), firmly adhering to what they read and meditate in the law of God, inculcating that which they believe, and putting into practice what they preach.[71]

The priests, prudent cooperators of the episcopal college[72] and its support and mouthpiece, called to the service of the People of God, constitute, together with their bishop, a unique sacerdotal college (*presbyterium*)[73] dedicated it is true to a variety of distinct duties. In each local assembly of the faithful they represent in a certain sense the bishop, with whom they are associated in all trust and generosity; in part they take upon themselves his duties and solicitude and in their daily toils discharge them. Those who, under the authority of the bishop, sanctify and govern that portion of the Lord's flock assigned to them render the universal Church visible in their locality and contribute ef-

---

67. Cf. Council of Trent. Session 22: *Denz.* 940 (1743). Pius XII, Encycl. *Mediator Dei*, 20 Nov. 1974: *AAS* 39 (1947) p. 553; *Denz.* 2300 (3850).
68. Cf. Council of Trent, Session 22: *Denz.* 938 (1739–40). Vatican Council II, Const. *De Sacra Liturgia*, no. 7 and no. 47.
69. Cf. Pius XII, Encycl. *Mediator Dei, loc. cit.*, under no. 67.
70. Cf. St. Cyprian, *Epist.* 11, 3: *PL* 4, 242B; Hartel, II, 2, p. 497.
71. *Order of priestly consecration*, at the clothing with the vestments.
72. *Order of priestly consecration*, the Preface.
73. Cf. St. Ignatius, Martyr, *Philad.* 4: ed. Funk, I, p. 266. St. Cornelius I *apud* St. Cyprian, *Epist.* 48, 2: Hartel, III, 2, p. 610.

ficaciously towards building up the whole body of Christ (cf. Eph. 4:12). And ever anxious for the good of the children of God they should be eager to lend their efforts to the pastoral work of the whole diocese, nay rather of the whole Church. By reason of this sharing in the priesthood and mission of the bishop the priests should see in him a true father and obey him with all respect. The bishop, on his side, should treat the priests, his helpers, as his sons and friends, just as Christ calls his disciples no longer servants but friends (cf. Jn. 15:15). All priests, then, whether diocesan or religious, by reason of the sacrament of Orders and of the ministry correspond to and cooperate with the body of bishops and, according to their vocation and the grace that is given them they serve the welfare of the whole Church.

In virtue of their sacred ordination and of their common mission all priests are united together by bonds of intimate brotherhood, which manifests itself in a spontaneously and gladly given mutual help, whether spiritual or temporal, whether pastoral or personal, through the medium of re-unions and community life, work and fraternal charity.

As to the faithful, they (the priests) should bestow their paternal attention and solicitude on them, whom they have begotten spiritually through baptism and instruction (cf. 1 Cor. 4:15; 1 Pet. 1:23). Gladly constituting themselves models of the flock (cf. 1 Pet. 5:3), they should preside over and serve their local community in such a way that it may deserve to be called by the name which is given to the unique People of God in its entirety, that is to say, the Church of God (cf. Cor. 1:2; 2 Cor. 1:1, and *passim*). They should be mindful that by their daily conduct and so-licitude they display the reality of a truly priestly and pas-toral ministry both to believers and unbelievers alike, to Catholics and non-Catholics; that they are bound to bear witness before all men of the truth and of the life, and as good shepherds seek after those too (cf. Lk. 15:4–7) who, whilst having been baptised in the Catholic Church, have given up the practice of the sacraments, or even fallen away from the faith.

Since the human race today is tending more and more to-wards civil, economic and social unity, it is all the more necessary that priests should unite their efforts and combine their resources under the leadership of the bishops and the Supreme Pontiff and thus eliminate division and dissension in every shape or form, so that all mankind may be led into the unity of the family of God.

29. At a lower level of the hierarchy are to be found deacons, who receive the imposition of hands "not unto the priesthood, but unto the ministry."[74] For, strengthened by sacramental grace they are dedicated to the People of God, in conjunction with the bishop and his body of priests, in the service of the liturgy, of the Gospel and of works of charity. It pertains to the office of a deacon, in so far as it may be assigned to him by the competent authority, to administer Baptism solemnly, to be custodian and distributor of the Eucharist, in the name of the Church, to assist at and to bless marriages, to bring Viaticum to the dying, to read the sacred scripture to the faithful, to instruct and exhort the people, to preside over the worship and the prayer of the faithful, to administer sacramentals, and to officiate at funeral and burial services. Dedicated to works of charity and functions of administration, deacons should recall the admonition of St Polycarp: "Let them be merciful, and zealous, and let them walk according to the truth of the Lord, who became the servant of all."[75]

Since, however, the laws and customs of the Latin Church in force today in many areas render it difficult to fulfil these functions, which are so extremely necessary for the life of the Church, it will be possible in the future to restore the diaconate as a proper and permanent rank of the hierarchy. But it pertains to the competent local episcopal conferences, of one kind or another, with the approval of the Supreme Pontiff, to decide whether and where it is opportune that such deacons be appointed. Should the Roman Pontiff think fit, it will be possible to confer this diaconal order even upon married men, provided they be of more mature age, and also on suitable young men, for whom, however, the law of celibacy must remain in force.

74. *Constitutions of the Egyptian Church*, III, 2: ed. Funk, *Didascalia*, II, p. 103, *Statuta Eccl. Ant.* 37–41: Mansi 3, 954.
75. St. Polycarp, *Ad Phil.* 5, 2: ed. Funk, I, p. 300: It is said that Christ "became the 'diaconus' of all." Cf. *Didachè*, 15, 1: ibid. p. 32. St. Ignatius, Martyr, *Trall.* 2, 3: ibid., p. 242. *Constitutiones Apostolorum* 8, 24, 4: ed. Funk, Didascalia, I, p. 580.

THE LAITY

30. Having made clear the functions of the hierarchy, the holy Council is pleased to turn its attention to the state of those Christians who are called the laity. Everything that has been said of the People of God is addressed equally to laity, religious and clergy. Because of their situation and mission, however, certain things pertain particularly to the laity, both men and women, the foundations of which must be more fully examined owing to the special circumstances of our time. The pastors, indeed, know well how much the laity contribute to the welfare of the whole Church. For they know that they themselves were not established by Christ to undertake alone the whole salvific mission of the Church to the world, but that it is their exalted office so to be shepherds of the faithful and also recognize the latter's contribution and charisms that everyone in his own way will, with one mind, cooperate in the common task. For all must "practise the truth in love, and so grow up in all things in him who is the head, Christ. For from him the whole body —being closely joined and knit together through every joint of the system according to the functioning in due measure of each single part—derives its increase to the building up of itself in love" (Eph. 4:15–16).

31. The term "laity" is here understood to mean all the faithful except those in Holy Orders and those who belong to a religious state approved by the Church. That is, the faithful who by Baptism are incorporated into Christ, are placed in the People of God, and in their own way share the priestly, prophetic and kingly office of Christ, and to the best of their ability carry on the mission of the whole Christian people in the Church and in the world.

Their secular character is proper and peculiar to the laity. Although those in Holy Orders may sometimes be engaged in secular activities, or even practice a secular profession, yet by reason of their particular vocation, they are principally and expressly ordained to the sacred ministry. At the same time, religious give outstanding and striking

a. This chapter has been translated by Father Christopher O'Donnell, O.CARM.

testimony that the world cannot be transfigured and offered to God without the spirit of the beatitudes. But by reason of their special vocation it belongs to the laity to seek the kingdom of God by engaging in temporal affairs and directing them according to God's will. They live in the world, that is, they are engaged in each and every work and business of the earth and in the ordinary circumstances of social and family life which, as it were, constitute their very existence. There they are called by God that, being led by the spirit to the Gospel, they may contribute to the sanctification of the world, as from within like leaven, by fulfilling their own particular duties. Thus, especially by the witness of their life, resplendent in faith, hope and charity they must manifest Christ to others. It pertains to them in a special way so to illuminate and order all temporal things with which they are so closely associated that these may be effected and grow according to Christ and may be to the glory of the Creator and Redeemer.

32. By divine institution holy Church is ordered and governed with a wonderful diversity. "For just as in one body we have many members, yet all the members have not the same function, so we the many, are one body in Christ, but severally members one of another" (Rom. 12:4–5).

There is, therefore, one chosen People of God: "one Lord, one faith, one baptism" (Eph. 4:5); there is a common dignity of members deriving from their rebirth in Christ, a common grace as sons, a common vocation to perfection, one salvation, one hope and undivided charity. In Christ and in the Church there is, then, no inequality arising from race or nationality, social condition or sex, for "there is neither Jew nor Greek; there is neither slave nor freeman; there is neither male nor female. For you are all 'one' in Christ Jesus" (Gal. 3:28 Greek; cf. Col. 3:11).

In the Church not everyone marches along the same path, yet all are called to sanctity and have obtained an equal privilege of faith through the justice of God (cf. 2 Pet. 1:1). Although by Christ's will some are established as teachers, dispensers of the mysteries and pastors for the others, there remains, nevertheless, a true equality between all with regard to the dignity and to the activity which is common to all the faithful in the building up of the Body of Christ. The distinction which the Lord has made between the sacred ministers and the rest of the People of God involves union, for the pastors and the other faithful are joined together by a close relationship: the pastors of the Church—following the example of the Lord—should minister to each other and to the rest of the faithful; the latter should eagerly collaborate with the pastors and teachers. And so amid variety all will bear witness to the wonderful unity in the Body of Christ: this very diversity of graces, of ministries and of works gathers the sons of God into one, for "all these things are the work of the one and the same Spirit" (1 Cor. 12:11).

As the laity through the divine choice have Christ as their brother, who, though Lord of all, came not to be served but to serve (cf. Mt. 20:28), they also have as brothers those in the sacred ministry who by teaching, by sanctifying and by ruling with the authority of Christ so nourish the family of God that the new commandment of love may be fulfilled by all. As St Augustine very beautifully puts it: "When I am frightened by what I am to you, then I am consoled by what I am with you. To you I am the bishop, with you I am a Christian. The first is an office, the second a grace; the first a danger, the second salvation.[1]

33. Gathered together in the People of God and established in the one Body of Christ under one head, the laity —no matter who they are—have, as living members, the vocation of applying to the building up of the Church and to its continual sanctification all the powers which they have received from the goodness of the Creator and from the grace of the Redeemer.

The apostolate of the laity is a sharing in the salvific mission of the Church. Through Baptism and Confirmation all are appointed to this apostolate by the Lord himself. Moreover, by the sacraments, and especially by the Eucharist, that love of God and man which is the soul of the apostolate is communicated and nourished. The laity, however, are given this special vocation: to make the Church present and fruitful in those places and circumstances where it is only through them that she can become the salt of the earth.[2] Thus, every lay person, through those gifts given to him, is at once the witness and the living instrument of the mission of the Church itself "according to the measure of Christ's bestowal" (Eph. 4:7).

1. St. Augustine, Sermon 340, 1: PL 38, 1438.
2. See Pius XI, Litt. Encycl. Quadragesimo anno, 15 May 1931: AAS 23 (1931) p. 221 s. 2 Pius XII, Alloc. De Quelle consolation, 14 Oct. 1951: AAS 43 (1951) p. 790 s.

Besides this apostolate which belongs to absolutely every Christian, the laity can be called in different ways to more immediate cooperation in the apostolate of the hierarchy,[3] like those men and women who helped the apostle Paul in the Gospel, laboring much in the Lord (cf. Phil. 4–3; Rom. 16:3 ff.). They have, moreover, the capacity of being appointed by the hierarchy to some ecclesiastical offices with a view to a spiritual end.

All the laity, then, have the exalted duty of working for the ever greater spread of the divine plan of salvation to all men, of every epoch and all over the earth. Therefore may the way be clear for them to share diligently in the salvific work of the Church according to their ability and the needs of the times.

34. Since he wishes to continue his witness and his service through the laity also, the supreme and eternal priest, Christ Jesus, vivifies them with his spirit and ceaselessly impels them to accomplish every good and perfect work.

To those whom he intimately joins to his life and mission he also gives a share in his priestly office, to offer spiritual worship for the glory of the Father and the salvation of man. Hence the laity, dedicated as they are to Christ and anointed by the Holy Spirit, are marvellously called and prepared so that even richer fruits of the Spirit may be produced in them. For all their works, prayers and apostolic undertakings, family and married life, daily work, relaxation of mind and body, if they are accomplished in the Spirit—indeed even the hardships of life if patiently borne —all these become spiritual sacrifices acceptable to God through Jesus Christ (cf. Pet. 2:5). In the celebration of the Eucharist these may most fittingly be offered to the Father along with the body of the Lord. And so, worshipping everywhere by their holy actions, the laity consecrate the world itself to God.

35. Christ is the great prophet who proclaimed the kingdom of the Father both by the testimony of his life and by the power of his word. Until the full manisfestation of his glory, he fulfills this prophetic office, not only by the hierarchy who teach in his name and by his power, but also by the laity. He accordingly both establishes them as witnesses and provides them with the appreciation of the faith

3. See Pius XII, Alloc. *Six ans sont écoulé*, 5 Oct. 1957: *AAS* 49 (1957) p. 927.

*(sensus fidei)** and the grace of the word (cf. Acts 2:17–18; Apoc. 19:10) so that the power of the Gospel may shine out in daily family and social life. They show themselves to be the children of the promise if, strong in faith and hope, they make the most of the present time (Eph. 5:16; Col. 4:5), and with patience await the future glory (cf. Rom. 8:25). Let them not hide this their hope then, in the depths of their hearts, but rather express it through the structure of their secular lives in continual conversion and in wrestling "against the world rulers of this darkness, against the spiritual forces of iniquity" (Eph. 6:12).

As the sacraments of the New Law, which nourish the life and the apostolate of the faithful, prefigure the new heaven and the new earth (cf. Apoc. 21:1), so too the laity become powerful heralds of the faith in things to be hoped for (cf. Heb. 11:1) if they join unhesitating profession of faith to the life of faith. This evangelization, that is, the proclamation of Christ by word and the testimony of life, acquires a specific property and peculiar efficacy because it is accomplished in the ordinary circumstances of the world.

The state of life that is sanctified by a special sacrament, namely, married and family life, has a special importance in this prophetic office. Where the Christian religion pervades the whole structure of life with a continuous and ever more profound transformation, there is both the practice and an outstanding school of the lay apostolate. In it the married partners have their own proper vocation: they must be witnesses of faith and love of Christ to one another and to their children. The Christian family proclaims aloud both the present power of the kingdom of God and the hope of the blessed life. Hence, by example and by their testimony, they convict the world of sin and give light to those who seek the truth.

Therefore, even when occupied by temporal affairs, the laity can, and must, do valuable work for the evangelization of the world. But if, when there are no sacred ministers or when these are impeded under persecution, some lay people supply sacred functions to the best of their ability, or if, indeed, many of them expend all their energies in apostolic work, nevertheless the whole laity must cooperate in spreading and in building up the kingdom of Christ. Let the laity, therefore, diligently apply themselves to a more pro-

---

* (See chapter 2, art. 12 of the constitution.—Translator.)

found knowledge of revealed truth and earnestly beg of God the gift of wisdom.

36. Christ, made obedient unto death and because of this exalted by the Father (cf. Ph. 2:8–9), has entered into the glory of his kingdom. All things are subjected to him until he subjects himself and all created things to the Father, so that God may be all in all (cf. 1 Cor. 15:27–28). He communicated this power to the disciples that they be constituted in royal liberty and, by self-abnegation of a holy life, overcome the reign of sin in themselves (cf. Rom. 6:12)— that indeed by serving Christ in others they may in humility and patience bring their brethren to that king to serve whom is to reign. The Lord also desires that his kingdom be spread by the lay faithful: the kingdom of truth and life, the kingdom of holiness and grace, the kingdom of justice, love and peace.[4] In this kingdom creation itself will be delivered from the slavery of corruption into the freedom of the glory of the sons of God (cf. Rom. 8:21). Clearly, a great promise, a great commission is given to the disciples: "all things are yours, you are Christ's, and Christ is God's" (1 Cor. 3:23).

The faithful must, then, recognize the inner nature, the value and the ordering of the whole of creation to the praise of God. Even by their secular activity they must aid one another to greater holiness of life, so that the world may be filled with the spirit of Christ and may the more effectively attain its destiny in justice, in love and in peace. The laity enjoy a principle role in the universal fulfillment of this task. Therefore, by their competence in secular disciplines and by their activity, interiorly raised up by grace, let them work earnestly in order that created goods through human labor, technical skill and civil culture may serve the utility of all men according to the plan of the creator and the light of his word. May these goods be more suitably distributed among all men and in their own way may they be conducive to universal progress in human and Christian liberty. Thus, through the members of the Church, will Christ increasingly illuminate the whole of human society with his saving light.

Moreover, by uniting their forces, let the laity so remedy the institutions and conditions of the world when the latter are an inducement to sin, that these may be conformed to

4. From the *Preface* of the Feast of Christ the King.

the norms of justice, favoring rather than hindering the practice of virtue. By so doing they will impregnate culture and human works with a moral value. In this way the field of the world is better prepared for the seed of the divine word and the doors of the Church are opened more widely through which the message of peace may enter the world.

Because of the very economy of salvation the faithful should learn to distinguish carefully between the rights and the duties which they have as belonging to the Church and those which fall to them as members of the human society. They will strive to unite the two harmoniously, remembering that in every temporal affair they are to be guided by a Christian conscience, since not even in temporal business may any human activity be withdrawn from God's dominion. In our times it is most necessary that this distinction and harmony should shine forth as clearly as possible in the manner in which the faithful act, in order that the mission of the Church may correspond more fully with the special circumstances of the world today. But just as it must be recognized that the terrestrial city, rightly concerned with secular affairs, is governed by its own principles, thus also the ominous doctrine which seeks to build society with no regard for religion, and attacks and utterly destroys the religious liberty of its citizens, is rightly to be rejected.[5]

37. Like all Christians, the laity have the right to receive in abundance the help of the spiritual goods of the Church, especially that of the word of God and the sacraments from the pastors.[6] To the latter the laity should disclose their needs and desires with that liberty and confidence which befits children of God and brothers of Christ. By reason of the knowledge, competence or pre-eminence which they have the laity are empowered—indeed sometimes obliged—to manifest their opinion on those things which pertain to the good of the Church.[7] If the occasion

5. See Leo XIII, Epist. Encycl. *Immortale Dei*, 1 Nov. 1885: *ASS* 18 (1885) p. 166 ss. *Idem.*, Litt. Encycl. *Sapientiae Christianae*, 10 Jan. 1890: *AAS* 22 (1889–90) p. 397 ss. Pius XII, Alloc. *Alla vostra filiale*, 23 March 1958: *AAS* 50 (1958) p. 220: *la legittima sana laicità dello Stato.*
6. *Code of Canon Law*, can. 682.
7. See Pius XII, Alloc. *De quelle Consolation, loc. cit.*, p. 789: *Dans les batailles dècisives, c'est parfois de front que partent les plus heureuses initiatives . . . Idem.*, Alloc. *L'importance de la presse catholique*, 17 Feb. 1950: *AAS* 42 (1950) p. 256.

should arise this should be done through the institutions established by the Church for that purpose and always with truth, courage and prudence and with reverence and charity towards those who, by reason of their office, represent the person of Christ.

Like all Christians, the laity should promptly accept in Christian obedience what is decided by the pastors who, as teachers and rulers of the Church, represent Christ. In this they will follow Christ's example who, by his obedience unto death, opened the blessed way of the liberty of the sons of God to all men. Nor should they fail to commend to God in their prayers those who have been placed over them, who indeed keep watch as having to render an account of our souls, that they may do this with joy and not with grief (cf. Heb. 13:17).

The pastors, indeed, should recognize and promote the dignity and responsibility of the laity in the Church. They should willingly use their prudent advice and confidently assign duties to them in the service of the Church, leaving them freedom and scope for acting. Indeed, they should give them the courage to undertake works on their own initiative. They should with paternal love consider attentively in Christ initial moves, suggestions and desires proposed by the laity.[8] Moreover the pastors must respect and recognize the liberty which belongs to all in the terrestrial city.

Many benefits for the Church are to be expected from this familiar relationship between the laity and the pastors. The sense of their own responsibility is strengthened in the laity, their zeal is encouraged, they are more ready to unite their energies to the work of their pastors. The latter, helped by the experience of the laity, are in a position to judge more clearly and more appropriately in spiritual as well as in temporal matters. Strengthened by all her members, the Church can thus more effectively fulfil her mission for the life of the world.

38. Each individual layman must be a witness before the world to the resurrection and life of the Lord Jesus, and a sign of the living God. All together, and each one to the best of his ability, must nourish the world with spiritual fruits (cf. Gal. 5:22). They must diffuse in the world the spirit

8. See 1 Th. 5:19 and 1 Jn. 4:1.

which animates those poor, meek and peace-makers whom
the Lord in the Gospel proclaimed blessed (cf. Mt. 5:3–9).
In a word: 'what the soul is in the body, let Christians be in
the world.'[9]

CHAPTER V

THE CALL TO HOLINESS[a]

39. The Church, whose mystery is set forth by this sacred Council, is held, as a matter of faith, to be unfailingly
holy. This is because Christ, the Son of God, who with the
Father and the Spirit is hailed as "alone holy,"[1] loved the
Church as his Bride, giving himself up for her so as to
sanctify her (cf. Eph. 5:25–26); he joined her to himself as
his body and endowed her with the gift of the Holy Spirit
for the glory of God. Therefore all in the Church, whether
they belong to the hierarchy or are cared for by it, are
called to holiness, according to the apostle's saying: 'For
this is the will of God, your sanctification' (1 Th. 4:3; cf.
Eph. 1:4). This holiness of the Church is constantly shown
forth in the fruits of grace which the Spirit produces in the
faithful and so it must be; it is expressed in many ways by
the individuals who, each in his own state of life, tend to
the perfection of love, thus sanctifying others; it appears in
a certain way of its own in the practice of the counsels
which have been usually called "evangelical." This practice
of the counsels prompted by the Holy Spirit, undertaken by
many Christians whether privately or in a form or state
sanctioned by the Church, gives and should give a striking
witness and example of that holiness.

40. The Lord Jesus, divine teacher and model of all

9. *Epist. ad Diognetum*, 6: ed. Funk, I, p. 400. See St. John Chrysostom, *In Matt.* Hom. 46 (47), 2: *PG* 58, 478, *de fermento in massa*.
a. This chapter has been translated by Father Joseph M. de Torre.
1. The Roman Missal, *Gloria in excelsis*. CF. Lk. 1:35, 4:34; Mk.
1:24; Jn. 6:69 (*ho hagios tou Theou*); Acts 3:14; 4:27 and 30;
Heb. 7:26; 1 Jn. 2:20; Apoc. 3:7.

perfection, preached holiness of life (of which he is the author and maker) to each and every one of his disciples
without distinction: "You, therefore, must be perfect, as
your heavenly Father is perfect" (Mt. 5:48).[2] For he sent
the Holy Spirit to all to move them interiorly to love God
with their whole heart, with their whole soul, with their
whole understanding, and with their whole strength (cf.
Mk. 12:30), and to love one another as Christ loved them
(cf. Jn. 13:34; 15:12). The followers of Christ, called by
God not in virtue of their works but by his design and
grace, and justified in the Lord Jesus, have been made sons
of God in the baptism of faith and partakers of the divine
nature, and so are truly sanctified. They must therefore
hold on to and perfect in their lives that sanctification
which they have received from God. They are told by the
apostle to live "as is fitting among saints" (Eph. 5:3), and
to put on "as God's chosen ones, holy and beloved, compassion, kindness, lowliness, meekness, and patience" (Col.
3:12), to have the fruits of the Spirit for their sanctification (cf. Gal. 5:22; Rom. 6:22). But since we all offend in
many ways (cf. Jas. 3:2), we constantly need God's mercy
and must pray every day: "And forgive us our debts" (Mt.
6:12)[3]

It is therefore quite clear that all Christians in any state
or walk of life are called to the fullness of Christian life
and to the perfection of love,[4] and by this holiness a more
human manner of life is fostered also in earthly society. In
order to reach this perfection the faithful should use the
strength dealt out to them by Christ's gift, so that, following
in his footsteps and conformed to his image, doing the will
of God in everything, they may wholeheartedly devote
themselves to the glory of God and to the service of their
neighbor. Thus the holiness of the People of God will grow

2. Cf. Origen, *Comm. Rom.* 7, 7: *PG* 14, 1122 B.; Ps.-Macarius, *De
Oratione*, 11: *PG* 34, 861 AB; St. Thomas, *Summa Theol.* II-II, q.
184, a. 3.
3. Cf. St. Augustine, *Retract.* II, 18: *PL* 32, 637 f.; Pius XII, Encycl.
Mystici Corporis, 29 June 1943: *AAS* 35 (1943) p. 225.
4. Cf. Pius XI, Encycl. *Rerum omnium*, 26 Jan. 1923: *AAS* 15
(1923) p. 50 and 59–60; Encycl. *Casti Connubii*, 31 Dec. 1930: *AAS*
22 (1930) p. 548; Pius XII, Apost. Const. *Provida Mater*, 2 Feb.
1947: *AAS* 30 (1947) p. 117; Address *Annus sacer*, 8 Dec. 1950: *AAS*
43 (1951) pp. 27–28; Address *Nel darvi*, 1 July 1956: *AAS* 48 (1956)
p. 574 f.

in fruitful abundance, as is clearly shown in the history of the Church through the life of so many saints.

41. The forms and tasks of life are many but holiness is one—that sanctity which is cultivated by all who act under God's Spirit and, obeying the Father's voice and adoring God the Father in spirit and in truth, follow Christ, poor, humble and cross-bearing, that they may deserve to be partakers of his glory. Each one, however, according to his own gifts and duties must steadfastly advance along the way of a living faith, which arouses hope and works through love.

In the first place, the shepherds of Christ's flock, in the image of the high and eternal priest, shepherd and bishop of our souls, should carry out their ministry with holiness and eagerness, with humility and fortitude; thus fulfilled, this ministry will also be for them an outstanding means of sanctification. Called to the fullness of the priesthood, they are endowed with a sacramental grace, so that by prayer, sacrifice and preaching, and through every form of episcopal care and service, they may fulfil the perfect duty of pastoral love.[5] They should not be afraid to lay down their life for their sheep and, being a model to their flock (cf. 1 Pet. 5:3), they must foster a growing holiness in the Church, also by their own example.

Priests, who resemble the episcopal rank, forming the spiritual crown of the bishops,[6] partake of their grace of office through Christ the eternal and only Mediator; they should grow in the love of God and of their neighbor by the daily exercise of their duty, should keep the bond of priestly fellowship, should abound in every spiritual good and bear a living witness of God to all,[7] imitating those priests who, in the course of centuries, left behind them an outstanding example of holiness, often in a humble and hidden service. Their praise lives on in God's Church. They have the duty to pray and offer sacrifice for their people and for the whole People of God, appreciating what they do and imitating what they touch with their hands.[8] Rather

5. Cf. St. Thomas, *Summa Theol.* II-II, q. 184, a. 5 and 6; *De perf. vitae spir.*, c. 18; Origen, *In Is.* Hom. 6, 1: *PG* 13, 239.
6. Cf. St. Ignatius Martyr, *Magn.* 13, 1: ed. Funk, I, p. 241.
7. Cf. St. Pius X, Exhort. *Haerent animo*, 4 Aug. 1908: *ASS* 41 (1908) p. 560 f.; Code of Canon Law, can. 124; Pius XI, Encycl. *Ad catholici sacerdotii*, 20 Dec. 1935: *AAS* 28 (1936) p. 22 f.
8. *Order of priestly consecration*, introductory exhortation.

than be held back by perils and hardships in their apostolic labors they should rise to greater holiness, nourishing and fostering their action with an overflowing contemplation, for the delight of the entire Church of God. Let all priests, especially those who by special title of ordination are called diocesan priests, remember that their faithful union and generous cooperation with their bishop greatly helps their sanctification.

The ministers of lesser rank also partake in a special way of the mission and grace of the high priest, and in the first place the deacons who, waiting upon the mysteries of Christ and of the Church,[9] should keep themselves free from every vice, should please God and give a good example to all in everything (cf. 1 Tim. 3: 8–10 and 12–13). Clerics, called by the Lord and set aside as his portion and preparing themselves for the ministerial duties under the watchful eye of the shepherds, are bound to conform their minds and hearts to such high calling, persevering in prayer, fervent in love, thinking about whatever is true, just and of good repute, doing everything for the glory and honor of God. Close to them are those laymen chosen by God, who are called by the bishop to give themselves fully to apostolic works, and carry out a very fruitful activity in the Lord's field.[10]

Christian married couples and parents, following their own way, should support one another in grace all through life with faithful love, and should train their children (lovingly received from God) in Christian doctrine and evangelical virtues. Because in this way they present to all an example of unfailing and generous love, they build up the brotherhood of charity, and they stand as witnesses and cooperators of the fruitfulness of mother Church, as a sign of, and a share in that love with which Christ loved his bride and gave himself for her.[11] In a different way, a similar example is given by widows and single people, who can also greatly contribute to the holiness and activity of the Church. And those who engage in human work, often of a heavy kind, should perfect themselves through it, help their

9. Cf. *St. Ignatius Martyr, Trall.* 2, 3: ed. Funk, I, p. 244.
10. Cf. Pius XII, Address *Sous la maternelle protection,* 9 Dec. 1957: *AAS* 50 (1958) p. 36.
11. Pius XI, Encycl. *Casti Connubii,* 31 Dec. 1930: *AAS* 22 (1930) p. 548 f.; cf. St. John Chrysostom, *In Ephes.* Hom. 20, 2: *PG* 62, 136 ff.

fellow-citizens, and promote the betterment of the whole of human society and the whole of creation; indeed, with their active charity, rejoicing in hope and bearing one another's burdens, they should imitate Christ who plied his hands with carpenter's tools and is always working with the Father for the salvation of all; and they should rise to a higher sanctity, truly apostolic, by their everyday work itself.

In a special way also, those who are weighed down by poverty, infirmity, sickness and other hardships should realize that they are united to Christ, who suffers for the salvation of the world; let those feel the same who suffer persecution for the sake of justice, those whom the Lord declared blessed in the Gospel and whom "the God of all grace, who has called us to his eternal glory in Christ Jesus, will himself restore, establish, strengthen and settle" (1 Pet. 5:10).

Accordingly all Christians, in the conditions, duties and circumstances of their life and through all these, will sanctify themselves more and more if they receive all things with faith from the hand of the heavenly Father and cooperate with the divine will, thus showing forth in that temporal service the love with which God has loved the world.

42. 'God is love, and he who abides in love abides in God, and God abides in him' (1 Jn. 4:16). God has poured out his love in our hearts through the Holy Spirit who has been given to us (cf. Rom. 5:5); therefore the first and most necessary gift is charity, by which we love God above all things and our neighbor because of him. But if charity is to grow and fructify in the soul like a good seed, each of the faithful must willingly hear the word of God and carry out his will with deeds, with the help of his grace; he must frequently partake of the sacraments, chiefly the Eucharist, and take part in the liturgy; he must constantly apply himself to prayer, self-denial, active brotherly service and the practice of all virtues. This is because love, as the bond of perfection and fullness of the law (cf. Col. 3:14; Rom. 13:10), governs, gives meaning to, and perfects all the means of sanctification.[12] Hence the true disciple of Christ is marked by love both of God and of his neighbor.

Since Jesus, the Son of God, showed his love by laying

12. Cf. St. Augustine, *Enchir.* 121, 32: *PL* 40, 288; St. Thomas, *Summa Theol.* II-II, q. 184, a. 1; Pius XII, Apost. Exhort. *Menti Nostrae*, 23 Sept. 1950: *AAS* 42 (1950) p. 660.

down his life for us, no one has greater love than he who lays down his life for him and for his brothers (cf. 1 Jn. 3:16, Jn. 15:13). Some Christians have been called from the beginning, and will always be called, to give this greatest testimony of love to all, especially to persecutors. Martyrdom makes the disciple like his master, who willingly accepted death for the salvation of the world, and through it he is conformed to him by the shedding of blood. Therefore the Church considers it the highest gift and supreme test of love. And while it is given to few, all however must be prepared to confess Christ before men and to follow him along the way of the cross amidst the persecutions which the Church never lacks.

Likewise the Church's holiness is fostered in a special way by the manifold counsels which the Lord proposes to his disciples in the Gospel for them to observe.[18] Towering among these counsels is that precious gift of divine grace given to some by the Father (cf. Mt. 19:11; 1 Cor. 7:7) to devote themselves to God alone more easily with an undivided heart (cf. 1 Cor 7: 32–34) in virginity or celibacy.[14] This perfect continence for love of the kingdom of heaven has always been held in high esteem by the Church as a sign and stimulus of love, and as a singular source of spiritual fertility in the world.

The Church bears in mind too the apostle's admonition when calling the faithful to charity and exhorting them to have the same mind which Christ Jesus showed, who "emptied himself, taking the form of a servant . . . and became obedient unto death" (Phil. 2:7–8) and for our sakes "became poor, though he was rich" (2 Cor. 8:9). Since the disciples must always imitate this love and humility of Christ and bear witness of it, Mother Church rejoices that she has within herself many men and women who pursue more closely the Saviour's self-emptying and show it forth more clearly, by undertaking poverty with the freedom of God's sons, and renouncing their own will: they subject

13. On the counsels in general cf. Origen, *Comm. Rom.* X, 14: *PG* 14, 1275B; St. Augustine, *De S. Virginitate*, 15, 15: *PL* 40, 403; St. Thomas, *Summa Theol.* I-II, q. 100, a. 2 c (end); II-II, q. 44, a. 4 ad 3.
14. On the excellence of holy virginity cf. Tertullian, *Exhort. Cast.* 10: *PL* 2, 925C; St. Cyprian, *Hab. Virg.* 3 and 22: *PL* 4, 443B and 461A f.; St. Athanasius (?), *De Virg.*: *PG* 28, 252 ff.; St. John Chrysostom, *De Virg.*: *PG* 48, 533 ff.

themselves to man for the love of God, thus going beyond what is of precept in the matter of perfection, so as to conform themselves more fully to the obedient Christ.[15]

Therefore all the faithful are invited and obliged to holiness and the perfection of their own state of life. Accordingly let all of them see that they direct their affections rightly, lest they be hindered in their pursuit of perfect love by the use of worldly things and by an adherence to riches which is contrary to the spirit of evangelical poverty, following the apostle's advice: Let those who use this world not fix their abode in it, for the form of this world is passing away (cf. 1 Cor. 7:31, Greek text).[16]

CHAPTER VI[a]

RELIGIOUS

43. The teaching and example of Christ provide the foundation for the evangelical counsels of chaste self-dedication to God, of poverty and of obedience. The Apostles and Fathers of the Church commend them as an ideal of life, and so do her doctors and pastors. They therefore constitute a gift of God which the Church has received from her Lord and which by his grace she always safeguards.

Guided by the Holy Spirit, Church authority has been at pains to give a right interpretation of the counsels, to regulate their practice, and also to set up stable forms of living embodying them. From the God-given seed of the counsels a wonderful and wide-spreading tree has grown up in the field of the Lord, branching out into various forms of reli-

15. On spiritual *poverty* cf. Mt. 5:3 and 19:21; Mk. 10:21; Lk. 18:22; *on obedience* Christ's example is presented in Jn. 4:34 and 6:38; Phil. 2:8–10; Heb. 10:5–7. Texts of Fathers and founders of orders are abundant.
16. On the effective practice of the counsels which is not imposed on everyone cf. St. John Chrysostom, *In Mt.* Hom 7, 7: *PG* 57, 81 s.; St. Ambrose, *De Viduis,* 4, 23; *PL* 16, 241 f.
a. This chapter was translated by Father Sean O'Riordan, CSSR.

gious life lived in solitude or in community. Different religious families have come into existence in which spiritual resources are multiplied for the progress in holiness of their members and for the good of the entire Body of Christ.[1]

Members of these families enjoy many helps towards holiness of life. They have a stable and more solidly based way of Christian life. They receive well-proven teaching on seeking after perfection. They are bound together in brotherly communion in the army of Christ. Their Christian freedom is fortified by obedience. Thus they are enabled to live securely and to maintain faithfully the religious life to which they have pledged themselves. Rejoicing in spirit they advance on the road of love.[2]

This form of life has its own place in relation to the divine and hierarchical structure of the Church. Not, however, as though it were a kind of middle way between the clerical and lay conditions of life. Rather it should be seen as a form of life to which some Christians, both clerical and lay, are called by God so that they may enjoy a special gift of grace in the life of the Church and may contribute, each in his own way, to the saving mission of the Church.[3]

44. The Christian who pledges himself to this kind of life binds himself to the practice of the three evangelical counsels by vows or by other sacred ties of a similar nature. He consecrates himself wholly to God, his supreme love. In a new and special way he makes himself over to God, to serve and honor him. True, as a baptized Christian he is dead to sin and dedicated to God; but he desires to derive still more abundant fruit from the grace of his baptism. For this purpose he makes profession in the Church of the evangelical counsels. He does so for two reasons: first, in order to be set free from hindrances that could hold him back from loving God ardently and worshipping him per-

---

1. Cf. Rosweyde, *Vitae Patrum* (Antwerp, 1628); *Apophtegmata Patrum (PG* 65); Palladius, *Historia Lausiaca (PG* 34, 995 ff), ed. C. Butler (Cambridge, 1898: 1904); Pius XI, Apostolic Constitution *Umbratilem,* 8 July 1924 *(AAS* 16 [1924] pp. 386–387); Pius XII, Allocution *Nous sommes heureux,* 11 April 1958 *(AAS* 50 [1958] p. 283).

2. Paul VI, Allocution *Magno gaudio,* 23 May 1964 *(AAS* 56 [1964] p. 566).

3. Cf. *Code of Canon Law,* can. 487 and 488, 4; Pius XII, Allocution *Annus sacer,* 8 December 1950 *(AAS* 43 [1951] p 27 f.); Pius XII, Apostolic Constitution *Provida Mater,* 2 February 1947 *(AAS* 39 [1947] p. 120 ff.).

fectly, and secondly, in order to consecrate himself in a more thoroughgoing way to the service of God.[4] The bonds by which he pledges himself to the practice of the counsels show forth the unbreakable bond of union that exists between Christ and his bride the Church. The more stable and firm these bonds are, then, the more perfect will the Christian's religious consecration be.

Being means to and instruments of love,[5] the evangelical counsels unite those who practice them to the Church and her mystery in a special way. It follows that the spiritual life of such Christians should be dedicated also to the welfare of the entire Church. To the extent of their capacities and in keeping with the particular kind of religious life to which they are individually called, whether it be one of prayer or of active labor as well, they have the duty of working for the implanting and strengthening of the kingdom of Christ in souls and for spreading it to the four corners of the earth. It is for this reason that the distinctive character of various religious institutes is preserved and fostered by the Church.

All the members of the Church should unflaggingly fulfil the duties of their Christian calling. The profession of the evangelical counsels shines before them as a sign which can and should effectively inspire them to do so. For the People of God has here no lasting city but seeks the city which is to come, and the religious state of life, in bestowing greater freedom from the cares of earthly existence on those who follow it, simultaneously reveals more clearly to all believers the heavenly goods which are already present in this age, witnessing to the new and eternal life which we have acquired through the redemptive work of Christ and preluding our future resurrection and the glory of the heavenly kingdom. Furthermore the religious state constitutes a closer imitation and an abiding reenactment in the Chruch of the form of life which the Son of God made his own when he came into the world to do the will of the Father and which he propounded to the disciples who followed him. Finally this state manifests in a special way the transcendence of the kingdom of God and its requirements over all earthly things and the highest kind of bonds within it, bring-

4. Paul VI, *loc. cit.* p. 567.
5. Cf. St. Thomas, *Summa Theol.* II-II, q. 184, a. 3 and q. 188, a. 2; St. Bonaventure, Opusc. XI, *Apologia Pauperum*, c. 3, 3 (Quaracchi, ed. of *Opera*, vol. 8, 1898, p. 245a).

ing home to all men the immeasurable greatness of the power of Christ in his sovereignty and the infinite might of the Holy Spirit which works so marvelously in the Church.

The state of life, then, which is constituted by the profession of the evangelical counsels, while not entering into the hierarchical structure of the Church, belongs undeniably to her life and holiness.

45. It is the task of the Church's hierarchy to feed the People of God and to lead them to good pasture (cf. Ezek. 34:14). Accordingly it is for the hierarchy to make wise laws for the regulation of the practice of the counsels whereby the perfect love of God and of our neighbor is fostered in a unique way.[6] Again, in docile response to the promptings of the Holy Spirit the hierarchy accepts rules of religious life which are presented for its approval by outstanding men and women, improves them further and then officially authorizes them. It uses its supervisory and protective authority too to ensure that religious institutes established all over the world for building up the Body of Christ may develop and flourish in accordance with the spirit of their founders.

With a view to providing better for the needs of the whole of the Lord's flock and for the sake of the general good, the Pope, as primate over the entire Church, can exempt any institute of Christian perfection and its individual members from the jurisdiction of local ordinaries and subject them to himself alone.[7] Similarly they can be left or entrusted to the care of the appropriate patriarchal authorities. Members of these institutes, however, in fulfilling the duty towards the Church inherent in their particular form of life must show respect and obedience towards bishops in accordance with canon law, both because these exercise pastoral authority in their individual churches and because this is necessary for unity and harmony in the carrying out of apostolic work.[8]

6. Cf. Vatican Council I, schema De Ecclesia Christi, cap. XV and adnot. 48 (Mansi 51, 549 f. and 619 f.); Leo XIII, Letter Au Milieu des consolations, 23 December 1900 (AAS 33 [1900–1901] p. 361); Pius XII, Apostolic Constitution Provida Mater, loc. cit., p. 114 f.
7. Cf. Leo XIII, Constitution Romanos Pontifices, 8 May 1881 (ASS 13 [1880–1881] p. 483); Pius XII, Allocution Annus sacer, 8 December 1950 (ASS 43 [1951] p. 28 f.).
8. Cf. Pius XII, Allocution Annus sacer, loc. cit., p. 28; Pius XII, Apostolic Constitution Sedes Sapientiae, 31 May 1956 (ASS 48 [1956] p. 355); Paul VI, loc. cit., pp. 570–571).

Besides giving legal sanction to the religious form of life and thus raising it to the dignity of a canonical state, the Church sets it forth liturgically also as a state of consecration to God. She herself, in virtue of her God-given authority, receives the vows of those who profess this form of life, asks aid and grace for them from God in her public prayer, commends them to God and bestows on them a spiritual blessing, associating their self-offering with the sacrifice of the Eucharist.

46. Let religious see well to it that the Church truly show forth Christ through them with every-increasing clarity to believers and unbelievers alike—Christ in contemplation on the mountain, or proclaiming the kingdom of God to the multitudes, or healing the sick and maimed and converting sinners to a good life, or blessing children and doing good to all men, always in obedience to the will of the Father who sent him.[9]

At the same time let all realize that while the profession of the evangelical counsels involves the renunciation of goods that undoubtedly deserve to be highly valued, it does not constitute an obstacle to the true development of the human person but by its nature is supremely beneficial to that development. For the counsels, when willingly embraced in accordance with each one's personal vocation, contribute in no small degree to the purification of the heart and to spiritual freedom: they continually stimulate one to ardour in the life of love; and above all they have the power to conform the Christian man more fully to that kind of poor and virginal life which Christ the Lord chose for himself and which his Virgin Mother embraced also. This is proved by the example of the many holy founders of religious institutes.

Let no one think either that their consecrated way of life alienates religious from other men or makes them useless for human society. Though in some cases they have no direct relations with their contemporaries, still in a deeper way they have their fellow men present with them in the heart of Christ and cooperate with them spiritually, so that the building up of human society may always have its foun-

9. Cf. Pius XII, Encyclical *Mystici Corporis,* 29 June 1943 (*AAS* 35 [1943] p. 214 f.).

dation in the Lord and have him as its goal: otherwise those who build it may have labored in vain.[10]

For this reason, then, this sacred council gives its support and praise to men and women, brothers and sisters, who in monasteries or in schools and hospitals or in missions adorn the bride of Christ by the steadfast and humble fidelity of their consecrated lives and give generous service of the most varied kinds to all manner of men.

47. Let everyone who has been called to the profession of the counsels take earnest care to preserve and excel still more in the life in which God has called him, for the increase of the holiness of the Church, to the greater glory of the one and undivided Trinity, which in Christ and through Christ is the source and origin of all holiness.

CHAPTER VII[a]

THE PILGRIM CHURCH

48. The Church, to which we are all called in Christ Jesus, and in which by the grace of God we acquire holiness, will receive its perfection only in the glory of heaven, when will come the time of the renewal of all things (Acts 3:21). At that time, together with the human race, the universe itself, which is so closely related to man and which attains its destiny through him, will be perfectly reestablished in Christ (cf. Eph. 1:10; Col. 1:20; 2 Pet. 3:10–13).

Christ lifted up from the earth, has drawn all men to himself (cf. Jn. 12:32). Rising from the dead (cf. Rom. 6:9) he sent his life-giving Spirit upon his disciples and through him set up his Body which is the Church as the universal sacrament of salvation. Sitting at the right hand

---

10. Cf. Pius XII, Allocution *Annus sacer, loc. cit.,* p. 30; Allocution *Sous la maternelle protection,* 9 December 1957 (*AAS* 50 [1958] p. 39 f.).

a. This chapter was translated by Father Thomas McInerney, O.P.

of the Father he is continually active in the world in order
to lead men to the Church and, through it, join them more
closely to himself; and, by nourishing them with his own
Body and Blood, make them partakers of his glorious life.
The promised and hoped for restoration, therefore, has already begun in Christ. It is carried forward in the sending
of the Holy Spirit and through him continues in the Church
in which, through our faith, we learn the meaning of our
earthly life, while we bring to term, with hope of future
good, the task allotted to us in the world by the Father, and
so work out our salvation (cf. Phil. 2:12).

Already the final age of the world is with us (cf. 1 Cor.
10:11) and the renewal of the world is irrevocably under
way; it is even now anticipated in a certain real way, for
the Church on earth is endowed already with a sanctity that
is real though imperfect. However, until there be realized
new heavens and a new earth in which justice dwells (cf. 2
Pet. 3:13) the pilgrim Church, in its sacraments and institutions, which belong to this present age, carries the mark
of this world which will pass, and she herself takes her
place among the creatures which groan and travail yet and
await the revelation of the sons of God (cf. Rom.
8:19–22).

So it is, united with Christ in the Church and marked
with the Holy Spirit "who is the guarantee of our inheritance" (Eph. 1:14) that we are truly called and indeed are
children of God (cf. 1 Jn. 3:1) though we have not yet appeared with Christ in glory (cf. Col. 3:4) in which we will
be like to God, for we will see him as he is (cf. 1 Jn. 3:2).
"While we are at home in the body we are away from the
Lord" (2 Cor. 5:6) and having the firstfruits of the Spirit
we groan inwardly (cf. Rom. 8:23) and we desire to be
with Christ (cf. Phil. 1:23). That same charity urges us to
live more for him who died for us and who rose again (cf.
2 Cor. 5:15). We make it our aim, then, to please the Lord
in all things (cf. 2 Cor. 5:9) and we put on the armor of
God that we may be able to stand against the wiles of the
devil and resist in the evil day (cf. Eph. 6:11–13). Since
we know neither the day nor the hour, we should follow the
advice of the Lord and watch constantly so that, when the
single course of our earthly life is completed (cf. Heb.
9:27), we may merit to enter with him into the marriage
feast and be numbered among the blessed (cf. Mt.
25:31–46) and not, like the wicked and slothful servants

(cf. Mt. 25:26), be ordered to depart into the eternal fire (cf. Mt. 25:41), into the outer darkness where "men will weep and gnash their teeth" (Mt. 22:13 and 25:30). Before we reign with Christ in glory we must all appear "before the judgment seat of Christ, so that each one may receive good or evil, according to what he has done in the body" (2 Cor. 5:10), and at the end of the world "they will come forth, those who have done good, to the resurrection of life, and those who have done evil, to the resurrection of judgment" (Jn. 5:29; cf. Mt. 25:46). We reckon then that "the sufferings of this present time are not worth comparing with the glory that is to be revealed to us" (Rom. 8:18; cf. 2 Tim. 2:11–12), and strong in faith we look for "the blessed hope, the appearing of the glory of our great God and Savior Jesus Christ" (Tit. 2:13) "who will change our lowly body to be like his glorious body" (Phil. 3:21) and who will come "to be glorified in his saints, and to be marvelled at in all who have believed" (2 Th. 1:10).

49. When the Lord will come in glory, and all his angels with him (cf. Mt. 25:31), death will be no more and all things will be subject to him (cf. 1 Cor. 15:26–27). But at the present time some of his disciples are pilgrims on earth. Others have died and are being purified, while still others are in glory, contemplating "in full light, God himself triune and one, exactly as he is."[1] All of us, however, in varying degrees and in different ways share in the same charity towards God and our neighbors, and we all sing the one hymn of glory to our God. All, indeed, who are of Christ and who have his Spirit form one Church and in Christ cleave together (Eph. 4:16). So it is that the union of the wayfarers with the brethren who sleep in the peace of Christ is in no way interrupted, but on the contrary, according to the constant faith of the Church, this union is reinforced by an exchange of spiritual goods.[2] Being more closely united to Christ, those who dwell in heaven fix the whole Church more firmly in holiness, add to the nobility of the worship that the Church offers to God here on earth,

---

1. Council of Florence, *Decretum pro Graecis, Denz.* 693 (1305).
2. Besides older documents against any kind of invocation of spirits, from the time of Alexander IV (27 Sept. 1258), cf. Encyclical S.S.C.S. Officii, *Concerning the Abuse of Magnetism,* 4 Aug. 1856 (*ASS* [1865] pp. 177–178), *Denz.* 1653–1654 (2823–2852); reply of the Holy Office, 24 April 1917 (*AAS* [1917] p. 268), *Denz.* 2182 (3642).

and in many ways help in a broader building up of the Church (cf. 1 Cor. 12:12–27).[3] Once received into their heavenly home and being present to the Lord (cf. 2 Cor. 5:8), through him and with him and in him they do not cease to intercede with the Father for us,[4] as they proffer the merits which they acquired on earth through the one mediator between God and men, Christ Jesus (cf. 1 Tim. 2:5), serving God in all things and completing in their flesh what is lacking in Christ's afflictions for the sake of his Body, that is, the Church (cf. Col. 1:24).[5] So by their brotherly concern is our weakness greatly helped.

50. In full consciousness of this communion of the whole Mystical Body of Jesus Christ, the Church in its pilgrim members, from the very earliest days of the Christian religion, has honored with great respect the memory of the dead;[6] and, "because it is a holy and a wholesome thought to pray for the dead that they may be loosed from their sins" (2 Mac. 12:46) she offers her suffrages for them. The Church has always believed that the apostles and Christ's martyrs, who gave the supreme witness of faith and charity by the shedding of their blood, are closely united with us in Christ; she has always venerated them, together with the Blessed Virgin Mary and the holy angels, with a special love,[7] and has asked piously for the help of their intercession. Soon there were added to these others who had chosen to imitate more closely the virginity and poverty of Christ,[8] and still others whom the outstanding practice of the Christian virtues[9] and the wonderful graces of God recommended to the pious devotion and imitation of the faithful.[10]

3. A synthesis of this pauline doctrine may be seen in: Pius XII, Encyclical *On the Mystical Body* (*AAS* 35 [1943] p. 200) *et passim*.
4. Cf. *inter al.*, St. Augustine, *Enarr. in Ps. 85*, 24: *PL* 37, 1099. St. Jerome, *Liber contra Vigilantium*, 6: *PL* 23, 344. St. Thomas, *In 4m Sent.*, d. 45, q. 3, a. 2. St. Bonaventure, *In 4m Sent.*, d. 45, a. 3, 2; etc.
5. Cf. Pius XII, Encyclical *On the Mystical Body* (*AAS* 35 [1943] p. 245).
6. Cf. a great many inscriptions in the catacombs of Rome.
7. Cf. Gelasius I, Decretalis *De Libris Recipiendis*, 3: *PL* 59, 160, *Denz.* 165 (353).
8. St. Methodius, *Symposium*, VII, 3: G.C.S. (Bonwetsch), p. 74.
9. Cf. Benedict XV, *Decretum approbationis virtutum in Causa beatificationis et canonizationis Servi Dei Joannis Nepomuceni Newmann* (*AAS* 14 [1922] p. 23); many allocutions of Pius XI on the saints: *Inviti all'eroismo*. Discorsi . . . t. I-III, Rome 1941–1942, *passim;* Pius XII, *Discorsi e Radiomessaggi*, t. 10, 1949, pp. 37–43.
10. Cf. Pius XII, Encyclical *Mediator Dei* (*AAS* 39 [1947] p. 581).

To look on the life of those who have faithfully followed Christ is to be inspired with a new reason for seeking the city which is to come (cf. Heb. 13:14 and 11:10), while at the same time we are taught to know a most safe path by which, despite the vicissitudes of the world, and in keeping with the state of life and condition proper to each of us, we will be able to arrive at perfect union with Christ, that is, holiness.[11] God shows to men, in a vivid way, his presence and his face in the lives of those companions of ours in the human condition who are more perfectly transformed into the image of Christ (cf. 2 Cor. 3:18). He speaks to us in them and offers us a sign of this kingdom,[12] to which we are powerfully attracted, so great a cloud of witnesses is there given (cf. Heb. 12:1) and such a witness to the truth of the Gospel.

It is not merely by the title of example that we cherish the memory of those in heaven; we seek, rather, that by this devotion to the exercise of fraternal charity the union of the whole Church in the Spirit may be strengthened (cf. Eph. 4:1-6). Exactly as Christian communion between men on their earthly pilgrimage brings us closer to Christ, so our community with the saints joins us to Christ, from whom as from its fountain and head issues all grace and the life of the People of God itself.[13] It is most fitting, therefore, that we love those friends and co-heirs of Jesus Christ who are also our brothers and outstanding benefactors, and that we give due thanks to God for them,[14] "humbly invoking them, and having recourse to their prayers, their aid and help in obtaining from God through his Son, Jesus Christ, Our Lord, our only Redeemer and Savior, the benefits we need."[15] Every authentic witnesss of love, indeed, offered by us to those who are in heaven tends to and terminates in Christ, "the crown of all the saints,"[16] and

---

11. Cf. Heb. 13:7; Eccl. 44-50; Heb. 2:3-40. Cf. also Pius XII, Encyclical *Mediator Dei* (*AAS* 39 [1947] pp. 582-583).

12. Cf. Vatican Council I, Constitution *De fide catholica*, cap. 3, *Denz.* 1794 (3013).

13. Cf. Pius XII, Encyclical *On the Mystical Body* (*AAS* 35 [1943] p. 216).

14. On the question of gratitude to the saints, cf. E. DIEHL, *Inscriptiones latinae christianae veteres*, I, Berolini, 1925, nn. 2008, 2382 and *passim*.

15. Council of Trent, session 25, *De invocatione . . . Sanctorum*, *Denz.* 984 (1821).

16. Roman Breviary, *Invitatory for the feast of All Saints*.

through him in God who is wonderful in his saints and is glorified in them.[17]

It is especially in the sacred liturgy that our union with the heavenly Church is best realized; in the liturgy, through the sacramental signs, the power of the Holy Spirit acts on us, and with community rejoicing we celebrate together the praise of the divine majesty,[18] when all those of every tribe and tongue and people and nation (cf. Apoc. 5:9) who have been redeemed by the blood of Christ and gathered together into one Church glorify, in one common song of praise, the one and triune God. When, then, we celebrate the eucharistic sacrifice we are most closely united to the worship of the heavenly Church; when in the fellowship of communion we honor and remember the glorious Mary ever virgin, St Joseph, the holy apostles and martyrs and all the saints.[19]

51. This sacred council accepts loyally the venerable faith of our ancestors in the living communion which exists between us and our brothers who are in the glory of heaven or who are yet being purified after their death; and it proposes again the decrees of the Second Council of Nicea,[20] of the Council of Florence,[21] and of the Council of Trent.[22] At the same time, in keeping with its pastoral preoccupations, this council urges all concerned to remove or correct any abuses, excesses or defects which may have crept in here or there, and so restore all things that Christ and God be more fully praised. Let us teach the faithful, therefore, that the authentic cult of the saints does not consist so much in a multiplicity of external acts, but rather in a more intense practice of our love, whereby, for our own greater good and that of the Church, we seek from the saints "example in their way of life, fellowship in their communion, and the help of their intercession."[23] On the other hand, let the faithful be taught that our communion with these in heaven, provided that it is understood in the

17. Cf. v.g., 2 Th. 1:10.
18. Vatican Council II, Constitution *De Sacra Liturgia*, c. 5, n. 104.
19. Canon of the Roman Mass.
20. Second Council of Nicea, Act. VII, *Denz.* 302 (600).
21. Council of Florence, *Decretum pro Graecis, Denz.* 693 (1304).
22. Council of Trent, Session 25, *De invocatione, veneratione et reliquiis Sanctorum et sacris imaginibus, Denz.* 984–988 (1821–1824); Session 25, *Decretum de Purgatorio, Denz.* 983 (1820); Session 6, *Decretum de justificatione*, can. 30, *Denz.* 840 (1580).
23. From the Mass preface granted to some dioceses.

full light of faith, in no way diminishes the worship of adoration given to God the Father, through Christ, in the Spirit; on the contrary, it greatly enriches it.[24]

For if we continue to love one another and to join in praising the Most Holy Trinity—all of us who are sons of God and form one family in Christ (cf. Heb. 3:6)—we will be faithful to the deepest vocation of the Church and will share in a foretaste of the liturgy of perfect glory.[25] At the hour when Christ will appear, when the glorious resurrection of the dead will occur, the glory of God will light up the heavenly city, and the Lamb will be its lamp (cf. Apoc. 21:24). Then the whole Church of the saints in the supreme happiness of charity will adore God and "the Lamb who was slain" (Apoc. 5:12), proclaiming with one voice: "To him who sits upon the throne and to the Lamb be blessing and honor and glory and might for ever and ever" (Apoc. 5:13–14).

CHAPTER VIII[a]

OUR LADY

I. INTRODUCTION

52. Wishing in his supreme goodness and wisdom to effect the redemption of the world, "when the fullness of time came, God sent his Son, born of a woman . . . that we might receive the adoption of sons" (Gal. 4:4). "He for us men, and for our salvation, came down from heaven, and was incarnated by the Holy Spirit from the Virgin Mary."[1] This divine mystery of salvation is revealed to us and continued in the Church, which the Lord established as

24. Cf. St. Peter Canisius, *Catechismus Maior seu Summa Doctrinae christianae*, c. III (ed. crit. F. Streicher), Paris I, pp. 15–16, n. 44 and pp. 100–101, n. 49.
25. Cf. Vatican Council II, Constitution *De Sacra Liturgia*, c. 1, n. 8.
a. The chapter was specially translated.
1. Creed of the Roman mass; Symbol of Constantinople: Mansi 3, 566. Cf. Council of Ephesus; ibid. 4, 1130 (*et ibid.* 2, 665 and 4, 1071); Council of Chalcedon, ibid. 7, 111–116; Council of Constantinople II. ibid. 9, 375–396.

his body. Joined to Christ the head and in communion with all his saints, the faithful must in the first place reverence the memory "of the glorious ever Virgin Mary, Mother of God and of our Lord Jesus Christ."[2]

53. The Virgin Mary, who at the message of the angel received the Word of God in her heart and in her body and gave Life to the world, is acknowledged and honored as being truly the Mother of God and of the redeemer. Redeemed, in a more exalted fashion, by reason of the merits of her Son and united to him by a close and indissoluble tie, she is endowed with the high office and dignity of the Mother of the Son of God, and therefore she is also the beloved daughter of the Father and the temple of the Holy Spirit. Because of this gift of sublime grace she far surpasses all creatures, both in heaven and on earth. But, being of the race of Adam, she is at the same time also united to all those who are to be saved; indeed, "she is clearly the mother of the members of Christ . . . since she has by her charity joined in bringing about the birth of believers in the Church, who are members of its head."[3] Wherefore she is hailed as pre-eminent and as a wholly unique member of the Church, and as its type and outstanding model in faith and charity. The Catholic Church taught by the Holy Spirit, honors charity. The Catholic Church taught by the Holy Spirit, honors her with filial affection and devotion as a most beloved mother.

54. Wherefore this sacred synod, while expounding the doctrine on the Church, in which the divine Redeemer brings about our salvation, intends to set forth painstakingly both the role of the Blessed Virgin in the mystery of the Incarnate Word and the Mystical Body, and the duties of the redeemed towards the Mother of God, who is mother of Christ and mother of men, and most of all those who believe. It does not, however, intend to give a complete doctrine on Mary, nor does it wish to decide those questions which the work of theologians has not yet fully clarified. Those opinions therefore may be lawfully retained which are propounded in Catholic schools concerning her, who occupies a place in the Church which is the highest after Christ and also closest to us.[4]

2. Canon of the Roman Mass.
3. Cf. St. Augustine, *De S. Virginitate*, 6: *PL* 40, 399.
4. Cf. Paul VI, *Allocution to the Council*, 4 December 1963: *AAS* 56 (1964), p. 37.

II. THE FUNCTION OF THE BLESSED VIRGIN IN THE PLAN OF SALVATION

55. The sacred writings of the Old and New Testaments, as well as venerable tradition, show the role of the Mother of the Saviour in the plan of salvation in an ever clearer light and call our attention to it. The books of the Old Testament describe the history of salvation, by which the coming of Christ into the world was slowly prepared. The earliest documents, as they are read in the Church and are understood in the light of a further and full revelation, bring the figure of a woman, Mother of the Redeemer, into a gradually clearer light. Considered in this light, she is already prophetically foreshadowed in the promise of victory over the serpent which was given to our first parents after their fall into sin (cf. Gen. 3:15). Likewise she is the virgin who shall conceive and bear a son, whose name shall be called Emmanuel (cf. Is. 7:14; Mic. 5:2-3; Mt. 1:22-23). She stands out among the poor and humble of the Lord, who confidently hope for and receive salvation from him. After a long period of waiting the times are fulfilled in her, the exhalted Daughter of Sion and the new plan of salvation is established, when the Son of God has taken human nature from her, that he might in the mysteries of his flesh free man from sin.

56. The Father of mercies willed that the Incarnation should be preceed by assent on the part of the predestined mother, so that just as a woman had a share in bringing about death, so also a woman should contribute to life. This is preeminently true of the Mother of Jesus, who gave to the world the Life that renews all things, and who was enriched by God with gifts appropriate to such a role. It is no wonder then that it was customary for the Fathers to refer to the Mother of God as all holy and free from every stain of sin, as though fashioned by the Holy Spirit and formed as a new creature.[5] Enriched from the first instant of her conception with the splendor of an entirely unique holiness, the virgin of Nazareth is hailed by the heralding angel, by divine command, as "full of grace" (cf. Lk. 1:28, and to the

5. Cf. Germanus of Constantinople, *Hom. in Annunt. Deiparae: PG* 98, 328A; *In Dorm.* 2, Col. 357. Anastasius of Antioch. *Serm.* 2 *de Annunt.* 2: *PG* 89, 1377 AB; *Serm.* 3. 2: Col. 1388 C. St. Andrew of Crete, *Can. in B.V. Nat.* 4: *PG* 97, 1321 B. *In B.V. Nat.* 1: Col. 812 A. *Hom. in Dorm.* 1: Col. 1068C. St. Sophronius, *Or.* 2 *in Annunt.* 18: *PG* 87 (3), 3237 BD.

heavenly messenger she replies: "Behold the handmaid of the Lord, be it done unto me according to thy word" (Lk. 1:38). Thus the daughter of Adam, Mary, consenting to the word of God, became the Mother of Jesus. Committing herself whole-heartedly and impeded by no sin to God's saving will, she devoted herself totally, as a handmaid of the Lord, to the person and work of her Son, under and with him, serving the mystery of redemption, by the grace of Almighty God. Rightly, therefore, the Fathers see Mary not merely as passively engaged by God, but as freely cooperating in the work of man's salvation through faith and obedience. For, as St Irenaeus says, she "being obedient, became the cause of salvation for herself and for the whole human race."[6] Hence not a few of the early Fathers gladly assert with him in their preaching: "the knot of Eve's disobedience was untied by Mary's obedience: what the virgin Eve bound through her disbelief, Mary loosened by her faith."[7] Comparing Mary with Eve, they call her "Mother of the living,"[8] and frequently claim: "death through Eve, life through Mary."[9]

57. This union of the mother with the Son in the work of salvation is made manifest from the time of Christ's virginal conception up to his death; first when Mary, arising in haste to go to visit Elizabeth, is greeted by her as blessed because of her belief in the promise of salvation and the precursor leaped with joy in the womb of his mother (cf. Lk. 1:41–45); then also at the birth of Our Lord, who did not diminish his mother's virginal integrity but sanctified it,[10] the Mother of God joyfully showed her firstborn son to the shepherds and the Magi: when she presented him to the Lord in the temple, making the offering of the poor, she heard Simeon foretelling at the same time that her Son

---

6. St. Irenaeus, *Adv. Haer.* III, 22, 4: *PG* 7, 959 A, Harvey, 2, 123.
7. St. Irenaeus, ibid.: Harvey 2, 124.
8. St. Epiphanius, *Haer.* 78, 18: *PG* 42, 728 CD–729 AB.
9. St. Jerome, *Epist.* 22, 21: *PL* 22, 408. Cf. St. Augustine, *Serm.* 51, 2, 3: *PL* 38, 335; *Serm.* 232, 2: Col. 1108. St. Cyril of Jerusalem, *Catech.* 12, 15: *PG* 33, 741 AB. St. John Chrysostom, *In Ps.* 44, 7: *PG* 55, 193. St. John Damascene, *Hom. 2 in dorm. B.M.V.*, 3: *PG* 96, 728.
10. Cf. Council of Lateran A.D. 649, Can. 3: Mansi 10, 1151. St. Leo the Great, *Epist. ad Flav.*: *PL* 54, 759. Council of Chalcedon: Mansi 7, 462. St. Ambrose, *De instit. virg.*: *PL* 16, 320.

would be a sign of contradiction and that a sword would pierce the mother's soul, that out of many hearts thoughts might be revealed (cf. Lk. 2:34–35); when the child Jesus was lost and they had sought him sorrowing, his parents found him in the temple, engaged in the things that were his Father's, and they did not understand the words of their Son. His mother, however, kept all these things to be pondered in her heart (cf. Lk. 2:41–51).

58. In the public life of Jesus Mary appears prominently; at the very beginning when at the marriage feast of Cana, moved with pity, she brought about by her intercession the beginning of miracles of Jesus the Messiah (cf. Jn. 2:1–11). In the course of her Son's preaching she received the words whereby, in extolling a kingdom beyond the concerns and ties of flesh and blood, he declared blessed those who heard and kept the word of God (cf. Mk. 3:35; par. Lk. 11:27–27) as she was faithfully doing (cf. Lk. 2:19; 51). Thus the Blessed Virgin advanced in her pilgrimage of faith, and faithfully persevered in her union with her Son unto the cross, where she stood, in keeping with the divine plan, enduring with her only begotten Son the intensity of his suffering, associated herself with his sacrifice in her mother's heart, and lovingly consenting to the immolation of this victim which was born of her. Finally, she was given by the same Christ Jesus dying on the cross as a mother to his disciple, with these words: "Woman, behold thy son" (Jn. 19:26–27).[11]

59. But since it had pleased God not to manifest solemnly the mystery of the salvation of the human race before he would pour forth the Spirit promised by Christ, we see the apostles before the day of Pentecost "persevering with one mind in prayer with the women and Mary the Mother of Jesus, and with his brethren" (Acts 1:14), and we also see Mary by her prayers imploring the gift of the Spirit, who had already overshadowed her in the Annunciation. Finally the Immaculate Virgin preserved free from all stain of original sin,[12] was taken up body and soul into heavenly

11. Cf. Pius XII, Encycl. *Mystici Corporis*, 29 June 1943: *AAS* 35 (1943), pp. 247–248.
12. Cf. Pius IX, Bull *Ineffabilis*, 8 Dec. 1854: *Acta Pii IX*, 1, 1, p. 616; *Denz.* 1641 (2803).

glory,[13] when her earthly life was over, and exalted by the Lord as Queen over all things, that she might be the more fully conformed to her Son, the Lord of lords, (cf. Apoc. 19:16) and conqueror of sin and death.[14]

III. THE BLESSED VIRGIN AND THE CHURCH

60. In the words of the apostle there is but one mediator: "for there is but one God and one mediator of God and men, the man Christ Jesus, who gave himself a redemption for all" (1 Tim. 2:5–6). But Mary's function as mother of men in no way obscures or diminishes this unique mediation of Christ, but rather shows its power. But the Blessed Virgin's salutary influence on men originates not in any inner necessity but in the disposition of God. It flows forth from the superabundance of the merits of Christ, rests on his mediation, depends entirely on it and draws all its power from it. It does not hinder in any way the immediate union of the faithful with Christ but on the contrary fosters it.

61. The predestination of the Blessed Virgin as Mother of God was associated with the incarnation of the divine word: in the designs of divine Providence she was the gracious mother of the divine Redeemer here on earth, and above all others and in a singular way the generous associate and humble handmaid of the Lord. She conceived, brought forth, and nourished Christ, she presented him to the Father in the temple, shared her Son's sufferings as he died on the cross. Thus, in a wholly singular way she cooperated by her obedience, faith, hope and burning charity in the work of the Savior in restoring supernatural life to souls. For this reason she is a mother to us in the order of grace.

62. This motherhood of Mary in the order of grace continues uninterruptedly from the consent which she loyally

---

13. Cf. Pius XII, Const. Apost. *Munificentissimus,* 1 Nov. 1950: *AAS* 42 (1950): *Denz.* 2333 (3903). Cf. St. John Damascene, *Enc. in dorm. Dei Genitricis, Hom.* 2 and 3: *PG* 96, 722–762, esp. Col. 728 B. St. Germanus of Constantinople, *In S. Dei gen. dorm. Serm.* 1: *PG* 78 (6), 340–348; *Serm.* 3: Col. 362. St. Modestus of Jerusalem, *In dorm. SS. Deiparae: PG* 86 (2), 3277–3312.

14. Cf. Pius XII, Encycl. *Ad coeli Reginam,* 11 Oct. 1954: *AAS* 46 (1954), pp. 633–636: *Denz.* 3914 ff. Cf. St. Andrew of Crete, *Hom. 3 in dorm. SS Deiparae: PG* 97, 1090–1109. St. John Damascene, *De fide orth.,* IV, 14: *PG* 94, 1153–1168.

gave at the Annunciation and which she sustained without wavering beneath the cross, until the eternal fulfilment of all the elect. Taken up to heaven she did not lay aside this saving office but by her manifold intercession continues to bring us the gifts of eternal salvation.[15] By her maternal charity, she cares for the brethren of her Son, who still journey on earth surrounded by dangers and difficulties, until they are led into their blessed home. Therefore the Blessed Virgin is invoked in the Church under the titles of Advocate, Helper, Benefactress, and Mediatrix.[16] This, however, is so understood that it neither takes away anything from nor adds anything to the dignity and efficacy of Christ the one Mediator.[17]

No creature could ever be counted along with the Incarnate Word and Redeemer; but just as the priesthood of Christ is shared in various ways both by his ministers and the faithful, and as the one goodness of God is radiated in different ways among his creatures, so also the unique mediation of the Redeemer does not exclude but rather gives rise to a manifold cooperation which is but a sharing in this one source.

The Church does not hesitate to profess this subordinate role of Mary, which it constantly experiences and recommends to the heartfelt attention of the faithful, so that encouraged by this maternal help they may the more closely adhere to the Mediator and Redeemer.

63. By reason of the gift and role of her divine motherhood, by which she is united with her Son, the Redeemer, and with her unique graces and functions, the Blessed Virgin is also intimately united to the Church. As St. Ambrose taught, the Mother of God is a type of the Church in the order of faith, charity, and perfect union with Christ.[18] For in the mystery of the Church, which is

---

15. Cf. Kleutgen, corrected text *De mysterio verbi incarnati*, ch. IV: Mansi 53, 290. Cf. St. Andrew of Crete, *In nat. Mariae, Serm.* 4: *PG* 97, 865 A. St. Germanus of Constantinople, *In ann. Deiparae: PG* 93, 322 BC. *In dorm. Deiparae* III: Col. 362 D. St. John Damascene, *In dorm B.V.M., Hom.* 1, 8: *PG* 96, 712 BC-713 A.

16. Cf. Leo XIII, Encycl. *Adjutricem populi*, 5 Sept. 1895: *AAS* 15 (1895-1896), p. 303. St. Pius X, Encycl. *Ad diem illum*, 2 Feb. 1904: *Acta* 1, p. 154; *Denz.* 1978a (3370). Pius XI, Encycl. *Miserentissimus*, 8 May 1928; *AAS* 20 (1928), p. 178. Pius XII, Radio Message, 13 May 1946: *AAS* 38 (1946), p. 268.

17. St. Ambrose, *Epist.* 63: *PL* 16, 1218.

18. Ambrose, *Expos. Lc. II.* 7: *PL* 15, 1555.

itself rightly called mother and virgin, the Blessed Virgin stands out in eminent and singular fashion as exemplar both of virgin and mother.[19] Through her faith and obedience she gave birth on earth to the very Son of the Father, not through the knowledge of man but by the overshadowing of the Holy Spirit, in the manner of a new Eve who placed her faith, not in the serpent of old but in God's messenger without waivering in doubt. The Son whom she brought forth is he whom God placed as the first born among many brethren (Rom. 8:29), that is, the faithful, in whose generation and formation she cooperates with a mother's love.

64. The Church indeed contemplating her hidden sanctity, imitating her charity and faithfully fulfilling the Father's will, by receiving the word of God in faith becomes herself a mother. By preaching and baptism she brings forth sons, who are conceived of the Holy Spirit and born of God, to a new and immortal life. She herself is a virgin, who keeps in its entirety and purity the faith she pledged to her spouse. Imitating the mother of her Lord, and by the power of the Holy Spirit, she keeps intact faith, firm hope and sincere charity.[20]

65. But while in the most Blessed Virgin the Church has already reached that perfection whereby she exists without spot or wrinkle (cf. Eph. 5:27), the faithful still strive to conquer sin and increase in holiness. And so they turn their eyes to Mary who shines forth to the whole community of the elect as the model of virtues. Devoutly meditating on her and contemplating her in the light of the Word made man, the Church reverently penetrates more deeply into the great mystery of the Incarnation and becomes more and more like her spouse. Having entered deeply into the history of salvation, Mary, in a way, unites in her person and re-echoes the most important doctrines of the faith: and when she is the subject of preaching and worship she prompts the faithful to come to her Son, to his sacrifice and

19. Cf. Pseudo Peter Damien, *Serm.* 63: *PL* 144, 861 AB. Geoffrey (de Breteuil) of St. Victor, *In nat. b.m.*, MS. Paris, Mazarine, 1002, fol. 109. Gerhoch of Reichersberg, *De gloria et honore Filii hominis* 10: *PL* 194, 1105AB.

20. St. Ambrose, l.c., and *Expos. Lc. X*, 24–25: *PL* 15, 1810. St. Augustine, *In Io. Tr.* 13. 12: *PL* 35, 1499. Cf. *Serm.* 191, 2, 3: *PL* 38, 1010, etc. Cf. also Ven. Bede, *In Lc. Expo.*, 1, ch. II: 92, 330. Isaac of Stella, *Serm.* 31: *PL* 194, 1863 A. 21. *"Sub tuum praesidium."*

to the love of the Father. Seeking after the glory of Christ, the Church becomes more like her lofty type, and continually progresses in faith, hope and charity, seeking and doing the will of God in all things. The Church, therefore, in her apostolic work too, rightly looks to her who gave birth to Christ, who was thus conceived of the Holy Spirit and born of a virgin, in order that through the Church he could be born and increase in the hearts of the faithful. In her life the Virgin has been a model of that motherly love with which all who join in the Church's apostolic mission for the regeneration of mankind should be animated.

IV. THE CULT OF THE BLESSED VIRGIN IN THE CHURCH

66. Mary has by grace been exalted above all angels and men to a place second only to her Son, as the most holy mother of God who was involved in the mysteries of Christ: she is rightly honored by a special cult in the Church. From the earliest times the Blessed Virgin is honored under the title of Mother of God, whose protection the faithful take refuge together in prayer in all their perils and needs.[21] Accordingly, following the Council of Ephesus, there was a remarkable growth in the cult of the People of God towards Mary, in veneration and love, in invocation and imitation, according to her own prophetic words: "all generations shall call me blessed, because he that is mighty hath done great things to me" (Lk. 1:48). This cult, as it has always existed in the Church, for all its uniqueness, differs essentially from the cult of adoration, which is offered equally to the Incarnate Word and to the Father and the Holy Spirit, and it is most favorable to it. The various forms of piety towards the Mother of God, which the Church has approved within the limits of sound and orthodox doctrine, according to the dispositions and understanding of the faithful, ensure that while the mother is honored, the Son through whom all things have their being (cf. Col. 1:15-16) and in whom it has pleased the Father that all fullness should dwell (cf. Col. 1:19) is rightly known, loved and glorified and his commandments are observed.

67. The sacred synod teaches this Catholic doctrine ad-

21. *"Sub tuum praesidium."*

visedly and at the same time admonishes all the sons of the Church that the cult, especially the liturgical cult, of the Blessed Virgin, be generously fostered, and that the practices and exercises of devotion towards her, recommended by the teaching authority of the Church in the course of centuries be highly esteemed, and that those decrees, which were given in the early days regarding the cult images of Christ, the Blessed Virgin and the saints, be religiously observed.[22] But it strongly urges theologians and preachers of the word of God to be careful to refrain as much from all false exaggeration as from too summary an attitude in considering the special dignity of the Mother of God.[23] Following the study of Sacred Scripture, the Fathers, the doctors and liturgy of the Church, and under the guidance of the Church's magisterium, let them rightly illustrate the duties and privileges of the Blessed Virgin which always refer to Christ, the source of all truth, sanctity, and devotion. Let them carefully refrain from whatever might by word or deed lead the separated brethren or any others whatsoever into error about the true doctrine of the Church. Let the faithful remember moreover that true devotion consists neither in sterile or transistory affection, nor in a certain vain credulity, but proceeds from true faith, by which we are led to recognize the excellence of the Mother of God, and we are moved to a filial love towards our mother and to the imitation of her virtues.

V. MARY, SIGN OF TRUE HOPE AND COMFORT FOR THE PILGRIM PEOPLE OF GOD

68. In the meantime the Mother of Jesus in the glory which she possesses in body and soul in heaven is the image and beginning of the Church as it is to be perfected in the world to come. Likewise she shines forth on earth, until the day of the Lord shall come (cf. 2 Pet. 3:10), a sign of certain hope and comfort to the pilgrim People of God.

69. It gives great joy and comfort to this sacred synod that among the separated brethren too there are those who give due honor to the Mother of Our Lord and Saviour, especially among the Easterns, who with devout mind and

---

22. Council of Nicea II. A.D. 787: Mansi 13, 378–379; *Denz.* 302 (600-601). Council of Trent, Session 25: Mansi 33, 171–172.
23. Cf. Pius XII, radio message, 24 Oct. 1954: *AAS* 46 (1954), p. 679 Encycl. *Ad coeli Reginam*, 11 Oct. 1954. *AAS* 46 (1954), p. 637.

fervent impulse give honor to the Mother of God, ever virgin.[24] The entire body of the faithful pours forth urgent supplications to the Mother of God and of men that she, who aided the beginnings of the Church by her prayers, may now, exalted as she is above all the angels and saints, intercede before her Son in the fellowship of all the saints, until all families of people, whether they are honored with the title of Christian or whether they still do not know the Saviour, may be happily gathered together in peace and harmony into one People of God, for the glory of the Most Holy and Undivided Trinity.

THE EXPLANATORY NOTE[a]

ANNOUNCEMENT MADE BY THE SECRETARY GENERAL OF THE COUNCIL AT THE ONE HUNDRED AND TWENTY-THIRD GENERAL CONGREGATION 16 NOVEMBER, 1964

A query has been made as to what is the *theological qualification* to be attached to the teaching put forward in the schema *The Church*, on which a vote is to be taken.

The doctrinal commission has replied to this query in appraising the *modi* proposed to the third chapter of the schema *The Church:*

As is self-evident, the conciliar text is to be interpreted in accordance with the general rules which are known to all.

On this occasion the doctrinal commission referred to its *Declaration* of 6 March, 1964, which we reproduce here:

Taking into account conciliar practice and the pastoral purpose of the present council, the sacred synod defined as binding on the Church only those matters of faith and morals which it has expressly put forward as such.

Whatever else it proposes as the teaching of the supreme

---

24. Cf. Pius XI, Encycl. *Ecclesiam Dei*, 12 Nov. 1923: *AAS* 15 (1923), p. 581; Pius XII, Encycl. *Fulgens corona*, 8 Sept. 1953: *AAS* 45 (1953), p. 590–591.

a. The following was published as an appendix to the official Latin version of the Constitution on the Church.

magisterium of the Church is to be acknowledged and accepted by each and every member of the faithful according to the mind of the Council which is clear from the subject matter and its formulation, following the norms of theological interpretation.

The following explanatory note prefixed to the *modi* of chapter three of the schema *The Church* is given to the Fathers, and it is according to the mind and sense of this note that the teaching contained in chapter three is to be explained and understood.

PRELIMINARY EXPLANATORY NOTE

The commission has decided to preface its assessment of the *modi* with the following general observations.

1. The word *College* is not taken in the *strictly juridical* sense, that is as a group of equals who transfer their powers to their chairman, but as a permanent body whose form and authority is to be ascertained from revelation. For this reason it is explicitly said about the twelve apostles in the reply to modus 12 that Our Lord constituted them "as a college or *permanent group*" (cf. modus 53, c). In the same way the words *Order* or *Body* are used at other times for the college of bishops. The parallel between Peter and the apostles on the one hand and the Pope and the bishops on the other does not imply the transmission of the extraordinary power of the apostles to their successors, nor obviously does it imply *equality* between the head and members of the college, but only a *proportion* between the two relationships: Peter—apostles and pope—bishops. And therefore the commission decided to write in Art. 22 not "in the same manner" (*eadem* ratione) but "in like manner" (*pari* ratione).

2. A man becomes a *member* of the college through episcopal consecration and hierarchical communion with the head of the college and its members (cf. art. 22, end of par. 1).

It is the unmistakable teaching of tradition, including liturgical tradition, that an *ontological* share in the *sacred* functions is given by *consecration*. The word *function* is deliberately used in preference to *powers* which can have the sense of power *ordered to action*. A *canonical* or *juridical* *determination* through hierarchical authority is required for such power ordered to action. A determination of this kind can come about through appointment to a particular office or the assignment of subjects, and is conferred according to norms approved by the supreme authority. The need for a further norm follows from the nature of the case, because it is a question of functions to be discharged by *more than one subject*, who work together in the hierarchy of functions intended by Christ. "Communion" of this kind was in fact a feature abiding in the varying circumstances *of the life* of the Church through the ages, before it was endorsed and codified *by law*.

For this reason it is expressly stated that *hierarchical* communion with the head and members is req ♦ ed. The idea of *communion* was highly valued in the early Church, as indeed it is today especially in the East. It is not to be understood as some vague sort of *goodwill*, but as *something organic* which calls for a juridical structure as well as being enkindled by charity. The commission, therefore, agreed, almost unanimously, on the wording "in *hierarchical* communion" (cf. modus 40 and the statements about canonical mission in art. 24).

The documents of recent Popes dealing with episcopal jurisdiction are to be interpreted as referring to this necessary determination of powers.

3. There is no such thing as the college without its head: it is "*The subject of supreme and entire power* over the whole Church." This much must be acknowledged lest the fullness of the Pope's power be jeopardized. The idea of college necessarily and at all times involves a head and *in the college the head preserves intact his function as Vicar of Christ and pastor of the universal Church*. In other words it is not a distinction between the Roman Pontiff and the bishops taken together but between the Roman Pontiff by himself and the Roman Pontiff along with the bishops. The Pope alone, in fact, being *head* of the college, is qualified to perform certain actions in which the bishops have no competence whatsoever, for example, the convocation and direction of the college, approval of the norms of its activity, and so on (cf. modus 18). It is for the Pope, to whom the care of the whole flock of Christ has been entrusted, to decide the best manner of implementing this care, either personal or collegiate, in order to meet the changing needs of the Church in the course of time. The Roman Pontiff undertakes the regulation, encouragement, and approval of the exercise of collegiality as he sees fit.

4. The Pope, as supreme pastor of the Church, may exercise his power at any time, as he sees fit, by reason of the demands of his office. But as the Church's tradition attests, the college, although it is always in existence, is not for that reason continually engaged in *strictly* collegiate activity. In other words it is not always "in full activity" (*in actu pleno*); in fact it is only occasionally that it engages in strictly collegiate activity and that only *with the consent of the head* (*nonnisi consentiente capite*). The phrase *with the consent of the head* is used in order to exclude the impression of *dependence* on something *external*: but the word "consent" entails *communion* between head and members and calls for this *action* which is exclusive to the head. The point is expressly stated in art. 22, par. 2 and it is explained at the end of the same article. The negative formulation "only with" (*nonnisi*) covers all cases: consequently it is evident that the norms approved by the supreme authority must always be observed (cf. modus 84).

Clearly it is the *connection* of bishops *with their head* that is in question throughout and not the activity of bishops *independently* of the Pope. In a case like that, in default of the Pope's action, the bishops cannot act as a college, for this is obvious from the idea of "college" itself. This hierarchical communion of all bishops with the Pope is unmistakably hallowed by tradition.

N.B.—The ontologico-sacramental function, which must be distinguished from the juridico-canonical aspect, *cannot* be discharged without hierarchical communion. It was decided in the commission not to enter into questions of *liceity* and *validity*, which are to be left to theologians, particularly in regard to the power exercised *de facto* among separated Eastern Christians, about which there are divergent opinions.

29

APOSTOLIC LETTER ON FIRST TONSURE, MINOR ORDERS AND THE SUBDIACONATE[a]

Paul VI, *Ministeria Quaedam*, 15 August, 1972

Certain ministries were established by the Church from earliest times for the proper ordering of worship and for the service of God's people as the need arose. By this means, certain liturgical and charitable duties suited to varying circumstances were entrusted to the faithful. The conferring of these ministries was frequently accompanied by a special rite, in which God's blessing was invoked, and which established the person designated in a special rank or class for the performance of some ecclesiastical function.

Some of these functions were more closely connected with the liturgy and gradually these came to be regarded as preparatory stages in the reception of sacred orders. Thus it came about that in the Latin Church the offices of porter, lector, exorcist and acolyte were called minor orders in comparison with the subdiaconate, the diaconate and the priesthood, which were called major orders. As a general rule, though not everywhere, minor orders were reserved to those who received them as preparatory stages on the way to the priesthood.

Minor orders have not always remained the same, however. At one time many functions which went with them were in fact exercised by the laity, as is now happening once again. It seems opportune, therefore, to reform this discipline and to adapt it to present-day needs, eliminating what is obsolete, retaining what is useful and determining what is necessary; and at the same time setting out what is required of candidates for holy orders.

a. The full title is "An apostolic letter, from Paul VI, given *motu proprio*, by which the discipline of first tonsure, minor orders and subdiaconate in the Latin Church is reformed." The translation is by A.F. Latin text in *AAS*, 64 (1972) pp. 529–534.

While the Second Council of the Vatican was in preparation many pastors of the Church requested the revision of minor orders and the subdiaconate. Although the Council made no decision on the matter, it did enunciate certain principles which opened the way to a solution.[1] Clearly, the norms laid down by the Council for the general ordering and renewal of the liturgy apply also to ministries in the liturgical assembly, to the end that the very arrangement of the celebration will show the Church constituted in its different orders and ministries.[2] The Second Vatican Council decreed that: "in liturgical celebrations each person, minister or layman, who has an office to perform, should carry out all and only those parts which pertain to his office by the nature of the rite and the principles of the liturgy."[3]

A little earlier in the same constitution there is an assertion in similar vein: "Mother Church earnestly desires that all the faithful should be led to that full, conscious and active participation in liturgical celebrations which is demanded by the very nature of the liturgy, and to which the Christian people, 'a chosen race, a royal priesthood, a holy people' (1 Pet. 2:9, 4–5), have a right and obligation by reason of their baptism. In the restoration and promotion of the sacred liturgy the full and active participation by all the people is the aim to be considered before all else, for it is the primary and indispensable source from which the faithful are to derive the true Christian spirit. Therefore, pastors of souls must earnestly strive to achieve it, by an adequate formation, in all their pastoral work."[4]

Among the special offices which are to be retained and adapted to present-day needs there are some which are especially connected with the ministries of the word and of the altar. In the Latin Church they are the office of lector, the office of acolyte and the subdiaconate. These offices will now be reduced to two, that of lector and that of acolyte, and the functions of the subdiaconate will be divided between them.

There is nothing to prevent episcopal conferences from requesting the establishment of other offices from the Holy See, over and above those which are common to the whole Church, if they decide that this is necessary or very helpful

1. See Constitution on the Sacred Liturgy, n. 62. See also n. 21.
2. See Ordo Missae, *Institutio Generalis Missalis Romani,* 58.
3. Constitution on the Sacred Liturgy, D.*I*), n. 28.
4. Ibid., n. 14.

for reasons peculiar to their own territories. Examples of such offices are those of porter, exorcist and catechist,[5] as well as other offices to be conferred on those who are engaged in charitable activities, where these are not committed to the care of deacons.

It is more in keeping with the nature of the case and with contemporary attitudes that such ministries should no longer be called "minor orders." Their conferring will no longer be called "ordination," but "installation." Only those who have received the diaconate will be, and will be called, clerics. The distinction between clergy and laity will thus emerge with greater clarity, the distinction between what belongs to the clergy and is reserved to them and what can be entrusted to the laity. Their respective natures will thus be more clearly understood: "though they differ essentially and not only in degree, the common priesthood of the faithful and the ministerial or hierarchical priesthood are nonetheless ordered one to another; each of them in its own proper way shares in the one priesthood of Christ."[6]

Having given due consideration to every aspect of the problem, having sought the opinion of experts, having consulted the episcopal conferences and noted their views, and having consulted our venerable brothers who are members of the sacred congregations whom this matter concerns, we prescribe with this letter the following norms by our apostolic authority, modifying if and insofar as it is necessary, provisions of the code of canon law now in force:

1. First tonsure is no longer conferred. Entrance into the clerical state is joined to the diaconate.

2. Orders which up to now have been called "minor," will henceforth be known as "ministries."

3. Ministries may be committed to lay Christians. They are thus no longer to be regarded as reserved to candidates for the sacrament of orders.

4. The ministries which are to be retained in the Latin Church as a whole, but adapted to today's needs, are two, that of lector and that of acolyte. The major order of subdiaconate no longer exists in the Latin Church. There is nothing to prevent acolytes being called subdeacons in this or that region, should the conference of bishops judge this opportune.

5. See Decree *Ad Gentes divinitus*, n. 15 and n. 17.
6. Dogmatic Constitution on the Church, n. 10.

5. The office of the lector, and it is proper to him, is to read the word of God in the liturgical assembly. Accordingly, it will be his task to read the lessons from the scripture (but not the gospel) at Mass and at other sacred functions; when there is no psalmist, he will recite the psalm between the readings; he will announce the intentions at the prayers of the faithful when the deacon or cantor is not present; he will direct the singing and the participation of the faithful; he is to instruct the faithful in the worthy reception of the sacraments. He may also, when necessary, prepare the faithful who are temproarily appointed to read the scriptures in liturgical celebrations. He should meditate assiduously on the sacred scriptures so that he may more fittingly and perfectly fulfil these functions.

The lector should be mindful of the office he has undertaken and should do all in his power to acquire increasingly that sweet and living love and knowledge of the scriptures that will make him a more perfect disciple of the Lord.[7]

6. An acolyte is appointed to assist the deacon and to minister to the priest. It is his duty therefore to attend to the service of the altar, to assist the deacon and the priest in liturgical celebrations, especially in the celebration of Mass. It also falls to him to distribute holy communion, as an extraordinary minister, whenever the ministers listed in Canon 845[8] of the code of canon law are not present, or are themselves unable to distribute holy communion because of sickness or old age, or because they have to perform some other pastoral function at the same time. It can also fall to the acolyte to distribute holy communion when the number of communicants would otherwise be considerable enough to prolong the celebration of Mass unduly. It is also permissible to entrust to him, in similar extraordinary circumstances, the task of exposing the Blessed Sacrament for the veneration of the faithful and of replacing it subsequently. He may not, however, bless the people. He may also, as the need arises, instruct those of the faithful who are temporarily appointed to assist the priest and deacon by carrying the missal, the cross or the candles or by performing other similar duties in liturgical celebrations. He will

7. See Constitution on the Sacred Liturgy, n. 24.
b. In that canon the ordinary minister of holy communion is given as the priest, while a deacon is listed as an extraordinary minister. —[Editor].

perform these duties more worthily if he participates in the holy Eucharist with ever-increasing fervor, is nourished by it and deepens his understanding of it.

Since an acolyte is especially destined for the service of the altar, he should familiarize himself with everything which pertains to divine worship and should endeavor to understand its spirit and its inner meaning. He will thus be able to offer himself entirely to God and in church will be an example of gravity and reverence to all. He will also have a sincere love for the mystical body of Christ, the people of God, especially for the weak and the sick.

7. The offices of lector and acolyte are reserved to men, in keeping with the venerable tradition of the Church.

8. Before a person can be admitted to these ministries, he must fulfil the following conditions:

(a) He must freely draw up and present a signed petition to the ordinary who has the right to acceptance. The ordinary is the bishop or, in the case of clerical institutes of perfection, the major superior.

(b) He must have attained the age and must possess the qualities determined by the episcopal conference.

(c) He must have the firm intention of serving God and the Christian people.

9. The ministries are conferred by the ordinary (the bishop or, in clerical institutes of perfection, the major superior) in the liturgical rites, "The Installation of a Lector" and "The Installation of an Acolyte," which are to be revised by the Holy See.

10. An interval of time, to be determined by the Holy See or the episcopal conference, must elapse between the conferring of the ministry of lector and the conferring of the ministry of acolyte, whenever both ministries are conferred on the same candidate.[c]

11. Candidates for the diaconate and the priesthood must receive the ministries of lector and acolyte and must exercise them for a suitable length of time so as to be better fitted for the future service of the word and of the altar. Dispensation from the reception of the ministries by these candidates is reserved to the Holy See.

c. The Latin text, in fact, has *"interstita . . . serventur"* and the English translation published by the Vatican Press also puts this in the plural. We have taken the liberty of putting it in the singular, which seems more accurate, since only two ministries are mentioned. [Editor].

12. The conferring of ministries does not carry with it the right to sustenance or salary from the Church.

13. The rites of installation of lector and acolyte will be published soon by the competent department of the Roman Curia.

These norms shall come into effect on 1 January, 1973. We order that what we have decreed in this letter, given *motu proprio*, be established and ratified, notwithstanding anything to the contrary.

30

APOSTOLIC LETTER CONTAINING NORMS FOR THE ORDER OF DIACONATE[a]

Paul VI, *Ad Pascendum*, 15 August, 1972

For the nurturing and constant growth of the people of God, Christ the Lord instituted in the Church a variety of ministries, which work for the good of the whole body.[1]

From the apostolic age the diaconate has had a clearly outstanding position among these ministries, and it has always been held in great honor by the Church. Explicit testimony of this is given by the Apostle Paul both in his letter to the Philippians, in which he sends his greetings not only to the bishops but also to the deacons,[2] and in a letter to Timothy, in which he illustrates the qualities and virtues that deacons must have in order to be worthy of their ministry.[3]

Later, when the early writers of the Church acclaim the dignity of deacons, they do not fail to extol also the spiritual qualities and virtues that are required for the performance of that ministry, namely, fidelity to Christ, moral integrity, and obedience to the bishop.

St. Ignatius of Antioch declares that the office of the deacon is nothing other than "the ministry of Jesus Christ, who was with the Father before all ages and has been manifested in the final time."[4] He also made the following observation: "The deacons too, who are ministers of the mysteries of Jesus Christ, should please all in every way; for they are

a. Translation by Vatican Press office. Latin text in *AAS* 64 (1972) pp 534–540.
1. Cf. Vatican II, Dogmatic Constitution on the Church, n. 18: *AAS* 57 (1965), pp. 21–22.
2. Cf. Phil. 1:1.
3. Cf. 1 Tim. 3:8–13.
4. *Ad Magnesios*, VI, 1: Funk, *Patres Apostolici* 1, p. 235.

not servants of food and drink, but ministers of the Church of God."[5]

St. Polycarp of Smyrna exhorts deacons to "be moderate in all things, merciful, diligent, living according to the truth of the Lord, who became the servant of all."[6] The author of the *Didascalia Apostolorum*, recalling the words of Christ, "Anyone who wants to be great among you must be your servant,"[7] addresses the following fraternal exhortation to deacons: "Accordingly you deacons also should behave in such a way that, if your ministry obliges you to lay down your lives for a brother, you should do so. . . . If the Lord of heaven and earth served us and suffered and sustained everything on our behalf, should not this be done for our brothers all the more by us, since we are imitators of him and have been given the place of Christ?"[8]

DEACON'S MINISTRY

Furthermore, when the writers of the first centuries insist on the importance of the ministry of deacons, they give many examples of the manifold important tasks entrusted to them, and clearly show how much authority they held in the Christian communities and how great was their contribution to the apostolate. The deacon is described as "the bishop's ear, mouth, heart and soul."[9] The deacon is at the disposal of the bishop in order that he may serve the whole people of God and take care of the sick and the poor;[10] he is correctly and rightly called "one who shows love for orphans, for the devout and for the widowed, one who is fervent in spirit, one who shows love for what is good."[11] Furthermore, he is entrusted with the mission of taking the holy Eucharist to the sick confined to their homes,[12] of

5. *Ad Trallianos*, II, 3: ibid., p. 245.
6. *Ad Philippenses*, V, 2: ibid., pp. 301–303.
7. Mt. 20:26–27.
8. *Didascalia Apostolorum* III, 13, 2–4: Funk, *Didascalia et Constitutiones Apostolorum* I, p. 214.
9. *Didascalia Apostolorum* II, 44, 4; ibid., p. 138.
10. Cf. *Traditio Apostolica*, 39 and 34; *La Tradition Apostolique de St. Hippolyte. Essai de reconstitution* by B. Botte (Münster, 1963), pp. 87, 91.
11. *Testamentum D.N. Iesu Christi* I, 38, ed. and translated into Latin by I. E. Rahmani (Mainz, 1899), p. 93.
12. Cf. St. Justin, *Apologia* I, 65, 5, and 67, 5; St. Justin, *Apologiae duae*, ed. G. Rauschen (Bonn, 1911), pp. 107, 111.

conferring baptism,[13] and of attending to preaching the Word of God in accordance with the express will of the bishop.

Accordingly, the diaconate flourished in a wonderful way in the Church, and at the same time gave an outstanding witness of love for Christ and the brethren through the performance of works of charity,[14] the celebration of sacred rites,[15] and the fulfilment of pastoral duties.[16]

PROFOUND EXAMINATION

The exercise of the office of deacon enabled those who were to become priests to give proof of themselves, to display the merit of their work, and to acquire preparation—all of which were requirements for receiving the dignity of the priesthood and the office of pastor.

As time went on, the discipline concerning this sacred order was changed. The prohibition against conferring ordination without observing the established sequence of orders was strengthened, and there was a gradual decrease in the number of those who preferred to remain deacons all their lives instead of advancing to a higher order. As a consequence, the permanent diaconate almost entirely disappeared in the Latin Church. It is scarcely the place to mention the decrees of the Council of Trent proposing to restore the sacred orders in accordance with their own nature as ancient functions within the Church;[17] it was much later that the idea matured of restoring this important sacred order also as a truly permanent rank. Our predecessor Pius XII briefly alluded to this matter.[18] Finally, the Second Vatican Council supported the wishes and requests that, where such would lead to the good of souls, the permanent diaconate should be restored as an intermediate order between the higher ranks of the Church's hierarchy and the

13. Cf. Tertullian, *De Baptismo* XVII, 1; *Corpus Christianorum* I, *Tertulliani Opera*, Turnholt (1954), p. 291.
14. Cf. *Didascalia Apostolorum* II, 31, 2: Funk I, p. 112; *Testamentum D.N. Iesu Christi* I, 31: Rahmani, p. 75.
15. Cf. *Didascalia Apostolorum* II, 57, 6, and 58, 1: Funk I, pp. 162, 166.
16. Cf. St. Cyprian, *Epist.* 15, 16, ed. G. Hartel (Vienna, 1871), pp. 513–520; cf. St. Augustine, *De catechezandis rudibus* I, cap. I, 1; *PL* 40, 309–310.
17. Session 23: Mansi, *Collectio* 33, 138–140.
18. Address to the Participants in the Second International Congress of the Lay Apostolate, 5 Oct. 1957: *AAS* 49 (1957), p. 925.

rest of the people of God, as an expression of the needs and desires of the Christian communities, as a driving force for the Church's service or *diaconia* towards the local Christian communities, and as a sign or sacrament of the Lord Christ himself, who "came not to be served but to serve."[19]

CONSTITUTION "LUMEN GENTIUM"

For this reason, at the third session of the Council, in October 1964, the Fathers ratified the principle of the renewal of the diaconate, and in the following November the Dogmatic Constitution on the Church, *Lumen Gentium*, was promulgated. In the 19th article of this document a description is given of the principal characteristics proper to that state: "At a lower level of the hierarchy are deacons, who receive the imposition of hands 'not unto the priesthood, but unto the ministry.' For strengthened by sacramental grace they are dedicated to the people of God, in conjunction with the bishop and his body of priests, in the service of the liturgy, of the Gospel, and of works of charity."[20]

The same constitution made the following declaration about permanency in the rank of deacon: "These duties (of deacons), so very necessary for the life of the Church, can in many areas be fulfilled only with difficulty according to the prevailing discipline of the Latin Church. For this reason, the diaconate can in the future be restored as a proper and permanent rank of the hierarchy."[21]

RESTORING THE DIACONATE

However, this restoration of the permanent diaconate required that the instructions of the Council be more profoundly examined and that there be mature deliberation concerning juridical status both of the celibate and married deacon. Similarly it was necessary that matters connected with the diaconate of those who are to become priests should be adapted to contemporary conditions, so that the time of diaconate would furnish that proof of life, of maturity and of aptitude for the priestly ministry, which ancient disciples demanded from candidates for the priesthood.

19. Mt. 20:28.
20. *AAS* 57 (1965), p. 36.
21. Ibid.

Thus on 18 June 1967 we issued in *motu proprio* form, the Apostolic Letter *Sacrum Diaconatus Ordinem*, by which suitable canonical norms for the permanent diaconate were established.[22] On June 17 of the following year, through the Apostolic Constitution *Pontificalis Romani Recognito*,[23] we authorized the new rite for the conferring of the sacred orders of diaconate, priesthood and episcopacy, and at the same time defined the matter and the form of the ordination itself.

Now that we are proceeding further and are today promulgating the Apostolic Letter *Ministeria Quaedam*, we consider it fitting to issue certain norms concerning the diaconate. We also desire that candidates for the diaconate should know what ministries they are to exercise before sacred ordination and when and how they are to take upon themselves the responsibilities of celibacy and liturgical prayer.

Since entrance into the clerical state is deferred until diaconate, there no longer exists the rite of first tonsure, by which a layman used to become a cleric. But a new rite is introduced, by which one who aspires to the diaconate or priesthood publicly manifests his will to offer himself to God and the Church, so that he may exercise a sacred order. The Church, accepting this offering, selects and calls him to prepare himself to receive a sacred order, and in this way he is properly numbered among candidates for the diaconate or priesthood.

It is especially fitting that the ministries of lector and acolyte should be entrusted to those who, as candidates for the order of diaconate or priesthood, desire to devote themselves to God and to the Church in a special way. For the Church, which "does not cease to take the bread of life from the table of the word of God and the body of Christ and offer it to the faithful,"[24] considers it to be very opportune that both by study and by gradual exercise of the ministry of the word and of the altar, candidates for sacred orders should through intimate contact understand and reflect upon the double aspect of the priestly office. Thus it comes about that the authenticity of the ministry shines out with the greatest effectiveness. In this way the candidates accede

22. *AAS* 59 (1967), pp. 697–704.
23. *AAS* 60 (1968), pp. 369–373.
24. Cf. Vatican II, Dogmatic Constitution on Divine Revelation, n. 21: *AAS* 58 (1966), p. 827.

to sacred orders fully aware of their vocation, fervent in spirit, serving the Lord, constant in prayer and aware of the needs of the faithful.[25]

NORMS PROMULGATED

Having weighed every aspect of the question well, having sought the opinion of experts, having consulted with the episcopal conferences and taken their views into account, and having taken council with our Venerable Brothers who are members of the Sacred Congregations competent in this matter, by our apostolic authority we enact the following norms, derogating—if and insofar as necessary—from provisions of the Code of Canon Law until now in force, and we promulgate them with this letter.

1. (a) A rite of admission for candidates to the diaconate and to the priesthood is introduced. In order that this admission be properly made, the free petition of the aspirant, made out and signed in his own hand, is required, as well as the written acceptance of the competent ecclesiastical superior, by which the selection by the Church is brought about.

Professed members of clerical congregations who seek the priesthood are not bound to this rite.

(b) The competent superior for this acceptance is the ordinary (the bishop and, in clerical institutes of perfection, the major superior). Those can be accepted who give signs of an authentic vocation and, endowed with good moral qualities and free from mental and physical defects, wish to dedicate their lives to the service of the Church for the glory of God and the good of souls. It is necessary that those who aspire to the transitional diaconate will have completed at least their twentieth year and have begun their course of theological studies.

(c) In virtue of the acceptance the candidate must care for his vocation in a special way and foster it. He also acquires the right to the necessary spiritual assistance by which he can develop his vocation and submit unconditionally to the will of God.

2. Candidates for the permanent or transitional diaconate and for the priesthood are to receive the ministries of lector and acolyte, unless they have already done so, and are to

25. Cf. Rom. 12:11–13.

exercise them for a fitting time, in order to be better disposed for the future service of the word and of the altar.

Dispensation from the reception of these ministries on the part of such candidates is reserved to the Holy See.

SIGNED DECLARATIONS

3. The liturgical rites by which admission of candidates for the diaconate and the priesthood takes place and the above-mentioned ministries are conferred should be performed by the ordinary of the aspirant (the bishop and, in clerical institutes of perfection, the major superior).

4. The intervals established by the Holy See or by the episcopal conferences between the conferring—during the course of theological studies—of the ministry of lector and that of acolyte, and between the ministry of acolyte and the order of deacon must be observed.

5. Before ordination candidates for the diaconate shall give to the ordinary (the bishop and, in clerical institutes of perfection, the major superior) a declaration made out and signed in their own hand, by which they testify that they are about to receive the sacred order freely and of their own accord.

6. The special consecration of celibacy observed for the sake of the kingdom of heaven and its obligation for candidates to the priesthood and for unmarried candidates to the diaconate are indeed linked with the diaconate. The public commitment to holy celibacy before God and the Church is to be celebrated in a particular rite, even by religious, and it is to precede ordination to the diaconate. Celibacy taken on in this way is a diriment impediment to entering marriage.

In accordance with the traditional discipline of the Church, a married deacon who has lost his wife cannot enter a new marriage.[26]

7. (a) Deacons called to the priesthood are not to be ordained until they have completed the course of studies prescribed by the norms of the Apostolic See.

(b) In regard to the course of theological studies to precede the ordination of permanent deacons, the episcopal conferences, with attention to the local situation, will issue

---

26. Cf. Paul VI, Apostolic Letter *Sacrum Diaconatus Ordinem*, n. 16: *AAS* 59 (1967), p. 701.

the proper norms and submit them for the approval of the Sacred Congregation for Catholic Education.

LITURGY OF THE HOURS

8. In accordance with norms 29-30 of the General Instruction for the Liturgy of the Hours:

(a) Deacons called to the priesthood are bound by their sacred ordination by the obligation of celebrating the liturgy of the hours;

(b) It is most fitting that permanent deacons should recite daily at least a part of the liturgy of the hours, to be determined by the episcopal conference.

9. Entrance into the clerical state and incardination into a diocese are brought about by ordination to the diaconate.

10. The rite of admission for candidates to the diaconate and priesthood and of the special consecration of holy celibacy is to be published soon by the competent department of the Roman Curia.

Transitional Norms. Candidates for the sacrament of Orders who have already received first tonsure before the promulgation of this letter, retain all the duties, rights and privileges of clerics. Those who have been promoted to the order of subdiaconate are held to the obligations taken on in regard to both celibacy and the liturgy of the hours. But they must celebrate once again their public commitment to celibacy before God and the Church by the new special rite preceding ordination to the diaconate.

All that has been decreed by us in this letter, in *motu proprio* form, we order to be confirmed and ratified, anything to the contrary notwithstanding. We also determine that it shall come into force on 1 January 1973.

31

DECREE ON THE CATHOLIC EASTERN CHURCHES[a]

Vatican II, *Orientalium Ecclesiarum*, 21 November, 1964

INTRODUCTION

1. The Catholic Church values highly the institutions of the Eastern Churches, their liturgical rites, ecclesiastical traditions and their ordering of Christian life. For in those churches, which are distinguished by their venerable antiquity, there is clearly evident the tradition which has come from the apostles through the Fathers[1] and which is part of the divinely revealed, undivided heritage of the Universal Church. This holy, ecumenical synod, therefore, has a special care for the Eastern Churches, which are living witnesses of this tradition, and wishes them to flourish and to fulfil with new apostolic strength the task entrusted to them. Accordingly it has decided to set down some guiding principles for these churches, in addition to those which refer to the Church universal, leaving all else to be cared for by the Eastern synods and the Apostolic See.

THE PARTICULAR CHURCHES OR RITES

2. The holy Catholic Church, which is the Mystical Body of Christ, is made up of the faithful who are organically united in the Holy Spirit by the same faith, the same sacraments and the same government. They combine into different groups, which are held together by their hierarchy, and so form particular churches or rites. Between those churches there is such a wonderful bond of union that this variety in the Universal Church, so far from diminishing its unity, rather serves to emphasize it. For the Catholic Church

a. Translated by P.A. O'Connell, S.J.
1. Leo XIII, Apostolic Letter *Orientalium dignitas*, 30 Nov. 1894: *Acta Leonis XIII*, vol. XIV, pp. 201–202.

wishes the traditions of each particular church or rite to remain whole and entire, and it likewise wishes to adapt its own way of life to the needs of different times and places.[2]

3. These individual churches both Eastern and Western, while they differ somewhat among themselves in what is called "rite," namely in liturgy, in ecclesiastical discipline and in spiritual tradition, are none the less all equally entrusted to the pastoral guidance of the Roman Pontiff, who by God's appointment is successor to Blessed Peter in primacy over the Universal Church. Therefore these churches are of equal rank, so that none of them is superior to the others because of its rite. They have the same rights and obligations, even with regard to the preaching of the Gospel in the whole world (cf. Mk. 16:15), under the direction of the Roman Pontiff.

4. Provision must be made therefore everywhere in the world to protect and advance all these individual churches. For this purpose, each should organize its own parishes and hierarchy, where the spiritual good of the faithful requires it. Prelates of the various individual churches who have jurisdiction in the same territory should meet at regular intervals for consultation, and thus foster unity of action and strive together to meet their common tasks, so as better to further the good of religion and to safeguard more effectively the discipline of their clergy.[8] All clerics and those who are to receive sacred orders should be well instructed concerning rites and particularly in practical rules for inter-ritual questions. Lay people also should receive instruction concerning rites and their rules in their catechetical formation.

2. St. Leo IX, Letter *In terra pax*, 1053, *Ut enim;* Innocent III, Fourth Lateran Council, 1215, ch. IV, *Licet Graecos;* Letter *Inter quattuor*, 2 Aug. 1206, *Postulasti Postmodum;* Innocent IV, Letter *Cum de cetero*, 27 Aug. 1247; Letter *Sub catholicae*, 6 March 1254, introd.; Nicholas III, Instruction *Istud est memoriale*, 9 Oct. 1278; Leo X, Apostolic Letter *Accepimus nuper*, 18 May 1521; Paul III, Apostolic Letter *Dudum*, 23 Dec. 1534; Pius IV, Constitution *Romanus Pontifex*, 16 Feb. 1564, sec. 5; Clement VIII, Constitution *Magnus Dominus*, 23 Dec. 1595, sec. 10; Paul V, Constitution *Solet circumspecta*, 10 Dec. 1615, sec. 3; Benedict XIV, Encyclical Letters *Demandatam*, 24 Dec. 1943, sec. 3; *Allatae sunt*, 26 June 1755, sec. 3, 6–19, 32; Pius VI, Encyclical Letter *Catholicae communionis*, 24 May 1787; Pius IX, Letter *In suprema*, 6 Jan. 1848, sec. 3; Apostolic Letter *Ecclesiam Christi*, 26 Nov. 1853; Constitution *Romani Pontificis*, 6 Jan. 1862; Leo XIII, Apostolic Letters *Praeclara*, 20 June 1894, n. 7; *Orientalium dignitas*, 30 Nov. 1894, introd.; etc.
3. Pius XII, Motu proprio *Cleri sanctitati*, 2 June 1957, Can. 4.

Finally, each and every Catholic, as also the baptized members of any non-Catholic church or community who come to the fulness of Catholic communion, must retain each his own rite wherever he is, and follow it to the best of his ability,[4] without prejudice to the right of appealing to the Apostolic See in special cases affecting persons, communities or districts. The Apostolic See which is the supreme arbiter of inter-Church relations will provide for all such needs in an ecumenical spirit, acting directly or through other authorities, giving suitable rules, decrees or rescripts.

PRESERVATION OF THE SPIRITUAL HERITAGE OF THE EASTERN CHURCHES

5. History, tradition and very many ecclesiastical institutions give clear evidence of the great debt owed to the Eastern Churches by the Church Universal.[5] Therefore the holy council not merely praises and appreciates as is due this ecclesiastical and spiritual heritage, but also insists on viewing it as the heritage of the whole Church of Christ. For that reason this Council solemnly declares that the churches of the East like those of the West have the right and duty to govern themselves according to their own special disciplines. For these are guaranteed by ancient tradition, and seem to be better suited to the customs of their faithful and to the good of their souls.

6. All members of the Eastern Churches should be firmly convinced that they can and ought always preserve their own legitimate liturgical rites and ways of life, and that changes are to be introduced only to forward their own organic development. They themselves are to carry out all these prescriptions with the greatest fidelity. They are to aim always at a more perfect knowledge and practice of their rites, and if they have fallen away due to circumstances of times or persons, they are to strive to return to their ancestral traditions.

Those who by reason of their office or apostolic ministry

4. Ibid. Can. 8: *Sine licentia Sedis Apostolicae,* following the practice of preceding centuries. Similarly, with regard to baptized non-Catholics, Can. 11 states: *Ritum quem maluerint amplecti possunt.* In the text as proposed there is a positive ruling on the observance of rite for all persons and places.

5. Cf. Leo XIII, Apostolic Letters *Orientalium dignitas,* 30 Nov. 1894; *Praeclara gratulationis,* 20 June 1894; and the Documents cited in note 2, above.

have frequent dealings with the Eastern Churches or their faithful should be instructed as their office demands in theoretical and practical knowledge of the rites, discipline, doctrine, history and character of the members of the Eastern Churches.[6] It is recommended strongly to religious orders and associations of the Latin rite, which are working in Eastern countries or among the Eastern faithful, that they should set up, so far as is possible, houses or even provinces of the Eastern rite to make their apostolic work more effective.[7]

THE EASTERN PATRIARCHS

7. The patriarchate as an institution has existed in the Church from the earliest times, and was already recognized by the first ecumenical councils.[8]

By the term "Eastern patriarch" is meant the bishop who has jurisdiction over all the bishops, metropolitans not excepted, clergy and people of his own territory or rite, according to the rules of canon law and without prejudice to the primacy of the Roman Pontiff.[9]

Wherever a prelate of any rite is appointed outside the territory of his patriarchate, he remains attached to the hierarchy of his rite, in accordance with canon law.[b]

8. The patriarchs of the Eastern Churches, although some are of later date than others, are all equal in patriarchal rank, without prejudice to their legitimately established precedence of honor.[10]

6. BENEDICT XV, Motu proprio *Orientis catholici,* 15 Oct. 1917; Pius XI, Encyclical Letter *Rerum orientalium,* 8 Sept. 1928, etc.
7. The practice of the Catholic Church in the time of Pius XI, Pius XII, John XXIII abundantly shows this tendency.
8. Cf. First Council of Nicea, Can. 6; First Council of Constantinople, Can. 2 and 3; Chalcedon, Can. 28 and 9; Fourth Council of Constantinople, Can 17 and 21; Fourth Lateran Council, Can 5 and 30; Florence, decree *Pro Graecis,* etc.
9. First Council of Nicea, Can. 6; First Council of Constantinople, Can. 3; Fourth Council of Constantinople, Can. 17; Pius XII, Motu proprio *Cleri sanctitati,* Can. 216, Sec. 2, n. 1.
b. "Prelate" in the Latin Code means "ordinary," strictly speaking (cf. *Codex Juris Canonici,* Can. 110), and has been used twice to translate *hierarcha,* where "Ordinary" would have sufficed.—Translator.
10. In the Ecumenical Councils: First Council of Nicea, Can. 6; First Council of Constantinople, Can. 3; Fourth Council of Constantinople, Can. 21; Fourth Lateran Council, Can. 5; Florence, decree *Pro Graecis,* 6 July 1439, sec. 9. Cf. Pius XII, Motu proprio *Cleri sanctitati,* 2 June 1957, Can. 219, etc.

9. Following the most ancient tradition of the Church, special honor is to be given to the patriarchs of the Eastern Churches, since each is set over his patriarchate as father and head. Therefore this holy council enacts that their rights and privileges be restored in accordance with the ancient traditions of each church and the decrees of the ecumenical councils.[11]

These rights and privileges are those which existed in the time of union between East and West, although they must be adapted somewhat to present-day conditions.

The patriarchs with their synods are the highest authority for all business of the patriarchate, not excepting the right of setting up new eparchies (dioceses) and appointing bishops of their rite within the patriarchal territory, without prejudice to the inalienable right of the Roman Pontiff to intervene in any particular case.

10. What is laid down concerning patriarchs applies also, in accordance with canon law, to major archbishops who rule the whole of some individual church or rite.[12]

11. Since the patriarchal system is the traditional form of government in the Eastern Churches, the holy ecumenical council wishes, where there is need, new patriarchates to be set up. This is reserved to an ecumenical council or to the Roman Pontiff.[13]

SACRAMENTAL DISCIPLINE

12. The holy ecumenical council confirms and approves the ancient discipline concerning the sacraments which exist in the Eastern Churches, and also the ritual observed in their celebration and administration, and wishes this to be restored where such a case arises.

13. The established practice with regard to the minister of Confirmation, which has existed among Eastern Chris-

11. Cf. above, note 8.
12. Cf. Council of Ephesus, Can. 8; Clement VIII, *Decet Romanum Pontificem*, 23 Feb. 1596; Pius VII, Apostolic Letter *In universalis Ecclesiae*, 22 Feb. 1807; Pius XII, Motu proprio *Cleri sanctitati*, 2 June 1957, Can. 324–339; Council of Carthage, 419, Can. 17.
13. Council of Carthage, 419, Can. 17, 57; Chalcedon, 451, Can. 12; St. Innocent I, Letter *Et onus et honor*, about 415: *Nam quid sciscitaris:* St. Nicholas I, Letter *Ad consulta vestra*, 13 Nov. 866: *A quo autem:* Innocent III, Letter *Rex requm*, 25 Feb. 1204; Leo XII, Apostolic Constitution *Petrus Apostolorum Princeps*, 15 Aug. 1824; Leo XIII, Apostolic Letter *Christi Domini*, 1895; Pius XII, Motu proprio *Cleri sanctitati*, 2 June 1957, Can. 159.

tians from ancient times, is to be fully restored. Accordingly priests are able to confer this sacrament, using chrism blessed by their patriarch or bishop.[14]

14. All priests of an Eastern rite can confer this sacrament validly, either in conjunction with baptism or separately, on all the faithful of any rite, including the Latin rite.[15] For liceity, however, they must follow what is laid down by their common and particular canon law. Priests also of the Latin rite, in accordance with the faculties which they have in regard to the administration of this sacrament, may administer it also to the faithful of the Eastern Churches, without prejudice to the rite. For liceity they must follow the prescriptions of common and particular canon law.[16]

15. The faithful are obliged to take part in the Divine Liturgy on Sundays and feast days or, according to the regulations or custom of their own rite, in the celebration of the Divine Office.[17] To enable the faithful to fulfil more easily this obligation, it is laid down that the time for fulfilling this precept extends from Vespers of the vigil to the end of the Sunday or feast day.[18] The faithful are strongly

14. Innocent IV, Letter *Sub catholicae*, 6 March 1254, sec. 3, n. 4; Second Council of Lyons, 1274 (Profession of Faith presented by Michael Palaeologus to Gregory X); Eugene IV, in Council of Florence, Constitution *Exsultate Deo*, 22 Nov. 1439, sec. 11; Clement VIII, Instruction *Sanctissimus*, 31 Aug. 1595; Benedict XIV, Constitution *Etsi pastoralis*, 26 May 1742, sec. II, n. 1, sec. III, n. 1, etc.; Council of Laodicea, 347-381, Can. 48; Council of Sis of the Armenians, 1342; Council of Lebanon of the Maronites, 1736, Pt. II, ch. III, n. 2, and other particular Councils.
15. Cf. Instruction of the Holy Office to the Bishop of Spis, 1783; the Sacred Congregation of Propaganda, for the Copts, 15 March 1790, n. XIII; Decree of 6 Oct. 1863, C, a; the Sacred Congregation for the Eastern Church, 1 May 1948; the Reply of the Holy Office, 22 April 1896, with the letter of 19 May 1896.
16. Code of Canon Law, Can. 782, sec. 4; Decree of the Sacred Congregation for the Eastern Church *de Sacramento Confirmationis administrando etiam fidelibus orientalibus a presbyteris latini ritus, qui hoc indulto quadent pro fidelibus sui ritus*, 1 May 1948.
17. Cf. Council of Laodicea, 347-381, Can. 29; St. Nicephorus of Constantinople, ch. 14; Council of Duin of the Armenians, 719, Can. 31; St. Theodore Studites, serm. 21; St. Nicholas I, Letter *Ad consulta vestra*, 13 Nov. 866: *In quorum Apostolorum, Nos cupitis, Quod interrogatis, Praeterea consulitis, Si die Dominico;* and particular Councils.
18. This is something new, at least where there is an obligation of assisting at the Sacred Liturgy. However, it does correspond to the liturgical day among the Orientals.

recommended to receive the Sacred Eucharist on these days, and to do so even more frequently, even every day.[19]

16. In view of the fact that the faithful of the different individual churches are constantly intermingled in the same district or Eastern territory, the faculties for hearing confessions given to priests of any rite by their own ordinaries[c] duly and without any restriction extend to the whole territory of him who grants them, and also to the places and faithful of any rite in the same territory, unless an ordinary of the place explicity refuses this for places of his own rite.[20]

17. The holy council wishes the institution of the permanent diaconate to be restored where it has fallen into disuse, in order that the ancient discipline of the Sacrament of Orders may flourish once more in the Eastern Churches.[21] For the subdiaconate and the lesser orders, their rights and obligations, the legislative authority of each individual church should make provision.[22]

18. In order to provide against invalid marriages, when Eastern Catholics marry baptized Eastern non-Catholics, and also in order to promote the permanence and sanctity of marriage as well as peace in the home, the holy council determines that the canonical form of celebration for these marriages is of obligation only for liceity. For their validity

19. Cf. Canons of the Apostles, 8 and 9; Council of Antioch, 341, Can. 2; Timothy of Alexandria, interr. 3; Innocent III, Constitution *Quia divinae*, 4 Jan. 1215; and very many more recent particular Councils of the Eastern Churches.

c. *Hierarcha* in Eastern terminology means "ordinary"; *loci* has to be added to indicate "local ordinary."—Translator.

20. While safeguarding the principle of territorial jurisdiction, the Canon wishes, for the good of souls, to make provision for the situation which arises from plurality of jurisdiction over the same territory.

21. Cf. First Council of Nicea, Can. 18; Council of Neocaesarea, 314–325, Can. 12; Council of Sardica, 343, Can. 8; St. Leo the Great, Letter *Omnium quidem*, 13 Jan. 444; Chalcedon, Can. 6; Fourth Council of Constantinople, Can. 23, 26; etc.

22. The Subdiaconate is considered a minor Order by many of the Eastern Churches, but by the Motu proprio *Cleri sanctitati* of Pius XII there are prescribed in its regard the obligations of major Orders. The Canon here proposes a return to the ancient discipline of each of the Churches regarding the obligations of subdeacons, thus derogating from the common law laid down in *Cleri sanctitati*.

the presence of a sacred minister is sufficient, provided that the other prescriptions of canon law are observed.[23]

DIVINE WORSHIP

19. For the future the setting up, transference or suppression of feast days common to all the Eastern Churches is reserved solely to an ecumenical council or the Apostolic See. On the other hand, the setting up, transference or suppression of feast days for any of the individual churches is within the competence not only of the Apostolic See but also of patriarchal or archiepiscopal synods, due regard being had for the whole area affected as also for the other individual churches.[24]

20. Until all Christians agree, as is hoped, on one day for the celebration of Easter by all, in the meantime as a means of fostering unity among Christians who live in the same area or country, it is left to the patriarchs or to the supreme ecclesiastical authorities of the place to consult all parties involved and so come to an unanimous agreement to celebrate the feast of Easter on the same Sunday.[25]

21. Regarding the law of the seasons of the Church's year, individual faithful who live outside the area or territory of their own rite may follow in all points the discipline in force in the place where they are living. In families of mixed rite this law may be observed according to one and the same rite.[26]

23. Cf. Pius XII, Motu proprio *Crebrae allatae*, 22 Feb. 1949, Can. 32, sec. 2, n. 5 (power of the patriarchs to dispense from the form); *Cleri sanctitati*, 2 June 1957, Can. 267 (power of the patriarchs regarding *sanatio in radice*); the Holy Office and the Sacred Congregation for the Eastern Church granted in 1957 the power of dispensing from the form and of applying *sanatio* because of defect of form, for five years: "Outside the patriarchates, to metropolitans and to other local ordinaries . . . who have no superior beneath the Holy See."
24. Cf. St. Leo the Great, Letter *Quod saepissime*, 15 April 454: *Petitionem quem*; St. Nicephorus of Constantinople, ch. 13; Council of Patriarch Sergius, 18 Sept. 1596, Can. 17; Pius VI, Apostolic Letter *Assueto paterne*, 8 April 1775; etc.
25. Constitution on the Sacred Liturgy (D.*1*).
26. Cf. Clement VIII, Instruction *Sanctissimus*, 31 Aug. 1595, sec. 6: *Si ipsi graeci;* the Holy Office, 7 June 1673, ad 1, 3; 13 March 1727, ad 1; the Sacred Congregation of Propaganda, Decree, 18 Aug. 1913, Art. 33; Decree, 14 Aug. 1914, Art. 27; Decree, 27 March 1916, Art. 14; Sacred Congregation for the Eastern Church, Decree, 1 March 1929, Art. 36; Decree, 4 May 1930, Art. 41.

22. Eastern clerics and religious should celebrate according to the prescriptions and traditions of their own particular discipline the Divine Office, which has been held in great honor in all the Eastern Churches from ancient times.[27] The faithful also, following the example of their forefathers, should take part devoutly and as much as they can in the Divine Office.

23. The patriarch with his synod, or the supreme authority of each church with his council of prelates, has the right to regulate the languages to be used in the sacred liturgical functions, and also, after reference to the Apostolic See, to approve translations of texts into the vernacular.[28]

RELATIONS WITH THE BRETHREN OF THE SEPARATED CHURCHES

24. The Eastern Churches in communion with the Apostolic See of Rome have the special duty of fostering the unity of all Christians, in particular of Eastern Christians, according to the principles laid down in the decree of this holy council, "On Ecumenism," by prayer above all, by their example, by their scrupulous fidelity to the ancient traditions of the East, by better knowledge of each other, by working together, and by a brotherly attitude towards persons and things.[29]

25. Nothing more should be demanded of separated Eastern Christians who come to Catholic unity under the influence of the grace of the Holy Spirit than what the simple profession of the Catholic faith requires. And since a valid priesthood has been preserved among them, Eastern clerics who come to Catholic unity may exercise their own Orders, in accordance with the regulations laid down by the competent authority.[30]

27. Cf. Council of Laodicea, 347–381, Can. 18; Council of Mar Isaac of the Chaldeans, 410, Can. 15; St. Nerses Glaien of the Armenians, 1166; Innocent IV, Letter *Sub catholicae*, 6 March 1254, sec. 8; Benedict XIV, Constitution *Etsi pastoralis*, 26 May 1742, sec. 7, n. 5; Instruction *Eo quamvis tempore*, 4 May 1745 sec. 42 ff.; and more recent particular Councils: Armenians (1911), Copts (1898), Maronites (1736), Rumanians (1872), Ruthenians (1891), Syrians (1888).
28. From Eastern tradition.
29. From the sense of the Bulls of union of the different Catholic Eastern Churches.
30. An obligation established by the Council regarding our separated Eastern brethren and all Orders or whatever degree, whether of divine or ecclesiastical right.

26. A mutual sharing in sacred things (*communicatio in sacris*), which runs counter to the unity of the Church, or which involves formal adhesion to error or the danger of aberration in the faith,[d] of scandal and of indifferentism, is forbidden by the law of God.[81] However, with regard to our Eastern brethren, pastoral experience shows that various circumstances affecting individuals can and ought to be taken into account, where the unity of the Church is not harmed nor are there dangers to be guarded against, but where the need of salvation and the spiritual good of souls are prime considerations. Therefore, the Catholic Church, by reason of circumstances of time, place and persons, has often followed and still follows a less rigorous course of action, offering to all the means of salvation and a witness to charity among Christians, through a common sharing in the sacraments and in other sacred functions and things.

In view of this,"lest we be an obstacle to the salvation of men through the harshness of our judgment,"[82] and in order to further union with the Eastern Churches separated from us, the holy council has laid down the following lines of action:

27. In view of the principles just noted, Eastern Christians who are separated in good faith from the Catholic Church, if they are rightly disposed and make such request of their own accord, may be given the Sacraments of Penance, the Eucharist and the Anointing of the Sick. Moreover, Catholics also may ask for those same sacraments from non-Catholic ministers in whose church there are valid sacraments, as often as necessity or true spiritual benefit recommends such action, and access to a Catholic priest is physically or morally impossible.[33]

28. Further, given the same principles, a common sharing in sacred functions, things and places, is permitted for a

d. *AAS* 57 (1965), p. 84: *periculum aberrationis in fiede*. The Latin text of this document published separately by the Vatican has misprint here: *periculum aberrationis in fine*, p. 11.—Translator.
31. This doctrine is also held in the separated Chruches.
32. St. Basil the Great, *Canonical Letter to Amphilochius, PG* 32, 669 B.
33. As foundation for this moderation of the law are considered the following: (a) validity of the sacraments; (b) good faith and good disposition; (c) the necessity of eternal salvation; (d) the absence of one's own priest; (e) the exclusion both of the dangers to be avoided and of formal adhesion to error.

just cause between Catholics and their separated Eastern brethren.[34]

29. This more relaxed regulation concerning common sharing in sacred things (*communicatio in sacris*) with our brethren of the separated Eastern Churches is entrusted to the watchfulness and control of local ordinaries. They should consult together, and if it seems good also consult the ordinaries of the separated churches, and so direct relations among Christians by timely and effective precepts and regulations.

CONCLUSION

30. The holy council finds great joy in the earnest and fruitful collaboration of the Eastern and Western Catholic Churches, and at the same time makes the following declaration: All these legal arrangements are made in view of present conditions, until such time as the Catholic Church and the separated Eastern Churches unite together in the fulness of communion.

In the meantime, however, all Christians, Eastern and Western, are strongly urged to pray to God daily with fervor and constancy in order that, by the help of God's most holy Mother, all may be one. They should pray also that the fulness of the strength and consolation of the Holy Spirit the Paraclete may be given to those many Christians, whatever church they belong to, who for their courageous profession of the name of Christ endure suffering and privation. "Let us all love one another with brotherly affection, out-doing one another in showing honor" (Rom. 12:10).

Each and all of these matters which are laid down in the decree have been approved by the Fathers. And we, by the apostolic power given by Christ to us, and in union with the venerable Fathers, approve, decree and prescribe them in the Holy Spirit, and we order that what has been laid down by the Council is to be promulgated to the glory of God.

34. There is question here of so-called "extra-sacramental *communicatio in sacris.*" It is the Council which grants this mitigation, while maintaining what should be maintained.

32

DECREE ON ECUMENISM

Vatican II, *Unitatis Redintegratio*, 21 November, 1964

INTRODUCTION

1. The restoration of unity among all Christians is one of the principal concerns of the Second Vatican Council. Christ the Lord founded one Church and one Church only. However, many Christian communions present themselves to men as the true inheritors of Jesus Christ; all indeed profess to be followers of the Lord but they differ in mind and go their different ways, as if Christ himself were divided.[1] Certainly, such division openly contradicts the will of Christ, scandalizes the world, and damages that most holy cause, the preaching of the Gospel to every creature.

The Lord of Ages nevertheless wisely and patiently follows out the plan of his grace on our behalf, sinners that we are. In recent times he has begun to bestow more generously upon divided Christians remorse over their divisions and longing for unity.

Everywhere large numbers have felt the impulse of this grace, and among our separated brethren also there increases from day to day a movement, fostered by the grace of the Holy Spirit, for the restoration of unity among all Christians. Taking part in this movement, which is called ecumenical, are those who invoke the Triune God and confess Jesus as Lord and Saviour. They do this not merely as individuals but also as members of the corporate groups in which they have heard the Gospel, and which each regards as his Church and indeed, God's. And yet, almost everyone, though in different ways, longs for the one visible Church of God, a Church truly universal and sent forth to the whole world that the world may be converted to the Gospel and so be saved, to the glory of God.

1. Cf. 1 Cor. 1:13.

452

The sacred Council gladly notes all this. It has already declared its teaching on the Church, and now, moved by a desire for the restoration of unity among all the followers of Christ, it wishes to set before all Catholics guidelines, helps and methods, by which they too can respond to the grace of this divine call.

CHAPTER I

CATHOLIC PRINCIPLES ON ECUMENISM

2. What has revealed the love of God among us is that the only-begotten Son of God has been sent by the Father into the world, so that, being made man, he might by his redemption of the entire human race give new life to it and unify it.[2] Before offering himself up as a spotless victim upon the altar of the cross, he prayed to his Father for those who believe: "that all may be one, as you, Father, are in me, and I in you; I pray that they may be one in us, that the world may believe that you sent me" (Jn. 17:21). In his Church he instituted the wonderful sacrament of the Eucharist by which the unity of the Church is both signified and brought about. He gave his followers a new commandment to love one another,[3] and promised the Spirit, their Advocate,[4] who, as Lord and life-giver, should remain with them forever.

After being lifted up on the cross and glorified, the Lord Jesus poured forth the Spirit whom he had promised, and through whom he has called and gathered together the people of the New Covenant, which is the Church, into a unity of faith, hope and charity, as the Apostle teaches us: "There is one body and one Spirit, just as you were called to the one hope of your calling; one Lord, one faith, one baptism" (Eph. 4:4-5). For "all you who have been baptized into Christ have put on Christ . . . for you are all

2. Cf. 1 Jn. 4:9; Col. 1:18–20; Jn. 11:52.
3. Cf. Jn. 13:34.
4. Cf. Jn. 16:7.

one in Christ Jesus" (Gal. 3:27-28). It is the Holy Spirit, dwelling in those who believe and pervading and ruling over the entire Church, who brings about that wonderful communion of the faithful and joins them together so intimately in Christ that he is the principle of the Church's unity. By distributing various kinds of spiritual gifts and ministries,[5] he enriches the Church of Jesus Christ with different functions "in order to equip the saints for the work of service, so as to build up the body of Christ" (Eph. 4:12).

In order to establish this his holy Church everywhere in the world till the end of time, Christ entrusted to the College of the Twelve the task of teaching, ruling and sanctifying.[6] Among their number he chose Peter. And after Peter's confession of faith, he determined that on him he would build his Church; to him he promised the keys of the kingdom of heaven,[7] and after his profession of love, entrusted all his sheep to him to be confirmed in faith[8] and shepherded in perfect unity,[9] with himself, Christ Jesus, forever remaining the chief corner-stone[10] and shepherd of our souls.[11]

It is through the faithful preaching of the Gospel by the Apostles and their successors—the bishops with Peter's successor at their head—through their administering the sacraments, and through their governing in love, that Jesus Christ wishes his people to increase, under the action of the Holy Spirit; and he perfects its fellowship in unity: in the confession of one faith, in the common celebration of divine worship, and in the fraternal harmony of the family of God.

The Church, then, God's only flock, like a standard lifted on high for the nations to see it,[12] ministers the Gospel of peace to all mankind,[13] as it makes its pilgrim way in hope toward its goal, the fatherland above.[14]

5. Cf. 1 Cor. 12:4-11.
6. Cf. Mt. 28:18-20, in conjunction with Jn. 20:21-23.
7. Cf. Mt. 16:19, in conjunction with Mt. 18:18.
8. Cf. Lk. 22:32.
9. Cf. Jn. 21:15-18.
10. Cf. Eph. 2:20.
11. Cf. 1 Pet. 2:25; Vatican Council I, Session 4 (1870), the Constitution *Pastor Aeternus:* Coll. Lac. 7, 482a.
12. Cf. Is. 11:10-12.
13. Cf. Eph. 2:17-18, in conjunction with Mk. 16:15.
14. Cf. 1 Pet. 1:3-9.

This is the sacred mystery of the unity of the Church, in Christ and through Christ, with the Holy Spirit energizing its various functions. The highest exemplar and source of this mystery is the unity, in the Trinity of Persons, of one God, the Father and the Son in the Holy Spirit.

3. In this one and only Church of God from its very beginnings there arose certain rifts,[15] which the Apostle strongly censures as damnable.[16] But in subsequent centuries much more serious dissensions appeared and large communities became separated from full communion with the Catholic Church—for which, often enough, men of both sides were to blame. However, one cannot charge with the sin of the separation those who at present are born into these communities and in them are brought up in the faith of Christ, and the Catholic Church accepts them with respect and affection as brothers. For men who believe in Christ and have been properly baptized are put in some, though imperfect, communion with the Catholic Church. Without doubt, the differences that exist in varying degrees between them and the Catholic Church—whether in doctrine and sometimes in discipline, or concerning the structure of the Church—do indeed create many obstacles, sometimes serious ones, to full ecclesiastical communion. The ecumenical movement is striving to overcome these obstacles. But even in spite of them it remains true that all who have been justified by faith in baptism are incorporated into Christ;[17] they therefore have a right to be called Christians, and with good reason are accepted as brothers by the children of the Catholic Church.[18]

Moreover, some, even very many, of the most significant elements and endowments which together go to build up and give life to the Church itself, can exist outside the visible boundaries of the Catholic Church: the written Word of God; the life of grace; faith, hope and charity, with the other interior gifts of the Holy Spirit, as well as visible elements. All of these, which come from Christ and lead back to him, belong by right to the one Church of Christ.

The brethren divided from us also carry out many liturgical actions of the Christian religion. In ways that vary ac-

15. Cf. 1 Cor. 11:18-19; Gal. 1:6-9; 1 Jn. 2:18-19.
16. Cf. 1 Cor. 1:11 ff.; 11:22.
17. Cf. Council of Florence, Session 8 (1439), the Decree *Exultate Deo:* Mansi 31, 1055 A.
18. Cf. St. Augustine, *In Ps. 32, Enarr. II, 29: PL* 36, 299.

cording to the condition of each Church or community, these liturgical actions most certainly can truly engender a life of grace, and, one must say, can aptly give access to the communion of salvation.

It follows that the separated Churches[19] and communities as such, though we believe they suffer from the defects already mentioned, have been by no means deprived of significance and importance in the mystery of salvation. For the Spirit of Christ has not refrained from using them as means of salvation which derive their efficacy from the very fullness of grace and truth entrusted to the Catholic Church.

Nevertheless, our separated brethren, whether considered as individuals or as communities and Churches, are not blessed with that unity which Jesus Christ wished to bestow on all those to whom he has given new birth into one body, and whom he has quickened to newness of life—that unity which the Holy Scriptures and the ancient Tradition of the Church proclaim. For it is through Christ's Catholic Church alone, which is the universal help towards salvation, that the fullness of the means of salvation can be obtained. It was to the apostolic college alone, of which Peter is the head, that we believe that Our Lord entrusted all the blessings of the New Covenant, in order to establish on earth the one Body of Christ into which all those should be fully incorporated who belong in any way to the people of God. During its pilgrimage on earth, this people, though still in its members liable to sin, is growing in Christ and is guided by God's gentle wisdom, according to his hidden designs, until it shall happily arrive at the fullness of eternal glory in the heavenly Jerusalem.

4. Today, in many parts of the world, under the influence of the grace of the Holy Spirit, many efforts are being made in prayer, word and action to attain that fullness of unity which Jesus Christ desires. The sacred Council exhorts, therefore, all the Catholic faithful to recognize the signs of the times and to take an active and intelligent part in the work of ecumenism.

The term "ecumenical movement" indicates the initiatives and activities encouraged and organized, according to

19. Cf. Lateran Council IV (1215), Constitution IV: Mansi 22, 990; II Council of Lyons (1274), Profession of faith of Michael Palaeologus: Mansi 24, 71 E; Council of Florence, Session 6 (1439), Definition *Laetentur caelis* Mansi 31, 1026 E.

the various needs of the Church and as opportunities offer, to promote Christian unity. These are: first, every effort to avoid expressions, judgments and actions which do not represent the condition of our separated brethren with truth and fairness and so make mutual relations with them more difficult. Then, "dialogue" between competent experts from different Churches and communities; in their meetings, which are organized in a religious spirit, each explains the teaching of his communion in greater depth and brings out clearly its distinctive features. Through such dialogue everyone gains a truer knowledge and more just appreciation of the teaching and religious life of both communions. In addition, these communions engage in that more intensive cooperation in carrying out any duties for the common good of humanity which are demanded by every Christian conscience. They also come together for common prayer, where this is permitted. Finally, all are led to examine their own faithfulness to Christ's will for the Church and, wherever necessary, undertake with vigor the task of renewal and reform.

Such actions, when they are carried out by the Catholic faithful with prudent patience and under the attentive guidance of their bishops, promote justice and truth, concord and collaboration, as well as the spirit of brotherly love and unity. The results will be that, little by little, as the obstacles to perfect ecclesiastical communion are overcome, all Christians will be gathered, in a common celebration of the Eucharist, into the unity of the one and only Church, which Christ bestowed on his Church from the beginning. This unity, we believe, subsists in the Catholic Church as something she can never lose, and we hope that it will continue to increase until the end of time.

However, it is evident that the work of preparing and reconciling those individuals who wish for full Catholic communion is of its nature distinct from ecumenical action. But there is no opposition between the two, since both proceed from the marvellous ways of God.

In ecumenical work, Catholics must assuredly be concerned for their separated brethren, praying for them, keeping them informed about the Church, making the first approaches toward them. But their primary duty is to make a careful and honest appraisal of whatever needs to be renewed and done in the Catholic household itself, in order that its life may bear witness more clearly and faithfully to the teachings and institutions which have been handed down from Christ through the apostles.

For although the Catholic Church has been endowed with all divinely revealed truth and with all means of grace, yet its members fail to live by them with all the fervor that they should. As a result the radiance of the Church's face shines less brightly in the eyes of our separated brethren and of the world at large, and the growth of God's kingdom is retarded. Every Catholic must therefore aim at Christian perfection[20] and, each according to his station, play his part, that the Church, which bears in her own body the humility and dying of Jesus,[21] may daily be more purified and renewed, against the day when Chirst will present her to himself in all her glory without spot or wrinkle.[22]

While preserving unity in essentials, let everyone in the Church, according to the office entrusted to him, preserve a proper freedom in the various forms of spiritual life and discipline, in the variety of liturgical rites, and even in the theological elaborations of revealed truth. In all things let charity prevail. If they are true to this course of action, they will be giving ever richer expression to the authentic catholicity and apostolicity of the Church.

On the other hand, Catholics must gladly acknowledge and esteem the truly Christian endowments for our common heritage which are to be found among our separated brethren. It is right and salutary to recognize the riches of Christ and virtuous works in the lives of others who are bearing witness to Christ, sometimes even to the shedding of their blood. For God is always wonderful in his works and worthy of all praise.

Nor should we forget that anything wrought by the grace of the Holy Spirit in the hearts of our separated brethren can contribute to our own edification. Whatever is truly Christian is never contrary to what genuinely belongs to the faith; indeed, it can always bring a more perfect realization of the very mystery of Christ and the Church.

Nevertheless, the divisions among Christians prevent the Church from realizing the fullness of catholicity proper to her in those of her sons who, though joined to her by baptism, are yet separated from full communion with her. Furthermore, the Church herself finds it more difficult to

20. Cf. Jas. 1:4; Rom. 12:1–2.
21. Cf. 2 Cor. 4:10; Phil. 2:5–8.
22. Cf. Eph. 5:27.

express in actual life her full catholicity in all its aspects.

This sacred Council is gratified to note that the participation by the Catholic faithful in ecumenical work is growing daily. It commends this work to the bishops everywhere in the world for their diligent promotion and prudent guidance.

CHAPTER II

THE PRACTICE OF ECUMENISM

5. The concern for restoring unity involves the whole Church, faithful and clergy alike. It extends to everyone, according to the talent of each, whether it be exercised in daily Christian living or in theological and historical studies. This concern itself already reveals to some extent the bond of brotherhood existing among all Christians, and it leads toward full and perfect unity, in accordance with what God in his kindness wills.

6. Every renewal of the Church[23] essentially consists in an increase of fidelity to her own calling. Undoubtedly this explains the dynamism of the movement toward unity.

Christ summons the Church, as she goes her pilgrim way, to that continual reformation of which she always has need, insofar as she is an institution of men here on earth. Consequently, if, in various times and circumstances, there have been deficiencies in moral conduct or in Church discipline, or even in the way that Church teaching has been formulated—to be carefully distinguished from the deposit of faith itself—these should be set right at the opportune moment and in the proper way.

Church renewal therefore has notable ecumenical importance. Already this renewal is taking place in various spheres of the Church's life: the biblical and liturgical movements, the preaching of the Word of God and catechetics, the apostolate of the laity, new forms of religious life and the spirituality of married life, and the Church's social teaching and activity. All these should be considered as

23. Cf. V Lateran Council, Session 12 (1517), Constitution *Constituti:* Mansi 32, 988 B-C.

promises and guarantees for the future progress of ecumenism.

7. There can be no ecumenism worthy of the name without interior conversion. For it is from newness of attitudes of mind,[24] from self-denial and unstinted love, that desires of unity take their rise and develop in a mature way. We should therefore pray to the Holy Spirit for the grace to be genuinely self-denying, humble, gentle in the service of others and to have an attitude of brotherly generosity toward them. The Apostle of the Gentiles says: "I, therefore, a prisoner for the Lord, beg you to lead a life worthy of the calling to which you have been called, with all humility and meekness, with patience, forbearing one another in love, eager to maintain the unity of the spirit in the bond of peace" (Eph. 4:1-3). This exhortation is directed especially to those raised to sacred orders in order that the mission of Christ may be continued. He came among us "not to be served but to serve" (Mt. 20:28).

St. John has testified: "If we say we have not sinned, we make him a liar, and his word is not in us" (1 Jn. 1:10). This holds good for sins against unity. Thus, in humble prayer we beg pardon of God and of our separated brethren, just as we forgive them that offend us.

The faithful should remember that they promote union among Christians better, that indeed they live it better, when they try to live holier lives according to the Gospel. For the closer their union with the Father, the Word, and the Spirit, the more deeply and easily will they be able to grow in mutual brotherly love.

8. This change of heart and holiness of life, along with public and private prayer for the unity of Christians, should be regarded as the soul of the whole ecumenical movement, and merits the name, "spiritual ecumenism."

It is a recognized custom for Catholics to meet for frequent recourse to that prayer for the unity of the Church with which the Saviour himself on the eve of his death so fervently appealed to his Father: "That they may all be one" (Jn. 17:20).

In certain circumstances, such as in prayer services "for unity" and during ecumenical gatherings, it is allowable, indeed desirable that Catholics should join in prayer with their separated brethren. Such prayers in common are cer-

24. Cf. Eph. 4:23.

tainly a very effective means of petitioning for the grace of unity, and they are a genuine expression of the ties which still bind Catholics to their separated brethren. "For where two or three are gathered together in my name, there am I in the midst of them" (Mt. 18:20).

Yet worship in common (*communicatio in sacris*) is not to be considered as a means to be used indiscriminately for the restoration of unity among Christians. There are two main principles upon which the practice of such common worship depends: first, that of the unity of the Church which ought to be expressed; and second, that of the sharing in the means of grace. The expression of unity very generally forbids common worship. Grace to be obtained sometimes commends it. The concrete course to be adopted, when all the circumstances of time, place and persons have been duly considered, is left to the prudent decision of the local episcopal authority, unless the bishops' conference according to its own statutes, or the Holy See, has determined otherwise.

9. We must become familiar with the outlook of our separated brethren. Study is absolutely required for this, and it should be pursued in fidelity to the truth and with a spirit of good will. Catholics who already have a proper grounding need to acquire a more adequate understanding of the respective doctrines of our separated brethren, their history, their spiritual and liturgical life, their religious psychology and cultural background. Most valuable for this purpose are meetings of the two sides—especially for discussion of theological problems—where each can treat with the other on an equal footing, provided that those who take part in them under the guidance of the authorities are truly competent. From such dialogue will emerge still more clearly what the situation of the Catholic Church really is. In this way, too, we will better understand the outlook of our separated brethren and more aptly present our own belief.

10. Sacred theology and other branches of knowledge, especially those of a historical nature, must be taught with due regard for the ecumenical point of view, so that they may correspond as exactly as possible with the facts.

It is important that future pastors and priests should have mastered a theology that has been carefully elaborated in this way and not polemically, especially in what concerns the relations of separated brethren with the Catholic

Church. For it is upon the formation which priests receive that so largely depends the necessary instruction and spiritual formation of the faithful and of religious.

Moreover, Catholics engaged in missionary work in the same territories as other Christians ought to know, particularly in these times, the problems and the benefits which affect their apostolate because of the ecumenical movement.

11. The manner and order in which Catholic belief is expressed should in no way become an obstacle to dialogue with our brethren. It is, of course, essential that the doctrine be clearly presented in its entirety. Nothing is so foreign to the spirit of ecumenism as a false irenicism which harms the purity of Catholic doctrine and obscures its genuine and certain meaning.

At the same time, Catholic belief must be explained more profoundly and precisely, in such a way and in such terms that our separated brethren can also really understand it.

Furthermore, in ecumenical dialogue, Catholic theologians, standing fast by the teaching of the Church yet searching together with separated brethren into the divine mysteries, should do so with love for the truth, with charity, and with humility. When comparing doctrines with one another, they should remember that in Catholic doctrine there exists an order or "hierarchy" of truths, since they vary in their relation to the foundation of the Christian faith. Thus the way will be opened whereby this kind of "fraternal rivalry" will incite all to a deeper realization and a clearer expression of the unfathomable riches of Christ.[25]

12. Before the whole world let all Christians confess their faith in God, one and three, in the incarnate Son of God, our Redeemer and Lord. United in their efforts, and with mutual respect, let them bear witness to our common hope which does not play us false. Since cooperation in social matters is so widespread today, all men without exception are called to work together; with much greater reason is this true of all who believe in God, but most of all, it is especially true of all Christians, since they bear the seal of Christ's name. Cooperation among Christians vividly expresses that bond which already unites them, and it sets in clearer relief the features of Christ the Servant. Such cooperation, which has already begun in many countries, should

25. Cf. Eph. 3:8.

be developed more and more, particularly in regions where social and technological evolution is taking place. It should contribute to a just appreciation of the dignity of the human person, to the promotion of the blessings of peace, the application of Gospel principles to social life, and the advancement of the arts and sciences in a truly Christian spirit. It should use every possible means to relieve the afflictions of our times, such as famine and natural disasters, illiteracy and poverty, lack of housing, and the unequal distribution of wealth. Through such cooperation, all believers in Christ are able to learn easily how they can understand each other better and esteem each other more, and how the road to the unity of Christians may be made smooth.

Chapter III

CHURCHES AND ECCLESIAL COMMUNITIES SEPARATED FROM THE ROMAN APOSTOLIC SEE

13. We now turn our attention to the two principal types of division which affect the seamless robe of Christ.

The first divisions occurred in the East, either because of the dispute over the dogmatic formulae of the Councils of Ephesus and Chalcedon, or later by the dissolving of ecclesiastical communion between the Eastern Patriarchates and the Roman See.

Still other divisions arose in the West more than four centuries later. These stemmed from the events which are commonly referred to as the Reformation. As a result, many communions, national or confessional, were separated from the Roman See. Among those in which Catholic traditions and institutions in part continue to exist, the Anglican communion occupies a special place.

These various divisions, however, differ greatly from one another not only by reason of their origin, place and time, but still more by reason of the nature and seriousness of questions concerning faith and Church order. Therefore, without minimizing the differences between the various Christian bodies, and without overlooking the bonds which continue to exist among them in spite of the division, the Council has decided to propose the following considerations for prudent ecumenical action.

I. THE SPECIAL POSITION OF THE EASTERN CHURCHES

14. For many centuries the Churches of the East and of the West went their own ways, though a brotherly communion of faith and sacramental life bound them together. If disagreements in faith and discipline arose among them, the Roman See acted by common consent as moderator.

This Council gladly reminds everyone of one highly significant fact among others: in the East there flourish many particular local Churches; among them the Patriarchal Churches hold first place, and of them many glory in taking their origins from the apostles themselves. Hence, of primary concern and care among the Orientals has been, and still is, the preservation in a communion of faith and charity of those family ties which ought to exist between local Churches, as between sisters.

From their very origins the Churches of the East have had a treasury from which the Church of the West has drawn largely for its liturgy, spiritual tradition and jurisprudence. Nor must we underestimate the fact that the basic dogmas of the Christian faith concerning the Trinity and the Word of God made flesh from the Virgin Mary were defined in Ecumenical Councils held in the East. To preserve this faith, these Churches have suffered, and still suffer much.

However, the heritage handed down by the apostles was received differently and in different forms, so that from the very beginnings of the Church its development varied from region to region and also because of differing mentalities and ways of life. These reasons, plus external causes, as well as the lack of charity and mutual understanding, left the way open to divisions.

For this reason the Council urges all, but especially those who commit themselves to the work for the restoration of the full communion that is desired between the Eastern Churches and the Catholic Church, to give due consideration to this special feature of the origin and growth of the Churches of the East, and to the character of the relations which obtained between them and the Roman See before

the separation, and to form for themselves a correct evaluation of these facts. The careful observation of this will
greatly contribute to the dialogue in view.

15. Everyone knows with what love the Eastern Christians
celebrate the sacred liturgy, especially the eucharistic mystery, source of the Church's life and pledge of future glory.
In this mystery the faithful, united with their bishops, have
access to God the Father through the Son, the Word made
flesh who suffered and was glorified, in the outpouring of
the Holy Spirit. And so, made "sharers of the divine nature" (2 Pet. 1:4), they enter into communion with the
most holy Trinity. Hence, through the celebration of the
Eucharist of the Lord in each of these Churches, the
Church of God is built up and grows in stature,[26] and
through concelebration, their communion with one another
is made manifest.

In this liturgical worship, the Eastern Christians pay high
tribute, in beautiful hymns of praise, to Mary ever Virgin,
whom the ecumenical Synod of Ephesus solemnly proclaimed to be the holy Mother of God in order that Christ
might be truly and properly acknowledged as Son of God
and Son of Man, according to the scriptures. They also give
homage to the saints, among them the Fathers of the universal Church.

These Churches, although separated from us, yet possess
true sacraments, above all—by apostolic succession—the
priesthood and the Eucharist, whereby they are still joined
to us in closest intimacy. Therefore some worship in common (*communicatio in sacris*), given suitable circumstances and the approval of Church authority, is not merely
possible but is encouraged.

Moreover, in the East are to be found the riches of those
spiritual traditions which are given expression in monastic
life especially. From the glorious times of the holy Fathers,
that monastic spirituality flourished in the East which later
flowed over into the Western world, and there provided a
source from which Latin monastic life took its rise and has
often drawn fresh vigor ever since. Therefore, it is earnestly
recommended that Catholics avail themselves more often of
the spiritual riches of the Eastern Fathers which lift up the
whole man to the contemplation of divine mysteries.

Everyone should realize that it is of supreme importance

26. Cf. St. John Chrysostom, *In Ioannem Homelia XLVI*, PG 59,
260–262.

to understand, venerate, preserve and foster the rich liturgical and spiritual heritage of the Eastern Churches in order faithfully to preserve the fullness of Christian tradition, and to bring about reconciliation between Eastern and Western Christians.

16. From the earliest times the Churches of the East followed their own disciplines, sanctioned by the holy Fathers, by Synods, and even by Ecumenical Councils. Far from being an obstacle to the Church's unity, such diversity of customs and observances only adds to her beauty and contributes greatly to carrying out her mission, as has already been stated. To remove all shadow of doubt, then, this holy Synod solemnly declares that the Churches of the East, while keeping in mind the necessary unity of the whole Church, have the power to govern themselves according to their own disciplines, since these are better suited to the character of their faithful and better adapted to foster the good of souls. The perfect observance of this traditional principle—which indeed has not always been observed—is a prerequisite for any restoration of union.

17. What has already been said about legitimate variety we are pleased to apply to differences in theological expressions of doctrine. In the study of revealed truth East and West have used different methods and approaches in understanding and confessing divine things. It is hardly surprising, then, if sometimes one tradition has come nearer to a full appreciation of some aspects of a mystery of revelation than the other, or has expressed them better. In such cases, these various theological formulations are often to be considered complementary rather than conflicting. With regard to the authentic theological traditions of the Orientals, we must recognize that they are admirably rooted in Holy Scripture, are fostered and given expression in liturgical life, are nourished by the living tradition of the apostles and by the works of the Fathers and spiritual writers of the East; they are directed toward a right ordering of life, indeed, toward a full contemplation of Christian truth.

This sacred Council thanks God that many Eastern children of the Catholic Church preserve this heritage and wish to express it more faithfully and completely in their lives, and are already living in full communion with their brethren who follow the tradition of the West. But it declares that this entire heritage of spirituality and liturgy, of discipline and theology, in the various traditions, belongs to the full catholic and apostolic character of the Church.

18. After taking all these factors into consideration, this sacred Council confirms what previous Councils and Roman Pontiffs have proclaimed: in order to restore communion and unity or preserve them, one must "impose no burden beyond what is indispensable" (Acts 15:28). It is the Council's urgent desire that every effort should be made toward the gradual realization of this unity in the various organizations and living activities of the Church, especially by prayer and by fraternal dialogue on points of doctrine and the more pressing pastoral problems of our time. Similarly, to the pastors and faithful of the Catholic Church, it commends close relations with those no longer living in the East but far from their homeland, so that friendly collaboration with them may increase in a spirit of love, without bickering or rivalry. If this task is carried on wholeheartedly, the Council hopes that with the removal of the wall dividing the Eastern and Western Church at last there may be but one dwelling, firmly established on the cornerstone, Christ Jesus, who will make both one.[27]

II. THE SEPARATED CHURCHES AND ECCLESIAL COMMUNITIES IN THE WEST

19. The Churches and ecclesial communities which were separated from the Apostolic See of Rome during the grave crisis that began in the West at the end of the Middle Ages or in later times, are bound to the Catholic Church by a specially close relationship as a result of the long span of earlier centuries when the Christian people had lived in ecclesiastical communion.

But since these Churches and ecclesial communities differ considerably not only from us, but also among themselves, due to their different origins and convictions in doctrine and spiritual life, the task of describing them adequately is extremely difficult; we do not propose to do it here.

Although the ecumenical movement and the desire for peace with the Catholic Church have not yet taken hold everywhere, it is nevertheless our hope that the ecumenical

27. Cf. Council of Florence, Sess. VI (1439), Definition *Laetentur caeli:* Mansi 31, 1026 E.

spirit and mutual esteem will gradually increase among all men.

At the same time, however, one should recognize that between these Churches and ecclesial communities, on the one hand, and the Catholic Church on the other, there are very weighty differences not only of a historical, sociological, psychological and cultural character, but especially in the interpretation of revealed truth. To facilitate entering into the ecumenical dialogue in spite of those differences, we wish to set down in what follows some considerations which can, and indeed should serve as a basis and encouragement for such dialogue.

20. Our thoughts are concerned first of all with those Christians who openly confess Jesus Christ as God and Lord and as the only Mediator between God and man for the glory of the one God, the Father, the Son and the Holy Spirit. We are indeed aware that there exist considerable differences from the doctrine of the Catholic Church even concerning Christ the Word of God made flesh and the work of redemption, and thus concerning the mystery and ministry of the Church and the role of Mary in the work of salvation. But we rejoice that our separated brethren look to Christ as the source and center of ecclesiastical communion. Their longing for union with Christ impels them ever more to seek unity, and also to bear witness to their faith among the peoples of the earth.

21. A love and reverence—almost a cult—of Holy Scripture leads our brethren to a constant and diligent study of the sacred text. For the Gospel "is the power of God for salvation to everyone who has faith, to the Jew first and then to the Greek" (Rom. 1:16).

While invoking the Holy Spirit, they seek in these very scriptures God as he speaks to them in Christ, the one whom the prophets foretold, the Word of God made flesh for us. In the scriptures they contemplate the life of Christ, as well as the teachings and the actions of the Divine Master for the salvation of men, in particular the mysteries of his death and resurrection.

But when Christians separated from us affirm the divine authority of the sacred books, they think differently from us—different ones in different ways—about the relationship between the scriptures and the Church. For in the Church, according to Catholic belief, its authentic teaching office has a special place in expounding and preaching the written Word of God.

Nevertheless, in the dialogue itself, the sacred Word is a precious instrument in the mighty hand of God for attaining to that unity which the Saviour holds out to all men.

22. By the sacrament of Baptism, whenever it is properly conferred in the way the Lord determined and received with the proper dispositions of soul, man becomes truly incorporated into the crucified and glorified Christ and is reborn to a sharing of the divine life, as the Apostle says: "For you were buried together with him in baptism, and in him also rose again through faith in the working of God who raised him from the dead."[28]

Baptism, therefore, constitutes the sacramental bond of unity existing among all who through it are reborn. But baptism, of itself, is only a beginning, a point of departure, for it is wholly directed toward the acquiring of fullness of life in Christ. Baptism is thus ordained toward a complete profession of faith, a complete incorporation into the system of salvation such as Christ himself willed it to be, and finally, toward a complete integration into eucharistic communion.

Although the ecclesial communities separated from us lack the fullness of unity with us which flows from baptism, and although we believe they have not preserved the proper reality of the eucharistic mystery in its fullness, especially because of the absence of the sacrament of Orders, nevertheless when they commemorate the Lord's death and resurrection in the Holy Supper, they profess that it signifies life in communion with Christ and await his coming in glory. For these reasons, the doctrine about the Lord's Supper, about the other sacraments, worship, and ministry in the Church, should form subjects of dialogue.

23. The Christian way of life of these brethren is nourished by faith in Christ. It is strengthened by the grace of baptism and the hearing of the Word of God. This way of life expresses itself in private prayer, in meditation on the scriptures, in the life of a Christian family, and in the worship of the community gathered together to praise God. Furthermore, their worship sometimes displays notable features of a liturgy once shared in common.

28. Cf. Rom. 6:4.

The faith by which they believe in Christ bears fruit in praise and thanksgiving for the benefits received from the hands of God. Joined to it is a lively sense of justice and a true charity toward others. This active faith has been responsible for many organizations for the relief of spiritual and material distress, the furtherance of education of youth, the improvement of social conditions of life, and the promotion of peace throughout the world.

And if in moral matters there are many Christians who do not always understand the Gospel in the same way as Catholics, and do not admit the same solutions for the more difficult problems of modern society, they nevertheless want to cling to Christ's word as the source of Christian virtue and to obey the command of the Apostle: "Whatever you do in word or in work, do all in the name of the Lord Jesus, giving thanks to God the Father through him" (Col. 3:17). Hence, the ecumenical dialogue could start with the moral application of the Gospel.

24. Now, after this brief exposition of the conditions under which ecumenical activity may be practiced, and of the principles by which it is to be guided, we confidently look to the future, This sacred Council urges the faithful to abstain from any frivolous or imprudent zeal, for these can cause harm to true progress toward unity. Their ecumenical activity cannot be other than fully and sincerely Catholic, that is, loyal to the truth we have received from the Apostles and the Fathers, and in harmony with the faith which the Catholic Church has always professed, and at the same time tending toward that fullness in which our Lord wants his Body to grow in the course of time.

This sacred Council firmly hopes that the intiatives of the sons of the Catholic Church, joined with those of the separated brethren, will go forward, without obstructing the ways of divine Providence, and without prejudging the future inspirations of the Holy Spirit. Further, this Council declares that it realizes that this holy objective—the reconciliation of all Christians in the unity of the one and only Church of Christ—transcends human powers and gifts. It therefore places its hope entirely in the prayer of Christ for the Church, in the love of the Father for us, and in the power of the Holy Spirit. "And hope does not disappoint, because God's love has been poured forth in our hearts through the Holy Spirit who has been given to us" (Rom. 5:5).

33

THE COMMON DECLARATION OF POPE PAUL VI AND PATRIARCH ATHENAGORAST[a]

Paul VI and Athenagoras I, 7 December, 1965

1. Full of gratitude to God for the favor which is mercifully granted them in their brotherly meeting in those holy places where the mystery of our salvation was accomplished by the death and resurrection of the Lord Jesus, and where the Church was born by the outpouring of the Holy Spirit, Pope Paul VI and Patriarch Athenagoras I have not lost sight of the intention which they held from then onwards, each for his part, never to omit in the future any of those gestures inspired by charity which might contribute towards the fraternal relationships thus initiated between the Roman Catholic Church and the Orthodox Church of Constantinople. They believe that they are thus responding to the call of divine grace, which today requires that the Roman Catholic Church and the Orthodox Church, as well as all Christians, overcome their differences, so as to be once again "one" as the Lord Jesus asked of his Father for them.

2. Among the obstacles to be found in the way of the development of these brotherly relationships of trust and esteem, there is the memory of those painful decisions, acts and incidents which led in 1054 to the sentence of excommunication delivered against Patriarch Michael Cerularius and two other persons by the legates of the Roman See led by Cardinal Humbert, legates who were themselves in turn objects of a similar sentence on the side of the Patriarch and the Synod of Constantinople.

3. One cannot pretend that these events were not what they were in that particularly troubled period of history. But now that today a more calm and equitable judgment

a. Translated from the French text in *AAS* 58 (1966) pp. 20–21.

has been brought to bear on them, it is important to recognize the excesses with which they were tainted and which later led to consequences which, as far as we can judge, went much further than their authors had intended or expected. Their censures were aimed at the persons concerned and not the Churches; they were not meant to break ecclesiastical communion between the sees of Rome and Constantinople.

4. This is why Pope Paul VI and Patriarch Athenagoras I with his synod, certain that they are expressing the common desire for justice and the unanimous sentiment of charity on the part of their faithful, and remembering the command of the Lord: "If you are offering your gift at the altar, and there remember that your brother has something against you, leave your gift before the altar and go first to be reconciled to your brother" (Mt. 5:23–24), declare with one accord that:

(a) They regret the offensive words, the reproaches without foundation and the reprehensible gestures which on both sides marked or accompanied the sad events of that period;

(b) They also regret and wish to erase from the memory and midst of the Church the sentences of excommunication which followed them, and whose memory has acted as an obstacle to a rapprochement in charity down to our own day, and to consign them to oblivion;

(c) Finally they deplore the troublesome precedents and the later events which, under the influence of various factors, among them lack of understanding and mutual hostility, eventually led to the effective rupture of ecclesiastical communion.

5. This reciprocal act of justice and forgiveness, as Pope Paul VI and Patriarch Athenagoras I with his synod are aware, cannot suffice to put an end to the differences, ancient or more recent, which remain between the Roman Catholic Church and the Orthodox Church and which, by the action of the Holy Spirit, will be overcome, thanks to the purification of hearts, regret for historical errors, and an effective determination to arrive at a common understanding and expression of the apostolic faith and its demands.

In accomplishing this act, however, they hope that it will be pleasing to God, who is prompt to pardon us when we forgive one another, and recognized by the whole Christian world, but especially by the Roman Catholic Church and the Orthodox Church together, as the expression of a sincere mutual desire for reconciliation and as an invitation to pursue, in a spirit of mutual trust, esteem and charity, the dialogue which will lead them, with the help of God, to live once again for the greater good of souls and the coming of the Kingdom of God, in the full communion of faith, of brotherly concord and of a sacramental life which existed between them throughout the first millenium of the life of the Church.

34

INSTRUCTION ON MIXED MARRIAGES[a]

S.C.D.F., *Matrimonii Sacramentum,* 18 March, 1966

The sacrament of matrimony was established by Christ as a symbol of his own union with the Church, to give full scope to its sacred power and to enable it truly to become for husband and wife a great mystery (see Eph. 5:32), whereby they might express in their own lives the love by which Christ gave himself for the Church. For this reason, marriage demands the fullest and most perfect agreement between the partners, especially where religion is concerned. "The link between souls weakens, or they drift apart, when they cease to be of one mind and heart with regard to the ultimate and highest values—with regard to religious truth and sentiment, that is to say."[1] This is why the Catholic Church takes with the utmost seriousness its obligation to guard the faith both of the marriage partners and of their children. It does its best to ensure that Catholics marry Catholics.

The Church's discipline with regard to mixed marriages, as laid down in Canon Law, clearly demonstrates this careful vigilance. It takes the form of two impediments to marriage: mixed religion and disparity of worship. The first of these forbids marriage between a Catholic and a baptized non-Catholic, while not taking from the validity of such a marriage.[2] The second renders invalid a marriage between a Catholic and a non-baptized person.[3] Another proof of the Church's solicitude for the holiness of Christian marriage is the juridical form by which consent is manifested. It is true that in the past several forms were permitted, but care was always taken to rule out clandestine marriages.

Pastors should be guided by this tradition and should

a. Translated by A.F. from *AAS* 58 (1966), pp. 235–239.
1. Pius XI, Encyclical Letter *Casti Connubii.*
2. Canons 1060–1064.
3. Canons 1070–1071.

teach the faithful the religious value and the worth of this sacrament. They should seriously warn them of the difficulties and the dangers involved in marrying a non-Catholic Christian and, much more so, a non-Christian. They should employ all appropriate means to ensure that their young people marry Catholics.

At the same time it must be borne in mind that in a short space of time great changes have taken place in social and family life. These have made more difficult the observance of the canonical discipline with regard to mixed marriages, more difficult than in former times.

Nowadays there is more frequent contact between Catholics and non-Catholics, many of whom share a common life-style and customs. Friendships can more easily develop among them, and it is a fact of experience that mixed marriages become more common.

Today more than ever the Church's pastoral solicitude demands that in mixed marriages the sanctity of marriage according to Catholic teaching and the faith of the partners should be safeguarded. It demands, too, that the Catholic education of the children be safeguarded with the greatest possible diligence and effectiveness.

Such pastoral care is made even more necessary in view of the fact that among non-Catholics there is a diversity of views with regard both to the essence of matrimony and its properties, especially indissolubility, and thus also with regard to indissolubility, divorce and remarriage after a (civil) divorce.

The Church therefore deems it her duty to protect her members lest their faith be endangered or lest they suffer spiritual or material damage.

Those who intend to get married therefore should be carefully instructed about the nature, the properties and the obligations of marriage, and the dangers to be avoided.

Further, in this context we must not lose sight of the code of behavior toward our separated brethren which has been solemnly established by the Second Vatican Council in the Decree on Ecumenism. This would seem to suggest a mitigation of the rigor of the existing discipline on mixed marriages, not with regard to what is of divine law, but with regard to certain ecclesiastical regulations which our separated brethren find offensive.

It will be readily appreciated that this grave question did not escape the attention of the Second Ecumenical Council of the Vatican, which was called by Pope John XXIII of happy memory to discuss the problems of our time. In fact the Council Fathers had a number of things to say on the matter which, as is right, have been attentively considered.

We therefore consulted the pastors concerned with these matters and considered all things very carefully. The two impediments, of mixed religion and disparity of worship, remain in force, though local ordinaries have been granted the faculty of dispensing from them, in accordance with the Apostolic Letter, *Pastorale Munus*, nn. 19 and 20, for a grave cause and provided the law is otherwise observed. The law of the Oriental Churches remains likewise unaffected. The following provisions have been established, by the authority of Pope Paul VI, to be inserted into the revised code of Canon Law if they stand the test of experience:

I

1. The need to safeguard the faith of the Catholic partner must be kept constantly in mind and the children's education in the Catholic faith must be ensured.[4]

2. The Catholic partner's local ordinary or parish priest must be careful to impress on him or her seriously the obligation of ensuring the baptism and education in the Catholic religion of the children. The Catholic party will make an express promise that he or she will fulfil the obligation.

3. The non-Catholic partner should, with due delicacy, but clearly, be informed of the Catholic teaching on the dignity of marriage and especially with regard to its principal characteristics, unity and dissolubility.

The non-Catholic party should also be informed of the grave obligation on the Catholic party to safeguard, preserve and profess his or her faith and to baptize and educate in it such children as may be born.

In order to ensure the fulfilment of this obligation, the non-Catholic party is to be invited to promise, sincerely and openly, that at the very least he or she will not impede it. If, however, the non-Catholic party feels that such a promise would go against his or her own conscience, the ordinary should refer the matter to the Holy See, with all the details.

4. See Canon 1060.

4. Ordinarily these promises should be given in writing. However, it is for the ordinary to decide whether, as a general rule or in individual instances, the promises should be made in writing or not, by the Catholic party, the non-Catholic party, or both. It is also for the ordinary to decide how they are to be inserted in the marriage documents.

II

It does happen in some places that the Catholic education of the children is impeded, not so much by the free choice of the parents as by the people's laws and customs, which those intending to marry have to obey. In that case the local ordinary may, all things considered, dispense from that impediment provided that the Catholic partner is prepared, to the best of his or her knowledge and ability, to ensure Catholic baptism and a Catholic education for all the children, and that the good will of the non-Catholic partner is guaranteed.

In granting this concession, the Church is moved by the hope of the repeal of civil laws which run counter to human liberty, such as those which forbid the Catholic education of children or the practice of the Catholic religion, and that thus the natural law will come into force in these matters.

III

The canonical form, prescribed in Canon 1094, must be observed in mixed marriages. This is necessary for validity. If difficulties should arise, the ordinary should refer the matter to the Holy See, outlining all the circumstances.

IV

With regard to the liturgical form, setting Canon 1103, par. 2, and Canon 1109, par. 3, to one side, local ordinaries may permit the celebration of mixed marriages with sacred rites and with the customary blessings and sermon.

V

It is absolutely forbidden to celebrate marriage before a Catholic priest and a non-Catholic minister, each of them performing his own rite, at the same time.

However, when the religious ceremony has been finished, there is no reason why the non-Catholic minister should not deliver an address of congratulation and encouragement and recite some prayers with the non-Catholics. All this, however, needs the approval of the local ordinary, and care must be taken to avoid the danger of provoking comment.

VI

Local ordinaries and parish priests should be careful to ensure that mixed-marriage families should lead holy lives, in keeping with the promises given, especially in the matter of imparting Catholic doctrine and morality to the children.

VII

The excommunication incurred, according to Canon 2319, par. 1, n. 1, by those who marry before a non-Catholic minister, is now abolished. The effects of this abolition are retroactive.

The thought and intention behind these regulations is as we described above: to meet the needs of the faithful in our day and to promote cordial relations between Catholics and non-Catholics.

Those who are charged with imparting Catholic doctrine to the faithful, and this is especially true of parish priests, should devote themselves wholeheartedly and constantly to this.

This they should endeavor to do, in all charity toward Catholics and with due reverence for the others, for the non-Catholics, that is to say, and for those honestly persuaded of their own position.

Catholics should endeavor to strengthen and increase their own faith; following the path of Christian virtue in their family lives, they should afford a shining example to their non-Catholic partner and to their children.

35

THE JOINT DECLARATION ON COOPERATION[a]

Paul VI and Archbishop Michael Ramsey, 22 March, 1966

In this city of Rome, from which St. Augustine was sent by St. Gregory to England and there founded the cathedral see of Canterbury, towards which the eyes of all Anglicans now turn as the center of their Christian Communion, His Holiness Pope Paul VI and His Grace Michael Ramsey, Archbishop of Canterbury, representing the Anglican Communion, have met to exchange fraternal greetings.

At the conclusion of their meeting they give thanks to Almighty God who by the action of his Spirit has in these latter years created a new atmosphere of Christian fellowship between the Roman Catholic Church and the Churches of the Anglican Communion.

This encounter of 23 March 1966 marks a new stage in the development of fraternal relations, based upon Christian charity, and of sincere efforts to remove the causes of conflict and reestablish unity.

In willing obedience to the command of Christ who bade his disciples love one another, they declare that, with his help, they wish to leave in the hands of the God of mercy all that in the past has been opposed to this precept of charity, and that they make their own the mind of the apostle which he expresses in these words: "Forgetting those things which are behind, and reaching forth unto those things which are before, I press towards the mark for the prize of high calling of God in Christ Jesus." (Phil. 3:13–14).

They affirm their desire that all those Christians who belong to these two Communions may be animated by these same sentiments of respect, esteem and fraternal love; and in order to help these develop to the full, they intend to in-

a. English text from *AAS* 58 (1966) pp. 286–288.

augurate between the Roman Catholic Church and the whole Anglican Communion a serious dialogue which, founded on the Gospels and on the ancient common traditions may lead to unity in truth for which Christ prayed.

The dialogue should include not only theological matters such as scripture, tradition and liturgy, but also matters of practical difficulty felt on either side. His Holiness the Pope and His Grace the Archbishop of Canterbury are, indeed, aware that serious obstacles stand in the way of a restoration of complete communion of faith and sacramental life; nevertheless, they are of one mind in their determination to promote responsible contacts between their Communions in all those spheres of Church life where collaboration is likely to lead to greater understanding and a deeper charity, and to strive in common to find solutions for all the great problems that face the Church in the world of today.

Through such collaboration, by the grace of God the Father and in the light of the Holy Spirit, may the prayer of our Lord Jesus Christ for unity among his disciples be brought nearer to fulfilment, and with progress towards unity may there be a strengthening of peace in the world, the peace that only he can grant who gives, "the peace that passeth all understanding," together with the blessing of Almighty God, Father, Son and Holy Spirit, that it may abide with all men for ever.

36

MARRIAGES BETWEEN ROMAN CATHOLICS AND ORTHODOX[a]

S.C.O.C., *Crescens Matrimoniorum,* 22 February, 1967

Because of the increasing frequency of mixed marriages between Oriental Catholics and non-Catholic Oriental Christians in the Eastern patriarchates and eparchies as well as in Latin dioceses, and the necessity of coping with the inconveniences resulting from this, the Second Vatican Ecumenical Council decreed: "When Oriental Catholics enter into marriage with baptized non-Catholic Orientals the canonical form for the celebration of such marriages obliges only for lawfulness: for their validity, the presence of a sacred minister suffices, as long as the other requirements of the law are observed." (Decree on the Eastern Catholic Churches, n. 18).

In the exceptional circumstances of today, mixed marriages between the Catholic faithful of the Latin rite and non-Catholic Oriental faithful are taking place, and the variety in canonical disciplines has brought about many grave difficulties both in the East and the West. For this reason petitions from various regions have been addressed to the Supreme Pontiff asking that he unify canonical discipline in this matter by permitting to Catholics of the Latin rite too what has been decreed for Catholics of the Eastern rite.

His Holiness Pope Paul VI, after mature reflection and diligent investigation, has resolved to agree to the petitions and desires addressed to him and, as a means of preventing invalid marriages between the faithful of the Latin rite and the non-Catholic Christian faithful of the Oriental rites, of showing proper regard for the permanence and sanctity of marriages, and of promoting charity between the Catholic faithful and the non-Catholic Oriental faithful, has kind-

a. Translation by Vatican Press office. Latin text *AAS* 59 (1967) pp. 165–166.

481

ly granted that, when Catholics, whether Orientals or Latins, contract marriage with non-Catholic Oriental faithful, the canonical form for the celebration of these marriages obliges only for lawfulness; for validity the presence of a sacred minister suffices, as long as the other requirements of law are observed.

All care should be taken that, under the guidance of the pastors such marriages be carefully entered into the prescribed registers as soon as possible. This prescription also holds when Catholic Orientals enter marriage with baptized non-Catholic Orientals according to the norm of the concilar decree, "On the Catholic Eastern Churches," n. 18.

In conformity with the holiness of marriage itself, non-Catholic ministers are reverently and earnestly requested to cooperate in the task of registering marriages in the books of the Catholic party, whether of the Latin or Oriental rite.

Ordinaries who grant the dispensation from the impediment of mixed religion are likewise given the faculty of dispensing from the obligation of observing canonical form for lawfulness, if there exist difficulties which, according to their prudent judgment, require this dispensation.

The same Supreme Pontiff has ordered the Sacred Congregation for the Oriental Church, of which he himself is the prefect, to make this resolution and concession known to all. Wherefore, the Sacred Congregation, after consulting the Sacred Doctrinal Congregation, at the order of His Holiness, has composed the present decree to be published in the *Acta Apostolicae Sedis*.

Meanwhile, in order that this new statute may be brought to the attention of those whom it concerns, whether they be Catholics of any rite or Orthodox, the present decree will go into effect 25 March 1967, the feast of the Annunciation of the Blessed Virgin Mary.

Anything to the contrary notwithstanding.

37

DIRECTORY CONCERNING ECUMENICAL MATTERS: PART ONE[a]

S.P.U.C., *Ad Totam Ecclesiam,* 14 May, 1967

INTRODUCTION

1. "The concern for restoring unity involves the whole Church, faithful and clergy alike. It extends to everyone, according to the talent of each . . ." (Decree on Ecumenism *Unitatis Redintegratio,* n. 5). The ecumenical directory is being published to encourage and guide this concern for untiy, so that what was promulgated in this field by the decrees of the Second Vatican Council may be better put into practice throughout the Catholic Church. This must be done in a manner faithful to the mind of the Church. "Ecumenical activity cannot be other than fully and sincerely Catholic, that is loyal to the truth we have received from the apostles and the fathers, and in harmony with the faith which the Catholic Church has always professed, and at the same time tending towards the fullness in which Our Lord wants his body to grow in the course of time" (Decree on Ecumenism, n. 24).

2. The Decree on Ecumenism insists in a number of places that it is the business of the Apostolic See and the bishops, with due regard for the rights of patriarchs and their synods, to decide ecumenical policy after taking all circumstances into account (cf. n. 4, n. 8, n. 9). Proper care must be taken in these matters so that the ecumenical movement itself is not impeded and the faithful do not suffer harm due to the danger of false irenicism or indifferentism. This is a pastoral care, which will be the more effective as the faithful become more solidly and fully instructed in the teaching and authentic tradition both of the Catholic

---

a. Translation put out by the SPUC. Latin text in *AAS* 59 (1967) pp. 574–592.

Church and of the churches and communities separated from her. Against the dangers and harm that may arise, this accurate knowledge of teachings and traditions will be a better safeguard than the kind of ignorance which is often reinforced by false fear: fear of those adjustments which, in accordance with the spirit and decisions of the Second Vatican Council, are necessary to any genuine renewal of the Church.

Ecumenical movement begins with the renewal by which the Church expresses more fully and perfectly the truth and holiness which comes from Christ our Lord. Every one of the faithful, as a member of the Church, should share in this renewal in truth and charity so as to grow in faith, hope and charity and bear witness in the Church to God and our saviour Jesus Christ by his own Christian life.

Since this movement has been set on foot by the Holy Spirit, what follows here is put forward with the intention and in a manner to be of service to the bishops in putting into effect the Decree on Ecumenism, "without obstructing the ways of divine providence, and without prejudging the future inspirations of the Holy Spirit" (Decree on Ecumenism, n. 24).

I. THE SETTING UP OF ECUMENICAL COMMISSIONS

A. The Diocesan Commission

3. It seems very suitable to set up a council, commission, or secretariat, either for several dioceses grouped together or, where circumstances call for it, in each diocese, charged to promote ecumenical activity by the episcopal conference or of the local ordinary. In those dioceses which cannot have their own commission there should at least be one person delegated by the bishop for these duties.

4. This commission should cooperate with such ecumenical institutions or enterprises as already exist or may be launched, making use of their help where occasion offers. It should also be prompt to help other diocesan work and individual initiative, by exchanging information and ideas with those concerned, to mutual advantage. This should all be done in harmony with the principles and general norms already existing in this matter.

5. To make clearer and foster better the concern for unity which belongs to the Church as a whole, where possible

the commission should include among its members not only diocesan clergy but also religious of both sexes and suitable laymen and women.

6. Besides the other functions assigned to it, the commission should

(a) put into practice, according to local situations, the decisions of Vatican II on ecumenical affairs;

(b) foster spiritual ecumenism according to the principles laid down in the Decree on Ecumenism (see especially n. 8) about public and private prayer for the unity of Christians;

(c) promote friendliness, cooperation and charity between Catholics and their brothers who are not in their communion;

(d) initiate and guide dialogue with them, bearing in mind the adaptation to be made to the types of participants according to nn. 9 and 11 of the Decree on Ecumenism;

(e) promote in common with our separated brethren joint witness to the Christian faith as well as cooperate in such areas as e.g. in education, morality, social and cultural matters, learning and the arts (cf. Decree on Ecumenism, n. 12, also the Decree *Ad gentes*, n. 12);

(f) appoint experts to undertake discussions and consultations with the other churches and communities in the diocese;

(g) offer help and encouragement for the instruction and education to be given to clergy and laity and for conducting one's life in an ecumenical spirit, with special emphasis being given to preparing seminary students, to preaching, catechetics and other kinds of teaching dealt with in the Decree on Ecumenism, n. 10;

(h) maintain relations with the territorial ecumenical commission (see below) adapting the latter's advice and recommendations to local diocesan conditions, and, in addition, when circumstances suggest, useful information should be sent to the Secretariat for Promoting Christian Unity in Rome, which can help the latter in carrying on its own work.

B. The Territorial Commission

7. Each national episcopal conference[1] and also those which, according to circumstances, include more than one nation, should establish in accordance with their own statutes a commission of bishops for ecumenical affairs assisted by experts. This commission should have a mandate from the episcopal conference of the territory to give guidance in ecumenical affairs and determine concrete ways of acting in accordance with the Decree on Ecumenism and with other ordinances and legitimate customs, taking account of the time, place and persons they are concerned with but also of the good of the universal Church. If possible, this commission should be assisted by a permanent secretariat.

8. The functions of this commission will include all those listed under n. 6 insofar as they enter into the competence of a territorial episcopal conference. In addition let it carry out other tasks, of which some examples are given here:

(a) putting into practice the rules and instructions issued by the Apostolic See in these matters;

(b) giving advice and assistance to the bishops who are setting up an ecumenical commission in their own dioceses;

(c) giving spiritual and material help where possible to both existing ecumenical institutions and to ecumenical enterprises to be promoted either in the field of instruction and research or in that of pastoral care and the promotion of Christian life according to the principles set out in the Decree on Ecumenism, nn. 9 to 11;

(d) establishing dialogue and consultation with the leaders and with ecumenical councils of other churches and communities which exist on a national or territorial (as distinct from diocesan) scale;

(e) appointing of those experts who, by a public mandate of the Church are designated for the conversations and consultations with experts of the communities referred to under (d) above;

(f) setting up, if need be, a special subcommission for ecumenical relations with the Easterns;

1. References in this directory to "Episcopal Conference" also apply, *servatis de jure servandis* with due consideration for the requirements of law, to the patriarchal synods and synods of major archbishops in the Catholic Eastern Churches.

(g) maintaining relations between the territorial hierarchy and the Holy See.

II. THE VALIDITY OF BAPTISM CONFERRED BY MINISTERS OF CHURCHES AND ECCLESIAL COMMUNITIES SEPARATED FROM US

9. The Church's practice in this matter is governed by two principles: that baptism is necessary for salvation, and that it can be conferred only once.

10. The eccumenical importance of baptism is clear from documents of the Second Vatican Council: "He himself (Jesus Christ) explicitly asserted the necessity of faith and baptism (cf. Mk. 16:16; Jn. 3:15), and thereby affirmed also the necessity of the Church, which men enter through baptism as through a door." (Dogmatic Constitution on the Church, (D. 28), n. 14).

"The Church knows that she is joined in many ways to the baptized who are honored with the name of Christian, but who do not profess the faith in its entirety or do not preserve unity or communion with the successor of Peter" (ibid., n. 15).

"For men who believe in Christ and have been properly baptized are brought into a certain, though imperfect, communion with the Catholic Church . . . all who have been justified by faith in baptism are incorporated into Christ; they therefore have a right to be called Christians, and with good reason are accepted as brothers by the children of the Catholic Church." (Decree on Ecumenism, n. 3).

"On the other hand, Catholics must gladly acknowledge and esteem the truly Christian endowments from our common heritage which are to be found among our separated brethren." (Ibid., n. 4).

11. Baptism is, then, the sacramental bond of unity, indeed the foundation of communion among all Christians. Hence its dignity and the manner of administering it are matters of great importance to all Christ's disciples. Yet a just evaluation of the sacrament and the mutual recognition of each other's baptisms by different communities is sometimes hindered because of a reasonable doubt about the baptism conferred in some particular case. To avoid difficulties which may arise when some Christian separated from us, led by the grace of the Holy Spirit and by his con-

science, seeks full communion with the Catholic Church, the following guiding principles are put forward:

12. There can be no doubt cast upon the validity of baptism as conferred among separated Eastern Christians.[2] It is enough therefore to establish the fact that baptism was administered. Since in the Eastern Churches the sacrament of confirmation (chrism) is always lawfully administered by the priest at the same time as baptism, it often happens that no mention is made of the confirmation in the canonical testimony of baptism. This does not give grounds for doubting that the sacrament was conferred.

13. In respect of other Christians a doubt can sometimes arise:

(a) concerning *matter and form*. Baptism by immersion, pouring or sprinkling, together with the trinitarian formula, is of itself valid. (Cf. *CIC* Canon 758). Therefore if the rituals and liturgical books or established customs of a church or community prescribe one of these ways of baptizing, doubt can only arise if it happens that the minister does not observe the regulations of his own community or church. What is necessary and sufficient, therefore, is evidence that the minister of baptism was faithful to the norms of his own community or church. For this purpose generally one should obtain a written baptismal certificate with the name of the minister. In many cases the other community may be asked to cooperate in establishing whether or not, in general or in a particular case, a minister is to be considered as having baptised according to the approved ritual.

(b) Concerning *faith and intention*. Because some consider that insufficiency of faith or intention in a minister can create a doubt about baptism, these points should be noted:

The minister's insufficient faith never of itself makes baptism invalid.

Sufficient intention in a baptizing minister is to be presumed unless there is serious ground for doubting that he intends to do what Christians do. (Cf. Response of the Holy Office, 30 January 1833: "It is sufficient to do what

2. With regard to all Christians, consideration should be given to the danger of invalidity when baptism is administered by sprinkling, especially of several people at once.

Christians do"; Sacred Congregation of the Council. Decrees approved by Pius V, 19 June 1570, cited by the Provincial Council of Evreux, France, 1576).

(c) Concerning the *application of the matter*. Where doubt arises about the application of the matter, both reverence for the sacrament and respect for the ecclesial nature of the other communities demand that a serious investigation of the community's practice and of the circumstances of the particular baptism be made before any judgment is passed on the validity of a baptism by reason of its manner of administration (cf. *CIC* Canon 73781).

14. Indiscriminate conditional baptism of all who desire full communion with the Catholic Church cannot be approved. The sacrament of baptism cannot be repeated (cf. Code of Canon Law, Can. 732, 1), and therefore to baptize again conditionally is not allowed unless there is prudent doubt of the fact, or of the validity, of a baptism already administered. (Cf. Council of Trent, Session 7, Can. 4; Code of Canon Law, Can. 732, 2).

15. If after serious investigation as to whether the baptism was properly administered, a reasonable doubt persists, and it is necessary to baptize conditionally, the minister should maintain proper regard for the doctrine that baptism is unique by (a) suitably explaining both why he is in this case baptising conditionally and what is the significance of the rite of conditional baptism; (b) carrying out the rite according to the private form (cf. *CIC* Can. 737, 52).

16. The whole question of the theology and practice of baptism should be brought up in dialogue between the Catholic Church and the other separated churches or communities. It is recommended that ecumenical commissions should hold such discussions with churches or councils of churches in various regions and, where convenient, come to a common agreement in this matter.

17. Out of reverence for the sacrament of initiation which the Lord instituted for the new covenant, and in order to clarify what is necessary for its proper administration, it is most desirable that dialogue with our separated brethren be not restricted to the sole question of what elements are absolutely necessary for valid baptism. Attention should also be given to the fullness of the sacramental sign and of the reality signified (or *res sacramentum*), as these emerge

from the New Testament; this will make it easier for churches to reach an agreement on mutual recognition of baptism.

18. Placing a proper value on the baptism conferred by ministers of the churches and ecclesial communities separated from us has ecumenical importance; baptism is thereby really revealed as the "sacramental bond of unity binding all who are regenerated by it." (Decree on Ecumenism, n. 22; Dogmatic Constitution on the Church, n. 15).[3] Therefore it is to be hoped that all Christians will grow continually more reverent and faithful in their regard for what the Lord instituted concerning its celebration.

19. The Decree on Ecumenism makes clear that the brethren born and baptized outside the visible communion of the Catholic Church should be carefully distinguished from those who, though baptized in the Catholic Church, have knowingly and publicly abjured her faith. According to the decree (n. 3) "one cannot charge with the sin of separation those who at present are born into these communities and in them are brought up in the faith of Christ." Hence, in the absence of such blame, if they freely wish to embrace the Catholic faith, they have no need to be absolved from excommunication, but after making profession of their faith according to the regulations set down by the ordinary of the place they should be admitted to the full communion of the Catholic Church. What Canon 2314 prescribes is only applicable to those who, after culpably giving up the Catholic faith or communion, repent and ask to be reconciled with mother Church.

20. What has just been said of absolution from censures obviously applies for the same reason to the abjuring of heresy.

III. FOSTERING SPIRITUAL ECUMENISM IN THE CATHOLIC CHURCH

21. "This change of heart and holiness of life, along with public and private prayer for the unity of Christians, should be regarded as the soul of the whole ecumenical move-

3. Cf. also the Report of the Mixed Commission between the Roman Catholic Church and the World Council of Churches (*L'Osservatore Romano*, 20 Feb. 1966, p. 7): The Report of the Fourth International Conference on "Faith and Order," Montreal 1963, nn. 111, 113, 154.

ment, and merits the name, 'spiritual ecumenism' " (Decree on Ecumenism, n. 8).

In these few words the decree defines spiritual ecumenism and stresses its importance in order that Christians may, both in prayer and in celebration of the Eucharist and indeed in their entire daily life, carefully keep in view the aim of unity. Every Christian, even though he does not live among separated brethren, always and everywhere has his part in this ecumenical movement, through restoring the whole Christian life according to the spirit of the Gospel, as has been taught by the Second Vatican Council—leaving out nothing of the common Christian heritage. (Cf. Decree on Ecumenism, n. 6: Decree on the Church's Missionary Activity, n. 36).

22. It is fitting that prayers for unity be offered regularly at fixed times, for example:

(a) the week from 18-25 January, called the Week of Prayer for Christian Unity, in which often many churches and communities join in praying to God for unity;

(b) the days from the Ascension to Pentecost, which commemorate the community at Jerusalem waiting and praying for the coming of the Holy Spirit to confirm them in unity and universal mission.

Additional examples are:

(a) the days about the Epiphany, when we commemorate the manifestation of Christ in the world and the link connecting the Church's function with unity;

(b) Maundy Thursday, when we commemorate the institution of the Eucharist, the sacrament of unity, and Christ our Savior's prayer in the supper room for the Church and for her unity;

(c) Good Friday, or the Feast of the Exaltation of the Holy Cross, when we commemorate the mystery of the Holy Cross by which the scattered sons of God are re-united:

(d) Easter, when all Christians share with one another the joy of Our Lord's resurrection;

(e) on the occasion of meetings or other important events of ecumenical origin or specially likely to serve ecumenical purposes.

23. "It is a recognized custom for Catholics to meet for frequent recourse to prayer for the unity of the Church with which the Savior himself on the eve of his death so fervently appealed to his Father 'That they may all be one'" (Decree on Ecumenism, n. 8). Therefore, let all pray for unity in a way consonant with Christ's prayer at the Last Supper: that all Christians may achieve "that fullness of unity which Jesus Christ wishes." (Ibid., n. 4).

24. Pastors should see to it that, as circumstances of places and persons suggest, gatherings of Catholic faithful are arranged to pray for unity; and since the holy Eucharist is that marvellous sacrament "by which the unity of the Church is signified and brought about," (Decree on Eumenism, n. 2) it is very valuable to remind the faithful of its importance; public prayers for Christian unity should be encouraged at Mass (for example, during the Prayer of the Faithful or in the litanies called *Ecteniae*) as well as the celebration of votive Masses for Christian unity. Further, those rites which have special liturgical prayers of petition like the *Litia* and *Moleben* and similar supplications can properly use them to pray for unity.

IV. SHARING OF SPIRITUAL ACTIVITY AND RE- SOURCES WITH OUR SEPARATED BRETHREN

A. Introduction

25. Fraternal charity in the relations of daily life is not enough to foster the restoration of unity among all Christians. It is right and proper that there should also be allowed a certain *communicatio in spiritualibus*—i.e., that Christians should be able to share that spiritual heritage they have in common, in a manner and to a degree permissible and appropriate in their present divided state. From those elements and endowments which together go to build up and give life to the Church herself, some, even very many, can exist outside the visible boundaries of the Catholic Church (Decree on Ecumenism, n. 3). These elements "which come from Christ and lead to him rightly belong to the one Church of Christ" (ibid.), they can contribute appropriately to our petitioning for the grace of unity; they can manifest and strengthen the bonds which still bind Catholics to their separated brethren.

26. But these spiritual endowments are found in different ways in the several Christian communities, and sharing in

spiritual activity and resources cannot be independent of this diversity; its treatment must vary according to the conditions of the people, Churches and communities involved. For present conditions the following guiding principles are offered:

27. There should be regard for a certain give-and-take ("reciprocity") if sharing in spiritual activity and resources, even within defined limits, is to contribute, in a spirit of mutual goodwill and charity, to the growth of harmony among Christians. Dialogues and consultations on the subject between Catholic local or territorial authorities and those of other communions are strongly recommended.

28. In some places and with some communities, sects and persons, the ecumenical movement and the wish for peace with the Catholic Church have not yet grown strong (cf. Decree on Ecumenism, n. 19), and so this reciprocity and mutual understanding are more difficult; the local ordinary or, if need be, the episcopal conference may indicate suitable measures for preventing the dangers of indifferentism and proselytism[4] among their faithful in these circumstances. It is to be hoped, however, that through the grace of the Holy Spirit and the prudent pastoral care of bishops, ecumenical feeling and mutual regard will so increase both among Catholics and among their separated brethren that the need for these special measures will gradually vanish.

29. The term, sharing of spiritual activity and resources (*communicatio in spiritualibus*) is used to cover all prayer offered in common, common use of sacred places and objects, as well as all sharing in liturgical worship (*communicatio in sacris*) in the strict sense.

30. There is *communicatio in sacris* when anyone takes part in the liturgical worship or in the sacraments of another church or ecclesial community.

31. By "liturgical worship" is meant worship carried out according to the books, prescriptions or customs of a church or community, celebrated by a minister or delegate of such church or community, in his capacity as minister of that community.

---

4. The word "proselytism" is here used to mean a manner of behaving, contrary to the spirit of the Gospel, which makes use of dishonest methods to attract men to a community—for example, by exploiting their ignorance or poverty. (Cf. Declaration on Religious Liberty, n. 4).

B. Prayer in Common

32. "In certain special circumstances, such as prayer services 'for unity' and during ecumenical gatherings, it is allowable, indeed desirable that Catholics should join in prayer with their separated brethren. Such prayers in common are certainly a very effective means of petitioning for the grace of unity, and they are a genuine expression of the ties which still bind Catholics to their separated brethren" (Decree on Ecumenism, n. 8). The decree is dealing with prayers in which members and even ministers of different communities take an "active" part. Where Catholics are concerned, this kind of participation is committed to the guidance and encouragement of local ordinaries. The following points should be noted.

33. It is to be hoped that Catholics and their other brethren will join in prayer for any common concern in which they can and should cooperate—e.g., peace, social justice, mutual charity among men, the dignity of the family, and so on. The same may be said of occasions when according to circumstances a nation or community wishes to make a common act of thanksgiving or petition to God, as on a national feast day, at a time of public disaster or mourning, on a day set aside for remembrance of those who have died for their country. This kind of prayer is also recommended so far as is possible at times when Christians hold meetings for study or common action.

34. However, common prayer should particularly be concerned with the restoration of Christian unity. It can center on, e.g., the mystery of the Church and her unity, baptism as a sacramental bond of unity however incomplete, the renewal of personal and social life as a necessary way to achieving unity, and the other themes set out under n. 22.

35. The form of the service.

(a) Representatives of the Churches or communities concerned should agree and cooperate in arranging such prayer—in deciding who should take part, what themes, hymns, scripture readings, prayers and the like should be used.

(b) In such a service there is room for any reading, prayer and hymn which manifests the faith or spiritual life shared by all Christians. There is a place for exhortations, address or biblical meditation drawing on the common Christian inheritance which may lead to mutual good will and promote unity among Christians.

(c) It is desirable that the structure of services of this kind, whether confined to Catholics, or held in common with our separated brethren, should conform to the pattern of community prayer recommended by the liturgical revival. (Cf. Constitution on the Sacred Liturgy, for example nn. 30, 34, 35.)

(d) When services are arranged to take place in an Eastern Church, it should be borne in mind that an official liturgical form is considered among orientals as particularly well adapted to prayer of petition; particular consideration should therefore be given to the liturgical order of this Church.

36. The place.

(a) A place should be chosen which is acceptable to all those taking part. Care should be taken that everything is properly prepared and conducive to devotion.

(b) Although a church building is the place in which a community is normally accustomed to celebrating its own liturgy, there is nothing which in itself prevents holding the common services mentioned in nn. 32–35, in the church of one or other of the communities concerned, if there is need for this and the local ordinary approves. In fact the situation may make this the suitable thing.

(c) It should be remembered, when arranging prayer services with the Eastern Orthodox brethren, that all Eastern Christians regard the church as far and away the most suitable place for public prayer.

37. Dress. There is nothing against the use of choir dress, where circumstances may indicate this and there is common agreement among the participants.

C. Sharing in Liturgical Worship

38. "Yet sharing in liturgical worship (*communicatio in sacris*) is not to be considered as a means to be used indiscriminately for the restoration of unity among Christians. There are two main principles upon which the practice of such common worship depends; first, that of the unity of

the Church which ought to be expressed; and second, that of the sharing in means of grace. The expression of unity very generally forbids common worship. Grace to be obtained sometimes commends it" (Decree on Ecumenism, n. 8).

1. Sharing in Liturgical Worship with Our Separated Eastern Brothers

39. "Although these (Eastern) Churches are separated from us, yet they possess true sacraments, above all—by apostolic succession—the priesthood and the Eucharist, whereby they are still joined to us in closest intimacy. Therefore some sharing in liturgical worship (*communicatio in sacris*), given suitable circumstances and the approval of church authority, is not merely possible but is encouraged (Ibid., n. 15; cf. also the Decree on the Catholic Eastern Churches, nn. 24–29).

40. Between the Catholic Church and the Eastern Churches separated from us there is still a very close communion in matters of faith (cf. Decree on Ecumenism, n. 44); moreover, "through the celebration of the Eucharist of the Lord in each of these Churches, the Church of God is built up and grows in stature" and "although separated from us, yet these Churches possess true sacraments, above all—by apostolic succession—the priesthood and the Eucharist . . ." (Ibid., n. 15).

This offers ecclesiological and sacramental grounds for allowing and even encouraging some sharing in liturgical worship—even eucharistic—with these churches "given suitable circumstances and the approval of church authority" (Decree on Ecumenism, n. 15).

Pastors should carefully instruct the faithful so that they will be clearly aware of the proper reasons for this kind of sharing in liturgical worship.

41. The principles governing this sharing set out in the Decree on the Catholic Eastern Churches (cf. nn. 26–29) should be observed with the prudence that the decree recommends; the norms which apply to oriental Catholics apply equally to the faithful of any rite, including the Latin.

42. It is particularly opportune that the Catholic authority, whether the local one, the synod or the episcopal conference, does not extend permission for sharing in the reception or administration of the sacraments of penance, holy

Eucharist or anointing the sick except after satisfactory consultations with the competent authorities (at least local ones) of the separated Oriental Church.

44. Besides cases of necessity, there would be reasonable grounds for encouraging sacramental sharing if special circumstances make it materially or morally impossible over a long period for one of the faithful to receive the sacraments in his own Church, so that in effect he would be deprived without legitimate reason, of the spiritual fruit of the sacraments.

45. Since practice differs between Catholics and other Eastern Christians in the matter of frequent communion, confession before communion and the eucharistic fast, care must be taken to avoid scandal and suspicion among the Orthodox, created by Catholics not following the Orthodox usage. A Catholic who legitimately communicates with the Orthodox in the cases envisaged here must observe the Orthodox discipline as much as he can.

46. Those Eastern Christians who, in the absence of sufficient confessors of their own Church, spontaneously desire to do so may go to a Catholic confessor. In similar circumstances a Catholic may approach a confessor of an Eastern Church which is separated from the apostolic Roman see. Reciprocity should be maintained here too. Both sides should of course take care to arouse no suspicion of proselytizing.[5]

47. A Catholic who occasionally, for reasons set out below (cf. n. 50) attends the holy liturgy (Mass) on a Sunday or holiday of obligation in an Orthodox Church is not then bound to assist at Mass in a Catholic Church. It is likewise a good thing if on such days Catholics, who for just reasons cannot go to Mass in their own church, attend the holy liturgy of their separated oriental brethren, if this is possible.

48. Because of the close communion between the Catholic Church and the separated Eastern Churches, as described above (n. 40), it is permissible for a member of one of the latter to act as godparent, together with a Catholic godparent, at the baptism of a Catholic infant or adult so long as there is provision for the Catholic education of the person being baptized, and it is clear that the godparent is a suitable one. A Catholic is not forbidden to stand as godparent in an Orthodox church, if he is so invited. In this

5. Cf. note on n. 28.

case, the duty of providing for the Christian education of the baptized person binds in the first place the godparent who belongs to the Church in which the child is baptized.

49. Brethren of other Churches may act as bridesmaid or best man at a wedding in a Catholic Church. A Catholic too can be best man or bridesmaid at a marriage properly celebrated among separated brethren.

50. Catholics may be allowed to attend Orthodox liturgical services if they have reasonable grounds, e.g. arising out of a public office or function, blood relationships, friendships, desire to be better informed, etc. In such cases there is nothing against their taking part in the common responses, hymns, and actions of the Church in which they are guests. Receiving Holy Communion however, will be governed by what is laid down above, nn. 42 and 44. Because of the close communion referred to earlier (n. 40) local ordinaries can give permission for a Catholic to read lessons at a liturgical service, if he is invited. These same principles govern the manner in which an Orthodox may assist at services in Catholic churches.

51. Regarding participation in ceremonies which do not call for sacramental sharing the following should be observed:

(a) In ceremonies carried out by Catholics, an oriental clergyman who is representing his Church should have the place and the liturgical honors which Catholics of equal rank and dignity have.

(b) A Catholic clergyman present in an official capacity at an Orthodox service can, if it is acceptable to his hosts, wear choir dress or the insignia of his ecclesiastical rank.

(c) There should be meticulous regard for the outlook of the clergy and faithful of the Eastern Churches, as well as for their customs which may vary according to time, place, persons and circumstances.

52. Because sharing in sacred functions, objects and places with all the separated Eastern brethren is allowed for a reasonable cause (cf. Decree on Eastern Catholic Churches, n. 28), it is recommended that with the approval of the local ordinary separated Eastern priests and communities be allowed the use of Catholic churches, buildings and cemeteries and other things necessary for their religious rites, if

they ask for this, and have no place in which they can celebrate sacred functions properly and with dignity.

53. The authorities of Catholic schools and institutions
should take care to offer Orthodox clergy every facility for
giving spiritual and sacramental ministration to their own
faithful who attend such schools and institutions. As far as
circumstances allow, and with the local ordinary's permission, these facilities can be offered on the Catholic premises, including the church.

54. In hospitals and similar institutions conducted by
Catholics, the authorities should promptly advise the Orthodox priest of the presence of his faithful, and give him facilities to visit the sick and administer the sacraments to
them in dignified and reverent conditions.

2. Sharing in Liturgical Worship with Other Separated Brethren

55. Celebration of the sacraments is an action of the celebrating community, carried out within the community, signifying the oneness in faith, worship and life of the community. Where this unity of sacremental faith is deficient,
the participation of the separated brethren with Catholics,
especially in the sacraments of the Eucharist, penance and
anointing of the sick, is forbidden. Nevertheless, since the
sacraments are both signs of unity and sources of grace (cf.
Decree on Ecumenism, n. 8) the Church can for adequate
reasons, allow access to those sacraments to a separated
brother. This may be permitted in danger of death or in urgent need (during persecution, in prisons) if the separated
brother has no access to a minister of his own communion,
and spontaneously asks a Catholic priest for the sacraments
—so long as he declares a faith in these sacraments in harmony with that of the Church, and is rightly disposed. In
other cases the judge of this urgent necessity must be the
diocesan bishop or the episcopal conference. A Catholic in
similar circumstances may not ask for these sacraments except from a minister who has been validly ordained.

56. A separated brother is not to act as a scripture reader or to preach during the celebration of the Eucharist. The
same is to be said of a Catholic at the celebration of the
Lord's Supper or at the principal liturgical service of the
Word held by the Christians who are separated from us. At

other services, even liturgical ones, it is allowable to exercise some functions, with the previous permission of the local ordinary and the consent of the authorities of the community concerned.

57. With the exception already dealt with above (n. 48) it is not permissible for a member of a separated community to act as godparent in the liturgical and canonical sense at baptism or confirmation. The reason is that a godparent is not merely undertaking his responsibility for the Christian education of the person baptized or confirmed as a relation or friend—he is also, as a representative of a community of faith, standing as sponsor for the faith of the candidate. Equally a Catholic cannot fulfil this function for a member of a separated community. However, because of ties of blood or friendship, a Christian of another communion, since he has faith in Christ, can be admitted with a Catholic godparent as a Christian witness of the baptism. In comparable circumstances a Catholic can do the same for a member of a separated community. In these cases the responsibility for the Christian education of the candidate belongs of itself to the godparent who is a member of the Church in which the candidate is baptised. Pastors should carefully explain to the faithful the evangelical and ecumenical reasons for this regulation, so that all misunderstanding of it may be prevented.

58. The separated brethren may act as "official" witness (bridesmaid or best man) at a Catholic marriage, and Catholics at a marriage which is properly celebrated between our separated brethren.

59. Catholics may be allowed to attend occasionally the liturgical services of other brethren if they have reasonable ground, e.g., arising out of a public office or function, blood relationship or friendship, desire to be better informed, an ecumenical gathering, etc. In these cases, with due regard to what has been said above—there is nothing against Catholics taking some part in the common responses, hymns and actions of the community of which they are guests—so long as they are not at variance with Catholic faith. The same principles govern the manner in which our separated brethren may assist at services in Catholic churches. This participation, from which reception of the Eucharist is always excluded, should lead the participants to esteem the spiritual riches we have in common and at the same time make them more aware of the gravity of our separations.

60. When taking part in services which do not call for sacramental sharing, ministers of other communions may, by mutual consent, take a place suitable to their dignity. So, too, Catholic ministers who are present at ceremonies celebrated by other communions may, with due regard for local customs, wear choir dress.

61. If the separated brethren have no place in which to carry out their religious rites properly and with dignity, the local ordinary may allow them the use of a Catholic building, cemetery or church.

62. The authorities of Catholic schools and institutions should take care to offer to ministers of other communions every facility for giving spiritual and sacramental ministration to their own communicants who attend Catholic institutions. These ministrations may be given in Catholic buildings, in accordance with the above, n. 61.

63. In hospitals and similar institutions conducted by Catholics, the authorities in charge should promptly advise ministers of other communions of the presence of their communicants and afford them every facility for visiting the sick and giving them spiritual and sacramental ministrations.

38

**DECLARATION ON THE POSITION OF
THE CATHOLIC CHURCH ON THE
CELEBRATION OF THE EUCHARIST
IN COMMON BY CHRISTIANS OF
DIFFERENT CONFESSIONS**[a]

S.P.U.C., *Dans ces derniers temps,* 7 January, 1970

1. Recently, in various parts of the world, certain intiatives have been taken with regard to common participation
in the Eucharist. They have involved, on the one hand,
faithful and clergy of the Catholic Church and, on the other, laity and pastors of other Christian Churches and ecclesial communities. At times there is question of the admission of Catholic faithful to a Protestant or Anglican
eucharistic communion; at other times, participation by Protestants and Anglicans in the eucharistic communion in a
Catholic church; or again, there are common acts of eucharistic worship jointly celebrated by ministers belonging to
Churches and ecclesial communities still separated from
one another, and in these the laity of the communities concerned take part.

This subject is of great theological, pastoral and, above
all, ecumenical importance, and we desire to recall the
Church's recently formulated norms concerning it.

2. The Second Vatican Council addressed itself to this
subject in the Decree on Ecumenism, *Unitatis Redintegratio.* After having called to mind that common prayers for
unity are an efficacious means for asking for the grace of
unity and constitute an authentic expression of the bonds
by which Catholics remain united with other Christians, the
Decree continues: "As for common worship, however, it
may not be regarded as a means to be used indiscriminately
for the restoration of unity among Christians. Such worship

a. Translation by SPUC. French text in AAS 62 (1970) pp. 184–188.

depends chiefly on two principles: it should signify the unity of the Church; it should provide a sharing in the means of grace. The fact that it should signify unity generally rules out common worship. Yet the gaining of needed grace sometimes commends it. The practical course to be adopted, after due regard has been given to all the circumstances of time, place, and persons, is left to the prudent decision of the local episcopal authority, unless the bishop's conference according to its own statutes, or the Holy See, has determined otherwise." (Decree on Ecumenism, D. *32*, n. 8).

3. In applying these general principles, the Council asks us to consider well "the particular situations of the Churches of the East."(Decree on Ecumenism, n. 14) and to draw the appropriate consequences from these facts: "Although these Churches are separated from us, they possess true sacraments, above all—by apostolic succession—the priesthood and the Eucharist, whereby they are still joined to us in a very close relationship Therefore, given suitable circumstances and the approval of Church authority, some worship in common is not merely possible but is recommended" (Decree on Ecumenism, n. 15).

The Decree on the Catholic Eastern Churches, *Orientalium Ecclesiarum,* makes some applications. It permits Eastern Christians not in full communion with the Apostolic See of Rome to be admitted to the Sacraments of Penance, of the Eucharist and of the Anointing of the Sick when they find themselves in the specified circumstances. It equally authorizes Catholics to request these same sacraments from Eastern priests whenever necessity or a genuine spiritual benefit call for it and access to a Catholic priest is physically or morally impossible. It also recommends that the authorities of the Churches involved contact each other about the matter (cf. Decree on the Catholic Eastern Churches, nn. 27, 29).

4. The section of the Decree on Ecumenism devoted to "the separated Churches and ecclesial communities in the West" includes Christian confessions of great variety. In it the Council treated the theological problem which underlies eucharistic sacramental relations with Christian communities where those conditions found in the Churches of the East are lacking: "The ecclesial communities separated from us lack that fullness of unity with us which should flow from Baptism, and we believe that especially because of a deficiency of the Sacrament of Order they have not

preserved the genuine and total reality of the eucharistic mystery. Nevertheless when they commemorate the Lord's death and resurrection in the Holy Supper, they profess that it signifies life in communion with Christ and they await his coming in glory. For these reasons, dialogue should be undertaken concerning the true meaning of the Lord's Supper, the other sacraments, and the Church's worship and ministry." (Decree on Ecumenism, n. 22).

It should be noted that the doctrinal appreciation of the Eucharist of these communities is bound up with an appeal for dialogue about the Eucharist and the entire sacramental life, and a special mention is made of the ministries of the Church.

It is well known that the Catholic Church attaches a decisive importance to the traditional teaching about the necessity of the ministerial priesthood connected with the apostolic succession, and the conditions in which it exists.

5. The dispositions of the Second Vatican Council were applied through the Ecumenical Directory which was approved by the Holy Father on 22 April 1967 and published in the *Acta Apostolicae Sedis* on 5 July of the same year.

For eucharistic relations with Eastern Christians not in full communion with the Apostolic See of Rome, the Directory reproduces the dispositions of the Council and determines in a precise way certain useful points especially in what concerns reciprocity and previous agreement between the ecclesiastical authorities of the Churches concerned (Directory Concerning Ecumenical Matters, Part One, nn. 39–47).

6. The Directory went more into detail when treating of those Christian communities with which we do not share the same ecclesiological and sacramental bases that particularly unite us to the Churches of the East. After giving doctrinal justifications of its norms, it formulates these in the following way: "Celebration of the sacraments is an action of the celebrating community, signifying the oneness in faith, worship and life of the community. Where this unity of sacramental faith is deficient, the participation of the separated with Catholics, especially in the Sacraments of the Eucharist, Penance and Anointing of the Sick, is forbidden. Nevertheless, since the sacraments are both signs of unity and sources of grace (cf. Decree on Ecumenism, n. 8), the Church can for adequate reasons allow access to those sacraments to a separated brother. This may be per-

mitted in danger of death or in urgent need (during persecution, in prisons) if the separated brother has no access to a minister of his own communion, and spontaneously asks for a Catholic priest for the sacraments—so long as he declares a faith in these sacraments in harmony with that of the Church, and is rightly disposed. In other cases the judge of this urgent necessity must be the diocesan bishop or the episcopal conference. A Catholic in similar circumstances may not ask for these sacraments except from a minister who has been validly ordained" (Directory concerning Ecumenical Matters, Part One, nn. 55).

7. In commenting on this passage, one month before his death, Cardinal Bea, President of the Secretariat for the Promotion of the Unity of Christians, endeavored to throw light on its exact meaning. "These texts determine precisely the conditions required for admitting an Anglican or a Protestant to eucharistic communion in the Catholic Church. It is not enough, then, that one of these Christians be spiritually well disposed and that he spontaneously request communion from a Catholic minister. In the first place two other conditions must be verified: that they hold the faith that the Catholic Church herself professes concerning the Eucharist, and that they are unable to approach a minister of their own confession.

"The Directory cites as examples three very special cases, where these conditions can be verified: danger of death, persecution, imprisonment. In other cases the ordinary of the place or the episcopal conference will be able to give the permission, if it is asked. The condition must be, however, that urgent necessity similar to that in cases cited as examples and the same conditions must be verified.

"When one of these conditions is lacking, admission to eucharistic communion in the Catholic Church is not possible" (Note on application of Directory concerning Ecumenical Matters, *L'Osservatore Romano*, 6 October 1968).

8. With regard to the role which the Directory plays in the pastoral action of the Church, it is useful to recall the words addressed by the Holy Father on 13 November 1968 to the members of the Secretariat for the Promotion of the Unity of Christians: "We need not tell you that, to promote ecumenism in an efficacious way, one must also guide it, submit it to the rules that are quite precise. We regard the Ecumenical Directory not as a collection of advisory principles which one can freely accept or ignore, but as an au-

thentic instruction, an exposition of the discipline to which all those who wish truly to serve ecumenism should submit themselves" (*L'Osservatore Romano*, 14 November 1968).

9. The Secretariat for the Promotion of the Unity of Christians is following this question very closely and itself has taken various initiatives concerning it. Recently, during its plenary assembly (*Congregatio plenaria* of which forty bishops from all over the world are members), held in Rome from 18 to 28 November, it devoted a great deal of attention to it. At the same time the Secretariat particularly appreciates the work being done all over the world to deepen the theology of the Church, of ministry and of the Eucharist, both as sacrament and sacrifice, done within the historical context of the division among Christians. It is following with interest and profit the efforts being made to clarify the problem in all its dimensions and to work out a more precise vocabulary. Above all it is pleased with the interconfessional dialogue on this subject which is now taking place at both local and international levels. The Secretariat hopes that these conversations will help to bring about a convergence of positions on the subject. Still, it must be pointed out that, up to the present, these dialogues have not yet produced results which can be adopted on both sides by those who have responsibility in the Churches and ecclesial communities involved.

The Catholic Church, then, is not at present in a position to modify the norms of the Directory concerning Ecumenical Matters as given above. The line of conduct traced out there results from the Church reflecting on her own faith and considering the pastoral needs of the faithful. Before considering another way of acting in the matter of a common Eucharist, it will be necessary to establish clearly that any change to be made will remain totally in conformity with the Church's profession of faith and that it will be a service to the spiritual life of her members.

10. At this time when the Week of Prayer for Unity is about to begin, we are taking into account the extent to which the desire for a common Eucharist powerfully stimulates the search for that perfect ecclesial unity among all Christians willed by Christ. This desire can be expressed very appropriately in the celebrations which will take place during this Week of Prayer. As well as the reading of and meditation upon holy Scripture, these celebrations could in fact include elements which point towards the common Eu-

charist so much desired: our gratitude for the partial unity already obtained, our regret for the divisions which still remain and our firm resolve to do everything possible to overcome them, and finally our humble petition to the Lord to hasten the day when we will be able to celebrate together the mystery of the Body and the Blood of Christ.

39

APOSTOLIC LETTER ON MIXED MARRIAGES[a]

Paul VI, *Matrimonia Mixta*, 7 January, 1970

Mixed marriages, that is to say marriages in which one party is a Catholic and the other a non-Catholic, whether baptized or not, have always been given careful attention by the Church in pursuance of her duty. Today the Church is constrained to give even greater attention to them, owing to the conditions of present times. In the past Catholics were separated from members of other Christian confessions and from non-Christians, by their situation in their community or even by physical boundaries. In more recent times, however, not only has this separation been reduced, but communication between men of different regions and religions has greatly developed, and as a result there has been a great increase in the number of mixed marriages. Also a great influence in this regard has been exercised by the growth and spread of civilization and industry, urbanization and consequent rural depopulation, migrations in great numbers and the increase in numbers of exiles of every kind.

The Church is indeed aware that mixed marriages, precisely because they admit differences of religion and are a consequence of the division among Christians, do not, except in some cases, help in re-establishing unity among Christians. There are many difficulties inherent in a mixed marriage, since a certain division is introduced into the living cell of the Church, as the Christian family is rightly called, and in the family itself the fulfilment of the gospel teachings is more difficult because of diversities in matters of religion, especially with regard to those matters which concern Christian worship and the education of the children.

a. Translation by Vatican Press office. Latin text in AAS 62 (1970) pp. 257–263.

For these reasons the Church, conscious of her duty, discourages the contracting of mixed marriages, for she is most desirous that Catholics be able in matrimony to attain to perfect union of mind and full communion of life. However, since man has the natural right to marry and beget children, the Church, by her laws, which clearly show her pastoral concern, makes such arrangements that on the one hand the principles of Divine law be scrupulously observed and that on the other the said right to contract marriage be respected.

The Church vigilantly concerns herself with the education of the young and their fitness to undertake their duties with a sense of responsibility and to perform their obligations as members of the Church, and she shows this both in preparing for marriage those who intend to contract a mixed marriage and in caring for those who have already contracted such a marriage. Although in the case of baptized persons of different religious confessions, there is less risk of religious indifferentism, it can be more easily avoided if both husband and wife have a sound knowledge of the Christian nature of marital partnership, and if they are properly helped by their respective Church authorities. Even difficulties arising in marriage between a Catholic and an unbaptized person can be overcome through pastoral watchfulness and skill.

Neither in doctrine or in law does the Church place on the same level a marriage between a Catholic and a baptized non-Catholic, and one between a Catholic and an unbaptized person; for, as the Second Vatican Council declared, men who, though they are not Catholics "believe in Christ and have been properly baptized are brought into a certain, though imperfect communion with the Catholic Church."[1] Moreover, although Eastern Christians who have been baptized outside the Catholic Church are separated from communion with us, they possess true sacraments, above all the Priesthood and the Eucharist, whereby they are joined to us in a very close relationship.[2]

Undoubtedly there exists in a marriage between baptized persons, since such a marriage is a true sacrament, a certain communion of spiritual benefits which is lacking in a marriage entered into by a baptized person and one who is not baptized.

1. The Constitution on the Church, n. 15.
2. The Decree on Ecumenism, n. 14.

Nevertheless, one cannot ignore the difficulties inherent even in mixed marriages between baptized persons. There is often a difference of opinion on the sacramental nature of matrimony, on the special significance of marriage celebrated within the Church, on the interpretation of certain moral principles pertaining to marriage and the family, on the extent to which obedience is due to the Catholic Church, and on the competence that belongs to ecclesiastical authority. From this it is clear that difficult questions of this kind can only be fully resolved when Christian unity is restored.

The faithful must therefore be taught that, although the Church somewhat relaxes ecclesiastical discipline in particular cases, she can never remove the obligation of the Catholic party, which, by divine law, namely by the plan of salvation instituted by Christ, is imposed according to the various situations.

The faithful should therefore be reminded that the Catholic party to a marriage has the duty of preserving his or her own faith; nor is it ever permitted to expose oneself to a proximate danger of losing it.

Furthermore, the Catholic partner in a mixed marriage is obliged, not only to remain steadfast in the faith, but also, as far as possible, to see that the children be baptized and brought up in that same faith and receive all those aids to eternal salvation which the Catholic Church provides for her sons and daughters.

The problem of the children's education is a particularly difficult one, in view of the fact that both husband and wife are bound by that responsibility and may by no means ignore it or any of the obligations connected with it. However the church endeavors to meet this problem, just as she does the others, by her legislation and pastoral care.

With all this in mind, no one will be really surprised to find that even the canonical discipline on mixed marriages cannot be uniform and that it must be adapted to the various cases in what pertains to the juridical form of contracting marriage, its liturgical celebration, and, finally, the pastoral care to be given to the married people, and the children of the marriage, according to the distinct circumstances of the married couple and the differing degrees of their ecclesiastical communion.

It was altogether fitting that so important a question should receive the attention of the Second Vatican Council. This occured several times as occasion arose. Indeed, in the third session the Council Fathers voted to entrust the question to us in its entirety.

To meet their desire, the Sacred Congregation for the Doctrine of the Faith, on the 18th March, 1966, promulgated an Instruction on mixed marriages, entitled "Matrimonii Sacramentum,"[3] which provided that, if the norms laid down therein stood the test of experience, they should be introduced in a definite and precise form into the Code of Canon Law which is now being revised.

When certain questions on mixed marriages were raised in the first General Meeting of the Synod of Bishops, held in October 1967 and many useful observations had been made upon them by the Fathers, we decided to submit those questions to examination by a special Commission of Cardinals which, after diligent consideration, presented us with its conclusions.

At the outset we state that Eastern Catholics contracting marriage with baptized non-Catholics or with unbaptized persons are not subject to the norms established by this Letter. With regard to the marriage of Catholics of whatsoever rite with Eastern non-Catholic Christians, the Church has recently issued certain norms,[4] which we wish to remain in force.

Accordingly, in order that ecclesiastical discipline on mixed marriages be more perfectly formulated and that, without violating divine law, canonical law should have regard for the differing circumstances of married couples, in accordance with the mind of the Second Vatican Council expressed especially in the Decree *Unitatis Redintegratio*[5] and in the Declaration *Dignitatis Humanae,*[6] and also in careful consideration of the wishes expressed in the Synod of Bishops, we, by our own authority, and after mature deliberation, establish and decree the following norms:

1. A marriage between two baptized persons, of whom one is a Catholic, while the other is a non-Catholic, may not licitly be contracted without the previous dispensation of the local Ordinary, since such a marriage is by its nature an obstacle to the full spiritual communion of the married parties.

2. A marriage between two persons, of whom one has

3. D. *34* in this collection.
4. D. *36* in this collection.
5. D. *32* in this collection.
6. D. *60* in this collection.

been baptized in the Catholic Church or received into it, while the other is unbaptized, entered into without previous dispensation by the local Ordinary, is invalid.

3. The Church, taking into account the nature and circumstances of times, places and persons, is prepared to dispense from both impediments, provided there is a just cause.

4. To obtain from the local Ordinary dispensation from an impediment, the Catholic party shall declare that he is ready to remove dangers of falling away from the faith. He is also gravely bound to make a sincere promise to do all in his power to have all the children baptized and brought up in the Catholic Church.

5. At an opportune time the non-Catholic party must be informed of these promises which the Catholic party has to make, so that it is clear that he is cognisant of the promise and obligation on the part of the Catholic.

6. Both parties are to be clearly instructed on the ends and essential properties of marriage, not to be excluded by either party.

7. Within its own territorial competence, it is for the Bishops' Conference to determine the way in which these declarations and promises, which are always required, shall be made: whether by word of mouth alone, in writing, or before witnesses; and also to determine what proof of them there should be in the external forum, and how they are to be brought to the knowledge of the non-Catholic party, as well as to lay down whatever other requirements may be opportune.

8. The canonical form is to be used for contracting mixed marriages, and is required for validity, without prejudice, however, to the provisions of the Decree *Crescens Matrimoniorum* published by the Sacred Congregation for the Eastern Churches on 22nd February, 1967.[7]

9. If serious difficulties stand in the way of observing the canonical form, local Ordinaries have the right to dispense from the canonical form in any mixed marriage; but the Bishops' Conference is to determine norms according to which the said dispensation may be granted licitly and uniformly within the region or territory of the Conference, with the provision that there should always be some public form of ceremony.

7. D. *36* in this collection.

10. Arrangements must be made that all validly contracted marriages be diligently entered in the books prescribed by canon law. Priests responsible should make sure that non-Catholic ministers also assist in recording in their own books the fact of a marriage with a Catholic.

Episcopal Conferences are to issue regulations determining, for their region or territory, a uniform method by which a marriage that has been publicly contracted after a dispensation from the canonical form was obtained, is registered in the books prescribed by canon law.

11. With regard to the liturgical form of the celebration of a mixed marriage, if it is to be taken from the Roman Ritual, use must be made of the ceremonies in the *Rite of Celebration of Marriage* promulgated by our authority, whether it is a question of a marriage between a Catholic and a baptized non-Catholic (39–54) or of a marriage between a Catholic and an unbaptized person (55–66). If, however, the circumstances justify it, a marriage between a Catholic and a baptized non-Catholic can be celebrated, subject to the local Ordinary's consent; according to the rites for the celebration of marriage within Mass (19–38), while respecting the prescription of general law with regard to Eucharistic Communion.

12. The Episcopal Conferences shall inform the Apostolic See of all decisions which, within their competence, they make concerning mixed marriages.

13. The celebration of marriage before a Catholic priest or deacon and a non-Catholic minister, performing their respective rites together, is forbidden; nor is it permitted to have another religious marriage ceremony before or after the Catholic ceremony, for the purpose of giving or renewing matrimonial consent.

14. Local Ordinaries and parish priests shall see to it that the Catholic husband or wife and the children born of a mixed marriage do not lack spiritual assistance in fulfilling their duties of conscience. They shall encourage the Catholic husband or wife to keep ever in mind the divine gift of the Catholic faith and to bear witness to it with gentleness and reverence, and with a clear conscience. They are to aid the married couple to foster the unity of their conjugal and family life, a unity which, in the case of Christians, is based on their baptism too. To these ends it is to be desired that those pastors should establish relationships of sincere

openness and enlightened confidence with ministers of other religious communities.

15. The penalties decreed by canon 2319 of the Code of Canon Law are all abrogated. For those who have already incurred them the effects of those penalties cease, without prejudice to the obligations mentioned in number 4 of these norms.

16. The local Ordinary is able to give a "sanatio in radice" of a mixed marriage, when conditions spoken of in numbers 4 and 5 of these norms have been fulfilled, and provided that the conditions of law are observed.

17. In the case of a particular difficulty or doubt with regard to the application of these norms, recourse is to be made to the Holy See.

We order that what we have decreed in this Letter, given in the form of "Motu Proprio," be regarded as established and ratified, notwithstanding any measure to the contrary, and is to take effect from the first day of October of this year.

40

DIRECTORY CONCERNING ECUMENICAL MATTERS: PART TWO: ECUMENISM IN HIGHER EDUCATION[a]

S.P.U.C., *Spiritus Domini*, 16 April, 1970

INTRODUCTION

64. The spirit of the Lord is at work in the present-day ecumenical movement in order that, when the obstacles hindering perfect ecclesiastical communion have been surmounted,[1] the unity of all Christians may at last be restored and shine forth,[2] for all peoples are called to be a single new people, confessing one Jesus, Savior and Lord, professing one faith, celebrating one eucharistic mystery.[3] "that the world may believe that thou hast sent me," as the Lord said (Jn. 17:21).

All Christians should be of an ecumenical mind, but especially those entrusted with particular duties and responsibilities in the world and in society; hence the principles of ecumenism sanctioned by the Second Vatican Council should be appropriately introduced in all institutions of advanced learning.[4] In fact, many have asked for some principles and lines of action which would help everybody to cooperate for the common good of the Catholic Church and the other Churches and ecclesial communities.

65. Bishops have a special responsibility for promoting the ecumenical movement and it is for them to lay down

a. Translation put out by the S.P.U.C.
1. Vatican II, Decree on Ecumenism, n. 4.
2. Cf. ibid., n. 1.
3. Cf. ibid., n. 4.
4. The term "institutions of advanced learning" in this Document covers all university faculties, academic institutes, diocesan seminaries, institutes or centers or houses for the training of religious, men and women; it excludes therefore grammar and secondary schools or (in American usage) high schools.

the required guiding principles. But because of the great variety of institutions of advanced learning it is far from easy to prescribe such guiding principles; there are differences between various nations and regions, differences deriving from varying individual maturity and experience, differences also resulting from the varying state of relationships whether in the ecclesiological sphere or in that of cooperation between the Catholic Church and other churches or ecclesial communities. It belongs, therefore, to bishops and episcopal conferences both to translate general principles into practice[5] and to adjust undertakings already on foot to existing conditions as these affect men and matters—and even, as occasion offers, to start new undertakings. It is strongly suggested that episcopal authorities should associate with themselves in this task an appropriate number of religious superiors, men and women, as well as rectors and administrators, specialists in religious education and practicing teachers—and should bring representatives of the students into consultation when necessary.

66. Since, moreover, all ecumenical work is conditioned by the abnormal situation that the Churches and ecclesial communities involved in it are divided and at the same time their efforts are directed to restoring unity, the principles set out below will sometimes, because of changed circumstances, be newly applied in practice by competent authority, and the lines of policy will be adapted so as always to go on serving the purpose for which they were put out.

I. GENERAL PRINCIPLES AND AIDS TO ECUMENICAL EDUCATION

67. Though some undertakings for fostering ecumenical education mainly concern theological faculties and colleges —which will be treated further on—there are some forms of ecumenical action which are applicable to all higher education. Students and teachers who take part in this kind of undertaking are reminded that they must willingly and generously equip themselves with that solid religious training, maturity of mind and real skill which the nature of the project demands.

5. According to the directives laid down in the Directory Concerning Ecumenical Matters, Part One, nn. 2, 6–8.

A. The Purpose of Ecumenical Programs

68. The purpose of programs of this type is to increase among students a deeper knowledge of the faith, the spirituality and the entire life and doctrine of the Catholic Church, so that they may wisely and fruitfully take part in ecumenical dialogue each according to his capabilities,[6] to direct their attention both to that inward renewal of the Catholic Church itself which will help so much to promote unity among Christians, and to those things in their own lives or in the life of the Church which hinder or slow down progress towards unity;[7] a further purpose is that teachers and students should learn more about other Churches and communities, and so understand better and assess more correctly what unites Christians and what divides them;[8] finally, since these efforts are not to be mere intellectual exercises, the aim is that those taking part in them should better realize the obligation of fostering unity between Christians and so be led to apply themselves more effectively to achieving it. They will also be led to do what is in their power to give joint Christian witness to the contemporary world.

B. Aids to Achieving This Purpose

69. (a) Since various academic subjects may have a connection with ecumenism, the following points, which may serve as examples, should be borne in mind:

Where courses or lectures on religion are given in various forms to students, whether as part of the syllabus or occasionally, those who give them should take note of what is said below about the ecumenical aspects of theological teaching.[9]

Courses in philosophy, while providing a solid and coherent understanding of man, of the world and of God based on a philosophical heritage of lasting value, should also take account of contemporary philosophical investigations, and pupils should properly be made aware of the principles which govern these.[10] This because they ought to know

6. Cf. Decree on Ecumenism, nn. 3, 5.
7. Cf. ibid., nn. 4, 6, 7.
8. Cf. ibid., n. 3.
9. Cf. pp. 7–9, ch. II, nn. 2–5.
10. Cf. Vatican II, Decree on the Training of Priests, n. 15.

and assess properly the philosophical principles which often underlie existing theological and exegetical views among the various Churches and Christian communities.

The style and ways of teaching history should be reviewed so that in dealing with Christian society due consideration is given to the different Christian communities and their whole way of life understood. The events and personalities involved in the various religious divisions should be dealt with fairly, and the many attempts to restore unity and bring about renewal in the Church should not be overlooked.

In the other subjects, attention can be paid to those spiritual elements which are part of the common Christian inheritance and are to be found among various Christian communities e.g., in the field of literature, the arts, music.

(b) As far as possible, properly instructed Catholics, so long as they firmly maintain their Catholic heritage, should be encouraged to support undertakings in the field if religious studies proposed by non-confessional universities.

(c) Among the various types of activites usually associated with academic institutions, some are more specially suited to promoting the ecumenical movement. These are some examples:

Conferences or study-days dealing with specifically ecumenical themes.

Meetings or associations for study, for joint work or for social welfare work which may provide occasion for ecumenical discussion, or for examining Christian principles of this social action and aids to putting those principles into practice. Those meetings and associations, whether confined to Catholics or including other Christians, should do all they can to cooperate with existing student societies.

In halls of residence attached to academic establishments, circumstances may suggest exchanges between Catholics, faithfully witnessing to their own belief, and other Christian students, by means of which both, with suitable guidance, may live their lives together in a deeper ecumenical spirit.

In university journals and reviews, space may be assigned for ecumenical news and at least occasionally for more serious articles on ecumenical subjects.

(d) Among activities to which special attention should be paid, we should include prayer for unity, not only during the Week of Prayer for Christian Unity, but at other appropriate times during the year.[11] Subject to local and personal circumstances, and to the rules laid down about liturgical worship in common, joint retreats may well be organised for one or more days under a reliable retreat master.[12]

(e) There is a wider field for joint witness in social and welfare work. Students should be prepared for this kind of cooperation and exhorted to take part in it. This will have greater and more precise effect if students not only of theology but of other facilities (e.g., law, sociology, political economy) join forces to promote and carry out the work.

(f) Priests engaged in some ministry in these various institutions (chaplains, teachers, student advisers) have a special duty in the matter of ecumenical relations. This duty demands of them both a deeper knowledge of the Church's doctrine and a particular qualification and experience in academic subjects, as well as steady prudence and moderation, if they are to be useful guides to students who want to combine full and genuine loyalty to their own Christian community with a positive and open bearing towards their fellow students.

II. THE ECUMENICAL DIMENSION OF RELIGIOUS AND THEOLOGICAL EDUCATION

A. Spiritual Formation

70. Since the Holy Spirit must be regarded as at work in the ecumenical movement, the first thing to be attended to in ecumenical education is conversion of heart—spiritual life and its renewal, for "from newness of mind, from self-denial and from the freest outpouring of charity, desires for unity proceed and mature."[13] This renewal should be rooted in the life of the Church itself, in its liturgy and sacraments; it should be directed to prayer for the unity of all Christians and to the fulfilling of the Church's function in the world. The spiritual life of Catholics must be genuine: centered on Christ the Saviour and looking to the glory of God the Father, it will assign to the whole range of religious acts and exercises their due and proper importance.

11. Cf. Directory Concerning Ecumenical Matters, Part One, nn. 22, 32–34.
12. According to the directive laid down by competent authority, cf. Introduction.
13. Cf. Decree on Ecumenism, n. 7.

To give adequate emphasis to the Catholic and apostolic character of the Church,[14] the ecumenical spiritual life of Catholics should also be nourished from the treasures of the many traditions, past and present, which are alive in other Churches and ecclesial communities; such are the treasures found in the liturgy, monasticism and mystical tradition of the Christian East; in Angelican worship and piety; in the evangelical prayer and spirituality of Protestants.

But this linking with other spiritual traditions, if it is not to remain in the realm of theory, should be perfected by practical acquaintance with them where circumstances favor this. Hence some prayer in common and sharing in public worship are to be promoted in harmony with the rules laid down by competent authority.[15]

B. Doctrinal Education

Ecumenism should bear on all theological disciplines as one of its necessary determining factors,[16] making for the richer manifestation of the fullness of Christ. Nevertheless, ecumenism as a separate question may either provide the material of a special course of lectures, if opportunity offers, or at least be the theme of some lectures given in the chief dogma courses.

C. The Ecumenical Aspect in All Theological Teaching

72. Ecumenism should embrace these aspects:

(a) those elements of the Christian heritage both of truth and of holiness which are found in common in all Churches and Christian communities,[17] though they are sometimes given different theological expression;[18]

(b) the spiritual treasury and wealth of doctrine which each Christian community has for its own, and which can lead all Christians to a deeper understanding of the nature of the Church;[19]

14. Cf. ibid., n. 3.
15. Cf. Directory Concerning Ecumenical Matters, Part One, nn. 25–63. Cf. also "A Declaration of the Secretariat for Promoting Christian Unity on the Position of the Catholic Church Concerning a Common Eucharist between Christians of Different Confessions," *L'Osservatore Romano*, 12–13 Jan. 1970, p. 3.
16. Cf. Decree on Ecumenism, nn. 9, 10.
17. Cf. ibid., n. 3.
18. Cf. ibid., n. 17.
19. Cf. ibid., n. 4; also Paul VI, Encycl. *Ecclesiam suam: AAS* 66 (1964), pp. 609 ff.

(c) whatever in matters of faith causes dissension and division, yet can stimulate a profounder examination of the word of God, aimed at manifesting what in proclaiming truth are real contraditions and what only seem to be.

D. The Ecumenical Aspect in the Branches of Theology

73. In every branch of theology the ecumenical standpoint should make for consideration of the link between the subject and the existing mystery of the unity of the Church. Moreover, when the subject is expounded, pupils should be given a sense of the fullness of Christian tradition in doctrine, spirituality and Church discipline. They will become aware of this when their own tradition is related to the riches of other Christian traditions of East and West, both in their classical forms and in their modern expressions.

This way of paying attention to the patrimonies of other Christian Churches and ecclesial communities is undoubtedly important: in studying Scripture, the common source of the faith of all Christians; in studying apostolic tradition as it is to be found in the Fathers and ecclesiastical writers of the Eastern and Western Church; in liturgical teaching which presents a scholarly comparison of various forms of divine worship and of their doctrinal and spiritual significance; in expounding dogmatic and moral theology, with particular regard for questions raised by the ecumenical movement; in Church history, when it carefully traces the unity of the Church itself through the changes brought about by time, and the causes of division among Christians; in teaching canon law, where elements of divine law are to be diligently distinguished from elements of merely ecclesiastical law which can be exposed to change by reason of the passage of time or because of temperament, culture or tradition;[20] finally, in pastoral and missionary training and in social studies, in which particularly careful attention is due to the situation in which all Christians find themselves when facing the requirements of the contemporary world. In this way the fullness of divine revelation is expressed better and more completely and the task which Christ entrusted his Church to fulfil in the world is carried out.[21]

---

20. Cf. Vatican II, Dogmatic Constitution on the Church, n. 13; cf. also Decree on Ecumenism, nn. 4, 16.
21. Cf. Decree on Ecumenism, n. 12; also Vatican II, Decree on the Church's Missionary Activity, nn. 12, 36.

E. Conditions of a Genuine Ecumenical Mind in Theology

74. Ecumenical action "cannot but be fully and sincerely Catholic—faithful, that is, to the truth which we have received from the apostles and fathers, and in harmony with the faith which the Catholic Church has always confessed."[22] But we should always preserve the sense of an order based on degree, of a "hierarchy" in the truths of Catholic doctrine which, although they all demand a due assent of faith, do not all occupy the same principal or central place in the mystery revealed in Jesus Christ, since they vary in their relationship to the foundation of the Christian faith.[23]

Students should learn to distinguish between revealed truths, which all require the same assent of faith, and theological doctrines. Hence they should be taught to distinguish between "the deposit of faith itself, or the truths which are contained in our venerable doctrine," and the way in which they are enunciated,[24] between the truth to be enunciated and the various ways of perceiving and more clearly illustrating it,[25] between apostolic tradition and merely ecclesiastical traditions. Already, from the time of their philosophical training, students should be put in a frame of mind to recognize that different ways of stating things in theology too are legitimate and reasonable, because of the diversity of methods or ways by which theologians understand and express divine relevation. Thus it is that these various theological formulae are often complementary rather than conflicting.[26]

F. Ecumenism as a Special Branch of Study

75. Even though all theological training has an ecumenical aspect, courses on ecumenism are not therefore superflous. The following may be regarded as elements for such courses, leaving room for development as circumstances and time suggest:

22. Decree on Ecumenism, n. 24.
23. Cf. ibid., n. 11.
24. Cf. Pope John XXIII, Allocution, 11 Oct. 1962 in *Constitutiones, Decreta, etc.*, ed. Polyglotta Vaticana, p. 865; also Decree on Ecumenism, n. 6, and the Pastoral Constitution on the Church in the Modern World, n. 62.
25. Cf. Decree on Ecumenism, n. 17.
26. Cf. ibid., n. 17.

(a) *Oecumene,* "ecumenism"—historical origins and present meaning;

(b) The doctrinal foundations of ecumenism, with special reference to the bonds of communion still holding between Churches and ecclesial communities;

(c) The aim and method of ecumenism, the various forms of union and cooperation, the hope of restoring unity, the conditions for unity, full and perfect unity, the practice of ecumenism, especially in the sphere of social action;

(d) The history of ecumenism, especially of the various attempts made in the course of time to restore unity, and a consideration of their positive and negative features;

(e) An account of the "institutional" aspect and present life of the different Christian communions: their doctrinal tendencies, the true causes of divisions, missionary effort, spirtuality, forms of divine worship;

(f) A number of questions to do with ecumenism; special questions which the ecumenical movement gives rise to about hermeneutics, ministry, divine worship, "intercommunion," tradition, "proselytism" and true evangelization, false irenicism, the laity, the ministry of women in the Church and so on;

(g) The spiritual approach to ecumenism, especially the significance of prayer for unity and the various forms of spiritual ecumenism;

(h) Existing relations between the Catholic Church and other Churches and ecclesial communities or federations of Churches, as well as the relations which all these have with each other;

(i) The importance of the special role which the World Council of Churches has in the ecumenical movement, and the relationships which exist between the Roman Catholic Church and the World Council of Churches.

III. PARTICULAR GUIDELINES FOR ECUMENICAL EDUCATION

A. Dialogue Between Christians in Higher Education

76. Careful examination of the general principles governing dialogue between Christians makes it very clear that seminaries, theological faculties and the other institutions of higher education have their own particular role to play in ecumenical dialogue, and that dialogue itself in these insti-

tutions is a help towards their fulfilling their function regarding the education of the young.

But dialogue as an element of education demands:

(a) sincere and firm fidelity to one's own faith, without which dialogue is reduced to a conversation in which neither side is genuinely engaged;

(b) a mind open and ready to base life more deeply on one's own faith because of the fuller knowledge derived from dialogue with others, who are to be reckoned as sharing with us the true name of Christian;

(c) investigation of ways and means of concerted effort to establish relations and restore a unity which will not rest on indifference or false irenicism of facile accommodation to the demands of the age, but on a greater fidelity to the Gospel and an authentic profession of the Christian religion which satisfies the demands both of truth and of charity;

(d) consultation and cooperation with the pastors of the Church and a due deference for their directions and advice, for dialogue is never a mere exchange between persons and institutions, but of its very nature engages the whole Church;[27]

(e) readiness to acknowledge that the members of the various Churches and ecclesial communities are generally best equipped to expound properly the doctrine and life of their own communion;

(f) respect for conscience and for the convictions of others in explaining the outlook and doctrine of one's own Church or one's own way of understanding divine revelation;

(g) Readiness to acknowledge that not everyone is equally equipped for dialogue—there are differences of intellectual training, maturity of mind, spiritual development; hence syllabuses and lectures should be revised so as to correspond to the real needs of the students.

B. Those Who Have Special Ecumenical Tasks

77. To fulfil her ecumenical responsibility, the Church must have at her disposal an adequate number of experts in ecumenical matters—clergy and religious, lay men and women. They are needed everywhere—even in regions where Catholics form the greater part of the population.

Among the tasks that may be assigned to them are these:

27. Cf. Decree on Ecumenism, n. 4.

to help bishop and clergy and regional authorities to prepare the faithful to acquire truly ecumenical mentality; to assist or direct the various diocesan and regional ecumenical commissions; to establish suitable relations with other Christian communities; to give special lectures on ecumenism in seminaries and other educational establishments; to organize ecumenical activity in Catholic schools and institutions; to foster the training of missionaries for their own special kind of ecumenical work.[28]

Besides their solid general theological training, it is desirable that these experts:

(a) should have special advanced training in some branch of study—such as theology, exegesis, history, philosophy, religious sociology;

(b) should be properly instructed in the principles of the present-day ecumenical movement, in the questions which occupy it, in what it has achieved and has still to achieve. Over and above what they can learn from lectures and research, they should be strongly urged to take every possible part in ecumenical relationships, which they can do by means of meetings, conferences, centers or institutes for ecumenical studies and so on;

(c) should be properly instructed in the traditions of those Christians, side by side with whom they live and work. Studies of this sort should as far as possible be done by regular contact with those who know and live such traditions.

C. Those Already Working in a Pastoral Ministry

78. In carrying out the established policy of pastoral training for the clergy through clergy councils, special institutes, retreats, days of recollection or pastoral discussion, bishops and religious superiors are earnestly exhorted to make sure that the necessary care is devoted to ecumenism, and also to bear in mind these particular points.[29]

As opportunity offers, special instruction should be provided for priests, religious and laity on the present stage of the ecumenical movement so that they may learn to bring an ecumenical point of view into preaching, into divine worship, into catechism and into Christian life at large. Fur-

28. Cf. Directory Concerning Ecumenical Matters, Part One, nn. 3–8.
29. Cf. Vatican II, Decree on the Pastoral Office of Bishops, n. 16; also Decree on the Ministry and Life of Priests, n. 9.

ther, as far as it is possible and prudent, a minister of another Church or community should be invited to explain his own tradition or talk on pastoral problems, which are very often common to all Christian ministers.

Where it seems advisable and the ordinary agrees, the Catholic clergy should be invited to attend special meetings with ministers of other Churches and communities—for the purpose of getting to know each other better and of solving pastoral problems by a joint Christian effort. This sort of activity often goes best when associations are set up, such as local or regional clergy councils, "clergy fraternals" etc., or when people join existing associations of the kind.

Theology faculties, seminaries and other seats of learning can make a great contribution to ecumenical effort both by arranging courses of study for clergy doing pastoral work and by urging their own teaching staff to take a ready share in studies and courses organized by others.

D. Concerning Superiors and Teaching Staff in Institutions for Theological Education

79. The general principles set out in Chapter II should shape, guide and give stimulus to the training of all those who are intended to teach theology and related subjects, so that they will be adequately learned and fitted for the office of educating younger priests, students of the sacred sciences, religious and laity.

To help teaching staff to satisfy their ecumenical responsibilities, bishops, whether in their own diocese or together with the bishops of the region or country, religious superiors and those in authority in seminaries, universities and similar institutions should take pains to promote the ecumenical movement and spare no effort to see that their teachers keep in touch with advances in ecumenical thought and action. Moreover, care must be taken to maintain an adequate supply of books, reviews, periodicals and similar publications, Catholic and non-Catholic.

In planning studies, the following points should be given the fullest attention:

(a) It seems appropriate to give a special course on ecumenism shortly after theological studies have begun: a broad knowledge of ecumenical matters will help students to a deeper understanding of particular subjects.

(b) To intensify devotion to ecumenism and promote familiarity with the whole ecumenical movement, it will be useful from the beginning to take opportunities of providing conferences for pupils. Teachers in class may also usefully set pupils essays and other exercises on ecumenical themes.

(c) Textbooks and other teaching aids should be chosen or written with due care. These works should faithfully set out the opinions of other Christians on matters of theology, history and spirituality, which moreover should not be considered in isolation from life but as embodied in a tradition by which men live.

(d) It is most important that students who are being trained for the priesthood or the religious life should learn fully how to conduct themselves in future pastoral dealings with other Christians—e.g., how they may help them in some spiritual need and yet at the same time respect their freedom of conscience and the grace of the Holy Spirit in them.

(e) The libraries of seminaries and other institutions of higher education should be kept well supplied with books and periodicals, both those which deal with ecumenism in general and those which give particular treatment to questions of local ecumenical concern or of importance for the special purpose of the institution.

IV. INSTITUTIONAL AND PERSONAL COOPERATION BETWEEN CATHOLICS AND OTHER CHRISTIANS

80. Subject to conditions which vary from place to place, and to the principles already put forward,[30] cooperation between institutions of higher education and relationships on various levels between teachers and students of different Churches and communities can be of the greatest advantage not only to the ecumenical movement at large but to the ecumenical education of teachers and pupils concerned.

81. Such cooperation between Christians in the sphere of higher education can greatly profit the institutions involved; it contributes, in fact:

to fuller knowledge of theology (especially in the matter of useful aids for the science of hermeneutics), and also of other subjects which are treated in institutions of advanced learning;

30. Cf. ch. III, n. 1, above.

to assisting the academic faculty, through the shared use
of books and libraries, by providing a greater number of
qualified teachers; by cutting down useless or duplicated
courses, subject to directions given below;

to increasing material resources where necessary, e.g. by
shared use of buildings, especially libraries and class-
rooms;

by multiplying the assistance which the institution can afford to society as a whole: for men will more freely pay
attention to the authority and influence of some joint
Christian action than to that of single institutions operat-
ing in isolation;

to reinforcing the witness offered to other Christians of
the proved worth of the institutions—something which
men look for from such training over and above the
merely academic quality of the teaching.

82. This cooperation and habit of exchanges with their
colleagues of other Christian communities continually
opens up new paths of scholarly enquiry to teachers, and
helps them to fulfil their teaching function better. Furthermore, the students can to some degree already be prepared
throughout their period of training for future ecumenical
work, and with the help of really expert Catholic instructors they can better learn to overcome such intellectual and
spiritual difficulties as might perhaps arise from exchanges
of this kind.

83. In this cooperation two classes of persons should be
distinguished:

(a) graduates and those who have completed a general
theological training,

(b) those who have not yet completed the ordinary curriculum.

84. Episcopal conferences, in drawing up a program of
training for the priesthood according to the decree *Optatam
Totius*, should issue general rules, on lines to be laid down
later, about particular cases of cooperation between Catholic seminaries and those of other Christians. But since institutions for training members of religious orders can also
take part in this cooperation, major superiors or their delegates should contribute towards drawing up rules in accordance with the decree *Christus Dominus*, n. 35, Arts. 5 and
6. If particular questions arise about some seminary or institution, the ordinary who has jurisdiction over it must de-

cide, according to the lines laid down by the episcopal conference, which undertakings require his approval and which can be left simply to those in charge of the seminary.

A. Graduates and Others Who Have Finished a General Theological Training

85. Ecumenical dialogue and action should be advanced by setting up ecumenical institutes and centers in various places and countries and, as circumstances demand, with the approval of lawful authority. These institutes, or "centers" as they are called, can be established separately, or as part of some faculty or by cooperation between existing faculties or universities. The structure and aims of these centers can vary. But when they are planned and their programs arranged, it is most desirable to keep in mind the whole ecumenical concern in all its aspects.

B. Of Such Institutes These Types May Be Distinguished

86. (a) Centers of ecumenical research in which theological questions on a particular theme are thoroughly thrashed out, and directed towards ecumenical dialogue through enquiry into sources, scholarly exchange and published writings.

(b) Ecumenical theological institutes in which students who have finished their general theological training can be set aside to do specialized work in ecumenical theology by means of special courses and seminars. Such institutes may be either designed for general ecumenical affairs, or devoted to special study in some one subject (e.g., the theology of the Oriental Churches, Protestant theology, Anglican theology, etc.), but this should by no means involve neglecting the ecumenical problem as a whole.

(c) Associations for the joint study of theological and pastoral questions by ministers of different Churches and communities who meet to discuss the theoretical and practical aspects of their ministry among their own people as well as their common witness to the world.

(d) Federations of universities and other institutions to facilitate the shared use of libraries and other resources and to establish closer links between their teachers and students in planning study programs.

C. Interconfessional Institutes

87. Subject to conditions of time and pláce, the institutes and centers just referred to may be conducted either by Catholics or by several confessions simultaneously. Joint institutes are particularly useful where Churches or ecclesial communities need to examine certain questions together (e.g., mission work, dealings with non-Christian religions, questions about atheism and unbelief, the use of media of social communication, architecture and sacred art and, in the province of theology, explanation of Holy Scripture, salvation history, pastoral theology, etc.) which if they are properly resolved can very much advance Christian unity. The setting-up and administration of these institutes should normally be entrusted to those who conduct them, saving the rights of competent ecclesiastical authority.

88. Where it seems advisable, Catholic institutes can, in accordance with n. 84 above, become members of associations designed to promote raising the standard of theological education, better training of those intended for the pastoral ministry, better cooperation between religious institutions for advanced learning. Care should however be taken that joining such an association leaves intact the autonomy of the Catholic institute in matters of the program of studies, of the doctrinal content of subjects to be taught, of the spiritual and priestly training of the students in so far as these things are determined by the institute's own purpose and by rules laid down by legitimate ecclesiastical authority.

D. Those Who Have Not Yet Finished General Theological Training

89. Throughout the whole period of their general theological training, whenever there is question of Catholic students cooperating in their intellectual formation with other Christian students, the principles set out in Ch. III, n. 1, must be especially borne in mind. For these exchanges (arising from joint study, prayer, social action, etc.) will be fruitful in proportion as everybody involved is firmly founded in his own faith and tradition as well as being aware of the purpose of ecumenism and the requirements of ecumenical dialogue.

90. Catholic seminaries, theological schools, houses and training colleges for religious men and women can collabo-

rate with other Christian institutions of a similar kind. This cooperation may take various forms according to local conditions and the character of the institutions concerned; for example, occasional exchange of teachers, mutual recognition of certain courses, various kinds of federation, affiliation to a university. In all this, care should be taken that the native character of the Catholic institution is preserved together with its right to train its own students and expound Catholic doctrine, taking account of what is said below, n. 13.

91. Experts in ecumenism from other communities may be invited to hold conferences in Catholic institutions and even to conduct some courses, so long as the proper character of the institution concerned is respected. Catholic teachers should by all means be ready to do the same for others if they are asked.

92. Catholic students may be allowed to attend lectures at institutions, even seminaries, of other Christians, according to the following guiding principles. These things should be kept in view: (a) the usefulness of the course and the solid help it will afford in their training as a whole; (b) the public reputation, mastery of his subject and ecumenical mind of the teacher; (c) the previous preparation of the pupils; (d) their spiritual and phychological maturity; and, above all, (e) the very nature of the branches of study concerned: for the more the doctrinal aspect enters into the subject matter, the more caution should be exercised in allowing pupils to attend. Hence, while ordinary or systematic instruction should be given by Catholic teachers, especially where exegesis, dogmatic and moral theology are concerned, Catholic pupils can attend classes dealing with practical subjects, such as biblical languages, communications media, religious sociology in so far as this new science is based on observation of facts, etc. Subject to the judgment of their superiors, who, as was said earlier, should weigh their scientific and spiritual preparedness, students may also attend lectures of common usefulness even though these have a certain doctrinal aspect—examples are church history and patrology. It is the office of superiors to take decisions in these matters, after consulting with the students, according to the general regulations of the seminary and the directions given by the ordinary who has jurisdiction over it.[31]

31. Cf. ch. IV, n. 5, above.

It will do much to make such programs really fruitful in practice if Catholic teachers have a fuller knowledge of the writings, opinions, and ecumenical outlook of those teachers from other Christian communities whose classes pupils are allowed to attend. This will be easier if they meet them often and visit their institutions. Further, it is strongly recommended that seminary superiors periodically hold discussions with their staff and spiritual directors, to review the program of studies, suggest changes, deal with difficulties that may have arisen. Similar meetings and discussions with colleagues from other Christian seminaries are also recommended.

93. In various parts of the world, the pattern of higher education is very much in a state of transition and many proposals are being put forward for amalgamating the different institutes for the study of religion in public and nondenominational universities. It belongs to episcopal conferences to judge, by appropriate means and with appropriate advice, what part clerical students may take in these schemes. In carefully examining this question, they should pay particular regard to the right and proper intellectual and spiritual education of students for the priesthood as well as of other pupils under the guidance of Catholic authority; also to the active involvement of Catholic teachers in these programs; and finally to the complete and assured freedom of the Church's magisterium to determine genuine Catholic doctrines and traditions.

If these joint enterprises are to give useful results, it is to be wished that the governing bodies of universities and faculties shall have as active members Catholic (laymen, clerics, religious) who are really expert in their own field and in ecumenical dialogue.

94. Other Catholic institutions which supply religious instruction both to students working for theology degrees and for those from other faculties should be guided by these same principles, but adapted to their own character and to the condition and requirements of their students. What has been said already about the previous religious training and maturity of mind of pupils, and of the special competence and general ability of teachers, is equally applicable to these institutions.

41

JOINT DECLARATION ON UNITY[a]

Paul VI and Vasken I Catholicos, Supreme Patriarch of the Armenians, 12 May, 1970

Paul VI, Bishop of Rome, Pope of the Catholic Church, and Vasken I Catholicos, Supreme Patriarch of all the Armenians, thank the Lord for permitting them to pray together, to meet and to exchange the kiss of peace, particularly in this period of preparation for the great feast of the descent of the Holy Spirit on the apostles.

Conscious of their duty as pastors, they invite all Christians and especially those of the Catholic Church and of the apostolic Armenian Church to be still more responsive to the Holy Spirit who calls them to the more profound unity, which is the will of our common Saviour and will make their service of the world more effective.

This unity can be realized only if all, pastors and faithful, try really to know one another. To that end, they appeal to theologians to deepen, by study in common, their knowledge of the mystery of Jesus Christ and of the revelation made in him. Let them be faithful to the tradition handed on from the apostles and the fathers, and at the same time let them be aware of the needs of a world which searches for God in the new developments of our time. They will thus be able to discover new ways of overcoming the differences which still exist and of leading their churches to more perfect unity, professing their faith before the world. For their part, the Pope and the Catholicos shall do all they can to support their efforts and they give them their pastoral blessing.

At the same time, the quest runs the danger of futility unless it takes in the life of the entire Church. For this reason they hope that close collaboration will develop in all

a. Translated by A.F. from the French in *AAS* LXII (1970), 416–417.

possible areas of the Christian life. There are precious steps towards that unity which is so desirable. They are prayer in common, reciprocal spiritual aid, combined efforts to discover the principles of a truly Christian solution to today's problems.

This common quest and collaboration must be based on reciprocal acknowledgement of a common Christian faith and of a common sacramental life, on mutual respect for persons and churches. If the disinterested efforts, which with all their hearts they wish to encourage, are inspired by this spirit and conducted in this way, they are confident that the Spirit of truth and love will give to the members of the Catholic Church and of the apostolic Armenian Church that truly Christian brotherhood which is the fruit of his action in them.

In the name of that brotherhood, Pope Paul VI and Catholicos Vasken I raise their voices in a solemn appeal to those who influence the lives of nations and peoples to do all in their power to put an end to wars, hatred, physical and moral violence, and to all oppression of man by man. May he who is our peace grant that this appeal may be heard.

42

REFLECTIONS AND SUGGESTIONS CONCERNING ECUMENICAL DIALOGUE[a]

S.P.U.C., 15 August, 1970

We give below the full text of the document entitled "Reflections and Suggestions concerning Ecumenical Dialogue" issued by the Secretariat for the Promotion of the Unity of Christians in September 1970. It is preceded by an explanatory note by Cardinal Willebrands, President of the S.P.U.C., concerning the nature of the document.

Introduction

"In March 1966, His Eminence Augustin Cardinal Bea, President of the Secretariat for the Promotion of the Unity of Christians, wrote to the Episcopal Conferences to inform them that the Secretariat was preparing the Ecumenical Directory requested by the Second Vatican Council. Among the subjects which would possibly be treated was "Ecumenical Dialogue." The bishops, in their responses, offered many helpful suggestions concerning this very important aspect of the whole movement for Christian unity.

On the basis of these first indications, the Secretariat held a consultation in February, 1967, to which were invited experts from many parts of the world actively engaged in ecumenical dialogue. The results of their deliberations were communicated to the Plenary Session of the bishops members of the Secretariat in April 1967. The Plenary, after having discussed the first project, remanded it to the Secretariat staff for further elaboration and revision.

a. Translation issued by S.P.U.C. Text does not appear in *AAS*.

In the meantime, the Joint Working Group between the Roman Catholic Church and the World Council of Churches has authorized a small interconfessional team to study the question of ecumenical dialogue and prepare a working paper on the subject. This paper, published in 1967, had no pretentions to laying down rules. However, it had the merit of being a cooperative effort, written in a language which was not confessional, but intelligible to all Christians. It was meant to stimulate personal reflection and invited analysis, discussion and criticism.

The Plenary Session of the Secretariat, in its meeting of November 1968, thoroughly revised its first project for a directory concerning ecumenical dialogue. Of particular importance to this discussion were the comments made about the project by many experts consulted as well as the reactions to the paper published under the authorization of the Joint Working Group.

As a result of the widespread discussion concerning the proposed document on ecumenical dialogue, the question began to be raised as to whether it should become an integral part of the Ecumenical Directory published by the Secretariat. The Directory is a normative text clothed with the highest approval. For certain situations (e.g., the organization of ecumenical works, worship in common, education for ecumenism) a document on this level is by all means appropriate. But given the wide variety which can be included in the term ecumenical dialogue with regard to the levels of persons who take part in it, the conditions under which it takes place, the subjects which can be treated, etc., it was asked whether norms similar to those given in Parts One and Two of the Ecumenical Directory were the most apt way for encouraging, developing and guiding this type of dialogue. What seemed more useful was a working instrument, a qualified and sure guide, which carries weight without, however, being based upon any authority in the juridical sense of the word. Such a document would be an aid particularly to the ecclesiastical authorities for application of the Decree on Ecumenism according to concrete circumstances and possibilities.

At the Plenary Session in November 1969, therefore, the cardinals and bishops members of the Secretariat resolved that the document approved by the Plenary *should not be published as a part of the Ecumenical Directory* but should be sent to the Episcopal Conferences accompanied by an explanatory introduction written by the Cardinal President. The Holy Father gave the matter serious consideration and approved the resolution of the Plenary Meeting of the Secretariat.

The document presented here does not have strict juridical authority. Entitled "Reflections and Suggestions concerning Ecumenical Dialogue," its authority resides uniquely in the fact that it is the result of prolonged reflection made on many levels by those engaged in ecumenical dialogue.

Although composed under the auspices of the Secretariat for the Promotion of the Unity of Christians and directed to the Pastors of the Roman Catholic Church, it has profited from wide discussions and experiences with members of other Christian Churches and ecclesial communities. It has been carefully reviewed by the cardinals and bishops members of the Secretariat, and has met with the approval of the Plenary Session in November 1969.

The document is now offered to the Episcopal Conferences of the Roman Catholic Church. It seeks to offer some orientations for an important modern phenomenon (the development of dialogue in the modern world, and especially among Christians) in the light of various conciliar documents, of statements of the Holy Father and of experience gained over the past few years both within the Roman Catholic Church and in the growing relationships among all Christians. It seeks to indicate pastoral orientations which have doctrinal foundations. It recognizes the complexities which are connected with various types of ecumenical dialogue and the elements required for a sincere dialogue which seeks truth in charity. It offers recommendations based on theoretical reflection and practical experience. It thus hopes to assist all Catholics who, according to the Council, are called to work for restoring Christian unity (cf. Decree on Ecumenism, n. 5), by rendering particular service to bishops everywhere to whom the Second Vatican Council recommended this work for their skilful promotion and prudent guidance (cf. *ibid.*, n. 4).

I. INTRODUCTION

This document concerns only ecumenical dialogue, that is to say, dialogue which is established between the "Christians of different Churches or Communions."[1] The principles on which it rests and the themes with which it deals are in part different from those which characterize the dialogue which the Catholic Church wishes to establish, and in fact does establish, with Judaism, the major religions, with non-believers and with the world. In fact, "we for our part should not wish to exclude anybody from such a dialogue, prompted only by charity and directed towards truth. . . ."[2] These various forms of dialogue cannot be dissociated one from the other; the dialogue which is dealt with here is not unconnected with those forms of dialogue which are the concern of the Secretariats for Non-Christian Religions and for Unbelievers.

In spite of certain contrary appearances, modern man seeks for dialogue as a privileged means of establishing and developing mutual understanding, esteem, respect and love, whether between groups or between individuals. For this reason he is eager to make ever greater use of it at all levels of his life, political, social, economic, educational and religious.

The same is true when individual Christians and Churches or ecclesial communities concern themselves with ecumenical matters. Dialogue is the indispensable means for their meeting and their witness, at the levels both of thought and action. Thus there have grown up interconfessional groups of the most varied composition and aims, and the need has made itself felt of establishing dialogue structures, as seen in the local and regional ecumenical commissions, the World Council of Churches and the Secretariat for the Promotion of the Unity of Christians.

Being aware of these facts, the Second Vatican Council stressed the importance of dialogue between the Catholic

1. Vatican II, Decree on Ecumenism, n. 4.
2. Vatican II, Pastoral Constitution on the Church in the Modern World, n. 92.

538

Church and the other churches and ecclesial communities.[3]
The Secretariat for the Promotion of the Unity of Christians, taking its inspiration from the concerns, orientations and motives of the Council, proposes to show the nature and aim of this ecumenical dialogue, together with its bases, its conditions, its method, the themes it handles and the forms it takes with a view to favoring and developing it in the present situation.

If concern for the reestablishment of Christian unity involves all the members of the Church, both the faithful and their pastors, each according to his own condition, it belongs to the bishops to be the promoters and guides of ecumenical dialogue.[4] As such, they will also exercise their pastoral vigilance in order to keep the dialogue on the exact lines laid down for it by the Second Vatican Council in the Decree on Ecumenism.

This pastoral vigilance will take into account the double aspect of ecumenical action envisaged by the Council. For if ecumenical action must remain "loyal to the truth we have received from the apostles and the fathers, and in harmony with the faith which the Catholic Church has always professed, and at the same time tending towards that fullness with which our Lord wants his body to be endowed in the course of time,"[5] nevertheless the Council expresses the desire "that the initiatives of the sons of the Catholic Church, joined with those of the separated brethren, go forward without obstructing the ways of divine Providence and without prejudging the future inspiration of the Holy Spirit."[6]

II. NATURE AND AIM OF ECUMENICAL DIALOGUE

1. In general terms, dialogue exists between individuals and groups from the moment when each party begins both to listen and reply, to seek to understand and to be understood, to pose questions and to be questioned in turn, to be freely forthcoming himself and receptive to the other party,

---

3. Cf. Decree on Ecumenism, nn. 4, 9, 11, 18–23; Pastoral Constitution on the Church in the Modern World, n. 92; Decree on the Church's Missionary Activity, n. 15.
4. Cf. Decree on Ecumenism, nn. 4, 5, 9; Decree on the Church's Missionary Activity, n. 15.
5. Decree on Ecumenism, n. 24.
6. Ibid.

concerning a given situation, research project or course of action, with the aim of progressing in unison towards a greater community of life, outlook and accomplishment. Each of the parties to the dialogue is ready to clarify further his ideas and his ways of living and acting, if it appears that truth is leading him in this direction. Thus reciprocity and a mutual commitment are essential elements of dialogue.[7]

2. The ecumenical dialogue demands all these elements, which will be made more specific by the aim pursued. This aim has several aspects:

(a) Through dialogue, Christians must learn to advance together in their sharing in the reality of the mystery of Christ and of his Church. In this way, they will be able to discern the common elements in their different ways of approaching the revealed mystery and of translating it into their thought, life and witness.

(b) Through dialogue, Christians must learn to give common witness to the mission which Jesus Christ confided to his Church, so that all may "before the whole world . . . profess their faith in God, one and three, in the incarnate Son of God, our Redeemer and Lord,"[8] and that thus the world may come to believe.

(c) Since the world poses the same questions to all the Churches and ecclesial communities, the latter, listening to the questions together and understanding them through dialogue, and being attentive to the Holy Spirit, will seek together the response that the Lord expects of them in order to serve the world, especially in those places where the Gospel has not been preached.[9]

(d) In the sphere of their internal life, a large number of Christian communions are face to face with the same questions, which however they may each find posed at different levels. Such questions are those concerning the laity, the ministry, liturgy, catechetics, the Christian family, and so on. Does not the Holy Spirit urge Christians to approach jointly these questions also?

Thus it becomes apparent that ecumenical dialogue is not limited to an academic or purely conceptual level, but striving for a more complete communion between the Christian communities, a common service of the Gospel and closer

7. Cf. Dialogue with Unbelievers, I, 1: AAS 60 (1968), pp. 695–696.
8. Decree on Ecumenism, n. 12.
9. Cf. Decree on the Church's Missionary Activity, nn. 15, 29.

collaboration on the level of thought and action, it serves to transform modes of thought and behavior and the daily life of those communities. In this way, it aims at preparing the way for their unity of faith in the bosom of a Church one and visible: thus "little by little, as the obstacles to perfect ecclesial communion are overcome, all Christians will be gathered, in a common celebration of the Eucharist, into that unity of the one and only Church which Christ bestowed on his Church from the beginning. This unity, we believe, dwells in the Catholic Church as something she can never lose, and we hope that it will continue to increase until the end of time."[10]

It is true that dialogue by itself does not suffice to bring about the fullness of unity that Christ wishes; nevertheless, that unity is the ultimate aim of the thoughts and desires of those engaged in dialogue, who are preparing themselves to receive it as the great gift that God alone will bestow, in the way and at the time that he wishes.[11]

III. BASES OF DIALOGUE

Ecumenical dialogue is rooted in a number of doctrinal and pastoral facts.

1. First, since "the brethren who believe in Christ are Christ's disciples, reborn in baptism, sharers with the People of God in very many riches,"[12] and since these riches, such as "the written word of God, the life of grace, faith, hope and charity, along with other interior gifts of the Holy Spirit and visible elements,[13] are accessible to all those who have been baptized, Christians are in a position to communicate to each other the riches that the Holy Spirit develops within them. This community of spiritual goods is the first basis upon which ecumenical dialogue rests.

2. But it is inside their Churches and ecclesial communities that Christians enjoy these spiritual goods; the Churches and communities which are separated from the Catholic Church enjoy "a significance and a value in the mystery of salvation. . . . Many of the sacred actions" that they per-

---

10. Decree on Ecumenism, n. 4.
11. Cf. "A Working Paper on Ecumenical Dialogue," prepared by the Joint Working Group between the World Council of Churches and the Roman Catholic Church, 1: S.P.U.C. *Information Service,* 1967, Eng. ed., p. 34.
12. Decree on the Church's Missionary Activity, n. 15.
13. Decree on Ecumenism, n. 3.

form are to be recognized as "capable of providing access to the community of salvation."[14] Between them and the Catholic Church therefore there is a certain communion already existing which must be the starting point for dialogue. This latter will tend towards a more perfect sharing by each Church and ecclesial community in the very mystery of Christ and his Church,[15] which is the foundation of their communion among themselves.

3. "Our common reference is Revelation as expressed in the witness of the Holy Scriptures. . . . Their witness is centered in Jesus Christ and has meaning through relation to him."[16] The Holy Spirit in fact is always acting in such a way as to lead the Christian people to live it and to understand it better and so to accomplish its prophetic role. Ecumenical dialogue therefore allows each one to communicate to his brethren the riches of Christ whereby he lives and to accept the riches whereby the others live.

4. Since "every renewal in the Church essentially consists in an increase of fidelity to her own calling, undoubtedly this explains the dynamism of the movement towards unity."[17] In a like manner, all communions in their effort to renew themselves are normally led to enter into dialogue, in order to question themselves on "their own faithfulness to Christ's will."[18]

IV. CONDITIONS FOR DIALOGUE

1. Before it can begin, all dialogue presupposes that an attitude of sympathy and openness between those who will take part has been brought about by more or less spontaneous contacts and exchanges, in the details of ordinary daily life. It is in such a context of human relationships, which can be very varied, that dialogue of whatever sort usually takes its origin and form.

2. Ecumenical dialogue will be conducted between the participants as between equals.[19] Everything that has been said about the nature, aim and bases of this dialogue, notably concerning reciprocity and mutual commitment, provides a basis for this attitude of equality.

14. Ibid.
15. Cf. ibid., n. 4.
16. "A Working Paper on Ecumenical Dialogue," p. 34.
17. Decree on Ecumenism, n. 6.
18. Ibid., n. 4.
19. Ibid., n. 9: *par cum pari.*

(a) In ecumenical dialogue, those who take part recognize honestly that because of existing differences there is an inequality between the different Christian communions. Hence they reject on the one hand that doctrinal indifferentism which would claim that, before the mystery of Christ and the Church, all positions are equivalent. On the other hand they do not pass any judgment regarding the willingness of one side or the other to be faithful to the Gospel. The Catholic participant, believing as he does that the Lord has confided to the Catholic Church the fullness of the means of salvation and all truth revealed by God, will be ready to give an account of his faith.[20]

(b) In ecumenical dialogue, those who take part recognize one another as existing in Christ, since they have been baptized in him, born again "not from any mortal seed but from the everlasting word of the living and eternal God" (1 Pet. 1:23), and able through the Holy Spirit to hear their brethren tell them of the marvellous works of God.

In this dialogue, they recognize together that a certain communion exists between the Christian communities; nevertheless, they are anxious not to conceal from one another the fact that in the content, development and expression of the faith of the Churches there exist certain differences which must become the object of their dialogue, so that they may attain a more perfect communion.

Each of those taking part will give the others, in a form that they will be really able to grasp and in the most genuine way, witness to the Gospel of Christ as his Church wishes to bear it; he in his turn will listen to the witness expressed by the others.

In brotherly emulation, those taking part become aware that God is calling them to an ever deeper faithfulness to himself and to the revelation made by him.

(c) On a practical level, equality between the participants in dialogue implies equality of standard in sacred and secular learning and equality in the level of responsibilities held.

3. To be genuine and fruitful, all dialogue requires that those who direct it, if not all those taking part, possess a certain degree of ability. This required competence will vary according to the forms of dialogue and the themes dealt with, but will always presuppose the religious forma-

20. Cf. ibid., nn. 3, 4, 11.

tion demanded by all dialogue which has as its aim the unity of Christians. Yet, competence in the theological field cannot be the only requirement; there is a place for practical skills in all subjects, whether professional, technical, apostolic or spiritual.

Without pretending to say everything that there is to be said on training for ecumenical dialogue, it will be useful here to recall the following considerations.

(a) Though it is not required that all Catholic participants should have the same degree of preparation for such dialogue, it is very much to the point that some of them, whether they be clerics or laymen, should have received an adequate training in this field. Among other things, an effective contribution can be made by ecumenical training sessions, programs for reading, correspondence courses, ecumenical centers and chairs of ecumenism in theological faculties. Through these and parallel ways, attention will be given to learning the art of dialogue, to understanding the thought of others and to becoming acquainted with their spiritual life.[21]

Within the framework of this training, it would be a good thing for Catholics taking part in ecumenical meetings to reflect together on the dialogue in which they participate, both beforehand, in order to prepare themselves for it, and also afterwards, to assess its development and results.

(b) Given that the Church "has always regarded the Scriptures together with sacred tradition as the supreme rule of faith, and will ever do so . . . all the preaching of the Church must, like the Christian religion itself, be nourished and ruled by sacred Scripture."[22] Care must therefore be taken to acquire a culture, theology and spirituality of biblical inspiration. It must not be forgotten that "the sacred utterances are precious instruments in the mighty hand of God."[23]

(c) The opportunities for encounter between Christians are becoming more numerous as a result of the circumstances of modern life. It is necessary that the faithful and their pastors should fully appreciate their responsibilities in this field and should take pains to be well informed and constantly alert about theological and spiritual matters.

21. Cf. ibid., n. 9.
22. Vatican II, Dogmatic Constitution on Divine Revelation, n. 21.
23. Decree on Ecumenism, n. 21.

4. With regard to the presentation of doctrine, a few remarks are necessary.

(a) On the one hand, dialogue leads to a more exact knowledge of our brethren,[24] to which they will normally be able to open the way for us. On the other hand, the Catholic participant must carefully inform himself of the content of his Church's faith, without either overstating or minimizing it, remembering that ecumenical encounter is not merely an individual work, but also a task of the Church, which takes precedence over all individual opinions.

(b) It will be borne in mind that "in Catholic teaching there exists an order of hierarchy of truths, since they vary in their relationship to the foundation of the Christian faith."[25] Neither in the life nor in the teaching of the whole Church is everything presented on the same level. Certainly all revealed truths demand the same acceptance of faith, but according to the greater or lesser proximity that they have to the basis of the revealed mystery, they are variously placed with regard to one another and have varying connections among themselves. For example, the dogma of Mary's Immaculate Conception, which may not be isolated from what the Council of Ephesus declares about Mary, the Mother of God, presupposes, before it can be properly grasped in a true life of faith, the dogma of grace to which it is linked and which in its turn necessarily rests upon the redemptive incarnation of the World.

(c) Approaching together the mystery of Christ, men discover the difficulty of speaking the same Christian language. By language is meant not just vocabulary, but above all mentality, the genius of a culture, philosophical tools, traditions and style of life.

With each one using the language of his own communion, the same words may signify quite different realities in one Church and in another, while different words may express the same reality. Since it is a question of establishing real and complete communication, of eliminating the risk of misunderstandings and of not travelling unware along parallel ways, it is absolutely necessary that those taking part in dialogue, even though they be formed by the spirit of the Scriptures and express themselves in a language in-

24. Cf. ibid., n. 9.
25. Ibid., n. 11.

spired by the Scriptures, should submit the language they use to a hermeneutic, a critical study.

5. In order to foster in themselves a spirit of true dialogue, and in order to prepare themselves for engaging in dialogue with their Christian brethren, Catholics will take careful note of the legitimate diversity within the Church's unity. Let them take care to promote "mutual esteem, reverence, and harmony, allowing for every legitimate difference, so that we can begin a dialogue among the People of God, pastors or faithful, which may become steadily more fruitful. The things that unite the faithful are stronger than those that divide them. Let there be unity in things essential, liberty in things doubtful, charity in all things."[26]

If Christians are prepared for dialogue within their own Communities, they are equipped to receive the fruits of an interconfessional dialogue. It is important that those who take part in the latter should consider themselves as the voice which must pass on to their own community the benefits they have received on its behalf during that dialogue.

6. The Catholic will be careful to check his manner of procedure in the ecumenical dialogue. In particular he will examine how closely he follows the directives and orientations given by the pastors of the Church regarding both the ecumenical task taken as a whole and dialogue in particular. He will normally become acquainted with these directives through the territorial commission for ecumenical questions or the diocesan commission.

Further, since ecumenical dialogue demands a very close fidelity to the life and faith of his Church, he must also be careful to share in the authentic renewals which develop within the Church, considering them "as favorable pledges and signs of ecumenical progress in the future."[27]

His commitment to dialogue can only be lived in a spirit of renunication, not only of any seeking for personal advantage, but also of confessional triumphalism or the appearance of it. This demands a spiritual climate which disposes the heart and mind to remain, in Christ, attentive to God and to the impulses of his Spirit. The essential qualities here are purity of intention, desire for holiness, an attitude of humility and repentance, and above all prayer.

Thanks to this atmosphere, the conviction strengthens

26. Pastoral Constitution on the Church in the Modern World, n. 92; cf. Decree on Ecumenism, n. 4.
27. Decree on Ecumenism, n. 6.

"that it will be possible to overcome the disagreements in an atmosphere of active patience, accepting the fact that time will be needed for ideas to mature and to make progress, and retaining at the same time a keen sense of the importance of the dialogue and of its efficacy."[28]

V. METHOD OF DIALOGUE

1. General remarks. Whether dialogue deals with questions of ecumenism or not, its method includes several elements, which appear either in succession or concurrently:

(a) exchange of ideas, whereby each participant explains his point of view on the subject of the meeting. This exchange has the aspect both of information, calling for competence in the participants and a desire to learn from the others, and of witness, when the facts or ideas set forth evoke in the speakers a religious attitude of faith and piety. It requires on both sides a resolve to be frank in expounding the truth and a resolve to welcome the truth one listens to;

(b) the comparing of ideas, whereby the participants try to bring to light the points of divergence, similarity and convergence in the ideas expounded. This demands attentive sympathy for persons and ideas, without which one cannot understand others' positions;

(c) research, by reflecting upon and discussing shared positions; all dialogue, even of the most elementary kind, always has this goal in view;

(d) the bringing to light of aspects previously unnoticed; in fact, as dialogue proceeds, the shared positions to which it leads become the starting point for fresh researches and further advances.

2. More specifically, attention is drawn to the following points concerning ecumenical dialogue:

(a) Each of the participants, starting from the understanding he has of the revealed mystery, should try to discover, evaluate and take into serious consideration everything in what the other says that seems to him to be of genuine value. The list of such things might be long. Here are a few useful indications for lines of enquiry:

truths confessed in common;

truths which have been allowed to become obscured in this or that community as a result of divisions and histor-

28. "A Working Paper on Ecumenical Dialogue," p. 36.

ical circumstances, and which may be better preserved and sometimes better developed in some other community;

true religious insights, valid theological intentions, even in areas of divergence; particular forms of worship, stresses laid on certain aspects of the Christian life, etc.

(b) Each partner should seek to expound the doctrine of his own community in a constructive manner, putting aside the tendency to define by opposition, which generally results in certain positions becoming overstressed or unduly hardened. This is a purifying process; the warping from which our respective theologies suffer can only be corrected at this price.

(c) The partners will work together towards a constructive synthesis, in such a way that every legitimate contribution is made use of, in a joint research aimed at the complete assimilation of the revealed datum. This research involves an effort to return to the sources, going back to Christian origins before the appearance of subsequent disagreements. It also calls for an effort at discovery, looking to the future for solutions that will transcend present historical differences.

(d) As the ecumenical dialogue proceeds, it opens up new perspectives for those taking part, leads them on to deeper research starting from the points of agreement they have recognized, and helps them to become aware of what adjustments of behavior and thought may seem necessary. "To seek in order to find, to find in order to seek still further": this saying of St. Augustine[29] comes home to them. Thus, thanks to that "brotherly emulation" that dialogue creates, they will be led "to a deeper realization and a clearer expression of the unfathomable riches of Christ."[30]

VI. SUBJECTS FOR DIALOGUE

1. Ecumenical dialogue may cover the content of faith, theological questions, subjects connected with liturgical and spiritual life, history, religious psychology, as well as anything that has to do with the presence, witness and mission of Christians in the world.

2. Subjects will be chosen by the participants taking into

29. *De Trinitate XV*, II, 2: *PL* 42, 1057: *Et quaeritur ut inveniatur dulcius et invenitur ut quaeratur avidius.*
30. Decree on Ecumenism, n. 11.

account local situations, the degree of specialized knowledge actually available, the qualifications of the participants or their involvement in the world, bearing in mind their confessional allegiance and also real questions that present themselves variously according to country or region and to historical, economic and sociological context. If dialogue is to be really effective at the level of the Christian people, a place must be given not only to the theologian but also to the sociologist, religious psychologist, anthropologist, historian—and above all to the pastor of souls.

3. Since dialogue is not an end in itself, the more experienced groups should be careful not to choose subjects which are too technical. Dialogue must spring from a legitimate desire for shared knowledge of an event or a situation. It is not just an academic discussion. For highly specialized subjects recourse will have to be made to experts who can provide the necessary information. But if the subjects were too technical for a group insufficiently prepared for them, or if specialists were continually called in, there would be a risk of bringing the dialogue to an end, because the participants would no longer be capable of expressing themselves to one another.

4. Attention to real life is fundamental as a guide in the choice of subjects and the way of tackling them. Certain subjects suggested in the Decree on Ecumenism will be the object of special attention, for example: the study of Scripture, the sacramental and liturgical life, notably on occasions of common prayer or attendance at the liturgical celebrations of the Churches.[31]

Further themes may be found in other documents of the Council or of the World Council of Churches: Revelation, the Church, Mission, the Church in the World, etc; also in questions raised by modern life, such as the problems of peace, overpopulation, marriage and birth, etc.; further, certain currents of contemporary thought: the philosophy of the "death of God," Marxism, encounter with non-Christian religions, the secularization phenomenon, etc. Whatever they may be, the subjects will be dealt with, in the light of the Gospel, as they affect and make demands upon the present-day life of Christians.

5. In some countries, the questions raised during the cris-

31. Cf. Decree on Ecumenism, ch. 3; Directory concerning Ecumenical Matters, Part One, nn. 50, 59: *AAS* 59 (1967), pp. 589, 591.

es of the eleventh and sixteenth centuries are today no longer the problem that they once were. Without forgetting historical origins, dialogue about such questions should focus
attention on the way they pose themselves here and now,
Particularly when dialogue hinges upon a subject relating to
faith, it will be a fruitful exercise to begin from the ecclesial witness of those taking part, so as to obtain a clearer
picture of how this faith is lived by them today within their
communities.

6. Dialogue, however, like all human effort, has its limits.
Certain differences between the Churches rest on data of a
historical, psychological and sociological order. They are
felt to be still irreducible. Other, deeper ones depend on the
way in which one conceives one's own faith and lives it.
Dialogue seems powerless here. The participants realize
that God is calling them to turn to him in prayer and that
he is teaching them to place their confidence in the power
of the Holy Spirit alone.

VII. FORMS OF DIALOGUE

1. The most frequent form of dialogue is the one which
springs up spontaneously when Christians meet one another. It is here that the desire makes itself felt to get to know
others better, and that the necessary contacts are made for
more organized meetings. It is impossible to regulate such
contacts, which are an integral part of the style of modern
life. But Christians must be helped to make use of them for
acquiring a better knowledge of one another's situation,
problems and doctrinal positions.

2. In particular, dialogue is carried on in a spontaneous
and unstructured way in many centers of education and
study. It is a means of education that allows the participants to get to know and understand better others' opinions
and convictions, to see more exactly their way of life and to
compare the various options open to men. It is therefore a
good thing to encourage young Catholics to take part in
such meetings, at the same time training them and giving
them support, so that they may be enriched by contact with
others and may bring to such meetings their own witness.

3. Groups of lay people will also meet to face in the light
of Christian faith the questions raised by their profession or
occupation: problems of law, medicine, politics, business,
technology, scientific research, the social sciences, trade un-

ion questions, and so on. The initiative for such meetings is the responsibility of the laymen themselves. They will readily call upon experts for questions which are beyond the competence of non-specialist participants.

4. In these various groups, Christians who are deeply aware of present-day problems often make them the subject of conversations, as country, particular time or the professional interests may suggest. Examples of such problems are peace, social justice, hunger, the problems of the underdeveloped countries, the running of cities, the difficulties of young households, etc. If they are attentive to the spirit of the Gospel, the participants are naturally led to joint enquiry, with a view to taking joint action in and for the world; here will be an opportunity for individual Christians and Christian Communions to bear a common witness.

5. As a consequence of these meetings, the legitmate desire to get to know other Christians better in their faith and their ecclesial and liturgical life may lead some people to form more specifically ecumenical groups, or to take part in already exsiting ones. It is to be desired that these groups should spring from friendly and fraternal personal contacts between Christians of the various communities. The Catholics will take pains to deepen their faith and to remain in communion of thought and desire with their Church. It will not be forgotten that the Holy Spirit can implant within the faithful charisms through which he means to act for the good of the Church and the world. The organization and conduct of such meetings can of course be entrusted to specially trained laymen, who will, where necessary, call upon theologians.

6. In mixed marriage households, ecumenical dialogue can have its place, with the attendance when desired of the pastors of the communities concerned. Such dialogue can serve to strengthen the religious life of the family and will in addition be an example of ecumenical charity

7. It is natural that the clergy of the different churches and communities should wish to meet one another for an exchange of views on the pastoral problems they have to face, so as to get to know the experiences of others, look for the best solutions to problems, take up common attitudes as far as the circumstances and the nature of the problem allow, and, when the occasion offers, decide on a practical course of joint action. Bishops will make a point of taking part in these meetings from time to time and of recom-

mending them to their priests. Such meetings will in fact
help to create an atmosphere favorable to the brotherhood
of all Christians. They will also help to replace the rivalries
of former times by ties of mutual help and collaboration. In
some countries these meetings often take place within recognized organizations, such as councils of churches and
ministerial associations.

8. Ecumenical dialogue can take place between theologians, for example members of ecumenical institutes, universities, faculties of theology and seminars. It goes without
saying that such dialogue requires of the Catholic participants a very serious, specific preparation for the questions
on the agenda. Care will be taken to note the necessary differences between the Church's dogma, the great spiritual
and liturgical traditions, and the legitimate options in the
matter of free discussion and research.

9. Dialogues may be two-sided or many-sided. The number and the confessional allegiance of those taking part will
be decided according to the subjects studied and to local
possibilities. In any event, during the dialogue those taking
part must bear in mind the Christian traditions not represented among them. It will often be a good idea to pass on
information concerning these meetings to the local ecumenical organizations and, in the case of more international
meetings, to the Secretariat for the Promotion of the Unity
of Christians.

10. In some theological dialogues, the participants are
appointed by the hierarchy to attend not in a personal capacity but as delegated representatives of their Church.
Such mandates can be given by the local ordinary, the episocopal conference within its territory or by the Holy See.
In these cases the Catholic participants have a special responsibility towards the authority that has sent them.

11. Ecumenical meetings at all levels will take account of
the existence of a body of literature which, taken as a
whole, amounts to a written form of dialogue between
Christians. This written dialogue is particularly fruitful
when the publications are interconfessional. Bishops will
encourage Catholic publications which, with regard to other
confessions, are marked by qualities of understanding and
esteem and have a keen sense of truth. These are the qualities that must mark any ecumenical undertaking.

12. Since the participants have a duty to see that the experience gained in these meetings benefit the members of

the Church, they will take care to communicate with the pastors of the Church, passing on information regarding their activities to the various commissions for ecumenism (the Secretariat for the Promotion of the Unity of Christians, national, regional or diocesan commissions). They will take an active part in initiatives of ecumenical interest, such as societies, libraries, reviews, publications, etc., and do their best to help these towards wider influence and circulation.

43

ON ADMITTING OTHER CHRISTIANS TO EUCHARISTIC COMMUNION IN THE CATHOLIC CHURCH[a]

S.P.U.C., *In Quibus Rerum Circumstantiis*, 1 June, 1972

I. THE QUESTION

We are often asked the question: "In what circumstances and on what conditions can members of other Churches and ecclesial communities be admitted to Eucharistic Communion in the Catholic Church?"

The question is not a new one. The Second Vatican Council (in the Decree on Ecumenism, *Unitatis Redintegratio*) and the *Ecumenical Directory* dealt with it.

The pastoral guidance offered here is not intended to change the existing rules but to explain them, bringing out the doctrinal principles on which the rules rest and so making their application easier.

II. THE EUCHARIST AND THE MYSTERY OF THE CHURCH

There is a close link between the mystery of the Church and the mystery of the Eucharist.

1. The Eucharist really contains what is the very foundation of the being and unity of the Church: the Body of Christ, offered in sacrifice and given to the faithful as the bread of eternal life. The sacrament of the Body and Blood of Christ, given to the Church so as to constitute the Church, of its nature carries with it:

(a) the ministerial power which Christ gave to his apostles and to their successors, the bishops along with the priests, to make effective sacramentally his own priestly act—that act by which once and forever he offered him-

a. The translation is that of the Secretariat. Latin text *AAS* 64 (1972) pp 518–525.

self to the Father in the Holy Spirit, and gave himself to his faithful that they might be one in him;

(b) the unity of the ministry, which is to be exercised in the name of Christ, Head of the Church, and hence in the hierarchial communion of ministers;

(c) the faith of the Church, which is expressed in the Eucharistic action itself—the faith by which she responds to Christ's gift in its true meaning.

The sacrament of the Eucharist, understood in its entirety with these three elements, signifies an existing unity brought about by him, the unity of the visible Church of Christ which cannot be lost.

2. "The celebration of Mass, the action of Christ and of the people of God hierarchically ordered, is the center of the whole Christian life, for the Universal Church as for the local Church and for each Christian." Celebrating the mystery of Christ in the Mass, the Church celebrates her own mystery and manifests concretely her unity.

The faithful assembled at the altar offer the sacrifice through the hands of the priest acting in the name of Christ, and they represent the community of the people of God united in the profession of one faith. Thus they constitute a sign and a kind of delegation of a wider assembly.

The celebration of Mass is of itself a profession of faith in which the whole Church recognizes and expresses itself. If we consider the marvellous meaning of the eucharistic prayers as well as the riches contained in the other parts of the Mass, whether they are fixed or vary with the liturgical cycle; if at the same time we bear in mind that the liturgy of the word and the eucharistic liturgy make up a single act of worship, then we can see here a striking illustration of the principle *lex orandi lex credendi*. Thus the Mass has a catechetical power which the recent liturgical renewal has emphasized. Again, the Church has in the course of history been careful to introduce into liturgical celebration the main themes of the common faith, the chief fruits of the experience of that faith. This she has done either by means of new texts or by creating new feasts.

3. The relation between local celebration of the Eucharist and universal ecclesial communion is stressed also by the special mention in the eucharistic prayers of the Pope, the local bishop and the other members of the Episcopal College.

What has been said here of the Eucharist as center and

summit of the Christian life holds for the whole Church
and for each of its members, but particularly for those who
take an active part in the celebration of Mass and above all
for those who receive the Body of Christ. Communion during Mass is indeed the most perfect way of participating in
the Eucharist, for it fulfils the Lord's command, "take and
eat."

III. THE EUCHARIST AS SPIRITUAL FOOD

The effect of the Eucharist is also to nourish spiritually
those who receive it as what the faith of the Church says it
truly is—the Body and Blood of the Lord given as the food
of eternal life (cf. Jn. 6:54–58). For the baptized, the Eucharist is spiritual food, a means by which they are brought
to live the life of Christ himself, are incorporated more profoundly in Him and share more intensely in the whole
economy of his saving mystery. "He who eats my flesh and
drinks my blood abides in me and I in him" (Jn. 6:56).

1. As the sacrament of full union with Christ and of the
perfection of spiritual life, the Eucharist is necessary to every Christian: in our Lord's words, ". . . unless you eat
the flesh of the Son of Man and drink his blood, you have
no life in you" (Jn. 6:53). Those who live intensely the life
of grace feel a compelling need for this spritual sustenance,
and the Church herself encourages daily communion.

2. Yet though it is a spiritual food whose effect is to unite
the Christian man to Jesus Christ, the Eucharist is far from
being simply a means of satisfying exclusively personal aspirations, however lofty these may be. The union brings
about the union of the faithful themselves with each other.
It is on their sharing of the Eucharist bread that St. Paul
bases the union of all the faithful: "Because there is one
loaf, we who are many are one body, for we all partake of
the same loaf" (1 Cor. 10:17). By this sacrament man is
incorporated in Christ and united with his members. By frequent receiving of the Eucharist the faithful are incorporated more and more in the Body of Christ and share increasingly in the mystery of the Church.

3. Spiritual need of the Eucharist is not therefore merely
a matter of personal spiritual growth: simultaneously, and
inseparably, it concerns our entering more deeply into
Christ's Church, "which is his body, the fullness of him who
fills all in all" (Eph. 1:23).

IV. GENERAL PRINCIPLES GOVERNING ADMIS-SION TO COMMUNION

Where members of the Catholic Church are concerned, there is a perfect parallel between regarding the Eucharist as the celebration of the entire ecclesial community united in one faith and regarding it as sustenance, as a response to the spiritual needs, personal and ecclesial, of each member. It will be the same when, in the Lord's good time, all the followers of Christ are reunited in one and the same Church. But what are we to say today, when Christians are divided? Any baptized person has a spiritual need for the Eucharist. Those who are not in full communion with the Catholic Church have recourse to the ministers of their own communities, as their conscience dictates. But what about those who cannot do this, and who for that or other reasons come and ask for communion from a Catholic priest?

The Ecumenical Directory (D. 37 and 40) has already shown how we must safeguard simultaneously the integrity of ecclesial communion and the good of souls. Behind the Directory lie two main governing ideas:

1. The strict relationship between the mystery of the Church and the mystery of the Eucharist can never be altered, whatever pastoral measures we may be led to take in given cases. Of its very nature, celebration of the Eucharist signifies the fullness of profession of faith and the fullness of ecclesial communion. This principle must not be obscured and must remain our guide in this field.

2. The principle will not be obscured if admission to Catholic eucharistic communion is confined to particular cases of those Christians who have a faith in the sacrament in conformity with that of the Church, who experience a serious spiritual need for the eucharistic sustenance, who for a prolonged period are unable to have recourse to a minister of their own community, and who ask for the sacrament of their own accord; all this provided that they have proper dispositions and lead lives worthy of a Christian. This spiritual need should be understood in the sense defined above: a need for an increase in spiritual life and a need for a deeper involvement in the mystery of the Church and of its unity.

Further, even if those conditions are fulfilled, it will be a pastoral responsibility to see that the admission of these other Christians to communion does not endanger or disturb the faith of Catholics.

V. DIFFERENCES, IN VIEW OF THESE PRINCIPLES, BETWEEN MEMBERS OF THE ORIENTAL CHURCHES AND OTHER CHRISTIANS

The Ecumenical Directory gives different directions for the admission to holy communion of separated Eastern Christians and of others. The reason is that the Eastern Churches, though separated from us, have true sacraments, above all because of the apostolic succession, the priesthood, and the Eucharist, which unite them to us by close ties, so that the risk of obscuring the relation between eucharistic communion and ecclesial communion is somewhat reduced. Recently the Holy Father recalled that: "between our Church and the venerable Orthodox Churches there exists already an almost total communion, though it is not yet perfect: it results from our joint participation in the mystery of Christ and of his Church."

With Christians who belong to communities whose eucharistic faith differs from that of the Church and which do not have the Sacrament of Orders, admitting them to the Eucharist entails the risk of obscuring the essential relation between eucharistic communion and ecclesial communion. This is why the Directory treats their case differently from that of the Eastern Christians and envisages admission only in exceptional cases of "urgent necessity." In cases of this kind the person concerned is asked to manifest a faith in the Eucharist in conformity with that of the Church, i.e., in the Eucharist as Christ instituted it and as the Catholic Church hands it on. This is not asked of an orthodox person, because he belongs to a Church whose faith in the Eucharist is conformable to our own.

VI. WHAT AUTHORITY DECIDES PARTICULAR CASES: THE MEANING OF NO. 55 OF THE ECUMENICAL DIRECTORY

No. 55 of the Directory allows fairly wide discretionary power to the episcopal authority in judging whether the necessary conditions are present for these exceptional cases. If cases of the same pattern recur often in a given region, episcopal conferences can give general directions. More often, however, it falls to the bishop of the diocese to make a decision. He alone will know all the circumstances of particular cases.

Apart from danger of death, the Directory mentions two examples, people in prison and those suffering persecution, but it then speaks of "other cases of such urgent necessity." Such cases are not confined to situations of suffering and danger. Christians may find themselves in grave spiritual necessity and with no chance of recourse to their own community. For example, in our time, which is one of large-scale movements of population, it can happen much more often than before that non-Catholic Christians are scattered in Catholic regions. They are often deprived of the help of their own communion and unable to get in touch with it except at great trouble and expense. If the conditions set out in the Directory are verified, they can be admitted to eucharistic communion, but it will be for the bishop to consider each case.

44

NOTE INTERPRETING THE "INSTRUCTION ON ADMITTING OTHER CHRISTIANS TO EUCHARISTIC COMMUNION IN THE CATHOLIC CHURCH UNDER CERTAIN CIRCUMSTANCES"[a]

S.P.U.C., *Dopo le publicazione,* 17 October, 1973

1. After the publication of the "Instruction on Admitting Other Christians to Eucharistic Communion in the Catholic Church" on 1 June 1972, various interpretations of it were given, some of which depart from the letter and the spirit of the document. To prevent the spread of such inaccurate interpretations and their consequences, we think it useful to recall to mind a few points.

2. With this Instruction, pastoral in character, the Secretariat for Promotion of the Unity of Christians had no intention of changing the rules laid down by the Vatican Council's Decree on Ecumenism and further explained by the Ecumenical Directory (D. *37* and *40*). The intention was to explain that the existing discipline derives from the requirements of the faith and so retains its full vigor.

3. The basic principles of the Instruction are:

(a) There is an indissoluble link between the mystery of the Church and the mystery of the Eucharist or between ecclesial and eucharistic communion; the celebration of the Eucharist of itself signifies the fullness of profession of faith and ecclesial communion (cf. Instruction, Pt. II, 1, 2, 3)

(b) The Eucharist is for the baptized a spiritual food which enables them to live with Christ's own life, to be incorporated more profoundly in him and share more intensely in the whole economy of the Mystery of Christ (cf. Instruction, (D. *43*), Pt. II).

a. Translation from *L'Osservatore Romano,* 15 Nov. 1973. Italian original in *AAS* 55 (1973) pp. 616–619.

4. Within the full communion of faith, eucharistic communion is the expression of this full communion and therefore of the unity of the faithful; at the same time it is the means of maintaining and reinforcing this unity. But eucharistic communion practiced by those who are not in full ecclesial communion with each other cannot be the expression of that full unity which the Eucharist of its nature signifies and which in this case does not exist; for this reason such communion cannot be regarded as a means to be used to lead to full ecclesial communion.

5. All the same, both the Ecumenical Directory and the Instruction, on the strength of what has already been said in the Vatican Council's Decree on Ecumenism, allow the possibility of exceptions insofar as the Eucharist is necessary spiritual nourishment for the Christian life.

6. It is the local ordinary's responsibility to examine these exceptional cases and make concrete decisions. The Instruction (n. 6) recalls that the Ecumenical Directory gives the episcopal authority power to decide whether in these rare cases the required conditions are present or not. The episcopal authority's faculty of examining and deciding is governed by criteria laid down in the Ecumenical Directory (n. 55) and further explained in the Instruction (Pt. IV, 2): ". . . admission to Catholic eucharistic communion is confined to particular cases of those Christians who have a faith in the sacrament in conformity with that of the Church, who experience a serious spiritual need for the eucharistic sustenance, who for a prolonged period are unable to have recourse to a minister of their own community, and who ask for the sacrament of their own accord; all this provided that they have proper dispositions and lead lives worthy of a Christian."

This criterion is observed if all the required conditions are verified. An objective, pastorally responsible examination does not allow any of the conditions to be ignored.

It must also be noted that the Instruction speaks of particular cases, which are to be examined individually. Hence a general regulation cannot be issued which makes a category out of an exceptional case, nor is it possible to legitimize on the basis of *epikeia* by turning this latter into a general rule.

Nevertheless, the bishop can in the various situations decide what are the needs that make exceptions applicable, that is to say, what constitutes a special case, and they can determine the manner of verifying whether all the required conditions are fulfilled in such a particular case. When particular cases present themselves fairly often in one region, following a recurrent pattern, episcopal conferences can issue some guiding principles for ascertaining that all the conditions are verified in particular cases. Normally however it will be within the competence of the local ordinary to judge such cases.

7. For other Christians to be admitted to the Eucharist in the Catholic Church the Instruction requires that they manifest a faith in the sacrament in conformity with that of the Catholic Church. This faith is not limited to a mere affirmation of the "real presence" in the Eucharist, but implies the doctrine of the Eucharist as taught in the Catholic Church.

8. It is to be noted that the Instruction (Pt. V) calls to mind the fact that the *Directorium Oecumenicum* (par. 34–54) provides for the Orientals not in full communion with the Catholic Church rules different from those regarding other Christians (par. 55–63). For example:

(a) since they belong to a community whose eucharistic faith is in conformity with that of the Catholic Church, a personal declaration of faith in the sacrament will not be required of them when they are admitted: in an Orthodox Christian this faith is taken for granted;

(b) since the Orthodox Churches have true sacraments and, above all, by virtue of apostolic succession, the priesthood and the Eucharist, concessions for sacramental communion must take account of legitimate reciprocity (n. 43);

(c) justifiable reasons for advising sacramental sharing are considerably more extensive.

9. The question of reciprocity arises only with these Churches which have preserved the substance of the Eucharist, the Sacrament of Orders and apostolic succession. Hence a Catholic cannot ask for the Eucharist except from a minister who has been validly ordained (*Directorium Oecumenicum*, n. 55).

10. The desire to share the Eucharist fundamentally expresses the desire of the perfect ecclesial unity of all Christians which Christ willed. Interconfessional dialogue on the theology of the Eucharist (as sacrament and sacrifice), on the theology of ministry and of the Church is pursuing its course within the ambit of the ecumenical movement, sup-

ported by the promises and prayer of our Lord; it is stimulated and enlivened by the charity, poured into our hearts by the Holy Spirit who has been given to us. We express the hope that the ecumenical movement will lead to a common profession of faith among Christians, and so allow us to celebrate the Eucharist in ecclesial unity, giving fulfilment to the words "Because there is one bread, we who are many are one body" (1 Cor. 10:17).

45

DECREE ON THE PASTORAL OFFICE OF BISHOPS IN THE CHURCH[a]

Vatican II, *Christus Dominus*, 28 October, 1965

INTRODUCTION

1. Christ the Lord, the Son of the living God, came to redeem his people from their sins[1] that all mankind might be sanctified. Having been sent by the Father, he in turn sent his apostles[2] whom he sanctified by conferring on them the Holy Spirit so that they also might glorify the Father on earth and procure the salvation of men "for the building up of the Body of Christ" (Eph. 4:12) which is the Church.

2. In this Church of Christ the Roman Pontiff, as the successor of Peter, to whom Christ entrusted the care of his sheep and his lambs, has been granted by God supreme, full, immediate and universal power in the care of souls. As pastor of all the faithful his mission is to promote the common good of the universal Church and the particular good of all the churches. He is therefore endowed with the primacy of ordinary power over all the churches.

The bishops also have been designated by the Holy Spirit to take the place of the apostles as pastors of souls[3] and, together with the Supreme Pontiff and subject to his authority, they are commissioned to perpetuate the work of Christ, the eternal Pastor.[4] For Christ commanded the apostles and their successors and gave them the power to

---

a. Translated by Matthew Dillon, o.s.b., Edward O'Leary, o.p. and A.F. The references to D. *46* at the end of certain sections indicate where the norms for their implementation may be found, in *Ecclesiae Sanctae*, 1.

1. Cf. Mt. 1:21.
2. Cf. Jn. 20:21.
3. Cf. VAT. I, fourth session, part 1 of Dogm. Const. on the Church of Christ, ch. 3, *Denz.* 1828 (306).
4. Cf. VAT.I, fourth session, Introd. to Dogm. Const. on the Church of Christ: *Denz.* 1821 (3050).

teach all peoples, to sanctify men in truth and to give them spiritual nourishment. By virtue, therefore, of the Holy Spirit who has been given to them, bishops have been constituted true and authentic teachers of the faith and have been made pontiffs and pastors.[5]

3. United in one college or body for the instruction and direction of the universal Church, the bishops, sharing in the solicitude of all the churches, exercise this their episcopal function, which they have received by virtue of their episcopal consecration[6] in communion with the Supreme Pontiff and subject to his authority. They exercise this function individually as regards that portion of the Lord's flock which has been entrusted to each one of them, each bishop having responsibility for the particular church assigned to him. On occasion a number of bishops will cooperate to provide for the common needs of their churches.

Accordingly the sacred Synod, having regard to the conditions of human society which have brought about a new order of things, has promulgated the following decrees in order to determine more exactly the pastoral functions of bishops.[7]

CHAPTER I

THE BISHOPS IN THEIR RELATION TO THE UNIVERSAL CHURCH

I. THE ROLE OF THE BISHOPS IN THE UNIVERSAL CHURCH

4. The bishops, by virtue of their sacramental consecration and their hierarchical communion with the head of the college and its other members, are constituted members of

5. Cf. VAT. II, Dogm. Const. on the Church, ch. 3, nn. 21, 24, 25: *AAS* 57 (1965) pp. 24–25, 29–31.
6. Cf. VAT. II, Dogm. Const. on the Church, ch. 3, n. 21: *AAS* 57 (1965) pp. 24–25.
7. Cf. John XXIII, apost. const. *Humanae Salutis*, Dec. 25, 1961: *AAS* 54 (1962) p. 6.

the episcopal body.[1] "The order of bishops is the successor to the college of the apostles in their role as teachers and pastors, and in it the apostolic college is perpetuated. Together with their head, the Supreme Pontiff, and never apart from him, they have supreme and full authority over the universal Church, but this power cannot be exercised without the agreement of the Roman Pontiff."[2] This authority "is exercised in a solemn way in an ecumenical council."[3] Accordingly the sacred Synod decrees that all bishops who are members of the episcopal college have the right to take part in an ecumenical council. "This same collegiate power can be exercised in union with the Pope by the bishops whilst living in different parts of the world, provided the head of the college summon them to collegiate action, or at least approve or freely admit the corporate action of the unassembled bishops, so that a truly collegiate action may result."[4]

5. Bishops chosen from different parts of the world in a manner and according to a system determined or to be determined by the Roman Pontiff will render to the Supreme Pastor a more effective auxiliary service in a council which shall be known by the special name of Synod of Bishops.[5] This council, as it will be representative of the whole Catholic episcopate, will bear testimony to the participation of all the bishops in hierarchical communion in the care of the universal Church.[6]

6. Bishops, as legitimate successors of the apostles and members of the episcopal college, should appreciate that they are closely united to each other and should be solicitous for all the churches. By divine institution and by virtue of their apostolic office, all of them jointly are responsible for the Church.[7]

They should be especially solicitous for those parts of the

1. Cf. VAT. II, Dogm. Const. on the Church, ch. 3, n. 22: *AAS* 57 (1965) pp. 25–27.
2. Ibid.
3. Ibid.
4. Ibid.
5. Cf. Paul VI, motu proprio *Apostolica Solicitudo*, 15 Sept. 1965: *AAS* 57 (1965) pp. 775–780.
6. Cf. VAT. II, Dogm. Const. on the Church, ch. 3, n. 23: *AAS* 57 (1965) pp. 27–28.
7. Cf. Pius XII, encycl. letter *Fidei Donum*, 21 Apr. 1957: *AAS* 49 (1957) p. 27. Cf. also Benedict XV, apost. letter *Maximum Illud*, 30 Nov. 1919: *AAS* 11 (1919) p. 440; Pius XI, encycl. letter *Rerum Ecclesiae*, 28 Feb. 1926: *AAS* 18 (1926) pp. 68 ff.

world in which the word of God has not yet been proclaimed or in which, especially on account of the scarcity
of priests, the faithful are in danger of falling away from
the obligations of the Christian life or even of losing the
faith itself. Bishops should, therefore, do their utmost to ensure that the activities of evangelization and the apostolate
are zealously supported and promoted by the faithful. It
should, moreover, be their special care that suitable priests,
as well as lay and religious auxiliaries, be trained for those
missions and regions suffering from a lack of clergy. They
should arrange also, as far as it is possible, that some of
their priests should go to these missions or dioceses to exercise the sacred ministry there, either permanently or for a
fixed period.

Furthermore, bishops should bear it in mind that in the
expenditure of ecclesiastical resources they must take into
account the needs not only of their own dioceses but of other individual churches, since they too form part of the one
Church of Christ. Let it be their care also to give help according to their resources when other dioceses or regions
are afflicted by disaster. (See D. 46, 1–5.)

7. Above all, they should extend their brotherly care to
those bishops who are harassed by calumny and hardship
for the name of Christ, who are detained in prison or prevented from exercising their ministry. They should manifest
an active fraternal interest in them so that their sufferings
may be lessened and alleviated by the prayers and works of
their brethren.

II. BISHOPS AND THE APOSTOLIC SEE

8. (a) Bishops, as the successors of the apostles, enjoy as
of right in the dioceses assigned to them all ordinary, special and immediate power which is necessary for the exercise of their pastoral office, but always without prejudice to
the power which the Roman Pontiff possesses, by virtue of
his office, of reserving certain matters to himself or to some
other authority.

(b) Individual diocesan bishops have the power to dispense from the general law of the Church in particular cases those faithful over whom they normally exercise authority. It must, however, be to their spiritual benefit and may
not cover a matter which has been specially reversed by the
supreme authority of the Church.

9. In exercising his supreme, full and immediate authority over the universal Church the Roman Pontiff employs the various departments of the Roman Curia, which act in his name and by his authority for the good of the churches and in the service of the sacred pastors. It is the earnest desire of the Fathers of the sacred Council that these departments, which have indeed rendered excellent service to the Roman Pontiff and to the pastors of the Church, should be reorganized and modernized, should be more in keeping with different regions and rites, especially in regard to their number, their names, their competence, their procedures and methods of coordination.[b] It is hoped also that, in view of the pastoral role proper to bishops, the functions of the legates of the Roman Pontiff should be more precisely determined.

10. Furthermore, as these departments have been instituted for the good of the universal Church it is hoped that their members, officials and consultors, as well as the legates of the Roman Pontiff, may be chosen, as far as it is possible, on a more representative basis, so that the offices or central agencies of the Church may have a truly universal spirit. It is urged also that more bishops, especially diocesan bishops, be co-opted to membership of these departments, who will be better able to inform the Supreme Pontiff on the thinking, the hopes and the needs of all the churches.[c] Finally, the Fathers of the Council judge that it would be most advantageous if these departments were to have more frequent recourse to the advice of laymen of virtue, knowledge and experience so that they also may have an appropriate role in the affairs of the Church.

b. This has since been done. See Appendix: full list of documents at the end of this volume, section on the Church.
c. See A. 23.

CHAPTER II

BISHOPS IN RELATION TO THEIR OWN
CHURCHES OR DIOCESES

I. DIOCESAN BISHOPS

11. A diocese is a section of the People of God entrusted to a bishop to be guided by him with the assistance of his clergy so that, loyal to its pastor and formed by him into one community in the Holy Spirit through the Gospel and the Eucharist, it constitutes one particular church in which the one, holy, catholic and apostolic Church of Christ is truly present and active.

Individual bishops to whom the care of particular dioceses is committed care for their flocks under the authority of the Supreme Pontiff, in the name of God, as their proper, ordinary and immediate pastors, sanctifying and governing them. They should, however, recognize the rights which are conferred by law on Patriarchs or other hierarchial authorities.[1]

Bishops should devote themselves to their apostolic office as witnesses of Christ to all men. They should not limit themselves to those who already acknowledge the Prince of Pastors but should also devote their energies wholeheartedly to those who have strayed in any way from the path of truth or who have no knowledge of the gospel of Christ and of his saving mercy, so that ultimately all men may walk "in all goodness, justice and truth." (Eph. 5:9)

12. When they exercise their teaching role, bishops should proclaim the gospel of Christ to men. This is one of the principal duties of bishops.[2] Fortified by the Spirit they should call on men to believe or should strengthen them when they already have a living faith. They should expound to them the whole mystery of Christ, that is, all those truths ignorance of which means ignorance of Christ. They should

1. Cf. VAT. II, Decree on Eastern Catholic Churches, 21 Nov. 1964, nn. 7–11: *AAS* 57 (1965) pp. 29 ff.
2. Cf. Council of Trent, fifth session, Decree *De reform*. ch. 2, Mansi 33, 30; twenty-fourth session, Decree *De reform*. ch. 4, Mansi 33, 159; VAT. II, Dogm. Const. on the Church, ch. 3, art. 25: *AAS* 57 (1965) pp. 29 ff.

show them, likewise, the way, divinely revealed, to give glory to God and thus attain eternal beatitude.[3]

They should demonstrate that worldly things and human institutions are ordered, according to the plan of God the Creator, towards the salvation of men, and that they can therefore make no small contribution to the building up of the Body of Christ.

Let them explain also how high a value, according to the doctrine of the Church, should be placed on the human person, on his liberty and bodily life; how highly we should value the family, its unity and stability, the procreation and education of children, human society with its laws and professions, its labor and leisure, its arts and technical inventions, its poverty and abundance. They should expound likewise the principles governing the solution of those very grave problems concerning the possession, increase and just distribution of material goods, concerning peace and war, and the fraternal coexistence of all peoples.[4]

13. Bishops should present the doctrine of Christ in a manner suited to the needs of the times, that is, so it may be relevant to those difficulties and questions which men find especially worrying and intimidating. They should also safeguard this doctrine, teaching the faithful themselves to defend it and propagate it. In presenting this doctrine they should proclaim the maternal solicitude of the Church for all men, whether they be Catholics or not, and should be especially solicitous for the poor and weaker brethren whom the Lord has commissioned them to evangelize.

Since it is the mission of the Church to maintain close relation with the society in which she lives[5] the bishops should make it their special care to approach men and to initiate and promote dialogue with them. These discussions on religious matters should be marked by charity of expression as well as by humility and courtesy, so that truth may be combined with charity, and understanding with love. The discussions should likewise be characterized by due prudence allied, however, with sincerity which by promoting friendship is conducive to a union of minds.[6]

3. Cf. VAT. II, Dogm. Const. on the Church, ch. 3, n. 25: *AAS* 57 (1965) pp. 29–31.
4. Cf. John XXIII, Encycl. letter *Peace on Earth,* 11 Apr. 1963 passim: *AAS* 55 (1963) pp. 257–304.
5. Cf. Paul VI, Encycl. letter *Ecclesiam suam,* 6 Aug. 1964: *AAS* 56 (1964) p. 639.
6. Cf. Paul VI, ibid. *AAS* 56 (1964) pp. 644–645.

Bishops should also endeavor to use the various methods available nowadays for proclaiming Christian doctrine. There are, first of all, preaching and catechetical instruction, which always hold pride of place. There is also doctrinal instruction in schools, universities, conferences and meetings of every kind. Finally, there are public statements made by way of comment on events, as well as the press and other media of public communication, all of which should be employed for the promulgation of the gospel of Christ.[7]

14. Bishops should be especially concerned about catechetical instruction. Its function is to develop in men a living, explicit and active faith, enlightened by doctrine. It should be very carefully imparted, not only to children and adolescents but also to young people and even to adults. In imparting this instruction the teachers must observe an order and method suited not only to the matter in hand but also to the character, the ability, the age and the life-style of their audience. This instruction should be based on holy scripture, tradition, liturgy, and on the teaching authority and life of the Church.

They should, furthermore, ensure that catechists are adequately prepared for their task, being well-instructed in the doctrine of the Church and possessing both a practical and theoretical knowledge of the laws of psychology and of educational method.

They should take steps to reestablish or to modernize the adult catechumenate.

15. In exercising their mission of sanctification bishops should be mindful of the fact that they have been chosen from among men and made their representatives before God to offer gifts and sacrifices in expiation of sins. It is the bishops who enjoy the fullness of the sacrament of orders, and both priests and deacons are dependent on them in the exercise of their power. The former, in order that they may be prudent cooperators with the episcopal order, have also been consecrated as true priests of the New Testament; the latter, having been ordained for the ministry, serve the people of God in union with the bishop and his clergy. It is therefore bishops who are the principal dispensers of the mysteries of God, and it is their function to control, pro-

7. Cf. VAT. II, Decree on the Instruments of Social Communication, 4 Dec. 1963: *AAS* 56 (1964) pp. 145–153.

mote and protect the entire liturgical life of the Church entrusted to them.[8]

They should therefore see to it that the faithful know and live the paschal mystery more deeply through the Eucharist, forming one closely-knit body, united by the charity of Christ;[9] "devoting themselves to prayer and the ministry of the word" (Acts 6:4).[10] They should aim to make of one mind in prayer all who are entrusted to their care, and to ensure their advancement in grace through the reception of the sacraments, and that they become faithful witnesses to the Lord.

As spiritual guides of their flocks, bishops should be zealous in promoting the sanctity of their clergy, their religious and their laity according to the vocation of each indivdual,[11] remembering that they are under an obligation to give an example of sanctity in charity, humility and simplicity of life. Let them so sanctify the churches entrusted to them that the mind of the universal Church of Christ may be fully reflected in them. They should, therefore, make every effort to foster vocations to the priesthood and to the religious life, and encourage missionary vocations especially.

16. In exercising his office of father and pastor the bishop should be with his people as one who serves,[12] as a good shepherd who knows his sheep and whose sheep know him, as a true father who excels in his love and solicitude for all, to whose divinely conferred authority all readily submit. He should so unite and mold his flock into one family that all, conscious of their duties, may live and act in the communion of charity.

In order to accomplish these things effectively the bishop "being ready for every good work" (2 Tim. 2:21) and "enduring all things for the sake of the elect" (2 Tim. 2:10) should so arrange his own life s to accommodate it to the needs of the times. His priests, who assume a part of his

8. Cf. VAT. II, Const. on the Sacred Liturgy, 4 Dec. 1963: *AAS* 56 (1964) pp. 97 ff; Paul VI, motu proprio *Sacram Liturgiam,* 25 Jan. 1964. *AAS* 56 (1964) pp. 139 ff.
9. Cf. Pius XII, Encycl. letter *Mediator Dei,* 20 Nov. 1947: *AAS* 39 (1947) pp. 97 ff; Paul VI, Encycl. *Mysterium Fidei,* 3 Sept. 1965: *AAS* 57 (1965) pp. 753–774.
10. Cf. Acts 1:14 and 2:46.
11. Cf. VAT. II, Dogm. Const. on the Church, ch. 6, nn. 44–45: *AAS* 57 (1965) pp. 50–52.
12. Lk. 22:26, 27.

duties and concerns, and who are ceaselessly devoted to their work, should be the objects of his particular affection. He should regard them as sons and friends.[13] He should always be ready to listen to them and cultivate an atmosphere of easy familiarity with them, thus facilitating the pastoral work of the entire diocese.

A bishop should be solicitious for the welfare—spiritual, intellectual, and material—of his priests, so that they may live holy and pious lives, and exercise a faithful and fruitful ministry. With this end in view he should encourage courses and arrange for special conferences for his priests from time to time. These could take the form of extended retreats for the renewal of their spiritual lives or courses intended to deepen their knowledge of ecclesiastical studies, especially of sacred scripture and theology, of the more important social questions, or of new methods of pastoral activity. (See D. *46*, 7 and 8.)

A bishop should be compassionate and helpful to those priests who are in any kind of danger or who have failed in some respect.

In order to be able to provide for the welfare of the faithful as their individual circumstances demand, he should try to keep himself informed of their needs in the social circumstances in which they live. To this end he should employ suitable methods, especially social research. He should be solicitious for all men whatever their age, condition or nationality, whether they are natives, visitors or foreign immigrants. In exercising his ministry he should ensure that the faithful are duly involved in Church affairs; he should recognize their right and duty to play their part in building up the Mystical Body of Christ.

Bishops should show affectionate consideration in their relations with the separated brethren and should urge the faithful also to exercise all kindness and charity in their regard, encouraging ecumenism as it is understood by the Church.[14] The non-baptized also should be the object of their solicitude so that on them too may shine the charity of Christ of whom bishops are the witnesses before all men.

17. The various forms of the apostolate should be encouraged. Close collaboration and the coordination of all the apostolic works under the direction of the bishop

---

13. Jn. 15:15.
14. Cf. VAT. II, Decree on Ecumenism: *AAS* 57 (1965) pp. 90–107.

should be promoted in the diocese as a whole or in parts of it. Thus all the undertakings and organizations, whether their object be catechetical, missionary, charitable, social, family, educational, or any other pastoral end, will act together in harmony, and the unity of the diocese will be more closely demonstrated.

The faithful should be carefully reminded of their obligation to promote the apostolate according to their state of life and aptitudes, and they should be urged to participate in or assist the various works of the lay apostolate, especially Catholic action. Those associations also should be inaugurated or encouraged which have, either directly or indirectly, a supernatural object such as the attainment of a more perfect life, the preaching of the gospel of Christ to all men, the promotion of Christian doctrine or of public worship, the pursuit of social aims, or the practice of works of piety or charity.

The forms of the apostolate should be duly adapted to the needs of the times, taking into account the human conditions, not merely spiritual and moral but also social, demographic and economic. This can be done effectively with the help of social and religious research conducted by institutes of pastoral sociology, the establishment of which is strongly recommended.

18. Special concern should be shown for those members of the faithful who, on account of their way of life are not adequately catered for by the ordinary pastoral ministry of the parochial clergy or are entirely deprived of it. These include the many migrants, exiles and refugees, sailors and airmen, itinerants and others of this kind. Suitable pastoral methods should be developed to provide for the spiritual life of people on holidays.

Conferences of bishops, and especially national conferences, should give careful consideration to the more important questions relating to these categories. They should determine and provide by common agreement and united effort suitable means and directives to cater for their spiritual needs. In doing this they should give due consideration especially to the norms determined,[15] or to be deter-

15. Cf. St. Pius X, motu proprio *Iampridem,* 19 Mar. 1914: *AAS* 6 (1914) pp. 173 ff; Pius XII, Apost. Const. *Exsul Familia,* 1 Aug. 1952: *AAS* 44 (1952) pp. 649 ff; Pius XII, *Regulations for the Apostolate of the Sea,* 21 Nov. 1957: *AAS* 50 (1958) pp. 375–383.

mined, by the Holy See, adapting them to their own times, places and people.[d] (See D. *46*, 9.)

19. In the exercise of their apostolic function, which is directed towards the salvation of souls, bishops enjoy as of right full and perfect freedom and independence from all civil authority. It is, therefore, unlawful to obstruct them directly or indirectly in the exercise of their ecclesiastical office or to prevent them from communicating freely with the Apostolic See and other ecclesiastical authorities or with their subjects.

In fact, the sacred pastors in devoting themselves to the spiritual care of their flock are in fact promoting social and civil progress and prosperity. With this end in view they co-operate actively with the public authorities in a manner consonant with their office and fitting for bishops, enjoining obedience to just laws and prescribing reverence for legitimately constituted authority.

20. Since the apostolic office of bishops was instituted by Christ the Lord and is directed to a spiritual and supernatural end, the sacred Ecumenical Council asserts that the competent ecclesiastical authority has the proper, special, and, as of right, exclusive power to appoint and install bishops. Therefore in order to safeguard the liberty of the Church and the better and more effectively to promote the good of the faithful, it is the desire of the sacred Council that for the future no rights or privileges be conceded to the civil authorities in regard to the election, nomination or presentation to bishoprics. The civil authorities in question, whose good will towards the Church the sacred Synod gratefully acknowledges and highly appreciates, are respectfully asked to initiate discussions with the Holy See with the object of freely waiving the aforesaid rights and privileges which they at present enjoy by agreement or custom. (see D. *46*, 10.)

21. As the pastoral office of bishops is so important and onerous, diocesan bishops and others whose juridical position corresponds to theirs are earnestly requested to resign from their office if on account of advanced age or from any other grave cause they become less able to carry out their duties. This they should do on their own initiative or when invited to do so by the competent authority. If the com-

---

d. Directories on migrants and tourists have since been published by the Holy See and are reproduced in this volume.

petent authority accepts the resignation it will make provision for the suitable support of those who have retired and for the special rights to be accorded to them. (See D. 46, 11.)

II. DIOCESAN BOUNDARIES

22. For a diocese to fulfill its purpose it is necessary that the nature of the Church be clearly manifested in the People of God belonging to the diocese. Bishops must be able to carry out their pastoral function effectively among their people, and finally the spiritual welfare of the People of God must be catered for as perfectly as possible. This requires not only a proper determination of the territorial limits of the diocese but also a reasonable distribution of clergy and resources in accordance with the needs of the apostolate. All these things contribute to the good, not only of the clergy and the faithful who are directly involved, but also of the whole Church.

Therefore as regards diocesan boundaries the sacred Synod decrees that, insofar as the good of souls requires it, a prudent revision of diocesan boundaries be undertaken as soon as possible. This can be done by dividing, distributing or uniting dioceses, changing their boundaries, or appointing a more suitable place for the episcopal see, or finally, and especially in those dioceses which comprise larger cities, by establishing a new internal organization. (See D. 46, 12.)

23. In revising diocesan boundaries a first care should be the preservation of the organic unity of each diocese, as in a healthy living body. This applies to persons, offices and institutions. Due weight being given in individual cases to the particular circumstances, the following general criteria should be borne in mind:

(1) In determining diocesan boundaries the variety of the composition of the People of God should be taken into consideration as far as possible, since this may materially contribute to more effective pastoral care.

At the same time an effort should be made to ensure as far as possible that the demographic groupings remain united with the civil offices and institutions which constitute their organic structure. For this reason the territory of each diocese should be continuous.

The limits of civil boundaries should also be taken into account where they occur, as well as the special characteristics—psychological, economic, geographical or historical—of people and regions.

(2) The size of the diocesan territory and the number of its inhabitants should as a general rule be such that on the one hand the bishop himself, assisted perhaps by others, is able to duly exercise his pontifical functions and carry out his pastoral visitations in it. He should also be in a position to control and coordinate effectively all the apostolic activities in his diocese, and especially to know his priests and all the religious and laymen who are involved in diocesan activities. On the other hand a diocese should provide sufficient and suitable scope for the bishop and his priests to employ usefully all their energies in the ministry, taking into account the needs of the universal Church.

(3) Finally, for the more effective exercise of the ministry of salvation, each diocese should normally have enough priests capable of looking after the People of God. Those offices, institutions and activities should not be lacking which are suited to a particular diocese and which experience shows to be necessary for its efficient administration and for its apostolate. Lastly, resources for the care of personnel and the maintenance of instituions should be already in hand or at least it should be foreseen that they will be provided from elsewhere.

Accordingly, where there are believers of different rites, the bishop of that diocese should make provision for their spiritual needs either by providing priests of those rites, or special parishes, or by appointing episcopal vicars, with the necessary faculties. If necessary, such a vicar may be ordained bishop. Alternatively, the bishop himself may perform the functions of an Ordinary for each of the different rites. And if the Apostolic See judges that, on account of some special circumstances, none of these alternatives are practicable, a special hierarchy should be established for each different rite.[16]

Likewise in similar circumstances provision should be made for the faithful of a different language group either by appointing priests who speak that language, or by creating special parishes, or by appointing an episcopal vicar well versed in it. If it is deemed suitable he may be ordained

16. Cf. VAT. II, Decree on Eastern Catholic Churches, n. 4: *AAS* 57 (1965) p. 77.

bishop, or the matter may be dealt with in some other appropriate way. (See D. *46*, 12.)

24. The competent episcopal conferences should examine all matters relating to the changes and alterations to be made in dioceses in their territories, in accordance with nn. 22, 23. This is without prejudice to the discipline of the Oriental Church. A special episcopal commission may be established for the purpose, but the views of the bishops of the provinces or regions involved should always be taken especially into consideration. Finally, they should present their recommendations and wishes to the Apostolic See. (See D. *46*, 12.)

III. THOSE WHO COOPERATE WITH THE DIOCESAN BISHOP IN HIS PASTORAL TASK

A. Coadjutor and auxiliary bishops

25. In governing their dioceses, bishops must take the good of the Lord's flock as their highest objective. This will often demand the appointment of auxiliary bishops, the bishop of the diocese being unable to perform his duty sufficiently well for the good of souls on his own, either because of the great size of the diocese, the number of inhabitants, some special pastoral problem, or for some other reasons. Sometimes indeed special circumstances may require that a coadjutor bishop be appointed to assist the diocesan bishop. Suitable faculties should be conferred on these coadjutors and auxiliary bishops so that, without prejudice to the untiy of the diocesan administration or to the authority of the diocesan bishop, their labors may be more effective and the dignity of the episcopal office duly safeguarded.

Since coadjutors and auxiliary bishops are chosen to share the burdens of the diocesan bishop, they should so perform their ministry that in all matters they act in single-minded accord with him. They should show all respect and reverence for the bishop of the diocese, who for his part should have a fraternal affection for his coadjutors or auxiliaries and should hold them in esteem. (See D *46*, 13.)

26. When the good of souls requires it the diocesan bishop should not hesitate to ask for one or more auxiliaries, who will be appointed for the diocese, however, without any right of succession.

If it is not expressly provided in the letters of nomination, the diocesan bishop should appoint his auxiliary—or each of his auxiliaries—vicar general or at least episcopal vicar. They will, however, be dependent on his authority. He may think it well to consult them in deciding matters of greater importance, especially questions of pastoral significance.

Unless it has been otherwise provided by the competent authority, the powers and faculties conferred by law on auxiliary bishops are not terminated by the departure from office of the diocesan bishop. It is indeed desirable, unless there are grave reasons to the contrary, that the responsibility of governing the diocese during the vacancy of the see should be entrusted to the auxiliary bishop, or if there are several, to one of them.

A coadjutor bishop, that is, one nominated with the right of succession, should always be appointed vicar general by the diocesan bishop. More extensive faculties may, in particular cases, be granted to him by the competent authority.

For the greater present and future good of the diocese the diocesan bishop and his coadjutor should consult each other on matters of major importance. (See D. *46*, 13.)

B. The diocesan curia and councils

27. In the diocesan curia the office of vicar general is preeminent. When, however, the good government of the diocese requires it, the bishop may appoint one or more episcopal vicars who by the very fact of their appointment will enjoy in specified parts of the diocese, or in specific types of affairs, or in regard to the faithful of particular rites, that authority which is conferred by the general law on the vicar general.

Among the cooperators of the bishop in the governing of the diocese are included the priests who constitute his senate or council, such as the cathedral chapter, the council of consultors, or other committees according to the circumstances and character of different localities. These councils, and especially the cathedral chapters, should be reorganized, as far as is necessary, to suit contemporary needs.

Priests and laymen who are attached to the diocesan curia should be mindful that they are collaborating in the pastoral work of the bishop.

The diocesan curia should be so organized that it may be

a useful medium for the bishop, not only for diocesan administration, but also for pastoral activity.

It is highly desirable that in every diocese a special pastoral council be established, presided over by the diocesan bishop himself, in which clergy, religious, and laity specially chosen for the purpose will participate. It will be the function of this council to investigate and consider matters relating to pastoral activity and to formulate practical conclusions concerning them. (See D. 46, 14–17.)

C. The diocesan clergy

28. All priests, whether diocesan or religious, share and exercise with the bishop the one priesthood of Christ. They are thus constituted providential cooperators of this episcopal order. The diocesan clergy have, however, a primary role in the care of souls because, being incardinated in or appointed to a particular church, they are wholly dedicated in its service to the care of a particular section of the Lord's flock, and accordingly form one priestly body and one family of which the bishop is the father. In order to allot the sacred ministries more suitably and more equitably among his priests, the bishop must have the requisite liberty in making appointments to ministries and benefices. All rights and privileges which in any way restrict that liberty should accordingly be abrogated.

The relations between the bishop and the diocesan clergy should be based before all else on supernatural charity, so that their unity of purpose will make their pastoral activity more effective. Therefore, to ensure an increasingly effective apostolate, the bishop should be willing to engage in dialogue with his priests, individually and collectively, not merely occasionally, but if possible, regularly. Furthermore, the diocesan priests should be united among themselves and should be genuinely zealous for the spiritual welfare of the whole diocese. They should bear in mind that the worldly goods which they acquire through their ecclesiastical functions are closely connected with their sacred office, and they should therefore contribute liberally to the material needs of the diocese, according to the bishop's directives. (See D. 46, 18.)

29. Priests to whom the bishop entrusts a pastoral duty or apostolic work of a trans-parochial nature collaborate even more closely with him, whether they are assigned to a

certain portion of the diocese, a special group of the faithful, or a particular kind of work.

Outstanding assistance is rendered also by those priests to whom the bishop entrusts various apostolic activities in schools or in other institutions or associations.

Moreover, those priests who are involved in trans-diocesan activities should be shown particular solicitude especially by the bishop in whose diocese they reside, since they are engaged in apostolic work of great importance.

30. Parish priests are in a special sense collaborators with the bishop. They are given, in a specific section of the diocese, and under the authority of the bishop, the care of souls as their particular shepherd.

(1) In exercising the care of souls parish priests and their assistants should carry out their work of teaching, sanctifying and governing in such a way that the faithful and the parish communities may feel that they are truly members both of the diocese and of the universal Church. They should therefore collaborate both with other parish priests and with those priests who are exercising a pastoral function in the district (such as vicars forane and deans) or who are engaged in works of an extra-parochial nature, so that the pastoral work of the diocese may be rendered more effective by a spirit of unity. Furthermore, the care of souls should always be inspired by a missionary spirit, so that it extends with due prudence to all those who live in the parish. And if the parish priest cannot make contact with certain groups of people he should call to his aid others, including laymen, to assist him in matters relating to the apostolate.

For the better ordering of the care of souls priests are strongly recommended to live in common, especially those attached to the same parish. This on one hand is helpful to their apostolate work, and on the other gives to the faithful an example of charity and unity.

(2) In their role as teachers it is the duty of parish priests to preach the word of God to all the faithful so that they, being firmly rooted in faith, hope and charity, may grow in Christ, and the Christian community may give that witness to charity which the Lord commended.[17] They should likewise by means of catechetical instruction lead all the faithful, according to their capacity, to a full knowl-

17. Cf. Jn. 13:35.

edge of the mystery of salvation. In providing this instruction, they should invoke the help not only of religious, but of the laity by establishing the Confraternity of Christian Doctrine.

In carrying out their work of sanctification parish priests should ensure that the celebration of the Eucharistic Sacrifice is the center and culmination of the entire life of the Christian community. It should also be their aim to ensure that the faithful receive spiritual nourishment from a frequent and devout reception of the sacraments and from an attentive and fervent participation in the liturgy. Parish priests must bear it constantly in mind how much the sacrament of penance contributes to the development of the Christian life and should therefore be readily available for the hearing of the confessions of the faithful. If necessary they should call on other priests who are fluent in different languages to help in this work.

In carrying out their duties as pastors parish priests should make it their special concern to know their parishioners. Since they are the shepherds of all the individual sheep they should endeavor to stimulate a growth of the Christian life in each one of the faithful, in families, in associations, especially those dedicated to the apostolate, and, finally, in the parish as a whole. They should, therefore, visit the homes and the schools as their pastoral function requires of them. They should manifest a special interest in adolescents and young people; they should exercise a paternal charity towards the poor and the sick. Finally, they should have a special care for the workers, and should urge the faithful to give their support to apostolic activities.

(3) Curates, as co-workers with the parish priest, should be eager and fervent in their daily exercise of their pastoral ministry under the authority of the parish priest. There should therefore be a fraternal relationship between the parish priest and his curates; mutual charity and respect should prevail, and they should assist each other by advice, practical help and example, providing with harmonious will and a common zeal for the needs of the parish. (See D. *46, 19*.)

31. In forming a judgment as to the suitability of a priest for governing a parish, the bishop should take into consideration not only his learning but also his piety, his zeal for the apostolate, and those other gifts and qualities which are necessary for the proper care of souls.

Basically, however, parochial responsibility has to with the good of souls. It follows that, if a bishop is more easily and efficiently to make provision for the parishes, all rights whatsoever of presentation, nomination and reservation should be abrogated, without prejudice, however, to the rights of religious. Regulations for *concursus*,[e] whether general or particular, should also be rescinded where they exist.

Each parish priest should enjoy that security of tenure in his parish as the good of souls requires. Therefore the distinction between removable and irremovable parish priests should be abandoned and the procedure for the transfer or removal of a parish priest should be reexamined and simplified so that the bishop, while observing the principles of natural and canonical justice, may more suitably provide for the good of souls.

Parish priests who on account of advanced years or for some other grave reason are unable to perform their duties adequately and fruitfully are earnestly requested to tender their resignation spontaneously, or when the bishop invites them to do so. The bishop will make suitable provision for the support of those who retire. (See D. 46, 20.)

32. Finally, the same concern for the salvation of souls should be the motive for determining or reconsidering the erection or suppression of parishes and other changes of this kind. The bishop may act in these matters on his own authority. (See D. *46*, 21.)

D. Religious

33. All religious (including for the purposes of this section members of other institutes professing the evangelical counsels) are under an obligation, in accordance with the particular vocation of each, to work zealously and diligently for the building up and growth of the whole Mystical Body of Christ and for the good of the particular churches. It is their duty to promote these objectives primarily by means of prayer, works of penance, and by the example of their own lives. The sacred Synod earnestly exhorts them to develop an ever-increasing esteem and zeal for these practices. But, with due consideration for the special character

[e] Literally, a competition. In this context it refers to a custom prevailing in some countries not in English-speaking countries, of appointing parish priests after a competitive examination. See CIC 459, 3, 4.–Ed.

of each religious institute, they should apply themselves more zealously to the external works of the apostolate.

34. Religious priests, who have been raised to the priesthood to be prudent cooperators with the episcopal order, are able nowadays to give more help to bishops in view of the more pressing needs of souls. Thus they may be said in a certain sense to belong to the diocesan clergy inasmuch as they share in the care of souls and in the practice of apostolic works under the authority of the bishops. The other members, too, of religious institutes, both men and women, also belong in a special sense to the diocesan family and render valuable help to the sacred hierarchy, and in view of the growing needs of the apostolate they can and should constantly increase the aid they give.

35. In order, however, that the works of the apostolate may always be carried out harmoniously in the individual dioceses and that the unity of diocesan discipline be preserved intact, the following fundamental principles are decreed:

(1) Religious should at all times treat the bishops, as the successors of the apostles, with loyal respect and reverence. Moreover, whenever legitimately called upon to do apostolic work, they must carry out these duties in such a way as to be the auxiliaries of the bishop and subject to him. Furthermore, religious should comply promptly and faithfully with the requests or desires of the bishops when they are asked to undertake a greater share in the ministry of salvation. Due consideration should be given to the character of the particular institute and to its constitutions, which may, if necessary, be adapted for this purpose in accord with the principles of this decree of the Council.

Especially in view of the urgent needs of souls and of the lack of diocesan clergy, those religious institutes which are not dedicated to a purely contemplative life may be called upon by the bishop to help in various pastoral ministries. The special character of each religious institute should be taken into consideration. Superiors should make every effort to cooperate, even taking responsibility for parishes on a temporary basis.

(2) Religious who are engaged in the external apostolate should be inspired by the spirit of their own institute, should remain faithful to the observance of their rule, and should be obedient to their superiors. Bishops should not fail for their part to insist on this obligation.

(3) The privilege of exemption whereby religious are reserved to the control of the Supreme Pontiff, or of some other ecclesiastical authority, and are exempted from the jurisdiction of bishops, relates primarily to the internal organization of their institutes. Its purpose is to ensure that everything is suitably and harmoniously arranged within them, and the perfection of the religious life promoted.[18] The privilege ensures also that the Supreme Pontiff may employ these religious for the good of the universal Church,[19] or that some other competent authority may do so for the good of the churches under its jurisdiction. This exemption, however, does not prevent religious being subject to the jurisdiction of the bishops in the individual dioceses in accordance with the general law, insofar as is required for the performance of their pastoral duties and the proper care of souls.[20]

(4) All religious, whether exempt or non-exempt, are subject to the authority of the local ordinary in the following matters: public worship, without prejudice, however, to the diversity of rites; the care of souls; preaching to the people; the religious and moral education, catechetical instruction and liturgical formation of the faithful, especially of children. They are also subject to diocesan rules regarding the comportment proper to the clerical state and also the various activities relating to the exercise of their sacred apostolate. Catholic schools conducted by religious are also subject to the local ordinaries as regards their general policy and supervision without prejudice, however, to the right of the religious to manage them. Likewise, religious are obliged to observe all those prescriptions which episcopal councils or conferences legitimately decree as binding on all.

(5) Organized cooperation should be encouraged between the various religious institutes and between them and the diocesan clergy. There should be the closest possible coordination of all apostolic works and activities. This will depend mainly on a supernatural attitude of heart and mind grounded on charity. It is the responsibility of the Apostolic See to foster this coordination in regard to the universal

18. Cf. Leo XIII, Apost. Const. *Romanos Pontifices*, 8 May 1881: *Acta Leonis* XIII, vol. 2, 1882, p. 234.
19. Cf. Paul VI, Allocution, 23 May 1964: *AAS* 56 (1965) pp. 570-571.
20. Cf. Pius XII, Allocution, 8 Dec. 1950: *AAS* 43 (1951) p. 28.

Church; it is for each bishop to do so in his own diocese, and for the patriarchs and episcopal synods and conferences in their territories.

There should be consultations beforehand between bishops or episcopal conferences and religious superiors or conferences of major superiors, with regard to apostolic activities to be undertaken by religious.

(6) In order to promote harmonious and fruitful relations between the bishops and religious, the bishops and superiors should meet at regular intervals and as often as seems opportune to discuss business matters of general concern in their territory. (See D. *46*, 22–40.)

CHAPTER III

CONCERNING THE COOPERATION OF BISHOPS FOR THE COMMON GOOD OF MANY CHURCHES

I. SYNODS, COUNCILS AND ESPECIALLY EPISCOPAL CONFERENCES

36. From the earliest ages of the Church, bishops in charge of particular churches, inspired by a spirit of fraternal charity and by zeal for the universal mission entrusted to the apostles, have pooled their resources and their aspirations in order to promote both the common good and the good of individual churches. With this end in view synods, provincial councils and, finally, plenary councils were established in which the bishops determined on a common program to be followed in various churches both for teaching the truths of the faith and for regulating ecclesiastical discipline.

This sacred Ecumenical Synod expresses its earnest hope that these admirable institutions—synods and councils— may flourish with renewed vigor so that the growth of religion and the maintenance of discipline in the various churches may increasingly be more effectively provided for in accordance with the needs of the times.

37. It is often impossible, nowadays especially, for bishops to exercise their office suitably and fruitfully unless they establish closer understanding and cooperation with other bishops. Since episcopal conferences—many such have already been established in different countries—have produced outstanding examples of a more fruitful apostolate, this sacred Synod judges that it would be in the highest degree helpful if in all parts of the world the bishops of each country or region would meet regularly, so that by sharing their wisdom and experience and exchanging views they may jointly formulate a program for the common good of the Church.

Therefore, the sacred Synod makes the following decrees concerning episcopal conferences:

38. (1) An episcopal conference is a form of assembly in which the bishops of a certain country or region exercise their pastoral office jointly in order to enhance the Church's beneficial influence on all men, especially by devising forms of the apostolate and apostolic methods suitably adapted to the circumstances of the times.

(2) Members of the episcopal conferences include all local ordinaries of whatever rite (but not vicars general), coadjutor and auxiliary bishops and other titular bishops to whom the Apostolic See or the episcopal conferences have entrusted some special work. Other titular bishops and legates of the Roman Pontiff, in view of their special position in the region, are not *de jure* members of the conference.

The local ordinaries and coadjutors have a deliberative vote. The statutes of the conference will determine whether auxiliary bishops and other bishops entitled to attend the conference be given a deliberative or consultative voice.

(3) Each episcopal conference will draw up its own statutes, which will be subject to the approval of the Apostolic See. These statutes will provide, among other things, for the setting up of those offices which are requisite for the effectiveness of the conference, for example, a permanent council of bishops, episcopal commissions and a general secretariat.

(4) Decisions of the episcopal conference, provided they have been legitimately approved by at least two thirds of the votes of the prelates who have a deliberative vote in the conference, and provided they have been confirmed by the Apostolic See, shall have the force of law, but only in those cases in which it it so prescribed by the common law, or

when it has been so declared by a special mandate of the Apostolic See promulgated on its own initiative or at the request of the conference itself.

(5) When the special circumstances require it, bishops of different countries may, subject to the approval of the Apostolic See, establish one joint conference. Moreover, contacts between episcopal conferences of different countries are to be encouraged for the promotion of the common good.

(6) It is earnestly recommended to prelates of the Oriental Churches that when engaged in the improvement of morals in their own Church and in the promotion of activities beneficial to religion, they should take into consideration the common good of the whole of a region in which there happen to be Churches of different rites. They should meet representatives of other rites and discuss matters with them, in accordance with rules to be determined by the competent authority. (See D. 46, 41.)

II. THE BOUNDARIES OF ECCLESIASTICAL PROVINCES AND THE ERECTION OF ECCLESIASTICAL REGIONS

39. The good of souls requires well-adjusted boundaries, not only of dioceses, but also of ecclesiastical provinces; it may indeed call for the establishment of ecclesiastical regions in order that better provision may be made for the needs of the apostolate in accordance with social and local circumstances. In this way easier and more fruitful relations may be established between bishops themselves and between them and their Metropolitans and other bishops of the same country, and also between bishops and the civil authorities.

40. Therefore, in order to achieve these objectives, the sacred Synod decrees the following:

(1) The boundaries of ecclesiastical provinces should be reviewed as soon as is practicable, and the rights and privileges of Metropolitans should be determined according to new and well-devised regulations.

(2) As a general rule all dioceses, and other territorial divisions which in law are equivalent to dioceses, should be incorporated in an ecclesiastical province. Thus those dioceses which are now immediately subject to the Apostolic See and which are not united with any other diocese should ei-

ther be consolidated into new ecclesiastical provinces, if that is practicable, or should be joined to the nearest and most suitable provinces. They should be made subject to the authority of the metropolitan archbishops in accordance with the norm of the common law.

(3) Whenever it seems expedient, ecclesiastical provinces should be consolidated into ecclesiastical regions, the organization of which is to be determined by law.

41. The competent episcopal conferences should examine the question of the boundaries of provinces of this kind and the establishment of regions in accordance with the provisions concerning the boundaries of dioceses in nn. 23, 24, and should submit their decisions to the Apostolic See. (See D. 46, 42.)

III. BISHOPS DISCHARGING AN INTER-DIOCESAN FUNCTION

42. As the needs of the apostolate make joint control and promotion of certain pastoral activities increasingly necessary, it is desirable that some offices be established for the service of all or several dioceses in a particular region or nation, and these may be entrusted to a bishop.

The sacred Synod recommends also that fraternal relations and unity of purpose in their pastoral zeal for souls should prevail between the prelates or bishops exercising these functions and the diocesan bishops and the episcopal conferences. These relations should be determined by the common law.

43. The spiritual welfare of military personnel, on account of the special nature of their life, should be the object of particular solicitude. A special military vicariate should therefore, if possible, be established in every country. Both the vicar and his chaplains should devote themselves with all zeal to this difficult work in harmonious cooperation with diocesan bishops.[1]

1. Cf. Sac. Consist. Congr., Instruction to Military Ordinaries, 23 April 1951: *AAS* 43 (1951), pp. 562–565; also Formula Regarding the Conferring of the Status of Military Ordinariates, 20 Oct. 1956; *AAS* 49 (1957), pp. 150–163; also Decree on *Ad Limina* Visits of Military Ordinariates, 28 Feb. 1959: *AAS* 51 (1959), pp. 272–274; also Decree on the Granting of Faculties for Confessions to Military Chaplains, 27 Nov. 1960: *AAS* 53 (1961), pp. 49–50; also Instruction of Sac. Congr. of Religious on Religious Military Chaplains, 2 Feb. 1955: *AAS* 47 (1955), pp. 93–97.

Diocesan bishops should for this purpose release to the military vicar a sufficient number of priests well-fitted for this difficult work. They should also give every encouragement to undertakings intended to promote the spiritual welfare of the military personnel.[2]

GENERAL DIRECTIVE

44. The sacred Synod prescribes that in the revision of the Code of Canon Law, suitable laws should be drawn up in conformity with the principles enunciated in this decree, due consideration being given to the comments made by individual commissions or the Fathers of the Council.

The sacred Synod further decrees that general directories concerning the care of souls be compiled for the use both of bishops and parish priests so that they may have definite directives to guide them in the discharge of their particular pastoral function.

A special directory should also be compiled concerning the pastoral care of special groups of the faithful according to the various circumstances of different countries or regions, and also a directory for the catechetical instruction of the Christian people in which the fundamental principles of this instruction and its organization will be dealt with and the preparation of books relating to it. In the preparation of these directories due consideration should be given to the views expressed both by the commissions and by the Conciliar Fathers.

2. Cf. Sac. Consist. Congr., *Letter to the cardinals, archbishops, bishops, and other ordinaries of Spanish-speaking nations*, 21 June 1951: *AAS* 43 (1951) p. 566.

46

APOSTOLIC LETTER, WRITTEN MOTU PROPRIO, ON THE IMPLEMENTATION OF THE DECREES CHRISTUS DOMINUS, PRESBYTERORUM ORDINIS AND PERFECTAE CARITATIS

Paul VI, *Ecclesiae Sanctae I*[a], 6 August, 1966

Now that the Second Ecumenical Council of the Vatican is over, the government of the holy Church requires the framing of new norms and the setting up of new organisms,[1] which would meet the needs created by the Council and which would be better adapted to the new apostolic aims and the new fields of apostolate in the modern world disclosed by the work of the Council. This world is greatly changed and it needs enlightenment and the warmth of supernatural charity.

It was these considerations which led us, as soon as the Ecumenical Council had finished, to establish commissions which applying their knowledge and experience, would prepare definite norms for the implementation of the Council's decrees, these having been declared not binding in the meantime. These commissions, as we were happy to say in our *Motu Proprio* MUNUS APOSTOLICUM, promulgated on 10 August last, went about their work with a will and made their conclusions known to us at the appointed time.

When we had examined their recommendations attentively we decided that the time had come to promulgate the aforesaid norms. However, we thought it wiser and more prudent to promulgate them on an experimental basis. Our reasons for this were: first, that one is here dealing with matters of discipline and that many more suggestions may still be forthcoming in the light of experience; second, the fact that a special commission is at present engaged in the

a. Translated from Latin text in *AAS* 58 (1966) pp. 757–758 by A.F.

reform and emendation of the Code of Canon Law, bringing the laws of the universal Church up to date and setting them out more clearly and in better order.

During this interval episcopal conferences will be entitled to communicate to us their observations and the conclusions they may have reached in the course of putting the norms into practice. They may also submit new recommendations.

Having given the matter mature consideration, of our own volition (*motu proprio*) and with our apostolic authority, we decree and promulgate the following norms for the implementation of the following conciliar decrees: *Christus Dominus* (On the Pastoral Office of Bishops in the Church), *Presbyterorum Ordinis* (On the Life and Ministry of Priests), *Perfectae Caritatis* (On the Up-to-date Renewal of Religious Life), *Ad gentes divinitus* (On the Missionary Activity of the Church). We order that they be observed on an experimental basis—until, that is to say, the new Code of Canon Law shall have been promulgated, unless the Holy See should decided otherwise in the meantime.

These norms shall take effect from 11 October next. It was on this day, the feast of Our Lady's maternity, four years ago, that the sacred Council was solemnly inaugurated by our predecessor of venerable memory, John XXIII.

NORMS FOR THE IMPLEMENTATION OF THE DECREES[a]

The office of bishop, which the sacred Council of Vatican II set in a clearer light in the Dogmatic Constitution *Lumen gentium* and in the Decree *Christus Dominus* for the edification of the Mystical Body of Christ, is of divine institution.

For this reason sacred pastors are obliged to fulfil each day with care their task of teaching, sanctifying and nourishing the People of God, by generously sharing with the Roman Pontiff the care for all the Churches, by making earnest and right provisions for the diocese committed to their charge, and finally, by actively cooperating with one another for the common good of the Churches.

In governing their dioceses, however, bishops have need

a. Translated from the French by J. G. McGarry. Latin text in *AAS* 58 (1966), pp. 758–775.

of helpers and advisers, of priests especially to whom for that reason they should be glad to listen and even to consult, without prejudice always to the right which bishops have of acting with freedom, of making such laws and regulations as consciousness of their obligations, duty and of the principles of government of the Church will suggest (cf. Dogmatic Constitution, *Lumen gentium*, no. 27).

To enable bishops to fulfil their office with greater facility and accommodation and to apply more effectively the principles solemnly approved by the sacred council in the Decrees *Christus Dominus* and *Presbyterorum Ordinis* the following norms are laid down.

DISTRIBUTION OF THE CLERGY AND ASSISTANCE OF DIOCESES (Christus Dominus, no. 6; Presbyterorum Ordinis, no. 10)[b]

1. A special council shall be instituted at the Apostolic See to lay down general principles to secure, taking account of the needs of the various Churches, a more suitable distribution of clergy.

2. It will be the duty of patriarchal synods and episcopal conferences, while taking account of the prescriptions of the Apostolic See, to make laws and regulations for bishops to secure a suitable distribution of clergy, both of the clergy of their own territory and of those coming to it from abroad, and also to make provision for the Churches in mission territories and in countries suffering from a shortage of priests. For this purpose there shall be erected in each episcopal conference a special commission to study the needs of the various dioceses of the territory and their potential for helping other Churches, and to apply the definite and tested conclusions arrived at by the conference and bring them before the bishops of the territory.

3. To facilitate the transfer (*transitus*) of clerics from one diocese to another the following regulations are to be observed. In the meantime the law of incardination and excardination remains in existence, to be adapted to the new circumstances.

(1) Clerics are to be trained in seminaries to feel concern not only for the affairs of the diocese they are to serve but for the whole Church, with the result that, with the approv-

b. *Christus Dominus* is D. 45 in this collection; *Presbyterorum Ordinis* is D. 63.

al of their bishop they should show themselves ready to devote their services to particular Churches in grave need.

(2) Apart from the case of true need in their own dioceses, ordinaries or hierarchs shall not refuse permission to clerics to emigrate to regions suffering from grave shortage of priests and exercise their ministry there, provided they know of their willingness to go and consider them suitable to work there.

(3) These ordinaries, however, shall see that clerics intending to leave their own diocese to serve in another country shall be suitably prepared for their ministry there; they should acquire the language of the region and an understanding of its institutions, social conditions, practices and customs.

(4) Ordinaries may give permission to their clerics to transfer to another diocese for a prescribed time, a permission which could be renewed many times, with the result however that these clerics remain incardinated in their own diocese and on returning to it enjoy all the rights they would have if they had been ministering there.

(5) If, however, a cleric has lawfully transferred from his own diocese, after five years he becomes incardinated by law into this diocese, provided he has manifested his wish to do so in writing both to the ordinary of the diocese which received him and to his own ordinary and that niether of these has within four months signified to him his disapproval.

4. Furthermore, in order to accomplish special pastoral or missionary tasks for various regions or social groups requiring special assistance, prelatures may usefully be established by the Apostolic See. These would consist of the secular clergy specially trained and under the rule of a prelate of their own and governed by statutes of their own.

It would be the duty of such a prelate to erect and govern a seminary for the suitable training of students. He would have the right to incardinate such students under the title of service to the prelature and to promote them to Orders.

The prelate should show care for the spiritual life of those he promoted under the title mentioned above, and for the continuance of their special formation and their particular ministry, by making arrangements with the local ordinaries to whom they are sent. He should also make provision for suitable means of living either by such agreements as are mentioned above or out of the resources of the prelature or by appropriate subsidies. He should also make provision for those who through illness or other reasons are obliged to relinquish their post.

There is no reason why laymen, whether celibate or married, should not dedicate their professional service, through contracts with the prelature, to its works and enterprises.

Such prelatures shall not be erected without first hearing the views of the episcopal conferences of the territory in which they will serve. In the exercise of their function care is to be shown that the rights of the local ordinaries are not infringed and that close relations are kept with the episcopal conferences at all times.

5. Finally, patriarchal synods and episcopal conferences alone can make opportune laws concerning the use of ecclesiastical goods, whereby, remembering first of all the needs of the territory itself, certain levies are imposed on the dioceses for works of apostolate or charity or for those Churches of small resources which because of their peculiar circumstances are in financial need.

THE POWER OF DIOCESAN BISHOPS (Christus Dominus, no. 8)

6. The norms for fulfilling prescription no. 8 are laid down in the Apostolic Letters given *motu proprio* on 15 June, 1966, *De Episcoporum muneribus.*

THE ENCOURAGEMENT OF STUDY AND PASTORAL SCIENCE (Christus Dominus, no. 16; Presbyterorum Ordinis, no. 19)

7. Bishops, either individually or in collaboration with other bishops, shall arrange that all priests, even if they are actually serving in the ministry, shall follow a course of pastoral lectures for a year after ordination and shall at stated intervals attend other lectures which will provide them with the opportunity of acquiring a fuller knowledge of pastoral matters, of the science of theology, of moral theology and of liturgy, of strengthening their spiritual life and of communicating their apostolic experience with one another.

Bishops or episcopal conferences shall also see to it that, in accordance with the conditions in each territory, one or more priests known for their learning and virtue shall be chosen as directors of studies to promote and direct pastoral lectures and other means considered necessary to encourage the scientific and pastoral formation of priests in the territory: study centers, travelling libraries, congresses on catechectics, homiletics, liturgy and such matters.

EQUITABLE REMUNERATION AND SOCIAL INSURANCE FOR PRIESTS (Christus Dominus, no. 16; Presbyterorum Ordinis, nn. 20-21)

8. Patriarchal synods and episcopal conferences will see that, whether in each individual diocese or for several dioceses in common or for the whole territory, norms shall be laid down for the provision of a proper living for all clerics who are, or have been, engaged in ministering to the People of God. The remuneration of the clergy shall be first of all on the same scale for all in identical circumstances, taking account of the nature of the office and of the conditions of time and place. The living should be sufficient to permit clerics a decent sustenance and to enable them to assist the poor. The reform of the system of benefices is entrusted to the Commission for the Revision of the Code of Canon Law. In the meantime bishops, having heard the views of the councils of priests, are to see that revenues are equitably distributed, even those revenues deriving from benefices.

The conferences shall take care that at least in those regions where the revenues of the clergy derive entirely or in great part from the offerings of the faithful, a special agency (*institutum*) shall be established in each diocese to collect the offerings made for this purpose. The bishop of the diocese is himself to administer it and he is to have the assistance of delegated priests and, where it seems useful, of laymen expert in economic matters as well.

These episcopal conferences will also see that, always observing ecclesiastical and civil laws, there shall be established in each country either diocesan institutes, even federated with one another, or institutes established at the same time for various dioceses, or an association serving the whole country, in which under the vigilance of the hierarchy adequate provision will be made for insurance, for health assistance, as it is called, and for the maintenance of the clergy in sickness and old age.

It will be for the Revised Code of Canon Law to determine the conditions for the establishment in each diocese or region another common fund to enable bishops to meet other obligations towards deserving persons in the Church and towards various needs in the diocese and by means of which also richer dioceses may be able to assist poorer ones.

CONCERN FOR PARTICULAR GROUPS OF THE FAITHFUL (Christus Dominus, no. 18)

9. In view of the great numbers of migrants and of travellers in our times, episcopal conferences are asked to entrust all that concerns their care and spiritual guidance to a priest delegated for this purpose or to a special commission.

THE NOMINATION OF BISHOPS (Christus Dominus, no. 20)

10. While the right of the Roman Pontiff freely to nominate and institute bishops remains intact and without prejudice to the discipline of the Eastern Churches, episcopal conferences in accordance with the laws laid down by the Apostolic See, or yet to be laid down, shall after taking prudent counsel each year propose in secret to the Apostolic See the names of candidates among ecclesiastical persons to be promoted to the office of bishop in their territory.

RESIGNATION OF BISHOPS (Christus Dominus, no. 21)

11. In order that prescription number 21 of the Decree *Christus Dominus* may be put into force, all diocesan bishops and others equiparated with them in law are earnestly requested voluntarily to submit their resignation not later than the completion of their seventy-fifth year to the competent authority, who will examine the circumstances of each case and make suitable provision.

A bishop, whose resignation from office has been accepted, may retain a place of residence in the diocese if he wishes. The diocese must besides provide for the bishop who resigns a worthy and appropriate living. It is the duty of the episcopal conference of the territory by means of general norms to determine the way dioceses should fulfil this obligation.

DIOCESAN BOUNDARIES (Christus Dominus, nn. 22-24)

12. (1) To secure a proper revision of the boundaries of dioceses, episcopal conferences shall, each for its own territory, examine the existing territorial division of Churches and, if necessary, set up a special commision for the purpose. Consequently, the status of dioceses with regard to territory, personnel and possessions are to be properly investigated; the opinion is to be sought of each individual bishop directly involved as well as of the bishops of the entire province or ecclesiastical region within whose limits the revision of dioceses is being considered; the assistance of those who are truly expert, whether ecclesiastics or laymen, is to be invited as far as possible; reasons based on nature which would perhaps provide reasons for a change of boundaries are to be considered in an objective spirit; all changes which might perhaps be introduced, to which there is reference in numbers 22–23 of the Decree *Christus Dominus*, are to be put forward; in the division or dismemberment of dioceses there should be an equitable and suitable distribution of priests and seminarians, taking account of the requirements of the ministry of salvation to be exercised in each diocese as well as of special conditions and desires.

(2) It is desirable, however, that in the case of the Eastern Churches in defining the limits of eparchs account be taken of the greater propinquity of those places where the faithful of the same rite live together.

THE FACULTIES OF AUXILIARY BISHOPS (Christus Dominus, nn. 25-26)

13. (1) Auxiliary bishops should be appointed for a diocese whenever the real necessity of the apostolate to be exercised there demands it. The chief principles to be kept in mind regarding the power to be given to an auxiliary bishop are: the good of the flock which is to be nourished, the achievement of unity in the government of the diocese, membership of the episcopal college which the auxiliary enjoys, and effective cooperation with the bishop of the diocese.

(2) The bishop of the diocese should appoint the auxiliary either vicar general (or syncellus) or episcopal vicar, but in such a manner that he is subordinate only to the authority of the bishop of the diocese.

BISHOPS IN THE CHURCH 599

(3) To make adequate provision for the common good of the diocese and protect the dignity of the auxiliary bishop the Council wished to express its desire that when a see falls vacant the auxiliary or one of the auxiliaries, if there are more than one, should in the interim be charged with the government of the diocese by those who have authority to do so. An auxiliary bishop, however, unless it is otherwise determined by the competent authority in a particular case, does not when the see falls vacant lose the powers and faculties he enjoyed by law as vicar general or episcopal vicar during the lifetime of the bishop. But in these circumstances the auxiliary who has not been elected vicar capitular shall exercise his power, given to him in fact by law, until the new bishop shall take possession of his see, in full accord with the vicar capitular, who is responsible for the government of the diocese.

EPISCOPAL VICARS (Christus Dominus, no. 27)

14. (1) The new office of episcopal vicar was established in law by the council in order that the bishop with the assistance of new helpers may be enabled to exercise the pastoral care of the diocese in the best possible manner. For this reason the bishop of the diocese is free to choose one or more episcopal vicars in accordance with the particular needs of the place; and he also retains the power to nominate one or more vicars general in accordance with canon 366 of the Code of Canon Law.

(2) Episcopal vicars enjoy the ordinary vicarious power which common law gives to the vicar general in a determined part of the diocese or with regard to certain areas of business or certain groups of persons, according as the bishop of the diocese has specified. Consequently they possess, within the limits of their competence, the habitual faculties given by the Apostolic See to bishops and they have the power to execute rescripts unless other provision has been expressly made or the bishop has been personally chosen to do so. The bishop of the diocese is free, however, to reserve to himself or to his vicar general matters which he chooses, and he may confer on the vicar general the special mandate, prescribed by common law for certain matters.

(3) As cooperator in the episcopal office the episcopal vicar should refer all that he has done or is going to do to the bishop of the diocese, and he should never act against

his mind and will. Furthermore, he should not omit to have frequent exchange of views with the other episcopal vicars —and particularly with the vicar general in ways to be determined by the bishop of the diocese—in order that unity of discipline among clergy and people should be strengthened and that greater spiritual fruits should result for the diocese.

(4) A favor (*gratia*) which has been refused by a vicar general (syncellus) or by an episcopal vicar and later obtained form the bishop without mention having been made of the earlier refusal is invalid; a favor which has been refused by the bishop cannot be validly given by the vicar general or episcopal vicar even if the refusal by the bishop is reported, without the bishop's consent.

(5) Episcopal vicars, who are not auxiliary bishops, shall be nominated for a limited period to be determined in the deed of nomination; they may however be removed from office at the wish (*ad nutum*) of the bishop. Their office ceases when the see falls vacant, unless they be auxiliary bishops. It is proper, however, that the vicar capitular should engage them as his delegates, lest the good of the diocese should suffer as a result.

COUNCIL OF PRIESTS AND PASTORAL COUNCIL
(Christus Dominus, no. 27; Presbyterorum Ordinis, no. 7)

15. Regarding the council of priests:

(1) There is to be in each diocese a council of priests, a group or senate of priests, representing the presbyterium, which by its advice will give effective assistance to the bishop in ruling the diocese. The manner and forms of its working are to be determined by the bishop. In this council the bishop shall hear the views of his priests and discuss with them the pastoral needs and the good of the diocese.

(2) Religious also may be co-opted as members of the council of priests insofar as they share in the care of souls and the works of the apostolate.

(3) The council of priests has a merely consultative voice.

(4) When the see falls vacant the council of priests ceases to exist, unless, in special circumstances to be recognized by the Holy See, the vicar capitular or apostolic administrator confirms it in existence.

The new bishop shall himself establish a new council of priests.

16. With regard to the pastoral council, which the Decree *Christus Dominus* strongly commended:

(1) The work of the pastoral council is to examine and consider all that relates to pastoral work and to offer practical conclusions on these matters, so that the life and activity of the People of God may be brought into greater conformity with the Gospel.

(2) The pastoral council, which enjoys only a consultative voice, may be established in different ways. Although of its nature it is ordinarily a permanent institution, it may be temporary as regards membership and activity and exercise its function as occasion arises. The bishop may convene it whenever he considers it advisable.

(3) Clerics, religious and laity, specially delegated by the bishop, take part in the work of the pastoral council.

(4) To achieve the real objective of this council, study must prepare the way for common work and the services of institutes and offices working in this field should be sought if possible.

(5) Where hierarchies of different rites are in existence in the same territory, it is strongly recommended that where possible the pastoral council should be inter-ritual, that is, consisting of clerics, religious and laity of the different rites.

(6) The regulation of other matters is left to the free decision of the bishop, keeping in mind what is set down in no. 17.

17. (1) In matters affecting the council of priests and the pastoral council and the relations of these councils with each other and with the councils of the bishop established in virtue of existing law, bishops, especially when they come together in conferences, should take counsel together and issue common regulations for the dioceses of the territory. The bishops shall also see that all the councils of the diocese are co-ordinated as well as possible, through precise definition of their competence, mutual participation of their members, through common or continuing sessions or by other means.

(2) In the meantime those councils of the bishop established by virtue of existing law, that is, the chapter of the cathedral, consultors and other existing bodies of this na-

ture, shall preserve their proper function and competence until they are revised.

SUPPRESSION OF RIGHTS AND PRIVILEGES IN CONFERRING OFFICES AND BENEFICES (Christus Dominus, no. 28)

18. (1) The good of souls demands that the bishop should enjoy appropriate liberty to bestow offices and benefices, even those without the care of souls attached, on more suitable clerics in accordance with their merits and aptitude. The Apostolic See no longer reserves to itself benefices, whether with the care of souls attached or not, unless they are consistorial; those clauses in the foundation law of any benefice which restricted the bishop in conferring it are forbidden in future; privileges without obligation which up to now may have been given to physical or moral persons with the right to elect, nominate or present to any non-consistorial benefice when it fell vacant are abrogated; also abrogated are customs, and the rights taken away, of nominating, electing or presenting priests to a parochial office or benefice; the law of concursus, even for benefices not having the care of souls, is suppressed.

Regarding popular elections, as they are called, where they continue to exist episcopal conferences will propose to the Apostolic See the course that seems best to them with a view to their abolition if possible.

(2) Should the rights and privileges in this matter be established by convention between the Apostolic See and the State or by agreement with individuals, either physical or moral persons, their termination should be discussed with the interested parties.

VICARS FORANE (Christus Dominus, no. 30)

19. (1) Amongst those who assist the bishop of the diocese in a more intimate manner are those priests who exercise a pastoral duty of a supraparochial nature. Included in this class are vicars forane, also called archpriests, deans and, in the Eastern Church, proto-presbyters. To this office priests shall be appointed outstanding for learning and for apostolic zeal who through the necessary powers conferred on them by the bishop will promote and direct common pastoral activity in the district assigned to them. For this reason the office is not attached to any particular parish.

(2) Vicars forane, archpriests or deans shall be established for a period of time to be determined by special law; they may, however, be removed at the wish of the bishop. The bishop of the diocese should hear their views whenever there is question of nominating, transferring or removing parish priests in the territory over which they preside.

REMOVAL, TRANSFER AND RESIGNATION OF PARISH PRIESTS (Christus Dominus, no. 31)

20. (1) The bishop may, without prejudice to the existing law concerning religious, lawfully remove any parish priest from his parish whenever his ministry, even without grave fault on his part, suffers injury or is rendered ineffective by reason of any of the causes recognized in law or for some other similar reason in the judgment of the bishop, provided that the form of procedure laid down for irremovable parish priests (canons 2157–2161) is followed, until the revision of the Code of Canon Law and without interference with the rights of the Eastern Churches.

(2) Should the good of souls or the need or advantage of the Church require it, the bishop may transfer a parish priest from his parish, in which he renders useful service, to another parish or to any other ecclesiastical office whatsoever. If the parish priest should refuse to obey in order that his transfer should be considered valid, the bishop should follow the procedure mentioned above.

(3) In execution of prescription number 31 of the Decree Christus Dominus all parish priests are requested voluntarily to submit their resignation to their own bishop not later than the completion of their seventy-fifth year. The bishop having considered all the circumstances of place and person shall decide whether to accept, or defer acceptance of, the resignation. The bishop shall make appropriate provision for the living and residence of those who resign.

ERECTION, SUPPRESSION AND CHANGE OF PARISHES (Christus Dominus, no. 32)

21. (1) Every possible effort should be made that parishes where, because of too great a population or too large a territory or for any cause whatsoever, apostolic activity can be exercised only with difficulty and less effectively, should be suitably divided or dismembered, as the circumstances

require. And likewise parishes which are too small should be united as conditions and circumstances demand.

(2) Parishes may no longer be united to canonical chapters *pleno jure.* If there are any such in existence, after the views both of the chapter and the council of priests have been heard, they are to be separated and a parish priest appointed, whether selected from among the members of the chapter or not, who will enjoy all the faculties a parish priest has by prescription of law.

(3) The bishop of the diocese has power by his own authority to erect, suppress or change parishes in any way whatever after he has heard the views of the council of priests; but should there be agreements in force between the Apostolic See and the civil government or should there be question of rights acquired in this matter by persons, either physical or moral persons, the matter is to be arranged with those parties by the competent authority.

RELIGIOUS (Christus Dominus, nn. 33-35)

22. The norms laid down here affect all religious, both men and women, of whatever rite, without interference however with the rights of patriarchs among those of Eastern rite.

23. (1) All religious, even exempt, working in places where there is only one rite, and that different from their own, or where the number of the faithful is so great that in the common opinion there is considered to be only one rite, are under the authority of the ordinary or hierarch of this rite in all matters concerning external works of the ministry and shall be subject to him according to the prescriptions of law.

(2) Where, however, there are several local ordinaries or hierarchs, these religious in their work among faithful of different rites are bound by the rules which these ordinaries and hierarchs impose in common council.

24. Even if a recognized exemption of religious, within the limits of law, should exist in mission territories, yet because of the special circumstances affecting the exercise of the sacred ministry in these places, in accordance with the Decree *Ad gentes divinitus,* the special statutes given or approved by the Apostolic See should be observed regarding relations between the local ordinary and the religious supe-

rior, particularly in the matter of a mission entrusted to a particular institute.

25. (1) All religious, even exempt, are bound by the laws, decrees and ordinances laid down by the local ordinary affecting various works, in those matters which concern the exercise of the sacred apostolate as well as the pastoral and social activity prescribed or recommended by the local ordinary.

(2) They are also bound by the laws, decrees and ordinances of the local ordinary or the episcopal conference which, among other things, deal with:

(a) the public use of all the instruments of social communication, in accordance with nn. 20 and 21 of the Decree *Inter mirifica*.

(b) attendance at public shows.

(c) membership of, or cooperation with, societies or associations which the local ordinary or the episcopal conference has issued a warning against.

(d) ecclesiastical dress, while observing canon 596 CIC and canon 139 CIC *de Religiosis,* and in accordance with the following rule: the local ordinary or the episcopal conference to prevent scandal to the faithful can prohibit clerics, both secular and religious, even exempt religious, from wearing lay dress in public.

26. Religious are also bound by the laws and decrees laid down in accordance with law by the local ordinary regarding public worship in their churches and public oratories and in their semi-public oratories if the faithful ordinarily attend there, without prejudice however to the right to use its own rite for its community service and while respecting the order of choral Divine Office and of other sacred functions related to the special purpose of the institute.

27. (1) The episcopal conference in each country, having heard the views of religious superiors with an interest in the matter, may lay down rules concerning soliciting financial help. These rules are to be obeyed by all religious orders, including those who in their title of foundation are called and are in fact mendicant, without prejudice however to their right to quest.

(2) Religious shall not proceed to invite financial assistance by public subscription without the consent of the local ordinaries where the subscriptions are collected.

28. Religious shall promote with zeal the proper or par-

ticular works of each institute, that is those which with the approval of the Apostolic See are theirs from their foundation or have behind them a venerable tradition and have been recognized and prescribed in the institutions and particular laws of the institute. Religious shall pay special attention to the spiritual needs of the dioceses and foster brotherly relations with the diocesan clergy and with other institutes engaged upon work similar to their own.

29. (1) The proper or special works carried on in the houses of an institute, even in houses which are leased, are under the government of the superiors of the institute, who shall carry out their task of ruling them and directing them in accordance with the constitutions.

(2) Those works, however, even though they be proper and special to the institute, which are entrusted by the local ordinary shall be subject to his authority and direction, without prejudice to the right of religious superiors to supervise the way of life of the members and even, together with the local ordinary, the execution of the task entrusted to them.

30. (1) Whenever a work of the apostolate is entrusted to any religious institute by a local ordinary in accordance with the prescriptions of law, a written agreement shall be made between the local ordinary and the competent superior of the institute which will, amongst other things, set down precisely all that concerns the work to be done, the members of the institute assigned to it and the finances.

(2) For works of this nature members of the religious institute who are really suitable should be selected by the religious superior after discussion with the local ordinary and, where an ecclesiastical office is to be conferred on a member of the institute, the religious should be nominated by the local ordinary himself for a definite time decided upon by mutual agreement, his own superior presenting the candidate or at least assenting to the nomination.

31. Even when a task is assigned to a religious by the local ordinary or by the episcopal conference, it shall be done with the consent of his superior and by means of a written agreement.

32. Any religious member of an institute may for a grave cause be removed from an office entrusted to him either at the wish of the authority who entrusted him with the office, who should inform the religious superior, or by the superior, who should inform the authority who entrusted the of-

fice; this by equal right, the consent of the other party being required in neither case. Neither party is required to reveal to the other reasons for his action, much less to justify them. There remains the right to appeal *in devolutivo* to the Apostolic See.

33. (1) The local ordinary may by his own authority, with the consent of the competent superior, entrust a parish to a religious institute, even erecting it in the religious church of the institute itself. A parish may be entrusted in this way either in perpetuity or for a certain fixed time; in either case it should be effected by means of a written agreement between the ordinary and the competent superior of the institute, which would, amongst other things, indicate accurately and with precision the work to be undertaken, the persons assigned to it and the finances involved.

(2) The local ordinary may also, with the approval of his superior, appoint a religious as parish priest of a parish which is not entrusted to a religious institute. This is to be done by special and appropriate agreement with the competent superior of the same institute.

34. (1) A religious house, whether it be a *domus formata* or not, belonging to an exempt religious group cannot be suppressed without the approval of the Apostolic See and without consulting the local ordinary.

(2) Religious superiors who wish to suppress any religious house or undertaking, for whatever reason, shall not do so hastily; they are to remember that the duty lies upon all religious of working with zeal and energy not only for the edification and building up of the whole Mystical Body of Christ but also for the good of particular Churches.

(3) However when the suppression of any house or undertaking is sought by superiors, particularly becuse of shortage of personnel, the local ordinary shall give the request sympathetic consideration.

35. Associations of the faithful which are under the direction and control of a religious order, even if they have been erected by the Apostolic See, are subject in accordance with the sacred canons to the jurisdiction and supervision of the local ordinary, who has the right and duty to inspect them.

If they are concerned with external works of the apostolate or the promotion of divine worship they are to observe the laws laid down in this matter by the local ordinary or by the episcopal conference.

36. (1) The apostolic zeal of the members of institutes of perfection who do not pursue the purely contemplative life is not so circumscribed by activities whether those proper to the institute or others undertaken upon occasion, that they—not only priests but all members of an institute, both men and women—cannot be summoned by the local ordinaries to help in the ministry in its various forms in the dioceses or regions where the urgent needs of the Church or shortage of clergy requires it.

(2) If in the judgment of the local ordinary the help of religious is considered necessary or very useful to support the manifold works of apostolate and assist pastoral and charitable work in secular parishes and in diocesan associations, religious superiors should, as far as they can, give the assistance requested by the ordinary.

37. The local ordinary may order that episcopal documents be read in public, that catechetical instruction be given, and that a special collection be taken for particular parochial, national or worldwide undertakings, to be carefully forwarded afterwards to the episcopal curia, in all churches belonging to religious and in all public and semi-public oratories of religious which are in fact habitually open to the faithful.

38. The local ordinary has the right of visitation of churches of exempt religious and of their oratories, even semi-public ones—if the faithful ordinarily have access to them—in matters relating to the observance of general laws and episcopal decrees regarding divine worship. Should he discover abuses in this matter, he may, if he has admonished the religious superior without avail, himself make provision by his own authority.

39. (1) In accordance with number 35 of the Decree *Christus Dominus* the general regulation of the Catholic schools of religious institutes, without prejudice to their rights in the government of these schools and while observing the norms laid down there [no. 35, (5)] concerning previous consultation between bishops and religious superiors, involve the general distribution of all the Catholic schools of the diocese, their cooperation with one another and their supervision, so that they shall be no less adapted than other schools to cultural and social objectives.

(2) The local ordinary may visit, in person or by a deputy, in accordance with the sacred canons, all schools of religious institutes, their colleges, oratories, recreational cen-

ters, clubs, hospitals, orphanages or other institutions of this nature engaged upon works of religion or of charity whether of a spiritual or temporal kind.

40. The rules governing the sending of members of a religious institute into diocesan works and ministries under the control of the bishop, applies also to works and ministries which extend beyond diocesan limits, with the appropriate adjustments.

EPISCOPAL CONFERENCES (Christus Dominus, no. 38)

41. (1) The bishops of countries or territories which have not yet established an episcopal conference, in accordance with the law of the Decree *Christus Dominus,* should take steps as quickly as possible to do so and draw up its statutes which are to be approved by the Apostolic See.

(2) Episcopal conferences already in existence should prepare their own statutes in accordance with the prescriptions of the sacred council; statutes already in existence shall be revised in accordance with the mind of the council and submitted to the Apostolic See for approval.

(3) Bishops of countries where it is difficult to establish conferences, shall, after consulting the Apostolic See, join the conference which best meets the requirements of the apostolate in their country.

(4) Episcopal conferences of many nations or international conferences can be established only with the approval of the Apostolic See, whose duty it will be to lay down special laws governing them. Whenever actions or procedures are being undertaken by the conferences which have an international character the Holy See should be informed beforehand.

(5) Episcopal conferences, especially those of neighboring countries, will be able to establish relations with one another in suitable and opportune ways through the secretariates of these conferences, regarding the following matters amongst others:

(a) communicating the principal decisions, especially in pastoral life and action.

(b) sending texts or reports of the decisions of the conference or the *acts* and documents by the bishops collectively.

(c) reporting the various apostolic enterprises proposed or recommended by the episcopal conference which could be of use in similar circumstances.

(d) proposing these questions of grave import which in our times and in particular circumstances seem of the greatest importance.

(e) indicating the dangers or errors making ground in their own country which might also creep into other nations, so that suitable means should be taken in good time to prevent them or remove or confine them.

LIMITS OF ECCLESIASTICAL PROVINCES OR RE-GIONS (Christus Dominus, nn. 39-41)

42. Episcopal conferences shall carefully study whether the further advancement of the good souls in the territory requires (a) a more suitable determination of the limits of ecclesiastical provinces or (b) the erection of ecclesiastical regions. If this should be so, they shall report to the Apostolic See on the revision of the limits or provinces and on the regions to be constituted. They should also signify to the Apostolic See how those dioceses in the territory are to be associated which hitherto were immediately subject to the Apostolic See.

PREPARATION OF PASTORAL DIRECTORIES (Christus Dominus, no. 44)

43. Regarding pastoral directories, patriarchal synods and episcopal conferences are requested to undertake without delay a study of those questions to be treated in the directories, both general and special ones, and communicate their views and requests to the Apostolic See as soon as possible.

47

DECREE ON THE UP-TO-DATE RENEWAL OF RELIGIOUS LIFE[a]

Vatican II, *Perfectae Caritatis*, 28 October, 1965

1. In the constitution, *Lumen Gentium*, the holy synod has already shown that the pursuit of perfect charity by means of the evangelical counsels traces its origins to the teaching and the example of the Divine Master, and that it is a very clear symbol of the heavenly kingdom. Now however it proposes to deal with the life and discipline of those institutes whose members make profession of chastity, poverty and obedience, and to make provision for their needs, as our times recommend.

From the very beginning of the Church there were men and women who set out to follow Christ with greater liberty, and to imitate him more closely, by practicing the evangelical counsels. They led lives dedicated to God, each in his own way. Many of them, under the inspiration of the Holy Spirit, became hermits or founded religious families. These the Church, by virtue of her authority, gladly accepted and approved. Thus, in keeping with the divine purpose, a wonderful variety of religious communities came into existence. This has considerably contributed towards enabling the Church not merely to be equipped for every good work (cf. 2 Tim. 3:17) and to be prepared for the work of the ministry unto the building-up of the Body of Christ (cf. Eph. 4:12), but also to appear adorned with the manifold gifts of her children, like a bride adorned for her husband (cf. Apoc. 21:2), and to manifest in herself the multiform wisdom of God (cf. Eph. 3:10).

Amid such a great variety of gifts, however, all those who are called by God to the practice of the evangelical

a. Translated by A. F. References to D. *48* after certain sections indicate where the norms for this implementation are to be found in *Ecclesiae Sanctae* 2.

counsels, and who make faithful profession of them, bind themselves to the Lord in a special way. They follow Christ who, virginal and poor (cf. Mt. 8:20; Lk. 9:58), redeemed and sanctified men by obedience unto death on the cross (cf. Phil. 2:8). Under the impulse of love, which the Holy Spirit pours into their hearts (cf. Rom. 5:5), they live more and more for Christ and for his Body, the Church (cf. Col. 1:24). The more fervently, therefore, they join themselves to Christ by this gift of their whole life, the fuller does the Church's life become and the more vigorous and fruitful its apostolate.

In order that the Church of today may benefit more fully from lives consecrated by the profession of the counsels and from the vital function which they perform, the holy synod makes the following provisions. They deal only with the general principles of the up-to-date renewal of the life and discipline of religious orders and, while leaving their special characters intact, of societies of common life without vows, and of secular institutes. Particular norms for their exposition and application will be determined after the council by the competent authority.

2. The up-to-date renewal of the religious life comprises both a constant return to the sources of the whole of the Christian life and to the primitive inspiration of the institutes, and their adaption to the changed conditions of our time. This renewal, under the impulse of the Holy Spirit and with the guidance of the Church, must be promoted in accordance with the following principles:

(a) Since the final norm of the religious life is the following of Christ as it is put before us in the Gospel, this must be taken by all institutes as the supreme rule.

(b) It is for the good of the Church that institutes have their own proper characters and functions. Therefore the spirit and aims of each founder should be faithfully accepted and retained, as indeed should each institute's sound traditions, for all of these constitute the patrimony of an institute.

(c) All institutes should share in the life of the Church. They should make their own and should foster to the best of their ability, in a manner consonant with their own natures, its initiatives and undertakings in biblical, liturgical, dogmatic, pastoral, ecumenical, missionary and social matters.

(d) Institutes should see to it that their members have a

proper understanding of men, of the conditions of the times and of the needs of the Church, this to the end that, making wise judgments about the contemporary world in the light of faith, and burning with apostolic zeal, they may be able to help men more effectively.

(e) Before all else, religious life is ordered to the following of Christ by its members and to their becoming united with God by the profession of the evangelical counsels. For this reason, it must be seriously and carefully considered that even the best-contrived adaptations to the needs of our time will be of no avail unless they are animated by a spiritual renewal, which must always be assigned primary importance even in the active ministry.

3. The manner of life, of prayer and of work should be in harmony with the present-day physical and psychological condition of the members. It should also be in harmony with the needs of the apostolate, in the measure that the nature of each institute requires, with the requirements of culture and with social and economic circumstances. This should be the case everywhere, but especially in mission territories.

The mode of government of the institutes should also be examined according to the same criteria.

For this reason, constitutions, directories, books of customs, of prayers, of ceremonies and such like should be properly revised, obsolete prescriptions being suppressed, and should be brought into line with conciliar documents. (See D. 48, 20.)

4. Effective renewal and right adaptation cannot be achieved save with the cooperation of all the members of an institute.

However, it is for the competent authorities, alone, and especially for general chapters, to establish the norms for appropriate renewal and to legislate for it, as also to provide for sufficient prudent experimentation. The approval of the Holy See and of the local ordinaries must be sought when the law requires this. Superiors, however, in matters which concern the destiny of the entire institute, should find appropriate means of consulting their subjects, and should listen to them.

For the appropriate renewal of convents of nuns suggestions and advice may be obtained also from assemblies of federations or from other lawfully convened assemblies.

All should remember, however, that hope for renewal

lies more in greater diligence in the observance of the rule and constitutions than in the multiplication of laws.

5. The members of each institute should recall, first of all, that when they made professions of the evangelical counsels they were responding to a divine call, to the end that, not merely being dead to sin (cf. Rom. 6:11) but renouncing the world also, they might live for God alone. They have dedicated their whole lives to his service. This constitutes a special consecration, which is deeply rooted in their baptismal consecration and is a fuller expression of it. Since this gift of themselves has been accepted by the Church, they should be aware that they are dedicated to its service also. This service of God should stimulate and foster the exercise of the virtues by them, especially the virtues of humility and obedience, fortitude and chastity, by which they share in Christ's emptying of himself (cf. Phil. 2:7–8) and at the same time in his life in the spirit (cf. Rom. 9:1–13).

Religious, therefore, faithful to their profession and leaving all things for Christ's sake (cf. Mk. 10:28), should follow him, regarding this as the one thing that is necessary (cf. Lk. 10:39) and should be solicitous for all that is his (cf. Cor. 7:32).

The members of each institute, therefore, ought to seek God before all else, and solely; they should join contemplation, by which they cleave to God by mind and heart, to apostolic love, by which they endeavor to be associated with the work of redemption and to spread the kingdom of God. (See D. 48, 22.)

6. They who make profession of the evangelical counsels should seek and love above all else God who has first loved us (cf. 1 Jn. 4:10). In all circumstances they should take care to foster a life hidden with Christ in God (cf. Col. 3:3), which is the source and stimulus of love of the neighbor, for the salvation of the world and the building-up of the Church. Even the very practice of the evangelical counsels is animated and governed by this charity.

For this reason, members of institutes should assiduously cultivate the spirit of prayer and prayer itself, drawing on the authentic sources of Christian spirituality. In the first place, let them have the sacred scripture at hand daily, so that they might learn "the surpassing worth of knowing Christ Jesus" (Phil. 3:8) by reading and meditating on the divine scriptures. They should perform the sacred liturgy, especially the holy mystery of the Eucharist, with their hearts and their lips, according to the mind of the Church, and they should nourish their spiritual lives from this richest of sources.

Thus, refreshed at the table of the divine law and of the sacred altar, let them love the members of Christ as brothers, let them reverence and love their pastors in a filial spirit; let them more and more live and think with the Church, and let them dedicate themselves wholeheartedly to its mission. (See D. *48*, 21.)

7. There are institutes which are entirely ordered towards contemplation, in such wise that their members give themselves over to God alone in solitude and silence, in constant prayer and willing penance. These will always have an honored place in the mystical Body of Christ, in which "all the members do not have the same function" (Rom. 12:4), no matter how pressing may be the needs of the active ministry. For they offer to God an exceptional sacrifice of praise, they lend luster to God's people with abundant fruits of holiness, they sway them by their example, and they enlarge the Church by their hidden apostolic fruitfulness. They are thus an ornament to the Church and a fount of heavenly graces. However, their way of life should be revised in accordance with the aforesaid principles and criteria of up-to-date renewal, the greatest care being taken to preserve their withdrawal from the world and the exercises which belong to the contemplative life.

8. In the Church there are very many institutes, clerical and lay, engaged in different kinds of apostolic work and endowed with gifts which vary according to the grace that is given to them. Administrators are given the gift of administration, the teacher the gift of doctrine, the preacher persuasiveness. Liberality is given to those who give to others, and cheerfulness to those who perform works of mercy (cf. Rom. 12:5–8). "There are varieties of gifts, but the same Spirit" (1 Cor. 12:4).

In these institutes, apostolic and charitable activity is of the very nature of religious life, as their own holy ministry and work of charity, entrusted to them by the Church and to be performed in its name. For this reason, the entire religious life of the members should be imbued with an apostolic spirit, and all their apostolic activity with a religious spirit. In order, therefore, that the members may first answer their call to follow Christ and to serve Christ himself in his members, their apostolic activity must needs have its source in intimate union with him. It is thus that their very love for God and their neighbor is fostered.

Consequently, these institutes should adjust their observances and customs to the needs of their particular apostolate. Since however the active religious life takes many forms, this diversity should be taken into account when its up-to-date renewal is being undertaken, and in the various institutes the members' life in the service of Christ should be sustained by means which are proper and suitable to each institute.

9. The venerable institution of monastic life must be carefully preserved and must shine forth increasingly in its true spirit in both East and West. Through long centuries it has deserved well of the Church and of human society. The principal duty of monks is to present to the divine majesty a service at once humble and noble within the walls of the monastery. This is true whether they dedicate themselves entirely to divine worship in the contemplative life, or have legitimately undertaken some apostolic or charitable activity. While preserving, therefore, the nature of their own institutions, they should renovate their ancient beneficent traditions and should so adapt them to the present-day needs of souls that monasteries will, as it were, carry in themselves the seeds of the growth of the Christian people.

There are religious orders which, from their rule or institution, unite the apostolic life with choral office and monastic observances. These should adapt their way of life to the needs of their proper apostolate, at the same time loyally preserving their form of life, for it has been of considerable service to the Church.

10. Lay religious life, for men and for women, is a state for the profession of the evangelical counsels which is complete in itself. The holy synod holds it in high esteem, for it is so useful to the Church in the exercise of its pastoral duty of educating the young, caring for the sick, and in its other ministries. It confirms the members in their vocation and urges them to adapt their life to modern requirements.

The holy synod declares that there is nothing to prevent some members of institutes of brothers being admitted to holy orders—the lay character of the institutes remaining intact—by provision of their general chapter and in order to meet the need for priestly ministration in their houses.

11. While it is true that secular institutes are not religious

institutes, at the same time they involve a true and full profession of the evangelical counsels in the world, recognized by the Church. This profession confers a consecration on people living in the world, men and women, laymen and clerics. Therefore they should make it their chief aim to give themselves to God totally in perfect charity. The institutes themselves ought to preserve their own special character—their secular character, that is to say—to the end that they may be able to carry on effectively and everywhere the apostolate in the world and, as it were, from the world, for which they were founded.

Let them know quite clearly, at the same time, that they will be unable to accomplish so great a task unless the members have so thorough a grounding in matters divine and human that they will be truly leaven in the world, for the strengthening and increase of the Body of Christ. Superiors therefore should devote great care to the formation, especially the spiritual formation, of their subjects, and also to the promotion of their higher studies.

12. Chastity "for the sake of the kingdom of heaven" (Mt. 19:22), which religious profess, must be esteemed an exceptional gift of grace. It uniquely frees the heart of man (cf. 1 Cor. 7:32–35), so that he becomes more fervent in love for God and for all men. For this reason it is a special symbol of heavenly benefits, and for religious it is a most effective means of dedicating themselves wholeheartedly to the divine service and the works of the apostolate. Thus for all Christ's faithful religious recall that wonderful marriage made by God, which will be fully manifested in the future age, and in which the Church has Christ for her only spouse.

Religious, therefore, at pains to be faithful to what they have professed, should believe our Lord's words and, relying on God's help, they should not presume on their own strength. They should practice mortification and custody of the senses. Nor should they neglect the natural means which promote health of mind and body. Thus, they should not be influenced by the false doctrines which allege that perfect continence is impossible or inimical to human development and, by a kind of spiritual instinct, they should reject whatever endangers chastity. Further, let all, and especially superiors, remember that chastity is preserved more securely when the members live a common life in true brotherly love.

The observance of perfect continence touches intimately the deeper inclinations of human nature. For this reason, candidates ought not to go forward, nor should they be admitted, to the profession of chastity except after really adequate testing, and unless they are sufficiently mature, psychologically and affectively. Not only should they be warned against the dangers to chastity which they may encounter, they should be taught to see that the celibacy they have dedicated to God is beneficial to their whole personality. (See D. *48*, 22.)

13. Voluntary poverty, in the footsteps of Christ, is a symbol of Christ which is much esteemed, especially nowadays. Religious should cultivate it diligently and, if needs be, express it in new forms. It enables them to share in the poverty of Christ who for our sake became poor, though he was rich, so that we might become rich through his poverty (cf. 2 Cor. 8:9; Mt. 8:20).

With regard to religious poverty it is by no means enough to be subject to superiors in the use of property. Religious should be poor in fact and in spirit, having their treasures in heaven (cf. Mt. 6:20).

They should, each in his own assigned task, consider themselves bound by the common law of labor, and while by this means they are provided with whatever they need for their sustenance or their work, they should reject all undue solicitude, putting their trust in the providence of the heavenly Father (cf. Mt. 6:25).

Religious congregations may, in their constitutions, permit their members to renounce their inheritances, both those which have already been acquired and those which may be acquired in the future.

The institutes themselves should endeavor, taking local conditions into account, to bear a quasi-collective witness to poverty. They should willingly contribute part of what they possess for the other needs of the Church and for the support of the poor, whom all religious should love with the deep yearning of Christ (cf. Mt. 19:21; 25:34–46; Jas. 2:15–15; 1 Jn. 3:17). Provinces and houses of the different institutes should share their poverty with one another, those who have more helping those who are in need.

While institutes have the right, provided this is allowed by their rules and constitutions, to possess whatever they need for their temporal life and work, they should avoid any semblance of luxury, excessive wealth and accumulation of property. (See D. *48*, 23 and 24.)

14. By their profession of obedience, religious offer the full dedication of their own wills as a sacrifice of themselves to God, and by this means they are united more permanently and securely with God's saving will. After the example of Jesus Christ, who came to do his Father's will (cf. Jn. 4:34; 5:30; Heb. 10:7; Ps. 39:9) and "taking the form of a servant" (Phil. 2:7) learned obedience through what he suffered (cf. Heb. 10:8), religious moved by the Holy Spirit subject themselves in faith to those who hold God's place, their superiors. Through them they are led to serve all their brothers in Christ, just as Christ ministered to his brothers in submission to the Father and laid down his life for the redemption of many (cf. Mt. 20:28; Jn. 10:14–18). They are thus bound more closely to the Church's service and they endeavor to attain to the measure of the stature of the fullness of Christ (cf. Eph. 4:13).

Religious, therefore, should be humbly submissive to their superiors, in a spirit of faith and of love for God's will, and in accordance with their rules and constitutions. They should bring their powers of intellect and will and their gifts of nature and grace to bear on the execution of commands and on the fulfilment of the tasks laid upon them, realizing that they are contributing towards the building up of the Body of Christ, according to God's plan. In this way, far from lowering the dignity of the human person, religious obedience leads it to maturity by extending the freedom of the sons of God.

Superiors will have to render an account of the souls committed to their care (Heb. 13:17). They should be docile to God's will in performing the task laid upon them and should exercise authority in a spirit of service of the brethren, thus giving expression to God's love for them.

They should govern their subjects in the realization that they are sons of God and with respect for them as human persons, fostering in them a spirit of voluntary subjection. In particular, therefore, they should allow them due liberty with regard to the sacrament of penance and the direction of conscience. They should train their subjects to cooperate with them by applying themselves to their ordinary duties and to new undertakings with an active and responsible obedience. Superiors therefore ought to listen to their subjects willingly and ought to promote cooperation between them for the good of the institute and of the Church, retaining however their own authority to decide and to prescribe what is to be done.

Chapters and councils should faithfully discharge the role committed to them in government and, each of them in its own way, should give expression to the involvement and the concern of all the members of the community for the good of the whole.

15. Common life, in prayer and the sharing of the same spirit (Acts 2:42), should be constant, after the example of the early Church, in which the company of believers were of one heart and soul. It should be nourished by the teaching of the Gospel and by the sacred liturgy, especially by the Eucharist. Religious, as members of Christ, should live together as brothers and should give pride of place to one another in esteem (cf. Rom. 12:10), carrying one another's burdens (cf. Gal. 6:12). A community gathered together as a true family in the Lord's name enjoys his presence (cf. Mt. 18:20), through the love of God which is poured into their hearts by the Holy Spirit (cf. Rom. 5:5). For love sums up the law (cf. Rom. 13:10) and is the bond which makes us perfect (cf. Col. 3:14); by it we know that we have crossed over from death to life (cf. 1 Jn. 3:14). Indeed, the unity of the brethren is a symbol of the coming of Christ (cf. Jn. 13:35; 17:21) and is a source of great apostolic power.

In order to strengthen the bond of brotherhood between the members of an institute, those who are called lay brothers, cooperators, or some such name should be associated more closely with the life and work of the community. Unless circumstances do really suggest otherwise, it should be the aim to arrive at but one category of sisters in women's institutes. The only distinction between persons that should then be retained is that demanded by the different tasks to which sisters are assigned by God's special vocation or by reason of their special aptitudes.

However, men's monasteries and institutes which are not entirely lay can, of their very nature, admit clerics and laymen, in accordance with the constitutions, on an equal footing and with equal rights and obligations, apart from those arising out of sacred orders. (See D. *48*, 25–29.)

16. Papal cloister is to be maintained for nuns whose life is wholly contemplative. However, it should be adjusted to

suit the conditions of time and place, abolishing obsolete practices after consultation with the monasteries themselves. Other nuns, however, who are engaged in the external apostolate by virtue of their own rule are to be exempted from papal cloister so that they can the better fulfil their apostolic tasks. The cloister prescribed by the constitutions must be maintained, however. (See D. *48*, 30–32.)

17. The religious habit, as a symbol of consecration, must be simple and modest, at once poor and becoming. In addition, it must be in keeping with the requirements of health and it must be suited to the times and place and to the needs of the apostolate. The habits, both of men and of women, which are not in conformity with these norms ought to be changed.

18. The up-to-date renewal of institutes depends very much on the training of the members. For this reason, nonclerical religious men, and religious women, should not be assigned to apostolic tasks immediately after the novitiate. Their religious, apostolic, doctrinal and technical training should, rather, be continued, as is deemed appropriate, in suitable establishments. They should also acquire whatever degrees they need.

Lest the adaptation of religious life to the needs of our time be merely external and lest those whose rule assigns them to the active ministry should prove unequal to the task, they should be properly instructed—each according to his intellectual calibre and personal bent—concerning the behavior-patterns, the emotional attitudes, and the thought-processes of modern society. The elements of the education should be so harmoniously fused that it will help to integrate the lives of the religious.

All through their lives, religious should endeavor assiduously to perfect this spiritual, doctrinal and technical culture. Superiors, as far as they are able, should provide for them the opportunity, assistance and the time for this.

It is also the task of superiors to see to it that directors, spiritual masters and professors are chosen to best advantage and are carefully trained. (See D. *48*, 33–38.)

19. When it is proposed to found new religious institutes the question must be seriously pondered, whether they are necessary, or even very useful, and whether it will be possible for them to increase. Otherwise, institutes may be imprudently brought into being which are useless or lacking in sufficient resources. In areas where the Church has re-

cently been established particular attention should be paid to the promotion and culitivation of forms of religious life which take into account the character and way of life of the inhabitants, and the local customs and conditions.

20. Institutes should faithfully maintain and accomplish the tasks that are theirs. Further mindful of what is useful for the universal Church and for the dioceses, they should adapt their ministry to the needs of time and place. They should employ appropriate and even new means, rejecting those which nowadays are less suited to the spirit and native genius of their institute.

The missionary spirit must, absolutely, be preserved in religious institutes and must be adapted to modern conditions, in keeping with the character of each, so that the preaching of the Gospel to all nations may be more effective.

21. Institutes and monasteries, however, which the Holy See, having consulted the local ordinaries concerned, judges not to offer any reasonable hope of further development, are to be forbidden to receive any more novices. If possible, they are to be amalgamated with more flourishing institutes or monasteries whose aims and spirit differ little from their own. (See D. 48, 39–41.)

22. Institutes and independent monasteries should, as opportunity offers and with the approval of the Holy See, form federations, if they belong in some measure, to the same religious family. Failing this, they should form unions, if they have almost identical constitutions and customs, have the same spirit, and especially if they are few in numbers. Or they should form associations if they have the same or similar active apostolates. (See ibid.)

23. Conferences or councils of major superiors, erected by the Holy See, are to be welcomed. They can contribute a great deal towards the fuller achievement of the purpose of the individual institutes, towards fostering more effective cooperation for the good of the Church, towards a more equitable distribution of ministers of the Gospel in a given territory, and towards treating the problems which are common to all religious. They should establish suitable coordination and cooperation with episcopal conferences with regard to the exercise of the apostolate.

Conferences of this type can also be established for secular institutes. (See D. 48, 42, 43.)

24. Priests and Christian educators should seriously set

about meeting fully the Church's need of a new increase4, through religious vocations carefully and suitably screened. Even ordinary preaching should deal more frequently with the evangelical counsels and with choosing the religious state. Parents should nurture and protect religious vocations in their children by educating them in Christian virtues.

Religious institutes have the right to publicize themselves in order to foster vocations, and they also have the right to seek candidates. However, they must do this with due prudence and they must observe the norms laid down by the Holy See and the local ordinary.

Religious should remember that the example of their own lives is the best commendation of their institutes and is an invitation to others to take on the religious life.

25. Religious institutes, for which these norms of up-to-date renewal have been established, should respond generously to the divine call and should be prompt in performing the task allotted to them in the Church today. The holy synod holds in high esteem their way of life in chastity, poverty and obedience, a way of life of which Christ the Lord himself is the exemplar. It places great hope in their work, which is so fruitful, whether it be hidden or in public. All religious, therefore, with undiminished faith, with charity towards God and their neighbor, with love for the cross and with the hope of future glory, should spread the good news of Christ throughout the whole world, so that their witness will be seen by all men and our Father, who is in heaven will be glorified (Mt. 5:16). Thus, through the prayers of the gentle Virgin Mary, Mother of God, "whose life is a model for all" (St. Ambrose, *De Virginitate*, 2, 2, n. 15) may they increase daily and may they bring more abundant fruits of salvation.

48

NORMS FOR IMPLEMENTING THE DECREE: ON THE UP-TO-DATE RENEWAL OF RELIGIOUS LIFE[a]

Paul VI, *Ecclesiae Sanctae II,* 6 August, 1966

If the fruits of the Council are to come to maturity, religious institutes must, first of all, promote a renewal of spirit. Then they should endeavor to effect the renewal and adaptation of their way of life and of their discipline, acting prudently but, at the same time, with energy. To this end they should study carefully the Dogmatic Constitution *Lumen Gentium* (chapters five and six) and the Decree *Perfectae Caritatis*—these especially—and they should endeavor to put the Council's teaching and directives into effect.

The norms which now follow apply, with the requisite distinctions, to all religious, both of the Eastern and of the Latin rites. They indicate the procedure to be followed and they include a number of prescriptions on how the Decree *Perfectae Caritatis* is to be applied and put into execution.

PART I

HOW TO PROMOTE RENEWAL AND ADAPTATION

I. THOSE RESPONSIBLE FOR RENEWAL

1. It is the institutes themselves which have the main responsibility for renewal and adaptation. They shall accomplish this especially by means of general chapters or, in the

---

a. Translated by Gilbert Volery, M.S.F.S., and Austin Flannery, O.P. These "norms" were published as part of a larger document which also included norms for the implementation of three other decrees, those on bishops, priests, and missions (See D. 46 and 62). The whole and any of the parts are often referred to under the title *Ecclesiae sanctae.*

Eastern rite, by *synaxes*. The task of general chapters is not limited to making laws; they should also foster spiritual and apostolic vitality.

2. The cooperation of all superiors and subjects is necessary for the renewal of their own religious lives, for the preparation of the spirit which should animate the chapters, for the accomplishment of their task, and for the faithful observance of the laws and norms laid down by the chapters.

3. In each institute, in order to put renewal and adaptation into effect, a special general chapter is to be summoned within two or, at most, three years. This can be the ordinary general chapter, or an extraordinary one.

This chapter can be divided into two separate sessions, provided that not more than a year elapses between one session and the next, and provided that the chapter itself so decides by a secret vote.

4. In preparation for this chapter, the general council must arrange, by some suitable means, for an ample and free consultation of all the subjects. The results of this consultation should be made available in good time so as to guide and assist the work of the chapter. The consultation may be done at the level of conventual or provincial chapters, by setting up commissions, by sending out questionnaires, etc.

5. In the case of monasteries directly dependent on a patriarch (*pro monasteriis stauropegiacis,* lit., enclosed monasteries), it will be his duty to define the norms which must guide this consultation.

6. This general chapter has the right to alter, temporarily, certain prescriptions of the constitutions—or, in Eastern rites, of the "typica"—by way of experiment, provided that the purpose, nature and character of the institute are safeguarded. Experiments which run counter to common law —and they should be embarked upon with prudence—will be readily authorized by the Holy See as the need arises.

Such experiments may be continued until the next ordinary general chapter, which will be empowered to grant a further prolongation but not beyond the date of the subsequent chapter.

7. The same faculty is granted to the general council for the space of time between the said chapters, according to the norms which they themselves shall decide. For those who belong to the Eastern rite, in monasteries *sui juris* of

that rite, this faculty is granted to the *hegumenus* (superior) with the minor *synaxis* (committee).

8. The final approval of constitutions is reserved to the competent authority.

9. With regard to the revision of nuns',[b] constitutions, the individual monasteries, through their chapters, or even the individual nuns, should offer their suggestions. In the interests of the preservation of the unity of each religious family, and in keeping with the character of each, these should be collected by the supreme authority in each order, if such there be; if not, by the delegate of the Holy See— or, in Eastern Churches, by the patriarch or *hierarch*. Views and suggestions from councils of federations or any similar lawfully constituted bodies can be sought as well. The bishops, in their pastoral solicitude, will give their kind help in this matter.

10. If in monasteries of nuns experiments relating to observance are judged necessary for a certain length of time, they may be authorized by the superiors general, the delegate of the Holy See or, in the East, by the local patriarch or hierarch. But one must bear in mind the particular mentality and psychology of enclosed communities, for they have a special need of stability and security.

11. It shall be the responsibility of the above mentioned authorities to see to the revision of the texts of the constitutions, in consultation and in collaboration with the monasteries themselves, and to submit them for approval to the Holy See or to the competent hierarchy.

II. REVISION OF CONSTITUTIONS AND TYPICA

12. The general laws of every institute (constitutions, typica, rules or whatever other name is given to these) must, generally speaking, contain the following elements:

(a) the evangelical and theological principles concerning religious life and its incorporation in the Church, and an apt and accurate formulation in which "the spirit and aims of the founder should be clearly recognized and faithfully preserved, as indeed should each institute's sound traditions, for all of these constitute the patrimony of an institute" (*Perfectae Caritatis*, no. 2b).

b. "Nuns" in the strict canonical sense of *moniales,* i.e. religious women with solemn vows. The word "nun" is used in this sense throughout.

(b) the juridical norms necessary to define the character, aims and means employed by the institute. Such rules must not be multiplied unduly, but should always be clearly formulated.

13. A combination of both elements, the spiritual and the juridical, is necessary, so as to ensure that the principal codes of each institute will have a solid foundation and be permeated by a spirit which is authentic and a law which is alive. Care must be taken not to produce a text either purely juridical or merely hortatory.

14. From the basic text of the rules one shall exclude anything which is now out of date, or anything which may change with the conditions of time, or which is of purely local application. These norms which are linked with present-day life or with the physical and psychical conditions or situations of the subjects, should be entered in separate books, such as directories, books of customs or similiar documents, whatever be their name.

III. CRITERIA FOR RENEWAL AND ADAPTATION

15. The norms and spirit according to which renewal and adaptation must be affected are not to be found solely in the Decree *Perfectae Caritatis,* but ought to be sought also in other conciliar documents, specially in chapters five and six of the Dogmatic Constitution *Lumen Gentium.*

16. Institutes should see to it that the principles formulated in no. 2 of the Decree *Perfectae Caritatis* do really inspire the renewal of their own religious life. To that end:

(1) The study and meditation of the Gospel and of the whole of Holy Scripture by all religious, from the time of the novitiate, should be more strongly encouraged. Further, care should be taken that all of them share, in whatever ways are most suitable, in the mystery and life of the Church.

(2) The doctrine of religious life must be examined and expounded under all its aspects (theological, historical, canonical, etc).

(3) For the good of the Church, institutes must seek after a genuine understanding of their original spirit, so that they will preserve it faithfully when deciding on adaptations, will purify their religious life from alien elements, and will free it from what is obsolete.

17. Those elements are to be considered obsolete which

do not pertain to the nature and purpose of the institute and which, having lost their meaning and impact, are of no further assistance to religious life. But the idea of witness, which religious life has for its function to show forth, must be kept in mind.

18. The mode of government should be such that "chapters and councils should express, each one at its own level, the involvement and the concern of all the members of the community for the good of the whole" (*Perfectae Caritatis*, no. 14). This will be the case, especially, if the members have a real and effective part in the choice of chapter and council officials. Again, the mode of government should be such that the exercise of authority is rendered more effective and expeditious, as our times demand. Superiors, therefore, at every level should be given appropriate powers, so as to minimize unnecessary or too frequent recourse to higher authority.

19. Besides, suitable renewal cannot be achieved once for all: it needs to be fostered continually, with the help of the fervor of members and the solicitude of chapters and superiors.

PART II

SOME PARTICULAR POINTS REGARDING RENEWAL AND ADAPTATIONS IN RELIGIOUS LIFE

I. THE DIVINE OFFICE OF BROTHERS AND SISTERS (Perfectae Caritatis, no. 3)

20. Although religious who recite a Little Office truly approved, perform the public prayer of the Church (cf. Constitution on the Liturgy, no. 98), it is recommended that religious institutes should recite, in full or in part, the Divine Office, instead of a Little Office. They will thus share more intimately in the liturgical life of the Church. Eastern subjects should recite the doxologies and the divine praises according to their typica and customs.

II. MENTAL PRAYER (Perfectae Caritatis, no. 6)

21. In order that religious may share more intimately and with greater profit in the holy mystery of the Eucharist, and in the public prayer of the Church, and that their interior

life be more abundantly nourished, priority should be given to mental prayer over a multiplicity of other prayers. However, those community exercises which are traditional in the Church should be preserved and care taken that religious be rightly instructed in the ways of spiritual life.

III. MORTIFICATION (Perfectae Caritatis, nn. 5 and 12)

22. Religious, more so than the rest of the faithful, should engage in acts of penance and mortification. The penitential practices proper to the various institutes should be revised whenever there is need, so that with due reference to the traditions of the Eastern or Western Church and to the conditions of our times, religious may be able to follow such observances. New forms of penance may also be derived from the circumstances of modern life.

IV. POVERTY (Perfectae Caritatis, no. 13)

23. Religious institutes, mainly through their general chapters, must with diligence and in concrete form promote the spirit and practice of poverty, according to the mind of no. 13 of the Decree *Perfectae Caritatis*. Here too, in keeping with the character of each institute, new forms should be devised and put into effect, forms which may render more effective the practice and witness of poverty today.

24. It belongs to the institutes of simple vows in their general chapters to define whether renunciation of inheritances—those which religious may already possess, and those which may come to them later—should be entered in the constitutions; and, if so, whether this renunciation should be compulsory or left to choice. They should state when such renunciation should take place, whether before the perpetual vows or after some years.

V. LIFE IN COMMON (Perfectae Caritatis, no. 15)

25. In institutes dedicated to apostolic activities, community life must be encouraged by all possible means, and in ways suitable to the vocation of each institute. It is of the greatest importance that the members should establish a fraternal life in common (*commercium fraternum*), as a family united in Christ.

26. In such institutes, it will often happen that the order of the day cannot be identical in all the houses, not even

sometimes within the same house for all the religious. But in all cases the order of the day must be arranged in such a way as to provide for the religious, besides the time given to spiritual exercises and apostolic activities, a little free time for themselves and sufficient time also for legitimate recreation.

27. General chapters and synaxes must study the manner in which religious who are called lay-brothers (and lay-sisters), cooperators or any similar name, may, gradually, obtain a vote in specified community activities and in elections, and may even become eligible for certain offices. They will thus become more directly involved in the life and activities of the community and the priests will have greater freedom to perform those ministries which are reserved to them.

28. In monasteries which have eliminated differences in category of nuns, choral obligations must be clearly defined in the constitutions: the differentiation of persons, demanded by the diversity of activities or by vocation, should be taken into consideration.

29. The sisters who are attending to the external duties of the monasteries, whether they are called oblates or any other name, should be ruled by special statutes. These rules must take account of the fact that their vocation is not purely contemplative, and also of the implications of the vocation of the enclosed nuns with whom the sisters live in close contact, though not being nuns themselves.

The superioress of the monastery has the grave obligation of looking after them, of providing a suitable training in religious life for them, of treating them with a true spirit of charity and of fostering ties of sisterly love with the community of the nuns.

VI. THE ENCLOSURE OF NUNS (Perfectae Caritatis, no. 16)

30. The papal enclosure of monasteries must be considered as an ascetical institution which is singularly appropriate to the particular vocation of nuns, and as one which stands as a sign and a protection; it is the particular form which their withdrawal from the world takes.

In the same manner, nuns of the Eastern Church must keep their enclosure.

31. This enclosure must be so adapted that the material separation from the outside world is always preserved. The individual religious families are left free, in pursuance of their own spirit, to set out and define in their constitutions the particular norms of the material separation.

32. The minor enclosure is suppressed. Those nuns who from their institution are dedicated to external activities, must define their enclosure in their constitutions. But those nuns who, though contemplative from their institution have adopted external works, must, after a suitable space of time left to them for deliberation, either abandon external works and retain the papal enclosure, or maintain these activities and define the nature of their enclosure in their constitutions, while still remaining nuns.

VII. THE FORMATION OF RELIGIOUS (Perfectae Caritatis, no. 18)

33. The formation of religious from the novitiate onwards need not be planned according to the same pattern for all institutes, but account must be taken of the specific character of each institute. In revising and adapting this formation, a sufficient measure of prudent experimentation should take place.

34. What is stated in the Decree *Optatam totius* (On Priestly Formation) must be carefully observed in the formation of religious clerics, with the necessary adaptations demanded by the particular character of each institute.

35. Post-novitiate formation, adapted to the character of each institute, is absolutely necessary for all subjects, not excepting contemplatives. For institutes of brothers and for the sisters in institutes dedicated to apostolic work, the formation must normally cover the entire period of temporary vows, as is the case already in many institutes, under the name of juniorate or scholasticate or similar terms.

36. This formation must be given in houses which are suitable for the purpose. It must not be merely theoretical but should be also practical, involving, for their educational value, various activities and duties which fit in with the character and circumstances of each institute. Thus the candidates will be gradually introduced to the kind of life that later on shall be theirs.

37. Due regard must be had for the kind of training

which is proper to the individual institute. But, since all institutes are not able to impart in a satisfactory manner a doctrinal and technical formation, they can make up for this by fraternal collaboration. This can be done on a variety of levels and can assume different forms: lectures or courses in common, the lending of teachers, even by pooling teachers and resources in a common school attended by members of several institutes.

The institutes which are well-provided as regards means of training should be willing to help other institutes.

38. After a due measure of experimentation, each institute must draw up proper and suitable rules for the training of its subjects.

VIII. UNIFICATION AND SUPPRESSION OF INSTITUTES (Perfectae Caritatis, nn. 21-22)

39. The project for a union between institutes—whatever its nature may be—supposes an adequate preparation, spiritual, psychological, juridical, according to the mind of the Decree *Perfectae Caritatis*. For this, it is often desirable that the institutes should have the help of some assistant approved by the competent authority.

40. In such cases and circumstances, the good of the Church must be kept in view, as also the particular character of each institute and the freedom of choice left to each individual religious.

41. In attempting to reach a decision concerning the suppression of an institute or monastery, the following are the criteria which, taken together, one should retain, after one has taken all the circumstances into consideration: the number of members remains small, even though the institute or monastery has been in existence for many years, candidates have not been forthcoming for a long time past and most members are advanced in years. If a suppression is finally decided upon, provision must be made that 'if possible (the institute) be amalgamated with a more flourishing (institute) whose aim and spirit differ little from its own' (*Perfectae Caritatis,* no. 21). Each religious must be individually consulted beforehand, and all must be done with perfect charity.

IX. CONFERENCES OR UNIONS OF MAJOR RELIGIOUS SUPERIORS (MEN AND WOMEN) (Perfectae Caritatis, no. 23)

42. Care must be taken that the union of major religious superiors, men and women, should have access to some council attached to the Sacred Congregation of Religious and should be able to be consulted by the said council.

43. It is of the utmost importance that the national unions of major religious superiors, men and women, should cooperate with confidence and reverence, with the episcopal conferences (cf. *Christus Dominus*, nn. 35, 50, and *Ad gentes divinitus*, no. 33).

To this end, it is desirable that questions having reference to both bishops and religious should be dealt with by mixed commissions consisting of bishops and major religious superiors, men or women.

CONCLUSION

44. These norms apply to all religious in the Church. They leave in full vigor the general laws of the Church, both of the Latin and Eastern rites, as also the laws proper to the religious orders themselves, unless the present norms explicitly or implicitly change them.

49

INSTRUCTION ON THE RENEWAL OF RELIGIOUS LIFE[a]

S.C.R.S.I., *Renovationis Causam,* 6 January 1969

INTRODUCTION

When the Second Ecumenical Council of the Vatican examined the problem of renewal—how to strengthen the Church spiritually and ensure that it be better prepared to proclaim the message of salvation to modern man—it devoted a good deal of attention to religious. It set forth in a clearer light the nature, structure and importance of their way of life.[1] Concerning their place in the body of the Church the Council affirmed: 'While it is true that the state constituted by profession of the evangelical counsels has no bearing on the hierarchical structure of the Church, it has an undeniable relevance to her life and holiness'.[2]

Besides, 'it is the task of the Church's Hierarchy to make wise laws for the regulation of the practice of the counsels whereby the perfect love of God and of our neighbor is fostered in a unique way; for the function of the Hierarchy is to feed the People of God and to bring them to richer pastures (cf. Ezek 34:14). In response to the urging of the Holy Spirit, the Hierarchy accepts the rules proposed by eminent men and women, and when they have been made more precise gives them authentic approval. Moreover, its supervisory and protective authority lends its presence to the Institutes set up in many places for the building up of Christ's Body, to see that they grow and flourish in accordance with the spirit of the founders.'[3]

a. Translation based on that in *OSS. Rom.,* 13 Feb. 1969, Latin text in *AAS* 51 (1969) pp. 103–120. (See A. 188.)
1. Cf. Vatican Council II, Dogmatic Constitution on the Church, *Lumen gentium,* (D. *28*). n. 43 ff.; Decree on the Renewal and Adaptation of the Religious Life, *Perfectae caritatis* (D. *47*).
2. *Lumen gentium,* n. 44.
3. *Lumen gentium,* n. 45.

It is no less true that the generous vitality, and especially the renewal of the spiritual, evangelical and apostolic life which must animate the various Institutes in the untiring pursuit of an ever greater charity is the responsibility chiefly of those who have received the mission, in the name of the Church and with the grace of the Lord, to govern these Institutes. And it also requires the generous collaboration of all their members. It is of the very nature of the religious life, just as it is of the very nature of the Church, to have that structure without which no society, not even a supernatural one, would be able to achieve its end, or be in a position to provide the best means to attain it.

Wherefore, having learned also from centuries of experience, the Church was led gradually to the formulation of a body of canonical norms, which have contributed in no small degree to the solidity and vitality of religious life in the past. Everyone recognizes that the renewal and adaptation of different Institutes, as demanded by actual circumstances, cannot be implemented without a revision of the canonical prescriptions dealing with the structure and the means of the religious life.

As 'the adaptation and renewal of Religious Institutes depends to a very large extent on the formation of its members,'[4] several Congregations both of men and of women, anxious to work out the renewal desired by the Council, have endeavoured by serious inquiries and have often taken advantage of the preparation of the special General Chapter prescribed by the Motu Proprio *Ecclesiae sanctae*[5] in order to discover the best conditions for a suitable renewal of the various phases of the formation of their members to the religious life.

Thus, it was that a certain number of requests were formulated and transmitted to the Sacred Congregation for Religious and for Secular Institutes, especially through the 'Union of Superiors General.' These requests were intended to secure a broadening of the canonical norms actually governing religious formation in order to permit the various Institutes, comformably to the instructions of the Decree *Perfectae caritatis*,[6] to make a better adaptation of the entire formation cycle to the mentality of younger generations

---

4. *Perfectae caritatis*, n. 18.
5. Cf. Motu Proprio *Ecclesiae sanctae*, II, (D. *48*), Part I, n. 3.
6. Cf. *Perfectae caritatis*, n. 3 ff.

and modern living conditions, as also to the present demands of the apostolate, while remaining faithful to the nature and the special aim of each Institute.

It is evident that no new clear and definitive legislation can be formulated except on the basis of experiments carried out on a sufficiently vast scale and over a sufficiently long period of time to make it possible to arrive at an objective judgment based on facts. This is most true since the complexity of situations, their variations according to localities and the rapidity of the changes which affect them make it impossible for those charged with the formation of the youth of today to an authentic religious life to determine *a priori* which solutions might be best.

This is why this Sacred Congregation for Religious and for Secular Institutes, after careful examination of the proposals submitted regarding the different phases of religious formation, has deemed it opportune to broaden the canonical rules now in force in order to permit these necessary experiments. Nevertheless, although the juridical norms are being eased, it is important that this be not to the detriment of those basic values which the prevailing legislation undertook to safeguard. 'It is therefore of the greatest importance that no adaptation to modern requirements should be put into effect, which is not inspired by a spiritual renewal.'[7]

In order to be authentic, every revision of the means and the rules of the religious life presupposes at the same time a redefining of the values which are essential to the religious life, since the safeguarding of these values is the aim of these norms. For this reason and in order to permit a clearer understanding of the significance of the new rulings set forth in this present Instruction, the Sacred Congregation has deemed it useful to preface them with certain explanatory remarks.

PART I

SOME GUIDELINES AND PRINCIPLES

RENEWAL OF INDIVIDUAL INSTITUTES

1. Not only the complexity of the situations alluded to previously, but also especially the growing diversity of Institutes and their activities, makes it increasingly difficult to

7. *Perfectae caritatis*, n. 2 (e).

formulate any useful set of directives equally applicable to all Institutes everywhere. Hence the much broader norms set forth in this Instruction give to individual Institutes the possibility of prudently choosing the solution best suited to their needs.

It is especially important, particularly with reference to formation and education, to remember that not even the best solutions can be absolutely identical both for Institutes of men and those of women. Similarly, the framework and the means of formation must vary according as an Institute is dedicated to contemplation or is committed to apostolic activities.

THE NATURE OF RELIGIOUS PROFESSION

2. Questions raised by the faculty granted in this present Instruction to those Institutes which might deem it opportune, to replace temporary vows with some other kind of commitment, emphasize the necessity of recalling here the nature and the proper value of religious profession. Such profession, whereby the members 'with the help of vows or other sacred obligations which resemble vows in their nature,'[8] bind themselves to living the three evangelical counsels, brings about a total consecration to God, who alone is worthy of such a sweeping gift on the part of a human person. It is more in keeping with the nature of such a gift to find its culmination and its most eloquent expression in perpetual profession, whether simple or solemn. In fact, 'the perfection of the consecration is proportionate to the strength and stability of the bonds which enable Christ to be seen more clearly in his indissoluble union with his bride, the Church.'[9] Thus it is that religious profession is an act of religion and a special consecration whereby a person dedicates himself to God.

Not only according to the teaching of the Church but likewise by the very nature of this consecration, the vows of obedience, whereby a religious consummates the complete renunciation of himself and, along with the vows of religious chastity and poverty, offers to God as it were a perfect sacrifice, belongs to the essence of religious profession.[10]

8. *Lumen gentium*, n. 44.
9. *Lumen gentium*, n. 44.
10. Cf. *Perfectae caritatis*, n. 14.

Thus consecrated to Christ, the religious is at the same time bound to the service of the Church and, according to his vocation, is led to the realization of the perfection of that apostolic charity which must animate and impel him, whether in a life entirely given over to contemplation or in different apostolic activities. This notwithstanding, it is important to note that, even though in Institutes dedicated to the apostolate 'apostolic and charitable works are essential to the religious life,'[11] this apostolic activity is not the primary aim of religious profession. Besides, the same apostolic works could be carried out quite well without the consecration deriving from the religious state although, for one who has taken on its obligations, this religious consecration can and must contribute to greater dedication to the apostolate.

Hence, although it is in order to renew religious life in its means and its forms of expression, it cannot be asserted that the very nature of religious profession must be changed or that there should be a lessening of the demands proper to it. The youth of today who are called by God to the religious state are not less desirous than before, rather they ardently desire to live up to this vocation in all its requirements, provided these be certain and authentic.

OTHER INSTITUTES

3. Nevertheless, in addition to the religious vocation strictly and properly so called, the Holy Spirit does not cease to stir up in the Church, especially in these latter times, numerous Institutes, whose members, whether bound or not by sacred commitments, undertake to live in common and to practice the evangelical counsels in order to devote themselves to various apostolic or charitable activities. The Church has sanctioned the authentic nature of these different modes of life and has approved them. Still, these modes do not constitute the religious state even though up to a certain point, they have often been likened to religious life in canonical legislation. Therefore, the norms and directives contained in this present Instruction deal directly with religious Institutes in the strict sense. Other Institutes, however, if they so wish, are free to follow them in the proper organization of their formation programme and in whatever is best suited to the nature of their activities.

11. *Perfectae caritatis*, n. 8.

PREPARATION FOR THE NOVITIATE

4. The faculties granted to religious Institutes by this present Instruction have been suggested by a certain number of considerations based on experience which it is here in order to explain briefly.

It would appear that in our day and age genuine religious formation should proceed more by stages and be extended over a longer period of time, since it must embrace both the time of the novitiate and the years following upon the first temporary commitment. In this formation cycle the novitiate must retain its irreplaceable and privileged role as the first initiation into religious life. This goal cannot be attained unless the future novice possesses a minumum of human and spiritual preparation which must not only be verified but, very often, also completed.

In fact, for each candidate the novitiate should come at the moment when, aware of God's call, he has reached that degree of human and spiritual maturity which will allow him to decide to respond to this call with sufficient and proper responsibility and freedom. No one should enter religious life without this choice being freely made, and without the separation from men and things which this entails being accepted. Nevertheless, this first decision does not necessarily demand that the candidate be then able to measure up immediately to all the demands of the religious and apostolic life of the Institute, but he must be judged capable of reaching this goal by stages. Most of the difficulties encountered today in the formation of novices are usually due to the fact that when they were admitted they did not have the required maturity.

Thus, preparation for entrance into the novitiate proves to be increasingly necessary as the world becomes less Christian in outlook. In most cases, in fact, a gradual spiritual and psychological adjustment appears to be indispensable in order to prepare the way for certain breaks with one's social milieu and even worldly habits. Young people today who are attracted by the religious life are not looking for an easy life; indeed their thirst for the absolute is consuming. But their life of faith is oftentimes based on merely elementary knowledge of doctrine, in sharp contrast to the development of their knowledge of profane subjects.

Hence it follows that all Institutes, even those whose formation cycle includes no postulancy, must attach great importance to this preparation for the novitiate. In Institutes having minor seminaries, seminaries or colleges, candidates for the religious life usually go directly to the novitiate. It will be worthwhile to reconsider if this policy should be maintained, or if it is not more advisable, in order to assure better preparation for a fully responsible choice of the religious life, to prepare for the novitiate by a fitting period of probation in order to develop the human and emotional maturity of the candidate. Moreover, while it must be recognized that problems vary according to countries, it must be affirmed that the age required for admission to the novitiate should be higher than heretofore.

DEEPENING OF UNITY WITH GOD

5. As regards the formation to be imparted in the novitiate in Institutes dedicated to the works of the apostolate, it is evident that greater attention should be paid to preparing the novices, in the very beginning and more directly, for the type of life or the activities which will be theirs in the future, and to teaching them how to realize in their lives in progressive stages that cohesive unity whereby contemplation and apostolic activity are closely linked together, a unity which is one of the most fundamental and primary values of these same societies. The achievement of this unity requires a proper understanding of the realities of the supernatural life and of the paths leading to a deepening of union with God in the unity of one same supernatural love for God and for men, finding expression at times in the solitude of intimate communing with the Lord and at others in the generous giving of self to apostolic activity. Young religious must be taught that this unity so eagerly sought and towards which all life tends in order to find its full development, cannot be attained on the level of activity alone, or even be psychologically experienced, for it resides in that divine love which is the bond of perfection and which surpasses all understanding.

The attainment of this unity, which cannot be achieved without long training in self-denial or without persevering efforts towards purity of intention in action, demands in those Institutes faithful compliance with the basic law of all spiritual life, which consists in arranging a proper balance of periods set aside for solitude with God and others devoted to various activities and to the human contacts which these involve.

Consequently, in order that novices, while acquiring experience in certain activities proper to their Institute, may discover the importance of this law and make it habitual, it has seemed advisable to grant to those Institutes which might regard it as opportune, the faculty of introducing into the novitiate formative activity and experimental periods in keeping with their activities and their type of life.

It must be emphasized that this formative activity, which complements novitiate teaching, is not intended to provide the novices with the technical or professional training required for certain apostolic activities, training which will be afforded to them later on, but rather to help them, in the very midst of these activities to better discover the exigencies of their vocation as religious and how to remain faithful to them.

In fact, confronted with the diversity of apostolic activities available to them, let religious not forget that, differently from secular Institutes, whose specific activity is carried out with the means of the world or in the performance of temporal tasks, religious must, above all, according to the teaching of the Council, be in a special manner witnesses to Christ within the Church: 'Religious must make it their careful aim that their efforts improve the Church's real and daily presentation, to believers and non-believers, of Christ as he meditated on the hillside, proclaimed to the crowds the kingdom of God, healed the sick and the injured, turning sinners to repentance, blessing children, doing good to all, and continually obeying the will of the Father who sent him.'[12]

There is a diversity of gifts. Wherefore, each one must stand firm in the vocation to which he has been called, since the mission of those called to the religious state in the Church is one thing; the mission of secular Institutes is another thing; the temporal and apostolic mission of the laity not especially consecrated to God in an Institute, is quite another.

It is in line with this perspective on his vocation that whoever is called by God to the religious state must understand the meaning of the formation which is begun in the novitiate.

12. *Lumen gentium*, n. 46.

Therefore, the nature and the educational value of these periods, as well as the timeliness of introducing them into the novitiate, will be evaluated differently in congregations of men or of women, in Institutes dedicated to contemplation or to apostolic activities.

Indeed, the effectiveness of this formation, while it is imparted in an atmosphere of greater freedom and flexibility, will also depend largely on the firmness and the wisdom of the guidance afforded by the Novice Master and by all those who share in the formation of young religious after the novitiate. It is extremely important also to recall the importance of the role played in such formation by the atmosphere of generosity provided by a fervent and united community, in the midst of which young religious will be enabled to learn by experience the value of mutual fraternal assistance as an element of readier progress and perseverance in their vocation.

GRADUAL FORMATION

6. In order then to respond to this same need of gradual formation the question has arisen concerning the extension of the period prior to perpetual profession in which a candidate is bound by temporary vows or by some other form of commitment.

It is proper that when he pronounces his perpetual vows, the religious should have reached the degree of spiritual maturity required in order that the religious state to which he is committing himself in stable and certain fashion may really be for him a means of perfection and greater love, rather than a burden too heavy to carry. Nevertheless, in certain cases the extension of temporary probation can be an aid to this maturity, while in others it can involve drawbacks which it will not be out of place to point out. The fact of remaining for too long a time in a state of uncertainty is not always a contribution to maturity, and this situation may in some cases encourage a tendency to instability. It should be added that in the case of non-admission to perpetual profession, the return to lay life will often entail problems of readjustment, which will be all the more serious and trying according as the time spent in temporary commitment has been longer. Superiors, consequently, must be aware of their grave responsibilities in this field and should not put off until the last minute a decision which could and should have been taken earlier.

TEMPORARY VOWS

7. No institute should decide to use the faculty granted by this Instruction to replace temporary vows by some other form of commitment without having clearly considered and weighed the reasons for and the nature of this commitment. For him who has heeded the call of Jesus to leave everything to follow Him there can be no question of how important it is to respond generously and wholeheartedly to this call from the very outset of his religious life; the making of temporary vows is completely in harmony with this requirement. For, while still retaining its probationary character by the fact that it is temporary, the profession of first vows makes the young religious share in the consecration proper to the religious state.

Yet, perpetual vows can be prepared for without making temporary vows. In fact, more frequently now than in the past, a certain number of young candidates come to the end of their novitiate without having acquired the religious maturity sufficient to bind themselves immediately by religious vows, although no prudent doubt can be raised regarding their generosity or their authentic vocation to the religious state. This hesitancy in pronouncing vows is frequently accompanied by a great awareness of the exigencies and the importance of the perpetual religious profession to which they aspire and wish to prepare themselves. Thus it has seemed desirable in a certain number of Institutes that at the end of their novitiate the novices should be able to bind themselves by a temporary commitment different from vows, yet answering their twofold desire to give themselves to God and the Institute and to pledge themselves to a fuller preparation for perpetual profession.

Whatever form such a temporary commitment may take, fidelity to a genuine religious vocation demands that it should in some way be based on the requirements of the three evangelical counsels, and should thus be already entirely orientated toward the one perpetual profession, for which it must be, as it were an apprenticeship and a preparation.

SOLUTIONS TO PERSONAL DIFFICULTIES

8. He who commits himself to walk in the path of the Saviour in the religious life, must bear in mind our Lord's own words that "no one who puts his hand to the plough and looks back is fit for the kingdom of God" (Luke 9:62). Just the same, the psychological and emotional difficulties encountered by some individuals in their progressive adaptation to the religious life are not always resolved upon the termination of the novitiate, and at the same time there is no doubt that their vocation can be authentic. In many cases, the permission for absence provided for by Canon Law will allow Superiors to make it possible for these religious to spend some time outside a house of the Institute in order to be the better able to resolve their problems. But in some more difficult cases, this solution will be inadequate. Superiors can then persuade such candidates to return to lay life, using if necessary, the faculty granted n. 38 of this Instruction.

PREPARATION FOR PERPETUAL VOWS

9. Lastly, a religious formation more based on stages and judiciously extended over the different periods of the life of a young religious should find its culmination in a serious preparation for perpetual vows. It is in fact desirable that this unique and essential act whereby a religious is consecrated to God forever should be preceded by a sufficiently long immediate preparation, spent in retreat and prayer, a preparation which could be like a second novitiate.

PART II

SPECIAL NORMS

The Sacred Congregation for Religious and for Secular Institutes, in its desire to promote necessary and useful experiments in view of the adaptation and renewal of religious formation, having examined these questions in its plenary meetings of 25–26 June, 1968, by virtue of a special mandate from the Sovereign Pontiff, Pope Paul VI, has seen fit, by this Instruction, to formulate and to publish the following norms:

PHASES OF RELIGIOUS FORMATION

10. (1) Religious formation comprises two essential phases: the novitiate and the probationary period which follows the novitiate and lasts for a period adapted to the nature of the Institute, during which the members are bound by vows or other commitments.

(2) A preliminary period of varying duration, obligatory in certain Institutes under the name of postulance, usually precedes admission to the novitiate.

PROBATIONARY PERIOD

11. (1) This preliminary probation has as its purpose not merely to formulate a tentative judgment on the aptitudes and vocation of the candidate, but also to verify the extent of his knowledge of religions subjects and, where need be, to complete it in the degree judged necessary and, lastly, to permit a gradual transition from lay life to the life proper to the novitiate.

(2) During this probationary period it is particularly necessary to secure assurance that the candidate for religious life be endowed with such elements of human and emotional maturity as will afford grounds for hope that he is capable of undertaking properly the obligations of the religious state and that, in the religious life and especially in the novitiate, he will be able to progress towards fuller maturity.

(3) If in certain more difficult cases, the Superior feels, with the free agreement of the subject, that he should have recourse to the services of a prudent and qualified psychologist known for his moral principles, it is desirable, in order that this examination may be fully effective, that it should take place after an extended period of probation, so as to enable the specialist to formulate a diagnosis based on experience.

ADAPTATION OF THE POSTULANCY

12. (1) In Institutes where a postulancy is obligatory, whether by common law or in virtue of the Constitutions, the General Chapter may follow the norms of this present Instruction for a better adaptation of the period of postulancy to the requirements of a more fruitful preparation for the novitiate.

(2) In other Institutes it belongs to the General Chapter to determine the nature and the length of this preliminary probation, which can vary according to candidates. Nevertheless, if it is to be genuinely effective, this period should neither be too brief nor, as a general rule, be extended beyond two years.

(3) It is preferable that this probation should not take place in the novitiate house. It could even be helpful that, either in whole or in part, it be organized outside a house of the Institute.

(4) During this preliminary probation, even if it takes place outside a house of the Institute, the candidates will be placed under the direction of qualified religious and there should be sufficient collaboration between these latter and the Novice Master, with a view to assuring the continuity of formation.

PURPOSE OF NOVITIATE

13. (1) Religious life begins with the novitiate. Whatever may be the special aim of the Institute, the principal purpose of the novitiate is to initiate the novice into the essential and primary requirements of the religious life and also, in view of a greater charity, to implement the evangelical counsels of chastity, poverty, and obedience of which he will later make profession, 'with the help of vows or other sacred obligations which resemble vows in their nature.'[13]

(2) In those Institutes where 'apostolic and charitable works are essential to the religious life,'[14] the novices are to be gradually trained to dedicate themselves to activities in keeping with the purpose of their Institute, while developing that intimate union with Christ whence all their apostolic activity must flow.[15]

SUITABLE CANDIDATES

14. Superiors responsible for the admission of candidates to the novitiate will take care to accept only those giving proof of the aptitudes and elements of maturity regarded as necessary for commitment to the religious life as lived in the Institute.

13. *Lumen gentium*, n. 44.
14. *Perfectae caritatis*, n. 8.
15. Cf. *Perfectae caritatis*, n. 8.

NOVICE FORMATION

15. (1) In order to be valid, the novitiate must be made in the house legitimately designated for his purpose.

(2) It should be made in the community or group of novices, fraternally united under the direction of the Novice Master. The program as well as the nature of the activities and work of the novitiate must be organized in such a way as to contribute to novice formation.

(3) This formation, conformable to the teachings of our Lord in the Gospel and the demands of the particular aim and spirituality of the Institute, consists mainly in initiating the novices gradually into detachment from everything not connected with the kingdom of God, the practice of obedience, poverty, prayer, habitual union with God in availability to the Holy Spirit, in order to help one another spiritually in frank and open charity.

(4) The novitiate will also include study and meditation on Holy Scripture, the doctrinal and spiritual formation indispensable for the development of a supernatural life of union with God and an understanding of the religious state and, lastly an initiation to liturgical life and the spirituality proper to the Institute.

AUTHORITY OF THE SUPERIOR GENERAL

16. (1) The erection of a novitiate does not require the authorization of the Holy See. It belongs to the Superior General, with the consent of his council and conformably to the norms laid down in the Constitutions, to erect or to authorize the erection of a novitiate, to determine the special details of the program and to decide on its location in a given house of the Institute.

(2) If necessary, in order to make more effective provision for the formation of the novices, the Superior General may authorize the transfer of the novitiate community during certain periods to another residence designated by himself.

INSTITUTING NOVITIATES

17. In case of necessity, the Superior General, with the consent of his council and after consultation with the interested Provincial, may authorize the erection of several novitiates within the same province.

THE IMPORTANCE OF COMMUNITY LIFE

18. In view of the very important role of community life in the formation of the novices, and when the small number of the novices would prevent the creation of conditions favorable to genuine community life, the Superior General should, if possible, organize the novitiate in another community of the Institute able to assist in the formation of this small group of novices.

SPECIAL CASES

19. In special cases and by way of exception, the Superior General, with the consent of his council, is empowered to allow a candidate to make his novitiate validly in some house of the Institute other than the novitiate, under the responsibility of an experienced religious acting as Novice Master.

FIRST PROFESSION OUTSIDE THE NOVITIATE HOUSE

20. For a reason which he regards as just, the major Superior may allow first profession to be made outside the novitiate house.

REQUIREMENT FOR VALIDITY

21. In order to be valid, the novitiate as described above must last twelve months.

ABSENCES FROM THE NOVITIATE

22. (1) Absences from the novitiate group and house which, either at intervals or continuously, exceed three months render the novitiate invalid.

(2) As for absences lasting less than three months, it pertains to the major Superiors, after consultation with the Novice Master, to decide in each individual case, taking into account the reasons for the absence, whether this absence should be made up by demanding an extension of the novitiate, and to determine the length of the eventual prolongation. The Constitutions of the Institute may also provide directives on this point.

EXPERIMENTATION

23. (1) The General Chapter, by at least a two-thirds majority, may decide, on an experimental basis, to integrate into novitiate formation one or several periods involving activities in line with the character of the Institute and away from the novitiate, in the degree in which, in the judgment of the Novice Master and with the consent of the major Superior, such an experiment would seem to be a useful contribution to formation.

(2) These formation stages may be used for one or several novices or for the novitiate community as a whole. Wherever possible, it would be preferable that the novices take part in these stages in groups of two or more.

(3) During these stages away from the novitiate community, the novices remain under the responsibility of the Novice Master.

FORMATIVE PERIODS

24. (1) The total length of the periods spent by a novice outside the novitiate will be added to the twelve months of presence required by n. 21 for the validity of the novitiate, but in such a way that the total duration of the novitiate thus expanded does not exceed two years.

(2) These formative apostolic periods may not begin until after a minimum of three months in the novitiate and will be distributed in such a way that the novice will spend at least six continuous months in the novitiate and return to the novitiate for at least one month prior to first vows or temporary commitment.

(3) In cases where Superiors would deem it useful for a future novice to have a period of experience before beginning the three months of presence required at the start of the novitiate, this period could be regarded as a probation period and only after its completion would the novitiate begin.

NOVITIATE PLANNING FOR THE INDIVIDUAL

25. (1) The nature of experimental periods outside the novitiate can vary according to the aims of various Institutes and the nature of their activities. Still, they must always be planned and carried out in view of forming the

novice or, in certain cases, testing his aptitude for the life of the Institute. Besides gradual precaution for apostolic activities, they can also have as their purpose to bring the novice into contact with certain concrete aspects of poverty or of labour, to contribute to character formation, a better knowledge of human nature, the strengthening of the will, the development of personal responsibility and, lastly, to provide occasions for effort at union with God in the context of the active life.

(2) This balancing of periods of activity and periods of retreat consecrated to prayer, meditation or study, which will characterize the formation of the novices, should stimulate them to remain faithful to it through the whole of their religious life. It would also be well for such period of retreat to be regularly planned during the years of formation preceding perpetual profession.

ANTICIPATING FIRST PROFESSION

26. The major Superior may, for a just cause, allow first profession to be anticipated, but not beyond fifteen days.

VALID NOVITIATE

27. In Institutes having different novitiates for different categories of religious, and unless the Constitutions stipulate otherwise, the novitiate made for one category is valid likewise for the other. It belongs to the Constitutions to determine eventual conditions regulating this passage from one novitiate to the other.

CONTACTS WITH THE COMMUNITY

28. The special nature and aim of the novitiate, as also the close bonds which should be found among the novices, really demand a certain separation of the novice group from the other members of the Institute. Nevertheless the novices may, according to the judgment of the Novice Master, have contacts with other communities or religious. Hence it will be the task of the General Chapter, taking into consideration the spirit of the Institute and the demands of special circumstances, to decide what kind of contacts the novices may have with the other members of the Institute.

USEFUL STUDIES

29. (1) The General Chapter may permit or even impose during the regular novitiate year certain studies which may be useful for the formation of the novices. Doctrinal studies must be put at the service of a loving knowledge of God and a deepening of the life of faith.

(2) Excluded from the novitiate year described in n. 21 are all formal study programs, even of theology or philosophy, as also studies directed toward the obtaining of diplomas or in view of professional training.

ROLE OF THE NOVICE MASTER

30. All tasks and work entrusted to novices will be under the responsibility and direction of the Novice Master, who nevertheless may seek the aid of competent persons. The chief aim of these various tasks must be the formation of the novices, not the interests of the Congregation.

THE TEACHING OF THE VATICAN COUNCIL

31. (1) In the direction of the novices, particularly during the periods of formative activity, the Novice Master will base his direction on the teaching so clearly enunciated by the Second Vatican Council: 'In order, therefore, that members may respond to their call to follow Christ above all and to serve Christ himself in his members, their apostolic activities must stem from an intimate union with him.'[16]

'And so members of any Religious Institute must seek God alone and above all else; they should combine contemplation, by which they become united to him in mind and heart, with apostolic love by which they strive to join in the work of the Redemption and spread the kingdom of God.'[17]

(2) With this in mind he should teach the novices:

(a) to seek in all things, as well in apostolic activities or the service of men as in the times consecrated to silent prayer or study, purity of intention and the unity of charity towards God and towards men;

16. *Perfectae caritatis*, n. 8.
17. *Perfectae caritatis*, n. 5.

(b) when the apostolic activities of their Institute lead them to become involved in human affairs, to learn how to use this world as though not using it;

(c) to understand the limitations of their own activity without being discouraged and to work at the ordering of their own life, bearing in mind that no one can give himself authentically to God and his brethren without first getting possession of himself in humility;

(d) to bring about in their lives, along with a will which is firm and rich in intiative, and conformable to the demands of a vocation to an Institute dedicated to the apostolate, the indisspensible balance on both the human and the supernatural level between times consecrated to the apostolate and the service of men and more or less lengthy periods, in solitude or in community, devoted to prayer and meditative reading of the Word of God;

(e) in fidelity to this program which is essential to every consecrated life, to ground their hearts gradually in union with God and that peace which comes from doing the divine will, whose demands they will have learned to discover in the duties of their state and in the promptings of justice and charity.

UNITY WITH SUPERIORS

32. (1) Unity of heart and mind must reign between Superiors, the Novice Master and the novices. This union, which is the fruit of genuine charity, is necessary for religious formation.

(2) Superiors and the Novice Master must always show towards the novices evangelical simplicity, kindness coupled with gentleness and respect for their personality, in order to build up a climate of confidence, docility and openness in which the Novice Master will be able to orientate their generosity toward a complete gift of themselves to the Lord in faith, and gradually lead them by word and example to learn in the mystery of Christ Crucified the exigencies of authentic religious obedience. Thus, let the Novice Master teach his novices 'that the obedience with which they fulfil their duties and perform their tasks allotted them is active and responsible.'[18]

18. *Perfectae caritatis*, n. 14.

THE RELIGIOUS HABIT

33. As for the habit of the novices and other candidates to the religious life, the decision rests with the General Chapter.

TEMPORARY COMMITMENT

34. (1) The General Chapter, by a two-thirds majority, may decide to replace temporary vows in the Institute with some other kind of commitment as, for example, a promise made to the Institute.

(2) This commitment will be made at the end of the novitiate and for the duration of the probationary period extending to the perpetual profession or to the sacred commitments which are its equivalent in certain Institutes.[19] This temporary commitment may also be made for a briefer period and be renewed at stated intervals, or even be followed by the making of temporary vows.

BASED ON EVANGELICAL COUNSELS

35. (1) It is altogether proper that this temporary bond should have reference to the practice of the three evangelical counsels, in order to constitute a genuine preparation for perpetual profession. It is of the utmost importance to safeguard unity of religious formation. Although the practice of this life is realized definitively at perpetual profession, it must begin quite a long time before this profession.

(2) Since, therefore, the one perpetual profession assumes its full significance, it is fitting that it should be preceded by a period of immediate preparation lasting for a certain length of time, and serving as a kind of second novitiate. The duration and details will be determined by the General Chapter.

COMMITMENT TO THE INSTITUTE

36. Whatever may be the nature of this temporary commitment, its effect will be to bind whoever makes it to his Congregation or his Institute and it will entail the obligation of observing the Rule, Constitutions and other regula-

---

19. Cf. *Perfectae caritatis*, n. 3.

tions of the Institute. The General Chapter will determine other aspects and consequences of this commitment.

THE DURATION OF TEMPORARY VOWS

37. (1) The General Chapter, after careful consideration of all the circumstances, shall decide on the length of the period of temporary vows or commitments which is to extend from the end of the novitiate until the making of perpetual vows. This period shall last for no less than three years and no more than nine, counting the time continuously.

(2) The prescription still stands that perpetual profession must be made before the reception of Holy Orders.

CIRCUMSTANCES REQUIRED FOR RE-ADMISSION

38. (1) When a member has left his Institute legitimately, either at the expiration of his temporary profession or commitment or after dispensation from these obligations, and later requests re-admission, the Superior General, with the consent of his council, may grant this re-admission without the obligation of prescribing the repetition of the novitiate.

(2) The Superior General must, none the less, impose on him a certain period of probation, upon the completion of which the candidate may be admitted to temporary vows or commitment for a period of no less than one year, or no less than the period of temporary probation which he would have had to complete before profession at the time he left the Institute. The Superior may also demand a longer period of trial.

PART III

APPLICATION OF THE SPECIAL NORMS

In the implementation of these present decisions the following directives shall be observed:

(1) The prescriptions of common law remain in force except in so far as this present instruction may derogate therefrom.

(2) The faculties granted by this Instruction may not in any way be delegated.

(3) The term Superior General also includes the Abbot President of a Monastic Congregation.

(4) In case the Superior General is incapacitated or legitimately impeded from acting, these same faculties are granted to the one who is legitimately designated by the Constitutions to replace him.

(5) In the case of nuns, dedicated exclusively to contemplative life, special regulations shall be inserted into the Constitutions and submitted for approval. Nevertheless, the norms indicated in nn. 22, 26 and 27 may be applied to them.

(6) (a) If the special General Chapter prescribed by the Motu Proprio *Ecclesiae sanctae* has already been held, it will belong to the Superior General and his council, acting as a body, after due consideration of all the circumstances, to decide if it is advisable to convoke a General Chapter to decide the questions reserved to it, or to await the next ordinary General Chapter.

(b) Should the Superior General with his council, as above, deem it too difficult or even impossible to convoke a new General Chapter and if, at the same time, the implementation of the faculties reserved to the decision of the Chapter is regarded as urgent for the welfare of the Institute, the Superior General and his council, as before, is hereby authorized to implement some or all of these faculties until the next General Chapter, provided that he previously consult the other major Superiors with their councils and obtain the consent of at least two-thirds of their number. The major Superiors in turn should make it a point to consult first their perpetually professed religious. In Institutes having no provinces, the Superior General must consult the perpetually professed and obtain the consent of two-thirds.

(7) These directives, issued on an experimental basis, take effect as of the date of the promulgation of the present Instruction.

50

INSTRUCTION ON THE CONTEMPLATIVE LIFE AND ON THE ENCLOSURE OF NUNS[a]

S.C.R.S.I., *Venite Seorsum*, 15 August, 1969

"Come away by yourselves to a lonely place" (Mk. 6:31). Numerous are those who have heard this call and have followed Christ, withdrawing into solitude to worship the Father there.

It was by this inspiration of the Spirit[1] that some were led to establish institutions dedicated to contemplation alone, among which convents of nuns occupy a position of great distinction.

With vigilant and maternal care the Church has always watched over virgins consecrated to God, considered by St. Cyprian as "a more illustrious part of Christ's flock,"[2] and it is particularly on this account that she has defended their separation from the affairs of the world by issuing a considerable number of regulations regarding papal enclosure.[3]

Since the Second Vatican Council likewise manifested its concern about this matter,[4] it is the purpose of this Instruction to continue its work by legislating the norms which in the future will regulate the enclosure of nuns wholly dedi-

---

[a] Translation by Vatican Press Office. Latin text in *AAS* 61 (1969), 674–690. See A. 192.

1. Cf. Pachomius, *Vies Coptes*, Cod. Bo. n. 17 (Lefort, p. 91). *Gaudium et spes*, n. 38, and Mt. 4:1.

2. Cyprian, *De habitu virginum* 3, *ML* 4, 455.

3. Already from the sixth century; cf. Caesarius of Arles, *Reg. ad Virg.* (approved by Pope Hormisdas) 1, *ML* 67, 1107; Conc. Epaonen. (517 A.D.) c. 38, CC ser. Lat. 148 A, p. 34. Cf. also Boniface VIII, Const. *Periculoso* (1298 A.D.); Council of Trent, Session 25, Decree *de Regularibus*, c. 5; *CIC* cc. 597–603; 2342; Pius XII, Apost. Const. *Sponsa Christi*; S.C.R. Instructions *Inter praeclara* and *Inter cetera*.

4. Vatican II, Decree *Perfectae Caritatis*, (D. 47), n. 16.

cated to contemplation. These norms are prefaced by certain fundamental consideration regarding enclosure itself.

I

Withdrawal from the world for the sake of leading a more intense life of prayer in solitude is nothing other than a very particular way of living and expressing the paschal mystery of Christ, which is death ordained toward resurrection.

This mystery is portrayed in Holy Scripture in terms of a passage or exodus, which without doubt constitutes the most important event in the development of Israelite history, inasmuch as it forms the basis of Israel's faith[5] and of her more intimate life with God,[6] an event which the Church recognizes as a certain prefiguration of Christian salvation.[7]

5. Cf. *Decalogue*: "I am Yahweh your God who brought you out of the land of Egypt, out of the house of slavery. You shall have no gods except me" (Ex. 20:2-3). And with reference to the convenant made at Shechem: "We have no intention of deserting Yahweh and serving other gods. Was it not Yahweh our God who brought us and our ancestors out of the land of Egypt, the house of slavery, who worked those great wonders before our eyes and preserved us all along the way we traveled and among all the peoples through whom we journeyed?" (Jos. 24:16-17). Idolatry, on the contrary, consists in saying: "Here is your god Israel, who brought you out of the land of Egypt" (Ex. 32:4). Expressions of this type are frequent.
6. Thus in the prayer of Israel, as may be inferred from the Psalms. Likewise anniversary feasts commemorating episodes of the exodus became liturgical celebrations. The promise or covenant was made in the desert, during the exodus. When hardships were inflicted on Israel because of her sins, she remembered the miracles performed by God in the past and placed her hope in them, since God who does not change is always capable of repeating the same miracles. Cf. Dt. 20:1; Is. 43:16-21, 63:10-14; Bar. 2:11; Sir. 36:5. But it will be necessary to pass again through the desert that purifies (Hos. 2:16-25): then it will no longer be a question of delivering the people from external enemies, but from the slavery of sin. The real exodus is a spiritual conversion.
7. Vatican II, Decree *Nostra aetate*, no. 4: "(The Church) professes that all who believe in Christ, Abraham's sons according to the faith, are included in the same patriarch's call, and likewise that the salvation of the Church was mystically foreshadowed by the chosen people's exodus from the land of bondage." Cf. 1 Cor. 10:11: "All this happened to them as a warning, and it was written down to be a lesson for us who are living at the end of the age." And Irenaeus: "The departure from Egypt that God made His people undertake was in all its detail an image and prefiguration of the exodus through which the Church of the future was to evolve out of paganism" (*Adv. haer.* 4, 30—*S. Ch.* 100, p. 784).

Certainly no one is unaware to what degree the sacred liturgy and the tradition of the Fathers—as the Apostles and Evangelists themselves had already done—evoked biblical themes of exodus in order to penetrate and expound the mystery of Christ.[8] From the dawn of the Chosen People's history, Abraham is depicted as being called to leave his country, his family and his father's house, while the Apostle repeatedly teaches that the same calling was the beginning of a long mystical journey to a homeland which is not of this world.[9]

What in this way was merely prefigured in the Old Testament, becomes a reality in the New. Coming from the Father and entering the world (cf. Jn. 16:28) to arouse a people "that walked in darkness" (Is. 9:2; Mt. 4:16), the Word of God delivered us from the domination of darkness (cf. Col. 1:13), that is from sin, and through His death (cf. Jn. 13:1; 16:28; and Heb. 9:11–12; 10:19–20), He set us on the return road to the Father, who "raised us up with Him and made us sit with Him in the heavenly places in Christ Jesus" (Eph. 2:6; cf. Col. 2:12–13; 3:1). Herein lies the true essence of the paschal mystery of Christ and the Church.

But the death of Christ demands a real type of solitude, as the Apostle himself understood it,[10] and many Fathers and Doctors of the Church after him.[11] They attributed in fact this significance to certain episodes in Christ's life: while considering Him withdrawing into solitude or into the desert to engage in battle with "the ruler of this world" (cf. Mt. 4:1; Jn. 12:31; 14:30),[12] but especially when He

8. According to the New Testament: (a) Christ puts into effect the new exodus: Mt. 2:15, 4:4 (cf. Ex. 16); 4:7 (cf. Ex. 17); 4:10 (cf. Dt. 32:48–53); 5:21–22 ff., 11:10 (cf. Mal. 3:1–2 and Ex. 23:20); 26:28 (cf. Mk. 10:38; Ex. 24:8; Heb. 9:18–28). Lk. 9:31, 12:50 (Mk. 10:38; cf. 1 Cor. 10:2); Jn. 1:17, 3:14, 3:14, 6:31, 49–50, 58; 7:37–39 (cf. Ex. 17:1–7); 19:36. (b) The Christian life as a new exodus: 1 Cor. 10:1–11; 2 Cor. 3:6–18; Heb. 4:1–9, 8:1–13, 9:12, 18–24; 1 Pet. 1:16, 2:9; Apoc. 1:6, 15:3, 2:17, 21:2–3 (cf. Hos. 2:14–24; Ex. 25:8).

For the evidence of the Fathers and the liturgy, cf. R. Le Deaut and J. Lecuyer, *Exode,* in *Dict. de Spirit,* 4, 1973–1995.

9. Heb. 11:13–16.

10. Heb. 13:12–14.

11. "My God, my God, why have you deserted me?" (Mt. 27:46). "Truly the Cross of Christ is called a desert because it is inhabited by a few, and Christ our God is a true hermit by Whom the Cross is carried" (author from the beginning of the 13th century, in *Arch. d'histoire doctr. et litt. du Moyen Age* 31, 1964, 41).

12. Cf. Origen, *In Matth.* 12, 8–9, *CGS* 10, 200.

withdrew to pray to His Father, to whose will He was totally submitted.[13] In this way He presignified the solitude of His passion,[14] which the Evangelists represent to us as a new exodus.[15]

Hence to withdraw into the desert is for the Christian tantamount to associating himself more intimately with Christ's passion, and it enables him, in a very special way, to share in the paschal mystery and in the passage of Our Lord from this world to the heavenly homeland. It was precisely on this account that monasteries were founded, situated as they are in the very heart of the mystery of Christ.

Certainly the faithful are called to follow Christ in the proclamation of His gospel of salvation, and they should at the same time contribute to the construction of the earthly city, thus becoming, as it were, a leaven by which it is transformed into the household of God.[16] It is in this sense that the follower of Christ is said to remain in the world (cf. Jn. 17:15). Yet with this mission the fulness of the mystery of the Church is not expressed, since the Church, though established for the service of God and man[17] is likewise—and even more especially—the aggregate of all who are redeemed, that is, of those who through Baptism and the other sacraments have already passed from this

---

13. Cf. Mt. 14:23 (Mk. 6:46); Mk. 1:35; Lk. 5:16, 6:12, 9:18, 28 (Mt. 17:1); 11:1, esp. Lk. 2:41-44: "Then He withdrew from them, about a stone's throw away, and knelt down and prayed. 'Father,' He said, 'If you are willing, take this cup away from me. Nevertheless let your will be done, not mine. . . .' In His anguish He prayed even more earnestly." The prayer of Moses on the hilltop, isolated from the battle which was being waged on the plain (Ex. 17:8-13), is, according to the Fathers, a foreshadowing of Christ on the Cross outside the gates of Jurusalem. Cf. *Epist. Barnabae* 12, 2-4 (Hemmer 74); Justin, *Dial. cum Triph.* 90, 4-5; 91, 3; 97, 1; 111, 1-2; 112, 2; Irenaeus, *Demonstrat.*, 46.
14. Hilary: "(The Evangelist says that) when evening came He was alone: this presignifies Christ's solitude during His passion," In Mt. alone: this presignifies Christ's solitude during His passion," *In Matth.* 14, 23, *ML* 9, 1001.
15. Cf. above note 8.
16. Vatican II, Past. Const. *Gaudium et Spes*, (D. 64), n. 40.
17. The Church is at the service of men in their earthly undertakings: Vatican II, Const. *Gaudium et spes*, 3 and 40-45; Decree *Ad gentes*, n. 12: "She claims no other authority than that of ministering to men with the help of God, in a spirit of charity and faithful service." But it is especially in view of their eternal salvation that she serves them: cf. *Lumen gentium* 38: "Christ . . . has established His body, the Church, as the universal sacrament of salvation." Cf. n. 5.

world to the Father.[18] The Church is indeed "eager to act," yet at the same time she is no less "devoted to contemplation," in such a way that in her "the human is directed and subordinated to the divine, the visible likewise to the invisible, action to contemplation."[19]

It is therefore both legitimate and necessary that some of Christ's followers, those upon whom this particular grace has been conferred by the Holy Spirit,[20] should give expression to this contemplative character of the Church by actually withdrawing into solitude to lead this particular type of life, in order that "through constant prayer and ready penance they give themselves to God alone" (*Perfectae Caritatis*, 7).[21]

18. Cf. Vatican II, Const. *Lumen gentium*, n. 2, 7, etc.
19. Cf. Vatican II, Const. *Sacrosanctum Concilium*, n. 2.
20. Cf. Vatican II, Const. *Gaudium et spes*, (D. *64*), n. 38.
21. According to the tradition of the Fathers, the contemplative life portrays the prayer of Christ in solitude or on the mountain top, which in its turn prefigured the contemplative life. Cf. Cassian: "Yet He withdrew into the hills by Himself to pray, thus giving us an example of withdrawal . . . so that we likewise retire into solitude" (*Conlat.* 10, 6, 4, *ML* 49, 826); Jerome: "Seek them Christ in solitude, and pray alone with Jesus in the hills" (*Epist. ad Paulinum*, 58, 4, 2, *CSEL* 54, 532); Isidore: "But the fact that He passed the night praying in the hills, entails a foreshadowing of the contemplative life" (*Different.* lib. 2, 2, 34, *ML* 83, 91); pseudo-Jerome: "When He prayed, He typified the contemplative life; when He sat to teach, He exemplified the active life . . . Going out to the hills to pray and going out toward the multitude, He portrayed the union of both lives"(*ML* 30, 571); Walafrid Strabo: "When He ascended the mountain, He typified the contemplative life" (*Expos. in IV Evangel. ML* 114, 872); Paschasius Radbertus: "In order that we attend to God alone in contemplation, that is on the mountain top" (*Expos. in Matth., ML* 120, 523); William of St. Thierry: "(The solitary life) was intimately patronized by our Lord Himself and longed for in His presence by His disciples. When they who were in His company on the holy mountain saw the glory of His transfiguration, immediately Peter . . . decided that it would be good for him to stay there forever" (*Ad fratres de Monte Dei*, I, 1, *ML* 184, 310); Amadeus of Lausanne: "(God) established for us a vantage-point on the mountain top with Moses and Elias, thus enabling us to see unveiled what we are seeking" (Homily 3, ed. Bavaud, *Sources Chrét.* 72, 90–92); Vatican II Const. *Lumen gentium* n. 46: Religious should carefully consider that through them, to believers and non-believers alike, the Church truly wishes to give an increasingly clear revelation of Christ. Through them Christ should be shown contemplating on the mountain . . . and always obeying the will of the Father who sent Him."
The exodus theme is likewise applied to the monastic life by John Climacus for the East (*Scala Paradisi*, 1st step, *MG* 88, 632–644),

On the other hand, it should be quite evident that a certain degree of withdrawal from the world and some measure of contemplation must necessarily be present in every form of Christian life, as the Second Vatican Council rightly declared in reference to priests and religious dedicated to the apostolate.[22] Indeed it is true that even outside the monastic setting there are some who through the grace of the Holy Spirit are elevated to contemplation. But just as a certain invitation of this type is extended to all Christians, so too a certain degree of separation from the affairs of this world is necessary to all, even though all do not withdraw to the desert in the same way. Monks and nuns, however, retiring to a cloistered life, put into practice in a more absolute and exemplary way an element essential to every Christian life: "From now on . . . let those who deal with the world (live) as if they had no dealings with it. For the form of this world is passing away" (1 Cor. 7:29, 31).[23]

II

To the foregoing concepts, elicited from the paschal mystery of Christ in the way that the Church participates in it, those must be added which bring to light the importance of recollection and silence in rendering intimacy with God in prayer safer and easier.[24] The way of life of those who are

---

and from the time of Ambrose for the West (*Epist.* 27, 1–2, and 28, 1, 8, *ML* 16, 1047, 1051, 1053). Cf. also Jerome *ad Eustochium:* "Follow Moses into the desert, and you will enter the promised land" (*Epist.* 22, 24, *ML* 22, 410).

22. Cf. Vatican II, Const. *Lumen gentium*, n. 41: "(The priest must not) be undone by his apostolic cares, dangers, and toils, but rather led by them to higher sanctity. His activities should be fed and fostered by a wealth of meditation"; Decree *Perfectae Caritatis*, n. 5: "Therefore the members of each institute, as they seek God before all things and only Him, should combine contemplation with apostolic love. By the former they adhere to God in mind and heart."

23. The text is cited in Const. *Lumen gentium*, n. 42. Cf. the same Const. n. 44: "For the people of God has no lasting city here below but looks forward to one which is to come. . . ."; n. 6: "The Church on earth while journeying in a foreign land away from her Lord, regards herself as an exile. . . ."

24. Hos. 2:14: "I am going to lure her and lead her out into the wilderness and speak to her heart." Augustine: "It is difficult to see Christ in the crowd: a certain degree of solitude is necessary for our spirit; God is seen in a certain undistracted seclusion. The crowd is noisy; this vision demands isolation" (*In Io. Tract.* 17, 5, *ML* 35, 1533); Guigues the *Carthusians*: "Who, when His passion was immi-

totally dedicated to contemplation, aiming as it does at eliminating all that might divide the spirit against itself in any way, enables them to achieve that fulness of their personalities whose hallmark is unity, and permits them to devote themselves more thoroughly to the quest for God their goal,[25] to attend to Him more perfectly.

Such a quest for God, moreover, for which man should renounce everything he possesses (cf. Lk. 14:33), is furthered to the utmost by reading and meditating on Holy Scripture (cf. *Perfectae Caritatis*, nt. 6). Reading of the Bible should therefore accompany prayer, "so that God and man may talk together; for 'we speak to Him when we pray; we hear Him when we read the divine sayings'" (cf. Const. *Dei Verbum*, n. 25; St. Ambrose, *De Officiis Ministrorum*, I, 20, 88; *ML* 16, 50).

And by studying Holy Scripture, which is "like a mirror in which the pilgrim Church on earth looks at God, from whom she has received everything" (*Dei Verbum*, n. 7), each one "inflamed with love of God burns to contemplate His beauty" (II, II, Q. 180, Art. 1, *in corpore*).

In such a way love and contemplation aid one another reciprocally. "The love of God is understanding Him: He is not known unless He is loved, nor is He loved unless He is known; and in reality He is known only to the degree that He is loved, and loved to the degree that He is known"

---

nent, left His apostles to pray alone, showing us particularly with this example how much solitude favors prayer, since He did not want to pray in anyone's company, not even the apostles'" (*Consuetudines* 80, 10, *ML* 153, 758).

John of the Cross: "(For prayer) it is good to choose a place that is solitary, and even wild, so that the spirit may resolutely and directly soar upward to God, and not be hindered or detained by visible things. . . . For this reason our Saviour was wont to choose solitary places for prayer, and such as occupied the senses but little, in order to give us an example. He chose places that lifted up the soul to God, such as mountains, which are lifted up above the earth." (*Ascent* III, 39, 2; *Canticle* B, 35, 1).

25. Cf. Paul VI, Allocution, 24 October 1964: "May St. Benedict return to help us to recuperate the personal type of life which today we anxiously long for; which the development of modern-day living, on whose account we feel the exasperated desire to be ourselves, suffocates while promoting, deludes while making us conscious of it. . . . Commotion, din, feverish activity, outward appearances and the crowd all threaten man's inner awareness. He lacks silence with its genuine voice speaking in the depths of his being; he lacks order, he lacks prayer, he lacks peace, he lacks himself": *AAS* 56 (1964), p. 987.

(William of St. Thierry, *Expositio in Cant.*, c. I: *ML* 180, 499, C).

Thus in silence and solitude "resolute men are able to recollect themselves and, so to speak, to dwell within themselves as much as they please, cultivating the buds of virtue and feeding happily on the fruits of paradise. Here one strives to acquire that eye by whose limpid glance the bridegroom is wounded with love, and in whose purity alone may God be seen. Here one is occupied in busy leisure, and rests in quiet activity. Here, for fatigue undergone in strife, God grants His athletes the reward they have longed for, namely a peace unknown to the world and the joy of the Holy Spirit. . . . This is the better part that Mary chose, that shall not be taken away from her."[26]

III

It must not be thought, however, that monks and nuns, because they are separated from the rest of mankind, are cut off, at it were, from the world and the Church and are aloof from them. On the contrary, they are united with them "in a more profound sense in the heart of Christ,"[27] since we are all one in Christ (cf. 1 Cor. 10:17; Jn. 17:20–22).[28]

26. Bruno, *Ad Radulphum* 6 (*S. Ch.* 88, p. 70).
27. Vatican II, Const. *Lumen gentium*, n. 46. Cf. Evagrius: "The monk is he who is separated from all and united to all" (*De Oratione* 124; for French *text see* I. Hausherr, *Les leçons d'un contemplatif*, p. 158); Peter Damian: "Though we seem to be separated far from the Church through physical solitude, we are forever and most intimately in her presence through the inviolable mystery of unity" (*Opusc. XI, L. qui appellatur Dominus vobiscum*, 10, *ML* 145, 239). With words of great fervor Ste. Teresa presented that ideal to the nuns of the first convent she founded: "Oh my sisters in Christ. Help me to entreat this of the Lord, Who has brought you together here for that very purpose . . . this is your vocation; this must be your business; these must be your desires; these your tears; these your petitions" (*Way of Perfection* 1, 5).
28. Cf. Peter Damian: "Therefore, if all who believe in Christ are one in Him, wherever any member is bodily present, there too will the entire body be by reason of the sacramental mystery. . . . Hence if we all form the same body of Christ, even though we appear to be scattered physically, spiritually however, it is impossible that we be separated one from the other since we remain in Him" (*Opusc. XI L. qui appellatur Dominus vobiscum*, 6, *ML* 145, 236–238); Paul VI: "You are not separated from the great communion of Christ's family, you are specialists; and your specialty is today, no less than

Apart from the traditional contribution of monasteries in the cultural and social domain, conclusive and unshakable evidence exists bearing witness to the great love with which men and women dedicated to contemplation alone harbor in their hearts the sufferings and anguish of all men.

From Scripture, moreover, it is evident that it was in the desert or in mountain solitude that God revealed hidden truths to man (cf. Gen. 32:25–31; Ex. 3; 24:1–8; 34:5–9 1 Kg. 19:8–13; Lk. 2:7–9; Mt. 17:1–8). These in fact are places in which heaven and earth seem to merge, where the world, in virtue of Christ's presence, rises from its condition of arid earth and becomes paradise anew (cf. Mk. 1:13).[29] How then can contemplatives be considered alien to mankind, if in them mankind achieves its fulfilment?

But however much contemplatives are entrenched, so to speak, in the heart of the world, still more so are they in the heart of the Church.[30] Their prayers, particularly their participation in the Eucharistic Sacrifice of Christ and their liturgical recitation of the Divine Office, constitute the fulfilment of a function essential to the ecclesial community, namely, the glorification of God. This in fact is the prayer that renders to the Father, through the Son and in the Holy Spirit, "a choice sacrifice of praise."[31] Those who worship

---

yesterday, beneficial and edifying for the entire Church, and indeed even for the whole of society" (*Allocutio* to the superiors of the Benedictine nuns, 28 Sept. 1966, *AAS* 58 (1966), pp. 1159–1160).

29. Cf. Is. 11:6–9; in the opposite sense, Gen. 9:2. For the comparison of the monastery with paradise, cf. Jerome: "You have a cell for paradise: pick the various fruits of the Scriptures" (Epist. 125 *ad Rusticum* 7, *ML* 22, 1075): Anselm, Epist. 3, 102, ML 159, 140; Peter Damian, Epist. 6, 3, *ML* 144, 374; William of Malmesbury, *De qestis Pont. Angliae* 4, *ML* 179, 1612–1613; Bernard, *Sermo de diver.* 42, 4, *ML* 183, 663; William of St. Thierry, *De natura et dignitate amoris*, 25, *ML* 184, 396; Peter of Celle, Epist. 75, *ML* 202, 522. Cf. J. Leclerq, *La vie parfaite*, Turnhout 1948; G. M. Colombas, *Paraiso y vida angelica*, Montserrat 1958.

30. Cf. Paul VI: "We want these islands of withdrawal, of penance, and of meditation to bear in mind . . . that they are neither forgotten nor detached from the communion of God's Church, but rather that they make up its heart, they multiply its spiritual wealth, they render its prayer sublime, they sustain its charity, they participate in its suffering, its fatigue, its apostolate, its hopes, they increase its merits" (*Allocutio* of 2 Feb. 1966, *Insegnamenti di Paolo VI*, VI [1966] p. 56).

31. Vatican II, Decree *Perfectae Caritatis*, n. 7. John of the Cross: "A little of this pure love, is more precious before God and the soul, more beneficial for the Church, than all those works together. For

in this way are admitted to the intimacy of the ineffable conversation which Our Lord has unendingly with His heavenly Father, and in whose bosom He pours out His infinite love. This, in a word, is the prayer which is like an apex toward which converges the universal activity of the Church.[32] In this way contemplative religious, bearing witness to the intimate life of the Church, are indispensable to the fulness of its presence.[33]

Furthermore, by vivifying the entire Mystical Body by the fervor of their love, and by bolstering the various efforts of the apostolate, which are indeed nothing without charity (cf. 1 Cor. 13:1–3), contemplatives raise the level of the spiritual life of the whole Church. "In the heart of the Church, my Mother, I shall be love," exclaimed the saint who, without ever having stepped outside of her convent, was nevertheless declared by Pope Pius XI Patroness of all the Missions.[34] Did not God through His charity, manifested in such proportion as to entail the sacrifice of His Son on the cross, deliver all men from sin? Therefore, when one steeps himself in this paschal mystery of the supreme love of God for man (cf. Jn. 13:1; 15:13), he nec-

---

this reason Mary Magdalen . . . hid herself in the desert for thirty years to dedicate herself wholly to this love . . . in view of how much a little of this love benefits the Church and is important to Her . . . In a word, it was for this love that we were created" (Canticle B, 29, 2–3).

32. Vatican II, Const. *Sacrosanctum Concilium* 10: "The glorification of God, to which all other activities of the Church are directed as toward their goal"; cf. also Const. *Gaudium et spes*, n. 76: Decree *Apostolicam actuositatem*, n. 2.

33. Vatican II, Decree *Ad gentes*, n. 18: "For the contemplative life belongs to the fulness of the Church's presence, and should therefore be everywhere established." Cf. John XXIII: "The contemplative life! . . . It constitutes one of the fundamental structures of the Holy Church, it has been present during all the phases of her bimillenary history": *Allocutio* of 20 Sept. 1960, *AAS* 52 (1960), p. 896.

34. "Charity gave me the key to my vocation. I understood that if the Church had a body, composed of different members, the most necessary, the noblest of all, would not be lacking. I understood that the Church had a heart and that this heart was burning with love. I understood that love alone makes the members of the Church act, that if love should be extinguished the apostles would no longer preach the Gospel, the martyrs would refuse to shed their blood. . . . Yes, I have found my place in the Church . . . in the heart of the Church, my Mother, I shall be love" (*Autobiographical manuscripts*, ms. B, Lisieux 1957, p. 229).

essarily participates in the redemptive mission of Christ's passion, which is the beginning of every apostolate.[35]

Finally, religious engaged in contemplation alone sustain through their prayers the missionary activity of the Church, "for it is God who sends workers into His harvest when He is asked to do so, who opens the minds of non-Christians to hear the Gospel, and who makes the word of salvation fruitful in their hearts."[36] In solitude, where they are devoted to prayer, contemplatives are never forgetful of their brothers. If they have withdrawn from frequent contact with their fellow men, it is not because they were seeking themselves and their own comfort, or peace and quiet for their own sake, but because, on the contrary, they were intent on sharing to a more universal degree the fatigue, the misery and the hopes of all mankind.[37]

35. Cf. John XIII: "For the apostolate, in the true sense of the word, consists in participation in the salvific work of Christ, which is possible only through assiduous prayer and personal sacrifice. In fact, it was particularly through His prayer to the Father and through His self-immolation that the Saviour redeemed the human race which was bound and crushed by sin. Hence it is that whoever endeavors to follow Christ in this essential aspect of His saving mission, even though he abstains from external action, exercises the apostolate nevertheless in a most excellent way": Epist. *Causa praeclara* 16 July 1962: *AAS* 54 (1962), p. 568.

36. Vatican II, Decree *Ad gentes*, n. 40. Cf. Const. *Umbratilem: AAS* 16 (1924), p. 389 and S.C.R. Decree *Super tuto* for the canonzation of B. Teresa Margaret Redi, 18 Feb. 1934: ". . . the soul truly crucified with Christ in the supreme martyrdom of the spirit, acquires for itself and for others the superabundant fruits of redemption. Such are the purest and most exalted souls in the Church who by suffering, loving and praying exercise an apostolate which, though silent, benefits everyone to the utmost": *AAS* 26 (1934) p. 106.

37. Cf. Paul VI: "Does this material, external and social reclusion separate you from the Church? I am here to tell you that the Church keeps you in mind. You are not forgotten, and for this reason that separation which would be the most desolating—the spiritual kind—does not exist. Why? Because you are the objects of special attention, of particular awareness, and even more yet. The Church is watching you, you have dedicated yourselves to this kind of life in order to speak unendingly with our Lord, to be able to understand His voice better, and—to sum up our poor human words with greater clarity and emphasis—you have turned this contact between heaven and earth into the one and only program of your entire life. You as contemplatives have dedicated yourselves to this absorption of your souls by God. You see, the Church perceives in you the fullest expression of itself; in a certain way you are placed at its peak" (*Allocutio* of 23 Feb. 1966, in *Vita Monastica*, n. 85, p. 68); "In

IV

Truly great, therefore, is the mystery of the contemplative life. And whereas its eminent role in the economy of salvation emerges along general lines from the foregoing remarks, the mystery is seen to be enacted in a very special way in the case of cloistered nuns. These women, in fact, by their very nature, portray in a more meaningful way the mystery of the Church, the "spotless spouse of the spotless Lamb,"[38] and, seated at the Lord's feet and listening to His teaching (cf. Lk. 10:39) in silence and withdrawal, seek and savor the things that are above where their lives are hidden with Christ in God, until they appear in glory with their Spouse.[39] It is woman's role to receive the word rather than to carry it to the far ends of the earth, even though she can be summoned successfully to the latter vocation. It is her place to become thoroughly and intimately acquainted with the word and to render it fruitful, in a very clear, vivid and feminine way. For in fact, once she has attained full maturity, woman intuits more keenly the needs of others and the assistance which they hope for. Hence, she ex-

the Catholic Church you have been assigned not only a place but also a function, as the Council says; you are not separated from the great communion of Christ's family, you are specialists. . . .": *Allocutio* of 28 Oct. 1966, *AAS* 58 (1966) pp. 1159–1160. And the Second Vatican Council firmly declares: "Let no one think that by their consecration religious have become strangers to their fellow men or useless citizens of this earthly city. For even though in some instances religious do not directly mingle with their contemporaries, yet in a more profound sense these same religious are united with them in the heart of Christ and cooperate with them spiritually. In this way the work of building up the earthly city can always have its foundation in the Lord and can tend toward Him. Otherwise, those who build the city will perhaps have labored in vain" (Const. *Lumen gentium*, n. 46). Such is the apostolic content of the contemplative ideal according to Ste. Teresa of Jesus: "Persaude the sisters to busy themselves constantly in beseeching God to help those who work for the Church" (*Way of Perfection*, title to chapter 3). "If we can prevail with God in the smallest degree about this, we shall be fighting His battle even while living a cloistered life. . . . If your prayers and desires and disciplines and fasts are not performed for the intention of which I have spoken, reflect and believe that you are not carrying out the work or fulfilling the object for which the Lord has brought you here" (Ibid, ch. 3, pars. 5, 10).
38. Vatican II, Const. *Lumen gentium*, n. 6.
39. Ibid.

presses more clearly the fidelity[40] of the Church toward her Spouse, and at the same time is endowed with a more acute sense of the fruitfulness of the contemplative life. On this account the Church, as is apparent from her Liturgy,[41] has always had particular regard for the Christian virgin. Highlighting the divine jealousy surrounding her,[42] the Church has safeguarded with special solicitude her withdrawal from the world and the enclosure of her convent.[43]

At this point it is impossible to pass over in silence the Blessed Virgin Mary, who welcomed into her bosom the Word of God. "Full of faith, and conceiving Christ first in her mind before in her womb,"[44] a garden enclosed, a sealed fountain, a closed gate (cf. S. of S. 4:12; Ezek. 44:1–2), "in faith and charity she is the Church's model and excellent exemplar."[45] The Blessed Virgin exhibits herself as a splendid model of the contemplative life, and a venerable liturgical tradition, both in the Eastern Church and the Western, appropriately applies to her these words from the Gospel: "Mary has chosen the better part" (Lk. 10:38–42).[46]

---

40. Cf. Vatican II, Const. *Lumen gentium*, n. 6: "The Church . . . whom He unites to Himself by an unbreakable covenant . . . once she had been purified, He willed her to be joined unto Himself and to be subject to Him in love and fidelity."
41. The liturgy in the West adapts and applies nuptial metaphors only to holy women, illustrating their holiness as the splendor of the spiritual betrothals plighted with our Lord their Spouse. Conversely, never for them—as for men—does it ever employ themes relating to the new man, or to other motifs indicating a relationship with Christ as priest, pastor or prophet. Likewise, from the 4th century, the religious profession of women entailed a special ceremony distinct from that used by monks: this was the taking of the virginal veil, thought to have been adopted from the marriage veiling of brides, and which therefore signified a form of marriage.
42. Cf. Dt. 4:24; 2 Cor. 11:2: "The jealousy that I feel for you is God's own jealousy: I arranged for you to marry Christ so that I might give you away as a chaste virgin to this one husband."
43. Cf. the citations in note 3.
44. Cf. Augustine, *Sermones* 215, 4, ML 38, 1074.
45. Vatican II, Const. *Lumen gentium*, n. 53.
46. Such New Testament pericopes, like the gospel selections for certain solemnities of our Lady, are used from the 6th century, e.g., for the feast of the Dormition or Assumption, both in the East and the West; cf. B. Capelle, *La fête de l'Assomption dans l'histoire liturgique*, in *Ephemer. theol. Lovan*, 3(1926) 33–45.

V

Still another aspect intrinsic to the mystery of the contemplative life must be illustrated, namely the importance of the sign and witness by which contemplatives, though especially commissioned by God to pray, are not for that reason excluded from the "apostolate of the word,"[47] even though they do not engage in direct public preaching.

In present-day society, which so easily rejects God and denies His existence, the life of men and women completely dedicated to the contemplation of eternal truth constitutes an open profession of the reality of both His existence and His presence, since such a life seeks that loving intimacy with God which "bears witness with our spirit that we are children of God" (Rom. 8:16). Hence, whoever leads such a life can efficaciously reassure both those who suffer temptations against faith and those who through error are led to be skeptical as to whatever possibility man might have of conversing with the transcendent God.[48]

Through such wondrous conversation with God, men and women dedicated exclusively to contemplation in silence and solitude, and to the practice of charity and the other Christian virtues, proclaim the death of the Lord until He comes. And indeed, so much the more do they proclaim it, since their entire life, dedicated to an unremitting quest for God, is nothing other than a journey to the heavenly Jerusalem and an anticipation of the eschatological Church immutable in its possession and contemplation of God. Furthermore, contemplatives do not only preach to the world the goal to be reached, that is eternal life, but they likewise indicate the way that leads to it. If the spirit of the beatitudes, which animates the discipleship of Christ, is to vivify any and every form of Christian life,[49] the life of the contemplative testifies that such can be put into practice even during one's earthly existence. This witness will exercise a more forceful influence on men of our times to the degree that it is collective, or rather, social. It is not, in fact, the

47. Cf. Acts 6:2–4: "It would not be right for us to neglect the word of God so as to give out food . . . we will continue to devote ourselves to prayer and to the service of the word."
48. Cf. Message of contemplative monks to the 1st synod of bishops in *L'Osservatore Romano* of 12 Sept. 1967.
49. Cf. Vatican II, Const. *Gaudium et spes*, n. 72.

witness of the individual that attracts the men of today, but the witness, fruit of a life led together with others, of a given community, or better still, of a virgin society already firmly established, which, in virtue of its continuity and vigor, confirms the validity of the contemplative community, which Paul VI appropriately described at Monte Cassino, speaking of "a small, ideal society in which at last reign love, obedience, innocence, freedom from created things, and the art of turning them to good use, in which prevail the spirit, peace, and—in a word—the Gospel."[50]

VI

Yet it is easy to understand that the specific and definite commitment which is assumed in the cloistered life cannot originate from, and still less thrive in, any ephemeral type of fervor whatever. On the contrary, it must be the product of mature reflection and unfaltering decisiveness which enable one to renounce certain social advantages known and esteemed at their true value. Such maturity is required in order that this type of life be chosen with perfect liberty of spirit so that one lives for Christ alone and is occupied with the affairs of heaven. On this account, vocations for the cloistered life of nuns must be placed under lenghty and careful probation, in order that the motives by which they are led become clearly discerned, and those candidates be duly excluded who, perhaps unknowingly, are not inspired by sufficiently clear and supernatural considerations, which as a result may well stand in the way of their spiritual and human development.[51] The useful precautions prescribed by the statutes of each Institute are to be observed, not only for admission of postulants but especially before the religious pronounce their perpetual vows.

All that is set forth in this Instruction is applicable to ev-

---

50. "A small, ideal society in which at last reign love, obedience, innocence, freedom from created things, and the art of turning them to good use, in which prevail the spirit, peace, and—in a world—the Gospel": *AAS* 56 (1964), p. 987.
51. Cf. Vatican II, Const. *Lumen gentium*, n. 46: "Finally, everyone should realize that the profession of the evangelical counsels, though entailing the renunciation of certain values which undoubtedly merit high esteem, does not detract from a genuine development of the human person. Rather, by its very nature it is most beneficial to that development." Cf. also Decree *Perfectae caritatis*, n. 12.

ery Institute dedicated wholly to the contemplative life. Every religious family, nevertheless, has its own particular characteristics, determined in many instances by the Founder himself, and these must be faithfully respected. Nor is the possibility denied that within the Church, through the inspiration of the Holy Spirit, new forms of the contemplative life may originate in the future.

Thus the elements that distinguish one Institute from another are indeed recognized as legitimate, since they constitute a splendid array of variety, arising principally, as is evident, from the practical importance which each Institute attributes to mental prayer or to liturgical worship, to life led in common or characterized by elements of eremitical solitude, these being factors of diversity readily compatible with the structures of monasticism. Differences without doubt further depend on the manner in which each Institute conceives and observes material separation from the world by means of enclosure.

VII

Confirming, then, the prescriptions of the Second Vatican Council regarding the observance and adaptation of the enclosure, which is a tried and unquestionable advantage for the contemplative life, the Sacred Congregation for Religious and Secular Institutes has undertaken to legislate the following norms approved by Pope Paul VI on 12 July, 1969, for cloistered nuns dedicated wholly to contemplation.

NORMS REGULATING PAPAL ENCLOSURE OF NUNS

"The papal enclosure of convents is to be regarded as an ascetical regulation particularly consistent with the special vocation of nuns, in that it is the sign, the safeguard and the characteristic form of their withdrawal from the world" (Motu Proprio *Ecclesiae Sanctae*, II, (D. *48*), n. 30).

1. The enclosure reserved for nuns totally dedicated to contemplation (*Perfectae Caritatis*, n. 16) is called papal since the norms which govern it must be sanctioned by apostolic authority, even though they are established by particular law, by which are fitly expressed the characteristics proper to each Institute.

2. The law of papal enclosure applies to all that part of the house inhabited by the nuns, together with the gardens and orchards, access to which is reserved to the nuns themselves.

3. The area of the convent subject to the law of enclosure must be circumscribed in such a way that material separation be ensured (*Ecclesiae Sanctae*, II, n. 31) that is, all coming in and going out must be thereby rendered impossible (e.g., by a wall or some other effective means, such as a fence of planks or heavy iron mesh, or a thick and firmly rooted hedge). Only through doors kept regularly locked may one enter or leave the enclosure.

4. The mode of ensuring this effective separation, especially as far as the choir and parlor are concerned, is to be specified in the Constitutions and in supplementary legislative documents, particular consideration being given to the diversity of each Institute's traditions and to the various circumstances of time and place (e.g., grates, lattice-work, stationary partitions, etc.). In conformity with Article 1, however, the means of separation mentioned above must be previously submitted for the approval of the Sacred Congregation for Religious and for Secular Institutes.

5. In virtue of the law of enclosure, the nuns, novices and postulants must live within the confines of the convent prescribed by the enclosure itself, nor may they licitly go beyond them, except in the cases provided for by law (cf. Art. 7).

6. The law of enclosure likewise forbids anyone, of whatever class, condition, sex or age, to enter the cloistered area of the convent, except in the cases provided for by law (cf. Articles 8 and 9).

7. Besides cases provided for by particular indults from the Holy See, those mentioned in Article 5 may leave the enclosure:

(a) In case of very grave and imminent danger;

(b) With permission of the Superior, and with at least habitual consent of the local Ordinary and of the regular superior, if there is one:

(1) To consult physicians or to undergo medical treatment, provided that this is done locally or in the vicinity of the covent;

(2) To accompany a sick nun, if real necessity so demands;

(3) To perform manual labor or to exercise necessary

surveillance in places situated outside the enclosure, yet on the premises of the convent;

(4) To exercise one's civil rights;

(5) To conduct business transactions which cannot be handled otherwise.

Except for purposes of medical treatment, if absence from the enclosure is to be prolonged for more than one week, the Superior must previously obtain the consent of the local Ordinary and of the regular superior, if there is one.

(c) Except in the cases referred to under (b), the Superior must seek permission from the local Ordinary, and, if there is one, from the regular superior, by whom such permission may be granted only if there is really a serious reason, and then for just as brief a period as is necessary;

(d) All absences permitted in accordance with clauses (a), (b) and (c) of this article may not be prolonged beyond three months without the authorization of the Holy See.

8. Besides cases provided for by particular indults of the Holy See, the following are permitted to enter the cloister:

(a) Cardinals, who may likewise introduce their retinue, nuncios and apostolic delegates, in their areas of their own jurisdiction;

(b) Reigning sovereigns or heads of State, together with their wives and retinue;

(c) The local Ordinary and the regular superior, for a reasonable motive;

(d) Canonical visitors at the time of the visitation, but only for inspection, and provided that they be accompanied by a male religious;

(e) A priest, together with servers, to administer the sacraments to the sick or to hold funeral services. A priest may likewise be admitted to assist those religious suffering from a chronic or grave illness;

(f) A priest, together with servers, to conduct liturgical processions, if such is requested by the Superior;

(g) Physicians and all others whose work or skill is required to provide for the needs of the convent, with the permission of the Superior and under the surveillance of the local Ordinary and, if there is one, of the regular superior;

(h) Sisters employed in the external service of the convent, in accordance with the statutes of each Institute.

9. Any particular law approved by the Holy See in accordance with Article 1 may, in conformity with the spirit and characteristics of each Institute, either determine stricter prescriptions regarding enclosure, or sanction other instances in which one may enter or leave the enclosure legitimately, in order to provide for the needs of the convent or to further the good of the nuns themselves.

10. The use of the radio and television, in convents of nuns dedicated totally to the contemplative life, may be permitted only in circumstances of a religious nature.

11. Newspapers, magazines and other publications must not be either too numerous or admitted indiscriminately (cf. *Inter Mirifica*, n. 4). By such means, in fact, even the best religious communities can be permeated with and disturbed by the spirit of worldliness.

12. Meetings and conventions of any kind which can hardly be reconciled with the cloistered life are to be prudently avoided. If, however, the present circumstances seem to justify it, nuns might sometimes, after having obtained the necessary permission, be authorized to assist at those meetings which will truly benefit the cloistered life, provided such absences from the convent do not become too frequent. The Superiors are to bear in mind that the purity and fervor of the cloistered life depend to a great extent on the strict observance of the rules of enclosure. On this account, leaving the premises of the convent must always remain an exception.

13. The law of enclosure entails a serious obligation in conscience, for both the nuns and outsiders.

14. During the canonical visitation, whereas the visitor must inspect the material cloister, the Superior is to report to him on the observance of the cloister prescriptions, presenting for his examination the book in which must be faithfully recorded all the instances of entering and leaving the enclosure.

15. Since the Church holds the cloistered contemplative life in great esteem, she highly praises those nuns who, though updating their cloistered life in ways ever more consistent with their contemplative vocation, maintain, nevertheless, full and reverent respect for their withdrawal from the world (*Perfectae Caritatis*, n. 7). Those, on the other hand, who have both the right and the duty to supervise observance of the cloister laws, namely the local Ordinary and, if there is one, the regular superior, are earnestly exhorted by

the Church to safeguard such observance with the greatest diligence, and to lend, in accordance with their duty, their valuable assistance to the Superior, who is directly responsible for the enforcement of the enclosure laws.

16. Until the promulgation of the new Code of Canon Law, the penalties established for those who violate the nuns' enclosure will be inoperative.

17. Regarding the mode of procedure in updating the cloistered life, let the norms specified in part II, Numbers 9, 10 and 11 of the Motu Proprio *Ecclesiae Sanctae* be faithfully observed. With reference to Number 6 of the same Motu Proprio, however, experiments contrary to what is established by the present norms, which are to constitute the general law, cannot be undertaken without permission previously obtained from the Holy See.

Furthermore, those convents which have already introduced certain innovations with a view to updating papal enclosure are hereby obliged to submit such modifications to the judgment of the Sacred Congregation for Religious and for Secular Institutes within six months from the date of publication of the present Instruction.

51

DECREE ON CONFESSION FOR RELIGIOUS[a]

S.C.R.S.I., *Dum Canonicarum*, 8 December, 1970

The Sacred Congregation for Religious and for Secular Institutes has decided, for a number of urgent reasons, since the revision of the canon law is still in progress, to examine in plenary assembly certain questions concerning the use and administration of the sacrament of Penance, especially for women religious. A particular problem with regard to fitness for the religious life was also examined.

After careful examination, the Fathers in the Plenary Assembly held on October 26 and 27, 1970, made the following decisions:

(1) The Church is 'continually engaged in repentance and renewal' (*Lumen Gentium*, n. 8) and religious, because of their special union with the Chruch, should value highly the sacrament of Penance. The sacrament of Penance restores and strengthens in members of the Church who have sinned the fundamental gift of 'metanoia', of conversion to the kingdom of Christ, which is first received in Baptism (cf. Ap. Const. *Paenitemini*, A.A.S., 58 [1966], pp. 179–180). Those who approach this sacrament receive from God's mercy the pardon of their offenses and at the same time they are reconciled to the Church which they have wounded by their sins (cf. Const. *Lumen Gentium*, n. 11).

(2) Religious should likewise hold in high esteem the frequent use of this sacrament. It is a practice which increases true knowledge of one's self, favors Christian humility and offers the occasion for salutary spiritual direction and the increase of grace. These and other wonderful effects not only contribute greatly to daily and more rapid

a. Translated by A.F. from *AAS* 63 (1971) pp. 318–319.

growth in virtue, but are likely beneficial to the common good of the whole community (cf. Encyclical *Mystici Corporis*, AAS 35 [1943], p. 235).

(3) Therefore, religious, desiring closer union with God, should endeavor to receive the sacrament of penance frequently, that is twice a month. Superiors, on their part, should encourage them in this effort and should make it possible for the members to go to confession at least every two weeks and even oftener, if they wish to do so.

(4) With specific reference to the confessions of women religious, the following provisions are made:

(a) To ensure legitimate liberty, all women religious and novices may make their confession validly and licitly to any priest approved for hearing confessions in the locality. For this, no special jurisdiction (can. 876) or designation is henceforth required.

(b) However, in order to make better provision for the needs of communities an ordinary confessor shall be named for monasteries of contemplative nuns, for houses of formation and for large communities. An extraordinary confessor shall also be appointed for the monasteries mentioned above and for houses of formation. However, there is no question of obliging the religious to present themselves to him.

(c) For other communities, an ordinary confessor may be named at the request of the community itself or after consultation with its members if, in the judgment of the Ordinary, special circumstances justify such an appointment.

(d) The local Ordinary should choose confessors carefully. They should be priests of sufficient maturity and possess the other necessary qualities. The Ordinary may determine the number, age and term of office of the confessors, and may name them or renew their appointment, after consultation with the community concerned.

(e) The prescriptions of canon law which are contrary to the foregoing dispositions, or which are incompatible with them, are revoked. The same holds true of prescriptions which, because of this new legislation, are no longer applicable.

(5) The provisions of the preceding paragraph (n. 4) hold also for lay communities of men in so far as they are applicable.

52

DECLARATION ON COEDUCATION IN SCHOOLS RUN BY RELIGIOUS[a]

S.C.C.E., *Instructio a Sacra Congregatione,* 1 February, 1971

The Sacred Congregation for Religious and Secular Institutes published an Instruction on 8 December, 1957, after a meeting of male and female religious which had been held by the order of the Sovereign Pontiff. That Instruction decreed: "religious may not be authorized to direct a mixed secondary school except rarely, and then because of extreme necessity and after having received an apostolic indult from this Sacred Congregation."[1]

A number of ordinaries and religious superiors have asked the Holy See if that provision still held, after the declarations of the Second Council of the Vatican. The question was submitted to the plenary assembly of the Sacred Congregation for Catholic Education, with the agreement of the Sacred Congregation for Religious and Secular Institutes. The Sacred Congregation for Catholic Education held a plenary session on 16–17 October, 1970, and gave the following reply to the query. The reply was later approved by the Holy Father.

(1) According to the decree, *Christus Dominus,* "all religious, exempt and non-exempt, are subject to the authority of local ordinaries, in all that concerns . . . the religious and moral education of the faithful, especially children, catechetical instruction. . . . Catholic schools belonging to religious are also subject to the local ordinaries as regards their general organization and supervision, without, however, infringing the rights of religious in the running of them."[2]

(2) The Motu Proprio, *Ecclesiae Sanctae,* gives the fol-

a. Latin text in *AAS,* 63 (1971) 250–251. The translation is by A.F.
1. *AAS* 50 (1958), p. 100.
2. D. *45,* No. 35, 4.

lowing interpretation of the application of that passage of the decree: "In accordance with number 35 of the decree *Christus Dominus,* the general regulation of Catholic schools of religious institutes, without prejudice to their rights in the goverment of these schools and while observing the norms laid down there (n. 35, 5) concerning previous consultation between bishops and religious superiors, involves the general distribution of all the Catholic schools of the diocese, their cooperation with one another and their supervision, so that they shall be no less adapted than other schools to cultural and social objectives."[3]

(3) If therefore a secondary school directed by religious is led to open a coeducational school for the reasons outlined in the Motu Proprio, *Ecclesiae Sanctae* or for other good reasons, it is no longer necessary to have recourse to the Holy See. It is sufficient, as with the other Catholic schools, that it conform with the instructions given on this score by the local ordinary or the conference of bishops.

3. No. 39, 1.

53

APOSTOLIC EXHORTATION ON THE RENEWAL OF RELIGIOUS LIFE[a]

S.C.R.S.I., *Evangelica Testificatio*, 29 June, 1971

1. Evangelical witness

The evangelical witness of the religious life clearly manifests to men the primacy of the love of God; it does this with a force for which we must give thanks to the Holy Spirit. In all simplicity—following the example given by our venerated predecessor, John XXIII, on the eve of the Council[1]—we would like to tell you what hope is stirred up in us, as well as in all pastors and faithful of the Church, by the spiritual generosity of those men and women who have consecrated their lives to the Lord in the spirit and practice of the evangelical counsels. We wish also to assist you to continue in your path of following Christ in faithfulness to the Council's teaching.

2. The Council

By doing this, we wish to respond to the anxiety, uncertainty and instability shown by some; at the same time we wish to encourage those who are seeking the true renewal of the religious life. The boldness of certain arbitrary transformations, an exaggerated distrust of the past—even when it witnesses to the wisdom and vigor of ecclesial traditions— and a mentality excessively preoccupied with hastily conforming to the profound changes which disturb our times, have succeeded in leading some to consider as outmoded the specific forms of religious life. Has not appeal even un-

---

[a] Translation by Vatican Press Office. Latin text in *AAS* 63 (1971), 497–526.
1. Exhortation, 2 July 1962.

justly been made to the Council to cast doubt on the very principle of religious life? And yet it is well known that the Council recognized "this special gift" as having a place in the life of the Church, because it enables those who have received it to be more closely conformed to "that manner of virginal and humble life which Christ the Lord elected for himself, and which his Virgin Mother also chose."[2] The Council has also indicated the ways for the renewal of religious life in accordance with the Gospel.[3]

3. The tradition of the Church

From the beginning, the tradition of the Church—is it perhaps necessary to recall it?—presents us with this privileged witness of a constant seeking for God, of an undivided love for Christ alone, and of an absolute dedication to the growth of his kingdom. Without this concrete sign there would be a danger that the charity which animates the entire Church would grow cold, that the salvific paradox of the Gospel would be blunted, and that the "salt" of faith would lose its savor in a world undergoing secularization.

From the first centuries, the Holy Spirit has stirred up, side by side with the heroic confession of the martyrs, the wonderful strength of disciples and virgins, of hermits and anchorites. Religious life already existed in germ, and progressively it felt the growing need of developing and of taking on different forms of community or solitary life, in order to respond to the pressing invitation of Christ: "There is no one who has left house, wife, brothers, parents or children for the sake of the kingdom of God who will not be given repayment many times over in this present time, and in the world to come, eternal life."[4]

Who would venture to hold that such a calling today no longer has the same value and vigor? That the Church could do without these exceptional witnesses of the transcendence of the love of Christ? Or that the world without damage to itself could allow these lights to go out? They are lights which announce the kingdom of God with a liberty which knows no obstacles and is daily lived by thousands of sons and daughters of the Church.

2. Dogmatic Constitution on the Church, (D. 28), n. 46.
3. Decree on the Up-to-date Renewal of Religious Life (D. 47).
4. Lk. 18:29–30.

4. Esteem and affection

Dear sons and daughters, you have wished by means of the practice of the evangelical counsels to follow Christ more freely and to imitate him more faithfully, dedicating your entire lives to God with a special consecration rooted in that of baptism and expressing it with greater fullness: could you but understand all the esteem and the affection that we have for you in the name of Christ Jesus! We commend you to our most dear brothers in the episcopate who, together with their collaborators in the priesthood, realize their own responsibility in regard to the religious life. And we ask all the laity to whom "secular duties and activities belong properly, although not exclusively"[5] to understand what a strong help you are for them in the striving for that holiness, to which they also are called by their baptism in Christ, to the glory of the Father.[6]

5. Renewal

Certainly many exterior elements, recommended by founders of orders or religious congregations, are seen today to be outmoded. Various encumberances or rigid forms accumulated over the centuries need to be curtailed. Adaptations must be made. New forms can even be sought and instituted with the approval of the Church. For some years now the greater part of religious institutes have been generously dedicating themselves to the attainment of this goal, experimenting—sometimes too hardily—with new types of constituitions and rules. We know well and we are following with attention this effort at renewal which was desired by the Council.[7]

6. Necessary discernment

How can we assist you to make the necessary discernment in this dynamic process itself, in which there is the constant risk that the spirit of the world will be intermingled with the action of the Holy Spirit? How can what is essential be safeguarded or attained? How can benefit be obtained from past experience and from present reflection, in order to

---

5. Pastoral Constitution on the Church in the Modern World, n. 43.
6. Dogmatic Constitution on the Church, ch. V.

strengthen this form of evangelical life? According to the singular responsibility which the Lord has given us in his Church—that of confirming our brethren[8]—we would like to encourage you to proceed with greater sureness and with more joyful confidence along the way that you have chosen. In the "pursuit of perfect charity"[9] which guides your existence, what attitude could you have other than a total surrender to the Holy Spirit who, working in the Church, calls you to the freedom of the sons of God?[10]

7. The teaching of the Council

Dear sons and daughters, by a free response to the call of the Holy Spirit you have decided to follow Christ, consecrating yourselves totally to him. The evangelical counsels of chastity vowed to God, of poverty and of obedience have now become the law of your existence. The Council reminds us that "the authority of the Church has taken care, under the inspiration of the Holy Spirit, to interpret these evangelical counsels, to regulate their practice, and also to establish stable forms of living according to them."[11] In this way, the Church recognizes and authenticates the state of life established by the profession of the evangelical counsels: "The faithful of Christ can bind themselves to the three previously mentioned counsels either by vows, or by other sacred bonds which are like vows in their purpose. Through such a bond a person is totally dedicated to God by an act of supreme love. . . . It is true that through baptism he has died to sin and has been consecrated to God. However, in order to derive more abundant fruit from his baptismal grace, he intends, by the profession of the evangelical counsels in the Church, to free himself from those obstacles which might draw him away from the fervor of charity and the perfection of divine worship. Thus he is more intimately consecrated to divine service. This consecration will be the more perfect to the extent that, through more firm and stable bonds, the indissoluble union of Christ with his Spouse the Church is more perfectly represented."[12]

This teaching of the Council illustrates well the grandeur

---

8. Lk. 22:32.
9. Decree on the Up-to-date Renewal of Religious Life.
10. Gal. 5:13; 2 Cor. 3:17.
11. Dogmatic Constitution on the Church, n. 43.
12. Ibid., n. 44.

of this self-giving, freely made by yourselves, after the pattern of Christ's self-giving to his Church; like his, yours is total and irreversible. It is precisely for the sake of the kingdom of heaven that you have vowed to Christ, generously and without reservation, that capacity to love, that need to possess, and that freedom to regulate one's own life which are so precious to man. Such is your consecration, made within the Chruch and through her ministry—both that of her representatives who receive your profession and that of the Christian community itself, whose love recognizes, welcomes, sustains and embraces those who within it make an offering of themselves as a lving sign "which can and ought to attract all the members of the Church to an effective and prompt fulfilment of the duties of their Christian vocation . . .more adequately manifesting to all believers the presence of heavenly goods already possessed in this world."[13]

I. FORMS OF THE RELIGIOUS LIFE

8. Contemplative life

Some of you have been called to the life which is termed "contemplative." An irresistible attraction draws you to the Lord. Held in God's grasp, you abandon yourselves to his sovereign action, which draws you toward him and transforms you into him, as it prepares you for that eternal contemplation which is the common vocation of us all. How could you advance along this road and be faithful to the grace which animates you if you did not respond with all your being, through a dynamism whose driving force is love, to that call which directs you unswervingly toward God? Consider, therefore, every other immediate activity to which you must devote yourselves—fraternal relationships, disinterested or renumerative work, necessary recreation— as a witness rendered to the Lord of your intimate communion with him, so that he may grant you that unifying purity of intention which in so necessary for encountering him in prayer itself. In this way you will contribute to the building up of the kingdom of God by the witness of your lives and with a "hidden apostolic fruitfulness."[14]

13. Dogmatic Constitution on the Church.
14. Decree on the Up-to-date Renewal of the Religious Life, n. 7.

9. Apostolic life

Others are consecrated to the apostolate in its essential mission, which is the proclaiming of the Word of God to those whom he places along their path, so as to lead them toward faith. Such a grace requires a profound union with the Lord, one which will enable you to transmit the message of the Incarnate Word in terms which the world is able to understand. How necessary it is therefore that your whole existence should make you share in his passion, death and glory.[15]

10. Contemplation and apostolate

When your vocation destines you for other tasks in the service of men—pastoral life, missions, teaching, works of charity and so on—is it not above all the intensity of your union with the Lord that will make them fruitful, in proportion to that union "in secret?"[16] In order to be faithful to the teaching of the Council, must not "the members of each community who are seeking God before all else combine contemplation with apostolic love? By the former they cling to God in mind and heart; by the latter they strive to associate themselves with the work of redemption and to spread the kingdom of God."[17]

11. The charisms of founders

Only in this way you will be able to reawaken hearts to truth and to divine love in accordance with the charisms of your founders who were raised up by God within his Church. Thus the Council rightly insists on the obligation of religious to be faithful to the spirit of their founders, to their evangelical intentions and to the example of their sanctity. In this it finds one of the principles for the present renewal and one of the most secure criteria for judging what each institute should undertake.[18] In reality, the charism of the religious life, far from being an impulse born of flesh and blood[19] or one derived from a mentality which

15. Phil. 3:10–11.
16. Mt. 6:6.
17. Decree on the Up-to-date Renewal of Religious Life, n. 5.
18. Dogmatic Constitution on the Church, n. 45; Decree on the Up-to-date Renewal of Religious Life, n. 2b.
19. Jn. 1:13.

conforms itself to the modern world,[20] is the fruit of the Holy Spirit, who is always at work within the Church.

12. External forms and interior driving force

It is precisely here that the dynamism proper to each religious family finds its origin. For while the call of God renews itself and expresses itself in different ways according to changing circumstances of place and time, it nevertheless requires a certain constancy of orientation. The interior impulse which is the response to God's call stirs up in the depth of one's being certain fundamental options. Fidelity to the exigencies of these fundamental options is the touchstone of authenticity in religious life. Let us not forget that every human institution is prone to become set in its ways and is threatened by formalism. It is continually necessary to revitalize external forms with this interior driving force, without which these external forms would very quickly become an excessive burden.

Through the variety of forms which give each institute its own individual character and which have their root in the fullness of the grace of Christ,[21] the supreme rule of the religious life and its ultimate norm is that of following Christ according to the teaching of the Gospel. Is it not perhaps this preoccupation which in the course of the centuries has given rise in the Church to the demand for a life which is chaste, poor and obedient?

II. ESSENTIAL COMMITMENTS

13. Consecrated chastity

Only the love of God—it must be repeated—calls in a decisive way to religious chastity. This love moreover makes so uncompromising a demand for fraternal charity that the religious will live more profoundly with his contemporaries in the heart of Christ. On this condition, the gift of self, made to God and to others, will be the source of deep peace. Without in any way undervaluing human love and marriage—is not the latter, according to faith, the image and sharing of the union of love joining Christ and

20. Rom. 12:2.
21. 1 Cor. 12:12–30.

the Church?[22]—consecrated chastity evokes this union in a more immediate way and brings that surpassing excellence to which all human love should tend. Thus, at the very moment that human love is more than ever threatened by a "ravaging eroticism,"[23] consecrated chastity must be today more than ever understood and lived with uprightness and generosity. Chastity is decisively positive, it witnesses to preferential love for the Lord and symbolizes in the most eminent and absolute way the mystery of the union of the Mystical Body with its Head, the union of the Bride with her eternal Bridegroom. Finally, it reaches, transforms and imbues with a mysterious likeness to Christ man's being in its most hidden depths.

14. A source of spiritual fruitfulness

Thus, dear brothers and sisters, it is necessary for you to restore to the Christian spirituality of consecrated chastity its full effectiveness. When it is truly lived, for the sake of the kingdom of heaven, consecrated chastity frees man's heart and thus becomes "a sign and stimulus of charity as well as a special source of spiritual fruitfulness in the world."[24] Even if the world does not always recognize it, consecrated chastity remains in every case effective in a mystical manner in the world.

15. A gift of God

For our part, we must be firmly and surely convinced that the value and the fruitfulness of chastity observed for love of God in religious celibacy find their ultimate basis in nothing other than the Word of God, the teachings of Christ, the life of his Virgin Mother, and also the apostolic tradition, as it has been unceasingly affirmed by the Church. We are in fact dealing here with a precious gift which the Father imparts to certain people. This gift, fragile and vulnerable because of human weakness, remains open to the contradictions of mere reason and is in part incomprehensible to those to whom the light of the Word In-

---

22. Pastoral Constitution on the Church in the Modern World, n. 48; Eph. 5:25, 32.
23. Address to the *Equipes Notre Dame*, 4 May 1970.
24. Dogmatic Constitution on the Church, n. 42.

carnate has not revealed how he who loses his life for him will find it.[25]

16. Consecrated poverty

Observing chastity as you do in the following of Christ, you desire also, according to his example, to live in poverty in the use of this world's goods which are necessary for your daily sustenance. On this point, moreover, our contemporaries question you with particular insistence. It is certainly true that religious institutes have an important role to fulfil in the sphere of works of mercy, assistance and social justice; it is clear that in carrying out this service they must be always attentive to the demands of the Gospel.

17. The cry of the poor

You hear rising up, more pressing than ever, from their personal distress and collective misery, "the cry of the poor."[26] Was it not in order to respond to their appeal as God's privileged ones that Christ came,[27] even going as far as to identify himself with them?[28] In a world experiencing the full flood of development this persistence of poverty-stricken masses and individuals constitutes a pressing call for "a conversion of minds and attitudes,"[29] especially for you who follow Christ more closely in this earthly condition of self-emptying.[30] We know that this call resounds within you in so dramatic a fashion that some of you even feel on occasion the temptation to take violent action. As disciples of Christ, how could you follow a way different from his? This way is not, as you know, a movement of the political or temporal order; it calls rather for the conversion of hearts, for liberation from all temporal encumbrances. It is a call to love.

18. Poverty and justice

How then will the cry of the poor find an echo in your lives? That cry must, first of all, bar you from whatever

25. Mt. 10:39, 16:25; Mk. 8:35; Lk. 9:24; Jn. 12:25.
26. Ps. 9:13; Job 34:28; Prov. 21:13.
27. Lk. 4:18, 6:20.
28. Mt. 25:35–40.
29. Pastoral Constitution on the Church in the Modern World, n. 63.
30. Mt. 19:21; 2 Cor. 8:9.

would be a compromise with any form of social injustice. It obliges you also to awaken consciences to the drama of misery and to the demands of social justice made by the Gospel and the Church. It leads some of you to join the poor in their situation and to share their bitter cares. Furthermore, it calls many of your institutes to rededicate for the good of the poor some of their works—something which many have already done with generosity. Finally, it enjoins on you a use of goods limited to what is required for the fulfilment of the functions to which you are called. It is necessary that in your daily lives you should give proof, even externally, of authentic poverty.

19. Use of the world's goods

In a civilization and a world marked by a prodigious movement of almost indefinite material growth, what witness would be offered by a religious who let himself be carried away by an uncurbed seeking for his own ease, and who considered it normal to allow himself without discernment or restraint everything that is offered him? At a time when there is an increased danger for many of being enticed by the alluring security of possessions, knowledge and power, the call of God places you at the pinnacle of the Christian conscience. You are to remind men that their true and complete progress consists in responding to their calling "to share as sons in the life of the living God, the Father of all men."[31]

20. Life of work

You will likewise be able to understand the complaints of so many persons who are drawn into the implacable process of work for gain, of profit for enjoyment, and of consumption, which in its turn forces them to a labor which is sometimes inhuman. It will therefore be an essential aspect of your poverty to bear witness to the human meaning of work which is carried out in liberty of spirit and restored to its true nature as the source of sustenance and of service. Did not the Council stress—in a very timely way—your necessary submission to "the common law of labor?"[32] Earning your own living and that of your brothers or sis-

31. P. P., n. 21.
32. Decree on the Up-to-date Renewal of Religious Life, n. 13.

ters, helping the poor by your work—these are duties incumbent upon you. But your activities cannot derogate from the vocation of your various institutes, nor habitually involve work such as would take the place of their specific tasks. Nor should these activities in any way lead you toward secularization, to the detriment of your religious life. Be watchful therefore regarding the spirit which animates you: what a failure it would be if you felt yourselves valued solely by the payment you receive for worldly work!

21. Fraternal sharing

The necessity, which is so imperative today, of fraternal sharing must preserve its evangelical value. According to the expression in the Didache, "If you share eternal goods, with all the more reason should you share the goods that perish."[33] Poverty really lived by pooling goods, including pay, will testify to the spiritual communion uniting you; it will be a living call to all the rich and will also bring relief to your needy brothers and sisters. The legitimate desire of exercising personal responsibility will not find expression in enjoyment of one's own income but in fraternal sharing in the common good. The forms of poverty of each person and of each community will depend on the type of institute and on the form of obedience practised in it. Thus will be brought to realization, in accordance with particular vocations, the character of dependence which is inherent in every form of poverty.

22. Evangelical exigency

You are aware, dear sons and daughters, that the needs of today's world, if you experience them in heart-to-heart union with Christ, make your poverty more urgent and more deep. If, as is evident, you must take account of the human surroundings in which you live, in order to adapt your life style to them, your poverty cannot be purely and simply a conformity to the manners of those surroundings. Its value as a witness will derive from a generous response to the exigencies of the Gospel, in total fidelity to your vocation—not just from an excessively superficial preoccupation for appearing to be poor—and in avoiding those ways

33. *Didache, IV,* 8; Acts 4:32.

of life which would denote a certain affectedness and vanity. While we recognize that certain situations can justify the abandonment of a religious type of dress, we can not pass over in silence the fittingness that the dress of religious men and women should be, as the Council wishes, a sign of their consecration[84] and that it should be in some way different from the forms that are clearly secular.

23. Consecrated obedience

Is it not the same fidelity which inspires your profession of obedience, in the light of faith and in accordance with the very dynamism of the charity of Christ? Through this profession, in fact, you make a total offering of your will and enter more decisively and more surely into his plan of salvation. Following the example of Christ, who came to do the will of the Father, and in communion with him who "learned to obey through suffering" and "ministered to the brethren," you have assumed a firmer commitment to the ministry of the Church and of your brethren.[35]

24. Evangelical fraternity and sacrifice

The evangelical aspiration to fraternity was forcefully expressed by the Council. The Church was defined as the People of God, in which the hierarchy is at the service of the members of Christ united by the same charity.[36] The same paschal mystery of Christ is lived in the religious state as in the whole Church. The profound meaning of obedience is revealed in the fullness of this mystery of death and resurrection in which the supernatural destiny of man is brought to realization in a perfect manner. It is in fact through sacrifice, suffering and death that man attains true life.

Exercising authority in the midst of your brethren means therefore being their servants,[37] in accordance with the example of him who gave "his life as a ransom for many."[38]

34. Decree on the Up-to-date Renewal of Religious Life, n. 17.
35. Ibid., 14; Jn. 4:34, 5:30, 10:15–18; Heb. 5:8, 10:7; Ps. 40(39): 8–9.
36. Dogmatic Constitution on the Church, ch. I-III.
37. Lk. 22:26–27; Jn. 13:14.
38. Mt. 20:28; Phil. 2:8.

25. Authority and obedience

Consequently, authority and obedience are exercised in the service of the common good as two complementary aspects of the same participation in Christ's offering. For those in authority, it is a matter of serving in their brothers the design of the Father's love; while, in accepting their directives, the religious follow our Master's example[39] and cooperate in the work of salvation. Thus, far from being in opposition to one another, authority and individual liberty go together in the fulfilment of God's will, which is sought fraternally through a trustful dialogue between the superior and his brother, in the case of a personal situation, or through a general agreement regarding what concerns the whole community. In this pursuit the religious will be able to avoid both an excessive agitation and a preoccupation for making the attraction of current opinion prevail over the profound meaning of the religious life. It is the duty of everyone, but especially of superiors and those who exercise responsibility among their brothers or sisters, to awaken in the community the certainties of faith which must be their guide. This pursuit has the aim of giving depth to these certainties and translating them into practice in everyday living in accordance with the needs of the moment; its aim is not in any way to cast doubt on them. This labor of seeking together must end, when it is the moment, with the decision of the superiors whose presence and acceptance are indispensable in every community.

26. In the needs of daily life

Modern conditions of life naturally have their effect on the way you live your obedience. Many of you carry out part of your activity outside your religious houses, performing a function in which you have special competence. Others join together in work teams having their own pattern of life and action. Is not the risk which is inherent in such situations a call to reassert and reexamine in depth the sense of obedience? If the risk is to have good results, certain conditions must be respected. First of all, it is necessary to see whether the work undertaken conforms with the institute's vocation. The two spheres ought also to be clearly marked off. Above all, it must be possible to pass from ex-

39. Lk. 2:51.

ternal activity to the demands of common life, taking care to ensure full effectiveness to the elements of the strictly religious life. One of the principal duties of superiors is that of ensuring that their brothers and sisters in religion should have the indispensable conditions for their spiritual life. But how could they fulfil this duty without the trusting collaboration of the whole community?

27. Freedom and obedience

Let us add this: the more you exercise your responsibility, the more you must renew your self-giving in its full significance. The Lord obliges each one to "lose his life" if he is to follow him.[40] You will observe this precept by accepting the directives of your superiors as a guarantee of your religious profession, through which you offer to God a total dedication of your own wills as a sacrifice of yourselves.[41] Christian obedience is unconditional submission to the will of God. But your obedience is more strict because you have made it the object of a special giving, and the range of your choices is limited by your commitment. It is a full act of your freedom that is at the origin of your present position: your duty is to make that act ever more vital, both by your own initiative and by the cordial assent you give the directives of your superiors. Thus it is that the Council includes among the benefits of the religious state "liberty strengthened by obedience,"[42] and stresses that such obedience "does not diminish the dignity of the human person but rather leads it to maturity through that enlarged freedom which belongs to the sons of God."[43]

28. Conscience and obedience

And yet, is it not possible to have conflicts between the superior's authority and the conscience of the religious, the "sanctuary of a person where he is alone with God, whose voice echoes in the depths of his being?"[44] Need we repeat that conscience on its own is not the arbiter of the moral worth of the actions which it inspires? It must take account

40. Lk. 9:23–24.
41. Decree on the Up-to-date Renewal of Religious Life, n. 14.
42. Dogmatic Constitution on the Church, n. 43.
43. Decree on the Up-to-date Renewal of Religious Life, n. 14.
44. Pastoral Constitution on the Church in the Modern World, n. 16.

of objective norms and, if necessary, reform and rectify itself. Apart from an order manifestly contrary to the laws of God or the constitutions of the institute, or one involving a serious and certain evil—in which case there is no obligation to obey—the superior's decisions concern a field in which the calculation of the greater good can vary according to the point of view. To conclude from the fact that a directive seems objectively less good that it is unlawful and contrary to conscience would mean an unrealistic disregard of the obscurity and ambivalence of many human realities. Besides, refusal to obey involves an often serious loss for the common good. A religious should not easily conclude that there is a contradiction between the judgment of his conscience and that of his superior. This exceptional situation will sometimes involve true interior suffering, after the pattern of Christ himself "who learned obedience through suffering."[45]

29. The Cross—proof of the greatest love

What has been said indicates what degree of renunciation is demanded by the practice of the religious life. You must feel something of the force with which Christ was drawn to his Cross—that baptism he had still to receive, by which that fire would be lighted which sets you too ablaze[46]—something of that "foolishness" which Saint Paul wishes we all had, because it alone makes us wise.[47] Let the Cross be for you, as it was for Christ, proof of the greatest love. Is there not a mysterious relationship between renunciation and joy, between sacrifice and magnanimity, between discipline and spiritual freedom?

III. LIFE STYLE

30. A witness to give

Let us admit, sons and daughters in Jesus Christ, that at the present moment it is difficult to find a life style in harmony with this exigency. Too many contrary attractions lead one to seek first of all for a humanly effective activity. But is it not for you to give an example of joyful, well-balanced austerity, by accepting the difficulties inherent in

45. Heb. 5:8.
46. Lk. 12:49–50.
47. 1 Cor. 3:18–19.

work and in social relationships and by bearing patiently the trials of life with its agonizing insecurity, as renunciations indispensable for the fullness of the Christian life? Religious, in fact, are "striving to attain holiness by a narrower path."[48] In the midst of troubles, great or small, your interior fervor enables you to recognize the Cross of Christ and assists you to accept these troubles with faith and love.

31. Following Christ's example

It is on this condition that you will give the witness which the People of God expect. It is the witness of men and women capable of accepting the abnegation of poverty, and of being attracted by simplicity and humility; it is that of those who love peace, who are free from compromise and set on complete self-denial—of those who are at the same time free and obedient, spontaneous and tenacious, meek and strong in the certainty of the faith. This grace will be given to you by Christ Jesus in proportion to the fundamental gift which you have made of yourselves and which you do not retract. The recent history of many religious in various countries who have suffered generously for Christ gives eloquent proof of this. While we express to them our admiration, we hold them up as an example for all.

32. Strengthening the inner man

Along this path a precious aid is offered you by the forms of life which experience, faithful to the charisms of the various institutes, has given rise to. Experience has varied the combinations of these forms, never ceasing to put forward new developments. No matter how different their expressions are, these forms are always ordered to the formation of the inner man. And it is the care you have for strengthening the inner man which will help you to recognize, in the midst of so many different and attractive possibilities, the most suitable forms of life. An excessive desire for flexibility and creative spontaneity can in fact give rise to accusations of rigidity directed against that minimum of regularity in activities which community life and personal maturity ordinarily require. Disorderly outbursts, which appeal to fraternal charity or to what one believes to be inspi-

---

48. Dogmatic Constitution on the Church, n. 13.

rations of the Spirit, can also lead to the breakup of communities.

33. Importance of life surroundings

As you know from experience, the importance of the surroundings in which one lives should not be underestimated either in relation to the habitual orientation of the whole person—so complex and divided—in the direction of God's call, or in relation to the spiritual integration of the person's tendencies. Does not the heart often let itself cling to what is passing? Many of you will in fact be obliged to lead your lives, at least in part, in a world which tends to exile man from himself and to compromise both his spiritual unity and his union with God. You must therefore learn to find God even under those conditions of life which are marked by an increasingly accelerated rhythm and by the noise and the attraction of the ephemeral.

34. Being strengthened in God

Everyone can see how much the fraternal setting of an ordered existence with freely undertaken discipline of life helps you to attain union with God. This discipline is increasingly necessary for anyone who "returns to the heart,"[49] in the biblical sense of the term, something deeper than our feelings, ideas and wishes, something inbued with the idea of the infinite, the absolute, or eternal destiny. In the present disarray it is especially necessary for religious to give witness as persons whose vital striving to attain their goal—the living God—has effectively created unity and openness in the depth and steadfastness of their life in God. This is accomplished by the integration of all their faculties, the purification of their thoughts and the spiritualization of their senses.

35. Necessary withdrawal from the world

To the extent therefore that you carry on external activities, it is necessary that you should learn to pass from these activities to the life of recollection, in which the vigor of your souls is renewed. If you truly do the work of God, you will of your own accord feel the need for times of retreat

49. Is. 46:8.

which, together with your brothers and sisters in religion, you will transform into times of fullness. In view of the hectic pace and tensions of modern life it is appropriate to give particular importance—over and above the daily rhythm of prayer—to those more prolonged moments of prayer, which can be variously spread out in different periods of the day, according to the possibilities and the nature of your vocation. If according to your constitutions the houses to which you belong widely practise fraternal hospitality, it will be for you to regulate the frequency and mode of that hospitality, so that all unnecessary disturbance is avoided, and so that your guests are helped to attain close union with God.

36. Spiritual initiation

This is the meaning of the observances which mark the rhythm of your daily life. An alert conscience, far from looking upon them solely as obligations imposed by a rule, judges them from the benefits that they bring, inasmuch as they ensure a greater spiritual fullness. It must be affirmed that religious observances demand, far more than intellectual instruction or training of the will, a true initiation with the purpose of deeply christianizing the individual in the spirit of the evangelical beatitudes.

37. Doctrine of life

The Council considers "a proven doctrine of acquiring perfection"[50] as one of the inherited riches of religious institutes and one of the greatest benefits that they must guarantee. And since this perfection consists in advancing ever further in the love of God and of our brethren, it is necessary to understand this doctrine in a very concrete way, that is as a doctrine of life that must be effectively lived. This means that the pursuit to which the institutes devote themselves cannot consist only in certain adaptations to be carried out in relation to the changing circumstances of the world; they must instead assist the fruitful rediscovery of the means essential for leading a life completely permeated with love of God and of men.

50. Dogmatic Constitution on the Church, n. 43.

38. Forming the new person

In consequence the necessity makes itself felt, both for the communities and for those who constitute them, of passing from the psychological level to the level of that which is truly "spiritual."[51] Is not the "New Man" spoken of by St. Paul perhaps like the ecclesial fullness of Christ and at the same time the sharing by each Christian in this fullness? Such an aim will make of your religious families the vital environment which will develop the seed of divine life—the seed which was planted in each of you at baptism and which your consecration, if lived to the full, will enable to bear its fruits in the greatest abundance.

39. Cheerful simplicity of community life

Even if—like every Christian—you are imperfect, you nevertheless intend to create surroundings which are favorable to the spiritual progress of each member of the community. How can this result be attained, unless you deepen in the Lord your relationships, even the most ordinary ones, with each of your brethren? Let us not forget that charity must be as it were an active hope for what others can become with the help of our fraternal support. The mark of its genuineness is found in a joyful simplicity, whereby all strive to understand what each one has at heart.[52] If certain religious give the impression of having allowed themselves to be crushed by their community life, which ought instead to have made them expand and develop, does this perhaps happen because this community life lacks that understanding cordiality which nourishes hope? There is no doubt that community spirit, relationships of friendship and fraternal cooperation in the same apostolate, as well as mutual support in a shared life chosen for a better service of Christ, are so many valuable factors in this daily progress.

40. Small communities

From this point of view there are emerging certain tendencies aiming at the establishment of smaller communities. A sort of spontaneous reaction against the anonymity of the great urban centers, the necessity of adapting the living

51. 1 Cor. 2:14–15.
52. Gal. 6:2.

quarters of a community to the cramped environment of modern cities and the very need to be closer, in one's living conditions, to the people to be evangelized—these are among the reasons that lead certain institutes to plan by preference the foundation of communities with a small number of members. Such small communities can in addition favor the development of closer relationships between the religious and a shared and more fraternal undertaking of responsibility. Nevertheless, while a certain structure can in fact favor the creation of a spiritual environment, it would be vain to imagine that it is sufficient for making it develop. Small communities, instead of offering an easier form of life, prove on the contrary to make greater demands on their members.

41. Large communities

On the other hand it remains true that communities containing many members particularly suit many religious. Communities of this sort may likewise be called for by the nature of a charitable service, by certain tasks of an intellectual nature or by the contemplative or monastic life. May perfect unity of hearts and minds be always found there, in exact correspondence to the spiritual and supernatural goal which is pursued. Besides, whatever their size, communities large or small will not succeed in helping their members unless they are constantly animated by the Gospel spirit, nourished by prayer, and distinguished by generous mortification of the old man, by the discipline necessary for forming the new man, and by the fruitfulness of the sacrifice of the Cross.

IV. RENEWAL AND SPIRITUAL GROWTH

42. Desire for God

Dear religious, how could you fail to desire to know better him whom you love and whom you wish to make manifest to men? It is prayer that unites you to him. If you have lost the taste for prayer, you will regain the desire for it by returning humbly to its practice. Do not forget, moreover, the witness of history: faithfulness to prayer or its abandonment are the test of the vitality or decadence of the religious life.

43. Prayer

The discovery of intimacy with God, the necessity for adoration, the need for intercession—the experience of Christian holiness shows us the fruitfulness of prayer, in which God reveals himself to the spirit and heart of his servants. The Lord gives us this knowledge of himself in the fervor of love. The gifts of the Spirit are many, but they always grant us a taste of that true and intimate knowledge of the Lord. Without it we shall not succeed either in understanding the value of the Christian and religious life or in gaining the strength to advance in it with the joy of a hope that does not deceive.

44. The spirit of prayer permeating fraternal life

The Holy Spirit also gives you the grace to discover the image of the Lord in the hearts of men, and teaches you to love them as brothers and sisters. Again, he helps you to see the manifestations of his love in events. If we are humbly attentive to men and things, the Spirit of Jesus enlightens us and enriches us with his wisdom, provided that we are imbued with the spirit of prayer.

45. Need for interior life

Is not perhaps one of the miseries of our times to be found in the imbalance "between the conditions of collective existence and the requisite of personal thought and even of contemplation?"[53] Many people, including many of the young, have lost sight of the meaning of their lives and are anxiously searching for the contemplative dimension of their being. They do not realize that Christ, through his Church, can respond to their expectations. Facts of this kind should cause you to reflect seriously on what men have the right to expect of you—you who have formally committed yourselves to a life in the service of the Word, "the true light that enlightens all men."[54] Be conscious, then, of the importance of prayer in your lives and learn to devote yourselves to it generously. Faithfulness to daily prayer always remains for each one of you a basic ne-

53. Pastoral Constitution on the Church in the Modern World, n. 8.
54. Jn. 1:9.

cessity. It must have a primary place in your constitutions and in your lives.

46. Silence

The interior man is aware that times of silence are demanded by love of God. As a rule he needs a certain solitude so that he may hear God "speaking to his heart."[55] It must be stressed that a silence which is a mere absence of noise and words, in which the soul cannot renew its vigor, would obviously lack any spiritual value. It could even be harmful to fraternal charity, if at that moment it were essential to have contact with others. On the contrary, the search for intimacy with God involves the truly vital need of a silence embracing the whole being, both for those who must find God in the midst of noise and confusion and for contemplatives.[56] Faith, hope and a love for God which is open to the gifts of the Spirit, and also a brotherly love which is open to the mystery of others, carry with them an imperative need for silence.

47. Liturgical life

Finally, there is surely no need to remind you of the special place occupied in your community life by the Church's liturgy, the center of which is the Eucharistic Sacrifice, in which interior prayer is linked to external worship.[57] At the moment of your religious profession you were offered to God by the Church, in close union with the Eucharistic Sacrifice.[58] Day after day this offering of yourselves must become a reality, concretely and continuously renewed. Communion in the Body and Blood of Christ is the primary source of this renewal;[59] by it may your will to love truly, and even to the sacrifice of your lives, be unceasingly confirmed.

48. The Eucharist as the heart of the community and source of life

Your communities, since they are united in Christ's name, naturally have as their center the Eucharist, "the

55. Hos. 2:16(14).
56. Instruction on the Contemplative Life.
57. *Sacramentali communione.*
58. O.P.R.
59. Decree on the Up-to-date Renewal of Religious Life, n. 15.

Sacrament of love, the sign of unity and the bond of charity."[60] It is therefore normal that these communities should be visibly united around an oratory, in which the presence of the Holy Eucharist expresses and at the same time makes real that which must be the principal mission of every religious family, as also of every Christian assembly. The Eucharist, through which we do not cease to proclaim the death and resurrection of the Lord and to prepare ourselves for his coming again in glory, brings back constantly to mind the physical and moral sufferings by which Christ was afflicted, and which he had indeed freely accepted, even to his agony and death on the Cross. May the trials which you encounter be for you an opportunity for bearing in union with the Lord, and of offering to the Father, the many misfortunes and unjust sufferings which weigh upon our brothers and sisters; to these the sacrifice of Christ can alone, in faith, give meaning.

49. Spiritual fruitfulness for the world

In this way, the world too is present at the center of your life of prayer and offering, as the Council has explained with force: "Let no one think that religious by their consecration have become strangers to their fellowmen or useless citizens of this earthly city. For even though in some instances religious do not directly serve their contemporaries, yet in a more profound sense these same religious are united with them in the heart of Christ and spiritually collaborate with them. In this way the work of building up the earthly city can always have its foundation in the Lord and can tend toward him in such a way that those who build this city will not have labored in vain."[61]

50. Sharing in the Church's mission

This sharing in the Church's mission, the Council insists, cannot take place without openness to collaboration in "her enterprises and objectives in such fields as the scriptural, liturgical, doctrinal, pastoral, ecumenical, missionary and social."[62] While anxious to take part in the pastoral activity of the whole, you will surely do so keeping in mind the par-

60. *Sacramentali communione*, n. 47.
61. Dogmatic Constitution on the Church, n. 46.
62. Decree on the Up-to-date Renewal of Religious Life, n. 2c.

ticular character of each institute. And you will always recall that exemption applies chiefly to internal structure; it does not dispense you from submission to the jurisdiction of the bishops in charge, "insofar as the performance of their pastoral office and the right ordering of the care of souls require."[63] Besides, must not you more than others untiringly recall that the Church's activity continues that of the Saviour, for the good of men, only by entering into the activity of Christ himself, who brings all back to his Father: "All are yours; and you are Christ's; and Christ is God's?"[64] God's call in fact orients you, in the most direct and effective manner, toward the eternal kingdom. Through the spiritual tensions which are inevitable in every truly religious life, you "give splendid and striking testimony that the world cannot be transfigured and offered to God without the spirit of the beatitudes."[65]

V. CONCLUDING APPEAL

51. For authentic renewal of the religious life

Dear sons and daughters in Christ, the religious life, if it is to be renewed, must adapt its accidental forms to certain changes which are affecting with growing rapidity and to an increasing extent the conditions of life of every human being. But how is this to be attained while maintaining those "stable forms of living"[66] recognized by the Church, except by a renewal of the authentic and integral vocation of your institutes? For a living being, adaptation to its surroundings does not consist in abandoning its true identity, but rather in asserting itself in the vitality that is its own. Deep understanding of present tendencies and of the needs of the modern world should cause your own sources of energy to spring up with renewed vigor and freshness. It is a sublime task in the measure that it is a difficult one.

52. Need for evangelical witness in today's world

A burning question of the present day preoccupies us: how can the message of the Gospel penetrate the world?

63. Decree on the Pastoral Office of Bishops on the Church, n. 35.
64. 1 Cor. 3:22–23; Pastoral Constitution on the Church in the Modern World, n. 37.
65. Dogmatic Constitution on the Church, n. 31.
66. Ibid., n. 43.

What can be done at those levels in which a new culture is unfolding, where a new type of man is emerging, a man who no longer believes he needs redemption? Since all men are called to the contemplation of the mystery of salvation, you can understand how these questions create such a serious obligation in your lives and such a challenge to your apostolic zeal! Dear religious, according to the different ways in which the call of God makes demands upon your spiritual families, you must give your full attention to the needs of men, their problems and their searchings; you must give witness in their midst, through prayer and action, to the Good News of love, justice and peace. The aspirations of men to a more fraternal life among individuals and nations require above all a change in ways of living, in mentality and in hearts. Such a mission, which is common to all the People of God, belongs to you in a special way. How can that mission ever be fulfilled if there is lacking an appreciation of the absolute, which results from a certain experience of God? This does but emphasize the fact that authentic renewal of the religious life is of capital importance for the very renewal of the Church and of the world.

53. Living witnesses of the love of the Lord

Today more than ever, the world needs to see in you men and women who have believed in the Word of the Lord, in his resurrection and in eternal life, even to the point of dedicating their lives to witnessing to the reality of that love, which is offered to all men. In the course of her history, the Church has ever been quickened and gladdened by many holy religious who, in the diversity of their vocations, have been living witnesses to love without limit and to the Lord Jesus. Is not this grace, for the man of today, a refreshing breeze coming from infinity itself, and foreshadowing man's liberation in eternal and absolute joy? Open to this divine joy, live generously the demands of your vocation, renewing the affirmation of the realities of faith and in its light interpreting in a Christian way the needs of the world. The moment has come, in all seriousness, to bring about a rectification, if need be, of your consciences, and also a transformation of your whole lives, in order to attain greater fidelity.

54. Appeal to all religious

As we contemplate the tenderness of the Lord when he referred to his followers as the "little flock" and reassured them that his Father was pleased to grant them the kingdom,[67] we make this appeal to you: keep the simplicity of the "least ones" of the Gospel. May you succeed in discovering this anew in an interior and closer relationship with Christ and in your direct contact with your brethren. You will then experience through the action of the Holy Spirit the joyful exultation of those who are introduced into the secrets of the kingdom. Do not seek to be numbered among the "learned and clever" whose numbers seem inclined by a combination of circumstances to increase. Such secrets are hidden from these.[68] Be truely poor, meek, eager for holiness, merciful and pure of heart. Be among those who will bring to the world the peace of God.[69]

55. Fruitful radiation of joy

The joy of always belonging to God is an incomparable fruit of the Holy Spirit, and one which you have already tasted. Filled with the joy which Christ will preserve in you even in the midst of trial, learn to face the future with confidence. To the extent that this joy radiates from your communities, it will be a proof to everyone that the state of life which you have chosen is helping you by the threefold renunciation of your religious profession to realize the greatest possible expansion of your life in Christ. Seeing you and the life you lead, the young will be able to understand well the appeal that Jesus never ceases to make among them.[70] The Council, in fact, brings this to mind: "The example of your life constitutes the finest recommendation of the institute and the most effective invitation to embrace the religious life."[71] There is no doubt, moreover, that by showing you profound esteem and great affection, bishops, priests, parents and Christian educators will awaken in many the desire to follow in your footsteps, in response to that call of Jesus which never ceases to be heard among his followers.

67. Lk. 12:32.
68. Lk. 10:21.
69. Mt. 5:3–11.
70. Mt. 19:11–12; 1 Cor. 7:34.
71. Decree on the Up-to-date Renewal of Religious Life, n. 24.

56. Prayer to Mary

May the most beloved Mother of the Lord, after whose example you have consecrated your lives to God, obtain for you in your daily journeying that lasting joy which Jesus alone can give. May your life, following her example, give witness to that "maternal love, which should animate all those who, associated in the apostolic mission of the Church, collaborate in the regeneration of men."[72] Beloved sons and daughters, may the joy of the Lord transfigure your consecrated life and may his love make it fruitful. With deep affection we bless you in his name.

72. Dogmatic Constitution on the Church, n. 65.

54

DECREE ON THE TRAINING OF PRIESTS[a]

Vatican II, *Optatan Totius,* 28 October, 1965

INTRODUCTION

The Council is fully aware that the desired renewal of the whole Church depends in great part upon a priestly ministry animated by the spirit of Christ[1] and it solemnly affirms the critical importance of priestly training. It lays down certain fundamental principles, wherein regulations already tested by the experience of centuries are reaffirmed, and new regulations are introduced, in harmony with the constitutions and decrees of the sacred Council and the changed conditions of our times. Because of the unity of the Catholic priesthood, this priestly formation is required for all priests, secular, religious and of every rite. Hence, although these directives are immediately concerned with the diocesan clergy, they should with due qualification be adapted to all.

a. This translation has been done by Fathers B. Hayes, s.м., S. Fagan, s.м., and Austin Flannery, o.p.
1. It is clear from the words by which our divine Lord appointed the apostles, with their successors and fellow workers, to be the preachers of the Gospel, the leaders of the new chosen people and the dispensers of the mysteries of God, that according to the will of Christ himself the progress of the whole People of God depends in the highest degree on the ministry of priests. This is supported by the statements of the Fathers and saints and by a whole series of papal documents. Cf. especially:

St. Pius X, Exhortation to the Clergy *Haerent animo,* 4 August 1908: St. Pii X Acta IV, pp. 237–264.

Pius XI, Encycl. Letter *Ad catholici Sacerdotii,* 20 December 1935: *AAS* 28 (1936), especially pp. 37–52.

Pius XII, Apostolic Exhortation *Menti Nostrae,* 23 September 1950: *AAS* 42 (1950), pp. 657–702.

John XXIII, Encycl. Letter *Sacerdotii Nostri primordia,* 1 August 1959: *AAS* 51 (1959), pp. 545–579.

Paul VI, Apostolic Letter *Summi Dei Verbum,* 4 November 1963: *AAS* 55 (1963), pp. 979–995.

I. PRIESTLY TRAINING IN DIFFERENT COUNTRIES

1. Since only regulations of a general nature can be made, owing to the wide diversity of peoples and countries, each nation or rite should have its own *Program of Priestly Training*. This should be drawn up by the episcopal conference[2] and should be revised at regular intervals and approved by the Holy See. In every such program, the general regulations will be adapted to the circumstances of time and place, so that priestly training will always answer the pastoral requirements of the particular area in which the ministry is to be exercised.

II. MORE INTENSIVE FOSTERING OF PRIESTLY VOCATIONS

2. The duty of fostering vocations[3] falls on the whole Christian community, and they should discharge it principally by living full Christian lives. The greatest contribution is made by families which are animated by a spirit of faith, charity and piety and which provide, as it were, a first seminary, and by parishes in whose abundant life the young people themselves take an active part. Teachers and all who are in any way involved in the education of boys and young men—and this applies especially to Catholic societies—should endeavor to train the young entrusted to them to recognize a divine vocation and to follow it willingly. All

2. The whole course of priestly training, i.e. the organization of the seminary, spiritual formation, course of studies, the common life and rule of the students, and pastoral practice, should be adapted to local conditions. The general principles of this adaptation should be decided by episcopal conferences for the diocesan clergy and in a similar manner by the competent superiors for religious (cf. the General Statutes attached to the Apostolic Constitution *Sedes Sepientiae*, art. 19).

3. Almost everywhere one of the chief anxieties of the Church today is the dearth of vocations.

Cf. Pius XII, Apostolic Exhortation *Menti Nostrae:* ". . . both in Catholic countries and in mission territories, the number of priests is insufficient to cope with the increasing demands" (*AAS* 42 [1950], p. 682).

John XXIII: "The problem of ecclesiastical and religious vocations is a daily preoccupation with the Pope. . . . Vocations are the object of his prayer, the ardent longing of his soul" (from the Allocution to the First International Congress on Religious Vocations, 16 December 1961: *L'Osservatore Romano,* 17 December 1961).

priests should show their apostolic zeal by fostering vocations as much as possible, and should draw the hearts of young men to the priesthood by the example of their humble, hardworking and happy lives, as well as by their mutual charity and fraternal cooperation.

It is the duty of bishops to encourage their people to foster vocations, and to see that all their energies and undertakings are closely coordinated, sparing themselves no sacrifice in their efforts to help, as fathers, those who in their judgment have been called to God's service.

Such active collaboration by all God's people in the task of fostering vocations is a response to the action of divine Providence, which endows with appropriate qualities and helps with divine grace those who have been chosen by God to share in the hierarchical priesthood of Christ. Divine Providence entrusts to the lawful ministers of the Church the task of judging the suitability of candidates seeking this exalted office with right intention and full liberty, and, after they have been approved, of calling and consecrating them with the seal of the Holy Spirit to the worship of God and the service of the Church.[4]

The Council, first of all, recommends the traditional aids towards this general cooperation, such as: unceasing prayer,[b] Christian penance and progressively more advanced instruction for the faithful, wherein the necessity, nature and excellence of the priestly vocation will be set forth by preaching, catechetics and the various means of social communication. The Council also directs that the organizations for promoting vocations which have been—or are about to be—set up in the various dioceses, regions or countries, in accordance with the relevant pontifical documents, should coordinate and systematize all pastoral work for vocations and develop them with as much discretion as zeal, making full use of the aids provided by modern psychological and sociological teaching.[5]

4. Pius XII, Apost. Const. *Sedes Sapientiae*, 31 May 1956: *AAS* 48 (1956), p. 357. Paul VI, Apost. Letter *Summi Dei Verbum*, 4 November 1963: *AAS* 55 (1963), pp. 984 ff.
b. This could also be rendered "fervent prayer" (*instans oratio*). Several translators have given that rendering.
5. Cf. especially: Pius XII, Motu proprio *Cum nobis*, on the establishment of the Pontifical Work for priestly vocations, 4 November 1941: *AAS* 33 (1941), p. 479; with the attached statutes and rules promulgated by the Sacred Congregation for Seminaries and Universities, 8 September 1943. The Motu proprio *Cum supremae*, on

The work of fostering vocations should be done generously. It should cross the boundaries of individual dioceses, countries, religious congregations and rites and, with the needs of the universal Church in view, should assist especially those areas for which workers are required with special urgency for the Lord's vineyard.

3. In minor seminaries founded to nurture the seeds of vocation, students should be prepared by a special religious formation and, especially, by suitable spiritual direction, to follow Christ the Redeemer with generous souls and pure hearts. Under the fatherly supervision of the superiors, the parents too playing their appropriate part, let them lead lives suited to the age, mentality and development of young people. Their way of life should be fully in keeping with the standards of sound psychology and should include suitable experience of the ordinary affairs of daily life and contact with their own families.[6] Furthermore, all that is laid down in the following paragraphs for major seminaries should be adapted to the minor seminary also as far as is suitable to its purpose and character. Courses of studies should be so arranged that pupils may be able to continue them elsewhere without inconvenience, should they embrace another state of life.

The same care should be taken to foster the seeds of vocations in those special institutes which, in keeping with local conditions, take the place of minor seminaries, and also among boys educated in other schools or according to other systems. Colleges for late vocations and other undertakings for the same purpose should be diligently promoted.

III. MAJOR SEMINARIES

4. Major seminaries are necessary for priestly training. In them the whole training of the students should have as its object to make them true shepherds of souls after the example of our Lord Jesus Christ, teacher, priest and shepherd.[7]

the Pontifical Work for religious vocations, 11 February 1955: *AAS* 47 (1955), p. 266; with the attached statutes and rules promulgated by the Sacred Congregation for Religious (*ibid.*, pp. 298–301); Vatican Council II, Decree on the Renewal of Religious Life, n. 24; Decree on the Pastoral Function of Bishops in the Church, n. 15.
6. Cf. Pius XII, Apostolic Exhortation *Menti Nostrae,* 23 September 1950: *AAS* 42 (1950), p. 685.
7. Cf. Vatican Council II, Dogmatic Constitution *De Ecclesia, n.* 28: *AAS* 57 (1965), p. 34.

Hence, they should be trained for the ministry of the Word, so that they may gain an ever increasing understanding of the revealed Word of God, making it their own by meditation, and giving it expression in their speech and in their lives. They should be trained for the ministry of worship and sanctification, so that by prayer and the celebration of the sacred liturgical functions they may carry on the work of salvation through the eucharistic sacrifice and the sacraments. They should be trained to undertake the ministry of the shepherd, that they may know how to represent Christ to men, Christ who "did not come to have service done to him, but to serve others and to give his life as a ransom for the lives of many" (Mk. 10:45; Jn. 13:12–17), and that they may win over many by becoming the servants of all (1 Cor. 9:19).

Hence, all the elements of their training, spiritual, intellectual, disciplinary, should be coordinated with this pastoral aim in view, and all superiors and teachers should zealously cooperate to carry out this program in loyal obedience to the bishop's authority.

5. The training of students depends not only on wise regulations but also, and especially, on competent educators. Seminary superiors and professors should therefore be chosen from among the best[8] and should receive a careful preparation in sound doctrine, suitable pastoral experience and special training in spirituality and teaching methods. To provide this training, special colleges should be established, or at least suitable courses should be organized, as well as regular meetings of seminary directors.

Superiors and professors should be keenly aware of the extent to which their mental outlook and conduct affects the formation of their students. Under the guidance of the rector they should cultivate the closest harmony of spirit and action, and should form with one another and with the students such a family as corresponds to our divine Lord's

8. Cf. Pius XI, Encycl. Letter *Ad Catholici Sacerdotii*, 20 December 1935: *AAS* 28 (1936), p. 37: "In the first place let careful choice be made of superiors and professors. . . . Give these sacred colleges priests of the greatest virtue, and do not hesitate to withdraw them from tasks which seem indeed to be of greater importance, but which cannot be compared with this supremely important matter, the place of which nothing else can supply." This principle of choosing the best men for the seminaries is again insisted on by Pius XII in his Apostolic Letter to the hierarchy of Brazil, 23 April 1947, *Discorsi e Radiomessaggi* IX, pp. 579–580.

prayer: "that they may be one" (cf. Jn. 17:11), and quickens in the students' hearts a sense of joy in their vocation. The bishop with his constant and affectionate interest should encourage those engaged in seminary work and show himself a true father in Christ to the students. Furthermore, all priests should regard the seminary as the very heart of the diocese and give it their willing support.[9]

6. Each candidate should be subjected to vigilant and careful enquiry, keeping in mind his age and development, concerning his right intention and freedom of choice, his spiritual, moral and intellectual fitness, adequate physical and mental health, and possible hereditary traits. Account should also be taken of the candidate's capacity for undertaking the obligations of the priesthood and carrying out his pastoral duties.[10]

Notwithstanding the regrettable shortage of priests,[11] due strictness should always be brought to bear on the choice and testing of students. God will not allow his Church to lack ministers if the worthy are promoted and those who are not suited to the ministry are guided with fatherly kindness and in due time to adopt another calling. These should be directed in such a way that, conscious of their Christian vocation, they will zealously engage in the lay apostolate.

7. Where individual dioceses are unable to provide adequate separate seminaries out of their own resources, common seminaries should be established and maintained. These common seminaries could meet the needs of a group of dioceses or of an entire region or nation. By their means better provision will be made for the solid training of the students, which is of paramount importance in this matter. These seminaries, regional or national, are to be controlled

9. With regard to this general duty of priests to give their support to seminaries, see Paul VI, Apostolic Letter *Summi Dei Verbum*, 4 November 1963: *AAS* 53 (1963), p. 984.
10. Cf. Pius XII, Apost. Exhortation *Menti Nostrae*, 23 September 1950. *AAS* 42 (1950), p. 684; cf. also the Sacred Congregation for the Sacraments, circular letter *Magna equidem* to Bishops, 27 December 1935, n. 10. For religious cf. the General Statutes attached to the Apostolic Constitution *Sedes Sapientiae*, 31 May 1956, art. 33. Paul VI, Apostolic Letter *Summi Dei Verbum*, 4 November 1963: *AAS* 55 (1963), pp. 987 f.
11. Cf. Pius XI, Encycl. Letter *Ad Catholici Sacerdotii*, 20 December 1935: *AAS* 28 (1936), p. 41.

according to regulations drawn up by the bishops concerned,[12] and approved by the Holy See.

In large seminaries, the students should be suitably organized in smaller groups, to enable more personal attention to be given to each student, while retaining unity of discipline and scientific training.

IV. GREATER ATTENTION TO SPIRITUAL TRAINING

8. Spiritual formation should be closely associated with doctrinal and pastoral formation, and, with the assistance of the spiritual director in particular,[13] should be conducted in such a way that the students may learn to live in intimate and unceasing union with God the Father through his Son Jesus Christ, in the Holy Spirit. Those who are to take on the likeness of Christ the priest by sacred ordination should form the habit of drawing close to him as friends in every detail of their lives.[14] They should live his Paschal Mystery in such a way that they will know how to initiate into it the people committed to their charge. They should be taught to seek Christ in faithful meditation on the Word of God and in active participation in the sacred mysteries of the Church, especially the Eucharist and the Divine Office,[15] to seek him in the bishop by whom they are sent and in the people to whom they are sent, especially the poor, little children, the weak, sinners and unbelievers.

---

12. It is decreed that in drawing up the statutes of regional or national seminaries, all bishops concerned will take part, setting aside canon 1357, par. 4, of the Code of Canon Law.

13. Cf. Pius XII, Apost. Exhortation *Menti Nostrae,* 23 September 1950: *AAS* 42 (1950), p. 674; Sacred Congregation of Seminaries and Universities, *La Formazione spirituale del candidato al sacerdozio,* Vatican City, 1965.

14. Cf. St. Pius X, Exhortation to the Catholic clergy, *Haerent animo,* 4 August 1908: *St. Pii X Acta,* IV, pp 242–244; Pius XII, Apost. Exhort. *Menti Nostrae,* 23 September 1950: *AAS* 42 (1950), pp. 659–661; John XXIII, Encycl. Letter *Sacerdotii Nostri Primordia,* 1 August 1959: *AAS* 51 (1959), pp. 550 f.

15. Cf. Pius XII, Encycl. Letter *Mediator Dei,* 20 November 1947: *AAS* 39 (1947), pp. 547 ff. and 572 f.; John XXIII, Apostolic Exhortation *Sacrae Laudis,* 6 January 1962: *AAS* 54 (1962), p. 69; Vatican Council II, Const. *De Sacra Liturgia,* art. 16 and 17: *AAS* 56 (1964), p. 104 f.; Sacred Congregation of Rites, *Instructio ad exsecutionem Constitutionis de Sacra Liturgia recte ordinandam,* 26 September 1964, nn 14–17: *AAS* 56 (1964), pp. 880 f.

With the confidence of sons they should love and reverence the most blessed virgin Mary, who was given as a mother to the disciples by Jesus Christ as he was dying on the cross.

The exercises of piety which are commended by the venerable practice of the Church should be strongly encouraged, but care must be taken that spiritual formation does not consist in these alone, nor develop religious sentiment, merely. The students should learn, rather, to live according to the standard of the Gospel, to be firmly established in faith, hope and charity, so that the practice of these virtues may develop in them a spirit of prayer,[16] may strengthen and protect their vocation and invigorate their other virtues, intensifying their zeal for winning all men to Christ.

9. The students should be thoroughly penetrated with a sense of the Mystery of the Church, which this holy Council has set particularly in relief. Their sense of the Church will find expression in a humble and filial attachment to the Vicar of Christ and, after ordination, in their loyal cooperation with the bishop, in harmony with their fellow-priests. By this means they will bear witness to that unity which draws men to Christ.[17] They should learn to participate with enthusiasm in the life of the Church as a whole, keeping in mind the words of St. Augustine: "A man possesses the Holy Spirit in the measure in which he loves the Church."[18] Students must clearly understand that it is not their lot in life to lord it over others and enjoy honors, but to devote themselves completely to the service of God and the pastoral ministry. With special care they should be so trained in priestly obedience, poverty and a spirit of self-denial,[19] that they may accustom themselves to living in conformity with the crucified Christ and to giving up willingly even those things which are lawful, but not expedient.

Students should be informed of the obligations which they are undertaking, and no difficulty of the priestly life

16. Cf. John XXIII, Encycl. Letter *Sacerdotii Nostri Primordia: AAS* 51 (1959), pp. 559 f.
17. Cf. Vatican Council II, Dogmatic Constitution *De Ecclesia*, n. 28: *AAS* 57 (1965), pp. 35 f.
18. St. Augustine, *In Ioannem tract.* 32, 8: *PL* 35, 1646.
19. Cf. Pius XII, Apostolic Exhortation *Menti Nostrae: AAS* 42 (1950), pp. 626 f., 685, 690; John XXIII, Encycl. Letter *Sacerdotii Nostri Primordia: AAS* 51 (1959), pp. 551–553, 556 f.; Paul VI, Encycl. Letter *Ecclesiam suam,* 6 August 1964: *AAS* 56 (1964), pp. 634 f.; Vatican Council II, Dogmatic Constitution *De Ecclesia*, especially n. 8: *AAS* 57 (1965), p. 12.

should be concealed from them. They should not, however, be almost completely taken up with the element of danger in their future apostolate, but should rather be trained to strengthen their spiritual life as fully as possible in the very exercise of their pastoral activity.

10. Students who follow the venerable tradition of priestly celibacy as laid down by the holy and permanent regulations of their own rite should be very carefully trained for this state. In it they renounce marriage for the sake of the kingdom of heaven (cf. Mt. 19:12) and hold fast to their Lord with that undivided love[20] which is profoundly in harmony with the New Covenant; they bear witness to the resurrection in a future life (cf. Lk. 20:36)[21] and obtain the most useful assistance towards the constant exercise of that perfect charity by which they can become all things to all men in their priestly ministry.[22] They should keenly realize with what a sense of gratitude they should embrace this state, not only as a precept of ecclesiastical law, but as a precious gift of God which they should ask for humbly and to which they should hasten to respond freely and generously, under the inspiration and with the assistance of the Holy Spirit.

Students should have a proper knowledge of the duties and dignity of Christian marriage, which represents the love which exists between Christ and the Church (cf. Eph. 5:32). They should recognize the greater excellence of virginity consecrated to Christ,[23] however, so that they may offer themselves to the Lord with fully deliberate and generous choice, and a complete surrender of body and soul.

They should be put on their guard against the dangers which threaten their chastity, especially in present-day society.[24] They should learn how, with suitable natural and supernatural safeguards, to weave their renunciation of marriage into the pattern of their lives, so that not only will their daily conduct and activities suffer no harm from celi-

---

20. Cf. Pius XII, Encycl. Letter *Sacra Virginitas*, 25 March 1954: *AAS* 46 (1954), pp. 165 ff.
21. Cf. St. Cyprian, *De habitu virginum*, 22: *PL* 4, 475; St. Ambrose, *De virginibus*, I, 8, 52: *PL* 16, 202 f.
22. Cf. Pius XII, Apostolic Exhortation *Menti Nostrae: AAS* 42 (1950), p. 663.
23. Cf. Pius XII, Encycl. Letter *Sacra Virginitas*, *loc. cit.*, pp. 170–174.
24. Cf. Pius XII, Apostolic Exhortation *Menti Nostrae, loc. cit.*, pp. 664 and 690 f.

bacy, but they themselves will acquire greater mastery of mind and body, will grow in maturity and receive greater measure of the blessedness promised by the Gospel.

11. The standards of Christian education should be faithfully maintained and they should be supplemented by the lastest findings of sound psychology and pedagogy. A prudent system of training will therefore aim at developing in the students a proper degree of human maturity. This will be chiefly attested by a certain stability of character, the ability to make carefully weighed decisions, and a sound judgment of events and people. The students should learn self-control,[c] develop strength of character, and in general value those good qualities which are esteemed by men and made Christ's minister acceptable.[25] Such qualities are sincerity, a constant love of justice, fidelity to one's promises, courtesy in deed, modesty and charity in speech.

The discipline of seminary life should be regarded not only as a strong protection for community life and charity, but as a necessary part of the complete system of training. Its purpose is to inculcate self-control, to promote solid maturity of personality and the formation of those other traits of character which are most useful for the ordered and fruitful activity of the Church. But it should be applied in such a way as to develop in the students a readiness to accept the authority of superiors out of deep conviction—because of the dictates of their conscience, that is to say (cf. Rom. 13:5)—and for supernatural reasons. Standards of discipline should be applied with due regard for the age of the students, so that while they gradually acquire self-mastery, they will at the same time form the habit of using

c. The Latin of the phrase is: '*Alumni propriam indolem recte componere assuescant*'. Translators seem divided as to what exactly it means. Some take it, as we have done, to refer to self-control—thus, the translation published in French by Editions du Cerf: '*Que les seminaristes prennent l'habitude de dominer leur tempérament*'. Others, however, take it to refer to the development of their abilities by the students—thus, the translation edited by Father Walter M. Abbott, s.J. (*The Documents of Vatican II*): 'They should be practised in an intellegent organization of their proper talents' and that published by the English Catholic Truth Society: 'The students should know how to make the most of their own abilities', and the Italian translation published by the *L'Osservatore Romano*: '*Gli alunni si abituino a perfezionare come si deve la propria indole*'.
25. Cf. Paul VI, Apostolic Letter *Summi Dei Verbum*, 4 November 1963: *AAS* 55 (1963), p. 991.

their freedom with discretion, of acting on their own initiative and energetically,[26] and of working harmoniously with their confreres and with the laity.

The whole program of the seminary should be so organized that, with its atmosphere of piety and silence and its concern for mutual cooperation, it should already be an initiation to the students' future lives as priests.

12. To provide a more solid foundation for the students' spiritual formation, and enable them to decide upon their vocation with full deliberation, it will rest with the bishops to set apart a suitable interval of time for a more intensive spiritual preparation. It is for them also to consider carefully the advantage of arranging some interruption of studies, or of providing suitable training in pastoral work, so that better provision can be made for testing the fitness of candidates for the priesthood. It will be for the bishops likewise, keeping in mind the special conditions of each country, to determine if the age at present required by the common law for the reception of sacred orders should be raised, and to discuss whether it be opportune to make a ruling that at the end of the theological course students should work for a time as deacons before being raised to the priesthood.

V. THE REVISION OF ECCLESIASTICAL STUDIES

13. Before seminarians commence their specifically ecclesiastical studies, they should already have received that literary and scientific education which is a prerequisite to higher studies in their country. In addition they should acquire a knowledge of Latin which will enable them to understand and make use of so many scientific sources and of the documents of the Church.[27] The study of the liturgical language of their own rite should also be considered a necessity and the acquisition of an adequate knowledge of the languages of holy Scripture and Tradition should be warmly encouraged.

14. In the revision of ecclesiastical studies the main object to be kept in mind is a more effective coordination of philosophy and theology so that they supplement one another in revealing to the minds of the students with ever in-

26. Cf. Pius XII, Apostolic Exhortation *Menti Nostrae, loc. cit.*, p. 686.
27. Cf. Paul VI, Apostolic Letter *Summi Dei Verbum, loc. cit.*, p. 993.

creasing clarity the Mystery of Christ, which affects the whole course of human history, exercises an unceasing influence on the Church, and operates mainly through the ministry of the priest.[28]

This vision should be communicated to the students from the very first moment of their training; their ecclesiastical studies, therefore, should begin with an introductory course of appropriate duration. In this course the mystery of salvation should be presented in such a way that the students may understand the meaning, arrangement and pastoral aim of ecclesiastical studies, and may be helped at the same time to make faith the foundation and inner principle of their entire personal lives, and be strengthened in their resolve to accept their vocation with joyful heart and complete personal dedication.

15. Philosophical subjects should be taught in such a way as to lead the students gradually to a solid and consistent knowledge of man, the world and God. The students should rely on that philosophical patrimony which is forever valid,[29] but should also take account of modern philosophical studies, especially those which have greater influence in their own country, as well as recent progress in the sciences. Thus, by correctly understanding the modern mind, students will be prepared to enter into dialogue with their contemporaries.[30]

The history of philosophy should be taught in such a manner that students may grasp the fundamental principles of the various systems, retaining those elements which are proved to be true, while being able to detect and refute those which are false.

The teaching method adopted should stimulate in the students a love of rigourous investigation, observation and demonstration of the truth, as well as an honest recognition of the limits of human knowledge. Careful attention should be paid to the bearing of philosophy on the real problems of life, as well as to the questions which engage the minds of the students. The students themselves should be helped to perceive the connection between philosophical arguments

28. Cf. Vatican Council II, Dogmatic Constitution *De Ecclesia*, nn. 7 and 28: *AAS* 57 (1965), pp. 9–11, 33 f.
29. Cf. Pius XII, Encycl. Letter *Humani Generis*, 12 August 1950: *AAS* 42 (1950), pp. 571–575.
30. Cf. Paul VI, Encycl. Letter *Ecclesiam suam*, 6 August 1964: *AAS* 56 (1964), pp. 637 ff.

and the mysteries of salvation which theology considers in the higher light of faith.

16. Theological subjects should be taught in the light of faith, under the guidance of the magisterium of the Church,[31] in such a way that students will draw pure Catholic teaching from divine revelation, will enter deeply into its meaning, make it the nourishment of their spiritual life,[32] and learn to proclaim, explain, and defend it in their priestly ministry.

Students should receive a most careful training in holy Scripture, which should be the soul, as it were, of all theology.[33] After a suitable introductory course, they should receive an accurate initiation in exegetical method. They should study closely the principal themes of divine revelation and should find inspiration and nourishment in daily reading and meditation upon the sacred books.[34]

The following order should be observed in the treatment of dogmatic theology: biblical themes should have first place; then students should be shown what the Fathers of the Church, both of the East and West, have contributed towards the faithful transmission and elucidation of each of the revealed truths; then the later history of dogma, including its relation to the general history of the Church;[35] lastly, in order to throw as full a light as possible on the mysteries of salvation, the students should learn to examine more deeply, with the help of speculation and with St.

---

31. Cf. Pius XII, Encycl. Letter *Humani Generis: AAS* 42 (1950), pp. 567–569; Allocution *Si diligis,* 31 May 1954: *AAS* 46 (1954), pp. 314 f.; Paul VI, Allocution in the Pontifical Gregorian University, 12 March 1964: *AAS* 56 (1964), pp. 364 f.; Vatican Council II, Dogmatic Constitution *De Ecclesia,* n. 25: *AAS* 57 (1965), pp. 29–31.
32. Cf. St. Bonaventure, *Itinerarium mentis in Deum,* Prol., n. 4: "Let no one think he will find sufficiency in a reading which lacks unction, an enquiry which lacks devotion, a search which arouses no wonder, a survey without enthusiasm, industry without piety, knowledge without love, intelligence without humility, application without grace, contemplation without wisdom inspired by God" (St. Bonaventure, *Opera Omnia,* V, Quaracchi 1891, p. 296).
33. Cf. Leo XIII, Encycl. *Providentissimus Deus,* 18 November 1893: *AAS* 26 (1893–94), p. 283.
34. Cf. Pontifical Biblical Commission, *Instructio de Sacra Scriptura recte docenda,* 13 May 1950: *AAS* 42 (1950), p. 502.
35. Cf. Pius XII, Encycl. Letter *Humani Generis,* 12 August 1950: *AAS* 42 (1950), p. 568 f.: "The sacred sciences are being constantly rejuvenated by the study of their sacred sources, while on the other hand that speculation which neglects the deeper examination of the sacred deposit becomes sterile, as we know from experience."

Thomas as teacher, all aspects of these mysteries, and to perceive their interconnection.[36] They should be taught at all times in the ceremonies of the liturgy,[37] and in the whole life of the Church. They should learn to seek the solution of human problems in the light of revelation, to apply its eternal truths to the changing conditions of human affairs, and to express them in language which people of the modern world will understand.[38]

In like manner the other theological subjects should be renewed through a more vivid contact with the Mystery of Christ and the history of salvation. Special care should be given to the perfecting of moral theology. Its scientific presentation should draw more fully on the teaching of holy Scripture and should throw light upon the exalted vocation of the faithful in Christ and their obligation to bring forth fruit in charity for the life of the world. In the same way the teaching of canon law and Church history should take into account the mystery of the Church, as it was set forth in the Dogmatic Constitution *De Ecclesia*, promulgated by this Council. Sacred liturgy, which is to be regarded as the first and indispensable source of the true Christian spirit, should be taught as prescribed in articles 15 and 16 of the Constitution on Sacred Liturgy.[39]

With due regard to the conditions of different countries,

36. Cf. Pius XII, Address to Seminarians, 24 June 1939: *AAS* 31 (1939), p. 247: "Emulation in seeking and propagating the truth is not suppressed, but is rather stimulated and given its true direction by commending the teaching of St. Thomas." Paul VI, Address in Gregorian Univ ersity, 12 March 1964: *AAS* 56 (1964), p. 365: "Let (teachers) listen with respect to the Doctors of the Church, among whom St. Thomas Aquinas holds the principal place. For so great is the power of the angelic Doctor's genius, so sincere his love of truth, and so great his wisdom in investigating the deepest truths, in illustrating them, and linking them together with a most fitting bond of unity, that his teaching is a most efficacious instrument not only for safeguarding the foundations of the faith, but also in gaining the fruits of healthy progress with profit and security." Cf. also his Allocution to the Sixth International Thomistic Congress, 10 September 1965.
37. Cf. Vatican Council II, Const. *De Sacra Liturgia*, nn. 7 and 16: *AAS* 56 (1964), pp. 100 f. and 104 f.
38. Cf. Paul VI, Encycl. Letter *Ecclesiam suam*, 6 August 1964: *AAS* 56 (1964), p. 640 f.
39. Cf. Vatican Council II, Const. *De Sacra Liturgia*, nn. 10, 14, 15, 16; Sacred Congregation of Rites, *Instructio ad exsecutionem Constitutionis de Sacra Liturgia recte ordinandam*, 26 September 1964, nn. 11 and 12: *AAS* 56 (1964), p. 879 f.

students should be introduced to a fuller knowledge of the Churches and ecclesial communities separated from the Holy See, so that they may be able to take part in promoting the restoration of unity between all Christians according to the decisions of the Council.[40]

40. Cf. Vatican Council II, Decree *De Oecumenismo*, nn. 1, 9, 10: *AAS* 57 (1965), pp. 90 and 98 f.

They should also be introduced to a knowledge of whatever other religions are most commonly encountered in this or that region, so that they may recognize more clearly how much goodness and truth they possess through the Providence of God, and learn how to refute their errors and bring the light of truth to those who are without it.

17. Doctrinal training should not have the mere communication of ideas as its objective, but a genuine and profound formation of the students. Teaching methods, consequently, should be revised. This applies to lectures, discussions and seminars and involves encouraging the students themselves to study, whether privately or in small groups. Great care should be taken to achieve an overall training which is coherent and solid, avoiding over-multiplication of subjects and lectures and omitting problems which have little importance today or which should be left to higher academic studies.

18. It is the bishops' responsibility to send young men of suitable character, virtue and ability to special institutes, faculties or universities, so that the various needs of the apostolate may be met by priests trained to a higher scientific standard in the sacred sciences and in other appropriate subjects. But the spiritual and pastoral training of these young men, especially if they have not yet been raised to the priesthood, should by no means be neglected.

VI. ATTENTION TO STRICTLY PASTORAL TRAINING

19. The pastoral preoccupation which should characterize every feature of the students' training[41] also requires

41. The perfect ideal of the pastor can be seen in the recent documents of the popes dealing specifically with the life, qualities and training of priests, especially:
St. Pius X, Exhortation to the Clergy *Haerent animo*, St. Pii X Acta, IV, pp. 237 ff.;

that they should be carefully instructed in all matters which are especially relevant in the sacred ministry. These are, principally, catechetics, preaching, liturgical worship and the administration of the sacraments, works of charity, their duty to contact those in error and the unbelievers, and other pastoral duties. They should receive precise instruction in the art of directing souls. They will thus be able, first of all, to form all the members of the Church in a Christian life which is fully conscious and apostolic. They will also instill in them a sense of the obligation of fulfilling the duties of their state. With equal solicitude they should learn how to help religious men and women to persevere in the grace of their vocation and to make progress, according to the spirit of their respective institutes.[42]

In general those aptitudes should be cultivated in the students which are most conducive to dialogue amongst men. They include the willingness to listen to others and the capacity to open their hearts in a spirit of charity to the various needs of their fellow men.[43]

20. They should be taught to use correctly the aids provided by pedagogy, psychology and sociology,[44] in keeping with the regulations of ecclesiastical authority. They should also be carefully taught how to inspire and encourage apos-

Pius XI, Encycl. Letter *Ad Catholici Sacerdotii: AAS* 28 (1936), pp. 5 ff.;

Pius XII, Apostolic Exhortation *Menti Nostrae: AAS* 42 (1950), pp. 657 ff.;

John XXIII, Encycl. Letter *Sacerdotii Nostri primordia: AAS* 51 (1959), pp. 545 ff.;

Paul VI, Apostolic Letter *Summi Dei Verbum: AAS* 55 (1963), pp. 979 ff.

Much information about pastoral training is also given in the encyclicals *Mystici Corporis* (1943); *Mediator Dei* (1947); *Evangelii Praecones* (1951); *Sacra Virginitas* (1954); *Musicae Sacrae Disciplina* (1955); *Princeps Pastorum* (1959), and in the Apostolic Constitution *Sedes Sapientiae* (1956) for religious.

Pius XII, John XXIII and Paul VI have often thrown light on the ideal of the good shepherd in their allocutions to seminarians and priests.

42. As regards the importance of that state which is set up by the profession of the evangelical counsels, see the Dogmatic Constitution *De Ecclesia* of the Second Vatican Council, chapter VI: *AAS* 57 (1965), pp. 49–55; Decree on the Renewal of Religious Life.

43. Cf. Paul VI, Encycl. Letter *Ecclesiam suam: AAS* 56 (1964), *passim*, especially pp. 635 f. and 640 ff.

44. Cf. especially John XXIII, Encycl. Letter *Mater et Magistra*, 15 May 1961: *AAS* 53 (1961), pp. 401 ff.

tolic action among the laity,[45] and to promote various and more effective forms of apostolate; and they should be filled with that truly Catholic spirit which habitually looks beyond the boundaries of diocese, country or rite, to meet the needs of the whole Church, being prepared in spirit to preach the Gospel everywhere.[46]

21. Students must learn the art of exercising the apostolate not only in theory but in practice and should be able to act on their own initiative and in cooperation with others. To this end, they should be initiated to pastoral work as a part of their course of studies, and also in holiday time, in suitable undertakings. These enterprises should be carried out methodically and under the direction of experts in pastoral work, according to the prudent judgment of the bishops, taking into account the age of the students and local conditions, and always keeping in mind the outstanding power of supernatural helps.[47]

VII. LATER STUDIES

22. Since priestly training, especially in view of the circumstances of modern society, should be continued and perfected after the completion of the seminary course,[48] it will be the task of episcopal conferences in each country to provide the appropriate means for its continuation. Examples of such means are: pastoral institutes cooperating with certain parishes selected for the purpose, the holding of meetings at stated times, and suitable projects by which the

45. Cf. especially Vatican Council II, Dogmatic Const. *De Ecclesia*, n. 33: *AAS* 57 (1965), p. 39.
46. Cf. Vatican Council II, Dogmatic Const. *De Ecclesia*, n. 17: *AAS* 57 (1965), p. 20 f.
47. Very many papal documents sound a warning against the danger of neglecting the supernatural goal in pastoral activity, and of minimizing the value of supernatural means, at least in practice; see especially the documents recommended in note 41.
48. More recent documents of the Holy See urge that special attention be paid to newly ordained priests. The following are specially recommended:
Pius XII, Motu proprio *Quandoquidem*, 2 April 1949: *AAS* 41 (1949), pp. 165–167; Apostolic Exhortation *Menti Nostrae*, 23 September 1950: *AAS* 42 (1950); Apostolic Constitution (for religious) *Sedes Sapientiae*, 31 May 1956, and the General Statutes attached to it; Address to the priests of the 'Convictus Barcinonensis,' 14 June 1957, *Discorsi e Radiomessaggi*, XIX, pp. 271–273.
Paul VI, address to the priests of the Gian Matteo Giberti Institute, of the diocese of Verona, 11 March 1964.

junior clergy will be gradually introduced to priestly life and apostolic activity in their spiritual, intellectual and pastoral aspects, with opportunities for constant renewal and progress.

CONCLUSION

The Fathers of the Council, continuing the work begun by the Council of Trent, confidently entrust to superiors and professors in seminaries the duty of training Christ's future priests in the spirit of that renewal promoted by the Council itself. At the same time, they most strongly exhort those who are preparing for the sacred ministry to develop a keen awareness that the hopes of the Church and the salvation of souls are being committed to them, and urge them by their joyful acceptance of the regulations in this Decree to bring forth most abundant and lasting fruit.

55

DECLARATION ON CHRISTIAN EDUCATION[a]

Vatican II, *Gravissimum Educationis,* 28 October, 1965

PREFACE

The sacred ecumenical Council has given careful consideration to the paramount importance of education in the life of men and its ever-growing influence on the social progress of the age.[1] In fact the education of youth, and indeed a certain continuing education of adults, have been rendered both easier and more necessary by the circumstances of our times. For men, as they become more conscious of their own dignity and responsibility, are eager to take an ever more active role in social life and especially in the economic and political spheres.[2] The wonderful progress in technical skill and scientific enquiry and the new means of social communication give men the opportunity of enjoying more leisure—and many of them take advantage of it—and of availing themselves of their birthright of culture of mind and spirit and of finding fulfilment in closer

a Translated by Matthew Dillon, O.S.B.
1. Among many documents, see especially: Benedict XV, Apost. Letter *Communes Litteras,* 10 April 1919: *AAS* 11 (1919) p. 172; Pius XI, Encycl. Letter *Divini Illius Magistri,* 31 Dec. 1929: *AAS* 22 (1930) pp. 49–86; Pius XII, *Allocutio* to youths of Ital. Cath. Action, 20 April 1946: Cf. *Discorsi e Radiomessaggi,* vol. 8, pp. 53–57; Pius XII, *Allocutio* to fathers of Families of France, 18 Sept. 1951: *Discorsi et Radiomessaggi,* vol. 13, pp. 241–245; John XXIII, message on 30th anniv. of *Divini Illius Magistri,* 30 Dec. 1959: *AAS* 52 (1960) pp. 57–59; Paul VI, *Allocutio* to Fed. Instits., 30 Dec. 1963: *Encicliche e Discorsi de Paulo VI,* vol. I, Rome 1964, pp. 601–603; there may be consulted also *Acta et Documenta Conc. Cecum. Vat. II apprando,* series I, *Antepraeparatoria,* vol. 3, pp. 363–364, 370–371, 373, 374.
2. Cf. John XXIII, Encycl. *Mater et Magistra,* 15 May 1961: *AAS* 53 (1961) p. 402, 413, 415–417, 424; and Encycl. *Pacem in terris,* 11 April 1963: *AAS* 55 (1963) pp. 278 ff.

relations both with other groups and even other nations.
Accordingly, efforts are being made everywhere to ensure
an ever increasing development of education. The fundamental rights in regard to the education of men, and especially of children and of parents, are being enunciated and
made a matter of public record.[3] As the number of pupils
is rapidly increasing, schools are being established far and
wide, and other scholastic institutions are being opened.
Methods of education and instruction are being developed
by new experiments, and great efforts are being made to
provide these services for all men, although many children
and young people are still without even elementary education, and many others are deprived of a suitable education
—one inculcating simultaneously truth and charity.

For her part Holy Mother Church, in order to fulfil the
mandate she received from her divine founder to announce
the mystery of salvation to all men and to renew all things
in Christ, is under an obligation to promote the welfare of
the whole life of man, including his life in this world insofar as it is related to his heavenly vocation;[4] she has therefore a part to play in the development and extension of education. Accordingly the sacred Synod hereby promulgates
some fundamental principles concerning Christian education, especially in regard to schools. These principles should
be more fully developed by a special postconciliar commission and should be adapted to the different local circumstances by episcopal conferences.

1. All men of whatever race, condition or age, in virtue
of their dignity as human persons, have an inalienable right
to education.[5] This education should be suitable to the particular destiny of the individuals,[6] adapted to their ability,
sex and national cultural traditions, and should be condu-

3. Cf. *United Nations' Universal Profession of the Rights of Man,* 10
Dec. 1948; and, in conjunction, John XXIII, Encycl. *Pacem in
Terris,* 11 April 1963: *AAS* 55 (1963) pp. 295 ff; also *UN Declaration on the Rights of the Child,* 20 Nov. 1959; also *Protocole
additionnel à la convention de sauvegarde des droits de l'homme et
des libertés fondamentales,* Paris, 20 March 1952.
4. Cf. John XXIII, Encycl. *Mater et Magistra,* 15 May 1961: *AAS* 53
(1961) p. 402; also VAT. II, Dogm. Const. on the Church, n. 17:
AAS 57 (1965) p. 21.
5. Cf. Pius XII, Radio message 24 Dec. 1924: *AAS* 35 (1943) pp. 12,
19; John XXIII, Encycl. *Pacem in Terris,* 11 Apr. 1963: *AAS* 55
(1963) p. 259 ff.; also cf. declarations in note (3) above.
6. Cf. Pius XI, Encycl. *Divini Illius Magistri,* 31 Dec. 1929: *AAS* 22
(1930) p. 50 ff.

cive to fraternal relations with other nations in order to promote true unity and peace in the world. True education is directed towards the formation of the human person in view of his final end and the good of that society to which he belongs and in the duties of which he will, as an adult, have a share.

Due weight being given to the advances in psychological, pedagogical and intellectual sciences, children and young people should be helped to develop harmoniously their physical, moral and intellectual qualities. They should be trained to acquire gradually a more perfect sense of responsibility in the proper development of their own lives by constant effort and in the pursuit of liberty, overcoming obstacles with unwavering courage and perseverance. As they grow older they should receive a positive and prudent education in matters relating to sex. Moreover, they should be so prepared to take their part in the life of society that, having been duly trained in the necessary and useful skills, they may be able to participate actively in the life of society in its various aspects. They should be open to dialogue with others and should willingly devote themselves to the promotion of the common good.

Similarly the sacred Synod affirms that children and young people have the right to be stimulated to make sound moral judgments based on a well-formed conscience and to put them into practice with a sense of personal commitment, and to know and love God more perfectly. Accordingly, it earnestly requests all those who are in charge of civil administration or in control of education to make it their care to ensure that young people are never deprived of this sacred right. It therefore exhorts the sons of the Church to assist in a spirit of generosity in the whole field of education, especially with the aim of extending more rapidly the benefits of suitable education and instruction throughout the world.[7]

2. All Christians—that is, all those who having been reborn in water and the Holy Spirit[8] are called and in fact are children of God—have a right to a Christian education. Such an education not only develops the maturity of the human person in the way we have described, but is espe-

---

7. Cf. John XXIII, Encycl. *Mater et Magistra*, 15 May 1961; *AAS* 53 (1961) p. 441 ff.
8. Cf. Pius XI, Encycl. *Divini Illius Magistri, loc. cit.*, p. 83.

cially directed towards ensuring that those who have been baptized, as they are gradually introduced to a knowledge of the mystery of salvation, become daily more appreciative of the gift of faith which they have received. They should learn to adore God the Father in spirit and in truth (Jn. 4:23), especially through the liturgy. They should be trained to live their own lives in the new self, justified and sanctified through the truth (Eph. 4:22–24). Thus they should come to true manhood, which is proportioned to the completed growth of Christ (cf. Eph. 4:13), and make their contribution to the growth of the Mystical Body. Moreover, conscious of their vocation they should learn to give witness to the hope that is in them (cf. 1 Pet. 3:15) and to promote the Christian concept of the world whereby the natural values, assimilated into the full understanding of man redeemed by Christ, may contribute to the good of society as a whole.[9] Accordingly the sacred Synod directs the attention of pastors of souls to their very grave obligation to do all in their power to ensure that this Christian education is enjoyed by all the faithful and especially by the young who are the hope of the church.[10]

3. As it is the parents who have given life to their children, on them lies the gravest obligation of educating their family.[11] They must therefore be recognized as being primarily and principally responsible for their education. The role of parents in education is of such importance that it is almost impossible to provide an adequate substitute. It is therefore the duty of parents to create a family atmosphere inspired by love and devotion to God and their fellow-men which will promote an integrated, personal and social education of their children. The family is therefore the principal school of the social virtues which are necessary to every society. It is therefore above all in the Christian family, inspired by the grace and the responsibility of the sacrament of matrimony, that children should be taught to know and worship God and to love their neighbor, in accordance with the faith which they have received in earliest infancy in the

9. Cf. VAT. II Dogm. Const. on the Church, n. 36: *AAS* 57 (1965) p. 41 ff.
10. Cf. VAT. II, Decree on Pastoral Function of Bishops, n. 12–14.
11. Cf. Pius XI, Encycl. *Divini Illius Magistri, loc. cit.,* p. 50 ff.; encycl. *Mit brennender Sorge,* 14 March 1937: *AAS* 29 (1937) p. 164 ff.; also Pius XII, *Allocutio* to Ital. Cath. Teachers, 8 Sept. 1946: *Discorsi e Radiomessaggi,* vol. 8, p. 218.

sacrament of Baptism. In it, also, they will have their first experience of a well-balanced human society and of the Church. Finally it is through the family that they are gradually initiated into association with their fellow-men in civil life and as members of the people of God. Parents should, therefore, appreciate how important a role the truly Christian family plays in the life and progress of the whole people of God.[12]

The task of imparting education belongs primarily to the family, but it requires the help of society as a whole. As well as the rights of parents, and of those others to whom the parents entrust some share in their duty to educate, there are certain duties and rights vested in civil society inasmuch as it is its function to provide for the common good in temporal matters. It is its duty to promote the education of youth in various ways. It should recognize the duties and rights of parents, and of those others who play a part in education, and provide them with the requisite assistance. In accordance with the principle of subsidiarity, when the efforts of the parents and of other organizations are inadequate it should itself undertake the duty of education, with due consideration, however, for the wishes of the parents. Finally, insofar as the common good requires it, it should establish its own schools and institutes.[13]

Education is, in a very special way, the concern of the Church, not only because the Church must be recognized as a human society capable of imparting education, but especially it has the duty of proclaiming the way of salvation to all men, of revealing the life of Christ to those who believe, and of assisting them with unremitting care so that they may be able to attain to the fulness of that life.[14]

The Church as a mother is under an obligation, therefore, to provide for its children an education by virtue of which their whole lives may be inspired by the spirit of

12. Cf. VAT. II, Dogm. Const. on the Church, n. 11, 35: *AAS* 57 (1965) pp. 16, 40 ff.

13. Cf. Pius XI, Encycl. *Divini Illius Magistri, loc. cit.* p. 63 ff.; Pius XII, Radio Message 1 June 1941: *AAS* 33 (1941) p. 200; *Allocutio* to Cath. Teachers, 8 Sept. 1946: *Discorsi e Radiomessaggi*, vol. 8, p. 218; re principle of subsidiarity, cf. John XXIII, Encycl. *Pacem in Terris*, 11 April 1963: *AAS* 44 (1963) p. 294.

14. Cf. Pius XI, Encycl. *Divini Illius Magistri, loc. cit.* p. 53 ff. and 56 ff., also Encycl. *Non abbiamo bisogno*, 29 June 1931: *AAS* 23 (1931) p. 311 ff.; Pius XII, Letter to Italian Social Week, 20 Sept. 1955: *L'Osservatore Romano*, 29 Sept. 1955.

Christ. At the same time it will offer its assistance to all peoples for the promotion of a well-balanced perfection of the human personality, for the good of society in this world and for the development of a world more worthy of man.[15]

4. In the exercise of its functions in education the Church is appreciative of every means that may be of service, but it relies especially on those which are essentially its own. Chief among these is catechetical instruction,[16] which illumines and strengthens the faith, develops a life in harmony with the spirit of Christ, stimulates a conscious and fervent participation in the liturgical mystery[17] and encourages men to take an active part in the apostolate. The Church values highly those other educational media which belong to the common patrimony of men and which make a valuable contribution to the development of character and to the formation of men. These it seeks to ennoble by imbuing them with its own spirit. Such are the media of social communication,[18] different groups devoted to the training of mind and body, youth associations, and especially schools.

5. Among the various organs of education the school is of outstanding importance.[19] In nurturing the intellectual faculties which is its special mission, it develops a capacity for sound judgment and introduces the pupils to the cultural heritage bequeathed to them by former generations. It fosters a sense of values and prepares them for professional life. By providing for friendly contacts between pupils of different characters and backgrounds it encourages mutual understanding. Furthermore it constitutes a center in whose activity and growth not only the families and teachers but

15. The Church praises civil authorities—civil, national and international—who, through an awareness of the urgent needs of the present age, work indefatigably so that all people may enjoy a fuller education and human culture. Cf. Paul VI, Allocutio to U.N. Assembly, 4 Oct. 1965: AAS 57 (1965) pp. 877–885.
16. Cf. Pius XI, Motu Proprio Orbem Catholicum, 29 June 1923: AAS 15 (1923) pp. 327–329; Decree Provido sane, 12 Jan. 1935: AAS 27 (1935) pp. 145–152; VAT. II, Decree on the Pastoral Function of Bishops in the Church, nn. 13–14.
17. Cf. VAT. II, Const. on the Sacred Liturgy, n. 14: AAS 56 (1964) p. 104.
18. Cf. VAT. II, Decree on the Means of Social Communication, nn. 13–14: AAS 56 (1964) pp. 149 ff.
19. Cf. Pius XI, Encycl. Divini Illius Magistri, loc. cit. p. 76; Pius XII, Allocutio to Assoc. of Cath. Teachers of Bavaria, 31 Dec. 1956: Discorsi e Radiomessaggi, vol. 18, p. 746.

also the various associations for the promotion of cultural, civil and religious life, civic society, and the entire community should take part.

Splendid, therefore, and of the highest importance is the vocation of those who help parents in carrying out their duties and act in the name of the community by undertaking a teaching career. This vocation requires special qualities of mind and heart, most careful preparation and a constant readiness to accept new ideas and to adapt the old.

6. Parents, who have a primary and inalienable duty and right in regard to the education of their children, should enjoy the fullest liberty in their choice of school. The public authority, therefore, whose duty it is to protect and defend the liberty of the citizens, is bound according to the principles of distributive justice to ensure that public subsidies to schools are so allocated that parents are truly free to select schools for their children in accordance with their conscience.[20]

But it is the duty of the state to ensure that all its citizens have access to an adequate education and are prepared for the proper exercise of their civic rights and duties. The state itself, therefore, should safeguard the rights of children to an adequate education in schools. It should be vigilant about the ability of the teachers and the standard of teaching. It should watch over the health of the pupils and in general promote the work of the schools in its entirety. In this, however, the principle of subsidiarity must be borne in mind, and therefore there must be no monopoly of schools which would be prejudicial to the natural rights of the human person and would militate against the progress and extension of education, and the peaceful coexistence of citizens. It would, moreover, be inconsistent with the pluralism which exists today in many societies.[21]

Accordingly the sacred Synod urges the faithful to cooperate readily in the development of suitable methods of education and systems of study and in the training of teachers competent to give a good education to their pupils.

20. Cf. III Prov. Council of Cincinnati (1861); Pius XI, Encycl. *Divini Illius Magistri, loc. cit.,* p. 60, 63 ff.
21. Cf. Pius XI, Encycl. *Divini Illius Magistri, loc. cit.* p. 63; also Encycl. *Non abbiamo bisogno,* 29 June 1931: *AAS* 23 (1931) p. 305; also Pius XII, Letter to 28th Ital. Social Week, 20 Sept. 1955; *L'Osservatore Romano,* 29 Sept. 1955; also Paul VI *Allocutio* to Chr. Assoc. of Ital. Workers, 6 Oct. 1963: *Encicliche e Discorsi di Paolo VI,* vol. 1, Rome, 1964, p. 230.

They are urged also to further by their efforts, and especially by associations of parents, the entire activity of the
schools and in particular the moral education given in
them.[22]

7. Acknowledging its grave obligation to see to the moral
and religious education of all its children, the Church
should give special attention and help to the great number
of them who are being taught in non-Catholic schools. This
will be done by the living example of those who teach and
have charge of these children and by the apostolic action of
their fellow-students,[23] but especially by the efforts of
those priests and laymen who teach them Christian doctrine
in a manner suited to their age and background and who
provide them with spiritual help by means of various activities adapted to the requirements of time and circumstance.

Parents are reminded of their grave obligation to make
all necessary arrangements and even to insist that their children may be able to take advantage of these services and
thus enjoy a balanced progress in their Christian formation
and their preparation for life in the world. For this reason
the Church is deeply grateful to those public authorities
and associations which, taking into consideration the pluralism of contemporary society, and showing due respect for
religious liberty, assist families to ensure that the education
of their children in all schools is given in accordance with
the moral and religious principles of the family.[24]

8. The Church's role is especially evident in Catholic
schools. These are no less zealous than other schools in the
promotion of culture and in the human formation of young
people. It is, however, the special function of the Catholic
school to develop in the school community an atmosphere
animated by a spirit of liberty and charity based on the
Gospel. It enables young people, while developing their
own personality, to grow at the same time in that new life
which has been given them in baptism. Finally it so orients
the whole of human culture to the message of salvation that
the knowledge which the pupils acquire of the world, of life

22. Cf. John XXIII, Message for 30th Anniv. of *Div. Illius Magistri*,
30 Dec. 1959: *AAS* 52 (1960) p. 57.
23. The Church places a high value upon the apostolic action which
Catholic teachers and those associated with them are able to perform even in these schools.
24. Cf. Pius XII, *Allocutio* to Assoc. of Cath. Teachers of Bavaria,
31 Dec. 1956: *Discorsi e Radiomessaggi*, vol. 18, pp. 745 ff.

and of men is illumined by faith.[25] Thus the Catholic school, taking into consideration as it should the conditions of an age of progress, prepares its pupils to contribute effectively to the welfare of the world of men and to work for the extension of the kingdom of God, so that by living an exemplary and apostolic life they may be, as it were, a saving leaven in the community.

Accordingly, since the Catholic school can be of such service in developing the mission of the People of God and in promoting dialogue between the Church and the community at large to the advantage of both, it is still of vital importance even in our times. The sacred Synod therefore affirms once more the right of the Church freely to establish and conduct schools of all kinds and grades, a right which has already been asserted time and again in many documents of the Magisterium.[26] It emphasizes that the exercise of this right is of the utmost importance for the preservation of liberty of conscience, for the protection of the rights of parents, and for the advancement of culture itself.

Teachers must remember that it depends chiefly on them whether the Catholic school achieves its purpose.[27] They should therefore be prepared for their work with special care, having the appropriate qualifications and adequate learning both religious and secular. They should also be skilled in the art of education in accordance with the discoveries of modern times. Possessed by charity both towards each other and towards their pupils, and inspired by an apostolic spirit, they should bear testimony by their lives and their teaching to the one Teacher, who is Christ. Above all they should work in close cooperation with the parents. In the entire educational program they should, together

25. Cf. First Prov. Council of Westminster (1852), *Collectio* Lacensis, vol. 3, col. 1334, a/b; also Pius XI, Encycl. *Div. Illius Magistri*, loc. cit., pp. 77 ff.; also Pius XII, *Allocutio* to Assoc. of Cath. Teachers of Bavaria, *loc. cit.* p. 746; also Paul VI, *Allocutio* to Federated Institutes, 30 Dec. 1963: *Encicliche e Discorsi di Paolo VI*, vol. 1, Rome, 1964, pp. 602 ff.

26. Cf. most importantly the documents recommended in (1); in addition, this right of the Church is proclaimed by many provincial councils and in the most recent declarations of many episcopal conferences.

27. Cf. Pius XI, Encycl. *Div. Illius Magistri, loc. cit.*, pp. 80 ff.; also Pius XII, *Allocutio* to Ital. Secondary Teachers, 5 Jan. 1954: *Discorsi e Radiomessaggi*, vol. 15, pp. 551–556; also John XXIII, Allocutio to Ital. Assoc. of Cath. Teachers, 5 Sept. 1959: *Discorsi, Messaggi, Colloqui*, vol. 1, Rome, 1960, pp. 427–431.

with the parents, make full allowance for the difference of sex and for the particular role which providence has appointed to each sex in the family and in society. They should strive to awaken in their pupils a spirit of personal initiative and, even after they have left school, they should continue to help them with their advice and friendship and by the organization of special groups imbued with the true spirit of the Chruch. The sacred Synod declares that the services of such teachers constitute an active apostolate, one which is admirably suited to our times and indeed is very necessary. At the same time they render a valuable service to society. Catholic parents are reminded of their duty to send their children to Catholic schools wherever this is possible, to give Catholic schools all the support in their power, and to cooperate with them in their work for the good of their children.[28]

9. Although Catholic schools may assume various forms according to local circumstances, all schools which are in any way dependent on the Church should conform as far as possible to this prototype.[29] Furthermore the Church attaches particular importance to those schools, especially in the territories of newly founded Churches, which include non-Catholics among their pupils.

Moreover, in establishing and conducting Catholic schools one must keep modern developments in mind. Accordingly, while one may not neglect primary and intermediate schools, which provide the basis of education, one should attach considerable importance to those establishments which are particularly necessary nowadays, such as: professional[30] and technical colleges, institutes for adult education and for the promotion of social work, institutions for those who require special care on account of some natural handicap, and training colleges for teachers, of religion and of other branches of education.

The sacred Synod earnestly exhorts the pastors of the Church and all the faithful to spare no sacrifice in helping Catholic schools to become increasingly effective, especially

28. Cf. Pius, *Allocutio* to Ital. Secondary Teachers, 5 Jan. 1954 *loc. cit.* p. 555.
29. Cf. Paul VI, *Allocutio* to Internat. Office of Cath. Education, 25 Feb. 1964: *Encicliche e Discorsi* di Paolo VI, vol. 2, Rome, 1964, p. 232.
30. Cf. Paul VI, *Allocutio* to Ital. Workers, 6 Oct. 1963: *loc. cit.* vol. 1, Rome, 1964, p. 229.

in caring for the poor, for those who are without the help and affection of family, and those who do not have the Faith.

10. The Church likewise devotes considerable care to higher-level education, especially in universities and faculties. Indeed, in the institutions under its control the Church endeavors systematically to ensure that the treatment of the individual disciplines is consonant with their own principles, their own methods, and with a true liberty of scientific enquiry. Its object is that a progressively deeper understanding of them may be achieved, and by a careful attention to the current problems of these changing times and to the research being undertaken, the convergence of faith and reason in the one truth may be seen more clearly. This method follows the tradition of the doctors of the Church and especially St. Thomas Aquinas.[31] Thus the Christian outlook should acquire, as it were, a public, stable and universal influence in the whole process of the promotion of higher culture. The graduates of these institutes should be outstanding in learning, ready to undertake the more responsible duties of society, and to be witnesses in the world to the true faith.[32]

In Catholic universities in which there is no faculty of Sacred Theology there should be an institute or course of theology in which lectures may be given suited also to the needs of lay students. Since the advance of knowledge is secured especially by research into matters of major scientific importance, every effort should be made in Catholic universities and faculties to develop departments for the advancement of scientific research.

The sacred Synod earnestly recommends the establishment of Catholic universities and faculties strategically distributed throughout the world, but they should be noteworthy not so much for their numbers as for their high standards. Entry to them should be made easy for students of

---

31. Cf. Paul VI, *Allocutio* to 6th Internat. Thomistic Congr., 10 Sept. 1965: *AAS* 57 (1965) pp. 788–792.
32. Cf. Pius XII, *Allocutio* to Higher Institutes of France, 21 Sept. 1950: *Discorsi e Radiomessaggi*, vol. 12, pp. 219–221; Letter to 22nd Congr. of *Pax Romana*, 12 Aug. 1952: *loc. cit.*, vol. 14 pp. 567–569; John XXIII, *Allocutio* to Fed. of Cath. Universities, 1 April 1959: *Discorsi, Messaggi, Colloqui*, vol. 1, Roma, 1960, pp. 226–229; Paul VI, *Allocutio* to Acad. Senate of University of Milan, 5 April 1964: *Encicliche e Discorsi di Paolo VI*, vol. 2, Rome, 1964, pp. 438–443.

great promise but of modest resources, and especially for those from newly developed countries.

Since indeed the well-being of society and of the Church herself is intimately related to the development of students pursuing higher studies,[33] the pastors of the Church should not only be assiduous in their care for the spiritual life of students attending Catholic universities but, in their solicitude for the spiritual formation of all their flock, they should provide by joint episcopal action the establishment of Catholic residences and centers even in the non-Catholic universities. In these, priests, religious and laymen, carefully chosen and prepared for the task, should provide permanent centers of guidance, spiritual and intellectual, for the students. Special interest should be taken in young men of outstanding ability, whether they be students of Catholic or other universities, who seem to be suited to teaching or research, and they should be encouraged to adopt an academic career.

11. The Church anticipates great benefits from the activities of the faculties of the sacred sciences.[34] For to them she confides the very grave responsibility of preparing her own students, not only for the priestly ministry, but especially either for teaching in the institutes of higher ecclesiastical study, or for the advancement of learning by their own investigations, or finally by undertaking the even more exacting duties of the intellectual apostolate. It is the function also of these faculties to promote research in the different fields of sacred learning. Their object will be to ensure that an ever-growing understanding of sacred revelation be achieved, that the inheritance of Christian wisdom handed down by former generations be more fully appreciated, that dialogue with our separated brethren and with non-Christians be promoted, and that questions arising from the development of thought be duly solved.[35]

Therefore the ecclesiastical faculties, having made such

33. Cf. Pius XII, *Allocutio* to Acad. Senate of Univ. of Rome, 15 June 1952, *Discorsi e Radiomessaggi*, vol. 14, p. 208: "The direction which society will take tomorrow will be largely decided by the mind and heart of university students of today."
34. Cf. Pius XI, Apost. Constit. *Deus Scientiarum Dominus*, 24 May, 1931: *AAS* 23 (1931) pp. 245–247.
35. Cf. Pius XII, Encycl. *Humani Generis*, 12 Aug. 1950: *AAS* 42 (1950) pp. 568 ff., 578; also Paul VI, Encycl. *Ecclesiam suam*, Part 3, 6 Aug. 1964: *AAS* 56 (1964) pp. 637–659; also VAT. II Decree on Ecumenism: *AAS* 57 (1965) pp. 90–107.

revision of their own statutes as seems opportune, should do all in their power to promote the sacred sciences and related branches of learning, and by the employment of modern methods and aids they should train their students for higher research.

12. As cooperation, which is becoming daily more important and more effective at diocesan, national and international levels, is very necessary also in the educational sphere, every care should be taken to encourage suitable coordination between Catholic schools. Such collaboration between these and other schools as the welfare of the whole community requires should also be developed.[36]

A greater measure of coordination and the undertaking of joint activities will be especially fruitful in the sphere of academic institutes. In every university, therefore, the various faculties should assist each other insofar as their particular provinces permit. The universities also should combine for purposes of joint enterprises, such as organizing international congresses and allotting scientific research among themselves. They should also communicate the results of their research to each other, interchange professors on a temporary basis, and in general promote all measures which may be mutually helpful.

CONCLUSION

The sacred Synod earnestly exhorts the students themselves to appreciate the excellence of the teaching vocation and to show a readiness to undertake it generously, especially in those countries where the education of young people is at risk because of a shortage of teachers.

The sacred Synod furthermore affirms its deep gratitude to those priests, religious, nuns and laity who in a spirit of evangelical dedication have devoted themselves to the all-important work of education and schools of all kinds and grades. It exhorts them to persevere generously in the work they have undertaken, and to strive so to excel in inspiring their pupils with the spirit of Christ, in their mastery of the art of teaching, and in their zeal for learning that they may not only promote the internal renewal of the Church but also maintain and augment its beneficial presence in the world today and especially in the intellectual sphere.

36. Cf. John XXIII, Encycl. *Pacem in Terris*, 11 April 1963: *AAS* 55 (1963) p. 284 and *passim*.

56

DECLARATION ON THE RELATION OF THE CHURCH TO NON-CHRISTIAN RELIGIONS[a]

Vatican II, *Nostra Aetate*, 28 October, 1965

1. In this age of ours, when men are drawing more closely together and the bonds of friendship between different peoples are being strengthened, the Church examines with greater care the relation which she has to non-Christian religions. Ever aware of her duty to foster unity and charity among individuals, and even among nations, she reflects at the outset on what men have in common and what tends to promote fellowship among them.

All men form but one community. This is so because all stem from the one stock which God created to people the entire earth (cf. Acts 17:26), and also because all share a common destiny, namely God. His providence, evident goodness, and saving designs extend to all men (cf. Wis. 8:1; Acts 14:17; Rom. 2:6–7; 1 Tim. 2:4) against the day when the elect are gathered together in the holy city which is illumined by the glory of God, and in whose splendor all peoples will walk(cf. Apoc. 21:23 ff.).

Men look to their different religions for an answer to the unsolved riddles of human existence. The problems that weigh heavily on the hearts of men are the same today as in the ages past. What is man? What is the meaning and purpose of life? What is upright behavior, and what is sinful? Where does suffering originate, and what end does it serve? How can genuine happiness be found? What happens at death? What is judgment? What reward follows death? And finally, what is the ultimate mystery, beyond human explanation, which embraces our entire existence, from which we take our origin and towards which we tend?

2. Throughout history even to the present day, there is

a. Translated by Father Killian, o.c.s.o.

found among different peoples a certain awareness of a hidden power, which lies behind the course of nature and the events of human life. At times there is present even a recognition of a supreme being, or still more of a Father. This awareness and recognition results in a way of life that is imbued with a deep religious sense. The religions which are found in more advanced civilizations endeavor by way of well-defined concepts and exact language to answer these questions. Thus, in Hinduism men explore the divine mystery and express it both in the limitless riches of myth and the accurately defined insights of philosophy. They seek release from the trials of the present life by ascetical practices, profound meditation and recourse to God in confidence and love. Buddhism in its various forms testifies to the essential inadequacy of this changing world. It proposes a way of life by which men can, with confidence and trust, attain a state of perfect liberation and reach supreme illumination either through their own efforts or by the aid of divine help. So, too, other religions which are found throughout the world attempt in their own ways to calm the hearts of men by outlining a program of life covering doctrine, moral precepts and sacred rites.

The Catholic Church rejects nothing of what is true and holy in these religions. She has a high regard for the manner of life and conduct, the precepts and doctrines which, although differing in many ways from her own teaching, nevertheless often reflect a ray of that truth which enlightens all men. Yet she proclaims and is in duty bound to proclaim without fail, Christ who is the way, the truth and the life (Jn. 1:6). In him, in whom God reconciled all things to himself (2 Cor. 5:18–19), men find the fulness of their religious life.

The Church, therefore, urges her sons to enter with prudence and charity into discussion and collaboration with members of other religions. Let Christians, while witnessing to their own faith and way of life, acknowledge, preserve and encourage the spiritual and moral truths found among non-Christians, also their social life and culture.

3. The Church has also a high regard for the Muslims. They worship God, who is one, living and subsistent, merciful and almighty, the Creator of heaven and earth,[1] who

1. Cf. St. Gregory VII, Letter 21 to Anzir (Nacir), King of Mauretania (*PL* 148, col. 450 ff.).

has also spoken to men. They strive to submit themselves without reserve to the hidden decress of God, just as Abraham submitted himself to God's plan, to whose faith Muslims eagerly link their own. Although not acknowledging him as God, they venerate Jesus as a prophet, his virgin Mother they also honor, and even at times devoutly invoke. Further, they await the day of judgment and the reward of God following the resurrection of the dead. For this reason they highly esteem an upright life and worship God, especially by way of prayer, alms-deeds and fasting.

Over the centuries many quarrels and dissensions have arisen between Christians and Muslims. The sacred Council now pleads with all to forget the past, and urges that a sincere effort be made to achieve mutual understanding; for the benefit of all men, let them together preserve and promote peace, liberty, social justice and moral values.

4. Sounding the depths of the mystery which is the Church, this sacred Council remembers the spiritual ties which link the people of the New Covenant to the stock of Abraham.

The Church of Christ acknowledges that in God's plan of salvation the beginning of her faith and election is to be found in the patriarchs, Moses and the prophets. She professes that all Christ's faithful, who as men of faith are sons of Abraham (cf. Gal. 3:7), are included in the same patriarch's call and that the salvation of the Church is mystically prefigured in the exodus of God's chosen people from the land of bondage. On this account the Church cannot forget that she received the revelation of the Old Testament by way of that people with whom God in his inexpressible mercy established the ancient covenant. Nor can she forget that she draws nourishment from that good olive tree onto which the wild olive branches of the Gentiles have been grafted (cf. Rom. 11:17–24). The Church believes that Christ who is our peace has through his cross reconciled Jews and Gentiles and made them one in himself (cf. Eph. 2:14–16).

Likewise, the Church keeps ever before her mind the words of the apostle Paul about his kinsmen: "they are Israelites, and to them belong the sonship, the glory, the covenants, the giving of the law, the worship, and the promises; to them belong the patriarchs, and of their race according to the flesh, is the Christ" (Rom. 9:4–5), the son of the virgin Mary. She is mindful, moreover, that the apostles, the pillars on which the Church stands, are of Jewish descent, as are many of those early disciples who proclaimed the Gospel of Christ to the world.

As holy Scripture testifies, Jerusalem did not recognize God's moment when it came (cf. Lk. 19:42). Jews for the most part did not accept the Gospel; on the contrary, many opposed the spreading of it (cf. Rom. 11:28). Even so, the apostle Paul maintains that the Jews remain very dear to God, for the sake of the patriarchs, since God does not take back the gifts he bestowed or the choice he made.[2] Together with the prophets and that same apostle, the Church awaits the day, known to God alone, when all peoples will call on God with one voice and "serve him shoulder to shoulder" (Soph. 3:9; cf. Is. 66:23; Ps. 65:4; Rom. 11:11–32).

Since Christians and Jews have such a common spiritual heritage, this sacred Council wishes to encourage and further mutual understanding and appreciation. This can be obtained, especially, by way of biblical and theological enquiry and through friendly discussions.

Even though the Jewish authorities and those who followed their lead pressed for the death of Christ (cf. John 19:6), neither all Jews indiscriminately at that time, nor Jews today, can be charged with the crimes committed during his passion. It is true that the Church is the new people of God, yet the Jews should not be spoken of as rejected or accursed as if this followed from holy Scripture. Consequently, all must take care, lest in catechizing or in preaching the Word of God, they teach anything which is not in accord with the truth of the Gospel message or the spirit of Christ.

Indeed, the Church reproves every form of persecution against whomsoever it may be directed. Remembering, then, her common heritage with the Jews and moved not by any political consideration, but solely by the religious motivation of Christian charity, she deplores all hatreds, persecutions, displays of antisemitism leveled at any time or from any source against the Jews.[b]

The Church always held and continues to hold that Christ out of infinite love freely underwent suffering and

2. Cf. Rom. 11:28–29; cf. Dogm. Const. *Lumen Gentium* (*AAS* 57, 1965, 20.
[b] See D. 57.

death because of the sins of all men, so that all might attain salvation. It is the duty of the Church, therefore, in her preaching to proclaim the cross of Christ as the sign of God's universal love and the source of all grace.

5. We cannot truly pray to God the Father of all if we treat any people in other than brotherly fashion, for all men are created in God's image. Man's relation to God the Father and man's relation to his fellow-men are so dependent on each other that the Scripture says "he who does not love, does not know God" (1 Jn. 4:8).

There is no basis therefore, either in theory or in practice for any discrimination between individual and individual, or between people and people arising either from human dignity or from the rights which flow from it.

Therefore, the Church reproves, as foreign to the mind of Christ, any discrimination against people or any harassment of them on the basis of their race, color, condition in life or religion. Accordingly, following the footsteps of the holy apostles Peter and Paul, the sacred Council earnestly begs the Christian faithful to "conduct themselves well among the Gentiles" (1 Pet. 2:12) and if possible, as far as depends on them, to be at peace with all men (cf. Rom. 12:18) and in that way to be true sons of the Father who is in heaven (cf. Mt. 5:45).

57

GUIDELINES ON RELIGIOUS RELATIONS WITH THE JEWS (N. 4)[a]

C.R.R.J., 1 December, 1974

The Declaration *Nostra Aetate,* issued by the Second Vatican Council on 28 October, 1965, "on the relationship of the Church to non-Christian religions" (n. 4), marks an important milestone in the history of Jewish-Christian relations.

Moreover, the step taken by the Council finds its historical setting in circumstances deeply affected by the memory of the persecution and massacre of Jews which took place in Europe just before and during the Second World War.

Although Christianity sprang from Judaism, taking from it certain essential elements of its faith and divine worship, the gap dividing them was deepened more and more, to such an extent that Christian and Jew hardly knew each other.

After two thousand years, too often marked by mutual ignorance and frequent confrontation, the Declaration *Nostra Aetate* provides an opportunity to open or to continue a dialogue with a view to better mutual understanding. Over the past nine years, many steps in this direction have been taken in various countries. As a result, it is easier to define the conditions under which a new relationship between Jews and Christians may be worked out and developed. This seems the right moment to propose, following the guidelines of the Council, some concrete suggestions born of experience, hoping that they will help to bring into actual existence in the life of the Church the intentions expressed in the conciliar document.

While referring the reader back to this document, we may simply restate here that the spiritual bonds and histori-

a. The English text was issued by the Commission. An Italian text was published in *L'Osservatore Romano,* 4 Jan. 1975.

cal links binding the Church to Judaism condemn (as opposed to the very spirit of Christianity) all forms of antisemitism and discrimination, which in any case the dignity of the human person alone would suffice to condemn. Further still, these links and relationships render obligatory a better mutual understanding and renewed mutual esteem. On the practical level in particular, Christians must therefore strive to acquire a better knowledge of the basic components of the religious tradition of Judaism; they must strive to learn by what essential traits the Jews define themselves in the light of their own religious experience.

With due respect for such matters of principle, we simply propose some first practical applications in different essential areas of the Church's life, with a view to launching or developing sound relations between Catholics and their Jewish brothers.

I. DIALOGUE

To tell the truth, such relations as there have been between Jew and Christian have scarcely ever risen above the level of monologue. From now on, real dialogue must be established.

Dialogue presupposes that each side wishes to know the other, and wishes to increase and deepen its knowledge of the other. It constitutes a particularly suitable means of favoring a better mutual knowledge and, especially in the case of dialogue between Jews and Christians, of probing the riches of one's own tradition. Dialogue demands respect for the other as he is; above all, respect for his faith and his religious convictions.

In virtue of her divine mission, and her very nature, the Church must preach Jesus Christ to the world (*Ad Gentes*, n. 2). Lest the witness of Catholics to Jesus Christ should give offence to Jews, they must take care to live and spread their Christian faith while maintaining the strictest respect for religious liberty in line with the teaching of the Second Vatican Council (Declaration *Dignitatis Humanae*). They will likewise strive to understand the difficulties which arise for the Jewish soul—rightly imbued with an extremely high, pure notion of the divine transcendence—when faced with the mystery of the incarnate Word.

While it is true that a widespread air of suspicion, inspired by an unfortunate past, is still dominant in this particular area, Christians, for their part, will be able to see to what extent the responsibility is theirs and deduce practical conclusions for the future.

In addition to friendly talks, competent people will be encouraged to meet and to study together the many problems deriving from the fundamental convictions of Judaism and of Christianity. In order not to hurt (even involuntarily) those taking part, it will be vital to guarantee, not only tact, but a great openness of spirit and diffidence with respect to one's own prejudices.

In whatever circumstances as shall prove possible and mutually acceptable, one might encourage a common meeting in the presence of God, in prayer and silent meditation—a highly efficacious way of finding that humility, that openness of heart and mind, necessary prerequisites for a deep knowledge of oneself and of others. In particular, that will be done in connection with great causes such as the struggle for peace and justice.

II. LITURGY

The existing links between the Christian liturgy and the Jewish liturgy will be borne in mind. The idea of a living community in the service of God, and in the service of men for the love of God, such as it is realized in the liturgy, is just as characteristic of the Jewish liturgy as it is of the Christian one. To improve Jewish-Christian relations, it is important to take cognizance of those common elements of the liturgical life (formulas, feasts, rites, etc.) in which the Bible holds an essential place.

An effort will be made to acquire a better understanding of whatever in the Old Testament retains its own perpetual value (cf. *Dei Verbum,* n. 14-15), since that has not been cancelled by the later interpretation of the New Testament. Rather, the New Testament brings out the full meaning of the Old, while both Old and New illumine and explain each other (cf. *ibid.,* n. 16). This is all the more important since liturgical reform is now bringing the text of the Old Testament ever more frequently to the attention of Christians.

When commenting on biblical texts, emphasis will be laid on the continuity of our faith with that of the earlier Covenant, in the perspective of the promises, without minimizing those elements of Christianity which are original. We believe that those promises were fulfilled with the first coming of Christ. But it is none the less true that we still await their perfect fulfilment in his glorious return at the end of time.

With respect to liturgical readings, care will be taken to see that homilies based on them will not distort their meaning, especially when it is a question of passages which seem to show the Jewish people as such in an unfavorable light. Efforts will be made so to instruct the Christian people that they will understand the true interpretation of all the texts and their meaning for the contemporary believer.

Commissions entrusted with the task of liturgical translation will pay particular attention to the way in which they express those phrases and passages which Christians, if not well informed, might misunderstand because of prejudice. Obviously, one cannot alter the text of the Bible. The point is that, with a version destined for liturgical use, there should be an overriding preoccupation to bring out explicitly the meaning of a text,[1] while taking scriptural studies into account.

The preceding remarks also apply to introductions to biblical readings, to the Prayer of the Faithful, and to commentaries printed in missals used by the laity.

III. TEACHING AND EDUCATION

Although there is still a great deal of work to be done, a better understanding of Judaism itself and its relationship to Christianity has been achieved in recent years thanks to the teaching of the Church, the study and research of scholars, and also to the beginning of dialogue. In this respect, the following facts deserve to be recalled.

It is the same God, "inspirer and author of the books of both Testaments," (*Dei Verbum*, n. 16), who speaks both in the old and new Covenants.

Judaism in the time of Christ and the Apostles was a complex reality, embracing many different trends, many spiritual, religious, social and cultural values.

The Old Testament and the Jewish tradition founded

---

1. Thus the formula "the Jews," in St. John, sometimes according to the context means "the leaders of the Jews," or "the adversaries of Jesus," terms which express better the thought of the evangelist and avoid appearing to arraign the Jewish people as such. Another example is the use of the words "pharisee" and "pharisaism," which have taken on a largely pejorative meaning.

upon it must not be set against the New Testament in such a way that the former seems to constitute a religion of only justice, fear and legalism, with no appeal to the love of God and neighbor (cf. Deut. 6:5, Lev. 19:18, Matt. 22:34-40).

Jesus was born of the Jewish people, as were his Apostles and a large number of his first disciples. When he revealed himself as the Messiah and Son of God (cf. Mt. 16:16), the bearer of the new Gospel message, he did so at the fulfilment and perfection of the earlier Revelation. And, although his teaching had a profoundly new character, Christ nevertheless, in many instances, took his stand on the teaching of the Old Testament. The New Testament is profoundly marked by its relation to the Old. As the Second Vatican Council declared: "God, the inspirer and author of the books of both Testaments, wisely arranged that the New Testament be hidden in the Old and the Old be made manifest in the New" (*Dei Verbum*, n. 16). Jesus also used teaching methods similar to those employed by the rabbis of his time.

With regard to the trial and death of Jesus, the Council recalled that "what happened in his passion cannot be blamed upon all the Jews then living, without distinction, nor upon the Jews of today" (*Nostra Aetate*, n. 4).

The history of Judaism did not end with the destruction of Jerusalem, but rather went on to develop a religious tradition. And, although we believe that the importance and meaning of that tradition were deeply affected by the coming of Christ, it is still nonetheless rich in religious values.

With the prophets and the apostle Paul, "the Church awaits the day, known to God alone, on which all peoples will address the Lord in a single voice and 'serve him with one accord'" (Soph. 3:9) (*Nostra Aetate*, n. 4).

Information concerning these questions is important at all levels of Christian instruction and education. Among sources of information, special attention should be paid to the following:

catechisms and religious textbooks
history books
the mass-media (press, radio, cinema, television)

The effective use of these means presupposes the thorough formation of instructors and educators in training schools, seminaries and universities.

Research into the problems bearing on Judaism and Jewish-Christian relations will be encouraged among specialists, particularly in the fields of exegesis, theology, history and sociology. Higher institutions of Catholic research, in association if possible with other similar Christian institutions and experts, are invited to contribute to the solution of such problems. Wherever possible, chairs of Jewish studies will be created, and collaboration with Jewish scholars encouraged.

IV. JOINT SOCIAL ACTION

Jewish and Christian tradition, founded on the Word of God, is aware of the value of the human person, the image of God. Love of the same God must show itself in effective action for the good of mankind. In the spirit of the prophets, Jews and Christians will work willingly together, seeking social justice and peace at every level—local, national and international.

At the same time, such collaboration can do much to foster mutual understanding and esteem.

CONCLUSION

The Second Vatican Council has pointed out the path to follow in promoting deep fellowship between Jews and Christians. But there is still a long road ahead.

The problem of Jewish-Christian relations concerns the Church as such, since it is when "pondering her own mystery" that she encounters the mystery of Israel. Therefore, even in areas where no Jewish communities exist, this remains an important problem. There is also an ecumenical aspect to the question: the very return of Christians to the sources and origins of their faith, grafted on to the earlier Covenant, helps the search for unity in Christ, the cornerstone.

In this field, the bishops will know what best to do on the pastoral level, within the general disciplinary framework of the Church and in line with the common teaching of her magisterium. For example, they will create some suitable commissions or secretariats on a national or regional level, or appoint some competent person to promote the implementation of the conciliar directives and the suggestions made above.

On 22 October, 1974, the Holy Father instituted for the universal Church this Commission for Religious Relations with the Jews, joined to the Secretariat for Promoting

Christian Unity. This special Commission, created to encourage and foster religious relations between Jews and Catholics—and to do so eventually in collaboration with other Christians—will be, within the limits of its competence, at the service of all interested organizations, providing information for them, and helping them to pursue their task in conformity with the instructions of the Holy See.

The Commission wishes to develop this collaboration in order to implement, correctly and effectively, the express intentions of the Council.

58

DOGMATIC CONSTITUTION ON DIVINE REVELATION[a]

Vatican II, *Dei Verbum,* 18 November, 1965

PROLOGUE

1. Hearing the Word of God with reverence, and proclaiming it with faith, the sacred Snyod assents to the words of St. John, who says: "We proclaim to you the eternal life which was with the Father and was made manifest to us—that which we have seen and heard we proclaim also to you, so that you may have fellowship with us; and our fellowship is with the Father and with his Son Jesus Christ." (1 Jn. 1:2–3). Following, then, in the steps of the Councils of Trent and Vatican I, this Synod wishes to set forth the true doctrine on divine Revelation and its transmission. For it wants the whole world to hear the summons to salvation, so that through hearing it may believe, through belief it may hope, through hope it may come to love.[1]

CHAPTER I

DIVINE REVELATION ITSELF

2. It pleased God, in his goodness and wisdom, to reveal himself and to make known the mystery of his will (cf. Eph. 1:9). His will was that men should have access to the Father, through Christ, the Word made flesh, in the Holy

---

a. Prologue and Chapters 1, 2, 6 translated by Liam Walsh, o.p., chapters 3, 4, 5 by Wilfred Harrington, o.p.
1. St. Augustine, *De Catechizandis rudibus,* c. 4, 8: *PL* 40, 316.

Spirit, and thus become sharers in the divine nature (cf. Eph. 2:18; 2 Pet. 1:4). By this revelation, then, the invisible God (cf. Col. 1:15; 1 Tim. 1:17), from the fullness of his love, addresses men as his friends (cf. Ex. 33:11; Jn. 15; 14–15), and moves among them ((cf. Bar. 3:38), in order to invite and receive them into his own company. This economy of Revelation is realized by deeds and words, which are intrinsically bound up with each other. As a result, the works performed by God in the history of salvation show forth and bear out the doctrine and realities signified by the words; the words, for their part, proclaim the works, and bring to light the mystery they contain. The most intimate truth which this revelation gives us about God and the salvation of man shines forth in Christ, who is himself both the mediator and the sum total of Revelation.[2]

3. God, who creates and conserves all things by his Word, (cf. Jn. 1:3), provides men with constant evidence of himself in created realities (cf. Rom. 1:19–20). And furthermore, wishing to open up the way to heavenly salvation, he manifested himself to our first parents from the very beginning. After the fall, he buoyed them up with the hope of salvation, by promising redemption (cf. Gen. 3:15); and he has never ceased to take care of the human race. For he wishes to give eternal life to all those who seek salvation by patience in well-doing (cf. Rom. 2:6–7). In his own time God called Abraham, and made him into a great nation (cf. Gen. 12:2). After the era of the patriarchs, he taught this nation, by Moses and the prophets, to recognize him as the only living and true God, as a provident Father and just judge. He taught them, too, to look for the promised Saviour. And so, throughout the ages, he prepared the way for the Gospel.

4. After God had spoken many times and in various ways through the prophets, "in these last days he has spoken to us by a Son" (Heb. 1:1–2). For he sent his Son, the eternal Word who enlightens all men, to dwell among men and to tell them about the inner life of God. Hence, Jesus Christ, sent as "a man among men,"[3] "speaks the words of God" (Jn. 3:34), and accomplishes the saving work which the Father gave him to do(cf. Jn. 5:36; 17:4). As a result,

---

2. Cf. Mt. 11:27; Jn. 1:14 and 17; 14:6; 17:1–3; 2 Cor. 3:16 and 4:6; Eph. 1:3–14.
3. *Epistle to Diognetus*, c. 7, 4: Funk, *Patres Apostolici*, I, p. 403.

he himself—to see whom is to see the Father (cf. Jn. 14:9)—completed and perfected Revelation and confirmed it with divine guarantees. He did this by the total fact of his presence and self-manifestation—by words and works, signs and miracles, but above all by his death and glorious resurrection from the dead, and finally by sending the Spirit of truth. He revealed that God was with us, to deliver us from the darkness of sin and death, and to raise us up to eternal life.

The Christian economy, therefore, since it is the new and definitive covenant, will never pass away; and no new public revelation is to be expected before the glorious manifestation of our Lord, Jesus Christ (cf. 1 Tim. 6:14 and Tit. 2:13).

5. "The obedience of faith" (Rom. 16:26; cf. Rom. 1:5; 2 Cor. 10:5–6) must be given to God as he reveals himself. By faith man freely commits his entire self to God, making "the full submission of his intellect and will to God who reveals,"[4] and willingly assenting to the Revelation given by him. Before this faith can be exercised, man must have the grace of God to move and assist him; he must have the interior helps of the Holy Spirit, who moves the heart and converts it to God, who opens the eyes of the mind and "makes it easy for all to accept and believe the truth."[5] The same Holy Spirit constantly perfects faith by his gifts, so that Revelation may be more and more profoundly understood.

6. By divine Revelation God wished to manifest and communicate both himself and the eternal decrees of his will concerning the salvation of mankind. He wished, in other words, "to share with us divine benefits which entirely surpass the powers of the human mind to understand."[6]

The sacred Synod professes that "God, the first principle and last end of all things, can be known with certainty from the created world, by the natural light of human reason" (cf. Rom. 1:20). It teaches that it is to his Revelation that we must attribute the fact "that those things, which in themselves are not beyond the grasp of human reason, can,

4. First Vatican Council, *Dogm. Const. on Cath. Faith*, c. 3 (on Faith): *Denz.* 189 (3008).
5. Second Council of Orange, can. 7: *Denz.* 180 (377). First Vatican Council, *loc. cit.: Denz.* 1791 (3010).
6. First Vatican Council, *Dogm. Const. on Cath. Faith*, c. 2 (on Revelation): *Denz.* 1786 (3005).

in the present condition of the human race, be known by all men with ease, with firm certainty, and without the contamination of error."[7]

CHAPTER II

THE TRANSMISSION OF DIVINE REVELATION

7. God graciously arranged that the things he had once revealed for the salvation of all peoples should remain in their entirety, throughout the ages, and be transmitted to all generations. Therefore, Christ the Lord, in whom the entire Revelation of the most high God is summed up (cf. 2 Cor. 1:20; 3:16-4, 6) commanded the apostles to preach the Gospel, which had been promised beforehand by the prophets, and which he fulfilled in his own person and promulgated with his own lips. In preaching the Gospel they were to communicate the gifts of God to all men. This Gospel was to be the source of all saving truth and moral discipline.[1] This was faithfully done: it was done by the apostles who handed on, by the spoken word of their preaching, by the example they gave, by the institutions they established, what they themselves had received—whether from the lips of Christ, from his way of life and his works, or whether they had learned it at the prompting of the Holy Spirit; it was done by those apostles and other men associated with the apostles who, under the inspiration of the same Holy Spirit, committed the message of salvation to writing.[2]

In order that the full and living Gospel might always be preserved in the Church the apostles left bishops as their successors. They gave them "their own position of teaching

7. Ibid.: *Denz.* 1785 and 1786 (3004 and 3005).
1. Cf. Mt. 28:19-20 and Mk. 16:15. Council of Trent, Session IV, Decree *On the Canonical Scriptures: Denz.* 783 (1501).
2. Cf. Council of Trent, *loc. cit.;* First Vatican Council, Session III, *Dogm. Const on the Catholic Faith,* c. 2 (on Revelation): *Denz.* 1787 (3006).

authority."[3] This sacred Tradition, then, and the sacred Scripture of both Testaments, are like a mirror, in which the Church, during its pilgrim journey here on earth, contemplates God, from whom she receives everything, until such time as she is brought to see him face to face as he really is (cf. Jn. 3:2).

8. Thus, the apostolic preaching, which is expressed in a special way in the inspired books, was to be preserved in a continuous line of succession until the end of time. Hence the apostles, in handing on what they themselves had received, warn the faithful to maintain the traditions which they had learned either by word of mouth or by letter (cf. 2 Th. 2:15); and they warn them to fight hard for the faith that had been handed on to them once and for all (cf. Jude 3).[4] What was handed on by the apostles comprises everything that serves to make the People of God live their lives in holiness and increase their faith. In this way the Church, in her doctrine, life and worship, perpetuates and transmits to every generation all that she herself is, all that she believes.

The Tradition that comes from the apostles makes progress in the Church, with the help of the Holy Spirit.[5] There is a growth in insight into the realities and words that are being passed on. This comes about in various ways. It comes through the contemplation and study of believers who ponder these things in their hearts (cf. Lk. 2:19 and 51). It comes from the intimate sense of spiritual realities which they experience. And it comes from the preaching of those who have received, along with their right of succession in the episcopate, the sure charism of truth. Thus, as the centuries go by, the Church is always advancing towards the plenitude of divine truth, until eventually the words of God are fulfilled in her.

The sayings of the Holy Fathers are a witness to the life-giving presence of this Tradition, showing how its riches are poured out in the practice and life of the Church, in her belief and her prayer. By means of the same Tradition the full canon of the sacred books is known to the Church and the holy Scriptures themselves are more thor-

3. St. Irenaeus, *Adv. Haer.*, III, 3, 1: *PG* 7, 848; Harvey, 2, p. 9.
4. Cf. Council of Nicea II: *Denz.* 303 (602). Council of Constantinople IV, Session X, can. 1: *Denz.* 336 (650–652).
5. Cf. First Vatican Council, *Dogm. Const. on the Catholic Faith*, c. 4 (on Faith and Reason): *Denz.* 1800 (3020).

oughly understood and constantly actualized in the Church. Thus God, who spoke in the past, continues to converse with the spouse of his beloved Son. And the Holy Spirit, through whom the living voice of the Gospel rings out in the Church—and through her in the world—leads believers to the full truth, and makes the Word of Christ dwell in them in all its richness (cf. Col. 3:16).

9. Sacred Tradition and sacred Scripture, then, are bound closely together, and communicate one with the other. For both of them, flowing out from the same divine well-spring, come together in some fashion to form one thing, and move towards the same goal. Sacred Scripture is the speech of God as it is put down in writing under the breath of the Holy Spirit. And Tradition transmits in its entirety the Word of God which has been entrusted to the apostles by Christ the Lord and the Holy Spirit. It transmits it to the successors of the apostles so that, enlightened by the Spirit of truth, they may faithfully preserve, expound and spread it abroad by their preaching. Thus it comes about that the Church does not draw her certainty about all revealed truths from the holy Scriptures alone. Hence, both Scripture and Tradition must be accepted and honored with equal feelings of devotion and reverence.[6]

10. Sacred Tradition and sacred Scripture make up a single sacred deposit of the Word of God, which is entrusted to the Church. By adhering to it the entire holy people, united to its pastors, remains always faithful to the teaching of the apostles, to the brotherhood, to the breaking of bread and the prayers (cf. Acts 2:42 Greek). So, in maintaining, practicing and professing the faith that has been handed on there should be a remarkable harmony between the bishops and the faithful.[7]

But the task of giving an authentic interpretation of the Word of God, whether in its written form or in the form of Tradition,[8] has been entrusted to the living teaching office of the Church alone.[9] Its authority in this matter is exer-

6. Cf. Council of Trent, Session IV, *loc. cit.*: *Denz.* 783 (1501).
7. Cf. Pius XII, Apost. Const. *Munificentissimus Deus*, 1 Nov. 1950: *AAS* 42 (1950) 756, taken along with the words of St. Cyprian, *Epist.* 66, 8; Hartel, III, B, p. 733: "The Church is the people united to its Priests, the flock adhering to its shepherd."
8. Cf. First Vatican Council, *Dogm. Const. on the Catholic Faith*, c. 3 (on Faith): *Denz.* 1972 (3011).
9. Cf. Pius XII, Encycl. *Humani Generis*, 12 Aug. 1950: *AAS* 42 (1950) 568–569: *Denz.* 2314 (3886).

cised in the name of Jesus Christ. Yet this Magisterium is not superior to the Word of God, but is its servant. It teaches only what has been handed on to it. At the divine command and with the help of the Holy Spirit, it listens to this devotedly, guards it with dedication and expounds it faithfully. All that it proposes for belief as being divinely revealed is drawn from this single deposit of faith.

It is clear, therefore, that, in the supremely wise arrangement of God, sacred Tradition, sacred Scripture and the Magisterium of the Church are so connected and associated that one of them cannot stand without the others. Working together, each in its own way under the action of the one Holy Spirit, they all contribute effectively to the salvation of souls.

CHAPTER III

SACRED SCRIPTURE: ITS DIVINE INSPIRATION AND ITS INTERPRETATION

11. The divinely revealed realities, which are contained and presented in the text of sacred Scripture, have been written down under the inspiration of the Holy Spirit. For Holy Mother Church relying on the faith of the apostolic age, accepts as sacred and canonical the books of the Old and the New Testaments, whole and entire, with all their parts, on the grounds that, written under the inspiration of the Holy Spirit (cf. Jn. 20:31; 2 Tim. 3:16; 2 Pet. 1:19–21; 3:15-16), they have God as their author, and have been handed on as such to the Church herself.[1] To compose the sacred books, God chose certain men who, all the while he employed them in this task, made full use of their powers and faculties[2] so that, though he acted in them and by

1. Cf. Vatican Council I, *Const. dogm. de fide catholica*, c. 2 (de revelatione): *Denz.* 1787 (3006). *Bibl. Commission*, Decr. 18 June 1915: *Denz.* 2180 (3629); EB 420; Holy Office, *Letter*, 22 Dec. 1923: EB 499.
2. Cf. Pius XII, Encycl. *Divino Afflante Spiritu*, 30 Sept. 1943: *AAS* 35 (1943), p. 314; EB 556.

them,[3] it was as true authors that they consigned to writing whatever he wanted written, and no more.[4]

Since, therefore, all that the inspired authors, or sacred writers, affirm should be regarded as affirmed by the Holy Spirit, we must acknowledge that the books of Scripture, firmly, faithfully and without error, teach that truth which God, for the sake of our salvation, wished to see confided to the sacred Scriptures.[5] Thus "all Scripture is inspired by God, and profitable for teaching, for reproof, for correction and for training in righteousness, so that the man of God may be complete, equipped for every good work" (2 Tim. 3:16-17, Gk. text).

12. Seeing that, in sacred Scripture, God speaks through men in human fashion,[6] it follows that the interpreter of sacred Scriptures, if he is to ascertain what God has wished to communicate to us, should carefully search out the meaning which the sacred writers really had in mind, that meaning which God had thought well to manifest through the medium of their words.

In determining the intention of the sacred writers, attention must be paid, *inter alia*, to "literary forms for the fact is that truth is differently presented and expressed in the various types of historical writing, in prophetical and poetical texts," and in other forms of literary expression. Hence the exegete must look for that meaning which the sacred writer, in a determined situation and given the circumstances of his time and culture, intended to express and did in fact express, through the medium of a contemporary literary form.[7] Rightly to understand what the sacred author wanted to affirm in his work, due attention must be paid both to the customary and characteristic patterns of perception, speech and narrative which prevailed at the age of the

3. *In* and *by* man: cf. Heb. 1:1; 4:7 (*in*); 2 Sam. 23:2; Mt. 1:22 and *passim* (*by*); Vatican Council I, *Schema de doctr. cath.*, note 9; Coll. Lac., VII, 522.

4. Leo XIII, Encycl. *Providentissimus Deus*, 18 Nov. 1893: Denz. 1952 (3293); EB 125.

5. Cf. St. Augustine, *Gen. ad Litt.*, 2, 9, 20: *PL* 34, 270-271; *Epist.* 82, 3: *PL* 33, 277; *CSEL* 34, 2, p. 354.—St. Thomas. *De Ver.* q. 12, a. 2, C.— Council of Trent, Session IV, *de canonicis Scripturis*: Denz. 783 (1501)—Leo XIII, Encycl. *Providentissimus*: EB 121, 124, 126-127.—Pius XII, Encycl. *Divino Afflante*: EB 539.

6. St. Augustine, *De Civ. Dei*, XVII, 6, 2: *PL* 41, 537: *CSEL* XL, 2, 228.

7. St. Augustine, *De Doctr. Christ.*, III, 18, 26; *PL* 34, 75-76.

sacred writer, and to the conventions which the people of his time followed in their dealings with one another.[8]

But since sacred Scripture must be read and interpreted with its divine authorship in mind,[9] no less attention must be devoted to the content and unity of the whole of Scripture, taking into account the Tradition of the entire Church and the analogy of faith, if we are to derive their true meaning from the sacred texts. It is the task of exegetes to work, according to these rules, towards a better understanding and explanation of the meaning of sacred Scripture in order that their research may help the Church to form a firmer judgment. For, of course, all that has been said about the manner of interpreting Scripture is ultimately subject to the judgment of the Church which exercises the divinely conferred commission and ministry of watching over and interpreting the Word of God.[10]

13. Hence, in sacred Scripture, without prejudice to God's truth and holiness, the marvellous "condescension" of eternal wisdom is plain to be seen "that we may come to know the ineffable loving-kindness of God and see for ourselves how far he has gone in adapting his language with thoughtful concern for our nature."[11] Indeed the words of God, expressed in the words of men, are in every way like human language, just as the Word of the eternal Father, when he took on himself the flesh of human weakness, became like men.

CHAPTER IV

THE OLD TESTAMENT

14. God, with loving concern contemplating, and making preparation for, the salvation of the whole human race, in a singular undertaking chose for himself a people to whom

---

8. Pius XII, *loc. cit.*: *Denz.* 2294 (3829–2830); EB 557–562.
9. Cf. Benedict XV, Encycl. *Spiritus Paraclitus,* 15 Sept. 1920: EB 469. St. Jerome. *In Gal.* 5, 19–21: *PL* 26, 417 A.
10. Cf. Vatican Council I, *Const. dogm. de fide catholica,* c. 2 (de revelatione): *Denz.* 1788 (3007).
11. St. John Chrysostom, *In Gen.* 3, 8 (hom. 17, 1): *PG* 53, 134. *Attemperatio* corresponds to the Greek *synkatábasis.*

he would entrust his promises. By his covenant with Abraham (cf. Gen. 15:18) and, through Moses, with the race of Israel (cf. Ex. 24:8), he did acquire a people for himself, and to them he revealed himself in words and deeds as the one, true, living God, so that Israel might experience the ways of God with men. Moreover, by listening to the voice of God speaking to them through the prophets, they had daily to understand his ways more fully and more clearly, and make them more widely known among the nations (cf. Ps. 21:28-29; 95:1-3; Is. 2:1-4; Jer. 3:17). Now the economy of salvation, foretold, recounted and explained by the sacred authors, appears as the true Word of God in the books of the Old Testament, that is why these books, divinely inspired, preserve a lasting value: "For whatever was written in former days was written for our instruction, that by steadfastness and the encouragement of the Scriptures we might have hope" (Rom. 15:4).

15. The economy of the Old Testament was deliberately so orientated that it should prepare for and declare in prophecy the coming of Christ, redeemer of all men, and of the messianic kingdom (cf. Lk. 24:44; Jn. 5:39; 1 Pet. 1:10), and should indicate it by means of different types (cf. 1 Cor. 10:11). For in the context of the human situation before the era of salvation established by Christ, the books of the Old Testament provide an understanding of God and man and make clear to all men how a just and merciful God deals with mankind. These books, even though they contain matters imperfect and provisional, nevertheless show us authentic divine teaching.[1] Christians should accept with veneration these writings which give expression to a lively sense of God, which are a storehouse of sublime teaching on God and of sound wisdom on human life, as well as a wonderful treasury of prayers; in them, too, the mystery of our salvation is present in a hidden way.

16. God, the inspirer and author of the books of both Testaments, in his wisdom has so brought it about that the New should be hidden in the Old and that the Old should be made manifest in the New.[2] For, although Christ founded the New Covenant in his blood (cf. Lk. 22:20; 1 Cor. 11:25), still the books of the Old Testament, all of them

---

1. Pius XI, Encycl. *Mit brennender Sorge*, 14 March 1937: *AAS* 29 (1937), p. 151.
2. St. Augustine, *Quaest. in Hept.* 2, 73: *PL* 34, 623.

caught up into the Gospel message,[3] attain and show forth
their full meaning in the New Testament (cf. Mt. 5:17; Lk.
24·27; Rom. 16:25-26; 2 Cor. 3:14-16) and, in their turn,
shed light on it and explain it.

CHAPTER V

THE NEW TESTAMENT

17. The Word of God, which is the power of God for
salvation to everyone who has faith (cf. Rom. 1:16), is set
forth and displays its power in a most wonderful way in the
writings of the New Testament. For when the time had fully come (cf. Gal. 4:4), the Word became flesh and dwelt
among us full of grace and truth (cf. Jn. 1:14). Christ established on earth the kingdom of God, revealed his Father
and himself by deeds and words; and by his death, resurrection and glorious ascension, as well as by sending the Holy
Spirit, completed his work. Lifted up from the earth he
draws all men to himself (cf. Jn. 10:32, Gk. text), for he
alone has the words of eternal life (cf. Jn. 6:68). This mystery was not made known to other generations as it has now
been revealed to his holy apostles and prophets by the Holy
Spirit (cf. Eph. 3:4-6, Gk. text), that they might preach
the Gospel, stir up faith in Jesus Christ and the Lord, and
bring together the Church. The writings of the New Testament stand as a perpetual and divine witness to these realities.

18. It is common knowledge that among all the inspired
writings, even among those of the New Testament, the Gospels have a special place, and rightly so, because they are
our principal source for the life and teaching of the Incarnate Word, our Saviour.

The Church has always and everywhere maintained, and

3. St. Irenaeus, *Adv. Haer*, III, 21, 3: *PG* 7, 950 (–25, 1; Harvey 2,
p. 115). St. Cyril of Jerusalem, *Catech*. 4, 35: *PG* 33, 497. Theodore
of Mopsuestia, *In Soph*. 1, 4–6: *PG* 66, 452D–453A.

continues to maintain, the apostolic origin of the four Gospels. The apostles preached, as Christ had charged them to do, and then, under the inspiration of the Holy Spirit, they and others of the apostolic age handed on to us in writing the same message they had preached, the foundation of our faith: the fourfold Gospel, according to Matthew, Mark, Luke and John.[1]

19. Holy Mother Church has firmly and with absolute constancy maintained and continues to maintain, that the four Gospels just named, whose historicity she unhesitatingly affirms, faithfully hand on what Jesus, the Son of God, while he lived among men, really did and taught for their eternal salvation, until the day when he was taken up (cf. Acts 1:1-2). For, after the ascension of the Lord, the apostles handed on to their hearers what he had said and done, but with that fuller understanding which they, instructed by the glorious events of Christ and enlightened by the Spirit of truth,[2] now enjoyed.[3] The sacred authors, in writing the four Gospels, selected certain of the many elements which had been handed on, either orally or already in written form, others they synthesized or explained with an eye to the situation of the churches, the while sustaining the form of preaching, but always in such a fashion that they have told us the honest truth about Jesus.[4] Whether they relied on their own memory and recollections or on the testimony of those who "from the beginning were eyewitnesses and ministers of the Word," their purpose in writing was that we might know the "truth" concerning the things of which we have been informed (cf. Lk. 1:2-4).

20. Besides the four Gospels, the New Testament also contains the Epistles of St. Paul and other apostolic writings composed under the inspiration of the Holy Spirit. In accordance with the wise design of God these writings firmly establish those matters which concern Christ the Lord, formulate more and more precisely his authentic teaching, preach the saving power of Christ's divine work and foretell its glorious consummation.

---

1. Cf. St. Irenaeus, *Adv. Haer.* III, 11, 8: *PG* 7, 885; ed. Sagnard, p. 194.
2. Cf. Jn. 14:26; 16:13.
3. Jn. 2:22; 12–16; cf. 14:26; 16:12–13; 7:39.
4. Cf. The Instruction *Sacra Mater Ecclesia* of the Pontifical Biblical Commission: *AAS* 56 (1964), p. 715.

For the Lord Jesus was with his apostles as he had promised (cf. Mt. 28:20) and he had sent to them the Spirit, the Counsellor, who would guide them into all the truth (cf. Jn. 16:13).

CHAPTER VI

SACRED SCRIPTURE IN THE LIFE OF THE CHURCH

21. The Church has always venerated the divine Scriptures as she venerated the Body of the Lord, in so far as she never ceases, particularly in the sacred liturgy, to partake of the bread of life and to offer it to the faithful from the one table of the Word of God and the Body of Christ. She has always regarded, and continues to regard the Scriptures, taken together with sacred Tradition, as the supreme rule of her faith. For, since they are inspired by God and committed to writing once and for all time, they present God's own Word in an unalterable form, and they make the voice of the Holy Spirit sound again and again in the words of the prophets and apostles. It follows that all the preaching of the Church, as indeed the entire Christian religion, should be nourished and ruled by sacred Scripture. In the sacred books the Father who is in heaven comes lovingly to meet his children, and talks with them. And such is the force and power of the Word of God that it can serve the Church as her support and vigor, and the children of the Church as strength for their faith, food for the soul, and a pure and lasting fount of spiritual life. Scripture verifies in the most perfect way the words: "The Word of God is living and active" (Heb. 4:12), and "is able to build you up and to give you the inheritance among all those who are sanctified" (Acts 20:32; cf. 1 Th. 2:13).

22. Access to sacred Scripture ought to be open wide to the Christian faithful. For this reason the Church, from the very beginning, made her own the ancient translation of the

Old Testament called the Septuagint; she honors also the other Eastern translations, and the Latin translations, especially that which is called the Vulgate. But since the Word of God must be readily available at all times, the Church, with motherly concern, sees to it that suitable and correct translations are made into various languages, especially from the original texts of the sacred books. If it should happen that, when the opportunity presents itself and the authorities of the Church agree, these translations are made in a joint effort with the separated brethren, they may be used by all Christians.

23. The spouse of the incarnate Word, which is the Church, is taught by the Holy Spirit. She strives to reach day by day a more profound understanding of the sacred Scriptures, in order to provide her children with food from the divine words. For this reason also she duly fosters the study of the Fathers, both Eastern and Western, and of the sacred liturgies. Catholic exegetes and other workers in the field of sacred theology should zealously combine their efforts. Under the watchful eye of the sacred Magisterium, and using appropriate techniques they should together set about examining and explaining the sacred texts in such a way that as many as possible of those who are ministers of the divine Word may be able to distribute fruitfully the nourishment of the Scriptures of the People of God. This nourishment enlightens the mind, strengthens the will and fires the hearts of men with the love of God.[1] The sacred Synod encourages those sons of the Church who are engaged in biblical studies constantly to renew their efforts, in order to carry on the work they have so happily begun, with complete dedication and in accordance with the mind of the Church.[2]

24. Sacred theology relies on the written Word of God, taken together with sacred Tradition, as on a permanent foundation. By this Word it is most firmly strengthened and constantly rejuvenated, as it searches out, under the light of faith, the full truth stored up in the mystery of Christ. The Sacred Scriptures contain the Word of God, and, because they are inspired, they are truly the Word of God. Therefore, the "study

1. Cf. Pius XII, Encycl. *Divino Afflante:* EB 551, 553, 567. Biblical Commission, Instruction on the Teaching of S. Scripture in Seminaries of Clerics and Religious, 13 May 1950: *AAS* 42 (1950), pp. 495–505.
2. Cf. Pius XII, ibid.: EB 569.

of the sacred page" should be the very soul of sacred theology.[3] The ministry of the Word, too—pastoral preaching, catechetics and all forms of Christian instruction, among which the liturgical homily should hold pride of place—is healthily nourished and thrives in holiness through the Word of Scripture.

25. Therefore, all clerics, particularly priests of Christ and others who, as deacons or catechists, are officially engaged in the ministry of the Word, should immerse themselves in the Scriptures by constant sacred reading and diligent study. For it must not happen that anyone becomes "an empty preacher of the Word of God to others, not being a hearer of the Word in his own heart,"[4] when he ought to be sharing the boundless riches of the divine Word with the faithful committed to his care, especially in the sacred liturgy. Likewise, the sacred Synod forcefully and specifically exhorts all the Christian faithful, especially those who live the religious life, to learn "the surpassing knowledge of Jesus Christ" (Phil. 3:8) by frequent reading of the divine Scriptures. "Ignorance of the Scriptures is ignorance of Christ."[5] Therefore, let them go gladly to the sacred text itself, whether in the sacred liturgy, which is full of the divine words, or in devout reading, or in such suitable exercises and various other helps which, with the approval and guidance of the pastors of the Church, are happily spreading everywhere in our day. Let them remember, however, that prayer should accompany the reading of sacred Scripture, so that a dialogue takes place between God and man. For, "we speak to him when we pray; we listen to him when we read the divine oracles."[6]

It is for the bishops, "with whom the apostolic doctrine resides"[7] suitably to instruct the faithful entrusted to them in the correct use of the divine books, especially of the New Testament, and in particular of the Gospels. They do this by giving them translations of the sacred texts which are equipped with necessary and really adequate explanations. Thus the children of the Church can familiarize themselves

3. Cf. Leo XIII, Encycl. *Providentissimus: EB* 114; Benedict XV, Encycl. *Spiritus Paraclitus:* EB 483.
4. St. Augustine, *Serm.* 179: *PL* 38, 966.
5. St. Jerome, *Comm. in Isaias,* Prol.: *PL* 24, 17. Cf. Benedict XV, Encycl. *Spiritus Paraclitus:* EB 475–480; Pius XII, Encycl. *Divino Afflante:* EB 544.
6. St. Ambrose, *De Officiis ministrorum* I, 20, 88: *PL* 16, 50.
7. St. Irenaeus, *Adv. Haer.* IV, 32, 1: *PG* 7, 1071; (=49, 2) Harvey, 2, p. 255.

safely and profitably with the sacred Scriptures, and become steeped in their spirit.

Moreover, editions of sacred Scripture, provided with suitable notes, should be prepared for the use of even non-Christians, and adapted to their circumstances. These should be prudently circulated, either by pastors of souls, or by Christians of any rank.

26. So may it come that, by the reading and study of the sacred books "the Word of God may speed on and triumph" (2 Th. 3:1) and the treasure of Revelation entrusted to the Church may more and more fill the hearts of men. Just as from constant attendance at the eucharistic mystery the life of the Church draws increase, so a new impulse of spiritual life may be expected from increased veneration of the Word of God, which "stands forever" (Is. 40:8; cf. 1 Pet. 1:23-25).

59

DECREE ON THE APOSTOLATE OF LAY PEOPLE[a]

Vatican II, *Apostolicam Actuositatem*, 18 November, 1965

INTRODUCTION

1. In its desire to intensify the apostolic activity of the People of God[1] the Council now earnestly turns its thoughts to the Christian laity. Mention has already been made in other documents of the laity's special and indispensable role in the mission of the Church.[2] Indeed, the Church can never be without the lay apostolate; it is something that derives from the layman's very vocation as a Christian. Scripture clearly shows how spontaneous and fruitful was this activity in the Church's early days (cf. Act 11:19-21; 18:26; Rom. 16:1-16; Phil. 4:3).

No less fervent a zeal on the part of lay people is called for today; present circumstances, in fact, demand from them an apostolate infinitely broader and more intense. For the constant increase in population, the progress in science and technology, the shrinking of the gaps that have kept men apart, have immensely enlarged the field of the lay apostolate, a field that is in great part open to the laity alone; they have in addition given rise to new problems which require from the laity an intelligent attention and ex-

---

a. Translated by Father Finnian, o.c.s.o.
1. Cf. John XXIII, Apostolic Constitution *Humanae Salutis*, 25 Dec. 1961: *AAS* 54 (1962) p. 7-10.
2. Cf. Dogmatic Constitution *De Ecclesia*, ch. IV, no. 33 ff.: *AAS* 57 (1965) p. 39 ff.; cf. Constitution *De Sacra Liturgia*, nos. 26-40: *AAS* 56 (1964) pp. 107 111; cf. Decree *De instrumentis communicationis socialis*: *AAS* 56 (1964) pp. 143-153; cf. Decree *De Oecumenismo*: *AAS* 57 (1965) pp. 90-107; cf. Decree *De pastorali Episcoporum munere in Ecclesia*, nos. 16, 17, 18; cf. Declaration *De educatione Christiana*, nos. 3, 5, 7.

amination. All the more urgent has this apostolate become, now that autonomy—as is only right—has been reached in numerous sectors of human life, sometimes with a certain relinquishing of moral and religious values, seriously jeopardizing the Christian life. Besides, in many regions where priests are very scarce or (as is sometimes the case) deprived of the freedom they need for their ministry, it is hard to see how the Church could make her presence and action felt without the help of the laity.

The need for this urgent and many-sided apostolate is shown by the manifest action of the Holy Spirit moving laymen today to a deeper and deeper awareness of their responsibility and urging them on everywhere to the service of Christ and the Church.[3]

The Council will explain in this Decree the nature of the lay apostolate, its character and the variety of its forms; it will state fundamental principles and give pastoral directives for its more effective exercise. These are all to serve as norms in the revision of Canon Law concerned with the lay apostolate.

Chapter I

THE VOCATION OF LAY PEOPLE TO THE APOSTOLATE

PARTICIPATION OF LAITY IN THE CHURCH'S MISSION

2. The Church was founded to spread the kingdom of Christ over all the earth for the glory of God the Father, to make all men partakers in redemption and salvation,[1] and through them to establish the right relationship of the entire

3. Cf. Pius XII, *Alloc. ad Cardinales,* 18 Feb. 1946: *AAS* 38 (1946) pp. 101–102; *idem., Sermo ad Iuvenes Operarios Catholicos,* 25 Aug. 1957: *AAS* 49 (1957) p. 843.
1. Cf. Pius XI, Encyclical Letter *Rerum Ecclesiae: AAS* 18 (1926) p. 65.

world to Christ. Every activity of the Mystical Body with this in view goes by the name of "apostolate"; the Church exercises it through all its members, though in various ways. In fact, the Christian vocation is, of its nature, a vocation to the apostolate as well. In the organism of a living body no member plays a purely passive part, sharing in the life of the body it shares at the same time in its activity. The same is true for the Body of Christ, the Church: "the whole Body achieves full growth in dependence on the full functioning of each part" (Eph. 4:16). Between the members of this body there exists, further, such a unity and solidarity (cf. Eph. 4:16) that a member who does not work at the growth of the body to the extent of his possibilities must be considered useless both to the Church and to himself.

In the Church there is diversity of ministry but unity of mission. To the apostles and their successors Christ has entrusted the office of teaching, sanctifying and governing in his name and by his power. But the laity are made to share in the priestly, prophetical and kingly office of Christ; they have therefore, in the Church and in the world, their own assignment in the mission of the whole People of God.[2] In the concrete, their apostolate is exercised when they work at the evangelization and sanctification of men; it is exercised too when they endeavor to have the Gospel spirit permeate and improve the temporal order, going about it in a way that bears clear witness to Christ and helps forward the salvation of men. The characteristic of the lay state being a life led in the midst of the world and of secular affairs, laymen are called by God to make of their apostolate, through the vigor of their Christian spirit, a leaven in the world.

FOUNDATIONS OF THE LAY APOSTOLATE

3. From the fact of their union with Christ the head flows the laymen's right and duty to be apostles. Inserted as they are in the Mystical Body of Christ by baptism and strengthened by the power of the Holy Spirit in confirmation, it is by the Lord himself that they are assigned to the apostolate. If they are consecrated a kingly priesthood and a holy nation (cf. 1 Pet. 2:4-10), it is in order that they may in all their actions offer spiritual sacrifices and bear witness to Christ all the world over. Charity, which is, as it

2. Cf. Dogmatic Constitution *De Ecclesia*, chap. IV, no. 33: *AAS* 57 (1965) p. 37.

were, the soul of the whole apostolate, is given to them and nourished in them by the sacraments, the Eucharist above all.[3]

The apostolate is lived in faith, hope and charity poured out by the Holy Spirit into the hearts of all the members of the Church. And the precept of charity, which is the Lord's greatest commandment, urges all Christians to work for the glory of God through the coming of his kingdom and for the communication of eternal life to all men, that they may know the only true God and Jesus Christ whom he has sent (cf. Jn. 17:3).

On all Christians, accordingly, rests the noble obligation of working to bring all men throughout the whole world to hear and accept the divine message of salvation.

The Holy Spirit sanctifies the People of God through the ministry and the sacraments. However, for the exercise of the apostolate he gives the faithful special gifts besides (cf. 1 Cor. 12:7), "allotting them to each one as he wills" (1 Cor. 12:11), so that each and all, putting at the service of others the grace received may be "as good stewards of God's varied gifts," (1 Pet. 4:10), for the building up of the whole body in charity (cf. Eph. 4:16). From the reception of these charisms, even the most ordinary ones, there arises for each of the faithful the right and duty of exercising them in the Church and in the world for the good of men and the development of the Church, of exercising them in the freedom of the Holy Spirit who "breathes where he wills" (Jn. 3:8), and at the same time in communion with his brothers in Christ, and with his pastors especially. It is for the pastors to pass judgment on the authenticity and good use of these gifts, not certainly with a view to quenching the Spirit but to testing everything and keeping what is good (cf. 1 Th. 5:12, 19, 21).[4]

THE SPIRITUALITY OF LAY PEOPLE

4. Christ, sent by the Father, is the source of the Church's whole apostolate. Clearly then, the fruitfulness of the apostolate of lay people depends on their living union with Christ; as the Lord said himself: "Whoever dwells in me and I in him bears much fruit, for separated from me

---

3. Cf. Dogmatic Constitution *De Ecclesia*, chap. IV, no. 33: *AAS* 57 (1965) p. 39. Cf. also no. 10, ibid., p. 14.
4. Cf. ibid., no. 12: *AAS* 57 (1965) p. 16.

you can do nothing" (Jn. 15:5). This life of intimate union with Christ in the Church is maintained by the spiritual helps common to all the faithful, chiefly by active participation in the liturgy.[5] Laymen should make such a use of these helps that, while meeting their human obligations in the ordinary conditions of life, they do not separate their union with Christ from their ordinary life; but through the very performance of their tasks, which are God's will for them, actually promote the growth of their union with him. This is the path along which laymen must advance, fervently, joyfully, overcoming difficulties with prudent patient efforts.[6] Family cares should not be foreign to their spirituality, nor any other temporal interest; in the words of the apostle: "Whatever you are doing, whether speaking or acting, do everything in the name of the Lord Jesus Christ, giving thanks to God the Father through him" (Col. 3:17).

A life like this calls for a continuous exercise of faith, hope and charity.

Only the light of faith and meditation on the Word of God can enable us to find everywhere and always the God "in whom we live and exist" (Acts 17:28); only thus can we seek his will in everything, see Christ in all men, acquaintance or stranger, make sound judgments on the true meaning and value of temporal realities both in themselves and in relation to man's end.

Those with such a faith live in the hope of the revelation of the sons of God, keeping in mind the cross and resurrection of the Lord.

On life's pilgrimage they are hidden with Christ in God, are free from the slavery of riches, are in search of the goods that last for ever. Generously they exert all their energies in extending God's kingdom, in making the Christian spirit a vital energizing force in the temporal sphere. In life's trials they draw courage from hope, "convinced that present sufferings are no measure of the future glory to be revealed in us" (Rom. 8:18).

With the love that comes from God prompting them, they do good to all, especially to their brothers in the faith

---

5. Cf. Constitution *De Sacra Liturgia,* chap. I, no. 11: *AAS* 56 (1964) pp. 102–103.
6. Cf. Dogmatic Constitution *De Ecclesia,* chap. IV, no. 32: *AAS* 57 (1965) p. 38. Cf. also chap. V, nos. 40–41, ibid., pp. 45–47.

(cf. Gal. 6:10), putting aside "all ill will and deceit, all hypocrisy, envy and slander" (1 Pet. 2:1), in this way attracting men to Christ. Divine love, "poured into our hearts by the Holy Spirit who has been given to us" (Rom. 5:5), enables lay people to express concretely in their lives the spirit of the Beatitudes. Following in his poverty, Jesus, they feel no depression in want, no pride in plenty: imitating the humble Christ, they are not greedy for vain show (cf. Gal. 5:26). They strive instead to please God rather than men, always ready to abandon everything for Christ (cf. Lk. 14:26) and to endure persecution in the cause of right (cf. Mt. 5:10), having in mind the Lord's saying: "If any man wants to come my way let him renounce self and take up his cross and follow me" (Mt. 16:24). Preserving a Christian friendship with one another, they afford mutual support in all needs.

This lay spirituality will take its particular character from the circumstances of one's state in life (married and family life, celibacy, widowhood), from one's state of health and from one's professional and social activity. Whatever the circumstances, each one has received suitable talents and these should be cultivated, as should also the personal gifts he has from the Holy Spirit.

Similarly laymen who have followed their particular vocation and become members of any of the associations or institutions approved by the Church, aim sincerely at making their own the forms of spirituality proper to these bodies.

They should also hold in high esteem professional competence, family and civic sense, and the virtues related to social behavior such as honesty, sense of justice, sincerity, courtesy, moral courage; without them there is no true Christian life.

Perfect model of this apostolic spiritual life is the Blessed Virgin Mary, Queen of Apostles. While on earth her life was like that of any other, filled with labors and the cares of the home; always, however, she remained intimately united to her Son and cooperated in an entirely unique way in the Saviour's work. And now, assumed into heaven, "her motherly love keeps her attentive to her Son's brothers, still on pilgrimage amid the dangers and difficulties of life, until they arrive at the happiness of the fatherland."[7] Everyone should have a genuine devotion to her and entrust his life to her motherly care.

CHAPTER II

OBJECTIVES

5. The work of Christ's redemption concerns essentially the salvation of men; it takes in also, however, the renewal of the whole temporal order. The mission of the Church, consequently, is not only to bring men the message and grace of Christ but also to permeate and improve the whole range of the temporal. The laity, carrying out this mission of the Church, exercise their apostolate therefore in the world as well as in the Church, in the temporal order as well as in the spiritual. These orders are distinct; they are nevertheless so closely linked that God's plan is, in Christ, to take the whole world up again and make of it a new creation, in an initial way here on earth, in full realization at the end of time. The layman, at one and the same time a believer and a citizen of the world, has only a single conscience, a Christian conscience; it is by this that he must be guided continually in both domains.

THE APOSTOLATE OF EVANGELIZATION AND SANCTIFICATION

6. The Church's mission is concerned with the salvation of men; and men win salvation through the grace of Christ and faith in him. The apostolate of the Church therefore, and of each of its members, aims primarily at announcing to the world by word and action the message of Christ and communicating to it the grace of Christ. The principal means of bringing this about is the ministry of the word and of the sacraments. Committed in a special way to the

7. Cf. ibid., chap. VIII, no. 62: *AAS* 57 (1965) p. 63. Cf. also no. 65, ibid., pp. 64–65.

clergy, it leaves room however for a highly important part for the laity, the part namely of "helping on the cause of truth" (3 Jn. 8). It is in this sphere most of all that the lay apostolate and the pastoral ministry complete each other.

Laymen have countless opportunities for exercising the apostolate of evangelization and sanctification. The very witness of a Christian life, and good works done in a supernatural spirit, are effective in drawing men to the faith and to God; and that is what the Lord has said: "Your light must shine so brightly before men that they can see your good works and glorify your Father who is in heaven" (Mat. 5:16).

This witness of life, however, is not the sole element in the apostolate; the true apostle is on the lookout for occasions of announcing Christ by word, either to unbelievers to draw them towards the faith, or to the faithful to instruct them, strengthen them, incite them to a more fervent life; "for Christ's love urges us on" (2 Cor. 5:14), and in the hearts of all should the apostle's words find echo: "Woe to me if I do not preach the Gospel" (1 Cor. 9:16).[1]

At a time when new questions are being put and when grave errors aiming at undermining religion, the moral order and human society itself are rampant, the Council earnestly exhorts the laity to take a more active part, each according to his talents and knowledge and in fidelity to the mind of the Church, in the explanation and defense of Christian principles and in the correct application of them to the problems of our times.

THE RENEWAL OF THE TEMPORAL ORDER

7. That men, working in harmony, should renew the temporal order and make it increasingly more perfect: such is God's design for the world.

All that goes to make up the temporal order: personal and family values, culture, economic interests, the trades and professions, institutions of the political community, international relations, and so on, as well as their gradual development—all these are not merely helps to man's last end; they possess a value of their own, placed in them by God, whether considered individually or as parts of the in-

1. Cf. Pius XI, Encyclical Letter *Ubi arcano*, 23 Dec. 1922: *AAS* 14 (1922) p. 659; Pius XII, Encyclical Letter *Summi Pontificatus*, 20 Oct. 1939: *AAS* 31 (1939) pp. 442–443.

tegral temporal structure: "And God saw all that he had made and found it very good" (Gen. 1:31). This natural goodness of theirs receives an added dignity from their relation with the human person, for whose use they have been created. And then, too, God has willed to gather together all that was natural, all that was supernatural, into a single whole in Christ, "so that in everything he would have the primacy" (Col. 1:18). Far from depriving the temporal order of its autonomy, of its specific ends, of its own laws and resources, or its importance for human well-being, this design, on the contrary, increases its energy and excellence, raising it at the same time to the level of man's integral vocation here below.

In the course of history the use of temporal things has been tarnished by serious defects. Under the influence of original sin men have often fallen into very many errors about the true God, human nature and the principles of morality. As a consequence human conduct and institutions became corrupted, the human person itself held in contempt. Again in our own days not a few, putting an immoderate trust in the conquests of science and technology, turn off into a kind of idolatry of the temporal; they become the slaves of it rather than the masters.

It is the work of the entire Church to fashion men able to establish the proper scale of values on the temporal order and direct it towards God through Christ. Pastors have the duty to set forth clearly the principles concerning the purpose of creation and the use to be made of the world, and to provide moral and spiritual helps for the renewal of the temporal order in Christ.

Laymen ought to take on themselves as their distinctive task this renewal of the temporal order. Guided by the light of the Gospel and the mind of the Church, prompted by Christian love, they should act in this domain in a direct way and in their own specific manner. As citizens among citizens they must bring to their cooperation with others their own special competence, and act on their own responsibility; everywhere and always they have to seek the justice of the kingdom of God. The temporal order is to be renewed in such a way that, while its own principles are fully respected, it is harmonized with the principles of the Christian life and adapted to the various conditions of times, places and peoples. Among the tasks of this apostolate Christian social action is preeminent. The Council desires to see it extended today to every sector of life, not forgetting the cultural sphere.[2]

CHARITABLE WORKS AND SOCIAL AID

8. While every activity of the apostolate should find in charity its origin and driving force, certain works are of their nature a most eloquent expression of this charity; and Christ has willed that these should be signs of his messianic mission (cf. Mt. 11:4-5).

The greatest commandment of the law is to love God with one's whole heart and one's neighbor as oneself (cf. Mt. 22:37-40). Christ has made this love of the neighbor his personal commandment and has enriched it with a new meaning when he willed himself, along with his brothers, to be the object of this charity saying: "When you showed it to one of the least of my brothers here, you showed it to me" (Mt. 25:40). In assuming human nature he has united to himself all humanity in a supernatural solidarity which makes of it one single family. He has made charity the distinguishing mark of his disciples, in the words: "By this will all men know you for my disciples, by the love you bear one another" (Jn. 13:35).

In the early days the Church linked the "agape" to the eucharistic supper, and by so doing showed itself as one body around Christ united by the bond of charity. So too, in all ages, love is its characteristic mark. While rejoicing at initiatives taken elsewhere, it claims charitable works as its own mission and right. That is why mercy to the poor and the sick, and charitable works and works of mutual aid for the alleviation of all kinds of human needs, are held in special honor in the Church.[3]

Today these activities and works of charity have become much more urgent and worldwide, now that means of communication are more rapid, distance between men has been more or less conquered, people in every part of the globe have become as members of a single family. Charitable action today can and should reach all men and all needs.

---

2. Cf. Leo XIII, Encyclical Letter *Rerum Novarum: AAS* 23 (1890-1891) p. 647; Pius XI, Encyclical Letter *Quadragesimo Anno: AAS* 23 (1931) p. 190; Pius XII, *Nuntius Radiophonicus*, 1 June 1941: *AAS* 33 (1941) p. 207.
3. Cf. John XXIII, Encyclical Letter *Mater et Magistra: AAS* 53 (1961) p. 402.

Wherever men are to be found who are in want of food and drink, of clothing, housing, medicine, work, education, the means necessary for leading a truly human life, wherever there are men racked by misfortune or illness, men suffering exile or imprisonment, Christian charity should go in search of them and find them out, comfort them with devoted care and give them the helps that will relieve their needs. This obligation binds first and foremost the more affluent individuals and nations.[4]

If this exercise of charity is to be above all criticism, and seen to be so, one should see in one's neighbor the image of God to which he has been created, and Christ the Lord to whom is really offered all that is given to the needy. The liberty and dignity of the person helped must be respected with the greatest sensitivity. Purity of intention should not be stained by any self-seeking or desire to dominate.[5] The demands of justice must first of all be satisfied; that which is already due in justice is not to be offered as a gift of charity. The cause of evils, and not merely their effects, ought to disappear. The aid contributed should be organized in such a way that beneficiaries are gradually freed from their dependence on others and become self-supporting.

The laity should therefore highly esteem, and support as far as they can, private or public works of charity and social assistance movements, including international schemes. By these channels effective help is brought to individuals and nations in need. They should collaborate in this with all men of good will.[6]

CHAPTER III

THE VARIOUS FIELDS OF THE APOSTOLATE

9. The lay apostolate, in all its many aspects, is exercised both in the Church and in the world. In either case differ-

4. Cf. ibid., pp. 440–441.
5. Cf. ibid., pp. 442–443.
6. Cf. Pius XII, *Alloc. ad Pax Romana M.I.I.C.*, 25 April 1957: *AAS* 49 (1957) pp. 298–299; and especially John XXIII, *Conventum Consilii 'Food and Agriculture Organization'* (F.A.O.), 10 Nov. 1959: *AAS* 51 (1959) pp. 856, 866.

ent fields of apostolic action are open to the laity. We propose to mention here the chief among them: Church communities, the family, the young, the social environment, national and international spheres. Since in our days women are taking an increasingly active share in the whole life of society, it is very important that their participation in the various sectors of the Church's apostolate should likewise develop.

CHURCH COMMUNITIES

10. Participators in the function of Christ, priest, prophet and king, the laity have an active part of their own in the life and action of the Church. Their action within the Church communities is so necessary that without it the apostolate of the pastors will frequently be unable to obtain its full effect. Following in the footsteps of the men and women who assisted Paul in the proclamation of the Gospel (cf. Acts 18:18-26; Rom. 16:3), lay persons of a genuinely apostolic spirit supply the needs of their brothers and are a source of consolation no less to the pastors than to the rest of the faithful (cf. 1 Cor. 16:17-18). Nourished by their active participation in the liturgical life of their community, they engage zealously in its apostolic works; they draw men towards the Church who had been perhaps very far away from it; they ardently cooperate in the spread of the Word of God, particularly by catechetical instruction; by their expert assistance they increase the efficacy of the care of souls as well as of the administration of the goods of the Church.

The parish offers an outstanding example of community apostolate, for it gathers into a unity all the human diversities that are found there and inserts them into the universality of the Church.[1] The laity should develop the habit of working in the parish in close union with their priests,[2] of bringing before the ecclesial community their own problems, world problems, and questions regarding man's salvation, to examine them together and solve them by general

1. Cf. Pius X, Apostolic Letter *Creationis duarum novarum paroeciarum*, 1 June 1905: *ASS* 3 (1905) pp. 65–67; Pius II, *Alloc. ad fideles Paroeciae S. Saba*, 11 Jan. 1953. *Discorsi e Radiomessaggi di S.S. Pio XII*, 14 (1952–1953) pp. 449–454; John XXIII, *Alloc. Clero et christifidelibus e diocesi suburbicaria Albanensi, ad Arcem Gandulfi habita*, 16 Aug. 1962: *AAS* 54 (1962) pp. 656–660.
2. Cf. Leo XIII, *Alloc.*, 28 Jan. 1894: *Acts* 14 (1894) pp. 424–425.

discussion. According to their abilities the laity ought to cooperate in all the apostolic and missionary enterprises of their ecclesial family.

The laity will continuously cultivate the "feeling for the diocese," of which the parish is a kind of cell; they will be always ready on the invitation of their bishop to make their own contribution to diocesan undertakings. Indeed, they will not confine their cooperation within the limits of the parish or diocese, but will endeavor, in response to the needs of the towns and rural districts,[3] to extend it to inter-parochial, interdiocesan, national and international spheres. This widening of horizons is all the more necessary in the present situation, in which the increasing frequency of population shifts, the development of active solidarity and the ease of communications no longer allow any one part of society to live in isolation. The laity will therefore have concern for the needs of the People of God scattered throughout the world. Especially will they make missionary works their own by providing them with material means and even with personal service. It is for Christians a duty and an honor to give God back a portion of the goods they have received from him.

THE FAMILY

11. The Creator of all made the married state the beginning and foundation of human society; by his grace he has made of it too a great mystery in Christ and in the Church (cf. Eph. 5:32), and so the apostolate of married persons and of families has a special importance for both Church and civil society.

Christian couples are, for each other, for their children and for their relatives, cooperators of grace and witnesses of the faith. They are the first to pass on the faith to their children and to educate them in it. By word and example they form them to a Christian and apostolic life; they offer them wise guidance in the choice of vocation, and if they discover in them a sacred vocation they encourage it with all care.

To give clear proof in their own lives of the indissolu-

3. Cf. Pius XII, *Alloc. ad Parochos, etc.*, 6 Feb. 1951: *Discorsi e Radiomessaggi di S.S. Pio XII*, 12 (1950–1951) pp. 437–443; 8 March 1952: ibid., 14 (1952–1953) pp. 5–10; 27 March 1953: ibid., 15 (1953–1954) pp. 27–35; 28 Feb. 1954: ibid., pp. 585–590.

bility and holiness of the marriage bond; to assert with vigor the right and duty of parents and guardians to give their children a Christian upbringing; to defend the dignity and legitimate autonomy of the family: this has always been the duty of married persons; today, however, it has become the most important aspect of their apostolate. They and all the faithful, therefore, should collaborate with men of good will in seeing that these rights are perfectly safeguarded in civil legislation; that in social administration consideration is given to the requirements of families in the matter of housing, education of children, working conditions, social security and taxes; and that in emigration regulations family life is perfectly safeguarded.[4]

The mission of being the primary vital cell of society has been given to the family by God himself. This mission will be accomplished if the family, by the mutual affection of its members and by family prayer, presents itself as a domestic sanctuary of the Church; if the whole family takes its part in the Church's liturgical worship; if, finally, it offers active hospitality, and practises justice and other good works for the benefit of all its brothers suffering from want. Among the various works of the family apostolate the following may be listed: adopting abandoned children, showing a loving welcome to strangers, helping with the running of schools, supporting adolescents with advice and help, assisting engaged couples to make a better preparation for marriage, taking a share in catechism-teaching, supporting married people and families in a material or moral crisis, and in the case of the aged not only providing them with what is indispensable but also procuring for them a fair share of the fruits of economic progress.

Everywhere and always, but especially in regions where the first seeds of the Gospel are just being sown, or where the Church is still in its infancy or finds itself in a critical situation, Christian families bear a very valuable witness to Christ before the world when all their life they remain at-

---

4. Pius XI, Encyclical Letter *Casti Connubii: AAS* 22 (1930) p. 554; Pius XII, *Nuntius Radiophonicus*, 1 June 1941: *AAS* 33 (1941) p. 203; *idem., Delegatis ad Conventum Unionis Internationalis sodalitatum ad iura familiae tuenda*, 20 Sept. 1949: *AAS* 41 (1949) p. 552; idem., *AD patresfamilias e Gallia Roman peregrinantes*, 18 Sept. 1951, p. 731: *AAS* 45 (1953) p. 41; idem., *Numtius Radiophonicus in Natali Domini*, 1952: *AAS* 45 (1953) p. 41; John XXIII, Encyclical Letter *Mater et Magistra*, 15 May 1961: *AAS* 53 (1961) pp. 429, 439.

tached to the Gospel and hold up the example of Christian marriage.[5]

To attain the ends of their apostolate more easily it can be of advantage for families to organize themselves into groups.[6]

YOUNG PEOPLE

12. Young people exert a very important influence in modern society:[7] The circumstances of their life, their habits of thought, their relations with their families, have been completely transformed. Often they enter too rapidly a new social and economic environment. While their social and even political importance is on the increase day by day, they seem unequal to the weight of these new responsibilities.

The growth of their social importance demands from them a corresponding apostolic activity; and indeed their natural character inclines them in this direction. Carried along by their natural ardor and exuberant energy, when awareness of their own personality ripens in them they shoulder responsibilities that are theirs and are eager to take their place in social and cultural life. If this enthusiasm is penetrated with the spirit of Christ, animated by a sense of obedience and love towards the pastors of the Church, a very rich harvest can be expected from it. The young should become the first apostles of the young, in direct contact with them, exercising the apostolate by themselves among themselves, taking account of their social environment.[8]

Adults should be anxious to enter into friendly dialogue with the young, where, despite the difference in age, they could get to know one another and share with one another their own personal riches. It is by example first of all and, on occasion, by sound advice and practical help that adults should persuade the young to undertake the apostolate. The

---

5. Cf. Pius XII, Encyclical Letter *Evangelii Praecones*, 2 June 1951: *AAS* 43 (1951) p. 514.

6. Cf. Pius XII, *Delegatis ad Conventum Unionis Internationalis sodalitatum ad iura familiae tuenda*, 20 Sept. 1949: *AAS* 41 (1949) p. 552.

7. Cf. Pius X, *Alloc. ad catholicam Associationem Iuventutis Gallicae de pietate, scientia et actione*, 25 Sept. 1904: *AAS* 37 (1904–1905) pp. 296–300.

8. Cf. Pius XII, *Ad Conventum J.O.C. Montreal*, 24 May 1947; *AAS* 39 (1974) p. 257; *Nuntius Radiophonicus ad J.O.C. Bruxelles*, 3 Sept. 1950: *AAS* 42 (1950) pp. 640–641.

young, on their side, will treat their elders with respect and confidence; and though by nature inclined to favor what is new, they will have due esteem for praiseworthy traditions.

Children too have an apostolate of their own. In their own measure they are true living witnesses of Christ among their companions.

APOSTOLATE OF LIKE TOWARDS LIKE

13. The apostolate in one's social environment endeavors to infuse the Christian spirit into the mentality and behavior, laws and structures of the community in which one lives. To such a degree is it the special work and responsibility of lay people, that no one else can ever properly supply for them. In this area laymen can conduct the apostolate of like towards like. There the witness of their life is completed by the witness of their word.[9] It is amid the surroundings of their work that they are best qualified to be of help to their brothers, in the surroundings of their profession, of their study, residence, leisure or local group.

The laity accomplish the Church's mission in the world principally by that blending of conduct and faith which makes them the light of the world; by that uprightness in all their dealings which is for every man such an incentive to love the true and the good and which is capable of inducing him at last to go to Christ and the Church; by that fraternal charity that makes them share the living conditions and labors, the sufferings and yearnings of their brothers, and thereby prepare all hearts, gently, imperceptibly, for the action of saving grace; by that full awareness of their personal responsibility in the development of society, which drives them on to perform their family, social and professional duties with Christian generosity. In this way their conduct makes itself gradually felt in the surroundings where they live and work.

This apostolate should reach out to every single person in that environment; and it must not exclude any good, spiritual or temporal, that can be done for them. Genuine apostles are not content, however, with just this: they are earnest also about revealing Christ by word to those around them. It is a fact that many men cannot hear the Gospel

9. Cf. Pius XI, Encyclical Letter *Quadragesimo Anno,* 15 May 1931: *AAS* 23 (1931) pp. 225–226.

and come to acknowledge Christ except through the laymen they associate with.

THE NATIONAL AND INTERNATIONAL LEVELS

14. On the national and international planes the field of the apostolate is vast; and it is there that the laity more than others are the channels of Christian wisdom. In their patriotism and in their fidelity to their civic duties Catholics will feel themselves bound to promote the true common good; they will make the weight of their convictions so influential that as a result civil authority will be justly exercised and laws will accord with the moral precepts and the common good. Catholics versed in politics and, as should be the case, firm in the faith and Christian teaching, should not decline to enter public life; for by a worthy discharge of their functions, they can work for the common good and at the same time prepare the way for the Gospel.

Catholics are to be keen on collaborating with all men of good will in the promotion of all that is true, just, holy, all that is worthy of love (cf. Phil. 4:8). They are to enter into dialogue with them, approaching them with understanding and courtesy; and are to search for means of improving social and public institutions along the lines of the Gospel.

Among the signs of our times, particularly worthy of note is the ever growing and inescapable sense of the solidarity of all peoples. It is the task of the lay apostolate to take pains in developing this sense and transforming it into a really sincere desire for brotherly union. The laity should have an awareness also of the international sector, of the doctrinal and practical problems and solutions that are brought forward there, in particular those concerned with newly-developing nations.[10]

Everyone who works in foreign nations or brings them aid must remember that relations among peoples should be a real fraternal interchange in which both parties give and at the same time receive. Those who travel abroad, for international activities, on business or on holiday, should keep in mind that no matter where they may be they are the travelling messengers of Christ, and should bear themselves really as such.

10. Cf. John XXIII, Encyclical Letter *Mater et Magistra*, 15 May 1961: *AAS* 53 (1961) pp. 448–450.

Chapter IV

THE DIFFERENT FORMS OF THE APOSTOLATE

15. The laity can exercise their apostolic activity either singly or grouped in various communities or associations.

INDIVIDUAL APOSTOLATE

16. The apostolate to be exercised by the individual—which flows abundantly from a truly Christian life (cf. Jn. 4:11)—is the starting point and condition of all types of lay apostolate, including the organized apostolate; nothing can replace it.

The individual apostolate is everywhere and always in place; in certain circumstances it is the only one appropriate, the only one possible. Every lay person, whatever his condition, is called to it, is obliged to it, even if he has not the opportunity or possibility of collaborating in associations.

The apostolate, through which the laity build up the Church, sanctify the world and get it to live in Christ, can take on many forms.

A special form of the individual apostolate is the witness of a whole lay life issuing from faith, hope and charity; it is a sign very much in keeping with our times, and a manifestation of Christ living in his faithful. Then, by the apostolate of the word, which in certain circumstances is absolutely necessary, the laity proclaim Christ, explain and spread his teachings, each one according to his condition and competence, and profess those teachings with fidelity.

Moreover, cooperating as citizens of this world in all that has to do with the constructing and conducting of the temporal order, the laity should, by the light of faith, try to find the higher motives that should govern their behavior in the home and in professional, cultural and social life; they should too, given the opportunity, let these motives be seen by others, conscious that by so doing they become cooperators with God the creator, redeemer and sanctifier, and give him glory.

Finally, the laity should vitalize their lives with charity and, to the extent of the capability of each give concrete expression to it in works.

All should remember that by public worship and by prayer, by penance and the willing acceptance of the toil and hardships of life by which they resemble the suffering Christ (cf. 2 Cor. 4:10; Col. 1:24), they can reach all men and contribute to the salvation of the entire world.

INDIVIDUAL APOSTOLATE IN CERTAIN CIRCUMSTANCES

17. There is an imperative need for the individual apostolate in those areas where the Church's freedom is seriously hampered. In such difficult circumstances the laity take over as far as possible the work of priests, jeopardizing their own freedom and sometimes their lives; they teach Christian doctrine to those around them, train them in a religious way of life and in Catholic attitudes, encourage them to receive the sacraments frequently and to cultivate piety, especially eucharistic piety.[1] The Council renders God most heartfelt thanks that even in our own times he is still raising up laymen with heroic courage in the midst of persecutions; the Council embraces them with gratitude and fatherly affection.

The individual apostolate has a special field in regions where Catholics are few and scattered. In such circumstances the laity who exercise only the personal apostolate —whether from the reasons mentioned above or from particular motives arising, among other things, from their professional activity—can gather for discussion into small groups with no rigid form of rules or organization. This is particularly appropriate in the present instance, for it ensures the continual presence before the eyes of others of a sign of the Church's community, a sign that will be seen as a genuine witness of love. Thus, by affording mutual spiritual aid by friendship and the exchange of personal experiences, they get the courage to surmount the difficulties of too isolated a life and activity and can increase the yield of their apostolate.

GROUP APOSTOLATE

18. The faithful are called as individuals to exercise an apostolate in the various conditions of their life. They must,

1. Cf. Pius XII, *Alloc. ad I Conventum ex Omnibus Gentibus Laicorum Apostolatui provehendo*, 15 Oct. 1951: *AAS* 43 (1951) p. 788.

however, remember that man is social by nature and that it has been God's pleasure to assemble those who believe in Christ and make of them the People of God (cf. 1 Pet. 2:5-10), a single body (cf. 1 Cor. 12:12). The group apostolate is in happy harmony therefore with a fundamental need in the faithful, a need that is both human and Christian. At the same time it offers a sign of the communion and unity of the Church in Christ, who said: "Where two or three are gathered together in my name, I am there in the midst of them" (Mt. 18:20).

For that reason Christians will exercise their apostolate in a spirit of concord.[2] They will be apostles both in their families and in the parishes and dioceses, which already are themselves expressions of the community character of the apostolate; apostles too in the free associations they will have decided to form among themselves.

The group apostolate is very important also for another reason: often, either in ecclesial communities or in various other environments, the apostolate calls for concerted action. Organizations created for group apostolate afford support to their members, train them for the apostolate, carefully assign and direct their apostolic activities; and as a result a much richer harvest can be hoped for from them than if each one were to act on his own.

In present circumstances it is supremely necessary that wherever the laity are at work the apostolate under its collective and organized form should be strengthened. In actual fact only a well-knit combination of efforts can completely attain all the aims of the modern apostolate and give its fruits good protection.[3] From this point of view it is particularly important for the apostolate to establish contact with the group attitudes and social conditions of the persons who are its object; otherwise these will often be incapable of withstanding the pressure of public opinion or of social institutions.

2. Cf. Pius XII, *Alloc. ad I Conventum ex Omnibus Gentibus Laicorum Apostolatui provehendo*, 15 Oct. 1951: *AAS* 43 (1951) pp. 787–788.
3. Cf. Pius XII, Encyclical Letter *Le pèlerinage de Lourdes*, 2 July 1957: *AAS* 49 (1957) p. 615.

VARIOUS TYPES OF GROUP APOSTOLATE

19. Great variety is to be found in apostolic associations.[4] Some look to the general apostolic end of the Church; others aim specifically at evangelization and sanctification; others work for the permeation of the temporal order by the Christian spirit; and others engage in works of mercy and of charity as their special way of bearing witness to Christ.

First among these associations to be given consideration should be those which favor and promote a more intimate unity between the faith of the members and their everyday life. Associations are not ends in themselves; they are meant to be of service to the Church's mission to the world. Their apostolic value depends on their conformity with the Church's aims, as well as on the Christian witness and evangelical spirit of each of their members and of the association as a whole.

As a consequence of the progress of institutions and the rapid evolution of modern society, the universal nature of the Church's mission requires that the apostolic initiatives of Catholics should more and more perfect the various types of international organizations. Catholic international organizations will the more surely gain their object, the more intimately the groups that compose them, as well as their members, are united to them.

While preserving intact the necessary link with ecclesiastical authority,[5] the laity have the right to establish and direct associations,[6] and to join existing ones. Dissipation of forces must, however, be avoided; this would happen if new associations and works were created without sufficient reason, if old ones now grown useless were held on to, if out-of-date methods continued to be employed. It will not always be a wise procedure, either, to transfer indiscriminately into some particular country forms that have arisen in another.[7]

---

4. Cf. Pius XII, *Alloc. ad Consilium Foederationis internationalis virorum catholicorum*, 8 Dec. 1956: *AAS* 49 (1957) pp. 26–27.
5. Cf. below, chap. V, no. 24.
6. Cf. Decree of the Sacred Congregation of the Council, *Corrienten.*, 13 Nov. 1920: *AAS* 13 (1921) p. 139.
7. Cf. John XXIII, Encyclical Letter *Princeps Pastorum*, 10 Dec. 1959. AAS 51 (1959) p. 836.

CATHOLIC ACTION

20. Several decades ago lay people, dedicating themselves increasingly to the apostolate, in many countries formed themselves into various kinds of movements and societies which, in closer union with the hierarchy, have pursued and continue to pursue ends properly apostolic. Among these institutions, as indeed among other similar older ones, special mention must be made of those which, though using differing methods, have yielded abundant fruit for the kingdom of Christ. Deservedly praised and promoted by the popes and numerous bishops, they have received from them the name of Catholic Action, and have most often been described by them as a collaboration of the laity in the hierarchical apostolate.[8]

These types of apostolate, whether or not they go by the name of Catholic Action, are today doing a work of much value. They are constituted by the combination of all the following characteristics:

(a) The immediate end of organizations of this class is the apostolic end of the Church; in other words: the evangelization and sanctification of men and the Christian formation of their conscience, so as to enable them to imbue with the Gospel spirit the various social groups and environments.

(b) The laity, cooperating in their own particular way with the hierarchy, contribute their experience and assume responsibility in the direction of these organizations, in the investigation of the conditions in which the Church's pastoral work is to be carried on, in the elaboration and execution of their plan of action.

(c) The laity act in unison after the manner of an organic body, to display more strikingly the community aspect of the Church and to render the apostolate more productive.

(d) The laity, whether coming of their own accord or in response to an invitation to action and direct cooperation with the hierarchical apostolate, act under the superior direction of the hierarchy, which can authorize this cooperation, besides, with an explict mandate.

Organizations which, in the judgment of the hierarchy,

8. Cf. Pius XI, Letter *Quae nobis*, to Cardinal Bertram, 13 Nov. 1928: *AAS* 20 (1928) p. 385. Cf. also Pius XII, *Alloc. ad A.C. Italicam*, 4 Sept. 1940: *AAS* 32 (1940) p. 362.

combine all these elements should be regarded as Catholic
Action, even if they have forms and names that vary according to the requirements of localities and peoples.

The Council most earnestly commends those institutions
which certainly meet the requirements of the Church's
apostolate in many countries; it invites the priests and laity
working in them to develop more and more the characteristics mentioned above, and always to give brotherly cooperation in the Church to all other forms of the apostolate.

SPECIAL COMMENDATION

21. Proper esteem is to be shown to all associations of
the apostolate; those, however, which the hierarchy has
praised, commended, or decided to found as more urgent to
meet the needs of times and places, should be valued most
by priests, religious and lay people, and developed each in
its own way. And among these organizations today especially
must be numbered the international associations or societies
of Catholics.

22. Worthy of special respect and praise in the Church
are the laity, single or married, who, in a definitive way or
for a period, put their person and their professional competence at the service of institutions and their activities. It is a
great joy to the Church to see growing day by day the number of lay people who are offering their personal service to
associations and works of the apostolate, whether within
the confines of their own country, or in the international
field, or, above all, in the Catholic communities of the missions and of the young Churches.

Pastors are to welcome these lay persons with joy and
gratitude. They will see to it that their conditions of life satisfies as perfectly as possible the requirements of justice,
equity and charity, chiefly in the matter of resources necessary for the maintenance of themselves and their families.
They should too be provided with the necessary training
and with spiritual comfort and encouragement.

Chapter V

THE ORDER TO BE OBSERVED

23. The lay apostolate, individual or collective, must be set in its true place within the apostolate of the whole Church. Union with those whom the Holy Spirit has appointed to rule the Church of God (cf. Acts 20:28) is an essential element of the Christian apostolate. Not less necessary is collaboration among the different undertakings of the apostolate; it is the hierarchy's place to put proper system into this collaboration.

Mutual esteem for all forms of the Church's apostolate, and good coordination, preserving nevertheless the character special to each, are in fact absolutely necessary for promoting that spirit of unity which will cause fraternal charity to shine out in the Church's whole apostolate, common aims to be reached and ruinous rivalries avoided.[1]

This is appropriate most of all when some particular action in the Church calls for the agreement and apostolic cooperation of both classes of the clergy, of religious and of the laity.

RELATIONS WITH THE HIERARCHY

24. The hierarchy's duty is to favor the lay apostolate, furnish it with principles and spiritual assistance, direct the exercise of the apostolate to the common good of the Church, and see to it that doctrine and order are safeguarded.

Yet the lay apostolate allows of different kinds of relations with the hierarchy, depending on the various forms and objects of this apostolate.

In the Church are to be found, in fact, very many apostolic enterprises owing their origin to the free choice of the laity and run at their own discretion. Such enterprises enable the Church, in certain circumstances, to fulfil her mission more effectively; not seldom, therefore, are they praised and commended by the hierarchy.[2] But no enter-

---

1. Cf. Pius XI, Encyclical Letter *Quamvis Nostra*, 30 April 1936: *AAS* 28 (1936) pp. 160-161.
2. Cf. Sacred Congregation of the Council, Resolution *Corrienten.*, 13 Nov. 1920: *AAS* 13 (1921) pp. 137-140.

prise must lay claim to the name "Catholic" if it has not the approval of legitimate ecclesiastical authority.

Certain types of the lay apostolate are explicitly recognized by the hierarchy though in different ways.

Ecclesiastical authority, looking to the needs of the common good of the Church, may also, from among apostolic associations and undertakings aiming immediately at a spiritual goal, pick out some which it will foster in a particular way; in these it assumes a special responsibility. And so, organizing the apostolate differently according to circumstances, the hierarchy brings into closer conjunction with its own apostolic functions such-and-such a form of apostolate, without, however, changing the specific nature of either or the distinction between the two, and consequently without depriving the laity of their rightful freedom to act on their own initiative. This act of the hierarchy has received the name of "mandate" in various ecclesiastical documents.

Finally, the hierarchy entrusts the laity with certain charges more closely connected with the duties of pastors: in the teaching of Christian doctrine, for example, in certain liturgical actions, in the care of souls. In virtue of this mission the laity are fully subject to superior ecclesiastical control in regard to the exercise of these charges.

As for works and institutions of the temporal order, the duty of the ecclesiastical hierarchy is the teaching and authentic interpretation of the moral principles to be followed in this domain. It is also in its province to judge, after mature reflection and with the help of qualified persons, of the conformity of such works or institutions with moral principles, and to pronounce in their regard concerning what is required for the safeguard and promotion of the values of the supernatural order.

RELATIONS WITH THE CLERGY AND WITH RELIGIOUS

25. Bishops, parish priests and other priests of the secular and regular clergy will remember that the right and duty of exercising the apostolate are common to all the faithful, whether clerics or lay; and that in the building up of the Church the laity too have parts of their own to play.[3] For

3. Cf. Pius XII, *Ad II Conventum ex Omnibus Gentibus Laicorum Apostolatui provehendo,* 5 Oct. 1957: *AAS* 49 (1957) p. 927.

this reason they will work as brothers with the laity in the Church and for the Church, and will have a special concern for the laity in their apostolic activities.[4]

A careful choice will be made of priests with the ability and appropriate training for helping special forms of the lay apostolate.[5] Those who take part in this ministry in virtue of a mission received from the hierarchy represent the hierarchy in this pastoral action of theirs. Ever faithfully attached to the spirit and teaching of the Church they will promote good relations between laity and hierarchy, they will devote their energies to fostering the spiritual life and the apostolic sense of the Catholic associations confided to them; their wise advice will be there to help these along in their apostolic labors; their encouragement will be given to their enterprises. In constant dialogue with the laity they will make painstaking search for methods capable of making apostolic action more fruitful; they will develop the spirit of unity within the association, and between it and others.

Lastly, religious Brothers and Sisters will hold lay apostolic works in high regard; and will gladly help in promoting them in accordance with the spirit and rules of their institute;[6] they will strive to support, assist and complete the ministrations of the priest.

SPECIAL COUNCILS

26. In dioceses, as far as possible, councils should be set up to assist the Church's apostolic work, whether in the field of evangelization and sanctification or in the fields of charity, social relations and the rest; the clergy and religious working with the laity in whatever way proves satisfactory. These councils can take care of the mutual coordinating of the various lay associations and undertakings, the autonomy and particular nature of each remaining untouched.[7]

Such councils should be found too, if possible, at paro-

---

4. Cf. Dogmatic Constitution *De Ecclesia,* chap. IV, no. 37: *AAS* 57 (1965) pp. 42–43.
5. Cf. Pius XII, Apostolic Exhortation *Menti Nostrae,* 23 Sept. 1950: *AAS* 42 (1950) p. 660.
6. Cf. Decree *De Accomodata renovatione vitae religiosae,* no. 8.
7. Cf. Benedict XIV, *De Synodo Dioecesana,* book III, chap. IX, no. VII.

chial, inter-parochial, inter-diocesan level, and also on the national and international plane.[8]

In addition, a special secretariat should be established at the Holy See for the service and promotion of the lay apostolate. This secretariat will act as a center which, with the proper equipment, will supply information about the different apostolic initiatives of the laity. It will undertake research on the problems arising today in this domain; and with its advice will assist the hierarchy and laity in the field of apostolic activities. The various apostolic movements and institutes of the lay apostolate all the world over should be represented in this secretariat. Clerics and religious should also be there to collaborate with the laity.

COOPERATION WITH OTHER CHRISTIANS AND NON-CHRISTIANS

27. The common patrimony of the Gospel and the common duty resulting from it of bearing a Christian witness make it desirable, and often imperative, that Catholics cooperate with other Christians, either in activities or in societies; this collaboration is carried on by individuals and by ecclesial communities, and at national or international level.[9]

Not seldom also do human values common to all mankind require of Christians working for apostolic ends that they collaborate with those who do not profess Christianity but acknowledge these values.

Through this dynamic, yet prudent, cooperation,[10] which is of great importance in temporal activities, the laity bears witness to Christ the Saviour of the world, and to the unity of the human family.

8. Cf. Pius XI, Encyclical Letter *Quamvis Nostra*, 30 April 1936; *AAS* 28 (1936) pp. 160–161.
9. Cf. John XXIII, Encyclical Letter *Mater et Magistra*, 15 May 1961: *AAS* 53 (1961) pp. 456–457; cf. Decree *De Oecumenismo*, chap. II, no. 12: *AAS* 57 (1965) pp. 99–100.
10. Cf. Decree *De Oecumenismo*, chap. II, no. 12: *AAS* 57 (1965) p. 100; cf. also Dogmatic Constitution *De Ecclesia*, chap. II, no. 15: *AAS* 57 (1965) pp. 19–20.

CHAPTER VI

TRAINING FOR THE APOSTOLATE

THE NEED FOR TRAINING

28. A training, at once many-sided and complete, is indispensable if the apostolate is to attain full efficacy. This is required, not only by the continuous spiritual and doctrinal progress of the layman himself, but also by the variety of circumstances, persons and duties to which he should adapt his activity. This education to the apostolate must rest on those foundations which the Council has in other places set down and expounded.[1] Not a few types of apostolate require, besides the education common to all Christians, a specific and individual training, by reason of the diversity of persons and circumstances.

PRINCIPLES OF TRAINING

29. Since the laity participate in the Church's mission in a way that is their own, their apostolic training acquires a special character precisely from the secularity proper to the lay state and from its particular type of spirituality.

Education for the apostolate presupposes an integral human education suited to each one's abilities and conditions. For the layman ought to be, through an intimate knowledge of the contemporary world, a member well integrated into his own society and its culture.

But in the first place he should learn to accomplish the mission of Christ and the Church, living by faith in the divine mystery of creation and redemption, moved by the Holy Spirit who gives life to the People of God and urges all men to love God the Father, and in him to love the world of men. This education must be considered the foundation and condition of any fruitful apostolate.

Besides spiritual formation, solid grounding in doctrine is required: in theology, ethics and philosophy, at least, proportioned to the age, condition and abilities of each one. The importance too of a general culture linked with a prac-

---

1. Cf. Dogmatic Constitution *De Ecclesia*, chaps. II, IV, V: *AAS* 57 (1965) pp. 12–21, 37–49; cf. also Decree *De Oecumenismo*, nos. 4, 6, 7, 12: *AAS* 57 (1965) pp. 94, 96, 97, 99, 100; cf. also above, no. 4.

tical and technical training is something which should by no means be overlooked.

If good human relations are to be cultivated, then it is necessary for genuine human values to stand at a premium, especially the art of living and working on friendly terms with others and entering into dialogue with them.

Training for the apostolate cannot consist in theoretical teaching alone; on that account there is need, right from the start of training, to learn gradually and prudently to see all things in the light of faith, to judge and act always in its light, to improve and perfect oneself by working with others, and in this manner to enter actively into the service of the Church.[2] Inasmuch as the human person is continuously developing and new problems are forever arising, this education should be steadily perfected; it requires an ever more thorough knowledge and a continual adaptation of action. While meeting all its demands, concern for the unity and integrity of the human person must be kept always in the foreground, in order to preserve and intensify its harmony and equilibrium.

In this way the layman actively inserts himself deep into the very reality of the temporal order and takes his part competently in the work of the world. At the same time, as a living member and witness of the Church, he brings its presence and its action into the heart of the temporal sphere.[3]

THOSE WHO TRAIN OTHERS FOR THE APOSTOLATE

30. Training for the apostolate should begin from the very start of a child's education. But it is more particularly adolescents and youth who should be initiated into the apostolate and imbued with its spirit. This training should be continued all through life, to fit them to meet the demands of fresh duties. It is clear, then, that those with responsibility for Christian education have also the duty of attending to this apostolic education.

It rests with parents to prepare their children from an

2. Cf. Pius XII, *Ad I Conferentiam internationalem 'boy-scouts,'* 6 June 1952: *AAS* 44 (1952) pp. 579–580; John XXIII, Encyclical Letter *Mater et Magistra,* 15 May 1961: *AAS* 53 (1961) p. 456.
3. Cf. Dogmatic Constitution *De Ecclesia,* chap. IV, no. 33: *AAS* 57 (1965) p. 39.

early age, within the family circle, to discern God's love for all men; they will teach them little by little—and above all by their example—to have concern for their neighbors' needs, material and spiritual. The whole family, accordingly, and its community life should become a kind of apprenticeship to the apostolate.

Children must be trained, besides, to go beyond the confines of the family and take an interest in both ecclesial and temporal communities. Their integration into the local parish community should succeed in bringing them the awareness of being living, active members of the People of God. Priests, for their part, should not lose sight of this question of training for the apostolate when catechizing, preaching and directing souls, and in other functions of the pastoral ministry.

Schools and colleges and other Catholic educational institutions should foster in the young a Catholic outlook and apostolic action. If the young do not get this type of education, either because they do not attend these schools, or for some other reason, all the greater is the responsibility for it that devolves upon parents, pastoral and apostolic bodies. As for teachers and educators, who by their calling and position practice an outstanding form of lay apostolate, adequate learning and a thorough grasp of pedagogy is a prerequisite to any success in this branch of education.

The various lay groups and associations dedicated to the apostolate or to any other supernatural end should look after this education to the apostolate with care and constancy, in ways consistent with their objectives and limits.[4] Frequently they are the ordinary channel of adequate apostolic training; doctrinal, spiritual and practical. The members, gathered in small groups with their companions or friends, evaluate the methods and results of their apostolic action, and measure their everyday behavior by the Gospel.

The training should be pursued in such a way as to take account of the entire range of the lay apostolate, an apostolate that is to be exercised in all circumstances and in every sector of life—in the professional and social sectors especially—and not confined within the precincts of the associations. In point of fact, every single lay person should himself actively undertake his own preparation for the aposto-

---

4. Cf. John XXIII, Encyclical Letter *Mater et Magistra,* 15 May 1961: *AAS* 53 (1961) p. 455.

late. Especially for adults does this hold true; for as the years pass, self-awareness expands and so allows each one to get a clearer view of the talents with which God has enriched his life and to bring in better results from the exercise of the charisms given him by the Holy Spirit for the good of his brothers.

FIELDS CALLING FOR SPECIALIZED TRAINING

31. Different types of apostolate require their own appropriate method of training:

(a) The apostolate of evangelization and sanctification: the laity are to be specially trained for engaging in dialogue with others, believers or non-believers, their aim being to set the message of Christ before the eyes of all.[5] But as materialism under various guises is today spreading far and wide, even among Catholics, the laity should not only make a careful study of Catholic doctrine, especially points that are called into question, but should confront materialism of every type with the witness of evangelical life.

(b) The Christian renewal of the temporal order: the laity are to be instructed in the true meaning and value of temporal goods, both in themselves and in their relation to all the aims of the human person. The laity should gain experience in the right use of goods and in the organization of institutions, paying heed always to the common good in the light of the principles of the Church's moral and social teaching. They should acquire such a knowledge of social teaching especially, its principles and conclusions, as will fit them for contributing to the best of their ability to the progress of that teaching, and for making correct application of these same principles and conclusions in individual cases.[6]

(c) Works of charity and mercy bear a most striking testimony to Christian life; therefore, an apostolic training which has as its object the performance of these works should enable the faithful to learn from very childhood

5. Cf. Pius XII, Encyclical Letter *Sertum laetitiae,* 1 Nov. 1939: *AAS* 31 (1939) pp. 635–644; cf. idem., *Ad 'Laureati' Act. Cath. It.,* 24 May 1953.
6. Cf. Pius XII, *Ad congressum Universalem Foederationis Juventutis Femininae Catholicae,* 18 April 1952: *AAS* 44 (1952) pp. 414–419; cf. idem., *Ad Associationem Christianam Operariorum Italiae (A.C.L.I.),* 1 May 1955: *AAS* 47 (1955) pp. 403–404.

how to sympathize with their brothers, and help them generously when in need.[7]

AIDS TO TRAINING

32. Many aids are now at the disposal of the laity who devote themselves to the apostolate: namely, sessions, congresses, recollections, retreats, frequent meetings, conferences, books and periodicals; all these enable them to deepen their knowledge of holy scripture and Catholic doctrine, nourish the spiritual life, and become acquainted also with world conditions and discover and adopt suitable methods.[8]

8. Cf. John XXIII, Encyclical Letter *Mater et Magistra,* 15 May 1961: *AAS* 53 (1961) p. 454.

These educational aids take into account the various types of apostolate exercised in this or that particular area.

With this end in view higher centers or institutes have been created; these have already given excellent results.

The Council rejoices at initiatives of this kind now flourishing in certain regions; it desires to see them take root in other places too, wherever the need for them makes itself felt.

Moreover, centers of documentation and research should be established, not only in theology but also in anthropology, psychology, sociology, methodology, for the benefit of all fields of the apostolate. The purpose of such centers is to create a more favorable atmosphere for developing the aptitudes of the laity, men and women, young and old.

EXHORTATION

33. The Council, then, makes to all the laity an earnest appeal in the Lord to give a willing, noble and enthusiastic response to the voice of Christ, who at this hour is summoning them more pressingly, and to the urging of the Holy Spirit. The younger generation should feel this call to be addressed in a special way to themselves; they should welcome it eagerly and generously. It is the Lord himself, by this Council, who is once more inviting all the laity to unite themselves to him ever more intimately, to consider his interests as their own (cf. Phil. 2:5), and to join in his mis-

7. Cf. Pius XII, *Ad Delegatos Conventus Sodalitatum Caritas,* 27 April 1952: *AAS,* pp. 470–471.

sion as Saviour. It is the Lord who is again sending them into every town and every place where he himself is to come (cf. Lk. 10:1). He sends them on the Church's apostolate, an apostolate that is one yet has different forms and methods, an apostolate that must all the time be adapting itself to the needs of the moment; he sends them on a apostolate where they are to show themselves his cooperators, doing their full share continually in the work of the Lord, knowing that in the Lord their labor cannot be lost (cf. Cor. 15:58).

60

DECLARATION ON RELIGIOUS LIBERTY[a]

Vatican II, *Dignitatis Humanae,* 7 December, 1965

ON THE RIGHT OF THE PERSON AND COMMUNITIES TO SOCIAL AND CIVIL LIBERTY IN RELIGIOUS MATTERS

1. Contemporary man is becoming increasingly conscious of the dignity of the human person;[1] more and more people are demanding that men should exercise fully their own judgment and a responsible freedom in their actions and should not be subject to the pressure of coercion but be inspired by a sense of duty. At the same time they are demanding constitutional limitation of the powers of goverment to prevent excessive restriction of the rightful freedom of individuals and associations. This demand for freedom in human society is concerned chiefly with man's spiritual values, and especially with what concerns the free practice of religion in society. This Vatican Council pays careful attention to these spiritual aspirations and, with a view to declaring to what extent they are in accord with the truth and justice, searches the sacred tradition and teaching of the Church, from which it draws forth new things that are always in harmony with the old.

The sacred Council begins by professing that God himself has made known to the human race how men by serving him can be saved and reach happiness in Christ. We believe that this one true religion continues to exist in the Catholic and Apostolic Church, to which the Lord Jesus entrusted the task of spreading it among all men when he said to the apostles: "Go therefore and make disciples of all nations baptizing them in the name of the Father and of the Son and of the Holy Spirit, teaching them to observe all that I have commanded you" (Mt. 18:19–20). All men are

---

a. Translated by Laurence Ryan.
1. Cf. John XXIII, Encyc. *Pacem in Terris,* 11 April 1963: *AAS* 55 (1963), p. 279; ibid., p. 265; Pius XII, Radio message, 24 Dec. 1944: *AAS* 37 (1945), 14.

bound to seek the truth, especially in what concerns God and his Church, and to embrace it and hold on to it as they come to know it.

The sacred Council likewise proclaims that these obligations bind man's conscience. Truth can impose itself on the mind of man only in virtue of its own truth, which wins over the mind with both gentleness and power. So while the religious freedom which men demand in fulfilling their obligation to worship God has to do with freedom from coercion in civil society, it leaves intact the traditional Catholic teaching on the moral duty of individuals and societies towards the true religion and the one Church of Christ. Furthermore, in dealing with this question of liberty the sacred Council intends to develop the teaching of recent popes on the inviolable rights of the human person and on the constitutional order of society.

CHAPTER I

THE GENERAL PRINCIPLE OF RELIGIOUS FREEDOM

2. The Vatican Council declares that the human person has a right to religious freedom. Freedom of this kind means that all men should be immune from coercion on the part of individuals, social groups and every human power so that, within due limits, nobody is forced to act against his convictions nor is anyone to be restrained from acting in accordance with his convictions in religious matters in private or in public, alone or in associations with others. The Council further declares that the right to religious freedom is based on the very dignity of the human person as known through the revealed word of God and by reason itself.[2] This right of the human person to religious freedom must be given such recognition in the constitutional order of society as will make it a civil right.

2. Cf. John XXIII, Encycl. *Pacem in Terris*, 11 April 1963: *AAS* 55 (1963), pp. 260–261; Pius XII, Radio message, 24 Dec. 1942: *AAS* 35 (1943), p. 19; Pius XI, Encyc. *Mit brennender Sorge*, 14 March 1937: *AAS* 29 (1937), p. 160; Leo XIII, Encyc. *Libertas Praestantissimum*, 20 June 1888: *Acta Leonis XIII*, 8, 1888, pp. 237–238.

It is in accordance with their dignity that all men, because they are persons, that is, beings endowed with reason and free will and therefore bearing personal responsibility, are both impelled by their nature and bound by a moral obligation to seek the truth, especially religious truth. They are also bound to adhere to the truth once they come to know it and direct their whole lives in accordance with the demands of truth. But men cannot satisfy this obligation in a way that is in keeping with their own nature unless they enjoy both psychological freedom and immunity from external coercion. Therefore the right to religious freedom has its foundation not in the subjective attitude of the individual but in his very nature. For this reason the right to this immunity continues to exist even in those who do not live up to their obligation of seeking the truth and adhering to it. The exercise of this right cannot be interfered with as long as the just requirements of public order are observed.

3. This becomes even clearer if one considers that the highest norm of human life is the divine law itself—eternal, objective and universal, by which God orders, directs and governs the whole world and the ways of the human community according to a plan conceived in his wisdom and love. God has enabled man to participate in this law of his so that, under the gentle disposition of divine providence, many may be able to arrive at a deeper and deeper knowledge of unchangeable truth. For this reason everybody has the duty and consequently the right to seek the truth in religious matters so that, through the use of appopriate means, he may prudently form judgments of conscience which are sincere and true.

The search for truth, however, must be carried out in a manner that is appropriate to the dignity of the human person and his social nature, namely, by free enquiry with the help of teaching or instruction, communication and dialogue. It is by these means that men share with each other the truth they have discovered, or think they have discovered, in such a way that they help one another in the search for truth. Moreover, it is by personal assent that men must adhere to the truth they have discovered.

It is through his conscience that man sees and recognizes the demands of the divine law. He is bound to follow this conscience faithfully in all his activity so that he may come to God, who is his last end. Therefore he must not be forced to act contrary to his conscience. Nor must he be prevented from acting according to his conscience, especially in religious matters. The reason is because the practice of religion of its very nature consists primarily of those voluntary and free internal acts by which a man directs himself to God. Acts of this kind cannot be commanded or forbidden by any merely human authority.[3] But his own social nature requires that man give external expression to these internal acts of religion, that he communicate with others on religious matters, and profess his religion in community. Consequently to deny man the free exercise of religion in society, when the just requirements of public order are observed, is to do an injustice to the human person and to the very order established by God for men.

Furthermore, the private and public acts of religion by which men direct themselves to God according to their convictions transcend of their very nature the earthly and temporal order of things. Therefore the civil authority, the purpose of which is the care of the common good in the temporal order, must recognize and look with favor on the religious life of the citizens. But if it presumes to control or restrict religious activity it must be said to have exceeded the limits of its power.

4. The freedom or immunity from coercion in religious matters which is the right of individuals must also be accorded to men when they act in community. Religious communities are a requirement of the nature of man and of religion itself.

Therefore, provided the just requirements of public order are not violated, these groups have a right to immunity so that they may organize themselves according to their own principles. They must be allowed to honor the supreme Godhead with public worship, help their members to practice their religion and strengthen them with religious instruction, and promote institutions in which members may work together to organize their own lives according to their religious principles.

Religious communities also have the right not to be hindered by legislation or administrative action on the part of the civil authority in the selection, training, appointment and transfer of their own ministers, in communicating with religious authorities and communities in other parts of the

3. Cf. John XXIII, Encyc. *Pacem in Terris,* 11 April 1963: *AAS* 55 (1963), p. 270; Paul VI, Radio message 22 Dec. 1964: *AAS* 57 (1965), pp. 181–182.

world, in erecting buildings for religious purposes, and in the acquisition and use of the property they need.

Religious communities have the further right not to be prevented from publicly teaching and bearing witness to their beliefs by the spoken or written word. However, in spreading religious belief and in introducing religious practices everybody must at all times avoid any action which seems to suggest coercion or dishonest or unworthy persuasion especially when dealing with the uneducated or the poor. Such a manner of acting must be considered an abuse of one's own right and an infringement of the rights of others.

Also included in the right to religious freedom is the right of religious groups not to be prevented from freely demonstrating the special value of their teaching for the organization of society and the inspiration of all human activity. Finally, rooted in the social nature of man and in the very nature of religion is the right of men, prompted by their own religious sense, freely to hold meetings or establish educational, cultural, charitable and social organizations.

5. Every family, in that it is a society with its own basic rights, has the right freely to organize its own religious life in the home under the control of the parents. These have the right to decide in accordance with their own religious beliefs the form of religious upbringing which is to be given to their children. The civil authority must therefore recognize the right of parents to choose with genuine freedom schools or other means of education. Parents should not be subjected directly or indirectly to unjust burdens because of this freedom of choice. Furthermore, the rights of parents are violated if their children are compelled to attend classes which are not in agreement with the religious beliefs of the parents or if there is but a single compulsory system of education from which all religious instruction is excluded.

6. The common good of society consists in the sum total of those conditions of social life which enable men to achieve a fuller measure of perfection with greater ease. It consists especially in safeguarding the rights and duties of the human person.[4] For this reason the protection of the

4. Cf. John XXIII, Encyc. *Mater et Magistra*, 15 May 1961: *AAS* 53 (1961), p. 417; Id., Encyc. *Pacem in Terris*, 11 April 1963: *AAS* 55 (1963), p. 273.

right to religious freedom is the common responsibility of individual citizens, social groups, civil authorities, the Church and other religious communities. Each of these has its own special responsibility in the matter according to its particular duty to promote the common good.

The protection and promotion of the inviolable rights of man is an essential duty of every civil authority.[5] The civil authority therefore must undertake to safeguard the religious freedom of all the citizens in an effective manner by just legislation and other appropriate means. It must help to create conditions favorable to the fostering of religious life so that the citizens will be really in a position to exercise their religious rights and fulfil their religious duties and so that society itself may enjoy the benefits of justice and peace, which result from man's faithfulness to God and his holy will.[6]

If because of the circumstances of a particular people special civil recognition is given to one religious community in the constitutional organization of a State, the right of all citizens and religious communities to religious freedom must be recognized and respected as well.

Finally, the civil authority must see to it that the equality of the citizens before the law, which is itself an element of the common good of society, is never violated either openly or covertly for religious reasons and that there is no discrimination among citizens.

From this it follows that it is wrong for a public authority to compel its citizens by force or fear or any other means to profess or repudiate any religion or to prevent anyone from joining or leaving a religious body. There is even more serious transgression of God's will and of the sacred rights of the individual person and the family of nations when force is applied to wipe out or repress religion either throughout the whole world or in a single region or in a particular community.

7. The right to freedom in matters of religion is exercised in human society. For this reason its use is subject to certain regulatory norms.

---

5. Cf. John XXIII, Encyc. *Pacem in Terris,* 11 April 1963: *AAS* 55 (1963), pp. 273–274; Pius XII, Radio message, 1 June 1941: *AAS* 33 (1941), p. 200.
6. Cf. Leo XIII, Encyc. *Immortale Dei,* 1 Nov. 1885: *AAS* 18 (1885), p. 165.

In availing of any freedom men must respect the moral principle of personal and social responsibility: in exercising their rights individual men and social groups are bound by the moral law to have regard for the rights of others, their own duties to others and the common good of all. All men must be treated with justice and humanity.

Furthermore, since civil society has the right to protect itself against possible abuses committed in the name of religious freedom the responsibility of providing such protection rests especially with the civil authority. However, this must not be done in an arbitrary manner or by the unfair practice of favoritism but in accordance with legal principles which are in conformity with the objective moral order. These principles are necessary for the effective protection of the rights of all citizens and for peaceful settlement of conflicts of rights. They are also necessary for an adequate protection of that just public peace which is to be found where men live together in good order and true justice. They are required too for the necessary protection of public morality. All these matters are basic to the common good and belong to what is called public order. For the rest, the principle of the integrity of freedom in society should continue to be upheld. According to this principle man's freedom should be given the fullest possible recognition and should not be curtailed except when and in so far as is necessary.

8. Modern man is subjected to a variety of pressures and runs the risk of being prevented from following his own free judgment. On the other hand, there are many who, under the pretext of freedom, seem inclined to reject all submission to authority and make light of the duty of obedience.

For this reason this Vatican Council urges everyone, especially those responsible for educating others, to try to form men with a respect for the moral order who will obey lawful authority and be lovers of true freedom—men, that is, who will form their own judgments in the light of truth, direct their activities with a sense of responsibility, and strive for what is true and just in willing cooperation with others.

Religious liberty therefore should have this further purpose and aim of enabling men to act with greater responsibility in fulfilling their own obligations in society.

CHAPTER II

RELIGIOUS FREEDOM IN THE LIGHT OF REVELATION

9. The Declaration of this Vatican Council on man's right to religious freedom is based on the dignity of the person, the demands of which have become more fully known to human reason through centuries of experience. Furthermore, this doctrine of freedom is rooted in divine revelation, and for this reason Christians are bound to respect it all the more conscientiously. Although revelation does not affirm in so many words the right to immunity from external coercion in religious matters, it nevertheless shows forth the dignity of the human person in all its fullness. It shows us Christ's respect for the freedom with which man is to fulfill his duty of believing the word of God, and it teaches us the spirit which disciples of such a Master must acknowledge and follow in all things. All this throws light on the general principles on which the teaching of this Declaration on Religious Freedom is based. Above all, religious freedom in society is in complete harmony with the act of Christian faith.

10. One of the key truths in Catholic teaching, a truth that is contained in the word of God and constantly preached by the Fathers,[7] is that man's response to God by faith ought to be free, and that therefore nobody is to be forced to embrace the faith against his will.[8] The act of

7. Cf. Lactantius, *Divinarum Institutionum*, v. 19, *CSEL* 19, pp. 463–464, 465; *PL* 6, 614 and 616 (cap. 20); St. Ambrose, *Epistola ad Valentinianum Imp.*, Ep. 21: *PL* 16, 1005; St. Augustine, *Contra Litteras Petiliani*, II, 83: *CSEL* 52 p. 112; *PL* 43, 315; cf. C.3, q.5, c.33 (ed. Friedberg, col. 939); Id., Ep. 23: *PL* 33, 98; Id., Ep. 34: *PL* 33, 132, Id., Ep. 35: *PL* 33, 135; St. Gregory the Great, *Epistola ad Virgilium et Theodorum Episcopos Massiliae Galliarum*, Registrum Epistolarum I, 45: MGH Ep. 1, p. 72: *PL* 77, 510–511 (lib. 1, ep. 47); Id., *Epistola ad Iohannem Episcopum Constantinopilitanum*, Registrum Epistolarum III, 52; MGH Ep. 1, p. 210; *PL* 77, 649 (lib. III, ep. 53); cf. D. 45, c.1 (ed. Friedberg, col. 160); Conc. Tolet. IV, c.57: Mansi 10, 633; cf. D.45, c.5 (ed. Friedberg, col. 161–162); Clement III: X., V, 6, 9: ed. Friedberg, col. 774; Innocent III, *Epistola ad Arelatensem Archiepiscopum*, X., III, 42, 3: ed. Friedberg, col. 646.
8. Cf. *C.I.C.*, c. 1351; Pius XII, Allocution to the Prelates, Auditors

faith is of its very nature a free act. Man, redeemed by Christ the Saviour and called through Jesus Christ to be an adopted son of God,[9] cannot give his adherence to God when he reveals himself unless, drawn by the Father,[10] he submits to God with a faith that is reasonable and free. It is therefore fully in accordance with the nature of faith that in religious matters every form of coercion by men should be excluded. Consequently the principle of religious liberty contributes in no small way to the development of a situation in which men can without hindrance be invited to the Christian faith, embrace it of their own free will and give it practical expression in every sphere of their lives.

11. God calls men to serve him in spirit and in truth. Consequently they are bound to him in conscience but not coerced. God has regard for the dignity of the human person which he himself created; the human person is to be guided by his own judgment and to enjoy freedom. This fact received its fullest manifestation in Christ Jesus in whom God revealed himself and his ways in a perfect manner. For Christ, who is our master and Lord[11] and at the same time is meek and humble of heart,[12] acted patiently in attracting and inviting his disciples.[13] He supported and confirmed his preaching by miracles to arouse the faith of his hearers and give them assurance, but not to coerce them.[14] He did indeed denounce the unbelief of his listeners but he left vengeance to God until the day of judgment.[15] When he sent his apostles into the world he said to them: "He who believes and is baptized will be saved; he who does not believe will be condemned" (Mk. 16:16). He himself recognized that weeds had been sown through the wheat but ordered that both be allowed to grow until the harvest which will come at the end of the world.[16]

and other Ministers of the Tribunal of the Sacred Roman Rota, 6 Oct. 1943, p. 394; Id., Encyc. *Mystici Corporis*, 29 June 1943, *AAS* 1943 p. 243.
9. Cf. Eph. 1:5.
10. Cf. Jn. 6:44.
11. Cf. Jn. 13:13.
12. Cf. Mt. 11:29.
13. Cf. Mt. 11:28–30; Jn. 6:67–68.
14. Cf. Mt. 9:28–29; Mk. 9:23–24; 6:5–6; Paul V, Encyc. *Ecclesiam Suam*, 6 Aug. 1964: *AAS* 56 (1964), pp. 642–643.
15. Cf. Mt. 11:20–24; Rom. 12:19–20; 2 Th. 1:8.
16. Cf. Mt. 13:30 and 40–42.

He did not wish to be a political Messiah who would dominate by force[17] but preferred to call himself the Son of
Man who came to serve, and "to give his life as a ransom
for many" (Mk. 10:45). He showed himself as the perfect
Servant of God[18] who "will not break a bruised reed or
quench a smouldering wick" (Mt. 12:20). He recognized
civil authority and its rights when he ordered tribute to be
paid to Caesar, but he gave clear warning that the higher
rights of God must be respected: "Render therefore to Caesar the things that are Caesar's, and to God, the things that
are God's" (Mt. 22:21). Finally, he brought his revelation
to perfection when he accomplished on the cross the work
of redemption by which he achieved salvation and true freedom for men. For he bore witness to the truth[19] but refused to
use force to impose it on those who spoke out against it.
His kingdom does not make its claims by blows,[20] but is
established by bearing witness to and hearing the truth and
grows by the love with which Christ, lifted up on the cross,
draws men to himself.[21]

Taught by Christ's word and example the apostles followed the same path. From the very beginnings of the
Church the disciples of Christ strove to convert men to confess Christ as Lord, not however by applying coercion or
with the use of techniques unworthy of the Gospel but,
above all, by the power of the word of God.[22] They steadfastly proclaimed to all men the plan of God the Saviour,
"who desires all men to be saved and to come to the knowledge of the truth" (1 Tim. 2:4). At the same time, however,
they showed respect for the weak even though they were in
error, and in this way made it clear how "each of us shall
give account of himself to God" (Rom. 14:12)[23] and for
that reason is bound to obey his conscience. Like Christ,
the apostles were constantly bent on bearing witness to the
truth of God and they showed the greatest courage in
speaking "the word of God with boldness" (Acts 4:31)[24]
before people and rulers. With a firm faith they upheld the

17. Cf. Mt. 4:8–10; Jn. 6:15.
18. Cf. Is. 42:1–4.
19. Cf. Jn. 18:37.
20. Cf. Mt. 26:51–53; Jn. 18:36.
21. Cf. Jn. 12:32.
22. Cf. 1 Cor. 2:3–5; 1 Th. 2:3–5.
23. Cf. Rom. 14:1–23; 1 Cor. 8:9–13; 10:23–33.
24. Cf. Eph. 6:19–20.

truth that the Gospel itself is indeed the power of God for the salvation of all who believe.[25] They therefore despised "all worldly weapons"[26] and followed the example of Christ's meekness and gentleness as they preached the word of God with full confidence in the divine power of that word to destroy those forces hostile to God[27] and lead men to believe in and serve Christ.[28] Like their Master, the apostles too recognized legitimate civil authority: "Let every person be subject to the governing authorities . . . he who resists the authorities resists what God has appointed" (Rom. 13:1–2).[29] At the same time they were not afraid to speak out against public authority when it opposed God's holy will: "We must obey God rather than men" (Acts 5:29).[30] This is the path which innumerable martyrs and faithful have followed through the centuries all over the world.

12. The Church, therefore, faithful to the truth of the Gospel, is following in the path of Christ and the apostles when she recognizes the principle that religious liberty is in keeping with the dignity of man and divine revelation and gives it her support. Throughout the ages she has preserved and handed on the doctrine which she has received from her Master and the apostles. Although in the life of the people of God in its pilgrimage through the vicissitudes of human history there has at times appeared a form of behavior which was hardly in keeping with the spirit of the Gospel and was even opposed to it, it has always remained the teaching of the Church that no one is to be coerced into believing.

Thus the leaven of the Gospel has long been at work in the minds of men and has contributed greatly to a wider recognition by them in the course of time of their dignity as persons. It has contributed too to the growth of the conviction that in religous matters the human person should be kept free from all manner of coercion in civil society.

13. Among those things which pertain to the good of the Church and indeed to the good of society here on earth, things which must everywhere and at all times be safe-

25. Cf. Rom. 1:16.
26. Cf. 2 Cor. 10:4; 1 Th. 5:8–9.
27. Cf. Eph. 6:11–17.
28. Cf. 2 Cor. 10:3–5.
29. Cf. 1 Pet. 2:13–17.
30. Cf. Acts 4:19–20.

guarded and defended from all harm, the most outstanding surely is that the Church enjoy that freedom of action which her responsibility for the salvation of men requires.[31] This is a sacred liberty with which the only-begotten Son of God endowed the Church which he purchased with his blood. Indeed it belongs so intimately to the Church that to attack it is to oppose the will of God. The freedom of the Church is the fundamental principle governing relations between the Church and public authorities and the whole civil order.

As the spiritual authority appointed by Christ the Lord with the duty, imposed by divine command, of going into the whole world and preaching the Gospel to every creature,[32] the Church claims freedom for herself in human society and before every public authority. The Church also claims freedom for herself as a society of men with the right to live in civil society in accordance with the demands of the Christian faith.[33]

When the principle of religious freedom is not just proclaimed in words or incorporated in law but is implemented sincerely in practice, only then does the Church enjoy in law and in fact those stable conditions which give her the independence necessary for fulfilling her divine mission. Ecclesiastical authorities have been insistent in claiming this independence in society.[34] At the same time the Christian faithful, in common with the rest of men, have the civil right of freedom from interference in leading their lives according to their conscience. A harmony exists therefore between the freedom of the Church and that religious freedom which must be recognized as the right of all men and all communities and must be sanctioned by constitutional law.

14. In order to satisfy the divine command: "Make disciples of all nations" (Mt. 28:19), the Catholic Church must spare no effort in striving "that the word of the Lord may speed on and triumph" (2 Th. 3:1).

The Church therefore earnestly urges her children first of

31. Cf. Leo XIII, *Officio Sanctissimo,* 22 Dec. 1887: *AAS* 20 (1887), p. 269; Id., *Ex Litteris,* 7 April 1887: *AAS* 19 (1886), p. 465.
32. Cf. Mk. 16:15; Mt. 28:18–20; Pius XII, Encyc. *Summi Pontificatus,* 20 Oct. 1939: *AAS* 31 (1939), pp. 445–446.
33. Cf. Pius XI, *Firmissimam Constantiam,* 28 Mar. 1937: *AAS* 29 (1937), p. 196.
34. Cf. Pius XII, Allocution *Ci riesce,* 6 Dec. 1953: *AAS* 45 (1953), p. 802.

all that "supplications, prayers, intercessions and thanksgivings be made for all men. . . . This is good and is acceptable in the sight of God our Savior, who desires all men to be saved and to come to the knowledge of the truth" (1 Tim. 2:1-4).

However, in forming their consciences the faithful must pay careful attention to the sacred and certain teaching of the Church.[35] For the Catholic Church is by the will of Christ the teacher of truth. It is her duty to proclaim and teach with authority the truth which is Christ and, at the same time, to declare and confirm by her authority the principles of the moral order which spring from human nature itself. In addition, Christians should approach those who are outside wisely, "in the holy Spirit, genuine love, truthful speech" (2 Cor. 6:6-7), and should strive, even to the shedding of their blood, to spread the light of life with all confidence[36] and apostolic courage.

The disciple has a grave obligation to Christ, his Master, to grow daily in his knowledge of the truth he has received from him, to be faithful in announcing it and vigorous in defending it without having recourse to methods which are contrary to the spirit of the Gospel. At the same time the love of Christ urges him to treat with love, prudence and patience[37] those who are in error or ignorance with regard to the faith. He must take into account his duties towards Christ, the life-giving Word whom he must proclaim, the rights of the human person and the measure of grace which God has given to each man through Christ in calling him freely to accept and profess the faith.

15. It is certain therefore that men of the present day want to profess their religion freely in private and in public. Indeed it is a fact that religious freedom has already been declared a civil right in most constitutions and has been given solemn recognition in international documents.[38]

But there are forms of government under which, despite constitutuional recognition of the freedom of religious worship, the public authorities themselves strive to deter the citi-

35. Cf. Pius XII, Radio message, 23 Mar. 1952: *AAS* 44 (1952), pp. 270-278.
36. Cf. Acts 4:29.
37. Cf. John XXIII, Encyc. *Pacem in Terris*, 11 April 1963: *AAS* 55 (1963), pp. 299-300.
38. See John XXIII, Encycl. *Pacem in Terris*, 11 April 1963: *AAS* 55 (1963), pp. 295-296.

zens from professing their religion and make life particularly difficult and dangerous for religious bodies.

This sacred Council gladly welcomes the first of these two facts as a happy sign of the times. In sorrow however it denounces the second as something deplorable. The Council exhorts Catholics and directs an appeal to all men to consider with great care how necessary religious liberty is, especially in the present condition of the human family.

It is clear that with the passage of time all nations are coming into a closer unity, men of different cultures and religions are being bound together by closer links, and there is a growing awareness of individual responsibility. Consequently, to establish and strengthen peaceful relations and harmony in the human race, religious freedom must be given effective constitutional protection everywhere and that highest of man's rights and duties—to lead a religious life with freedom in society—must be respected.

May God, the Father of all, grant that the human family by carefully observing the principle of religious liberty in society may be brought by the grace of Christ and the power of the holy Spirit to that "glorious freedom of the children of God" (Rom. 8:21) which is sublime and everlasting.

61

DECREE ON THE CHURCH'S MISSIONARY ACTIVITY[a]

Vatican II, *Ad Gentes Divinitus,* 7 December, 1965

INTRODUCTION

1. Having been divinely sent to the nations that she might be "the universal sacrament of salvation,"[1] the Church, in obedience to the command fo her founder (Mt. 16:15) and because it is demanded by her own essential universality, strives to preach the Gospel to all men. The apostles, on whom the Church was founded, following the footsteps of Christ "preached the word of truth and begot churches."[2] It is the duty of their successors to carry on this work so that "the word of God may run and be glorified" (2 Th. 3:1), and the kingdom of God proclaimed and renewed throughout the whole world.

In the present state of things which gives rise to a new situation for mankind, the Church, the salt of the earth and the light of the world (cf. Mt. 5:13–14), is even more urgently called upon to save and renew every creature, so that all things might be restored in Christ, and so that in him men might form one family and one people of God.

And so this sacred Synod, while it thanks God for the outstanding work done through the generous labor of the whole Church, proposes to outline the principles of missionary activity. It wishes to unite the efforts of all the faithful, so that the people of God, following the narrow way of the cross, might everywhere spread the kingdom of Christ, the Lord and beholder of the ages (cf. Eccl. 36:19), and prepare the way for his coming.

a. Translated by Redmond Fitzmaurice, o.p. The references to D.62 at the end of certain sections indicate where the norms for their implementations are to be found.
1. Cf. Dogm. Const. *Lumen Gentium,* 48.
2. St. Augustine, *Enarr. in Ps. 44,* 23 (*PL* 36, 508; CChr. 38, 510).

CHAPTER I

DOCTRINAL PRINCIPLES

2. The Church on earth is by its very nature missionary since, according to the plan of the Father, it has its origin in the mission of the Son and the Holy Spirit.[1] This plan flows from "fountain-like love," the love of God the Father. As the principle without principle from whom the Son is generated and from whom the Holy Spirit proceeds through the Son, God in his great and merciful kindness freely creates us and moreover, graciously calls us to share in his life and glory. He generously pours out, and never ceases to pour out, his divine goodness, so that he who is creator of all things might at last become "all in all" (1 Cor. 15:28), thus simultaneously assuring his own glory and our happiness. It pleased God to call men to share in his life and not merely singly, without any bond between them, but he formed them into a people, in which his children who had been scattered were gathered together (cf. Jn. 11:52).

3. This universal plan of God for salvation of mankind is not carried out solely in a secret manner, as it were, in the minds of men, nor by the efforts, even religious, through which they in many ways seek God in an attempt to touch him and find him, although God is not far from any of us (cf. Acts 17:27); their efforts need to be enlightened and corrected, although in the loving providence of God they may lead one to the true God and be a preparation for the Gospel.[2] However, in order to establish a relationship of peace and communion with himself, and in order to bring about brotherly union among men, and they sinners, God decided to enter into the history of mankind in a new and definitive manner, by sending his own Son in human flesh,

1. Cf. Dogm. Const. *Lumen Gentium*, 1.
2. Cf. St. Irenaeus, *Adv. Haer.* III, 18, 1: "The Word existing with God, through whom everything was made and who was always present to the human race . . ." (*PG* 7, 932); id. IV, 6, 7: "From the beginning, the Son, being present in his creation, reveals the Father to all whom the Father desires, at the time and in the manner desired by the Father" (id. 990); cf. IV, 20, 6 and 7 (id. 1037); Demonstratio n. 34 (*Patr. Or.* XII, 773; *Sources Chret.* 62, Paris 1958, p. 87); Clement of Alex., *Protrept.* 112, 1 (G.C.S. Clement I, 79); *Strom.* VI, 6, 44, 1 (G.C.S. Clement II, 453); 13, 106, 3 and 4 (id. 485). For the same doctrine cf. Pius XII, Radio message, 31 Dec. 1952; Dogm. Const. *Lumen Gentium*, 16.

so that through him he might snatch men from the power of darkness and of Satan (cf. Col. 1:13; Acts 10:38) and in him reconcile the world to himself. He appointed him, through whom he made the world,[4] to be heir of all things, that he might restore all things in him (cf. Eph. 1:10).

Jesus Christ was sent into the world as the true Mediator between God and men. Since he is God, all the fullness of the divine nature dwells in him bodily (Col. 2:9); as man he is the new Adam, full of grace and truth (Jn. 1:14), who has been constituted head of a restored humanity. So the Son of God entered the world by means of a true incarnation that he might make men sharers in the divine nature; though rich, he was made poor for our sake, that by his poverty we might become rich (2 Cor. 8:9). The Son of man did not come to be served, but to serve and to give his life as a ransom for many, that is for all (cf. Mk. 10:45). The fathers of the Church constantly proclaim that what was not assumed by Christ was not healed.[4] Now Christ took a complete human nature just as it is found in us poor unfortunates, but one that was without sin (cf. Heb. 4:15; 9:28). Christ, whom the Father sanctified and sent into the world (cf. Jn. 10:36), said of himself: "The Spirit of the Lord is upon me, because he annointed me; to bring good news to the poor he sent me, to heal the broken-hearted, to proclaim to the captive release, and sight to the blind" (Lk. 4:8); and on another occasion: "The Son of man has come to seek and to save what was lost " (Lk. 9:10).

Now, what was once preached by the Lord, or fulfilled in him for the salvation of mankind, must be proclaimed and spread to the ends of the earth (Acts 1:8), starting from Jerusalem (cf. Lk. 24:27), so that what was accomplished for the salvation of all men may, in the course of time, achieve its universal effect.

3. Cf. Heb. 1:2; Jn. 1:3 and 10; 1 Cor. 8:6; Col. 1:16.
4. Cf. St. Athanasius, *Ep. ad Epictetum*, I (*PG* 26, 1060); St. Cyril of Jerusalem, *Catech.* 4, 9 (*PG* 33, 465); Marius Victorinus, *Adv. Arium*, 3, 3 (*PL* 8, 1101); St. Basil, *Epist.* 261, 2 (*PG* 32, 969); St. Gregory Naz. *Epist. 101* (*PG* 37, 181); St. Gregory of Nyssa, *Antirrheticus, Adv. Apollin.*, 17 (*PG* 45, 1156); St. Ambrose, *Epist.* 48, 5 (*PL* 16, 1153); St. Augustine, *In Joann. Ev.*, tr. XXIII, 6 (*PL* 35, 1585; CChr. 36. 236); besides in this way, he shows, that he holy Spirit did not redeem us because he was not made flesh: *De Agone* Christ. 22, 24 (*PL* 40, 302); St. Cyril of Alex, *Adv. Nestor.* I, 1 (*PG* 76, 20); St. Fulgentius, *Epist. 17*, 3, 5 (*PL* 65, 284); *Ad Trasimundum*, III, 21 (*PL* 65, 284: *de tristitia et timore*).

4. To do this, Christ sent the Holy Spirit from the Father to exercise inwardly his saving influence, and to promote the spread of the Church. Without doubt, the Holy Spirit was at work in the world before Christ was glorified.[5] On the day of Pentecost, however, he came down on the disciples that he might remain with them forever (cf. Jn. 14:16); on that day the Church was openly displayed to the crowds and the spread of the Gospel among the nations, through preaching, was begun. Finally, on that day was foreshadowed the union of all peoples in the catholicity of the faith by means of the Church of the New Alliance, a Church which speaks every language, understands and embraces all tongues in charity, and thus overcomes the dispersion of Babel.[6] The "acts of the apostles" began with Pentecost, just as Christ was conceived in the Virgin Mary with the coming of the Holy Spirit and was moved to begin his ministry by the descent of the same Holy Spirit, who came down upon him while he was praying.[7] Before freely laying down his life for the world, the Lord Jesus organized

5. It is the Spirit who spoke through the prophets: *Symb. Constantinopol.* Denz.-Schoenmetzer, 150): St. Leo the Great, *Sermon 76* (*PL* 54, 405-406): "When the holy Spirit filled the Lord's disciples on the day of Pentecost, this was not the first exercise of his role but an extension of his bounty, because the patriarchs, prophets, priests, and all the holy men of the previous ages were nourished by the same sanctifying Spirit . . . although the measure of the gifts was not the same." Also *Sermon 77*, 1 (*PL* 54, 412); Leo XIII,, Encyc. *Divinum illud* (*AAS* 1897, 650-651). Also St. John Chrysostom, although he insisted on the newness of the mission of the holy Spirit on the day of Pentecost: *In Eph.* c. 4, Hom. 10, 1 (*PG* 62, 75).

6. The fathers of the Church often speak of Babel and Pentecost: Origen, *in Genesim*, c. 1 (*PG* 12, 112); St. Gregory Naz. *Oratio* 41, 16 (*PG* 36, 449); St. John Chrysostom, *Hom. in Pentec.*, 2 (*PG* 50, 467); St. Augustine, *Enn. in Ps.* 54, 11 (*PL* 36, 636; CChr. 39, 664 ff.); *Sermon 271* (*PL* 38, 1245); St. Cyril of Alex., *Glaphyra in Genesim* II (*PG* 69, 79); St. Gregory the Great, *Hom. in Evang.*, Lib. II, Hom. 30, 4 (*PL* 76, 1222); St. Bede, *in Hexaem.*, lib. III (*PL* 91, 125). See also the image in the porch of the Basilica of St. Mark, Venice.

The Church speaks all languages and so gathers men into the catholicity of the faith: St. Augustine, *Sermons 266, 267, 268, 269* (*PL* 38, 1225-1237), *Sermon 165*, 3 (*PL* 38, 946); St. John Chrysost., *In Ep. I ad Cor.*, Hom. 35 (*PG* 74, 758); St. Fulgentius, *Sermon 8*, 2-3 (*PL* 65, 743-744).

On Pentecost as the consecration of the apostles for their mission cf. J. A. Cramer, *Catena in Acta SS. Apostolorum*, Oxford 1838, p. 24 ff.

7. Cf. Lk. 3:22; 4:1; Acts 10:38.

the apostolic ministry and promised to send the Holy Spirit, in such a way that both would be always and everywhere associated in the fulfilment of the work of salvation.[8] Throughout the ages the Holy Spirit makes the entire Church "one in communion and ministry; and provides her with different hierarchical and charismatic gifts,"[9] giving life to ecclesiastical structures, being as it were their soul,[10] and inspiring in the hearts of the faithful that same spirit of mission which impelled Christ himself. He even at times visibly anticipates apostolic action,[11] just as in various ways he unceasingly accompanies and directs it.[12]

5. From the beginning of his ministry the Lord Jesus "called to himself those whom he wished and he caused twelve of them to be with him and to be sent out preaching" (Mk. 3:13; cf. Mt. 10:1-42). Thus the apostles were both the seeds of the new Israel and the beginning of the sacred hierarchy. Later, before he was assumed into heaven (cf. Acts 1:11), after he had fulfilled in himself the mysteries of our salvation and the renewal of all things by his death and resurrection, the Lord, who had received all power in heaven and on earth (cf. Mt. 28:18), founded his Church as the sacrament of salvation; and just as he had been sent by the Father (cf. Jn. 20:21), so he sent the apostles into the whole world, commanding them: "Go, therefore, and make disciples of all nations, baptizing them in the name of the Father and of the Son and of the Holy Spirit; teaching them to observe all that I have commanded you" (Mt. 28:19 ff.); "Go into the whole world, preach the Gospel to every creature. He who believes and is baptized shall be saved; but he who does not believe, shall be condemned" (Mk. 16:15 ff.). Hence the Church has an obligation to proclaim the faith and salvation which comes from Christ, both by reason of the express command which the order of bishops inherited from the apostles, an obligation in the discharge of which they are assisted by priests, and one which they share with the successor of St. Peter, the supreme pastor of the

8. Cf. Jn. ch. 14–17; Paul VI, Allocution delivered in the Council on 14 September 1964: *AAS* (1964), 807.
9. Cf. Dogm. Const. *Lumen Gentium*, 4.
10. St. Augustine, *Sermon* 267, 4 (*PL* 38, 1231): "The holy Spirit does for the whole Church what the soul does for all the members of one body." Cf. Dogm. Const. *Lumen Gentium*, 7 (also note 8).
11. Cf. Acts 10:44–47; 11:15; 15:8.
12. Cf. Acts 4:8; 5:32; 8:26, 29, 39; 9:31; 10; 11:24, 28; 13:2, 4, 9; 16:6–7; 20:22–23; 21:11 etc.

Church, and also by reason of the life which Christ infuses into his members: "From him the whole body, being closely joined and knit together through every joint of the system, according to the functioning in due measure of each single part, derives its increase to the building up of itself in love" (Eph. 4:16). The mission of the Church is carried out by means of that activity through which, in obedience to Christ's command and moved by the grace and love of the Holy Spirit, the Church makes itself fully present to all men and peoples in order to lead them to the faith, freedom and peace of Christ by the example of its life and teaching, by the sacraments and other means of grace. Its aim is to open up for all men a free and sure path to full participation in the mystery of Christ.

Since this mission continues and, in the course of history, unfolds the mission of Christ, who was sent to evangelize the poor, then the Church, urged on by the Spirit of Christ, must walk the road Christ himself walked, a way of poverty and obedience, of service and self-sacrifice even to death, a death from which he emerged victorious by his resurrection. So it was that the apostles walked in hope and by much trouble and suffering filled up what was lacking in the sufferings of Christ for his body, which is the Church. Often, too, the seed was the blood of Christians.[18]

6. This task which must be carried out by the order of bishops, under the leadership of Peter's successor and with the prayers and cooperation of the whole Church, is one and the same everywhere and in all situations, although, because of circumstances, it may not always be exercised in the same way. The differences which must be recognized in this activity of the Church, do not flow from the inner nature of the mission itself, but from the circumstances in which it is exercised.

These circumstances depend either on the Church itself or on the peoples, classes or men to whom its mission is directed. Although the Church possesses in itself the totality and fullness of the means of salvation, it does not always, in fact cannot, use every one of them immediately, but it has to make beginnings and work by slow stages to give effect to God's plan. Sometimes after a successful start it has cause to mourn a setback, or it may linger in a state of semi-fulfilment and insufficiency. With regard to peoples,

13. Tertullian, *Apologeticum*, 50, 13 (*PL* 1, 534); (CChr. 1, 171).

classes and men it is only by degrees that it touches and penetrates them and so raises them to a catholic perfection. In each situation and circumstance a proper line of action and effective means should be adopted.

The special undertakings in which preachers of the Gospel, sent by the Church, and going into the whole world, carry out the work of preaching the Gospel and implanting the Church among people who do not yet believe in Christ, are generally called "missions." Such undertakings are accomplished by missionary activity and are, for the most part, carried out in defined territories recognized by the Holy See. The special end of this missionary activity is the evangelization and the implanting of the Church among peoples or groups in which it has not yet taken root.[14] All over the world indigenous particular churches ought to grow from the seed of the word of God, churches which would be adequately organized and would possess their own proper strength and maturity. With their own hierarchy and faithful, and sufficiently endowed with means adapted to the living of a full Christian life, they should contribute to the good of the whole Church. The principal instrument in this work of implanting the Church is the preaching of the Gospel of Jesus Christ. It was to announce this Gospel that the Lord sent his disciples into the whole world, that men, having been reborn by the word of God (cf. 1 Pet. 1:23), might through baptism, be joined to the Church which, as the Body of the Word Incarnate, lives and is nourished by the word of God and the Eucharist (cf. Acts 4:23).

Various stages, which are sometimes intermingled, are to

14. St. Thomas Aquinas already speaks of the apostolic duty to implant the Church: cf. *Sent.* Lib. I, dist. 16, q.1, a.2 ad 2 et ad 4; a.3 sol.; *Summa Theol.* Ia, q.43, a.7, ad 6; Ia IIae q.106, a.4 ad 4. Cf. Benedict XV, *Maximum illud*, 30 Nov. 1919 (*AAS* 1919, 445 and 453); Pius XI, *Rerum Ecclesiae*, 28 Feb. 1926 (*AAS* 1926, 74); Pius XII, 30 April 1939 to the Directors OO.PP.MM.; id., 24 June 1944, to the Directors OO.PP.MM. (*AAS* 1944, 210; also in *AAS* 1950, 727 and 1951, 508); id., 29 June 1948 to the indigenous clergy (*AAS* 1948, 374); id., *Evangelii Praecones*, 2 June 1951 (*AAS* 1951, 507); id., *Fidei Donum*, 15 Jan. 1957 (*AAS* 1957, 236); John XXIII, *Princeps Pastorum*, 28 Nov. 1959 (*AAS* 1959, 835); Paul VI, Hom. 18 Oct. 1964 (*AAS* 1964, 911).

The popes, fathers and scholastics often speak of the "spreading" (*dilatio*) of the Church: St. Thomas Aquinas, *Comm. in Matth.* 16, 28; Leo XIII, Encyc. *Sancta Dei Civitas* (*AAS* 1880, 241); Benedict XV, Encyc. *Maximum illud* (*AAS* 1919, 442); Pius XI, Encyc. *Rerum Ecclesiae* (*AAS* 1926, 65).

be found in this missionary activity of the Church; first there is the beginning or planting and then a time of freshness and youthfulness. Nor does the Church's missionary activity cease once this point has been passed; the obligation to carry on the work devolves on the particular churches already constituted, an obligation to preach the Gospel to all who are still outside.

Moreover, it often happens that, owing to various cases, the groups among whom the Church operates are utterly changed so that an entirely new situation arises. Then the Church must consider whether these new circumstances require that she should once again exercise her missionary activity. The situation, however, is often of such a nature that for the time being there is no possibility of directly and immediately preaching the Gospel. In that case missionaries, patiently, prudently, and with great faith, can and ought at least bear witness to the love and kindness of Christ and thus prepare a way for the Lord, and in some way make him present.

It is clear, therefore, that missionary activity flows immediately from the very nature of the Church. Missionary activity extends the saving faith of the Church, it expands and perfects its catholic unity, it is sustained by its apostolicity, it activates the collegiate sense of its hierarchy, and bears witness to its sanctity which it both extends and promotes. Missionary work among the nations differs from the pastoral care of the faithful and likewise from efforts aimed at restoring Christian unity. Nevertheless, these two latter are very closely connected with the Church's missionary endeavor[15] because the division of Christians is injurious to the holy work of preaching the Gospel to every creature,[16] and deprives many people of access to the faith. Because of the Church's mission, all baptized people are called upon to come together in one flock that they might bear unanimous witness to Christ their Lord before the nations. And if they

15. Obviously included in this concept of missionary activity are in fact those parts of Latin America where there is no proper hierarchy, nor maturity of Christian life, nor sufficient preaching of the Gospel. Whether these territories are in fact recognized by the Holy See as missionary is not a matter for the Council. This is why with regard to the connection between the concept of missionary activity and definite areas, it is rightly said that such activity is "for the most part" exercised in definite geographical areas recognized by the Holy See.

16. Decree *Unitatis Redintegratio*, 1.

cannot yet fully bear witness to one faith, they should at least be imbued with mutual respect and love.

7. The reason for missionary activity lies in the will of God, "who wishes all men to be saved and to come to the knowledge of the truth. For there is one God and one Mediator between God and men, himself a man, Jesus Christ, who gave himself as a ransom for all" (1 Tim. 2:4–5), "neither is their salvation in any other" (Acts 4:12). Everyone, therefore, ought to be converted to Christ, who is known through the preaching of the Church, and they ought, by baptism, become incorporated into him, and into the Church which is his body. Christ himself explicitly asserted te necesity of faith and baptism (cf. Mk. 16:16; Jn. 3:5), and thereby affirmed at the same time the necessity of the Church, which men enter through baptism as through a door. Hence those cannot be saved, who, knowing that the Catholic Church was founded through Jesus Christ, by God, as something necessary, still refuse to enter it, or to remain in it.[17] So, although in ways known to himself God can lead those who, through no fault of their own, are ignorant of the Gospel to that faith without which it is impossible to please him (Heb. 11:6), the Church, nevertheless, still has the obligation and also the sacred right to evangelize. And so, today as always, missionary activity retains its full force and necessity.

By means of this activity the mystical Body of Christ unceasingly gathers and directs its energies towards its own increase (Eph. 4:11–16). The members of the Church are impelled to engage in this activity because of the charity with which they love God and by which they desire to share with all men in the spiritual goods of this life and the life to come.

Finally, by this missionary activity God is fully glorified, when men fully and consciously accept the work of salvation which he accomplished in Christ. By means of it God's plan is realized, a plan to which Christ lovingly and obediently submitted for the glory of the Father who sent him[18] in order that the whole human race might become one people of God, form one body of Christ, and be built up into one temple of the Holy Spirit; all of which, as an expression of brotherly concord, answers to a profound longing in

17. Cf. Dogm. Const. *Lumen Gentium*, 14.
18. Cf. Jn. 7:18; 8:30 and 44; 8:50; 17:1.

all men. And thus, finally, the intention of the creator in creating man in his own image and likeness will be truly realized, when all who possess human nature, and have been regenerated in Christ through the Holy Spirit, gazing together on the glory of God, will be able to say "Our Father."[19]

8. Missionary activity is intimately bound up with human nature and its aspirations. In manifesting Christ, the Church reveals to men their true situation and calling, since Christ is the head and exemplar of that renewed humanity, imbued with that brotherly love, sincerity and spirit of peace, to which all men aspire. Both Christ and the Church which bears witness to him transcend the distinctions of race and nationality, and so cannot be considered as strangers to anyone or in any place.[20] Christ is the Truth and the Way which the preaching of the Gospel lays open to all men when it speaks those words of Christ in their ear: "Repent, and believe the Gospel" (Mk. 1:15). Since he who does not believe is already judged (cf. Jn. 3:18), the words of Christ are at once words of judgment and grace, of life and

19. As regards this synthetic idea see the doctrine of St. Irenaeus on the Recapitulation. Cf. also Hippolytus, *De Antichristo*, 3: "Loving all men and desiring to save all, wishing to make of them sons of God and calling all the saints to form one perfect man . . ." (*PG* 10, 732; G.C.S. Hippolyt. I, 2 p. 6); *Benedictiones Jacob*, 7 (T.U., 38–1 p. 18, lin. 4 ff.); Origen, *In Ioann.* tom. 1, n. 16: "For those who have come to God, led by the Word who is with God, there is only one act of knowing God, that as sons they might be carefully formed in the knowledge of God, as at present the Son alone knows the Father" (*PG* 14, 49; G.C.S. Origen IV, 20); St. Augustine, *De Sermone Domini in monte*, I, 41: "Let us love that which can lead us to those kingdoms where no one says: my Father, but all say to the one God: our Father" (*PL* 34, 1250); St. Cyril of Alex., *In Ioann.*: "We are all in Christ, and our common human nature is revitalized in him. This is why he is called the new Adam . . . He who is by nature both Son and God, dwells in us and so in his Spirit we call Abba Father! The Word dwells in all, in one temple, that is to say in that temple which he has taken for us and from us in order that having all men in himself, he might, as St. Paul says, reconcile all men to the Father in one body" (*PG* 73, 161–165).
20. Benedict XV, *Maximum illud* (*AAS* 1919, 445): "As the Church of God is Catholic, it is never a stranger to any race or nation" Cf. John XXIII, Encyc. *Mater et Magistra*: "by divine right the Church extends to all peoples . . . since it injects its power into the veins, as it were, of a people, it is not, therefore, nor does it consider itself as just an institution which is imposed on this people from without . . . So all that appears to it as good and honest it strengthens and brings to perfection" (i.e. those who are reborn in Christ) (*AAS* 1961, 444).

death. For it is only by putting to death that which is old that we can come to newness of life. Now although this refers primarily to people, it is also true of various worldly goods which bear the mark both of man's sin and the blessing of God: "For all have sinned and have need of the glory of God" (Rom. 3:23). No one is freed from sin by himself or by his own efforts, no one is raised above himself or completely delivered from his own weakness, solitude or slavery; all have need of Christ who is the model, master, liberator, saviour, and giver of life.[21] Even in the secular history of mankind the Gospel has acted as a leaven in the interests of liberty and progress, and it always offers itself as a leaven with regard to brotherhood, unity and peace. So it is not without reason that Christ is hailed by the faithful as "the hope of the nations and their saviour."[22]

9. The period, therefore, between the first and second coming of the Lord is the time of missionary activity, when, like the harvest, the Church will be gathered from the four winds into the kingdom of God.[23] For the Gospel must be preached to all peoples before the Lord comes (cf. Mk. 13:10).

Missionary activity is nothing else, and nothing less, than the manifestation of God's plan, its epiphany and realization in the world and in history; that by which God, through mission, clearly brings to its conclusion the history of salvation. Through preaching and the celebration of the sacraments, of which the holy Eucharist is the center and summit, missionary activity makes Christ present, he who is the author of salvation. It purges of evil associations those elements of truth and grace which are found among peoples, and which are, as it were, a secret presence of God; and it restores them to Christ their source who overthrows the rule of the devil and limits the manifold malice of evil. So whatever goodness is found in the minds and hearts of men, or in the particular customs and cultures of peoples, far from being lost is purified, raised to a higher level and reaches its perfection, for the glory of God, the confusion of the demon, and the happiness of men.[24] Thus mission-

---

21. Cf. Irenaeus, *Adv. Haer.* III, 15, n. 3 (*PG* 7, 919): "They were preachers of truth and apostles of liberty."
22. Ant. *O diei* 23 December.
23. Cf. Mt. 24:31; *Didache* 10, 5 (Funk I, p. 32).
24. Dogm. Const. *Lumen Gentium*, 17. St. Augustine, *De Civitate Dei* 19, 17 (*PL* 41, 646). Instr. S.C.P.F. (*Collectanea* I, n. 135, p. 42).

ary acitivity tends towards eschatological fullness;[25] by it the people of God is expanded to the degree and until the time that the Father has fixed by his own authority (cf. Acts 1:7); of it was it said in prophecy: "Enlarge the space for your tent and spread out your tent clothes unsparingly" (Is. 54:2).[26] By missionary activity the mystical Body is enlarged until it reaches the mature fullness of Christ (cf. Eph. 4:13); the spiritual temple where God is adored in spirit and truth (cf. Jn. 4:23) grows and is built up on the foundation of the apostles and prophets, Jesus Christ himself being the chief cornerstone (Eph. 2:20). (See D. 62, 1.)

Chapter II

MISSIONARY WORK

10. The Church, which has been sent by Christ to reveal and communicate the love of God to all men and to all peoples, is aware that for her a tremendous missionary work still remains to be done. There are two billion people —and their number is increasing day by day—who have never, or barely, heard the Gospel message; they constitute large and distinct groups united by enduring cultural ties, ancient religious traditions, and strong social relationships. Of these, some belong to one or other of the great religions, others have no knowledge of God, while others expressly deny the existence of God and sometimes even attack it. If the Church is to be in a position to offer all men the mystery of salvation and the life brought by God, then it must implant itself among all these groups in the same way that

25. According to Origen the Gospel ought to be preached before the consummation of this world: *Hom. in Lc.* XXI (G.C.S. *Orig.* IX, 136, 21 ff.); *In Matth. comm.* ser. 39 (XI, 75, 25, FF; 76, 4 ff); St. Thomas Aquinas *Summa Theol.* Ia IIae, q. 106, a.4 ad 4.
26. Hilary of Poitiers, *In Ps.* 14 (*PL* 9, 301); Eusebius of Caes., *In Isaiam* 54, 2–3 (*PG* 24, 462–463); Cyril of Alex., *In Isaiam* V, ch. 54, 1–3 (*PG* 70, 1193).

Christ by his incarnation committed himself to the particular social and cultural circumstances of the men among who he lived.

ARTICLE 1: CHRISTIAN WITNESS

11. The Church must be present to these groups through those of its members who live among them or have been sent to them. All Christians by the example of their lives and the witness of the word, wherever they live, have an obligation to manifest the new man which they put on in baptism, and to reveal the power of the Holy Spirit by whom they were strengthened at confirmation, so that others, seeing their good works, might glorify the Father (cf. Matt. 5:16) and more perfectly perceive the true meaning of human life and the universal solidarity of mankind. In order to bear witness to Christ, fruitfully, they should establish relationships of respect and love with those men, they should acknowledge themselves as members of the group in which they live, and through the various undertakings and affairs of human life they should share in their social and cultural life. They should be familiar with their national and religious traditions and uncover with gladness and respect those seeds of the Word which lie hidden among them. They must look to the profound transformation which is taking place among nations and work hard so that modern man is not turned away from the things of God by an excessive preoccupation with modern science and technology, but rather aroused to desire, even more intensely, that love and truth which have been revealed by God. Just as Christ penetrated to the hearts of men and by a truly human dialogue led them to the divine light, so too his disciples, profoundly pervaded by the Spirit of Christ, should know and converse with those among whom they live, that through sincere and patient dialogue these men might learn of the riches which a generous God has distributed among the nations. They must at the same time endeavor to illuminate these riches with the light of the Gospel, set them free, and bring them once more under the dominion of God the saviour.

12. The presence of Christians among these human groups should be one that is animated by that love with which we are loved by God, who desires that we should love each other with that self-same love (cf. 1 Jn 4:11).

Christian charity is extended to all without distinction of race, social condition, or religion, and seeks neither gain nor gratitude. Just as God loves us with a gratuitous love, so too the faithful, in their charity, should be concerned for mankind, loving it with that same love with which God sought man. As Christ went about all the towns and villages healing every sickness and infirmity, as a sign that the kingdom of God had come (cf. Mt. 9:35 ff.; Acts 10:38), so the Church, through its children, joins itself with men of every condition, but especially with the poor and afflicted, and willingly spends herself for them (cf. 2 Cor. 12:15). It shares their joys and sorrows, it is familiar with the hopes and problems of life, it suffers with them in the anguish of death. It wishes to enter into fraternal dialogue with those who are working for peace, and to bring them the peace and light of the Gospel.

Christians ought to interest themselves, and collaborate with others, in the right ordering of social and economic affairs. They should apply themselves with special care to the education of children and young people through various types of schools, and these are not to be considered solely as an outstanding means for forming and developing a Christian youth, but as a service of great value to men, especially in the developing countries, one that is ordered to raising human dignity and promoting more human conditions. They should, furthermore, share in the efforts of those people who, in fighting against famine, ignorance and disease, are striving to bring about better living conditions and bring about peace in the world. In this work the faithful, after due consideration, should be eager to collaborate in projects initiated by private, public, state, or international bodies, or by other Christian or even non-Christian communities.

The Church, nevertheless, has no desire to become involved in the government of the temporal order. It claims no other competence besides that of faithfully serving men in charity with the help of God (cf. Mt. 20:26; 23:11).[1]

The disciples of Christ, being in close contact with men through their life and work, hope to offer them an authentic Christian witness and work for their salvation, even in those places where they cannot preach Christ in full. They

---

1. Cf. the allocution given by Paul VI in the Council, 21 Nov. 1964 (*AAS* 1964, 1013).

are not working for the merely material progress or prosperity of men; but in teaching the religious and moral truths, which Christ illumined with his light, they seek to enhance the dignity of men and promote fraternal unity, and, in this way, are gradually opening a wider approach to God. So men are aided in attaining salvation by love of God and love of men; the mystery of Christ begins to shine out, that mystery in which has appeared the new man created in the likeness of God (cf. Eph. 4:24) and in whom the charity of God is revealed.

ARTICLE 2: PREACHING THE GOSPEL AND ASSEMBLING THE PEOPLE OF GOD

13. Wherever God opens a door for the word in order to declare the mystery of Christ (cf. Col. 4:3) then the living God, and he whom he has sent for the salvation of all, Jesus Christ (cf. 1 Th. 1:9–10; 1 Cor. 1:18–21; Gal. 1:31; Acts 14:15–17; 17:22–31), are confidently and perseveringly (cf. Acts 4:13, 29, 31; 9:27, 28; 13:40; 14:3; 19:8; 26:26; 28:31; 1 Th. 2:2; 2 Cor. 3:12; 7:4; Phil. 1:20; Eph. 3:12; 6:19–20) proclaimed (cf. 1 Cor. 9:15; Rom. 10:14) to all men (cf. Mk. 16:15). And this is in order that non-Christians, whose heart is being opened by the Holy Spirit (cf. Acts 16:4), might, while believing, freely turn to the Lord who, since he is the "way, the truth and the life" (Jn. 14:6), will satisfy all their inner hopes, or rather infinitely surpass them.

This conversion is, indeed, only initial; sufficient however to make a man realize that he has been snatched from sin, and is being led into the mystery of God's love, who invites him to establish a personal relationship with him in Christ. Under the movement of divine grace the new convert sets out on a spiritual journey by means of which, while already sharing through faith in the mystery of the death and resurrection, he passes from the old man to the new man who has been made perfect in Christ (cf. Col. 3:5–10; Eph. 4:20–24). This transition, which involves a progressive change of outlook and morals, should be manifested in its social implications and effected gradually during the period of catechumenate. Since the Lord in whom he believes is a sign of contradiction (cf. Lk. 2:34; Mt. 10:34–39) the convert often has to suffer misunderstanding and separation, but he also experiences those joys which are generously granted by God.

The Church strictly forbids that anyone should be forced to accept the faith, or be induced or enticed by unworthy devices; as it likewise strongly defends the right that no one should be frightened away from the faith by unjust persecutions.[2]

In accordance with the very ancient practice of the Church, the motives for the conversion should be examined and, if necessary, purified. (See D. 62, 12.)

14. Those who have received from God the gift of faith in Christ, through the Church,[3] should be admitted with liturgical rites to the catechumenate which is not a mere exposition of dogmatic truths and norms of morality, but a period of formation in the whole Christian life, an apprenticeship of sufficient duration, during which the disciples will be joined to Christ their teacher. The catechumens should be properly initiated into the msytery of salvation and the practice of the evangelical virtues, and they should be introduced into the life of faith, liturgy and charity of the People of God by successive sacred rites.[4]

Then, having been delivered from the powers of darkness through the sacraments of Christian initiation (cf. Col. 1:13),[5] and having died, been buried, and risen with Christ (cf. Rom. 6:4–11; Col. 2:12–13; 1 Pet. 3:21–22; Mk. 16:16), they receive the Spirit of adoption of children (cf. 1 Th. 3:5–7; Acts 8:14–17) and celebrate with the whole people of God the memorial of the Lord's death and resurrection.

It is desirable that the liturgy of Lent and Paschal time should be restored in such a way that it will serve to prepare the hearts of the catechumens for the celebration of the Paschal Mystery, at whose solemn ceremonies they are reborn to Christ in baptism.

This Christian initiation, which takes place during the catechumenate, should not be left entirely to the priests and catechists, but should be the concern of the whole Christian

---

2. Cf. Decl. on Religious Freedom, 2, 4, 10; Const. on the Church in the Modern World.
3. Cf. Dogm. Const. *Lumen Gentium*, 17.
4. Cf. Const. on the Sacred Liturgy, 64–65.
5. On this deliverance from the slavery of the devil and of darkness in the Gospel, cf. Mt. 12:28; Jn. 8:44; 12:31 (cf. Jn. 3:8; Eph. 2:1–2). On the liturgy of Baptism cf. Roman Ritual.

community, especially of the sponsors, so that from the beginning the catechumens will feel that they belong to the people of God. Since the life of the Church is apostolic, the catechumens must learn to cooperate actively in the building up of the Church and in its work of evangelization, both by the example of their lives and the profession of their faith.

The juridical status of catechumens should be clearly defined in the new Code of Canon Law. Since they are already joined to the Church[6] they are already of the household of Christ[7] and are quite frequently already living a life of faith, hope and charity. (See D. *62*, 12.)

ARTICLE 3: FORMING THE CHRISTIAN COMMUNITY

15. When the Holy Spirit, who calls all men to Christ and arouses in their hearts the submission of faith by the seed of the word and the preaching of the Gospel, brings those who believe in Christ to a new life through the womb of the baptismal font, he gathers them into one people of God which is a "chosen race, a royal priesthood, a holy nation, a purchased people" (1 Pet. 2:9).[8]

Therefore, missionaries, the fellow workers of God (cf. 1 Cor. 3:9), should raise up communities of the faithful, so that walking worthy of the calling to which they have been called (cf. Eph. 4:1) they might carry out the priestly, prophetic and royal offices entrusted to them by God. In this way the Christian community will become a sign of God's presence in the world. Through the eucharistic sacrifice it goes continually to the Father with Christ,[9] carefully nourished with the word of God[10] it bears witness to Christ,[11] it walks in charity and is enlivened by an apostolic spirit.[12]

From the start the Christian community should be so organized that it is able to provide for its own needs as far as possible.

6. Cf. Dogm. Const. *Lumen Gentium*, 14.
7. Cf. St. Augustine, *Tract. in Ioann.* 11, 4 (*PL* 35, 1476).
8. Cf. Dogm. Const. *Lumen Gentium*, 9.
9. Cf. Dogm. Const. *Lumen Gentium*, 10, 11, 34.
10. Cf. Dogm. Const. on Divine Revelation, 21.
11. Cf. Dogm. Const. *Lumen Gentium*, 12, 35.
12. Cf. ibid., 23, 26.

This community of the faithful, endowed with the cultural riches of its own nation, must be deeply rooted in the people; families imbued with the spirit of the Gospel should flourish[13] and be helped with suitable schools; groups and associations should be set up so that the spirit of the lay apostolate might pervade the whole of society. Finally, let charity shine out between Catholics of different rites.[14]

The ecumenical spirit should be nourished among neophytes; they must appreciate that their brothers who believe in Christ are disciples of Christ, and having been reborn in baptism share in many of the blessings of the people of God. Insofar as religious conditions permit, ecumenical action should be encouraged, so that, while avoiding every form of indifferentism or confusion and also senseless rivalry, Catholics might collaborate with their separated brethren, insofar as it is possible, by a common profession before the nations of faith in God and in Jesus Christ, and by a common, fraternal effort in social, cultural, technical and religious matters, in accordance with the Decree on Ecumenism. Let them cooperate, especially, because of Christ their common Lord. May his name unite them! There should be collaboration of this type not only between private persons, but also, subject to the judgment of the local ordinary, between churches or ecclesiastical communities in their undertakings.

The Christian faithful who have been gathered into the Church from every nation and "are not marked off from the rest of men either by country, by language, or by political institutions,"[15] should live for God and Christ according to the honorable usages of their race. As good citizens they should sincerely and actively foster love of country and, while utterly rejecting racial hatred or exaggerated nationalism, work for universal love among men.

In achieving all this, the laity, that is Christians who have been incorporated into Christ and live in the world, are of primary importance and worthy of special care. It is for them, imbued with the Spirit of Christ, to be a leaven animating and directing the temporal order from within, so

13. Cf. ibid., 11, 35, 41.
14. Cf. Decree on the Catholic Eastern Churches, 30.
15. *Epist. ad Diognetum*, 5 (*PG* 2, 1173); cf. Dogm. Const. *Lumen Gentium*, 38.

that everything is always carried out in accordance with the will of Christ.[16]

However, it is not sufficient for the Christian people to be present or established in a particular nation, nor sufficient that it should merely exercise the apostolate of good example; it has been established and it is present so that it might by word and deed proclaim Christ to non-Christian fellow countrymen and help them towards a full reception of Christ.

Various types of ministry are necessary for the implanting and growth of the Christian community, and once these forms of service have been called forth from the body of the faithful, by the divine call, they are to be carefully fostered and nurtured by all. Among these functions are those of priests, deacons and catechists, and also that of Catholic Action. Brothers and nuns, likewise, play an indispensable role in planting and strengthening the kingdom of Christ in souls, and in the work of further extending it, both by their prayers and active work.

16. The Church, with great joy, gives thanks for the priceless gift of the priestly vocation which God has given to so many young men from among those peoples but recently converted to Christ. For the Church is more firmly rooted in a people when the different communities of the faithful have ministers of salvation who are drawn from their own members—bishops, priests and deacons, serving their own brothers—so that these young churches gradually acquire a diocesan structure with their own clergy.

Those things which have been decreed by this Council concerning the priestly vocation and priestly formation are to be religiously observed wherever the Church is being planted for the first time and also by the young churches. Special importance is to be attached to what has been said about closely combining spiritual, doctrinal and pastoral formation; about living a life in accordance with the Gospel without any thought of personal or family advantage; about fostering a deep appreciation of the mystery of the Church. In this way they will learn, in a wonderful manner, to give themselves fully to the service of Christ's Body, and to the work of the Gospel; they will learn to adhere to their bish-

16. Cf. Dogm. Const. *Lumen Gentium*, 32; Decree on the Lay Apostolate.

op as loyal fellow workers, and to collaborate with their brothers.[17]

To attain this general end, the whole of the student's formation is to be organized in the light of the mystery of salvation, as it is revealed in the Scriptures. They must discover and live this mystery of Christ and of human salvation as it is present in the liturgy.[18]

These general requirements for priestly training, both pastoral and practical, which have been laid down by the Council,[19] must be accompanied with a desire to face up to the particular nation's own way of thinking and acting. Therefore, the minds of the students must be opened and refined so that they will better understand and appreciate the culture of their own people; in philosophy and theology they should examine the relationship between the traditions and religion of their homeland and Christianity.[20] In the same way, priestly formation must take account of the pastoral needs of the region; the students must learn the history, goal and method of missionary activity, as well as the peculiar social, economic and cultural conditions of their own people. They should be formed in the spirit of ecumenism and properly prepared for fraternal dialogue with non-Christians.[21] All this demands that, as far as possible, studies for the priesthood should be undertaken in close contact with the way of life of their own people.[22] Finally, care must be taken to train them in proper ecclesiastical and financial administration.

Suitable priests should be selected, who, after a period of pastoral work, would pursue higher studies even at foreign universities, especially at Rome, or at other institutes of learning. As members of the local clergy, with their learning and experience, they should be a great asset to these young churches in discharging the more difficult ecclesiastical duties.

Wherever it appears opportune to episcopal conferences, the diaconate should be restored as a permanent state of life, in accordance with the norms of the Constitution on

---

17. Cf. Decree on the Training of Priests, 4, 8, 9.
18. Cf. Const. on the Sacred Liturgy, 17.
19. Cf. Decree on the Training of Priests, 1.
20. Cf. John XXIII, *Princeps Pastorum* (*AAS* 1959, 843–844).
21. Cf. Decree on Ecumenism, 4.
22. Cf. John XXIII, *Princeps Pastorum* (*AAS* 1959, 842).

the Church.[23] It would help those men who carry out the ministry of a deacon—preaching the word of God as catechists, governing scattered Christian communities in the name of the bishop or parish priest, or exercising charity in the performance of social or charitable works—if they were to be strengthened by the imposition of hands which has come down from the apostles. They would be more closely bound to the altar and their ministry would be made more fruitful through the sacramental grace of the diaconate. (See D. *62*, 18.)

17. Also worthy of praise is that army of catechists, both men and women, to whom missionary work among the nations is so indebted; who imbued with an apostolic spirit make an outstanding and absolutely necessary contribution to the spread of the faith and the Church by their great work.

In our days, when there are so few clerics to evangelize such great multitudes and to carry out the pastoral ministry, the role of catechists is of the highest importance. Therefore, their training must be in keeping with cultural progress and such that, as true co-workers of the priestly order, they will be able to perform their task as well as possible, a task which involves new and greater burdens.

The number of diocesan and regional schools should be increased where future catechists, while studying Catholic doctrine with special reference to the Bible and the liturgy, and also catechetical method and pastoral practice, would at the same time model themselves on the lives of Christian men,[24] and tirelessly strive for piety and holiness of life. There should be conventions and courses where at certain times catechists would be brought up to date in those sciences and skills which are useful for their ministry, and where their spiritual life would be nourished and strengthened. In addition, those who give themselves fully to this work should be assured, by being paid a just wage, of a decent standard of living and social security.[25]

It is desirable that the sacred Congregation for the Propagation of the Faith should, in some suitable manner, provide special aids for the training and upkeep of catechists.

---

23. Cf. Dogm. Const. *Lumen Gentium,* 29.
24. Cf. John XXIII, *Princeps Pastorum (AAS* 1959, 855).
25. It is a question of so called "full-time catechists."

If it seems necessary and right an institute for catechists should be founded.

The churches should also gratefully acknowledge the generous work of auxiliary catechists of whose help they have such need. These preside at prayers in their communities and also teach sacred doctrine. Proper care should be taken regarding their doctrinal and spiritual formation. It would be desirable too, wherever it seems opportune, to confer the canonical mission on properly trained catechists in the course of a public liturgical celebration, so that in the eyes of the people they might serve the cause of the faith with greater authority. (See D. 62, 19.)

18. Right from the planting of the Church the religious life should be carefully fostered, because not only does it provide valuable and absolutely necessary help for missionary activity, but through the deeper consecration made to God in the Church it clearly shows and signifies the intimate nature of the Christian vocation.[26]

Religious institutes which are working for the implanting of the Church and which are deeply imbued with those mystical graces which are part of the Church's religious tradition, should strive to give them expression and to hand them on in a manner in keeping with the character and outlook of each nation. They should carefully consider how traditions of asceticism and contemplation, the needs of which have been sown by God in certain ancient cultures before the preaching of the Gospel, might be incorporated into the Christian religious life.

Different forms of relegous life should be promoted in the new churches, so that they might manifest different aspects of Christ's mission and the life of the Church, devote themselves to various pastoral works, and prepare their members to exercise them properly. However, episcopal conferences should take care that congregations pursuing the same apostolic end are not multiplied, with consequent damage to the religious life and the apostolate.

The various undertakings aimed at establishing the contemplative life are worthy of special mention; some aim at implanting the rich tradition of their own order and retaining the essential elements of the monastic life, others are returning to the more simple forms of early monasticism. All, however, are eagerly seeking a real adaptation to local con-

26. Cf. Dogm. Const. *Lumen Gentium*, 31, 44.

ditions. The contemplative life should be restored everywhere, because it belongs to the fullness of the Church's
presence.

CHAPTER III

PARTICULAR CHURCHES

19. This work of implanting the Church in a particular
human community reaches a definite point when the assembly of the faithful, already rooted in the social life of the
people and to some extent conformed to its culture, enjoys
a certain stability and permanence; when it has its own
priests, although insufficient, its own religious and laity, and
possesses those ministries and institutions which are required for leading and spreading the life of the people of
God under the leadership of their own bishop.

In these young churches the life of the people of God
ought to mature in all those spheres of the Christian life
which are to be renewed in accordance with the norms of
this Council. Assemblies of the faithful must daily become
more conscious of themselves as living communities of
faith, liturgy and charity; lay people should strive to establish in the state an order of love and justice by means of
civil and apostolic action; by living a true Christian life
families should become seminaries for lay apostles and indeed of priestly and religious vocations. The faith should be
imparted by means of a well adapted catechesis and celebrated in a liturgy that is in harmony with the character of
the people; it should also be embodied by suitable canonical
legislation in the healthy institutions and customs of the locality.

Bishops and their priests must feel and live with the universal Church, becoming more and more imbued with a
sense of Christ and the Church. The communion of the
young churches with the whole Church must remain intimate, they must graft elements of its tradition on to their

own culture and thus, by a mutual outpouring of energy, increase the life of the mystical Body.[1] To this end, those theological, psychological and human elements which would contribute to this sense of communion with the whole Church should be fostered.

These churches, which are often situated in the poorer parts of the world, still suffer from a serious shortage of priests and a lack of material resources. Therefore, they are extremely dependent on the continued missionary activity of the whole Church to supply that assistance which is necessary for the growth of the Church and the full development of Christian life. This missionary activity should also help those churches which, although long established, are in a state of decline or weakness.

However, these churches should renew their common pastoral zeal and set up suitable joint projects so that vocations to both the diocesan clergy and religious institutes might be increased, assessed with greater certainty, and more effectively fostered,[2] that gradually these churches might be able to provide for themselves and help others. (See D. 62, 18, 19.)

20. As the local church must represent the universal Church as perfectly as possible, it must remember that it has been sent to those who live in the same territory as itself, but do not believe in Christ so that it might be for them, by the example of the lives of the faithful and of the whole community, a sign indicating Christ.

The ministry of the word is also necessary so that the Gospel might reach all men. The bishop should be, above all, a preacher of the faith who brings new disciples to Christ.[3] To fulfil this noble task as he ought he must be fully acquainted with conditions among his flock and also with those notions about God which are current among his countrymen. He must take special account of those changes which have been brought about through urbanization, migration and religious indifferentism.

In the young churches the local priests should give themselves generously to the work of evangelization. They should work with the foreign missionaries, with whom they form one priestly body under the authority of the bishop, not

---

1. Cf. John XXIII, *Princeps Pastorum* (*AAS* 1959, 838).
2. Cf. Decree on the Life and Ministry of Priests, 11; Decree on the Training of Priests, 2.
3. Cf. Dogm. Const. *Lumen Gentium*, 25.

only in ministering to the faithful and in celebrating divine worship, but also in preaching the Gospel to those who are outside. They should show themselves ready and eagerly offer themselves to their bishop to undertake missionary work in distant and abandoned areas of their own or other dioceses when the occasion arises.

Brothers and nuns should be on fire with this same zeal, and likewise lay-people with regard to their fellow countrymen, especially those who are poorer.

Episcopal conferences should ensure that periodically there are refresher courses on the Bible and in spiritual and pastoral theology, so that amid all the change and flux the clergy will acquire a deeper knowledge of theology and of pastoral methods.

For the rest, everything that the Council has enacted, especially in the Decree on the Life and Ministry of Priests, should be religiously observed.

Qualified ministers are needed to carry out the missionary program of a particular church; they must be prepared in good time and in a manner that is in keeping with the needs of each church. Since men are more and more coming together in associations, it would be a good thing for episcopal conferences to draw up a common plan for dialogue with these groups. If it happens that in certain regions there is a group of men which is impeded from accepting the Catholic faith because they cannot adapt themselves to the particular guise in which the Church presents itself in that place, then it is desirable that this situation should be specially[4] provided for, until all Christians can gather together in one community. If the Holy See is able to provide missionaries, then bishops should invite them to their dioceses, they should welcome them and actively assist them in their undertakings.

In order that this missionary zeal might flourish among their fellow countrymen it would help greatly if the young churches took part in the universal mission of the Church as soon as possible and sent missionaries to preach the Gospel throughout the whole world, even though they are themselves short of clergy. In a sense, their communion with the universal Church will be perfect when they them-

---

4. Cf. Decree on the Life and Ministry of Priests, 10, where the institution of personal "prelatures" is foreseen to facilitate special pastoral projects aimed at particular social categories insofar as it is demanded for the better exercise of the apostolate.

selves take an active part in missionary work on behalf of other nations.

21. The Church is not truly established and does not fully live, nor is a perfect sign of Christ unless there is a genuine laity existing and working alongside the hierarchy. For the Gospel cannot become deeply rooted in the mentality, life and work of a people without the active presence of lay people. Therefore, from the foundation of a church very special care must be taken to form a mature Christian laity.

The lay faithful belong fully both to the people of God and civil society. They belong to the nation into which they were born, they begin to share in its cultural riches by their education, they are linked to its life by many social ties, they contribute to its progress by personal effort in their professions, they feel its problems to be their own and they try to solve them. They belong also to Christ because by faith and baptism they have been reborn in the Church, so that by newness of life and work they might belong to Christ (cf. 1 Cor. 15:23), in order that all things might be subjected to God in Christ and that God might be all in all (cf. 1 Cor. 15:28).

The principal duty of both men and women is to bear witness to Christ, and this they are obliged to do by their life and their words, in the family, in their social group, and in the sphere of their profession. In them must be seen the new man who has been created according to God in justice and holiness of truth (cf. Eph. 4:24). They must give expression to this newness of life in their own society and culture and in a manner that is in keeping with the traditions of their own land. They must be familiar with this culture, they must purify and guard it, they must develop it in accordance with present-day conditions, they must perfect it in Christ so that the faith of Christ and the life of the Church will not be something foreign to the society in which they live, but will begin to transform and permeate it. They should be linked with their fellow countrymen by ties of sincere charity so that their manner of life reveals the new bond of unity and universal solidarity which derives from the mystery of Christ. They should spread the faith of Christ among those with whom they are connected by social and professional ties, and this obligation is all the more urgent since so many men can only come to hear the Gospel and recognize Christ through lay people who are their neighbors. Indeed wherever possible lay people should be ready to carry out the special mission of preaching the Gospel and teaching Christian doctrine so that they might strengthen the young church by a more immediate coöperation with the hierarchy.

Ministers of the Church should greatly value this arduous apostolate of the laity. They should so train them as members of Christ that they would become conscious of their responsibility for all men. They should instruct them deeply in the mystery of Christ, teach them practical techniques, and help them in their difficulties, all according to the spirit of the Constitution on the Church and the Decree on the Lay Apostolate.

And so while both pastors and laity each retain their own special functions and obligations, the whole of the young church will bear a simple, living, strong witness to Christ, that it might become a bright token of that salvation which comes to us in Christ.

22. The seed which is the word of God grows out of good soil watered by the divine dew, it absorbs moisture, transforms it, and makes it part of itself, so that eventually it bears much fruit. So too indeed, just as happened in the economy of the incarnation, the young churches, which are rooted in Christ and built on the foundations of the apostles, take over all the riches of the nations which have been given to Christ as an inheritance (cf. Ps. 2:8). They borrow from the customs, traditions, wisdom, teaching, arts and sciences of their people everything which could be used to praise the glory of the Creator, manifest the grace of the saviour, or contribute to the right ordering of Christian life.[5]

To achieve this, it is necessary that in each of the great socio-cultural regions, as they are called, theological investigation should be encouraged and the facts and words revealed by God, contained in sacred Scripture, and explained by the Fathers and Magisterium of the Church, submitted to a new examination in the light of the tradition of the universal Church. In this way it will be more clearly understood by what means the faith can be explained in terms of the philosophy and wisdom of the people, and how their customs, concept of life and social structures can be reconciled with the standard proposed by divine revelation. Thus a way will be opened for a more profound adaptation

5. Cf. Dogm. Const. *Lumen Gentium*, 13.

in the whole sphere of Christian life. This manner of acting will avoid every appearance of syncretism and false exclusiveness; the Christian life will be adapted to the mentality and character of each culture,[6] and local traditions together with the special qualities of each national family, illumined by the light of the Gospel, will be taken up into a Catholic unity. So new particular churches, each with its own traditions, have their place in the community of the Church, the primacy of Peter which presides over this universal assembly of charity[7] all the while remaining intact.

And so it is to be hoped, and indeed it would be a very good thing, that episcopal conferences should come together within the boundaries of each great socio-cultural region and by a united and coordinated effort pursue this proposal of adaptation. (See D. *62*, 18.)

CHAPTER IV

MISSIONARIES

23. Although the obligation of spreading the faith falls individually on every disciple of Christ,[1] still the Lord Christ has always called from the number of his disciples those whom he has chosen that they might be with him so that he might send them to preach to the nations (cf. Mk. 3:13 ff). So the Holy Spirit, who shares his gifts as he wills for the common good (cf. 1 Cor. 12:11), implants in the hearts of individuals a missionary vocation and at the same time raises up institutes in the Church[2] who take on the duty of evangelization, which pertains to the whole Church, and make it as it were their own special task.

6. Cf. The allocution of Paul VI at the canonization of the Ugandan Martyrs (*AAS* 1964, 908).
7. Cf. Dogm. Const. *Lumen Gentium*, 13.
1. Dogm. Const. *Lumen Gentium*, 17.
2. By "institutes" are meant the orders, congregations, institutes and association which work in the missions.

Those people who are endowed with the proper natural temperament, have the necessary qualities and outlook, and are ready to undertake missionary work, have a special vocation,[3] whether they are natives of the place or foreigners, priests, religious or lay people. Having been sent by legitimate authority they go forth in faith and obedience to those who are far from Christ, as ministers of the Gospel, set aside for the work to which they have been called (cf. Acts 13:2) "that the offering up of the Gentiles may become acceptable, being sanctified by the Holy Spirit" (Rom. 16:16). (See D. *62*, 11.)

24. When God calls, a man must reply without taking counsel with flesh and blood (cf. Gal. 1:16) and give himself fully to the work of the Gospel. However, such an answer can only be given with the encouragement and help of the Holy Spirit. The one who is sent enters upon the life and mission of him "who emptied himself, taking the nature of a slave" (Phil. 2:7). Therefore, he must be prepared to remain faithful to his vocation for life, to renounce himself and everything that up to this he possessed as his own, and "to make himself all things to all men" (1 Cor. 9:22).

In preaching the Gospel to the nations he will proclaim with confidence the mystery of Christ whose legate he is, so that in him he will dare to speak as he ought (cf. Eph. 6:19 ff.; Acts 4:31), not being ashamed of the scandal of the Cross. Meek and humble, following in the footsteps of his master, he will show that his yoke is sweet and his burden light (Mt. 11:29 ff.). By a truly evangelical life,[4] with great patience and longanimity, in kindness and unfeigned love (cf. 2 Cor. 6:4 ff.) he will bear witness to his Lord, if necessary to the shedding of his blood. He will ask God for strength and courage and in the midst of great affliction and abject poverty he will know abundance of joy (cf. 2 Cor. 8:2). Let him be convinced that obedience is the special virtue of a minister of Christ who by his obedience redeemed the human race.

Preachers of the Gospel should be renewed in spirit day by day, lest they should neglect the grace that is in them (cf. 1 Tim. 4:14; Eph. 4:23; 2 Cor. 4:16). Ordinaries and

---

3. Cf. Pius XI, *Rerum Ecclesiae* (*AAS* 1926, 69–71); Pius XII, *Saeculo exeunte* (*AAS* 1940, 256); *Evangelii Praecones* (*AAS* 1951, 506).

4. Cf. Benedict XV, *Maximum illud* (*AAS* 1919, 449–450).

superiors should gather the missionaries together from time to time, so that they might be strengthened in the hope of their calling and renewed in the apostolic ministry. Special houses should be provided for this purpose.

25. The future missionary must be prepared for such an important task by a special spiritual and moral formation.[5] He must be prompt to take the initiative, constant in carrying out an undertaking, persevering in difficulties, patient and strong of heart in bearing loneliness, exhaustion, and fruitless labor. He must approach men with an open mind and heart, he must willingly accept the duties entrusted to him; and generously accommodate himself to the different customs and the changing circumstances of other peoples. In harmony and mutual love he will cooperate with his brethren and with all who dedicate themselves to this work, so that together with the faithful, and imitating the apostolic community, they might be of one heart and soul (cf. Acts 2:42; 4:32).

These interior dispositions should be diligently developed and fostered during the time of formation; they should be elevated and nourished by the spiritual life. With a living faith and an inexhaustible hope, the missionary should be a man of prayer; he should burn with a spirit of power, of love and of self control (cf. 2 Tim. 1:7). Let him learn to be content with the circumstances in which he finds himself (Phil. 4:11); let him carry about with him the death of Jesus, in a spirit of sacrifice, that the life of Jesus might work on those to whom he has been sent (cf. 2 Cor. 4:10 ff.); let him willingly give all out of zeal for others; let him spend himself for souls (cf. 2 Cor. 12:15 ff.) so that "by the daily exercise of his duty he might grow in the love of God and of his neighbor."[6] Thus united with Christ in obedience to the will of the Father he will continue his mission under the authority of the hierarchy of the Church and collaborate in the mystery of salvation.

26. Those who are sent to the different nations should, as worthy ministers of Christ, be nourished by the "words of faith and with good doctrine" (1 Tim. 4:6) which they will will be.

---

5. Cf. Benedict XV, *Maximum illud* (*AAS* 1919, 448–449); Pius XII, *Evangelii Praecones* (*AAS* 1951, 507). In the formation of missionary priests account must also be taken of what has been said in the Decree on the Training of Priests.
6. Dogm. Const. *Lumen Gentium,* 41.

draw mainly from sacred Scripture while they are studying the mystery of Christ, whose preachers and witnesses they

So all missionaries—priests, brothers, sisters and lay people—should be trained and formed, each according to their state, lest they be found unequal to the demands of their future task.[7] From the very beginning their doctrinal training should be such that they understand both the universality of the Church and the diversity of peoples. This holds for all the studies which prepare them for their future ministry, and indeed for other sciences in which they might usefully be instructed so that they might have a general knowledge of peoples, cultures and religions, not only with regard to the past but also with respect to the present time. Whoever is to go among another people must hold their inheritance, language and way of life in great esteem. It is very necessary for the future missionary that he undertake missiological studies, that he know, that is, the teaching and the laws of the Church regarding missionary activity, that he be aware of the paths which have been followed by the messengers of the Gospel down through the centuries, and that he be familiar with the present state of the missions and with the methods considered most effective in the present time.[8]

If this full training is to be pervaded by a sense of pastoral solicitude, then a special and ordered apostolic formation should be imparted, both by means of instruction and practical exercises.[9]

The greatest possible number of brothers and sisters should be well instructed and prepared in the art of catechetics, so that they might be of even greater assistance in the work of the apostolate.

It is necessary that those who engage in missionary activity, even for a time, should receive a training suited to their condition.

These different forms of training should be undertaken in the countries to which they are to be sent, so that the missionary might more fully understand the history, social

---

7. Cf. Benedict XV, *Maximum illud* (*ASS* 1919, 440); Pius XII, *Evangelii Praecones* (*AAS* 1951, 507).

8. Benedict XV, *Maximum illud* (*AAS* 1919, 448); Decr. S.C.P.F., 20 May 1923 (*AAS* 1923, 369–370); Pius XII, *Saeculo exeunte* (*AAS* 1940, 256); *Evangelii Praecones* (*AAS* 1951, 507); John XXIII, *Princeps Pastorum* (*AAS* 1959, 843–844).

9. Decree on the Training of Priests, 19–21; Apost. Const. *Sedes Sapientiae* with the general statutes.

structures and customs of the people, that they might have an insight into their moral outlook, their religious precepts, and the intimate ideas which they form of God, the world and men according to their own sacred traditions.[10] They should learn their language so that they can speak it easily and correctly and so be able to enter more easily into the minds and hearts of the people.[11] They should, besides, be properly instructed as regards special pastoral needs.

Some should be more thoroughly prepared in missiological institutes, and other faculties and universities, that they might exercise certain special duties more effectively,[12] and by their learning be a help to other missionaries in carrying out missionary work which, in our time especially, presents so many difficulties and opportunities. It is also extremely desirable that regional conferences of bishops should have available a goodly number of such experts and that they should make fruitful use of their knowledge and experience in the problems which attach to their office. Experts in the use of technical instruments and in social communication, whose importance all should greatly appreciate, should not be lacking.

27. Now, although all these things are really necessary for each person sent to the nations, yet in fact, they can scarcely be acquired by individuals. Since, however, it is clear from experience that the missionary task cannot be accompanied by lone individuals, a common vocation has gathered these individuals into institutes where, having combined their strength, they are properly trained and will carry out this work in the name of the Church and under the direction of the hierarchy. These institutes have borne the burden and heat of the day for many centuries, devoting themselves fully or in part to this missionary work. Often vast territories to be evangelized were committed to them by the Holy See in which they assembled a new people of God, and established a local church around its own pastors. By their zeal and experience, and in brotherly collaboration, they will serve those churches which were established by their sweat and even in their blood, either by undertaking the care of souls, or by fulfilling certain special tasks for the common good.

10. Pius XII, *Evangelii Praecones* (*AAS* 1951, 523–524).
11. Benedict XV, *Maximum illud* (*AAS* 1919, 448); Pius XII, *Evangelii Praecones* (*AAS* 1951, 507).
12. Cf. Pius XII, *Fidei Donum* (*AAS* 1957, 234).

Sometimes they undertake more urgent tasks throughout a particular region, for example the evangelization of groups or peoples who for some special reason have not yet, perhaps, accepted the Gospel message or have so far resisted it.[13]

If necessary, let them from their experience be ready to train and help those who engage in missionary activity for a time.

For these reasons, and since there are still many nations to be brought to Christ, these institutes are still extremely necessary. (See D. 62, 10.)

CHAPTER V

THE ORGANIZATION OF MISSIONARY ACTIVITY

28. Since Christians have different gifts (cf. Rom. 12:6) they should collaborate in the work of the Gospel, each according to his opportunity, ability, charism and ministry (cf. 1 Cor. 3:10); all who sow and reap (cf. Jn. 4:37), plant and water, should be one (cf. 1 Cor. 3:8) so that "working together for the same end in a free and orderly manner"[1] they might together devote their powers to the building up of the Church.

For this reason, the labors of those who preach the Gospel, and the assistance given by other Christians, should be so organized and coordinated that "all may be done in order" (1 Cor. 14:40) in every sphere of missionary activity and cooperation.

29. Since the responsibility of preaching the Gospel throughout the whole world falls primarily on the body of bishops,[2] then the synod of bishops, or the "permanent

13. Cf. Decree on the Life and Ministry of Priests, 10, where it speaks of dioceses, personal prelatures and such matters.
1. Cf. Dogm. Const. *Lumen Gentium*, 18.
2. Cf. Dogm. Const. *Lumen Gentium*, 23.

commission of bishops for the universal Church,"[3] among matters of general importance,[4] should pay special attention to missionary activity which is the greatest and holiest duty of the Church.[5]

There should be only one competent congregation for all missions and missionary activity, namely that of the "Propagation of the Faith," which would direct and coordinate missionary work and missionary cooperation throughout the world. The rights of the Eastern Churches must, however, be safeguarded.[6]

Although the Holy Spirit arouses a missionary spirit in the Church in many ways, and indeed often anticipates the work of those whose task it is to guide the life of the Church, nevertheless, this congregation should itself promote missionary vocations and spirituality, as also zeal and prayer for the missions, and it should furnish genuine and adequate information about them. It should raise up missionaries and distribute them according to the more urgent needs of certain regions. It should draw up an organized plan of action, issue directives and principles adapted to the work of evangelization and give the work impulse. It is its job to encourage and coordinate the effective collection of funds which will be distributed according to need and utility, the size of the area, the numbers of believers and non-believers, undertakings and institutes, ministers and missionaries.

In collaboration with the Secretariat for the Promotion of Christian Unity it will seek ways and means for attaining and organizing fraternal cooperation and harmonious relations with the missionary undertakings of other Christian communities, so that as far as possible the scandal of division might be removed.

It is therefore necessary that this congregation should be both an instrument of administration and an organ of dynamic direction, that it should use scientific methods and

---

3. Cf. Motu Proprio *Apostolica Sollicitudo,* 15 September 1965.
4. Cf. Paul VI allocution given in the Council, 21 Nov. 1964 (*AAS* 1964).
5. Cf. Benedict XV, *Maximum illud* (*AAS* 1919, 39–40).
6. If for special reasons some missions are for the time being under the control of other congregations, it is desirable that those congregations should be in contact with the sacred Congregation for the Propagation of the Faith so that it will be possible to maintain a completely constant and uniform rule and purpose in organizing and governing all missions.

instruments adapted to modern conditions, that it be guided by present-day research in theology, methodology and pastoral missionary work.

In a manner and according to norms which should be laid down by the Pope, selected representatives of all those who are engaged in missionary work should have an active part in the direction of this congregation and also a deliberative vote: that is, bishops from all over the world, after consultation with episcopal conferences, and also the heads of institutes and pontifical agencies. These should all be called together at set times and, subject to the authority of the Pope, should exercise supreme control over all missionary work.

There should be a permanent body of consultors and experts, noted for their learning and experience, attached to this congregation, whose task it will be to gather useful information as to the actual situation in various regions and as to the mental outlook of different groups, and so make scientifically-based proposals for missionary work and cooperation.

Institutes of nuns, regional missionary undertakings and lay organizations, especially those which are international, should also be suitably represented. (See D. *62*, 2, 13, 14, 16, 18.)

30. In order that the goal might be attained and results obtained in working for the missions, all missionary workers must be of "one heart and one soul" (Acts 4:32).

It is the responsibility of the bishop, as the head of the diocesan apostolate and its center of unity, to promote missionary activity, guide and coordinate it, so that the spontaneous zeal of those who engage in this work may be safeguarded and fostered. All missionaries, even exempt religious, are subject to this authority in all the various activities which have to do with the exercise of the sacred apostolate.[7] For better coordination, the bishop should, as far as possible, establish a pastoral council in which clergy, religious and lay people would have a part through elected delegates. He should also take care that apostolic action is not entirely restricted to those who have already been converted, but that a fair proportion of workers and funds is directed to the evangelization of non-Christians. (See D. *62*, 20.)

---

7. Cf. Decree on the Pastoral Office of Bishops in the Church, 36–38.

31. Graver questions and more urgent problems should be considered by episcopal conferences in common, without however, neglecting local differences.[8] In order that the insufficient supply of personnel and funds might not be wasted, and in order that undertakings might not be unnecessarily multiplied, it is recommended that resources should be pooled and projects initiated which would serve the common good of all as, for example, seminaries, higher and technical schools, pastoral, catechetical and liturgical centers, and centers devoted to the means of social communication.

Similar cooperation should even be established between different episcopal conferences, wherever it is considered opportune.

32. It would also be useful to coordinate the work being done by institutes and ecclesiastical associations. They should all, of whatever type, submit to the local ordinary in everything that concerns missionary activity. Therefore, it would be very helpful to draw up contracts which would regulate relations between the local ordinary and the head of the institute.

When a territory is committed to the care of a particular institute, it should be the one concern of the ecclesiastical superior and the institute to organize everything to this end: that the new Christian community might grow into a local church which will, in due course, be ruled by its own pastor and have its own clergy.

A new situation arises when the mandate to care for a particular territory expires. Then the conferences of bishops and the institutes will come together and draw up norms which will regulate relations between the local ordinaries and the institutes. It will be the responsibility of the Holy See to outline the general principles in accordance with which regional or even local contracts will be drawn up.

Although the institutes will be prepared to continue the work which they have begun, collaborating in the ordinary care of souls, yet as the number of local clergy increases, it should be arranged that the institutes, insofar as it is in keeping with their end, would remain faithful to the diocese and generously undertake special work in it, or the care of some particular area of it. (See D. 62, 17.)

---

8. Cf. Decree on the Pastoral Office of Bishops in the Church, 35, 5–6.

33. Institutes which are engaged in missionary activity in the same territory should find ways and means of coordinating their work. So conferences of religious and unions of nuns, in which all the institutes of a particular nation or region would have a part, would be extremely helpful. These conferences would investigate what could be done by a common effort and would be closely linked with the conferences of bishops.

With equal reason, all these things could be usefully extended to collaboration between missionary institutes at home, so that common difficulties and projects might be more easily resolved and with less cost. For instance, the doctrinal formation of future missionaries, courses for missionaries, relations with the civil authorities and with international or supernational organizations. (See D. *62*, 21.)

34. Since the proper and methodical exercise of missionary activity demands that those who work for the Gospel should be scientifically prepared for their tasks, especially for dialogue with non-Christian religions and cultures, and should be effectively assisted in carrying them out, it is desirable that for the good of the missions there should be fraternal collaboration among certain scientific institutes which specialize in missiology and in other sciences and arts useful for the missions, such as ethnology, linguistics, the history and science of religious, sociology, pastoral techniques and the likes. (See D. *62*, 22.)

CHAPTER VI

COOPERATION

35. Since the whole Church is missionary, and the work of evangelization the fundamental task of the people of God, this sacred Synod invites all to undertake a profound interior renewal so that being vitally conscious of their responsibility for the spread of the Gospel they might play their part in missionary work among the nations.

36. As members of the living Christ, incorporated into him and made like him by baptism, confirmation and the Eucharist, all the faithful have an obligation to collaborate in the expansion and spread of his Body, so that they might bring it to fullness as soon as possible (cf. Eph. 4:13).

So all the children of the Church should have a lively consciousness of their own responsibility for the world, they should foster within themselves a truly Catholic spirit, they should spend themselves in the work of the Gospel. However, let everyone be aware that the primary and most important contribution he can make to the spread of the faith is to lead a profound Christian life. Their fervor in the service of God and their love for others will be like a new spiritual breeze throughout the whole Church, which will appear as the sign raised up among the nations (cf. Is. 11:12), "the light of the world" (Mt. 5:14) and "the salt of the earth" (Mt. 5:13). This witness of their life will achieve its effect more easily if it is borne in union with other christian bodies, according to the norms of the Decree on Ecumenism, 12.[1]

From this renewed spirit prayers and works of penance will be spontaneously offered to God that by his grace he might make fruitful the work of missionaries, that there might be missionary vocations, and the support of which the missions stand in need might be forthcoming.

So that each and every one of the Christian faithful might be well acquainted with the present state of the Church in the world and might hear the voice of the multitudes crying "help us" (cf. Acts 16:9), information regarding the missions should be published so as to make them feel they have a part to play in missionary activity, and make them open their hearts to the immense and deep needs of men, and come to their assistance.

Coordination of information and cooperation with national and international bodies is also necessary. (See D. 62, 3, 7.)

37. Since the people of God live in communities especially in dioceses and parishes by means of which, in a certain sense, they become manifest, it belongs to such communities to bear witness to Christ before the nations.

The grace of renewal cannot grow in communities unless each of them expands the range of its charity to the ends of

1. Cf. Decree on Ecumenism, 12.

the earth, and has the same concern for those who are far away as it has for its own members.

Through those of its sons whom God has chosen for this very special work the whole community prays, collaborates and works among the nations.

It would be advantageous, provided the worldwide missionary effort is not neglected, to establish contacts with missionaries from the community, or with some diocese or parish in the missions, so that the union between the communities might be visible and contribute to their mutual development. (See D. *62*, 11.)

38. All bishops, as members of the body of bishops which succeeds the college of the apostles, are consecrated not for one diocese alone, but for the salvation of the whole world. The command of Christ to preach the Gospel to every creature (Mk. 16:15) applies primarily and immediately to them—with Peter, and subject to Peter. From this arises that communion and cooperation of the churches which is so necessary today for the work of evangelization. Because of this communion, each church cares for all the others, they make known their needs to each other, they share their possessions, because the spread of the Body of Christ is the responsibility of the whole college of bishops.[2]

By arousing, fostering and directing missionary work in his own diocese, with which he is one, the bishop makes present and, as it were, visible the missionary spirit and zeal of the people of God, so that the whole diocese becomes missionary.

It is the task of the bishop to raise up among his people, especially among those who are sick or afflicted, souls who with a generous heart will offer prayers and works of penance to God for the evangelization of the world. He should gladly foster vocations to missionary institutes among young people and clerics, and be grateful if God should choose some of them to play a part in the missionary activity of the Church. He should exhort and assist diocesan congregations to undertake their own work in the missions; he should promote the works of missionary institutes among his people, especially the pontifical works for the missions. It is right that these works should be given first place, because they are a means by which Catholics are imbued from infancy with a truly universal and missionary

2. Cf. Dogm. Const. *Lumen Gentium*, 23–24.

outlook and also a means for instigating an effective collecting of funds for all the missions, each according to its needs.[3]

Since the need for workers in the vineyard of the Lord grows from day to day; and since diocesan priests themselves wish to play a greater part in the evangelization of the world, this sacred Synod desires that bishops, being conscious of the very grave shortage of priests which impedes the evangelization of many regions, would, after a proper training, send to those dioceses which lack clergy some of their best priests who offer themselves for mission work, where at least for a time they would exercise the missionary ministry in a spirit of service.[4]

In order that the missionary activity of bishops might be more effectively exercised for the good of the whole Church, it is desirable that episcopal conferences should regulate all those matters which concern organized cooperation in their own regions.

In their conferences the bishops should consider the question of sending diocesan priests for the evangelization of the nations; the particular contribution, in proportion to its income, which each diocese will be obliged to make every year for the work of the missions;[5] the direction and organization of ways and means for directly helping or, if need be, founding missionary institutes and seminaries of diocesan clergy for the missions; the fostering of closer links betwen such institutes and the dioceses.

It likewise pertains to episcopal conferences to found and promote agencies which will fraternally receive those who immigrate from missionary territories for reasons of work or study, and which will aid them by suitable pastoral attention. By means of these immigrants people who are distant become, in a sense, neighbors, while a wonderful opportunity is offered to communities which have long been Christian to speak with nations which have not yet heard the Gospel, and of showing them the true face of Christ by their own acts of kindness and assistance.[6] (See D. *62*, 4–6, 8, 9, 11, 23.)

---

3. Cf. Benedict XV, *Maximum illud* (*AAS* 1919, 453–454); Pius XI, *Rerum Ecclesiae* (*AAS* 1926, 71–73); Pius XII, *Evangelii Praecones* (*AAS* 1951, 525–526); id., *Fidei Donum* (*AAS* 1957, 241).
4. Cf. Pius XII, *Fidei Donum* (*AAS* 1957, pp. 245–246).
5. Decree on the Pastoral Office of Bishops, 6.
6. Cf. Pius XII, *Fidei Donum* (*AAS* 1957, 245).

39. Priests represent Christ and are the collaborators of the order of bishops in that threefold sacred duty which, of its nature, pertains to the mission of the Church.[7] They must be profoundly aware of the fact that their very life is consecrated to the service of the missions. Since by their own ministry—which consists mainly in the Eucharist, which gives the Church its perfection—they are in communion with Christ the head, and are leading others to this communion, they cannot but be aware of how much is still lacking to the fullness of the Body, and of how much must therefore be done that it might grow from day to day. They will therefore so organize their pastoral care that it will contribute to the spread of the Gospel among non-Christians.

In their pastoral work priests will stimulate and maintain among the faithful a zeal for the evangelization of the world by teaching them through preaching and religious instruction of the Church's duty to proclaim Christ to the nations; by impressing on Christian families the honor and the need for fostering missionary vocations among their own sons and daughters; by promoting missionary fervor among young people from Catholic schools and associations so that future preachers of the Gospel might spring from them. They should teach them to pray for the missions and should not be ashamed to ask them for alms, being made beggars for Christ and the salvation of souls.[8]

University and seminary professors will instruct the young as to the true condition of the world and the Church, so that the need for a more intense evangelization of non-Christians will be clear to them and feed their zeal. In teaching dogmatic, biblical, moral and historical subjects, they should focus attention on their missionary aspects, so that in this way a missionary awareness will be formed in future priests.

40. Religious institutes of the contemplative and active life have up to this time played, and still play, the greatest part in the evangelization of the world. This sacred Synod willingly acknowledges their merits and thanks God for all that has been done for the glory of God and the service of souls; it exhorts them to continue untiringly in the work they have begun, since they know that the virtue of charity which they are obliged to practice more perfectly because

---

7. Cf. Dogm. Const. *Lumen Gentium*, 28.
8. Cf. Pius XI, *Rerum Ecclesiae (AAS* 1926, 72).

of their vocation, impels and obliges them to a spirit and a work that is truly Catholic.[9]

Institutes of the contemplative life, by their prayers, penances and trials, are of the greatest importance in the conversion of souls since it is in answer to prayer that God sends workers into his harvest (cf. Mt. 9:38), opens the minds of non-Christians to hear the Gospel (cf. Acts 16:14), and makes fruitful the word of salvation in their hearts (cf. 1 Cor. 3:7). Indeed these institutes are requested to establish houses in missionary territories, as quite a few have already done, so that by living their life there in a manner adapted to the genuinely religious traditions of the people, they might bear an outstanding witness among non-Christians to the majesty and love of God, and to union in Christ.

Institutes of the active life, whether or not they pursue a strictly missionary ideal, should sincerely examine themselves before God as to whether they might be able to extend their work for the expansion of the kingdom of God among the nations; whether they might be able to leave certain ministries to others so as to spend their strength for the missions; whether they might be able to begin work in the missions, adapting their constitutions if necessary, in accordance, however, with the mind of the founder; whether their members engage in missionary work to the full extent of their possibilities; whether their form of life bears witness to the Gospel in a manner adapted to the mentality and circumstances of the people.

Since, under the inspiration of the Holy Spirit, secular institutes are growing daily in the Church, their work, under the authority of the bishop, can be fruitful in many ways for the missions especially as an example of total dedication to the evangelization of the world.

41. Lay people should cooperate in the Church's work of evangelization and share in its saving mission both as witnesses and living instruments,[10] especially if having been called by God they are accepted by the bishop for this work.

In lands which are already Christian lay people can cooperate in the work of evangelization by fostering knowl-

9. Cf. Dogm. Const. *Lumen Gentium*, 44.
10. Cf. ibid., 33, 35.

edge and love of the missions in themselves and others, by encouraging vocations among their own families and in Catholic associations and schools, by offering aid of any description, so that the gift of faith which they have received freely might be bestowed on others.

In missionary lands, however, lay people, whether they are foreigners or inhabitants of the country, should teach in the schools, administer temporal affairs, collaborate in parochial and diocesan activity, establish and promote various forms of the lay apostolate, so that the faithful of the new churches might, as soon as possible, be able to play their own part in the life of the Church.[11]

Finally, lay people should willingly give socio-economic assistance to peoples in the process of development; such cooperation is the more praiseworthy according as it is more closely connected with establishing institutions which affect the fundamental structures of social life, or are directed to the training of those who will have charge of public affairs.

Those lay people who promote the knowledge of peoples and religions, by their historical or scientific-religious investigations in universities and scientific institutes, and so help the preachers of the Gospel and prepare for dialogue with non-Christians, are worthy of special praise.

In a spirit of brotherhood they should collaborate with other Christians, with non-Christians and especially with members of international associations, always bearing in mind that "the structure of the earthly city should be founded on the Lord and directed to him."[12]

To carry out all these tasks, lay people require the necessary technical and spiritual preparation which should be given in institutes designed for this purpose, so that their life might bear witness to Christ among non-Christians according to the words of the apostle: "Do not be a stumbling block to Jews and Greeks and to the Church of God, even as I myself in all things please all men, not seeking what is profitable to myself but to the many, that they may be saved" (1 Cor. 10:32–33). (See D. 62, 24.)

---

11. Cf. Pius XII, *Evangelii Praecones* (*AAS* 510–514); John XXIII, *Princeps Pastorum* (*AAS* 1959, 851–852).
12. Cf. Dogm. Const. *Lumen Gentium*, 46.

CONCLUSION

42. The fathers of the Council together with the Roman Pontiff, being deeply conscious of their duty to spread everywhere the kingdom of God, affectionately salute all preachers of the Gospel, and making themselves sharers in their sufferings, they especially salute those who suffer persecution for the name of Christ.[13]

13. Cf. Pius XII, *Evangelii Praecones* (*AAS* 1951, 527); John XXIII, *Princeps Pastorum* (*AAS* 1959, 864).

They are inflamed with the same love that inflamed the heart of God towards men. Aware that it is God who makes his kingdom-to-come on earth, they pour out their prayers, together with the Christian faithful, that through the intercession of the Virgin Mary, Queen of the Apostles, the nations might soon be led to the knowledge of the truth (1 Tim. 2:4) and that the glory of God, which shines in the face of Jesus Christ, might shed its light on all men through the Holy Spirit (2 Cor. 4:6).

62

NORMS FOR IMPLEMENTING THE DECREE ON THE CHURCH'S MISSIONARY ACTIVITY[a]

Paul VI, *Ecclesiae Sanctae III*, 6 August, 1966

Since the Decree *Ad gentes divinitus* (on the Missionary Activity of the Church) of the Second Vatican Council should come into force for the whole Church and be observed by all the faithful, so that the whole Church become missionary in fact and the entire People of God be made aware of its missionary obligation, local ordinaries will see to it that the decree is brought to the notice of all the faithful: conferences and sermons are to be preached to priests and people to illustrate and underline the obligation in conscience for all with regard to the work of the missions.

For the easier and more faithful application of the decree the following laws are laid down:

1. The theology of mission is to become so much a part of theology, in the teaching of it as well as in its advancement by study, that the missionary nature of the Church will be clearly understood. In addition the ways of the Lord for the preparation for the Gospel and the possibility of salvation for those who have not had the Gospel preached to them are to be considered and the necessity of evangelization and of incorporation in the Church is to be emphasized (chapter 1, *Ad gentes divinitus*).

All these matters are to be kept in mind again in determining the proper curriculum of studies in seminaries and universities.

2. Episcopal conferences are invited to propose to the Holy See as soon as possible the general questions affecting

a. Translated by J. G. McGarry. This is part of a larger Document, usually referred to as *Ecclesiae Sanctae,* containing the norms for three other decrees as well: bishops, priests, and religious. (See D *47* and *52*). Latin text in *AAS* 58 (1966), 783–787.

missions which could be dealt with in the next Synod of Bishops (no. 29).

3. To increase the missionary spirit among the Christian people, prayers and daily sacrifices are to be encouraged so that the annual mission day should become, as it were, the spontaneous expression of that spirit (no. 36).

Bishops or episcopal conferences shall prepare various invocations for the missions to be included in the Prayers of the Faithful.

4. A priest shall be appointed in each diocese to effectively promote the work of the missions. He will also take part in the pastoral council (no. 38).

5. In order to foster the missionary spirit, seminarians and members of Catholic youth organizations are to be encouraged to establish and maintain relations with seminarians and members of similar youth organizations in the missions, so that through mutual understanding missionary consciousness and the sense of the Church may grow among the Christian people (no. 38).

6. Bishops, realizing how urgent the need is for spreading the Gospel in the world, shall promote vocations among their own clergy and their young people, and shall provide institutes working in the mission fields with the means and opportunity to make the needs of the mission known in the diocese and to foster vocations (no. 38).

In promoting vocations for the missions both the mission of the Church to all peoples and the various ways in which different groups seek to fulfil this mission (institutes, priests, religious and lay people of both sexes) should be carefully explained. But the special missionary vocation "for life" (nn. 23, 24) is to be especially singled out for praise and illustrated by examples.

7. The pontifical work of the missions is to be promoted in all dioceses and its statutes faithfully observed, especially those regarding the transmission of subsidies (no. 36).

8. Since the voluntary offerings of the faithful for the missions are by no means adequate, it is recommended that as soon as possible a certain sum be fixed to be paid each year out of their own resources by the diocese itself and by the parishes and the other diocesan communities, to be distributed by the Holy See, without diminution of the other offerings of the faithful (no. 38).

9. In episcopal conferences an episcopal commission for the missions shall be established to promote missionary con-

sciousness and activity and foster cooperative relationship between dioceses as well as good relations with other episcopal conferences and to seek out ways of securing as far as possible an equitable distribution of assistance to the missions (no. 38).

10. Since missionary institutes remain a first necessity, everyone must recognize that the task of spreading the Gospel has been assigned to them by the ecclesiastical authority in fulfilment of the missionary duty of the whole People of God (no. 27).

11. Bishops shall also make use of missionary institutes to develop concern for the missions among the faithful and, while observing a right order, they shall give them opportunity to stimulate and foster vocations for the missions among the youth and to seek financial assistance (nn. 23, 37, 38).

For greater unity and effectiveness bishops shall make use of the national or regional mission council, consisting of the directors of pontifical works and the missionary institutes in the country or region.

12. Each missionary institute shall take steps as soon as possible to effect its own adaptation and renewal, especially with regard to methods of evangelization and Christian initiation (nn. 13, 14) and the way of life of communities (no. 3, *Perfectae caritatis*).

13. (1). The Sacred Congregation for the Propagation of the Faith shall be the sole competent curial office for all missions. But since some missions shall be subject for the time being to other offices, in the meantime, for special reasons, those offices shall have a special mission section in close relationship with the Sacred Congregation for the Propagation of the Faith, so that there shall be complete stability, uniformity of law and procedure (no. 29) in all matters regarding the regulation and direction of the missions.

(2) The pontifical work for the missions, namely the Pontifical Work for the Propagation of the Faith, the Work of St. Peter for Native Clergy, the Union of the Clergy for the Missions, and the Work of the Holy Infancy, are subject to the authority of the Sacred Congregation for the Propagation of the Faith.

14. The President of the Secretariat for Christian Unity is by reason of his office a member of the Sacred Congregation for the Propagation of the Faith; the Secretary of the same secretariat is coopted as a consultor to the Sacred

Congregation for the Propagation of the Faith (no. 29).

Similarly the Sacred Congregation for the Propagation of the Faith is to be represented on the Secretariat for Christian Unity.

15. Twenty-four representatives shall take part with a deliberative vote, unless the Supreme Pontiff shall decree otherwise in individual instances, in the government of the Sacred Congregation for the Propagation of the Faith. These representatives shall be composed as follows: twelve prelates from the missions; four from other regions; four from the superiors of institutes; four from the pontifical works. All of these shall be summoned to meet twice a year. The members of this conference are nominated for a period of five years; about a fifth of the conference changes each year. At the expiry of the five-year period members may be nominated for another five years.

Episcopal conferences, however, institutes and pontifical works in accordance with norms to be communicated by the Apostolic See as soon as possible, shall propose to the Supreme Pontiff the names of those from whom the Supreme Pontiff will select the representatives mentioned above and the names of those from whom, even though now living in mission territories, consultors might be chosen.

16. The representatives of religious institutes on the missions and of regional works for the missions and of councils of laymen, especially of international councils, shall take part in the meetings of this office and have a consultative vote (no. 29).

17. The Sacred Congregation for the Propagation of the Faith, having consulted the episcopal conferences and missionary institutes, shall as soon as possible outline the general principles to guide the agreements entered into between local ordinaries and missionary institutes regarding their mutual relationship (no. 32).

In these agreements account must be taken both of the continuity of the missionary work and of the needs of the institute (no. 32).

18. Since it is desirable that episcopal conferences in mission territories should be coordinated into organic groups, according to socio-cultural areas, as they are called (cf. above, no. 9), the Sacred Congregation for the Propagation of the Faith (no. 29) shall promote such coordination of episcopal conferences.

The task of these conferences will be, in cooperation

(*connexione*) with the Sacred Congregation for the Propagation of the Faith:

(1) to seek out ways, even new ones, for the faithful and missionary institutes by joining forces to establish their presence (*inserere*) among the people or groups among whom they live or to whom they are sent (nn. 10, 11) and with whom it is necessary to initiate the dialogue of salvation.

(2) to set up study groups to examine the thought of the people on the universe, on man and on its attitude towards God, and to undertake theological reflection on what is good and true in their culture (no. 22).

Such theological study is a necessary foundation for deciding what adaptations are to be made and in the decision concerning these adaptations the study groups mentioned above will take part. These adaptations covers, amongst other things, methods of evangelization, forms of worship, religious life and ecclesiastical legislation (no. 19).

With regard to methods of evangelization or of catechesis (nn. 11, 13, 14) the Sacred Congregation for the Propagation of the Faith shall promote close cooperation among higher pastoral institutes.

Regarding forms of worship the study groups shall send documents and proposals to the Consilium for the Implementation of the Constitution on the Liturgy.

Regarding the religious state (no. 18) care must be taken that greater attention is not given to external forms (matters such as gesture, vestment and arts) than to the religious character of the people that is to be taken up into the Christian life or to be assimilated to the perfection of the Gospel.

(3) to promote at stated times meetings of seminary professors for adapting their program of studies and the exchange of information among themselves, through discussion with the study groups mentioned above, so that more suitable provision be made for the formation of priests according to the demands of our times (no. 16).

(4) to examine a more suitable manner of distributing resources (priests, catechists, institutes, etc.), especially so that assistance might be given to densely populated areas lacking sufficient personnel to minister to them.

19. In the distribution of aid an appropriate part shall be reserved each year for the formation and sustenance of the local clergy, missionaries, catechists and the study groups

mentioned above in no. 18. Bishops shall submit documentation relating to these matters to the Sacred Congregation for the Propagation of the Faith (nn. 17, 19).

20. The pastoral council shall be duly constituted. It will be its duty according to no. 27 of the Decree *Christus Dominus*, "to investigate, consider and come to practical conclusions about matters relating to pastoral work" and to assist in preparing for the diocesan synod and carrying out its statutes (no. 30).

21. Conferences of men religious and unions of sisters shall be set up in mission territories, in which the major superiors of all the institutes of the country or region shall take part and in which their enterprises shall be coordinated (no. 33).

22. Scientific institutes are to be greatly increased in mission territories, insofar as this is possible or necessary. They shall make proper arrangements for the work of investigation and specialization and take precautions against the duplication in the same region of undertakings of the same nature (no. 34).

23. In order that immigrants from mission lands may be properly received and given appropriate pastoral care by the bishops of older Christian lands, cooperation with missionary bishops is necessary (no. 38).

24. With regard to laymen on the missions:

(1) Stress should be laid on the sincere intention of serving the missions, on maturity, on suitable preparation, professional specialization, as it is called, and on the need for spending a suitable length of time on the mission.

(2) Lay associations for the missions should be effectively coordinated.

(3) The bishop of the place should be concerned about such lay missionaries.

(4) The social security of such laymen should be assured (no. 41).

63

DECREE ON THE MINISTRY AND LIFE OF PRIESTS[a]

Presbyterorum Ordinis, 7 December, 1965

INTRODUCTION

1. This sacred Council has already on several occasions drawn the attention of the world to the excellence of the order of priests in the Church.[1] Since however a most important and increasingly difficult role is being assigned to this order in the renewal of Christ's Church it has been thought that it would be extremely useful to treat of the priesthood at greater length and depth. What is said here applies to all priests. It refers in a special way to those who are engaged in the care of souls. It is to be applied to regular clergy insofar as its provisions suit their circumstances.

Through the sacred ordination and mission which they receive from the bishops priests are promoted to the service of Christ the Teacher, Priest and King; they are given a share in his ministry, through which the Church here on earth is being ceaselessly built up into the People of God, Christ's Body and the temple of the Spirit. For that reason the Council has made the following Decree with the aim of giving more effective support to the ministry of priests and making better provision for their life in the often vastly changed circumstances of the pastoral and human scene.

a. Translated by Archbishop Joseph Cunnane, of Tuam, and revised by Michael Mooney and Enda Lyons of St. Jarlath's College, Tuam, Co. Galway. The references to D. 46 at the end of certain sections indicate where the norms for their implementation are to be found, in *Ecclesiae Sanctae*, 1.
1. Conc. Vat. II, Const. *Sacrosanctum Concilium*, on the Sacred Liturgy, 4 December 1963: *AAS* 56 (1964), pp. 97 ff.; Const. dogm. *Lumen gentium*, 21 November 1964: *AAS* 57 (1965), pp. 5 ff.; Decree *Christus Dominus*, on the Pastoral Function of Bishops in the Church, 28 October 1965: Decree *Optatam totius*, on Priestly Training, 28 October 1965.

CHAPTER I

THE PRIESTHOOD IN THE CHURCH'S MISSION

Nature of the priesthood[a]

2. The Lord Jesus "whom the Father consecrated and sent into the world" (Jn. 10:36) makes his whole Mystical Body sharer in the anointing of the Spirit wherewith he has been anointed:[1] for in that Body all the faithful are made a holy and kingly priesthood, they offer spiritual sacrifices to God through Jesus Christ, and they proclaim the virtues of him who has called them out of darkness into his admirable light.[2] Therefore there is no such thing as a member that has not a share in the mission of the whole Body. Rather, every single member ought to reverence Jesus in his heart[3] and by the spirit of prophecy give testimony of Jesus.[4]

However, the Lord also appointed certain men as ministers, in order that they might be united in one body in which "all the members have not the same function" (Rom. 12:4). These men were to hold in the community of the faithful the sacred power of Order, that of offering sacrifice and forgiving sins,[5] and were to exercise the priestly office publicly on behalf of men in the name of Christ. Thus Christ sent the apostles as he himself had been sent by the Father,[6] and then through the apostles made their successors, the bishops,[7] sharers in his consecration and mission. The function of the bishops' ministry was handed over in a subordinate degree to priests[8] so that they might be ap-

---

a. The subheadings are those of the final draft of the Decree presented to the Council Fathers after the debate in the aula, October 1965.
1. Cf. Mt. 3:16; Lk. 4:18; Acts 4:27; 10:38.
2. Cf. 1 Pet. 2:5 and 9.
3. Cf. 1 Pet. 3:15.
4. Cf. Apoc. 19:10; Conc. Vat. II, Const. dogm. *Lumen gentium,* 21 November 1964, n. 35: *AAS* 57 (1965), pp. 40–41.
5. Conc. Trid., Session 23, cap. 1 and can. 1: *Denz.* 957 and 961 (1764 and 1771).
6. Cf. John 20:21; Conc. Vat. II, Const. dogm. *Lumen gentium,* 21 November 1964, n. 18: *AAS* 57 (1965), pp. 21–22.
7. Cf. Conc. Vat. II, Const. dogm. *Lumen gentium,* 21 November 1964, n. 28: *AAS* 57 (1965), pp. 33–36.
8. Cf. ibid.

pointed in the order of the priesthood and be co-workers of the episcopal order[9] for the proper fulfilment of the apostolic mission that had been entrusted to it by Christ.

Because it is joined with the episcopal order the office of priests shares in the authority by which Christ himself builds up and sanctifies and rules his Body. Hence the priesthood of priests, while presupposing the sacraments of initiation, is nevertheless conferred by its own particular sacrament. Through that sacrament priests by the anointing of the Holy Spirit are signed with a special character and so are configured to Christ the priest in such a way that they are able to act in the person of Christ the head.[10]

Since they share in the function of the apostles in their own degree, priests are given the grace by God to be the ministers of Jesus Christ among the nations, fulfilling the sacred task of the Gospel, that the oblation of the gentiles may be made acceptable and sanctified in the Holy Spirit.[11] For it is by the apostolic herald of the Gospel that the People of God is called together and gathered so that all who belong to this people, sanctified as they are by the Holy Spirit, may offer themselves "a living sacrifice, holy and acceptable to God" (Rom. 12:1). Through the ministry of priests the spiritual sacrifice of the faithful is completed in union with the sacrifice of Christ the only mediator, which in the Eucharist is offered through the priests' hands in the name of the whole Church in an unbloody and sacramental manner until the Lord himself come.[12] The ministry of priests is directed to this and finds its consummation in it. For their ministration, which begins with the announcement of the Gospel, draws its force and power from the sacrifice of Christ and tends to this, that "the whole redeemed city, that is, the whole assembly and community of the saints should be offered as a universal sacrifice to God through the High Priest who offered himself in

9. Cf. Roman Pontifical, "Ordination of a Priest," Preface. These words are already found in the *Sacramentary of Verona* (ed. L. C. Mohlberg, Rome 1956, p. 122); *Missale Francorum* (ed. L. C. Mohlberg, Rome 1957, p. 9); in the *Liber Sacramentorum Romanae Ecclesiae* (ed. L. C. Mohlberg, Rome 1960, p. 25); in the *Pontificale Romano-Germanicum* (ed. Vogel-Elze, Vatican City 1963, vol. 1, p. 34).
10. Cf. Conc. Vat. II, Const. dogm. *Lumen gentium*, 21 November 1964, n. 10: *AAS* 57 (1965), pp. 14–15.
11. Cf. Rom. 15:16 Gr.
12. Cf. 1 Cor. 11:26.

his passion for us that we might be the body of so great a Head."[13]

Therefore the object that priests strive for by their ministry and life is the procuring of the glory of God the Father in Christ. That glory consists in men's conscious, free, and grateful acceptance of God's plan as completed in Christ and their manifestation of it in their whole life. Thus priests, whether they devote themselves to prayer and adoration, or preach the Word, or offer the eucharistic sacrifice and administer the other sacraments, or exercise other services for the benefit of men, are contributing at once to the increase of God's glory and men's growth in the divine life. And all these activities, since they flow from the pasch of Christ, will find their consummation in the glorious coming of the same Lord, when he shall have delivered up the kingdom to God and the Father.[14]

Place of priests in the world

3. Priests, while being taken from amongst men and appointed for men in the things that appertain to God that they may offer gifts and sacrifices for sins,[15] live with the rest of men as with brothers. So also the Lord Jesus the Son of God, a man sent by the Father to men, dwelt amongst us and willed to be made like to his brothers in all things save only sin.[16] The apostles in their turn imitated him, and St. Paul the teacher of the gentiles, the man "set apart for the Gospel of God" (Rom. 1:1), declares that he became all things to all men that he might save all.[17]

The priests of the New Testament are, it is true, by their vocation to ordination, set apart in some way in the midst of the People of God, but this is not in order that they should be separated from that people or from any man, but that they should be completely consecrated to the task for which God chooses them.[18] They could not be the servants of Christ unless they were witnesses and dispensers of a life other than that of this earth. On the other hand they would be powerless to serve men if they remained aloof from their

13. St. Augustine, *De civitate Dei*, 10, 6: *PL* 41, 284.
14. Cf. 1 Cor. 15:24.
15. Cf. Heb. 5:1.
16. Cf. Heb. 2:17; 4–15.
17. Cf. 1 Cor. 9:19–23 Vg.
18. Cf. Acts 13:2.

life and circumstances.[19] Their very ministry makes a special claim on them not to conform themselves to this world;[20] still it requires at the same time that they should live among men in this world and that as good shepherds they should know their sheep and should also seek to lead back those who do not belong to this fold, so that they too may hear the voice of Christ and there may be one fold and one Shepherd.[21]

In the pursuit of this aim priests will be helped by cultivating those virtues which are rightly held in high esteem in human relations. Such qualities are goodness of heart, sincerity, strength and constancy of mind, careful attention to justice, courtesy and others which the apostle Paul recommends when he says: "Whatever is true, whatever is honorable, whatever is just, whatever is pure, whatever is lovely, whatever is gracious, if there is any excellence, if there is

---

19. "Such anxiety for religious and moral perfection is more and more demanded even by the external conditions in which the Church lives out her life. For she cannot remain immovable and indifferent to the changes in the human scene around her which in many ways influences her policy and imposes limits and conditions upon her. It is quite clear that the Church is not isolated from the human community, but is situated in it, and hence that her children are influenced and guided by it, and that they imbibe its culture, obey its laws, adopt its customs. Now this intercourse of the Church with human society is constantly giving rise to difficult problems. These are particularly serious at present . . . The Apostle of the Gentiles addressed this exhortation to the Christians of his time: 'Bear not the yoke with unbelievers. For what participation hath justice with injustice? Or what fellowship hath light with darkness? . . . Or what part hath the faithful with the unbeliever?' (2 Cor. 6:14–15). For this reason those who at present hold the position of educators and teachers in the Church must impress upon Catholic youth their outstanding dignity and the duty arising from this of living in this world but not according to the sentiments of this world. This will be in conformity with the prayer made by Christ for his disciples: 'I pray not that thou shouldst take them out of the world, but that thou shouldst keep them from evil. They are not of the world, as I am not of the world' (Jn. 17–16). The Church adopts this prayer as her own.

"At the same time however such a difference as this does not mean the same thing as separation. It does not profess neglect, nor fear, not contempt. For when the Church makes a distinction between herself and the human race, so far is she from setting herself in opposition to it that she rather is joined with it" (Paul VI, Litt. Encycl. *Ecclesiam suam*, 6 August 1964: *AAS* 56 (1964), pp. 627 and 638).
20. Cf. Rom. 12:2.
21. Cf. Jn. 10:14–16.

anything worthy of praise, think about these things" (Phil. 4:8).[22]

CHAPTER II

THE MINISTRY OF PRIESTS

I. FUNCTIONS OF PRIESTS

Priests as Ministers of God's Word

4. The People of God is formed into one in the first place by the Word of the living God,[1] which is quite rightly sought from the mouth of priests.[2] For since nobody can be saved who has not first believed,[3] it is the first task of priests as co-workers of the bishops to preach the Gospel of God to all men.[4] In this way they carry out the Lord's command "Go into all the world and preach the Gospel to every creature" (Mk. 16:15)[5] and thus set up and increase

---

22. Cf. St. Polycarp, *Epist. ad Philippenses*, VI, I: "Let priests also be disposed to pity, merciful to all, leading back the erring, visiting all the sick, not neglecting the widow, the orphan or the poor. Rather let them be always solicitous for good in the sight of God and men, refraining from all anger, acceptance of persons, unjust judgment, completely avoiding all avarice, slow to believe evil against anyone. Let them not be over-severe in judgment, knowing that we are all debtors of sin" (ed. F. X. Funk, *Patres Apostolici*, I, p. 303).

1. Cf. 1 Pet. 1:23; Acts 6:7; 12:24. "(The apostles) preached the Word of truth and produced churches." (St. Augustine, *Comments on Ps.*, 44, 23: *PL* 36, 508).

2. Cf. Mal. 2:7; 1 Tim. 4:11–13; 2 Tim. 4:5; Tit. 1:9.

3. Cf. Mk. 16:16.

4. Cf. 2 Cor. 11:7. What is said of bishops holds also for priests, since they are the co-workers of the bishops. Cf. *Statuta Ecclesiae Antiqua*, c. 3 (ed. Munier, Paris 1960, p. 79); *Decretum Gratiani*, C. 6, D. 88 (ed. Friedberg, I, 307); Conc. Trid., Decree *De reform.*, Session 5, c. 2, n. 9 (*Conc. Oec. Decreta*, ed. Herder, Rome 1963, p. 645); Session 24, c. 4 (p. 739); Conc. Vat. II, Const. dogm. *Lumen gentium*, 21 November 1964, n. 25: *AAS* 57 (1965), pp. 29–31

5. Cf. *Constitutiones Apostolorum*, II, 26, 7: "Let (priests) be the teachers of divine knowledge, since the Lord himself also commanded us, saying: Going teach ye, etc." (ed. F. X. Funk, *Diadascalia et Constitutiones Apostolorum*, I, Paderborn 1905, p. 105). *Leonine Sacramentary* and other sacramentaries down to the *Roman Pontifi-*

the People of God. For by the saving Word of God faith is aroused in the heart of unbelievers and is nourished in the heart of believers. By this faith then the congregation of the faithful begins and grows, according to the saying of the apostle: "Faith comes from what is heard, and what is heard comes by the preaching of Christ" (Rom. 10:17).

Priests then owe it to everybody to share with them the truth of the Gospel[6] in which they rejoice in the Lord. Therefore, whether by behaving honourably towards people they led people to glorify God;[7] or by openly preaching proclaim the mystery of Christ to unbelievers; or teach the Christian message or explain the Church's doctrine; or endeavor to treat of contemporary problems in the light of Christ's teaching—in every case their role is to teach not their own wisdom but the Word of God and to issue an urgent invitation to all men to conversion and to holiness.[8] Moreover, the priest's preaching, often very difficult in present-day conditions, if it is to become more effective in moving the minds of his hearers, must expound the Word of God not merely in a general and abstract way but by an application of the eternal truth of the Gospel to the concrete circumstances of life.

Thus the ministry of the Word is exercised in many different ways according to the needs of the hearers and the spiritual gifts of preachers. In non-Christian territories or societies people are led by the proclamation of the Gospel to faith and by the saving sacraments.[9] In the Christian

cal, Preface for the Ordination of a Priest: "By this providence, O Lord, you have added teachers of the faith to the apostles of your Son, and through them they filled the whole earth with preachers [or: preachings] of the second rank." *Book of Orders of the Mozarabic Liturgy*, Preface for the Ordination of a Priest: "The teacher of peoples and the ruler of subjects, let him keep the Catholic faith in well-ordered fashion, and announce true salvation to all" (ed. M. Ferotin, Paris 1904, col. 55).

6. Cf. Gal. 2:5.

7. Cf. 1 Pet. 2:12.

8. Cf. the Rite of Ordination of a Priest in the Alexandrian Church of the Jacobites: ". . . Gather your people to the word of doctrine like a nurse who cherishes her children" (H. Denzinger, *Ritus Orientalium*, vol. II, Wurzburg 1863, p. 14).

9. Cf. Mt. 28:19; Mk. 16:16; Tertullian, *On baptism*, 14, 2 (Corpus Christianorum, Latin series, 1, p. 289, 11–13); St. Athanasius, *Adv. Arianos*, 2, 42 (*PG* 26, 237); St. Jerome, *Comment. on Mat.*, 28, 19 (*PL* 26, 218 BC): "First they teach all nations, then they baptize with water those who have been taught. For it cannot be that the body should receive the sacrament of Baptism unless the soul has

community itself on the other hand, especially for those who seem to have little understanding or belief underlying their practice, the preaching of the Word is required for the sacramental ministry itself, since the sacraments are sacraments of faith, drawing their origin and nourishment from the Word.[10] This is of paramount importance in the case of the liturgy of the Word within the celebration of Mass where there is an inseparable union of the proclamation of the Lord's death and resurrection, the response of its hearers and the offering itself by which Christ confirmed the new covenant in his blood. In this offering the faithful share both by their sacrificial sentiments and by the reception of the sacrament.[11]

Priests as Ministers of the Sacraments and the Eucharist

5. God, who alone is the holy one and sanctifier, has willed to take men as allies and helpers to become humble servants in his work of sanctification. The purpose then for which priests are consecrated by God through the ministry of the bishop is that they should be made sharers in a special way in Christ's priesthood and, by carrying out sacred functions, act as his ministers who through his Spirit continually exercises his priestly function for our benefit in the liturgy.[12] By Baptism priests introduce men into the People of God; by the sacrament of Penance they reconcile sinners with God and the Church; by the Anointing of the Sick they relieve those who are ill; and especially by the celebration of Mass they offer Christ's sacrifice sacramentally. But in the celebration of all the sacraments—as St. Ignatius Martyr already asserted in the early Church[13]—priests are hierarchically united with the bishop in various ways and so

previously received the truth of the faith"; St. Thomas, *Expositio primae Decretalis*, §1: "When our Saviour was sending his disciples to preach he gave them three injunctions. First, that they should teach the faith; secondly that they should initiate believers through the sacraments" (ed. Marietti, *Opuscula Theologica*, Turin-Rome 1954, 1138).

10. Cf. Conc. Vat. II, Const. *Sacrosanctum Concilium*, on the Sacred Liturgy, 4 December 1963, n. 35, 2: *AAS* 56 (1964), p. 109.

11. Cf. ibid., nn. 33, 35, 48, 52 (pp. 108–109, 113, 114).

12. Cf. ibid., n. 7 (pp. 100–101); Pius XII, Encycl. *Mystici Corporis*, 29 June 1943: *AAS* 35 (1943), p. 230.

13. St. Ignatius Martyr, *Smyrn.*, 8, 1–2 (ed. F. X. Funk, p. 282, 6–15); *Constitutiones Apostolorum*, VIII, 12, 3 (ed. F. X. Funk, p. 496); VIII, 29, 2 (p. 532).

make him present in a certain sense in individual assemblies of the faithful.[14]

But the other sacraments, and indeed all ecclesiastical ministries and works of the apostolate are bound up with the Eucharist and are directed towards it.[15] For in the most blessed Eucharist is contained the whole spiritual good of the Church,[16] namely Christ himself our Pasch and the living bread which gives life to men through his flesh—that flesh which is given life and gives life through the Holy Spirit. Thus men are invited and led to offer themselves, their works and all creation with Christ. For this reason the Eucharist appears as the source and the summit of all preaching of the Gospel: catechumens are gradually led up to participation in the Eucharist, while the faithful who have already been consecrated in baptism and confirmation are fully incorporated in the Body of Christ by the reception of the Eucharist.

Therefore the eucharistic celebration is the center of the assembly of the faithful over which the priest presides. Hence priests teach the faithful to offer the divine victim to God the Father in the sacrifice of the Mass and with the victim to make an offering of their whole life. In the spirit of Christ the pastor, they instruct them to submit their sins to the Church with a contrite heart in the sacrament of Penance, so that they may be daily more and more converted to the Lord, remembering his words: "Repent, for the kingdom of heaven is at hand" (Mt. 4:17). They teach them to take part in the celebrations of the sacred liturgy in such a way as to achieve sincere prayer in them also. They guide them to the exercise of an ever more perfect spirit of prayer throughout their lives in proportion to each one's graces and needs. They lead all the faithful on to the observance of the duties of their particular state in life, and those who are more advanced to the carrying out of the evangelical counsels in the way suited to their individual cases. Finally they train the faithful so that they will be able to sing in their hearts to the Lord with psalms and hymns and spiritu-

---

14. Cf. Conc. Vat. II, Const. dogm. *Lumen gentium*, 21 November 1964, n. 28: *AAS* 57 (1965), pp. 33–36.
15. "The Eucharist is as it were the completion of the spiritual life and the end of all the sacraments" (St. Thomas, *Summa Theol.* III, q. 73, a. 3 c); cf. *Summa Theol.* III, q. 65, a. 3.
16. Cf. St. Thomas, *Summa Theol.* III, q. 65, a. 3, ad 1; q. 79, a. 1, c. et ad 1.

al canticles, giving thanks always for all things in the name of our Lord Jesus Christ to God the Father.[17]

By their fulfilment of the Divine Office priests themselves should extend to the different hours of the day the praise and thanksgiving they offer in the celebration of the Eucharist. By the Office they pray to God in the name of the Church for the whole people entrusted to them and in fact for the whole world.

The house of prayer in which the most holy Eucharist is celebrated and reserved, where the faithful assemble, and where is worshipped the presence of the Son of God our Saviour, offered for us on the sacrificial altar for the help and consolation of the faithful—this house ought to be in good taste and a worthy place for prayer and sacred ceremonial.[18] In it pastors and faithful are called upon to respond with grateful hearts to the gifts of him who through his humanity is unceasingly pouring the divine life into the members of his Body.[19] Priests ought to go to the trouble of properly cultivating liturgical knowledge and art so that by means of their liturgical ministry God the Father, Son, and Holy Spirit may be daily more perfectly praised by the Christian communities entrusted to their care.

Priests as Rulers of God's People

6. Priests exercise the function of Christ as Pastor and Head in proportion to their share of authority. In the name of the bishop they gather the family of God as a brotherhood endowed with the spirit of unity and lead it in Christ through the Spirit to God the Father.[20] For the exercise of

17. Cf. Eph. 5:19–20.
18. Cf. St. Jerome, *Epist.*, 114, 2: ". . . and consecrated chalices and sacred vestments and the other things that have to do with the worship of the Lord's passion . . . because of their association with the Body and Blood of the Lord are to be venerated with the same reverence as his Body and Blood" (*PL* 22, 934). See Conc. Vat. II, Const. *Sacrosanctum Concilium*, on Sacred Liturgy, 4 December 1963, nn. 122–127: *AAS* 56 (1964), pp. 130–132.
19. "Moreover, let them not omit to make each day a visit to the most blessed sacrament, which is to be reserved in the most noble place and in the most honorable way possible in churches, according to liturgical laws, since this visit will be at once a proof of gratitude, a pledge of love and an act of the adoration due to Christ present in this same sacrament" (Paul VI, Encycl. *Mysterium Fidei*, 3 September 1965: *AAS* 57 [1965], p. 771).
20. Cf. Conc. Vat. II, Const. dogm. *Lumen gentium*, 21 November 1964, n. 28: *AAS* 57 (1965), pp. 33–36.

this ministry, as for the rest of the priests' functions, a spiritual power is given them, a power whose purpose is to build up.[21] And in building up the Church priests ought to treat everybody with the greatest kindness after the model of our Lord. They should act towards people not according to what may please men,[22] but according to the demands of Christian doctrine and life. They should teach them and warn them as their dearest children,[23] according to the words of the apostle: "Be urgent in season and out of season, convince, rebuke, and exhort, be unfailing in patience and in teaching" (2 Tim. 4:2).[24]

For this reason it is the priests' part as instructors of the people in the faith to see to it either personally or through others that each member of the faithful shall be led in the Holy Spirit to the full development of his own vocation in accordance with the Gospel teaching, and to sincere and active charity and the liberty with which Christ has set us free.[25] Very little good will be achieved by ceremonies however beautiful, or societies however flourishing, if they are not directed towards educating people to reach Christian maturity.[26] To encourage this maturity priests will make their help available to people to enable them to determine the solution to their problems and the will of God in the crises of life, great or small. Christians must also be trained so as not to live only for themselves. Rather, according to the demands of the new law of charity every man as he has received grace ought to minister it one to another,[27] and in this way all should carry out their duties in a Christian way in the community of their fellow men.

Although priests owe service to everybody, the poor and the weaker ones have been committed to their care in a special way. It was with these that the Lord himself associated,[28] and the preaching of the Gospel to them is

21. Cf. 2 Cor. 10:8; 13:10.
22. Cf. Gal. 1:10.
23. Cf. 1 Cor. 4:14.
24. Cf. Didascalia, II, 34, 3; II, 46, 6; II, 47, 1; Constitutiones Apostolorum, II, 47, 1 (ed. F. X. Funk, Didascalia et Constitutiones, I, pp. 116, 142 and 143).
25. Cf. Gal. 4:3; 5:1 and 13.
26. Cf. St. Jerome, Epist., 58, 7: "What use is it that walls glitter with gems while Christ dies in the person of a poor man?" (PL 22, 584).
27. Cf. 1 Pet. 4:10 ff.
28. Cf. Mt. 25:34–35.

given as a sign of his messianic mission.[29] Priests will look after young people with special diligence. This applies also to married couples and parents. It is desirable that these should meet in friendly groups to help each other in the task of more easily and more fully living in a Christian way of life that is often difficult. Priests should keep in mind that all religious, men and women, being a particularly eminent group in the Lord's house, are deserving of having special care directed to their spiritual progress for the good of the whole Church. Finally, priests ought to be especially devoted to the sick and the dying, visiting them and comforting them in the Lord.[30]

The pastor's task is not limited to individual care of the faithful. It extends by right also to the formation of a genuine Christian community. But if a community spirit is to be properly cultivated it must embrace not only the local church but the universal Church. A local community ought not merely to promote the care of the faithful within itself, but should be imbued with the missionary spirit and smooth the path to Christ for all men. But it must regard as its special charge those under instruction and the newly converted who are gradually educated in knowing and living the Christian life.

However, no Christian community is built up which does not grow from and hinge on the celebration of the most holy Eucharist. From this all education for community spirit must begin.[31] This eucharistic celebration, to be full and sincere, ought to lead on the one hand to the various works of charity and mutual help, and on the other hand to missionary activity and the various forms of Christian witness.

In addition the ecclesial community exercises a truly

29. Cf. Lk. 4:18.
30. Other classes can be mentioned, e.g., migrants, itinerants, etc. These are dealt with in the Decree *Christus Dominus,* on the Pastoral Function of Bishops in the Church, 28 October 1965.
31. Cf. *Didascalia,* II, 59, 1–3: "In your teaching order and exhort the people to visit the church and never to be entirely absent, but to assemble always and not impoverish the church, by staying away, and make the Body of Christ less a member. . . . Therefore since you are members of Christ do not separate yourselves from the Church by failing to be united; for having Christ your head according to his promise present and communicating with you, do not neglect yourselves or alienate the Saviour from his members or divide or disperse his Body . . ." (ed. F. X. Funk, I, p. 170); Paul VI, *Allocution* to the Italian clergy at the 13th "Week of pastoral renewal," at Orvieto, 6 September 1963: *AAS* 55 (1963), pp. 750 ff.

motherly function in leading souls to Christ by its charity, its prayer, its example and its penitential works. For it constitutes an effective instrument for showing or smoothing the path towards Christ and his Church for those who have not yet found faith; while also encouraging, supporting and strengthening believers for their spiritual struggles.

In building up a community of Christians, priests can never be the servants of any human ideology or party. Rather their task as heralds of the Gospel and pastors of the Church is the attainment of the spiritual growth of the Body of Christ.

II. PRIESTS' RELATION WITH OTHERS

Relation between Bishops and the Priestly Body

7. All priests share with the bishops the one identical priesthood and ministry of Christ. Consequently the very unity of their consecration and mission requires their hierarchical union with the order of bishops.[32] This unity is best shown on some occasions by liturgical concelebration, and priests also affirm their union with the bishops in the eucharistic celebration.[33] Bishops, therefore, because of the gift of the Holy Spirit that has been given to priests at their ordination, will regard them as their indispensable helpers and advisers in the ministry and in the task of teaching, sanctifying and shepherding the People of God.[34] This has been forcefully emphasized from the earliest ages of the Church by the liturgical documents. These solemnly pray God for the pouring out upon the priest to be ordained of "the spirit of grace and counsel, that he may help and gov-

32. Cf. Conc. Vat. II, Const. dogm. *Lumen gentium*, 21 November 1964, n. 28: *AAS* 57 (1965), p. 35.
33. Cf. the so-called *Ecclesiastical Constitution of the Apostles*, XVIII: Priests are fellow-participants in the mysteries and fellow-soldiers of the bishops (ed. Th. Schermann, *Die allgemeine Kirchenordnung*, I, Paderborn 1914, p. 26; A. Harnack, T. u. U., II, 4, p. 13, n. 18 and 19); Pseudo-Jerome, *On the Seven Orders of the Church*: ". . . in the blessing, they are sharers in the mysteries with the bishops" (ed. A. W. Kalff, Wurzburg 1937, p. 45); St. Isidore of Seville, *On Ecclesiastical Offices*, c. VII: "They are set over the Church of God and in the celebration of the Eucharist they are the associates of the bishops, as they are also in teaching the people and in the office of preaching" (*PL* 83, 787).
34. Cf. *Didascalia*, II, 28, 4 (ed. F. X. Funk, p. 108); *Apostolic Constitutions*, II, 28– 4; II, 34, 3 (ibid., pp. 109 and 117).

ern the people in a pure heart,"[35] just as in the desert the spirit of Moses was made grow into the minds of the seventy wise men[36] "whom he employed as helpers and easily governed countless multitudes among the people."[37]

On account of this common sharing in the same priesthood and ministry then, bishops are to regard their priests as brothers and friends[38] and are to take the greatest interest they are capable of in their welfare both temporal and spiritual. For on their shoulders particularly falls the burden of sanctifying their priests:[39] therefore they are to exercise the greatest care in the progressive formation of their diocesan body of priests.[40] They should be glad to listen to their priests' views and even consult them and hold conference with them about matters that concern the needs of pastoral work and the good of the diocese. But for this to

35. *Apostolic Constitutions*, VIII, 16, 4 (ed. F. X. Funk, I, p. 522, 13); cf. *Summary of Apostolic Constitutions*, VI (ibid., 11, p. 80, 3–4); *Testament of the Lord:* ". . . give him the Spirit of grace, counsel, and magnanimity, the spirit of the priesthood . . . to help and govern your people in work, in fear, in a pure heart" (trans. I. E. Rahmani, Mainz 1899, p. 69). So also in *Apostolic Tradition* (ed. B. Botte, *La Tradition Apostolique*, Munster i. W. 1963, p. 20).

36. Cf. Num. 11:16–25.

37. *Roman Pontifical*, "Ordination of a Priest," Preface; these words are already contained in the *Leonine, Gelasian* and *Gregorian Sacramentaries*. Similar expressions are found in the eastern liturgies; cf. *Apost. Trad.:* ". . . look upon your servant and impart to him the spirit of grace and counsel, that he may aid the priests and rule your people in a clean heart, as you looked upon the people of your choice and commanded Moses to choose elders whom you filled with your spirit which you have given to your servant" (from the ancient Latin version of Verona, ed. B. Botte, *La Tradition Apostolique de S. Hippolyte. Essai de reconstruction*, Munster i. W. 1963, p. 20); *Apost. Const.* VIII, 16, 4 (ed. F. X. Funk, I, p. 522, 16–17); *Summary of Apost. Const.* 6 (ed. F. X. Funk, II, p. 20, 5–7); *Testament of the Lord* (trans. I. E. Rahmani, Mainz 1899, p. 69), *Euchology of Serapion*, XXVII (ed. F. X. Funk, *Didascalia et Constitutiones*, II, p. 190, lin. 1–7); *Rite of Ordination in the Maronite Liturgy* (trans. H. Denzinger, *Ritus Orientalium*, II, Wurzburg 1863, p. 161). Among the Fathers can be cited: Theodore of Mopsuesta, *In 1 Tim.* 3, 8 (ed. Swete, II, pp. 119–121); Theodore, *Questions on Numbers*, XVIII (*PG* 80, 372 b).

38. Cf. Conc. Vat. II, Const. dogm. *Lumen gentium*, 21 November 1964, n. 28: *AAS* 57 (1965), p. 35.

39. Cf. John XXIII, Encycl. *Sacerdotii Nostri primordia*, 1 August 1959: *AAS* 51 (1959), p. 576; St. Pius X, Exhortation to the Clergy *Haerent animo*, 4 August 1908: S. Pii X Acta, vol. IV (1908), pp. 237 ff.

40. Cf. Conc. Vat. II, Decree *Christus Dominus*, on the Pastoral Function of Bishops in the Church, 28 October 1965, nn. 15 and 16.

be reduced to practice a group or senate of priests[41] should be set up in a way suited to present-day needs,[42] and in a form and with rules to be determined by law. This group would represent the body of priests and by their advice could effectively help the bishop in the management of the diocese.

Priests for their part should keep in mind the fullness of the sacrament of Order which bishops enjoy and should reverence in their persons the authority of Christ the supreme Pastor. They should therefore be attached to their bishop with sincere charity and obedience.[43] That priestly obedience, inspired through and through by the spirit of cooperation, is based on that sharing of the episcopal ministry which is conferred on priests by the sacrament of Order and the canonical mission.[44]

There is all the more need in our day for union of priests

41. In established law the Cathedral Chapter is regarded as the bishop's "senate and council" *C.I.C.*, c. 391), or in its absence the group of diocesan consultors (cf. *C.I.C.*, cc. 423–428). But it is desirable to reform these institutions in such a way as to make better provision for present-day needs. Clearly this group of priests differs from the pastoral council spoken of in the Decree *Christus Dominus* on the Pastoral Function of Bishops in the Church, 28 October 1965, n. 27, which includes laymen and whose function is confined to investigating question of pastoral activity. On the question of priests as counsellors of bishops see *Didascalia*, II, 28, 4 (ed. F. X. Funk, I, p. 108); also *Apost. Const.*, II, 28, 4 (ed F. X. Funk, I, p. 109); St. Ignatius Martyr, *Magnesians*, 6, 1 (ed. F. X. Funk, p. 244, 10–12); Origen, *Against Celsus*, 3, 30: Priests are counsellors or *bouleutai* (*PG* 11, 157 d—960 a).

42. St. Ignatius Martyr, *Magnesians*, 6, 1: "I exhort you to strive to do all things in the peace of God, the bishop presiding in the place of God and the priests in the place of the senate of apostles, and the deacons who are so dear to me having entrusted to them the ministry of Jesus Christ who was with the Father before all ages and finally appeared" (ed F. X. Funk, p. 234, 10–13); St. Ignatius Martyr, *Trallians*, 3, 1: "Likewise let all reverence the deacons as Jesus Christ, as also the bishop who is the image of the Father, the priests as the senate of God and the council of apostles: without these one cannot speak of a church" (ibid., p. 244, 10–12); St. Jerome, *Commentary on Isaias*, II, 3 (*PL* 24, 61 A): "We also have in the Church our senate, the group of priests."

43. Cf. Paul VI, *Allocution* to the parish priests and Lenten preachers of Rome, in the Sistine Chapel, 1 March 1965: *AAS* 57 (1965), p. 326.

44. Cf. *Apost. Const.*, VIII, 47, 39: "Priests . . . should do nothing without the decision of the bishop; for it is to him that the people of the Lord has been entrusted and from him an account of their souls will be demanded" (ed. F. X. Funk, p. 577).

with bishops because in this age of ours apostolic enterprises must necessarily for various reasons take on many different forms. And not only that, but they must often overstep the bounds of one parish or diocese. Hence no priest is sufficiently equipped to carry out his own mission alone and as it were single-handed. He can only do so by joining forces with other priests, under the leadership of those who are rulers of the Church. (See D. *46*, 15–17.)

Brotherly Bond and Cooperation among Priests

8. All priests, who are constituted in the order of priesthood by the sacrament of Order, are bound together by an intimate sacramental brotherhood; but in a special way they form one priestly body in the diocese to which they are attached under their own bishop. For even though they may be assigned different duties, yet they fulfill the one priestly service for people. Indeed all priests are sent to cooperate in the same work. This is true whether the ministry they exercise be parochial or supra-parochial; whether their task be research or teaching, or even if they engage in manual labor and share the lot of the workers, where that appears to be of advantage and has the approval of the competent authority; or finally if they carry out other apostolic works or those directed towards the apostolate. They all contribute to the same purpose, namely the building up of the body of Christ, and this, especially in our times, demands many kinds of duties and fresh adaptations.

For this reason it is of great importance that all priests, whether diocesan or regular, should help each other, so that they may be fellow-helpers of the truth.[45] Each is joined to the rest of the members of this priestly body by special ties of apostolic charity of ministry and of brotherhood. This is signified liturgically from ancient times by the fact that the priests present at an ordination are invited to impose hands, along with the ordaining bishop, on the chosen candidate, and when priests concelebrate the sacred Eucharist in a spirit of harmony. So priests are all united with their brother-priests by the bond of charity, prayer, and total cooperation. In this way is shown forth that unity with which Christ willed his own to be perfected in one, that the world might know that the Son had been sent by the Father.[46]

45. Cf. 3 Jn. 8.
46. Cf. Jn. 17:23.

From this it follows that older priests should sincerely accept the younger ones as brothers and be a help to them in facing the first tasks and responsibilities of their ministry. They should make an effort also to understand their outlook even though it may be different from their own, and should give kindly encouragement to their projects. Young priests for their part are to respect the age and experience of their elders; they ought to consult with them on matters concerning the care of souls and willingly cooperate with them.

Under the influence of the spirit of brotherhood priests should not forget hospitality,[47] and should cultivate kindness and the sharing of goods.[48] They should be particularly concerned about those who are sick, about the afflicted, the overworked, the lonely, the exiled, the persecuted.[49] They should also be delighted to gather together for relaxation, remembering the words by which the Lord himself invited his weary apostles: "Come apart into a desert place and rest a little" (Mk. 6:31).

Moreover, in order to enable priests to find mutual help in cultivating the intellectual and spiritual life, to promote better cooperation amongst them in the ministry, to safeguard them from possible dangers arising from loneliness, it is necessary to foster some kind of community life or social relations with them. This however can take different forms according to varying personal and pastoral needs: by priests' living together where this is possible, or by their sharing a common table, or at least meeting at frequent intervals. Associations of priests are also to be highly esteemed and diligently promoted, when by means of rules recognized by the competent authority they foster priestly holiness in the exercise of the ministry through a suitable and properly approved rule of life and through brotherly help, and so aim at serving the whole order of priests.

Finally, because of the same brotherly bond of priesthood, priests ought to realize that they have an obligation towards those laboring under difficulties. They should offer timely help to them, even by discreetly warning them where necessary. They ought always to treat with fraternal charity and compassion those who have failed in certain ways.

47. Cf. Heb. 13:1–2.
48. Cf. Heb. 13:16.
49. Cf. Mt. 5:10.

They should pray earnestly to God for them and never cease to show themselves genuine brothers and friends to them.

Relation of Priests with Lay People

9. Even though the priests of the new law by reason of the sacrament of Order fulfill the preeminent and essential function of father and teacher among the People of God and on their behalf, still they are disciples of the Lord along with all the faithful and have been made partakers of his kingdom by God, who has called them by his grace.[50] Priests, in common with all who have been reborn in the font of baptism, are brothers among brothers[51] as members of the same Body of Christ which all are commanded to build up.[52]

Priests should, therefore, occupy their position of leadership as men who do not seek the things that are their own but the things that are Jesus Christ's.[53] They should unite their efforts with those of the lay faithful and conduct themselves among them after the example of the Master, who came amongst men "not to be served but to serve, and to give his life as a ransom for many" (Mt. 20:28). Priests are to be sincere in their appreciation and promotion of lay people's dignity and of the special role the laity have to play in the Church's mission. They should also have an unfailing respect for the just liberty which belongs to everybody in civil society. They should be willing to listen to lay people, give brotherly consideration to their wishes, and recognize their experience and competence in the different fields of human activity. In this way they will be able to recognize along with them the signs of the times.

While trying the spirits if they be of God,[54] they must discover with faith, recognize with joy, and foster with diligence the many and varied charismatic gifts of the laity,

---

50. Cf. 1 Th. 2:12; Col. 1:13.
51. Cf. Mt. 23:8. "From the very fact that we wish to be the pastors, fathers and teachers of men it follows that we must act as their brothers" (Paul VI, Encycl. *Ecclesiam suam*, 6 August 1964: *AAS* 58 [1964], p. 647).
52. Cf. Eph. 4:7 and 16; *Apost. Const.*, VIII, 1, 20: "The bishop moreover should not set himself up over the deacons or priests, nor the priests over the people; for the structure of the assembly is made up of members of both" (ed F. X. Funk, I, p. 467).
53. Cf. Phil. 2:21.
54. Cf. 1 Jn 4:1.

whether these be of a humble or more exalted kind. Among the other gifts of God which are found abundantly among the faithful, special attention ought to be devoted to those graces by which a considerable number of people are attracted to greater heights of the spiritual life. Priests should also be confident in giving lay people charge of duties in the service of the Church, giving them freedom and opportunity for activity and even inviting them, when opportunity occurs, to take the initiative in undertaking projects of their own.[65]

Finally, priests have been placed in the midst of the laity so that they may lead them all to the unity of charity, "loving one another with brotherly affection; outdoing one another in sharing honor" (Rom. 12:10). Theirs is the task, then, of bringing about agreement among divergent outlooks in such a way that nobody may feel a stranger in the Christian community. They are to be at once the defenders of the common good, for which they are responsible in the bishop's name; and at the same time the unwavering champions of truth lest the faithful be carried about with every wind of doctrine.[56] Those who have abandoned the practice of the sacraments, or even perhaps the faith, are entrusted to priests as special objects of their care. They will not neglect to approach these as good shepherds.

Priests should keep in mind what has been laid down in regard to ecumenism[57] and not forget those fellow Christians who do not enjoy complete ecclesiastical union with us.

They will regard as committed to their charge all those who fail to recognize Christ as their Saviour.

The faithful for their part ought to realize that they have obligations to their priests. They should treat them with filial love as being their fathers and pastors. They should also share their priests' anxieties and help them as far as possible by prayer and active work so that they may be better able to overcome difficulties and carry out their duties with greater success.[58]

55. Cf. Conc. Vat. II, Const. dogm. Lumen gentium, 21 November 1964, n. 37: AAS 57 (1965), pp. 42–43.
56. Cf. Eph. 4:14.
57. Cf. Conc. Vat. II, Decree Unitatis redintegratio, on Ecumenism, 21 November 1964: AAS 57 (1965), pp. 90 ff.
58. Cf. Conc. Vat. II, Const. Dogm. Lumen gentium, 21 November 1964, n. 37: AAS 57 (1965), pp. 42–43.

III. THE DISTRIBUTION OF PRIESTS, PRIESTLY VOCATIONS

Proper Distribution of Priests

10. The spiritual gift which priests have received in ordination does not prepare them merely for a limited and circumscribed mission, but for the fullest, in fact the universal mission of salvation "to the end of the earth" (Acts 1:8). The reason is that every priestly ministry shares in the fullness of the mission entrusted by Christ to the apostles. For the priesthood of Christ, of which priests have been really made sharers, is necessarily directed to all peoples and all times, and is not confined by any bounds of blood, race, or age, as was already typified in a mysterious way by the figure of Melchizedek.[59]

Priests, therefore, should recall that the solicitude of all the churches ought to be their intimate concern. For this reason priests of those dioceses which are blessed with greater abundance of vocations should be prepared gladly to offer themselves—with the permission or encouragement of their own ordinary—for the exercise of their ministry in countries or mission or tasks that are hampered by shortage of clergy.

In additon, the rules about incardination and excardination should be revised in such a way that, while this ancient institution remains intact, it will answer better to the pastoral needs of today. Where the nature of the apostolate demands this, not only the proper distribution of priests should be made easier but also the carrying out of special pastoral projects for the benefit of different social groups in any region or among any race in any part of the world. For this purpose there can with advantages be set up some international seminaries, special dioceses, or personal prelacies and other institutions to which, by methods to be decided for the individual undertaking and always without prejudice to the rights of local ordinaries, priests can be attached or incardinated for the common good of the whole Church.

As far as possible, however, priests are not to be sent alone into a new territory, especially if they are not yet well versed in its language and customs. Rather, after the

59. Cf. Heb. 7:3.

example of Christ's disciples,[60] they should be sent at least in groups of two or three so that they may be of mutual help to one another. It is advisable also to pay careful attention to their spiritual life and their mental and bodily health. Where possible, places and conditions of work are to be prepared for them to suit each one's personal circumstances.

It is also of the greatest advantage that those who go to a new territory should take the trouble to learn not only the language of the place but also the special psychological and social characteristics of the people they wish to serve in humility, and should establish the most perfect possible communication with them. In this way they will be following the example of St. Paul, who could say of himself: "For though I am free of all men, I made myself a slave to all, that I might win the more. To the Jews I became a Jew, in order to win Jews . . ." (1 Cor. 9:19–20). (See D. *46*, 1–5.)

Priests' Care for Priestly Vocations

11. The Shepherd and Bishop of our souls[61] set up his Church in such a way that the people whom he chose and acquired by his blood[62] should always and until the end of the world have its own priests, for fear Christians would ever be like sheep that have no shepherd.[63] The apostles realized this intention of Christ and under the guidance of the Holy Spirit considered it their duty to choose ministers who should "be able to teach others also" (Tim. 2:2). In fact this duty belongs to the very nature of the priestly mission which makes the priest share in the anxiety of the whole Church lest laborers should ever be wanting to the People of God here on earth.

However, since "a common interest exists . . . between the pilot of the ship and the passengers,"[64] the whole Christian people ought to be made aware that it is their duty to cooperate in their various ways, both by earnest prayer and by other means available to them,[65] to ensure that the Church will always have those priests who are

60. Cf. Lk. 10:1.
61. Cf. 1 Pet. 2:25.
62. Cf. Acts 20:28.
63. Cf. Mt. 9:36.
64. *Roman Pontifical*, "Ordination of a Priest."
65. Cf. Conc. Vat. II, Decree *Optatam totius*, on Priestly Training, 28 October 1965, n. 2.

needed for the fulfilment of her divine mission. First, then, priests are to make it their most cherished object to make clear to people the excellence and necessity of the priesthood. They do this by their preaching and by the personal witness of a life that shows clearly a spirit of service and a genuine paschal joy. Then they must spare no trouble or inconvenience in helping both youths and older men whom they prudently consider suitable for so great a ministry to prepare themselves properly so that they can be called at some time by the bishops—while preserving their full freedom, both external and internal. In the pursuit of this object diligent and prudent spiritual direction is of the greatest advantage.

Parents, teachers, and all who are in any way concerned in the education of boys and young men ought to train them in such a way that they will know the solicitude of the Lord for his flock and be alive to the needs of the Church. In this way they will be prepared when the Lord calls to answer generously with the prophet: "Here am I! Send me" (Is. 6:8). However, it is emphatically not to be expected that the voice of the Lord calling should come to the future priest's ears in some extraordinary way. Rather it must be perceived and judged through the signs by which God's will becomes known to prudent Christians in everyday life. And these signs are to be studied attentively by priests.[66]

Therefore organizations for the promotion of vocations, whether diocesan or national, are recommended highly to priests.[67] In sermons, in catechetical instruction and in periodicals the needs of the Church both local and universal are to be made known clearly. The meaning and excellence

66. "The voice of God which calls expresses itself in two different ways that are marvellous and converging: one interior, that of grace, that of the Holy Spirit, that inexpressible interior attraction which the silent and powerful voice of the Lord exercises in the unfathomable depths of the human soul; and the other one external, human, sensible, social, juridical, concrete, that of the qualified minister of the Word of God, that of the Apostle, that of the hierarchy, an indispensable instrument instituted and willed by Christ as a concrete means of translating into the language of experience the message of the Word and the divine precept. Such is the teaching of Catholic doctrine with St. Paul: *How shall they hear without a preacher . . . Faith comes from hearing* (Rom. 10:14 and 17)" (Paul VI, *Allocution,* 5 May 1965: *L'Osservatore Romano,* 6 May 1965, p. 1).

67. Cf. Conc. Vat. II, Decree *Optatam totius,* on Priestly Training, 28 October 1965, n. 2.

of the priestly ministry is to be highlighted—a ministry in which the many trials are balanced by such great joys, and especially one in which, as the Fathers teach, the greatest witness of love can be given to Christ.[68]

CHAPTER III

THE LIFE OF PRIESTS

I. PRIESTS' CALL TO PERFECTION

Call of Priests to Holiness

12. By the sacrament of Order priests are configured to Christ the priest as servants of the Head, so that as co-workers with the episcopal order they may build up the Body of Christ, the Church. Like all Christians they have already received in the consecration of baptism the sign and gift of their great calling and grace. So they are enabled and obliged even in the midst of human weakness[1] to seek perfection, according to the Lord's word: "You, therefore, must be perfect, as your heavenly Father is perfect" (Mt. 5:48).

But priests are bound by a special reason to acquire this perfection. They are consecrated to God in a new way in their ordination and are made the living instruments of Christ the eternal priest, and so are enabled to accomplish throughout all time that wonderful work of his which with supernatural efficacy restored the whole human race.[2] Since every priest in his own way assumes the person of Christ he is endowed with a special grace. By this grace the priest, through his service of the people committed to his care and

---

68. This is the teaching of the Fathers when they explain Christ's words to Peter: "Lovest thou me? . . . Feed my sheep" (Jn. 21:17): so St. John Chrysostom, *On the Priesthood*, II, 1–2 (*PG* 47–48, 633); St. Gregory the Great, *Pastoral Rule*, P. I. c. 5 (*PL* 77, 19 a).

1. Cf. 2 Cor. 12:9.

2. Cf. Pius XI, Encycl. *Ad catholici sacerdotii*, 20 December 1935: *AAS* 28 (1936), p. 10.

all the People of God, is able the better to pursue the
perfection of Christ, whose place he takes. The human
weakness of his flesh is remedied by the holiness of him
who became for us a high priest "holy, innocent, undefiled,
separated from sinners" (Heb. 7:26).

Christ, whom the Father sanctified or consecrated and
sent into the world,[3] "gave himself for us to redeem us
from all iniquity and to purify for himself a people of his
own who are zealous for good deeds" (Tit. 2:14), and in
this way through his passion entered into his glory.[4] In a
similar way, priests, who are consecrated by the anointing
of the Holy Spirit and sent by Christ, mortify the works of
the flesh in themselves and dedicate themselves completely
to the service of people, and so are able, in the holiness
with which they have been enriched in Christ, to make
progress towards the perfect man.[5]

In this way they are made strong in the life of the spirit
by exercising the ministration of the Spirit and of justice,[6]
provided they are prepared to listen to the inspiration of the
Spirit of Christ who gives them life and guidance. For it is
through the sacred actions they perform every day, as
through their whole ministry which they exercise in union
with the bishop and their fellow-priests, that they are set on
the right course to perfection of life. The very holiness of
priests is of the greatest benefit for the fruitful fulfilment of their ministry. While it is possible for God's grace
to carry out the work of salvation through unworthy ministers, yet God ordinarily prefers to show his wonders
through those men who are more submissive to the impulse
and guidance of the Holy Spirit and who, because of their
intimate union with Christ and their holiness of life, are
able to say with St. Paul: "It is no longer I who live, but
Christ who lives in me" (Gal. 2:20).

For this reason this sacred Council, in the hope of attaining its pastoral objectives of interior renewal, of worldwide
diffusion of the Gospel, and of dialogue with the modern
world, issues the strongest exhortation to all priests to strive
always by the use of all suitable means commended by the
Church[7] towards that greater holiness that will make them

3. Cf. Jn. 10:36.
4. Cf. Lk. 24:26.
5. Cf. Eph. 4:13.
6. Cf. 2 Cor. 3:8–9.
7. Cf. among others: St. Pius X, Exhortation to the Clergy, *Haerent*

daily more effective instruments for the service of all God's people.

The Exercise of the Threefold Priestly Function both Demands and Fosters Holiness

13. Priests will acquire holiness in their own distinctive way by exercising their functions sincerely and tirelessly in the Spirit of Christ.

Since they are ministers of the Word of God, they read and hear every day the Word of God which they must teach to others. If they strive at the same time to make it part of their own lives, they will become daily more perfect disciples of the Lord, according to the saying of the apostle Paul to Timothy: "Practice these duties, devote yourself to them; so that all may see your progress. Take heed to thyself and to your teaching; hold to that, for in doing so you will save both yourself and your hearers" (1 Tim. 4:15–16). For by seeking more effective ways of conveying to others what they have meditated on[8] they will savor more profoundly the "unsearchable riches of Christ" (Eph. 3:8) and the many-sided wisdom of God.[9] By keeping in mind that it is the Lord who opens hearts[10] and that the excellence comes not from themselves but from the power of God[11] they will be more intimately united with Christ the Teacher and will be guided by his Spirit in the very act of teaching the Word. And by this close union with Christ they share in the charity of God, the mystery of which was kept hidden from all ages[12] to be revealed in Christ.

Priests as ministers of the sacred mysteries, especially in the sacrifice of the Mass, act in a special way in the person of Christ who gave himself as a victim to sanctify men. And this is why they are invited to imitate what they handle, so that as they celebrate the mystery of the Lord's

---

animo, 4 August 1908: St. Pii X Acta, vol. IV (1908), p. 237 ff. Pius XI, Encycl. *Ad catholici sacerdotii*, 20 December 1935: *AAS* 28 (1936), p. 5 ff. Pius XII, Apostolic Exhortation, *Menti Nostrae*, 23 September 1950: *AAS* 42 (1950), p. 657 ff. John XXIII, Encycl. *Sacerdotii Nostri primordia*, 1 August 1959: *AAS* 51 (1959), p. 545 ff.

8. Cf. St. Thomas, *Summa Theol.*, II-II, q. 188, a. 7.
9. Cf. Heb. 3:9–10.
10. Cf. Acts 16:14.
11. Cf. 2 Cor. 4:7.
12. Cf. Eph. 3:9.

death they may take care to mortify their members from vices and concupiscences.[13]

In the mystery of the eucharistic sacrifice, in which priests fulfil their principal function, the work of our redemption is continually carried out.[14] For this reason the daily celebration of it is earnestly recommended. This celebration is an act of Christ and the Church even if it is impossible for the faithful to be present.[15] So when priests unite themselves with the act of Christ the Priest they daily offer themselves completely to God, and by being nourished with Christ's Body they share in the charity of him who gives himself as food to the faithful.

In the same way they are united with the intention and the charity of Christ when they administer the sacraments. They do this in a special way when they show themselves to be always available to administer the sacrament of Penance whenever it is reasonably requested by the faithful. In reciting the Divine Office they lend their voice to the Church which perseveres in prayer in the name of the whole human race, in union with Christ who "always lives to make intercession for them" (Heb. 7:25).

While they govern and shepherd the People of God they are encouraged by the love of the Good Shepherd to give their lives for their sheep.[16] They, too, are prepared for the supreme sacrifice, following the example of those priests who even in our own times have not shrunk from laying down their lives. Since they are the instructors in the faith and have themselves "confidence to enter the sanctuary by the blood of Jesus" (Heb. 10:19), they approach God

13. *Roman Pontifical*, "Ordination of a Priest."
14. Cf. *Roman Missal*, Prayer over the offerings, of Ninth Sunday after Pentecost.
15. "The Mass, even though it is celebrated privately is still not private, but is the act of Christ and the Church. The Church, in the sacrifice which she offers, learns to offer herself as a universal sacrifice and applies the unique and infinite redemptive power of the sacrifice of the cross to the whole world for its salvation. For every Mass that is celebrated is offered not merely for the salvation of some souls but for that of the whole world . . . Therefore we recommend with paternal insistence to priests, who are our especial joy and our crown in the Lord, that . . . they celebrate Mass worthily and devoutly every day" (Paul VI, Encycl. *Mysterium Fidei,* 3 September 1965: *AAS* 57 [1965], pp. 761–762). Cf. Conc. Vat. II, Const. *Sacrosanctum Concilium,* on the Sacred Liturgy, 4 December 1963, nn. 26 and 27: *AAS* 56 (1964), p. 107.
16. Cf. Jn. 10:11.

"with a true heart in full assurance of faith" (Heb. 10:22). They set up a steadfast hope for their faithful people,[17] so that they may be able to comfort all who are in distress by the exhortation wherewith God also exhorts them[18] As rulers of the community they cultivate the form of asceticism suited to a pastor of souls, renouncing their own convenience, seeking not what is to their own advantage but what will benefit the many for salvation,[19] always making further progress towards a more perfect fulfilment of their pastoral work and, where the need arises, prepared to break new ground in pastoral methods under the guidance of the Spirit of love who breaths where he will.[20]

Unity and Harmony of Priests

14. In the world of today, with so many duties which people must undertake and the great variety of problems vexing them and very often demanding a speedy solution, there is often danger for those whose energies are divided by different activities. Priests who are perplexed and distracted by the very many obligations of their position may be anxiously enquiring how they can reduce to unity their interior life and their program of external activity. This unity of life cannot be brought about merely by an outward arrangement of the works of the ministry nor by the practice of spiritual exercises alone, though this may help to foster such unity. Priests can however achieve it by following in the fulfilment of their ministry the example of Christ the Lord, whose meat was to do the will of him who sent him that he might perfect his work.[21]

The fact of the matter is that Christ, in order ceaselessly to do that same will of his Father in the world through the Church, is working through his ministers and therefore remains always the principle and source of the unity of their life. Therefore priests will achieve the unity of their life by joining themselves with Christ in the recognition of the Father's will and in the gift of themselves to the flock entrusted to them.[22] In this way, by adopting the role of the

17. Cf. 2 Cor. 1:7.
18. Cf. 2 Cor. 1:4.
19. Cf. 1 Cor. 10:33.
20. Cf. Jn. 3:8.
21. Cf. Jn. 4:34.
22. Cf. 1 Jn. 3:16.

good shepherd they will find in the practice of pastoral charity itself the bond of priestly perfection which will reduce to unity their life and activity. Now this pastoral charity[23] flows especially from the eucharistic sacrifice. This sacrifice is therefore the center and root of the whole life of the priest, so that the priestly soul strives to make its own what is enacted on the altar of sacrifice. But this cannot be achieved except through priests themselves penetrating ever more intimately through prayer into the mystery of Christ.

To enable them to make their unity of life a concrete reality they should consider all their projects to find what is God's will[24]—that is to say, how far their projects are in conformity with the standards of the Church's Gospel mission. Faithfulness to Christ cannot be separated from faithfulness to his Church. Hence pastoral charity demands that priests, if they are not to run in vain,[25] should always work within the bond of union with the bishops and their fellow priests. If they act in this manner, priests will find unity of life in the unity of the Church's own mission. In this way they will be united with their Lord and through him with the Father in the Holy Spirit, and can be filled with consolation and exceedingly abound with joy.[26]

II. SPECIAL SPIRITUAL REQUIREMENTS IN THE LIFE OF THE PRIEST

Humility and obedience

15. Among the virtues especially demanded by the ministry of priests must be reckoned that disposition of mind by which they are always prepared to seek not their own will but the will of him who has sent them.[27] The divine task for the fulfilment of which they have been set apart by the Holy Spirit[28] transcends all human strength and human wisdom; for "God chose what is weak in the world to shame the strong" (1 Cor. 1:27).

Therefore the true minister of Christ is conscious of his

23. "Let it be the duty of love to shepherd the Lord's flock" (St. Augustine, *Treatise on John*, 123, 5: *PL* 35, 1967).
24. Cf. Rom. 12:2.
25. Cf. Gal. 2:2.
26. Cf. 2 Cor. 7:4.
27. Cf. Jn 4:34; 5:30; and 6:38.
28. Cf. Acts. 13:2.

own weakness and labors in humility. He proves what is well-pleasing to God[29] and, bound as it were in the Spirit,[30] he is guided in all things by the will of him who wishes all men to be saved. He is able to discover and carry out that will in the course of his daily routine by humbly placing himself at the service of all those who are entrusted to his care by God in the office that has been committed to him and the variety of events that make up his life.

The priestly ministry, being the minstry of the Church itself, can only be fulfilled in the hierarchical union of the whole body of the Church. Hence pastoral charity urges priests to act within this communion and by obedience to dedicate their own will to the service of God and their fellow-Christians. They will accept and carry out in the spirit of faith the commands and suggestions of the Pope and of their bishop and other superiors. They will most gladly spend themselves and be spent[31] in whatever office is entrusted to them, even the humbler and poorer. By acting in this way they preserve and strengthen the indispensable unity with their brothers in the ministry and especially with those whom the Lord has appointed the visible rulers of his Church. They also work towards the building up of the Body of Christ, which grows "by what every joint supplieth."[32] This obedience, which leads to the more mature freedom of the sons of God, by its nature demands that priests in the exercise of their duties should be moved by charity prudently to seek new methods of advancing the good of the Church. At the same time it also demands that while putting forward their schemes with confidence and being insistent in making known the needs of the flock entrusted to them, they should always be prepared to submit to the judgment of those who exercise the chief function in ruling God's Church.

By this humility and by responsible and willing obedience priests conform themselves to Christ. They reproduce the sentiment of Jesus Christ who "emptied himself, taking the form of a servant . . . and became obedient unto death" (Phil. 2:7–9), and who by this obedience overcame and redeemed the disobedience of Adam, as the apostle de-

29. Cf. Eph. 5:10.
30. Cf. Acts 20:22.
31. Cf. 2 Cor. 12:15.
32. Cf. Eph. 4:11–16.

clares: "For as by one man's disobedience many were made sinners, so by one man's obedience many will be made righteous" (Rom. 5:19).

Celibacy to be embraced and esteemed as a gift

16. Perfect and perpetual continence for the sake of the kingdom of heaven was recommended by Christ the Lord.[33] It has been freely accepted and laudably observed by many Christians down through the centuries as well as in our own time, and has always been hightly esteemed in a special way by the Church as a feature of priestly life. For it is at once a sign of pastoral charity and an incentive to it as well as being in a special way a source of spiritual fruitfulness in the world.[34] It is true that it is not demanded of the priesthood by its nature. This is clear from the practice of the primitive Church[35] and the tradition of the Eastern Churches where in addition to those—including all bishops —who choose from the gift of grace to preserve celibacy, there are also many excellent married priests. While recommending ecclesiastical celibacy this sacred Council does not by any means aim at changing that contrary discipline which is lawfully practiced in the Eastern Churches. Rather the Council affectionately exhorts all those who have received the priesthood in the married state to persevere in their holy vocation and continue to devote their lives fully and generously to the flock entrusted to them.[36]

There are many ways in which celibacy is in harmony with the priesthood. For the whole mission of the priest is dedicated to the service of the new humanity which Christ, the victor over death, raises up in the world through his Spirit and which is born "not of blood nor of the will of the flesh nor of the will of man, but of God" (Jn 1:13). By preserving virginity or celibacy for the sake of the kingdome of heaven[37] priests are consecrated in a new and excellent way to Christ. They more readily cling to him with undivided heart[38] and dedicate themselves more freely in

33. Cf. Mt. 19:12.
34. Cf. Conc. Vat. II, Const. dogm. *Lumen gentium*, 21 November 1964, n. 42: *AAS* 57 (1965), pp. 47–49.
35. Cf. 1 Tim. 3:2–5; Tit. 1:6.
36. Cf. Pius XI, Encycl. *Ad catholici sacerdotii*, 20 December 1935: *AAS* 28 (1936), p. 28.
37. Cf. Mt. 19:12.
38. Cf. 1 Cor. 7:32–34.

him and through him to the service of God and of men. They are less encumbered in their service of his kingdom and of the task of heavenly regeneration. In this way they become better fitted for a broader acceptance of fatherhood in Christ.

By means of celibacy, then, priests profess before men their willingness to be dedicated with undivided loyalty to the task entrusted to them, namely that of espousing the faithful to one husband and presenting them as a chaste virgin to Christ.[39] They recall that mystical marriage, established by God and destined to be fully revealed in the future, by which the Church holds Christ as her only spouse.[40] Moreover they are made a living sign of that world to come, already present through faith and charity, a world in which the children of the resurrection shall neither be married nor take wives.[41]

For these reasons, based on the mystery of Christ and his mission, celibacy, which at first was recommended to priests, was afterwards in the Latin Church imposed by law on all who were to be promoted to holy Orders. This sacred Council approves and confirms this legislation so far as it concerns those destined for the priesthood, and feels confident in the Spirit that the gift of celibacy, so appropriate to the priesthood of the New Testament, is liberally granted by the Father, provided those who share Christ's priesthood through the sacrament of Order, and indeed the whole Church, ask for that gift humbly and earnestly.

This sacred Council also exhorts all priests who, with trust in God's grace, have of their own free choice accepted consecrated celibacy after the example of Christ, to hold fast to it with courage and enthusiasm, and to persevere faithfully in this state, appreciating that glorious gift that has been given them by the Father and is so clearly extolled by the Lord,[42] and keeping before their eyes the great mysteries that are signified and fulfilled in it. And the more that perfect continence is considered by many people to be im-

39. Cf. 2 Cor. 11:2.
40. Cf. Conc. Vat. II, Const. dogm. *Lumen gentium*, 21 November 1964, nn. 42 and 44: *AAS* 57 (1965), pp. 47–49 and 50–51; Decree *Perfectae caritatis*, on the Renewal of Religious Life, 28 October 1965, n. 12.
41. Cf. Lk. 20:35–36; Pius XI, Encycl. *Ad catholici sacerdotii*, 20 December 1935: *AAS* 28 (1936), pp. 24–28; Pius XII, Encycl. *Sacra Virginitas*, 25 March 1954: *AAS* 46 (1954), pp. 169–172.
42. Cf. Mt. 19:11.

possible in the world of today, so much the more humbly and perseveringly in union with the Church ought priests demand the grace of fidelity, which is never denied to those who ask.

At the same time they will employ all the helps to fidelity both supernatural and natural, which are available to everybody. Especially they should never neglect to follow the rules of ascetical practice which are approved by the experience of the Church and are as necessary as ever in the modern world. So this sacred Council asks that not only priests but all the faithful would cherish this precious gift of priestly celibacy, and that all of them would beg of God always to lavish this gift abundantly on his Church.

Relation with the world and worldly goods: voluntary poverty

17. Priests can learn, by brotherly and friendly association with each other and with other people, to cultivate human values and appreciate created goods as gifts of God. While living in the world they should still realize that according to the Word of our Lord and Master they are not of the world.[43] By using the world, then, as those who do not use it[44] they will come to that liberty by which they will be freed from all inordinate anxiety and will become docile to the divine voice in their daily life. From this liberty and docility grows that spiritual insight through which is found a right attitude to the world and to earthly goods.

This attitude is of great importance for priests for this reason, that the Church's mission is carried out in the midst of the world and that created goods are absolutely necessary for man's personal progress. Let priests be thankful then for everything that the heavenly Father has given them towards a proper standard of living. However, they ought to judge everything they meet in the light of faith, so that they will be guided towards the right use of things in accordance with God's will and will reject anything that is prejudicial to their mission.

Priests as men whose "portion and inheritance" (Num. 18:20) is the Lord ought to use temporal goods only for those purposes to which the teaching of Christ and the direction of the Church allow them to be devoted.

43. Cf. Jn. 17:14–16.
44. Cf. 1 Cor. 7:31.

Priests are to manage ecclesiastical property, properly so called, according to the nature of the case and the norm of ecclesiastical laws and with the help, as far as possible, of skilled laymen. They are to apply this property always to those purposes for the achievement of which the Church is allowed to own temporal goods. These are: the organization of divine worship, the provision of decent support for the clergy, and the exercise of works of the apostolate and of charity, especially for the benefit of those in need.[45]

Priests, just like bishops (without prejudice to particular law),[46] are to use moneys acquired by them on the occasion of their exercise of some ecclesiastical office primarily for their own decent support and the fulfilment of the duties of their state. They should be willing to devote whatever is left over to the good of the Church or to works of charity. So they are not to regard an ecclesiastical office as a source of profit, and are not to spend the income accruing from it for increasing their own private fortunes.[47] Hence priests, far from setting their hearts on riches,[48] must always avoid all avarice and carefully refrain from all appearance of trafficking.

In fact priests are invited to embrace voluntary poverty. By it they become more clearly conformed to Christ and more ready to devote themselves to their sacred ministry. For Christ being rich became poor for our sakes, that through his poverty we might be rich.[49] The apostles by their example gave testimony that the free gift of God was to be given freely.[50] They knew both how to abound and to suffer need.[51] Even some kind of use of property in common, like the community of goods which is extolled in the history of the primitive Church,[52] provides an excellent opening for pastoral charity. By this way of life priests can

45. Council of Antioch, can. 25: Mansi 2, 1328; *Decree of Gratian*, c. 23, C. 12, q. 1 (ed. Friedberg, I, pp. 684–685).
46. This is to be understood especially of the laws and customs in force in the Eastern Churches.
47. Council of Paris, a. 829, can. 15: M.G.H., sect. III, *Concilia*, t. 2, par. 6, 622; Council of Trent, Session 25, *De reform.*, cap. 1.
48. Cf. Ps. 62, 11 Vg. 61.
49. Cf. 2 Cor. 8:9.
50. Cf. Acts 8:9.
50. Cf. Acts 8:18–25.
51. Cf. Phil. 4:12.
52. Cf. Acts 2:42–47.

laudably reduce to practice the spirit of poverty commended by Christ.

Guided then by the Spirit of the Lord, who anointed the Saviour and sent him to preach the Gospel to the poor,[53] priests and bishops alike are to avoid everything that might in any way antagonize the poor. More than the rest of Christ's disciples they are to put aside all appearance of vanity in their surroundings. They are to arrange their house in such a way that it never appears unapproachable to anyone and that nobody, even the humblest, is ever afraid to visit it.

III. HELPS FOR THE PRIEST'S LIFE

Helps toward fostering interior life

18. To enable them to foster union with Christ in all circumstances of life, priests, in addition to the meaningful carrying out of their ministry, have at their disposal the means both common and particular, new and old, which the Holy Spirit has never ceased to raise up among the People of God and which the Church recommends and in fact sometimes commands[54] for the sanctification of her members. Those actions by which Christians draw nourishment through the Word of God from the double table of holy Scripture and the Eucharist hold a preeminent place above all spiritual aids.[55] Everybody knows how important their continuous use is for the personal sanctification of priests.

The ministers of sacramental grace are intimately united to Christ the Saviour and Pastor through the fruitful reception of Penance. If it is prepared for by a daily examination of conscience, it is a powerful incentive to the essential conversation of heart to the love of the Father of mercies. Under the light of a faith that has been nourished by spiritual reading, priests can diligently search for the signs of God's will and the inspirations of his grace in the varied events of life. In this way they will become daily more docile in the demands of the mission they have undertaken in the Holy Spirit. They always find a wonderful example of such docility in the Blessed Virgin Mary who under the guidance of

53. Cf. Lk. 4:18.
54. Cf. *C.I.C.*, can. 125 ff.
55. Cf. Conc. Vat. II, Decree *Perfectae caritatis*, on the Renewal of Religious Life, 28 October 1965, n. 6; Const. dogm. *Dei verbum*, on Divine Revelation, 18 November 1965, n. 21.

the Holy Spirit made a total dedication of herself for the mystery of the redemption of men.[56] Priests should always venerate and love her, with a filial devotion and worship, as the Mother of the supreme and eternal Priest, as Queen of Apostles, and as protectress of their ministry.

As a help towards faithful fulfilment of their ministry priests should love to talk daily with Christ the Lord in their visit to the most blessed sacrament and in their personal devotion to it. They should be glad to take time for spiritual retreat and should have a high regard for spiritual direction. In various ways, in particular through the approved practice of mental prayer and the different forms of vocal prayer which they freely choose to practice, priests are to seek and perseveringly ask of God the true spirit of adoration. By this spirit they themselves, and with them the people entrusted to their care, will unite themselves with Christ the Mediator of the New Testament, and will be able as adopted sons to cry, "Abba! Father!" (Rom. 8:15).

Study and pastoral knowledge

19. Priests are warned by the bishop in the ceremony of ordination that they are to be "mature in knowledge" and that their teaching should be "a spiritual medicine for the People of God."[57] Now a sacred minister's knowledge ought to be sacred in the sense of being derived from a sacred source and directed to a sacred purpose. Primarily, then, it is drawn from the reading and meditation of sacred Scripture.[58] It is also fruitfully nourished by the study of the Fathers and Doctors of the Church and the other ancient records of Tradition. Moreover, if priests are to give adequate answers to the problems discussed by people at the present time, they should be well versed in the statements of the Church's magisterium and especially those of the Councils and the Popes. They should also consult the best approved writers on the science of theology.

Secular culture and even sacred science are advancing at an unprecedented rate in our time. Priests are therefore urged to adequate and continuous perfection of their

---

56. Cf. Conc. Vat. II, Const. dogm. *Lumen gentium*, 21 November 1964, n. 65: *AAS* 57 (1965), pp. 64–65.
57. *Roman Pontifical*, "Ordination of a Priest."
58. Cf. Conc. Vat. II, Const. dogm., *Dei verbum*, on Divine Revelation, 18 November 1965, n. 25.

knowledge of things divine and human. In this way they will prepare themselves to enter with greater advantage into dialogue with their contemporaries.

To facilitate study and the more effective learning of methods of evangelization and the apostolate, every attention is to be given to providing priests with suitable helps. Examples of these are the organization according to the conditions of each territory of courses or congresses, the setting up of centers designed for pastoral studies, the founding of libraries, and the proper direction of studies by suitable persons.

In addition bishops, either individually or in collaboration with others, should consider more effective ways of arranging that their priests would be able to attend a course of study at certain times, especially for a few years after ordination.[59] The aim of the course would be to give them an opportunity of increasing their knowledge of pastoral methods and theological science, and at the same time of strengthening their spiritual life and sharing their pastoral experiences with their brother priests.[60] By these and other suitable aids special attention may be given to helping newly appointed parish priests also, as well as priests assigned to new pastoral work or sent to another diocese or country.

Finally, bishops should be careful to see that some priests devote themselves to deeper study of the sacred sciences. This will ensure that there will never be any lack of suitable teachers for the education of clerics. It will also ensure that the rest of the priests and the faithful will be helped to acquire the knowledge of religion necessary for them, and that the sound progress in sacred studies so very necessary for the Church will be encouraged. (See D. *46*, 7.)

The provision of just remuneration for priests

20. Completely devoted as they are to the service of God in the fulfilment of the office entrusted to them, priests are entitled to receive a just remuneration. For "the laborer deserves his wages" (Lk. 10:7),[61] and "the Lord commanded

59. This course is not the same as the pastoral course to be completed immediately after ordination and dealt with in the Decree *Optatam totius*, on Priestly Training, 28 October 1965, n. 22.
60. Cf. Conc. Vat. II, Decree *Christus Dominus*, on the Pastoral Function of Bishops in the Church, 28 October 1965, n. 16.
61. Cf. Mt. 10:10; 1 Cor. 9:7; 1 Tim. 5:18.

that they who proclaim the Gospel should get their living by the Gospel" (1 Cor. 9:14). For this reason, insofar as provision is not made from some other source for the just remuneration of priests, the faithful are bound by a real obligation of seeing to it that the necessary provision for a decent and fitting livelihood for the priests is available. This obligation arises from the fact that it is for the benefit of the faithful that priests are working. Bishops are bound to warn the faithful of their obligation in this connection. They should also, either individually for their own dioceses or better still by several acting together for a common territory, see to it that rules are drawn up by which due provision is made for the decent support of those who hold or have held any office in the serving of God.

Taking into consideration the conditions of different places and times as well as the nature of the office they hold, the remuneration to be received by each of the priests should be fundamentally the same for all living in the same circumstances. It should be in keeping with their status and in addition should give priests the means not only of providing properly for the salary of those who devote themselves to their service but also of personally assisting in some way those who are in need. The Church has always from its very beginnings held this ministry to the poor in great honor. Moreover, priests' remuneration should be such as to allow the priest a proper holiday each year. The bishop should see to it that priests are able to have this holiday.

It is, however, to the office that sacred ministers fulfil that the greatest importance must be attached. For this reason the so-called system of benefices is to be abandoned or else reformed in such a way that the part that has to do with the benefice—that is, the right to the revenues attached to the endowment of the office—shall be regarded as secondary and the principal emphasis in law given to the ecclesiastical office itself. This should in future be understood as any office conferred in a permanent fashion and to be exercised for a spiritual purpose. (See D. *46*, 8.)

Common funds to be set up: social security for priests to be organized

21. The example of the faithful in the primitive Church of Jerusalem should be always kept in mind. There "they

had everything in common" (Acts 4:32), and "distribution was made to each as any had need" (Acts 4:35). It is then an excellent arrangement, at least in places where the support of the clergy depends completely or to a great extent on the offerings of the faithful, that the money offered in this way should be collected by some kind of diocesan agency. The bishop would administer this agency with the help of priests appointed for this purpose and also lay experts in financial matters, where the advantage of such appointment may make it advisable.

It is also desirable that as far as possible there should be set up in each diocese or region a common fund to enable bishops to satisfy obligations to people employed in the service of the Church and to meet the various needs of the diocese. From this fund too, richer dioceses would be able to help poorer ones, so that the abundance of the one may supply the want of the other.[62] This common fund also should be made up mainly of moneys from the offerings of the faithful as well as from those coming from other sources to be determined by law.

Moreover, in countries where social security has not yet been adequately organized for the benefit of clergy, episcopal conferences are to make provision, in harmony with ecclesiastical and civil law, for the setting up of diocesan organizations (even federated with one another), or organizations for different dioceses grouped together, or an association catering for the whole territory: the purpose of these being that under the supervision of the hierarchy satisfactory provision should be made both for suitable insurance and what is called health assistance, and for the proper support of priests who suffer from sickness, ill health or old age.

Priests should assist this organization when it has been set up, moved by a spirit of solidarity with their brother priests, sharing their hardships,[63] and at the same time realizing that in this way they can, without anxiety for their future, practice poverty with a readier appreciation of the Gospel and devote themselves completely to the salvation of souls. Those responsible should do their utmost to have such organizations combined on an international scale, so as to give them more stability and strength and promote their wider diffusion. (See D. 46, 8.)

62. Cf. 2 Cor. 8:14.
63. Cf. Phil. 4:14.

CONCLUSION AND EXHORTATION

22. This sacred Council, while keeping in mind the joys of the priestly life, cannot pass over the difficulties too which priests encounter in the circumstances of their life today. It knows also how much economic and social conditions, and even men's morals, are being transformed, and how much men's sense of values is undergoing change. Hence it is that the Church's ministers, and even sometimes the faithful, in the midst of this world feel themselves estranged from it and are anxiously seeking suitable methods and words by which they may be able to communicate with it. The new obstacles opposing the faith, the apparent fruitlessness of the work done, the bitter loneliness they experience—these can bring for priests the danger of a feeling of frustration.

But this world as it is entrusted today to the Church as the object of its love and service, this is the world God has so loved as to give his only-begotten Son for it.[1] The truth is that this world, caught as it is in the grip of much sin yet enriched too with many possibilities, provides the Church with the living stones[2] which are built together into an habitation of God in the Spirit.[3] The same Holy Spirit, while urging the Church to open new avenues of approach to the modern world, also suggests and fosters suitable adaptations of the priestly ministry.

Let priests remember that in carrying out their task they are never alone but are supported by the almighty power of God. Believing in Christ who has called them to share in his priesthood, let them devote themselves to their office with all trust, knowing that God is powerful to increase charity in them.[4] Let them remember too that they have their brothers in the priesthood and indeed the faithful of the entire world, as allies.

For all priests are cooperating in carrying out God's saving plan, the mystery of Christ or the sacrament hidden from eternity in God.[5] Only gradually is this mystery carried into effect by the united efforts of the different minis-

1. Cf. Jn. 3:16.
2. Cf. 1 Pet. 2:5.
3. Cf. Eph. 2:22.
4. Cf. *Roman Pontifical*, "Ordination of a Priest."
5. Cf. Eph. 3:9.

tries for the building up of the Body of Christ until the measure of its age be fulfilled. Since all these truths are hidden with Christ in God[6] it is by faith especially that they can be perceived. For the leaders of the People of God must needs walk by faith, following the example of the faithful Abraham who by faith "obeyed when he was called to go out to a place which he was to receive as an inheritance; and he went out, not knowing where he was to go" (Heb. 11:8).

Indeed the dispenser of the mysteries of God can be compared to the man who cast the seed into the earth, of whom the Lord said that he "should sleep and rise night and day, and the seed should sprout and grow, he knows not how" (Mk. 4:27). The Lord Jesus who said "Be of good cheer, I have overcome the world" (Jn. 16:23), did not by these words promise complete victory to his Church in this world. This sacred Council rejoices that the earth which has been sown with the seed of the Gospel is now bringing forth fruit in many places under the guidance of the Spirit of the Lord. This Spirit is filling the world and has stirred up a truly missionary spirit in the hearts of many priests and faithful. For all this the sacred Council affectionately offers its thanks to all the priests of the world: "Now to him who by the power of work within us is able to do far more abundantly than all that we ask or think, to him be glory in the church and in Christ Jesus . . ." (Eph. 3:20–21).

Note: The regulations for the implementation of the Decree on *The Ministry and Life of Priests* form part of the Document which gives the regulations for the implementation of the Decree on *The Pastoral Office of Bishops in the Church*. That Document, usually referred to as *Ecclesiae Sanctae,* is printed after the Decree on *The Pastoral Office of Bishops*. It is D. 46 in this collection.

6. Cf. Col. 3:3.

64

PASTORAL CONSTITUTION ON THE CHURCH IN THE MODERN WORLD [a][1]

Vatican II, *Gaudium et Spes*, 7 December, 1965

PREFACE

Solidarity of the church with the whole human family

1. The joy and hope, the grief and anguish of the men of our time, especially of those who are poor or afflicted in any way, are the joy and hope, the grief and anguish of the followers of Christ as well. Nothing that is genuinely human fails to find an echo in their hearts. For theirs is a community composed of men, of men who, united in Christ and guided by the holy Spirit, press onwards towards the kingdom of the Father and are bearers of a message of salvation intended for all men. That is why Christians cherish

---

a. With the exception of Part I, chap. 1 (translated by Ambrose McNicholl, o.p.), the Constitution has been translated by Ronan Lennon, o.carm. The whole was revised by Senan Crowe, o.p.

1. Although it consists of two parts, the Pastoral Constitution "The Church in the World Today" constitutes an organic unity.

The Constitution is called "pastoral" because, while resting on doctrinal principles, it seeks to set forth the relation of the Church to the world and to the men of today. In Part I, therefore, the pastoral emphasis is not overlooked, nor is the doctrinal emphasis overlooked in Part II.

In Part I the Church develops her teaching on man, the world he inhabits, and her relationship to him. Part II treats at length of various aspects of life today and human society and in particular deals with those questions and problems which seem to have a greater urgency in our day. The result is that in Part II the subject matter which is viewed in the light of doctrinal principles consists of elements, some of which are permanent and some of which are contingent.

The Constitution is to be interpreted according to the general norms of theological interpretation, while taking into account, especially in Part II, the changing circumstances which the subject matter, by its very nature, involves.

a feeling of deep solidarity with the human race and its history.

The council addresses all men

2. Now that the Second Vatican Council has deeply studied the mystery of the Church, it resolutely addresses not only the sons of the Church and all who call upon the name of Christ, but the whole of humanity as well, and it longs to set forth the way it understands the presence and function of the Church in the world of today.

Therefore, the world which the Council has in mind is the whole human family seen in the context of everything which envelopes it: it is the world as the theatre of human history, bearing the marks of its travail, its triumphs and failures, the world, which in the Christian vision has been created and is sustained by the love of its maker, which has been freed from the slavery of sin by Christ, who was crucified and rose again in order to break the stranglehold of the evil one, so that it might be fashioned anew according to God's design and brought to its fulfilment.

An offer of service to mankind

3. In wonder at their own discoveries and their own might men are today troubled and perplexed by questions about current trends in the world, about their place and their role in the universe, about the meaning of individual and collective endeavor, and finally about the destiny of nature and of men. And so the Council, as witness and guide to the faith of the whole people of God, gathered together by Christ, can find no more eloquent expression of its solidarity and respectful affection for the whole human family, to which it belongs, than to enter into dialogue with it about all these different problems. The Council will clarify these problems in the light of the Gospel and will furnish mankind with the saving resources which the Church has received from its founder under the promptings of the Holy Spirit. It is man himself who must be saved: it is mankind that must be renewed. It is man, therefore, who is the key to this discussion, man considered whole and entire, with body and soul, heart and conscience, mind and will.

This is the reason why this sacred Synod, in proclaiming the noble destiny of man and affirming an element of the divine in him, offers to co-operate unreservedly with mankind in fostering a sense of brotherhood to correspond to this destiny of theirs. The Church is not motivated by an earthly ambition but is interested in one thing only—to carry on the work of Christ under the guidance of the Holy Spirit, for he came into the world to bear witness to the truth, to save and not to judge, to serve and not to be served.[1]

INTRODUCTION

THE SITUATION OF MAN IN THE WORLD TODAY

Hope and anguish

4. At all times the Church carries the responsibility of reading the signs of the time and of interpreting them in the light of the Gospel, if it is to carry out its task. In language intelligible to every generation, she should be able to answer the ever recurring questions which men ask about the meaning of this present life and of the life to come, and how one is related to the other. We must be aware of and understand the aspirations, the yearnings, and the often dramatic features of the world in which we live. An outline of some of the more important features of the modern world forms the subject of the following paragraphs.

Ours is a new age of history with critical and swift upheavals spreading gradually to all corners of the earth. They are the products of man's intelligence and creative activity, but they recoil upon him, upon his judgments and desires, both individual and collective, upon his ways of thinking and acting in regard to people and things. We are entitled then to speak of a real social and cultural transformation whose repercussions are felt too on the religious level.

A transformation of this kind brings with it the serious problems associated with any crisis of growth. Increase in power is not always accompanied by control of that power for the benefit of man. In probing the recesses of his own mind man often seems more uncertain than ever of himself: in the gradual and precise unfolding of the laws of social living, he is perplexed by uncertainty about how to plot its course.

2. Cf. Jn. 3:17; 18:37; Mt. 20:28; Mk. 10:45.

In no other age has mankind enjoyed such an abundance of wealth, resources and economic well-being; and yet a huge proportion of the people of the world is plagued by hunger and extreme need while countless numbers are totally illiterate. At no time have men had such a keen sense of freedom, only to be faced by new forms of slavery in living and thinking. There is on the one hand a lively feeling of unity and of compelling solidarity, of mutual dependence, and on the other a lamentable cleavage of bitterly opposing camps. We have not yet seen the last of bitter political, social, and economic hostility, and racial and ideological antagonism, nor are we free from the spectre of a war of total destruction. If there is a growing exchange of ideas, there is still widespread disagreement about the meaning of the words expressing our key concepts. There is lastly a painstaking search for a better material world, without a parallel spiritual advancement.

Small wonder then that many of our contemporaries are prevented by this complex situation from recognizing permanent values and duly applying them to recent discoveries. As a result they hover between hope and anxiety and wonder uneasily about the present course of events. It is a situation that challenges men to respond; they cannot escape.

Deep-seated changes

5. The spiritual uneasiness of today and the changing structure of life are part of a broader upheaval, whose symptoms are the increasing part played on the intellectual level by the mathematical and natural sciences (not excluding the sciences dealing with man himself) and on the practical level by their repercussions on technology. The scientific mentality has wrought a change in the cultural sphere and on habits of thought, and the progress of technology is now reshaping the face of the earth and has its sights set on the conquest of space.

The human mind is, in a certain sense, broadening its mastery over time—over the past through the insights of history, over the future by foresight and planning. Advances in biology, psychology, and the social sciences not only lead man to greater self-awareness, but provide him with the technical means of molding the lives of whole peoples as well. At the same time the human race is giving more and more thought to the forecasting and control of its own population growth.

The accelerated pace of history is such that one can scarcely keep abreast of it. The destiny of the human race is viewed as a complete whole, no longer, as it were, in the particular histories of various peoples: now it merges into a complete whole. And so mankind substitutes a dynamic and more evolutionary concept of nature for a static one, and the result is an immense series of new problems calling for a new endeavor of analysis and synthesis.

Changes in the social order

6. As a result the traditional structure of local communities—family, clan, tribe, village, various groupings and social relationships—is subjected to ever more sweeping changes. Industrialization is on the increase and has raised some nations to a position of affluence, while it radically transfigures ideas and social practices hallowed by centuries. Urbanization too is on the increase, both on account of the expanding number of city dwellers and the spread of an urban way of life into rural settings. Recent more efficient mass media are contributing to the spread of knowledge and the speedy diffusion far and wide of habits of thought and feeling, setting off chain reactions in their wake. One cannot underestimate the effect of emigration on those who, for whatever reason, are led to undertake a new way of life. On the whole, the bonds uniting man to his fellows multiply without ceasing, and "socialization" creates yet other bonds, without, however, a corresponding personal development, and truly personal relationships (personalization). It is above all in countries with advanced standards of economic and social progress that these developments are evident, but there are stirrings for advancement afoot among peoples eager to share in the benefits of industrialization and urbanization. Peoples like these, especially where ancient traditions are still strong, are at the same time conscious of the need to exercise their freedom in a more mature and personal way.

Changes in attitudes, morals and religion

7. A change in attitudes and structures frequently calls accepted values into question. This is true above all of

young people who have grown impatient at times and, indeed, rebellious in their distress. Conscious of their own importance in the life of society, they aspire to play their part in it all the sooner. Consequently, it frequently happens that parents and teachers face increasing difficulties in the performance of their tasks.

Traditional institutions, laws and modes of thought and emotion do not always appear to be in harmony with today's world. This has given rise to a serious disruption of patterns and even of norms of behavior.

As regards religion there is a completely new atmosphere that conditions its practice. On the one hand people are taking a hard look at all magical world-views and prevailing superstitions and demanding a more personal and active commitment of faith, so that not a few have achieved a lively sense of the divine. On the other hand greater numbers are falling away from the practice of religion. In the past it was the exception to repudiate God and religion to the point of abandoning them, and then only in individual cases; but nowadays it seems a matter of course to reject them as incompatible with scientific progress and a new kind of humanism. In many places it is not only in philosophical terms that such trends are expressed, but there are signs of them in literature, art, the humanities, the interpretation of history and even civil law: all of which is very disturbing to many people.

Imbalances in the world of today

8. The headlong development of the world and a keener awareness of existing inequalities make for the creation and aggravation of differences and imbalances. On the personal level there often arises an imbalance between an outlook which is practical and modern and a way of thinking which fails to master and synthesize the sum total of its ideas. Another imbalance occurs between concern for practicality and the demands of moral conscience, not to mention that between the claims of group living and the needs of individual reflection and contemplation. A third imbalance takes the form of conflict between specialization and an overall view of reality.

On the family level there are tensions arising out of demographic, economic and social pressures, out of conflicts between succeeding generations, and out of new social relationships between the sexes.

On the level of race and social class we find tensions between the affluent and the underdeveloped nations; we find them between international bodies set up in the interests of peace and the ambitions of ideological indoctrination along with national or bloc expansionism. In the midst of it all stands man, at once the author and the victim of mutual distrust, animosity, conflict and woe.

Broader aspirations of mankind

9. Meanwhile there is a growing conviction of mankind's ability and duty to strengthen its mastery over nature and of the need to establish a political, social, and economic order at the service of man to assert and develop the dignity proper to individuals and to societies.

Great numbers of people are acutely conscious of being deprived of the world's goods through injustice and unfair distribution and are vehemently demanding their share of them. Developing nations like the recently independent states are anxious to share in the political and economic benefits of modern civilization and to play their part freely in the world, but they are hampered by their economic dependence on the rapidly expanding richer nations and the ever widening gap between them. The hungry nations cry out to their affluent neighbors; women claim parity with men in fact as well as of rights, where they have not already obtained it; farmers and workers insist not just on the necessities of life but also on the opportunity to develop by their labor their personal talents and to play their due role in organizing economic, social, political, and cultural life. Now for the first time in history people are not afraid to think that cultural benefits are for all and should be available to everybody.

These claims are but the sign of a deeper and more widespread aspiration. Man as an individual and as a member of society craves a life that is full, autonomous, and worthy of his nature as a human being; he longs to harness for his own welfare the immense resources of the modern world. Among nations there is a growing movement to set up a worldwide community.

In the light of the foregoing factors there appears the dichotomy of a world that is at once powerful and weak, capable of doing what is noble and what is base, disposed to freedom and slavery, progress and decline, brotherhood and hatred. Man is growing conscious that the forces he has unleashed are in his own hands and that it is up to him to control them or be enslaved by them. Here lies the modern dilemma.

Man's deeper questionings

10. The dichotomy affecting the modern world is, in fact, a symptom of the deeper dichotomy that is in man himself. He is the meeting point of many conflicting forces. In his condition as a created being he is subject to a thousand shortcomings, but feels untrammeled in his inclinations and destined for a higher form of life. Torn by a welter of anxieties he is compelled to choose between them and repudiate some among them. Worse still, feeble and sinful as he is, he often does the very thing he hates and does not do what he wants.[1] And so he feels himself divided, and the result is a host of discords in social life. Many, it is true, fail to see the dramatic nature of this state of affairs in all its clarity for their vision is in fact blurred by materialism, or they are prevented from even thinking about it by the wretchedness of their plight. Others delude themselves that they have found peace in a world-view now fashionable. There are still others whose hopes are set on a genuine and total emancipation of mankind through human effort alone and look forward to some future earthly paradise where all the desires of their hearts will be fulfilled. Nor is it unusual to find people who having lost faith in life extol the kind of foolhardiness which would empty life of all significance in itself and invest it with a meaning of their own devising. Nonetheless, in the face of modern developments there is a growing body of men who are asking the most fundamental of all questions or are glimpsing them with a keener insight: What is man? What is the meaning of suffering, evil, death, which have not been eliminated by all this progress? What is the purpose of these achievements, purchased at so high a price? What can man contribute to society? What can he expect from it? What happens after this earthly life is ended?

1. Cf. Rom. 7:14 ff.

The Church believes that Christ, who died and was raised for the sake of all,[2] can show man the way and strengthen him through the Spirit in order to be worthy of his destiny: nor is there any other name under heaven given among men by which they can be saved.[3] The Church likewise believes that the key, the center and the purpose of the whole of man's history is to be found in its Lord and Master. She also maintains that beneath all that changes there is much that is unchanging, much that has its ultimate foundation in Christ, who is the same yesterday, and today, and forever.[4] And that is why the Council, relying on the inspiration of Christ, the image of the invisible God, the firstborn of all creation,[5] proposes to speak to all men in order to unfold the mystery that is man and cooperate in tackling the main problems facing the world today.

2. Cf. 2 Cor. 5:15.
3. Cf. Acts 4:12.
4. Cf. Heb. 13:8.
5. Cf. Col. 1:15.

PART ONE

The Church and Man's Vocation

WE MUST RESPOND TO THE PROMPTINGS OF THE HOLY SPIRIT

11. The people of God believes that it is led by the Spirit of the Lord who fills the whole world. Moved by that faith it tries to discern in the events, the needs, and the longings which it shares with other men of our time, what may be genuine signs of the presence or of the purpose of God. For faith throws a new light on all things and makes known the full ideal which God has set for man, thus guiding the mind towards solutions that are fully human.

In that light the Council intends first of all to assess those values which are most highly prized today and to relate them to their divine source. For such values, insofar as they stem from the natural talents given to man by God, are exceedingly good. Not seldom, however, owing to corruption of the human heart, they are distorted through lack of due order, so that they need to be set right.

What does the Church think of man? What measures are to be recommended for building up society today? What is the final meaning of man's activity in the universe? These questions call for a reply. From their answers it will be increasingly clear that the people of God, and the human race which is its setting, render service to each other; and the mission of the Church will show itself to be supremely human by the very fact of being religious.

CHAPTER I

THE DIGNITY OF THE HUMAN PERSON

MAN AS THE IMAGE OF GOD

12. Believers and unbelievers agree almost unanimously that all things on earth should be ordained to man as to their center and summit.

But what is man? He has put forward, and continues to put forward, many views about himself, views that are divergent and even contradictory. Often he either sets himself up as the absolute measure of all things, or debases himself to the point of despair. Hence his doubt and his anguish. The Church is keenly sensitive to these difficulties. Enlightened by divine revelation she can offer a solution to them by which the true state of man may be outlined, his weakness explained, in such a way that at the same time his dignity and his vocation may be perceived in their true light.

For sacred Scripture teaches that man was created "to the image of God," as able to know and love his creator, and as set by him over all earthly creatures[1] that he might rule them, and make use of them, while glorifying God.[2] "What is man that thou are mindful of him, and the son of man that thou dost care for him? Yet thou hast made him little less than God, and dost crown him with glory and honor. Thou hast given him dominion over the works of thy hands; thou hast put all things under his feet" (Ps. 8:5-8).

But God did not create man a solitary being. From the beginning "male and female he created them" (Gen. 1:27). This partnership of man and woman constitutes the first form of communion between persons. For by his innermost nature man is a social being; and if he does not enter into

1. Cf. Gen. 1:26; Wis. 2:23.
2. Cf. Ecclus. 17:3-10.

relations with others he can neither live nor develop his gifts.

So God, as we read again in the Bible, saw "all the things that he had made, and they were very good" (Gen. 1:31).

SIN

13. Although set by God in a state of rectitude, man, enticed by the evil one, abused his freedom at the very start of history. He lifted himself up against God, and sought to attain his goal apart from him. Although they had known God, they did not glorify him as God, but their senseless hearts were darkened, and they served the creature rather than the creator.[3] What Revelation makes known to us is confirmed by our own experience. For when man looks into his own heart he finds that he is drawn towards what is wrong and sunk in many evils which cannot come from his good creator. Often refusing to acknowledge God as his source, man has also upset the relationship which should link him to his last end; and at the same time he has broken the right order that should reign within himself as well as between himself and other men and all creatures.

Man therefore is divided in himself. As a result, the whole life of men, both individual and social, shows itself to be a struggle, and a dramatic one, between good and evil, between light and darkness. Man finds that he is unable of himself to overcome the assaults of evil successfully, so that everyone feels as though bound by chains. But the Lord himself came to free and strengthen man, renewing him inwardly and casting out the "prince of this world" (Jn. 12:31), who held him in the bondage of sin.[4] For sin brought man to a lower state, forcing him away from the completeness that is his to attain.

Both the high calling and the deep misery which men experience find their final explanation in the light of this Revelation.

THE ESSENTIAL NATURE OF MAN

14. Man, though made of body and soul, is a unity. Through his very bodily condition he sums up in himself the elements of the material world. Through him they are

3. Cf. Rom. 1:21–25.
4. Cf. Jn. 8:34.

thus brought to their highest perfection and can raise their voice in praise freely given to the creator.[5] For this reason man may not despise his bodily life. Rather he is obliged to regard his body as good and to hold it in honor since God has created it and will raise it up on the last day. Nevertheless man has been wounded by sin. He finds by experience that his body is in revolt. His very dignity therefore requires that he should glorify God in his body,[6] and not allow it to serve the evil inclinations of his heart.

Man is not deceived when he regards himself as superior to bodily things and as more than just a speck of nature or a nameless unit in the city of man. For by his power to know himself in the depths of his being he rises above the whole universe of mere objects.[b] When he is drawn to think about his real self he turns to those deep recesses of his being where God who probes the heart[7] awaits him, and where he himself decides his own destiny in the sight of God. So when he recognizes in himself a spiritual and immortal soul, he is not being led astray by false imaginings that are due to merely physical or social causes. On the contrary, he grasps what is profoundly true in this matter.

DIGNITY OF THE INTELLECT, OF TRUTH, AND OF WISDOM

15. Man, as sharing in the light of the divine mind, rightly affirms that by his intellect he surpasses the world of mere things. By diligent use of his talents through the ages he has indeed made progress in the empirical sciences, in technology, and in the liberal arts. In our time his attempts to search out the secrets of the material universe and to bring it under his control have been extremely successful. Yet he has always looked for, and found, truths of a higher order. For his intellect is not confined to the range

5. Cf. Dan. 3:57-90.
6. Cf. 1 Cor. 6:13-20.
b. The Latin text (*Interioritate enim sua universitatem rerum excedit: ad haec profunda redit, quando convertitur ad cor . . .*) here shows most closely its dependence on the French draft prepared under the direction of Abbé P. Haubtmann. I have had to render the French 'interiorité' and the semi-biblical 'revertitur ad cor' by paraphrasing. Similarly, in (15), with regard to the words 'ut humaniora fiant' as applied to what man has discovered.— (Translator).
7. Cf. 1 Kg. 16:7; Jer. 17:10.

of what can be observed by the senses. It can, with genuine certainty, reach to realities known only to the mind, even though, as a result of sin, its vision has been clouded and its powers weakened.

The intellectual nature of man finds at last its perfection, as it should, in wisdom, which gently draws the human mind to look for and to love what is true and good. Filled with wisdom man is led through visible realities to those which cannot be seen.

Our age, more than any of the past, needs such wisdom if all that man discovers is to be enobled through human effort. Indeed the future of the world is in danger unless provision is made for men of greater wisdom. It should also be pointed out that many nations, poorer as far as material goods are concerned yet richer as regards wisdom, can be of the greatest advantage to others.

It is by the gift of the Holy Spirit that man, through faith, comes to contemplate and savor the mystery of God's design.[8]

DIGNITY OF MORAL CONSCIENCE

16. Deep within his conscience man discovers a law which he has not laid upon himself but which he must obey. Its voice, ever calling him to love and to do what is good and to avoid evil, tells him inwardly at the right moment: do this, shun that. For man has in his heart a law inscribed by God. His dignity lies in observing this law, and by it he will be judged.[9] His conscience is man's most secret core, and his sanctuary. There he is alone with God whose voice echoes in his depths.[10] By conscience, in a wonderful way, that law is made known which is fulfilled in the love of God and of one's neighbor.[11] Through loyalty to conscience Christians are joined to other men in the search for truth and for the right solution to so many moral problems which arise both in the life of individuals and from social relationships. Hence, the more a correct conscience prevails, the more do persons and groups turn aside from blind choice and try to be guided by the objective

8. Cf. Eccl. 17:7–8.
9. Cf. Rom. 2:15–16.
10. Cf. Pius XII, *radio message* on rightly forming the Christian conscience in youth. 23 March 1952: *AAS* 44 (1952), p. 271.
11. Cf. Mt. 22:37–40; Gal. 5:14.

standards of moral conduct. Yet it often happens that conscience goes astray through ignorance which it is unable to avoid, without thereby losing its dignity. This cannot be said of the man who takes little trouble to find out what is true and good, or when conscience is by degrees almost blinded through the habit of committing sin.

THE EXCELLENCE OF FREEDOM

17. It is, however, only in freedom that man can turn himself towards what is good. The people of our time prize freedom very highly and strive eagerly for it. In this they are right. Yet they often cherish it improperly, as if it gave them leave to do anything they like, even when it is evil. But that which is truly freedom is an exceptional sign of the image of God in man. For God willed that man should "be left in the hand of his own counsel"[12] so that he might of his own accord seek his creator and freely attain his full and blessed perfection by cleaving to him. Man's dignity therefore requires him to act out of conscious and free choice, as moved and drawn in a personal way from within, and not by blind impulses in himself or by mere external constraint. Man gains such dignity when, ridding himself of all slavery to the passions, he presses forward towards his goal by freely choosing what is good, and, by his diligence and skill, effectively secures for himself the means suited to this end. Since human freedom has been weakened by sin it is only by the help of God's grace that man can give his actions their full and proper relationship to God. Before the judgment seat of God an account of his own life will be rendered to each one according as he has done either good or evil.[13]

THE MYSTERY OF DEATH

18. It is in regard to death that man's condition is most shrouded in doubt. Man is tormented not only by pain and by the gradual breaking-up of his body but also, and even more, by the dread of forever ceasing to be. But a deep instinct leads him rightly to shrink from and to reject the utter ruin and total loss of his personality. Because he bears in himself the seed of eternity, which cannot be reduced to

12. Cf. Eccl. 15:14.
13. Cf. 2 Cor. 5:10.

mere matter, he rebels against death. All the aids made available by technology, however useful they may be, cannot set his anguished mind at rest. They may prolong his life-span; but this does not satisfy his heartfelt longing, one that can never be stifled, for a life to come

While the mind is at a loss before the mystery of death, the Church, taught by divine Revelation, declares that God has created man in view of a blessed destiny that lies beyond the limits of his sad state on earth. Moreover, the Christian faith teaches that bodily death, from which man would have been immune had he not sinned,[14] will be overcome when that wholeness which he lost through his own fault will be given once again to him by the almighty and merciful Saviour. For God has called man, and still calls him, to cleave with all his being to him in sharing for ever a life that is divine and free from all decay. Christ won this victory when he rose to life, for by his death he freed man from death.[15] Faith, therefore, with its solidly based teaching, provides every thoughtful man with an answer to his anxious queries about his future lot. At the same time it makes him able to be united in Christ with his loved ones who have already died, and gives hope that they have found true life with God.

KINDS OF ATHEISM AND ITS CAUSES

19. The dignity of man rests above all on the fact that he is called to communion with God. The invitation to converse with God is addressed to man as soon as he comes into being. For if man exists it is because God has created him through love, and through love continues to hold him in existence. He cannot live fully according to truth unless he freely acknowledges that love and entrusts himself to his creator. Many however of our contemporaries either do not at all perceive, or else explicitly reject, this intimate and vital bond of man to God. Atheism must therefore be regarded as one of the most serious problems of our time, and one that deserves more thorough treatment.

The word atheism is used to signify things that differ considerably from one another. Some people expressly deny the existence of God. Others maintain that man cannot make any assertion whatsoever about him. Still others ad-

14. Cf. Wis. 1:13; 2:23–24; Rom. 5:21; 6:23; Jas. 1:15.
15. Cf. 1 Cor. 15:56–57.

mit only such methods of investigation as would make it seem quite meaningless to ask questions about God. Many, trespassing beyond the boundaries of the positive sciences, either contend that everything can be explained by the reasoning process used in such sciences, or, on the contrary, hold that there is no such thing as absolute truth. With others it is their exaggerated idea of man that causes their faith to languish; they are more prone, it would seem, to affirm man than to deny God. Yet others have such a faulty notion of God that when they disown this product of the imagination their denial has no reference to the God of the Gospels. There are also those who never enquire about God; religion never seems to trouble or interest them at all, nor do they see why they should bother about it. Not infrequently atheism is born from a violent protest against the evil in the world, or from the fact that certain human ideals are wrongfully invested with such an absolute character as to be taken for God. Modern civilization itself, though not of its very nature but because it is too engrossed in the concerns of this world, can often make it harder to approach God.

Without doubt those who wilfully try to drive God from their heart and to avoid all questions about religion, not following the biddings of their conscience, are not free from blame. But believers themselves often share some responsibility for this situation. For atheism, taken as a whole, is not present in the mind of man from the start (*Atheismus, integre consideratus, non est quid originarium*). It springs from various causes, among which must be included a critical reaction against religions and, in some places, against the Christian religion in particular. Believers can thus have more than a little to do with the rise of atheism. To the extent that they are careless about their instruction in the faith, or present its teaching falsely, or even fail in their religious, moral, or social life, they must be said to conceal rather than to reveal the true nature of God and of religion.

SYSTEMATIC ATHEISM

20. Modern atheism often takes on a systematic form also which, in addition to other causes, so insists on man's desire for autonomy as to object to any dependence on God at all. Those who profess this kind of atheism maintain that freedom consists in this, that man is an end to himself, and

the sole maker, with supreme control, of his own history (*propriae suae historae solus artifex et demiurgus*). They claim that this outlook cannot be reconciled with the assertion of a Lord who is author and end of all things, or that at least it makes such an affirmation altogether unnecessary. The sense of power which modern technical progress begets in man may encourage this outlook.

Among the various kinds of present-day atheism, that one should not go unnoticed which looks for man's autonomy through his economic and social emancipation. It holds that religion, of its very nature, thwarts such emancipation by raising man's hopes in a future life, thus both deceiving him and discouraging him from working for a better form of life on earth. That is why those who hold such views, wherever they gain control of the state, violently attack religion, and in order to spread atheism, especially in the education of young people, make use of all the means by which the civil authority can bring pressure to bear on its subjects.

THE ATTITUDE OF THE CHURCH TOWARDS ATHEISM

21. The Church, as given over to the service of both God and man, cannot cease from reproving, with sorrow yet with the utmost firmness, as she has done in the past,[16] those harmful teachings and ways of acting which are in conflict with reason and with common human experience, and which cast man down from the noble state to which he is born.

She tries nevertheless to seek out the secret motives which lead the atheistic mind to deny God. Well knowing how important are the problems raised by atheism, and urged by her love for all men, she considers that these motives deserve an earnest and more thorough scrutiny.

The Church holds that to acknowledge God is in no way to oppose the dignity of man, since such dignity is grounded and brought to perfection in God. Man has in fact been placed in society by God, who created him as an intelligent

16. Cf. Pius XI, Encyclical *Divini Redemptoris*, 19 March 1937: *AAS* 29 (1937), pp. 65–106; Pius XII, Encyclical *Ad Apostolorum Principis*, 29 June 1958: *AAS* 50 (1958), pp. 601–14; John XXIII, Encyclical *Mater et Magistra*, 15 May 1961: *AAS* 53 (1961), pp. 451–3; Paul VI, Encyclical *Ecclesiam Suam*, 6 August 1964: *AAS* 56 (1964), pp. 651–3.

and free being; but over and above this he is called as a
son to intimacy with God and to share in his happiness. She
further teaches that hope in a life to come does not take
away from the importance of the duties of this life on earth
but rather adds to it by giving new motives for fulfilling
those duties. When, on the other hand, man is left without
this divine support and without hope of eternal life his
dignity is deeply wounded, as may so often be seen today.
The problems of life and death, of guilt and of suffering,
remain unsolved, so that men are not rarely cast into despair.

Meanwhile, every man remains a question to himself,
one that is dimly perceived and left unanswered. For there
are times, especially in the major events of life, when no
man can altogether escape from such self-questioning. God
alone, who calls man to deeper thought and to more humble probing, can fully and with complete certainty supply
an answer to this questioning.

Atheism must be countered both by presenting true
teaching in a fitting manner and by the full and complete
life of the Church and of her members. For it is the function of the Church to render God the Father and his incarnate Son present and as it were visible, while ceaselessly renewing and purifying herself[c] under the guidance of the
Holy Spirit.[17] This is brought about chiefly by the witness
of a living and mature faith, one namely that is so well
formed that it can see difficulties clearly and overcome
them. Many martyrs have borne, and continue to bear, a
splendid witness to this faith. This faith should show its
fruitfulness by penetrating the whole life, even the worldly
activities, of those who believe, and by urging them to be
loving and just especially towards those in need. Lastly,
what does most to show God's presence clearly is the brotherly love of the faithful who, being all of one mind and
spirit, work together for the faith of the Gospel[18] and present themselves as a sign of unity.

c. Grammatically the text could read: *by* ceaselessly renewing and
purifying herself. But this would imply that the Church makes God
present only when she renews herself. The text, in trying to be
short, mixes two ideas, that of the presence of God in the world
through the Church, and that of a presence made more visible and
striking through a renewal of Christian life.
17. Cf. Vatican Council II, Dogmatic Constitution *Lumen Gentium*,
ch. 1, n. 8: *AAS* 57 (1965), p. 12.
18. Cf. Phil. 1:27.

Although the Church altogether rejects atheism, she nevertheless sincerely proclaims that all men, those who believe as well as those who do not, should help to establish right order in this world where all live together. This certainly cannot be done without a dialogue that is sincere and prudent. The Church therefore deplores the discrimination between believers and unbelievers which some civil authorities unjustly practice in defiance of the fundamental rights of the human person. She demands effective freedom for the faithful to be allowed to build up God's temple in this world also. She courteously invites atheists to weigh the merits of the Gospel of Christ with an open mind.

For the Church knows full well that her message is in harmony with the most secret desires of the human heart, since it champions the dignity of man's calling, giving hope once more to those who already despair of their higher destiny. Her message, far from impairing man, helps him to develop himself by bestowing light, life, and freedom. Apart from this message nothing is able to satisfy the heart of man: "Thou hast made us for thyself, O Lord, and our heart is restless until it rest in thee."[19]

CHRIST THE NEW MAN

22. In reality it is only in the mystery of the Word made flesh that the mystery of man truly becomes clear. For Adam, the first man, was a type of him who was to come,[20] Christ the Lord, Christ the new Adam, in the very revelation of the mystery of the Father and of his love, fully reveals man to himself and brings to light his most high calling. It is no wonder, then, that all the truths mentioned so far should find in him their source and their most perfect embodiment.

He who is the "image of the invisible God" (Col. 1:15),[21] is himself the perfect man who has restored in the children of Adam that likeness to God which had been disfigured ever since the first sin. Human nature, by the very fact that it was assumed, not absorbed, in him, has been

19. St. Augustine, *Confessions* I, 1: *PL* 32, 661.
20. Cf. Rom. 5:14. Cf. Tertullian, *De carnis resurrectione*, 6: "For in all the form which was moulded in the clay, Christ was in his thoughts as the man who to be":*PL* 2, 282; *CSEL*, 47, p. 33, 1. 12–13.
21. Cf. 2 Cor. 4:4.

raised in us also to a dignity beyond compare.[22] For, by his incarnation, he, the son of God, has in a certain way united himself with each man. He worked with human hands, he thought with a human mind. He acted with a human will,[23] and with a human heart he loved. Born of the Virgin Mary, he has truly been made one of us, like to us in all things except sin.[24]

As an innocent lamb he merited life for us by his blood which he freely shed. In him God reconciled us to himself and to one another,[25] freeing us from the bondage of the devil and of sin, so that each one of us could say with the apostle: the Son of God "loved me and gave himself for me" (Gal. 2:20). By suffering for us he not only gave us an example so that we might follow in his footsteps,[26] but he also opened up a way. If we follow this path, life and death are made holy and acquire a new meaning.

Conformed to the image of the Son who is the firstborn of many brothers,[27] the Christian man receives the "first fruits of the Spirit" (Rom. 8:23) by which he is able to fulfil the new law of love.[28] By this Spirit, who is the "pledge of our inheritance" (Eph. 1:14), the whole man is inwardly renewed, right up to the "redemption of the body" (Rom. 8:23). "If the Spirit of him who raised Jesus from the dead dwells in you, he who raised Christ Jesus from the dead will give life to your mortal bodies also through his Spirit who dwells in you" (Rom. 8:11).[29] The Christian is certainly bound both by need and by duty to struggle with evil through many afflictions and to suffer death; but, as one who has been made a partner in the paschal mystery,

22. Cf. Council Constantinople II, can. 7: "Neither was God the Word changed into the nature of flesh, nor his flesh changed into the nature of the word"; *Denz.* 219 (428); cf. also Council Constantinople III: "For as his all-holy and immaculate ensouled flesh was not destroyed (*theothesia ouk anèrethé*) by being deified, but persisted in its own state and sphere": *Denz.* 291 (556); cf. Council Chalcedon: "Recognized in two natures, without confusion, without change, without division, without separation": *Denz.* 291 (302).
23. Cf. Council Constantinople III: "So also his human will was not destroyed by being deified, but was rather preserved": *Denz.* 291 (556).
24. Cf. Heb. 4:15.
25. Cf. 2 Cor. 5:18–19; Col. 1:20–22.
26. Cf. 1 Pet. 2:21; Mt. 16:24; Lk. 14–27.
27. Cf. Rom. 8:29; Col. 3:10–14.
28. Cf. Rom. 8:1–11.
29. Cf. 2 Cor. 4:14.

and as one who has been configured to the death of Christ, he will go forward, strengthened by hope, to the resurrection.[30]

All this holds true not for Christians only but also for all men of good will in whose hearts grace is active invisibly.[31] For since Christ died for all,[32] and since all men are in fact called to one and the same destiny, which is divine, we must hold that the Holy Spirit offers to all the possibility of being made partners, in a way known to God, in the paschal mystery.

Such is the nature and the greatness of the mystery of man as enlightened for the faithful by the Christian revelation. It is therefore through Christ, and in Christ, that light is thrown on the riddle of suffering and death which, apart from his Gospel, overwhelms us. Christ has risen again, destroying death by his death, and has given life abundantly to us[33] so that, becoming sons in the Son, we may cry out in the Spirit: Abba, Father![34]

CHAPTER II

THE COMMUNITY OF MANKIND

INTENTION OF THE COUNCIL

23. One of the most striking features of today's world is the intense development of interpersonal relationships due in no small measure to modern technical advances. Nevertheless genuine fraternal dialogue is advanced not so much on this level as at the deeper level of personal fellowship, and this calls for mutual respect for the full spiritual dignity of men as persons. Christian revelation greatly fosters the establishment of such fellowship and at the same time

30. Cf. Phil. 3:10; Rom. 8:17.
31. Cf. Vatican Council II, Dogmatic Constitution *Lumen Gentium*, ch. 2, n. 16: *AAS* 57 (1965), p. 20.
32. Cf. Rom. 8:32.
33. Cf. *Byzantine Easter Liturgy*.
34. Cf. Rom. 8:15 and Gal. 4:6; cf. also Jn. 1:22 and Jn. 3:1-2.

promotes deeper understanding of the laws of social living with which the creator has endowed man's spiritual and moral nature.

Some recent pronouncements of the Church's teaching authority have dealt at length with Christian teaching on human society.[1] The Council, therefore, proposes to repeat only a few of the more important truths and outline the basis of these truths in the light of revelation. Later it will deal with some of their implications which have special importance for our day.

COMMUNITARIAN NATURE OF MAN'S VOCATION: DESIGN OF GOD

24. In his fatherly care for all of us, God desired that all men should form one family and deal with each other in a spirit of brotherhood. All, in fact, are destined to the very same end, namely God himself, since they have been created in the likeness of God who "made from one every nation of men who live on all the face of the earth" (Acts 17:26). Love of God and of one's neighbor, then, is the first and greatest commandment. Scripture teaches us that love of God cannot be separated from love of one's neighbor: "Any other commandment [is] summed up in this sentence: 'You shall love your neighbor as yourself . . .' therefore love is the fulfilling of the law" (Rom. 13:9–10; cf. 1 Jn. 4:20). It goes without saying that this is a matter of the utmost importance to men who are coming to rely more and more on each other and to a world which is becoming more unified every day

Furthermore, the Lord Jesus, when praying to the Father "that they may all be one . . . even as we are one" (Jn. 17:21–22), has opened up new horizons closed to human reason by implying that there is a certain parallel between the union existing among the divine persons and the union of the sons of God in truth and love. It follows, then, that if man is the only creature on earth that God has wanted for its own sake, man can fully discover his true self only in a sincere giving of himself.[2]

1. Cf. John XXIII, Litt. Encycl. *Mater et Magistra*, 15 May 1961: *AAS* 53 (1961), pp. 401–64, and Litt. Encycl. *Pacem in Terris*, 11 April 1963: *AAS* 55 (1963), pp. 257–304; Paul VI, Litt. Encycl. *Ecclesiam Suam*, 6 August 1964: *AAS* 56 (1964), pp. 609–59.
2. Cf. Lk. 17:33.

PERSON AND SOCIETY: INTERDEPENDENCE

25. The social nature of man shows that there is an interdependence between personal betterment and the improvement of society. Insofar as man by his very nature stands completely in need of life in society,[3] he is and he ought to be the beginning, the subject and the object of every social organization. Life in society is not something accessory to man himself: through his dealings with others, through mutual service, and through fraternal dialogue, man develops all his talents and becomes able to rise to his destiny.

Among the social ties necessary for man's development some correspond more immediately to his innermost nature—the family, for instance, and the political community; others flow rather from his free choice. Nowadays for various reasons mutual relationships and interdependence increase from day to day and give rise to a variety of associations and organizations, both public and private. Socialization, as it is called, is not without its dangers, but it brings with it many advantages for the strengthening and betterment of human qualities and for the protection of human rights.[4]

While on the one hand in fulfilling his calling (even his religious calling), man is greatly helped by life in society, on the other hand it cannot be denied that he is often turned away from the good and urged to evil by the social environment in which he lives and in which he is immersed since the day of his birth. Without doubt frequent upheavals in the social order are in part the result of economic, political, and social tensions. But at a deeper level they come from selfishness and pride, two things which contaminate the atmosphere of society as well. As it is, man is prone to evil, but whenever he meets a situation where the effects of sin are to be found, he is exposed to further inducements to sin, which can only be overcome by unflinching effort under the help of grace.

3. Cf. St. Thomas, I *Ethic.*, Lect. 1.
4. Cf. John XXIII, Litt. Encycl. *Mater et Magistra,* 15 May 1961: *AAS* 53 (1961), p. 418. Cf. also Pius XI, Litt. Encycl. *Quadragesimo Anno,* 15 May 1931: *AAS* 23 (1931), p. 222 ff.

THE COMMON GOOD

26. Because of the closer bonds of human interdependence and their spread over the whole world, we are today witnessing a widening of the role of the common good, which is the sum total of social conditions which allow people, either as groups or as individuals, to reach their fulfilment more fully and more easily. The whole human race is consequently involved with regard to the rights and obligations which result. Every group must take into account the needs and legitimate aspirations of every other group, and still more of the human family as a whole.[5]

At the same time, however, there is a growing awareness of the sublime dignity of the human person, who stands above all things and whose rights and duties are universal and inviolable. He ought, therefore, to have ready access to all that is necessary for living a genuinely human life: for example, food, clothing, housing, the right freely to choose his state of life and set up a family, the right to education, work, to his good name, to respect, to proper knowledge, the right to act according to the dictates of conscience and to safeguard his privacy, and rightful freedom even in matters of religion.

The social order and its development must constantly yield to the good of the person, since the order of things must be subordinate to the order of persons and not the other way around, as the Lord suggested when he said that the Sabbath was made for man and not man for the Sabbath.[6] The social order requires constant improvement: it must be founded in truth, built on justice, and enlivened by love: it should grow in freedom towards a more humane equilibrium.[7] If these objectives are to be attained there will first have to be a renewal of attitudes and far-reaching social changes.

The Spirit of God, who, with wondrous providence, directs the course of time and renews the face of the earth, assists at this development. The ferment of the Gospel has

5. Cf. John XXIII, Litt. Encycl. *Mater et Magistra: AAS* 53 (1961), p. 417.
6. Mk. 2:27.
7. Cf. John XXIII, Litt. Encycl. *Pacem in Terris: AAS* 55 (1963), p. 266.

aroused and continues to arouse in the hearts of men an unquenchable thirst for human dignity.

RESPECT FOR THE HUMAN PERSON

27. Wishing to come down to topics that are practical and of some urgency, the Council lays stress on respect for the human person: everyone should look upon his neighbor (without any exception) as another self, bearing in mind above all his life and the means necessary for living it in a dignified way[8] lest he follow the example of the rich man who ignored Lazarus, the poor man.[9]

Today there is an inescapable duty to make ourselves the neighbor of every man, no matter who he is, and if we meet him, to come to his aid in a positive way, whether he is an aged person abandoned by all, a foreign worker despised without reason, a refugee, an illegitimate child wrongly suffering for a sin he did not commit, or a starving human being who awakens our conscience by calling to mind the words of Christ: "As you did it to one of the least of these my brethren, you did it to me" (Mt. 25:40).

The varieties of crime are numerous: all offenses against life itself, such as murder, genocide, abortion, euthanasia and wilful suicide; all violations of the integrity of the human person, such as mutilation, physical and mental torture, undue psychological pressures; all offenses against human dignity, such as subhuman living conditions, arbitrary imprisonment, deportation, slavery, prostitution, the selling of women and children, degrading working conditions where men are treated as mere tools for profit rather than free and responsible persons: all these and the like are criminal: they poison civilization; and they debase the perpetrators more than the victims and militate against the honor of the creator.

RESPECT AND LOVE FOR ENEMIES

28. Those also have a claim on our respect and charity who think and act differently from us in social, political, and religious matters. In fact the more deeply we come to understand their ways of thinking through kindness and

8. Cf. Jas. 2:15–16.
9. Cf. Lk. 16:19–31.

love, the more easily will we be able to enter into dialogue with them.

Love and courtesy of this kind should not, of course, make us indifferent to truth and goodness. Love, in fact, impels the followers of Christ to proclaim to all men the truth which saves. But we must distinguish between the error (which must always be rejected) and the person in error, who never loses his dignity as a person even though he flounders amid false or inadequate religious ideas.[10] God alone is the judge and the searcher of hearts: he forbids us to pass judgment on the inner guilt of others.[11]

The teaching of Christ even demands that we forgive injury,[12] and the precept of love, which is the commandment of the New Law, includes all our enemies: "You have heard that it was said, 'You shall love your neighbor and hate your enemy.' But I say to you, love your enemies, do good to them that hate you; and pray for those who persecute and calumniate you" (Mt. 5:43-44).

ESSENTIAL EQUALITY OF ALL MEN: SOCIAL JUSTICE

29. All men are endowed with a rational soul and are created in God's image; they have the same nature and origin and, being redeemed by Christ, they enjoy the same divine calling and destiny; there is here a basic equality between all men and it must be given ever greater recognition.

Undoubtedly not all men are alike as regards physical capacity and intellectual and moral powers. But forms of social or cultural discrimination in basic personal rights on the grounds of sex, race, color, social conditions, language or religion, must be curbed and eradicated as incompatible with God's design. It is regrettable that these basic personal rights are not yet being respected everywhere, as is the case with women who are denied the chance freely to choose a husband, or a state of life, or to have access to the same educational and cultural benefits as are available to men.

Furthermore, while there are rightful differences between people, their equal dignity as persons demands that we

10. Cf. John XXIII, Litt. Encycl. *Pacem in Terris: AAS* 55 (1963), pp. 299 and 300.
11. Cf. Lk. 6:37-38; Mt. 7:1-11; 14:10-12.
12. Cf. Mt. 5:43-47.

strive for fairer and more humane conditions. Excessive economic and social disparity between individuals and peoples of the one human race is a source of scandal and militates against social justice, equity, human dignity, as well as social and international peace.

It is up to public and private organizations to be at the service of the dignity and destiny of man; let them spare no effort to banish every vestige of social and political slavery and to safeguard basic human rights under every political system. And even if it takes a considerable time to arrive at the desired goal, these organizations should gradually be brought into harmony with spiritual realities, which are the most sublime of all.

NEED TO TRANSCEND AN INDIVIDUALISTIC MORALITY

30. The pace of change is so far-reaching and rapid nowadays that no one can allow himself to close his eyes to the course of events or indifferently ignore them and wallow in the luxury of a merely individualistic morality. The best way to fulfil one's obligations of justice and love is to contribute to the common good according to one's means and the needs of others, even to the point of fostering and helping public and private organizations devoted to bettering the conditions of life. There is a kind of person who boasts of grand and noble sentiments and lives in practice as if he could not care less about the needs of society. There are many in various countries who make light of social laws and directives and are not ashamed to resort to fraud and cheating to avoid paying just taxes and fulfilling other social obligations. There are others who neglect the norms of social conduct, such as those regulating public hygiene and speed limits, forgetting that they are endangering their own lives and the lives of others by their carelessness.

Let everyone consider it his sacred duty to count social obligations among man's chief duties today and observe them as such. For the more closely the world comes together, the more widely do men's obligations transcend particular groups and gradually extend to the whole world. This will be realized only if individuals and groups practice moral and social virtues and foster them in social living. Then, under the necessary help of divine grace, there will arise a generation of new men, the molders of a new humanity.

RESPONSIBILITY AND PARTICIPATION

31. To achieve a greater fulfilment of their duties of conscience as individuals towards themselves and towards the various groups to which they belong, men have to be carefully educated to a higher degree of culture through the employment of the immense resources available today to the human race. Above all we must undertake the training of youth from all social backgrounds if we are to produce the kind of men and women so desperately needed by our age—men and women not only of high culture but of great personality as well.

But this sense of responsibility does not come unless circumstances are such as to allow man to be conscious of his dignity and to rise to his destiny in the service of God and of men. For freedom is often crippled by extreme destitution just as it can wither in an ivory-tower isolation brought on by overindulgence in the good things of life. It can, however, be strengthened by accepting the inevitable constraints of social life, by undertaking the manifold demands of human fellowship, and by service to the community at large.

It is necessary then to foster among all the will to play a role in common undertakings. One must pay tribute to those nations whose systems permit the largest possible number of the citizens to take part in public life in a climate of genuine freedom, although one must always keep in mind the concrete circumstances of each people and the decisiveness required of public authority. Nevertheless, if all citizens are to feel inclined to take part in the activities of the various constituent groups of the social structure, they must find motives in these groups which will attract members and dispose them to serve their fellow men. One is entitled to think that the future of humanity is in the hands of those men who are capable of providing the generations to come with reasons for life and optimism.

THE WORD MADE FLESH AND HUMAN SOLIDARITY

32. Just as God did not create men to live as individuals but to come together in the formation of social unity, so he "willed to make men holy and save them, not as individuals without any bond or link between them, but rather to make

them into a people who might acknowledge him and serve him in holiness."[13] At the outset of salvation history he chose certain men as members of a given community, not as individuals, and revealed his plan to them, calling them "his people" (Ex. 3:7-12) and making a covenant on Mount Sinai with them.[14]

This communitarian character is perfected and fulfilled in the work of Jesus Christ, for the Word made flesh willed to share in human fellowship. He was present at the wedding feast at Cana, he visited the house of Zacchaeus, he sat down with publicans and sinners. In revealing the Father's love and man's sublime calling he made use of the most ordinary things of social life and illustrated his words with expressions and imagery from everyday life. He sanctified those human ties, above all family ties, which are the basis of social structures. He willingly observed the laws of his country and chose to lead the life of an ordinary craftsman of his time and place.

In his preaching he clearly outlined an obligation on the part of the sons of God to treat each other as brothers. In his prayer he asked that all his followers should be "one." As the redeemer of all mankind he delivered himself even unto death for the sake of all: "Greater love has no man than this, that a man lay down his life for his friends" (Jn. 15:13). His command to the apostles was to preach the Gospel to all peoples in order that the human race would become the family of God, in which love would be the fullness of the law.

As the firstborn of many brethren, and by the gift of his Spirit, he established, after his death and resurrection, a new brotherly communion among all who received him in faith and love; this is the communion of his own body, the Church, in which everyone as members one of the other would render mutual service in the measure of the different gifts bestowed on each.

This solidarity must be constantly increased until that day when it will be brought to fulfilment; on that day mankind, saved by grace, will offer perfect glory to God as the family beloved of God and of Christ their brother.

13. Vatican Council II, Dogmatic Constitution *Lumen Gentium,* ch. 2, n. 9: *AAS* 57 (1965), pp. 12–13.
14. Cf. Ex. 24:1–8.

CHAPTER III

MAN'S ACTIVITY IN THE UNIVERSE

THE PROBLEM

33. Man has always striven to develop his life through his mind and his work; today his efforts have achieved a measure of success, for he has extended and continues to extend his mastery over nearly all spheres of nature thanks to science and technology. Thanks above all to an increase in all kinds of interchange between nations the human family is gradually coming to recognize itself and constitute itself as one single community over the whole earth. As a result man now produces by his own enterprise many things which in former times he looked for from heavenly powers.

In the face of this immense enterprise now involving the whole human race men are troubled by many questionings. What is the meaning and value of this feverish activity? How ought all of these things be used? To what goal is all this individual and collective enterprise heading? The Church is guardian of the heritage of the divine Word and draws religious and moral principles from it, but she does not always have a ready answer to every question. Still, she is eager to associate the light of revelation with the experience of mankind in trying to clarify the course upon which mankind has just entered.

VALUE OF HUMAN ACTIVITY

34. Individual and collective activity, that monumental effort of man through the centuries to improve the circumstances of the world, presents no problem to believers: considered in itself, it corresponds to the plan of God. Man was created in God's image and was commanded to conquer the earth with all it contains and to rule the world in justice and holiness:[1] he was to acknowledge God as maker

1. Cf. Gen. 1:26–27; 9:2–3; Wis. 9:2–3.

of all things and relate himself and the totality of creation to him, so that through the dominion of all things by man the name of God would be majestic in all the earth.[2]

This holds good also for our daily work. When men and women provide for themselves and their families in such a way as to be of service to the community as well, they can rightly look upon their work as a prolongation of the work of the creator, a service to their fellow men, and their personal contribution to the fulfilment in history of the divine plan.[3]

Far from considering the conquests of man's genius and courage as opposed to God's power as if he set himself up as a rival to the creator, Christians ought to be convinced that the achievements of the human race are a sign of God's greatness and the fulfilment of his mysterious design. With an increase in human power comes a broadening of responsibility on the part of individuals and communities: there is no question, then, of the Christian message inhibiting men from building up the world or making them disinterested in the good of their fellows: on the contrary it is an incentive to do these very things.[4]

REGULATION OF HUMAN ACTIVITY

35. Human activity proceeds from man: it is also ordered to him. When he works, not only does he transform matter and society, but he fulfils himself. He learns, he develops his faculties, and he emerges from and transcends himself. Rightly understood, this kind of growth is more precious than any kind of wealth that can be amassed. It is what a man is, rather than what he has, that counts.[5] Technical progress is of less value than advances towards greater justice, wider brotherhood, and a more humane social environment. Technical progress may supply the material for human advance but it is powerless to actualize it.

Here then is the norm for human activity—to harmonize with the authentic interests of the human race, in accor-

2. Cf. Ps. 8:7 and 10.
3. Cf. John XXIII, Litt. Encycl. *Pacem in Terris: AAS* 55 (1963), p. 297.
4. Cf. *Message to all Men*, issued by the Fathers at the beginning of Vatican Council II, October 1962: *AAS* 54 (1962), p. 823.
5. Cf. Paul VI, *Allocution to the Diplomatic Corps*, 7 January 1965: *AAS* 57 (1965), p. 232.

dance with God's will and design, and to enable men as individuals and as members of society to pursue and fulfil their total vocation.

RIGHTFUL AUTONOMY OF EARTHLY AFFAIRS

36. There seems to be some apprehension today that a close association between human activity and religion will endanger the autonomy of man, of organizations and of science. If by the autonomy of earthly affairs is meant the gradual discovery, exploitation, and ordering of the laws and values of matter and society, then the demand for autonomy is perfectly in order: it is at once the claim of modern man and the desire of the creator. By the very nature of creation, material being is endowed with its own stability, truth and excellence, its own order and laws. These man must respect as he recognizes the methods proper to every science and technique. Consequently, methodical research in all branches of knowledge, provided it is carried out in a truly scientific manner and does not override moral laws, can never conflict with the faith, because the things of the world and the things of faith derive from the same God.[6] The humble and persevering investigator of the secrets of nature is being led, as it were, by the hand of God in spite of himself, for it is God, the conserver of all things, who made them what they are. We cannot but deplore certain attitudes (not unknown among Christians) deriving from a shortsighted view of the rightful autonomy of science; they have occasioned conflict and controversy and have misled many into opposing faith and science.[7]

However, if by the term "the autonomy of earthy affairs" is meant that material being does not depend on God and that man can use it as if it had no relation to its creator, then the falsity of such a claim will be obvious to anyone who believes in God. Without a creator there can be no creature. In any case, believers, no matter what their religion, have always recognized the voice and the revelation of God in the language of creatures. Besides, once God is forgotten, the creature is lost sight of as well.

6. Cf. Vatican Council I, Dogmatic Constitution *De fide cath.*, ch. 3: *Denz.* 1785–1786 (3004–3005).
7. Cf. Pius Paschini, *Vita e opere di Galileo Galilei*, 2 vol., Vatic., 1964.

HUMAN ACTIVITY INFECTED BY SIN

37. Sacred Scripture teaches mankind what has also been confirmed by man's own experience, namely, that the great advantages of human progress are fraught with grave temptations: the hierarchy of values has been disordered, good and evil intermingle, and every man and every group is interested only in its own affairs, not in those of others. So it is that the earth has not yet become the scene of true brotherhood; rather, man's swelling power at the present time threatens to put an end to the human race itself.

The whole of man's history has been the story of dour combat with the powers of evil, stretching, so our Lord tells us,[8] from the very dawn of history until the last day. Finding himself in the midst of the battlefield man has to struggle to do what is right, and it is at great cost to himself, and aided by God's grace, that he succeeds in achieving his own inner integrity. Hence the Church of Christ, trusting in the design of the creator and admitting that progress can contribute to man's true happiness, still feels called upon to echo the words of the apostle: "Do not be conformed to this world" (Rom. 12:2). "World" here means a spirit of vanity and malice whereby human activity from being ordered to the service of God and man is distorted to an instrument of sin.

To the question of how this unhappy situation can be overcome, Christians reply that all these human activities, which are daily endangered by pride and inordinate self-love, must be purified and perfected by the cross and resurrection of Christ. Redeemed by Christ and made a new creature by the Holy Spirit, man can, indeed he must, love the things of God's creation: it is from God that he has received them, and it is as flowing from God's hand that he looks upon them and reveres them. Man thanks his divine benefactor for all these things, he uses them and enjoys them in a spirit of poverty and freedom: thus he is brought to a true possession of the world, as having nothing yet possessing everything:[9] "All [things] are yours; and you are Christ's; and Christ is God's" (1 Cor. 2:22–23).

8. Cf. Mt. 24:13; 13:24–30 and 36–43.
9. Cf. 2 Cor. 6:10.

HUMAN ACTIVITY: ITS FULFILMENT IN THE PASCHAL MYSTERY

38. The Word of God, through whom all things were made, became man and dwelt among men:[10] a perfect man, he entered world history, taking that history into himself and recapitulating it.[11] He reveals to us that "God is love" (1 Jn. 4:8) and at the same time teaches that the fundamental law of human perfection, and consequently of the transformation of the world, is the new commandment of love. He assures those who trust in the charity of God that the way of love is open to all men and that the effort to establish a universal brotherhood will not be in vain.

This love is not something reserved for important matters, but must be exercised above all in the ordinary circumstances of daily life. Christ's example in dying for us sinners[12] teaches us that we must carry the cross, which the flesh and the world inflict on the shoulders of all who seek after peace and justice. Constituted Lord by his resurrection and given all authority in heaven and on earth,[13] Christ is now at work in the hearts of men by the power of his Spirit; not only does he arouse in them a desire for the world to come but he quickens, purifies, and strengthens the generous aspirations of mankind to make life more humane and conquer the earth for this purpose. The gifts of the Spirit are manifold: some men are called to testify openly to mankind's yearning for its heavenly home and keep the awareness of it vividly before men's minds; others are called to dedicate themselves to the earthly service of men and in this way to prepare the way for the kingdom of heaven. But of all the Spirit makes free men, who are ready to put aside love of self and integrate earthly resources into human life, in order to reach out to that future day when mankind itself will become an offering accepted by God.[14]

Christ left to his followers a pledge of this hope and food for the journey in the sacrament of faith, in which natural elements, the fruits of man's cultivation, are changed into His glorified Body and Blood, as a supper of brotherly fellowship and a foretaste of the heavenly banquet.

10. Cf. Jn. 1:3 and 14.
11. Cf. Eph. 1:10.
12. Cf. Jn 3:16; Rom. 5:8–10.
13. Cf. Acts 2:36; Mt. 28:18.
14. Cf. Rom. 15:16.

39. We know neither the moment of the consummation of the earth and of man[15] nor the way the universe will be transformed. The form of this world, distorted by sin, is passing away[16] and we are taught that God is preparing a new dwelling and a new earth in which righteousness dwells,[17] whose happiness will fill and surpass all the desires of peace arising in the hearts of men.[18] Then with death conquered the sons of God will be raised in Christ and what was sown in weakness and dishonor will put on the imperishable:[19] charity and its works will remain[20] and all of creation,[21] which God made for man, will be set free from its bondage to decay.

We have been warned, of course, that it profits man nothing if he gains the whole world and loses or forfeits himself.[22] Far from diminishing our concern to develop this earth, the expectancy of a new earth should spur us on, for it is here that the body of a new human family grows, foreshadowing in some way the age which is to come. That is why, although we must be careful to distinguish earthy progress clearly from the increase of the kingdom of Christ, such progress is of vital concern to the kingdom of God, insofar as it can contribute to the better ordering of human society.[23]

When we have spread on earth the fruits of our nature and our enterprise—human dignity, brotherly communion, and freedom—according to the command of the Lord and in his Spirit, we will find them once again, cleansed this time from the stain of sin, illuminated and transfigured, when Christ presents to his Father an eternal and universal kingdom "of truth and life, a kingdom of holiness and grace, a kingdom of justice, love and peace."[24] Here on earth the kingdom is mysteriously present; when the Lord comes it will enter into its perfection.

---

15. Cf. Acts 1:7.
16. Cf. 1 Cor. 7:31; St. Irenaeus, *Adversus Haereses*, V, 36, 1: *PG* 7, 1222.
17. Cf. 2 Cor. 5:2; 2 Pet. 3:13.
18. Cf. 1 Cor. 2:9; Apoc. 21:4–5.
19. Cf. 1 Cor. 15:42 and 53.
20. Cf. 1 Cor. 13:8; 3:14.
21. Cf. Rom. 8:19–21.
22. Cf. Lk. 9:25.
23. Cf. Pius XI, Litt. Encycl. *Quadragesimo Anno: AAS* 23 (1931), p. 207.
24. Preface for the Feast of Christ the King.

CHAPTER IV

ROLE OF THE CHURCH IN THE MODERN WORLD

MUTUAL RELATIONSHIP OF CHURCH AND WORLD

40. All we have said up to now about the dignity of the human person, the community of mankind, and the deep significance of human activity, provides a basis for discussing the relationship between the Church and the world and the dialogue between them.[1] The Council now intends to consider the presence of the Church in the world, and its life and activity there, in the light of what it has already declared about the mystery of the Church.

Proceeding from the love of the eternal Father,[2] the Church was founded by Christ in time and gathered into one by the Holy Spirit.[3] It has a saving and eschatological purpose which can be fully attained only in the next life. But it is now present here on earth and is composed of men; they, the members of the earthly city, are called to form the family of the children of God even in this present history of mankind and to increase it continually until the Lord comes. Made one in view of heavenly benefits and enriched by them, this family has been "constituted and organized as a society in the present world"[4] by Christ and "provided with means adapted to its visible and social union."[5] Thus the Church, at once "a visible organization and a spiritual community,"[6] travels the

---

1. Paul VI, Litt. Encycl. *Ecclesiam Suam*, III: *AAS* 56 (1964), pp. 637-659.
2. Cf. Tit. 3:4; 'philantropia.'
3. Cf. Eph. 1:3; 5-6; 13-14; 23.
4. Vatican Council II, Dogmatic Constitution *Lumen Gentium*, ch. 1, n. 8: *AAS* 57 (1965), p. 12.
5. Ibid., ch. 2, n. 9: *AAS* 57 (1965), p. 14; cf. n. 8: *AAS loc. cit.*, p. 11.
6. Ibid., ch. 1, n. 8: *AAS* 57 (1965), p. 11.

same journey as all mankind and shares the same earthly lot with the world: it is to be a leaven and, as it were, the soul of human society in its renewal by Christ[7] and transformation into the family of God.

That the earthly and the heavenly city penetrate one another is a fact open only to the eyes of faith; moreover, it will remain the mystery of human history, which will be harassed by sin until the perfect revelation of the splendor of the sons of God. In pursuing its own salvific purpose not only does the Church communicate divine life to men but in a certain sense it casts the reflected light of that divine life over all the earth, notably in the way it heals and elevates the dignity of the human person, in the way it consolidates society, and endows the daily activity of men with a deeper sense and meaning. The Church, then, believes it can contribute much to humanizing the family of man and its history through each of its members and its community as a whole.

Furthermore, the Catholic Church gladly values what other Christian Churches and ecclesial communities have contributed and are contributing cooperatively to the realization of this aim. Similarly it is convinced that there is a considerable and varied help that it can receive from the world in preparing the ground for the Gospel, both from individuals and from society as a whole, by their talents and activity. The Council will now outline some general principles for the proper fostering of mutual exchange and help in matters which are in some way common to the Church and the world.

WHAT THE CHURCH OFFERS TO INDIVIDUALS

41. Modern man is in a process of fuller personality development and of a growing discovery and affirmation of his own rights. But the Church is entrusted with the task of opening up to man the mystery of God, who is the last end of man; in doing so it opens up to him the meaning of his own existence, the innermost truth about himself. The Church knows well that God alone, whom it serves, can satisfy the deepest cravings of the human heart, for the world and what it has to offer can never fully content it. It also realizes that man is continually being aroused by the Spirit

7. Ibid., ch. 4, 38: AAS 57 (1965), p. 43, with note 120.

of God and that he will never be utterly indifferent to religion—a fact confirmed by the experience of ages past and plentiful evidence at the present day. For man will ever be anxious to know, if only in a vague way, what is the meaning of his life, his activity, and his death. The very presence of the Church recalls these problems to his mind. The most perfect answer to these questionings is to be found in God alone, who created man in his own image and redeemed him from sin; and this answer is given in the revelation in Christ his Son who became man. Whoever follows Christ the perfect man become himself more a man.

Relying on this faith the Church can raise the dignity of human nature above all fluctuating opinions which, for example, would unduly despise or idolize the human body. There is no human law so powerful to safeguard the personal dignity and freedom of man as the Gospel which Christ entrusted to the Church; for the Gospel announces and proclaims the freedom of the sons of God, it rejects all bondage resulting from sin,[8] it scrupulously respects the dignity of conscience and its freedom of choice, it never ceases to encourage the employment of human talents in the service of God and man, and, finally, it commends everyone to the charity of all.[9] This is nothing other than the basic law of the Christian scheme of things. The fact that it is the same God who is at once saviour and creator, Lord of human history and of the history of salvation, does not mean that the autonomy of the creature, of man in particular, is suppressed; on the contrary, in the divine order of things all this redounds to the restoration and consolidation of this autonomy.

In virtue of the Gospel entrusted to it the Church proclaims the rights of man: she acknowledges and holds in high esteem the dynamic approach of today which is fostering these rights all over the world. But this approach needs to be animated by the spirit of the Gospel and preserved from all traces of false autonomy. For there is a temptation to feel that our personal rights are fully maintained only when we are exempt from every restriction of divine law. But this is the way leading to the extinction of human dignity, not its preservation.

8. Cf. Rom. 8:14–17.
9. Cf. Mt. 22:39.

WHAT THE CHURCH OFFERS TO SOCIETY

42. The union of the family of man is greatly consolidated and perfected by the unity which Christ established among the sons of God.[10]

Christ did not bequeath to the Church a mission in the political, economic, or social order: the purpose he assigned to it was a religious one.[11] But this religious mission can be the source of commitment, direction, and vigor to establish and consolidate the community of men according to the law of God. In fact, the Church is able, indeed it is obliged, if times and circumstances require it, to initiate action for the benefit of all men, especially of those in need, like works of mercy and similar undertakings.

The Church, moreover, acknowledges the good to be found in the social dynamism of today, particularly progress towards unity, healthy socialization, and civil and economic cooperation. The encouragement of unity is in harmony with the deepest nature of the Church's mission, for it "is in the nature of a sacrament—a sign and instrument —that is of communion with God and of unity among all men."[12] It shows to the world that social and exterior union comes from a union of hearts and minds, from the faith and love by which its own indissoluble unity has been founded in the Holy Spirit. The impact which the Church can have on modern society amounts to an effective living of faith and love, not to any external power exercised by purely human means.

By its nature and mission the Church is universal in that it is not committed to any one culture or to any political, economic or social system. Hence it can be a very close bond between the various communities of men and nations, provided they have trust in the Church and guarantee it true freedom to carry out its mission. With this in view the Church calls upon its members and upon all men to put aside, in the family spirit of the children of God, all conflict between nations and races and to consolidate legitimate human organizations in themselves.

10. Cf. Dogmatic Constitution *Lumen Gentium*, ch. 2, n. 9: *AAS* 57 (1965), pp. 12–14.
11. Cf. Pius XII, *Allocution to Historians and Artists*, 9 March 1956: *AAS* 48 (1956), p. 212.
12. Dogmatic Constitution *Lumen Gentium*, ch. 1, n. 1: *AAS* 57 (1965), p. 5.

Whatever truth, goodness, and justice is to be found in past or present human institutions is held in high esteem by the Council. In addition, the Council declares that the Church is anxious to help and foster these institutions insofar as it depends on it and is compatible with its mission. The Church desires nothing more ardently than to develop itself untrammelled in the service of all men under any régime which recognizes the basic rights of the person and the family, and the needs of the common good.

WHAT THE CHURCH OFFERS TO HUMAN ACTIVITY THROUGH ITS MEMBERS

43. The Council exhorts Christians, as citizens of both cities, to perform their duties faithfully in the spirit of the Gospel. It is a mistake to think that, because we have here no lasting city, but seek the city which is to come,[13] we are entitled to shirk our earthly responsibilities; this is to forget that by our faith we are bound all the more to fulfil these responsibilities according to the vocation of each one.[14] But it is no less mistaken to think that we may immerse ourselves in earthly activities as if these latter were utterly foreign to religion, and religion were nothing more than the fulfilment of acts of worship and the observance of a few moral obligations. One of the gravest errors of our time is the dichotomy between the faith which many profess and the practice of their daily lives. As far back as the Old Testament the prophets vehemently denounced this scandal,[15] and in the New Testament Christ himself with greater force threatened it with severe punishment.[16] Let there, then, be no such pernicious opposition between professional and social activity on the one hand and religious life on the other. The Christian who shirks his temporal duties shirks his duties towards his neighbor, neglects God himself, and endangers his eternal salvation. Let Christians follow the example of Christ who worked as a craftsman; let them be proud of the opportunity to carry out their earthly activity in such a way as to integrate human, domestic, professional, scientific and technical enterprises with religious values, under whose supreme direction all things are ordered to the glory of God.

13. Cf. Heb. 13:14.
14. Cf. 2 Th. 3:6–13; Eph. 4:28.
15. Cf. Is. 58:1–12.
16. Cf. Mt. 23:3–33; Mk. 7:10–13.

It is to the laity, though not exclusively to them, that secular duties and activity properly belong. When therefore, as citizens of the world, they are engaged in any activity either individually or collectively, they will not be satisfied with meeting the minimum legal requirements but will strive to become truly proficient in that sphere. They will gladly cooperate with others working towards the same objectives. Let them be aware of what their faith demands of them in these matters and derive strength from it; let them not hesitate to take the initiative at the opportune moment and put their findings into effect. It is their task to cultivate a properly informed conscience and to impress the divine law on the affairs of the earthly city. For guidance and spiritual strength let them turn to the clergy; but let them realize that their pastors will not always be so expert as to have a ready answer to every problem (even every grave problem) that arises; this is not the role of the clergy: it is rather up to the laymen to shoulder their responsibilities under the guidance of Christian wisdom and with eager attention to the teaching authority of the Church.[17]

Very often their Christian vision will suggest a certain solution in some given situation. Yet it happens rather frequently, and legitimately so, that some of the faithful, with no less sincerity, will see the problem quite differently. Now if one or other of the proposed solutions is too easily associated with the message of the Gospel, they ought to remember that in those cases no one is permitted to identify the authority of the Church exclusively with his own opinion. Let them, then, try to guide each other by sincere dialogue in a spirit of mutual charity and with anxious interest above all in the common good.

The laity are called to participate actively in the whole life of the Church; not only are they to animate the world with the spirit of Christianity, but they are to be witnesses to Christ in all circumstances and at the very heart of the community of mankind.

Bishops, to whom has been committed the task of directing the Church of God, along with their priests, are to preach the message of Christ in such a way that the light of the Gospel will shine on all activities of the faithful. Let all pastors of souls be mindful to build up by their daily be-

17. Cf. John XXIII, Litt. Encycl. *Mater et Magistra*, IV: *AAS* 53 (1961), pp. 456–7: cf. I: *AAS Loc. cit.*, pp. 407, 410–411.

havior and concern[18] an image of the Church capable of impressing men with the power and truth of the Christian message. By their words and example and in union with religious and with the faithful, let them show that the Church with all its gifts is, by its presence alone, an inexhaustible font of all those resources of which the modern world stands in such dire need. Let them prepare themselves by careful study to meet and play their part in dialogue with the world and with men of all shades of opinion: let them have in their hearts above all these words of the Council: "Since the human race today is tending more and more towards civil, economic, and social unity, it is all the more necessary that priests should unite their efforts and combine their resources under the leadership of the bishops and the supreme Pontiff and thus eliminate division and dissension in every shape and form, so that all mankind may be led into the unity of the family of God.[19]

By the power of the Holy Spirit the Church is the faithful spouse of the Lord and will never fail to be a sign of salvation in the world; but it is by no means unaware that down through the centuries there have been among its members,[20] both clerical and lay, some who were disloyal to the Spirit of God, Today as well, the Church is not blind to the discrepancy between the message it proclaims and the human weakness of those to whom the Gospel has been entrusted. Whatever is history's judgment on these shortcomings, we cannot ignore them and we must combat them earnestly, lest they hinder the spread of the Gospel. The Church also realizes how much it needs the maturing influence of centuries of past experience in order to work out its relationship to the world. Guided by the Holy Spirit the Church ceaselessly "exhorts her children to purification and renewal so that the sign of Christ may shine more brightly over the face of the Church."[21]

18. Dogmatic Constitution *Lumen Gentium*, ch. 3, n. 28: *AAS* 57 (1965), pp. 34-5.
19. Ibid., n. 28: *AAS loc. cit.*, pp. 35-6.
20. Cf. St. Ambrose, *De virginitate*, ch. VIII, n. 48: *PL* 16, 278.
21. Dogmatic Constitution *Lumen Gentium*, ch. 2, n. 15: *AAS* 57 (1965), p. 20.

WHAT THE CHURCH RECEIVES FROM THE MODERN WORLD

44. Just as it is in the world's interest to acknowledge the Church as a social reality and a driving force in history, so too the Church is not unaware how much it has profited from the history and development of mankind. It profits from the experience of past ages, from the progress of the sciences, and from the riches hidden in various cultures, through which greater light is thrown on the nature of man and new avenues to truth are opened up. The Church learned early in its history to express the Christian message in the concepts and language of different peoples and tried to clarify it in the light of the wisdom of their philosophers: it was an attempt to adapt the Gospel to the understanding of all men and the requirements of the learned, insofar as this could be done. Indeed, this kind of adaptation and preaching of the revealed Word must ever be the law of all evangelization. In this way it is possible to create in every country the possibility of expressing the message of Christ in suitable terms and to foster vital contact and exchange between the Church and different cultures.[22] Nowadays when things change so rapidly and thought patterns differ so widely, the Church needs to step up this exchange by calling upon the help of people who are living in the world, who are expert in its organizations and its forms of training, and who understand its mentality, in the case of believers and nonbelievers alike. With the help of the Holy Spirit, it is the task of the whole people of God, particularly of its pastors and theologians, to listen to and distinguish the many voices of our times and to interpret them in the light of the divine Word, in order that the revealed truth may be more deeply penetrated, better understood, and more suitably presented.

The Church has a visible social structure, which is a sign of its unity in Christ: as such it can be enriched, and it is being enriched, by the evolution of social life—not as if something were missing in the constitution which Christ gave the Church, but in order to understand this constitution more deeply, express it better, and adapt it more successfully to our times. The Church is happy to feel that, with regard to the community it forms and each of its

22. Dogmatic Constitution *Lumen Gentium*, ch. 2, n. 13: *AAS* 57 (1965), p. 17.

members, it is assisted in various ways by men of all classes and conditions. Whoever contributes to the development of the community of mankind on the level of family, culture, economic and social life, and national and international politics, according to the plan of God, is also contributing in no small way to the community of the Church insofar as it depends on things outside itself. The Church itself also recognizes that it has benefited and is still benefiting from the opposition of its enemies and persecutors.[23]

CHRIST: ALPHA AND OMEGA

45. Whether it aids the world or whether it benefits from it, the Church has but one sole purpose—that the kingdom of God may come and the salvation of the human race may be accomplished. Every benefit the people of God can confer on mankind during its earthly pilgrimage is rooted in the Church's being "the universal sacrament of salvation,"[24] at once manifesting and actualizing the mystery of God's love for men.

The Word of God, through whom all things were made, was made flesh, so that as a perfect man he could save all men and sum up all things in himself. The Lord is the goal of human history, the focal point of the desires of history and civilization, the center of mankind, the joy of all hearts, and the fulfilment of all aspirations.[25] It is he whom the Father raised from the dead, exalted and placed at his right hand, constituting him judge of the living and the dead. Animated and drawn together in his Spirit we press onwards on our journey towards the consummation of history which fully corresponds to the plan of his love: "to unite all things in him, things in heaven and things on earth" (Eph. 1:10).

The Lord himself said: "Behold, I am coming soon, bringing my recompense, to repay every one for what he has done. I am the alpha and the omega, the first and the last, the beginning and the end" (Apoc. 22:12–13).

23. Justin, *Dialogus cum Tryphone*, ch. 110, *PG* 6, 729: ed. Otto, 1897, pp. 391–393: ". . . sed quanto magis talia nobis infliguntur, tanto plures alii fideles et pii per nomen Iesu fiunt." Cf. Tertullian, *Apologeticus*, ch. L, 13: Corpus Christ. set. lat. 1, p. 171: "Etiam plures efficimur, quoties metimur a vobis: semen est sanguis Christianorum!" Cf. Dogmatic Constitution *Lumen Gentium*, ch. 2, n. 9: *AAS* 57 (1965), p. 14.
24. Dogmatic Constitution *Lumen Gentium*, ch. 7, n. 48: *AAS* 57 (1965), p. 53.
25. Cf. Paul VI, *Allocution*, Feb. 1965.

PART TWO

Some More Urgent Problems

PREFACE

46. Having set forth the dignity of the human person and his individual and social role in the universe, the Council now draws the attention of men to the consideration of some more urgent problems deeply affecting the human race at the present day in the light of the Gospel and of human experience.

Of the many problems which excite general concern nowadays it may be helpful to concentrate on the following: marriage and the family, culture, economic and social life, politics, the solidarity of peoples, and peace. We must seek light for each of these problems from the principles which Christ has given us; in this way the faithful will receive guidance and all men will be enlightened in their search for solutions to so many complex problems.

Chapter I

THE DIGNITY OF MARRIAGE AND THE FAMILY

MARRIAGE AND THE FAMILY IN THE MODERN WORLD

47. The well-being of the individual person and of both human and Christian society is closely bound up with the healthy state of conjugal and family life. Hence Christians today are overjoyed, and so too are all who esteem conjugal and family life highly, to witness the various ways in which progress is being made in fostering those partnerships of love and in encouraging reverence for human life; there is progress too in services available to married people and parents for fulfilling their lofty calling: even greater benefits are to be expected and efforts are being made to bring them about.

However, this happy picture of the dignity of these partnerships is not reflected everywhere, but is overshadowed by polygamy, the plague of divorce, so-called free love, and similar blemishes; furthermore, married love is too often dishonoured by selfishness, hedonism, and unlawful contraceptive practices. Besides, the economic, social, psychological, and civil climate of today has a severely disturbing effect on family life. There are also the serious and alarming problems arising in many parts of the world as a result of population expansion. On all of these counts an anguish of conscience is being generated. And yet the strength and vigor of the institution of marriage and family shines forth time and again: for despite the hardships flowing from the profoundly changing conditions of society today, the true nature of marriage and of the family is revealed in one way or another.

It is for these reasons that the Council intends to present certain key points of the Church's teaching in a clearer light; and it hopes to guide and encourage Christians and all men who are trying to preserve and to foster the dignity and supremely sacred value of the married state.

HOLINESS OF MARRIAGE AND THE FAMILY

48. The intimate partnership of life and the love which constitutes the married state has been established by the creator and endowed by him with its own proper laws: it is rooted in the contract of its partners, that is, in their irrevocable personal consent. It is an institution confirmed by the divine law and receiving its stability, even in the eyes of society, from the human act by which the partners mutually surrender themselves to each other; for the good of the partners, of the children, and of society this sacred bond no longer depends on human decision alone. For God himself is the author of marriage and has endowed it with various benefits and with various ends in view:[1] all of these have a very important bearing on the continuation of the human race, on the personal development and eternal destiny of every member of the family, on the dignity, stability, peace, and prosperity of the family and of the whole human race. By its very nature the institution of marriage and married love is ordered to the procreation and education of the offspring and it is in them that it finds its crowning glory. Thus the man and woman, who "are no longer two but one" (Mt. 19:6), help and serve each other by their marriage partnership; they become conscious of their unity and experience it more deeply from day to day. The intimate union of marriage, as a mutual giving of two persons, and the good of the children demand total fidelity from the spouses and require an unbreakable unity between them.[2]

Christ our Lord has abundantly blessed this love, which is rich in its various features, coming as it does from the spring of divine love and modeled on Christ's own union with the Church. Just as of old God encountered his people with a covenant of love and fidelity,[3] so our Saviour, the spouse of the Church,[4] now encounters Christian spouses through the sacrament of marriage. He abides with them in

1. St. Augustine, *De bono coniugii: PL* 40, 375–376 and 394; St. Thomas, *Summa Theol.*, Suppl. Quaest. 49, art. 3 ad 1; *Decretum pro Armenis: Denz.* 702 (1327); Pius XI, Litt. Encycl. *Casti Connubii: AAS* 22 (1930), pp. 543–545; *Denz.* 2227–2238 (3703–3714).
2. Cf. Pius XI, Litt. Encycl. *Casti Connubii: AAS* 22 (1930), pp. 546–7: *Denz*, 2231 (3706).
3. Cf. Hos. 2; Jer. 3:6–13; Eze. 16 and 23; Is. 54.
4. Cf. Mt. 9:15; Mk. 2:19–20; Lk. 5:34–35; Jn. 3:29; 2 Cor. 11:2; Eph. 5:27; Apoc. 19:7–8; 21:2 and 9.

order that by their mutual self-giving spouses will love each other with enduring fidelity, as he loved the Church and delivered himself for it.[5] Authentic married love is caught up into divine love and is directed and enriched by the redemptive power of Christ and the salvific action of the Church, with the result that the spouses are effectively led to God and are helped and strengthened in their lofty role as fathers and mothers.[6] Spouses, therefore, are fortified and, as it were, consecrated for the duties and dignity of their state by a special sacrament;[7] fulfilling their conjugal and family role by virtue of this sacrament, spouses are penetrated with the spirit of Christ and their whole life is suffused by faith, hope, and charity; thus they increasingly further their own perfection and their mutual sanctification, and together they render glory to God.

Inspired by the example and family prayer of their parents, children, and in fact everyone living under the family roof, will more easily set out upon the path of a truly human training, of salvation, and of holiness. As for the spouses, when they are given the dignity and role of fatherhood and motherhood, they will eagerly carry out their duties of education, especially religious education, which primarily devolves on them.

Children as living members of the family contribute in their own way to the sanctification of their parents. With sentiments of gratitude, affection and trust, they will repay their parents for the benefits given to them and will come to their assistance as devoted children in times of hardship and in the loneliness of old age. Widowhood, accepted courageously as a continuation of the calling to marriage, will be honored by all.[8] Families will generously share their spiritual treasures with other families. The Christian family springs from marriage,[9] which is an image and a sharing in the partnership of love between Christ and the Church; it will show forth to all men Christ's living presence in the world and the authentic nature of the Church by the love and generous fruitfulness of the spouses, by their unity and

5. Cf. Eph. 5:25.
6. Cf. Vatican Council II, Dogmatic Constitution *Lumen Gentium: AAS* 57 (1965), pp. 15–16; 40–41; 47.
7. Cf. Pius XI, Litt. Encycl. *Casti Connubii: AAS* (1930), p. 583.
8. Cf. 1 Tim. 5:3.
9. Cf. Eph. 5:32.

fidelity, and by the loving way in which all members of the family cooperate with each other.

MARRIED LOVE

49. On several occasions the Word of God invites the betrothed to nourish and foster their betrothal with chaste love, and likewise spouses their marriage.[10] Many of our contemporaries, too, have a high regard for true love between husband and wife as manifested in the worthy customs of various times and peoples. Married love is an eminently human love because it is an affection between two persons rooted in the will and it embraces the good of the whole person; it can enrich the sentiments of the spirit and their physical expression with a unique dignity and ennoble them as the special elements and signs of the friendship proper to marriage. The Lord, wishing to bestow special gifts of grace and divine love on it, has restored, perfected, and elevated it. A love like that, bringing together the human and the divine, leads the partners to a free and mutual giving of self, experienced in tenderness and action, and permeates their whole lives;[11] besides, this love is actually developed and increased by the exercise of it. This is a far cry from mere erotic attraction, which is pursued in selfishness and soon fades away in wretchedness.

Married love is uniquely expressed and perfected by the exercise of the acts proper to marriage. Hence the acts in marriage by which the intimate and chaste union of the spouses takes place are noble and honorable; the truly human performance of these acts fosters the self-giving they signify and enriches the spouses in joy and gratitude. Endorsed by mutual fidelity and, above all, consecrated by Christ's sacrament, this love abides faithfully in mind and body in prosperity and adversity and hence excludes both adultery and divorce. The unity of marriage, distinctly recognized by our Lord, is made clear in the equal personal dignity which must be accorded to man and wife in mutual and unreserved affection. Outstanding courage is required for the constant fulfilment of the duties of this Christian calling: spouses, therefore, will need grace for leading a

10. Cf. Gen. 2:22–24; Prov. 5:18–20; 31:10–31; Tob. 8:4–8; Cant. 1:1–3; 2:16; 7:8–11; Eph. 5:25–33.
11. Cf. Pius XI, Litt. Encycl. *Casti Connubii: AAS* 22 (1930), pp. 547 and 548; *Denz.* 2232 (3707).

holy life: they will eagerly practice a love that is firm, generous, and prompt to sacrifice and will ask for it in their prayers.

Authentic married love will be held in high esteem, and healthy public opinion will be quick to recognize it, if Christian spouses give outstanding witness to faithfulness and harmony in their love, if they are conspicuous in their concern for the education of their children, and if they play their part in a much needed cultural, psychological, and social renewal in matters of marriage and the family. It is imperative to give suitable and timely instruction to young people, above all in the heart of their own families, about the dignity of married love, its role and its exercise; in this way they will be able to engage in honorable courtship and enter upon marriage of their own.

THE FRUITFULNESS OF MARRIAGE

50. Marriage and married love are by nature ordered to the procreation and education of children. Indeed children are the supreme gift of marriage and greatly contribute to the good of the parents themselves. God himself said: "It is not good that man should be alone" (Gen. 2:18), and "from the beginning (he) made them male and female" (Mt. 19:4); wishing to associate them in a special way with his own creative work, God blessed man and woman with the words: "Be fruitful and multiply" (Gen. 1:28). Without intending to underestimate the other ends of marriage, it must be said that true married love and the whole structure of family life which results from it is directed to disposing the spouses to cooperate valiantly with the love of the Creator and Saviour, who through them will increase and enrich his family from day to day.

Married couples should regard it as their proper mission to transmit human life and to educate their children; they should realize that they are thereby cooperating with the love of God the Creator and are, in a certain sense, its interpreters. This involves the fulfilment of their role with a sense of human and Christian responsibility and the formation of correct judgments through docile respect for God and common reflection and effort; it also involves a consideration of their own good and the good of their children already born or yet to come, an ability to read the signs of the times and of their own situation on the material and spiritual level, and, finally, an estimation of the good of the family, of society, and of the Church. It is the married couple themselves who must in the last analysis arrive at these judgments before God. Married people should realize that in their behavior they may not simply follow their own fancy but must be ruled by conscience—and conscience ought to be conformed to the law of God in the light of the teaching authority of the Church, which is the authentic interpreter of divine law. For the divine law throws light on the meaning of married love, protects it and leads it to truly human fulfilment. Whenever Christian spouses in a spirit of sacrifice and trust in divine providence[12] carry out their duties of procreation with generous human and Christian responsibility, they glorify the Creator and perfect themselves in Christ. Among the married couples who thus fulfil their God-given mission, special mention should be made of those who after prudent reflection and common decision courageously undertake the proper upbringing of a large number of children.[13]

But marriage is not merely for the procreation of children: its nature as an indissoluble compact between two people and the good of the children demand that the mutual love of the partners be properly shown, that it should grow and mature. Even in cases where despite the intense desire of the spouses there are no children, marriage still retains its character of being a whole manner and communion of life and preserves its value and indissolubility.

MARRIED LOVE AND RESPECT FOR HUMAN LIFE

51. The Council realizes that married people are often hindered by certain situations in modern life from working out their married love harmoniously and that they can sometimes find themselves in a position where the number of children cannot be increased, at least for the time being: in cases like these it is quite difficult to preserve the practice of faithful love and the complete intimacy of their lives. But where the intimacy of married life is broken, it often happens that faithfulness is imperiled and the good of the children suffers: then the education of the children as well

12. Cf. 1 Cor. 7:5.
13. Cf. Pius XII, Allocution, *Tra le verità*, 20 Jan. 1958: *AAS* 50 (1958), p. 91.

as the courage to accept more children are both endangered.

Some of the proposed solutions to these problems are shameful and some people have not hesitated to suggest the taking of life: the Church wishes to emphasize that there can be no conflict between the divine laws governing the transmission of life and the fostering of authentic married love.

God, the Lord of life, has entrusted to men the noble mission of safeguarding life, and men must carry it out in a manner worthy of themselves. Life must be protected with the utmost care from the moment of conception: abortion and infanticide are abominable crimes. Man's sexuality and the faculty of reproduction wondrously surpass the endowments of lower forms of life; therefore the acts proper to married life are to be ordered according to authentic human dignity and must be honored with the greatest reverence. When it is a question of harmonizing married love with the responsible transmission of life, it is not enough to take only the good intention and the evaluation of motives into account; the objective criteria must be used, criteria drawn from the nature of the human person and human action, criteria which respect the total meaning of mutual self-giving and human procreation in the context of true love; all this is possible only if the virtue of married chastity is seriously practiced. In questions of birth regulation the sons of the Church, faithful to these principles, are forbidden to use methods disapproved of by the teaching authority of the Church in its interpretation of the divine law.[14]

Let all be convinced that human life and its transmission are realities whose meaning is not limited by the horizons of this life only: their true evaluation and full meaning can only be understood in reference to man's eternal destiny.

14. Cf. Pius XI, Litt. Encycl. *Casti Connubii: AAS* 22 (1930), pp. 559–561; *Denz.* 2239–2241 (3716–3718); Pius XII, *Allocution to the Congress of Italian Midwives*, 29 Oct. 1951: *AAS* 43 (1951), pp. 835–54; Paul VI, *Allocution to the Cardinals*, 23 June 1964: *AAS* 56 (1964), pp. 581–9. By order of the Holy Father, certain questions requiring further and more careful investigation have been given over to a commission for the study of population, the family, and births, in order that the Holy Father may pass judgment when its task is completed. With the teaching of the magisterium standing as it is, the Council has no intention of proposing concrete solutions at this moment.

FOSTERING MARRIAGE AND THE FAMILY: A DUTY FOR ALL

52. The family is, in a sense, a school for human enrichment. But if it is to achieve the full flowering of its life and mission, the married couple must practice an affectionate sharing of thought and common deliberation as well as eager cooperation as parents in the children's upbringing. The active presence of the father is very important for their training: the mother, too, has a central role in the home, for the children, especially the younger children, depend on her considerably; this role must be safeguarded without, however, underrating woman's legitimate social advancement. The education of children should be such that when they grow up they will be able to follow their vocation, including a religious vocation, and choose their state of life with full consciousness of responsibility; and if they marry they should be capable of setting up a family in favorable moral, social, and economic circumstances. It is the duty of parents and teachers to guide young people with prudent advice in the establishment of a family; their interest should make young people listen to them eagerly; and they should beware of exercising any undue influence, directly or indirectly, to force them into marriage or compel them in their choice of partner.

The family is the place where different generations come together and help one another to grow wiser and harmonize the rights of individuals with other demands of social life; as such it constitutes the basis of society. Everyone, therefore, who exercises an influence in the community and in social groups should devote himself effectively to the welfare of marriage and the family. Civil authority should consider it a sacred duty to acknowledge the true nature of marriage and the family, to protect and foster them, to safeguard public morality and promote domestic prosperity. The rights of parents to procreate and educate children in the family must be safeguarded. There should also be welfare legislation and provision of various kinds made for the protection and assistance of those who unfortunately have been deprived of the benefits of family life.

Christians, making full use of the times in which we live[15] and carefully distinguishing the everlasting from the

15. Cf. Eph. 5:16; Col. 4:5.

changeable, should actively strive to promote the values of marriage and the family; it can be done by the witness of their own lives and by concerted action along with all men of good will; in this way they will overcome obstacles and make provision for the requirements and the advantages of family life arising at the present day. To this end the Christian instincts of the faithful, the right moral conscience of man, and the wisdom and skill of persons versed in the sacred sciences will have much to contribute.

Experts in other sciences, particularly biology, medicine, social science and psychology, can be of service to the welfare of marriage and the family and the peace of mind of people, if by pooling their findings they try to clarify thoroughly the different conditions favoring the proper regulation of births.

It devolves on priests to be properly trained to deal with family matters and to nurture the vocation of married people in their married and family life by different pastoral means, by the preaching of the Word of God, by liturgy, and other spiritual assistance. They should strengthen them sympathetically and patiently in their difficulties and comfort them in charity with a view to the formation of truly radiant families.

Various organizations, especially family associations, should set out by their programs of instruction and activity to strengthen young people and especially young married people, and to prepare them for family, social, and apostolic life.

Let married people themselves, who are created in the image of the living God and constituted in an authentic personal dignity, be united together in equal affection, agreement of mind, and mutual holiness.[16] Thus, in the footsteps of Christ, the principle of life,[18] they will bear witness by their faithful love in the joys and sacrifices of their calling, to that mystery of love which the Lord revealed to the world by his death and resurrection.[18]

16. Cf. *Sacramentarium Gregorianum: PL* 78, 262.
17. Cf. Rom. 5:15 and 18; 6:5–11; Gal. 2:20.
18. Cf. Eph. 5:25–27.

Chapter II

PROPER DEVELOPMENT OF CULTURE

INTRODUCTION

53. It is one of the properties of the human person that he can achieve true and full humanity only by means of culture, that is through the cultivation of the goods and values of nature. Whenever, therefore, there is a question of human life, nature and culture are intimately linked together.

The word "culture" in the general sense refers to all those things which go to the refining and developing of man's diverse mental and physical endowments. He strives to subdue the earth by his knowledge and his labor; he humanizes social life both in the family and in the whole civic community through the improvement of customs and institutions; he expresses through his works the great spiritual experiences and aspirations of men throughout the ages; he communicates and preserves them to be an inspiration for the progress of many, even of all mankind.

Hence it follows that culture necessarily has historical and social overtones, and the word "culture" often carries with it sociological and ethnological connotations; in this sense one can speak about a plurality of cultures. For different styles of living and different scales of values originate in different ways of using things, of working and self-expression, of practicing religion and of behavior, of establishing laws and juridical institutions, of developing science and the arts and of cultivating beauty. Thus the heritage of its institutions forms the patrimony proper to each human community; thus, too, is created a well-defined, historical milieu which envelops the men of every nation and age, and from which they draw the values needed to foster humanity and civilization.

SECTION 1: CULTURAL SITUATION TODAY

NEW FORMS OF LIVING

54. The circumstances of life today have undergone such profound changes on the social and cultural level that one is entitled to speak of a new age of human history;[1] hence new ways are opened up for the development and diffusion of culture. The factors which have occasioned it have been the tremendous expansion of the natural and human sciences (including social sciences), the increase of technology, and the advances in developing and organizing media of communication. As a result modern culture is characterized as follows: the "exact" sciences foster to the highest degree a critical way of judging; recent psychological advances furnish deeper insights into human behavior; historical studies tend to make us view things under the aspects of changeability and evolution; customs and patterns of life tend to become more uniform from day to day; industrialization, urbanization, and other factors which promote community living create new mass-cultures which give birth to new patterns of thinking, of acting, and of use of leisure; heightened media of exchange between nations and different branches of society open up the riches of different cultures to each and every individual, with the result that a more universal form of culture is gradually taking shape, and through it the unity of mankind is being fostered and expressed in the measure that the particular characteristics of each culture are preserved.

MAN, AUTHOR OF CULTURE

55. In each nation and social group there is a growing number of men and women who are conscious that they themselves are the craftsmen and molders of their community's culture. All over the world the sense of autonomy and responsibility increases with effects of the greatest importance for the spiritual and moral maturity of mankind. This will become clearer to us if we place before our eyes the unification of the world and the duty imposed on us to Insert Footnote

build up a better world in truth and justice. We are witness-

1. Cf. The Introduction to this Constitution, nn. 4–10.

ing, then, the birth of a new humanism, where man is defined before all else by his responsibility to his brothers and
at the court of history.

DIFFICULTIES AND DUTIES

56. In circumstances such as these it is no wonder that
man feels responsible for the progress of culture and nourishes high hopes for it, but anxiously foresees numerous
conflicting elements which it is up to him to resolve.

What is to be done to prevent increased exchange between cultures (which ought to lead to genuine and fruitful
dialogue between groups and nations) from disturbing the
life of communities, overthrowing traditional wisdom and
endangering the character proper to each people?

How is the dynamism and expansion of the new culture
to be fostered without losing living fidelity to the heritage
of tradition? This question is of particular relevance in a
culture where the enormous progress of science and technique must be harmonized with a system where classical
studies according to various traditions have held sway.

As specialization in different branches of knowledge continues to increase so rapidly, how can the necessary synthesis of them be worked out, not to mention the need to
safeguard man's powers of contemplation and wonder
which lead to wisdom?

What can be done to enable everyone to share in the
benefits of culture, when the culture of specialists is becoming every day more complex and esoteric?

Finally, how are we to acknowledge as lawful the claims
of autonomy, which culture makes for itself, without falling
into a humanism which is purely earthbound and even hostile to religion?

In spite of these conflicting issues human culture must
evolve today in such a way that it will develop the whole
human person harmoniously and integrally, and will help
all men to fulfil the tasks to which they are called, especially Christians who are fraternally united at the heart of the
human family.

SECTION 2: SOME PRINCIPALS FOR PROPER CULTURAL DEVELOPMENT

FAITH AND CULTURE

57. In their pilgrimage to the heavenly city Christians are to seek and relish the things that are above:[2] this involves not a lesser, but rather a greater commitment to working with all men towards the establishment of a world that is more human. Indeed, the mystery of the Christian faith provides them with an outstanding incentive and encouragement to fulfil their role even more eagerly and to discover the full sense of the commitment by which human culture becomes important in man's total vocation.

By the work of his hands and with the aid of technical means man tills the earth to bring forth fruit and to make it a dwelling place fit for all mankind; he also consciously plays his part in the life of social groups; in so doing he is realizing the design, which God revealed at the beginning of time, to subdue the earth[3] and perfect the work of creation, and at the same time he is improving his own person: he is also observing the command of Christ to devote himself to the service of his fellow men.

Furthermore, when man works in the fields of philosophy, history, mathematics and science and cultivates the arts, he can greatly contribute towards bringing the human race to a higher understanding of truth, goodness, and beauty, to points of view having universal value; thus man will be more clearly enlightened by the wondrous Wisdom, which was with God from eternity, working beside him like a master craftsman, rejoicing in his inhabited world, and delighting in the sons of men.[4] As a consequence the human spirit, freed from the bondage of material things, can be more easily drawn to the worship and contemplation of the creator. Moreover, man is disposed to acknowledge, under the impulse of grace, the Word of God, who was in the world as "the true light that enlightens every man" (Jn. 1:9), before becoming flesh to save and gather up all things in himself.[5]

2. Cf. Col. 3:1–2.
3. Cf. Gen. 1:28.
4. Cf. Prov. 8:30–31.
5. Cf. St. Irenaeus, *Adv. Haer.*, III, 11, 8: ed. Sagnard, p. 200; cf. ibid., 16, 6, pp. 290–292; 21, 10–22, pp. 370–373; 22, 3, p. 378Q.

There is no doubt that modern scientific and technical progress can lead to a certain phenomenism or agnosticism; this happens when scientific methods of investigation, which of themselves are incapable of penetrating to the deepest nature of things, are unjustifiably taken as the supreme norm for arriving at truth. There is a further danger that in his excessive confidence in modern inventions man may think he is sufficient unto himself and give up the search for higher values.

But these drawbacks are not necessarily due to modern culture and they should not tempt us to overlook its positive values. Among these values we would like to draw attention to the following: study of the sciences and exact fidelity to truth in scientific investigation, the necessity of teamwork in technology, the sense of international solidarity, a growing awareness of the expert's responsibility to help and defend his fellow men, and an eagerness to improve the standard of living of all men, especially of those who are deprived of responsibility or suffer from cultural destitution. All these can afford a certain kind of preparation for the acceptance of the message of the Gospel and can be infused with divine charity by him who came to save the world.

RELATIONS BETWEEN CULTURE AND THE GOOD NEWS OF CHRIST

58. There are many links between the message of salvation and culture. In his self-revelation to his people culminating in the fullness of manifestation in his incarnate Son, God spoke according to the culture proper to each age. Similarly the Church has existed through the centuries in varying circumstances and has utilized the resources of different cultures in its preaching to spread and explain the message of Christ, to examine and understand it more deeply, and to express it more perfectly in the liturgy and in various aspects of the life of the faithful.

Nevertheless, the Church has been sent to all ages and nations and, therefore, is not tied exclusively and indissolubly to any race or nation, to any one particular way of life, or to any customary practices, ancient or modern. The Church is faithful to its traditions and is at the same time conscious of its universal mission; it can, then, enter into communion with different forms of culture, thereby enriching both itself and the cultures themselves.

The good news of Christ continually renews the life and culture of fallen man; it combats and removes the error and evil which flow from the ever-present attraction of sin. It never ceases to purify and elevate the morality of peoples. It takes the spiritual qualities and endowments of every age and nation, and with supernatural riches it causes them to blossom, as it were, from within; it fortifies, completes and restores them in Christ.[6] In this way the Church carries out its mission[7] and in that very act it stimulates and advances human and civil culture, as well as contributing by its activity, including liturgical activity, to man's interior freedom.

PROPER HARMONY BETWEEN FORMS OF CULTURE

59. For the reasons given above the Church recalls to mind that culture must be subordinated to the integral development of the human person, to the good of the community and of the whole of mankind. Therefore one must aim at encouraging the human spirit to develop its faculties of wonder, of understanding, of contemplation, of forming personal judgments and cultivating a religious, moral and social sense.

Culture, since it flows from man's rational and social nature, has continual need of rightful freedom of development and a legitimate possibility of autonomy according to its own principles. Quite rightly it demands respect and enjoys a certain inviolability, provided, of course, that the rights of the individual and the community, both particular and universal, are safeguarded within the limits of the common good.

Calling to mind the teaching of the first Vatican Council, this sacred Synod declares that "there are two orders of knowledge" distinct from one another, faith and reason, and that the Church is not against "the use of human arts and sciences of their own principles and methods in their

---

6. Cf. Eph. 1:10.
7. Cf. words of Pius XI to Mgr. M.-D. Roland-Gosselin: "One must never lose sight of the fact that the Church's objective is to evangelize, not to civilize. If it does civilize, it is done through evangelizing" (*Semaines sociales de France,* Versailles, 1936, pp. 461–462).

respective fields;" therefore, "it acknowledges this lawful freedom" and affirms the legitimate autonomy of culture and especially of the sciences.[8]

All this demands that man, provided he respects the moral order and the common interest, is entitled to seek after truth, express and make known his opinions; he may practice whatever art he pleases; and, finally, he ought to be truthfully informed about matters of public interest.[9]

The scope of public authority extends, not to determining the proper nature of cultural forms, but to building up the environment and the provision of assistance favorable to the development of culture, without overlooking minority groups in the nation.[10] This is the reason why one must avoid at all costs distorting culture from its proper purposes and its exploitation by political or economical forces.

SECTION 3: SOME MORE URGENT DUTIES OF CHRISTIANS IN REGARD TO CULTURE

RECOGNITION OF EVERYONE'S RIGHT TO CULTURE AND ITS IMPLEMENTATION

60. Man is now offered the possibility to free most of the human race from the curse of ignorance: it is, therefore, one of the duties most appropriate to our times, above all for Christians, to work untiringly for fundamental decisions to be taken in economic and political affairs, on the national as well as the international level, which will ensure the recognition and implementation everywhere of the right of every man to human and civil culture in harmony with the dignity of the human person, without distinction of race, sex, nation, religion, or social circumstances. Hence it is necessary to ensure that there is a sufficiency of cultural benefits available to everybody, especially the benefit of what is called "basic" culture, lest any be prevented by illiteracy and lack of initiative from contributing in an authentically human way to the common good.

8. Vatican Council I, Dogmatic Constitution De fide catholica, ch. IV: Denz., 1795, 1799 (3015, 3019). Cf. Pius XI, Litt. Encycl. Quadragesimo Anno: AAS 23 :1931), p. 190.
9. Cf. John XXIII, Litt. Encycl. Pacem in Terris: AAS 55 (1963), p. 260.
10. Cf. John XXIII, Litt. Encycl. Pacem in Terris: AAS 55 (1963), p. 283; Pius XII, radio message, 24 Dec. 1941: ASS 34 (1942), pp. 16–17.

Every effort should be made to provide for those who are capable of it the opportunity to pursue higher studies so that as far as possible they may engage in the functions and services, and play the role in society, most in keeping with their talents and the skills they acquire.[11] In this way all the individuals and social groups of a particular people will be able to attain a full development of their cultural life in harmony with their capabilities and their traditions.

We must do everything possible to make all persons aware of their right to culture and their duty to develop themselves culturally and to help their fellows. Sometimes conditions of life and work are such as to stifle man's cultural efforts and destroy this urge for culture. This holds true especially for those living in the country and for manual workers who ought to be provided with working conditions not unfavorable, but rather conducive to, their cultural development. At present women are involved in nearly all spheres of life: they ought to be permitted to play their part fully according to their own particular nature. It is up to everyone to see to it that woman's specific and necessary participation in cultural life be acknowledged and fostered.

CULTURAL EDUCATION

61. Nowadays much more than in the past it is difficult to form a synthesis of the arts and of the different branches of knowledge. While, in fact, the volume and diversity of the constituent elements of culture are on the increase, there is a decrease in the individual's capability to perceive and harmonize them, so that the picture of "a universal man" has almost disappeared. Still, it remains each man's duty to safeguard the notion of the human person as a totality in which predominate values of intellect, will, conscience, and brotherhood, since these values were established by the creator and wondrously restored and elevated by Christ.

Education of this kind has its source and its cradle, as it were, in the family: there, children in an atmosphere of love learn more quickly the true scale of values, and approved forms of culture are almost naturally assimilated by the developing minds of adolescents.

11. Cf. John XXIII, Litt. Encycl. *Pacem in Terris: AAS* 55 (1963), p. 260.

There are nowadays many opportunities favorable to the development of a universal culture, thanks especially to the boom in book publication and new techniques of cultural and social communication. Shorter working hours are becoming the general rule everywhere and provide greater opportunities for large numbers of people. May this leisure time be properly employed to refresh the spirit and strengthen the health of mind and body—by means of voluntary activity and study; of tourism to broaden the mind and enrich man with understanding of others; by means of physical exercise and sport, which help to create harmony of feeling even on the level of the community as well as fostering friendly relations between men of all classes, countries, and races. Christians, therefore, should cooperate in the cultural framework and collective activity characteristic of our times, to humanize them and imbue them with a Christian spirit. All these advantages, however, are insufficient to confer full cultural development, unless they are accompanied by a deeply thought out evaluation of the meaning of culture and knowledge of the human person.

PROPER HARMONY BETWEEN CULTURE AND CHRISTIAN FORMATION

62. Although the Church has contributed largely to the progress of culture, it is the lesson of experience that there have been difficulties in the way of harmonizing culture with Christian thought, arising out of contingent factors. These difficulties do not necessarily harm the life of faith, but can rather stimulate a more precise and deeper understanding of that faith. In fact, recent research and discoveries in the sciences, in history and philosophy bring up new problems which have an important bearing on life itself and demand new scrutiny by theologians. Furthermore, theologians are now being asked, within the methods and limits of the science of theology, to seek out more efficient ways—provided the meaning and understanding of them is safeguarded.[12]—of presenting their teaching to modern man: for the deposit and the truths of faith are one thing, the manner of expressing them is quite another. In pastoral care sufficient use should be made, not only of theological principles,

12. Cf. John XXIII, Speech delivered at the opening of the Council: *AAS* 54 (1962), p. 792.

but also of the findings of secular sciences, especially psychology and sociology: in this way the faithful will be brought to a purer and more mature living of the faith.

In their own way literature and art are very important in the life of the Church. They seek to give expression to man's nature, his problems and his experience in an effort to discover and perfect man himself and the world in which he lives; they try to discover his place in history and in the universe, to throw light on his suffering and his joy, his needs and his potentialities, and to outline a happier destiny in store for him. Hence they can elevate human life, which they express under many forms according to various times and places.

Every effort should be made, therefore, to make artists feel that they are understood by the Church in their artistic work and to encourage them, while enjoying a reasonable standard of freedom, to enter into happier relations with the Christian community. New art forms adapted to our times and in keeping with the characteristics of different nations and regions should be acknowledged by the Church. They may also be brought into the sanctuary whenever they raise the mind up to God with suitable forms of expression and in conformity with liturgical requirements.[13] Thus the knowledge of God will be made better known; the preaching of the Gospel will be rendered more intelligible to man's mind and will appear more relevant to his situation.

Therefore, the faithful ought to work in close conjunction with their contemporaries and try to get to know their ways of thinking and feeling, as they find them expressed in current culture. Let the faithful incorporate the findings of new sciences and teachings and the understanding of the most recent discoveries with Christian morality and thought, so that their practice of religion and their moral behavior may keep abreast of their acquaintance with science and of the relentless progress of technology: in this way they will succeed in evaluating and interpreting everything with an authentically Christian sense of values.

Those involved in theological studies in seminaries and universities should be eager to cooperate with men versed in

13. Cf. Constitution on the Sacred Liturgy, *Sacrosanctum Concilium*, n. 123: *AAS* 56 (1964), p. 131; Paul VI, *Address to Roman Artists*, 7 May 1964: *AAS* 56 (1964), pp. 439–442.

other fields of learning by pooling their resources and their points of view. Theological research, while it deepens knowledge of revealed truth, should not lose contact with its own times, so that experts in various fields may be led to a deeper knowledge of the faith. Collaboration of this kind will be beneficial in the formation of the sacred ministers; they will be able to present teaching on God, on man, and on the world, in a way more suited to our contemporaries, who will then be more ready to accept their worlds.[14] Furthermore, it is to be hoped that more of the laity will receive adequate theological formation and that some among them will dedicate themselves professionally to these studies and contribute to their advancement. But for the proper exercise of this role, the faithful, both clerical and lay, should be accorded a lawful freedom of inquiry, of thought, and of expression, tempered by humility and courage in whatever branch of study they have specialized.[15]

CHAPTER III

ECONOMIC AND SOCIAL LIFE

SOME CHARACTERISTICS OF ECONOMIC LIFE TODAY

63. In the sphere of economics and social life, too, the dignity and entire vocation of the human person as well as the welfare of society as a whole have to be respected and fostered; for man is the source, the focus and the end of all economic and social life.

Like all other areas of social life, the economy of today is marked by man's growing dominion over nature, by closer

14. Cf. Vatican Council II, Decree on Priestly Formation, *Optatam Totius*, and on Christian Education, *Gravissimum Educationis*.
15. Cf. Dogmatic Constitution *Lumen Gentium*, ch. 4, n. 37: *AAS* 57 (1965), pp. 42–43.

and keener relationships between individuals, groups and peoples, and by the frequency of state intervention. At the same time increased efficiency in production and improved methods of distribution, of productivity and services have rendered the economy an instrument capable of meeting the growing needs of the human family.

But the picture is not without its disturbing elements. Many people, especially in economically advanced areas, seem to be dominated by economics; almost all of their personal and social lives are permeated with a kind of economic mentality, and this is true of nations that favor a collective economy as well as of other nations. At the very same time when economic progress (provided it is directed and organized in a reasonable and human way) could do so much to reduce social inequalities, it serves all too often only to aggravate them; in some places it even leads to a decline in the position of the underprivileged and contempt for the poor. In the midst of huge numbers deprived of the absolute necessities of life there are some who live in riches and squander their wealth; and this happens in less developed areas as well. Luxury and misery exist side by side. While a few individuals enjoy an almost unlimited opportunity to choose for themselves, the vast majority have no chance whatever of exercising personal initiative and responsibility, and quite often have to live and work in conditions unworthy of human beings.

Similar economic and social imbalances exist between those engaged in agriculture, industry, and the service industries, and even between different areas of the same country. The growing contrast between the economically more advanced countries and others could well endanger world peace.

Our contemporaries are daily becoming more keenly aware of these discrepancies because they are thoroughly convinced that this unhappy state of affairs can and should be rectified by the greater technical and economic resources available in the world today. To achieve it much reform in economic and social life is required along with a change of mentality and of attitude by all men. It was for this reason that the Church in the course of centuries has worked out in the light of the Gospel principles of justice and equity demanded by right reason for individual and social life and also for international relations. The Council now intends to reiterate these principles in accordance with the situation of the world today and will outline certain guidelines, particularly with reference to the requirements of economic development.[1]

SECTION 1: ECONOMIC DEVELOPMENT

ECONOMIC DEVELOPMENT IN THE SERVICE OF MAN

64. Today more than ever before there is an increase in the production of agricultural and industrial goods and in the number of services available, and this is as it should be in view of the population expansion and growing human aspirations. Therefore we must encourage technical progress and the spirit of enterprise, we must foster the eagerness for creativity and improvement, and we must promote adaptation of production methods and all serious efforts of people engaged in production—in other words of all elements which contribute to economic progress. The ultimate and basic purpose of economic production does not consist merely in the increase of goods produced, nor in profit nor prestige; it is directed to the service of man, of man, that is, in his totality, taking into account his material needs and the requirements of his intellectual, moral, spiritual, and religious life; of all men whomsoever and of every group of men of whatever race or from whatever part of the world. Therefore, economic activity is to be carried out in accordance with techniques and methods belonging to the moral order,[2] so that God's design for man may be fulfilled.[3]

ECONOMIC DEVELOPMENT UNDER MAN'S DIRECTION

65. Economic development must remain under man's direction; it is not to be left to the judgment of a few individuals or groups possessing too much economic power, nor

1. Pius XII, *Message*, 23 March 1952: *AAS* 44 (1952), p. 273; John XXIII, *Allocution to the Italian Catholic Workers Association*, 1 May 1959: *AAS* 51 (1959), p. 358.
2. Pius XI, Litt. Encycl. *Quadragesimo Anno: AAS* 23 (1931), p. 190 f.; Pius XII, *Message*, 23 March 1952: *AAS* 44 (1952), p. 276 ff.; John XXIII, Litt. Encycl. *Mater et Magistra: AAS* 53 (1961), p. 450; Vatican Council II, Decree *Inter Mirifica*, ch. 1, n. 6: *AAS* 56 (1964), p. 147.
3. Cf. Mt. 16:26; Lk. 16:1–31; Col 3:17.

of the political community alone, nor of a few strong nations. It is only right that, in matters of general interest, as many people as possible, and, in international relations, all nations, should participate actively in decision making. It is likewise necessary that the voluntary initiatives of individuals and of free groups should be integrated with state enterprises and organized in a suitable and harmonious way. Nor should development be left to the almost mechanical evolution of economic activity nor to the decision of public authority. Hence we must denounce as false doctrines which stand in the way of all reform on the pretext of a false notion of freedom, as well as those which subordinate the basic rights of individuals and of groups to the collective organization of production.[4]

All citizens should remember that they have the right and the duty to contribute according to their ability to the genuine progress of their own community and this must be recognized by the civil authority. Above all in areas of retarded economic progress, where all resources must be urgently exploited, the common good is seriously endangered by those who hoard their resources unproductively and by those who (apart from the case of every man's personal right of migration) deprive their community of much needed material and spiritual assistance.

AN END TO EXCESSIVE ECONOMIC AND SOCIAL DIFFERENCES

66. To fulfil the requirements of justice and equity, every effort must be made to put an end as soon as possible to the immense economic inequalities which exist in the world and increase from day to day, linked with individual and social discrimination, provided, of course, that the rights of individuals and the character of each people are not disturbed. Likewise in many areas, in view of the special difficulties of production and marketing in agriculture, country people must be helped to improve methods of production and marketing, to introduce necessary developments and

4. Cf. Leo XIII, Litt. Encycl. *Libertas Praestantissimum,* 20 June 1888: *AAS* 20 (1887–1888), p. 597 ff.; Pius XI, Litt. Encycl. *Quadragesimo Anno: AAS* 23 (1931), p. 191 ff.; Pius XI, *Divini Redemptoris: AAS* 39 (1937), p. 65 ff.; Pius XII, *Christmas Message,* 1941: *AAS* 34 (1942), p. 10 ff.; John XXIII, Litt. Encycl. *Mater et Magistra: AAS* 53 (1961). pp. 401–464.

renewal, and to achieve a fair return for their products, lest they continue, as often happens, in the state of inferior citizens. Farmers themselves, especially young farmers, ought to apply themselves eagerly to bettering their professional skill, without which the advancement of farming is impossible.[5]

Justice and equity also demand that the livelihood of individuals and their families should not become insecure and precarious through a kind of mobility which is a necessary feature of developing economies. All kinds of discrimination in wages and working conditions should be avoided in regard to workers who come from other countries or areas and contribute their work to the economic development of a people or a region. Furthermore, no one, especially public authorities, should treat them simply as mere tools of production, but as persons; they should facilitate them in having their families with them and in obtaining decent housing conditions, and they should endeavor to integrate them into the social life of the country or area to which they have come. However, emploment should be found for them so far as possible in their own countries.

Nowadays when the economy is undergoing transition, as in new forms of industrialization, where, for example automation is being introduced, care must be taken to ensure that there is sufficient and suitable employment available; opportunities of appropriate technical and professional training should be provided, and safeguards should be placed so that the livelihood and human dignity should be protected of those who through age or ill health labor under serious disadvantages.

SECTION 2: SOME PRINCIPLES GOVERNING ECONOMIC AND SOCIAL LIFE AS A WHOLE

WORK, WORKING CONDITIONS, LEISURE

67. Human work which is exercised in the production and exchange of goods or in the provision of economic services, surpasses all other elements of economic life, for the latter are only means to an end.

Human work, whether exercised independently or in subordination to another, proceeds from the human person,

5. For the problem of agriculture cf. especially John XXIII, Litt. Encycl. *Mater et Magistra: AAS* 53 (1961), p. 341 ff.

who as it were impresses his seal on the things of nature and reduces them to his will. By his work a man ordinarily provides for himself and his family, associates with others as his brothers, and renders them service; he can exercise genuine charity and be a partner in the work of bringing divine creation to perfection. Moreover, we believe by faith that through the homage of work offered to God man is associated with the redemptive work of Jesus Christ, whose labor with his hands at Nazareth greatly ennobled the dignity of work. This is the source of every man's duty to work loyally as well as his right to work; moreover, it is the duty of society to see to it that, according to the prevailing circumstances, all citizens have the opportunity of finding employment. Finally, remuneration for work should guarantee man the opportunity to provide a dignified livelihood for himself and his family on the material, social, cultural and spiritual level to correspond to the role and the productivity of each, the relevant economic factors in his employment, and the common good.[6]

Since economic activity is, for the most part, the fruit of the collaboration of many men, it is unjust and inhuman to organize and direct it in such a way that some of the workers are exploited. But it frequently happens, even today, that workers are almost enslaved by the work they do. So-called laws of economics are no excuse for this kind of thing. The entire process of productive work, then, must be accommodated to the needs of the human person and the nature of his life, with special attention to domestic life and of mothers of families in particular, taking sex and age always into account. Workers should have the opportunity to develop their talents and their personalities in the very exercise of their work. While devoting their time and energy to the performance of their work with a due sense of responsibility, they should nevertheless be allowed sufficient rest and leisure to cultivate their family, cultural, social and religious life. And they should be given the opportunity to develop those energies and talents, which perhaps are not catered for in their professional work.

6. Cf. Leo XIII, Litt. Encycl. *Rerum Novarum: AAS* 23 (1890–1891), pp. 649–662; Pius XI, Litt. Encycl. *Quadragesimo Anno: AAS* 23 (1931), p. 200; Pius XI, Litt. Encycl. *Divini Redemptoris: AAS* 29 (1937), p. 92; Pius XII, *Christmas Message*, 1942: *AAS* 35 (1943); Pius XII, *radio message to Spanish workers*, 11 March 1951: *AAS* 43 (1951), p. 215; John XXIII, Litt. Encycl. *Mater et Magistra: AAS* 53 (1961), p. 419.

CO-RESPONSIBILITY IN ENTERPRISE AND IN THE ECONOMIC SYSTEM AS A WHOLE; LABOR DISPUTES

68. In business enterprises it is persons who associate together, that is, men who are free and autonomous, created in the image of God. Therefore, while taking into account the role of every person concerned—owners, employers, management, and employees—and without weakening the necessary executive unity, the active participation of everybody in administration is to be encouraged.[7] More often, however, decisions concerning economic and social conditions are made not so much within the business itself but by institutions at a higher level, and since it is on these that the future of the workers and their children depends, the latter ought to have a say in decision-making either in person or through their representatives.

Among the fundamental rights of the individual must be numbered the right of workers to form themselves into associations which truly represent them and are able to cooperate in organizing economic life properly, and the right to play their part in the activities of such associations without risk of reprisal. Thanks to such organized participation, along with progressive economic and social education, there will be a growing awareness among all people of their role and their responsibility, and, according to the capacity and aptitudes of each one, they will feel that they have an active part to play in the whole task of economic and social development and in the achievement of the common good as a whole.

In the event of economic-social disputes all should strive to arrive at peaceful settlements. The first step is to engage in sincere discussion between all sides; but the strike remains even in the circumstances of today a necessary (although an ultimate) means for the defense of workers' rights and the satisfaction of their lawful aspirations. As soon as possible, however, avenues should be explored to resume negotiations and effect reconciliation.

7. Cf. John XXIII, Litt. Encycl. *Mater et Magistra: AAS* 53 (1961), pp. 408, 424, 427; the word "curatione" used in the original text is taken from the Latin version of the Encyclical *Quadragesimo Anno: AAS* 23 (1931), p. 199. For the evolution of the question cf. also: Pius XII, *Allocution*, 3 June 1950: *AAS* 42 (1950), pp. 484–8; Paul VI, *Allocution*, 8 June 1964: *AAS* 56 (1964), pp. 574–9.

EARTHLY GOODS DESTINED FOR ALL MEN

69. God destined the earth and all it contains for all men and all peoples so that all created things would be shared fairly by all mankind under the guidance of justice tempered by charity.[8] No matter what the structures of property are in different peoples, according to various and changing circumstances and adapted to their lawful institutions, we must never lose sight of this universal destination of earthly goods. In his use of things man should regard the external goods he legitimately owns not merely as exclusive to himself but common to others also, in the sense that they can benefit others as well as himself.[9] Therefore every man has the right to possess a sufficient amount of the earth's goods for himself and his family. This has been the opinion of the Fathers and Doctors of the Church, who taught that men are bound to come to the aid of the poor and to do so not merely out of their superfluous goods.[10] When a person is in extreme necessity he has the right to supply himself with what he needs out of the riches of others." Faced

8. Cf. Pius XII, Litt. Encycl. *Sertum Laetitiae: AAS* 31 (1939), p. 642; John XXIII, *Consistorial Allocution: AAS* 52 (1969), pp. 5–11; John XXIII, Litt. Encycl. *Mater et Magistra; AAS* 53 (1961), p. 411.
9. Cf. St. Thomas, *Summa Theol.*, II-II, q.32, a.5 ad 2; ibid., q.66, a.2; cf. the explanation in Leo XIII, Litt. Encycl. *Rerum Novarum: AAS* 23 (1890–1891), p. 651; cf. also Pius XII, *Allocution*, 1 June 1941: *AAS* 33 (1941), p. 199; Pius XII, *Christmas Message*, 1954: *AAS* 47 (1955), p. 27.
10. Cf. St. Basil, *Hom. in illud Lucae "Destruam horrea mea,"* n. 2: *PG* 31, 263; Lactantius, *Divinarum Institutionum*, bk. V on justice: *PL* 6, 565 B; St. Augustine, *In Ioann. Ev.*, tr. 50, n. 6: *PL* 35, 1760; St. Augustine, *Enarratio in Ps. CXLVII*, 12: *PL* 37, 1922; St. Gregory the Great, *Homiliae in Ev.*, hom. 20: *PL* 76, 1165; St. Gregory the Great, *Regulae Pastoralis liber*, part III, c. 21: *PL* 77, 87; St. Bonaventure, *In III Sent.*, d. 33, dub. 1 (ed. Quaracchi III, 728); St. Bonaventure, *In IV Sent.*, d. 15, p. 11, a. 2, q. 1 (ed. cit. IV, 371 b); q. *de superfluo* (ms. *Assisi, Bibl, commun.* 186, ff. 112a-113a); St. Albert the Great, *In III Sent.*, d. 33, a. 3, sol. 1 (ed. Borgnet XXVIII, 611); St. Albert the Great, *In IV Sent.*, d. 15, a. 16 (ed. cit. XXIX, 494–497). As regards the determination of what is superflous today cf. John XXIII, *Radio-Television Message*, 11 Sept. 1962: *AAS* 54 (1962), p. 682: "It is the duty of every man, the compelling duty of Christians, to calculate what is superfluous by the measure of the needs of others and to see to it that the administration and distribution of created goods be utilized for the advantage of all."
11. In this case the old principle holds good: "In extreme necessity all goods are common, that is, they are to be shared." On the other

with a world today where so many people are suffering from want, the Council asks individuals and governments to remember the saying of the Fathers: "Feed the man dying of hunger, because if you do not feed him you are killing him,"[12] and it urges them according to their ability to share and dispose of their goods to help others, above all by giving them aid which will enable them to help and develop themselves.

In economically less developed societies it often happens that the common destination of goods is partly achieved by a system of community customs and traditions which guarantee a minimum of necessities to each one. Certain customs must not be considered sacrosanct if they no longer correspond to modern needs; on the other hand one should not rashly do away with respectable customs which if they are brought up to date can still be very useful. In the same way, in economically advanced countries the common destination of goods is achieved through a system of social institutions dealing with insurance and security. Family and social services, especially those providing for culture and education, should be further developed. In setting up these different organizations care must be taken to prevent the citizens from slipping into a kind of passivity vis-à-vis society, or of irresponsibility in their duty, or of a refusal to do their fair share.

INVESTMENT AND MONEY

70. Investment in its turn should be directed to providing employment and ensuring sufficient income for the people of today and of the future. Those responsible for investment and the planning of the economy (individuals, associations, public authority) must keep these objectives in mind; they must show themselves aware of their serious obligation, on the one hand, to see to it that the necessities for living a decent life are available to individuals and to the community as a whole, and, on the other hand, to provide

hand for the scope, the extension, and the way this principle is to be applied in the text, besides accepted modern authors, cf. St. Thomas, *Summa Theol.*, II-II. q.66, a.7. Clearly, for the correct application of the principle all the moral conditions required must be fulfilled.

12. Cf. Gratian, *Decretum*, c. 21, dist. LXXXVI: ed. Friedberg I, 302. This axiom is found already in *PL* 54, 591a and *PL* 56, 1132b; cf. *Antonianum*, 27 (1952), 349–366.

for the future and strike a rightful balance between the needs of present-day consumption, individual and collective, and the requirements of investment for future generations. Always before their eyes they must keep the pressing needs of underdeveloped countries and areas. In fiscal matters they must be careful not to do harm to their own country or to any other. Care must also be taken that economically weak countries do not unjustly suffer loss from a change in the value of money.

OWNERSHIP, PRIVATE PROPERTY, LARGE ESTATES

71. Property and other forms of private ownership of external goods contribute to the expression of personality and provide man with the opportunity of exercising his role in society and in the economy; it is very important, then, that the acquisition of some form of ownership of external goods by individuals and communities be fostered.

Private property or some form of ownership of external goods assures a person a highly necessary sphere for the exercise of his personal and family autonomy and ought to be considered as an extension of human freedom. Lastly, in stimulating exercise of responsibility, it constitutes one of the conditions for civil liberty.[13] Nowadays the forms of such ownership or property are varied and are becoming more diversified every day. In spite of the social security, the rights, and the services guaranteed by society, all these forms of ownership are still a source of security which must not be underestimated. And this applies not only to ownership of material goods but also to the possession of professional skills.

The lawfulness of private ownership is not opposed to the various forms of public ownership. But the transfer of goods from private to public ownership may be undertaken only by competent authority, in accordance with the demands and within the limits of the common good, and it

13. Cf. Leo XII, Litt. Encycl. *Rerum Novarum: AAS* 23 (1890–1891), pp. 643–6; Pius XI, Litt. Encycl. *Quadragesimo Anno: AAS* 23 (1931), p. 191; Pius XII, *Radio Message*, 1 June 1941: *AAS* 33 (1941), p. 199; Pius XII, *Christmas Message*, 1942: *AAS* 35 (1943), p. 17; Pius XII, *Radio Message*, 1 Sept. 1944: *AAS* 36 (1944), p. 253; John XXIII, Litt. Encycl. *Mater et Magistra: AAS* 53 (1961), pp. 428-fi.

must be accompanied by adequate compensation. Furthermore, the state has the duty to prevent anyone from abusing his private property to the detriment of the common good.[14] By its nature private property has a social dimension which is based on the law of common destination of earthly goods.[15] Whenever the social aspect is forgotten, ownership can often become the source of greed and serious disorder, so that its opponents easily find a pretext for calling the right itself into question.

In several economically retarded areas there exist large and sometimes very extensive rural estates which are only slightly cultivated or not cultivated at all for the sake of profit, while the majority of the population have no land or possess only very small holdings and the need to increase agricultural production is pressing and evident to all. Not infrequently those who are hired as labourers or who till a portion of the land as tenants receive a wage or income unworthy of the human being; they are deprived of decent living conditions and are exploited by middlemen. They lack all sense of security and live in such a state of personal dependence that almost all chance of exercising initiative and responsibility is closed to them and they are denied any cultural advancement or participation in social and political life. Reforms are called for in these different situations: incomes must be raised, working conditions improved, security in employment assured, and personal incentives to work encouraged; estates insufficiently cultivated must even be divided up and given to those who will be able to make them productive. In this event the necessary resources and equipment must be supplied, especially educational facilities and proper cooperative organizations. However, when the common good calls for expropriation, compensation must be made and is to be calculated according to equity, with all circumstances taken into account.

14. Cf. Pius XI, Litt. Encycl. *Quadragesimo Anno: AAS* 23 (1931), p. 214; John XXIII, Litt. Encycl. *Mater et Magistra: AAS* 53 (1961), p. 429.
15. Cf. Pius XII, *radio message* of Pentecost 1941: *AAS* 44 (1941), p. 199; John XXIII, Litt. Encycl. *Mater et Magistra: AAS* 53 (1961), p. 430.

ECONOMIC AND SOCIAL ACTIVITY AND THE KINGDOM OF CHRIST

72. Christians engaged actively in modern economic and social progress and in the struggle for justice and charity must be convinced that they have much to contribute to the prosperity of mankind and to world peace. Let them, as individuals and as group members, give a shining example to others. Endowed with the skill and experience so absolutely necessary for them, let them preserve a proper sense of values in their earthly activity in loyalty to Christ and his Gospel, in order that their lives, individual as well as social, may be inspired by the spirit of the Beatitudes, and in particular by the spirit of poverty.

Anyone who in obedience to Christ seeks first the kingdom of God will derive from it a stronger and purer love for helping all his brethren and for accomplishing the task of justice under the inspiration of charity.[16]

CHAPTER IV

THE POLITICAL COMMUNITY

MODERN PUBLIC LIFE

73. In our times profound transformations are to be noticed in the structure and institutions of peoples; they are the accompaniment of cultural, economic, and social development. These transformations exercise a deep influence on political life, particularly as regards the rights and duties of the individual in the exercise of civil liberty and in the achievement of the common good; and they affect the organization of the relations of citizens with each other and of their position vis-à-vis the state.

16. For the right use of goods according to the teaching of the New Testament cf. Lk. 3:11; 10:30 ff.; 11:41; Mk. 8:36; 12:29–31; 1 Pet. 5:3; Jas. 5:1–6; 1 Tim. 6:8; Eph. 4:28; 2 Cor. 8:13 f.; 1 Jn. 3:17–18.

A keener awareness of human dignity has given rise in various parts of the world to an eagerness to establish a politico-juridical order in which the rights of the human person in public life will be better protected—for example, the right of free assembly and association, the right to express one's opinions and to profess one's religion privately and publicly. The guarantee of the rights of the person is, indeed, a necessary condition for citizens, individually and collectively, to play an active part in public life and administration.

Linked with cultural, economic, and social progress there is a growing desire among many to assume greater responsibilities in the organization of political life. Many people are becoming more eager to ensure that the rights of minority groups in their country be safeguarded, without overlooking the duties of these minorities towards the political community; there is also an increase in tolerance for others who differ in opinion and religion; at the same time wider cooperation is taking place to enable all citizens, and not only a few privileged individuals, to exercise their rights effectively as persons.

Men are repudiating political systems, still prevailing in some parts of the world, which hinder civil and religious liberty or victimize their citizens through avarice and political crimes, or distort the use of authority from being at the service of the common good to benefiting the convenience of political parties or of the governing classes.

There is no better way to establish political life on a truly human basis than by encouraging an inward sense of justice of good will, and of service to the common good, and by consolidating the basic convictions of men as to the true nature of the political community and the aim, proper exercise, and the limits of public authority.

NATURE AND PURPOSE OF THE POLITICAL COMMUNITY

74. Individuals, families, and the various groups which make up the civil community, are aware of their inability to achieve a truly human life by their own unaided efforts; they see the need for a wider community where each one will make a specific contribution to an even broader implementation of the common good.[1] For this reason they set

1. Cf. John XXIII, Litt. Encycl. *Mater et Magistra: AAS* 53 (1961), p. 417.

up various forms of political communities. The political community, then, exists for the common good: this is its full justification and meaning and the source of its specific and basic right to exist. The common good embraces the sum total of all those conditions of social life which enable individuals, families, and organizations to achieve complete and efficacious fulfilment.[2]

The persons who go to make up the political community are many and varied; quite rightly, then, they may veer towards widely differing points of view. Therefore, lest the political community be ruined while everyone follows his own opinion, an authority is needed to guide the energies of all towards the common good—not mechanically or despotically, but by acting above all as a moral force based on freedom and a sense of responsibility. It is clear that the political community and public authority are based on human nature, and therefore that they need belong to an order established by God; nevertheless, the choice of the political régime and the appointment of rulers are left to the free decision of the citizens.[3]

It follows that political authority, either within the political community as such or through organizations representing the state, must be exercised within the limits of the moral order and directed toward the common good (understood in the dynamic sense of the term) according to the juridical order legitimately established or due to be established. Citizens, then, are bound in conscience to obey.[4] Accordingly, the responsibility, the dignity, and the importance of state rulers is clear.

When citizens are under the oppression of a public authority which oversteps its competence, they should still not refuse to give or to do whatever is objectively demanded of them by the common good; but it is legitimate for them to defend their own rights and those of their fellow citizens against abuses of this authority within the limits of the natural law and the law of the Gospel.

The concrete forms of structure and organization of public authority adopted in any political community may vary according to the character of various peoples and their historical development; but their aim should always be the for-

2. Cf. John XXIII, ibid.
3. Cf. Rom. 13:1–5.
4. Cf. Rom. 13:5.

mation of a human person who is cultured, peace-loving, and well disposed towards his fellow men with a view, to the benefit of the whole human race.

PARTICIPATION BY ALL IN PUBLIC LIFE

75. It is fully consonant with human nature that there should be politico-juridical structures providing all citizens without any distinction with ever improving and effective opportunities to play an active part in the establishment of the juridical foundations of the political community, in the administration of public affairs, in determining the aims and the terms of reference of public bodies, and in the election of political leaders.[5] Every citizen ought to be mindful of his right and his duty to promote the common good by using his vote. The Church praises and esteems those who devote themselves to the public good for the service of men and take upon themselves the burdens of public office.

If the citizens' cooperation and their sense of responsibility are to produce the favourable results expected of them in the normal course of public life, a system of positive law is required providing for a suitable division of the functions and organs of public authority and an effective and independent protection of citizens' rights. The rights of all individuals, families, and organizations and their practical implementation must be acknowledged, protected, and fostered,[6] together with the public duties binding on all citizens. Among these duties it is worth mentioning the obligation of rendering to the state whatever material and personal services are required for the common good. Governments should take care not to put obstacles in the way of family, cultural or social groups, or of organizations and intermediate institutions, nor to hinder their lawful and constructive activity; rather, they should eagerly seek to promote such orderly activity. Citizens, on the other hand, either individually or in association, should take care not to vest too much power in the hands of public authority nor to

5. Cf. Pius XII, *Christmas Message* 1942: *AAS* 35 (1043), pp. 9–24; *Christmas Message* 1944: *AAS* 37 (1945), pp. 11–17; John XXIII, Litt. Encycl. *Pacem in Terris*: *AAS* 55 (1963), pp. 263, 271, 277, 278.
6. Cf. Pius XII, *radio message*, 1 June 1941: *AAS* 33 (1941), p. 200; John XXIII, Litt. Encycl. *Pacem in Terris*: *AAS* 55 (1963), pp. 273, 274.

make untimely and exaggereated demands for favors and subsidies, lessening in this way the responsible role of individuals, families, and social groups.

The growing complexity of modern situations makes it necessary for public authority to intervene more often in social, cultural and economic matters in order to bring about more favorable conditions to enable citizens and groups to pursue freely and effectively the achievement of man's well-being in its totality. The understanding of the relationship between socialization[7] and personal autonomy and progress will vary according to different areas and the development of peoples. However, if restrictions are imposed temporarily for the common good on the exercise of human rights, these restrictions are to be lifted as soon as possible after the situation has changed. In any case it is inhuman for public authority to fall back on totalitarian methods or dictatorship which violate the rights of persons or social groups.

Citizens should cultivate a generous and loyal spirit of patriotism, but without narrow-mindedness, so that they will always keep in mind the welfare of the whole human family which is formed into one by various kinds of links between races, peoples, and nations.

Christians must be conscious of their specific and proper role in the political community: they should be a shining example by their sense of responsibility and their dedication to the common good; they should show in practice how authority can be reconciled with freedom, personal initiative and with the solidarity and the needs of the whole social framework, and the advantages of unity with profitable diversity. They should recognize the legitimacy of differing points of view about the organization of worldly affairs and show respect for their fellow citizens, who even in association defend their opinions by legitimate means. Political parties, for their part, must support whatever in their opinion is conducive to the common good, but must never put their own interests before the common good.

So that all citizens will be able to play their part in political affairs, civil and political education is vitally necessary for the population as a whole and for young people in particular, and must be diligently attended to. Those with a tal-

7. Cf. John XXIII, Litt. Encycl. *Mater et Magistra: AAS* 53 (1961), p. 415–418.

ent for the difficult yet noble art of politics,[8] or whose talents in this matter can be developed, should prepare themselves for it, and, forgetting their own convenience and material interests, they should engage in political activity. They must combat injustice and oppression, arbitrary domination and intolerance by individuals or political parties, and they must do so with integrity and wisdom. They must dedicate themselves to the welfare of all in a spirit of sincerity and fairness, of love and of the courage demanded by political life.

THE POLITICAL COMMUNITY AND THE CHURCH

76. It is of supreme importance, especially in a pluralistic society, to work out a proper vision of the relationship between the political community and the Church, and to distinguish clearly between the activities of Christians, acting individually or collectively in their own name as citizens guided by the dictates of a Christian conscience, and their activity acting along with their pastors in the name of the Church.

The Church, by reason of her role and competence, is not identified with any political community nor bound by ties to any political system. It is at once the sign and the safeguard of the transcendental dimension of the human person.

The political community and the Church are autonomous and independent of each other in their own fields. Nevertheless, both are devoted to the personal vocation of man, though under different titles. This service will redound the more effectively to the welfare of all insofar as both institutions practice better cooperation according to the local and prevailing situation. For man's horizons are not bounded only by the temporal order; living on the level of human history he preserves the integrity of his eternal destiny. The Church, for its part, being founded in the love of the Redeemer, contributes towards the spread of justice and charity among nations and within the borders of the nations themselves. By preaching the truths of the Gospel and clarifying all sectors of human activity through its teaching and

8. Cf. Pius XI, *Allocution to the Directors of the Catholic University Federation: Discorsi di Pio XI*, ed. Bertetto, Torino, vol. 1 (1960), p. 743.

the witness of its members, the Church respects and encourages the political freedom and responsibility of the citizen.

Since the apostles, their successors and all who help them have been given the task of announcing Christ, Saviour of the world, to man, they rely in their apostolate on the power of God, who often shows forth the force of the Gospel in the weakness of its witnesses. If anyone wishes to devote himself to the ministry of God's Word, let him use the ways and means proper to the Gospel, which differ in many respects from those obtaining in the earthly city.

Nevertheless, there are close links between the things of earth and those things in man's condition which transcend the world, and the Church utilizes temporal realities as often as its mission requires it. But it never places its hopes in any privileges accorded to it by civil authority; indeed, it will give up the exercise of certain legitimate rights whenever it becomes clear that their use will compromise the sincerity of its witness, or whenever new circumstances call for a revised approach. But at all times and in all places the Church should have true freedom to preach the faith, to proclaim its teaching about society, to carry out its task among men without hindrance, and to pass moral judgments even in matters relating to politics, whenever the fundamental rights of man or the salvation of souls requires it. The means, the only means, it may use are those which are in accord with the Gospel and the welfare of all men according to the diversity of times and circumstances.

With loyalty to the Gospel in the fulfilment of its mission in the world, the Church, whose duty it is to foster and elevate all that is true, all that is good, and all that is beautiful in the human community,[9] consolidates peace among men for the glory of God.[10]

9. Cf. Vatican Council II, Dogmatic Constitution *Lumen Gentium*, n. 13: *AAS* 57 (1965), p. 17.
10. Cf. Lk. 2:14.

CHAPTER V

FOSTERING OF PEACE AND ESTABLISHMENT
OF A COMMUNITY OF NATIONS

INTRODUCTION

77. In our generation, which has been marked by the persistent and acute hardships and anxiety resulting from the ravages of war and the threat of war, the whole human race faces a moment of supreme crisis in its advance towards maturity. Mankind has gradually come closer together and is everywhere more conscious of its own unity; but it will not succeed in accomplishing the task awaiting it, that is, the establishment of a truly human world for all men over the entire earth, unless everyone devotes himself to the cause of true peace with renewed vigor. Thus the message of the Gospel, which epitomizes the highest ideals and aspirations of mankind, shines anew in our times when it proclaims that the advocates of peace are blessed "for they shall be called sons of God" (Mt. 5:9).

Accordingly, the Council proposes to outline the true and noble nature of peace, to condemn the savagery of war, and earnestly to exhort Christians to cooperate with all in securing a peace based on justice and charity and in promoting the means necessary to attain it, under the help of Christ, author of peace.

NATURE OF PEACE

78. Peace is more than the absence of war: it cannot be reduced to the maintenance of a balance of power between opposing forces nor does it arise out of despotic dominion, but it is appropriately called "the effect of righteousness" (Is. 32:17). It is the fruit of that right ordering of things with which the divine founder has invested human society and which must be actualized by man thirsting after an

ever more perfect reign of justice. But while the common good of mankind ultimately derives from the eternal law, it depends in the concrete upon circumstances which change as time goes on; consequently, peace will never be achieved once and for all, but must be built up continually. Since, moreover, human nature is weak and wounded by sin, the achievement of peace requires a constant effort to control the passions and unceasing vigilance by lawful authority.

But this is not enough. Peace cannot be obtained on earth unless the welfare of man is safeguarded and people freely and trustingly share with one another the riches of their minds and their talents. A firm determination to respect the dignity of other men and other peoples along with the deliberate practice of fraternal love are absolutely necessary for the achievement of peace. Accordingly, peace is also the fruit of love, for love goes beyond what justice can ensure.

Peace on earth, which flows from love of one's neighbor, symbolizes and derives from the peace of Christ who proceeds from God the Father. Christ, the Word made flesh, the prince of peace, reconciled all men to God by the cross, and, restoring the unity of all in one people and one body, he abolished hatred in his own flesh,[1] having been lifted up through his resurrection he poured forth the Spirit of love into the hearts of men. Therefore, all Christians are earnestly to speak the truth in love (cf. Eph. 4:15) and join with all peace-loving men in pleading for peace and trying to bring it about. In the same spirit we cannot but express our admiration for all who forgo the use of violence to vindicate their rights and resort to those other means of defense which are available to weaker parties, provided it can be done without harm to the rights and duties of others and of the community.

Insofar as men are sinners, the threat of war hangs over them and will so continue until the coming of Christ; but insofar as they can vanquish sin by coming together in charity, violence itself will be vanquished and they will make these words come true: "They shall beat their swords into ploughshares, and their spears into pruning hooks; nation shall not lift up sword against nation, neither shall they learn war any more" (Is. 2:4).

1. Cf. Eph. 2:16; Col. 1:20–22.

SECTION 1: AVOIDANCE OF WAR

CURBING THE SAVAGERY OF WAR

79. Even though recent wars have wrought immense material and moral havoc on the world, the devastation of battle still rages in some parts of the world. Indeed, now that every kind of weapon produced by modern science is used in war, the savagery of war threatens to lead the combatants to barbarities far surpassing those of former ages. Moreover, the complexity of the modern world and the intricacy of international relations cause incipient wars to develop into full-scale conflict by new methods of infiltration and subversion. In many cases terrorist methods are regarded as new strategies of war.

Faced by this deplorable state of humanity the Council wishes to remind men that the natural law of peoples and its universal principles still retain their binding force. The conscience of mankind firmly and ever more emphatically proclaims these principles. Any action which deliberately violates these principles and any order which commands such actions is criminal and blind obedience cannot excuse those who carry them out. The most infamous among these actions are those designed for the reasoned and methodical extermination of an entire race, nation, or ethnic minority. These must be condemned as frightful crimes; and we cannot commend too highly the courage of the men who openly and fearlessly resist those who issue orders of this kind.

On the question of warfare, there are various international conventions, signed by many countries, aimed at rendering military action and its consequences less inhuman; they deal with the treatment of wounded and interned prisoners of war and with various kindred questions. These agreements must be honored; indeed public authorities and specialists in these matters must do all in their power to improve these conventions and thus bring about a better and more effective curbing of the savagery of war. Moreover, it seems just that laws should make humane provision for the case of conscientious objectors who refuse to carry arms, provided they accept some other form of community service.

War, of course, has not ceased to be part of the human scene. As long as the danger of war persists and there is no international authority with the necessary competence and power, governments cannot be denied the right of lawful self-defense, once all peace efforts have failed. State leaders and all who share the burdens of public administration have the duty to defend the interests of their people and to conduct such grave matters with a deep sense of responsibility. However, it is one thing to wage a war of self-defense; it is quite another to seek to impose domination on another nation. The possession of war potential does not justify the use of force for political or military objectives. Nor does the mere fact that war has unfortunately broken out mean that all is fair between the warring parties.

All those who enter the military service in loyalty to their country should look upon themselves as the custodians of the security and freedom of their fellow-countrymen; and when they carry out their duty properly, they are contributing to the maintenance of peace.

TOTAL WARFARE

80. The development of armaments by modern science has immeasurably magnified the horrors and wickedness of war. Warfare conducted with these weapons can inflict immense and indiscriminate havoc which goes far beyond the bounds of legitimate defense. Indeed if the kind of weapons now stocked in the arsenals of the great powers were to be employed to the fullest, the result would be the almost complete reciprocal slaughter of one side by the other, not to speak of the widespread devastation that would follow in the world and the deadly after-effects resulting from the use of such arms.

All these factors force us to undertake a completely fresh reappraisal of war.[2] Men of this generation should realize that they will have to render an account of their warlike behavior; the destiny of generations to come depends largely on the decisions they make today.

With these considerations in mind the Council, endorsing the condemnations of total warfare issued by recent popes,[3]

2. Cf. John XXIII, Litt. Encycl. *Pacem in Terris: AAS* 55 (1963), p. 291: "Therefore in this age of ours, which prides itself on its atomic power, it is irrational to think that war is a proper way to obtain justice for violated rights."
3. Cf. Pius XII, *Allocution*, 30 Sept. 1954: *AAS* 46 (1954), p. 589; *Christmas Message* 1954: *AAS* 47 (1955), pp. 15 ff.; John XXIII, Litt. Encycl. *Pacem in Terris: AAS* 55 (1963), pp. 286– 291; Paul VI,

declares: Every act of war directed to the indiscriminate destruction of whole cities or vast areas with their inhabitants is a crime against God and man, which merits firm and unequivocal condemnation.

The hazards peculiar to modern warfare consist in the fact that they expose those possessing recently developed weapons to the risk of perpetrating crimes like these and, by an inexorable chain of events, of urging men to even worse acts of atrocity. To obviate the possibility of this happening at any time in the future, the bishops of the world gathered together to implore all men, especially government leaders and military advisers, to give unceasing consideration to their immense responsibilities before God and before the whole human race.

THE ARMS RACE

81. Undoubtedly, armaments are not amassed merely for use in wartime. Since the defensive strength of any nation is thought to depend on its capacity for immediate retaliation, the stockpiling of arms which grows from year to year serves, in a way hitherto unthought of, as a deterrent to potential attackers. Many people look upon this as the most effective way known at the present time for maintaining some sort of peace among nations.

Whatever one may think of this form of deterrent, people are convinced that the arms race, which quite a few countries have entered, is no infallible way of maintaining real peace and that the resulting so-called balance of power is no sure and genuine path to achieving it. Rather than eliminate the causes of war, the arms race serves only to aggravate the position. As long as extravagant sums of money are poured into the development of new weapons, it is impossible to devote adequate aid in tackling the misery which prevails at the present day in the world. Instead of eradicating international conflict once and for all, the contagion is spreading to other parts of the world. New approaches, based on reformed attitudes, will have to be chosen in order to remove this stumbling block, to free the earth from its pressing anxieties, and give back to the world a genuine peace.

Address to the United Nations, 4 Oct. 1965: *AAS* 57 (1965), pp. 877–885.

Therefore, we declare once again: the arms race is one of the greatest curses on the human race and the harm it inflicts on the poor is more than can be endured. And there is every reason to fear that if it continues it will bring forth those lethal disasters which are already in preparation. Warned by the possibility of the catastrophes that man has created, let us profit by the respite we now enjoy, thanks to the divine favor, to take stock of our responsibilities and find ways of resolving controversies in a manner worthy of human beings. Providence urgently demands of us that we free ourselves from the age-old slavery of war. If we refuse to make this effort, there is no knowing where we will be led on the fatal path we have taken.

TOTAL OUTLAWING OF WAR: INTERNATIONAL ACTION TO PREVENT WAR

82. It is our clear duty to spare no effort in order to work for the moment when all war will be completely outlawed by international agreement. This goal, of course, requires the establishment of a universally acknowledged public authority vested with the effective power to ensure security for all, regard for justice, and respect for law. But before this desirable authority can be constituted, it is necessary for existing international bodies to devote themselves resolutely to the exploration of better means for obtaining common security. But since peace must be born of mutual trust between peoples instead of being forced on nations through dread of arms, all must work to put an end to the arms race and make a real beginning of disarmament, not unilaterally indeed but at an equal rate on all sides, on the basis of agreements and backed up by genuine and effective guarantees.[4]

In the meantime one must not underestimate the efforts already made or now under way to eliminate the danger of war. On the contrary, support should be given to the good will of numerous individuals who are making every effort to eliminate the havoc of war; these men, although burdened by the weighty responsibilities of their high office, are motivated by a consciousness of their very grave obligations, even if they cannot ignore the complexity of the situ-

---

4. Cf. John XXIII, Litt. Encycl. *Pacem in Terris,* where the reduction of arms is treated: *AAS* 55 (1963), p. 287.

ation as it stands. We must beseech the Lord to give them the strength to tackle with perseverance and carry out with courage this task of supreme love for man which is the building up of a lasting peace in a true spirit of manhood. In our times this work demands that they enlarge their thoughts and their spirit beyond the confines of their own country, that they put aside nationalistic selfishness and ambitions to dominate other nations, and that they cultivate deep reverence for the whole of mankind which is painstakingly advancing towards greater maturity.

The problems of peace and disarmament have been treated at length with courage and untiring consultation at negotiations and international meetings; these are to be considered as the first steps towards the solutions of such important questions and must be further pursued with even greater insistence, with a view to obtaining concrete results in the future. But people should beware of leaving these problems to the efforts of a few men without putting their own attitudes in order. For state leaders, who are at once the guardians of their own people and the promoters of the welfare of the whole world, rely to a large extent on public opinion and public attitudes. Their peace-making efforts will be in vain, as long as men are divided and warring among themselves through hostility, contempt, and distrust, as well as through racial hatred and uncompromising hostilities. Hence there is a very urgent need of re-education and a new orientation of public opinion. Those engaged in the work of education, especially youth education, and the people who mold public opinion, should regard it as their most important task to educate the minds of men to renewed sentiments of peace. Every one of us needs a change of heart; we must set our gaze on the whole world and look to those tasks we can all perform together in order to bring about the betterment of our race.

But let us not be buoyed up with false hope. For unless animosity and hatred are put aside, and firm, honest agreements about world peace are concluded, humanity may, in spite of the wonders of modern science, go from the grave crisis of the present day to that dismal hour, when the only peace it will experience will be the dread peace of death. The Church, however, living in the midst of these anxieties, even as it makes these statements, has not lost hope. The Church intends to propose to our age over and over again, in season and out of season, the apostle's message: "Behold, now is the acceptable time" for a change of heart; "behold, now is the day of salvation."[5]

SECTION 2: ESTABLISHMENT OF AN INTERNATIONAL COMMUNITY

CAUSES OF DISCORD: REMEDIES

83. If peace is to be established, the first condition is to root out the causes of discord among men which lead to wars— in the first place, injustice. Not a few of these causes arise out of excessive economic inequalities and out of hesitation to undertake necessary correctives. Some are due to the desire for power and to contempt for people, and at a deeper level, to envy, distrust, pride, and other selfish passions. Man cannot put up with such an amount of disorder; the result is that, even when war is absent, the world is constantly beset by strife and violence between men. Since the same evils are also to be found in the relations between nations, it is of the utmost importance, if these evils are to be overcome or forestalled and if headlong violence is to be curbed, for international bodies to work more effectively and more resolutely together and to coordinate their efforts. And finally, man should work unsparingly towards the creation of bodies designed to promote the cause of peace.

THE COMMUNITY OF NATIONS AND INTERNATIONAL ORGANIZATIONS

84. At the present time when close ties of dependence between individuals and peoples all over the world are developing, the universal common good has to be pursued in an appropriate way and more effectively achieved; it is now a necessity for the community of nations to organize itself in a manner suited to its present responsibilities, with special reference to its obligations towards the many areas of the world where intolerable want still prevails. To reach this goal, organizations of the international community, for their part, should set themselves to provide for the different needs of men; this will involve the sphere of social life to which belong questions of food, hygiene, education, em-

5. Cf. 2 Cor. 6:2.

ployment, and certain particular situations arising here and there, as for example a general need to promote the welfare of developing countries, to alleviate the miseries of refugees dispersed throughout the world, and to assist migrants and their families.

Already existing international and regional organizations certainly deserve well of the human race. They represent the first attempts at laying the foundations on an international level for a community of all men to work towards the solutions of the very serious problems of our times, and specifically towards the encouragement of progress everywhere and the prevention of wars of all kinds. The Church is glad to view the spirit of true brotherhood existing in all spheres between Christians and non-Christians as it seeks to intensify its untiring efforts to alleviate the enormity of human misery.

INTERNATIONAL COOPERATION IN ECONOMIC MATTERS

85. The present solidarity of mankind calls for greater international cooperation in economic matters. Indeed, although nearly all peoples have achieved political independence, they are far from being free from excessive inequalities and from every form of undue independence and far from being immune to serious internal difficulties.

The development of a nation depends on human and financial resources. The citizens of every nation must be prepared by education and professional training to undertake the various tasks of economic and social life. This involves the help of experts from abroad, who, while they are the bearers of assistance, should not behave as overlords but as helpers and fellow-workers. Material aid for developing nations will not be forthcoming unless there is a profound change in the prevailing conventions of commerce today. Other forms of aid from affluent nations should take the form of grants, loans, or investments; they should be given in a spirit of generosity and without greed on one side, and accepted with complete honesty on the other.

The establishment of an authentic economic order on a worldwide scale can come about only by abolishing profiteering, nationalistic ambitions, greed for political domination, schemes of military strategy, and intrigues for spreading and imposing ideologies. Different economic and social systems have been suggested; it is to be hoped that experts will find in them a common basis for a just world commerce; it will come about if all men forgo their own prejudices and show themselves ready to enter into sincere dialogue.

SOME USEFUL NORMS

86. The following norms seem useful for such cooperation:

(a) Developing nations should be firmly convinced that their express and unequivocal aim is the total human development of their citizens. They should not forget that progress has its roots and its strength before all else in the work and talent of their citizens. They should not forget that progress is based, not only on foreign aid, but on the full exploitation of native resources and on the development of their own talents and traditions. In this matter those who exert the greater influence on others should be the more outstanding by their example.

(b) The most important task of the affluent nations is to help developing nations to fulfil these commitments. Accordingly, they should undertake within their own confines the spiritual and material adjustments which are needed for the establishment of world-wide cooperation. They should look to the welfare of the weaker and poorer nations in business dealings with them, for the revenues the latter make from the sale of home-produced goods are needed for their own support.

(c) It is up to the international community to coordinate and stimulate development, but in such a way as to distribute with the maximum fairness and efficacy the resources set aside for this purpose. It is also its task to organize economic affairs on a worldwide scale, without transgressing the principle of subsidiarity, so that business will be conducted according to the norms of justice. Organizations should be set up to promote and regulate international commerce, especially with less developed nations, in order to compensate for losses resulting from excessive inequality of power between nations. This kind of organization accompanied by technical, cultural, and financial aid, should provide nations on the path of progress with all that is necessary for them to achieve adequate economic success.

(d) In many instances there exists a pressing need to

reassess economic and social structure, but caution must be exercised with regard to proposed solutions which may be untimely, especially those which offer material advantage while militating against man's spiritual nature and advancement. For "Man does not live on bread alone but on every word that comes from the mouth of God" (Mt. 4:4). Every branch of the human race possesses in itself and in its nobler traditions some part of the spiritual treasure which God has entrusted to men, even though many do not know the source of it.

87. International cooperation is vitally necessary in the case of those peoples who very often in the midst of many difficulties are faced with the special problems arising out of rapid increases in population. There is a pressing need to harness the full and eager cooperation of all, particularly of the richer countries, in order to explore how the human necessities of food and suitable education can be furnished and shared with the entire human community. Some peoples could improve their standard of living considerably if they were properly trained to substitute new techniques of agricultural production for antiquated methods and adapt them prudently to their own situation. The social order would also be improved and a fairer distribution of land ownership would be assured.

The government has, assuredly, in the matter of the population of its country, its own rights and duties, within the limits of its proper competence, for instance as regards social and family legislation, the migration of country-dwellers to the city, and information concerning the state and needs of the nation. Some men nowadays are gravely disturbed by this problem; it is to be hoped that there will be Catholic experts in these matters, particularly in universities, who will diligently study the problems and pursue their researches further.

Since there is widespread opinion that the population expansion of the world, or at least some particular countries, should be kept in check by all possible means and by every kind of intervention by public authority, the Council exhorts all men to beware of all solutions, whether uttered in public or in private or imposed at any time, which transgress the natural law. Because in virtue of man's inalienable right to marriage and the procreation of children, the decision regarding the number of children depends on the judgment of the parents and is in no way to be left to the decrees of public authority. Now, since the parents' judgment presupposes a properly formed conscience, it is of great importance that all should have an opportunity to cultivate a genuinely human sense of responsibility which will take account of the circumstances of time and situation and will respect the divine law; to attain this goal a change for the better must take place in educational and social conditions and, above all, religious formations, or at least full moral training, must be available. People should be discreetly informed of scientific advances in research into methods of birth regulation, whenever the value of these methods has been thoroughly proved and their conformity with the moral order established.

ROLE OF CHRISTIANS IN INTERNATIONAL AID

88. Christians should willingly and wholeheartedly support the establishment of an international order that includes a genuine respect for legitimate freedom and friendly sentiments of brotherhood towards all men. It is all the more urgent now that the greater part of the world is in a state of such poverty that it is as if Christ himself were crying out in the mouths of these poor people to the charity of his disciples. Let us not be guilty of the scandal of having some nations, most of whose citizens bear the name of Christians, enjoying an abundance of riches, while others lack the necessities of life and are tortured by hunger, disease, and all kinds of misery. For the spirit of poverty and charity is the glory and witness of the Church of Christ.

We must praise and assist those Christians, especially those young Christians, who volunteer their services to help other men and other peoples. Indeed it is a duty for the whole people of God, under the teaching and example of the bishops, to alleviate the hardships of our times within the limits of its means, giving generously, as was the ancient custom of the Church, not merely out of what is superflous, but also out of what is necessary.

Without being rigid and altogether uniform in the matter, methods of collection and distribution of aid should be systematically conducted in dioceses, nations, and throughout the world and in collaboration with suitable institutes.

EFFECTIVE PRESENCE OF THE CHURCH IN THE INTERNATIONAL COMMUNITY

89. The Church, in preaching the Gospel to all men and dispensing the treasures of grace in accordance with its divine mission, makes a contribution to the strengthening of peace over the whole world and helps to consolidate the foundations of brotherly communion among men and peoples. This it does by imparting the knowledge of the divine and the natural law. Accordingly, the Church ought to be present in the community of peoples, to foster and stimulate cooperation among men; motivated by the sole desire of serving all men, it contributes both by means of its official channels and through the full and sincere collaboration of all Christians. This goal will be more effectively brought about if all the faithful are conscious of their responsibility as men and as Christians and work in their own environments to arouse generous cooperation with the international community. In their religious and civil education special attention should be given to the training of youth in this matter.

ROLE OF CHRISTIANS IN INTERNATIONAL ORGANIZATIONS

90. For Christians one undoubtedly excellent form of international activity is the part they play, either individually or collectively, in organizations set up or on the way to being set up to foster cooperation between nations. Different Catholic international bodies can assist the community of nations on the way to peace and brotherhood; these bodies should be strengthened by enlarging the number of their well-trained members, by increasing the subsidies they need so badly, and by suitable coordination of their forces. Nowadays efficiency of action and the need for dialogue call for concerted effort. Organizations of this kind, moreover, contribute more than a little to the instilling of a feeling of universality, which is certainly appropriate for Catholics, and to the formation of truly wouldwide solidarity and responsibility.

Finally, it is to be hoped that, in order to fulfil their role in the international community properly, Catholics will seek to cooperate actively and positively with our separated brethern, who profess the charity of the Gospel along with us, and also with all men thirsting for true peace.

Taking into account the immensity of the hardships which still afflict a large section of humanity, and with a view to fostering everywhere the justice and love of Christ for the poor, the Council suggests that it would be most opportune to create some organization of the universal Church whose task it would be to arouse the Catholic community to promote the progress of areas which are in want and foster social justice between nations.

CONCLUSION

ROLE OF INDIVIDUAL CHRISTIANS AND OF LOCAL CHURCHES

91. Drawn from the treasures of the teaching of the Church, the proposals of this Council are intended for all men, whether they believe in God or whether they do not explicitly acknowledge him; they are intended to help them to a keener awareness of their own destiny, to make the world conform better to the surpassing dignity of man, to strive for a more deeply rooted sense of universal brotherhood, and to meet the pressing appeals of our times with a generous and common effort of love.

Faced with the wide variety of situations and forms of human culture in the world, this conciliar program is deliberately general on many points; indeed, while the teaching presented is that already accepted in the Church, it will have to be pursued further and amplified because it often deals with matters which are subject to continual development. Still, we have based our proposals on the Word of God and the Spirit of the Gospel. Hence we entertain the hope that many of our suggestions will succeed in effectively assisting all people, especially after they have been adapted to different nations and mentalities and put into practice by the faithful under the direction of their pastors.

DIOLOGUE BETWEEN ALL MEN

92. In virtue of its mission to enlighten the whole world with the message of the Gospel and gather together in one Spirit all men of every nation, race and culture, the Church

shows itself as a sign of the spirits of brotherhood which renders possible sincere dialogue and strengthens it.

Such a mission requires us first of all to create in the Church itself mutual esteem, reverence and harmony, and acknowledge all legitimate diversity; in this way all who constitute the one people of God will be able to engage in ever more fruitful dialogue, whether they are pastors or other members of the faithful. For the ties which unite the faithful together are stronger than those which separate them: let there be unity in what is necessary, freedom in what is doubtful, and charity in everything.[1]

At the same time our thoughts go out to those brothers and communities not yet living in full communion with us; yet we are united by our worship of the Father, the Son, and the Holy Spirit and the bonds of love. We are also mindful that the unity of Christians is today awaited and longed for by many non-believers. For the more this unity is realized in truth and charity under the powerful impulse of the Holy Spirit, the more it will be a harbinger of unity and peace throughout the whole world. Let us, then, join our forces and modify our methods in a way suitable and effective today for achieving this lofty goal, and let us pattern ourselves daily more and more after the spirit of the Gospel and work together in a spirit of brotherhood to serve the human family which has been called to become in Christ Jesus the family of the sons of God.

Our thoughts also go out to all who acknowledge God and who preserve precious religious and human elements in their traditions; it is our hope that frank dialogue will spur us all on to receive the impulses of the Spirit with fidelity and act upon them with alacrity.

For our part, our eagerness for such dialogue, conducted with appropriate discretion and leading to truth by way of love alone, excludes nobody; we would like to include those who respect outstanding human values without realizing who the author of those values is, as well as those who oppose the Church and persecute it in various ways. Since God the Father is the beginning and the end of all things, we are all called to be brothers; we ought to work together without violence and without deceit to build up the world in a spirit of genuine peace.

1. Cf. John XXIII, Litt. Encycl. *Ad Petri Cathedram*, 29 June 1959: *AAS* 55 (1959), p. 513.

A WORLD TO BE BUILT UP AND BROUGHT TO FULFILMENT

93. Mindful of the words of the Lord: "By this all men will know that you are my disciples, if you have love for one another" (Jn. 13:35), Christians can yearn for nothing more ardently than to serve the men of this age with an ever growing generosity and success. Holding loyally to the Gospel, enriched by its resources, and joining forces with all who love and practice justice, they have shouldered a weighty task here on earth and they must render an account of it to him who will judge all men on the last day. Not everyone who says "Lord, Lord," will enter the kingdom of heaven, but those who do the will of the Father,[2] and who manfully put their hands to the work. It is the Father's will that we should recognize Christ our brother in the persons of all men and love them with an effective love, in word and in deed, thus bearing witness to the truth; and it is his will that we should share with others the mystery of his heavenly love. In this way men all over the world will awaken to a lively hope (the gift of the Holy Spirit) that they will one day be admitted to the haven of surpassing peace and happiness in their homeland radiant with the glory of the Lord.

"Now to him who by the power at work within us is able to do far more abundantly than all that we ask or think, to him be glory in the Church and in Christ Jesus to all generations, for ever and ever. Amen" (Eph. 3:20–21).

2. Cf. Mt. 7:21.

56

ON DIALOGUE WITH UNBELIEVERS[a]

S.U., *Humanae Personae Dignitatem*, 28 August, 1968

The Document published by the Secretariat for Unbelievers
is intended, as the character of the Secretariat would suggest, to promote dialogue between believers and unbelievers
and to bring it to a successful conclusion, for this is in the
nature of dialogue. It thus explains the nature of dialogue,
as it is distinguished from other forms of contact between
believers and unbelievers. It outlines the essential conditions
of dialogue and the norms which this implies.

Dialogue as this Document understands it does not necessarily have an apostolic purpose. At the same time, for the
Christian it involves bearing witness to his own belief and
thus in its own way it is part of the Church's proclamation
of the Gospel. Further, it can happen that dialogue with
unbelievers can lead believers not only to a fuller knowledge of human values but also to a better understanding of
religious matters.

The Document is intended primarily for Christians, and
for that reason it draws a good deal on ecclesiastical documents which touch on our subject. However, it explains
what is involved in dialogue in a way that unbelievers can
understand and accept.

INTRODUCTION

1. Modern man increasingly acknowledges the dignity
and worth of the human person, in view of the general
progress of human culture and of society and in spite of
anxieties about the way the modern world is developing.

Largely because of more frequent contacts with each other, men have become aware of pluralism and indeed have
come to see it as the hallmark of our age. True pluralism,
however, is impossible unless men and communities of different origins and culture undertake dialogue.[1]

a. Translated by Austin Flannery, o.p., from *AAS* 60 (1968), pp.
692–704.
1. Constitution on the Church in the Modern World, n. 43.

As we read in the Encyclical *Ecclesiam suam*: dialogue "is demanded nowadays by the prevalent understanding of the relationship between the sacred and the profane. It is demanded by the dynamic course of action which is changing the face of modern society. It is demanded by the pluralism of society, and by the maturity man has reached in this day and age. Be he religious or not, his secular education has enabled him to think and speak, and to conduct a dialogue with dignity."[2]

Thus dialogue, insofar as it relies on mutual relationships between the participants, demands that each party acknowledge the dignity and worth of the other person.

Christians find a richer motivation, in man's supernatural vocation, for acknowledging his worth and dignity. Further, because of the Incarnation the Church is aware how important it is, indeed how much it is part of its own task, to humanize the temporal order.

All Christians should do their best to promote dialogue between men of every class, as a duty of fraternal charity suited to our progressive and adult age.[3]

"The Church," as the Second Vatican Council declares, "by virtue of its mission to enlighten the entire world by preaching the Gospel and to unify in spirit men of every nation, race and culture, is a sign of that brotherhood which makes sincere dialogue possible and strengthens it."[4]

However, the nature and purpose of dialogue does not exclude other forms of communication, such as, among others, apologetics, contention and controversy, nor does it rule out the defense of the rights of the human person. In general, however, an open and benevolent mind, which is the foundation of dialogue, is needed for all social contact.

Such an attitude demands that a person "show consideration and esteem for others, and understanding and kindness."[5] This cannot be unless the other person is freely seen and accepted as "other."

Lastly, the willingness to engage in dialogue is the measure and the strength of that general renewal which must be carried out in the Church, which implies a still greater appreciation of liberty. "The search for truth," as the Second

2. Ibid., ch. 3, n. 78.
3. Decree on the Apostolate of the Laity, n. 7.
4. Constitution on the Church in the Modern World, n. 92.
5. Encyclical Letter, *Ecclesiam suam*, n. 79.

Vatican Council teaches, "must be carried out in a manner that is appropriate to the dignity of the human person and his social nature, namely by free enquiry with the help of teaching or instruction, communication and dialogue. It is by these means that men share with each other the truth they have discovered or think they have discovered in such a way that they help one another in the search for truth. Moreover, it is by personal assent that men must adhere to the truth they have discovered."[6]

2. "The desire for such discussion," as we read in the Constitution on the Church in the Modern World, "which is motivated solely by love of truth, excludes nobody, as far as we are concerned, the dictates of prudence being observed."[7]

The Encyclical Letter *Ecclesiam suam* speaks of three kinds of groups in dialogue in terms of three concentric circles, of varying sizes: first, all mankind, many of whom profess no religion, then those who profess non-Christian religions, and lastly our brother Christians who are not Catholics. In order to institute dialogue with these three categories of people, Paul VI set up three Secretariats: one for the promotion of Christian unity, another for non-Christians, and a third for unbelievers.

If one is to embark on dialogue with unbelievers, special and, in part, new problems arise.[8] Thus at the commencement of dialogue, students of Catholic truth and the benefits of the Christian faith can experience certain difficulties, even though they pursue their enquiries diligently. For this reason, the Secretariat for Unbelievers wishes to offer some reflections and advice, relying on the documents of the Pope and the Council.

Paul VI wrote at length about dialogue under its apostolic aspect in the Encyclical Letter *Ecclesiam suam*. It is by means of dialogue in that sense that the Church performs its chief function in preaching the Gospel to all men, giving them in a spirit of reverence and love the gift of grace and truth which Christ deposited with it.

The Pastoral Constitution *Gaudium et spes* discusses dialogue with the world as such. The preaching of the Gospel is not immediately in question here. Rather it is the dia-

6. Declaration on Religious Liberty, n. 3.
7. Constitution on the Church in the Modern World, n. 92.
8. Ibid., n. 19.

logue which Christians wish to establish with men who do not share their faith, either in order to search together for the truth in different areas, or in order to solve the more urgent problems of our day by social action. The following is offered as an examination of dialogue between the Church and the world in that sense.

I. ON THE NATURE AND CONDITIONS OF DIALOGUE

1. On dialogue in general

In general, dialogue here means any form of getting together and communication between persons, groups or communities, in a spirit of sincerity, reverence for persons, and a certain trust, in order to achieve either a greater grasp of truth or more human relationships.

Dialogue is of greater importance and is more difficult when it takes place between people of different and even sometimes opposing opinions. They try to dispel each other's prejudiced opinions and to increase, as much as they are able, consensus between themselves. Their objective may be simply interrelationships between men, the search for truth, or cooperation in some activity.

All of these elements are present in every form of dialogue, but since one or other element can predominate, it is possible to distinguish three forms of dialogue, seen as attempting to reach:

an agreement, to be established only in terms of human relationships, destined to liberate those engaged in discussion from their solitude and their mutual distrust, and to induce a truer fellow-feeling, mutual reverence and esteem;

an agreement, to be established in the realm of truth, involving discussion of problems of the greatest importance to those engaged in dialogue, and the achievement by common effort of a better grasp of the truth and an extension of knowledge;

an agreement, to be reached in the realm of action, establishing the conditions under which certain set objectives may be achieved, in spite of ideological differences.

Although it is to be hoped that dialogue would be pursued for all three reasons at once, it remains true that each form retains its own power of establishing interpersonal relationships.

Every form of dialogue, insofar as the participants are involved in mutual give and take, involves a certain reciprocity. In this it differs from teaching, which enriches the pupil-partner to dialogue. However, dialogue can be called a true form of teaching, since it is able to provide the benefit of doctrine for very many men. Dialogue is also, implicitly, a proclamation of the Gospel.

Further, dialogue as here understood differs from contention and controversy, in which each participant aims to defend his own side and prove that the other side is in error.

Further, dialogue is not the same as confrontation. For the object of dialogue is that one side should come closer to the other side and should understand it better. Lastly, while each party to dialogue may legitimately hope to persuade the other that he is right, the fact remains that this is not the purpose of dialogue, but rather mutual enrichment.

II. ON DOCTRINAL DIALOGUE

1. Can such dialogue be justified?

The possibility of doctrinal dialogue is often doubted. The question is asked whether one has to set all truth aside in order to have sincere dialogue and whether one needs an indefinitely searching mind if dialogue is to be open. It is further asked whether, if one accepts absolute truth, dialogue is possible when one is persuaded of the possibility of possessing it. It would seem to be a prerequisite for dialogue that one doubts about absolute truth.

Further, can dialogue be instituted if the parties to it accept two different thought-systems? If every affirmation makes full sense only in the context of an integral system, can one have real scope for dialogue if the disputants speak in the context of different thought-systems?

Further, it follows from the analysis of truth which many hold today that truth is immanent to man and depends on man and on his liberty, in such wise that there is no place for truth which does not originate in man. In that situation dialogue can have no foundation, since Christians reject the principle of immanentism and accept a different notion, that of absolute truth.

Further, with regard to public dialogue, it is asked if it is permissible to expose the faith of the masses, who are insufficiently prepared for controversy, to danger.

We put forward the following remarks as a contribution toward solving these problems:

Doctrinal dialogue should be initiated with courage and sincerity, with the greatest freedom and with reference. It focuses on doctrinal questions which are of concern to the parties to dialogue. They have different opinions but by common effort they try to improve mutual understanding, to clarify matters on which they agree, and if possible to enlarge the areas of agreement. In this way the parties to dialogue can enrich each other.

On the other hand, it is characteristic of dialogue to direct its attention to those personal traits which affect men's grasp of truth. Thus there is need to take into account each participant's condition, his special characteristics, the limits within which his grasp of the truth is confined. Individuals and historical communities are limited in this way and an understanding of these limits will open men's hearts to a consideration of other men's opinions and strivings and to acceptance of what is true in every opinion.

On the other hand, dialogue as search for truth will be valueless unless the participants accept that the human mind can, at least to some extent, attain objective truth, that it is always capable of grasping some portion of the truth even if it is perhaps intertwined with error. Lastly, individual men grasp reality, each in his own and indeed unique way; consequently they are in a position to offer help in the search for truth, and others must rely on this help.

That truth is possible is an affirmation, therefore, which is not merely in harmony with dialogue, but is its necessary condition. When engaging in dialogue, there must be no ambiguity about truth, as though it could be postponed until after dialogue, as some false forms of irenicism seem to do. Indeed, dialogue should originate in the common moral obligation on all to seek the truth, especially in the realm of religious problems.

Further, although each of the participants thinks that he is in possession of the truth, this does not invalidate dialogue. Such conviction is not contrary to the nature of dialogue, for dialogue begins from two different positions, which it attempts to clarify and as far as possible to bring closer together. It is enough if each participant judges that his knowledge of the truth can increase as a result of dialogue with the other.

This attitude must be adopted and developed by believers with the utmost sincerity. The truths of faith, since they are revealed by God, are in themselves absolute and perfect. However, they are always imperfectly grasped by believers, who can increase their understanding of them and can meditate further on them. Further, not everything that Christians accept comes from revelation. Dialogue with unbelievers can help them to distinguish between what comes from revelation and what comes from elsewhere. It can also help them to examine the signs of the times in the light of revelation.

Nor does their Christian faith excuse believers from examining in the light of reason the rational presuppositions to belief. Indeed, the Christian is driven to accept whatever is rightly postulated by human reason, since his faith assures him that faith can never contradict reason. Lastly, the Christian knows that faith cannot supply all the answers to every question in dispute. But from faith he knows how such questions should be discussed and in what spirit, especially in temporal affairs, where the field is wide open for enquiry.[9]

With regard to the difficulty arising out of the internal cohesion of a system of thought: one must remember that one has dialogue where the participants agree on certain matters only. If in any system there are certain truths and values which do not necessarily derive their meaning and importance from the system itself and can be separated from it, it is enough if this is brought to light in order to have a certain consensus.

Even between men who are separated by the greatest diversity of opinion, it is possible to discover certain headings for agreement and communication. Taking the internal cohesion of systems into account, therefore, it is possible to distinguish degrees of dialogue, since dialogue can be undertaken in one area rather than in another. Specifically, it should be recalled that human affairs have their own legiti-

9. Ibid., n. 91.

mate autonomy[10] and that consequently disagreement on religious matters does not necessarily impede the emergence of a certain consensus on temporal matters.

It cannot, of course, be denied that dialogue is made more difficult if the parties to dialogue have different notions of truth and do not agree on the very principles of reason. If this happens, it will be the object of dialogue to try to arrive at whatever notion of truth and whatever principles all the participants can accept. If this cannot be achieved, it does not follow that the dialogue has been of no use. It is no small thing to establish the boundaries beyond which progress is impossible. For dialogue should not be initiated for just any reason.

The danger of confrontation can scarcely be avoided in today's pluralist society. Hence the need to prepare the faithful against this danger, especially in public discussion. If this is properly done, it can contribute in no small measure to building a more mature faith. Further, in public discussion the participants are given the opportunity of putting forward their teaching to the listeners, whom they could not have reached in any other way.

Dialogue between believers and unbelievers does indeed carry some danger. But it is not only possible, but to be encouraged. Dialogue can be undertaken with regard to all subjects which are open to human reason, such as philosophy, religion, morals, history, politics, social problems, economics, art and culture. The Christian accepts faithfully all spiritual and bodily values, and this bids him acknowledge them wherever he finds them.[11] There can even be dialogue about the values for man's life and culture which flow from truths of the supernatural order.

2. The conditions for doctrinal dialogue

If dialogue is to achieve its aims, it must obey the rules of truth and liberty. It needs sincere truth, thus excluding manipulated doctrinal discussion, discussion which is undertaken for political ends. Many difficulties arise with regard to dialogue with Communist Marxists, because of the close link which they can make between theory and practice. It thus becomes very difficult to distinguish the different

10. Ibid., nn. 36, 59.
11. Ibid., n. 57.

kinds of dialogue, doctrinal dialogue being changed into practical dialogue.

The search for truth also demands the greatest clarity on the part of the participants in stating their own positions and in their discussions, lest words which sound the same have different meanings, in fact, for different listeners, thus obscuring differences rather than settling them. It is essential that participants perceive clearly what sense is given to the same words by each side, so that the discussion can proceed without any ambiguity whatsoever.

Doctrinal discussion requires perceptiveness, both in honestly setting out one's own opinion and in recognizing the truth everywhere, even if the truth demolishes one so that one is forced to reconsider one's own position, in theory and in practice, at least in part.

Discussion is of little use unless it is undertaken by experts. Otherwise the ensuing benefits will not make up for the dangers involved. Lastly, in discussion the truth will prevail by no other means than by the truth itself.[12] Therefore the liberty of the participants must be ensured by law and reverenced in practice.

III. ON DIALOGUE IN PRACTICAL AFFAIRS

Dialogue can also be initiated in order to achieve cooperation between individuals, groups or communities who may at times differ in ideology.

It must be remembered that sometimes undertakings which had their origin in ideologies hostile to the Christian religion can arrive at a state which no longer corresponds with their beginnings.[13] Further, as we said above, differences which set systems at odds with each other when taken in their entirety, do not rule out agreement between the systems on some counts. It is especially true that differences with regard to religion do not exclude agreement on temporal matters which, as the Constitution *Gaudium et spes* has it, are autonomous in their own sphere.

Finally, where there can be no agreement on ideology, it is possible that agreement can be reached with regard to practical matters. Certain conditions must be fulfilled, however, before consensus and cooperation can legitimately be

---

12. Declaration on Religious Liberty, nn. 1, 3.
13. Encyclical Letters *Pacem in terris*, n. 160; *Ecclesiam suam*.

achieved: the object of the dialogue must be good in itself or must be such that good may come from it;[14] the agreement reached between the participants must not jeopardize a greater good, such as the integrity of doctrine, or personal rights such as civil, cultural and religious liberty. In order to establish whether or not such conditions are verified of the dialogue to be undertaken, one must examine what the participants propose to do in the present and in the future, and also what they did in the past.

The usefulness of such cooperation will have to be judged from the different circumstances of time and place. Although it will be for the laity, especially, to make such judgments, it will be for the hierarchy, with due regard for the laity's legitimate liberty and expertise, to oversee and to intervene when it becomes necessary for the defense of religious and moral values.

IV. PRACTICAL RULES

The rules which now follow have their justification in the nature and conditions of dialogue. However, they are of necessity general, because of the different circumstances prevailing in different regions and because it will be for the pastors and faithful to apply the rules to the different cases. For example, one must distinguish between people who still retain ancient Christian traditions, people to whom the Gospel has not yet been preached, and people the majority of whom are Christian but who are ruled by atheistic governments. Further, there will be more fruitful experiments in the future, and from them more suitable rules will be forthcoming. It will be the duty of the episcopal conference in each country to set out general rules adapted to local conditions.

1. Rules for promoting dialogue

In the light of the Second Vatican Council it is to be hoped that public opinion in the Church would present the opportunity, and indeed the very greatest opportunity, for establishing dialogue.

(a) Clerics should be so imbued with philosophy and theology during their period of formation that "by correctly understanding the modern mind they will be prepared to

14. Encyclical Letter, *Mater et Magistra.*

enter into dialogue with their contemporaries."[15] With regard to unbelievers, future priests should be properly informed about the principal forms of unbelief, especially those which are to be found in their own regions. They should also be taught the nature and the philosophical and theological foundations of dialogue. These should be imparted more fully and more fruitfully in universities and in faculties.

(b) In promoting the pastoral renewal of the clergy—by courses, study weeks, conferences, etc.—attention should be given to concrete questions concerning dialogue with unbelievers and which the clergy are liable to encounter.

(c) Further, courses of higher studies on dialogue with unbelievers, special courses for experts, study days or conferences for lay people should be promoted, with particular emphasis on youth and on those who are involved in the Christian apostolate.

(d) Preaching and catechetical formation should take account of this new climate, for which the Church today is especially prepared and ready.

(e) With regard to the study of atheism and the establishment of dialogue: national and diocesan offices should establish some link with the Roman Secretariat and should operate in collaboration with it and under the guidance of the hierarchy. These offices should look for experts among the clergy and laity of both sexes, inviting them to promote enquiries, studies, courses and conferences.

(f) It is to be hoped that true ecumenical cooperation between Catholics and other Christians would be instituted both nationally and internationally.

(g) It is also to be hoped that such cooperation would be forthcoming between Christians and members of non-Christian religions, especially Jews and Muslims.

2. Directives

First of all, one must distinguish between public and private dialogue.

No special ruling can be given on *private* dialogue, apart from prudence and courtesy, which should govern all activities which are truly human and worthy of the name of Christian. By private dialogue is meant a gathering made

15. Decree on Priestly Formation, n. 15.

up of a number of men or groups who come together spontaneously or by invitation. The following suggestions, however, seem helpful:

(a) If a dialogue is to be fully fruitful, the participants should be familiar with the subject under discussion, not only with regard to their own opinions, but also and especially with regard to Christian teaching.

(b) If, however, a Christian participant feels that he is not sufficiently informed, he should ask an expert or send another participant to him.

(c) The seduction of facile irenicism or syncretism should be resisted, lest a participant depart from the true deposit of faith and endanger his own beliefs.

(d) Nor should one underestimate the witness of integrity of life and belief in promoting effective agreement.

With regard to *public* dialogue, greater prudence is required because of its possible powerful effect on public opinion. A public meeting is one which is composed of people who represent the community (not necessarily having a mandate from the community), both the community of believers and of others who hold different or even opposite doctrines and customs. The following general remarks are offered:

(a) Christians who take part in these dialogues, whether they be clerics or laity, should have the qualities listed above for private dialogue. But they must also be expert in doctrine, have moral authority, and be good speakers, as such dialogue demands.

(b) If there is a question of a non-official public dialogue (non-official, in the sense that the authorities are not involved in its organization), it would seem better, to ensure the necessary liberty, that no official be present. The participants, however, must be faithful to the postulates of the communities whom they represent.

(c) An official dialogue (that is, organized by the authorities) cannot be excluded *a priori*. However, it is only rarely that conditions exist in which such dialogue can take place between Christians and unbelievers. The reasons are that often unbelievers represent nobody but themselves, or that there is no homogeneity between the Church on the one hand and a political faction or cultural group on the other. In these circumstances, one should take care that all equivocation is avoided with regard to the purpose and the nature of the dialogue and the willingness to cooperate.

(d) Dialogue is to be undertaken only if the circumstances of place and time favor true dialogue. One must therefore avoid making it too much of an occasion and having people present who are insufficiently prepared and who might disturb the serenity of the discussion, reducing it to laughter or comedy. In general, dialogue is more beneficial among a small group of experts. Sometimes the rules of dialogue should be laid down beforehand. Lastly, it is better not to engage in dialogue if it is obvious that a faction is using it for its own purposes.

(e) Similarly, to avoid dissensions and scandals, sometimes it will be proper to publish a declaration beforehand making clear in what sense, about what subject, and to what purpose the dialogue is initiated.

(f) Priests should obtain the consent of their own ordinary and of the ordinary of the place where the dialogue is scheduled. All Christians should obey the instructions of the ecclesiastical authority. The authority must respect the legitimate liberty of the laity in temporal affairs and in the general conditions of life in which they live.

Apart from spoken dialogue, there is also written dialogue, which can take place between believers and unbelievers in reviews and newspapers and in pamphlets.

That kind of public dialogue requires greater care because of the publicity and the greater diffusion of the written word: consequently, it places a greater onus on the conscience of the faithful who take part in it. On the other hand, it is easier here to guard against the dangers of ignorance and haste. It is to be hoped that when they engage in that sort of dialogue, all Christians involved would give their typescripts beforehand to experts. For the rest, all the faithful will observe the canonical regulations in this matter.

DESCRIPTIVE CATALOGUE OF THE MORE IMPORTANT POST-CONCILIAR DOCUMENTS

BISHOPS

See also A. 14, 15, 16, 21, 23.

1. *30 Nov., 1963*, Paul VI, Apostolic Letter, PASTOR-ALE MUNUS, given Motu Proprio, granting certain faculties and privileges to bishops, A.A.S., LVI (1964), 5–12.

2. *15 Sept., 1965*, Paul VI, Apostolic Letter, APOSTO-LICA SOLLICITUDO, given Motu Proprio, establishing the synod of bishops. A.A.S., LVII (1965), 775–778.

3. *15 June, 1966*, Paul VI, Apostolic Letter, DE EPIS-COPORUM MUNERIBUS, given Motu Proprio, containing the regulations governing the granting of dispensations by bishops in accordance with the decree on the Pastoral Office of Bishops, *Christus Dominus*, A.A.S., LVIII (1966), 467–472.

4. **6 August, 1966*, Paul VI, Apostolic Letter, ECCLE-SIAE SANCTAE, I, given Motu Proprio, with the norms for implementing the decree on the Pastoral Office of Bishops, *Christus Dominus*. There are three sections to *Ecclesiae Sanctae*, the norms for implementing the decrees on bishops and on priests together form the first section, (Ecclesiae Sanctae I), while sections two and three are on religious (E.S. II) and missions (E.S. III) respectively, A.A.S. LVII (1966), 757–775. (See A. 152, 182)

5. *8 Dec., 1966* S.S., regulations for conducting the synod of bishops, A.A.S., LIX (1967), 91–103.

6. *24 June, 1969*, C.C.P.A., revised and augmented regulations for conducting the synod of bishops, A.A.S. LXI (1969), 525–539.

7. *15 August, 1969*, Paul VI, Apostolic Letter, PASTOR-ALIS MIGRATORUM CURA, given Motu Proprio, promulgating new norms for the pastoral care of migrants (see A. 8), A.A.S., LXI (1969), 601–603.

8. *22 August, 1969*, S.C.B., Instruction, NEMO EST, on the Pastoral Care of Migrants. A.A.S. LXI (1969), 614–643 (See also A.1 and 28).

9. *27 March, 1969*, S.C.C., General Directory, PERE-GRINANS IN TERRA, on the Pastoral care of tourists, A.A.S., LXI (1969) 361–384. (See A. 132)

10. *28 December, 1970*, S.T.A.S., Circular Letter to Presidents of Episcopal Conferences on Ecclesiastical Tri-

bunals, INTER CETERA, A.A.S., LXIII (1971) 480–486.

11. *28 December, 1970,* S.T.A.S., Norms, UT CAUS-ARUM JUDICIALIUM, for interdiocesan or regional and for inter-regional tribunals: A.A.S. LXIII (1971), 436–492.

12. *11 April, 1971,* S.C.C., General Catechetical Directory, AD NORMAM DECRETI, A.A.S., LXIV (1972), 97–176.

13. *20 August, 1971,* C.C.P.A., Revisions and additions to the regulations for conducting the synod of bishops, A.A.S., LXIII (1971), 702–704.

CATHOLIC EASTERN CHURCHES

See also A. 2, 5, 6, 13, 202.

14. *11 Feb. 1965,* Paul VI, Apostolic Constitution, AD PURPURATORUM PATRUM, on the place of Oriental Patriarchs in the college of Cardinals, A.A.S. LVII (1965), 295–296.

15. *2 May, 1967,* Paul VI, Apostolic Letter, EPISCO-PALIS POTESTAS, given Motu Proprio, containing the regulations governing the granting of dispensations by Eastern bishops in accordance with the decree on the pastoral office of bishops, *CHRISTUS DOMINUS,* A.A.S., LIX (1967), 385–390.

16. *25 March, 1970,* S.C.O.C., declaration on relations between Eastern bishops and their patriarchs, A.A.S. LXII (1970) 179.

CURIA, THE ROMAN

17. *2 April, 1964,* Paul IV, Apostolic Letter, IN FRUC-TIBUS MULTIS, given Motu Proprio, establishing pontifical commission for means of social communication (the media). A.A.S. LVI (1964), 289–292.

18. *19 May, 1964,* S.S., Letter, PROGREDIENTE CONCILIO, from the Cardinal Secretary of State announcing that Pope Paul VI had established a secretariat for non-Christians, A.A.S., LVI (1964), 560.

19. *26 Feb. 1965,* Paul VI, Apostolic Letter, SACRO CARDINALIUM CONSILIO, stating that the dean and sub-dean of the college of Cardinals would be elected instead of the offices going to the next seniors, A.A.S., LVII (1965) 296–297.

20. *7 December, 1965.* Paul VI, Apostolic Letter, INTE-

GRAE SERVANDAE, reforming the Holy Office and changing its name to the Sacred Congregation for the Doctrine of the Faith, A.A.S., LVII (1965) 952–955. (See also A. 24)

21. *3 Jan., 1966,* Paul VI, Apostolic Letter, FINIS CONCILIO, given Motu Proprio, establishing five post-conciliar commissions: on bishops, religious, missions, Christian education, the apostolate of the laity. It recalls that the following bodies with similar objectives (the implementation of the council's directives) were already in existence and would continue to function: on the liturgy, the media, the reform of canon law, Christian unity, non-Christian religions, non-believers: A.A.S., LVIII (1966), 37–40.

22. *7 Jan. 1967,* Paul VI, Apostolic Letter, *CATHOLICAM CHRISTI ECCLESIAM,* establishing a Council on the Laity and a Commission of experts on Justice and Peace: A.A.S., LIX (1967), 25–28.

23. *6 Aug., 1967,* Paul VI, Apostolic Letter, PRO COMPERTO SANE, given Motu Proprio, co-opting diocesan bishops on to the Roman Curia: A.A.S., LIX, (1967), 881–884.

24. *15 August, 1967,* Paul VI, Apostolic Constitution, REGIMINI ECCLESIAE UNIVERSAE, one of two major documents reorganizing the Roman Curia. According to the document, there are two bodies with central competence, the Secretariat of State, or Papal Secretariat, and the Council for the Church's Public Affairs; there are nine "congregations", dealing respectively with "the Doctrine of the Faith", "Eastern Churches", "Bishops", "the discipline of the Sacraments", "Rites", "the Clergy", "Religious and Secular Institutes", "Catholic Education", "the Evangelization of Peoples, or Propaganda Fidei". Of these, "Rites" was later split in two (see A. 26). There are three "secretariats": "for promoting Christian Unity", "for non-Christians" and "for non-believers". There are the "Council on the Laity" and the "Commission for Justice and Peace" (see A. 22). The remaining bodies are: "The Supreme Tribunal of the Signatura Apostolica", which has a supervisory function with regard to legal processes, including marriage cases, and justice in general in the Church; it judges appeals against ecclesiastical decisions and adjudicates if there is a conflict with regard to the scope of different Roman congregations; the "Roman Rota" adjudicates on the nullity of marriages; the "Apostolic Penitentiary" is concerned with

matters of conscience—absolution, dispensations, indulgences, etc.; the "Apostolic Chancellery" (later merged with the Secretariat of State: see below, A. 32), sends out apostolic constitutions, decretal letters, apostolic letters, etc., and has charge of the "leaden seal" and the "fisherman's ring"; the "Prefecture for the Holy See's Economic Affairs" does as its title suggests; the "Apostolic Chamber" looks after the temporal affairs of the Holy See between the death of a Pope and the election of his successor; the "Administration of the Patrimony of the Apostolic See" administers the property of the Holy See—whereas the "Prefecture for economic affairs" is the ministry of finance; the "Prefecture of the Apostolic Palace" regulates audiences and protocol at home and away from the Vatican; the "Statistics Office" compiles and analyzes statistics on the life of the Church: A.A.S., LIX (1967), 885–928. (See also A. 20, 21, 22, 23, 25, 26, 28, 30, 31, 32, 33)

25. *22 Feb. 1968*, S.S.: The General Regulations for the Roman Curia—recruitment, promotion, transfers, holidays, discipline, types of meetings of congregations, etc. A.A.S., LX (1968) 129–176.

26. *7 May, 1969*, Paul VI: Apostolic Constitution, SACRA RITUUM CONGREGATIO, which divided the Congregation of Rites in two: The Sacred Congregation for Divine Worship and the Sacred Congregation for the Causes of the Saints (i.e. beatification, canonization): A.A.S., LXI (1969), 297–305.

27. *24 June, 1969*, Paul VI: Apostolic Constitution, SOLLICITUDO OMNIUM ECCLESIARUM, given Motu Proprio, on the duties of papal nuncios: A.A.S., LXI (1969), 473–484.

28. *19 March, 1970*, Paul VI, Apostolic Letter, APOSTOLICAE CARITATIS, given Motu Proprio, establishing a pontifical commission on the spiritual care of migrants and travellers: A.A.S., LXII (1970), 193–197. (See also A. 7 and 8)

29. *21 Nov., 1970*, Paul VI, Apostolic Letter, INGRAVESCENTEM AETATEM, given Motu Proprio, on retirement ages for cardinals: at 75, they are asked to offer to retire from the charge of Roman congregations, etc., if they are in charge, but not from membership of the Roman curia: it is for the Pope to accept their resignation or not; at 80 they cease to be members of the Roman curia (they do

not cease to be cardinals), but they may no longer vote in papal elections: A.A.S., LXII (1970), 810–813.

30. *15 July, 1971,* Paul VI, Letter, AMORIS OFFICIO, establishing Pontifical Council, "Cor Unum", for promoting human and Christian progress in Rome: A.A.S., LXIII (1971) 669–673.

31. *13 Jan., 1973,* S.S. Announcement that the Holy Father had established a "Committee on the Family", for an experimental period of three years, its task being "to study the spiritual, moral and social problems of the family, in a pastoral context." A.A.S., LXV (1973), 60–61.

32. *27 Feb., 1973,* Paul VI, Apostolic Letter, QUO APTIUS ROMANAE CURIAE, given Motu Proprio, transferring the Apostolic Chancellery (see above, A. 24) to the Secretariat of State: A.A.S., LXV (1973), 113–116.

33. *15 July, 1973,* S.S., Rescript announcing that the Congregation for the Discipline of the Sacraments, alone, would in future deal with petitions for nullity in cases of non-consummated marriage involving a baptized and a non-baptized partner: A.A.S., LXV (1973), 602.

34. *4 Feb., 1974,* S.S., Rescript describing the obligation not to divulge papal secrets and the extent of the obligation: A.A.S., LXVI (1974), 89–92.

34a. *21 July, 1975,* Paul VI, Apostolic Constitution, CONSTANS NOBIS, merging the S. Congregation for Divine Worship and the S. Congregation for the Discipline of the Sacraments into one, the S. Congregation for the Sacraments and Divine Worship, *Osservatore Romano,* 18 July, 1975.

THE DIVINE OFFICE

See also A. 106, 116, 124, 133, 137, 140, 141, 143, 205.

35. *1 Nov., 1970,* Paul VI, Apostolic Constitution, LAUDIS CANTICUM, announcing the completion of the reform of the divine office and approving it, A.A.S., LXIII (1971), 527–535.

36. *2 Feb., 1971,* S.C.D.W., Decree, CUM EDITIO, promulgating the General Instruction on the Liturgy of the Hours, published in the book containing the Latin original of the General Instruction.

37. *11 April, 1971,* S.C.D.W., Decree, HORARUM LITURGIA, announcing the publication of the "Liturgy of the Hours", *Liturgia Horarum,* and stating that it is the "editio typica", A.A.S., LXIII (1971) 712.

ECUMENISM

See also A. 21.

38. *7 December, 1965, Joint declaration by Pope Paul VI and Patriarch Athenagoras I, consigning to oblivion the excommunications of 1054 and lifting the anathemas between Rome and Constantinople: A.A.S. LVIII (1966), 20–21.

39. 7 December, 1965 Paul VI, Apostolic Letter, AMBULATE IN DILECTIONE, on the duty of charity to the Church of Constantinople: A.A.S., LVII (1966), 40–41.

40. *18 March, 1966, S.C.D.F.: Instruction, MATRIMONII SACRAMENTUM, on mixed marriages: A.A.S., LVIII (1966), 235–239.

41. *24 March, 1966, Joint declaration by Pope Paul VI and Michael Ramsey, Archbishop of Canterbury: A.A.S., LVII (1966), 286–288.

42. *22 Feb., 1967, S.C.O.C.: Decree, CRESCENTS MATRIMONIORUM, on mixed marriages between Roman Catholics and baptized oriental non-Catholics: A.A.S., LIX (1967), 165–166.

43. *14 May, 1967, S.P.U.C.: Directory on ecumenism, AD TOTAM ECCLESIAM, part one: A.A.S., LIX (1967), 574–592.

44. 25 July, 1967, Paul VI, Letter to the Patriarch Athenagoras, ANNO INEUNTE, on unity: A.A.S., LIX (1967), 652–654.

45. 28 October, 1967, Joint declaration by Pope Paul VI and the Patriarch Athenagoras on fostering unity: A.A.S., LIX (1967), 1054–1055.

46. *7 Jan., 1970, S.P.U.C.: Declaration, DANS CES DERNIERS TEMPS, on the position of the Catholic Church on the celebration of the Eucharist in common by Christians of different confessions. A.A.S., LXII (1970), 184–188.

47. *7 Jan., 1970, Paul VI, Apostolic Letter, MATRIMONIA MIXTA, given Motu Proprio, on mixed marriages: A.A.S., LXII (1970), 257–263.

48. *16 April, 1970, S.P.U.C.: Directory on ecumenism, part two, SPIRITUS DOMINI: Ecumenism in Higher Education: A.A.S., LXII (1970), 715–724.

49. *12 May, 1970, Joint declaration by Pope Paul VI and Vasken I Catholicos, Supreme Patriarch of the Arme-

nians, on the promotion of unity between their churches: A.A.S., LXII (1970), 416–417.

50. *15 August, 1970, S.P.U.C.: Reflections and suggestions concerning ecumenical dialogue, not published in the A.A.S., but issued to episcopal conferences by the Secretariat for Promoting Christian Unity.

51. *1 June, 1972, S.P.U.C.: Instruction on admitting other Christians to eucharistic communion in the Catholic Church, IN QUIBUS RERUM CIRCUMSTANTIIS, A.A.S., LXIV (1972), 518–525.

52. *17 October, 1973, S.P.U.C.: Note, DOPO LA PUBBLICAZIONE, interpreting the "Instruction on admitting other Christians to eucharistic communion": A.A.S., LXV (1973), 616–619.

52a. 22 Feb., 1975, S.P.U.C.: Ecumenical Collaboration at the Regional, National and Local Levels, document issued by the S.P.U.C. Italian Text in Oss. Rom., 7-8 July, 1975.

THE EUCHARIST

See also A. 46, 51, 52, 102, 103, 107, 112, 114, 122, 124, 125, 132, 133, 134, 138, 142, 144.

53. 25 April, 1964, S.C.R., Decree, QUO ACTUOSIUS, introducing the formula, "The Body of Christ" in the distribution of Holy Communion, A.A.S., LVI (964), 337–338.

54. 21 Nov., 1964, announcement, ATTENTIS MULTARUM, at a public session of the ecumenical council that the eucharistic fast had been reduced to one hour before Holy Communion, for priests and laity, A.A.S., LVII (1965), 186.

55. 27 Jan., 1965, S.C.R., Decree, NUPER EDITA INSTRUCTIO, announcing the publication of "The Order of the Mass and the Rite to be observed in the celebration of Mass" and "On defects occurring in the celebration of Mass". It incorporates the changes introduced in the instruction, Inter oecumenici, A.A.S., LVII (1965), 408–409.

56. *7 March, 1965, S.C.R., Decree, ECCLESIAESEMPER, announcing the publication of the rite of concelebration and of communion under both kinds, A.A.S., LVII (1965), 410–142. (See A. 79, 129).

57. 3 Sept., 1965, Paul VI, encyclical letter, MYSTERIUM FIDEI, on the doctrine and worship of the eucharist, A.A.S., LVII (1965), 753–774.

58. *25 Sept., 1965*, S.C.R., Letter, IMPETRATA PRIUS, that when the Mass of the Sunday or holyday obligation is celebrated the evening before, it should be the Mass of the Sunday or the holyday and there should be a homily and prayers of the faithful, Notitiae, 1966, 14.

59. *14 Feb., 1966*, S.C.R., Decree, CUM HAC NOS-TRA AETATE, on administering holy communion in hospitals, A.A.S., LVIII (1966), 525–526.

60. *24 Feb., 1967*, S.C.R., Declaration, TRICENARIO GREGORIANO, that a series of Gregorian Masses may be resumed, without repeating the Masses already celebrated, after an interruption caused by illness or pastoral duty, A.A.S., LIX (1967), 229–230.

61. *18 May, 1967*, S.C.R., Decree, PER INSTRUCTI-ONEM ALTERAM, announcing the publication of "Changes to be made in the order of the Mass", implementing the directives of the second instruction, *Tres abhinc annos*, Notitiae, 1967, 195.

62. *25 May, 1967*, S.C.R., Instruction, EUCHARISTI-CUM MYSTERIUM, on the worship of the eucharistic mystery, A.A.S., LIX (1967), 539–573.

63. *10 August, 1967*, C.P.I.C.L., Letter, AUSSITOT APRES, on translating the canon of the Mass, Notitiae, 1967, 326–327.

64. *23 May, 1968*, S.C.R., Decree, PRECE EUCHARIS-TICA, promulgating three new eucharistic prayers and eight new prefaces, Notitiae, 1968, 156.

65. *3 April, 1969*, Paul VI, Apostolic Constitution, MIS-SALE ROMANUM, announcing the reform of the Roman Missal, A.A.S., LXI (1969) 217–222.

66. *6 April, 1969*, S.C.R., Decree, ORDINE MISSAE, announcing the publication of the "Order of the Mass" and the General Instruction on the Roman Missal, Notitiae, 1969, 147.

67. *15 May, 1969*, S.C.D.W., Instruction, ACTIO PAS-TORALIS ECCLESIAE, on Masses for special gatherings, A.A.S., LXI (1969) 806–811.

68. *25 May 1969*, S.C.D.W., Decree, ORDINEM LEC-TIONUM, announcing the publication of the new series of readings at Mass, A.A.S. LXI (1969), 848–849.

69. *29 May, 1969*, S.C.D.W., Instruction, MEMORI-ALE DOMINI, on the manner of administering Holy Communion: A.A.S., LXI (1969), 541–547.

70. *20 Oct., 1969*, S.C.D.W.: Instruction, CONSTITU-

TIONE APOSTOLICA, on arranging the gradual implementation of the Apostolic Constitution, *Missale Romanum*: A.A.S., LXI (1969), 749–753.

71. *10 Nov., 1969*, S.C.D.W.: Letter, CUM NONNULLAE, stating it is no longer necessary to publish the Latin text of the Roman missal, as had been prescribed in the Instruction, Inter Oecumenici, n. 57(c), for missals for liturgical use. However, the letter says that as a help for priests who do not know the vernacular language, such missals should carry the ordinary of the Mass and some propers, in Latin: *Notitiae*, 1969, 442.

72. *20 March, 1970*, S.C.D.W.: Decree, CELEBRATIONIS EUCHARISTICAE, promulgating the Latin original of the Roman Missal and declaring it the "editio typica": A.A.S., LXII (1970), 554.

73. **29 June, 1970*, S.C.D.W.: Instruction, SACRAMENTALI COMMUNIONE, allowing more scope for administering Holy Communion under both kinds: A.A.S., LXII (1970) 664–667.

74. *30 Sept., 1970*, S.C.D.W.: Decree, ORDINE LECTIONUM, promulgating the Latin edition of the Lectionary and declaring it the "edito typica": A.A.S., LXII (1971), 710.

75. *25 July, 1970*, S.C.C.: Decree, LITTERIS APOSTOLICIS, stating that a pastor of souls is obliged to celebrate Mass for his people on Sundays and Holy Days of obligation: A.A.S., LXIII (1971), 943–944.

76. *11 Nov., 1971*, S.C.D.W.: Norms to be observed temporarily, pending the publication of the new Roman Missal in the vernacular, with regard to the texts to be used at Mass: *Notitiae*, December, 1971, 379–383.

77. *29 Nov., 1971*, S.S.: Note to the effect that the Holy Father had temporarily reserved to himself all decisions with regard to problems concerning Mass stipends: A.A.S., LXIII (1971), 841.

78. *2 May, 1972*, S.C.D.W.: Declaration on collecting fragments of the eucharist after the celebration of Mass: *Notitiae*, July-August, 1972, 227.

79. **7 August, 1972*, S.C.D.W.: Declaration, IN CELEBRATIONE MISSAE, on concelebration: A.A.S., LXIV (1972), 561–563. (See A. 56, 179)

80. *9 Oct., 1972*, S.C.D.W.: Decree, CUM DE NOMINE, on naming bishops in the eucharistic prayers: A.A.S., LXIV (1972), 692–694.

81. *23 Dec., 1972*, S.C.D.W.: Changes to be made in the General Instruction on the Roman Missal in view of the abolition of the order of subdeacon: *Notitiae,* January, 1973, 34–38. (See A. 170, D. 29)

82. **29 Jan., 1973*, S.C.D.W.: Instruction, IMMENSAE CARITATIS, on facilitating sacramental eucharistic communion in certain circumstances: A.A.S., LXV (1973), 264–271.

FAITH AND DOCTRINE

See also A. 20.

83. **27 April, 1973*, S.C.D.W., Circular Letter, EUCHARISTIAE PARTICIPATIONEM, to presidents of episcopal conferences on the eucharistic prayers: A.A.S., LXV (1973), 340–347.

84. **21 June, 1973*, S.C.D.W., Decree, EUCHARISTIAE SACRAMENTUM, announcing the publication of 'Holy Communion and the Worship of the Eucharist outside of Mass' in Latin and declaring that it is the 'editio typica': A.A.S., LXV (1973), 610.

85. **1 Nov., 1973*, S.C.D.W., Directory, PUEROS BAPTIZOS, on Masses for children: A.A.S., LXVI (1974), 30–46.

86. **13 June, 1974*, Paul VI, Apostolic Letter, FIRMA IN TRADITIONE, concerning Mass stipends: A.A.S., LXVI (1974), 303–311.

87. **28 Oct., 1974*, S.C.D.W., Note, CONFERENTIARUM EPISCOPALIUM, on the obligation to use the new Roman Missal: *Notitiae,* 1974, 353.

88. *1 Nov., 1974*, S.C.D.W., Norms, POSTQUAM DE PRECIBUS, for the use of the eucharistic prayers for children and of the eucharistic prayer for reconciliation: *Notitiae,* 1975, 4–12.

89. *14 June, 1966*, S.C.D.F.: Note, POST LITTERAS APOSTOLICAS, stating that the Index of Prohibited Books no longer has legal force, but retains moral force: A.A.S., LVIII (1966), 445.

90. *24 July, 1966*, S.C.D.F.: Letter to presidents of episcopal conferences, CUM OECUMENICUM CONCILIUM, on bishops' duty to oversee implementation of council and on current errors: A.A.S., LVIII (1966), 659–661.

91. *15 Nov., 1966,* S.C.D.F.: Decree, POST EDITAM NOTIFICATIONEM, on the abrogation of canons 1399 and 2318: A.A.S., LVIII (1966), 1186.

92. *23 Feb., 1967,* S.C.D.F.: Instruction, LITTERIS APOSTOLICIS, inviting bishops to set up doctrinal commissions to help them in judging publications and fostering true religious science: Text in *Vatican II: Pour Construire l'Eglise Nouvelle,* tome 2, 74–77, Cerf. Paris, 1970.

93. *1967* (no further date): S.C.D.F.: New formula for profession of faith, to replace Tridentine profession of faith and anti-modernist oath. Contains Creed and promise to accept the Church's teaching authority: A.A.S., LIX (1969), 1058.

9. *30 June, 1968,* Paul VI, solemn profession of faith (The Credo of the People of God) SOLLEMNI HAC LITURGIA: A.A.S., LX (1968), 433–445.

95. *12 July, 1969,* S.C.D.F.: Experimental statutes for newly-formed theological commission: A.A.S., LXI (1969), 540–541.

96. *15 Jan., 1971,* S.C.D.F.: New procedures for the Congregation of the Doctrine of the Faith in examining suspect teaching: A.A.S., LXIII (1971), 234–236.

97. *27 June, 1971,* Paul VI, Apostolic letter, SEDULA CURA, given Motu Proprio, establishing new regulations for the Pontifical Biblical Commission: A.A.S., LXIII (1971), 665–669.

98. *21 Feb., 1972,* S.C.D.F.: Declaration, MYSTERIUM FILII DEI, in defense of the mysteries of the Incarnation and of the Blessed Trinity against recent errors: A.A.S., LXIV (1972), 237–241.

99. *24 July, 1973,* S.C.D.F.: Declaration, MYSTERIUM ECCLESIAE, on the Catholic doctrine on the Church, against present-day errors: A.A.S., LXV (1973), 396–408.

100. *19 March, 1975,* S.C.D.F.: Decree, ECCLESIAE PASTORIBUS, on the previous censorship of books: *obligatory* for publication of bible, catechisms, text books on religious and moral matters for use in Catholic educational establishments, liturgical book, books on religion or morality displayed for sale or distributed in churches and oratories, obligatory too for priests or religious writing for newspapers or periodicals which clearly and habitually are hostile to the Church; *strongly recommended* to priests and religious writing on religion and morality outside of cases mentioned above (*Oss. Rom.* 5 April 1975).

LAITY, THE

See also A. 22.

101. *3 December, 1971*, C. L. Directory establishing criteria for defining international Catholic institutions, A.A.S. LXIII, (1971), 648–656.

LITURGICAL BOOKS

Note: the following is a list of the Latin originals of the major liturgical books in the order of their publication. The date of publication (of the Latin original) is as given in the decree of promulgation which is published in the book and also in the *Acta Apostolicae Sedis* or in *Notitiae*. However, some books did not actually become available until after the date of promulgation; the publication of the *Lectionary* and of the *Liturgy of the Hours*, each of which comprises several volumes, continued for more than a year in each case after the publication of the first volume.

We list only the complete and final editions of the liturgical books. The revision of the Mass, for example, unfolded gradually, as the number of "interim" liturgical books testify. Further excerpts from liturgical books have been published separately: a "Small Missal", for example, and "Night Prayer". Books like these are not listed.

The liturgico-pastoral introductions, called (in the main) *Praenotanda*, are especially valuable. This is the main reason for listing the liturgical books here, even though most of the introductions are not contained in this collection. They are however easily accessible in good English translations. We give the page references to the Latin originals for the introductions. All of the books are published and printed by the Vatican Polyglot Press.

All of them have been translated or are in process of being translated and published in English.

102. *14 Dec., 1964*, "A Simple Kyrial: *Simplex Kyriale*", a small collection of simple chants used at Mass.

103. *3 Sept., 1967*, "A Simple Gradual: *Simplex Graduale*", a larger collection of Gregorian chants for use in small churches. Praenotanda, pp. vii to xii.

104. *29 June, 1968*, "A Manual of Indulgences: *Enchiridion Indulgentiarum*," Praenotanda, pp. 11 and 12.

105. *15 August, 1968,* "The Ordination of a Deacon, Priest and Bishop: *De ordinatione diaconi, presbytri et episcopi.*"

106. *19 March, 1969,* "The Rite of the Celebration of Marriage: *Ordo celebrandi matrimonium.*" Praenotanda, pp. 7 to 10.

107. *21 March, 1969,* "The Roman Calendar: *Calendarium Romanum*". "Universal Norms on the Liturgical Year and the Calendar", pp. 11 to 22.

108. *15 May, 1969,* "The Rite of Infant Baptism: *Ordo baptismi parvulorum*" Praenotanda, pp. 7 to 22.

109. *25 May, 1969,* "The Order of the Readings at Mass: *Ordo lectionum missae*" (not texts, but references). Praenotanda, pp. ix to xxi.

110. *15 August, 1969,* "The Funeral Rite: *Ordo exsequiarum,*" Praenotanda, pp. 7 to 14.

111. *2 Feb., 1970,* "The Rite of Religious Profession: *Ordo professionis religiosae.*" Praenotanda, pp. 7 to 10.

112. **26 March, 1970,* "The Roman Missal: *Missale Romanum.*" General Instruction on the Roman Missal, pp. 19 to 92.

113. *31 May, 1970,* "The Rite of the Consecration of Virgins: *Ordo consecrationis virginum.*" Praenotanda, pp. 7 to 9.

114. *31 May, 1970,* "The Lectionary: *Lectionarium,*" in three volumes. Praenotanda, vol. 1, pp. 7 to 23.

115. *9 Nov., 1970,* "The Blessing of an Abbot and an Abbess: *Ordo benedictionis abbatis et abbatissae.*" Praenotanda, pp. 7 and 8.

116. *3 Dec., 1970,* "The Rite of the Blessing of the Oil of Catechumens, of the Sick and the Consecration of Chrism: *Ordo benedicendi oleum catechumenorum et infirmorum et conficiendi chrisma.*" Praenotanda, pp. 7 and 8.

117. *11 April, 1971,* "The Liturgy of the Hours: *Liturgia Horarum,*" in four volumes. General Instruction on the Liturgy of the Hours, pp. 19–92.

118. *22 August, 1971,* "The Rite of Confirmation: *Ordo confirmationis.*" Praenotanda, 16 to 22.

119. *6 Jan., 1972,* "The Rite of the Christian Initiation of Adults: *Ordo initiationis Christianae adultorum.*" Praenotanda, pp. 7 to 30.

120. *3 Dec., 1972,* "On instituting readers and acolytes, on admission to candidacy for diaconate and priesthood, on embracing celibacy: *De institutione lectorum et acolytho-*

rum, de admissione inter candidatos ad diaconatum et presbyteratum, de sacro caelibatu amplectendo.

121. *7 Dec., 1972,* "The Rite of Anointing of the Sick and their Pastoral Care: *Ordo unctionis infirmorum eorumque pastoralis curae."* Praenotanda, pp. 13 to 22.

122. **21 June, 1973,* "On Holy Communion and the Worship of the Eucharistic Mystery outside Mass: *De sacra communione et de cultu mysterii eucharistici extra missam."* Praenotanda, pp. 7 to 15, 36 to 40, 43 to 45.

123. *2 Dec., 1973,* "The Rite of Penance: *Ordo paenitentiae."* Praenotanda, pp. 9 to 25.

LITURGY: GENERAL AND MISCELLANEOUS

See also A. 26, 34a, 35–37, 53–88, 211–234, 155–161, 180, 102–123, 236–239, 247.

124 **25 Jan., 1964,* Paul VI, Apostolic Letter, SACRAM LITURGIAM, given Motu Proprio, on the reform of the liturgy, A.A.S. LVI (1964) 139–140.

125. **26 Sept., 1964,* S.C.R., Instruction, INTEROECUMENICI, on the Proper Implementation of the Constitution on the Sacred Liturgy, A.A.S., LVI (1964) 877–900.

126. *16 Oct., 1964,* Letter, CONSILIUM AD EXSEQUENDAM, to presidents of liturgical conferences stating it was preferable that there be only one translation in countries sharing the same language. *Notitiae,* 1965, 195–196.

127. *7 March, 1965,* S.C.R., Decree, QUAMPLURES EPISCOPI, announcing the publication of changes in the Holy Week services. A.A.S., LVII (1965) 412–413.

128. *25 March, 1965,* S.C.R., Decree, PLURES LOCORUM ORDINARII, granting permission for other clerics or laity to read the Gospel of the Passion in the absence of priests or deacons. A.A.S. LVII (1965) 13–414.

129. *30 June, 1965,* Letter, LE RENOUVEAU LITURGIQUE, to presidents of episcopal conferences on the liturgical reform. *Notitiae,* 1965, 257–264.

130. *25 Jan., 1966,* Letter, L'HEUREUX DEVELOPEMENT, to presidents of episcopal conferences on the liturgical reform, *Notitiae,* 1966, 157–161.

131. *27 Jan., 1966,* S.C.R., Decree, CUM NOSTRA AETATE, on the publication of liturgical books. A.A.S. LVIII (1966) 169–172.

132. *19 March, 1966,* S.C. Conc. Circular letter, OMNI-

BUS IN COMPERTO, to bishops on the need, in major tourist areas, for Masses and confessions etc., in the language of majority of tourists on Sundays and feast days. *Notitiae*, 1966, 185–189 (See A.9).

133. *29 Dec. 1966*, S.C.R., Declaration, DA QUALCHE TEMPO, on the application of the constitution of the sacred liturgy—warning against abuses in the celebration of Mass. A.A.S. LIX (1967), 85–86.

134. *4 May, 1967*, S.C.R. Second Instruction, TRES ABHINC ANNOS, on the Proper implementation of the Constitution on the Sacred Liturgy. A.A.S. LIX (1967) 442–448.

135. *21 June, 1967*, C.P.I.C.L., Letter, DANS SA RÉCENTE, to presidents of episcopal conferences on the liturgical reform. *Notitiae*, 1967, 289–296.

136. *2 June, 1968*, C.P.I.C.L., Letter, LA PUBLICATION, to presidents of episcopal conferences on the liturgy. *Notitiae*, 1968, 146–148.

137. *25 Jan., 1969*, C.P.I.C.L., Instruction, COMME LE PREVOIT, on the translation of liturgical texts for celebrations with the people. *Notitiae*, 1969, 3–12.

138. *14 Feb., 1969*, Paul VI. Apostolic Letter, MYSTERII PASCHALIS, given Motu Proprio, approving the new regulations of the liturgical year and the new Roman Calendar. A.A.S. LXI (1969) 222–226.

139. *19 March, 1969*, Paul VI. Apostolic Letter, SANCTITAS CLARIOR, given Motu Proprio, on the better arranging of beatification and canonization. A.A.S. LXI (1969) 149–153.

140. *3 April, 1970*, S.C.C.S. Decree NOVAE DE ACTORUM, giving practical regulations on preparing accounts of the lives of candidates for canonization. A.A.S. LXII (1970) 554–555.

141. *24 June, 1970*, S.C.R. Instruction, CALENDARIA PARTICULARIA, on the revision of special calendars, offices and Masses in dioceses and religious orders and congregations. A.A.S. LXII (1970) 651–663.

142. *5 Sept., 1970*, S.C.D.W.: Third Instruction, LITURGIAE INSTAURATIONES, on the Proper Implementation of the Constitution on the Sacred Liturgy: A.A.S., LXII (1970), 692–704.

143. *11 April, 1971*, S.C.C.: Letter, OPERA ARTIS, to presidents of episcopal conferences on the care of the his-

torico-artistic patrimony of the Church: A.A.S., LXIII (1971), 315–317.

144. *14 June, 1971,* S.C.D.W.: Note on the Roman Missal and the Liturgy of the Hours (bishops decide when vernacular editions become obligatory, decide on use of vernacular in all parts of the Mass, on advisability of some Masses in Latin; in private Masses, priests may use Latin or vernacular; the liturgy of the hours may be celebrated in Latin or vernacular, in private or in common) and on the calendar (bishops decide when general Roman calendar comes into use; certain problems with regard to the interim calendar): A.A.S., LXIII (1971) 712–715.

145. *19 March, 1973,* S.C.D.W.: Regulations for the formal choosing, approval and confirmation of a patron saint of a place, religious family, institute, etc and for liturgical celebration of a patron's feast: A.A.S., LXV (1973), 276–279.

146. *25 March, 1973,* S.C.D.W.: Regulations for the solemn crowning of a statue of Our Lady: A.A.S., LXV (1973), 280–281.

147. *25 Oct., 1973,* S.C.D.W.: Circular letter, DUM TOTO TERRARUM, on publishing liturgical books and on the translation of sacramental formulae: A.A.S., LXVI (1974), 98–99.

MARRIAGE CASES

See also A. 24, 33, 40, 42, 47.

148. *28 March 1971,* Paul VI, Apostolic Letter, CAUSAS MATRIMONIALES, given Motu Proprio, on expediting marriage cases: A.A.S., LXIII (1971), 441–446.

149. *7 March, 1972,* S.C.D.S.: Instruction, DISPENSATIONIS MATRIMONII RATI, on certain improvements in the legal process for non-consummated marriages: A.A.S., LXIV (1972), 244–252.

150. *8 Sept., 1973,* Paul VI, Apostolic Letter, CUM MATRIMONALIUM, given Motu Proprio, on expediting marriage cases in the Eastern Churches: A.A.S., LXV (1973), 577–581.

MEDIA, THE

See also A. 17.

151. *23 May, 1971, P.C.I.S.C.: Pastoral instruction, COMMUNIO ET PROGRESSIO, on the correct implementation of the Vatican Council's Decree on the Means of Social Communication: A.A.S., LXIII (1971), 593–656.

MISSIONS

See also A. 4, 21, 24, 244.

152. *6 August, 1966, Paul VI: Norms for implementing the decree on the missions, referred to as ECCLESIAE SANCTAE III, after the Apostolic Letter which prefaces them and the norms for bishops and priests (Ecclesiae Sanctae I) and the norms for religious (Ecclesiae Sanctae II): A.A.S., LVIII (1966), 783–787. (See A. 4, 182).

153. 24 Feb., 1969, S.C.E.P.: Instruction, QUO APTIUS, on missionary co-operation between bishops, the Congregation for the Evangelization of Peoples and the various Pontifical Missionary Works. A.A.S., LXI (1969), 276–281.

154. 24 Feb., 1969, S.C.E.P.: Instruction, RELATIONES IN TERRITORIIS, on relations between local ordinaries and missionary institutes: A.A.S., LXI (1969), 281–287.

MUSIC, SACRED

See also A. 102, 103.

155. 22 Nov., 1963, Paul VI: Hand-written letter, NOBILE SUBSIDIUM, establishing the International Association of Sacred Music: A.A.S., LVI (1964), 231–234.

156. 14 Dec., 1964, S.C.R.: Decree, QUUM CONSTITUTIO, announcing the publication of a simple "Kyriale": A.A.S., LVII (1965), 407.

157. 14 Dec., 1964, S.C.R.: Decree, EDITA INSTRUCTIONE, announcing the publication of the new chants needed for the celebration of Mass: A.A.S., LVII (1965), 408.

158 *5 March, 1967, S.C.R., Instruction, MUSICAM SACRAM, on music in the liturgy: A.A.S., LIX (1967), 300–320.

159. *3 Sept., 1967*, S.C.R.: Decree, SACROSANCTI OECUMENICI CONCILII, announcing the publication of a "Simple Gradual" for the use of smaller churches: *Notitiae*, 1967, 311.

160. *24 June, 1972*, S.C.R.: Decree, THESAURUM CANTUS GREGORIANI, on disposing the Latin chants in the Mass in a new way: A.A.S., LXV (1973), 274.

161. **April 1974*, S.C.D.W., Letter to bishops on the minimum repertoire of plain chant: *Notitiae*, April 1974, 123–126.

PRIESTS, DEACONS AND OTHER MINISTERS

See also A. 105, 120. (Norms for the implementation of the Decree on the Life and Ministry of Priests are included in Ecclesiae Sanctae I,—see A. 4 and D. 49.)

162. *18 June, 1967*, Paul VI, Apostolic Letter, SACRUM DIACONATUS ORDINEM, given Motu Proprio, prescribing regulations for the restoration of the permanent diaconate in the Latin Church: A.A.S., LIX (1967), 697–704.

163. *24 July, 1967,* Paul VI: Encyclical Letter, SACERDOTALIS CAELIBATUS, Reaffirming the Latin Church's discipline on priestly celibacy: A.A.S., LIX (1967) 657–697.

164. *4 Nov., 1969*, S.C.C.: Circular Letter, INTER EA, to presidents of episcopal conferences on the continuing formation and education of the clergy, especially the younger clergy: A.A.S., LXII (1970), 123–134.

165. *6 Jan., 1970*, S.C.C.E.: "The Fundametnal Principles of Priestly Formation," sent to episcopal conferences to guide them in the preparation of guide-lines for the program of education in their own seminaries: A.A.S., LXII (1970), 321–384.

166. *11 April, 1970*, S.C.C.: Circular Letter, PRESBYTERI SACRA ORDINATIONE, on priests' councils: A.A.S., LXII (1970), 459–465.

167. *13 Jan., 1971*, S.C.D.F.: Norms, for dioceses and religious orders, for the process of requesting laicization of priests and dispensation from the obligations that go with ordination: A.A.S., LXIII (1971), 303–308.

168. *13 Jan., 1971*, S.C.D.F.: Circular Letter, LITTERIS

ENCYCLICIS SACERDOTALIS CAELIBATUS, to all bishops and superiors general of clerical religious institutes, on the new norms for the process of laicization: A.A.S., LXIII (1971), 309–312.

169. *26 June, 1972*, S.C.D.F.: Declaration concerning the meaning of some of the norms issued on 13 Jan. 1971, on the process of laicization of priests: A.A.S., LXIV (1972), 641–643.

170 *15 August, 1972*, Paul VI: Apostolic Letter, MINISTERIA QUAEDAM, given Motu Proprio, on first tonsure, minor orders and the subdiaconate in the Latin Church: A.A.S., LXIV (1972), 529–534. (See A. 81).

171. *15 August, 1972*, Paul VI, Apostolic Letter, AD PASCENDUM, given Motu Proprio, containing norms for the order of the diaconate: A.A.S., LXIV (1972), 534–540.

RELATIONS WITH NON-CHRISTIAN RELIGIONS

172. *1 Dec., 1974*, C.R.R.J.: Guidelines on Religious relations with the Jews. *Oss Rom.* 4 Jan. 1975.

RELATIONS WITH UNBELIEVERS

173. *28 August, 1968*, S.U.: On dialogue with unbelievers. HUMANAE PERSONAE DIGNITATEM. A.A.S. LX (1968) 692–704.

RELIGIOUS

See also A. 111, 113, 115, 152, 154, 163–169, 219–221.

174. *2 August, 1962*, S.C. Rel.: Decree giving definitive approval to the statutes of the "Roman Union of Superiors General": C.R.M., 1963, 228. (See A. 175, 177, 178, 184, 203).

175. *2 August, 1962*, Statutes of the "Roman Union of Superiors General": C.R.M., 1963, 229–231. (see A. 174, 177, 178, 184, 203).

176. *6 Nov., 1964*, S.S.: Pontifical Rescript, CUM ADMOTAE, granting certain faculties to superiors general of clerical religious orders of pontifical right and to the abbots president of monastic congregations: A.A.S., LIX, (1967), 374–378.

177. *8 Dec., 1965*, S.C. Rel.: Decree approving the stat-

utes of the "International Union of Superioresses General":
C.R.M., 1966, 114, (See A. 174, 175, 178, 184, 203).

178. *18 Dec., 2965,* S.C. Rel.: Statutes of the "International Union of Superioresses General." C.M.R., 1966, 115–120. (See A. 174, 175, 177, 184, 203).

179. *12 Jan., 1966,* S.C. Rel., Decree on the powers of major religious superiors with regard to concelebration: C.R.M., 1966, 328. (See A. 56, 79).

180. *6 Feb., 1966,* S.C. Rel.: Instruction, IN EDICENDIS NORMIS, on religious and the use of the vernacular in the liturgy: the spread of the vernacular was largely to erode its significance in a comparatively short time, (See A. 144) A.A.S., LVII (1965), 1010–1013.

181. *31 May, 1966,* S.C. Rel.: Decree, RELIGIONUM LAICALIUM, granting certain faculties to superiors general of non-clerical religious congregations of pontifical right: A.A.S., LIX (1967), 362–364. (See A. 185).

182. **6 August, 1966,* Norms for implementing the decree on the renewal of religious life, usually referred to as ECCLESIAE SANCTAE II, after the Apostolic Letter of Paul VI which prefaces them and the norms for bishops and priests (Ecclesiae Sanctae I) and for missions (Ecclesiae Sanctae III): A.A.S., LVII (1966), 775–782. (See A. 4, 152).

183. *15 March, 1967,* S.C. Rel.: Letter abrogating canon 504 of the Code of Canon Law, which prohibited the election of an illegitimate person as major superior in a religious institute, the prohibition still to hold in the case of someone publicly known to be the offspring of an adulterous or sacrilegious union; (if not publicly known, the Holy See to be consulted): Italian text in *La Vita Religiosa: Documenti,* ed. Antonello Ravazzi, Ancora, Milan, p. 294; see C.R.M., 1967, 186–193.

184. *29 May, 1967,* S.C. Rel., Statutes of Union Superiors General approved: C.R.M., 1968, 66–69. (See A. 174, 175, 177, 178, 203).

185. *7 Sept., 1967,* S.C.E.P.: Certain faculties listed in *Religionum Laicalium* (see A. 181) are granted to religious institutes of women subject to the Congregation for the Evangelization of Peoples: C.R.M., 1968, 263–265.

186. *1967 (no further date),* S.A.P.: On revising the list of indulgences granted to religious institutes and pious associations. The Apostolic Penitentiary intends to grant plenary indulgences on following days: (a) for whole institute:

on Titular Feast or feast of principal patron; on feast of founder saint or blessed; on occasion of general chapter; (b) in individual houses: on feast of principal patron of house, on feasts of saints or blesseds whose body or notable relics conserved there; at the end of regular visitation; (c) for individual religious: on day of entry into novitiate; on day of first profession; on day of permanent profession; on 25th, 50th, 60th or 75th aniversary of first profession: C.R.M., 1968, 172–173.

187. *6 Jan., 1969, S.C.R.S.I.: Instruction, RENOVA-TIONIS CAUSAM, on the renewal of religious formation: A.A.S., LXI (1969), 103–120. (See A. 188)

188. 18 March, 1969, S.C.E.P.: Letter stating that the instruction, Renovations Causam, (see A. 187) has been adopted by the Congregation for the Evangelization of Peoples and applies also to institutes dependent on that congregation: C.R.M., 1970, 83.

189. *15 August, 1969, S.C.R.S.I.: Instruction, VENITE SEORSUM, on the comtemplative life and on nuns' cloister: A.A.S., LXI (1969), 674–690. (See A. 192).

190. 27 Nov., 1969, S.C.R.S.I.: Decree. CUM SUPER-IORES GENERALES, granting faculties to superiors general of non-clerical religious institutes to grant secularization to temporarily professed: A.A.S., LXI (1969), 738–739.

191. 27 Nov., 1969, S.C.R.S.I.: Decree, CLERICALIA INSTITUTA, on the role of non-clerical members in clerical institutes: General chapter may admit them to administrative and economic positions, to passive and active voice in all chapters, to be counsellors, but not to be superiors or vicars: A.A.S., LXI (1969), 739–740.

192. 2 Jan., 1970, S.C.R.S.I. Note on the status of the Instruction, Venite Seorsum (see A. 189): it was approved by the Pope as current legislation for contemplative nuns; if unacceptable to some, they may enter a different category of religious; local adaptations possible: C.R.M., 1970, 180–181.

193. 4 June, 1970, S.C.R.S.I.: Declaration, CLAUSUR-AM PAPALEM, that superiors general of canons regular, mendicants and clerics regular (but not monks) may modify their rule of cloister in accordance with canon 604 of the Code of Canon Law: A.A.S., LXII (1970), 548–549.

194. 4 June, 1970, S.C.R.S.I.: Decree, AD INSTITUEN-DA EXPERIMENTA, granting certain faculties to reli-

gious institutes to facilitate experimentation: A.A.S., LXII (1970), 549–550.

195. *12 Oct., 1970,* S.C.R.S.I.: Letter granting faculties to non-clerical religious men and to religious women, outside mission territories, to administer baptism, in the absence of priests and deacons, on the prior request of the bishop to the Holy See: C.R.M., 1971, 188–189.

196. *8 Dec., 1970,* S.C.R.S.I.: Decree, DUM CANONICARUM, on religious and the sacrament of penance and on professing sick religious: A.A.S., LXIII (1971), 318–319.

197. *1970 (no further date),* S.C.R.S.I.: Note on documents to be sent when requesting erection as congregation of diocesan right or "decree of praise": C.R.M., 1971, 191.

198. *1 Feb., 1971,* S.C.C.E.: Declaration, INSTRUCTIO A SACRA CONGREGATIONE, on co-education in schools run by religious: A.A.S., LXIII (1971), 250–251.

199. *29 June, 1971,* Paul VI: Apostolic Exhortation, EVANGELICA TESTIFICATIO, on the renewal of religious life according to Vatican II: A.A.S., LXIII (1971), 497–526.

200. *2 Feb. 1972,* S.C.R.S.: Decree, EXPERIMENTA CIRCA REGIMINIS, stating that collegial authority is not sufficient, superior must have personal authority, that religious dispensed from vows may retain certain offices, etc., hitherto forbidden by canon 642: A.A.S., LXIV (1972), 393–394.

201. *25 Feb., 1975,* S.C.R.S.I.: Letter, PERENGONO A QUESTO, on the religious habit: C.R.M., 1972, 179–180.

202. *27 June, 1972,* S.C.O.C.: Decree, ORIENTALIUM RELIGIOSORUM, granting certain faculties to Oriental religious: A.A.S., LXIV (1972), 738–743.

203. *28 June, 1972,* S.C.R.S.I.: Letter approving new statutes of Union of Superiors General: C.R.M., 1972, 262–263; The new Statutes: ibid., 263–267. (See A. 174, 175, 177, 178, 184).

204. *10 June, 1972,* S.C.R.S.I.: Circular Letter, PAR UNE LETTRE, on the Acts of the Special General Chapter: C.R.M., 1974, 76–80.

205. *6 August, 1972,* S.C.D.W.: Note, UNIVERSI QUI OFFICIUM DIVINUM, on certain religious orders and the divine office: C.R.M., 1972, 359–363.

206. *14 Feb., 1973,* S.C.R.S.I.: Reply, L'ORDO PUB-

LICATO, on the formula for religious profession: C.R.M., 1974, 179.

207. *1973 (no further date)* S.C.C.E.: Final document of the congress on vacations held in Rome, 20–24 November, 1973: C.R.M., 1974, 274–283.

208. *25 Jan., 1974,* S.C.R.S.I.: Decree, SACRA CONGREGATIO PRO RELIGIOSIS, on helping those who leave religious life: C.R.M., 1974, 73–75.

209. *2 March, 1974,* S.C.R.S.I.: Decree, PROCESSUS JUDICIALIS, on the expulsion of religious who have taken vows in an exempt religious institute: A.A.S., LXVI (1974), 215–216.

210. *1974 (no further date),* S.C.R.S.I.: Sample schema of the statutes of federation of nuns: C.R.M., 1974, 365–377.

SACRAMENTS (OTHER THAN THE EUCHARIST) AND SACRAMENTALS

211. *5 July, 1963,* S.S.C.H.O.: Instruction, DE CADAVERUM CREMATIONE, permitting cremation, since it is often necessary nowadays for hygienic, economic or other reasons, but stating that burial is preferable for a Christian: A.A.S., LVI (1964); 822–823.

212. *4 March, 1965,* S.C.R.: Decree, PIENTISSIMA MATER ECCLESIA, granting bishops the right to permit priests to carry the holy oils of the sick with them: A.A.S., LVII (1965), 409.

213. **1 Jan., 1967,* Paul VI: Apostolic Constitution, INDULGENTIARUM DOCTRINA, on the revision of indulgences: A.A.S., LIX (1967), 5–24.

214. *18 June, 1968,* Paul VI, Apostolic Constitution, PONTIFICALIS ROMANI, approving the new rites for the ordination of deacons, priests and bishops: A.A.S., LX (1968), 369–373.

215. *29 June, 1968,* S.A.P.: Decree, IN CONSTITUTIONE APOSTOLICA, promulgating the new "Enchiridion Indulgentiarum", or "Manual of Indulgences": A.A.S., LX (1968), 413–419.

216. *19 March, 1969,* S.C.R.: Decree, ORDO CELEBRANDI MATRIMONIUM, promulgating new rite of marriage, *Notitiae,* 1969, 203.

217. *15 May, 1969,* S.C.D.W.: Decree, ORDINEM

BAPTISMI PARVULORUM, promulgating new rite for infant baptism: A.A.S., LXI (1969), 448.

218. *15 August, 1969,* S.C.D.W.: Decree, RITIBUS EXSEQUIARUM, promulgating the new rite of burial: *Notitiae,* 1969, 423–424.

219. *2 Feb., 1970,* S.C.D.W.: Decree, PROFESSIONIS RITUS, promulgating the new rite of religious profession: A.A.S., LXII (1970), 553.

220. *31 May, 1970,* S.C.D.W.: Decree, CONSECRATIONIS VIRGINUM, promulgating the new rite of the consecration of virgins: A.A.S., LXII (1970), 650.

221. *9 Nov., 1970,* S.C.D.W.: Decree, BENEDICTIONIS ABBATIS, promulgating the new rite for the blessing of abbots and abbesses: A.A.S., LXIII (1971), 710–711.

222. *3 Dec., 1970,* S.C.D.W.: Decree, RITIBUS HEBDOMADAE, promulgating the new rite for the blessing of oil of catechumens and the oil of the sick and for making chrism: A.A.S., LXIII (1971), 711.

223. *15 August, 1971,* Paul VI, Apostolic Constitution, DIVINAE CONSORTIUM NATURAE, approving the revision of the rite for the sacrament of confirmation: A.A.S., LXIII (1971), 657–664.

224. *22 August, 1971,* S.C.D.W.: Decree, PECULIARE SPIRITUS SANCTI, promulgating the new rite of confirmation and declaring it the typical edition: A.A.S., LXIV (1972), 77.

225. *6 Jan., 1972,* S.C.D.W.: Decree, ORDINIS BAPTISMI ADULTORUM, promulgating the new rite for adult baptism: A.A.S., LXIV (1972), 252–253.

226. *16 June, 1972,* S.C.D.F.: Pastoral norms, SACRAMENTUM PAENITENTIAE, for the administration of general sacramental absolution: A.A.S., LXIV (1972), 510–514.

227. *30 Nov., 1972,* Paul VI, Apostolic Constitution, SACRAM UNCTIONEM INFIRMORUM, approving the revision of the rite of the sacrament of the sick: A.A.S., LXV (1973), 5–9.

228. *3 Dec., 1972,* S.C.D.W.: Decree, MINISTERIORUM DISCIPLINA, promulgating the rite of institution of lectors and acolytes, of admission among candidates for the diaconate and the priesthood and of embracing celibacy: A.A.S., LXV (1973), 274–275.

229. *7 Dec., 1972,* S.C.D.W.: Decree, INFIRMIS CUM ECCLESIA, promulgating the new rite of anointing of the

sick and of their pastoral care: A.A.S.: LXV (1973), 275–276.

230. *23 March, 1973,* S.C.D.F.: Declaration, SACRA CONGREGATIO, excommunicating anybody who, from contempt of the sacrament, records real or false confessions and divulges them, and anybody who co-operates in this: A.A.S., LXV (1973), 678.

231. **24 May, 1973,* S.C.C. and S.C.D.S.: Declaration, SANCTUS PONTIFEX PIUS X, on fiirst confession and first communion: A.A.S., LXV (1973), 410.

232. *20 Sept., 1973,* S.C.D.F.: Decree, PATRES SACRAE CONGREGATIONIS, stating that Christian burial is not to be denied to public sinners if they give some sign of repentence before death and there is no question of scandal for others: A.A.S., LXV (1973), 500.

233. *2 Dec., 1973,* S.C.D.W.: Decree, RECONCILIATIONEM INTER, approving the new order of penance: LXVI (1974), 172–173.

234. **25 Jan., 1974,* S.C.D.F.: Declaration, INSTAURATIO LITURGICA, on the meaning of sacramental formulae: A.A.S., LXVI (1974), 661.

SYNOD, THE ROMAN: DOCUMENTS

(See A. 2,5,6)

235. *30 Nov., 1971,* Published with a rescript from the Council for the Church's Public Affairs: "On the priestly ministry," and "On Justice in the World." A.A.S., LXIII (1971), 897–942.

VESTMENTS AND INSIGNIA OF CARDINALS, BISHOPS, etc.

236. *21 June, 1968,* S.C.R.: Instruction, PONTIFICALES RITUS, on simplifying pontifical rites and insignia: A.A.S., LX (1968), 406–412.

237. *21 June, 1968,* Paul VI, Apostolic Letter, PONTIFICALIA INSIGNIA, given Motu Proprio, on the revision of the use of pontifical insignia: A.A.S., LX (1968), 374–377.

238. *21 March, 1969,* S.S.: Instruction, UT SIVE SOLLICITE, on the vestments, titles and insignia of cardinals, bishops and lesser prelates: A.A.S., LXI (1969), 334–340.

239. *30 Oct., 1971*, S.C.C.: Circular Letter, PER IN-STRUCTIONEM, on the reform of choral dress: A.A.S., LXIII (1971), 314–315.

OTHER RELATED DOCUMENTS

240. *6 August 1964*, Paul VI, Encyclical Letter, EC-CLESIAM SUAM, on the Church in our day: A.A.S., LVI (1964), 609–659.

241. *17 Feb., 1966*, Paul VI, Apostolic Constitution, PAENITEMINI, given Motu Proprio, on the virtue and practice of penance: A.A.S., LVIII (1966), 177–198.

242. *26 March, 1967*, Paul VI, Encyclical Letter, POPU-LORUM PROGRESSIO, on promoting the development of peoples: A.A.S., LIX (1967), 257–299.

243. *13 May, 1967*, Paul VI, Apostolic Exhortation, SIGNUM MAGNUM, on our Lady, Mother of the Church: A.A.S., LIX (1967), 465–475.

244. *19 Oct., 1967*, Message given in writing, AFRICAE TERRARUM, to the African bishops and to the people of Africa: A.A.S., LIX (1967), 1073–1097.

245. *25 July, 1968*, Paul VI, Encyclical Letter, HU-MANAE VITAE, on the regulation of births: A.A.S., LX (1968), 481–503.

246 *14 May, 1971*, Paul VI, Apostolic Letter to Cardinal Roy, OCTOGESIMA ADVENIENS, on social justice: A.A.S., LXIII (1971), 401–441.

247. *11 Feb., 1974*, Paul VI, Apostolic Exhortation, MARIALIS CULTUS, on the worship of the Blessed Virgin Mary: A.A.S., LXVI, 113–168.

248. *30 June, 1974*, Paul VI, Apostolic Letter, APOSTO-LORUM LIMINA, given under his seal, on the Holy Year: A.A.S., LXVI, (1974), 289–307.

249. *18 Nov., 1974*, S.C.D.F.: Declaration, QUAESTIO DE ABORTU, on procured abortion, A.A.S., LXVI (1974), 730–747.

250. *8 Dec., 1974*, Paul VI, Apostolic Exhortation, PA-TERNA CUM BENEVOLENTIA, on reconciliation in the Church, Oss. Rom. 16–17 Dec., 1974.

INDEX OF FIRST WORDS OF ORIGINALS OF DOCUMENTS

INDEX

N.B.

The contents of this publication will be updated as new data is obtained.

Those persons who wish to be kept informed need only register with the distributor from whom this book was purchased or the publisher.

Furnish a complete address including Zip Code to:

EDITOR/VATICAN II DOCUMENTS
Costello Publishing Co., Inc.
Box 9
Northport, N.Y. 11768
or Your Local Catholic Book Store
or Church Goods Dealer